CURRENT ISSUES
AND
ENDURING QUESTIONS

*A Guide to
Critical Thinking and Argument,
with Readings*

FIFTH EDITION

SYLVAN BARNET
Professor of English, Tufts University

HUGO BEDAU
Professor of Philosophy, Tufts University

Bedford/St. Martin's   BOSTON   NEW YORK

For Bedford/St. Martin's
Developmental Editor: Stephen A. Scipione
Production Editors: Karen S. Baart, Stasia Zomkowski
Production Supervisor: Scott Lavelle
Marketing Manager: Karen Melton
Editorial Assistant: Maura Shea
Production Assistants: Coleen O'Hanley, Helaine Denenberg
Copyeditor: Lisa Wehrle
Text Design: Sandra Rigney
Cover Design: Donna Lee Dennison
Composition: Pine Tree Composition, Inc.
Printing and Binding: Haddon Craftsmen, Inc.

President: Charles H. Christensen
Editorial Director: Joan E. Feinberg
Director of Editing, Design, and Production: Marcia Cohen
Managing Editor: Elizabeth M. Schaaf

Library of Congress Catalog Card Number: 98–85187

For information, write: Bedford/St. Martin's, 75 Arlington Street, Boston, MA 02116 (617-426-7440)

ISBN: 0–312–17154–4

Acknowledgments

Preface

This book is a text—a book about reading other people's arguments and writing your own arguments—and it is also an anthology—a collection of more than a hundred selections, ranging from Plato to the present, with a strong emphasis on contemporary arguments. In a moment we will be a little more specific about what sorts of essays we include, but first we want to mention our chief assumptions about the aims of a course that might use *Current Issues and Enduring Questions: A Guide to Critical Thinking and Argument, with Readings.*

Probably most students and instructors would agree that, *as critical readers,* students should be able to

- summarize accurately an argument they have read;
- locate the thesis of an argument;
- locate the assumptions, stated and unstated;
- analyze and evaluate the strength of the evidence and the soundness of the reasoning offered in support of the thesis;
- analyze, evaluate, and account for discrepancies among various readings on a topic (for example, explain why certain facts are used or not used, why two sources might interpret the same facts differently) .

Probably, too, students and instructors would agree that, *as thoughtful writers,* students should be able to

- imagine an audience, and write effectively for it (by such means as using the appropriate tone and providing the appropriate amount of detail);
- present information in an orderly and coherent way;
- be aware of own assumptions;
- incorporate sources into their own writing, not simply by quoting extensively or by paraphrasing, but also by having digested materials so that they can present it in their own words;
- properly document all borrowings—not merely quotations and paraphrases but also borrowed ideas;

iii

- do all these things in the course of developing a thoughtful argument of their own.

ABOUT THE TEXT

Parts One and Two   Part One (Chapters 1–3) and Part Two (Chapters 4–6) taken together offer a short course in methods of thinking
about arguments and in methods of writing arguments. By "thinking"
we mean serious analytic thought, including analysis of one's own assumptions (Chapter 1); by "writing" we mean the use of effective, respectable techniques, not gimmicks such as the notorious note a politician scribbled in the margin of the text of his speech: "Argument weak;
shout here." For a delightfully wry account of the use of gimmicks, we
recommend that you consult "The Art of Controversy," in *The Will to
Live,* by the nineteenth-century German philosopher Arthur Schopenhauer. Schopenhauer reminds his reader that a Greek or Latin quotation
(however irrelevant) can be impressive to the uninformed, and that one
can knock down almost any argument by loftily saying, "That's all very
well in theory, but it won't do in practice."

We offer lots of advice about setting forth an argument, but we do
not offer instruction in one-upmanship. Rather, we discuss responsible
ways of arguing persuasively. We know, however, that before one can
write a persuasive argument one must clarify one's own ideas—and that
includes arguing with oneself—to find out what one really thinks about
a problem. Therefore we devote Chapter 1 to critical thinking, Chapters
2 and 3 to critical reading, and Chapters 4, 5, and 6 to critical writing.
These chapters are not all lecturing. Parts One and Two together contain
thirty-five readings (three are by students) for analysis and discussion.
Moreover, each of the three chapters in Part One contains a casebook, a
group of closely related readings. For instance, the casebook in Chapter 1
consists of a newspaper editorial on divorce, followed by five letters that
were written in response to the editorial.

All of the essays[1] in the book are accompanied by questions. This is
not surprising, given the emphasis we place on asking oneself questions
to get ideas for writing. Among the chief questions that writers should
ask, we suggest, are such matters as "What is *X*?" and "What is the value
of *X*?" (pp. 3–9). By asking such questions—for instance (to look only
at these two types of questions), "Is the fetus a person?" or "Is Arthur Miller a better playwright than Tennessee Williams?"—a writer
probably will find ideas coming, at least after a few moments of head-
scratching. The device of developing an argument by identifying issues
is, of course, nothing new; indeed, it goes back to an ancient method of

---

[1]With a few exceptions, the paragraphs in the essays are, for ease of reference, numbered
in increments of five (5, 10, 15, and so forth). The exceptions involve essays in which paragraphs are uncommonly long; in such cases, every paragraph is numbered.

argument used by classical rhetoricians, who proceeded by identifying a *stasis* (an issue) and then asked questions about it: Did *X* do such-and-such? If so, was the action bad? If bad, how bad? (Finding an issue or *stasis*—a position where one stands—by asking questions is discussed in Chapter 5.)

In keeping with our emphasis on writing as well as reading, we raise issues not only of what can roughly be called the "content" of the essays but also of what can (equally roughly) be called the "style"—that is, the ways in which the arguments are set forth. Content and style, of course, cannot finally be kept apart. As Cardinal Newman said, "Thought and meaning are inseparable from each other.... *Style is thinking out into language.*" In our questions we sometimes ask the student to evaluate the effectiveness of the opening paragraph, or to explain a shift in tone from one paragraph to the next, or to characterize the persona of the author as revealed in the whole essay. In short, the book is not designed as an introduction to some powerful ideas (though in fact it is that, too); it is designed as an aid to writing thoughtful, effective arguments on important political, social, scientific, ethical, and religious issues.

The essays reprinted in this book also illustrate different styles of argument that arise, at least in part, from the different disciplinary backgrounds of the various authors. Essays by journalists, lawyers, judges, social scientists, policy analysts, philosophers, critics, activists, and other writers—including undergraduates—will be found in these pages. The authors develop and present their views in arguments that have distinctive features reflecting their special training and concerns. The differences in argumentative styles found in these essays foreshadow the differences students will encounter in the readings assigned in many of their other courses. (Part Three, which offers a philosopher's view, a logician's view, a psychologist's view, a lawyer's view, and a literary critic's view, also reveals differences in argumentative styles.)

Parts One and Two, then, are a preliminary (but we hope substantial) discussion of such topics as *identifying assumptions, getting ideas by means of invention strategies, using sources, evaluating kinds of evidence,* and *organizing material,* as well as an introduction to some ways of thinking.

Part Three "Further Views on Argument" consists of Chapters 7–11. The first of these, Chapter 7, "A Philosopher's View: The Toulmin Model," is a summary of the philosopher Stephen Toulmin's method for analyzing arguments. This summary will assist those who wish to apply Toulmin's methods to the readings in our book. The next chapter, "A Logician's View," offering a more rigorous analysis of deduction, induction, and fallacies than is usually found in composition courses, reexamines from a logician's point of view material already treated briefly in Chapter 3. Chapter 9, with an essay by psychotherapist Carl R. Rogers, complements the discussion of audience, organization, and tone in Chapter 5. Chapter 10, "A Lawyer's View: Steps toward Civic Literacy," introduces students to some basic legal concepts, such as the distinction between civil and criminal cases, and then gives majority and minority decisions in three cases: searching students for drugs, burning the flag, protesting the draft. We accompany these decisions with questions that invite the student to participate in these exercises in democracy. The last chapter in Part Three, "A Literary Critic's View: Arguing about Literature," should help students to see what sorts of things literary critics argue about and *how* they argue. Students can apply what they learn not only to the literary readings that appear in the chapter (poems by Robert Frost and Andrew Marvell, stories by Kate Chopin and Jean Rhys, and a casebook concerning the national anthem) but also to the readings that appear in Part Six, "Enduring Questions," where we include eleven poems, two stories, and two plays.

ABOUT THE ANTHOLOGY

Part Four   "Current Issues: Pro-Con Debates" (Chapters 12–16) begins with a checklist for analyzing a debate, and then offers five pairs of arguments on such issues as affirmative action, gay marriage, and the distribution of condoms in school, all of which are accompanied by topics for critical thinking that widen the student's view of the issues. Here, as in Part Five, many of the selections (drawn from such sources as *The Nation, The National Review,* and the *New York Times*) are very short—scarcely longer than the 500-word essays that students are often asked to write.

Part Five   "Current Issues: Casebooks" (Chapters 17–25) gives the student nine casebooks—that is, several voices discussing an issue. For example, a casebook on whether human cloning is acceptable (Chapter 18) begins with a letter by Laurence Tribe, which is followed by a response that the letter evoked and then three additional essays concerned with cloning. The casebook on sexual harassment (Chapter 24) begins with one university's statement of policy—an opportunity to invite students to examine *their* school's statement—and then offers a wide range of voices in three essays by authors such as Ellen Goodman and Catharine A. MacKinnon.

Part Six   "Enduring Questions: Essays, Stories, Poems, and Plays" (Chapters 26–28) extends the arguments to three topics: "What Is the Ideal Society?" (the nine voices here range from Thomas More, Thomas Jefferson, and Martin Luther King, Jr., to literary figures W. H. Auden, Langston Hughes, and Ursula K. Le Guin); "How Free Is the Will of the Individual within Society?" (among the eleven authors are Plato, Susan Glaspell, George Orwell, and Stanley Milgram); and "What Are the Grounds of Religious Faith?" (among the selections are writings by Paul, Bertrand Russell, Emily Dickinson, and Judith Ortiz Cofer).

Appendices We include an appendix, "World Wide Web Sources for Current Issues," recognizing that many students use the vast resources of the World Wide Web in their research. This appendix, we hope, will help them focus more effectively on using the Internet as they develop their thoughts and research their papers on many of the current issues raised in this book.

The Instructor's Edition includes its own appendix, "Resources for Teaching," with detailed suggestions about ways in which the essays may be approached and with many additional suggestions for writing.

ABOUT WHAT'S NEW TO THE FIFTH EDITION

In the first edition of this book we quoted Edmund Burke and John Stuart Mill. Burke said, "He that wrestles with us strengthens our nerves, and sharpens our skill. Our antagonist is our helper." Mill said, "He who knows only his own side of the cause knows little." We can regret the aggressive language in Burke and the sexist language in Burke and Mill, but these two quotations continue to reflect the view of argument that underlies this text. When one writes an argument, one is not setting out to trounce an opponent, and that is partly why such terms as *marshaling evidence, attacking an opponent,* and *defending a thesis* are misleading. True, in television talk shows we see people who have made up their minds and who are concerned only with pushing their own view and brushing aside all other views. But in writing an essay one is engaging in a serious effort to know what one's own ideas are and, having found them, to contribute to a multisided conversation. We learn by listening to others and also by listening to ourselves; we draft a response to something we have read, and in the very act of drafting we may find—if we think critically about the words we are putting down on paper—we are changing (perhaps slightly, perhaps radically) our own position. Even if we do not drastically change our view, the reader at the very least comes to understand why we hold the view we do.

In preparing the fifth edition we were greatly aided by suggestions from instructors who were using the fourth edition. In line with their recommendations, in Part One, "Critical Thinking and Reading," we have added checklists to each of the three chapters (checklists for critical thinking, for examining assumptions, for getting started, for examining statistical evidence, and for analyzing an argument), and we have also added casebooks (on divorce, free speech, and bilingual education) to each chapter.

We have also added checklists to Part Two, "Critical Writing," and in the chapter on the research paper we now include advice on using electronic sources. We have somewhat heightened the reader's awareness of classical rhetoric by including discussion of topics such as *ethos, logos, pathos, stasis,* and, for that matter, *topos.*

In Part Three, we have increased the number of literary selections in "A Literary Critic's View," and in an effort to increase civic literacy, we have added "A Lawyer's View," with three legal cases (majority and minority opinions). We think that our prefatory material in "A Lawyer's View" concerning such matters as facts and the law and the balancing of interests will help students think not only about the legal cases included in Chapter 10 and in other chapters but also about cases they read in the daily newspaper.

In Parts Four and Five, "Current Issues: Pro-Con Debates" and "Current Issues: Casebooks," we have changed some of the readings in issues that we retained, and we have introduced new issues—censoring the Internet and cloning, for example.

Part Six, "Enduring Questions," also has new readings, with a new issue, "How Free Is the Will of the Individual within Society?"

There can be no argument about the urgency of the topics that we have added or about the need to develop civic literacy, but there can be lots of arguments about the merits of the positions offered in the selections. That's where the users of the book, students and instructors, come in.

Note: For instructors who do not require a text with a large number of essays, a shorter edition of this book, *Critical Thinking, Reading, and Writing: A Brief Guide to Argument,* Third Edition, is also available. The shorter version contains Parts One, Two, and Three (Chapters 1–11) of the present book as well as its own "Casebook on the State and the Individual," drawn from three Part Six readings in the longer edition.

ACKNOWLEDGMENTS

Finally, it is our pleasant duty to thank those who have strengthened the book by their advice: Alan Ainsworth, Houston Community College; Roy M. Anker, Calvin College; Jim Arlandson, California Baptist College; Robert Baird, University of Illinois; Claudia Basha, Victor Valley College; Mark Bedau; Frank Beesley, University of Nebraska at Lincoln; Donavin Bennes, University of North Dakota; Jack A. Bennett, Sinclair Community College; Laurie J. Bergamini, State University of New York at Plattsburgh; Jeffrey Berger, Community College of Philadelphia; B. J. Bowman, Radford University; Anthony Boyle, Fairleigh Dickinson University; Moana Boyle, Ricks College; Beverly M. Braud, Southwest Texas State University; Edward Brooks, Bergen Community College; Duane Bruce, University of Hartford; Jacintha Burke, King's College; Jim Butterfield, Western Michigan University; Mary Cantrell, Tulsa Community College; Janet Carter, Bridgewater State College; Brandon Cesmat, Palomar College; Claire Chantell, University of Illinois at Urbana–Champaign; Jo Chern, University of Wisconsin at Green Bay; Barbara G. Clark,

Adams State College; Denise Clark, Santa Clara University; Elsie Clark, Durham Technical Community College; James Clarke, Washington State University; Lorna Clymer, University of California at Santa Barbara; Sherill Cobb, Collin County Community College; Bobbie Cohen, Florida University; Paul Cohen, Southwest Texas State University; Minnie A. Collins, Seattle Central Community College; Marie Conte, California State University–Dominguez Hills; Genevieve Coogan, Houston Northwest Community College; Dr. Michael E. Cooley, Berry College; Marcia Corcoran, Evergreen Valley College; Susan Carolyn Cowan, University of Southern California; Jody Cross-Hansen, Hofstra University; Linda Daigle, Houston Central Community College; Anne D'Arcy, California State University–Hayward; Fara Darland, Scottsdale Community College; Robert Denham, Roanoke College; Kent R. DeVault, Central Washington University; Allen DiWederburg, Clackamas Community College; Carl Dockery, Tri-County Community College; Paula Doctor, Muskegon Community College; Alberta M. Dougan, Southeast Missouri State University; Elizabeth Elclepp, Rancho Santiago Community College; Diane El-Rouaiheb, University of Louisville; Hal Enger, San Diego Mesa College; Dianne Fallon, State University of New York at Binghamton; Amy Farmer, University of Illinois; Sister Isabella Ferrell, Cardinal Stritch College; John Finnegan, West Liberty Sate College; Jane Fischer, Southwest State University; Robert H. Fleeson, New Hampshire College; Anne Marie Frank, Elmhurst College; Amy Freed, Virginia Polytechnic Institute; Stephen Fullmer, Utah Valley State College; Michael J. Galgano, James Madison University; Joseph E. Geist, Central Methodist College; Sheryl Gobble, San Diego City College; Stuart Goodman, Duke University; Nathanael Gough, Forsyth Technical Community College; Mary Anne F. Grabarek, Durham Technical Community College; Tim Gracyk, Santa Clara University; Becky C. Graham, Livingston University; Rebecca Graham, University of Minnesota–Morris; Richard Grande, Pennsylvania State University; Mark A. Graves, Bowling Green State University; Kate Gray, Clackamas Community College; Verge Hagopian, Orange Coast College; Dennis R. Hall, University of Louisville; William M. Hamlin, Idaho State University; William Hampl, Bridgewater State College; Donald Heidt, College of the Canyons; Charles Heimler, California State University at Hayward; Janet Ruth Heller, Grand Valley State University; John C. Herold, Elon College; Edwin L. Hetfield, Jr., Onondaga Community College; Katherine Hoffman, Roanoke College; Pau-San Hoh, Marist College; Cathy Hope, Tarleton State University; Diane W. Howard, Valdosta State University; Rosemary T. Hunkeler, University of Wisconsin–Parkside; Barbara Hunter, Wright College; Joan Hutchison, Oakland Community College; Dr. Brian D. Ingraffia, Biola University; Shelly Jaffray, Rancho Santiago Community College; Bonita Nahoum Jaros, Rancho Santiago College; Alison Jasper, California Polytechnic State University; Janet Juhnke, Kansas Wesleyan University; Diane M. Kammeyer, Anoka-Ramsey Community College; Priscilla Kelly,

Slippery Rock University; Michael Kent, San Bernardino Valley College; Mary Jane Kinnebrew, San Jacinto College Central; Geoffrey Klinger, University of Iowa; Bobbie Knable, Tufts University; Prudence Kohl, Baldwin–Wallace College; Catherine W. Kroll, Sonoma State University; Elaine W. Kromhout, Indian River Community College; Lita A. Kurth, Santa Clara University; Brother Christopher Lambert, Quincy College; Richard L. Larson, Lehman College; John Lawing, Regent University; Erin Lebofsky, Temple University; J. N. Lee, Portland State University; Charles Lefcourt, State University of New York at Buffalo; Elizabeth Lewis, Manhattanville College; L. M. Lewis, University of Texas at Brownsville; Alex Liddie, Trenton State College; Miriam Lilley, College of the Canyons; John Little, James Madison University; Martin Litz, Raymond Walters College; Warren H. Loveless, Indiana State University; Christopher Lukasik, University of Washington; Tom Lynch, California State University at Hayward; Carter Lyons, James Madison University; Nelly McFeely, California State University and Merritt College; Ted McFerrin, Collin County Community College; Natalie McKnight, Boston University; Marcia MacLennan, Kansas Wesleyan University; Kelli Maloy, West Virginia University; Ruth E. Manson, South Dakota State University; Diane Marlett, University of Wisconsin at Green Bay; Brian Massey, Winthrop College; Alice Maudsley, Cleveland State University; James May, Pennsylvania State University; Carl E. Meacham, State University of New York–Oneonta; Dan C. Miller, University of Northern Colorado; Peggy A. Moore, College of Siskiyous; Richard Moore, Delgado Community College; Linda Morante, College of the Desert; Mary Munsil, University of Southern California; Cris Newport, New Hampshire Technical Institute; Melanie Ohler; Leonard Orr, Washington State University; Roswell Park, State University of New York at Buffalo; Scott Payne, University of Louisville; Robert Peltier, Trinity College; Nancy P. Pope, Washington University; Constance Putnam; Jan Rainbird, California State University at Fullerton; Sally Lynn Raines, West Virginia University; Carol Redmore, Highland Community College; Elaine Reed, Kutztown University; M. Resnick, State University of New York at Farmingdale; Dan Richards; Susan Roberson, Auburn University; Helen M. Robinette, Glassboro State College; Linda Rosekraus, State University of New York, College at Cortland; Jennifer O. Rosti, Roanoke College; Julie H. Rubio, University of Southern California at Long Beach; Rebecca Sabounchi, University of Texas; Suzette Schlapkohl, Scottsdale Community College; Henry Schwarzschild; Harsh Sharma, Buffalo State College; Hassell B. Sledd, Slippery Rock University; Sydney J. Slobodnik, University of Illinois at Urbana–Champaign; Andrew J. Smyth, St. Louis University; Daniel R. Snyder, Sagwan Valley University; Lynn Steiner, Cuesta College; Skaidrite Stelzer, University of Toledo; Elisabeth Stephens, University of North Carolina at Greensboro; Ed Stieve, Nova College; Barbara W. Stewart, Long Beach City College; Steven Strang, Massachusetts Institute of Technology; Suba Subbarao, Oakland Community

College; Catherine Sutton, University of Louisville; Richard C. Taylor, East Carolina University; Diane Thompson, Harrisburg Area Community College; Eve Thompson, College of the Siskiyons; Linda Toonen, University of Wisconsin at Green Bay; David Tumpleman, Monroe Community College; Pauline Uchmanowicz, University of Rhode Island; Lynn A. Walkiewicz, Cazenovia College; Kathleen Walsh, Central Oregon Community College; Nancy Weingart, John Carrol University; Stephen White; Phyllis C. Whitesoll, Franklin and Marshall College; Allen D. Widerburg, Clackamas Community College; Marilyn Wienk, Elmira College; Stephen Wilhoit, University of Dayton; Josie Williams, Durham Technical Community College; Joseph Wilson, Anna Maria College; Michelle L. Zath, Berry College; Bruce D. Zessin, University of Wisconsin at Waukesha.

We would like especially to thank Janet E. Gardner of the University of Massachusetts, Dartmouth, who revised the research chapter to encompass the latest advice and information on using electronic sources and who prepared the new appendix of Web sites. A timely conversation with Phyllis West of El Camino Community College prompted us to include Sophocles' classic play *Antigone* in the book; our thanks to her as well.

We are also indebted to the people at Bedford/St. Martin's, especially Charles H. Christensen, Joan E. Feinberg, Steve Scipione, Elizabeth M. Schaaf, Karen Baart, Stasia Zomkowski, and Maura Shea, who offered many valuable (and invaluable) suggestions. Intelligent, informed, firm yet courteous, they really know how to think, and how to argue.

Brief Contents

Contents

Part One

CRITICAL THINKING AND READING

1

Critical Thinking

The comedian Jack Benny cultivated the stage personality of a penny-pincher. In one of his skits a stickup man thrusts a gun into Benny's ribs and says, "Your money or your life." Utter silence. The robber, getting no response, and completely baffled, repeats, "Your money or your life." Short pause, followed by Benny's exasperated reply: "I'm *thinking*, I'm *thinking*!"

Without making too much of this gag, we want to point out that Benny is using the word *thinking* in the sense that we use it in *critical thinking*. *Thinking*, by itself, can mean almost any sort of mental activity, from idle daydreaming ("During the chemistry lecture I kept thinking about how I'd like to go camping") to careful analysis ("I'm thinking about whether I can afford more than one week—say two weeks—of camping in the Rockies," or even "I'm thinking about *why* Benny's comment strikes me as funny," or, "I'm thinking about why you find Benny's comment funny and I don't").

In short, when we add the adjective *critical* to the noun *thinking*, we pretty much eliminate reveries, just as we also eliminate snap judgments. We are talking about searching for hidden assumptions, noticing various facets, unraveling different strands, and evaluating what is most significant. (The word *critical* comes from a Greek word, *krinein*, meaning "to separate," "to choose"; it implies conscious, deliberate inquiry.)

THINKING ABOUT DRIVER'S LICENSES AND SCHOOL ATTENDANCE: IMAGINATION, ANALYSIS, EVALUATION

By way of illustration let's think critically about a law passed in West Virginia in 1989. The law provides that although students may drop out of school at the age of sixteen, no dropout younger than eighteen can hold a driver's license.

But what ought we to think of such a law? Is it fair? What is its purpose? Is it likely to accomplish its purpose? Might it unintentionally do some harm, and, if so, can we weigh the potential harm against the potential good? Suppose you had been a member of the West Virginia state legislature in 1989: How would you have voted?

In thinking critically about a topic, we try to see it from all sides before we come to our conclusion. We conduct an argument with ourselves, advancing and then questioning opinions. What can be said *for* the proposition, and what can be said *against* it? Our first reaction may be quite uncritical, quite unthinking: "What a good idea!" or "That's outrageous!" But critical thinking requires us to reflect further, trying to support our position *and also* trying to see the other side. One can almost say that the heart of critical thinking is a *willingness to face objections to one's own beliefs,* a willingness to adopt a skeptical attitude not only toward authority and toward views opposed to our own, but also toward common sense, that is, toward the views that seem obviously right to us. If we assume we have a monopoly on the truth and we dismiss as bigots those who oppose us, or if we say our opponents are acting merely out of self-interest, and we do not in fact analyze their views, we are being critical but we are not engaged in critical thinking.

Critical thinking requires us to use our *imagination,* seeing things from perspectives other than our own and envisioning the likely consequences of our position. (This sort of imaginative thinking—grasping a perspective other than our own, and considering the possible consequences of positions—is, as we have said, very different from daydreaming, an activity of unchecked fantasy.)

Thinking critically involves, along with imagination (so that we can see our own beliefs from another point of view), a twofold activity:

> **analysis,** separating the parts of the problem, trying to see how things fit together; and
>
> **evaluation,** judging the merit of our assumptions and the weight of the evidence in their favor.

If we engage in imaginative, analytic, and evaluative thought, we will have second and third ideas; almost to our surprise we may find ourselves adopting a position that we initially couldn't imagine we would hold. As we think about the West Virginia law, we might find ourselves coming up with a fairly wide variety of ideas, each triggered by the preceding idea but not necessarily carrying it a step further. For instance, we may think X, and then immediately think, "No, that's not quite right. In fact, come to think of it, the opposite of X is probably true." We haven't carried X further, but we have progressed in our thinking.

WRITING AS A WAY OF THINKING

"To learn to write," Robert Frost said, "is to learn to have ideas." But how do we get ideas? One way, practiced by the ancient Greeks and Romans and still regarded as among the best ways, is to consider what the ancients called **topics,** from the Greek word *topos,* meaning "place," as in our word *topography* (a description or representation of a place). For the ancients, certain topics, put into the form of questions, were in effect places where one went to find ideas. Among the classical *topics* were

- definition (What is it?);
- comparison (What is it like or unlike?);
- relationship (What caused it, and what will it cause?);
- testimony (What is said about it, for instance by experts?).

All of these topics or idea-generating places will be treated in detail in later chapters, but here we can touch briefly on a few of them.

If we are talking about the West Virginia law, it's true that we won't get ideas by asking questions concerning definition, but we may generate ideas by asking ourselves if this law is like any other (and, if so, how well did the corresponding law work), and by asking what caused this law, and what it may in turn cause. Similarly, if we go to the topic of testimony, we may want to find out what some students, teachers, parents, police officers, and lawmakers have to say.

If you think you are at a loss for ideas when confronted with an issue (and when confronted with an assignment to write about it), you probably will find ideas coming to you if you turn to the relevant classical topics and begin jotting down your responses. (In classical terminology, you are engaged in the process of **invention** (from the Latin *invenīre,* "to come upon," "to find.") Seeing your ideas on paper—even in the briefest form—will help bring other ideas to mind, and will also help you to evaluate them. For instance, after jotting down ideas as they come and responses to them,

1. you might go on to organize them into two lists, pro and con;
2. next, you might delete ideas that, when you come to think about them, strike you as simply wrong or irrelevant; and
3. then you might develop those ideas that strike you as pretty good.

You probably won't know where you stand until you have gone through some such process. It would be nice if we could make a quick decision and then immediately justify it with three excellent reasons, and could give three further reasons showing why the opposing view is inadequate. In fact, however, we almost never can come to a reasoned decision without a good deal of preliminary thinking.

Consider again the West Virginia law. Here is a kind of inner dialogue that you might engage in as you think critically about it.

The purpose is to give students an incentive to stay in school by making them pay a price if they choose to drop out.

Adolescents will get the message that education really is important.

But, come to think of it, *will* they? Maybe they will see this as just another example of adults bullying young people.

According to a newspaper article, the dropout rate in West Virginia decreased by 30 percent in the year after the bill was passed.

Well, that sounds good, but is there any reason to think that kids who are pressured into staying really learn anything? The *assumption* behind the bill is that if would-be dropouts stay in school, they—and society—will gain. But is the assumption sound? Maybe such students will become resentful, will not learn anything, and may even be so disruptive that they will interfere with the learning of other students.

Notice how part of the job is *analytic,* recognizing the elements or complexities of the whole, and part is *evaluative,* judging the adequacy of all of these ideas, one by one. Both tasks require *imagination.*

So far we have jotted down a few thoughts, and then immediately given some second thoughts contrary to the first. Of course, the counterthoughts might not immediately come to mind. For instance, they might not occur until we reread the jottings, or try to explain the law to a friend, or until we sit down and begin drafting an essay aimed at supporting or undermining the law. Most likely, in fact, some good ideas won't occur until a second or third or fourth draft.

Here are some further thoughts on the West Virginia law. We list them more or less as they arose and as we typed them into a word processor—not sorted out neatly into two groups, pro and con, nor evaluated as you would want to do in further critical thinking of your own. And of course a later step would be to organize the material into some useful pattern. As you read, you might jot down your own responses in the margin.

> Education is <u>not</u> optional, something left for the individual to take or not to take--like going to a concert, or jogging, or getting annual health checkups, or getting eight hours of sleep each night. Society has determined that it is <u>for the public good</u> that citizens have a substantial education, so we require education up to a certain age.

> Come to think about it, maybe the criterion of age doesn't make much sense. If we want an educated citizenry, it would make more sense to require people to attend school until they demonstrated competence in certain matters, rather than until they reached a certain age. Exceptions of course would be made for mentally retarded persons, and perhaps for certain other groups.

What is needed is not legal pressure to keep teenagers
   in school, but schools that hold the interest of
   teenagers.

A sixteen-year-old usually is not mature enough to make
   a decision of this importance.

Still, a sixteen-year-old who finds school unsatisfying
   and who therefore drops out may become a perfectly
   useful citizen.

Denying a sixteen-year-old a driver's license may work
   in West Virginia, but it would scarcely work in a
   state with great urban areas, where most high
   school students rely on public transportation.

We earn a driver's license by demonstrating certain
   skills. The state has no right to take away such a
   license unless we have demonstrated that we are
   unsafe drivers.

To prevent a person of sixteen from having a driver's
   license prevents that person from holding certain
   kinds of jobs, and that's unfair.

A law of this sort deceives adults into thinking that
   they have really done something constructive for
   teenage education, but it may work against improving the schools. If we are really serious about
   educating youngsters, we have to examine the curriculum and the quality of our teachers.

Doubtless there is much that we haven't said, on both sides, but we hope
you will agree that the issue deserves thought. (A number of state legislatures are indeed thinking about bills resembling the West Virginia law.)
And if you were a member of the legislature of West Virginia in 1989
you would have *had* to think about the issue.

One other point about this issue: *Today,* if you had to think about the
matter, you might also want to know whether the West Virginia legislation of 1989 is considered a success, and on what basis. That is, you
would want to get answers to such questions as the following:

1. What sort of evidence tends to support the law or tends to suggest that the law is a poor idea?
2. Did the reduction in the dropout rate continue, or did the reduction occur only in the first year following the passage of the law?
3. If indeed students did not drop out, was their presence in school a
   good thing, both for them and for their classmates?

4. Have some people emerged as authorities on this topic? What makes them authorities, and what do they have to say?

5. Has the constitutionality of the bill been tested? With what results?

Some of these questions require you to do **research** on the topic. The questions raise issues of fact, and some relevant evidence probably is available. If you are to arrive at a conclusion in which you can have confidence, you will have to do some research to find out what the facts are.

Even without doing any research, however, you might want to look over the ideas, pro and con, perhaps adding some totally new thoughts, or perhaps modifying or even rejecting (for reasons that you can specify) some of those already given. If you do think a bit further about this issue, and we hope that you will, notice an interesting point about *your own* thinking: It probably is not *linear* (moving in a straight line from A to B to C) but *recursive*, moving from A to C, back to B, or starting over at C and then back to A and B. By zigging and zagging almost despite yourself, you'll get to a conclusion that may finally seem correct. In retrospect it seems obvious; *now* you can chart a nice line from A to B to C—but that was not at all evident to you at the start.

A CHECKLIST FOR CRITICAL THINKING

Attitudes

✓ Does my thinking show imaginative open-mindedness and intellectual curiosity?

　✓ Am I willing to examine my assumptions?

　✓ Am I willing to entertain new ideas—both those that I encounter while reading and those that come to mind while writing?

✓ Am I willing to exert myself, for instance to do research in order to acquire information and to evaluate evidence?

Skills

✓ Can I summarize an argument accurately?

✓ Can I evaluate assumptions, evidence, and inferences?

✓ Can I present my ideas effectively—for instance by organizing and by writing in a manner appropriate to my imagined audience?

EXAMINING ASSUMPTIONS

In Chapter 3 we will discuss **assumptions** (normally, unexamined beliefs) in some detail, but here we want to emphasize the importance of *examining* assumptions, both those that you encounter when you read and those that underlie your own essays.

Let's think a bit further about the West Virginia driver's license law. What assumptions did the legislature make in enacting this statute? We earlier mentioned one such assumption: If the law helped to keep teenagers from dropping out of school, then that was a good thing for them and for society in general. Perhaps the legislature made this assumption *explicit* and its advocates defended it on this ground. Perhaps not; maybe the legislature just took this point for granted, leaving this assumption *implicit* (or *tacit*) and unargued, believing that everyone *shared* the assumption. But of course everyone didn't share it, in particular many teenagers who wanted to drop out of school at sixteen and get their driver's license immediately.

Consider, for instance, a newspaper article concerning antisocial activities on campus, ranging from boisterous behavior (including, say, the shouting of racial epithets) to vandalism, theft, and physical violence (perhaps stimulated by excessive drinking), including rape. Until thirty or so years ago, many colleges assumed that they stood *in loco parentis*, "in the place of a parent." What did this mean? Parents would be unlikely to turn over to the police a youngster who struck a sibling or who dipped into a family cookie jar that contained loose change but rather would handle the matter within the family; in similar manner, college administrators would seek to educate offenders, perhaps by reprimands, perhaps by probation or suspension, or in the most severe cases, by expulsion. But the assumption that colleges ought to engage in this sort of quasi-judicial activity when students are alleged to break the law on campus can be questioned. Should colleges be in the business of judging crimes? Or should they let the courts take care of the offenders?

On May 5 and May 6, 1996, the *New York Times* ran a two-part story on the topic of campus discipline. Newspaper stories of this sort are supposed to report the facts, but inevitably they stimulate responses; people want to offer their views on what they have been reading. They may want to argue that the newspaper report was inaccurate, or accurate so far as it went but missed the big issue, or—and here is our point—that it is not enough to report such things, "Something must be done!" One reader of the *Times* story was John Silber, who at that time was president of Boston University. He wrote the following Op-Ed piece (an essay of opinion, printed opposite the editorial page).

As your read Silber's piece, note his assumptions. Does he make any assumptions that you do not share? If so, what are they?

John Silber

Students Should Not Be above the Law

In medieval Europe, there were two parallel court systems: the church's and the king's. The big difference between them was that the church courts did not resort to capital punishment.

In an age when all felonies were capital crimes, the church court was, from the defendants' point of view, considerably more attractive.

Although in theory these courts were limited to clergymen, in practice one proved clerical status by being able to read. And this skill was indulgently tested. One had to read a verse of one's own choosing from the Bible. Hence, the foresighted felon memorized his verse. It assured him of what was known as "benefit of clergy."

This system now seems quaint. But today colleges and universities increasingly tend to circumvent the courts and bury serious criminal cases in their own judicial systems. For instance, a young man at Miami University in Oxford, Ohio, is being allowed to graduate this year even though he was put on "student conduct probation" after he was accused of sexually assaulting an eighteen-year-old freshman who was sleeping.

Colleges have a right to establish judicial codes to assure civility in   5
the classroom, on the campus, and in residences. But the administration of these codes should not give criminals sanctuary from the law.

Yet in many cases administrators successfully press students not to bring criminal behavior to the attention of the police and instead use campus disciplinary proceedings to judge charges of rape, arson, and assault.

No campus court can impose a fine or imprison anyone for a single day. The most serious sanction is expulsion. The penalty for criminal assault is often not much worse than being tossed out of a club.

College judicial systems were originally intended to deal with infractions that were neither felonies nor misdemeanors, perhaps not even torts. And most disciplinary proceedings don't have the basics required for a fair trial: a professional and independent judiciary, enforceable rules of procedure, effective and fairly applied sanctions.

But this is not the most serious problem. Once again, students are receiving special treatment. This treatment was the great scandal of the Vietnam War: The ability to gain entry to and finance college provided a "benefit of clergy" to middle-class young adults who avoided the draft.

Many administrators recoil from the idea that they should oper-   10
ate a collegiate criminal justice system. One can understand why. Outside of law school faculties, few academics have an interest in prosecution.

There is, of course, a simple way for administrators to avoid this entanglement. They can refer all criminal cases to the real criminal justice system. This is their obligation, not merely as administrators but as citizens. (Indeed, there is a name for a citizen who becomes aware of a crime and does not report it: an accessory after the fact.)

Students, predictably, don't like this idea. But in my twenty-five years as a college president, I have heard again and again that students wish to be treated as adults. But I have also heard their repeated demands that they be exempted from the laws of Boston, of Massachusetts, and of the United States.

These two demands are contradictory. Legally, college students are adults. There is, of course, a difference between legal adulthood and substantive adulthood. Some people achieve substantive adulthood at twelve; others never do. But except for the anomaly of the drinking age, everyone can claim legal adulthood at eighteen. And that includes the obligation to be held accountable for criminal behavior—not in juvenile courts or in the even more lenient courts of the academy but in the adult courts.

When colleges and universities usurp the role of the courts, they deny justice to victims. But they also do a terrible wrong to perpetrators, for they deny them entrance into the adult world of responsible action. And in this they fail utterly as educators.

Silber opens his essay by informing the reader about the medieval system of criminal justice, which exempted clerics from the risk of punishments handed out by the criminal courts. By the fourth paragraph we can see the point of this opening; it was to draw a parallel between the assumed unfairness of that medieval practice and (what Silber regards as) the unfair student disciplinary procedures in use by our colleges and universities. Thus, Silber in effect opens his essay on the basis of this crucial assumption:

> It was unfair to give advantages in medieval times to clerics when accused of crimes, and it is no less unfair to give advantages to college students today when they are accused of crimes.

Silber does not argue for this proposition; he does not even assert it explicitly. But he presupposes it as the launching pad for his criticism of today's college disciplinary practices.

In a similar manner, Silber closes his essay with another important assumption:

> College students who are legally adults (eighteen or over) ought to be given the same treatment when accused of crimes as other adults are.

Obviously, college faculty and administrators charged with the responsibility to cope with student misbehavior on campus do not accept this assumption; if they did, the problem that agitates Silber would never have arisen in the first place.

In other places he makes assumptions of no great importance, for instance this one in paragraph 10:

> Law school faculties have an interest in prosecution.

Whether or not this proposition is true makes little difference to Silber's overall argument; its role is the minor one of reinforcing Silber's claim (no doubt true) that college and university faculty and administrators are typically very uncomfortable when it comes to disciplinary sanctions for students guilty of serious wrongdoing.

In paragraph 8, Silber draws a contrast between the rough-and-ready disciplinary practices on campus and the strict by-the-rules procedures of the criminal courts. This position might stimulate the reader to wonder whether Silber assumes the following:

> College disciplinary practices would be much better if they incorporated the basic procedures that the criminal law requires for a fair trial.

However, by the time the reader reaches paragraph 11 (if not before) it becomes clear that Silber has no interest in this alternative; instead, this is what he assumes:

> There are only two alternatives: Either college authorities continue down the current unfair path, or they wash their hands of any attempt to deal with students accused of criminal behavior by turning them over to the mercies of the criminal courts.

The third alternative, of tightening up college disciplinary procedures, is never considered.

In other cases it is not entirely clear just what Silber assumes. He obviously assumes the following:

> College disciplinary practices usurp the role of the courts in the criminal justice system.

But does he also assume that this usurpation occurs only occasionally, or does he think that it happens quite often? Silber gives no statistical data to qualify his assumption, and so his readers are left uncertain whether they are worrying about a major problem affecting hundreds of college students every year, or whether Silber is riled up over events of no great frequency.

Do you agree with Silber's assertions

- that it is wrong (para. 6) for college officials in some circumstances to "press students not to bring criminal behavior to the attention of the police and instead use campus disciplinary proceedings to judge charges of rape, arson, and assault"?

- that administrators have an "obligation" (para. 11) to "refer all criminal cases to the real criminal justice system," and that their failure to do so makes them "an accessory after the fact"?

- that (para. 14) "When colleges and universities usurp the role of the courts, . . . they also do a terrible wrong to perpetrators, for they deny them entrance into the adult world of responsible action"?

You may agree or disagree, in whole or in part, with Silber's argument, but it is important to realize that he makes certain assumptions and to think about their implications. For instance, if you agree that administrators who fail to report actions that may later prove to be criminal behavior are "accessories after the fact" (persons who screen or assist felons), are you willing to concede that campus rape crisis centers and other counseling activities may find it impossible to function?

Consider, too, if assumptions allegedly founded on facts are indeed based on facts. Thus, Silber asserts in paragraph 6 that "in many cases administrators successfully press students not to bring criminal behavior to the attention of the police." "Many cases" indicates that he assumes the practice is widespread. If this assumption were questioned, and Silber offered as evidence solely his long experience as a college administrator, would you think that you had to accept the assumption? On the other hand, could you just brush off his assumption as merely the view of one person?

An Op-Ed piece such as Silber's is likely to set readers thinking—not merely thinking about direct replies or refutations but about related issues. For instance, it might stimulate a reader to respond with a letter to the editor, suggesting that college faculty and administrators have a duty to assist young people in understanding what it means to act responsibly, and this duty is not effectively fulfilled by handing them over to the police in borderline cases. Another letter-writer might argue that alcohol is the chief cause of most fraternity-related violence and crime, and colleges need to do more to educate students about drinking. Still another might argue that the real problem is that the *accused* may not get justice because college judicial boards are not restricted to the rules of evidence used by lawyers and judges in court.

One letter-writer was moved by Silber's essay to write about an aspect of the issue that she thought was important and that he had neglected. We reprint this letter here.

Judith H. Christie
What about the Faculty?

To the Editor:

Conspicuously absent from John Silber's argument that colleges not "usurp the role of courts" in dealing with student criminal behavior (Op-Ed, May 9) is any criticism of the manner in which college administrators routinely deal with student complaints of faculty misconduct.

With few exceptions, it has long been the practice of colleges to ignore female students' charges of sexual harassment by male faculty members or to deal with such accusations behind closed doors.

In the rare instances where faculty members are dismissed for sexual harassment, their records do not reflect the reason; that these teachers are free to seek positions at other institutions keeps academia's "dirty little secret" secret.

Faculty members, like students, should be held accountable for their behavior; they, too, are adults and have long enjoyed the "benefit of clergy" exemption Mr. Silber rightly deplores.

- Do you agree that Silber does not raise the point Christie makes?
- Do you think that Christie makes a good point?
- If you do agree that he does not raise her point and that her point is a good one, do you think the omission is a weakness in Silber's essay? Why, or why not?

A CHECKLIST FOR EXAMINING ASSUMPTIONS

✓ What assumptions does the writer's argument presuppose?

✓ Are these assumptions explicit or implicit?

✓ Are these assumptions important to the author's argument, or only incidental?

✓ Does the author give any evidence of being aware of the hidden assumptions in her or his argument?

✓ Would a critic be likely to share these assumptions, or are they exactly what a critic would challenge?

✓ What sort of evidence would be relevant to supporting or rejecting these assumptions?

✓ Are you willing to grant the author's assumptions?
   ✓ If not, why not?

Remember, also, to ask these questions (except the last two) when you are reading your own drafts. And remember to ask yourself why some people may *not* grant *your* assumptions.

A CASEBOOK ON EXAMINING ASSUMPTIONS: Should Divorce Be More Difficult?

Now let's turn to a second issue that is very much in the newspapers because it is very much a part of daily life: divorce. The United States has the world's highest divorce rate, and statisticians estimate that about half of today's marriages will end in divorce. It was not always so. Divorce was fairly unusual in the days when individuals seeking divorce were required to demonstrate the spouse's legally defined intolerable behavior, usually adultery, cruelty, or desertion. But in the 1960s "no-fault" divorce became popular, and today no state requires as a condition of granting a divorce that one party be guilty of a serious fault. It is enough for either party to allege "incompatibility."

No-fault divorce was hailed, perhaps especially by women, as a step forward, but recently it has come under attack. Some feminists argue that high-income husbands can now easily walk away from marriage, impoverishing their wives; some conservatives argue that no-fault divorce is immoral. It has especially come under attack when the couple has a dependent child. For instance, in her book, *It Takes a Village*, Hillary Rodham Clinton says she feels "ambivalent [about divorce] when children are involved." Her worry here is that divorce has a bad effect on children, and one sometimes hears of statistical studies that compare the well-being of children in two-parent families with the well-being of children brought up by one divorced parent. (Incidentally, does this sound like a valid comparison? Or should the comparison be between children of divorced parents and children of parents who, though deeply hostile to each other, for one reason or another remain married?) Some twenty state legislatures are considering proposals to repeal no-fault divorce in cases involving children, and there is now much talk about ways of reducing the divorce rate. We provide a tiny sample of such talk. Before you read any of these writings, however, you may want to find out where you stand on the following issues:

- Should it be harder than it is to get a divorce? In particular, should one party have to demonstrate that the other party is seriously at fault (for example, desertion, physical abuse)? If no fault is alleged, should there be a waiting period, and, if so, how long?

- Should it be harder than it is for couples with dependent children to get a divorce?

- Should there be a two-category system, one for couples without children and one for couples with children?

- In divorces where there are children, is the solution not to tighten the divorce law but to tighten child support laws?

- Should people be required to take a marriage education course before they can get a marriage license?

- Should the Louisiana law of 1997, allowing couples to choose between a no-fault marriage and a "covenant marriage," be enacted by other states? In a covenant marriage, the two participants agree to try to resolve disputes through counseling and to seek divorce only after a mutually agreed-on two-year separation, except for specified circumstances such as adultery, abuse, and imprisonment for a felony.

We begin with an unsigned editorial in the *New York Times*, February 15, 1996, and we follow it with some of the responses printed in subsequent issues.

The *New York Times*
The Divorce Debate

Led by conservative Christian groups, a new movement is afoot to toughen state divorce laws. Its main target is the "no-fault" divorce statutes adopted by every state over the last twenty-five years to make divorces easier, quicker, and less freighted with destructive recrimination.

There are powerful reasons to be alarmed about the impact of family breakups on children, and about the high incidence of poverty in single-parent households. But rolling back the clock to make the legal process of divorce more expensive and acrimonious is not a useful answer.

Supporters of tougher divorce laws complain that the current rules encourage a casual attitude toward the dissolution of marriage. But few people who have lived through a no-fault divorce, especially those with children, would say they took the step lightly.

Even though divorces have jumped about 30 percent in the last twenty-five years, blaming the new laws for a long-term upward trend confuses cause and effect. No-fault divorce was a response to changes already taking place in the family system.

Under the no-fault approach, a divorce is granted even if only one 5
spouse wants it. By contrast, a bill just introduced in the Michigan Legislature would deny a divorce when one spouse opposes it unless the
plaintiff could show that a spouse had been physically or mentally abusive, had a problem with alcohol or drugs, had committed adultery, had
deserted the home, or had been sentenced to prison.

The idea is to try to force couples to stay together. But a more likely
consequence would be a return to the perjuries, fabrications, and other
devices required to obtain divorces before no-fault. That would mean yet
more pain for children, as parents slug it out in a prolonged legal blame-
game, wasting scarce family resources in the process.

Another consequence would be to discourage couples from getting
married in the first place—thereby aggravating the already staggering
problem of unwed motherhood and the resulting social and financial
vulnerability of women and children.

The nation should be concentrating on ways to reduce the economic
stresses that experts say contribute both to the high divorce rate and to
the rising number of children born to unmarried couples. Absent fathers
should be required to live up to their child support obligations. But making it more difficult for people to escape a broken marriage seems cruel
and counterproductive.

The first response printed here, an Op-Ed piece by Maggie Gallagher,
does not directly address itself point by point to the preceding editorial,
but clearly it represents an opposing view. Gallagher, a scholar at the Institute for American Values, is the author of *The Abolition of Marriage:
How We Destroy Lasting Love* (1996).

Maggie Gallagher

Why Make Divorce Easy?

For all practical purposes, the debate is over. Almost all Americans
now agree that divorce is harmful to children. Now the question becomes: What, if anything, can we do about the fact that at least half of
our marriages fail?

Get rid of no-fault divorce, say some state legislators in Michigan,
one of several states with an active campaign to reform divorce laws.

Call it a delayed backlash. Unlike some European countries, which impose five-to-seven-year waits for contested no-fault divorces, Americans
in the late '60s and '70s opted for speedy spouse disposal. Almost every
state adopted some version of no-fault divorce, either by eliminating the
need to find marital wrongdoing or by speeding up the divorce process.

In short, no-fault divorce (or more accurately "unilateral divorce") allows one partner to dissolve a marriage at any time, for any reason, or for no reason at all.

No-fault was supposed to remake divorce into a kinder, gentler insti-   5
tution. It hasn't worked out that way. Under no-fault, divorces today are no less angry. In her book *Second Chances*, Judith Wallerstein found that about half of all the couples she studied were still locked in bitter conflict five years after divorcing.

Thanks to no-fault, divorces have also become more common. Between the late '60s and mid-'70s, the likelihood that a couple would divorce in the first five years of marriage jumped by one-third. A recent study in the *Journal of Marriage and the Family* suggests that no-fault pushed up the divorce rate anywhere from 15 to 25 percent.

Supporters of no-fault divorce argue that it strengthens marriage because couples can leave bad marriages and make better ones. But, as the University of Texas demographer Norval Glenn has pointed out, surveys suggest that the opposite has happened. After twenty-five years of no-fault, there are as many unhappy marriages as ever, and far fewer happy ones.

That no-fault divorce has led to a surge in the divorce rate should come as no surprise to anyone who has ever been married. Even the best marriages go through bleak times.

What would happen if courts treated business contracts as they now treat the marriage contract? What if our courts refused to enforce contracts and instead systematically favored the party that wished to withdraw, on the grounds that finding fault was messy, irrelevant, and acrimonious? Under such circumstances, the economy might collapse.

Imposing a five-to-seven-year waiting period for contested no-fault   10
divorces could raise the number of marriages that ultimately succeed while insuring that those who want a quick and easy divorce negotiate with their partners in order to get it.

Law is more than a system of punishments, as Mary Ann Glendon, a Harvard law professor, has pointed out. It is also one way we pass values from one generation to the next. Our divorce laws define what the marriage commitment is.

The purpose of making divorce more difficult is not to torment a couple into staying together but to give weight to the original contract, to put the law on the side of those who say: Wait, think, reconsider. Something of inestimable value—a commitment to love and care for another human being—is about to be lost. Is there really no way the marriage can be saved?

At this point you may want to take a sheet of paper, draw a vertical line down the middle, reread "The Divorce Debate," and in one column jot down a list of the chief points made by the editorial writer. Then reread Gallagher's essay and in the other column jot down her chief points; where she seems to be responding to a point in "The Divorce Debate," put your entry for Gallagher on the same line.

Do you find any shared assumptions? (By the way, one shared assumption of almost all people who publicly discuss the issue, whether they recommend easing or tightening the divorce laws, is that marriage is a good thing. Almost no one who writes on the subject suggests that marriage ought to be done away with.)

Here are four letters that were published in the *New York Times* in the days immediately following the editorial and the Op-Ed piece.

Letters from Patrick G. D. Riley, Lois M. Brenner, Allison Lassieur, and Rebecca Sawyer-Fay

To the Editor:

Re "The Divorce Debate" (editorial, Feb. 15): Nowhere do you mention the constitutional prohibition of laws "impairing the obligation of contracts," found in Article 1, Section 10.

Marriage, in the form recognized throughout the United States, can scarcely be construed as less than a contract binding both parties equally. The Supreme Court has touched on this matter more than once.

In *Dartmouth College v. Woodward,* famously argued by Daniel Webster, Chief Justice John Marshall observed: "When any state legislature shall pass an act annulling all marriage contracts, or allowing either party to annul it, without the consent of the other, it will be time enough to inquire whether such an act be constitutional."

According to the California Court of Appeals, that time arrived in 1888 when the Supreme Court opined that marriage is not a contract. Why not? Because, said the Court in *Maynard v. Hill,* marriage is "more than a contract." The logic of this has raised many an eyebrow.

The Supreme Court refused to revisit the question in 1992 when ⁵ James Sutherland, whose wife had won a divorce under California's no-fault divorce law, appealed the state court's ruling.

At present, marriage stands as the only contract that one party can nullify without evidence of breach by the other party. What makes this deplorable in the eyes of many is that marriage is sacred, as the state seems to grant when it recognizes the validity of religious marriage.

Patrick G. D. Riley
Wauwatosa, Wis., Feb. 15, 1996

To the Editor:

Re "The Divorce Debate" (editorial, Feb. 15): No-fault has indeed eliminated "perjuries" and "fabrications" in establishing grounds but has failed to dismantle the rest of the divorce meat grinder.

Divorce is more painful, protracted, and costly than ever. Until we make the process more humane, its laws will be vulnerable to "rolling back the clock."

Lois M. Brenner
New York, Feb. 16, 1996
The writer is a matrimonial lawyer.

To the Editor:

Re your Feb. 12 news article on the move to repeal no-fault divorce laws: The problem isn't that divorce is too easy. It's that marriage is.

Anyone, anywhere, for any reason can get married. In some states all that is needed is a justice of the peace and a few dollars. Some states don't even require blood tests.

What if getting married required a more stringent process? If couples had to work for the right to say "I do," more marriages might stay together.

Mandatory counseling that focused on goals would be a start. Required classes on money management and child care, checkups by a physician, counseling on sexual issues, and mandatory prenuptial agreements could help weed out those unions that may be happening for the wrong reasons.

Reinstituting fault divorce won't stop abuse or infidelity. What it will do is force people to drag each other through litigation to end something that should not have begun in the first place.

Allison Lassieur
Damascus, Pa., Feb. 15, 1996

To the Editor:

While not a scholar like Maggie Gallagher (Op-Ed, Feb. 20), I can tell you this: No five-year waiting period or law of any kind would have prevented my husband and me from leaving our former miserable marriages. What a harsher divorce law would have done is render our son illegitimate. When will our leaders stop legislating morality and let us live our lives as best we can?

Rebecca Sawyer-Fay
Hallowell, Me.

You may now want to go back to pages 15–16 and reread (and rethink) your responses to the questions that we asked concerning divorce laws. Has anything said in this six-way conversation caused you to change your mind, at least a little bit? If not, why not? (Religious principles? Experience as the child of divorced parents, or as a divorced person?)

Exercises

1. Think further about the West Virginia law, jotting down pros and cons, and then write a balanced dialogue between two imagined speakers who hold opposing views on the merits of the law. You'll doubtless have to revise your dialogue several times, and in revising your drafts you will find that further ideas come to you. Present *both* sides as strongly as possible. (You may want to give the two speakers distinct characters; for instance, one may be a student who has dropped out and the other a concerned teacher, or one a parent—who perhaps argues that he or she needs the youngster to work full-time driving a delivery truck—and one a legislator. But do not feel that the speakers must present the arguments they might be expected to hold. A student might argue *for* the law, and a teacher *against* it.)

2. With newspaper readers in mind, write (but don't mail) a letter of about 250 words (one double-spaced typed page) setting forth your response to at least one aspect of the arguments concerning divorce. You may want to provide additional evidence to support an argument, or provide counterevidence, or introduce an entirely new issue.

3. Take one of the following topics, and jot down all the pro and con arguments you can think of in, say, ten minutes. Then, at least an hour or two later, return to your jottings and see whether you can add to them. Finally, as in Exercise 1, write a balanced dialogue, presenting each idea as strongly as possible. (If none of these topics interests you, talk with your instructor about the possibility of choosing a topic of your own.) Suggested topics:

    a. Colleges should not award athletic scholarships.
    b. Bicyclists and motorcyclists should be required by law to wear helmets.
    c. High school teachers should have the right to search students for drugs on school grounds.
    d. Smoking should be prohibited in all parts of all college buildings.
    e. College administrators should take no punitive action against students who use racist language or language that offends any minority.
    f. Students should have the right to drop out of school at any age.
    g. In rape trials the names of the alleged victims should not be released to the public.

2

Critical Reading: Getting Started

Some books are to be tasted, others to be chewed, and some few to be chewed and digested. — FRANCIS BACON

ACTIVE READING

In the passage that we quote at the top of the page, Bacon makes at least two good points. One is that books are of varying worth; the second is that a taste of some books may be enough.

But even a book (or an essay) that you will chew and digest is one that you first may want to taste. How can you get a taste — that is, how can you get some sense of a piece of writing *before* you sit down to read it carefully?

Previewing

Even before you read the work you may have some ideas about it, perhaps because you already know something about the **author.** You know, for example, that a work by Martin Luther King, Jr., will probably deal with civil rights. You know, too, that it will be serious and eloquent. On the other hand, if you pick up an essay by Woody Allen you will probably expect it to be amusing. It may be serious — Allen has written earnestly about many topics, especially those concerned with the media — but it's your hunch that the essay will be at least somewhat entertaining and it probably will not be terribly difficult. In short, a reader who has some knowledge of the author probably has some idea of what the writing will be like, and so the reader reads it in a certain mood. Admittedly, most of the authors represented in this book are not widely known, but we give biographical notes that may provide you with some sense of what to expect.

The **place of publication** may also tell you something about the essay. For instance, *The National Review* (formerly edited by William F.

Buckley, Jr.) is a conservative journal. If you notice that an essay on affirmative action was published in *The National Review,* you are probably safe in tentatively assuming that the essay will not endorse affirmative action. On the other hand, *Ms.* is a liberal magazine for women, and an essay on affirmative action published in *Ms.* will probably be an endorsement.

The **title** of an essay, too, may give you an idea of what to expect. Of course a title may announce only the subject and not the author's thesis or point of view ("On Gun Control," "Should Drugs Be Legal?"), but fairly often it will indicate the thesis too, as in "Give Children the Vote" and "Gay Marriages: Make Them Legal." Knowing more or less what to expect, you can probably take in some of the major points even on a quick reading.

Skimming: Finding the Thesis

Although most of the material in this book is too closely argued to be fully understood by merely skimming, still, skimming can tell you a good deal. Read the first paragraph of an essay carefully, because it may announce the author's **thesis** (chief point, major claim), and it may give you some sense of how the argument for that thesis will be conducted. (What we call the thesis can also be called the main idea, or the point, or even the argument, but in this book we use *argument* to refer not only to the thesis statement but also to the entire development of the thesis in the essay.) Run your eye over the rest, looking for key expressions that indicate the author's conclusions, such as "It follows, then, that. . . ." Passages of this sort often occur as the first or last sentence in a paragraph. And of course pay attention to any headings within the text. Finally, pay special attention to the last paragraph because it probably will offer a summary and a brief restatement of the writer's thesis.

Having skimmed the work, you probably know the author's thesis, and you may detect the author's methods—for instance, whether the author supports the thesis chiefly by personal experience, or by statistics, or by ridicule of the opposition. You also have a clear idea of the length and some idea of the difficulty of the piece. You know, then, whether you can read it carefully now, before dinner, or whether you had better put off a careful reading until you have more time.

Reading with a Pencil: Underlining, Highlighting, Annotating

Once you have a general idea of the work—not only an idea of its topic and thesis but also a sense of the way in which the thesis is argued—you can then go back and start reading it carefully.

As you read, **underline** or **highlight** key passages and make **annotations** in the margins (but not in library books, please). Because you are reading actively, or interacting with the text, you will not simply let your eye rove across the page. You will underline or highlight what seem to be the chief points, so that later when you review the essay you can easily locate the main passages. But don't overdo a good thing. If you find yourself underlining or highlighting most of a page, you are probably not thinking carefully enough about what the key points are. Similarly, your marginal annotations should be brief and selective. Probably they will consist of hints or clues, things like "really?," "doesn't follow," "!!!," "???," "good," "compare with Jones," and "check this." In short, in a paragraph you might underline or highlight a key definition, and in the margin you might write "good" or, on the other hand, "?," if you think the definition is fuzzy or wrong. You are interacting with the text, and laying the groundwork for eventually writing your own essay on what you have read.

What you annotate will depend largely on your **purpose.** If you are reading an essay in order to see the ways in which the writer organizes an argument, you will annotate one sort of thing. If you are reading in order to challenge the thesis, you will annotate other things. Here is a passage from an essay entitled "On Racist Speech," with a student's rather skeptical, even aggressive annotations. But notice that at least one of the annotations — "Definition of 'fighting words'" — apparently was made chiefly in order to remind the reader of where an important term appears in the essay. The essay, printed in full on page 39, is by Charles R. Lawrence III, a professor of law at Stanford University. It originally appeared in *The Chronicle of Higher Education* (October 25, 1989), a publication read chiefly by college and university faculty members and administrators.

example of such a policy?

University officials who have formulated policies to respond to incidents of racial harassment have been characterized in the press as "thought police," but such policies generally do nothing more than impose sanctions against intentional face-to-face insults. When racist speech takes the form of face-to-face insults, catcalls, or other assaultive speech aimed at an individual or small group of persons, it falls directly within the "fighting words" exception to First Amendment protection. The Supreme Court has held that words which "by their very utterance inflict injury" or tend to incite an immediate breach of the peace" are not protected by the First Amendment.

?

example?

What about sexist speech?

Definition of "fighting words"

If the purpose of the First Amendment is to foster the greatest amount of speech, racial insults disserve that purpose. Assaultive racist speech functions as a preemptive strike. The invective is experienced as a blow, not as a proffered idea, and once the blow is struck, it is unlikely that a dialogue will follow. Racial insults are particularly undeserving of First Amendment protection because the perpetrator's intention is not to discover truth or initiate dialogue but to injure the victim. In most situations, members of minority groups realize that they are likely to lose if they respond to epithets by fighting and are forced to remain silent and submissive.

Why must speech always seek "to discover truth"?

Really? Probably depends on the individual.

How does he know?

This, Therefore That

In order to arrive at a coherent thought, or a coherent series of thoughts that will lead to a reasonable conclusion, a writer has to go through a good deal of preliminary effort; and if the writer is to convince the reader that the conclusion is sound, the reasoning that led to the conclusion must be set forth in detail, with a good deal of "This, therefore that," and "If this, then that." The arguments in this book require more comment than President Calvin Coolidge provided when his wife, who hadn't been able to go to church on a Sunday, asked him what the preacher's sermon was about. "Sin," he said. His wife persisted: "What did the preacher say about it?" Coolidge's response: "He was against it."

But, again, when we say that most of the arguments in this book are presented at length and require careful reading, we do not mean that they are obscure; we mean, rather, that the reader has to take the sentences one by one. And speaking of one by one, we are reminded of an episode in Lewis Carroll's *Through the Looking-Glass:*

> "Can you do Addition?" the White Queen asked. "What's one and one and one and one and one and one and one and one and one and one?"
> "I don't know," said Alice. "I lost count."
> "She can't do Addition," the Red Queen said.

It's easy enough to add one and one and one and so on, and Alice can, of course, do addition, but not at the pace that the White Queen sets. Fortunately, you can set your own pace in reading the cumulative thinking set forth in the essays we reprint. Skimming won't work, but slow reading—and thinking about what you are reading—will.

When you first pick up an essay, you may indeed want to skim it, for some of the reasons mentioned on page 23, but sooner or later you have to settle down to read it, and to think about it. The effort will be worthwhile. John Locke, the seventeenth-century English philosopher, said,

> *Reading* furnishes the mind with materials of knowledge; it is *thinking* [that] makes what we read ours. We are of the ruminating kind, and it is not enough to cram ourselves with a great load of collections; unless we chew them over again they will not give us strength and nourishment.

First, Second, and Third Thoughts

Suppose you are reading an argument about pornographic pictures. For the present purpose, it doesn't matter whether the argument favors or opposes censorship. As you read the argument, ask yourself whether "pornography" has been adequately defined. Has the writer taken the trouble to make sure that the reader and the writer are thinking about the same thing? If not, the very topic under discussion has not been adequately fixed, and therefore further debate over the issue may well be so unclear as to be futile. How, then, ought a topic such as this be fixed for effective critical thinking?

It goes without saying that pornography can't be defined simply as pictures of nude figures, or even of nude figures copulating, for such a definition would include not only photographs taken for medical, sociological, and scientific purposes but also some of the world's great art. Nobody seriously thinks pornography includes such things.

Is it enough, then, to say that pornography "stirs lustful thoughts" or "appeals to prurient interests"? No, because pictures of shoes probably stir lustful thoughts in shoe fetishists, and pictures of children in ads for underwear probably stir lustful thoughts in pedophiles. Perhaps, then, the definition must be amended to "material that stirs lustful thoughts in the average person." But will this restatement do? First, it may be hard to agree on the characteristics of "the average person." True, in other matters the law often assumes that there is such a creature as "the reasonable person," and most people would agree that in a given situation, there might be a reasonable response—for almost everyone. But we cannot be so sure that the same is true about the emotional responses of this "average person." In any case, far from stimulating sexual impulses, sadomasochistic pictures of booted men wielding whips on naked women probably turn off "the average person," yet this is the sort of material that most people would agree is pornographic.

Something must be wrong, then, with the definition that pornography is material that "stirs lustful thoughts in the average person." We began with a definition that was too broad ("pictures of nude figures"), but now we have a definition that is too narrow. We must go back to the drawing board. This is not nitpicking. The label "average person" was found to be inadequate in a pornography case argued before the Supreme Court; because the materials in question were aimed at a homosexual audience, it was agreed that the average person would not find them sexually stimulating.

One difficulty has been that pornography is often defined according to its effect on the viewer ("genital commotion," Father Harold Gardiner, S.J., called it, in *Catholic Viewpoint on Censorship*), but different people, we know, may respond differently. In the first half of the twentieth century, in an effort to distinguish between pornography and art—after all, most people don't want to regard Botticelli's *Venus* or Michelangelo's *David* as "dirty"—it was commonly said that a true work of art does not stimulate in the spectator ideas or desires that the real object might stimulate. But in 1956 Kenneth Clark, probably the most influential English-speaking art critic of our century, changed all that; in a book called *The Nude* he announced that "no nude, however abstract, should fail to arouse in the spectator some vestige of erotic feeling."

SUMMARIZING

Perhaps the best thing to do with a fairly difficult essay is, after a first reading, to reread it and simultaneously to take notes on a sheet of paper, perhaps summarizing each paragraph in a sentence or two. Writing a summary will help you

- to understand the contents, and
- to see the strengths and weaknesses of the piece.

Don't confuse a summary with a paraphrase; a **paraphrase** is a word-by-word or phrase-by-phrase rewording of a text, a sort of translation of the author's language into your own. A paraphrase is therefore as long as the original, or even longer; a **summary** is much shorter. Paraphrasing can be useful in helping you to grasp difficult passages; summarizing is useful in helping you to get the gist of the entire essay. (Caution: Do *not* incorporate a summary or a paraphrase into your own essay without acknowledging your source and stating that you are summarizing or paraphrasing.)

Summarizing each paragraph, or each group of closely related paragraphs, will help you to follow the thread of the discourse, and, when you are finished, will provide you with a useful map of the essay. Then, when you reread the essay yet again, you may want to underline passages that you now understand are the author's key ideas—for instance, definitions, generalizations, summaries—and you may want to jot notes in the margins, questioning the logic, or expressing your uncertainty, or calling attention to other writers who see the matter differently.

Here is a paragraph from a 1973 decision of the U.S. Supreme Court, written by Chief Justice Warren Burger, setting forth reasons why the government may censor obscene material. We follow it with a sample summary.

> If we accept the unprovable assumption that a complete education requires the reading of certain books, and the well-nigh universal belief that good books, plays, and art lift the spirit, improve the mind, enrich the human personality, and develop character, can we then say that a state legislature may not act on the corollary assumption that commerce in obscene books, or public exhibitions focused on obscene conduct, have a tendency to exert a corrupting and debasing impact leading to antisocial behavior? The sum of experience, including that of the past two decades, affords an ample basis for legislatures to conclude that a sensitive, key relationship of human existence, central to family life, community welfare, and the development of human personality, can be debased and distorted by crass commercial exploitation of sex. Nothing in the Constitution prohibits a State from reaching such a conclusion and acting on it legislatively simply because there is no conclusive empirical data.

Now for a student's summary. Notice that the summary does *not* include the reader's evaluation or any other sort of comment on the original; it is simply an attempt to condense the original. Notice too that, because its purpose is merely to assist the reader to grasp the ideas of the original by focusing on them, it is written in a sort of shorthand (not every sentence is a complete sentence), though of course if this summary were being presented in an essay it would have to be grammatical.

> Unprovable but acceptable assumption that good books etc. shape character, so that legislature can assume obscene works debase character. Experience lets one conclude that exploitation of sex debases the individual, family, and community. Though no conclusive evidence for this view, Constitution lets states act on it legislatively.

The first sentence of the original, some eighty words, is reduced in the summary to eighteen words. Of course the summary loses much of the detail and flavor of the original: "Good books etc." is not the same as "good books, plays, and art"; and "shape character" is not the same as "lift the spirit, improve the mind, enrich the human personality, and develop character." But the statement in the summary will do as a rough approximation, useful for a quick review. More important, of course, the act of writing a summary forces the reader to go slowly and to think about each sentence of the original. Such thinking may help the reader-writer to see the complexity—or the hollowness—of the original.

The sample summary in the preceding paragraph was just that, a summary; but when writing your summaries, it is often useful to inject your own thoughts ("seems far-fetched," "strong point," "I don't get it"), enclosing them within square brackets, [ ], or in some other way keeping these responses distinct from your summary of the writer's argument. Remember, however, that if your instructor asks you to hand in a summary, it should not contain ideas other than those found in the original piece. You can rearrange these, add transitions as needed, and so forth, but the summary should give the reader nothing but a sense of the original piece.

We don't want to nag you, but we do want to emphasize the need to read with a pencil in hand. If you read slowly and take notes, you will find that what you read will give you the strength and nourishment that Locke spoke of.

Having insisted that although skimming is a useful early step and that the essays in this book need to be read slowly because the writers build one reason upon another, we will now seem to contradict ourselves by presenting an essay that can *almost* be skimmed. Susan Jacoby's essay originally appeared in the *New York Times,* a thoroughly respectable newspaper but not one that requires its readers to linger over every sentence. Still, compared with most of the news accounts, Jacoby's essay requires close reading. When you read the essay you will notice that it zigs and zags, not because Jacoby is careless or wants to befuddle her readers but because she wants to build a strong case to support her point of view, and she must therefore look at some widely held views that she does *not* accept; she must set these forth, and must then give her reasons for rejecting them.

Susan Jacoby

Susan Jacoby (b. 1946), a journalist since the age of seventeen, is well known for her feminist writings. "A First Amendment Junkie" (our title) appeared in a "Hers" column in the New York Times *in 1978.*

A First Amendment Junkie

It is no news that many women are defecting from the ranks of civil libertarians on the issue of obscenity. The conviction of Larry Flynt, publisher of *Hustler* magazine — before his metamorphosis into a born-again Christian — was greeted with unabashed feminist approval. Harry Reems, the unknown actor who was convicted by a Memphis jury for conspiring to distribute the movie *Deep Throat,* has carried on his legal battles with almost no support from women who ordinarily regard themselves as supporters of the First Amendment. Feminist writers and scholars have even discussed the possibility of making common cause against pornography with adversaries of the women's movement — including opponents of the equal rights amendment and "right-to-life" forces.

All of this is deeply disturbing to a woman writer who believes, as I always have and still do, in an absolute interpretation of the First Amendment. Nothing in Larry Flynt's garbage convinces me that the late Justice Hugo L. Black was wrong in his opinion that "the Federal Government is without any power whatsoever under the Constitution to put any type of burden on free speech and expression of ideas of any kind (as distinguished from conduct)." Many women I like and respect tell me I am wrong; I cannot remember having become involved in so many heated discussions of a public issue since the end of the Vietnam War. A feminist writer described my views as those of a "First Amendment junkie."

Many feminist arguments for controls on pornography carry the implicit conviction that porn books, magazines, and movies pose a greater threat to women than similarly repulsive exercises of free speech pose to other offended groups. This conviction has, of course, been shared by everyone—regardless of race, creed, or sex—who has ever argued in favor of abridging the First Amendment. It is the argument used by some Jews who have withdrawn their support from the American Civil Liberties Union because it has defended the right of American Nazis to march through a community inhabited by survivors of Hitler's concentration camps.

If feminists want to argue that the protection of the Constitution should not be extended to *any* particularly odious or threatening form of speech, they have a reasonable argument (although I don't agree with it). But it is ridiculous to suggest that the porn shops on 42nd Street are more disgusting to women than a march of neo-Nazis is to survivors of the extermination camps.

The arguments over pornography also blur the vital distinction be-   5
tween expression of ideas and conduct. When I say I believe unreservedly in the First Amendment, someone always comes back at me with the issue of "kiddie porn." But kiddie porn is not a First Amendment issue. It is an issue of the abuse of power—the power adults have over children—and not of obscenity. Parents and promoters have no more right to use their children to make porn movies than they do to send them to work in coal mines. The responsible adults should be prosecuted, just as adults who use children for back-breaking farm labor should be prosecuted.

Susan Brownmiller, in *Against Our Will: Men, Women and Rape,* has described pornography as "the undiluted essence of antifemale propaganda." I think this is a fair description of some types of pornography, especially of the brutish subspecies that equates sex with death and portrays women primarily as objects of violence.

The equation of sex and violence, personified by some glossy rock record album covers as well as by *Hustler,* has fed the illusion that censorship of pornography can be conducted on a more rational basis than other types of censorship. Are all pictures of naked women obscene? Clearly not, says a friend. A Renoir nude is art, she says, and *Hustler* is trash. "Any reasonable person" knows that.

But what about something between art and trash—something, say, along the lines of *Playboy* or *Penthouse* magazines? I asked five women for their reactions to one picture in *Penthouse* and got responses that ranged from "lovely" and "sensuous" to "revolting" and "demeaning." Feminists, like everyone else, seldom have rational reasons for their preferences in erotica. Like members of juries, they tend to disagree when confronted with something that falls short of 100 percent vulgarity.

In any case, feminists will not be the arbiters of good taste if it becomes easier to harass, prosecute, and convict people on obscenity charges. Most of the people who want to censor girlie magazines are equally opposed to open discussion of issues that are of vital concern to women: rape, abortion, menstruation, contraception, lesbianism — in fact, the entire range of sexual experience from a women's viewpoint.

Feminist writers and editors and filmmakers have limited financial 10 resources: Confronted by a determined prosecutor, Hugh Hefner[1] will fare better than Susan Brownmiller. Would the Memphis jurors who convicted Harry Reems for his role in *Deep Throat* be inclined to take a more positive view of paintings of the female genitalia done by sensitive feminist artists? *Ms.* magazine has printed color reproductions of some of those art works; *Ms.* is already banned from a number of high school libraries because someone considers it threatening and/or obscene.

Feminists who want to censor what they regard as harmful pornography have essentially the same motivation as other would-be censors: They want to use the power of the state to accomplish what they have been unable to achieve in the marketplace of ideas and images. The impulse to censor places no faith in the possibilities of democratic persuasion.

It isn't easy to persuade certain men that they have better uses for $1.95 each month than to spend it on a copy of *Hustler*? Well, then, give the men no choice in the matter.

I believe there is also a connection between the impulse toward censorship on the part of people who used to consider themselves civil libertarians and a more general desire to shift responsibility from individuals to institutions. When I saw the movie *Looking for Mr. Goodbar,* I was stunned by its series of visual images equating sex and violence, coupled with what seems to me the mindless message (a distortion of the fine Judith Rossner novel) that casual sex equals death. When I came out of the movie, I was even more shocked to see parents standing in line with children between the ages of ten and fourteen.

I simply don't know why a parent would take a child to see such a movie, any more than I understand why people feel they can't turn off a television set their child is watching. Whenever I say that, my friends tell me I don't know how it is because I don't have children. True, but I do have parents. When I was a child, they did turn off the TV. They didn't expect the Federal Communications Commission to do their job for them.

I am a First Amendment junkie. You can't OD on the First Amend- 15 ment, because free speech is its own best antidote.

Suppose we want to make a rough summary, more or less paragraph by paragraph, of Jacoby's essay. Such a summary might look something like this. (The numbers refer to Jacoby's paragraphs.)

---

[1]**Hugh Hefner** Founder and longtime publisher of *Playboy* magazine. [Editors' note.]

1. Although feminists usually support the First Amendment, when it comes to pornography many feminists take pretty much the position of those who oppose ERA and abortion and other causes of the women's movement.

2. Larry Flynt produces garbage, but I think his conviction represents an unconstitutional limitation of freedom of speech.

3, 4. Feminists who want to control (censor) pornography argue that it poses a greater threat to women than similar repulsive speech poses to other groups. If feminists want to say that all offensive speech should be restricted they can make a case, but it is absurd to say that pornography is a "greater threat" to women than a march of neo-Nazis is to survivors of concentration camps.

5. Trust in the First Amendment is not refuted by kiddie porn; kiddie porn is not a First Amendment issue but an issue of child abuse.

6, 7, 8. Some feminists think censorship of pornography can be more "rational" than other kinds of censorship, but a picture of a nude woman strikes some women as base and others as "lovely." There is no unanimity.

9, 10. If feminists censor girlie magazines, they will find that they are unwittingly helping opponents of the women's movement to censor discussions of rape, abortion, and so on. Some of the art in the feminist magazine *Ms.* would doubtless be censored.

11, 12. Like other would-be censors, feminists want to use the power of the state to achieve what they have not achieved in "the marketplace of ideas." They display a lack of faith in "democratic persuasion."

13, 14. This attempt at censorship reveals a desire to "shift responsibility from individuals to institutions." The responsibility—for instance, to keep young people from equating sex with violence—is properly the parents'.

15. We can't have too much of the First Amendment.

Jacoby's **thesis,** or major claim, or chief proposition—that any form of censorship is wrong—is clear enough, even as early as the end of her first paragraph, but it gets its life or its force from the **reasons** offered throughout the essay. If we want to reduce our summary even further, we might say that Jacoby supports her thesis by arguing several subsidiary points. We will merely assert them briefly, but Jacoby **argues** them—that is, she gives reasons.

a. Pornography can scarcely be thought of as more offensive than Nazism.

b. Women disagree about which pictures are pornographic.

c. Feminists who want to censor pornography will find that they help antifeminists to censor discussions of issues advocated by the women's movement.

d. Feminist advocates are in effect turning to the government to achieve what they haven't achieved in the free marketplace.

e. One sees this abdication of responsibility in the fact that parents allow their children to watch unsuitable movies and television programs.

If we want to present a brief summary in the form of one coherent paragraph—perhaps as part of our own essay, in order to show the view we are arguing in behalf of or against—we might write something like this summary. (The summary would, of course, be prefaced by a **lead-in** along these lines: "Susan Jacoby, writing in the *New York Times,* offered a forceful argument against censorship of pornography. Jacoby's view, briefly, is . . .".)

> When it comes to censorship of pornography, some feminists take a position shared by opponents of the feminist movement. They argue that pornography poses a greater threat to women than other forms of offensive speech offer to other groups, but this interpretation is simply a mistake. Pointing to kiddie porn is also a mistake, for kiddie porn is an issue involving not the First Amendment but child abuse. Feminists who support censorship of pornography will inadvertently aid those who wish to censor discussions of abortion and rape, or art that is published in magazines such as Ms. The solution is not for individuals to turn to institutions (i.e., for the government to limit the First Amendment) but for individuals to accept the responsibility for teaching young people not to equate sex with violence.

Whether we agree or disagree with Jacoby's thesis, we must admit that the reasons she sets forth to support it are worth thinking about. Only a reader who closely follows the reasoning with which Jacoby buttresses her thesis is in a position to accept or reject it.

Topics for Critical Thinking and Writing

1. What does Jacoby mean when she says she is a "First Amendment junkie"?

2. The essay is primarily an argument against the desire of some feminists to try to censor pornography of the sort that appeals to some heterosexual adult males, but the next-to-last paragraph is about television and children. Is the paragraph connected to Jacoby's overall argument? If so, how?

3. Evaluate the final paragraph as a final paragraph. (Effective final paragraphs are not, of course, all of one sort. Some, for example, round off the essay by echoing something from the opening; others suggest that the reader, having now seen the problem, should think further about it or even act on it. But a good final paragraph, whatever else it does, should make the reader feel that the essay has come to an end, not just broken off.)

4. This essay originally appeared in the *New York Times.* If you are unfamiliar with this newspaper, consult an issue or two in your library. Next, in a paragraph, try to characterize the readers of the paper—that is, Jacoby's audience.

5. Jacoby claims in paragraph 2 that she "believes . . . in an absolute interpretation of the First Amendment." What does such an interpretation involve? Would it permit shouting "Fire!" in a crowded theater even though the shouter knows there is no fire? Would it permit shouting racist insults at blacks or immigrant Vietnamese? Spreading untruths about someone's past? If the "absolutist" interpretation of the First Amendment does permit these statements, does that argument show that nothing is morally wrong with uttering them? (*Does* the First Amendment, as actually interpreted by the Supreme Court today, permit any or all of these claims? Consult your reference librarian for help in answering this question.)

6. Jacoby implies that permitting prosecution of persons on obscenity charges will lead eventually to censorship of "open discussion" of important issues such as "rape, abortion, menstruation, contraception, lesbianism" (para. 9). Do you find her fears convincing? Does she give any evidence to support her claim?

A CHECKLIST FOR GETTING STARTED

✓ Have I adequately previewed the work?

✓ Can I state the thesis?

If I have jotted down a summary,

  ✓ is the summary accurate?

  ✓ does the summary mention all the chief points?

  ✓ if there are inconsistencies, are they in the summary or the original selection?

  ✓ will the summary be clear and helpful?

A CASEBOOK FOR
CRITICAL READING:
Should Some Kinds of Speech
Be Curtailed?

Now we present a series of essays that we think are somewhat more difficult than Jacoby's but that address in more detail some of the issues of free speech that she raises. We suggest you read each one through, to get its gist, and then read it a second time, jotting down after each paragraph a sentence or two summarizing the paragraph. Keep in mind the First Amendment to the Constitution, which reads, in its entirety,

> Congress shall make no law respecting an establishment of religion, or prohibiting the free exercise thereof; or abridging the freedom of speech, or of the press; or the right of the people peaceably to assemble, and to petition the government for a redress of grievances.

Susan Brownmiller

Susan Brownmiller (b. 1935), a graduate of Cornell University, is the founder of Women against Pornography, and the author of several books, including Against Our Will: Men, Women, and Rape *(1975). The essay reprinted here is from* Take Back the Night *(1980), a collection of essays edited by Laura Lederer. The book has been called "the manifesto of antipornography feminism."*

Let's Put Pornography Back in the Closet

Free speech is one of the great foundations on which our democracy rests. I am old enough to remember the Hollywood Ten, the screenwriters who went to jail in the late 1940s because they refused to testify before a congressional committee about their political affiliations. They tried to use the First Amendment as a defense, but they went to jail because in those days there were few civil liberties lawyers around who cared to champion the First Amendment right to free speech, when the speech concerned the Communist party.

The Hollywood Ten were correct in claiming the First Amendment. Its high purpose is the protection of unpopular ideas and political dissent. In the dark, cold days of the 1950s, few civil libertarians were willing to declare themselves First Amendment absolutists. But in the brighter, though frantic, days of the 1960s, the principle of protecting unpopular political speech was gradually strengthened.

It is fair to say now that the battle has largely been won. Even the American Nazi party has found itself the beneficiary of the dedicated,

tireless work of the American Civil Liberties Union. But—and please notice the quotation marks coming up—"To equate the free and robust exchange of ideas and political debate with commercial exploitation of obscene material demeans the grand conception of the First Amendment
and its high purposes in the historic struggle for freedom. It is a misuse
of the great guarantees of free speech and free press."

I didn't say that, although I wish I had, for I think the words are
thrilling. Chief Justice Warren Burger said it in 1973, in the United
States Supreme Court's majority opinion in *Miller v. California*. During
the same decades that the right to political free speech was being
strengthened in the courts, the nation's obscenity laws also were undergoing extensive revision.

It's amazing to recall that in 1934 the question of whether James   5
Joyce's *Ulysses* should be banned as pornographic actually went before
the Court. The battle to protect *Ulysses* as a work of literature with re-
deeming social value was won. In later decades, Henry Miller's *Tropic*
books, *Lady Chatterley's Lover*, and the *Memoirs of Fanny Hill* also were adjudged not obscene. These decisions have been important to me. As the
author of *Against Our Will*, a study of the history of rape that does contain explicit sexual material, I shudder to think how my book would
have fared if James Joyce, D. H. Lawrence, and Henry Miller hadn't gone
before me.

I am not a fan of *Chatterley* or the *Tropic* books, I should quickly mention. They are not to my literary taste, nor do I think they represent female sexuality with any degree of accuracy. But I would hardly suggest
that we ban them. Such a suggestion wouldn't get very far anyway. The
battle to protect these books is ancient history. Time does march on,
quite methodically. What, then, is unlawfully obscene, and what does
the First Amendment have to do with it?

In the *Miller* case of 1973 (not Henry Miller, by the way, but a porn
distributor who sent unsolicited stuff through the mails), the Court
came up with new guidelines that it hoped would strengthen obscenity
laws by giving more power to the states. What it did in actuality was
throw everything into confusion. It set up a three-part test by which
materials can be adjudged obscene. The materials are obscene if they depict patently offensive, hard-core sexual conduct; lack serious scientific,
literary, artistic, or political value; and appeal to the prurient interest of
an average person—as measured by contemporary community standards.

"Patently offensive," "prurient interest," and "hard-core" are indeed
words to conjure with. "Contemporary community standards" are what
we're trying to redefine. The feminist objection to pornography is not
based on prurience, which the dictionary defines as lustful, itching desire. We are not opposed to sex and desire, with or without the itch, and
we certainly believe that explicit sexual material has its place in litera-

ture, art, science, and education. Here we part company rather swiftly with old-line conservatives who don't want sex education in the high schools, for example.

No, the feminist objection to pornography is based on our belief that pornography represents hatred of women, that pornography's intent is to humiliate, degrade, and dehumanize the female body for the purpose of erotic stimulation and pleasure. We are unalterably opposed to the presentation of the female body being stripped, bound, raped, tortured, mutilated, and murdered in the name of commercial entertainment and free speech.

These images, which are standard pornographic fare, have nothing to 10 do with the hallowed right of political dissent. They have everything to do with the creation of a cultural climate in which a rapist feels he is merely giving in to a normal urge and a woman is encouraged to believe that sexual masochism is healthy, liberated fun. Justice Potter Stewart once said about hard-core pornography, "You know it when you see it," and that certainly used to be true. In the good old days, pornography looked awful. It was cheap and sleazy, and there was no mistaking it for art.

Nowadays, since the porn industry has become a multimillion dollar business, visual technology has been employed in its service. Pornographic movies are skillfully filmed and edited, pornographic still shots using the newest tenets of good design artfully grace the covers of *Hustler*, *Penthouse*, and *Playboy*, and the public—and the courts—are sadly confused.

The Supreme Court neglected to define "hard-core" in the *Miller* decision. This was a mistake. If "hard-core" refers only to explicit sexual intercourse, then that isn't good enough. When women or children or men—no matter how artfully—are shown tortured or terrorized in the service of sex, that's obscene. And "patently offensive," I would hope, to our "contemporary community standards."

Justice William O. Douglas wrote in his dissent to the *Miller* case that no one is "compelled to look." This is hardly true. To buy a paper at the corner newsstand is to subject oneself to a forcible immersion in pornography, to be demeaned by an array of dehumanized, chopped-up parts of the female anatomy, packaged like cuts of meat at the supermarket. I happen to like my body and I work hard at the gym to keep it in good shape, but I am embarrassed for my body and for the bodies of all women when I see the fragmented parts of us so frivolously, and so flagrantly, displayed.

Some constitutional theorists (Justice Douglas was one) have maintained that any obscenity law is a serious abridgement of free speech. Others (and Justice Earl Warren was one) have maintained that the First Amendment was never intended to protect obscenity. We live quite compatibly with a host of free-speech abridgements. There are restraints against false and misleading advertising or statements—shouting "fire" without cause in a crowded movie theater, etc.—that do not threaten, but strengthen, our societal values. Restrictions on the public display of pornography belong in this category.

The distinction between permission to publish and permission to dis-   15
play publicly is an essential one and one which I think consonant with First Amendment principles. Justice Burger's words which I quoted above support this without question. We are not saying "Smash the presses" or "Ban the bad ones," but simply "Get the stuff out of our sight." Let the legislatures decide—using realistic and humane contemporary community standards—what can be displayed and what cannot. The courts, after all, will be the final arbiters.

Topics for Critical Thinking and Writing

1. Objecting to Justice Douglas's remark that no one is "'compelled to look'" (para. 13), Brownmiller says, "This is hardly true. To buy a paper at the corner newsstand is to subject oneself to a forcible immersion in pornography, to be demeaned by an array of dehumanized, chopped-up parts of the female anatomy, packaged like cuts of meat at the supermarket." Is this true at your local newsstand, or are the sex magazines kept in one place, relatively remote from the newspapers?

2. When Brownmiller attempts to restate the "three-part test" for obscenity established by the Supreme Court in *Miller v. California*, she writes (para. 7): "The materials are obscene if they depict . . ." and so on. She should have written: "The materials are obscene if and only if they depict . . ." and so on. Explain what is wrong here with her "if," and why "if and only if" is needed.

3. In her next-to-last paragraph, Brownmiller reminds us that we already live quite comfortably with some "free-speech abridgements." The examples she gives are that we may not falsely shout "fire" in a crowded theater, and we may not issue misleading advertisements. Do you think that these widely accepted restrictions are valid evidence in arguing in behalf of limiting the display of what Brownmiller considers pornography? Why, or why not?

4. Brownmiller insists that defenders of the First Amendment, who will surely oppose laws that interfere with the freedom to publish, need not go on to condemn laws that regulate the freedom to "display publicly" pornographic publications. Do you agree? Suppose a publisher insists he cannot sell his product at a profit unless he is permitted to display it to advantage, and so restriction on the latter amounts to interference with his freedom to publish. How might Brownmiller reply?

5. In her last paragraph Brownmiller says that "contemporary community standards" should be decisive. Can it be argued that, because standards vary from one community to another, and from time to time even in the same place, her recommendation subjects the rights of a minority to the

whims of a majority? The Bill of Rights, after all, was supposed to safe-guard constitutional rights from the possible tyranny of the majority.

6. When Brownmiller accuses "the public . . . and the courts" of being "sadly confused" (para. 11), what does she think they are confused about? The definition of "pornography" or "obscenity"? The effects of such literature on men and women? Or is it something else?

Charles R. Lawrence III

Charles R. Lawrence III (b. 1943), author of numerous articles in law jour-nals and coauthor of The Bakke Case: The Politics of Inequality *(1979), teaches law at Stanford University. This essay originally appeared in* The Chronicle of Higher Education *(October 25, 1989), a publica-tion read chiefly by faculty and administrators at colleges and universities. An amplified version of the essay appeared in* Duke Law Journal, *Feb-ruary 1990.*

On Racist Speech

I have spent the better part of my life as a dissenter. As a high school student, I was threatened with suspension for my refusal to participate in a civil defense drill, and I have been a conspicuous consumer of my First Amendment liberties ever since. There are very strong reasons for protecting even racist speech. Perhaps the most important of these is that such protection reinforces our society's commitment to tolerance as a value, and that by protecting bad speech from government regulation, we will be forced to combat it as a community.

But I also have a deeply felt apprehension about the resurgence of racial violence and the corresponding rise in the incidence of verbal and symbolic assault and harassment to which blacks and other traditionally subjugated and excluded groups are subjected. I am troubled by the way the debate has been framed in response to the recent surge of racist inci-dents on college and university campuses and in response to some uni-versities' attempts to regulate harassing speech. The problem has been framed as one in which the liberty of free speech is in conflict with the elimination of racism. I believe this has placed the bigot on the moral high ground and fanned the rising flames of racism.

Above all, I am troubled that we have not listened to the real vic-tims, that we have shown so little understanding of their injury, and that we have abandoned those whose race, gender, or sexual preference con-tinues to make them second-class citizens. It seems to me a very sad irony that the first instinct of civil libertarians has been to challenge even the smallest, most narrowly framed efforts by universities to provide black and other minority students with the protection the Constitution guarantees them.

The landmark case of _Brown v. Board of Education_ is not a case that we normally think of as a case about speech. But _Brown_ can be broadly read as articulating the principle of equal citizenship. _Brown_ held that segregated schools were inherently unequal because of the _message_ that segregation conveyed—that black children were an untouchable caste, unfit to go to school with white children. If we understand the necessity of eliminating the system of signs and symbols that signal the inferiority of blacks, then we should hesitate before proclaiming that all racist speech that stops short of physical violence must be defended.

University officials who have formulated policies to respond to incidents of racial harassment have been characterized in the press as "thought police," but such policies generally do nothing more than impose sanctions against intentional face-to-face insults. When racist speech takes the form of face-to-face insults, catcalls, or other assaultive speech aimed at an individual or small group of persons, it falls directly within the "fighting words" exception to First Amendment protection. The Supreme Court has held that words which "by their very utterance inflict injury or tend to incite an immediate breach of the peace" are not protected by the First Amendment.

If the purpose of the First Amendment is to foster the greatest amount of speech, racial insults disserve that purpose. Assaultive racist speech functions as a preemptive strike. The invective is experienced as a blow, not as a proffered idea, and once the blow is struck, it is unlikely that a dialogue will follow. Racial insults are particularly undeserving of First Amendment protection because the perpetrator's intention is not to discover truth or initiate dialogue but to injure the victim. In most situations, members of minority groups realize that they are likely to lose if they respond to epithets by fighting and are forced to remain silent and submissive.

Courts have held that offensive speech may not be regulated in public forums such as streets where the listener may avoid the speech by moving on, but the regulation of otherwise protected speech has been permitted when the speech invades the privacy of the unwilling listener's home or when the unwilling listener cannot avoid the speech. Racist posters, fliers, and graffiti in dormitories, bathrooms, and other common living spaces would seem to clearly fall within the reasoning of these cases. Minority students should not be required to remain in their rooms in order to avoid racial assault. Minimally, they should find a safe haven in their dorms and in all other common rooms that are a part of their daily routine.

I would also argue that the university's responsibility for ensuring that these students receive an equal educational opportunity provides a compelling justification for regulations that ensure them safe passage in all common areas. A minority student should not have to risk becoming the target of racially assaulting speech every time he or she chooses to

walk across campus. Regulating vilifying speech that cannot be anticipated or avoided would not preclude announced speeches and rallies—
situations that would give minority-group members and their allies
the chance to organize counterdemonstrations or avoid the speech
altogether.

The most commonly advanced argument against the regulation of
racist speech proceeds something like this: We recognize that minority
groups suffer pain and injury as the result of racist speech, but we must
allow this hate mongering for the benefit of society as a whole. Freedom of speech is the lifeblood of our democratic system. It is especially
important for minorities because often it is their only vehicle for rally-
ing support for the redress of their grievances. It will be impossible to
formulate a prohibition so precise that it will prevent the racist speech
you want to suppress without catching in the same net all kinds of
speech that it would be unconscionable for a democratic society to
suppress.

Whenever we make such arguments, we are striking a balance on   10
the one hand between our concern for the continued free flow of ideas
and the democratic process dependent on that flow, and, on the other,
our desire to further the cause of equality. There can be no meaningful
discussion of how we should reconcile our commitment to equality and
our commitment to free speech until it is acknowledged that there is real
harm inflicted by racist speech and that this harm is far from trivial.

To engage in a debate about the First Amendment and racist speech
without a full understanding of the nature and extent of that harm is to
risk making the First Amendment an instrument of domination rather
than a vehicle of liberation. We have not known the experience of victim-
ization by racist, misogynist, and homophobic speech, nor do we equally
share the burden of the societal harm it inflicts. We are often quick to say
that we have heard the cry of the victims when we have not.

The *Brown* case is again instructive because it speaks directly to the
psychic injury inflicted by racist speech by noting that the symbolic message of segregation affected "the hearts and minds" of Negro children "in
a way unlikely ever to be undone." Racial epithets and harassment often
cause deep emotional scarring and feelings of anxiety and fear that per-
vade every aspect of a victim's life.

Brown also recognized that black children did not have an equal opportunity to learn and participate in the school community if they bore
the additional burden of being subjected to the humiliation and psychic
assault contained in the message of segregation. University students bear
an analogous burden when they are forced to live and work in an environment where at any moment they may be subjected to denigrating
verbal harassment and assault. The same injury was addressed by the
Supreme Court when it held that sexual harassment that creates a hostile or abusive work environment violates the ban on sex discrimination
in employment of Title VII of the Civil Rights Act of 1964.

Carefully drafted university regulations would bar the use of words as assault weapons and leave unregulated even the most heinous of ideas when those ideas are presented at times and places and in manners that provide an opportunity for reasoned rebuttal or escape from immediate injury. The history of the development of the right to free speech has been one of carefully evaluating the importance of free expression and its effects on other important societal interests. We have drawn the line between protected and unprotected speech before without dire results. (Courts have, for example, exempted from the protection of the First Amendment obscene speech and speech that disseminates official secrets, that defames or libels another person, or that is used to form a conspiracy or monopoly.)

Blacks and other people of color are skeptical about the argument that even the most injurious speech must remain unregulated because, in an unregulated marketplace of ideas, the best ones will rise to the top and gain acceptance. Our experience tells us quite the opposite. We have seen too many good liberal politicians shy away from the issues that might brand them as being too closely allied with us.

Whenever we decide that racist speech must be tolerated because of the importance of maintaining societal tolerance for all unpopular speech, we are asking blacks and other subordinated groups to bear the burden for the good of all. We must be careful that the ease with which we strike the balance against the regulation of racist speech is in no way influenced by the fact that the cost will be borne by others. We must be certain that those who will pay that price are fairly represented in our deliberations and that they are heard.

At the core of the argument that we should resist all government regulation of speech is the ideal that the best cure for bad speech is good, that ideas that affirm equality and the worth of all individuals will ultimately prevail. This is an empty ideal unless those of us who would fight racism are vigilant and unequivocal in that fight. We must look for ways to offer assistance and support to students whose speech and political participation are chilled in a climate of racial harassment.

Civil rights lawyers might consider suing on behalf of blacks whose right to an equal education is denied by a university's failure to ensure a nondiscriminatory educational climate or conditions of employment. We must embark upon the development of a First Amendment jurisprudence grounded in the reality of our history and our contemporary experience. We must think hard about how best to launch legal attacks against the most indefensible forms of hate speech. Good lawyers can create exceptions and narrow interpretations that limit the harm of hate speech without opening the floodgates of censorship.

Everyone concerned with these issues must find ways to engage actively in actions that resist and counter the racist ideas that we would have the First Amendment protect. If we fail in this, the victims of hate speech must rightly assume that we are on the oppressors' side.

Topics for Critical Thinking and Writing

1. Summarize Lawrence's essay in a paragraph. (You may find it useful first to summarize each paragraph in a sentence, and then to revise these summary sentences into a paragraph.)

2. In a sentence state Lawrence's thesis (his main point).

3. Why do you suppose Lawrence included his first paragraph? What does it contribute to his argument?

4. Paragraph 7 argues that "minority students" should not have to endure "racist posters, fliers, and graffiti in dormitories, bathrooms, and other common living spaces." Do you think that Lawrence would also argue that straight white men should not have to endure posters, fliers, or graffiti that speak of "honkies" or "rednecks"? On what do you base your answer?

5. In paragraph 8 Lawrence speaks of "racially assaulting speech" and of "vilifying speech." It is easy to think of words that fit these descriptions, but what about other words? Is *Uncle Tom*, used by an African American about another African American who is eager to please whites, an example? Or take the word *gay*. Surely this word is acceptable because it is widely used by homosexuals, but what about *queer* (used by some homosexuals, but usually derogatory when used by heterosexuals)? A third example: There can be little doubt that women are demeaned when males speak of them as *chicks* or *babes*, but are these terms "assaulting" and "vilifying"?

6. Find out if your college or university has a code governing hate speech. If it does, evaluate it. If your college has no such code, imagine that you are Lawrence, and draft one of about 250 words. (See especially his paras. 5, 7, and 14.)

Derek Bok

Derek Bok was born in 1930 in Bryn Mawr, Pennsylvania, and educated at Stanford University and Harvard University, where he received a law degree. From 1971 to 1991 he served as president of Harvard University. The following essay, first published in the Boston Globe *in 1991, was prompted by the display of Confederate flags hung from a window of a Harvard dormitory.*

Protecting Freedom of Expression on the Campus

For several years, universities have been struggling with the problem of trying to reconcile the rights of free speech with the desire to avoid racial tension. In recent weeks, such a controversy has sprung up at Harvard. Two students hung Confederate flags in public view, upsetting students who equate the Confederacy with slavery. A third student tried to protest the flags by displaying a swastika.

These incidents have provoked much discussion and disagreement. Some students have urged that Harvard require the removal of symbols that offend many members of the community. Others reply that such symbols are a form of free speech and should be protected.

Different universities have resolved similar conflicts in different ways. Some have enacted codes to protect their communities from forms of speech that are deemed to be insensitive to the feelings of other groups. Some have refused to impose such restrictions.

It is important to distinguish between the appropriateness of such communications and their status under the First Amendment. The fact that speech is protected by the First Amendment does not necessarily mean that it is right, proper, or civil. I am sure that the vast majority of Harvard students believe that hanging a Confederate flag in public view—or displaying a swastika in response—is insensitive and unwise because any satisfaction it gives to the students who display these symbols is far outweighed by the discomfort it causes to many others.

I share this view and regret that the students involved saw fit to be- 5 have in this fashion. Whether or not they merely wished to manifest their pride in the South—or to demonstrate the insensitivity of hanging Confederate flags, by mounting another offensive symbol in return— they must have known that they would upset many fellow students and ignore the decent regard for the feelings of others so essential to building and preserving a strong and harmonious community.

To disapprove of a particular form of communication, however, is not enough to justify prohibiting it. We are faced with a clear example of the conflict between our commitment to free speech and our desire to foster a community founded on mutual respect. Our society has wrestled with this problem for many years. Interpreting the First Amendment, the Supreme Court has clearly struck the balance in favor of free speech.

While communities do have the right to regulate speech in order to uphold aesthetic standards (avoiding defacement of buildings) or to protect the public from disturbing noise, rules of this kind must be applied across the board and cannot be enforced selectively to prohibit certain kinds of messages but not others.

Under the Supreme Court's rulings, as I read them, the display of swastikas or Confederate flags clearly falls within the protection of the free-speech clause of the First Amendment and cannot be forbidden simply because it offends the feelings of many members of the community. These rulings apply to all agencies of government, including public universities.

Although it is unclear to what extent the First Amendment is enforceable against private institutions, I have difficulty understanding why a university such as Harvard should have less free speech than the surrounding society—or than a public university.

One reason why the power of censorship is so dangerous is that it is 10 extremely difficult to decide when a particular communication is offensive enough to warrant prohibition or to weigh the degree of offensiveness against the potential value of the communication. If we begin to forbid flags, it is only a short step to prohibiting offensive speakers.

I suspect that no community will become humane and caring by restricting what its members can say. The worst offenders will simply find other ways to irritate and insult.

In addition, once we start to declare certain things "offensive," with all the excitement and attention that will follow, I fear that much ingenuity will be exerted trying to test the limits, much time will be expended trying to draw tenuous distinctions, and the resulting publicity will eventually attract more attention to the offensive material than would ever have occurred otherwise.

Rather than prohibit such communications, with all the resulting risks, it would be better to ignore them, since students would then have little reason to create such displays and would soon abandon them. If this response is not possible—and one can understand why—the wisest course is to speak with those who perform insensitive acts and try to help them understand the effects of their actions on others.

Appropriate officials and faculty members should take the lead, as the Harvard House Masters have already done in this case. In talking with students, they should seek to educate and persuade, rather than resort to ridicule or intimidation, recognizing that only persuasion is likely to produce a lasting, beneficial effect. Through such effects, I believe that we act in the manner most consistent with our ideals as an educational institution and most calculated to help us create a truly understanding, supportive community.

Topics for Critical Thinking and Writing

1. Bok sketches the following argument (paras. 8 and 9): The First Amendment protects free speech in public universities and colleges; Harvard is not a public university; therefore Harvard does not enjoy the protection of the First Amendment. This argument is plainly valid. But Bok clearly rejects this conclusion ("I have difficulty understanding why . . . Harvard should have less free speech . . . than a public university"). Therefore, he must reject at least one of the premises. But which one? And why?

2. Bok objects to censorship in order to prevent students from being "offended." He would not object to the campus police preventing students from being harmed. In an essay of 100 words, explain the difference between conduct that is *harmful* and conduct that is (merely?) *offensive.*

3. Bok advises campus officials (and students) simply to "ignore" offensive words, flags, and so forth (para. 13). Do you agree with this advice? Or do you favor a different kind of response? Write a 250-word essay on the theme "How We Ought to Respond to the Offensive Misconduct of Others."

Steven McDonald

Steven McDonald is an associate legal counsel at the Ohio State University. This selection was downloaded from Academe Today, The Chronicle of Higher Education*'s Web site, on October 28, 1997.*

The Laws of Cyberspace:
What Colleges Need to Know

Continued incidents of misuse of the Internet on college campuses suggest that we need to reexamine our existing approaches to the problem. For the most part, colleges and universities (much like legislators) have addressed misuse of the Internet as though it were an entirely new issue. In reality, however, it is simply a new form of an old problem: how to handle abuses of free speech and similar types of misconduct.

Hardly anyone uses computers to compute anymore. Instead, we use them to communicate. Every day on our campuses, students and faculty and staff members use our computer systems and networks to disseminate far more text and images than the *New York Times,* far more audio than NPR, and far more video than NBC. They are sending far more electronic mail than paper mail and are engaging in far more electronic discussions than telephone calls. And their electronic messages have a far wider audience than any of the more traditional forms of communications. In effect, people on our campuses are acting as international publishers and broadcasters.

If computer users are engaged in the same kinds of communications as the traditional media are, it should come as no surprise that they also face the same long-standing legal issues and have the same well-settled legal responsibilities and liabilities in connection with those communications that traditional media do. However, few of our users understand themselves to be publishers or broadcasters. At best, only a handful of them are aware of the libel, copyright, obscenity, and other laws applicable to their activities on the Internet—let alone the finer points of "actual malice" doctrine, the Supreme Court's latest pronouncement on the four factors to be considered in analyzing a claim of "fair use," or the scope of "local community standards" in the various jurisdictions through which their racier communications may pass. They also know virtually nothing about the potential legal consequences of violating the applicable laws.

Instead, to the extent that they consider legal issues at all, computer users typically view them through the lens of Internet folklore, which mistakenly conceives of cyberspace as a separate, law-free jurisdiction in which what is permissible is defined solely by the limits of users' technical capabilities. Unfortunately, that view recently has been reinforced by the widespread misconception that the Supreme Court's decision striking down the Communications Decency Act outlawed *all* regulation of the Net.

In fact, while that decision was indeed momentous, all that it really held was that government regulation of the Internet must be consistent with First Amendment principles, and that the C.D.A. was not, because it restricted far more speech than was necessary or appropriate to deal with the problem of minors' access to "indecency." The Supreme Court did not hold that the Internet could not be regulated at all—indeed, it expressly recognized that a more "narrowly tailored" approach to that problem would have been constitutional. Further, the Court certainly did not release computer users from their responsibilities and liabilities under existing, generally applicable laws, such as those governing libel, copyright, and obscenity.

The result of these misconceptions has been that our computer users increasingly, if unknowingly, are engaging in communications that are libelous or obscene, that infringe copyrighted works, and that violate other laws. And because those communications flow through and reside in our computer systems, colleges and universities are being asked and expected to do something about them.

Most commonly, our response to such expectations has been to adopt new, computer-specific codes of conduct, often expressed in long lists of "thou shalt nots." Such codes, however, can do more harm than good: They usually duplicate or conflict with—and therefore sometimes cause confusion about—other applicable laws and institutional policies. Moreover, they can encourage computer users to seek out and exploit the inevitable loopholes; they may infringe upon academic freedom by chilling legitimate expression; and, most important, they can actually increase institutions' liabilities for our users' communications, because they raise expectations about both our ability and our duty to police these communications.

Although the law is not completely settled, what is increasingly clear is that colleges and universities are not liable for an illegal communication solely because they own the system through which that communication flows. We will, of course, always be responsible for the communications of college and university employees on the Internet when they are acting within the scope of their employment. But with respect to the other, "personal" communications on our systems—including, in particular, most student communications—we are liable only when we know, or have good reason to know, of their illegal character but fail to stop them.

Thus, for example, if a student posts a libelous message to our Usenet server and we never learn of it, the student alone will be liable if the message results in a lawsuit. But if we become aware of the existence of the libel on our system, by complaint or any other means, and do nothing about it, we will be liable, along with the student.

The more that we specifically attempt to regulate the content of the personal communications on our systems, the more likely it is that we will be expected to know what that content is, and the more likely it is that we will be held liable for it when it is illegal, whether or not we actually know about the offense. In other words, if we act as if we were newspaper editors, imposing rigid, Internet-specific content guidelines or screening material before it is distributed publicly — or even if we just reserve the right to act in this way — we should not be surprised to find ourselves subjected to the same liabilities as newspapers are for their libelous or other illegal communications. If, however, we act more like a telephone company — that is, simply as the operator of a communications system, the content of which is determined by others — our liability for individuals' personal communications should be reduced.

That is not to say that we should abandon all responsibility. We can and should continue to enforce existing, generally applicable laws and policies in the context of the Internet, just as we would in any other context, when we learn that they have been violated. And, at least for now, the law also appears to require us to investigate in good faith whatever complaints about the legality of our computer users' communications are brought to our attention and — if the complaints are justified — to remove those communications from our systems.

Such after-the-fact enforcement of general laws and policies does not carry with it the legal risks associated with more active editorial control. But because it is impossible, as a practical matter, for us to keep track — let alone control the content — of all of the personal communications on our computer systems, we should be careful not to make it appear that we are doing so by adopting content regulations specific to the Internet.

A more productive approach to the problem of Internet misuse is one that, ironically, we often forget about: education. If, as our experience at the Ohio State University suggests, the primary problem is that our computer users do not understand their legal responsibilities online, rather than that they intend to act maliciously, surely the solution is to teach our users about the relevant legal issues.

For the past year, we have been doing just that at Ohio State. Each quarter, we teach all entering freshmen the basic principles of the laws and university policies relevant to their Internet communications, including libel, copyright, and obscenity laws. These are the areas in which problems arise most frequently, and existing laws and policies already address them quite well. Our main message is: Communications that would be illegal or that would violate university policy in the "off line" world are equally illegal or in violation of university policy when they occur online. We will soon be making our educational materials available to the rest of our computer users as well.

Informal educational efforts also can be extremely effective, particu-   15
larly when dealing with specific complaints of misuse. Nothing drives home the point so well to those accused of misusing the Internet as a discussion of the concept of *personal* liability — for example, the prospect of as much as $100,000 in statutory damages for a single instance of copyright infringement, as well as a demonstration of how easy it is for a

university administrator (or, say, the user's parents and prospective employers) to find a potentially embarrassing communication by means of Web-based search engines such as AltaVista or Deja News. It is only then that some students first understand the consequences of what they may have considered harmless fun.

As part of the same effort, we are also revising our computer-use policy at Ohio State to make it more of an educational tool than a mere list of regulations. To the extent possible, the policy will simply incorporate—and remind our users of—existing relevant laws, policies, and enforcement mechanisms, including our code of student conduct. The policy will include computer-specific rules only to the extent that computers pose unique issues not addressed by existing laws and policies—for example, the need to limit usage so as not to interfere with others' use of the computer resources that are available.

It is still too early to tell how effective our educational approach will be, but the results so far are promising. Our students have seemed eager to learn about "Internet law" (if only because they want to know what they can get away with), and it appears that the number of serious complaints about Internet misuse on our campus is dropping. If that reduction continues, not only should we see a corresponding reduction in potential legal claims against the university, but we will also be able to spend less time and effort on complaints. It seems that with the Internet, as with most things, an ounce of prevention is worth a pound of cure.

Topics for Critical Thinking and Writing

1. McDonald suggests (para. 2) that today's college students and faculties are acting as "international publishers and broadcasters" in their use of computers. Explain whether you think this is a helpful analogy.

2. What does McDonald say are the four factors the Supreme Court has decided must be considered in weighing a claim of "fair use" of printed matter?

3. What was the Supreme Court's holding in the case striking down the constitutionality of the Communications Decency Act?

4. Define each of the following ideas: copyright infringement, libel, obscenity. (Also construct a hypothetical example of each.)

5. Does McDonald believe that university administrations ought to approach the Internet more like newspaper editors or more like telephone operators? Can you tell? Explain why.

6. Consider the educational practices regarding computer use being taught at Ohio State (paras. 14–16). Does your college or university have a similar program? If so, compare it with the one at Ohio State. If not, arrange an interview with your college dean and ask the dean to explain why.

3

Critical Reading: Getting Deeper into Arguments

He that wrestles with us strengthens our nerves, and sharpens our skill.
Our antagonist is our helper. —EDMUND BURKE

PERSUASION, ARGUMENT, DISPUTE

When we think seriously about an argument (not name calling or mere rationalization), not only do we hear ideas that may be unfamiliar, but we are also forced to examine closely our own cherished opinions, and perhaps for the first time we really come to see the strengths and weaknesses of what we believe. As John Stuart Mill put it, "He who knows only his own side of the case knows little."

It is customary, and useful, to distinguish between persuasion and argument. **Persuasion** has the broader meaning. To persuade is to win over—whether by giving reasons (that is, by argument) or by appealing to the emotions, or, for that matter, by using torture. **Argument,** one form of persuasion, relies on reason; it offers statements as reasons for other statements. Rhetoricians often use the Greek word **logos,** which merely means "word," to denote this aspect of persuasive writing—the appeal to reason. (The appeal to the emotions is known as **pathos.** Strictly speaking, *pathos* is Greek for "suffering," but it now covers all sorts of emotional appeal, for instance to one's sense of pity or one's sense of patriotism.)

Notice that an argument, in the sense of statements that are offered as reasons for other statements, does not require two speakers or writers who represent opposed positions. The Declaration of Independence is an argument, setting forth the colonists' reasons for declaring their independence. In practice, of course, someone's argument usually advances reasons in opposition to someone else's position or belief. But even if one is writing only for oneself, trying to clarify one's thinking by setting forth reasons, the result is an argument. In a **dispute,** however, two or more people express views that are at odds.

Most of this book is about argument in the sense of the presentation of reasons, but of course reason is not the whole story. If an argument is to be effective, it must be presented persuasively. For instance, the writer's **tone** (attitude toward self, topic, and audience) must be appropriate if the discourse is to persuade the reader. The careful presentation of the self is not something disreputable, nor is it something that publicity agents or advertising agencies invented. Aristotle (384–322 B.C.) emphasized the importance of impressing upon the audience that the speaker is a person of good sense and high moral character. (He called this aspect of persuasion **ethos,** the Greek word for "character," as opposed to *logos,* which we have noted is the word for persuasion by appealing to reason.) We will talk at length about tone, along with other matters such as the organization of an argument, in Chapter 5, but here we deal with some of the chief devices used in reasoning, and we will glance at emotional appeals.

We should note at once, however, that an argument presupposes a fixed **topic.** Suppose we are arguing about Jefferson's assertion, in the Declaration of Independence, that "all men are created equal." Jones subscribes to this statement, but Smith says it is nonsense and argues that one has only to look around to see that some people are brighter than others, or healthier, or better coordinated, or whatever. Jones and Smith, if they intend to argue the point, will do well to examine what Jefferson actually wrote.

> We hold these truths to be self-evident, that all men are created equal: that they are endowed by their Creator with certain unalienable rights; and that among these are life, liberty, and the pursuit of happiness.

There is room for debate over what Jefferson really meant, and about whether he is right, but clearly he was talking about *equality of rights,* and if Smith and Jones wish to argue about Jefferson's view of equality — that is, if they wish to offer their reasons for accepting, rejecting, or modifying it — they will do well first to agree on what Jefferson said or what he probably meant to say. Jones and Smith may still hold different views; they may continue to disagree on whether Jefferson was right, and proceed to offer arguments and counterarguments to settle the point. But only if they can agree on *what* they disagree about will their dispute get somewhere.

REASON VERSUS RATIONALIZATION

Reason may not be our only way of finding the truth, but it is a way we often rely on. The subway ran yesterday at 6:00 A.M. and the day before at 6:00 A.M. and the day before, and so I infer from this evidence that it is also running today at 6:00 A.M. (a form of reasoning known as **induction**). Or: Bus drivers require would-be passengers to present the exact change; I do not have the exact change; therefore I infer I cannot ride on the bus (**deduction**). (The terms *induction* and *deduction* will be discussed shortly.)

We also know that, if we set our minds to a problem, we can often find reasons (not necessarily sound ones, but reasons nevertheless) for almost anything we want to justify. Here is an entertaining example from Benjamin Franklin's *Autobiography:*

> I believe I have omitted mentioning that in my first voyage from Boston, being becalmed off Block Island, our people set about catching cod and hauled up a great many. Hitherto I had stuck to my resolution of not eating animal food, and on this occasion, I considered with my master Tryon the taking of every fish as a kind of unprovoked murder, since none of them had or ever could do us any injury that might justify the slaughter. All this seemed very reasonable. But I had formerly been a great lover of fish, and when this came hot out of the frying pan, it smelt admirably well. I balanced some time between principle and inclination, till I recollected that when the fish were opened I saw smaller fish taken out of their stomachs. Then thought I, if you eat one another, I don't see why we mayn't eat you. So I dined upon cod very heartily and continued to eat with other people, returning only now and then occasionally to a vegetable diet. So convenient a thing it is to be a *reasonable creature,* since it enables one to find or make a reason for everything one has a mind to do.

Franklin of course is being playful; he is *not* engaging in critical thinking. He tells us that he loved fish, that this fish "smelt admirably well," and so we are prepared for him to find a reason (here one as weak as "Fish eat fish, so people may eat fish") to abandon his vegetarianism. (But think: Fish also eat their own young. May we therefore eat ours?) Still, Franklin touches on a truth: If necessary, we can find reasons to justify whatever we want. That is, instead of reasoning we may *rationalize* (devise a self-serving but dishonest reason), like the fox in Aesop's fables who, finding the grapes he desired were out of his reach, consoled himself with the thought they were probably sour.

Probably we can never be certain that we are not rationalizing, but—except when, like Franklin, we are being playful—we can seek to think critically about our own beliefs, scrutinizing our assumptions, looking for counterevidence, and wondering if different conclusions can reasonably be drawn.

SOME PROCEDURES IN ARGUMENT

Definition

Definition, we mentioned in our first chapter, is one of the classical *topics*, a "place" to which one goes with questions; in answering the questions, one finds ideas. When we define, we are answering the question "What is it?," and in answering this question as precisely as we can, we will find, clarify, and develop ideas.

We have already glanced at an argument over the proposition that "all men are created equal," and we saw that the words needed clarification. *Equal* meant, in the context, not physically or mentally equal but something like "equal in rights," equal politically and legally. (And of course "men" meant "men and women.") Words do not always mean exactly what they seem to: There is no lead in a lead pencil, and a standard 2-by-4 is 1⅝ inches in thickness and 3⅜ inches in width.

Definition by Synonym   Let's return, for a moment, to *pornography*, a word that, we saw, is not easily defined. One way to define a word is to offer a **synonym.** Thus, pornography can be defined, at least roughly, as "obscenity" (something indecent). But definition by synonym is usually only a start, because we find that we will have to define the synonym and, besides, very few words have exact synonyms. (In fact, *pornography* and *obscenity* are not exact synonyms.)

Definition by Example   A second way to define something is to point to an example (this is often called **ostensive definition,** from the Latin *ostendere*, "to show"). This method can be very helpful, ensuring that both writer and reader are talking about the same thing, but it also has its limitations. A few decades ago many people pointed to James Joyce's *Ulysses* and D. H. Lawrence's *Lady Chatterley's Lover* as examples of obscene novels, but today these books are regarded as literary masterpieces. Possibly they can be obscene and also be literary masterpieces. (Joyce's wife is reported to have said of her husband, "He may have been a great writer, but . . . he had a very dirty mind.")

One of the difficulties of using an example, however, is that the example is richer, more complex than the term it is being used to define, and this richness and complexity get in the way of achieving a clear definition. Thus, if one cites Lawrence's *Lady Chatterley's Lover* as an example of pornography, a listener may erroneously think that pornography has something to do with British novels or with heterosexual relationships outside of marriage. Yet neither of these ideas is part of the concept of pornography.

We are not trying here to formulate a satisfactory definition of *pornography;* our object is to say that an argument will be most fruitful if the participants first agree on what they are talking about, and that one way to secure such agreement is to define the topic ostensively. Choosing the right example, one that has all the central or typical characteristics, can make a topic not only clear but vivid.

Definition by Stipulation   In arguing, you can legitimately offer a **stipulative definition,** saying, perhaps, that by *Native American* you mean any person with any Native American blood; or you might say, "For the purpose of the present discussion, I mean by a *Native American* any person who has at least one grandparent of pure Native American blood." A stipulative definition is appropriate where no fixed or standard definition is available and where some arbitrary specification is necessary in order to fix the meaning of a key term in the argument. Not everyone may be willing to accept your stipulative definition, and alternatives can probably be defended. In any case, when you stipulate a definition, your audience knows what *you* mean by the term thus defined.

Of course it would *not* be reasonable to stipulate that by *Native American* you mean anyone with a deep interest in North American aborigines. That's just too idiosyncratic to be useful. Similarly, an essay on Jews in America will have to rely on some definition of the key idea. Perhaps the writer will stipulate the definition used in Israel: A Jew is any person with a Jewish mother, or, if not born of a Jewish mother, a person who has formally adopted the Jewish faith. Or perhaps the writer will stipulate another meaning: Jews are people who consider themselves to be Jews. Some sort of reasonable definition must be offered.

To stipulate, however, that by *Jews* you mean "persons who believe that the area formerly called Palestine rightfully belongs to the Jews" would hopelessly confuse matters. Remember the old riddle and the answer: If you call a dog's tail a leg, how many legs does a dog have? Answer: Four. Calling a tail a leg doesn't make it a leg.

Suppose someone says she means by a *Communist* "anyone who opposes the president, does not go to church, and favors a more nearly equal distribution of wealth and property." A dictionary or encyclopedia will tell us that a person is a Communist who accepts the main doctrines of Karl Marx (or perhaps of Marxism-Leninism). For many purposes, we may think of Communists as persons who belong to some Communist political party, by analogy with Democrats and Republicans. Or we may even think of a Communist as someone who supports what is common to the constitutions and governments currently in power in China and Cuba. But what is the point of the misleading stipulative definition of *Communist* given at the beginning of this paragraph, except to cast disapproval on everyone whose views bring them within the definition?

There is no good reason for offering this definition, and there are two goods reasons against it. The first is that we already have perfectly adequate definitions of *Communist,* and one should learn them and rely on them until the need to revise and improve them occurs. The second reason for refraining from using a misleading stipulative definition is that it is unfair to tar with a dirty and sticky brush nonchurchgoers and the rest by calling them derogatory names they do not deserve. Even if it is true that Communists favor more egalitarian distribution of wealth and property, the converse is *not* true: Not all egalitarians are Communists. Furthermore, if something is economically unsound or morally objectionable about such egalitarianism, the only responsible way to make that point is to argue against it.

A stipulation may be helpful and legitimate. Here is the opening paragraph of an essay by Richard B. Brandt titled "The Morality and Rationality of Suicide." Notice that the author first stipulates a definition and then, aware that the definition may strike some readers as too broad and therefore unreasonable or odd, he offers a reason on behalf of his definition:

> "Suicide" is conveniently defined, for our purposes, as doing something which results in one's death, either from the intention of ending one's life or the intention to bring about some other state of affairs (such as relief from pain) which one thinks it certain or highly probable can be achieved only by means of death or will produce death. It may seem odd to classify an act of heroic self-sacrifice on the part of a soldier as suicide. It is simpler, however, not to try to define "suicide" so that an act of suicide is always irrational or immoral in some way; if we adopt a neutral definition like the above we can still proceed to ask when an act of suicide in that sense is rational, morally justifiable, and so on, so that all evaluations anyone might wish to make can still be made.
> — (*A Handbook for the Study of Suicide,* ed. Seymour Perlin)

Sometimes a definition that at first seems extremely odd can be made acceptable, if strong reasons are offered in its support. Sometimes, in fact, an odd definition marks a great intellectual step forward. For instance, recently the Supreme Court recognized that *speech* includes symbolic nonverbal expression such as protesting against a war by wearing armbands or by flying the American flag upside down. Such actions, because they express ideas or emotions, are now protected by the First Amendment. Few people today would disagree that *speech* should include symbolic gestures. (We include an example of controversy over precisely this issue, in Derek Bok's "Protecting Freedom of Expression on the Campus," in Chapter 2.)

An example that seems notably eccentric to many readers and thus far has not gained much support is from page 94 of *Practical Ethics,* in which Peter Singer suggests that a nonhuman being can be a *person.* He admits that "it sounds odd to call an animal a person," but says that it seems so only because of our bad habit of sharply separating ourselves from other species. For Singer, *persons* are "rational and self-conscious beings, aware of themselves as distinct entities with a past and a future." Thus, although a newborn infant is a human being, it is not a person; on the other hand, an adult chimpanzee is not a human being but probably is a person. You don't have to agree with Singer to know exactly what he means and where he stands. Moreover, if you read his essay you may even find that his reasons are plausible and that by means of his unusual definition he has enlarged your thinking.

The Importance of Definitions   Trying to decide on the best way to define a key idea or a central concept is often difficult as well as controversial. *Death,* for example, has been redefined in recent years. Traditionally, a person was dead when there was no longer any heart-beat. But with advancing medical technology, the medical profession has persuaded legislatures to redefine *death* by reference to cessation of cere-bral and cortical functions—so-called brain death. Recently, some schol-ars have hoped to bring clarity into the abortion debate by redefining *life.*

Traditionally, human life begins at birth, or perhaps at viability (the capacity of a fetus to live independently of the uterine environment). Now, however, some are proposing a "brain birth" definition, in the hope of resolving the abortion controversy. A *New York Times* story of November 8, 1990, reported that these thinkers want abortion to be pro-hibited by law at the point where "integrated brain functioning begins to emerge—about seventy days after conception." Whatever the merits of such a redefinition, the debate is convincing evidence of just how impor-tant the definition of certain terms can be.

Last Words about Definition   Since Plato's time, in the fourth cen-tury B.C., it has often been argued that the best way to give a definition is to state the *essence* of the thing being defined. Thus, the classic example defines *man* as "a rational animal." (Today, to avoid sexist implications, instead of *man* we would say *human being* or *person.*) That is, the property of *rational animality* is taken to be the essence of every human creature, and so it must be mentioned in the definition of *man.* This statement guarantees that the definition is neither too broad nor too narrow. But philosophers have long criticized this alleged ideal type of definition, on several grounds, one of which is that no one can propose such defini-tions without assuming that the thing being defined has an essence in the first place—an assumption that is not necessary. Thus, we may want to define *causality,* or *explanation,* or even *definition* itself, but it is doubtful whether it is sound to assume that any of these things has an essence.

A much better way to provide a definition is to offer a set of **suffi-cient and necessary conditions.** Suppose we want to define the word *circle* and are conscious of the need to keep circles distinct from other geometrical figures such as rectangles and spheres. We might express our definition by citing sufficient and necessary conditions as follows: "Any-thing is a circle *if and only if* it is a closed plane figure, all points on the circumference of which are equidistant from the center." Using the con-nective "if and only if" (called the *biconditional*) between the definition and what is being defined helps to force into our consciousness the need to make the definition neither too exclusive (too narrow) nor too inclu-sive (too broad). Of course, for most ordinary purposes we don't require such a formally precise and explicit definition. Nevertheless, perhaps the best criterion to keep in mind when assessing a proposed definition is whether it can be stated in the "if and only if" form, and whether, if it is so stated, it is true; that is, if it truly specifies *all and only* the things cov-ered by the word being defined.

Definitions can be given by

- synonym,
- example,
- stipulation,
- mentioning the essence, and
- stating necessary and sufficient conditions.

Assumptions

In Chapter 1 we discussed the **assumptions** made by the authors of two essays on campus discipline. But we have more to say about assumptions. We have already said that in the form of discourse known as argument, certain statements are offered as reasons for other statements. But even the longest and most complex chain of reasoning or proof is fastened to assumptions, one or more *unexamined beliefs*. (Even if such a belief is shared by writer and reader, it is no less an assumption.) Benjamin Franklin argued against paying salaries to the holders of executive offices in the federal government on the grounds that men are moved by ambition and by avarice (love of power and of money), and that powerful positions conferring wealth incite men to do their worst. These assumptions he stated, though he felt no need to argue them at length because he assumed that his readers shared them.

An assumption may be unstated. For example, Elizabeth Whelan in her essay on legal prohibition of teenage drinking (p. 83) assumes without explicitly saying so that no matter what the law may be, today's teenagers will consume alcohol and some will do so to excess. A writer, painstakingly arguing specific points, may choose to keep one or more of the assumptions tacit. Or the writer may be as unaware of some underlying assumption as of the surrounding air. For example, Franklin didn't even bother to state another assumption. He assumed that persons of wealth who accept an unpaying job (after all, only persons of wealth could afford to hold unpaid government jobs) will have at heart the interests of all classes of people, not only the interests of their own class. If you think critically about this assumption, you may find reasons to doubt it. Surely one reason we pay our legislators is to make certain that the legislature does not consist only of people whose incomes may give them an inadequate view of the needs of others.

An Example: Assumptions in the Argument Permitting Abortion

1. Ours is a pluralistic society, in which we believe that the religious beliefs of one group should not be imposed on others.

2. Personal privacy is a right, and a woman's body is hers, not to be violated by laws that tell her she may not do certain things to her body.

But these (and other) arguments *assume* that a fetus is not—or not yet—a person, and therefore is not entitled to the same protection against assaults that we are. Virtually all of us assume that it is usually wrong to kill a human being. Granted, we may find instances in which we believe it is acceptable to take a human life, such as self-defense against a would-be murderer. But even here we find a shared assumption, that persons are ordinarily entitled not to be killed.

The argument about abortion, then, usually depends on opposed assumptions: For one group, the fetus is a human being and a potential person—and this potentiality is decisive. But for the other group it is not. Persons arguing one side or the other of the abortion issue ought to be aware that opponents may not share their assumptions.

Premises and Syllogisms

Premises are stated assumptions used as reasons in an argument. (The word comes from a Latin word meaning "to send before," or "to set in front.") A premise thus is a statement set down—assumed—before the argument is begun. The joining of two premises—two statements taken to be true—to produce a conclusion, a third statement, is called a **syllogism** (Greek for "a reckoning together"). The classic example is this:

Major Premise: All human beings are mortal.

Minor Premise: Socrates is a human being.

Conclusion: Socrates is mortal.

Deduction

The mental process of moving from one statement ("All human beings are mortal") through another ("Socrates is a human being") to yet a further statement ("Socrates is mortal") is called **deduction,** from Latin for "lead down from." In this sense, deductive reasoning does not give us any new knowledge, although it is easy to construct examples that have so many premises, or premises that are so complex, that the conclusion really does come as news to most who examine the argument. Thus, the great detective Sherlock Holmes was credited by his admiring colleague, Dr. Watson, with unusual powers of deduction. Watson meant in part that Holmes could see the logical consequences of apparently disconnected reasons, the number and complexity of which left others at a loss. What is common in all cases of deduction is that the reasons or premises offered are supposed to contain within themselves, so to speak, the conclusion extracted from them.

Often a syllogism is abbreviated. Martin Luther King, Jr., defending a protest march, wrote, in "Letter from Birmingham Jail":

> You assert that our actions, even though peaceful, must be condemned because they precipitate violence.

Fully expressed, the argument that King attributes to his critics would be stated thus:

> We must condemn actions (even if peaceful) that precipitate violence.
>
> This action (though peaceful) will precipitate violence.
>
> Therefore we must condemn this action.

An incomplete or abbreviated syllogism in which one of the premises is left unstated, of the sort found in King's original quotation, is called an **enthymeme** (Greek for "in the mind").

Here is another, more whimsical example of an enthymeme, in which both a premise and the conclusion are left implicit. Henry David Thoreau is said to have remarked that "Circumstantial evidence can be very strong, as when you find a trout in the milk." The joke, perhaps intelligible only to people born before 1930 or so, depends on the fact that milk used to be sold "in bulk," that is, ladled out of a big can directly to the customer by the farmer or grocer. This practice was finally prohibited in the 1930s because for centuries the sellers, in order to increase their profit, were known to dilute the milk with water. Thoreau's enthymeme can be fully expressed thus:

> Trout live only in water.
>
> This milk has a trout in it.
>
> Therefore this milk has water in it.

Sound Arguments

The purpose of a syllogism is to *prove* its conclusion from its premises. This is done by making sure that the argument satisfies both of two independent criteria:

> First, all of the premises must be *true*.
>
> Second, the syllogism must be *valid*.

Once these criteria are satisfied, the conclusion of the syllogism is guaranteed. Any such argument is said to prove its conclusion, or, to use another term, is said to be **sound.** Here's an example of a sound argument, a syllogism that proves its conclusion:

> No city in Nevada has a population over 200,000.
>
> Denver has a population over 200,000.
>
> Therefore Denver is not a city in Nevada.

Each premise is **true,** and the syllogism is **valid,** so it proves its conclusion.

But how do we tell in any given case that an argument is sound? We perform two different tests, one for the truth of each of the premises and another for the validity of the argument.

The basic test for the **truth** of a premise is to determine whether what it asserts corresponds with reality; if it does, then it is true, and if it doesn't, then it is false. Everything depends on the content of the premise—what it asserts—and the evidence for it. (In the preceding syllogism, the truth of the premises can be tested by checking population statistics in a recent almanac.)

The test for **validity** is quite different. We define a valid argument as one in which the conclusion follows from the premises, so that if all the premises are true then the conclusion *must* be true, too. The general test for validity, then, is this: If one grants the premises, one must also grant the conclusion. Or to put it another way, if one grants the premises but denies the conclusion, is one caught in a self-contradiction? If so, the argument is valid; if not, the argument is invalid.

The preceding syllogism obviously passes this test. If you grant the population information given in the premises but deny the conclusion, you have contradicted yourself. Even if the population information were in error, the conclusion in this syllogism would still follow from the premises—the hallmark of a valid argument! The conclusion follows because the validity of an argument is a purely formal matter concerning the *relation* between premises and conclusion given what they mean.

One can see this relationship more clearly by examining an argument that is valid but that does *not* prove its conclusion. Here is an example of such a syllogism:

The whale is a large fish.

All large fish have scales.

Therefore whales have scales.

We know that the premises and the conclusion are false: Whales are mammals, not fish, and not all large fish have scales (sharks have no scales, for instance). But where the issue is the validity of the argument, the truth of the premises and the conclusion is beside the point. Just a little reflection assures us that *if* both of these premises were true, then the conclusion would have to be true as well. That is, anyone who grants the premises of this syllogism and yet denies the conclusion has contradicted herself. So the validity of an argument does not in any way depend on the truth of the premises or the conclusion.

A sound argument, as we said, is an argument that passes both the test of true premises and the test of valid inference. To put it another way, a sound argument is one that passes the test of *content* (the premises are true, as a matter of fact) and the test of *form* (its premises and conclusion, by virtue of their very meanings, are so related that it is impossible for the premises to be true and the conclusion false).

Accordingly, an unsound argument, an argument that fails to prove its conclusion, suffers from one or both of two defects. First, not all of the premises are true. Second, the argument is invalid. Usually it is one or both of these defects that we have in mind when we object to someone's argument as "illogical." In evaluating someone's deductive argument, therefore, you must always ask: Is it vulnerable to criticism on the ground that one (or more) of its premises is false? Or is the inference itself vulnerable, because whether or not all the premises are all true, even if they were the conclusion still wouldn't follow?

A deductive argument *proves* its conclusion if and only if *two conditions* are satisfied: (1) All the premises are *true;* (2) it would be *inconsistent to assert the premises and deny the conclusions.*

A Word about False Premises   Suppose that one or more of the premises of a syllogism is false, but the syllogism itself is valid. What does that tell us about the truth of the conclusion? Consider this example:

All Americans prefer vanilla ice cream to other flavors.

Tiger Woods is an American.

Therefore Tiger Woods prefers vanilla ice cream to other flavors.

The first (or major) premise in this syllogism is false. Yet the argument passes our formal test for validity; it is clear that if one grants both premises, one must accept the conclusion. So we can say that the conclusion *follows from* its premises, even though the premises *do not prove* the conclusion. This is not as paradoxical as it may sound. For all we know, the conclusion of this argument may in fact be true; Tiger Woods may indeed prefer vanilla ice cream, and the odds are that he does, because consumption statistics show that *most* (even if not all) Americans prefer vanilla. Nevertheless, if the conclusion in this syllogism is true, it is not because this argument proved it.

A Word about Invalid Syllogisms   Usually, one can detect a false premise in an argument, especially when the suspect premise appears in someone else's argument. A trickier business is the invalid syllogism. Consider this argument:

All crows are black.

This bird is black.

Therefore this bird is a crow.

Let's assume that both of the premises are true. What does this tell us about the truth of the conclusion? Nothing, because the argument is invalid. The *form* of the reasoning, the structure of the argument, is such that its premises (whether true or false) do not guarantee the conclusion. Even if both the premises were true, the conclusion might still be false.

In the preceding syllogism, the conclusion may well be true. It could be that the bird referred to in the second (minor) premise is a crow. But the conclusion might be false, because not only crows are black; ravens and blackbirds are also black. If the minor premise is asserted on the strength of observing a blackbird, then the conclusion surely is false: *This* bird is *not* a crow. So the argument is invalid, since as it stands it would lead us from true premises to accept a false conclusion.

How do we tell, in general and in particular cases, whether a syllogism is valid? As you know, chemists use litmus paper to enable them to tell instantly whether the liquid in a test tube is an acid or a base. Unfortunately, logic has no litmus test to tell us instantly whether an argument is valid or invalid. Logicians beginning with Aristotle have developed techniques that enable them to test any given argument, no matter how complex or subtle, to determine its validity. But the results of their labors cannot be expressed in a paragraph or even a few pages; not for nothing are semester-long courses devoted to teaching formal deductive logic. Apart from advising you to consult Chapter 8 ("A Logician's View"), all we can do here is repeat two basic points.

First, validity of deductive arguments is a matter of their *form* or *structure*. Even syllogisms like the one on Denver on page 59 come in a large variety of forms (256 different ones, to be precise), and only some of these forms are valid. Second, all valid deductive arguments (and only such arguments) pass this test: If one accepts all the premises, then one must accept the conclusion as well. Hence, if it is possible to accept the premises but reject the conclusion (without self-contradiction, of course), then the argument is invalid.

Let us exit from further discussion of this important but difficult subject on a lighter note. Many illogical arguments masquerade as logical. Consider this example: If it takes a horse and carriage four hours to go from Pinsk to Chelm, does it follow that if you have a carriage with two horses you will get there in two hours? In Chapter 8, we discuss at some length other kinds of deductive arguments, as well as **fallacies,** which are kinds of invalid reasoning.

Induction

Whereas the purpose of deduction is to extract the hidden consequences of our beliefs and assumptions, the purpose of **induction** is to use information about observed cases in order to reach a conclusion about unobserved cases. (The word comes from Latin *in ducere,* "to lead into," or "to lead up to.") If we observe that the bite of a certain snake is poisonous, we may conclude on this evidence that another snake of the same general type is also poisonous. Our inference might be even broader. If we observe that snake after snake of a certain type has a poisonous bite, and that these snakes are all rattlesnakes, we are tempted to **generalize** that all rattlesnakes are poisonous.

By far the most common way to test the adequacy of a generalization is to confront it with one or more **counterexamples.** If the counterexamples are genuine and reliable, then the generalization must be false. For example, Ronald Takaki's essay on the "myth" of Asian racial superiority (p. 77) is full of examples that contradict the alleged superiority of Asians; they are counterexamples to that thesis and they help to expose it as a "myth." What is true of Takaki's reasoning is true generally in argumentative writing. We are constantly testing our generalizations against actual or possible counterexamples.

Unlike deduction, induction gives us conclusions that go beyond the information contained in the premises used in their support. Not surprisingly, the conclusions of inductive reasoning are not always true, even when all the premises are true. On page 57 we gave as an example the belief that the subway runs at 6:00 A.M. every day, based on our observation that on previous days it ran at 6:00 A.M. Suppose, following this reasoning, one arrives at the subway platform just before 6:00 A.M. on a given day only to discover after an hour of waiting that there still is no train. What inference should we draw to explain this? Possibly today is Sunday, and the subway doesn't run before 7:00 A.M. Or possibly there was a breakdown earlier this morning. Whatever the explanation, we relied on a sample that was not large enough (a larger sample might have included some early morning breakdowns), or not representative enough (a more representative sample would have included the later starts on holidays).

A Word about Samples   When we reason inductively, much depends on the size and the quality of the sample. We may interview five members of Alpha Tau Omega and find that all five are Republicans, yet we cannot legitimately conclude that all members of ATO are Republicans. The problem is not always one of failing to interview large numbers. A poll of ten thousand college students tells us very little about "college students" if all ten thousand are white males at the University of Texas. Such a sample, because it leaves out women and minority males, obviously is not sufficiently *representative* of "college students" as a group. Further, though not all of the students at the University of Texas are from Texas, or even from the Southwest, it is quite likely that the student body is not fully representative (for instance, in race and in income) of American college students. If this conjecture is correct, even a truly representative sample of University of Texas students would not allow one to draw firm conclusions about American college students.

In short: An argument that uses samples ought to tell the reader how the samples were chosen. If it does not provide this information, it may rightly be treated with suspicion.

Evidence

Induction is obviously of use in arguing. If, for example, one is arguing that handguns should be controlled, one will point to specific cases in which handguns caused accidents, or were used to commit crimes. If one is arguing that abortion has a traumatic effect on women, one will point to women who testify to that effect. Each instance constitutes **evidence** for the relevant generalization.

In a courtroom, evidence bearing on the guilt of the accused is introduced by the prosecution, and evidence to the contrary is introduced by the defense. Not all evidence is admissible (hearsay, for one, is not, even if it is true), and the law of evidence is a highly developed subject in jurisprudence. In the forum of daily life, the sources of evidence are less disciplined. Daily experience, a particularly memorable observation, an unusual event we witnessed—any or all of these may be used as evidence for (or against) some belief, theory, hypothesis, or explanation. The systematic study of what experience can yield is what science does, and one of the most distinctive features of the evidence that scientists can marshal on behalf of their claims is that it is the result of **experimentation.** Experiments are deliberately contrived situations, often quite complex in their technology, designed to yield particular observations. What the ordinary person does with unaided eye and ear, the scientist does, much more carefully and thoroughly, with the help of laboratory instruments.

The variety, extent, and reliability of the evidence obtained in daily life and in the laboratory are quite different. It is hardly a surprise that in our civilization, much more weight is attached to the "findings" of scientists than to the corroborative (much less the contrary) experiences of the ordinary person. No one today would seriously argue that the sun really does go around the earth, just because it looks that way; nor would we argue that because viruses are invisible to the naked eye they cannot cause symptoms such as swellings and fevers, which are quite plainly visible.

Examples

One form of evidence is the **example.** Suppose that we argue that a candidate is untrustworthy and should not be elected to public office. We point to episodes in his career—his misuse of funds in 1994, and the false charges he made against an opponent in 1997—as examples of his untrustworthiness. Or, if we are arguing that President Truman ordered the atom bomb dropped to save American (and, for that matter, Japanese) lives that otherwise would have been lost in a hard-fought invasion of Japan, we point to the stubbornness of the Japanese defenders in battles on the islands of Saipan, Iwo Jima, and Okinawa, where the Japanese fought to the death rather than surrender.

These examples, we say, show us that the Japanese defenders of the main islands would have fought to the end, even though they knew they would be defeated. Or, if we take a different view of Truman's action and argue that the war in effect was already won and that Truman had no justification for dropping the bomb, we can cite examples of the Japanese willingness to end the war, such as secret negotiations in which they sent out peace feelers.

An example is a sample; the two words come from the same Old French word, *essample,* from the Latin *exemplum,* which means "something taken out," that is, a selection from the group. A Yiddish proverb shrewdly says that "'For example' is no proof," but the evidence of well-chosen examples can go a long way toward helping a writer to convince an audience.

In arguments, three sorts of examples are especially common:

1. real events,
2. invented instances (artificial or hypothetical cases), and
3. analogies.

We will treat each of these briefly.

Real Events   In referring to Truman's decision to drop the atom bomb, we have already touched on examples drawn from real events, the battles at Saipan and elsewhere. And we have also seen Ben Franklin pointing to an allegedly real happening, a fish that had consumed a smaller fish. The advantage of an example drawn from real life, whether a great historical event or a local incident, is that its reality gives it weight. It can't simply be brushed off.

On the other hand, an example drawn from reality may not provide as clear-cut an instance as could be wished for. Suppose, for instance, that someone cites the Japanese army's behavior on Saipan and on Iwo Jima as evidence that the Japanese later would have fought to the death in an American invasion of Japan, and would therefore have inflicted terrible losses on themselves and on the Americans. This example is open to the response that in August 1945, when Truman dropped the bomb, the situation was very different. In June and July 1945, Japanese diplomats had already sent out secret peace feelers; Emperor Hirohito probably wanted peace by then; and so on.

Similarly, in support of the argument that nations will not resort to atomic weapons, some people have offered as evidence the fact that since World War I the great powers have not used poison gas. But the argument needs more support than this fact provides. Poison gas was not decisive or even highly effective in World War I. Moreover, the invention of gas masks made it obsolete.

In short, any *real* event is, so to speak, so entangled in its historical circumstances that one may question whether indeed it is adequate or even relevant evidence in the case being argued. In using a real event as an example (and real events certainly can be used), the writer ordinarily must demonstrate that the event can be taken out of its historical context and be used in the new context of argument. Thus, in an argument against any further use in warfare of atomic weapons, one might point to the example of the many deaths and horrible injuries inflicted on the Japanese at Hiroshima and Nagasaki, in the confident belief that these effects of nuclear weapons will invariably occur and did not depend on any special circumstances of their use in Japan in 1945.

Invented Instances   **Artificial** or **hypothetical cases, invented instances,** have the great advantage of being protected from objections of the sort just given. Recall Thoreau's trout in the milk; that was a colorful hypothetical case that nicely illustrated his point. An invented instance ("Let's assume that a burglar promises not to shoot a householder if the householder swears not to identify him. Is the householder bound by the oath?") is something like a drawing of a flower in a botany textbook, or a diagram of the folds of a mountain in a geology textbook. It is admittedly false, but by virtue of its simplifications it sets forth the relevant details very clearly. Thus, in a discussion of rights, the philosopher Charles Frankel says:

> Strictly speaking, when we assert a right for X, we assert that Y has a duty. Strictly speaking, that Y has such a duty presupposes that Y has the capacity to perform this duty. It would be nonsense to say, for example, that a nonswimmer has a moral duty to swim to the help of a drowning man.

This invented example is admirably clear, and it is immune to charges that might muddy the issue if Frankel, instead of referring to a wholly abstract person, Y, talked about some real person, Jones, who did not rescue a drowning man. For then he would get bogged down over arguing about whether Jones *really* couldn't swim well enough to help, and so on.

Yet invented cases have their drawbacks. First and foremost, they cannot be used as evidence. A purely hypothetical example can illustrate a point or provoke reconsideration of a generalization, but it cannot substitute for actual events as evidence supporting an inductive inference. Sometimes such examples are so fanciful, so remote from life that they fail to carry conviction with the reader. Thus the philosopher Judith Jarvis Thomson, in the course of an argument entitled "A Defense of Abortion," asks us to imagine that we wake up one day and find that against our will a celebrated violinist whose body is not adequately functioning has been hooked up into our body, for life-support. Do we have the right to unplug the violinist? Readers of the essays in this book will have to decide for themselves whether the invented cases proposed by various authors are helpful or whether they are so remote that they hinder thought. Readers will have to decide, too, about when they can use invented cases to advance their own arguments.

But we add one point: Even a highly fanciful invented case can have the valuable effect of forcing us to see where we stand. We may say that we are, in all circumstances, against vivisection. But what would we say if we thought that an experiment on one mouse would save the life of someone we love? Or, conversely, if one approves of vivisection, would one also approve of sacrificing the last giant panda in order to save the life of a senile stranger, a person who in any case probably would not live longer than another year? Artificial cases of this sort can help us to see that, well, no, we didn't really mean to say such-and-such when we said so-and-so.

Analogies   The third sort of example, **analogy,** is a kind of comparison. Strictly, an analogy is an extended comparison in which different things are shown to be similar in several ways. Thus, if one wants to argue that a head of state should have extraordinary power during wartime, one can argue that the state at such a time is like a ship in a storm: The crew is needed to lend its help, but the decisions are best left to the captain. (Notice that an analogy compares things that are relatively *un*like. Comparing the plight of one ship to another, or of one government to another, is not an analogy; it is an inductive inference from one case of the same sort to another such case.) Or take another analogy: We have already glanced at Judith Thomson's hypothetical case in which the reader wakes up to find himself or herself hooked up to a violinist. Thomson uses this situation as an analogy in an argument about abortion. The reader stands for the mother, the violinist for the unwanted fetus. Whether this analogy is close enough to pregnancy to help illuminate our thinking about abortion is something that you may want to think about.

The problem with argument by analogy is this: Two admittedly different things are agreed to be similar in several ways, and the arguer goes on to assert or imply that they are also similar in the point that is being argued. (That is why Thomson argues that if something is true of the reader-hooked-up-to-a-violinist, it is also true of the pregnant mother-hooked-up-to-a-fetus.) But of course despite some similarities, the two things which are said to be analogous and which are indeed similar in characteristics A, B, and C, are also different, let's say in characteristics D and E. As Bishop Butler said, about two hundred fifty years ago, "Everything is what it is, and not another thing."

Analogies can be convincing, especially because they can make complex issues simple ("Don't change horses in midstream" of course is not a statement about riding horses across a river, but about choosing leaders in critical times). Still, in the end, analogies can prove nothing. What may be true about riding horses across a stream need not be true about choosing leaders in troubled times, or not true about a given change of leadership. Riding horses across a stream and choosing leaders are, at bottom, different things, and however much these activities may be said to resemble one another, they remain different, and what is true for one need not be true for the other.

Analogies can be helpful in developing our thoughts. It is sometimes argued, for instance—on the analogy of the doctor-patient or the lawyer-client or the priest-penitent relationship—that newspaper and television reporters should not be required to reveal their confidential sources. That is worth thinking about: Do the similarities run deep enough, or are there fundamental differences? Or take another example: Some writers who support abortion argue that the fetus is not a person any more than the acorn is an oak. That is also worth thinking about. But one should also think about this response: A fetus is not a person, just as an acorn is not an oak, but an acorn is a potential oak, and a fetus is a potential person, a potential adult human being. Children, even newborn infants, have rights, and one way to explain this claim is to call attention to their potentiality to become mature adults. And so some people argue that the fetus, by analogy, has the rights of an infant, for the fetus, like the infant, is a potential adult.

While we're on this subject let's consider a very brief comparison made by Jill Knight, a member of the British Parliament, speaking about abortion:

> Babies are not like bad teeth, to be jerked out because they cause suffering.

Her point is effectively put; it remains for the reader to decide whether or not fetuses are *babies;* and, second, if a fetus is not a baby, *why* it can or can't be treated like a bad tooth. And yet a further bit of analogical reasoning, again about abortion: Thomas Sowell, an economist at the Hoover Institute, grants that women have a legal right to abortion, but he objects to the government's paying for abortions:

> Because the courts have ruled that women have a legal right to an abortion, some people have jumped to the conclusion that the government has to pay for it. You have a constitutional right to privacy, but the government has no obligation to pay for your window shades. . . . (*Pink and Brown People,* p. 57)

We leave it to the reader to decide if the analogy is compelling—that is, if the points of resemblance are sufficiently significant to allow one to conclude that what is true of people wanting window shades should be true of people wanting abortions.

Authoritative Testimony

Another form of evidence is **testimony,** the citation or quotation of authorities. In daily life we rely heavily on authorities of all sorts: We get a doctor's opinion about our health, we read a book because an intelligent friend recommends it, we see a movie because a critic gave it a good review, and we pay at least a little attention to the weather forecaster.

In setting forth an argument, one often tries to show that one's view is supported by notable figures, perhaps Jefferson, Lincoln, and Martin Luther King, Jr., or scientists who won the Nobel Prize. You may recall that in the second chapter, in talking about definitions of pornography, we referred to Kenneth Clark. To make certain that you were impressed by his testimony even if you had never heard of him, we described him as "probably the most influential English-speaking art critic of our century." But heed some words of caution:

- Be sure that the authority, however notable, is an authority on the topic in question (a well-known biologist on vitamins, yes, but not on the justice of a war).

- Be sure the authority is not biased. A chemist employed by the tobacco industry isn't likely to admit that smoking may be harmful, and a "director of publications" (that means a press agent) for a hockey team isn't likely to admit that watching or even playing ice hockey stimulates violence.

- Beware of nameless authorities: "a thousand doctors," "leading educators," "researchers at a major medical school."

- Be careful in using authorities who indeed were great authorities in their day but who now may be out of date (Adam Smith on economics, Julius Caesar on the art of war, Louis Pasteur on medicine).

- Cite authorities whose opinions your readers will value. William F. Buckley's opinion means a good deal to readers of *The National Review* but not to most feminists. Gloria Steinem's opinion carries weight with many feminists but not much with persons who support traditional family values. If you are writing for the general reader, your usual audience, cite authorities who are likely to be accepted by the general reader.

One other point: *You* may be an authority. You probably aren't nationally known, but on some topics you perhaps can speak with authority, the authority of personal experience. You may have been injured on a motorcycle while riding without wearing a helmet, or you may have escaped injury because you wore a helmet; you may have dropped out of school and then returned; you may have tutored a student whose native language is not English, or you may be such a student and you may have received tutoring. You may have attended a school with a bilingual education program. Your personal testimony on topics relating to these issues may be invaluable, and a reader will probably consider it seriously.

Statistics

The last sort of evidence we will discuss here is quantitative or statistical. The maxim More Is Better captures a basic idea of quantitative evidence. Because we know that 90 percent is greater than 75 percent, we are usually ready to grant that any claim supported by experience in 90 percent of the cases is more likely to be true than an alternative claim supported by experience only 75 percent of the time. The greater the difference, the greater our confidence. Consider an example. Honors at graduation from college are often computed on a student's cumulative grade-point average (GPA). The undisputed assumption is that the nearer a student's GPA is to a perfect record (4.0), the better scholar he or she is, and therefore the more deserving of highest honors. Consequently, a student with a GPA of 3.9 at the end of her senior year is a stronger candidate for graduating summa cum laude than another student with a GPA of 3.6. When faculty members on the honors committee argue over the relative academic merits of graduating seniors, we know that these quantitative, statistical differences in student GPAs will be the basic (even if not the only) kind of evidence under discussion.

Graphs, Tables, Numbers   Statistical information can be marshaled and presented in many forms, but it tends to fall into two main types: the graphic and the numerical. Graphs, tables, and pie charts are familiar ways of presenting quantitative data in an eye-catching manner. To prepare the graphics, however, one first has to get the numbers themselves under control, and for many purposes (such as writing argumentative essays) it is probably more convenient simply to stick with the numbers themselves.

But should the numbers be presented in percentages, or in fractions? Should one report, say, that the federal budget underwent a twofold increase over the decade, or that it increased by 100 percent, or that it doubled, or that the budget at the beginning of the decade was one-half what it was at the end? Taken strictly, these are equivalent ways of saying the same thing. Choice among them, therefore, in an example like this perhaps will rest on whether one's aim is to dramatize the increase (a 100 percent increase looks larger than a doubling) or to play down the size of the increase.

Thinking about Statistical Evidence   Statistics often get a bad name because it is so easy to misuse them, unintentionally or not, and so difficult to be sure that they have been correctly gathered in the first place. (We remind you of the old saw "There are lies, damned lies, and statistics.") Every branch of social science and natural science needs statistical information, and countless decisions in public and private life are based on quantitative data in statistical form. It is extremely important, therefore, to be sensitive to the sources and reliability of the statistics, and to develop a healthy skepticism when confronted with statistics whose parentage is not fully explained.

Consider, for instance, statistics that kept popping up during the baseball strike of 1994. The owners of the clubs said that the average salary of a major-league player was $1.2 million. (The **average** in this case is the result of dividing the total number of salary dollars by the number of players.) The players' union, however, did not talk about the average; rather, the union talked about the **median,** which was less than half of the average, a mere $500,000. (The *median* is the middle value in a distribution. Thus, of the 746 players, 363 earned less than $500,000, 361 earned more, and 22 earned exactly $500,000.) The union said, correctly, that *most* players earned a good deal less than the $1.2 million figure that the owners kept citing; but the $1.2 million average sounded more impressive to the general public, and that is the figure that the guy in the street mentioned when asked for an opinion about the strike.

Here is a more complicated example of the difficulty of interpreting statistics. Violent crime increased in the 1960s and early 1970s, then leveled off, and began to decline in 1981. Did America become more violent for a while, and then become more law-abiding? Bruce Jackson in *Law and Disorder* suggests that much of the rise in the 1960s was due to the baby boom of 1948 to 1952. Whereas in 1960 the United States had only about 11 million people aged twenty to twenty-four, by 1972 it had almost 18 million of them, and it is people in this age group who are most likely to commit violent crimes. The decline in the rate of violent crime in the 1980s was accompanied by a decline in the proportion of the population in this age group—though of course some politicians and law enforcement officers took credit for the reduction in violent crime.

One other example may help to indicate the difficulties of interpreting statistics. According to the San Francisco police department, in 1990 the city received 1,074 citizen complaints against the police. Los Angeles received only half as many complaints in the same period, and Los Angeles has five times the population of San Francisco. Does this mean that the police of San Francisco are much rougher than the police of Los Angeles? Possibly. But some specialists who have studied the statistics not only for these two cities but also for many other cities have concluded that a department with proportionately more complaints against it is not necessarily more abusive than a department with fewer complaints. According to these experts, the more confidence that the citizens have in their police force, the more the citizens will complain about police misconduct. The relatively small number of complaints against the Los Angeles police department thus may indicate that the citizens of Los Angeles are so intimidated and have so little confidence in the system that they do not bother to complain.

We are not suggesting, of course, that everyone who uses statistics is trying to deceive, or even that many who use statistics are unconsciously deceived by them. We mean only to suggest that statistics are open to widely different interpretations and that often those columns of numbers, so precise with their decimal points, are in fact imprecise and possibly even worthless because they may be based on insufficient or biased samples.

A CHECKLIST FOR EVALUATING STATISTICAL EVIDENCE

Regard statistical evidence (like all other evidence) cautiously, and don't accept it until you have thought about these questions:

✓ Was it compiled by a disinterested source? Of course, the name of the source does not always reveal its particular angle (for example, People for the American Way), but sometimes the name lets you know what to expect (National Rifle Association, American Civil Liberties Union).

✓ Is it based on an adequate sample? (A study pointed out that criminals have an average IQ of 91 to 93, whereas the general population has an IQ of 100. The conclusion drawn was that criminals have a lower IQ than the general population. This reading may be accurate, but some doubts have been expressed. For instance, because the entire sample of criminals consisted only of *convicted* criminals, this sample may be biased; possibly the criminals with higher IQs have enough intelligence not to get caught. Or, if they are caught, they are smart enough to hire better lawyers.)

✓ Is the statistical evidence recent enough to be relevant?

✓ How many of the factors likely to be relevant were identified and measured?

✓ Are the figures open to a different and equally plausible interpretation? (Remember the decline in violent crime, for which law enforcement officers took credit.)

Quiz

What is wrong with the following statistical proof that children do not have time for school?

One-third of the time they are sleeping (about 122 days);

One-eighth of the time they are eating (three hours a day, totaling 45 days);

One-fourth of the time is taken up by summer and other vacations (91 days);

Two-sevenths of the year is weekends (104 days).

Total: 362 days—so how can a kid have time for school?

SATIRE, IRONY, SARCASM

In talking about definition, deduction, and evidence, we have been talking about means of rational persuasion. But, as mentioned earlier, there are also other means of persuasion. Take force, for example. If X kicks Y, threatens to destroy Y's means of livelihood, or threatens Y's life, X may persuade Y to cooperate. As Al Capone noted, "You can get more out of people with a gun and a kind word than with just a kind word." One form of irrational but sometimes highly effective persuasion is **satire**— that is, witty ridicule. A cartoonist may persuade viewers that a politician's views are unsound by caricaturing (and thus ridiculing) the politician's appearance, or by presenting a grotesquely distorted (funny, but unfair) picture of the issue.

Satiric artists often use caricature; satiric writers, also seeking to persuade by means of ridicule, often use **verbal irony.** In irony of this sort there is a contrast between what is said and what is meant. For instance, words of praise may be meant to imply blame (when Shakespeare's Cassius says, "Brutus is an honorable man," he means his hearers to think that Brutus is dishonorable), and words of modesty may be meant to imply superiority ("Of course I'm too dumb to understand this problem"). Such language, when heavy-handed, is called **sarcasm** ("You're a great guy," said to someone who will not lend the speaker ten dollars). If it is witty—if the jeering is in some degree clever—it is called irony rather than sarcasm.

Although ridicule is not a form of argument (because it is not a form of reasoning), passages of ridicule, especially verbal irony, sometimes appear in essays that are arguments. These passages, like reasons, or for that matter like appeals to the emotions, are efforts to persuade the hearer to accept the speaker's point of view. For example, in Judy Brady's essay "I Want a Wife" (p. 91), the writer, a woman, cannot really mean that she wants a wife. The pretense that she wants a wife gives the essay a playful, joking quality; her words must mean something other than what they seem to mean. But that she is not merely joking (satire has been defined as "joking in earnest") is evident; she is seeking to persuade. She has a point, and she could argue it straight, but that would produce a very different sort of essay.

EMOTIONAL APPEALS

It is sometimes said that good argumentative writing appeals only to reason, never to emotion, and that any sort of emotional appeal is illegitimate, irrelevant. Logic textbooks may even stigmatize with Latin labels the various sorts of emotional appeal, for instance *argumentum ad populam* (appeal to the prejudices of the mob, as in "Come on, we all know

that schools don't teach anything anymore"), and *argumentum ad misericordiam* (appeal to pity, as in "No one can blame this poor kid for stab-
bing a classmate because his mother was often institutionalized for alcoholism and his father beat him").

True, appeals to emotion may get in the way of the facts of the case;
they may blind the audience by, in effect, throwing dust in its eyes or by
stimulating tears. A classic example is found in Shakespeare's *Julius
Caesar*, when Marc Antony addresses the Roman populace after Brutus,
Cassius, and others have assassinated Caesar. The real issue is whether
Caesar was becoming tyrannical (as the assassins claim) and would
therefore curtail the freedom of the people. Antony turns from the evidence and stirs the mob against the assassins by appealing to its emotions. In the ancient Roman biographical writing that Shakespeare drew
on, Sir Thomas North's translation of Plutarch's *Lives of the Noble Grecians
and Romans*, Plutarch says that Antony,

> perceiving that his words moved the common people to compassion, . . .
> framed his eloquence to make their hearts yearn [that is, grieve] the
> more, and, taking Caesar's gown all bloody in his hand, he laid it open
> to the sight of them all, showing what a number of cuts and holes it had
> upon it. Therewithal the people fell presently into such a rage and
> mutiny that there was no more order kept.

Here are a few extracts from Antony's speeches in Shakespeare's play.
Antony begins by asserting that he will speak only briefly:

> Friends, Romans, countrymen, lend me your ears;
> I come to bury Caesar, not to praise him.

After briefly offering some rather insubstantial evidence that Caesar gave
no signs of behaving tyrannically (for example, "When that the poor
have cried, Caesar hath wept"), Antony begins to play directly on the
emotions of his hearers. Descending from the platform so that he may be
in closer contact with his audience (like a modern politician, he wants to
work the crowd), he calls attention to Caesar's bloody toga:

> If you have tears, prepare to shed them now.
> You all do know this mantle; I remember
> The first time ever Caesar put it on:
> 'Twas on a summer's evening, in his tent,
> That day he overcame the Nervii.
> Look, in this place ran Cassius' dagger through;
> See what a rent the envious Casca made;
> Through this, the well-belovèd Brutus stabbed. . . .

In these few lines Antony first prepares the audience by suggesting to
them how they should respond ("If you have tears, prepare to shed
them now"), then flatters them by implying that they, like Antony, were
intimates of Caesar (he credits them with being familiar with Caesar's

garment), then evokes a personal memory of a specific time ("a summer's evening")—not just any old specific time, but a very important one, the day that Caesar won a battle against the Nervii (a particularly fierce tribe in what is now France). In fact, Antony was *not* at the battle, and he did not join Caesar until three years later, but Antony does not mind being free with the facts. His point here is not to set the record straight; rather, it is to stir the mob against the assassins. He goes on, daringly but successfully, to identify one particular slit in the garment with Cassius's dagger, another with Casca's, and a third with Brutus's. Antony of course cannot know which slit was made by which dagger, but his rhetorical trick works. Notice, too, that he arranges the three assassins in climactic order, since Brutus (Antony claims) was especially beloved by Caesar.

> Judge, O you gods, how dearly Caesar loved him!
> This was the most unkindest cut of all;
> For when the noble Caesar saw him stab,
> Ingratitude, more strong than traitor's arms,
> Quite vanquished him. Then burst his mighty heart. . . . (3.2.75–188)

Nice. According to Antony, the noble-minded Caesar—Antony's words have erased all thought of the tyrannical Caesar—died not from the wounds inflicted by daggers but from the heartbreaking perception of Brutus's ingratitude. Doubtless there was not a dry eye in the house. We can all hope that if we are ever put on trial, we have a lawyer as skilled in evoking sympathy as Antony.

The oration is obviously successful in the play and apparently was successful in real life, but it is the sort of speech that prompts logicians to write disapprovingly of attempts to stir feeling in an audience. (As mentioned earlier in this chapter, the evocation of emotion in an audience is called **pathos,** from the Greek word for emotion or suffering.) There is nothing inherently wrong in stimulating our audience's emotions, but when an emotional appeal confuses the issue that is being argued about or shifts the attention away from the facts of the issue, we can reasonably speak of the fallacy of emotional appeal.

No fallacy is involved, however, when an emotional appeal heightens the facts, bringing them home to the audience rather than masking them. If we are talking about legislation that would govern police actions, it is legitimate to show a photograph of the battered, bloodied face of an alleged victim of police brutality. Of course, such a photograph cannot tell the whole truth; it cannot tell us if the subject threatened the officer with a gun or repeatedly resisted an order to surrender. But it can tell us that the victim was severely beaten and (like a comparable description in words) evoke in us emotions that may properly enter into our decision about what sorts of limitations are appropriate. Similarly, an animal rights activist who is arguing that calves are cruelly confined might reasonably tell us about the size of the pen in which the beast—

unable to turn around or even to lie down—is kept. Others may argue that calves don't much care about turning around or have no right to turn around, but the verbal description, which unquestionably makes an emotional appeal, can hardly be called fallacious or irrelevant.

In appealing to emotions then, the important things are

- not to falsify (especially by oversimplifying) the issue, and
- not to distract attention from the facts of the case.

Focus on the facts and concentrate on offering reasons (essentially, statements linked with "because"), but you may also legitimately bring the facts home to your readers by seeking to induce in them the appropriate emotions. Your words will be fallacious only if you stimulate emotions that are not rightly connected with the facts of the case.

A CHECKLIST FOR ANALYZING AN ARGUMENT

✓ What is the writer's thesis? Ask yourself:

   ✓ What claim is being asserted?

   ✓ What assumptions are being made—and are they acceptable?

   ✓ Are important terms satisfactorily defined?

✓ What support is offered on behalf of the claim? Ask yourself:

   ✓ Are the examples relevant, and are they convincing?

   ✓ Are the statistics (if there are any) relevant, accurate, and complete? Do they allow only the interpretation that is offered in the argument?

   ✓ If authorities are cited, are they indeed authorities on this topic, and can they be regarded as impartial?

   ✓ Is this logic—deductive and inductive—valid?

   ✓ If there is an appeal to emotion—for instance, if satire is used to ridicule the opposing view—is this appeal acceptable?

✓ Does the writer seem to you to be fair? Ask yourself:

   ✓ Are counterarguments adequately considered?

   ✓ Is there any evidence of dishonesty or of a discreditable attempt to manipulate the reader?

ARGUMENTS FOR ANALYSIS

Ronald Takaki

Ronald Takaki, the grandson of agricultural laborers who had come from Japan, is professor of ethnic studies at the University of California at Berkeley. He is the editor of From Different Shores: Perspectives on Race and Ethnicity in America *(1987), and the author of (among other writings)* Strangers from a Different Shore: A History of Asian-Americans *(1989). The essay that we reprint appeared originally in the* New York Times, *June 16, 1990, page 21.*

The Harmful Myth of Asian Superiority

Asian Americans have increasingly come to be viewed as a "model minority." But are they as successful as claimed? And for whom are they supposed to be a model?

Asian Americans have been described in the media as "excessively, even provocatively" successful in gaining admission to universities. Asian American shopkeepers have been congratulated, as well as criticized, for their ubiquity and entrepreneurial effectiveness.

If Asian Americans can make it, many politicians and pundits ask, why can't African Americans? Such comparisons pit minorities against each other and generate African American resentment toward Asian Americans. The victims are blamed for their plight, rather than racism and an economy that has made many young African American workers superfluous.

The celebration of Asian Americans has obscured reality. For example, figures on the high earnings of Asian Americans relative to Caucasians are misleading. Most Asian Americans live in California, Hawaii, and New York—states with higher incomes and higher costs of living than the national average.

Even Japanese Americans, often touted for their upward mobility, 5 have not reached equality. While Japanese American men in California earned an average income comparable to Caucasian men in 1980, they did so only by acquiring more education and working more hours.

Comparing family incomes is even more deceptive. Some Asian American groups do have higher family incomes than Caucasians. But they have more workers per family.

The "model minority" image homogenizes Asian Americans and hides their differences. For example, while thousands of Vietnamese American young people attend universities, others are on the streets. They live in motels and hang out in pool halls in places like East Los Angeles; some join gangs.

Twenty-five percent of the people in New York City's Chinatown lived below the poverty level in 1980, compared with 17 percent of the city's population. Some 60 percent of the workers in the Chinatowns of Los Angeles and San Francisco are crowded into low-paying jobs in garment factories and restaurants.

"Most immigrants coming into Chinatown with a language barrier cannot go outside this confined area into the mainstream of American industry," a Chinese immigrant said. "Before, I was a painter in Hong Kong, but I can't do it here. I got no license, no education. I want a living; so it's dishwasher, janitor, or cook."

Hmong and Mien refugees from Laos have unemployment rates that 10 reach as high as 80 percent. A 1987 California study showed that three out of ten Southeast Asian refugee families had been on welfare for four to ten years.

Although college-educated Asian Americans are entering the professions and earning good salaries, many hit the "glass ceiling" — the barrier through which high management positions can be seen but not reached. In 1988, only 8 percent of Asian Americans were "officials" and "managers," compared with 12 percent for all groups.

Finally, the triumph of Korean immigrants has been exaggerated. In 1988, Koreans in the New York metropolitan area earned only 68 percent of the median income of non-Asians. More than three-quarters of Korean greengrocers, those so-called paragons of bootstrap entrepreneurialism, came to America with a college education. Engineers, teachers, or administrators while in Korea, they became shopkeepers after their arrival. For many of them, the greengrocery represents dashed dreams, a step downward in status.

For all their hard work and long hours, most Korean shopkeepers do not actually earn very much: $17,000 to $35,000 a year, usually representing the income from the labor of an entire family.

But most Korean immigrants do not become shopkeepers. Instead, many find themselves trapped as clerks in grocery stores, service workers in restaurants, seamstresses in garment factories, and janitors in hotels.

Most Asian Americans know their "success" is largely a myth. They 15 also see how the celebration of Asian Americans as a "model minority" perpetuates their inequality and exacerbates relations between them and African Americans.

Topics for Critical Thinking and Writing

1. What is the thesis of Takaki's essay? What is the evidence he offers for its truth? Do you find his argument convincing? Explain your answers to these questions in an essay of 500 words.

2. Takaki several times uses statistics to make a point. Do some of the statistics seem more convincing than others? Explain.

3. Consider Takaki's title. To what group(s) is the myth of Asian superiority harmful?

4. Suppose you believed that Asian Americans are economically more successful in America today, relative to white Americans, than African Americans are. Does Takaki agree or disagree with you? What evidence, if any, does he cite to support or reject the belief?

5. Takaki attacks the "myth" of Asian American "success," and thus rejects the idea that they are a "model minority" (recall the opening and closing paragraphs). What do you think a genuine model minority would be like? Can you think of any racial or ethnic minority in the United States that can serve as a model? Explain why or why not in an essay of 500 words.

James Q. Wilson

James Q. Wilson is Collins Professor of Management and Public Policy at the University of California at Los Angeles. Among his books are Thinking about Crime *(1975),* Bureaucracy *(1989),* The Moral Sense *(1993), and* Moral Judgment *(1997). The essay that we reprint appeared originally in the* New York Times Magazine, *March 20, 1994.*

Just Take Away Their Guns

The president wants still tougher gun control legislation and thinks it will work. The public supports more gun control laws but suspects they won't work. The public is right.

Legal restraints on the lawful purchase of guns will have little effect on the illegal use of guns. There are some 200 million guns in private ownership, about one-third of them handguns. Only about 2 percent of the latter are employed to commit crimes. It would take a Draconian, and politically impossible, confiscation of legally purchased guns to make much of a difference in the number used by criminals. Moreover, only about one-sixth of the handguns used by serious criminals are purchased from a gun shop or pawnshop. Most of these handguns are stolen, borrowed, or obtained through private purchases that wouldn't be affected by gun laws.

What is worse, any successful effort to shrink the stock of legally purchased guns (or of ammunition) would reduce the capacity of law-abiding people to defend themselves. Gun control advocates scoff at the importance of self-defense, but they are wrong to do so. Based on a household survey, Gary Kleck, a criminologist at Florida State University, has estimated that every year, guns are used—that is, displayed or fired—for defensive purposes more than a million times, not counting their use by the police. If his estimate is correct, this means that the number of people who defend themselves with a gun exceeds the number of arrests for violent crimes and burglaries.

Our goal should not be the disarming of law-abiding citizens. It should be to reduce the number of people who carry guns unlawfully, especially in places—on streets, in taverns—where the mere presence of a gun can increase the hazards we all face. The most effective way to reduce illegal gun-carrying is to encourage the police to take guns away from people who carry them without a permit. This means encouraging the police to make street frisks.

The Fourth Amendment to the Constitution bans "unreasonable   5 searches and seizures." In 1968 the Supreme Court decided (*Terry v. Ohio*) that a frisk—patting down a person's outer clothing—is proper if the officer has a "reasonable suspicion" that the person is armed and dangerous. If a pat-down reveals an object that might be a gun, the officer can enter the suspect's pocket to remove it. If the gun is being carried illegally, the suspect can be arrested.

The reasonable-suspicion test is much less stringent than the probable-cause standard the police must meet in order to make an arrest. A reasonable suspicion, however, is more than just a hunch; it must be supported by specific facts. The courts have held, not always consistently, that these facts include someone acting in a way that leads an experienced officer to conclude criminal activity may be afoot; someone fleeing at the approach of an officer; a person who fits a drug courier profile; a motorist stopped for a traffic violation who has a suspicious bulge in his pocket; a suspect identified by a reliable informant as carrying a gun. The Supreme Court has also upheld frisking people on probation or parole.

Some police departments frisk a lot of people, but usually the police frisk rather few, at least for the purpose of detecting illegal guns. In 1992 the police arrested about 240,000 people for illegally possessing or carrying a weapon. This is only about one-fourth as many as were arrested for public drunkenness. The average police officer will make *no* weapons arrests and confiscate *no* guns during any given year. Mark Moore, a professor of public policy at Harvard University, found that most weapons arrests were made because a citizen complained, not because the police were out looking for guns.

It is easy to see why. Many cities suffer from a shortage of officers, and even those with ample law-enforcement personnel worry about having their cases thrown out for constitutional reasons or being accused of police harassment. But the risk of violating the Constitution or engaging in actual, as opposed to perceived, harassment can be substantially reduced.

Each patrol officer can be given a list of people on probation or parole who live on that officer's beat and be rewarded for making frequent stops to insure that they are not carrying guns. Officers can be trained to recognize the kinds of actions that the Court will accept as providing the "reasonable suspicion" necessary for a stop and frisk. Membership in a gang known for assaults and drug dealing could be made the basis, by statute or Court precedent, for gun frisks.

The available evidence supports the claim that self-defense is a legiti- 10 mate form of deterrence. People who report to the National Crime Survey that they defended themselves with a weapon were less likely to lose property in a robbery or be injured in an assault than those who did not defend themselves. Statistics have shown that would-be burglars are threatened by gun-wielding victims about as many times a year as they are arrested (and much more often than they are sent to prison) and that the chances of a burglar being shot are about the same as his chances of going to jail. Criminals know these facts even if gun control advocates do not and so are less likely to burgle occupied homes in America than occupied ones in Europe, where the residents rarely have guns.

Some gun control advocates may concede these points but rejoin that the cost of self-defense is self-injury: Handgun owners are more likely to shoot themselves or their loved ones than a criminal. Not quite. Most gun accidents involve rifles and shotguns, not handguns. Moreover, the rate of fatal gun accidents has been declining while the level of gun ownership has been rising. There are fatal gun accidents just as there are fatal car accidents, but in fewer than 2 percent of the gun fatalities was the victim someone mistaken for an intruder.

Those who urge us to forbid or severely restrict the sale of guns ignore these facts. Worse, they adopt a position that is politically absurd. In effect, they say, "Your government, having failed to protect your person and your property from criminal assault, now intends to deprive you of the opportunity to protect yourself."

Opponents of gun control make a different mistake. The National Rifle Association and its allies tell us that "guns don't kill, people kill" and urge the Government to punish more severely people who use guns to commit crimes. Locking up criminals does protect society from future crimes, and the prospect of being locked up may deter criminals. But our experience with meting out tougher sentences is mixed. The tougher the prospective sentence the less likely it is to be imposed, or at least to be imposed swiftly. If the Legislature adds on time for crimes committed with a gun, prosecutors often bargain away the add-ons; even when they do not, the judges in many states are reluctant to impose add-ons.

Worse, the presence of a gun can contribute to the magnitude of the crime even on the part of those who worry about serving a long prison sentence. Many criminals carry guns not to rob stores but to protect themselves from other armed criminals. Gang violence has become more threatening to bystanders as gang members have begun to arm themselves. People may commit crimes, but guns make some crimes worse. Guns often convert spontaneous outbursts of anger into fatal encounters. When some people carry them on the streets, others will want to carry them to protect themselves, and an urban arms race will be underway.

And modern science can be enlisted to help. Metal detectors at air-   15
ports have reduced the number of airplane bombings and skyjackings to nearly zero. But these detectors only work at very close range. What is needed is a device that will enable the police to detect the presence of a large lump of metal in someone's pocket from a distance of ten or fifteen feet. Receiving such a signal could supply the officer with reasonable grounds for a pat-down. Underemployed nuclear physicists and electronics engineers in the post-cold-war era surely have the talents for designing a better gun detector.

Even if we do all these things, there will still be complaints. Innocent people will be stopped. Young black and Hispanic men will probably be stopped more often than older white Anglo males or women of any race. But if we are serious about reducing drive-by shootings, fatal gang wars and lethal quarrels in public places, we must get illegal guns off the street. We cannot do this by multiplying the forms one fills out at gun shops or by pretending that guns are not a problem until a criminal uses one.

Topics for Critical Thinking and Writing

1. If you had to single out one sentence in Wilson's essay as coming close to stating his thesis, what sentence would that be? Why do you think it states, better than any other sentence, the thesis of the essay?

2. In his third paragraph Wilson reviews some research by a criminologist purporting to show that guns are important for self-defense in American households. Does the research as reported show that displaying or firing guns in self-defense actually prevented crimes? Or wounded aggressors? Suppose you were also told that in households where guns may be used defensively, thousands of innocent people are injured, and hundreds are killed—for instance, children who find a loaded gun and play with it. Would you regard these injuries and deaths as a fair trade-off? Explain. What does the research presented by Wilson really show?

3. In paragraph 12 Wilson says that people who want to severely restrict the ownership of guns are in effect saying, "'Your government, having failed to protect your person and your property from criminal assault, now intends to deprive you of the opportunity to protect yourself.'" What reply might an advocate of severe restrictions make? (Even if you strongly believe Wilson's summary is accurate, try to put yourself in the shoes of an advocate of gun control, and come up with the best reply that you can.)

4. Wilson reports in paragraph 7 that the police arrest four times as many drunks on the streets as they do people carrying unlicensed firearms.

Does this strike you as absurd, reasonable, or mysterious? Does Wilson explain it to your satisfaction?

5. In his final paragraph Wilson grants that his proposal entails a difficulty: "Innocent people will be stopped. Young black and Hispanic men will probably be stopped more often than older white Anglo males or women of any race." Assuming that his predictions are accurate, is Wilson's proposal therefore fatally flawed and worth no further thought, or (to take the other extreme view) do you think that innocent people who fall into certain classifications will just have to put up with frisking, for the public good?

6. In an essay of no more than 100 words, explain the difference between the "reasonable-suspicion test" and the "probable-cause standard" that the courts use in deciding whether a street frisk is lawful. (You may want to organize your essay into two paragraphs, one on each topic, or perhaps into three if you want to use a brief introductory paragraph.)

7. Wilson criticizes both gun control advocates and the National Rifle Association for their ill-advised views. In an essay of 500 words, state his criticisms of each side and explain whether and to what extent you agree.

Elizabeth M. Whelan

Elizabeth M. Whelan is president of the American Council on Science and Health. This selection appeared in the May 29, 1995, issue of Newsweek.

Perils of Prohibition

My colleagues at the Harvard School of Public Health, where I studied preventive medicine, deserve high praise for their recent study on teenage drinking. What they found in their survey of college students was that they drink "early and . . . often," frequently to the point of getting ill.

As a public-health scientist with a daughter, Christine, heading to college this fall, I have professional and personal concerns about teen binge drinking. It is imperative that we explore *why* so many young people abuse alcohol. From my own study of the effects of alcohol restrictions and my observations of Christine and her friends' predicament about drinking, I believe that today's laws are unrealistic. Prohibiting the sale of liquor to responsible young adults creates an atmosphere where binge drinking and alcohol abuse have become a problem. American teens, unlike their European peers, don't learn how to drink gradually, safely, and in moderation.

Alcohol is widely accepted and enjoyed in our culture. Studies show that moderate drinking can be good for you. But we legally proscribe alcohol until the age of twenty-one (why not thirty or forty-five?). Christine and her classmates can drive cars, fly planes, marry, vote, pay taxes, take out loans, and risk their lives as members of the U.S. armed forces. But laws in all fifty states say that no alcoholic beverages may be sold to anyone until that magic twenty-first birthday. We didn't always have a national "twenty-one" rule. When I was in college, in the mid-'60s, the drinking age varied from state to state. This posed its own risks, with underage students crossing state lines to get a legal drink.

In parts of the Western world, moderate drinking by teenagers and even children under their parents' supervision is a given. Though the per capita consumption of alcohol in France, Spain, and Portugal is higher than in the United States, the rate of alcoholism and alcohol abuse is lower. A glass of wine at dinner is normal practice. Kids learn to regard moderate drinking as an enjoyable family activity rather than as something they have to sneak away to do. Banning drinking by young people makes it a badge of adulthood—a tantalizing forbidden fruit.

Christine and her teenage friends like to go out with a group to a   5
club, comedy show, or sports bar to watch the game. But teens today have to go on the sly with fake IDs and the fear of getting caught. Otherwise, they're denied admittance to most places and left to hang out on the street. That's hardly a safer alternative. Christine and her classmates now find themselves in a legal no man's land. At eighteen, they're considered adults. Yet when they want to enjoy a drink like other adults, they are, as they put it, "disenfranchised."

Comparing my daughter's dilemma with my own as an "underage" college student, I see a difference—and one that I think has exacerbated the current dilemma. Today's teens are far more sophisticated than we were. They're treated less like children and have more responsibilities than we did. This makes the twenty-one restriction seem anachronistic.

For the past few years, my husband and I have been preparing Christine for college life and the inevitable partying—read keg of beer—that goes with it. Last year, a young friend with no drinking experience was violently ill for days after he was introduced to "clear liquids in small glasses" during freshman orientation. We want our daughter to learn how to drink sensibly and avoid this pitfall. Starting at the age of fourteen, we invited her to join us for a glass of champagne with dinner. She'd tried it once before, thought it was "yucky" and declined. A year later, she enjoyed sampling wine at family meals.

When, at sixteen, she asked for a Mudslide (a bottled chocolate-milk-and-rum concoction), we used the opportunity to discuss it with her. We explained the alcohol content, told her the alcohol level is lower when the drink is blended with ice and compared it with a glass of wine. Since the drink of choice on campus is beer, we contrasted its potency with wine and hard liquor and stressed the importance of not drinking on an empty stomach.

Our purpose was to encourage her to know the alcohol content of what she is served. We want her to experience the effects of liquor in her own home, not on the highway and not for the first time during a college orientation week with free-flowing suds. Although Christine doesn't drive yet, we regularly reinforce the concept of choosing a designated driver. Happily, that already seems a widely accepted practice among our daughter's friends who drink.

We recently visited the Ivy League school Christine will attend in the   10 fall. While we were there, we read a story in the college paper about a student who was nearly electrocuted when, in a drunken state, he climbed on top of a moving train at a railroad station near the campus. The student survived, but three of his limbs were later amputated. This incident reminded me of a tragic death on another campus. An intoxicated student maneuvered himself into a chimney. He was found three days later when frat brothers tried to light a fire in the fireplace. By then he was dead.

These tragedies are just two examples of our failure to teach young people how to use alcohol prudently. If eighteen-year-olds don't have legal access to even a beer at a public place, they have no experience handling liquor on their own. They feel "liberated" when they arrive on campus. With no parents to stop them, they have a "let's make up for lost time" attitude. The result: binge drinking.

We should make access to alcohol legal at eighteen. At the same time, we should come down much harder on alcohol abusers and drunk drivers of all ages. We should intensify our efforts at alcohol education for adolescents. We want them to understand that it is perfectly OK not to drink. But if they do, alcohol should be consumed in moderation.

After all, we choose to teach our children about safe sex, including the benefits of teen abstinence. Why, then, can't we—schools and parents alike—teach them about safe drinking?

Topics for Critical Thinking and Writing

1. Whelan states (para. 3), "Studies show that moderate drinking can be good for you." Ask a reference librarian to help you find out more about these studies. How do they define "moderate drinking"? How does Whelan?

2. In paragraph 3 Whelan speaks, with a touch of mockery in her voice, about "that magic twenty-first birthday." Of course there is nothing magical about this birthday, but if an age must be set, what should the age be? Whelan points out that at eighteen one can vote, serve in the armed forces, drive, and so forth. Does it follow that one age should be set for all activities? Should eighteen be the "magic" age? Why, or why not?

3. Whelan says (para. 6) that her daughter's college generation is far more "sophisticated" than hers was in the mid-1960s. Does she offer any evidence to support this claim? What evidence (if any) could you cite concerning the difference in sophistication between your generation and that of your parents?

4. Also in paragraph 6 Whelan says that "today's teens . . . have more responsibilities than we did." Do you think such a statement can be verified? Explain.

5. Whelan ends her essay by arguing that if teachers, parents, and other authority figures can teach teenagers about "safe sex," then they certainly can teach them about "safe drinking." Do you think the parallel is a good one? Why, or why not?

6. Whelan relates in some detail how she and her husband introduced their daughter to the pleasures of moderate alcohol consumption. In an essay of 250 to 500 words, compare and contrast their daughter's experience with your own. Argue for one course or the other or for some entirely different course.

Robert H. Bork

Robert H. Bork (b. 1927) taught at Yale Law School, resigned to serve as Solicitor General of the United States, and was then appointed to the U.S. Court of Appeals. He is now a resident scholar at the American Enterprise Institute, Washington, D.C. This selection appeared in the July 28, 1997, issue of The National Review.

Addicted to Health

When moral self-righteousness, greed for money, and political ambition work hand in hand they produce irrational, but almost irresistible, policies. The latest example is the war on cigarettes and cigarette smokers. A proposed settlement has been negotiated among politicians, plaintiffs' lawyers, and the tobacco industry. The only interests left out of the negotiations were smokers', who will be ordered to pay enormous sums with no return other than the deprivation of their own choices and pleasures.

It is a myth that today's Americans are a sturdy, self-reliant folk who will fight any officious interference with their liberties. That has not been true at least since the New Deal. If you doubt that, walk the streets of any American city and see the forlorn men and women cupping their hands against the wind to light cigarettes so that they can get through a few more smokeless hours in their offices. Twenty-five percent of Americans smoke. Why can't they demand and get a compromise rather than accepting docilely the exile that employers and building managers impose upon them?

The answer is that they have been made to feel guilty by self-righteous nonsmokers. A few years back, hardly anyone claimed to be seriously troubled by tobacco smoke. Now, an entire class of the morally superior claim to be able to detect, and be offended by, tobacco smoke several offices away from their own. These people must possess the sense of smell of a deer or an Indian guide. Yet they will happily walk through suffocating exhaust smoke from buses rather than wait a minute or two to cross the street.

No one should assume that peace will be restored when the last cigarette smoker has been banished to the Alaskan tundra. Other products will be pressed into service as morally reprehensible. If you would know the future, look to California—the national leader in health fanaticism. After a long day in Los Angeles flogging a book I had written, my wife and I sought relaxation with a drink at our hotel's outdoor bar. Our anticipation of pleasure was considerably diminished by a sign: "Warning! Toxic Substances Served Here." They were talking about my martini!

And martinis *are* a toxic substance, taken in any quantity sufficient 5 to induce a sense of well-being. Why not, then, ban alcohol or at least require a death's head on every martini glass? Well, we did once outlaw alcohol; it was called Prohibition. The myth is that Prohibition increased the amount of drinking in this country; the truth is that it reduced it. There were, of course, some unfortunate side effects, like Al Capone and Dutch Schultz. But by and large the mobsters inflicted rigor mortis upon one another.

Why is it, then, that the end of Prohibition was welcomed joyously by the population? Not because alcohol is not dangerous. Not because the consumption of alcohol was not lessened. And not in order to save the lives of people with names like Big Jim and Ice Pick Phil. Prohibition came to an end because most Americans wanted to have a drink when and where they felt like it. If you insist on sounding like a law-and-economics professor, it ended because we thought the benefits of alcohol outweighed the costs.

That is the sort of calculation by which we lead our lives. Automobiles kill tens of thousands of people every year and disable perhaps that many again. We could easily stop the slaughter. Cars could be made with a top speed of ten miles an hour and with exteriors the consistency of marshmallows. Nobody would die, nobody would be disabled, and nobody would bother with cars very much.

There are, of course, less draconian measures available. On most highways, it is almost impossible to find anyone who observes the speed limits. On the theory of the tobacco precedent, car manufacturers should be liable for deaths caused by speeding; after all, they could build automobiles incapable of exceeding legal speed limits.

The reason we are willing to offer up lives and limbs to automobiles is, quite simply, that they make life more pleasant (for those who remain intact) — among other things, by speeding commuting to work, by making possible family vacations a thousand miles from home, and by lowering the costs of products shipped from a distance. The case for regulating automobiles far more severely than we do is not essentially different from the case for heavy regulation of cigarettes or, soon, alcohol.

But choices concerning driving, smoking, and drinking are the sort of things that ought to be left to the individual unless there are clear, serious harms to others.

The opening salvo in the drive to make smoking a criminal act is the proposed settlement among the cigarette companies, plaintiffs' lawyers, and the states' attorneys general. We are told that the object is to protect teenagers and children (children being the last refuge of the sanctimonious). But many restrictions will necessarily affect adults, and the tobacco pact contains provisions that can only be explained as punishment for selling to adults.

The terms of the settlement plainly reveal an intense hatred of smoking. Opposition to the pact comes primarily from those who think it is not severe enough. For example, critics say the settlement is defective in not restricting the marketing of cigarettes overseas by American tobacco companies. Connecticut's attorney general, Richard Blumenthal, defended the absence of such a provision: "Given our druthers we would have brought them to their knees all over the world, but there is a limit to our leverage." So much for the sovereignty of nations.

What the settlement does contain is bad enough. The pact would require the companies to pony up $60 billion; $25 billion of this would be used for public-health issues to be identified by a presidential panel and the rest for children's health insurance. Though the purpose of the entire agreement is punitive, this slice is most obviously so.

The industry is also required to pay $308 billion over twenty-five years, in part to repay states for the cost of treating sick smokers. There are no grounds for this provision. The tobacco companies have regularly won litigation against plaintiffs claiming injury on the grounds that everybody has known for the past forty years that smoking can cause health problems. This $308 billion, which takes from the companies what they have won in litigation, says, in effect, that no one assumed the risk of his own behavior.

The provision is groundless for additional reasons. The notion that the states have lost money because of cigarettes ignores the federal and state taxes smokers have paid, which cover any amount the states could claim to have lost. Furthermore, a percentage of the population dies early from smoking. Had these people lived longer, the drain on Medicare and Medicaid would have been greater. When lowered pension and Social Security costs are figured in, it seems certain that government is better off financially with smoking than without it. If we must reduce the issue to one of dollars, as the attorneys general have done, states have profited financially from smoking. If this seems a gruesome and heartless calculation, it is. But don't blame me. The state governments advanced the financial argument and ought to live with its consequences, however distasteful.

Other provisions of the settlement fare no better under the application of common sense. The industry is to reduce smoking by teenagers by 30 percent in five years, 50 percent in seven years, and 60 percent in ten years. No one knows how the industry is to perform this trick. But if those goals are not met, the industry will be amerced $80 million a year for each percentage point it falls short. The settlement assumes teenage smoking can be reduced dramatically by requiring the industry to conduct an expensive antismoking advertising campaign, banning the use of people and cartoon characters to promote cigarettes, and similar tactics. It is entirely predictable that this will not work. Other countries have banned cigarette advertising, only to watch smoking increase. Apparently the young, feeling themselves invulnerable, relish the risk of smoking. Studies have shown, moreover, that teenagers are drawn to smoking not because of advertising but because their parents smoke or because of peer pressure. Companies advertise to gain or maintain market share among those who already smoke.

To lessen the heat on politicians, the pact increases the powers of the Food and Drug Administration to regulate tobacco as an addictive drug, with the caveat that it may not prohibit cigarette smoking altogether before the year 2009. The implicit promise is that the complete prohibition of cigarettes will be seriously contemplated at that time. In the meantime, the FDA will subject cigarettes to stricter and stricter controls on the theory that tobacco is a drug.

Another rationale for prohibiting or sharply limiting smoking is the supposed need to protect nonsmokers from secondhand smoke. The difficulty is that evidence of causation is weak. What we see is a possible small increase in an already small risk which, as some researchers have pointed out, may well be caused by other variables such as misclassification of former smokers as nonsmokers or such lifestyle factors as diet.

But the tobacco companies should take little or no comfort from that. Given today's product-liability craze, scientific support is unnecessary to successful lawsuits against large corporations.

The pact is of dubious constitutionality as well. It outlaws the adver- 20 tising of a product it is legal to sell, which raises the problem of commercial speech protected by the First Amendment. The settlement also requires the industry to disband its lobbying organization, the Tobacco Institute. Lobbying has traditionally been thought to fall within the First Amendment's guarantee of the right to petition the government for the redress of grievances.

And who is to pay for making smoking more difficult? Smokers will have the price of cigarettes raised by new taxes and by the tobacco companies' costs of complying with the settlement. It is a brilliant strategy: Smokers will pay billions to have their pleasure taken away.

But if the tobacco settlement makes little sense as public policy, what can be driving it to completion? The motivations are diverse. Members of the plaintiffs' bar, who have signally failed in litigation against tobacco to date, are to be guaranteed billions of dollars annually. The states' attorneys general have a different set of incentives. They are members of the National Association of Attorneys General, NAAG, which is commonly, and accurately, rendered as the National Association of Aspiring Governors.

So far they have got what they wanted. There they are, on the front pages of newspapers all over the country, looking out at us, jaws firm, conveying images of sobriety, courage, and righteousness. They have, after all, done battle with the forces of evil, and won—at least temporarily.

Tobacco executives and their lawyers are said to be wily folk, however. They may find ways of defeating the strictures laid upon them. It may be too soon to tell, therefore, whether the tobacco settlement is a major defeat or a victory for the industry. In any case, we can live with it. But whenever individual responsibility is denied, government control of our behavior follows. After cigarettes it will be something else, and so on *ad infinitum.* One would think we would have learned that lesson many times over and that we would have had enough of it.

Topics for Critical Thinking and Writing

1. Bork refers to smokers as "ordered to pay" (para. 1) for the privilege of smoking and as enduring "exile" (para. 2) from their places of work if they want to enjoy a smoke. With these words, does Bork misrepresent the facts of the matter? Why, or why not?

2. Bork implies that today's "self-righteous nonsmokers" will "happily walk" through exhaust fumes without a second thought (para. 3). Interview six nonsmokers among your friends and ask them whether, in all honesty, Bork's generalization applies to their behavior. In any case, what evidence, if any, does Bork seem to have for his generalization?

3. In an essay of 500 words, explain whether you agree or disagree with Bork when he says "The case for regulating automobiles far more severely than we do is not essentially different from the case for heavy regulation of cigarettes or, soon, alcohol" (para. 9).

4. Bork evidently believes that cigarette smoking does not cause "clear, serious harms to others" (para. 10)—that is, to nonsmokers—or he would favor its prohibition. In an essay of 500 words, explain why you believe he is either right or wrong about the harm smoking causes nonsmokers.

5. Using the resources of your library, find out what the current status is of the "proposed settlement among the cigarette companies, plaintiffs' lawyers, and the states' attorneys general" (para. 11). How, if at all, does it differ from the provisions Bork describes?

6. Explain whether you agree with Bork that, given all the evidence currently available, the "government is better off financially with smoking than without it" (para. 15).

7. Bork invokes a slippery slope objection to the proposed tobacco settlement, suggesting in paragraphs 4 and 24 that soon after cigarettes, some other products will go on trial as "morally reprehensible." Is this just a scare tactic, or do you think he is right?

Judy Brady

Born in San Francisco in 1937, Judy Brady married in 1960 and two years later earned a bachelor's degree in painting at the University of Iowa. Active in the women's movement and in other political causes, she has worked as an author, an editor, and a secretary. The essay reprinted here, written before she and her husband separated, appeared originally in the first issue of Ms. *in 1971.*

I Want a Wife

I belong to that classification of people known as wives. I am A Wife. And, not altogether incidentally, I am a mother.

Not too long ago a male friend of mine appeared on the scene fresh from a recent divorce. He had one child, who is, of course, with his ex-wife. He is looking for another wife. As I thought about him while I was ironing one evening, it suddenly occurred to me that I, too, would like to have a wife. Why do I want a wife?

I would like to go back to school so that I can become economically independent, support myself, and, if need be, support those dependent upon me. I want a wife who will work and send me to school. And while I am going to school I want a wife to take care of my children. I want a wife to keep track of the children's doctor and dentist appointments. And to keep track of mine, too. I want a wife to make sure my children eat properly and are kept clean. I want a wife who will wash the children's clothes and keep them mended. I want a wife who is a good nurturant attendant to my children, who arranges for their schooling, makes sure that they have an adequate social life with their peers, takes them to the park, the zoo, etc. I want a wife who takes care of the children when they are sick, a wife who arranges to be around when the children need special care, because, of course, I cannot miss classes at school. My wife must arrange to lose time at work and not lose the job. It may mean a small cut in my wife's income from time to time, but I guess I can tolerate that. Needless to say, my wife will arrange and pay for the care of the children while my wife is working.

I want a wife who will take care of *my* physical needs. I want a wife who will keep my house clean. A wife who will pick up after my children, a wife who will pick up after me. I want a wife who will keep my clothes clean, ironed, mended, replaced when need be, and who will see to it that my personal things are kept in their proper place so that I can find what I need the minute I need it. I want a wife who cooks the meals, a wife who is a *good* cook. I want a wife who will plan the menus, do the necessary grocery shopping, prepare the meals, serve them pleasantly, and then do the cleaning up while I do my studying. I want a wife who will care for me when I am sick and sympathize with my pain and loss of time from school. I want a wife to go along when our family takes a vacation so that someone can continue to care for me and my children when I need a rest and change of scene.

I want a wife who will not bother me with rambling complaints   5
about a wife's duties. But I want a wife who will listen to me when I feel the need to explain a rather difficult point I have come across in my course of studies. And I want a wife who will type my papers for me when I have written them.

I want a wife who will take care of the details of my social life. When my wife and I are invited out by my friends, I want a wife who will take care of the babysitting arrangements. When I meet people at school that I like and want to entertain, I want a wife who will have the house clean, will prepare a special meal, serve it to me and my friends, and not interrupt when I talk about things that interest me and my friends. I want a wife who will have arranged that the children are fed and ready for bed before my guests arrive so that the children do not bother us. I want a wife who takes care of the needs of my guests so that they feel comfortable, who makes sure that they have an ashtray, that they are passed the hors d'oeuvres, that they are offered a second helping of the food, that their wine glasses are replenished when necessary, that their coffee is served to them as they like it. And I want a wife who knows that sometimes I need a night out by myself.

I want a wife who is sensitive to my sexual needs, a wife who makes love passionately and eagerly when I feel like it, a wife who makes sure that I am satisfied. And, of course, I want a wife who will not demand sexual attention when I am not in the mood for it. I want a wife who assumes the complete responsibility for birth control, because I do not want more children. I want a wife who will remain sexually faithful to me so that I do not have to clutter up my intellectual life with jealousies. And I want a wife who understands that *my* sexual needs may entail

more than strict adherence to monogamy. I must, after all, be able to relate to people as fully as possible.

If, by chance, I find another person more suitable as a wife than
the wife I already have, I want the liberty to replace my present wife
with another one. Naturally, I will expect a fresh, new life; my wife
will take the children and be solely responsible for them so that I am
left free.

When I am through with school and have a job, I want my wife to
quit working and remain at home so that my wife can more fully and
completely take care of a wife's duties.

My God, who *wouldn't* want a wife?   10

Topics for Critical Thinking and Writing

1. If one were to summarize Brady's first paragraph, one might say it adds
   up to "I am a wife and a mother." But analyze it closely. Exactly what
   does the second sentence add to the first? And what does "not altogether incidentally" add to the third sentence?

2. Brady uses the word *wife* in sentences where one ordinarily would use
   she or *her*. Why? And why does she begin paragraphs 4, 5, 6, and 7 with
   the same words, "I want a wife"?

3. In her second paragraph Brady says that the child of her divorced male
   friend "is, of course, with his ex-wife." In the context of the entire essay,
   what does this sentence mean?

4. Complete the following sentence by offering a definition: "According to
   Judy Brady, a wife is . . ."

5. Try to state the essential argument of Brady's essay in a simple syllogism. (*Hint:* Start by identifying the thesis or conclusion you think she is
   trying to establish, and then try to formulate two premises, based on
   what she has written, that would establish the conclusion.)

6. Drawing on your experience as observer of the world around you (and
   perhaps as husband, wife, or ex-spouse), do you think Brady's picture of
   a wife's role is grossly exaggerated? Or is it (allowing for some serious
   playfulness) fairly accurate, even though it was written in 1971? If
   grossly exaggerated, is the essay therefore meaningless? If fairly accurate, what attitudes and practices does it encourage you to support?
   Explain.

7. Whether or not you agree with Brady's vision of marriage in our society, write an essay (500 words) titled "I Want a Husband," imitating her
   style and approach. Write the best possible essay, and then decide which
   of the two essays—yours or hers—makes a fairer comment on current
   society. Or, if you believe Brady is utterly misleading, write an essay
   titled "I Want a Wife," seeing the matter in a different light.

8. If you feel that you have been pressed into an unappreciated, unreasonable role—built-in babysitter, listening post, or girl (or boy or man or woman) Friday—write an essay of 500 words that will help the reader to see both your plight and the injustice of the system. (*Hint:* A little humor will help to keep your essay from seeming to be a prolonged whine.)

A CASEBOOK FOR ANALYSIS:
Does Bilingual Education Make Sense?

Diane Ravitch

Diane Ravitch (b. 1938) has taught history and education at Teacher's College, Columbia University, and has served as assistant secretary of education. She is now a senior research scholar at New York University and a senior fellow at the Brookings Institution. We reprint an essay that originally appeared in the New York Times, *September 5, 1997, and we follow it with letters written in response.*

First Teach Them English

The Bilingual Education Act of 1968 was intended to help Hispanic children learn English. But nearly thirty years later, it is clear that bilingual education has been a dismal failure.

The United States Department of Education recently reported a dropout rate of 30 percent for Hispanics between the ages of sixteen and twenty-four, more than double the dropout rate for blacks or whites in the same age group. The report also found that Hispanic students who spoke English well were far less likely to drop out than those who did not.

In 1994, a New York City Board of Education study showed that more than 90 percent of the students who started bilingual education in the sixth grade were unable to pass an English-language test after three years of bilingual instruction. The students most likely to languish in bilingual classes for four or more years were Hispanic.

Despite the failure of bilingual education, the President and Congress have agreed to increase federal financing for it to $354 million. That's double the amount spent in 1996, and it will trigger even more spending at the state and local levels.

Moreover, the New York State Education Department is expanding   5
such programs. In June, the state issued new guidelines for students

from English-speaking Caribbean nations who speak or understand a Creole language. Many students from countries like Jamaica, Barbados, Antigua, and the Bahamas will be routed into bilingual classes if they score in the bottom 40 percent on an English-language test. The state has listed nearly two dozen distinct Creole languages—including Leeward Islands Creole, Kokoy, Papiamento, and Bermudian Creole—that must be taught when at least twenty students who speak the language are in the same building and the same grade.

If these students had never left their countries they would have been instructed in English, which is the official language of the Caribbean nations identified by the state in this bizarre initiative. Now that they are residents of New York, they will be taught in their native patois.

Apparently, the purpose of this state initiative is not to help students learn English but to maintain their culture. If this is so, then their parents should be told about the poor track record of bilingual education and asked if they want their children enrolled in such a program. Those who want their children to learn English should be allowed to withhold consent. Under existing regulations, parents must navigate an elaborate bureaucratic process to withdraw children from bilingual education.

If schools really want to teach English to children with limited proficiency, they can look to the Middlebury College Language Schools' intensive summer immersion program as a model. Students sign a pledge to communicate only in the new language. By summer's end, they are as fluent as someone who has just completed a first-year college course.

Structured immersion, as this approach is called, works so well that it is used exclusively by the Defense Language Institute in Monterey, Calif., where the Pentagon teaches twenty-four different languages to more than three thousand students each year. Last year, the City University of New York established six English-immersion centers, in which students study English intensively for twenty-five hours a week to prepare them for college-level classes. Many students in the university's English immersion program are New York public school graduates whose language skills are so poor that they are not ready for college.

The United States should not be an English-only society. We should 10 encourage the study of foreign languages in schools and universities. But unless students are fluent in English, they will not have a fair chance of graduating from high school, going to college, and getting good jobs. All students should learn two languages. In this society, one of them must be English.

Ravitch's essay evoked the following responses, all of which were printed in the *New York Times* on September 9, 1997.

Letters from Kendall A. King,
Jeffrey O. Jones, Lisa M. Garcia,
Mathilda Holzman, and Judith D. Wallach

To the Editor:

Re "First Teach Them English" (Op-Ed, Sept. 5): While Diane Ravitch is right about the high dropout rate among Hispanic students, the conclusion she draws is wrong. The problem is not that students receive too much bilingual education but that they receive too little high-quality bilingual instruction.

Good bilingual education programs teach English. They also allow children to keep up with English-speaking peers by teaching reading, writing, and content in the first language. Contrary to popular belief, a 1995 Education Department study found that less than half of the nation's youngest students classified as having limited English proficiency received reading and math instruction in their native language.

Yet there is substantial evidence that school use of the native language not only has positive academic benefits but also lowers dropout rates. Those children who benefit from academic instruction in their native language are significantly more likely to enroll in college.

Kendall A. King
New York, Sept. 6, 1997
The writer is an assistant professor, department of teaching and learning,
N.Y.U. School of Education.

To the Editor:

Diane Ravitch (Op-Ed, Sept. 5) cites a Department of Education study showing that Hispanic students who spoke English well were far less likely to drop out than those who did not. Contrary to Ms. Ravitch, this only confirms the importance of bilingual education.

A case in point is Miguel, a high school boy I mentored for some years. Miguel arrived in the Bronx from a rural town in the Dominican Republic at age fifteen speaking little English. A diligent student who in the Dominican Republic walked miles to school each day, here he was unable to understand those around him or to express his thoughts.

"In my country, I was smart," he told me in frustration.

Enrolled in a New York City high school, he studied English as a second language. While he learned this new tongue, he also had Spanish-language classes in subjects like math and chemistry. Today Miguel speaks English fluently and is a college freshman.

Jeffrey O. Jones
New York, Sept. 6, 1997

To the Editor:

Diane Ravitch (Op-Ed, Sept. 5) cites the dropout rates of Hispanic students as proof that bilingual education has failed. That Hispanic students with low English proficiency drop out at higher rates than Hispanic students with high English proficiency has been proved in education studies to result from differences in socioeconomic status.

Students with low English proficiency are most often children of immigrant parents who have been in this country for a short period of time. The parents tend to have less education and income than parents of Hispanic students born in the United States.

Ms. Ravitch suggests immersion programs as a preferred alternative to bilingual education. Most studies agree that how students adapt to the school environment has a lasting effect on success. Immersion can only make this adaptation more traumatic for non-English-speaking students, suggesting grave consequences for their future educational success.

Lisa M. Garcia

Washington, Sept. 5, 1997

The writer is an intern in education policy at the Rand Corporation.

To the Editor:

I agree with Diane Ravitch (Op-Ed, Sept. 5) that bilingual education has been a dismal failure and that we need to help immigrants become fluent in English and complete high school. I do not agree that structured immersion is a solution.

Ms. Ravitch, in advocating immersion in the new language, seems to have in mind people who are educated in their native language and who need only transfer their native-language literacy to English. While this may be true of the Russian and Asian immigrants in Lexington, Mass., where I live, it is not true of most immigrants who live in the poor neighborhoods of Boston, where I have worked.

When I was living in Paris in 1979, I found a system that worked well. All immigrant children in a neighborhood, whatever their native language, attended the same school. The language of instruction was French and the children were motivated to acquire it. As soon as a child became literate enough to participate in the regular class of French children at his grade level, he was transferred.

Mathilda Holzman

Medford, Mass., Sept. 5, 1997

The writer is professor emeritus of child development, Tufts University.

To the Editor:

Diane Ravitch (Op-Ed, Sept. 5) is right. All students need to know English as well as another language. But that is true only if they want to participate in the life of the community at large, not if their interest is limited to an insular subculture.

The underlying message of the bilingual model is that the particular group with which one identifies is the only one that matters, so why prepare to participate in a heterogeneous society? This is the postmodern message of which Jean Bethke Elshtain, in "Democracy on Trial," writes: "To the extent that there is a *we* in this world of *I*'s, it is that of the discrete group with whom the *I* identifies."

We are stuck in a fragmented world that Ms. Elshtain describes as "a world of many *I*'s who form a *we* only with others exactly like themselves." That being the case, why bother to learn to communicate with those with whom there is no commonality?

Judith D. Wallach
New York, Sept. 5, 1997

Topics for Critical Thinking and Writing

1. Cite the evidence that Ravitch relies on when she concludes that "bilingual education has been a dismal failure" (para. 1). Can you think of any evidence that would contradict her conclusion? Does the letter by Kendall King seriously undermine her view? The letter from Jeffrey Jones? Why, or why not?

2. Can you think of any reasonable explanation for why, as Ravitch reports it, Caribbean natives at home are taught in English, whereas if they come to New York "they will be taught in their native patois" (para. 6)?

3. What is Ravitch's alternative to continuing to fund bilingual education?

4. What is "structured immersion" in foreign-language teaching? Why is it an effective method of instruction? How might Ravitch respond to the criticism in Lisa Garcia's letter? Mathilda Holzman's letter?

5. Ravitch opposes making the United States "an English-only society" (para. 10). List three advantages and three disadvantages of such a development. Which side has the better of the argument, in your judgment?

6. Ravitch favors "the study of foreign languages in [our] schools and universities" (para. 10). How might she reply to the criticism in Judith Wallach's letter?

Part Two

CRITICAL WRITING

4

Writing an Analysis
of an Argument

ANALYZING AN ARGUMENT

Examining the Author's Thesis

Most of your writing in other courses will require you to write an analysis of someone else's writing. In a course in political science you may have to analyze, say, an essay first published in *Foreign Affairs,* perhaps reprinted in your textbook, that argues against raising tariff barriers to foreign trade; or a course in sociology may require you to analyze a report on the correlation between fatal accidents and drunk drivers under the age of twenty-one. Much of your writing, in short, will set forth reasoned responses to your reading, as preparation for making an argument of your own.

Obviously you must understand an essay before you can analyze it thoughtfully. You must read it several times—not just skim it—and (the hard part) you must think about it. Again, you'll find that your thinking is stimulated if you take notes and if you ask yourself questions about the material. Notes will help you to keep track of the writer's thoughts and also of your own responses to the writer's thesis. The writer probably *does* have a thesis, a point, and if so, you must try to locate it. Perhaps the thesis is explicitly stated in the title or in a sentence or two near the beginning of the essay or in a concluding paragraph, but perhaps you will have to infer it from the essay as a whole.

Notice that we said the writer *probably* has a thesis. Much of what you read will indeed be primarily an argument; the writer explicitly or implicitly is trying to support some thesis and to convince you to agree with it. But some of what you read will be relatively neutral, with the argument just faintly discernible—or even with no argument at all. A work may, for instance, chiefly be a report: Here are the data, or here is what X, Y, and Z said; make of it what you will. A report might simply state how various ethnic groups voted in an election. In a report of this sort, of course, the writer hopes to persuade readers that the facts are correct, but no thesis is advanced, at least not explicitly or perhaps even consciously; the writer is not evidently arguing a point and trying to change our minds. Such a document differs greatly from an essay by a political analyst who presents similar findings in order to persuade a candidate to sacrifice the votes of this ethnic bloc in order to get more votes from other blocs.

Examining the Author's Purpose

While reading an argument, try to form a clear idea of the author's **purpose.** Judging from the essay or the book, was the purpose to persuade, or was it to report? An analysis of a pure report (a work apparently without a thesis or argumentative angle) on ethnic voting will deal chiefly with the accuracy of the report. It will, for example, consider whether the sample poll was representative.

Much material that poses as a report really has a thesis built into it, consciously or unconsciously. The best evidence that the prose you are reading is argumentative is the presence of two kinds of key terms:

transitions that imply the drawing of a conclusion: *therefore, because, for the reason that, consequently;*

verbs that imply proof: *confirms, accounts for, implies, proves, disproves, is (in)consistent with, refutes, it follows that.*

Keep your eye out for such terms and scrutinize their precise role whenever they appear. If the essay does not advance a thesis, think of a thesis (a hypothesis) that it might support or some conventional belief that it might undermine.

Examining the Author's Methods

If the essay advances a thesis, you will want to analyze the strategies or methods of argument that allegedly support the thesis.

Does the writer quote authorities? Are these authorities really competent in this field? Are equally competent authorities who take a different view ignored?

If statistics are used, are they appropriate to the point being argued? Can they be interpreted differently?

Does the writer build the argument by using examples, or analogies? Are they satisfactory?

Are the writer's assumptions acceptable?

Are all relevant factors considered? Has the author omitted some points that you think should be discussed? For instance, should the author recognize certain opposing positions, and perhaps concede something to them?

Does the writer seek to persuade by means of ridicule? If so, is the ridicule fair—is it supported also by rational argument?

In writing your analysis, you will want to tell your reader something about the author's purpose and something about the author's **methods.** It is usually a good idea at the start of your analysis—if not in the first paragraph then in the second or third—to let the reader know the purpose (and thesis, if there is one) of the work you are analyzing, and then to summarize the work briefly.

Next you will probably find it useful (your reader will certainly find it helpful) to write out *your* thesis (your evaluation or judgment). You might say, for instance, that the essay is impressive but not conclusive, or is undermined by convincing contrary evidence, or relies too much on unsupported generalizations, or is wholly admirable, or whatever. Remember, because your paper is itself an argument, it needs its own thesis.

And then, of course, comes the job of setting forth your analysis and the support for your thesis. There is no one way of going about this work. If, say, your author gives four arguments (for example: an appeal to common sense, the testimony of authorities, the evidence of comparisons, an appeal to self-interest), you may want to take up these four arguments in sequence. Or you may want to begin by discussing the simplest of the four, and then go on to the more difficult ones. Or you may want first to discuss the author's two arguments that you think are sound and then turn to the two that you think are not. And, as you warm to your thesis, you may want to clinch your case by constructing a fifth argument, absent from the work under scrutiny but in your view highly important. In short, the organization of your analysis may or may not follow the organization of the work you are analyzing.

Examining the Author's Persona

You will probably also want to analyze something a bit more elusive than the author's explicit arguments: the author's self-presentation. Does the author seek to persuade readers partly by presenting himself or herself as conscientious, friendly, self-effacing, authoritative, tentative, or in some other light? Most writers do two things: They present evidence, and they present themselves (or, more precisely, they present the image of themselves that they wish us to behold). In some persuasive writing this **persona** or **voice** or presentation of the self may be no less important than the presentation of evidence.

In establishing a persona, writers adopt various rhetorical strategies, ranging from the use of characteristic words to the use of a particular form of organization. For instance, the writer who speaks of an opponent's "gimmicks" instead of "strategy" is trying to downgrade the opponent and also to convey the self-image of a streetwise person. On a larger scale, consider the way in which evidence is presented and the kind of evidence offered. One writer may first bombard the reader with facts and then spend relatively little time drawing conclusions. Another may rely chiefly on generalizations, waiting until the end of the essay to bring the thesis home with a few details. Another may begin with a few facts and spend most of the space reflecting on these. One writer may seem professorial or pedantic, offering examples of an academic sort; another, whose examples are drawn from ordinary life, may seem like a regular guy. All such devices deserve comment in your analysis.

The writer's persona, then, may color the thesis and help it develop in a distinctive way. If we accept the thesis, it is partly because the writer has won our goodwill.

The author of an essay may, for example, seem fair minded and open minded, treating the opposition with great courtesy and expressing interest in hearing other views. Such a tactic is, of course, itself a persuasive device. Or take an author who appears to rely on hard evidence such as statistics. This reliance on seemingly objective truths is itself a way of seeking to persuade—a rational way, to be sure, but a mode of persuasion nonetheless.

Especially in analyzing a work in which the author's persona and ideas are blended, you will want to spend some time commenting on the persona. Whether you discuss it near the beginning of your analysis or near the end will depend on your own sense of how you want to construct your essay, and this decision will partly depend on the work you are analyzing. For example, if the author's persona is kept in the background, and is thus relatively invisible, you may want to make that point fairly early, to get it out of the way, and then concentrate on more interesting matters. If, however, the persona is interesting—and perhaps seductive, whether because it seems so scrupulously objective or so engagingly subjective—you may want to hint at this quality early in your essay, and then develop the point while you consider the arguments.

Summary

In the last few pages we have tried to persuade you that, in writing an analysis of your reading, you must do the following:

1. Read and reread thoughtfully. Writing notes will help you to think about what you are reading.
2. Be aware of the purpose of the material to which you are responding.

We have also tried to point out these facts:

3. Most of the nonliterary material that you will read is designed to argue, or to report, or to do both.
4. Most of this material also presents the writer's personality, or voice, and this voice usually merits attention in an analysis. An essay on, say, nuclear war, in a journal devoted to political science, may include a voice that moves from an objective tone to a mildly ironic tone to a hortatory tone, and this voice is worth commenting on.

Possibly all this explanation is obvious. There is yet another point, though, equally obvious but often neglected by students who begin by writing an analysis and end up by writing only a summary, a shortened version of the work they have read:

5. Although your essay is an analysis of someone else's writing, and you may have to include a summary of the work you are writing about, your essay is *your* essay. The thesis, the organization, and the tone are yours. Your thesis, for example, may be that although the author is convinced she has presented a strong case, her case is far from proved. Your organization may be deeply indebted to the work you are analyzing, but it need not be. The author may have begun with specific examples and then gone on to make generalizations and to draw conclusions, but you may begin with the conclusions. Similarly, your tone may resemble your subject's (let's say the voice is Courteous Academic), but it will nevertheless have its own ring, its own tone of (say) urgency, or caution, or coolness.

AN ARGUMENT, ITS ELEMENTS, AND A STUDENT'S ANALYSIS OF THE ARGUMENT

Stanley S. Scott

Stanley S. Scott (1933–1992) was vice president and director of corporate affairs of Philip Morris Companies Inc. This essay originally appeared on December 29, 1984, in the Op-Ed page of the New York Times.

Smokers Get a Raw Deal

The Civil Rights Act, the Voting Rights Act, and a host of antidiscrimination laws notwithstanding, millions of Americans are still forced to sit in the back of planes, trains, and buses. Many more are subject to segregation in public places. Some are even denied housing and employment: victims of an alarming—yet socially acceptable—public hostility.

This new form of discrimination is based on smoking behavior.

If you happen to enjoy a cigarette, you are the potential target of violent antismokers and overzealous public enforcers determined to force their beliefs on the rest of society.

Ever since people began smoking, smokers and nonsmokers have been able to live with one another using common courtesy and common sense. Not anymore. Today, smokers must put up with virtually unenforceable laws regulating when and where they can smoke—laws intended as much to discourage smoking itself as to protect the rights of nonsmokers. Much worse, supposedly responsible organizations devoted to the "public interest" are encouraging the harassment of those who smoke.

This year, for example, the American Cancer Society is promoting   5 programs that encourage people to attack smokers with canisters of gas, to blast them with horns, to squirt them with oversized water guns, and burn them in effigy.

Harmless fun? Not quite. Consider the incidents that are appearing on police blotters across America:

> In a New York restaurant, a young man celebrating with friends was zapped in the face by a man with an aerosol spray can. His offense: lighting a cigarette. The aggressor was the head of a militant antismoker organization whose goal is to mobilize an army of two million zealots to spray smokers in the face.

> In a suburban Seattle drugstore, a man puffing on a cigarette while he waited for a prescription to be filled was ordered to stop by an elderly customer who pulled a gun on him.

> A twenty-three-year-old lit up a cigarette on a Los Angeles bus. A passenger objected. When the smoker objected to the objection, he was fatally stabbed.

> A transit policeman, using his reserve gun, shot and fatally wounded a man on a subway train in the Bronx in a shootout over smoking a cigarette.

The basic freedoms of more than 50 million American smokers are at risk today. Tomorrow, who knows what personal behavior will become socially unacceptable, subject to restrictive laws and public ridicule? Could travel by private car make the social engineers' hit list because it is less safe than public transit? Could ice cream, cake, and cookies become socially unacceptable because their consumption causes obesity? What about sky diving, mountain climbing, skiing, and contact sports? How far will we allow this to spread?

The question all Americans must ask themselves is: Can a nation that has struggled so valiantly to eliminate bias based on race, religion, and sex afford to allow a fresh set of categories to encourage new forms of hostility between large groups of citizens?

After all, discrimination is discrimination, no matter what it is based on.

Let's examine Scott's essay with an eye to identifying those elements we mentioned earlier in this chapter (pp. 101–04) that deserve notice when examining *any* argument: the author's *thesis, purpose, methods,* and *persona.* And, while we're at it, let's also notice some other features of Scott's essay that will help us appreciate its effects and evaluate its strengths and weaknesses. All this will put us in a better position to write an evaluation or to write an argument of our own confirming, extending, or rebutting Scott's argument.

Title   Scott starts off with a bang — no one likes a "raw deal," and if that's what smokers are getting, then they probably deserve better. So, already in his title, Scott has made a plea for the reader's sympathy. He has also indicated something about his *topic* and his *thesis,* and (in the words "raw deal") something of his *persona;* he is a regular guy, someone who does not use fancy language but who calls a spade a spade.

Thesis   What is the basic *thesis* Scott is arguing? By the end of the second paragraph his readers have a good idea, and surely by paragraph 7, they can state his thesis explicitly, perhaps in these words: *Smokers today are victims of unfair discrimination.* Writers need not announce their thesis in so many words, but they ought to have a thesis, a point they want to make, and they ought to make it evident fairly soon — as Scott does.

Purpose   There's really no doubt that Scott's *purpose* in this essay is to *persuade* the reader to adopt his view of the plight of today's smokers. This amounts to trying to persuade us that his thesis (stated above) is *true.* Scott, however, does not show that his essay is argumentative or persuasive by using any of the key terms that normally mark argumentative prose. He doesn't call anything his "conclusion," none of his statements is labeled "my reasons" or "my premises," and he doesn't connect any clauses or sentences with a "therefore" or a "because."

But this doesn't matter. The argumentative nature of his essay is revealed by the *judgment* he states in paragraph 2: Smokers are experiencing undeserved discrimination. This is, after all, his thesis in brief form.

Any author who has a thesis as obvious as Scott does is likely to want to persuade his readers to agree with it. To do that, he needs to try to *support* it; accordingly, the bulk of the rest of Scott's essay constitutes just such support.

Method   Scott's principal method of argument is to cite a series of *examples* (introduced by para. 6) in which the reader can see what Scott believes is actual discrimination against smokers. This is his *evidence* in support of his thesis. (Ought we to trust him here? He cites no sources for the events he reports. On the other hand, these examples sound plausible, and so we probably shouldn't demand documentation for them.) The nature of his thesis doesn't require experimental research or support from recognized authorities. All it requires is some *reported instances* that can properly be described as "harassment" (para. 4, end). Scott of course is relying here on an *assumption:* Harassment is unfair discrimination—but few would quarrel with that assumption.

Notice the *language* in which Scott characterizes the actions of the American Cancer Society ("blast," "squirt," "burn"—all in para. 5). He chose these verbs deliberately, to convey his disapproval of these actions and subtly to help the reader disapprove of them, too.

Another distinctive feature of Scott's method of argument is found in paragraph 7, after the examples. Here, he drives his point home by using the argumentative technique known as *the thin end of the wedge.* (We discuss it later on p. 285. The gist of the idea is that just as the thin end of the wedge makes a small opening that will turn into a larger one, so a small step may lead to a large step. The idea is also expressed in the familiar phrase, "Give him an inch and he'll take a mile.") Scott here argues that tolerating discrimination today against a vulnerable minority (smokers) could lead to tolerating widespread discrimination against other minorities (mountain climbers) tomorrow—perhaps even a minority that includes the reader. (Does he exaggerate by overstating his case? Or are his examples well chosen and plausible?)

Notice, finally, the role that *rhetorical questions* play in Scott's argument. (A **rhetorical question,** such as Scott's "How far will we allow this to spread?" in para. 7, is a question to which no answer is expected, because only one answer can reasonably be made.) Writers who use a rhetorical question save themselves the trouble of offering further evidence to support their claims; the person asking the rhetorical question assumes the reader understands and agrees with the questioner's unstated answer.

Persona   Scott presents himself as a no-nonsense defender of the rights of a beleaguered minority. This may add little or nothing to the soundness of his argument, but it surely adds to its persuasive effect. By presenting himself as he does—plain-speaking but righteously indignant—Scott effectively jars the reader's complacency (surely, all the good guys *oppose* smoking—or do they?), and he cultivates at least the reader's grudging respect (we all like to see people stand up for their rights, and the more unpopular the cause the more we respect the sincere advocate).

Closing Paragraph   Scott ends with one of those seeming platitudes that tolerates no disagreement—"discrimination is discrimination," thus making one last effort to enlist the reader on his side. We say "seeming platitudes," because, when you come to think about it, of course not all discrimination is morally objectionable. After all, what's unfair with "discriminating" against criminals by punishing them?

Consider a parallel case, that popular maxim "Business is business." What is it, really, but a disguised claim to the effect that *in business, unfair practices must be tolerated or even admired.* But as soon as this sentiment is reformulated by removing its disguise as a tautology, its controversial character is immediately evident. So with Scott's "discrimination is discrimination"; it is designed to numb the reader into believing that all discrimination is *objectionable* discrimination. The critic might reply to Scott in the same vein: There is discrimination, and there is discrimination.

Let's turn now to a student's analysis of Scott's essay—and then to our analysis of the student's analysis.

Tom Wu

English 2B

Professor McCabe

March 13, 1998

Is All Discrimination Unfair?

Stanley S. Scott's "Smokers Get a Raw
Deal," though a poor argument, is an extremely
clever piece of writing. Scott writes clearly
and he holds a reader's attention. Take his
opening paragraph, which evokes the bad old days
of Jim Crow segregation, when blacks were forced
to ride at the back of the bus. Scott tells us,
to our surprise, that there still are Americans
who are forced to ride at the back of the bus.
Who, we wonder, are the people who are treated
so unfairly--or we would wonder, if the title of
the essay hadn't let us make an easy guess. They
are smokers. Of course most Americans detest
segregation, and Scott thus hopes to tap our
feelings of decency and fair play, so that we
will recognize that smokers are people too, and
they ought not to be subjected to the same evil
that blacks were subjected to. He returns to
this motif at the end of his essay, when he
says, "After all, discrimination is discrimination, no matter what it is based on." Scott is,
so it seems, on the side of fair play.

But "discrimination" has two meanings. One
is the ability to make accurate distinctions,
as in "She can discriminate between instant
coffee and freshly ground coffee." The second
meaning is quite different: an act based on
prejudice, as in "She does not discriminate
against the handicapped," and of course this is

Scott's meaning. Blacks were the victims of
discrimination in this second sense when they
were forced to sit at the back of the bus simply because they were black, not because they
engaged in any action that might reasonably be
perceived as offensive or harmful to others.
That sort of segregation was the result of
prejudice; it held people accountable for something (their color) over which they had no control. But smokers voluntarily engage in an
action which can be annoying to others (like
playing loud music on a radio at midnight, with
the windows open), and which may have effects
that can injure others. In pursuing their
"right," smokers thus can interfere with the
rights of others. In short, the "segregation"
and "discrimination" against smokers is in no
way comparable to the earlier treatment of
blacks. Scott illegitimately--one might say
outrageously--suggests that segregating smokers
is as unjust, and as blindly prejudiced, as was
the segregating of blacks.

Between his opening and his closing paragraphs, which present smokers as victims of
"discrimination," he cites several instances of
smokers who were subjected to violence, including two smokers who were killed. His point is,
again, to show that smokers are being treated
as blacks once were, and are in effect subjected to lynch law. The instances of violence
that he cites are deplorable, but they scarcely
prove that it is wrong to insist that people do
not have the unrestricted right to smoke in

public places. It is clearly wrong to assault smokers, but surely these assaults do not therefore make it right for smokers to subject others to smoke that annoys and may harm.

Scott's third chief argument, set forth in the third paragraph from the end, is to claim that if today we infringe on "the basic freedoms of more than 50 million American smokers" we will perhaps tomorrow infringe on the freedom of yet other Americans. Here Scott makes an appeal to patriotism ("basic freedoms," "American") and at the same time warns the reader that the reader's innocent pleasures, such as eating ice cream or cake, are threatened. But this extension is preposterous: Smoking undoubtedly is greatly bothersome to many nonsmokers, and may even be unhealthy for them; eating ice cream cannot affect onlookers. If it was deceptive to classify smokers with blacks, it is equally deceptive to classify smoking with eating ice cream. Scott is trying to tell us that if we allow smokers to be isolated, we will wake up and find that we are the next who will be isolated by those who don't happen to like our habits, however innocent. The nation, he says, in his next-to-last paragraph, has "struggled so valiantly [we are to pat ourselves on the back] to eliminate bias based on race, religion, and sex." Can we, he asks, afford to let a new bias divide us? The answer, of course, is that indeed we should discriminate, not in Scott's sense, but in the sense of making distinctions. We discriminate, entirely

Wu 4

properly, between the selling of pure food and
of tainted food, between law-abiding citizens
and criminals, between licensed doctors and unlicensed ones, and so on. If smokers are a serious nuisance and a potential health hazard,
it is scarcely un-American to protect the innocent from them. That's not discrimination (in
Scott's sense) but is simply fair play.

AN ANALYSIS OF THE STUDENT'S ANALYSIS

Tom Wu's essay seems to us to be excellent, doubtless the product of a good deal of thoughtful revision. Of course he does not cover every possible aspect of Scott's essay—he concentrates on Scott's reasoning and he says very little about Scott's style—but we think that, given the limits of 500 to 750 words, he does a good job. What makes the student's essay effective? We can list the chief reasons:

- The essay has a title that is of at least a little interest, giving a hint of what is to follow. A title such as "An Analysis of an Argument" or "Scott on Smoking" would be acceptable, certainly better than no title at all, but in general it is a good idea to try to construct a more informative or a more interesting title that (like this one) arouses interest, perhaps by stirring the reader's curiosity.
- The author identifies his subject (he names the writer and the title of his essay) early.
- He reveals his thesis early. His topic is Scott's essay; his thesis or point is that it is clever but wrongheaded. Notice, by the way, that he looks closely at Scott's use of the word *discrimination*, and that he defines this word carefully. Defining terms is often essential in argumentative essays. Of course Scott did *not* define the word, probably because he hoped his misuse of it would be overlooked.
- He takes up all of Scott's main points.

- He uses a few brief quotations, to let us hear Scott's voice and to assure us that he is staying close to Scott, but he does not pad his essay with long quotations.

- The essay has a sensible organization. The student begins with the beginning of Scott's essay, and then, because Scott uses the opening motif again at the end, touches on the end. The writer is not skipping around; he is taking a single point (a "new discrimination" is upon us) and following it through.

- He turns to Scott's next argument, that smokers are subjected to violence. He doesn't try to touch on each of Scott's four examples — he hasn't room, in an essay of 500 to 750 words — but he treats their gist fairly.

- He touches on Scott's next point, that no one will be safe from other forms of discrimination, and shows that it is both a gross exaggeration and, because it equates utterly unlike forms of behavior, a piece of faulty thinking.

- He concludes (without the stiffness of saying "in conclusion") with some general comments on discrimination, thus picking up a motif he introduced early in his essay. His essay, like Scott's, uses a sort of frame, or, changing the figure, it finishes off by tying a knot that was begun at the start. He even repeats the words "fair play," which he used at the end of his first paragraph, and neatly turns them to his advantage.

- Notice, finally, that he sticks closely to Scott's essay. He does not go off on a tangent and talk about the harm that smokers do to themselves. Because the assignment was to analyze Scott's essay

---

A CHECKLIST FOR AN ESSAY ANALYZING AN ARGUMENT

✓ In your opening paragraph (or opening paragraphs) do you give the reader a good idea of what your essay will be doing? Do you identify the essay you will discuss, and introduce your subject?

✓ Is your essay fair? Does it face all of the strengths (and weaknesses) of the argument?

✓ Have you used occasional quotations, in order to let your reader hear the tone of the author, and in order to insure fairness?

✓ Is your analysis effectively organized? Probably you can't move through the original essay paragraph by paragraph, but have you created a coherent structure for your own essay?

✓ If the original essay relies partly on the writer's tone, have you sufficiently discussed this matter?

✓ Is your own tone appropriate?

(rather than to offer his own views on smoking) he confines himself to analyzing the essay.

Exercise

Take one of the essays not yet discussed in class, or an essay assigned now by your instructor, and in an essay of 500 words analyze and evaluate it.

ARGUMENTS FOR ANALYSIS

Rita Kramer

Rita Kramer, the author of At a Tender Age: Violent Youth and Juvenile Justice *(1988) and other books, published this article in the* Wall Street Journal *(May 27, 1992).*

Juvenile Justice Is Delinquent

Anyone who reads newspapers or watches TV is familiar with scenes of urban violence in which the faces of those who rob and rape, maim and kill get younger and younger. On the streets, in the subways, and even in the schools, juvenile crime has taken on a character unthinkable when the present justice system was set up to deal with it. That system, like so many of the ambitious social programs designed in the '60s, has had unintended results. Instead of solving society's ills, it has added to them.

The juvenile justice system now in place in most parts of the country is not very different from New York's Family Court. Originally conceived to protect children (defined by different states as those under age sixteen, seventeen, or eighteen) who ran afoul of the law, it was designed to function as a kind of wise parent providing rehabilitation.

The 1950s delinquent, who might have been a shoplifter, a truant, or a car thief, would not be treated like an adult criminal. He was held to be, in the wording of the New York statute, "not criminally responsible . . . by reason of infancy." He would be given a hearing (not a trial) closed to the press and public and the disposition (not a sentence) would remain sealed, so the juvenile would not be stigmatized by youthful indiscretion. The optimistic belief was that under the guidance of social workers he would undergo a change of character.

It was a dream destined to become a nightmare. In the early 1960s, the character of juvenile court proceedings underwent a radical transformation. Due process was interpreted to grant youthful "respondents" (not defendants) not only the services of a lawyer, but also the

protections the criminal justice system affords adults, who are liable to
serious penalties if found guilty.

In the hands of Legal Aid Society lawyers (and sometimes sympa-   5
thetic judges), the juvenile system focuses on the minutiae of procedural
technicalities at the expense of fact-finding, in order to achieve the goal
of "getting the kid off." The question is not whether a teenage boy has
beaten up a homeless old man, shot a storekeeper, or sodomized a little
girl. He may even admit the act. The question is whether his admission
can be invalidated because a police officer forgot to have him initial his
responses to the Miranda warnings in the proper place or whether the
arresting officer had probable cause to search him for the loaded gun
that was found on him.

It has become the lawyer's job not only to protect his young client
from punishment, but from any possibility of rehabilitation in the system's various facilities. The best interests of the child or adolescent have
been reinterpreted to mean his legal rights, even when the two are in
opposition. He now has the right to continue the behavior that brought
him into the juvenile court, which he leaves with the knowledge that his
behavior had no real negative consequences to him.

Even when there are consequences, they are mild indeed, a fact not
lost on his peers. Eighteen months in a facility that usually has TV, a basketball court, and better food and medical care than at home is the worst
that all but the most violent repeat offenders have to fear in New York.
The system, based on a person's age and not his crimes, fails either to restrain or retrain him.

As juvenile courts were changing, so were juvenile criminals. As recently as the early '70s, the majority of cases before children's and family
courts were misdemeanors. In New York City, the most common charge
was "jostling," pickpocketing without physical contact. By 1991, robbery—a charge that involves violence against people—had outpaced
drug-related offenses as the largest category of crimes by juveniles. Between 1987 and 1991, the fastest-growing crime by juveniles was loaded
gun possession, and metal detectors and spot police checks had become
routine in some inner-city high schools.

Cases of violent group assault—"kids" causing serious physical injury "for fun"—had increased dramatically. Predatory behavior was becoming a form of entertainment for some of the urban young, white as
well as black and Hispanic. Last year, according to Peter Reinharz, chief
of New York City's Family Court Division, 85 percent of the young offenders brought into Family Court were charged with felonies. "These
are dangerous people," Mr. Reinharz says. "We hardly ever see the nonviolent any more."

Nationwide figures compiled by the FBI's Uniform Crime Reporting   10
Program in 1990 showed the highest number of arrests of youth for violent offenses—homicide, armed robbery, rape, aggravated assault—in
the more than twenty-five years that the statistics have been compiled.
Juvenile arrest rates, after rising steadily from the mid-1960s through

the 1970s, remained relatively constant until the 1989–90 statistics revealed a 26 percent increase in the number of youths arrested for murder and non-negligent manslaughter, while arrests for robbery had increased by 16 percent, and those for aggravated assault by 17 percent.

But the system still defines juveniles as children rather than as criminals, a distinction that makes little sense to their victims or to the rest of the public. Family Court turns the worst juvenile offenders over to the adult system for trial, but they are still sentenced as juveniles.

When anything does happen it's usually so long after the event, so short in duration, and so ineffective that it's no wonder the young men who rob, maim, rape, and terrorize don't perceive those actions as having any serious consequences. Eighty percent of chronic juvenile offenders (five or more arrests) go on to adult criminal careers.

Is it possible to change these young criminals? And what should be done to protect the community from them?

The first necessity is legislation to open juvenile court proceedings to the public and the press. It makes no sense to protect the privacy of those who are a palpable menace to their neighbors or scruple about "stigmatizing" them. A repeat offender should know the authorities will make use of his past record in deciding what to do with him next time. At present, a young habitual criminal is born again with a virgin record when he reaches the age to be dealt with by the adult system.

Opening court records would also make it possible to undertake 15 follow-up studies to find out what works and what doesn't in the various detention facilities and alternative programs designed to rehabilitate. Taxpayers have a right to know what outcomes they are getting for the $85,000 a year it costs to keep a juvenile offender in a secure facility in New York state.

Intervention should occur early, while there is still time to try measures that might make a difference. First offenders should be required to make restitution to their victims or perform community service. A second arrest should be followed by stronger measures. For those who have families who undertake to be responsible for them, there should be intensive supervision by well-trained probation officers with manageable caseloads. For those who require placement out of the home, it should include intensive remedial schoolwork and practical training in some job-related skill. The youth should remain long enough for such efforts to have some hope of proving effective.

Sanctions should be swift and sure. Once arrested, a court appearance should follow without delay, preferably on the same day, so that there is a clear connection made between behavior and its consequences. Placement in appropriately secure institutions, locked away from the community for definite periods of time, should be the immediate and inevitable response to repeated acts of violence. And incarceration should involve some form of work that helps defray its cost to the community, not just a period of rest and recreation. Young criminals should know that is what they can expect.

A growing cadre of violent teenage boys are growing up with mothers who are children and no resident fathers. What they need most of all is structure and supervision. We may not be able to change attitudes, but we can change behavior. While there is no evidence that any form of therapy can really change a violent repeat offender into someone with empathy for others, it has been demonstrated that the one thing that can result in impulse control is the certainty of punishment.

The present system actually encourages the young to continue their criminal behavior by showing them that they can get away with it. No punishment means a second chance at the same crimes. A significant number of boys arrested for violent crimes were out on parole at the time of the arrest.

They think of the system as a game they can win. "They can't do   20
nothing to me, I ain't sixteen yet" is a repeated refrain in a system that breeds contempt for the law and for the other institutions of society. It is time to acknowledge its failure and restructure the system so that "juvenile justice" ceases to be an oxymoron. We owe it to the law-abiding citizens who share the streets and schools with the violent few to protect the rights of the community and not just those of its victimizers.

Topics for Critical Thinking and Writing

1. In her fifth paragraph Kramer indicates her distress with a system that allows a guilty juvenile to be released because the police failed to comply with some details. But the requirement that police comply with details was generated by police misconduct. If adults can be released because the police fail to act according to all of the standard procedures, why shouldn't juveniles also be released?

2 Kramer says (para. 6) that the current juvenile justice system has made it the defendant's lawyer's job "to protect his young client . . . from any possibility of rehabilitation." Explain her reasoning.

3. Kramer says (para. 7) that if a youthful offender is put away, it is "in a facility that usually has TV, a basketball court, and better food and medical care than at home." Let's assume she is right. Why do you suppose the government provides TV, a basketball court, and better food and medical care than the youth probably has at home? If you were running things, what would you change? Would you, for instance, do away with television sets, or provide medical care that is below the standard? Explain.

4. "But the system," Kramer says in paragraph 11, "still defines juveniles as children rather than as criminals, a distinction that makes little sense to their victims." Does she have a point here? Or might it also be said that of course the victims are distressed, but the feelings of the victims are irrelevant to a society that is trying to deal intelligently and humanely with youthful offenders? Explain.

5. In paragraph 18 Kramer says that "it has been demonstrated that the one thing that can result in impulse control is the certainty of punishment." She offers no evidence. Do you take her statement on trust? Or because it seems self-evident? Or do you assume it is true because it is a principle that guides your own life? Or what? Explain.

6. Kramer says (para. 19): "The present system actually encourages the young to continue their criminal behavior by showing them that they can get away with it." What evidence, if any, does she offer to support this sentence? If she does not support it, should she have, or is it self-evident?

7. In her final paragraph Kramer indicates that the reason we must reform the system is "to protect the rights of the community." Earlier in the essay, however, she also indicated the desirability of helping youthful offenders to reform their conduct. What do you make of the fact that she does not continue this point into her final paragraph?

8. Kramer reports a sudden increase (26 percent) in violent crimes by juveniles in the years 1989–90. If your library receives the FBI's annual *Uniform Crime Reports* or the *Sourcebook of Criminal Justice Statistics*, consult one of these sources and determine whether in the years since 1990 juvenile crime has continued to increase, has leveled off, or has decreased.

9. In paragraph 18 Kramer mentions the "growing cadre of violent teenage boys . . . growing up with . . . no resident fathers." She ends this paragraph insisting on the "certainty of punishment" for such boys. Why do you suppose she doesn't instead recommend measures to punish the fathers for neglecting their sons?

10. List the measures Kramer recommends to decrease juvenile crime. Does she cite any evidence to show that these reforms really would reduce such crime? Can you think of reasons to believe in or to doubt their efficacy?

Jeff Jacoby

Jeff Jacoby is a columnist for the Boston Globe, *where this essay was originally published on February 20, 1997.*

Bring Back Flogging

Boston's Puritan forefathers did not indulge miscreants lightly.

For selling arms and gunpowder to Indians in 1632, Richard Hopkins was sentenced to be "whipt, & branded with a hott iron on one of his cheekes." Joseph Gatchell, convicted of blasphemy in 1684, was ordered "to stand in pillory, have his head and hand put in & have his toung drawne forth out of his mouth, & peirct through with a hott iron." When Hannah Newell pleaded guilty to adultery in 1694, the court ordered "fifteen stripes Severally to be laid on upon her naked back at the Common Whipping post." Her consort, the aptly named Lambert Despair, fared worse: He was sentenced to 25 lashes "and that on the next Thursday Immediately after Lecture he stand upon the Pillory for . . . a full hower with Adultery in Capitall letters written upon his brest."

Corporal punishment for criminals did not vanish with the Puritans — Delaware didn't get around to repealing it until 1972 — but for all relevant purposes, it has been out of fashion for at least 150 years. The day is long past when the stocks had an honored place on the Boston Common, or when offenders were publicly flogged. Now we practice a more enlightened, more humane way of disciplining wrongdoers: We lock them up in cages.

Imprisonment has become our penalty of choice for almost every offense in the criminal code. Commit murder; go to prison. Sell cocaine; go to prison. Kite checks; go to prison. It is an all-purpose punishment, suitable — or so it would seem — for crimes violent and nonviolent, motivated by hate or by greed, plotted coldly or committed in a fit of passion. If anything, our preference for incarceration is deepening — behold the slew of mandatory minimum sentences for drug crimes and "three-strikes-you're-out" life terms for recidivists. Some 1.6 million Americans are behind bars today. That represents a 250 percent increase since 1980, and the number is climbing.

We cage criminals at a rate unsurpassed in the free world, yet few of us believe that the criminal justice system is a success. Crime is out of control, despite the deluded happy talk by some politicians about how "safe" cities have become. For most wrongdoers, the odds of being arrested, prosecuted, convicted, and incarcerated are reassuringly long. Fifty-eight percent of all murders do *not* result in a prison term. Likewise 98 percent of all burglaries.

Many states have gone on prison-building sprees, yet the penal system is choked to bursting. To ease the pressure, nearly all convicted felons are released early — or not locked up at all. "About three of every four convicted criminals," says John DiIulio, a noted Princeton criminologist, "are on the streets without meaningful probation or parole supervision." And while everyone knows that amateur thugs should be deterred before they become career criminals, it is almost unheard of for judges to send first- or second-time offenders to prison.

Meanwhile, the price of keeping criminals in cages is appalling — a common estimate is $30,000 per inmate per year. (To be sure, the cost to society of turning many inmates loose would be even higher.) For tens of thousands of convicts, prison is a graduate school of criminal studies: They emerge more ruthless and savvy than when they entered. And for many offenders, there is even a certain cachet to doing time — a stint in prison becomes a sign of manhood, a status symbol.

But there would be no cachet in chaining a criminal to an outdoor post and flogging him. If young punks were horsewhipped in public after their first conviction, fewer of them would harden into lifelong felons. A humiliating and painful paddling can be applied to the rear end of a crook for a lot less than $30,000—and prove a lot more educational than ten years' worth of prison meals and lockdowns.

Are we quite certain the Puritans have nothing to teach us about dealing with criminals?

Of course, their crimes are not our crimes: We do not arrest blasphe-   10
mers or adulterers, and only gun control fanatics would criminalize the sale of weapons to Indians. (They would criminalize the sale of weapons to anybody.) Nor would the ordeal suffered by poor Joseph Gatchell— the tongue "peirct through" with a hot poker—be regarded today as anything less than torture.

But what is the objection to corporal punishment that doesn't maim or mutilate? Instead of a prison term, why not sentence at least some criminals—say, thieves and drunk drivers—to a public whipping?

"Too degrading," some will say. "Too brutal." But where is it written that being whipped is more degrading than being caged? Why is it more brutal to flog a wrongdoer than to throw him in prison—where the risk of being beaten, raped, or murdered is terrifyingly high?

The *Globe* reported in 1994 that more than two hundred thousand prison inmates are raped each year, usually to the indifference of the guards. "The horrors experienced by many young inmates, particularly those who . . . are convicted of nonviolent offenses," former Supreme Court Justice Harry Blackmun has written, "border on the unimaginable." Are those horrors preferable to the short, sharp shame of corporal punishment?

Perhaps the Puritans were more enlightened than we think, at least on the subject of punishment. Their sanctions were humiliating and painful, but quick and cheap. Maybe we should readopt a few.

Topics for Critical Thinking and Writing

1. When Jacoby says (para. 3) that today we are more "enlightened" than our Puritan forefathers, because where they used flogging "We lock them up in cages," is he being ironic? Explain.

2. Suppose you agree with Jacoby; explain precisely (1) what you mean by *flogging* (does Jacoby explain what he means?) and (2) how much flogging is appropriate for the crimes of housebreaking, rape, robbery, and murder.

3. In an essay of 250 words, explain why you think that flogging would be more (or less) degrading and brutal than imprisonment.

4. At the end of his essay Jacoby draws to our attention the terrible risk of being raped in prison as an argument in favor of replacing imprisonment with flogging. Do you think he mentions this point at the end because he believes it is the strongest or most pervasive of all those he mentions? Why, or why not?

5. It is often said that corporal punishment does not have any effect or, if it does, the effect is the negative one of telling the recipient that violence is an acceptable form of behavior. But suppose it were demonstrated that the infliction of physical pain reduced at least certain kinds of crimes, perhaps shoplifting, or unarmed robbery. Should we adopt the practice?

6. Jacoby draws the line (para. 11) at punishment that would "maim or mutilate." Why draw the line here? Some societies punish thieves by amputating a hand. Suppose we knew that this practice really did seriously reduce theft. Should we adopt it? How about adopting castration (surgical or chemical?) for rapists? For child molesters?

Katha Pollitt

Katha Pollitt (b. 1949) often writes essays on literary, political, and social topics for The Nation, *a liberal journal that on January 30, 1995, published the essay that we reprint here. Some of Pollitt's essays have been collected and published in a volume called* Reasonable Creatures *(1994). Pollitt is also widely known as a poet; her first collection of poems,* Antarctic Traveller *(1982), won the National Book Critics Circle award for poetry.*

It Takes Two: A Modest Proposal for Holding Fathers Equally Accountable

"You start out with the philosophy that you can have as many babies as you want . . . if you don't ask the government to take care of them. But when you start asking the government to take care of them, the government ought to have some control over you. I would say, for people like that, if they want the government to take care of their children I would be for something like Norplant, mandatory Norplant."

What well-known politician made the above remarks? Newt Gingrich? Jesse Helms? Dan Quayle? No, it was Marion Barry, newly installed Democratic mayor of our nation's capital, speaking last November to Sally Quinn of the *Washington Post.* The same Marion Barry whose swearing-in on January 2 featured a poetry reading by Maya Angelou, who, according to the *New York Times,* "drew thunderous applause when she pointed at Mr. Barry and crooned: 'Me and my baby, we gonna shine, shine!'" Ms. Angelou sure knows how to pick them.

One of my neighbors told me in the laundry room that it wasn't very nice of me to have mentioned Arianna Huffington's millions when we "debated" spirituality and school prayer on *Crossfire* the other day. So I won't belabor Mayor Barry's personal history[1] here. After all, the great

---

[1]**Mayor Barry's personal history** Marion Barry served six months in prison for possessing drugs.

thing about Christianity, of which Mayor Barry told Ms. Quinn he is now a fervent devotee, is that you can always declare yourself reformed, reborn, and redeemed. So maybe Mayor ("Bitch set me up") Barry really is the man to "bring integrity back into government," as he is promising to do.

But isn't it interesting that the male politicians who go all out for family values—the deadbeat dads, multiple divorcers, convicted felons, gropers, and philanderers who rule the land—always focus on women's behavior and always in a punitive way? You could, after all, see the plethora of women and children in poverty as the fruits of male feckless-ness, callousness, selfishness, and sexual vanity. We hear an awful lot about pregnant teens, but what about the fact that 30 percent of fathers of babies born to girls under sixteen are men in their twenties or older? What about the fact that the condom is the only cheap, easy-to-use, ef-fective, side-effectless nonprescription method of contraception—and it is the male partner who must choose to use it? What about the 50 per-cent of welfare mothers who are on the rolls because of divorce—i.e., the failure of judges to order, or husbands to pay, adequate child support?

Marion Barry's views on welfare are shared by millions: Women   5
have babies by parthenogenesis or cloning, and then perversely demand that the government "take care of them." Last time I looked, taking care of children meant feeding, bathing, and singing the Barney song, and mothers, not government bureaucrats, were performing those tasks. It is not the mother's care that welfare replaces, but the father's cash. Newt Gingrich's Personal Responsibility Act is directed against unmarried moms, but these women are actually assuming a responsibility that their babies' fathers have shirked. It's all very well to talk about orphanages, but what would happen to children if mothers abandoned them at the rate fathers do? A woman who leaves her newborn in the hospital and never returns for it still makes headlines. You'd need a list as thick as the New York City phone book to name the men who have no idea where or how or who their children are.

My point is not to demonize men, but fair's fair. If we've come so far down the road that we're talking about mandatory Norplant, about starving women into giving up their kids to orphanages (Republican ver-sion) or forcing young mothers to live in group homes (Democratic ver-sion); if *The Bell Curve* coauthor Charles Murray elicits barely a peep when he suggests releasing men from financial obligations to out-of-wedlock children; and if divorced moms have to hire private detectives to get their exes to pay court-awarded child support, then it's time to en-sure that the Personal Responsibility Act applies equally to both sexes. For example:

1. A man who fathers a child out of wedlock must pay $10,000 a year or 20 percent of his income, whichever is greater, in child sup-port until the child reaches twenty-one. If he is unable to pay, the

government will, in which case the father will be given a workfare (no wage) job and a dorm residence comparable to those provided homeless women and children—i.e., curfews, no visitors, and compulsory group-therapy sessions in which, along with other unwed fathers, he can learn to identify the patterns of irresponsibility that led him to impregnate a woman so thoughtlessly.

2. A man who fathers a second child out of wedlock must pay child support equal to that for the first; if he can't, or is already on workfare, he must have a vasectomy. A sample of his sperm will be preserved so he can father more children if he becomes able to support the ones he already has.

3. Married men who father children out of wedlock or in sequential marriages have the same obligations to all their children, whose living standards must be as close to equal as is humanly possible. This means that some older men will be financially unable to provide their much-younger trophy wives with the babies those women often crave. Too bad!

4. Given the important role played by fathers in everything from up- 10 ping their children's test scores to teaching them the meaning of terms like "wide receiver" and "throw weight," divorced or unwed fathers will be legally compelled to spend time with their children or face criminal charges of child neglect. Absentee dads, not overburdened single moms, will be legally liable for the crimes and misdemeanors of their minor children, and their paychecks will be docked if the kids are truant.

5. In view of the fact that men can father children unknowingly, all men will pay a special annual tax to provide support for children whose paternity is unknown. Men wishing to avoid the tax can undergo a vasectomy at state expense, with sperm to be frozen at personal expense (Republican version) or by government subsidy (Democratic version).

As I was saying, fair's fair.

Topics for Critical Thinking and Writing

1. In paragraph 5 Pollitt sums up what she says is a common view of welfare: "Women have babies by parthenogenesis or cloning, and then perversely demand that the government 'take care of them.'" What absurdity is she calling to our attention?

2. In paragraph 4 Pollitt cites three important facts for her argument pointing to "male . . . selfishness" as a chief cause of women on welfare. Consult some reliable source—a word with the reference librarian will probably help guide you to the right place—and verify at least one of these facts.

3. In paragraph 5 Pollitt mentions "Newt Gingrich's Personal Responsibility Act." With the assistance of your college's librarian, locate the text, or at least a summary, of this proposed law. Then look up the Republi-

cans' *Contract with America,* edited by Ed Gillespie and Bob Schellhas (1994), and check out what is described there as the Family Reinforcement Act. How do these two proposed laws differ?

4. Reread the first five paragraphs. Do you think that Pollitt has helped you to think about a problem? Or has she muddied the waters? Explain.

5. Pollitt declares not only once but twice (paras. 6 and 12) that "fair's fair." People also sometimes say "business is business." Both expressions look like more tautologies (needless repetitions), explaining or justifying nothing—yet they aren't really tautologies at all. What do you think is the rhetorical or persuasive function of such expressions?

6. Do you think that any of Pollitt's five proposals might become law? If not, why not, and, further, what *is* her purpose in offering them?

7. If you have read Jonathan Swift's "A Modest Proposal" (p. 151), explain why Pollitt echoes Swift's title in her own title.

David Cole

David Cole, a professor at Georgetown University Law Center, is a volunteer staff attorney for the Center for Constitutional Rights. This essay originally appeared in The Nation *on October 17, 1994.*

Five Myths about Immigration

For a brief period in the mid-nineteenth century, a new political movement captured the passions of the American public. Fittingly labeled the "Know-Nothings," their unifying theme was nativism. They liked to call themselves "Native Americans," although they had no sympathy for people we call Native Americans today. And they pinned every problem in American society on immigrants. As one Know-Nothing wrote in 1856: "Four-fifths of the beggary and three-fifths of the crime spring from our foreign population; more than half the public charities, more than half the prisons and almshouses, more than half the police and the cost of administering criminal justice are for foreigners."

At the time, the greatest influx of immigrants was from Ireland, where the potato famine had struck, and Germany, which was in political and economic turmoil. Anti-alien and anti-Catholic sentiments were the order of the day, especially in New York and Massachusetts, which received the brunt of the wave of immigrants, many of whom were dirt-poor and uneducated. Politicians were quick to exploit the sentiment: There's nothing like a scapegoat to forge an alliance.

I am especially sensitive to this history: My forebears were among those dirt-poor Irish Catholics who arrived in the 1860s. Fortunately for them, and me, the Know-Nothing movement fizzled within fifteen years. But its pilot light kept burning, and is turned up whenever the American public begins to feel vulnerable and in need of an enemy.

Although they go by different names today, the Know-Nothings have returned. As in the 1850s, the movement is strongest where immigrants are most concentrated: California and Florida. The objects of prejudice are of course no longer Irish Catholics and Germans; 140 years later, "they" have become "us." The new "they"—because it seems "we" must always have a "they"—are Latin Americans (most recently, Cubans), Haitians, and Arab Americans, among others.

But just as in the 1850s, passion, misinformation and shortsighted   5
fear often substitute for reason, fairness, and human dignity in today's immigration debates. In the interest of advancing beyond knownothingism, let's look at five current myths that distort public debate and government policy relating to immigrants.

America is being overrun with immigrants. In one sense, of course, this is true, but in that sense it has been true since Christopher Columbus arrived. Except for the real Native Americans, we are a nation of immigrants.

It is not true, however, that the first-generation immigrant share of our population is growing. As of 1990, foreign-born people made up only 8 percent of the population, as compared with a figure of about 15 percent from 1870 to 1920. Between 70 and 80 percent of those who immigrate every year are refugees or immediate relatives of U.S. citizens.

Much of the anti-immigrant fervor is directed against the undocumented, but they make up only 13 percent of all immigrants residing in the United States, and only 1 percent of the American population. Contrary to popular belief, most such aliens do not cross the border illegally but enter legally and remain after their student or visitor visa expires. Thus, building a wall at the border, no matter how high, will not solve the problem.

Immigrants take jobs from U.S. citizens. There is virtually no evidence to support this view, probably the most widespread misunderstanding about immigrants. As documented by a 1994 A.C.L.U. Immigrants' Rights Project report, numerous studies have found that immigrants actually *create* more jobs than they fill. The jobs immigrants take are of course easier to see, but immigrants are often highly productive, run their own businesses, and employ both immigrants and citizens. One study found that Mexican immigration to Los Angeles County between 1970 and 1980 was responsible for 78,000 new jobs. Governor Mario Cuomo reports that immigrants own more than 40,000 companies in New York, which provide thousands of jobs and $3.5 billion to the state's economy every year.

Immigrants are a drain on society's resources. This claim fuels many of   10
the recent efforts to cut off government benefits to immigrants. However, most studies have found that immigrants are a net benefit to the economy because, as a 1994 Urban Institute report concludes, "immi-

grants generate significantly more in taxes paid than they cost in services received." The Council of Economic Advisers similarly found in 1986 that "immigrants have a favorable effect on the overall standard of living."

Anti-immigrant advocates often cite studies purportedly showing the contrary, but these generally focus only on taxes and services at the local or state level. What they fail to explain is that because most taxes go to the federal government, such studies would also show a net loss when applied to U.S. citizens. At most, such figures suggest that some redistribution of federal and state monies may be appropriate; they say nothing unique about the costs of immigrants.

Some subgroups of immigrants plainly impose a net cost in the short run, principally those who have most recently arrived and have not yet "made it." California, for example, bears substantial costs for its disproportionately large undocumented population, largely because it has on average the poorest and least educated immigrants. But that has been true of every wave of immigrants that has ever reached our shores; it was as true of the Irish in the 1850s, for example, as it is of Salvadorans today. From a long-term perspective, the economic advantages of immigration are undeniable.

Some have suggested that we might save money and diminish incentives to immigrate illegally if we denied undocumented aliens public services. In fact, undocumented immigrants are already ineligible for most social programs, with the exception of education for schoolchildren, which is constitutionally required, and benefits directly related to health and safety, such as emergency medical care and nutritional assistance to poor women, infants, and children. To deny such basic care to people in need, apart from being inhumanly callous, would probably cost us more in the long run by exacerbating health problems that we would eventually have to address.

Aliens refuse to assimilate, and are depriving us of our cultural and political unity. This claim has been made about every new group of immigrants to arrive on U.S. shores. Supreme Court Justice Stephen Field wrote in 1884 that the Chinese "have remained among us a separate people, retaining their original peculiarities of dress, manners, habits, and modes of living, which are as marked as their complexion and language." Five years later, he upheld the racially based exclusion of Chinese immigrants. Similar claims have been made over different periods of our history about Catholics, Jews, Italians, Eastern Europeans, and Latin Americans.

In most instances, such claims are simply not true; "American cul- 15 ture" has been created, defined, and revised by persons who for the most part are descended from immigrants once seen as anti-assimilationist. Descendants of the Irish Catholics, for example, a group once decried as separatist and alien, have become Presidents, senators, and representatives (and all of these in one family, in the case of the Kennedys). Our society exerts tremendous pressure to conform, and cultural separatism rarely survives a generation. But more important, even if this claim were true, is this a legitimate rationale for limiting immigration in a society built on the values of pluralism and tolerance?

Noncitizen immigrants are not entitled to constitutional rights. Our government has long declined to treat immigrants as full human beings, and nowhere is that more clear than in the realm of constitutional rights. Although the Constitution literally extends the fundamental protections in the Bill of Rights to all people, limiting to citizens only the right to vote and run for federal office, the federal government acts as if this were not the case.

In 1893 the executive branch successfully defended a statute that required Chinese laborers to establish their prior residence here by the testimony of "at least one credible white witness." The Supreme Court ruled that this law was constitutional because it was reasonable for Congress to presume that nonwhite witnesses could not be trusted.

The federal government is not much more enlightened today. In a pending case I'm handling in the Court of Appeals for the Ninth Circuit, the Clinton Administration has argued that permanent resident aliens lawfully living here should be extended no more First Amendment rights than aliens applying for first-time admission from abroad—that is, none. Under this view, students at a public university who are citizens may express themselves freely, but students who are not citizens can be deported for saying exactly what their classmates are constitutionally entitled to say.

Growing up, I was always taught that we will be judged by how we treat others. If we are collectively judged by how we have treated immigrants—those who would appear today to be "other" but will in a generation be "us"—we are not in very good shape.

Topics for Critical Thinking and Writing

1. What are the "five current myths" about immigration that Cole identifies? Why does he describe them as "myths" (rather than "errors," "mistakes," or "falsehoods")?

2. In an encyclopedia or other reference work in your college library, look up the Know-Nothings. What, if anything, of interest do you learn about the movement that is not mentioned by Cole in his opening paragraphs (1 to 4)?

3. Cole attempts to show how insignificant the immigrant population really is (in paras. 7 and 13) because it is such a small fraction (8 percent in 1990) of the total population. Suppose someone said to him, "That's all very well, but 8 percent of the population is still 20 million people—far more than the 15 percent of the population during the years from 1870 to 1920." How might he reply?

4. Suppose Cole is right, that most illegal immigration results from over-staying visitor and student visas (para. 8). Why not pass laws prohibiting foreign students from studying here, since so many abuse the privilege? Why not pass other laws forbidding foreign visitors?

5. Cole cites a study (para. 9) showing that Mexican immigration in Los Angeles County in the decade 1970–80 "was responsible for 78,000 new jobs." Suppose it were also true that this immigration was responsible for 78,000 other Mexican immigrants who joined criminal gangs or were otherwise not legally employed. How might Cole respond?

6. Cole admits (para. 12) that in California, the large population of undoc-umented immigrants imposes "substantial costs" on taxpayers. Does Cole offer any remedy for this problem? Should the federal government bear some or all of these extra costs that fall on California?

7. Cole thinks that "cultural separatism" among immigrants "rarely sur-vives a generation" (para. 15). His evidence? Look at the Irish Catholics. But suppose someone argued that this is weak evidence: Today's immi-grants are not Europeans, they are Asian and Hispanic; they will never assimilate to the degree that European immigrants did—their race, cul-ture, religion, and the trend toward "multiculturalism" all block the way. How might Cole reply?

8. Do you think that immigrants who are not citizens and not applying for citizenship ought to be allowed to vote in state and local elections (the Constitution forbids them to vote in federal elections, as Cole points out in para. 16)? Why, or why not? How about illegal immigrants?

Janet Radcliffe Richards

Janet Radcliffe Richards is lecturer in philosophy in England on the central faculty of the Open University, where she specializes in ethics, philosophy of science, and applied philosophy. The essay reprinted here was published in the Newsletter of the Voluntary Euthanasia Society of Scotland *in September 1994.*

Thinking Straight and Dying Well

Presumably you would not have invited me to give this lecture un-less you had thought I was on your side; and this puts us from the start in a situation of intellectual and moral danger. People are inclined to be very tolerant of arguments that seem to support conclusions they al-ready accept.

It is easy to think of this fact as just another symptom of the well-known irrationality of our species, but oddly enough, what appears as ir-rationality is often a sign of a deeper, underlying rationality. When people are careless about facts, or play fast and loose with logic, this is often because they are trying to make it seem (to themselves as well as others) as though various ideas to which they are strongly committed can be made to fit together. Think, for instance, of someone who refuses to give to a charity, asserting (without any investigation of the matter) that charities waste all the money given to them. Pretty obviously, the invented fact is there to allow the person to reach the desired conclusion (not giving money) without having to make an undesirable admission (not being generous).

This is a useful thing to bear in mind in any area where there are strong passions. They are breeding grounds for twisted arguments and invented facts, and identifying these not only clarifies the issues and sharpens political argument; it also offers important indications of what the real motivations are. This applies potentially as much to our own arguments as to our opponents', and provides a method of real progress in moral enquiry. But here I want to concentrate on arguments against euthanasia.

And the first thing to do is to qualify the little I have already said. I have referred to *sides* and *the euthanasia debate,* and *arguments against euthanasia.* But this is just where the trouble starts. A moment's thought shows that the word "euthanasia" is applied to a wide range of actions; not only the ones counted as voluntary euthanasia, but also such things as turning off life support machines, killing defective babies, and not trying to save the lives of people who are senile or badly damaged in accidents.

These are all different, and there is no reason to presume they must   5
be morally identical. Inevitably, however, whenever there is a single word people will tend to think of it as denoting a single thing, and this is always dangerous. In particular, people who think of themselves as against whatever it is will often pounce on arguments that seem to work against the most troubling cases, and wave them around as if they were objections to all.

The first thing to do, therefore, is to pull the issue out of the impressionistic blur produced by the word "euthanasia," and make sure that each issue is analyzed in its own right. We must make sure that the clearest cases are not weakened by spurious association with more difficult ones. And, of course, the other way round. We must not allow any relatively straightforward cases to disguise the difficulty of others.

Since this is a voluntary euthanasia society I shall keep to the range of issues that come up only under that heading. That will be more than enough to be going on with.

THE BASIC ISSUE:
MAKING SUICIDE POSSIBLE

Slippery slopes. Two years ago there occurred the much-publicized case of Dr. Cox, who eventually gave in to the pleadings of a patient in desperate, terminal pain, and who wanted to die. This led to the usual rush of public alarm. Euthanasia must not be allowed, it was protested, because if we gave doctors the right to kill we should be off on a slippery slope, turning off life support machines, clearing geriatric wards, and moving inexorably towards Hitlerian extermination camps. Hitler is always the bogey at the bottom of the slope; an awful warning to anyone tempted to set out on it. Dr. Cox was forced, like Galileo, to recant.

But the issue brought up by this case has nothing to do with allowing doctors to decide whom to kill. It is, quite differently, that of whether people trapped by disability or institutions should be denied the freedom the rest of us have to commit suicide. Many people are simply not able to kill themselves; and it is, incidentally, a striking fact that the very helplessness which makes suicide impossible does itself provide some of the most rational grounds for wanting to die. The present law, which does not forbid suicide, nevertheless ensures that such people must stay alive, because no one else may help them to do what they cannot do alone.

But, say the objectors, at this point it ceases to be suicide and becomes killing; and killing is wrong. But once again, it cannot be presumed that everything describable by a single word must fall into a single moral category.

Normally we regard it as charitable and generous when people put their own powers at the disposal of the powerless, to enable them to do what they otherwise could not, and we see this as morally quite different from doing the same things against their will. If your aunt whose fingers are crippled with arthritis cannot put the sugar in her tea, and you do it for her, we do not hesitate to distinguish it from malicious tea-sweetening (as from Cicely to Gwendolen in *The Importance of Being Earnest*). Why, then, if you get the pills she wants to make her escape from life, or manipulate the syringe because she cannot do it herself, should we put this in the same moral category as doing those things against her will? In any other case such a conflation would scream out its absurdity; and so it should in this one.

If assisting the suicide of the helpless is killing, we must insist that there are different kinds of killing, and that this kind bears no moral resemblance at all to murder, or even to justifiable forms of killing without consent.

When the matter is put this way, it provides an indication of what really lies behind the objections. When do we say that it is wrong to help other people to do what they want to do, but cannot? Only, surely, when what they want is itself wrong. You would not feel that kindness to your arthritic aunt should extend to putting poison on her behalf into her neighbor's tea. Surely, therefore, anyone who thinks it wrong to assist the suicide of the helpless must think suicide itself wrong. Conversely, if the law does not forbid suicide, it has no justification for its seeing the assisting of suicide as different from the assisting of anything else.

So we can start the clarification of the issues by resolutely detaching this most fundamental case—the desperate situation of people who want to die but cannot kill themselves—from anything else to which the label of euthanasia may have become attached. And when this is done, and (obviously most important) proper safeguards are in place to make sure that what is going on really is assisted suicide and not murder, the slippery-slope idea stands exposed for the irrelevance it is. There is no slope. Suicide is not a thing there is any danger of anyone's getting into a habit of.

Making life worth living. Needless to say, however, that will [15] not be the end of the argument, even when it is clear that the issue is the limited one of freedom to commit suicide. One of the commonest symptoms of deeply rooted attitudes, held not because of the arguments offered in their defense but for other, unstated, reasons, is the speed with which refuted arguments are replaced by others.

The next familiar line of argument is that euthanasia of this sort should not be necessary; that we should instead be making people's lives worth living, by controlling their pain and making them feel valued. And this argument is a good piece of strategy, because no one is going to rush in and deny that we should be doing these things. It also tends to divert supporters of euthanasia into arguments about the extent to which it is possible to control pain, when what they should really be doing is exposing this maneuver as a fudge of the first order, and a particularly dangerous one. To see this, all that is needed is a steady eye for the point at issue. It is claimed that we should make life worth living for the suffering, and *implied* that this is a reason for not allowing help with suicide. But how can a claim that something should not be needed be regarded as a reason for saying it should be forbidden? You might just as well say that because all children should learn to read at school, we should prohibit adult literacy classes.

If we could reliably make everyone's life worth living, no one would want to die, and laws preventing assistance would have no purpose. Conversely, to the extent that they have a purpose, *precisely* what they achieve is to force continuing life on people whose sufferings we have not managed to prevent. The claim that we should prevent suffering is being used to defend a law whose main effect is to perpetuate it.

This is a clear case of an argument so outrageously bad that it could not possibly be thought to work by anyone not already convinced of the conclusion on quite other grounds. It seems obvious, once again, that its proponents really disapprove of suicide altogether, but are unwilling to face the fact that this may mean forcing people to remain alive in agony.

To put the matter even more starkly, the prevention of suicide achieves nothing for the sufferers, but it does mean the rest of us can avoid having forced on our attention the knowledge of how many people there are who would rather be dead, and can more easily forget them. I do not think for a moment that that is the motive of the people who argue in this way, but it is the effect. Anyone who really wants to make people's lives worth living should be glad to allow suicide, as a reminder of the extent of failure.

The dangers of coercion. The final objection I want to consider 20 against allowing assistance with suicide is increasingly common, and widely accepted as conclusive. It is that if euthanasia were allowed, we could never be sure it was truly voluntary. Relatives and doctors might make people feel unwanted, or even (though I have not actually heard this suggested) leave them in more pain than necessary to coerce them into choosing death. And even if this did not happen, people might still feel burdensome and under an obligation to choose to go. We must therefore keep the option closed.

This issue is more complicated than the previous two, and there is no quick answer on the euthanasia side. But what can be shown is that the other side is even less entitled to its own quick answer.

It is necessary to get the form of the problem clear. We should not be thinking about wards full of old people and wondering what their relations would do if we decided to institute voluntary euthanasia. Rather the question is, for everyone in a democracy, about the kinds of institutions we should prefer to live by. Would we, individually, choose to live in a society which forbade voluntary euthanasia altogether, to protect ourselves from the risk of being put under pressure to choose it?

It is certainly true that making things impossible is one way to prevent our being coerced into doing them. This is a well understood maneuver (see, for instance, Thomas Schelling in *The Strategy of Conflict*). On the other hand, it is not one to be adopted lightly. Usually it is absurd to give up an option completely in order to avoid the chance of being put under pressure to use it in a particular way; you would hardly think of giving up the freedom to choose whom to marry in order to avoid the danger of being put under pressure to make the wrong choice. Such decisions can be made only through careful risk analysis, involving estimates of how bad the various possible outcomes are, and how likely they are to come about. How likely is it that our relatives would start putting pressure on us? Is it a severe enough danger to justify the sacrifice of the freedom to opt out if we are in terrible pain?

There is no algorithm for calculations of this sort, but a few comments may help to put the matter in perspective.

First, although this line of argument does not seem to be motivated 25 by a straightforward opposition to suicide, I think in fact it must be. Anyone who can see the anti-euthanasia conclusion as immediate and obvious, rather than as difficult and to be reached only after much agonizing, is willing to give up the suicide option to avoid any risk at all that anyone will be put under pressure to take it. No one who thought the option intrinsically valuable could give it up so quickly. And for anyone who would like to keep it, the case for giving it up need seem nothing like as strong.

For one thing, it is not at all obvious that allowing suicide will make it more likely that people are put under pressure to take that option. It could work quite the other way: Relatives and hospitals might become so afraid of being accused of driving anyone to euthanasia that they become assiduous in their attempts to prevent it. Until we try, we shall not know.

Furthermore, there is no reason to think of these probabilities, whatever they are, as fixed. We could try to influence them in various ways. Perhaps hospitals might deliberately develop a culture in which euthanasia was regarded as a failure, and patients were persuaded not to choose it. (Though that would, of course, create pressures the other way.)

And, finally, a most important point. If different people might have different preferences in this context, we should consider whether it might be possible to let people choose their own risks. Even if suicide were allowed, I do not see why people who did not want the risk of pressure could not (say) sign an anti-suicide pledge, and join societies and churches committed to the repudiation of this option.

That kind of possibility does, indeed, seem to me to settle the issue. But even if it does not, it still seems clear that we need not be bullied by what is widely regarded as a knock-down argument against euthanasia, but which, without the hidden presupposition that suicide is never morally acceptable, is nothing of the sort.

SECOND ISSUE: EASING DEATH

So far I have discussed only one part of the voluntary euthanasia 30 issue, that of making death possible for people who cannot choose to die, and considered three common arguments against it. But of course there are other issues, and a closely related one is that of making death pleasant. For many people suicide is not actually impossible, but can be achieved only by painful or distressing means. Many of us think everyone should have access to the means of dying painlessly.

The usual objection is that this makes suicide too easy, and people will do away with themselves during passing bouts of depression. That, however, confuses ease and pleasantness. Most of us probably think there should be a waiting time, perhaps longer for young people than old, and other safeguards. But that is quite compatible with making death painless for anyone who can show they really want it.

But still, it will be said, to make death less unpleasant is to make it more attractive, and more people will choose it than otherwise would have done. Surely we should keep death unattractive in order to discourage suicide?

If this sounds plausible, consider it in more detail. Think of life as measured against a scale of satisfaction, and each person as fixing a point on that scale at which life becomes not worth living. If we want to prevent people choosing suicide when they reach that point, there are two ways of doing it. One is to make life better, so that it rises again above the crisis point. The other is to make death so unpleasant that things have to get even worse before death becomes an attractive option. Either of these, therefore, would prevent suicides.

But why, exactly, do we want to prevent suicide? What is bad about it? Some people think it bad in itself, and probably as sinful; others think the ground for regret is that anyone's life should be not worth living. If you want to prevent suicide for this second reason, only the first way of proceeding—improving people's lives—makes any sense. Preventing suicide by making death unpleasant does not make anyone's life one scrap more worth living; it just gives them a reason to live with more misery.

In other words, the now-familiar background assumption appears 35 again, in yet another disguise. To oppose allowing people the means of painless suicide is to regard suicide as bad in itself, and to be discouraged whether life is worth living or not.

THIRD ISSUE: ADVANCE DIRECTIVES

Finally, many of us would like to be able to specify that if we became so ill or damaged that we could not make any wishes known, we should be actively killed. This is quite different from saying that everyone in a coma or irreversibly damaged by a stroke should be done away with; that is related, but it needs separate argument. Here the claim is only that we should be allowed to decide for ourselves. What reason could anyone offer for saying that we should not?

The usual line of argument here is that we can never be sure. We cannot be sure that the coma will not be emerged from, or that a new treatment will not be found. Furthermore, we cannot be sure about the state of mind of someone unable to communicate, and who may have undergone a change of mind since writing the directive.

All these arguments, however, make the same presuppositions. They all presuppose that in case of doubt we should err on the side of caution, and that caution means not killing unless we are absolutely certain. Since we can never be certain, we should never risk killing.

But this is another case where risk analysis is needed, and many of us would assess the situation in quite the opposite way. The worst imaginable outcome is not being killed when we might (conceivably) have changed our minds but be unable to say so; far worse than that would be the *unutterable horror* of being trapped for years in a dreadful, degrading existence, unable even to communicate a wish to escape. The same applies to the risk of dying when a cure might be found, as compared with that of being kept alive and its not being found.

This seems to me so clear that it seems also relevant to the involun- 40 tary euthanasia issue: Surely in any case of doubt it would be better to risk killing quickly someone who might not want to die than to leave in such an appalling existence someone who might want to. But the voluntary case seems quite unanswerable, because this is not a matter that needs to be settled for everybody or nobody. It is something that people can choose for themselves, and it seems quite outrageous that they should not be allowed to.

Once again, the opposition to this kind of euthanasia clearly has nothing to do with respect for choices and fears about mistakes. It must arise from a general conviction that no one should be able to choose to die; or at least, to have anyone else's assistance in doing so.

So it seems to me that all the standard arguments against the different forms of voluntary euthanasia are not only seriously mistaken, but mistaken in ways that could not deceive anyone in neutral contexts. The situation seems to be the one I described at the outset. Deep feelings that these things are wrong accompany a wish to justify them (at least in public) in terms that seem more humane and enlightened than a simple opposition to suicide, and the arguments are a valiant attempt to reconcile the irreconcilable. If this were better understood, I think it might be much easier to overcome the continuing resistance to voluntary euthanasia.

DOCTORS AND DYING

Finally, one note on a rather different matter. Advocates of euthanasia often seem to take for granted the idea that it can be justified only by terminal illness and intolerable pain. But this is odd, because there could be innumerable good reasons for wanting to die. Hopeless disability, simple old age that made impossible all the things that gave life purpose, or just not wanting to waste on a nursing home the money you hoped to leave to your children or vess,[1] might make it perfectly rational to wish to die. Why should we think some reasons, but not others, adequate for euthanasia?

My suspicion is that the idea of confining voluntary euthanasia to cases of terminal illness arises partly from political realism, but even more from assumptions about where doctors fit into all this.

A common line of argument against euthanasia is that doctors 45 should be committed to preserving life. Other people say that their duty of care should be understood more broadly than this, and that there is a

---

[1]vess Voluntary Euthanasia Society of Scotland. [Editors' note.]

duty to end suffering, even by death, when life is declining and has nothing more to offer. But even these people rarely go so far as to say that doctors should help anyone who simply wants to die.

Obviously any society needs to decide the use its doctors may make of their powers. However, there is no reason why their role, whatever it is, should define the boundaries of euthanasia. There are two aspects to being a doctor: technical knowledge, and a set of commitments about the use that may be made of it. But these two are separable; and even though we might agree that there were certain things doctors should not do, that would not be a reason for saying that no one else should do it either. The means of suicide could be available elsewhere.

If this possibility is widely overlooked, that may be another consequence of the way the euthanasia issue has been seen as the question of what doctors should be allowed to do to people. Voluntary euthanasia is anyway not about allowing doctors to decide when anyone shall die, but about the permissibility of providing technical help for people who are not adequately equipped themselves. But if technical help is the issue, it need not come from doctors at all, and voluntary euthanasia need not be limited to cases of pain and imminent death.

We can see the issue for what it is: the idea that an essential element of a good life is the freedom to leave it in peace and with dignity.

Topics for Critical Thinking and Writing

1. Write a 250-word summary of the main points of Richards's essay.

2. Richards mentions what she calls "the invented fact" (para. 2). What, if any, invented facts about euthanasia does she identify in the course of her essay?

3. Richards mentions having discussed "three common arguments against" voluntary euthanasia (para. 30). What are these three arguments?

4. Formulate as precisely as you can the "slippery slope" argument to which Richards alludes (para. 8). What is her view about this argument as applied to euthanasia? Richards says (para. 14), "Suicide is not a thing there is any danger of anyone's getting into a habit of." But does this show that *assisting* another to suicide is not something that an unscrupulous doctor might get into the habit of doing?

5. Richards reasons (para. 13) that "if the law does not forbid suicide, it has no justification for [making illegal] the assisting of suicide." Suppose someone objected, saying, "Well, if we were to abolish laws against prostitution, that doesn't mean we have to abolish laws against pimping and keeping a brothel." How might Richards reply?

6. Evaluate Richards's analogy in paragraph 16: Prohibiting euthanasia because it isn't needed is like prohibiting adult literacy classes because children ought to learn to read in school.

7. Richards refers (in para. 20) to worries over whether suicide is ever "truly voluntary." What do you think is required for an act to be truly voluntary?

8. Richards says (para. 24), "There is no algorithm for calculations of this sort." What is an "algorithm," and why do you think she asserts there is none of the required sort?

9. Richards refers (in para. 33) to an imaginary scale to measure the value or worth one attaches to going on living, and supposes that each of us might fix a point on that scale when our own "life becomes not worth living." In fifty words, write out what for you would make you conclude that your life was no longer "worth living."

10. Richards seems (in para. 35) to think that suicide is *not* "bad in itself," although it might be quite bad if unnecessary, or bad for other reasons. Can you think of any reasons why one might disagree with her, believing that suicide indeed is bad in itself?

11. In your library, look up (in *Facts on File* or some other source) the activities during the 1990s of Dr. Jack Kevorkian, famous for his role in making physician-assisted suicide a headline issue. Would Richards approve of what Kevorkian has done? Why, or why not?

Peter Singer

Educated at the University of Melbourne and at Oxford, Peter Singer (b. 1946) has taught at Oxford and now teaches at Monash University in Australia. He has written on a variety of ethical issues, but he is especially known for caring about the welfare of animals.

This essay originally appeared in the New York Review of Books *(April 5, 1973), as a review of* Animals, Men and Morals, *edited by Stanley and Roslind Godlovitch and John Harris.*

Animal Liberation

I

We are familiar with Black Liberation, Gay Liberation, and a variety of other movements. With Women's Liberation some thought we had come to the end of the road. Discrimination on the basis of sex, it has been said, is the last form of discrimination that is universally accepted and practiced without pretense, even in those liberal circles which have long prided themselves on their freedom from racial discrimination. But one should always be wary of talking of "the last remaining form of discrimination." If we have learned anything from the liberation movements, we should have learned how difficult it is to be aware of the ways in which we discriminate until they are forcefully pointed out to us. A liberation movement demands an expansion of our moral horizons, so that practices that were previously regarded as natural and inevitable are now seen as intolerable.

Animals, Men and Morals is a manifesto for an Animal Liberation movement. The contributors to the book may not all see the issue this way. They are a varied group. Philosophers, ranging from professors to graduate students, make up the largest contingent. There are five of them, including the three editors, and there is also an extract from the unjustly neglected German philosopher with an English name, Leonard Nelson, who died in 1927. There are essays by two novelist/critics, Brigid Brophy and Maureen Duffy, and another by Muriel the Lady Dowding, widow of Dowding of Battle of Britain fame and the founder of "Beauty without Cruelty," a movement that campaigns against the use of animals for furs and cosmetics. The other pieces are by a psychologist, a botanist, a sociologist, and Ruth Harrison, who is probably best described as a professional campaigner for animal welfare.

Whether or not these people, as individuals, would all agree that they are launching a liberation movement for animals, the book as a whole amounts to no less. It is a demand for a complete change in our attitudes to nonhumans. It is a demand that we cease to regard the exploitation of other species as natural and inevitable, and that, instead, we see it as a continuing moral outrage. Patrick Corbett, Professor of Philosophy at Sussex University, captures the spirit of the book in his closing words:

> We require now to extend the great principles of liberty, equality, and fraternity over the lives of animals. Let animal slavery join human slavery in the graveyard of the past.

The reader is likely to be skeptical. "Animal Liberation" sounds more like a parody of liberation movements than a serious objective. The reader may think: We support the claims of blacks and women for equality because blacks and women really are equal to whites and males— equal in intelligence and in abilities, capacity for leadership, rationality, and so on. Humans and nonhumans obviously are not equal in these respects. Since justice demands only that we treat equals equally, unequal treatment of humans and nonhumans cannot be an injustice.

This is a tempting reply, but a dangerous one. It commits the non- 5 racist and nonsexist to a dogmatic belief that blacks and women really are just as intelligent, able, etc., as whites and males—and no more. Quite possibly this happens to be the case. Certainly attempts to prove that racial or sexual differences in these respects have a genetic origin have not been conclusive. But do we really want to stake our demand for equality on the assumption that there are no genetic differences of this kind between the different races or sexes? Surely the appropriate response to those who claim to have found evidence for such genetic differences is not to stick to the belief that there are no differences, whatever the evidence to the contrary; rather one should be clear that the claim to equality does not depend on IQ. Moral equality is distinct from factual equality. Otherwise it would be nonsense to talk to the equality of human beings, since humans, as individuals, obviously differ in intelligence and almost any ability one cares to name. If possessing greater intelligence does not entitle one human to exploit another, why should it entitle humans to exploit nonhumans?

Jeremy Bentham expressed the essential basis of equality in his famous formula: "Each to count for one and none for more than one." In other words, the interests of every being that has interests are to be taken into account and treated equally with the like interests of any other being. Other moral philosophers, before and after Bentham, have made the same point in different ways. Our concern for others must not depend on whether they possess certain characteristics, though just what that concern involves may, of course, vary according to such characteristics.

Bentham, incidentally, was well aware that the logic of the demand for racial equality did not stop at the equality of humans. He wrote:

> The day *may* come when the rest of the animal creation may acquire those rights which never could have been withholden from them but by the hand of tyranny. The French have already discovered that the blackness of the skin is no reason why a human being should be abandoned without redress to the caprice of a tormentor. It may one day come to be recognized that the number of the legs, the villosity of the skin, or the termination of the *os sacrum,* are reasons equally insufficient for abandoning a sensitive being to the same fate. What else is it that should trace the insuperable line? Is it the faculty of reason, or perhaps the faculty of discourse? But a full-grown horse or dog is beyond comparison a more rational, as well as a more conversable animal, than an infant of a day, or a week, or even a month, old. But suppose they were otherwise, what would it avail? The question is not, Can they *reason?* nor Can they *talk?* but, Can they *suffer?*[1]

Surely Bentham was right. If a being suffers, there can be no moral justification for refusing to take that suffering into consideration, and, indeed, to count it equally with the like suffering (if rough comparisons can be made) of any other being.

So the only question is: Do animals other than man suffer? Most people agree unhesitatingly that animals like cats and dogs can and do suffer, and this seems also to be assumed by those laws that prohibit wanton cruelty to such animals. Personally, I have no doubt at all about this and find it hard to take seriously the doubts that a few people apparently do have. The editors and contributors of *Animals, Men and Morals*

---

[1] *The Principles of Morals and Legislation,* ch. XVII, sec. 1, footnote to paragraph 4. [All notes are the author's unless otherwise specified.]

seem to feel the same way, for although the question is raised more than once, doubts are quickly dismissed each time. Nevertheless, because this is such a fundamental point, it is worth asking what grounds we have for attributing suffering to other animals.

It is best to begin by asking what grounds any individual human has for supposing that other humans feel pain. Since pain is a state of consciousness, a "mental event," it can never be directly observed. No observations, whether behavioral signs such as writhing or screaming or physiological or neurological recordings, are observations of pain itself. Pain is something one feels, and one can only infer that others are feeling it from various external indications. The fact that only philosophers are ever skeptical about whether other humans feel pain shows that we regard such inference as justifiable in the case of humans.

Is there any reason why the same inference should be unjustifiable   10
for other animals? Nearly all the external signs which lead us to infer pain in other humans can be seen in other species, especially "higher" animals such as mammals and birds. Behavioral signs—writhing, yelping, or other forms of calling, attempts to avoid the source of pain, and many others—are present. We know, too, that these animals are biologically similar in the relevant respects, having nervous systems like ours which can be observed to function as ours do.

So the grounds for inferring that these animals can feel pain are nearly as good as the grounds for inferring other humans do. Only nearly, for there is one behavioral sign that humans have but nonhumans, with the exception of one or two specially raised chimpanzees, do not have. This, of course, is a developed language. As the quotation from Bentham indicates, this has long been regarded as an important distinction between man and other animals. Other animals may communicate with each other, but not in the way we do. Following Chomsky,[2] many people now mark this distinction by saying that only humans communicate in a form that is governed by rules of syntax. (For the purposes of this argument, linguists allow those chimpanzees who have learned a syntactic sign language to rank as honorary humans.) Nevertheless, as Bentham pointed out, this distinction is not relevant to the question of how animals ought to be treated, unless it can be linked to the issue of whether animals suffer.

This link may be attempted in two ways. First, there is a hazy line of philosophical thought, stemming perhaps from some doctrines associated with Wittgenstein, which maintains that we cannot meaningfully attribute states of consciousness to beings without language. I have not seen this argument made explicit in print, though I have come across it in conversation. This position seems to me very implausible, and I doubt

[2]**Chomsky** Noam Chomsky (b. 1928), a professor of linguistics and the author of (among other books) *Language and Mind* (1972). [Editors' note.]

that it would be held at all if it were not thought to be a consequence of a broader view of the significance of language. It may be that the use of a public, rule-governed language is a precondition of conceptual thought. It may even be, although personally I doubt it, that we cannot meaningfully speak of a creature having an intention unless that creature can use a language. But states like pain, surely, are more primitive than either of these, and seem to have nothing to do with language.

Indeed, as Jane Goodall points out in her study of chimpanzees, when it comes to the expression of feelings and emotions, humans tend to fall back on nonlinguistic modes of communication which are often found among apes, such as a cheering pat on the back, an exuberant embrace, a clasp of hands, and so on.[3] Michael Peters makes a similar point in his contribution to *Animals, Men and Morals* when he notes that the basic signals we use to convey pain, fear, sexual arousal, and so on are not specific to our species. So there seems to be no reason at all to believe that a creature without language cannot suffer.

The second, and more easily appreciated way of linking language and the existence of pain is to say that the best evidence that we can have that another creature is in pain is when he tells us that he is. This is a distinct line of argument, for it is not being denied that a non-language-user conceivably could suffer, but only that we could know that he is suffering. Still, this line of argument seems to me to fail, and for reasons similar to those just given. "I am in pain" is not the best possible evidence that the speaker is in pain (he might be lying) and it is certainly not the only possible evidence. Behavioral signs and knowledge of the animal's biological similarity to ourselves together provide adequate evidence that animals do suffer. After all, we would not accept linguistic evidence if it contradicted the rest of the evidence. If a man was severely burned, and behaved as if he were in pain, writhing, groaning, being very careful not to let his burned skin touch anything, and so on, but later said he had not been in pain at all, we would be more likely to conclude that he was lying or suffering from amnesia than that he had not been in pain.

Even if there were stronger grounds for refusing to attribute pain to those who do not have a language, the consequences of this refusal might lead us to examine these grounds unusually critically. Human infants, as well as some adults, are unable to use language. Are we to deny that a year-old infant can suffer? If not, how can language be crucial? Of course, most parents can understand the responses of even very young infants better than they understand the responses of other animals, and sometimes infant responses can be understood in the light of later development. 15

This, however, is just a fact about the relative knowledge we have of our own species and other species, and most of this knowledge is simply

[3]Jane van Lawick-Goodall, *In the Shadow of Man* (Houghton Mifflin, 1971), p. 225.

derived from closer contact. Those who have studied the behavior of other animals soon learn to understand their responses at least as well as we understand those of an infant. (I am not referring to Jane Goodall's and other well-known studies of apes. Consider, for example, the degree of understanding achieved by Tinbergen from watching herring gulls.[4]) Just as we can understand infant human behavior in the light of adult human behavior, so we can understand the behavior of other species in the light of our own behavior (and sometimes we can understand our own behavior better in the light of the behavior of other species).

The grounds we have for believing that other mammals and birds suffer are, then, closely analogous to the grounds we have for believing that other humans suffer. It remains to consider how far down the evolutionary scale this analogy holds. Obviously it becomes poorer when we get further away from man. To be more precise would require a detailed examination of all that we know about other forms of life. With fish, reptiles, and other vertebrates the analogy still seems strong, with molluscs like oysters it is much weaker. Insects are more difficult, and it may be that in our present state of knowledge we must be agnostic about whether they are capable of suffering.

If there is no moral justification for ignoring suffering when it occurs, and it does occur in other species, what are we to say of our attitudes toward these other species? Richard Ryder, one of the contributors to *Animals, Men and Morals,* uses the term "speciesism" to describe the belief that we are entitled to treat members of other species in a way in which it would be wrong to treat members of our own species. The term is not euphonious, but it neatly makes the analogy with racism. The nonracist would do well to bear the analogy in mind when he is inclined to defend human behavior toward nonhumans. "Shouldn't we worry about improving the lot of our own species before we concern ourselves with other species?" he may ask. If we substitute "race" for "species" we shall see that the question is better not asked. "Is a vegetarian diet nutritionally adequate?" resembles the slaveowner's claim that he and the whole economy of the South would be ruined without slave labor. There is even a parallel with skeptical doubts about whether animals suffer, for some defenders of slavery professed to doubt whether blacks really suffer in the way whites do.

I do not want to give the impression, however, that the case for Animal Liberation is based on the analogy with racism and no more. On the contrary, *Animals, Men and Morals* describes the various ways in which humans exploit nonhumans, and several contributors consider the defenses that have been offered, including the defense of meat-eating mentioned in the last paragraph. Sometimes the rebuttals are scornfully dismissive, rather than carefully designed to convince the detached critic.

[4]N. Tinbergen, *The Herring Gull's World* (Basic Books, 1961).

This may be a fault, but it is a fault that is inevitable, given the kind of book this is. The issue is not one on which one can remain detached. As the editors state in their Introduction:

> Once the full force of moral assessment has been made explicit there can be no rational excuse left for killing animals, be they killed for food, science, or sheer personal indulgence. We have not assembled this book to provide the reader with yet another manual on how to make brutalities less brutal. Compromise, in the traditional sense of the term, is simple unthinking weakness when one considers the actual reasons for our crude relationships with the other animals.

The point is that on this issue there are few critics who are genuinely 20 detached. People who eat pieces of slaughtered nonhumans every day find it hard to believe that they are doing wrong; and they also find it hard to imagine what else they could eat. So for those who do not place nonhumans beyond the pale of morality, there comes a stage when further argument seems pointless, a stage at which one can only accuse one's opponent of hypocrisy and reach for the sort of sociological account of our practices and the way we defend them that is attempted by David Wood in his contribution to his book. On the other hand, to those unconvinced by the arguments, and unable to accept that they are merely rationalizing their dietary preferences and their fear of being thought peculiar, such sociological explanations can only seem insultingly arrogant.

II

The logic of speciesism is most apparent in the practice of experimenting on nonhumans in order to benefit humans. This is because the issue is rarely obscured by allegations that nonhumans are so different from humans that we cannot know anything about whether they suffer. The defender of vivisection cannot use this argument because he needs to stress the similarities between man and other animals in order to justify the usefulness to the former of experiments on the latter. The researcher who makes rats choose between starvation and electric shocks to see if they develop ulcers (they do) does so because he knows that the rat has a nervous system very similar to man's, and presumably feels an electric shock in a similar way.

Richard Ryder's restrained account of experiments on animals made me angrier with my fellow men than anything else in this book. Ryder, a clinical psychologist by profession, himself experimented on animals before he came to hold the view he puts forward in his essay. Experimenting on animals is now a large industry, both academic and commercial. In 1969, more than 5 million experiments were performed in Britain, the vast majority without anesthetic (though how many of these involved pain is not known). There are no accurate U.S. figures, since there is no federal law on the subject, and in many cases no state law either. Estimates vary from 20 million to 200 million. Ryder suggests that 80 million may be the best guess. We tend to think that this is all for vital medical research, but of course it is not. Huge numbers of animals are used in university departments from Forestry to Psychology, and even more are used for commercial purposes, to test whether cosmetics can cause skin damage, or shampoos eye damage, or to test food additives or laxatives or sleeping pills or anything else.

A standard test for foodstuffs is the "LD50." The object of this test is to find the dosage level at which 50 percent of the test animals will die. This means that nearly all of them will become very sick before finally succumbing or surviving. When the substance is a harmless one, it may be necessary to force huge doses down the animals, until in some cases sheer volume or concentration causes death.

Ryder gives a selection of experiments, taken from recent scientific journals. I will quote two, not for the sake of indulging in gory details, but in order to give an idea of what normal researchers think they may legitimately do to other species. The point is not that the individual researchers are cruel men, but that they are behaving in a way that is allowed by our speciesist attitudes. As Ryder points out, even if only 1 percent of the experiments involve severe pain, that is 50,000 experiments in Britain each year, or nearly 150 every day (and about fifteen times as many in the United States, if Ryder's guess is right). Here then are two experiments:

> O. S. Ray and R. J. Barrett of Pittsburgh gave electric shocks to the feet of 1,042 mice. They then caused convulsions by giving more intense shocks through cup-shaped electrodes applied to the animals' eyes or through pressure spring clips attached to their ears. Unfortunately some of the mice who "successfully completed Day One training were found sick or dead prior to testing on Day Two." [*Journal of Comparative and Physiological Psychology*, 1969, vol. 67, pp. 110–116]
>
> At the National Institute for Medical Research, Mill Hill, London, W. Feldberg and S. L. Sherwood injected chemicals into the brains of cats—"with a number of widely different substances, recurrent patterns of reaction were obtained. Retching, vomiting, defecation, increased salivation and greatly accelerated respiration leading to panting were common features." . . .
>
> The injection into the brain of a large dose of Tubocuraine caused the cat to jump "from the table to the floor and then straight into its cage, where it started calling more and more noisily whilst moving about restlessly and jerkily . . . finally the cat fell with legs and neck flexed, jerking in rapid clonic movements, the condition being that of a major [epileptic] convulsion . . . within a few seconds the cat got up, ran for a few yards at high speed, and fell in another fit. The whole process was repeated several times within the next ten minutes, during which the cat lost faeces and foamed at the mouth."

This animal finally died thirty-five minutes after the brain injection.
[*Journal of Physiology*, 1954, vol. 123, pp. 148–167]

There is nothing secret about these experiments. One has only to 25
open any recent volume of a learned journal, such as the *Journal of Comparative and Physiological Psychology*, to find full descriptions of experiments of this sort, together with the results obtained — results that are
frequently trivial and obvious. The experiments are often supported by
public funds.

It is a significant indication of the level of acceptability of these practices that, although these experiments are taking place at this moment on
university campuses throughout the country, there has, so far as I know,
not been the slightest protest from the student movement. Students have
been rightly concerned that their universities should not discriminate on
grounds of race or sex, and that they should not serve the purposes of the
military or big business. Speciesism continues undisturbed, and many students participate in it. There may be a few qualms at first, but since everyone regards it as normal, and it may even be a required part of a course, the
student soon becomes hardened and, dismissing his earlier feelings as
"mere sentiment," comes to regard animals as statistics rather than sentient beings with interests that warrant consideration.

Argument about vivisection has often missed the point because it
has been put in absolutist terms: Would the abolitionist be prepared to
let thousands die if they could be saved by experimenting on a single animal? The way to reply to this purely hypothetical question is to pose another: Would the experimenter be prepared to experiment on a human
orphan under six months old, if it were the only way to save many lives?
(I say "orphan" to avoid the complication of parental feelings, although
in doing so I am being overfair to the experimenter, since the nonhuman
subjects of experiments are not orphans.) A negative answer to this
question indicates that the experimenter's readiness to use nonhumans
is simple discrimination, for adult apes, cats, mice, and other mammals
are more conscious of what is happening to them, more self-directing,
and, so far as we can tell, just as sensitive to pain as a human infant.
There is no characteristic that human infants possess that adult mammals do not have to the same or a higher degree.

(It might be possible to hold that what makes it wrong to experiment
on a human infant is that the infant will in time develop into more than
the nonhuman, but one would then, to be consistent, have to oppose
abortion, and perhaps contraception, too, for the fetus and the egg and
sperm have the same potential as the infant. Moreover, one would still
have no reason for experimenting on a nonhuman rather than a human
with brain damage severe enough to make it impossible for him to rise
above infant level.)

The experimenter, then, shows a bias for his own species whenever
he carries out an experiment on a nonhuman for a purpose that he

would not think justified him in using a human being at an equal or lower level of sentience, awareness, ability to be self-directing, etc. No one familiar with the kind of results yielded by these experiments can have the slightest doubt that if this bias were eliminated the number of experiments performed would be zero or very close to it.

III

If it is vivisection that shows the logic of speciesism most clearly, it is the use of other species for food that is at the heart of our attitudes toward them. Most of *Animals, Men and Morals* is an attack on meat eating—an attack which is based solely on concern for nonhumans, without reference to arguments derived from consideration of ecology, macrobiotics, health, or religion. 30

The idea that nonhumans are utilities, means to our ends, pervades our thought. Even conservationists who are concerned about the slaughter of wildfowl but not about the vastly greater slaughter of chickens for our tables are thinking in this way—they are worried about what we would lose if there were less wildlife. Stanley Godlovitch, pursuing the Marxist idea that our thinking is formed by the activities we undertake in satisfying our needs, suggests that man's first classification of his environment was into Edibles and Inedibles. Most animals came into the first category, and there they have remained.

Man may always have killed other species for food, but he has never exploited them so ruthlessly as he does today. Farming has succumbed to business methods, the objective being to get the highest possible ratio of output (meat, eggs, milk) to input (fodder, labor costs, etc.). Ruth Harrison's essay "On Factory Farming" gives an account of some aspects of modern methods, and of the unsuccessful British campaigns for effective controls, a campaign which was sparked off by her *Animal Machines* (London: Stuart, 1964).

Her article is in no way a substitute for her earlier book. This is a pity since, as she says, "Farm produce is still associated with mental pictures of animals browsing in the fields . . . of hens having a last forage before going to roost. . . ." Yet neither in her article nor elsewhere in *Animals, Men and Morals* is this false image replaced by a clear idea of the nature and extent of factory farming. We learn of this only indirectly, when we hear of the code of reform proposed by an advisory committee set up by the British government.

Among the proposals, which the government refused to implement on the grounds that they were too idealistic, were: *"Any animal should at least have room to turn around freely."*

Factory farm animals need liberation in the most literal sense. Veal calves are kept in stalls 5 feet by 2 feet. They are usually slaughtered when about four months old, and have been too big to turn in their 35 stalls for at least a month. Intensive beef herds, kept in stalls only proportionately larger for much longer periods, account for a growing percentage of beef production. Sows are often similarly confined when pregnant, which, because of artificial methods of increasing fertility, can be most of the time. Animals confined in this way do not waste food by exercising, nor do they develop unpalatable muscle.

"A dry bedded area should be provided for all stock." Intensively kept animals usually have to stand and sleep in slatted floors without straw, because this makes cleaning easier.

"Palatable roughage must be readily available to all calves after one week of age." In order to produce the pale veal housewives are said to prefer, calves are fed on an all-liquid diet until slaughter, even though they are long past the age at which they would normally eat grass. They develop a craving for roughage, evidenced by attempts to gnaw wood from their stalls. (For the same reason, their diet is deficient in iron.)

"Battery cages for poultry should be large enough for a bird to be able to stretch one wing at a time." Under current British practice, a cage for four or five laying hens has a floor area of 20 inches by 18 inches, scarcely larger than a double page of the *New York Review of Books*. In this space, on a sloping wire floor (sloping so the eggs roll down, wire so the dung drips through) the birds live for a year or eighteen months while artificial lighting and temperature conditions combine with drugs in their food to squeeze the maximum number of eggs out of them. Table birds are also sometimes kept in cages. More often they are reared in sheds, no less crowded. Under these conditions all the birds' natural activities are frustrated, and they develop "vices" such as pecking each other to death. To prevent this, beaks are often cut off, and the sheds kept dark.

How many of those who support factory farming by buying its produce know anything about the way it is produced? How many have heard something about it, but are reluctant to check up for fear that it will make them uncomfortable? To nonspeciesists, the typical consumer's mixture of ignorance, reluctance to find out the truth, and vague belief that nothing really bad could be allowed seems analogous to the attitudes of "decent Germans" to the death camps.

There are, of course, some defenders of factory farming. Their argu- 40 ments are considered, though again rather sketchily, by John Harris. Among the most common: "Since they have never known anything else, they don't suffer." This argument will not be put by anyone who knows anything about animal behavior, since he will know that not all behavior has to be learned. Chickens attempt to stretch wings, walk around, scratch, and even dustbathe or build a nest, even though they have never lived under conditions that allowed these activities. Calves can suffer from maternal deprivation no matter at what age they were taken from their mothers. "We need these intensive methods to provide protein for a growing population." As ecologists and famine relief organizations know, we can produce far more protein per acre if we grow the right vegetable crop, soy beans for instance, than if we use the land to grow crops to be converted into protein by animals who use nearly 90 percent of the protein themselves, even when unable to exercise.

There will be many readers of this book who will agree that factory farming involves an unjustifiable degree of exploitation of sentient creatures, and yet will want to say that there is nothing wrong with rearing animals for food, provided it is done "humanely." These people are saying, in effect, that although we should not cause animals to suffer, there is nothing wrong with killing them.

There are two possible replies to this view. One is to attempt to show that this combination of attitudes is absurd. Roslind Godlovitch takes this course in her essay, which is an examination of some common attitudes to animals. She argues that from the combination of "animal suffering is to be avoided" and "there is nothing wrong with killing animals" it follows that all animal life ought to be exterminated (since all sentient creatures will suffer to some degree at some point in their lives). Euthanasia is a contentious issue only because we place some value on living. If we did not, the least amount of suffering would justify it. Accordingly, if we deny that we have a duty to exterminate all animal life, we must concede that we are placing some value on animal life.

This argument seems to me valid, although one could still reply that the value of animal life is to be derived from the pleasures that life can have for them, so that, provided their lives have a balance of pleasure over pain, we are justified in rearing them. But this would imply that we ought to produce animals and let them live as pleasantly as possible, without suffering.

At this point, one can make the second of the two possible replies to the view that rearing and killing animals for food is all right so long as it is done humanely. This second reply is that so long as we think that a nonhuman may be killed simply so that a human can satisfy his taste for meat, we are still thinking of nonhumans as means rather than as ends in themselves. The factory farm is nothing more than the application of technology to this concept. Even traditional methods involve castration, the separation of mothers and their young, the breaking up of herds, branding or earpunching, and of course transportation to the abattoirs and the final moments of terror when the animal smells blood and senses danger. If we were to try rearing animals so that they lived and died without suffering, we should find that to do so on anything like the scale of today's meat industry would be a sheer impossibility. Meat would become the prerogative of the rich.

I have been able to discuss only some of the contributions to this book, saying nothing about, for instance, the essays on killing for furs and for sport. Nor have I considered all the detailed questions that need to be asked once we start thinking about other species in the radically different way presented by this book. What, for instance, are we to do about genuine conflicts of interest like rats biting slum children? I am not sure of the answer, but the essential point is just that we *do* see this as a conflict of interests, that we recognize that rats have interests too. Then we may begin to think about other ways of resolving the conflict — perhaps by leaving out rat baits that sterilize the rats instead of killing them.

I have not discussed such problems because they are side issues compared with the exploitation of other species for food and for experimental purposes. On these central matters, I hope that I have said enough to show that this book, despite its flaws, is a challenge to every human to recognize his attitudes to nonhumans as a form of prejudice no less objectionable than racism or sexism. It is a challenge that demands not just a change of attitudes, but a change in our way of life, for it requires us to become vegetarians.

Can a purely moral demand of this kind succeed? The odds are certainly against it. The book holds out no inducements. It does not tell us that we will become healthier, or enjoy life more, if we cease exploiting animals. Animal Liberation will require greater altruism on the part of mankind than any other liberation movement, since animals are incapable of demanding it for themselves, or of protesting against their exploitation by votes, demonstrations, or bombs. Is man capable of such genuine altruism? Who knows? If this book does have a significant effect, however, it will be a vindication of all those who have believed that man has within himself the potential for more than cruelty and selfishness.

Topics for Critical Thinking and Writing

1. In his fourth paragraph Singer formulates an argument on behalf of the skeptical reader. Examine that argument closely, restate it in your own words, and evaluate it. Which of its premises is most vulnerable to criticism? Why?

2. Singer quotes with approval (para. 7) Bentham's comment, "The question is not, Can they *reason?* nor Can they *talk?* but, Can they *suffer?*" Do you find this argument persuasive? Can you think of any effective challenge to it?

3. Singer allows that although developed linguistic capacity is not necessary for a creature to have pain, perhaps such a capacity is necessary for "having an intention" (para. 12). Do you think this concession is correct? Have you ever seen animal behavior that you would be willing to describe or explain as evidence that the animal has an intention to do something, despite knowing that the animal cannot talk?

4. Singer thinks that the readiness to experiment on animals cuts out the ground for believing that animals don't suffer pain (see para. 21). Do you agree with this reasoning?

5. Singer confesses (para. 22) to being made especially angry "with my fellow men" after reading the accounts of animal experimentation. What is

it that aroused his anger? Do such feelings, and the acknowledgment that one has them, have any place in a sober discussion about the merits of animal experimentation? Why, or why not?

6. What is "factory farming" (paras. 32–40)? Why is Singer opposed to it?

7. To the claim that there is nothing wrong with "rearing and killing animals for food," provided it is done "humanely," Singer offers two replies (paras. 42–44). In an essay of 250 words summarize them briefly and then indicate whether either persuades you, and why or why not.

8. Suppose someone were to say to Singer: "You claim that capacity to suffer is the relevant factor in deciding whether a creature deserves to be treated as my moral equal. But you're wrong—the relevant factor is whether the creature is *alive*. Being alive is what matters, not being capable of feeling pain." In one or two paragraphs declare what you think would be Singer's reply.

9. Do you think it is worse to kill an animal for its fur than to kill, cook, and eat an animal? Is it worse to kill an animal for sport than to kill it for medical experimentation? What is Singer's view? Explain your view, making use of Singer's if you wish, in an essay of 500 words.

10. Are there any arguments, in your opinion, that show the immorality of eating human flesh (cannibalism) but that do not show a similar objection to eating animal flesh? Write a 500-word essay in which you discuss the issue.

Jonathan Swift

Jonathan Swift (1667–1745) was born in Ireland of English stock. An Anglican clergyman, he became Dean of St. Patrick's in Dublin in 1723, but the post he really wanted, one of high office in England, was never given to him. A prolific pamphleteer on religious and political issues, Swift today is known not as a churchman but as a satirist. His best known works are Gulliver's Travels (1726, a serious satire but now popularly thought of as a children's book) and "A Modest Proposal" (1729). In "A Modest Proposal," which was published anonymously, Swift addresses the great suffering that the Irish endured under the British.

A Modest Proposal

For Preventing the Children of Poor People in Ireland from Being a Burden to Their Parents or Country, and for Making Them Beneficial to the Public

It is a melancholy object to those who walk through this great town or travel in the country, when they see the streets, the roads, and cabin doors, crowded with beggars of the female sex, followed by three, four, or six children, all in rags and importuning every passenger for an alms. These mothers, instead of being able to work for their honest livelihood, are forced to employ all their time in strolling to beg sustenance for their helpless infants: who as they grow up either turn thieves for want of work, or leave their dear native country to fight for the Pretender in Spain, or sell themselves to the Barbadoes.

I think it is agreed by all parties that this prodigious number of children in the arms, or on the backs, or at the heels of their mothers, and frequently of their fathers, is in the present deplorable state of the kingdom a very great additional grievance; and, therefore, whoever could find out a fair, cheap, and easy method of making these children sound, useful members of the commonwealth, would deserve so well of the public as to have his statue set up for a preserver of the nation.

But my intention is very far from being confined to provide only for the children of professed beggars; it is of a much greater extent, and shall take in the whole number of infants at a certain age who are born of parents in effect as little able to support them as those who demand our charity in the streets.

As to my own part, having turned my thoughts for many years upon this important subject, and maturely weighed the several schemes of our projectors,[1] I have always found them grossly mistaken in their computation. It is true, a child just dropped from its dam may be supported by her milk for a solar year, with little other nourishment; at most not above the value of 2s.,[2] which the mother may certainly get, or the value in scraps, by her lawful occupation of begging; and it is exactly at one year old that I propose to provide for them in such a manner as instead of being a charge upon their parents or the parish, or wanting food and raiment for the rest of their lives, they shall on the contrary contribute to the feeding, and partly to the clothing, of many thousands.

There is likewise another great advantage in my scheme, that it will   5 prevent those voluntary abortions, and that horrid practice of women murdering their bastard children, alas! too frequent among us! sacrificing the poor innocent babes I doubt more to avoid the expense than the shame, which would move tears and pity in the most savage and inhuman breast.

The number of souls in this kingdom being usually reckoned one million and a half, of these I calculate there may be about 200,000 couple whose wives are breeders; from which number I subtract 30,000 couple who are able to maintain their own children (although I apprehend there cannot be so many, under the present distress of the kingdom); but this being granted, there will remain 170,000 breeders. I again subtract 50,000 for those women who miscarry, or whose children die

---

[1]**projectors** Persons who devise plans. [All notes are the editors'.]
[2]**2s.** Two shillings. In paragraph 7, "£" is an abbreviation for pounds sterling and "d" for pence.

by accident or disease within the year. There only remain 120,000 children of poor parents annually born. The question therefore is, how this number shall be reared and provided for? which, as I have already said, under the present situation of affairs, is utterly impossible by all the methods hitherto proposed. For we can neither employ them in handicraft or agriculture; we neither build houses (I mean in the country) nor cultivate land; they can very seldom pick up a livelihood by stealing, till they arrive at six years old, except where they are of towardly parts; although I confess they learn the rudiments much earlier; during which time they can, however, be properly looked upon only as probationers; as I have been informed by a principal gentleman in the county of Cavan, who protested to me that he never knew above one or two instances under the age of six, even in a part of the kingdom so renowned for the quickest proficiency in that art.

I am assured by our merchants, that a boy or a girl before twelve years old is no salable commodity; and even when they come to this age they will not yield above 3£. or 3£. 2s. 6d. at most on the exchange; which cannot turn to account either to the parents or kingdom, the charge of nutriment and rags having been at least four times that value.

I shall now therefore humbly propose my own thoughts, which I hope will not be liable to the least objection.

I have been assured by a very knowing American of my acquaintance in London, that a young healthy child well nursed is at a year old a most delicious, nourishing, and wholesome food, whether stewed, roasted, baked, or broiled; and I make no doubt that it will equally serve in a fricassee or a ragout.

I do therefore humbly offer it to public consideration that of the 120,000 children already computed, 20,000 may be reserved for breed, whereof only one-fourth part to be males; which is more than we allow to sheep, black cattle, or swine; and my reason is, that these children are seldom the fruits of marriage, a circumstance not much regarded by our savages; therefore one male will be sufficient to serve four females. That the remaining 100,000 may, at a year old, be offered in sale to the persons of quality and fortune through the kingdom; always advising the mother to let them suck plentifully in the last month, so as to render them plump and fat for a good table. A child will make two dishes at an entertainment for friends; and when the family dines alone, the fore or hind quarter will make a reasonable dish, and seasoned with a little pepper or salt will be very good boiled on the fourth day, especially in winter.

I have reckoned upon a medium that a child just born will weigh twelve pounds, and in a solar year, if tolerably nursed, will increase to twenty-eight pounds.

I grant this food will be somewhat dear, and therefore very proper for landlords, who, as they have already devoured most of the parents, seem to have the best title to the children.

Infant's flesh will be in season throughout the year, but more plentiful in March, and a little before and after: for we are told by a grave author, an eminent French physician, that fish being a prolific diet, there are more children born in Roman Catholic countries about nine months after Lent than at any other season; therefore, reckoning a year after Lent, the markets will be more glutted than usual, because the number of popish infants is at least three to one in this kingdom: and therefore it will have one other collateral advantage, by lessening the number of papists among us.

I have already computed the charge of nursing a beggar's child (in which list I reckon all cottagers, laborers, and four-fifths of the farmers) to be about 2s. per annum, rags included; and I believe no gentleman would repine to give 10s. for the carcass of a good fat child, which, as I have said, will make four dishes of excellent nutritive meat, when he has only some particular friend or his own family to dine with him. Thus the squire will learn to be a good landlord, and grow popular among the tenants; the mother will have 8s. net profit, and be fit for work till she produces another child.

Those who are more thrifty (as I must confess the times require) 15 may flay the carcass; the skin of which artificially dressed will make admirable gloves for ladies, and summer boots for fine gentlemen.

As to our city of Dublin, shambles³ may be appointed for this purpose in the most convenient parts of it, and butchers we may be assured will not be wanting: although I rather recommend buying the children alive, and dressing them hot from the knife as we do roasting pigs.

A very worthy person, a true lover of his country, and whose virtues I highly esteem, was lately pleased in discoursing on this matter to offer a refinement upon my scheme. He said that many gentlemen of this kingdom, having of late destroyed their deer, he conceived that the want of venison might be well supplied by the bodies of young lads and maidens, not exceeding fourteen years of age nor under twelve; so great a number of both sexes in every country being now ready to starve for want of work and service; and these to be disposed of by their parents, if alive, or otherwise by their nearest relations. But with due deference to so excellent a friend and so deserving a patriot, I cannot be altogether in his sentiments; for as to the males, my American acquaintance assured me from frequent experience that their flesh was generally tough and lean, like that of our schoolboys by continual exercise, and their taste disagreeable; and to fatten them would not answer the charge. Then as to the females, it would, I think, with humble submission be a loss to the public, because they soon would become breeders themselves: and besides, it is not improbable that some scrupulous people might be apt to censure such a practice (although indeed very unjustly), as a little bor-

---

³**shambles** Slaughterhouses.

dering upon cruelty; which, I confess, has always been with me the strongest objection against any project, how well soever intended.

But in order to justify my friend, he confessed that this expedient was put into his head by the famous Psalmanazar[4] a native of the island Formosa, who came from thence to London about twenty years ago: and in conversation told my friend, that in his country when any young person happened to be put to death, the executioner sold the carcass to persons of quality as a prime dainty; and that in his time the body of a plump girl of fifteen, who was crucified for an attempt to poison the emperor, was sold to his imperial majesty's prime minister of state, and other great mandarins of the court, in joints from the gibbet, at 400 crowns. Neither indeed can I deny, that if the same use were made of several plump young girls in this town, who without one single groat to their fortunes cannot stir abroad without a chair, and appear at the playhouse and assemblies in foreign fineries which they never will pay for, the kingdom would not be the worse.

Some persons of a depending spirit are in great concern about the vast number of poor people, who are aged, diseased, or maimed, and I have been desired to employ my thoughts what course may be taken to ease the nation of so grievous an encumbrance. But I am not in the least pain upon that matter, because it is very well known that they are every day dying and rotting by cold and famine, and filth and vermin, as fast as can be reasonably expected. And as to the young laborers, they are now in as hopeful a condition: They cannot get work, and consequently pine away for want of nourishment, to a degree that if at any time they are accidentally hired to common labor, they have not strength to perform it; and thus the country and themselves are happily delivered from the evils to come.

I have too long digressed, and therefore shall return to my subject. I 20 think the advantages by the proposal which I have made are obvious and many, as well as of the highest importance.

For first, as I have already observed, it would greatly lessen the number of papists, with whom we are yearly overrun, being the principal breeders of the nation as well as our most dangerous enemies; and who stay at home on purpose to deliver the kingdom to the Pretender, hoping to take their advantage by the absence of so many good Protestants, who have chosen rather to leave their country than stay at home and pay tithes against their conscience to an Episcopal curate.

Secondly, The poor tenants will have something valuable of their own, which by law may be made liable to distress and help to pay their landlord's rent, their corn and cattle being already seized, and money a thing unknown.

[4]**Psalmanazar** George Psalmanazar (c. 1679–1763), a Frenchman who claimed to be from Formosa (now Taiwan); he wrote *An Historical and Geographical Description of Formosa* (1704). The hoax was exposed soon after publication.

Thirdly, Whereas the maintenance of 100,000 children from two years old and upward, cannot be computed at less than 10s. a-piece per annum, the nation's stock will be thereby increased £50,000 per annum, beside the profit of a new dish introduced to the tables of all gentlemen of fortune in the kingdom who have any refinement in taste. And the money will circulate among ourselves, the goods being entirely of our own growth and manufacture.

Fourthly, The constant breeders beside the gain of 8s. sterling per annum by the sale of their children, will be rid of the charge of maintaining them after the first year.

Fifthly, This food would likewise bring great custom to taverns, 25 where the vintners will certainly be so prudent as to procure the best receipts for dressing it to perfection, and consequently have their houses frequented by all the fine gentlemen, who justly value themselves upon their knowledge in good eating; and a skilful cook who understands how to oblige his guests, will contrive to make it as expensive as they please.

Sixthly, This would be a great inducement to marriage, which all wise nations have either encouraged by rewards or enforced by laws and penalties. It would increase the care and tenderness of mothers toward their children, when they were sure of a settlement for life to the poor babes, provided in some sort by the public, to their annual profit instead of expense. We should see an honest emulation among the married women, which of them would bring the fattest child to the market. Men would become as fond of their wives during the time of their pregnancy as they are now of their mares in foal, their cows in calf, their sows when they are ready to farrow; nor offer to beat or kick them (as is too frequent a practice) for fear of a miscarriage.

Many other advantages might be enumerated. For instance, the addition of some thousand carcasses in our exportation of barreled beef, the propagation of swine's flesh, and improvement in the art of making good bacon, so much wanted among us by the great destruction of pigs, too frequent at our table; which are no way comparable in taste or magnificence to a well-grown, fat, yearling child, which roasted whole will make a considerable figure at a lord mayor's feast or any other public entertainment. But this and many others I omit, being studious of brevity.

Supposing that 1,000 families in this city would be constant customers for infants' flesh, besides others who might have it at merry-meetings, particularly at weddings and christenings, I compute that Dublin would take off annually about 20,000 carcasses; and the rest of the kingdom (where probably they will be sold somewhat cheaper) the remaining 80,000.

I can think of no one objection that will possibly be raised against this proposal, unless it should be urged that the number of people will be thereby much lessened in the kingdom. This I freely own, and it was indeed one principal design in offering it to the world. I desire the reader will observe, that I calculate my remedy for this one individual kingdom of Ireland and for no other that ever was, is, or I think ever can be upon earth. Therefore let no man talk to me of other expedients: of taxing our absentees at 5s. a pound; of using neither clothes nor household furniture except what is of our own growth and manufacture; of utterly rejecting the materials and instruments that promote foreign luxury; of curing the expensiveness of pride, vanity, idleness, and gaming in our women; of introducing a vein of parsimony, prudence, and temperance; of learning to love our country, in the want of which we differ even from Laplanders and the inhabitants of Topinamboo; of quitting our animosities and factions, nor acting any longer like the Jews, who were murdering one another at the very moment their city was taken; of being a little cautious not to sell our country and conscience for nothing; of teaching landlords to have at least one degree of mercy toward their tenants; lastly, of putting a spirit of honesty, industry, and skill into our shopkeepers; who, if a resolution could now be taken to buy only our native goods, would immediately unite to cheat and exact upon us in the price the measure, and the goodness, nor could ever yet be brought to make one fair proposal of just dealing, though often and earnestly invited to it.

Therefore I repeat, let no man talk to me of these and the like expedients, till he has at least some glimpse of hope that there will be ever some hearty and sincere attempt to put them in practice. 30

But as to myself, having been wearied out for many years with offering vain, idle, visionary thoughts, and at length utterly despairing of success, I fortunately fell upon this proposal; which, as it is wholly new, so it has something solid and real, of no expense and little trouble, full in our own power, and whereby we can incur no danger in disobliging England. For this kind of commodity will not bear exportation, the flesh being of too tender a consistence to admit a long continuance in salt, although perhaps I could name a country which would be glad to eat up our whole nation without it.

After all, I am not so violently bent upon my own opinion as to reject any offer proposed by wise men, which shall be found equally innocent, cheap, easy, and effectual. But before something of that kind shall be advanced in contradiction to my scheme, and offering a better, I desire the author or authors will be pleased maturely to consider two points. First, as things now stand, how they will be able to find food and raiment for 100,000 useless mouths and backs. And secondly, there being a round million of creatures in human figure throughout this kingdom, whose subsistence put into a common stock would leave them in debt 2,000,000£. sterling, adding those who are beggars by profession to the bulk of farmers, cottagers, and laborers, with the wives and children who are beggars in effect; I desire those politicians who dislike my overture, and may perhaps be so bold as to attempt an answer, that they will first ask the parents of these mortals, whether they would not at this day think it a great happiness to have been sold for food at a year old in the manner I prescribe, and thereby have avoided such a perpetual scene of misfortunes as they have since gone through by the oppression of landlords, the impossibility of paying rent without money or trade, the want of common sustenance, with neither house nor clothes to cover them from the inclemencies of the weather, and the most inevitable prospect of entailing the like or greater miseries upon their breed for ever.

I profess, in the sincerity of my heart, that I have not the least personal interest in endeavoring to promote this necessary work, having no other motive than the public good of my country, by advancing our trade, providing for infants, relieving the poor, and giving some pleasure to the rich. I have no children by which I can propose to get a single penny; the youngest being nine years old, and my wife past childbearing.

Topics for Critical Thinking and Writing

1. In paragraph 4 the speaker of the essay mentions proposals set forth by "projectors," that is, by advocates of other proposals or projects. On the basis of the first two paragraphs of "A Modest Proposal," how would you characterize *this* projector, the speaker of the essay? Write your characterization in one paragraph. Then, in a second paragraph, characterize the projector as you understand him, having read the entire essay. In your second paragraph, indicate what *he thinks he is*, and also what the reader sees he really is.

2. The speaker or persona of "A Modest Proposal" is confident that selling children "for a good table" is a better idea than any of the then current methods of disposing of unwanted children, including abortion and infanticide. Can you think of any argument that might favor abortion or infanticide for parents in dire straits, rather than the projector's scheme?

3. In paragraph 29 the speaker considers, but dismisses out of hand, several other solutions to the wretched plight of the Irish poor. Write a 500-word essay in which you explain each of these ideas and their combined merits as an alternative solution to the one he favors.

4. What does the projector imply are the causes of the Irish poverty he deplores? Are there possible causes he has omitted? (If so, what are they?)

5. Imagine yourself as one of the poor parents to whom Swift refers, and write a 250-word essay explaining why you prefer not to sell your infant to the local butcher.

6. The modern version of the problem to which the proposal is addressed is called "population policy." How would you describe our nation's current population policy? Do we have a population policy, in fact? If not, what would you propose? If we do have one, would you propose any changes in it? Why, or why not?

7. It is sometimes suggested that just as persons need to get a license to drive a car, to hunt with a gun, or to marry, a husband and wife ought

to be required to get a license to have a child. Would you favor this idea, assuming that it applied to you as a possible parent? Would Swift? Explain your answers in an essay of 500 words.

8. Consider the six arguments advanced in paragraphs 21–26, and write a 1,000-word essay criticizing all of them. Or, if you find that one or more of the arguments is really unanswerable, explain why you find it so compelling.

5

Developing an Argument
of Your Own

PLANNING, DRAFTING, AND
REVISING AN ARGUMENT

First, hear the wisdom of Mark Twain: "When the Lord finished the world, He pronounced it good. That is what I said about my first work, too. But Time, I tell you, Time takes the confidence out of these incautious early opinions."

All of us, teachers and students, have our moments of confidence, but for the most part we know that we have trouble writing clear, thoughtful prose. In a conversation we can cover ourselves with such expressions as "Well, I don't know, but I sort of think . . . ," and we can always revise our position ("Oh, well, I didn't mean it that way"), but once we have handed in the final version of our writing we are helpless. We are (putting it strongly) naked to our enemies.

Getting Ideas

In Chapter 1 we quoted Robert Frost, "To learn to write is to learn to have ideas," and we offered suggestions about getting ideas, a process traditionally called **invention.** A moment ago we said that we often improve our ideas when we try to explain them to someone else. Partly, of course, we are responding to questions or objections raised by our companion in the conversation, but partly we are responding to ourselves; almost as soon as we hear what we have to say, we may find that it won't do, and, if we are lucky, we may find a better idea surfacing. One of the best ways of getting ideas is to talk things over.

The process of talking things over usually begins with the text that you are reading; your marginal notes, your summary, and your queries parenthetically incorporated within your summary are a kind of dialogue between you and the author you are reading. More obviously, when you talk with friends about your topic you are trying out and developing ideas. Finally, after reading, taking notes, and talking, you may feel that you now have clear ideas and you need only put them into writing. And so you take a sheet of blank paper, and perhaps a paralyzing thought suddenly strikes: "I have ideas but just can't put them into words."

Despite what many people believe, writing is not only a matter of putting one's ideas into words. Just as talking with others is a way of getting ideas, *writing is a way of getting and developing ideas.* Writing, in short, can be an important part of critical thinking. If fear of putting ourselves on record is one big reason we have trouble writing, another big reason is our fear that we have no ideas worth putting down. But by jotting down notes—or even free associations—and by writing a draft, however weak, we can help ourselves to think our way toward good ideas.

Freewriting   Writing for five or six minutes, nonstop, without censoring what you produce is one way of getting words down on paper that will help to lead to improved thoughts. Some people who write on a computer find it useful to dim the screen so they won't be tempted to look up and fiddle too soon with their words. Later they illuminate the screen, scroll back, and notice some key words or passages that can be used later in drafting a paper.

Listing   Jotting down items, just as you do when you make a shopping list, is another way of getting ideas. When you make a shopping list, you write *ketchup* and the act of writing it reminds you that you also need hamburger rolls—and *that* in turn reminds you (who knows how or why?) that you also need a can of tuna fish. Similarly, when you prepare a list of ideas for a paper, jotting down one item will generate another. Of course, when you look over the list you will probably drop some of these ideas—the dinner menu will change—but you are making progress.

Diagramming   Making some sort of visual representation of an essay is a kind of listing. Three methods of diagramming are especially common.

- *Clustering.* Write, in the middle of a sheet of paper, a word or phrase summarizing your topic (for instance, *health care*), circle it, and then write down and circle a related word (for example, *gov't-provided*). Perhaps this leads you to write *higher taxes,* and you then circle this phrase and connect it to *gov't-provided.* The next thing that occurs to you is *employer-provided*—and so you write this down and circle it. Obviously you will not connect this to *higher taxes,* but you will connect it to *health care* because it is a sort of parallel to *gov't-provided.* The next thing that occurs to you is *unemployed people.* Obviously this category does not connect easily with *employer-provided,* so you won't connect these two terms with a line, but you probably will connect *unemployed people* with *health care,* and maybe also with *gov't-provided.* Keep going, jotting down ideas, and making connections where possible, indicating relationships.

- *Branching.* Some writers find it useful to build a tree, moving from the central topic to the main branches (chief ideas) and then to the twigs (aspects of the chief ideas).

- *Comparing in columns.* Draw a line down the middle of the page, and then set up oppositions. For instance, if you are concerned with health care, you might head one column *gov't-provided* and the other *employer-provided,* and you might then, under the first column, write *covers unemployed* and under the second column, write *omits unemployed.* You might go on to write, under the first column, *higher taxes,* and under the second, *higher prices*—or whatever else relevant comes to mind.

All of these methods can of course be executed with pen and paper, but if you write on a computer you may also be able to use them, depending on the capabilities of your program.

Whether you are using a computer or a pen, you put down some words and almost immediately see that they need improvement, not simply a little polishing but a substantial overhaul. You write, "Truman was justified in dropping the atom bomb for two reasons," and as soon as you write these words, a third reason comes to mind. Or perhaps one of those "two reasons" no longer seems very good. As the little girl shrewdly replied when an adult told her to think before she spoke, "How do I know what I think before I hear what I say?" We have to see what we say, we have to get something down on paper, before we realize that we need to make it better.

Writing, then, is really **rewriting,** that is, **revising,** and a revision is a *re-vision,* a second look. The paper that you hand in should be clear and may even seem effortless to the reader, but in all likelihood the clarity and apparent ease are the result of a struggle with yourself, a struggle during which you greatly improved your first thoughts. You begin by putting down your ideas, such as they are, perhaps even in the random order in which they occurred, but sooner or later comes the job of looking at them critically, developing what is useful in them and chucking out what is not. If you follow this procedure you will be in the company of Picasso, who said that he "advanced by means of destruction."

Whether you advance bit by bit (writing a sentence, revising it, writing the next, and so on) or whether you write an entire first draft and then revise it and revise it again and again is chiefly a matter of temperament. Probably most people combine both approaches, backing up occasionally but trying to get to the end fairly soon so that they can see rather quickly what they know, or think they know, and can then start the real work of thinking, of converting their initial ideas into something substantial.

Getting Ideas by Asking Questions   Getting ideas, we said when we talked about **topics** and **invention** strategies in Chapter 1 (p. 5) is mostly a matter of asking (and then thinking about) questions. We append questions to the end of each argumentative essay in this book, not in order to torment you but in order to help you to think about the arguments, for instance to turn your attention to especially important matters. If your instructor asks you to write an answer to one of these questions, you are lucky: Examining the question will stimulate your mind to work in a definite direction. But if a topic is not assigned, and you are asked to write an argument, you will find that some ideas (possibly poor ones, at this stage, but that doesn't matter because you will soon revise) will come to mind if you ask yourself questions. Five basic questions by which you can begin finding where you stand on an issue (**stasis**) are:

1. What is *X?*
2. What is the value of *X?*
3. What are the causes (or the consequences) of *X?*
4. What should (or ought or must) we do about *X?*
5. What is the evidence for my claims?

Let's spend a moment looking at each of these questions.

1. **What is *X?*** We can hardly argue about the number of people sentenced to death in the United States in 1995—a glance at the appropriate government report will give the answer—but we can argue about whether or not capital punishment as administered in the United States is discriminatory. Does the evidence, we can ask, support the view that in the United States the death penalty is unfair? Similarly, we can ask whether a human fetus is a human being (in saying what something is, must we take account of its potentiality?), and, even if we agree that a fetus is a human being, we can further ask about whether it is a *person.* In *Roe v. Wade* the Supreme Court ruled that even the "viable" unborn human fetus is not a "person" as that term is used in the Fifth and Fourteenth Amendments. Here the question is this: Is the essential fact about the fetus that it is a person?

An argument of this sort makes a claim—that is, it takes a stand— but notice that it does not have to argue for an action. Thus, it may argue that the death penalty is administered unfairly—that's a big enough issue—but it need not therefore go on to argue that the death penalty should be abolished. After all, another possibility is that the death penalty should be administered fairly. The writer of the essay may be doing enough if he or she establishes the truth of the claim and leaves to others the possible courses of action.

2. **What is the value of** *X?* No one can argue with you if you say you prefer the plays of Tennessee Williams to those of Arthur Miller. But as soon as you say that Williams is a better playwright than Miller, you have based your preference on implicit standards, and it is incumbent on you to support your preference by giving evidence about the relative skill, insight, and accomplishments of Williams and Miller. Your argument is an evaluation. The question now at issue is the merits of the two authors and the standards appropriate for such an appraisal. (For a discussion of literary evaluations, see pp. 339–43.)

In short, an essay offering an evaluation normally has two purposes: (a) to set forth an assessment, and (b) to convince the reader that the assessment is reasonable. In writing an evaluation you will have to establish criteria, and these will vary depending on your topic. For instance, if you are comparing the artistic merit of the plays of Williams and Miller, you may want to talk about the quality of the characterization, the significance of the theme, and so on. But if the topic is, Which playwright is more suitable to be taught in high school?, other criteria may be appropriate, such as the difficulty of the language, the presence of obscenity, and so on.

3. **What are the causes (or the consequences) of** *X?* Why did the rate of auto theft increase during a specific period? If we abolish the death penalty, will that cause the rate of murder to increase? Notice, by the way, that such problems may be complex. The phenomena that people usually argue about—say, such things as inflation, war, suicide, crime—have many causes, and it is therefore often a mistake to speak of *the* cause of *X.* A writer in *Time* mentioned that the life expectancy of an average American male is about sixty-seven years, a figure that compares unfavorably with the life expectancy of males in Japan and Israel. The *Time* writer suggested that an important cause of the relatively short life span is "the pressure to perform well in business." Perhaps. But the life expectancy of plumbers is no greater than that of managers and executives. Nutrition authority Jean Mayer, in an article in *Life,* attributed the relatively poor longevity of American males to a diet that is "rich in fat and poor in nutrients." Doubtless other authorities propose other causes, and in all likelihood no one cause accounts for the phenomenon.

4. **What should (or ought or must) we do about** *X?* Must we always obey the law? Should the law allow eighteen-year-olds to drink alcohol? Should eighteen-year-olds be drafted to do one year of social service? Should pornography be censored? Should steroid use by athletes be banned? Ought there to be "Good Samaritan" laws, making it a legal duty to intervene to save a person from death or great bodily harm, when one might do so with little or no risk to oneself? These questions involve conduct and policy; how we answer them will reveal our values and principles.

An essay of this sort usually begins by explaining what the issue is—and why the reader should care about it—and then offers the proposal, paying attention to the counterarguments.

5. **What is the evidence for my claims?** Critical reading, writing, and thinking depend essentially on identifying and evaluating the evidence for and against the claims one makes and encounters in the writings of others. It is not enough to have an *opinion* or belief one way or the other; you need to be able to support your opinions—the bare fact of your sincere belief in what you say or write is not itself any *evidence* that what you believe is true.

So what are good reasons for opinions, adequate evidence for one's beliefs? The answer, of course, depends on what kind of belief or opinion, assertion or hypothesis, claim or principle, you want to assert. For example, there is good evidence that President John F. Kennedy was assassinated on November 22, 1963, because this is the date for his death reported in standard almanacs. You could further substantiate the date by checking the back issues of the *New York Times*. But a different kind of evidence is needed to support the proposition that the chemical composition of water is H_2O; and you will need still other kinds of evidence to support your beliefs about the likelihood of rain tomorrow, whether the Red Sox will win the pennant this year, the twelfth digit in the decimal expansion of pi, the average cumulative grades of the graduating seniors over the past three years in your college, whether *Hamlet* is greater than *Death of a Salesman*, and whether sexual harassment is morally wrong. None of these issues is merely a matter of opinion; yet on some of them, educated and informed people may disagree over the reasons and the evidence and what they show. Your job as a critical thinker is to be alert to the relevant reasons and evidence, and to make the most of them as you present your views.

Again, an argument may take in two or more of these five issues. Someone who argues that pornography should (or should not) be censored will have to mark out the territory of the discussion by defining pornography (our first issue: What is *X?*). The argument probably will also need to examine the consequences of adopting the preferred policy (our third issue), and may even have to argue about its value—our second issue. (Some people maintain that pornography produces crime, but others maintain that it provides a harmless outlet for impulses that otherwise might vent themselves in criminal behavior.) Further, someone arguing about the wisdom of censoring pornography might have to face the objection that censorship, however desirable on account of some of its consequences, may be unconstitutional, and that even if censorship were constitutional it would (or might) have undesirable side effects, such as repressing freedom of political opinion. And one will always have to keep asking oneself the fifth question, What is the evidence for my claims?

Thinking about one or more of these questions may get you going. For instance, thinking about the first question, What is *X?*, will require you to produce a definition, and as you work at producing a satisfactory definition, you may find new ideas arising. If a question seems relevant, start writing, even if you write only a fragmentary sentence. You'll probably find that one word leads to another and that ideas begin to appear. Even if these ideas seem weak as you write them, don't be discouraged; you have put something on paper, and returning to these words, perhaps in five minutes or perhaps the next day, you will probably find that some are not at all bad, and that others will stimulate you to better ones.

It may be useful to record your ideas in a special notebook reserved for the purpose. Such a **journal** can be a valuable resource when it comes time to write your paper. Many students find it easier to focus their thoughts on writing if during the period of gestation they have been jotting down relevant ideas on something more substantial than slips of paper or loose sheets. The very act of designating a notebook as your journal for a course can be the first step in focusing your attention on the eventual need to write a paper.

If what we have just said does not sound convincing, and you know from experience that you often have trouble getting started with your writing, don't despair; first aid is at hand in a sure-fire method that we will now explain.

The Thesis

Let's assume that you are writing an argumentative essay—perhaps an evaluation of an argument in this book—and you have what seems to be a pretty good draft, or at least a bunch of notes that are the result of hard thinking. You really do have ideas now, and you want to present them effectively. How will you organize your essay? No one formula works best for every essayist and for every essay, but it is usually advisable to formulate a basic **thesis,** a central point, a chief position, and to state it early. Every essay that is any good, even a book-length one, has a thesis, a main point, which can be stated briefly. Remember Coolidge's remark on the preacher's sermon on sin: "He was against it." Don't confuse the **topic** (here it is sin) with the thesis (opposition to sin). The thesis is the argumentative theme, the author's primary claim or contention, the proposition that the rest of the essay will explain and defend. Of course the thesis may sound commonplace, but the book or essay or sermon ought to develop it interestingly and convincingly.

Here are some sample theses:

Smoking should be prohibited in all enclosed public places.

Smoking should be limited to specific parts of enclosed public places and entirely prohibited in small spaces, such as elevators.

Proprietors of public places such as restaurants and sports arenas should be free to determine whether they wish to prohibit, limit, or impose no limitations on smokers.

Imagining an Audience

Of course the questions that you ask yourself, in order to stimulate your thoughts, will depend primarily on what you are writing about, but additional questions are always relevant:

- Who are my readers?
- What do they believe?
- How much common ground do we share?
- What do I want my readers to believe?
- What do they need to know?

These questions require a little comment. The literal answer to the first probably is "the teacher," but (unless you are given instructions to the contrary) you should not write specifically for the teacher; instead, you should write for an audience that is, generally speaking, like your classmates. In short, your imagined audience is literate, intelligent, and moderately well informed, but it does not know everything that you know, and it does not know your response to the problem that you are addressing.

The essays in this book are from many different sources, each with its own audience. An essay from the *New York Times* is addressed to the educated general reader; an essay from *Ms.* is addressed to readers sympathetic to the feminist movement. An essay from *Commonweal,* a Roman Catholic publication addressed to the nonspecialist, is likely to differ in point of view or tone from one in *Time,* even though both articles may advance approximately the same position. The writer of the article in *Commonweal* may, for example, effectively cite church fathers and distinguished Roman Catholic writers as authorities, whereas the writer of an article addressed largely to non-Catholic readers probably will cite few or even none of these figures because the audience might be unfamiliar with them or, even if familiar, might be unimpressed by their views.

The tone as well as the gist of the argument is in some degree shaped by the audience. For instance, popular journals, such as *The National Review* and *Ms.,* are more likely to use ridicule than are journals chiefly addressed to, say, an academic audience.

The Audience as Collaborator

If you imagine an audience, and keep asking yourself what this audience needs to be told and what it doesn't need to be told, you will find that material comes to mind, just as it comes to mind when a friend asks you what a film was about, and who was in it, and how you liked it. Your readers do not have to be told that Thomas Jefferson was an American statesman in the early years of this country's history, but they do have to be told that Thomas Huxley was a late-nineteenth-century

English advocate of Darwinism. You would identify Huxley because it's your hunch that your classmates never heard of him, or even if they may have heard the name, they can't quite identify it. But what if your class has been assigned an essay by Huxley? In that case your imagined reader knows Huxley's name and knows at least a little about him, so you don't have to identify Huxley as an Englishman of the nineteenth century. But you do still have to remind your reader about relevant aspects of his essay, and you do have to tell your reader about your responses to them.

After all, even if the instructor has assigned an essay by Huxley, you cannot assume that your classmates know the essay inside out. Obviously you can't say, "Huxley's third reason is also unconvincing," without reminding the reader, by means of a brief summary, of his third reason. Again, think of your classmates as your imagined readers; put yourself in their shoes, and be sure that your essay does not make unreasonable demands. If you ask yourself, "What do my readers need to know?" (and "What do I want them to believe?") you will find some answers arising, and you will start writing.

We have said that you should imagine your audience as your classmates. But this is not the whole truth. In a sense, your argument is addressed not simply to your classmates but to the world interested in ideas. Even if you can reasonably assume that your classmates have read only one work by Huxley, you will not begin your essay by writing "Huxley's essay is deceptively easy." You will have to name the work; it is possible that a reader has read some other work by Huxley. And by precisely identifying your subject you help to ease the reader into your essay.

Similarly, you won't begin by writing,

> The majority opinion in <u>Walker v. City of Birmingham</u> was that . . .

Rather, you'll write something like this:

> In <u>Walker v. City of Birmingham</u>, the Supreme Court ruled in 1966 that city authorities acted lawfully when they jailed Martin Luther King, Jr., and other clergymen in 1963 for marching in Birmingham without a permit. Justice Potter Stewart delivered the majority opinion, which held that . . .

By the way, if you think you suffer from a writing block, the mere act of writing out such obvious truths will help you to get started. You will find that putting a few words down on paper, perhaps merely copying the essay's title or an interesting quotation from the essay, will stimulate you to jot down thoughts that you didn't know you had in you.

Here, again, are the questions about audience. If you write with a word processor, consider putting these questions into a file. For each assignment, copy (with the "copy" command) the questions into the file you are currently working on, and then, as a way of generating ideas, *enter your responses, indented, under each question.*

- Who are my readers?
- What do they believe?
- How much common ground do we share?
- What do I want my readers to believe?
- What do they need to know?

Thinking about your audience can help you to put some words on paper; even more important, it can help you to get ideas. Our second and third questions about the audience ("What do they believe?" and "How much common ground do we share?") will usually help you get ideas flowing. Presumably your imagined audience does not share your views, or at least does not fully share them. But why? How can these readers hold a position that to you seems unreasonable? If you try to put yourself into your readers' shoes, and if you think about what your audience knows or thinks it knows, you will find yourself getting ideas.

You do not believe (let's assume) that people should be allowed to smoke in enclosed public places, but you know that some people hold a different view. Why do they hold it? Try to state their view in a way that would be satisfactory to them. Having done so, you may come to perceive that your conclusions and theirs differ because they are based on different premises, perhaps different ideas about human rights. Examine the opposition's premises carefully, and explain, first to yourself and ultimately to your readers, why you find some premises unsound.

Possibly some facts are in dispute, such as whether nonsmokers may be harmed by exposure to tobacco. The thing to do, then, is to check the facts. If you find that harm to nonsmokers has not been proved, but you nevertheless believe that smoking should be prohibited in enclosed public places, of course you can't premise your argument on the wrongfulness of harming the innocent (in this case, the nonsmokers). You will have to develop arguments that take account of the facts, whatever they are.

Among the relevant facts there surely are some that your audience or your opponent will not dispute. The same is true of the values relevant to the discussion; the two of you are very likely to agree, if only you stop to think about it, that you share belief in some of the same values (such as the principle mentioned above, that it is wrong to harm the innocent). These areas of shared agreement are crucial to effective persuasion in argument. If you wish to persuade, you'll have to begin by finding *premises you can share with your audience.* Try to identify and isolate these areas of agreement. There are two good reasons for doing so.

1. There is no point in disputing facts or values on which you and your readers really agree.
2. It usually helps to establish goodwill between you and your opponent when you can point to beliefs, assumptions, facts, and values that the two of you share.

In a few moments we will return to the need to share some of the opposition's ideas.

Recall that in writing college papers it is usually best to write for a general audience, an audience rather like your classmates but without the specific knowledge that they all share as students enrolled in one course. If the topic is smoking in public places, the audience presumably consists of smokers and nonsmokers. Thinking about our fifth question on page 167—What do the readers need to know?—may prompt you to give statistics about the harmful effects of smoking. Or, if you are arguing on behalf of smokers, it may prompt you to cite studies claiming that no evidence conclusively demonstrates that cigarette smoking is harmful to nonsmokers. If indeed you are writing for a general audience, and you are not advancing a highly unfamiliar view, our second question (What does the audience believe?) is less important here, but if the audience is specialized, such as an antismoking group, or a group of restaurant owners who fear that antismoking regulations will interfere with their business, or a group of civil libertarians, obviously an effective essay will have to address their special beliefs.

In addressing their beliefs (let's assume that you do not share them or do not share them fully), you must try to establish some common ground. If you advocate requiring restaurants to provide nonsmoking areas, you should at least recognize the possibility that this arrangement will result in inconvenience for the proprietor. But perhaps (the good news) it will regain some lost customers or will attract some new customers. This thought should prompt you to think of kinds of evidence, perhaps testimony or statistics.

When one formulates a thesis and asks questions about it, such as who the readers are, what do they believe, what do they know, and what do they need to know, one begins to get ideas about how to organize the material, or at least one begins to see that some sort of organization will have to be worked out. The thesis may be clear and simple, but the reasons (the argument) may take many pages. The thesis is the point; the argument sets forth the evidence that is offered to support the thesis.

The Title

It's not a bad idea to announce your thesis in your **title.** If you scan the table of contents of this book, you will notice that a fair number of essayists use the title to let the readers know, at least in a very general way, what position will be advocated. Here are a few examples:

Gay Marriages: Make Them Legal

Students Should Not Be above the Law

Why Handguns Must Be Outlawed

True, these titles are not especially engaging, but the reader welcomes them because they give some information about the writer's thesis.

Some titles do not announce the thesis but they at least announce the topic:

Is All Discrimination Unfair?

On Racist Speech

Why Make Divorce Easy?

Although not clever or witty, these titles are informative.

Some titles seek to attract attention or to stimulate the imagination:

A First Amendment Junkie

A Crime of Compassion

Addicted to Health

All of these are effective, but a word of caution is appropriate here. In your effort to engage your reader's attention, be careful not to sound like a wise guy. You want to engage your readers, not turn them off.

Finally, be prepared to rethink your title *after* you have finished the last draft of your paper. A title somewhat different from your working title may be an improvement because the emphasis of your finished paper may have turned out to be rather different from what you expected when you first thought of a title.

The Opening Paragraphs

A good introduction arouses the reader's interest and helps prepare the reader for the rest of the paper. How? Opening paragraphs usually do at least one (and often all) of the following:

- attract the reader's interest (often with a bold statement of the thesis, or with an interesting statistic, quotation, or anecdote);
- prepare the reader's mind by giving some idea of the topic, and often of the thesis;
- give the reader an idea of how the essay is organized;
- define a term.

You may not wish to announce your thesis in your title, but if you don't announce it there, you should set it forth very early in the argument, in your introductory paragraph or paragraphs. In her title "Human Rights and Foreign Policy," Jeanne J. Kirkpatrick merely announces her topic (subject) as opposed to her thesis (point), but she begins to hint at the thesis in her first paragraph, by deprecating President Jimmy Carter's policy:

> In this paper I deal with three broad subjects: first, the content and consequences of the Carter administration's human rights policy; second, the prerequisites of a more adequate theory of human rights; and third, some characteristics of a more successful human rights policy.

Or consider this opening paragraph from Peter Singer's "Animal Liberation":

> We are familiar with Black Liberation, Gay Liberation, and a variety of other movements. With Women's Liberation some thought we had come to the end of the road. Discrimination on the basis of sex, it has been said, is the last form of discrimination that is universally accepted and practiced without pretense, even in those liberal circles which have long prided themselves on their freedom from racial discrimination. But one should always be wary of talking of "the last remaining form of discrimination." If we have learned anything from the liberation movements, we should have learned how difficult it is to be aware of the ways in which we discriminate until they are forcefully pointed out to us. A liberation movement demands an expansion of our moral horizons, so that practices that were previously regarded as natural and inevitable are now seen as intolerable.

Although Singer's introductory paragraph nowhere mentions animal liberation, in conjunction with its title it gives us a good idea of what Singer is up to and where he is going. Singer knows that his audience will be skeptical, so he reminds them that many of us in previous years were skeptical of reforms that we now take for granted. He adopts a strategy used fairly often by writers who advance highly unconventional theses: Rather than beginning with a bold announcement of a thesis that may turn off some of his readers because it sounds offensive or absurd, Singer warms his audience up, gaining their interest by cautioning them politely that although they may at first be skeptical of animal liberation, if they stay with his essay they may come to feel that they have expanded their horizons.

Notice, too, that Singer begins by establishing common ground with his readers; he assumes, probably correctly, that they share his view that other forms of discrimination (now seen to be unjust) were once widely practiced and were assumed to be acceptable and natural. In this paragraph, then, Singer is not only showing himself to be fair-minded but is also letting us know that he will advance a daring idea. His opening wins our attention and our goodwill. A writer can hardly hope to do more. (In a few pages we will talk a little more about winning the audience.)

In your introductory paragraphs you may have to give some background informing or reminding your readers of material that they will have to be familiar with if they are to follow your essay. You may wish to define some terms, if the terms are unfamiliar or if you are using familiar terms in an unusual sense. In writing, or at least in revising these paragraphs, remember to keep in mind this question: What do my readers need to know? Remember, your aim throughout is to write *reader-friendly* prose, and keeping the needs and interests of your audience constantly in mind will help you achieve this goal.

After announcing the topic, giving the necessary background, and stating your position (and perhaps the opposition's) in as engaging a manner as possible, it is usually a good idea to give the reader an idea of how you will proceed. Look on the preceding page at Kirkpatrick's opening paragraph, for an obvious illustration. She tells us she will deal with three subjects, and she names them. Her approach in the paragraph is concise, obvious, and effective.

Similarly, you may, for instance, want to announce fairly early that there are four common objections to your thesis, and that you will take them up one by one, beginning with the weakest (or most widely held, or whatever) and moving to the strongest (or least familiar), after which you will advance your own view in greater detail. Of course not every argument begins with refuting the other side, though many arguments do. The point to remember is that you usually ought to tell your readers where you will be taking them and by what route.

Organizing and Revising the Body of the Essay

Most argumentative essays more or less follow this organization:

1. Statement of the problem
2. Statement of the structure of the essay
3. Statement of alternative solutions
4. Arguments in support of the proposed solution
5. Arguments answering possible objections
6. A summary, resolution, or conclusion

Let's look at each of these six steps.

1. **Statement of the problem.** Whether the problem is stated briefly or at length depends on the nature of the problem and the writer's audience. If you haven't already defined unfamiliar terms or terms you use in a special way, probably now is the time to do so. In any case, it is advisable here to state the problem objectively (thereby gaining the trust of the reader) and to indicate why the reader should care about the issue.

2. **Statement of the structure of the essay.** After stating the problem at the appropriate length, the writer often briefly indicates the structure of the rest of the essay. The commonest structure is suggested below, in points 3 and 4.

3. **Statement of alternative solutions.** In addition to stating the alternatives fairly, the writer probably conveys willingness to

recognize not only the integrity of the proposers but also the (partial) merit of at least some of the alternative solutions.

The point made in the previous sentence is important and worth amplifying. Because it is important to convey your goodwill—your sense of fairness—to the reader, it is advisable to let your reader see that you are familiar with the opposition, and that you recognize the integrity of those who hold that view. This you do by granting its merits as far as you can. (For more about this approach, see the essay by Carl Rogers on p. 301.)

The next stage, which constitutes most of the body of the essay, usually is this:

4. **Arguments in support of the proposed solution.** The evidence offered will, of course, depend on the nature of the problem. Relevant statistics, authorities, examples, or analogies may or may not come to mind or be available. This is usually the longest part of the essay.

5. **Arguments answering possible objections.** These arguments may suggest that

   a. the proposal won't work (perhaps it is alleged to be too expensive, or to make unrealistic demands on human nature, or to fail to get to the heart of the problem);

   b. the proposed solution will create problems greater than the difficulty to be resolved. (A good example of a proposal that produced dreadful unexpected results is the law mandating a prison term for anyone over eighteen in possession of an illegal drug. Heroin dealers then began to use children as runners, and cocaine importers followed the practice.)

6. **A summary, resolution, or conclusion.** Here the writer may seek to accommodate the views of the opposition as far as possible, but clearly suggests that the writer's own position makes good sense. A conclusion—the word comes from the Latin *claudere*, "to shut"—ought to provide a sense of closure, but it can be much more than a restatement of the writer's thesis. It can, for instance, make a quiet emotional appeal by suggesting that the issue is important and that the ball is now in the reader's court.

Of course not every essay will follow this six-part pattern, but let's assume that in the introductory paragraphs you have sketched the topic (and have shown or nicely said, or implied, that the reader doubtless is interested in it), and have fairly and courteously set forth the opposition's view, recognizing its merits and indicating the degree to which you can share part of that view. You now want to set forth your arguments explaining why you differ on some essentials.

In setting forth your own position, you can begin either with your strongest reasons or your weakest. Each method of organization has advantages and disadvantages. If you begin with your strongest, the essay may seem to peter out; if you begin with the weakest, you build to a climax but your readers may not still be with you because they may have felt at the start that the essay was frivolous. The solution to this last possibility is to make sure that even your weakest argument is an argument of some strength. You can, moreover, assure your readers that stronger points will soon be offered and you offer this point first only because you want to show that you are aware of it, and that, slight though it is, it deserves some attention. The body of the essay, then, is devoted to arguing a position, which means not only offering supporting reasons but also offering refutations of possible objections to these reasons.

Doubtless you will sometimes be uncertain, as you draft your essay, whether to present a given point before or after another point. When you write, and certainly when you revise, try to put yourself into your reader's shoes: Which point do you think the reader needs to know first? Which point *leads to* which further point? Your argument should not be a mere list of points, of course; rather, it should clearly integrate one point with another in order to develop an idea. But in all likelihood you won't have a strong sense of the best organization until you have written a draft and have reread it. You are likely to find that the organization needs some revising in order to make your argument clear to a reader.

Checking Paragraphs   When you revise your draft, watch out also for short paragraphs. Although a paragraph of only two or three sentences (like some in this chapter) may occasionally be helpful as a transition between complicated points, most short paragraphs are undeveloped paragraphs. (Newspaper editors favor very short paragraphs because they can be read rapidly when printed in the narrow columns typical of newspapers. Many of the essays reprinted in this book originally were published in newspapers, hence they're very short paragraphs. There is no reason for you to imitate this style in the argumentative essays you will be writing.)

In revising, when you find a paragraph of only a sentence or two or three, check first to see if it should be joined to the paragraph that precedes or follows. Second, if on rereading you are certain that a given paragraph should not be tied to what comes before or after, think about amplifying the paragraph with supporting detail (this is not the same as mere padding).

Checking Transitions   Make sure, too, in revising, that the reader can move easily from the beginning of a paragraph to the end, and from one paragraph to the next. Transitions help the reader to perceive the connections between the units of the argument. For example (that's a transition, of course), they may

illustrate: *for example, for instance, consider this case;*

establish a sequence: *a more important objection, a stronger example, the best reason;*

connect logically: *thus, as a result, therefore, so, it follows;*

compare: *similarly, in like manner, just as, analogously;*

contrast: *on the other hand, in contrast, however, but;*

summarize: *in short, briefly.*

Expressions such as these serve as guideposts that enable your reader to move easily through your essay.

When writers revise an early draft they chiefly

- unify the essay by eliminating irrelevancies;
- organize the essay by keeping in mind an imagined audience;
- clarify the essay by fleshing out thin paragraphs, by making certain that the transitions are adequate, and by making certain that generalizations are adequately supported by concrete details and examples.

We are not talking about polish or elegance; we are talking about fundamental matters. Be especially careful not to abuse the logical connectives (*thus, as a result,* and so on). If you write several sentences followed by *therefore* or a similar word or phrase, be sure that what you write after the *therefore* really *does follow* from what has gone before. Logical connectives are not mere transitional devices used to link disconnected bits of prose. They are supposed to mark a real movement of thought—the essence of an argument.

The Ending

What about concluding paragraphs, in which you try to summarize the main points and reaffirm your position? If you can look back over your essay and can add something that enriches it and at the same time wraps it up, fine, but don't feel compelled to say, "Thus, in conclusion, I have argued *X, Y,* and *Z,* and I have refuted Jones." After all, *conclusion* can have two meanings: (1) ending, or finish, as the ending of a joke or a novel; (2) judgment or decision reached after deliberation. Your essay should finish effectively (the first sense), but it need not announce a judgment (the second).

If the essay is fairly short, so that a reader can more or less keep the whole thing in mind, you may not need to restate your view. Just make sure that you have covered the ground, and that your last sentence is a good one. Notice that the essay printed later in this chapter (p. 187) does not end with a formal conclusion, though it ends conclusively, with a note of finality.

By a note of finality we do *not* mean a triumphant crowing. It's usually far better to end with the suggestion that you hope you have by now indicated why those who hold a different view may want to modify it and accept yours.

If you study the essays in this book, or, for that matter, the editorials and Op-Ed pieces in a newspaper, you will notice that writers often provide a sense of closure by using one of the following devices:

- a return to something in the introduction;
- a glance at the wider implications of the issue (for example, if smoking is restricted, other liberties are threatened);
- an anecdote that engagingly illustrates the thesis;
- a brief summary (but this sort of ending may seem unnecessary and even tedious, especially if the paper is short and if the summary merely repeats what has already been said).

The Uses of an Outline

Some writers find it useful to sketch an **outline** as soon as they think they know what they want to say, even before they write a first draft; others write an outline after a draft that has given them additional ideas. These procedures can be helpful in planning a tentative organization, but remember that in revising a draft new ideas will arise, and the outline may have to be modified. A preliminary outline is chiefly useful as a means of getting going, not as a guide to the final essay.

The Outline as a Way of Checking a Draft   Whether or not you use a preliminary outline, we suggest that after you have written what you hope is your last draft, you make an outline of it; there is no better way of finding out whether the essay is well organized.

Go through the draft and jot down the chief points, in the order in which you make them. That is, prepare a table of contents — perhaps a phrase for each paragraph. Next, examine your jottings to see what kind of sequence they reveal in your paper.

1. Is the sequence reasonable? Can it be improved?
2. Are any passages irrelevant?
3. Does something important seem to be missing?

If no structure or sequence clearly appears in the outline, then the full prose version of your argument probably doesn't have any, either. Therefore, produce another draft, moving things around, adding or subtracting paragraphs — cutting and pasting into a new sequence, with transitions as needed — and then make another outline to see if the sequence now is satisfactory.

You are probably familiar with the structure known as a **formal outline.** A major point is indicated by I, and points within this major point are indicated by A, B, C, and so on. Divisions within A, B, C, are indicated by 1, 2, 3, and so on, thus:

I. Arguments for opening all Olympic sports to professionals
   A. Fairness
      1. Some Olympic sports are already open to professionals
      2. Some athletes who really are not professionals are classified as professionals
   B. Quality (achievements would be higher)

You may want to outline your draft according to this principle, or it may be enough if you simply jot down a phrase for each paragraph and indent the subdivisions. But keep this point in mind: It is not enough for the parts to be ordered reasonably; the order must be made clear to the reader, probably by means of transitions such as *for instance, on the other hand, we can now turn to an opposing view,* and so on.

Tone and the Writer's Persona

Although this book is chiefly about argument in the sense of rational discourse—the presentation of reasons in support of a thesis or conclusion—the appeal to reason is only one form of persuasion. Another form is the appeal to emotion—to pity, for example. Aristotle saw, in addition to the appeal to reason and the appeal to emotion, a third form of persuasion, the appeal to the character of the speaker. He called it the **ethical appeal** (the Greek word for this kind of appeal is **ethos,** "character"). The idea is that effective speakers convey the suggestion that they are

- informed,
- intelligent,
- benevolent,
- honest.

Because they are perceived as trustworthy, their words inspire confidence in their listeners. It is, of course, a fact that when we read an argument we are often aware of the *person* or *voice* behind the words, and our assent to the argument depends partly on the extent to which we can share the speaker's assumptions, look at the matter from the speaker's point of view—in short, *identify* with this speaker.

How can a writer inspire the confidence that lets readers identify themselves with the writer? To begin with, the writer should possess the virtues Aristotle specified: intelligence or good sense, honesty, and benevolence or goodwill. As the Roman proverb puts it, "No one gives what he does not have." Still, possession of these qualities is not a guarantee that you will convey them in your writing. Like all other writers, you will have to revise your drafts so that these qualities become apparent, or, stated more moderately, you will have to revise so that nothing in the essay causes a reader to doubt your intelligence, honesty, and goodwill. A blunder in logic, a misleading quotation, a snide remark — all such slips can cause readers to withdraw their sympathy from the writer.

But of course all good argumentative essays do not sound exactly alike; they do not all reveal the same speaker. Each writer develops his or her own voice or (as literary critics and teachers call it) **persona.** In fact, one writer will have several voices or personae, depending on the topic and the audience. The president of the United States delivering an address on the State of the Union has one persona; chatting with a reporter at his summer home he has another. This change is not a matter of hypocrisy. Different circumstances call for different language. As a French writer put it, there is a time to speak of "Paris," and a time to speak of "the capital of the nation." When Lincoln spoke at Gettysburg, he didn't say "Eighty-seven years ago," but "Four score and seven years ago." We might say that just as some occasions required him to be the folksy Honest Abe, the occasion of the dedication of hallowed ground required him to be formal and solemn, and so the president of the United States appropriately used biblical language. The election campaigns called for one persona, and this occasion called for a different persona.

When we talk about a writer's persona, we mean the way in which the writer presents his or her attitudes:

> the attitude toward *the self,*
>
> toward *the audience*, and
>
> toward *the subject.*

Thus, if a writer says,

> I have thought long and hard about this subject, and I can say with assurance that . . .

we may feel that we are listening to a self-satisfied ass who probably is simply mouthing other people's opinions. Certainly he is mouthing other people's clichés: "long and hard," "say with assurance."

Let's look at a slightly subtler example of an utterance that reveals an attitude. When we read that

> President Nixon was hounded out of office by journalists

we hear a respectful attitude toward Nixon ("President Nixon") and a hostile attitude toward the press (they are beasts, curs who "hounded" our elected leader). If the writer's attitudes were reversed, she might have said something like this:

The press turned the searchlight on Tricky Dick's criminal shenanigans.

"Tricky Dick" and "criminal" are obvious enough, but notice that "shenanigans" also implies the writer's contempt for Nixon, and of course "turned the searchlight" suggests that the press is a source of illumination, a source of truth. The original version and the opposite version both say that the press was responsible for Nixon's resignation, but the original version ("President Nixon was hounded") conveys indignation toward journalists, whereas the revision conveys contempt for Nixon.

These two versions suggest two speakers who differ not only in their view of Nixon but also in their manner, including the seriousness with which they take themselves. Although the passage is very short, it seems to us that the first speaker conveys righteous indignation ("hounded"), whereas the second conveys amused contempt ("shenanigans"). To our ears the tone, as well as the point, differs in the two versions.

We are talking about **loaded words,** words that convey the writer's attitude and that by their connotations are meant to win the reader to the writer's side. Compare "freedom fighter" with "terrorist," "pro-choice" with "pro-abortion," or "pro-life" with "anti-abortion." "Freedom fighter," "pro-choice," and "pro-life" sound like good things; speakers who use these words are seeking to establish themselves as virtuous people who are supporting worthy causes. The **connotations** (associations, overtones) of these pairs of words differ, even though the **denotations** (explicit meanings, dictionary definitions) are the same, just as the connotations of "mother" and "female parent" differ, although the denotations are the same. Similarly, although "four score and seven" and "eighty-seven" both denote "thirteen less than one hundred," they differ in connotation.

Tone is not only a matter of connotations ("hounded out of office," versus, let's say, "compelled to resign," or "pro-choice" versus "pro-abortion"); it is also a matter of such things as the selection and type of examples. A writer who offers many examples, especially ones drawn from ordinary life, conveys a persona different from that of a writer who offers no examples, or only an occasional invented instance. The first of these probably is, one might say, friendlier, more down-to-earth.

Last Words on Tone   On the whole, in writing an argument it is advisable to be courteous, respectful of your topic, of your audience, and of people who hold views you are arguing against. It is rarely good for one's own intellectual development to regard as villains or fools persons who hold views different from one's own, especially if some of them are in the audience. Keep in mind the story of the two strangers on a train who, striking up a conversation, found that both were clergymen, though of different faiths. Then one said to the other, "Well, why shouldn't we be friends? After all, we both serve God, you in your way and I in His."

Complacency is all right when telling jokes but not in arguments. Recognize opposing views, assume they are held in good faith, state them fairly (if you don't, you do a disservice not only to the opposition but to your own position, because the perceptive reader will not take you seriously), and be temperate in arguing your own position: "If I understand their view correctly . . ."; "It seems reasonable to conclude that . . ."; "Perhaps, then, we can agree that . . ."

"We," "One," or "I"?

The use of *we* in the last sentence brings us to another point: May the first-person pronouns *I* and *we* be used? In this book, because two of us are writing, we often use *we* to mean the two authors. And we sometimes use *we* to mean the authors and the readers, as in phrases like the one that ends the previous paragraph. This shifting use of one word can be troublesome, but we hope (clearly the *we* here refers only to the authors) that we have avoided any ambiguity. But can, or should, or must, an individual use *we* instead of *I*? The short answer is no.

If you are simply speaking for yourself, use *I*. Attempts to avoid the first person singular by saying things like "This writer thinks . . . ," and "It is thought that . . . ," and "One thinks that . . . ," are far more irritating (and wordy) than the use of *I*. The so-called editorial *we* is as odd sounding in a student's argument as is the royal *we*. Mark Twain said that the only ones who can appropriately say *we* are kings, editors, and people with a tapeworm. And because one *one* leads to another, making the sentence sound (James Thurber's words) "like a trombone solo," it's best to admit that you are the author, and to use *I*. But of course there is no need to preface every sentence with "I think." The reader knows that the essay is yours; just write it, using *I* when you must, but not needlessly.

Avoiding Sexist Language

Courtesy (as well as common sense) requires that you respect the feelings of your readers. Many people today find offensive the implicit sexism in the use of male pronouns to denote not only men but also women ("As the reader follows the argument, he will find . . ."). And sometimes the use of the male pronoun to denote all people is ridiculous: "An individual, no matter what his sex, . . ."

In most contexts there is no need to use gender-specific nouns or pronouns. One way to avoid using *he* when you mean any person is to use *he or she* (or *she or he*) instead of *he*, but the result is sometimes a bit cumbersome—although it is superior to the overly conspicuous *he/she* and to *s/he*.

A PEER REVIEW CHECKLIST FOR A DRAFT OF AN ARGUMENT

Read the draft through, quickly. Then read it again, with the following questions in mind.

✓ Does the draft show promise of fulfilling the assignment?

✓ Looking at the essay as a whole, what thesis (main idea) is advanced?

✓ Are the needs of the audience kept in mind? For instance, do some words need to be defined? Is the evidence (for instance, the examples, and the testimony of authorities) clear and effective?

✓ Can you accept the assumptions? If not, why not?

✓ Is any obvious evidence (or counterevidence) overlooked?

If the writer is proposing a solution,

   ✓ Are other equally attractive solutions adequately examined?

   ✓ Has the writer overlooked some unattractive effects of the proposed solution?

Here are two simple ways to solve the problem:

1. *use the plural* ("As readers follow the argument, they will find . . ."), or
2. *recast the sentence* so that no pronoun is required ("Readers following the argument will find . . .").

Because *man* and *mankind* strike many readers as sexist when used in such expressions as "Man is a rational animal" and "Mankind has not yet solved this problem," consider using such words as *human being, person, people, humanity,* and *we.* (*Examples:* "Human beings are rational animals"; "We have not yet solved this problem.")

PEER REVIEW

Your instructor may suggest—or may even require—that you submit an early draft of your essay to a fellow student or small group of students for comment. Such a procedure benefits both author and readers: You get the responses of a reader, and the student-reader gets experience in thinking about the problems of developing an argument, especially in thinking about such matters as the degree of detail that a writer needs to offer to a reader, and the importance of keeping the organization evident to a reader.

Looking at each paragraph separately:

✓ What is the basic point?

✓ How does each paragraph relate to the essay's main idea or to the previous paragraph?

✓ Should some paragraphs be deleted? Be divided into two or more paragraphs? Be combined? Be put elsewhere? (If you outline the essay by jotting down the gist of each paragraph, you will get help in answering these questions.)

✓ Is each sentence clearly related to the sentence that precedes and to the sentence that follows?

✓ Is each paragraph adequately developed? Are there sufficient details, perhaps brief supporting quotations from the text?

✓ Are the introductory and concluding paragraphs effective?

✓ What are the paper's chief strengths?

✓ Make at least two specific suggestions that you think will assist the author to improve the paper.

A STUDENT'S ESSAY, FROM ROUGH NOTES TO FINAL VERSION

While we were revising this textbook we asked the students in one of our classes to write a short essay (500–750 words) on some ethical problem that concerned them. Because this assignment was the first writing assignment in the course, we explained that a good way to get ideas is to ask oneself some questions, jot down responses, question those responses, and write freely for ten minutes or so, not worrying about contradictions. We invited our students to hand in their initial jottings along with the finished essay, so that we could get a sense of how they proceeded as writers. Not all of them chose to hand in their jottings, but we were greatly encouraged by those who did. What was encouraging was the confirmation of an old belief, the belief — we call it a fact — that students will hand in a thoughtful essay if before they prepare a final version they nag themselves, ask themselves *why* they think this or that, jot down their responses, and are not afraid to change their minds as they proceed.

Here are the first jottings of a student, Emily Andrews, who elected to write about whether to give money to street beggars. She simply put down ideas, one after the other.

```
Help the poor? Why do I (sometimes) do it?

I feel guilty, and think I should help them: poor,
    cold, hungry (but also some of them are thirsty
```

for liquor, and will spend the money on liquor, not on food).

I also feel annoyed by them--most of them:

Where does the expression "the deserving poor" come from?

And "poor but honest"? Actually, that sounds a bit odd. Wouldn't "rich but honest" make more sense?

Why don't they work? Fellow with red beard, always by bus stop in front of florist's shop, always wants a handout. He is a regular, there all day every day, so I guess he is in a way "reliable," so why doesn't he put the same time in on a job?

Or why don't they get help? Don't they know they need it? They <u>must</u> know they need it.

Maybe that guy with the beard is just a con artist. Maybe he makes more money by panhandling than he would by working, and it's a lot easier!

Kinds of poor--how to classify??
        drunks, druggies, etc.
        mentally ill (maybe drunks belong here too)
        decent people who have had terrible luck
                            .

Why private charity?

Doesn't it makes sense to say we (fortunate individuals) should give something--an occasional handout-- to people who have had terrible luck? (I suppose some people might say that there is no need for any of us to give anything--the government takes care of the truly needy--but I <u>do</u> believe in giving charity. A month ago a friend of the family passed away, and the woman's children suggested that people might want to make a donation in her name, to a shelter for battered women. I know my parents made a donation.)

BUT how can I tell who is who, which are which? Which of these people asking for "spare change" really need (deserve???) help, and which are phonies? Impossible to tell.

Possibilities:
        Give to no one
        Give to no one but make an annual donation, maybe to United Way
        Give a dollar to each person who asks. This would probably not cost me even a dollar a day

Occasionally do without something--maybe a CD--or
a meal in a restaurant--and give the money I save
to people who seem worthy.

WORTHY? What am I saying? How can I, or anyone, tell?
The neat-looking guy who says he just lost his job
may be a phony, and the dirty bum--probably a
drunk--may desperately need food. (OK, so what if
he spends the money on liquor instead of food? At
least he'll get a little pleasure in life. No!
It's not all right if he spends it on drink.)

Other possibilities:
Do some volunteer work?
To tell the truth, I don't want to put in the
time. I don't feel that guilty.

So what's the problem?

Is it, How I can help the very poor (handouts, or
through an organization)? or

How I can feel less guilty about being lucky enough to
be able to go to college, and to have a supportive
family?

I can't quite bring myself to believe I should help
every beggar who approaches, but I also can't
bring myself to believe that I should do nothing,
on the grounds that:

a. it's probably their fault

b. if they are deserving, they can get gov't help.
No, I just can't believe that. Maybe some are
too proud to look for government help, or don't
know that they are entitled to it.

What to do?

On balance, it seems best to
a. give to United Way
b. maybe also give to an occasional individual, if
I happen to be moved, without worrying about
whether he or she is "deserving" (since it's
probably impossible to know).

A day after making these notes Emily reviewed them, added a few
points, and then made a very brief selection from them, to serve as an
outline for her first draft.

Opening para.: "poor but honest"? Deserve "spare
change"?

```
Charity: private or through organizations?
         pros and cons
         guy at bus
         it wouldn't cost me much, but . . . better to
         give through organizations


Concluding para.: still feel guilty?
                  maybe mention guy at bus again?
```

After writing and revising a draft, Emily Andrews submitted her essay to a fellow student for peer review. She then revised her work in light of the suggestions she received, and in light of her own further thinking.

On the next page we give the final essay. If after reading the final version you reread the early jottings, you will notice that some of the jottings never made it into the final version. But without the jottings, the essay probably could not have been as interesting as it is. When the writer made the jottings, she was not so much putting down her ideas as *finding* ideas by the process of writing.

Andrews 1

Emily Andrews

Professor Barnet

English 102

January 13, 1998

Why I Don't Spare "Spare Change"

"Poor but honest." "The deserving poor." I
don't know the origin of these quotations, but
they always come to mind when I think of "the
poor." But I also think of people who, perhaps
through alcohol or drugs, have ruined not only
their own lives but also the lives of others in
order to indulge in their own pleasure. Perhaps
alcoholism and drug addiction really are "diseases," as many people say, but my own feeling--
based, of course, not on any serious study--is
that most alcoholics and drug addicts can be
classified with the "<u>un</u>deserving poor." And that
is largely why I don't distribute spare change
to panhandlers.

But surely among the street people there
are also some who can rightly be called "deserving." Deserving what? <u>My</u> spare change? Or simply
the government's assistance? It happens that I
have been brought up to believe that it is appropriate to make contributions to charity--
let's say a shelter for battered women--but if I
give some change to a panhandler, am I making a
contribution to charity and thereby helping
someone, or, on the contrary, am I perhaps simply encouraging someone not to get help? Or,
maybe even worse, am I supporting a con artist?

If one believes in the value of private
charity, one can either give to needy individu-

als or to charitable organizations. In giving
to a panhandler one may indeed be helping a
person who badly needs help, but one cannot be
certain that one is giving to a needy individual. In giving to an organization such as the
United Way, on the other hand, one can feel
that one's money is likely to be used wisely.
True, confronted by a beggar one may feel that
this particular unfortunate individual needs
help at this moment--a cup of coffee, or a
sandwich--and the need will not be met unless I
put my hand in my pocket right now. But I have
come to think that the beggars whom I encounter
can get along without my spare change, and indeed perhaps they are actually better off for
not having money to buy liquor or drugs.

It happens that in my neighborhood I encounter few panhandlers. There is one fellow
who is always by the bus stop where I catch the
bus to the college, and I never give him anything precisely because he is always there. He
is such a regular that, I think, he ought to be
able to hold a regular job. Putting him aside,
I probably don't encounter more than three or
four beggars in a week. (I'm not counting
street musicians. These people seem quite able
to work for a living. If they see their "work"
as playing or singing, let persons who enjoy
their performances pay them. I do not consider
myself among their audience.) The truth of the
matter is that, since I meet so few beggars, I
could give each one a dollar and hardly feel
the loss. At most, I might go without seeing a

Andrews 3

movie some week. But I know nothing about these
people, and it's my impression--admittedly
based on almost no evidence--that they simply
prefer begging to working. I am not generalizing about street people, and certainly I am not
talking about street people in the big urban
centers. I am talking only about the people
whom I actually encounter.

That's why I usually do not give "spare
change," and I don't think I will in the future.
These people will get along without me. Someone
else will come up with money for their coffee or
their liquor, or, at worst, they will just have
to do without. I will continue to contribute occasionally to a charitable organization, not
simply (I hope) to salve my conscience but because I believe that these organizations actually do good work. But I will not attempt to be
a mini-charitable organization, distributing
(probably to the unworthy) spare change.

Finally, here are a few comments about the essay:

The title is informative, alerting the reader to the topic and the author's
position. (By the way, the student told us that in her next-to-last
draft the title was "Is It Right to Spare 'Spare Change'?" This title,
like the revision, introduces the topic but not the author's position.
The revised version seems to us to be more striking.)

The opening paragraph holds a reader's interest, partly by alluding to the
familiar phrase, "the deserving poor," and partly by introducing the
*un*familiar phrase, "the *un*deserving poor." Notice, too, that this
opening paragraph ends by clearly asserting the author's thesis. Of
course writers need not always announce their thesis early, but it is

usually advisable to do so. Readers like to know where they are going.

The second paragraph begins by voicing what probably is the reader's somewhat uneasy—perhaps even negative—response to the first paragraph. That is, *the writer has a sense of her audience;* she knows how her reader feels, and she takes account of the feeling.

The third paragraph clearly sets forth the alternatives. A reader may disagree with the writer's attitude, but the alternatives seem to be stated fairly.

The last two paragraphs are more personal than the earlier paragraphs. The writer, more or less having stated what she takes to be the facts, now is entitled to offer a highly personal response to them.

The final paragraph nicely wraps things up by means of the words *spare change,* which go back to the title and to the end of the first paragraph. The reader thus experiences a sensation of completeness. The essayist of course has not solved the problem for all of us for all time, but she presents a thoughtful argument and she ends the essay effectively.

Exercise

In an essay of 500 words state a claim and support it with evidence. Choose an issue in which you are genuinely interested and about which you already know something. You may want to interview a few experts and do some reading, but don't try to write a highly researched paper. Sample topics:

1. Students in laboratory courses should not be required to participate in the dissection of animals.
2. Washington, D.C., should be granted statehood.
3. Puerto Rico should be granted statehood.
4. Women should, in wartime, be exempted from serving in combat.
5. The annual Miss America contest is an insult to women.
6. The government should not offer financial support to the arts.
7. The chief fault of the curriculum in high school was . . .
8. Grades should be abolished in college and university courses.
9. No specific courses should be required in colleges or universities.

6

Using Sources

WHY USE SOURCES?

We have pointed out that one gets ideas by writing; in the exercise of writing a draft, ideas begin to form, and these ideas stimulate further ideas, especially when one questions—when one *thinks* about—what one has written. But of course in writing about complex, serious questions, nobody is expected to invent all the answers. On the contrary, a writer is expected to be familiar with the chief answers already produced by others, and to make use of them through selective incorporation and criticism. In short, writers are not expected to reinvent the wheel; rather, they are expected to make good use of it, and perhaps round it off a bit or replace a defective spoke. In order to think out your own views in writing, you are expected to do some preliminary research into the views of others.

We use the word *research* broadly. It need not require taking copious notes on everything written on your topic; rather, it can involve no more than familiarizing yourself with at least some of the chief responses to your topic. In one way or another, almost everyone does some research. If we are going to buy a car, we may read an issue or two of a magazine or visit a Web site that rates cars, or we may talk to a few people who own models that we are thinking of buying, and then we visit a couple of dealers to find out who is offering the best price.

Research, in short, is not an activity conducted only by college professors or by students who visit the library in order to write research papers. It is an activity that all of us engage in to some degree. In writing a research paper, you will engage in it to a great degree. But doing research is not the whole of a research paper. The reader expects the writer to have *thought* about the research, and to develop an argument based on the findings. Many businesses today devote an entire section to research and development. That's what is needed in writing, too. The reader wants not only a lot of facts but also a developed idea, a point to which the facts lead. Don't let your reader say of your paper what Gertrude Stein said of Oakland, California: "When you get there, there isn't any there there."

Consider arguments about whether athletes should be permitted to take anabolic steroids, drugs that supposedly build up muscle, restore energy, and enhance aggressiveness. A thoughtful argument on this subject will have to take account of information that the writer can gather only by doing some research. Do steroids really have the effects commonly attributed to them? And are they dangerous? If they are dangerous, how dangerous are they? (After all, competitive sports are inherently dangerous, some of them highly so. Many boxers, jockeys, and football players have suffered severe injury, even death, from competing. Does anyone believe that anabolic steroids are more dangerous than the contests themselves?) Obviously, again, a respectable argument about steroids will have to show awareness of what is known about them.

Or take this question: Why did President Truman order that atomic bombs be dropped on Hiroshima and Nagasaki? The most obvious answer is, to end the war, but some historians believe he had a very different purpose. In their view, Japan's defeat was ensured before the bombs were dropped, and the Japanese were ready to surrender; the bombs were dropped not to save American (or Japanese) lives, but to show Russia that we were not to be pushed around. Scholars who hold this view, such as Gar Alperovitz in *Atomic Diplomacy*, argue that Japanese civilians in Hiroshima and Nagasaki were incinerated not to save the lives of American soldiers who otherwise would have died in an invasion of Japan, but to teach Stalin a lesson. Dropping the bombs, it is argued, marked not the end of the Pacific War but the beginning of the cold war.

One must ask: What evidence supports this argument or claim or thesis, which assumes that Truman could not have thought the bomb was needed to defeat the Japanese because the Japanese knew they were defeated and would soon surrender without a hard-fought defense that would cost hundreds of thousands of lives? What about the momentum that had built up to use the bomb? After all, years of effort and $2 billion had been expended to produce a weapon with the intention of using it to end the war against Germany. But Germany had been defeated without the use of the bomb. Meanwhile, the war in the Pacific continued unabated. If the argument we are considering is correct, all this background counted for little or nothing in Truman's decision, a decision purely diplomatic and coolly indifferent to human life. The task for the writer is to evaluate the evidence available, and then to argue for or against the view that Truman's purpose in dropping the bomb was to impress the Soviet government.

A student writing on the topic will certainly want to read the chief books on the subject (Alperovitz's, cited above, Martin Sherwin's *A World Destroyed*, and John Toland's *The Rising Sun*), and perhaps reviews of them, especially the reviews in journals devoted to political science. (Reading a searching review of a serious scholarly book is a good way to identify quickly some of the book's main contributions and controversial claims.) Truman's letters and statements, and books and articles about Truman, are also clearly relevant, and doubtless important articles are to be found in recent issues of scholarly journals. In fact, even an essay on such a topic as whether Truman was morally justified in using the atomic bomb for *any* purpose will be a stronger essay if it is well informed about such matters as the estimated loss of life that an invasion would have cost, the international rules governing weapons, and Truman's own statements about the issue.

How does one go about finding the material needed to write a well-informed argument? We will provide help, but first we want to offer a few words about choosing a topic.

CHOOSING A TOPIC

We will be brief. If a topic is not assigned, choose one that

1. interests you, and that
2. can be researched with reasonable thoroughness in the allotted time.

Topics such as censorship, the environment, and sexual harassment obviously impinge on our lives, and it may well be that one such topic is of especial interest to you. But of course the scope of these topics makes researching them potentially overwhelming. Type the word *censorship* into an **Internet** search engine and you might be referred to thousands of information sources.

This brings us to our second point — a compassable topic. Any of the topics above would need to be narrowed substantially before you could begin searching in earnest. Similarly, a topic such as the causes of World War II can hardly be mastered in a few weeks or argued in a ten-page paper. It is simply too big.

You can, however, write a solid paper analyzing, evaluating, and arguing for or against General Eisenhower's views on atomic warfare. What were they, and when did he hold them? (In his books of 1948 and 1963 Eisenhower says that he opposed the use of the bomb before Hiroshima, and that he argued with Secretary of War Henry Stimson against dropping it, but what evidence supports these claims? Was

Eisenhower attempting to rewrite history in his books?) Eisenhower's own writings, and books on Eisenhower, will of course be the major sources for a paper on this topic, but you will also want to look at books and articles about Stimson, and at publications that contain information about the views of other generals, so that, for instance, you can compare Eisenhower's view with Marshall's or MacArthur's.

Your instructor understands that you are not going to spend a year writing a 200-page book, but you should understand that you must do more than consult the article on Eisenhower in one encyclopedia and the article on atomic energy in another encyclopedia.

FINDING MATERIAL

Your sources will of course depend on your topic. Some topics will require no more than a trip to the library or an afternoon spent at your personal computer, but others may require interviews. If you are writing about some aspect of AIDS, for instance, you probably will find it useful to consult your college or community health center.

For facts, you ought to try to consult experts—for instance, members of the faculty or other local authorities on art, business, law, and so forth; for opinions and attitudes, you will usually consult interested laypersons. Remember, however, that experts have their biases, and that "ordinary" people may have knowledge that experts lack. When interviewing experts, keep in mind Picasso's comment: "You musn't always believe what I say. Questions tempt you to tell lies, particularly when there is no answer."

INTERVIEWING PEERS
AND LOCAL AUTHORITIES

If you are interviewing your peers, you will probably want to make an effort to get a representative sample. Of course, even within a group not all members share a single view—many African Americans favor affirmative action but not all do, and many gays favor legalizing gay marriage but, again, some don't. Make an effort to talk to a range of people who might be expected to offer varied opinions. You may learn some unexpected things.

Here we will concentrate, however, on interviews with experts.

1. **Finding subjects for interviews.** If you are looking for expert opinions, you may want to start with a faculty member on your campus. You may already know the instructor, or you may have to scan the catalog to see who teaches courses relevant to your topic. Department secretaries are good sources of information about the special interests of the faculty, and also about lecturers who will be visiting the campus.

2. **Doing preliminary homework.** (1) Know something about the person whom you will be interviewing. Biographical reference works such as *Who's Who in America, Who's Who Among Black Americans, Who's Who of American Women,* and *Directory of American Scholars* may include your interviewee, or, again, a departmental secretary may be able to provide a vita for a faculty member. (2) In requesting the interview, make evident your interest in the topic and in the person. (If you know something about the person, you will be able to indicate why you are asking him or her.) (3) Request the interview, preferably in writing, a week in advance, and ask for ample time—probably half an hour to an hour. Indicate whether or not the material will be confidential, and (if you want to use a recorder) ask if you may record the interview. (4) If the person accepts the invitation, ask if he or she recommends any preliminary reading, and establish a time and a suitable place, preferably not the cafeteria during lunchtime.

3. **Preparing thoroughly.** (1) If your interviewee recommended any reading, or has written on the topic, read the material. (2) Tentatively formulate some questions, keeping in mind that (unless you are simply gathering material for a survey of opinions) you want more than "yes" or "no" answers. Questions beginning with "Why" and "How" will usually require the interviewee to go beyond "yes" and "no."

Even if your subject has consented to let you bring a recorder, be prepared to take notes on points that strike you as especially significant; without written notes, you will have nothing if the recorder has malfunctioned. Further, by taking occasional notes you will give the interviewee some time to think, and perhaps to rephrase or to amplify a remark.

4. **Conducting the interview.** (1) Begin by engaging in brief conversation, without taking notes. If the interviewee has agreed to let you use a recorder, settle on the place where you will put the recorder. (2) Come prepared with an opening question or two, but as the interview proceeds don't hesitate to ask questions that you had not anticipated asking. (3) Near the end—you and your subject have probably agreed on the length of the interview—ask the subject if he or she wishes to add anything, perhaps by way of clarifying some earlier comment. (4) Conclude by thanking the interviewee, and by offering to provide a copy of the final version of your paper.

5. **Writing up the interview.** (1) As soon as possible—certainly within twenty-four hours after the interview—review your notes and clarify them. At this stage, you can still remember the meaning of your abbreviated notes and shorthand devices (maybe you have been using *n* to stand for *nurses* in clinics where abortions are performed), but if you wait even a whole day you may be puzzled by your own notes. If you have recorded the interview, you may want to transcribe all of it—the laboriousness of this task is one good reason why many interviewers do not use recorders—and you may then want to scan the whole and mark

the parts that now strike you as especially significant. If you have taken notes by hand, type them up, along with your own observations, for example, "Jones was very tentative on this matter, but she said she was inclined to believe that . . . ." (2) Be especially careful to indicate which words are direct quotations. If in doubt, check with the interviewee.

USING THE LIBRARY

Most topics, as we have said, will require research in the library. Notice that we have spoken of a topic, not of a thesis or even of a *hypothesis* (tentative thesis). Advanced students, because they are familiar with the rudiments of a subject (say, the origins of the cold war) usually have not only a topic but also a hypothesis or even a thesis in mind. Less experienced students are not always in this happy position: Before they can offer a hypothesis, they have to find a problem. Some instructors assign topics; others rely on students to find their own topics, based on readings in the course or in other courses.

When you have a *topic* ("Eisenhower and the atomic bomb"), and perhaps a *thesis* (an attitude toward the topic, a claim that you want to argue, such as "Eisenhower's disapproval of the bomb was the product of the gentleman-soldier code that he had learned at West Point"), it is often useful to scan a relevant book. You may already know of a relevant book, and it is likely in turn to cite others. If, however, you don't know of any book, you can find one by consulting the catalog in the library, which lists books not only by author and by title but also by subject. There are many computerized cataloguing systems; your librarian can teach you how to use the one in your college or university library.

If there are many books on the topic, how do you choose just one? Choose first a fairly thin one, of fairly recent date, published by a reputable publisher. You may even want to jot down two or three titles and then check reviews of these books before choosing one book to skim. Five indexes enable you easily to locate book reviews in newspapers and periodicals:

Book Review Digest (1905–)

Book Review Index (1965–)

Humanities Index (1974–)

Index to Book Reviews in the Humanities (1960–)

Social Sciences Index (1974–)

Book Review Digest includes brief extracts from the reviews, and so look there first, but its coverage is not as broad as the other indexes.

Skimming a recent academic book is a good way to get an overview of a topic, and it may help you to form a tentative thesis and focus your research further. But because the publication process takes a year or more, even a book with a publication date of this year may have been written at least a year earlier (and on some issues, for instance regulations concerning cloning or censorship of the Internet, some of the information in the source may be outdated). Articles in academic journals, too, usually are written many months before they are published, but magazines and newspapers can provide you with up-to-date information. Articles, whether in academic journals or in current magazines, have the further advantage of being short, so they are likely to be more focused than a book; they therefore may speak more directly to your tentative thesis.

To find articles in periodicals, begin with the computerized search tools that now are available in most college and university libraries. The two most popular search tools are *InfoTrac* and the *Readers' Guide to Periodical Literature*. Your library probably has at least one of these CD-ROM systems, each of which indexes several hundred popular and semi-popular magazines (like *Time* and *Scientific American*) and well-respected newspapers (like the *New York Times* and the *Washington Post*). If your topic is one in which there is wide public interest, these **databases** will point you toward many potential research sources. Using these systems is simply a matter of launching the appropriate software, typing in one or two key words related to your topic, and perhaps narrowing the search with additional words if the database turns up more than a few references to the terms you enter.

Even better than *InfoTrac* and the *Readers' Guide*, however, are the many specialized academic indexes now available on CD-ROM. These indexes, which list scholarly books and articles in specialized academic journals, are up-to-date and therefore are among the most valued tools. To find articles in journals, consult the *Humanities Index* and the *MLA International Bibliography* for topics in the humanities; for topics in psychology and other social sciences, consult *PsycLit* and the *Social Science Index*. Your college librarian can guide you to indexes for engineering and hard sciences, business and industry, education, the arts, or whatever field you are working in. Some of these indexes (such as the popular education index ERIC and the *Newspaper Abstracts*) not only provide bibliographic information but also include abstracts, or short summaries, of the articles they index. Which search tools you use will depend, obviously, both on your topic and on what is available in your library. All of the major systems are designed to be easy to use, but if you experience difficulty don't hesitate to ask the librarian for advice about which system to use and how to use it.

Annual print versions of many of these bibliographies and indexes also exist. If you prefer to use a print document or if your library doesn't have the CD-ROM database you need, ask your librarian for advice about using a more traditional search method.

FINDING INFORMATION ONLINE

If you have an Internet connection, you don't have to go any further than your personal computer to access a wealth of information for your research paper. This information may come from a number of online sources, including text archives, listservs (e-mail discussion groups), and Usenet newsgroups. But unless you already know of a particular source for your paper, the best place to begin an Internet search is with the hypertext and hypermedia portion of the Internet known as the **World Wide Web**. The Web is the largest and fastest-growing portion of the Net, as well as the easiest to use. In addition, a good Web site will often, along with providing information, point to other on- and offline sources of related interest.

All popular Internet browsers (the software, such as Netscape or Internet Explorer, through which you access the Web) have a "search" feature that hooks you up with a range of Internet search engines, programs to search the Net for relevant documents and provide you with hypertext links to those documents. These search engines are of two basic types. With most engines — some popular examples are Excite, Lycos, and InfoSeek — you type in a key word or words and the software scans the Net for documents containing those words. If your topic is highly focused and you have clear and specific search terms, a key word may work well, but if you enter a broad topic like "affirmative action" or "euthanasia" you will turn up thousands of "hits," leaving you overwhelmed with choices. The other sort of engine allows you to start with a very broad topic area, such as "government" or "entertainment," and narrow the topic through a series of menus until you reach a more specific topic, like "divorce law" or "television violence." The most popular engine of this type is called Yahoo!, and many researchers find it a good first choice.

We have two words of caution if you plan to use the Internet for serious research. First, the early stages of your research may take longer than planned. The Net is huge, fast-changing, and chaotic, and navigating it is not easy. Computer systems crash, Web pages move or disappear altogether, and the discourse surrounding a controversial topic like censorship or abortion can change overnight. Second, remember that the Net is highly democratic; anyone who can get online can express an opinion. The advantage is that knowledgeable people can offer information quickly, but the disadvantage is that careless scholars, blowhards, and liars can shed misinformation. It is always important for researchers to evaluate their sources, but evaluation is especially important when the source is online.

In the Appendix you will find reference to a few Web sites that provide reliable information on many of the topics in this book.

EVALUATING SOURCES

Finding a source of information related to your topic is not sufficient; you must be sure that the source is both valid and appropriate for your purposes. A quick evaluation of your sources before you begin carefully reading and taking notes on them may save you an enormous amount of time and frustration. Skim each source quickly, and keep the following in mind as you skim.

A recent book or article is usually preferable to an older one. Not only should your information be as up-to-date as possible, but recent works often effectively summarize previous research. (An exception to the rule "newer is better" would be if you have chosen an older work for a specific purpose, such as to compare it to more recent work to demonstrate changing attitudes.) In the case of Internet sources, sites will often indicate when they were last updated; if the one you use doesn't, you have no way of knowing reliably how fresh the information is.

A CHECKLIST FOR EVALUATING SOURCES

For Books (also useful for CD-ROMs and published databases):

✓ Is the book recent? If not, is the information you will be using from it unlikely to change over time?

✓ How credible is the author?

✓ Is the book published by a respectable press?

✓ Is the book broad enough in its focus, and written in a style you can understand?

✓ Does the book relate directly to your tentative thesis, or is it of only tangential interest?

✓ Do the arguments in the book seem sound, based on what you have learned about skillful critical reading and writing?

For Articles from Periodicals:

✓ Is the periodical recent?

✓ Is the author's name given? Does he or she seem a credible source?

✓ Is the periodical respectable and serious?

✓ How directly does the article speak to your topic and tentative thesis?

✓ If the article is from a scholarly journal, are you sure you understand it?

For Internet Sources:

✓ How up-to-date is the site?

✓ Is there an author listed for the site or document?

✓ Is the information associated with a reliable host site?

✓ Does the site rely on substance — or on flash alone?

As far as possible, try to determine the credibility of the author. The author's credentials are often briefly described on the book jacket or at the back of the book; these may reveal if the author is indeed an expert in the field, and even his or her possible biases about the topic. But what if the work is anonymous, as many newspaper articles and Internet sources are? Anonymous articles are not necessarily bad sources, but approach them with a bit of caution; why might an author not have put his or her name on a piece?

You will also want to determine the credibility of the publisher (especially in the case of anonymous works). Though publisher credibility may be difficult for you to judge, you can usually trust large, nationally recognized companies and presses associated with universities more than smaller, less well-known publishers. (If you have doubts, ask your instructor or librarian about a particular publisher.) Remember that academic journals tend to be more respectable than popular magazines, and that among magazines a hierarchy exists; an article from *Newsweek* usually is more credible than one from *People*. A similar hierarchy exists for newspapers: the *Washington Post* is powerfully credible, while tabloids such as the *Midnight Globe* are not. With online sources you often can tell, either from the document itself or from a close look at the Internet address, if a Web site, archive, or other source is associated with a reliable institution, such as a university, library, or government agency. While this does not guarantee accuracy, it does help to establish the credibility of the information. A final word about Internet sources: Don't let a flashy, expensive-looking Web site distract you from thinking critically about the site's content. While graphics, fancy fonts, audio and video clips, and the like can enhance a good site, a reliable source must offer more than a good show.

TAKING NOTES

When it comes to taking notes, all researchers have their own habits that they swear by, and they can't imagine any other way of working. Some people prefer to take notes by hand, others on a computer. Possibly you already are fixed in your habits, but if not, you may want to borrow ours. We use 4-by-6-inch index cards. Smaller cards don't have space for enough notes, and larger cards have space for too much. We recommend the following techniques.

1. Write in ink (pencil gets smudgy).
2. Put only one idea on each card (though an idea may include several facts).
3. Write on only one side of the card (notes on the back usually get lost).
4. Summarize, for the most part, rather than quote at length.

5. Quote only passages in which the writing is especially effective, or passages that are in some way crucial.

6. Make sure that all quotations are exact. Enclose quoted words within quotation marks, indicate omissions by ellipses (three spaced periods: . . .), and enclose within square brackets ([ ]) any insertions or other additions you make.

7. *Never* copy a passage, changing an occasional word. *Either* copy it word for word, with punctuation intact, and enclose it within quotation marks, *or* summarize it drastically. If you copy a passage but change a word here and there, you may later make the mistake of using your note verbatim in your essay, and you will be guilty of plagiarism.

8. Give the page number of your source, whether you summarize or quote. If a quotation you have copied runs in the original from the bottom of page 210 to the top of page 211, in your notes put a diagonal line (/) after the last word on page 210, so that later, if in your paper you quote only the material from page 210, you will know that you must cite 210 and not 210–11.

9. Indicate the source. The author's last name is enough if you have consulted only one work by the author; but if you consult more than one work by an author, you need further identification, such as the author's name and a short title.

10. Add your own comments about the substance of what you are recording. Such comments as "but contrast with Sherwin" or "seems illogical" or "evidence?" will ensure that you are thinking as well as writing, and will be of value when you come to transform your notes into a draft. Be sure, however, to enclose such notes within double diagonals (//), or to mark them in some other way, so that later you will know they are yours and not your source's.

11. Put a brief heading on the card, such as "Truman's last words on A-bomb."

12. Write a bibliographic card for each source. The information on this card will vary, depending on whether the source is a book, a periodical, an electronic document, and so forth. The kind of information (for example, author and title) needed for each type of source can be found in the sections on Works Cited or References (pp. 216, 227).

A WORD ABOUT PLAGIARISM

Plagiarism is the unacknowledged use of someone else's work. The word comes from a Latin word for "kidnapping," and plagiarism is indeed the stealing of something engendered by someone else. We won't deliver a sermon on the dishonesty (and folly) of plagiarism; we intend only to help you understand exactly what plagiarism is. The first thing to say is that plagiarism is not limited to the unacknowledged quotation of words.

A *paraphrase* is a sort of word-by-word or phrase-by-phrase translation of the author's language into your language. True, if you paraphrase you are using your own words, but you are also using someone else's ideas, and, equally important, you are using this other person's sequence of thoughts. Even if you change every third word in your source, and you do not give the author credit, you are plagiarizing. Here is an example of this sort of plagiarism, based on the previous sentence:

> Even if you alter every third or fourth word from your source, and you fail to give credit to the author, you will be guilty of plagiarism.

Even if the writer of this paraphrase had cited a source after it, the writer would still be guilty of plagiarism, because the passage borrows not only the idea but the shape of the presentation, the sentence structure. The writer of this passage hasn't really written anything; he or she has only adapted something. What the writer needs to do is to write something like this:

> Changing an occasional word does not free the writer from the obligation to cite a source.

And the source would still need to be cited, if the central idea were not a commonplace one.

You are plagiarizing if without giving credit you use someone else's ideas — even if you put these ideas entirely into your own words. When you use another's ideas, you must indicate your indebtedness by saying something like "Alperovitz points out that . . ." or "Secretary of War Stimson, as Martin Sherwin notes, never expressed himself on this point." Alperovitz and Sherwin pointed out something that you had not thought of, and so you must give them credit if you want to use their findings.

Again, even if after a paraphrase you cite your source, you are plagiarizing. How, you may wonder, can you be guilty of plagiarism if you cite a source? Easy. A reader assumes that the citation refers to information or an opinion, *not* to the presentation or development of the idea; and of course in a paraphrase you are not presenting or developing the material in your own way.

Now consider this question: *Why* paraphrase? Often there is no good answer. Since a paraphrase is as long as the original, you may as well quote the original, if you think that a passage of that length is worth quoting. Probably it is *not* worth quoting in full; probably you should *not* paraphrase but rather should drastically *summarize* most of it, and perhaps quote a particularly effective phrase or two.

Generally what you should do is to take the idea and put it entirely into your own words, perhaps reducing a paragraph of a hundred words to a sentence of ten words, but of course you must still give credit for the idea. If you believe that the original hundred words are so perfectly put that they cannot be transformed without great loss, you'll have to quote them, and cite your source. But clearly there is no point in paraphrasing the author's hundred words into a hundred of your own. Either quote or summarize, but cite the source.

Keep in mind, too, that almost all generalizations about human nature, no matter how common and familiar (for instance, "males are innately more aggressive than females") are not indisputable facts; they are at best hypotheses on which people differ and therefore should either not be asserted at all or should be supported by some cited source or authority. Similarly, because nearly all statistics (whether on the intelligence of criminals or the accuracy of lie detectors) are the result of some particular research and may well have been superseded or challenged by other investigators, it is advisable to cite a source for any statistics you use unless you are convinced they are indisputable, such as the number of registered voters in Memphis in 1988.

On the other hand, there is something called **common knowledge,** and the sources for such information need not be cited. The term does not, however, mean exactly what it seems to. It is common knowledge, of course, that Ronald Reagan was an American president (so you don't cite a source when you make that statement), and under the conventional interpretation of this doctrine, it is also common knowledge that he was born in 1911. In fact, of course, few people other than Reagan's wife and children know this date. Still, information that can be found in many places and that is indisputable belongs to all of us; therefore a writer need not cite her source when she says that Reagan was born in 1911. Probably she checked a dictionary or an encyclopedia for the date, but the source doesn't matter. Dozens of sources will give exactly the same information and, in fact, no reader wants to be bothered with a citation on such a point.

Some students have a little trouble developing a sense of what is and what is not common knowledge. Although, as we have just said, readers don't want to hear about the sources for information that is indisputable and can be documented in many places, if you are in doubt about whether to cite a source, cite it. Better risk boring the reader a bit than risk being accused of plagiarism.

COMPILING AN ANNOTATED BIBLIOGRAPHY

When several sources have been identified and gathered, many researchers prepare an annotated bibliography. This is a list providing all relevant bibliographic information (just as it will appear in your Works Cited or Reference list) as well as a brief descriptive and evaluative summary of each source — perhaps one to three sentences. Your instructor may ask you to provide an annotated bibliography for your research project.

An annotated bibliography serves three main purposes. First, constructing such a document helps you to master the material contained in any given source. To find the heart of the argument presented in an article or book, phrase it briefly, and comment on it, you must understand it fully. Second, creating an annotated bibliography helps you to think about how each portion of your research fits into the whole of your project, how you will use it, and how it relates to your topic and thesis. Finally, in constructing an annotated bibliography at this early stage, you will get some hands-on practice at bibliographic format, thereby easing the job of creating your final bibliography (the Works Cited or Reference list for your paper).

Below are two examples of entries for an annotated bibliography in MLA (Modern Language Association) format for a project on the effect of violence in the media. The first is for a book, the second for an article from a periodical. Notice that each

- begins with a bibliographic entry (author — last name first — title, and so forth), and then
- provides information about the content of the work under consideration, suggesting how each may be of use to the final research paper.

Clover, Carol J. <u>Men, Women, and Chain Saws: Gender in the Modern Horror Film</u>. Princeton: Princeton UP, 1992. The author focuses on Hollywood horror movies of the 1970s and 1980s. She studies representations of women and girls in these movies and the responses of male viewers to female characters, suggesting that this relationship is more complex and less exploitative than the common wisdom claims.

Winerip, Michael. "Looking for an 11 O'Clock Fix." <u>New York Times Magazine</u>. 11 Jan. 1998: 30-40. The article focuses on the rising levels of violence on local television news and highlights a station in Orlando, Florida, that tried to reduce its depictions of violence and lost viewers as a result. Winerip suggests that people only claim to be against media violence, while their actions prove otherwise.

WRITING THE PAPER

Organizing Your Notes

If you have read thoughtfully and taken careful (and, again, thoughtful) notes on your reading, and then (yet again) have thought about these notes, you are well on the way to writing a good paper. You have, in fact, already written some of it, in your notes. By now you should clearly have in mind the thesis you intend to argue. But of course you still have to organize the material, and, doubtless, even as you set about organizing it you will find points that will require you to do some additional research and much additional thinking.

Sort the index cards into packets, each packet devoted to one theme or point (for instance, one packet on the extent of use of steroids, another on evidence that steroids are harmful, yet another on arguments that even if harmful they should be permitted). Put aside all notes that—however interesting—you now see are irrelevant to your paper.

Next, arrange the packets into a tentative sequence. In effect, you are preparing a **working outline.** At its simplest, say, you will give three arguments on behalf of *X*, and then three counterarguments. (Or you might decide that it is better to alternate material from the two sets of three packets each, following each argument with an objection. At this stage, you can't be sure of the organization you will finally use, but make a tentative decision.)

The First Draft

Draft the essay, without worrying much about an elegant opening paragraph. Just write some sort of adequate opening that states the topic and your thesis. When you revise the whole later, you can put some effort into developing an effective opening. (Most experienced writers find that the opening paragraph in the final version is almost the last thing they write.)

If your notes are on cards, carefully copy into the draft all quotations that you plan to use. If your notes are in a computer, you may simply cut and paste them from one file to another. Do keep in mind, however, that rewriting or retyping quotations will make you think carefully about them, and may result in a more focused and thoughtful paper. (In the next section of this chapter we will talk briefly about leading into quotations, and about the form of quotations.) Be sure to include citations in your drafts, so that if you must check a reference later it will be easy to do so.

Later Drafts

Give the draft, and yourself, a rest, perhaps for a day or two, and then go back to it, read it over, make necessary revisions, and then

outline it. That is, on a sheet of paper chart the organization and development, perhaps by jotting down a sentence summarizing each paragraph or each group of closely related paragraphs. Your outline or map may now show you that the paper obviously suffers from poor organization. For instance, it may reveal that you neglected to respond to one argument, or that one point is needlessly treated in two places. It may also help you to see that if you gave three arguments and then three counterarguments, you probably should instead have followed each argument with its rebuttal. Or, on the other hand, if you alternated arguments and objections, it may now seem better to use two main groups, all the arguments and then all the criticisms.

No one formula is always right. Much will depend on the complexity of the material. If the arguments are highly complex, it is better to respond to them one by one than to expect a reader to hold three complex arguments in mind before you get around to responding. If, however, the arguments can be stated briefly and clearly, it is effective to state all three, and then to go on to the responses. If you write on a word processor you will find it easy, even fun, to move passages of text around. Even so, you will probably want to print out a hard copy from time to time to review the structure of your paper. Allow enough time to produce several drafts.

A few more words about organization: There is a difference between

a. a paper that *has* an organization and
b. a paper that *shows* what the organization is.

Write papers of the second sort, but (there is always a "but") take care not to belabor the obvious. Inexperienced writers sometimes either hide the organization so thoroughly that a reader cannot find it, or, on the other hand, they so ploddingly lay out the structure ("Eighth, I will show . . .") that the reader becomes impatient. Yet it is better to be overly explicit than to be obscure.

The ideal, of course, is the middle route. Make the overall strategy of your organization evident by occasional explicit signs at the beginning of a paragraph ("We have seen . . . ," "It is time to consider the objections . . . ," "By far the most important . . ."); elsewhere make certain that the implicit structure is evident to the reader. When you reread your draft, if you try to imagine that you are one of your classmates, you will probably be able to sense exactly where explicit signs are needed and where they are not needed. Better still, exchange drafts with a classmate in order to exchange (tactful) advice.

Choosing a Tentative Title

By now a couple of tentative titles for your essay should have crossed your mind. If possible, choose a title that is both interesting and informative. Consider these three titles:

```
Are Steroids Harmful?
The Fuss over Steroids
Steroids: A Dangerous Game
```

"Are Steroids Harmful?" is faintly interesting, and it lets the reader know the gist of the subject, but it gives no clue about the writer's thesis, the writer's contention or argument. "The Fuss over Steroids" is somewhat better, for it gives information about the writer's position. "Steroids: A Dangerous Game" is still better; it announces the subject ("steroids") and the thesis ("dangerous"), and it also displays a touch of wit, because "game" glances at the world of athletics.

Don't try too hard, however; better a simple, direct, informative title than a strained, puzzling, or overly cute one. And remember to make sure that everything in your essay is relevant to your title. In fact, your title should help you to organize the essay and to delete irrelevant material.

The Final Draft

When at last you have a draft that is for the most part satisfactory, check to make sure that **transitions** from sentence to sentence and from paragraph to paragraph are clear ("Further evidence," "On the other hand," "A weakness, however, is apparent"), and then worry about your opening and your closing paragraphs. Your **opening paragraph** should be clear, interesting, and focused; if neither the title nor the first paragraph announces your thesis, the second paragraph probably should do so.

The **final paragraph** need not say, "In conclusion, I have shown that . . . ." It should effectively end the essay, but it need not summarize your conclusions. We have already offered a few words about final paragraphs (p. 174), but the best way to learn how to write such paragraphs is to study the endings of some of the essays in this book, and to adopt the strategies that appeal to you.

Be sure that all indebtedness is properly acknowledged. We have talked about plagiarism; now we will turn to the business of introducing quotations effectively.

QUOTING FROM SOURCES
The Use and Abuse of Quotations

When is it necessary, or appropriate, to quote? Sometimes the reader must see the exact words of your source; the gist won't do. If you are arguing that Z's definition of *rights* is too inclusive, your readers have to know exactly how Z defined *rights*. Your brief summary of the definition may be unfair to Z; in fact, you want to convince your readers that you are being fair, and so you quote Z's definition, word for word. More-over, if the passage is only a sentence or two long, or even if it runs to a paragraph, it may be so compactly stated that it defies summary. And to attempt to paraphrase it—substituting *natural* for *inalienable*, and so forth—saves no space and only introduces imprecision. There is nothing to do but to quote it, word for word.

Second, you may want to quote a passage that could be summarized but that is so effectively stated that you want your readers to have the pleasure of reading the original. Of course readers will not give you credit for writing these words, but they will give you credit for your taste, and for your effort to make especially pleasant the business of reading your paper.

In short, use (but don't overuse) quotations. Speaking roughly, quo-tations should occupy no more than 10 or 15 percent of your paper, and they may occupy much less. Most of your paper should set forth your ideas, not other people's ideas.

How to Quote

Long and Short Quotations   **Long quotations** (five or more lines of typed prose, or three or more lines of poetry) are set off from your text. To set off material, start on a new line, indent one inch from the left margin and type the quotation double-spaced. Do not enclose quota-tions within quotation marks if you are setting them off.

Short quotations are treated differently. They are embedded within the text; they are enclosed within quotation marks but otherwise they do not stand out.

All quotations, whether set off or embedded, must be exact. If you omit any words, you must indicate the ellipsis by substituting three spaced periods for the omission; if you insert any words or punctuation, you must indicate the addition by enclosing it within square brackets, not to be confused with parentheses.

Leading into a Quotation   Now for a less mechanical matter, the way in which a quotation is introduced. To say that it is "introduced" implies that one leads into it, though on rare occasions a quotation ap-pears without an introduction, perhaps immediately after the title. Nor-mally one leads into a quotation by giving the name of the author and (no less important) clues about the content of the quotation and the purpose it serves in the present essay. For example:

```
William James provides a clear answer to Huxley when he
says that ". . ."
```

The writer has been writing about Huxley, and now is signaling readers that they will be getting James's reply. The writer is also signaling (in "a clear answer") that the reply is satisfactory. If the writer believed that James's answer was not really acceptable, the lead-in might have run thus:

> William James attempts to answer Huxley, but his re-
> sponse does not really meet the difficulty Huxley calls
> attention to. James writes, ". . ."

Or:

> William James provided what he took to be an answer to
> Huxley when he said that ". . ."

In this last example, clearly the words "what he took to be an answer" imply that the essayist will show, after the quotation from James, that the answer is in some degree inadequate. Or the essayist may wish to suggest the inadequacy even more strongly:

> William James provided what he took to be an answer to
> Huxley, but he used the word "religion" in a way that
> Huxley would not have allowed. James argues that ". . ."

If after reading something by Huxley the writer had merely given us "William James says . . . ," we wouldn't know whether we were getting confirmation, refutation, or something else. The essayist would have put a needless burden on the readers. Generally speaking, the more difficult the quotation, the more important is the introductory or explanatory lead-in, but even the simplest quotation profits from some sort of brief lead-in, such as "James reaffirms this point when he says . . ."

DOCUMENTATION

In the course of your essay, you will probably quote or summarize material derived from a source. You must give credit, and although there is no one form of documentation to which all scholarly fields subscribe, you will probably be asked to use one of two. One, established by the Modern Language Association (MLA), is used chiefly in the humanities; the other, established by the American Psychological Association (APA), is used chiefly in the social sciences.

We include two papers that use sources. "Why Trials Should Not Be Televised" (p. 232), uses the MLA format. (You may notice that various styles are illustrated in other selections we have included.)

A Note on Footnotes (and Endnotes)

Before discussing these two formats a few words about footnotes are in order. Before the MLA and the APA developed their rules of style, citations commonly were given in footnotes. Although today footnotes are not so frequently used to give citations, they still may be useful for another purpose. (The MLA suggests endnotes rather than footnotes, and of course endnotes are easier to type, unless you use a word processing program, but all readers know that in fact footnotes are preferable to endnotes. After all, who wants to keep shifting from a page of text to a page of notes at the rear?) If you want to include some material that may seem intrusive in the body of the paper, you may relegate it to a footnote. For example, in a footnote you might translate a quotation given in a foreign language, or you might demote from text to footnote a paragraph explaining why you are not taking account of such-and-such a point. By putting the matter in a footnote you are signaling the reader that it is dispensable; it is something relevant but not essential, something extra that you are, so to speak, tossing in. Don't make a habit of writing this sort of note, but there are times when it is appropriate.

MLA Format

This discussion is divided into two parts, a discussion of citations within the text of the essay, and a discussion of the list of references, called Works Cited, that is given at the end of the essay.

Citations within the Text   Brief citations within the body of the essay give credit, in a highly abbreviated way, to the sources for material you quote, summarize, or make use of in any other way. These *in-text citations* are made clear by a list of sources, titled Works Cited, appended to the essay. Thus, in your essay you may say something like this:

```
Commenting on the relative costs of capital punishment
and life imprisonment, Ernest van den Haag says that he
doubts "that capital punishment really is more expen-
sive" (33).
```

The **citation,** the number 33 in parentheses, means that the quoted words come from page 33 of a source (listed in Works Cited) written by van den Haag. Without Works Cited, a reader would have no way of knowing that you are quoting from page 33 of an article that appeared in the February 8, 1985, issue of *The National Review*.

Usually the parenthetic citation appears at the end of a sentence, as in the example just given, but it can appear elsewhere; its position will depend chiefly on your ear, your eye, and the context. You might, for example, write the sentence thus:

```
Ernest van den Haag doubts that "capital punishment
really is more expensive" than life imprisonment (33),
but other writers have presented figures that contra-
dict him.
```

Five points must be made about these examples:

1. **Quotation marks.** The closing quotation mark appears after the last word of the quotation, *not* after the parenthetic citation. Since the citation is not part of the quotation, the citation is not included within the quotation marks.

2. **Omission of words (ellipsis).** If you are quoting a complete sentence or only a phrase, as in the examples given, you do not need to indicate (by three spaced periods) that you are omitting material before or after the quotation. But if for some reason you want to omit an interior part of the quotation, you must indicate the omission by inserting an *ellipsis,* the three spaced dots. To take a simple example, if you omit the word "really" from van den Haag's phrase, you must alert the reader to the omission:

```
Ernest van den Haag doubts that "capital punishment
. . . is more expensive" than life imprisonment (33).
```

Suppose you are quoting a sentence but wish to omit material from the end of the sentence. Suppose, also, that the quotation forms the end of your sentence. Write a lead-in phrase, then quote as much from your source as you need, then type three spaced periods for the omission, close the quotation, give the parenthetic citation, and finally type a fourth period to indicate the end of your sentence.

Here's an example. Suppose you want to quote the first part of a sentence that runs, "We could insist that the cost of capital punishment be reduced so as to diminish the differences." Your sentence would incorporate the desired extract as follows:

```
Van den Haag says, "We could insist that the cost of
capital punishment be reduced . . ." (33).
```

3. **Punctuation with parenthetic citations.** In the preceding examples, the punctuation (a period or a comma in the examples) *follows* the citation. If, however, the quotation ends with a question mark, include the question mark *within* the quotation, since it is part of the quotation, and put a period *after* the citation.

```
Van den Haag asks, "Isn't it better--more just and
more useful--that criminals, if they do not have the
```

> certainty of punishment, at least run the risk of suf-
> fering it?" (35).

But if the question mark is your own, and not in the source, put it after the citation, thus:

> What answer can be given to van den Haag's doubt that
> "capital punishment really is more expensive" (33)?

4. **Two or more works by an author.** If your list of Works Cited includes two or more works by an author, you cannot, in your essay, simply cite a page number, because the reader will not know which of the works you are referring to. You must give additional information. You can give it in your lead-in, thus:

> In "New Arguments against Capital Punishment," van den
> Haag expresses doubt "that capital punishment really is
> more expensive" than life imprisonment (33).

Or you can give the title, in a shortened form, within the citation:

> Van den Haag expresses doubt that "capital punishment
> really is more expensive" than life imprisonment ("New
> Arguments" 33).

5. **Citing even when you do not quote.** Even if you don't quote a source directly, but use its point in a paraphrase or a summary, you will give a citation:

> Van den Haag thinks that life imprisonment costs more
> than capital punishment (33).

Note that in all of the previous examples, the author's name is given in the text (rather than within the parenthetic citation). But there are several other ways of giving the citation, and we shall look at them now. (We have already seen, in the example given under paragraph 4, that the title and the page number can be given within the citation.)

AUTHOR AND PAGE NUMBER IN PARENTHESES

> It has been argued that life imprisonment is more
> costly than capital punishment (van den Haag 33).

AUTHOR, TITLE, AND PAGE NUMBER IN PARENTHESES

We have seen that if Works Cited includes two or more works by an author, you will have to give the title of the work on which you are drawing, either in your lead-in phrase or within the parenthetic citation. Similarly, if you are citing someone who is listed more than once in Works Cited, and for some reason you do not mention the name of the author or the work in your lead-in, you must add the information in your citation:

> Doubt has been expressed that capital punishment is as costly as life imprisonment (van den Haag, "New Arguments" 33).

A GOVERNMENT DOCUMENT OR A WORK
OF CORPORATE AUTHORSHIP

Treat the issuing body as the author. Thus, you will write something like this:

> The Commission on Food Control, in Food Resources Today, concludes that there is no danger (37–38).

A WORK BY TWO OR MORE AUTHORS

If a work is by *two or three authors,* give the names of all authors, either in the parenthetic citation (the first example below) or in a lead-in (the second example below):

> There is not a single example of the phenomenon (Smith, Dale, and Jones 182–83).

> Smith, Dale, and Jones insist there is not a single example of the phenomenon (182–83).

If there are *more than three authors,* give the last name of the first author, followed by "et al." (an abbreviation for *et alii,* Latin for "and others"), thus:

> Gittleman et al. argue (43) that . . .

Or:

> On average, the cost is even higher (Gittleman et al. 43).

PARENTHETIC CITATION OF AN INDIRECT SOURCE
(CITATION OF MATERIAL THAT ITSELF WAS QUOTED
OR SUMMARIZED IN YOUR SOURCE)

Suppose you are reading a book by Jones, in which she quotes Smith, and you wish to use Smith's material. Your citation must refer the reader to Jones—the source you are using—but of course you cannot attribute the words to Jones. You will have to make it clear that you are quoting Smith, and so, after a lead-in phrase like "Smith says," followed by the quotation, you will give a parenthetic citation along these lines:

```
(qtd. in Jones 324-25).
```

PARENTHETIC CITATION OF TWO OR MORE WORKS

```
The costs are simply too high (Smith 301; Jones 28).
```

Notice that a semicolon, followed by a space, separates the two sources.

A WORK IN MORE THAN ONE VOLUME

This is a bit tricky. If you have used only one volume, in Works Cited you will specify the volume, and so in the parenthetic in-text citation you will not need to specify the volume. All that you need to include in the citation is a page number, as illustrated by most of the examples that we have given.

If you have used more than one volume, your parenthetic citation will have to specify the volume as well as the page, thus:

```
Jackson points out that fewer than one hundred fifty
people fit this description (2: 351).
```

The reference is to page 351 in volume 2 of a work by Jackson.

If, however, you are citing not a page but an entire volume—let's say volume 2—your parenthetic citation will look like this:

```
Jackson exhaustively studies this problem (vol. 2).
```

Or:

```
Jackson (vol. 2) exhaustively studies this problem.
```

Notice the following points:

1. In citing a volume and page, the volume number, like the page number, is given in arabic (not roman) numerals, even if the original used roman numerals.
2. The volume number is followed by a colon, then a space, then the page number.
3. If you cite a volume number without a page number, as in the last example quoted, the abbreviation is "vol." Otherwise do *not* use such abbreviations as "vol." and "p." and "pg."

AN ANONYMOUS WORK

For an anonymous work, give the title in your lead-in, or give it in a
shortened form in your parenthetic citation:

```
A Prisoner's View of Killing includes a poll taken of
the inmates on death row (32).
```

Or:

```
A poll is available (Prisoner's View 32).
```

AN INTERVIEW

Probably you won't need a parenthetic citation, because you'll say
something like

```
Vivian Berger, in an interview, said . . .
```

or

```
According to Vivian Berger, in an interview . . .
```

and when your reader turns to Works Cited, he or she will see that
Berger is listed, along with the date of the interview. But if you do not
mention the source's name in the lead-in, you will have to give it in the
parentheses, thus:

```
Contrary to popular belief, the death penalty is not
reserved for serial killers and depraved murderers
(Berger).
```

AN ELECTRONIC SOURCE

Electronic sources, such as those found on CD-ROMs or the Internet,
are generally not divided into pages. Therefore, the in-text citation for
such sources cite the author's name (or, if a work is anonymous, the
title) only:

```
According to the World Wide Web site for the American
Civil Liberties Union . . .
```

If the source does use pages, or breaks down further into paragraphs or
screens, insert the appropriate identifier or abbreviation (*p.* or *pp.* for
page or pages; *par.* or *pars.* for paragraph or paragraphs; *screen* or *screens*)
before the relevant number:

```
The growth of day care has been called "a crime against
posterity" by a spokesman for the Institute for the
American Family (Terwilliger, screens 1-2).
```

The List of Works Cited (MLA Format)

As the previous pages explain, parenthetic documentation consists of references that become clear when the reader consults the list titled Works Cited, given at the end of an essay.

The list of Works Cited continues the pagination of the essay; if the last page of text is 10, then Works Cited begins on its own page, in this case page 11. Type the page number in the upper right corner, a half inch from the top of the sheet and flush with the right margin. Next, type the heading: Works Cited (*not* enclosed within quotation marks), centered, one inch from the top, then double-space and type the first entry.

An Overview   Here are some general guidelines.

FORM ON THE PAGE

1. Begin each entry flush with the left margin, but if an entry runs to more than one line, indent five spaces, or a half inch, for each succeeding line of the entry.
2. Double-space each entry, and double-space between entries.
3. Underline titles of works published independently — for instance, books, pamphlets, and journals. Enclose within quotation marks a work not published independently — for instance, an article in a journal, or a short story.
4. If you are citing a book that includes the title of another book, underline the main title but do *not* underline the title mentioned. Example:

```
A Study of Mill's On Liberty
```

5. In the sample entries below, pay attention to the use of commas, colons, and the space after punctuation.

ALPHABETIC ORDER

1. Arrange the list alphabetically by author, with the author's last name first.
2. For information about anonymous works, works with more than one author, and two or more works by one author, see below.

A Closer Look   Here is more detailed advice.

THE AUTHOR'S NAME

Notice that the last name is given first, but otherwise the name is given as on the title page. Do not substitute initials for names written out on the title page.

If your list includes two or more works by an author, do not repeat the author's name for the second title but represent it by three hyphens followed by a period. The sequence of the works is determined by the alphabetic order of the titles. Thus, Smith's book titled *Poverty* would be listed ahead of her book *Welfare*. See the example on page 218, listing two works by Roger Brown.

Anonymous works are listed under the first word of the title, or the second word if the first is *A, An,* or *The,* or a foreign equivalent. In a few moments we will discuss books by more than one author, government documents, and works of corporate authorship.

THE TITLE

After the period following the author's name, allow one space and then give the title. Take the title from the title page, not from the cover or the spine, but disregard any unusual typography such as the use of all capital letters or the use of the ampersand (&) for *and.* Underline the title and subtitle (separate them by a colon) with one continuous underline, to indicate italics, but do not underline the period that concludes this part of the entry.

Capitalize the first and the last word.

Capitalize all nouns, pronouns, verbs, adjectives, adverbs, and subordinating conjunctions (for example, *although, if, because*).

Do not capitalize (unless it's the first or last word of the title) articles (*a, an, the*), prepositions (for instance, *in, on, toward, under*), coordinating conjunctions (for instance, *and, but, or, for*), or the *to* in infinitives.

Examples:

The Death Penalty: A New View

On the Death Penalty: Toward a New View

On the Penalty of Death in a Democracy

PLACE OF PUBLICATION, PUBLISHER, AND DATE

For the place of publication, provide the name of the city; you can usually find it either on the title page or on the reverse of the title page. If a number of cities are listed, provide only the first. If the city is not likely to be known, or if it may be confused with another city of the same name (as is Oxford, Mississippi with Oxford, England), add the name of the state, abbreviated (use the newer two-letter postal code: IL, not Ill.).

The name of the publisher is abbreviated. Usually the first word is enough (Random House becomes Random), but if the first word is a first name, such as in Alfred A. Knopf, the surname (Knopf) is used instead. University presses are abbreviated thus: Yale UP, U of Chicago P, State U of New York P.

The date of publication of a book is given when known; if no date appears on the book, write n.d. to indicate "no date."

SAMPLE ENTRIES   Here are some examples, illustrating the points we have covered thus far:

Brown, Roger. Social Psychology. New York: Free, 1965.

---. Words and Things. Glencoe, IL: Free, 1958.

Douglas, Ann. The Feminization of American Culture. New
    York: Knopf, 1977.

Hartman, Chester. The Transformation of San Francisco.
    Totowa: Rowman, 1984.

Kellerman, Barbara. The Political Presidency: Practice
    of Leadership from Kennedy through Reagan. New
    York: Oxford UP, 1984.

Notice that a period follows the author's name, and another period follows the title. If a subtitle is given, as it is for Kellerman's book, it is separated from the title by a colon and a space. A colon follows the place of publication, a comma follows the publisher, and a period follows the date.

A BOOK BY MORE THAN ONE AUTHOR

The book is alphabetized under the last name of the first author named on the title page. If there are *two or three authors*, the names of these are given (after the first author's name) in the normal order, *first name first.*

Gilbert, Sandra M., and Susan Gubar. The Madwoman in
    the Attic: The Woman Writer and the Nineteenth-
    Century Literary Imagination. New Haven: Yale UP,
    1979.

Notice, again, that although the first author's name is given *last name first,* the second author's name is given in the normal order, first name

first. Notice, too, that a comma is put after the first name of the first author, separating the authors.

If there are *more than three authors,* give the name only of the first
and then add (but *not* enclosed within quotation marks) "et al." (Latin
for "and others").

> Altshuler, Alan, et al. The Future of the Automobile.
>   Cambridge: MIT P, 1984.

GOVERNMENT DOCUMENTS

If the writer is not known, treat the government and the agency as
the author. Most federal documents are issued by the Government Printing Office (abbreviated to GPO) in Washington, D.C.

> United States Congress. Office of Technology Assess-
>   ment. Computerized Manufacturing Automation:
>   Employment, Education, and the Workplace. Washing-
>   ton: GPO, 1984.

WORKS OF CORPORATE AUTHORSHIP

Begin the citation with the corporate author, even if the same body
is also the publisher, as in the first example:

> American Psychiatric Association. Psychiatric Glossary.
>   Washington: American Psychiatric Association,
>   1984.

> Carnegie Council on Policy Studies in Higher Education.
>   Giving Youth a Better Chance: Options for Educa-
>   tion, Work, and Service. San Francisco: Jossey,
>   1980.

A REPRINT, FOR INSTANCE A PAPERBACK VERSION
OF AN OLDER CLOTHBOUND BOOK

> Gray, Francine du Plessix. Divine Disobedience: Pro-
>   files in Catholic Radicalism. 1970. New York: Vin-
>   tage, 1971.

After the title, give the date of original publication (it can usually be
found on the reverse of the title page of the reprint you are using), then
a period, and then the place, publisher, and date of the edition you are
using. The example indicates that Gray's book was originally published
in 1970 and that the student is using the Vintage reprint of 1971.

A BOOK IN SEVERAL VOLUMES

If you have used more than one volume, in a citation within your essay you will (as explained on p. 214) indicate a reference to, say, page 250 of volume 3 thus: (3: 250).

If, however, you have used only one volume of the set—let's say volume 3—in your entry in Works Cited, specify which volume you used, as in the next example:

```
Friedel, Frank. Franklin D. Roosevelt. Vol. 3. Boston:
     Little, 1973. 4 vols.
```

With such an entry in Works Cited, the parenthetic citation within your essay would be to the page only, not to the volume and page, because a reader who consults Works Cited will understand that you used only volume 3. In Works Cited, you may specify volume 3 and not give the total number of volumes, or you may add the total number of volumes, as in the example above.

ONE BOOK WITH A SEPARATE TITLE
IN A SET OF VOLUMES

Sometimes a set with a title makes use also of a separate title for each book in the set. If you are listing such a book, use the following form:

```
Churchill, Winston. The Age of Revolution. New York:
     Dodd, 1957. Vol. 3 of History of the English-
     Speaking Peoples. 4 vols. 1956-58.
```

A BOOK WITH AN AUTHOR AND AN EDITOR

```
Churchill, Winston, and Franklin D. Roosevelt. The Com-
     plete Correspondence. Ed. Warren F. Kimball. 3
     vols. Princeton: Princeton UP, 1985.

Kant, Immanuel. The Philosophy of Kant: Immanuel Kant's
     Moral and Political Writings. Ed. Carl J.
     Friedrich. New York: Modern, 1949.
```

If the book has one editor, the abbreviation is "ed."; if two or more editors, "eds."

If you are making use of the editor's introduction or other editorial material rather than of the author's work, list the book under the name of the editor rather than of the author, as shown below under "An Introduction, Foreword, or Afterword."

A REVISED EDITION OF A BOOK

Arendt, Hannah. Eichmann in Jerusalem. Rev. and en-
    larged ed. New York: Viking, 1965.

Honour, Hugh, and John Fleming. The Visual Arts: A His-
    tory. 2nd ed. Englewood Cliffs: Prentice, 1986.

A TRANSLATED BOOK

Franqui, Carlos. Family Portrait with Fidel: A Memoir.
    Trans. Alfred MacAdam. New York: Random, 1984.

AN INTRODUCTION, FOREWORD, OR AFTERWORD

Goldberg, Arthur J. Foreword. An Eye for an Eye? The
    Morality of Punishing by Death. By Stephen
    Nathanson. Totowa: Rowman, 1987. v-vi.

Usually a book with an introduction or some such comparable material
is listed under the name of the author of the book (here Nathanson)
rather than under the name of the writer of the foreword (here Goldberg), but if you are referring to the apparatus rather than to the book itself, use the form just given. The words *Introduction, Preface, Foreword,*
and *Afterword* are neither enclosed within quotation marks nor underlined.

A BOOK WITH AN EDITOR BUT NO AUTHOR

Let's assume that you have used a book of essays written by various
people but collected by an editor (or editors), whose name appears on
the collection.

LaValley, Albert J., ed. Focus on Hitchcock. Englewood
    Cliffs: Prentice, 1972.

A WORK WITHIN A VOLUME OF WORKS BY ONE AUTHOR

The following entry indicates that a short work by Susan Sontag, an
essay called "The Aesthetics of Silence," appears in a book by Sontag
titled *Styles of Radical Will.* Notice that the inclusive page numbers of the
short work are cited, not merely page numbers that you may happen to
refer to but the page numbers of the entire piece.

Sontag, Susan. "The Aesthetics of Silence." In Styles
    of Radical Will. New York: Farrar, 1969. 3-34.

A BOOK REVIEW

Here is an example, citing Gerstein's review of Walker's book. Gerstein's review was published in a journal called *Ethics*.

Gerstein, Robert S. Rev. of <u>Punishment, Danger and</u>
        <u>Stigma: The Morality of Criminal Justice</u>, by Nigel
        Walker. <u>Ethics</u> 93 (1983): 408-10.

If the review has a title, give the title between the period following the reviewer's name and "Rev."

If a review is anonymous, list it under the first word of the title, or under the second word if the first word is *A, An,* or *The.* If an anonymous review has no title, begin the entry with "Rev. of" and then give the title of the work reviewed; alphabetize the entry under the title of the work reviewed.

AN ARTICLE OR ESSAY—NOT A REPRINT— IN A COLLECTION

A book may consist of a collection (edited by one or more persons) of new essays by several authors. Here is a reference to one essay in such a book. (The essay by Balmforth occupies pages 19–35 in a collection edited by Bevan.)

Balmforth, Henry. "Science and Religion." <u>Steps to</u>
        <u>Christian Understanding</u>. Ed. R. J. W. Bevan. London: Oxford UP, 1958. 19-35.

AN ARTICLE OR ESSAY REPRINTED IN A COLLECTION

The previous example (Balmforth's essay in Bevan's collection) was for an essay written for a collection. But some collections reprint earlier material, such as essays from journals or chapters from books. The following example cites an essay that was originally printed in a book called *The Cinema of Alfred Hitchcock.* This essay has been reprinted in a later collection of essays on Hitchcock, edited by Arthur J. LaValley, and it was LaValley's collection that the student used.

Bogdanovich, Peter. "Interviews with Alfred Hitchcock."
        <u>The Cinema of Alfred Hitchcock</u>. New York: Museum
        of Modern Art, 1963. 15-18. Rpt. in <u>Focus on</u>
        <u>Hitchcock</u>. Ed. Albert J. LaValley. Englewood
        Cliffs: Prentice, 1972. 28-31.

The student has read Bogdanovich's essay or chapter, but not in Bogdanovich's book, where it occupied pages 15–18. The material was actually read on pages 28–31 in a collection of writings on Hitchcock, edited by LaValley. Details of the original publication—title, date, page numbers, and so forth—were found in LaValley's collection. Almost all editors will include this information, either on the copyright page or at the foot of the reprinted essay, but sometimes they do not give the original page numbers. In such a case, you need not include the original numbers in your entry.

Notice that the entry begins with the author and the title of the work you are citing (here, Bogdanovich's interviews), not with the name of the editor of the collection or the title of the collection.

AN ENCYCLOPEDIA OR OTHER ALPHABETICALLY ARRANGED REFERENCE WORK

The publisher, place of publication, volume number, and page number do *not* have to be given. For such works, list only the edition (if it is given) and the date.

For a *signed* article, begin with the author's last name. (If the article is signed with initials, check elsewhere in the volume for a list of abbreviations, which will inform you who the initials stand for, and use the following form.)

```
Williams, Donald C. "Free Will and Determinism." Ency-
     clopedia Americana. 1987 ed.
```

For an *unsigned article,* begin with the title of the article:

```
"Automation." The Business Reference Book. 1977 ed.

"Tobacco." Encyclopaedia Britannica: Macropaedia. 1988
     ed.
```

A TELEVISION OR RADIO PROGRAM

```
"Back to My Lai." Narr. Mike Wallace. 60 Minutes. CBS.
     29 Mar. 1998.

"Juvenile Justice." Narr. Ray Suarez. Talk of the Na-
     tion. Natl. Public Radio. WBUR, Boston. 15 Apr.
     1998.
```

AN ARTICLE IN A SCHOLARLY JOURNAL   The title of the article is enclosed within quotation marks, and the title of the journal is underlined to indicate italics.

Some journals are paginated consecutively; the pagination of the second issue begins where the first issue leaves off. Other journals begin each issue with page 1. The forms of the citations differ slightly.

A JOURNAL THAT IS PAGINATED CONSECUTIVELY

> Vilas, Carlos M. "Popular Insurgency and Social Revolu-
>   tion in Central America." <u>Latin American Perspec-
>   tives</u> 15 (1988): 55-77.

Vilas's article occupies pages 55–77 in volume 15, which was published in 1988. (Notice that the volume number is followed by a space, and then by the year, in parentheses, and then by a colon, a space, and the page numbers of the entire article.) Because the journal is paginated consecutively, the issue number does *not* need to be specified.

A JOURNAL THAT BEGINS EACH ISSUE WITH PAGE 1

If the journal is, for instance, a quarterly, there will be four page 1's each year, so the issue number must be given. After the volume number, type a period and (without hitting the space bar) the issue number, as in the next example:

> Greenberg, Jack. "Civil Rights Enforcement Activity of
>   the Department of Justice." <u>The Black Law Journal</u>
>   8.1 (1983): 60-67.

Greenberg's article appeared in the first issue of volume 8 of *The Black Law Journal.*

AN ARTICLE IN A WEEKLY, BIWEEKLY, OR MONTHLY PUBLICATION

> Lamar, Jacob V. "The Immigration Mess." <u>Time</u> 27 Feb.
>   1989: 14-15.

AN ARTICLE IN A NEWSPAPER

Because a newspaper usually consists of several sections, a section number or a capital letter may precede the page number. The example indicates that an article begins on page 1 of section 2 and is continued on a later page.

> Chu, Harry. "Art Thief Defends Action." <u>New York Times</u>
>   8 Feb. 1989, sec. 2: 1+.

AN UNSIGNED EDITORIAL

> "The Religious Tyranny Amendment." Editorial. <u>New York
>   Times</u> 15 Mar. 1998, sec. 4: 16.

A LETTER TO THE EDITOR

Lasken, Douglas. "Teachers Reject Bilingual Education."
      Letter. New York Times 15 Mar. 1998, sec. 4: 16.

AN INTERVIEW

Jevgrafovs, Alexandre L. Personal [or Telephone] inter-
      view. 14 Dec. 1997.

PERSONAL CORRESPONDENCE

Raso, Robert. Letter [or E-mail] to the author. 6 Jan.
      1998.

CD-ROM

CD-ROMs are cited very much like their printed counterparts. To the usual print citation information, add (1) the title of the database, underlined; (2) the medium ("CD-ROM"); (3) the vendor's name; and (4) the date of electronic publication.

Louisberg, Margaret. Charlie Brown Meets Godzilla: What
      Are Our Children Watching? Urbana: ERIC Clearing-
      house on Elementary and Early Childhood Educ.,
      1990. ERIC. CD-ROM. SilverPlatter. May 1997.

"Pornography." The Oxford English Dictionary. 2nd ed.
      CD-ROM. Oxford: Oxford UP, 1992.

THE INTERNET

Include as much of the following information as is available, in the order and format specified: (1) author's name, last name first; (2) title of section (subject lines for e-mails and newsgroup postings) in quotation marks; (3) title of the full document or site, underlined or in italics; (4) date of publication or most recent update; (5) protocol (World Wide Web, FTP, Usenet newsgroup, listserv, and so forth); (6) date of access; (7) electronic address (URL) or path, in angle brackets. Break the URL only after a slash (or, for a double slash, after the second slash).

Ricci, Paul. "Global Warming." Online posting. 10 June
      1996. Global Electronic Science Conference. 22
      Sept. 1997 <http://www.science.envir/earth>.

Trammell, George W. "Cirque du O. J." Court Technology
      Bulletin July/Aug. 1995. World Wide Web. 12 Sept.

```
1995 <http://www.ncsc.dni.us/ncsc/bulletin/
     v07n04.htm>.
```

A DATABASE SOURCE

Treat material obtained from a computer service, such as Bibliographies Retrieval Service (BRS), like other printed material, but at the end of the entry add (if available) the title of the database (underlined), publication medium (*Online*), name of the computer service, and date of access.

```
Jackson, Morton. "A Look at Profits." Harvard Business
     Review 40 (1962): 106-13. Online. BRS. 23 Dec.
     1995.
```

Caution: Although we have covered the most usual kinds of sources, it is entirely possible that you will come across a source that does not fit any of the categories that we have discussed. For approximately two hundred pages of explanations of these matters, covering the proper way to cite all sorts of troublesome and unbelievable (but real) sources, see Joseph Gibaldi, *MLA Handbook for Writers of Research Papers,* Fourth Edition (New York: Modern Language Association of America, 1995).

APA Format

Your paper will conclude with a separate page headed "References," in which you list all of your sources. If the last page of your essay is numbered 10, number the first page of references 11.

Citations within the Text   The APA style emphasizes the date of publication; the date appears not only in the list of references at the end of the paper, but also in the paper itself, when you give a brief parenthetic citation of a source that you have quoted or summarized or in any other way used. Here is an example:

```
Statistics are readily available (Smith, 1989, p. 20).
```

The title of Smith's book or article will be given at the end of your paper, in the list titled "References." We will discuss the form of the material listed in References in a moment, but first we will look at some typical citations within the text of a student's essay.

A SUMMARY OF AN ENTIRE WORK

```
Smith (1988) holds the same view.
```

Or

```
Similar views are held widely (Smith, 1988; Jones &
Metz, 1990).
```

A REFERENCE TO A PAGE OR TO PAGES

```
Smith (1988) argues that "the death penalty is a lot-
tery, and blacks usually are the losers" (p. 17).
```

A REFERENCE TO AN AUTHOR WHO IN THE
LIST OF REFERENCES IS REPRESENTED BY
MORE THAN ONE WORK

If in References you list two or more works that an author published in the same year, the works are listed in alphabetic order, by the first letter of the title. The first work is labeled *a,* the second *b,* and so on. Here is a reference to the second work that Smith published in 1989:

```
Florida presents "a fair example" of how the death
penalty is administered (Smith, 1989b, p. 18).
```

References   Your brief parenthetic citations are made clear when the reader consults the list you give in References. Type this list on a separate page, continuing the pagination of your essay.

AN OVERVIEW   Here are some general guidelines.

FORM ON THE PAGE
1. Begin each entry flush with the left margin, but if an entry runs to more than one line, indent five spaces for each succeeding line of the entry.
2. Double-space each entry, and double-space between entries.

ALPHABETIC ORDER
1. Arrange the list alphabetically by author.
2. Give the author's last name first, then the initial of the first and of the middle name (if any).
3. If there is more than one author, name all of the authors, again inverting the name (last name first) and giving only initials for first and middle names. (But do not invert the editor's name when the entry begins with the name of an author who has written an article in an edited book.) When there are two or more authors, use an ampersand (&) before the name of the last author. Example (here, of an article in the tenth volume of a journal called *Developmental Psychology*):

Drabman, R. S., & Thomas, M. H. (1974). Does media violence increase children's tolerance of real-life
aggression? <u>Developmental Psychology, 10</u>, 418–421.

4. If you list more than one work by an author, do so in the order of
   publication, the earliest first. If two works by an author were
   published in the same year, give them in alphabetic order by the
   first letter of the title, disregarding *A, An,* or *The,* and their foreign
   equivalent. Designate the first work as "a," the second as "b." Repeat the author's name at the start of each entry.

Donnerstein, E. (1980a). Aggressive erotica and violence against women. <u>Journal of Personality and
Social Psychology, 39</u>, 269–277.

Donnerstein, E. (1980b). Pornography and violence
against women. <u>Annals of the New York Academy of
Sciences, 347</u>, 227–288.

Donnerstein, E. (1983). Erotica and human aggression.
In R. Green and E. Donnerstein (Eds.), <u>Aggression:
Theoretical and empirical reviews</u> (pp. 87–103).
New York: Academic Press.

FORM OF TITLE

1. In references to books, capitalize only the first letter of the first
   word of the title (and of the subtitle, if any) and capitalize proper
   nouns. Underline the complete title (but not the period at the
   end).
2. In references to articles in periodicals or in edited books, capitalize only the first letter of the first word of the article's title (and
   subtitle, if any), and all proper nouns. Do not put the title within
   quotation marks. Type a period after the title of the article. For
   the title of the journal, and the volume and page numbers, see
   the next instruction.
3. In references to periodicals, give the volume number in arabic
   numerals, and underline it. Do *not* use *vol.* before the number,
   and do not use *p.* or *pg.* before the page numbers.

Sample References   Here are some samples to follow.

A BOOK BY ONE AUTHOR

Pavlov, I. P. (1927). <u>Conditioned reflexes</u> (G. V.
Anrep, Trans.). London: Oxford University Press.

A BOOK BY MORE THAN ONE AUTHOR

Belenky, M. F., Clinchy, B. M., Goldberger, N. R., & Torule, J. M. (1986). Women's ways of knowing: The development of self, voice, and mind. New York: Basic Books.

A COLLECTION OF ESSAYS

Christ, C. P., & Plaskow, J. (Eds.). (1979). Womanspirit rising: A feminist reader in religion. New York: Harper & Row.

A WORK IN A COLLECTION OF ESSAYS

Fiorenza, E. (1979). Women in the early Christian movement. In C. P. Christ & J. Plaskow (Eds.), Womanspirit rising: A feminist reader in religion (pp. 84–92). New York: Harper & Row.

GOVERNMENT DOCUMENTS

If the writer is not known, treat the government and the agency as the author. Most federal documents are issued by the Government Printing Office in Washington, D.C. If a document number has been assigned, insert that number in parentheses between the title and the following period.

United States Congress. Office of Technology Assessment. (1984). Computerized manufacturing automation: Employment, education, and the workplace. Washington, DC: U.S. Government Printing Office.

AN ARTICLE IN A JOURNAL WITH CONTINUOUS PAGINATION

Tversky, A., & Kahneman, D. (1981). The framing of decisions and the psychology of choice. Science, 211, 453–458.

AN ARTICLE IN A JOURNAL THAT PAGINATES EACH ISSUE SEPARATELY

Foot, R. J. (1988-89). Nuclear coercion and the ending of the Korean conflict. International Security, 13(4), 92–112.

The reference informs us that the article appeared in issue number 4 of volume 13.

AN ARTICLE FROM A MONTHLY OR WEEKLY MAGAZINE

Greenwald, J. (1989, February 27). Gimme shelter. Time, 133, 50-51.

Maran, S. P. (1988, April). In our backyard, a star explodes. Smithsonian, 19, 46-57.

AN ARTICLE IN A NEWSPAPER

Connell, R. (1989, February 6). Career concerns at heart of 1980s' campus protests. Los Angeles Times, pp. 1, 3.

(*Note:* If no author is given, simply begin with the title followed by the date in parentheses.)

A BOOK REVIEW

Daniels, N. (1984). Understanding physician power [Review of the book, The social transformation of American medicine]. Philosophy and Public Affairs, 13, 347-356.

Daniels is the reviewer, not the author of the book. The book under review is called *The Social Transformation of American Medicine,* but the review, published in volume 13 of *Philosophy and Public Affairs,* had its own title, "Understanding Physician Power."

If the review does not have a title, retain the square brackets and use the material within as the title. Proceed as in the example just given.

For a full account of the APA method of dealing with all sorts of unusual citations, see the fourth edition (1994) of the APA manual, *Publication Manual of the American Psychological Association.*

AN ANNOTATED
STUDENT RESEARCH PAPER

The following argument makes good use of sources. Early in the semester the students were asked to choose one topic from a list of ten, and to write a documented argument of 750 to 1,250 words (three to five pages of double-spaced typing). The completed paper was due two weeks after the topics were distributed. The assignment, a prelude to working on a research paper of 2,500 to 3,000 words, was in part designed to give students practice in finding and in using sources. Citations are given in the MLA form.

A CHECKLIST FOR PAPERS USING SOURCES

✓ All borrowed words and ideas credited?

✓ Quotations and summaries not too long?

✓ Quotations accurate?

✓ Quotations provided with helpful lead-ins?

✓ Documentation in proper form?

And of course you will also ask yourself the questions that you would ask of a paper that did not use sources, such as:

✓ Topic sufficiently narrowed?

✓ Thesis (to be advanced or refuted) stated early and clearly, perhaps even in title?

✓ Audience kept in mind? Opposing views stated fairly and as sympathetically as possible? Controversial terms defined?

✓ Assumptions likely to be shared by readers? If not, are they argued rather than merely asserted?

✓ Focus clear (for example, evaluation, or recommendation of policy)?

✓ Evidence (examples, testimony, statistics) adequate and sound?

✓ Inferences valid?

✓ Organization clear? (Effective opening, coherent sequence of arguments, unpretentious ending?)

✓ All worthy opposition faced?

✓ Tone appropriate?

✓ Has the paper been carefully proofread?

✓ Is the title effective?

✓ Is the opening paragraph effective?

✓ Is the structure reader-friendly?

✓ Is the closing paragraph effective?

The *MLA Handbook* does not insist on a title page and outline, but many instructors prefer them.

Title one-third down page.

Why Trials Should Not Be Televised

By

Theresa Washington

All lines centered.

Professor Wilson

English 102

December 12, 1997

Washington i

Outline

Thesis: The televising of trials is a bad idea because it has several negative effects on the First Amendment: it gives viewers a deceptive view of particular trials and of the judicial system in general, and it degrades the quality of media reporting outside the courtroom.

I. Introduction
   A. Trend toward increasing trial coverage
   B. First Amendment versus Sixth Amendment
II. Effect of televising trials on First Amendment
   A. Provides deceptive version of truth
      1. Confidence in verdicts misplaced
         a. Willie Smith trial
         b. Rodney King trial
      2. Nature of TV as a medium
         a. Distortion in sound bites
         b. Stereotyping trial participants
         c. Misleading camera angles
         d. Commentators and commercials
   B. Confuses viewers about judicial system
      1. Contradicts basic concept "innocent until proven guilty"
      2. Can't explain legal complexities
   C. Contributes to media circus outside of court
      1. Blurs truth and fiction
      2. Affects print media in negative ways
      3. Media makes itself the story
      4. Distracts viewers from other issues
III. Conclusion

Small roman numerals for page with outline.

Roman numerals for chief units (I, II, etc.); capital letters for chief units within these largest units; then, for smaller and smaller units, arabic numerals and lowercase letters.

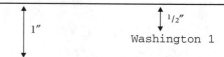

Title is focused
and announces
the thesis.

Double-space
between title and
first paragraph—
and throughout
the essay.

1″ margin on each
side and at
bottom.

Summary of
opposing
positions.

Parenthetic
reference to an
anonymous
source and also to
a source with a
named author.

Superscript
numerals indicate
endnotes.

Why Trials Should Not Be Televised

Although trials have been televised on and off since the 1950s,[1] in the last few years the availability of trials for a national audience has increased dramatically.[2] Media critics, legal scholars, social scientists, and journalists continue to debate the merits of this trend.

Proponents of cameras in the courtroom argue, falsely, I believe, that confidence in the fairness of our institutions, including the judicial system, depends on a free press, guaranteed by the First Amendment. Keeping trials off television is a form of censorship, they say. It limits the public's ability to understand (1) what is happening in particular trials, and (2) how the judicial system operates, which is often confusing to laypeople. Opponents claim that televising trials threatens the defendant's Sixth-Amendment rights to a fair trial because it can alter the behavior of the trial participants, including the jury ("Tale"; Thaler).

Regardless of its impact on due process of law,[3] TV in court does not serve the First Amendment well. Consider the first claim, that particular trials are easier to understand when televised. But does watching trials on television really allow the viewer to "see it like it is," to get the full scope and breadth of a trial? Steven Brill, founder of Court TV, would like us to believe so. He points out that most high-profile defendants in televised trials

Washington 2

have been acquitted; he names William Kennedy
Smith, Jimmy Hoffa, John Connally, and John
Delorean as examples (Clark 821). "Imagine if
[Smith's trial] had not been shown and he got
off. Millions of people would have said the
Kennedys fixed the case" (Brill qtd. in "Tale"
29). Polls taken after the trial seem to confirm this claim, since they showed the public
by and large agreed with the jury's decision to
acquit (Quindlen).

    However, Thaler points out that the public
can just as easily disagree with the verdict as
agree, and when this happens, the effects can
be catastrophic. One example is the Rodney King
case. Four white Los Angeles police officers
were charged in 1991 with severely beating
African American Rodney King, who, according to
the officers, had been resisting arrest. At
their first trial, all four officers were acquitted. This verdict outraged many African
Americans throughout the country; they felt the
evidence from watching the trial overwhelmingly
showed the defendants to be guilty. The black
community of south-central Los Angeles expressed its feelings by rioting for days
(Thaler 50-51).

    Clearly the black community did not expe-
rience the trial the same way the white community and the white jury did. Why? Marty Rosen-
baum, an attorney with the New York State
Defenders Association, points out that viewers
cannot experience a trial the same way trial
participants do. "What you see at home 'is not

Parenthetic reference to author and page.

Parenthetic reference to an indirect source (a borrowed quotation).

what jurors see'" (qtd. in Thaler 70). The
trial process is slow, linear, and methodical,
as the defense and prosecution each build their
case, one piece of information at a time

Although no
words are quoted,
the idea is
borrowed and so
the source is cited.

(Thaler 11). The process is intended to be
thoughtful and reflective, with the jury weighing all the evidence in light of the whole
trial (Altheide 299-301). And it emphasizes
words--both spoken and written--rather than images (Thaler 11).

Clear transition
("In contrast").

     In contrast, TV's general strength is in
handling visual images that entertain or that
provoke strong feelings. News editors and reporters choose footage for its assumed visual
and emotional impact on viewers. Words are made
to fit the images, not the other way around,
and they tend to be short catchy phrases, easy
to understand (Thaler 4, 7). As a result, the
15- to 30-second "sound bites" in nightly news-
casts often present trial events out of con-

Parenthetic
citation of two
sources.

text, emphasizing moments of drama rather than
of legal importance (Thaler 7; Zoglin 62).

     Furthermore, this emphasis on emotional
visuals leads to stereotyping the participants,
making larger-than-life symbols out of them,
especially regarding social issues (Thaler 9):
abused children (the Menendez brothers), the
battered wife (Hedda Nussbaum), the abusing
husband (Joel Steinberg, O. J. Simpson), the
jealous lover (Amy Fisher), the serial killer
(Jeffrey Dahmer), and date rapist (Willie
Smith). It becomes difficult for viewers to see
defendants as ordinary human beings.

Washington 4

One can argue, as Brill has done, that gavel-to-gavel coverage of trials counteracts the distortions in sound-bite journalism (Clark 821). Yet even here a number of editorial assumptions and decisions affect what viewers see. Camera angles and movements reinforce in the viewer differing degrees of intimacy with the trial participant; close-ups are often used for sympathetic witnesses, three-quarter shots for lawyers, and profile shots for defendants (Entner 73-75).[4]

On-air commentators also shape the viewers' experience. Several media critics have noted how much commentators' remarks often have the play-by-play tone of sportscasters informing viewers of what each side (the defense and the prosecution) needs in order to win (Cole 245; Thaler 71, 151). Continual interruptions for commercials add to the impression of watching a spectacle. "The CNN coverage [of the Smith trial] isn't so much gavel-to-gavel, actually, as gavel-to-commercial-to-gavel, with former CNN Gulf War correspondent Charles Jaco acting more as ringleader than reporter" (Bianculli 60). This encourages a sensationalistic tone to the proceedings that the jury does not experience. In addition, breaking for ads frequently occurs at important points in the trial (Thaler 48).

In-court proponents also believe that watching televised trials will help viewers understand the legal aspects of the judicial system. In June 1991, a month before Court TV went

Summary of an opposing view, then countered with a clear transition ("Yet").

Author lets reader
hear the opposi-
tion by means of a

on the air, Vincent Blasi, a law professor at
Columbia University, told Time magazine, "Today
most of us learn about judicial proceedings
from lawyers' sound bites and artists'

Omitted material
indicated by three
periods, with a
fourth to mark
the end of a
sentence.

sketches. . . . Televised proceedings [such as
Court TV] ought to dispel some of the myth and
mystery that shroud our legal system" (qtd. in
Zoglin 62).

But after several years of Court TV and
CNN, we can now see this is not so. As a
medium, TV is not good at educating the general
public, either about concepts fundamental to
our judicial system or about the complexities
in particular cases.

For example, one basic concept--"innocent
until proven guilty"--is contradicted in televised trials in numerous subtle ways: Commentators sometimes make remarks about (or omit
comment on) actions of the defense or prosecution that show a bias against the defendant.

Media critic Lewis Cole, watching the trial
of Lorena Bobbitt on Court TV in 1994, observed:

Quotation of
more than four
lines, indented 1″
from left margin
(ten spaces),
double-spaced,
parenthetic
reference set off
from quotation.

> Court TV commentators rarely challenged the
> state's characterization of what it was
> doing, repeating without comment, for in-
> stance, the prosecution's claims about pro-
> tecting the reputation of Lorena Bobbitt
> and concentrating on the prosecution deci-
> sion to pursue both cases as a tactical
> matter, rather than inquiring how the pros-
> ecution's view of the incident as a "bar-
> room brawl" had limited its approach to and
> understanding of the case. (245)

Washington 6

Camera angles play a role also: Watching the defendant day after day in profile, which makes him or her seem either vulnerable or remote, tends to reinforce his or her guilt (Entner 158).

Thaler points out that these editorial effects arise because the goals of the media (print as well as electronic) differ from the goals of the judicial system. His argument runs as follows: The court is interested in determining only whether the defendant broke the law. The media (especially TV) focus on acts in order to reinforce social values, whether they're codified into law or not. This can lead viewers to conclude that a defendant is guilty because pretrial publicity or courtroom testimony reveals he or she has transgressed against the community's moral code, even when the legal system later acquits. This happened in the case of Claus von Bulow, who between 1982 and 1985 was tried and acquitted twice for attempting to murder his wife, and who clearly had behaved in reprehensible ways in the eyes of the public (35). It also happened in the case of Joel Steinberg, who was charged with murdering his daughter. Extended televised testimony by his ex-partner, Hedda Nussbaum, helped paint a portrait of "a monster" in the eyes of the public (140-42). Yet the jury chose to convict him on the lesser charge of manslaughter. When many viewers wrote to the prosecutor, Peter Casolaro, asking why the verdict was not first-degree murder, he had to conclude that TV does

Argument supported by specific examples.

Washington 7

not effectively teach about due process of law
(176).

In addition to being poor at handling
basic judicial concepts, television has difficulty conveying more complex and technical aspects of the law. Sometimes the legal nature of
the case makes for a poor translation to the
screen. Brill admitted that, despite attempts
at hourly summaries, Court TV was unable to
convey to its viewers any meaningful understanding of the case of Manuel Noriega (Thaler
61), the Panamanian leader who was convicted by
the United States in 1992 of drug trafficking
and money laundering ("Former"). In other
cases, like the Smith trial, the "civics lesson" gets swamped by its sensational aspects
(Thaler 45). In most cases print media are better at exploring and explaining legal issues
than is TV (Thaler 4).

Transition (briefly summarizes, then moves to a new point).

In addition to shaping the viewer's per-
ceptions of trial reality directly, in-court TV
also negatively affects the quality of trial
coverage outside of court, which in turn limits
the public's "right to know." Brill likes to
claim that Court TV helps to counteract the
sensationalism of such tabloid TV shows as A
Current Affair and Hard Copy, which pay trial
participants to tell their stories and publish
leaks from the prosecution and defense. "I
think cameras in the courtroom is [sic] the
best antidote to that garbage" (Brill qtd. in
Clark 821). However, as founder and editor of
Court TV, he obviously has a vested interest in

Author uses "[*sic*]" (Latin for "thus") to indicate that the oddity is in the source and is not by the author of the paper.

Washington 8

affirming his network's social and legal worth.
There are several ways that in-court TV, rather
than supplying a sobering contrast, helps to
feed the media circus surrounding high-profile
trials (Thaler 43).

One way is by helping to blur the line between reality and fiction. This is an increasing trend among all media, but is especially
true of TV, whose footage can be combined and
recombined in so many ways. An excellent example of this is the trial of Amy Fisher, who
pleaded guilty in September 1992 to shooting
her lover's wife, and whose sentencing was
televised by Court TV (Thaler 83). Three TV
movies about this love triangle appeared on
network TV in the same week, just one month
after she had been sentenced to five to fifteen
years of jail (Thaler 82). Then Geraldo Rivera,
the syndicated TV talk-show host, held a mock
grand jury trial of her lover, Joey Buttafuoco;
even though Buttafuoco had not at that point
been charged with a crime, Geraldo felt many
viewers thought he ought to have been (Thaler
83). Then A Current Affair had a series that
"tried" Fisher for events and behaviors that
never got resolved in the actual trial. The an-
nouncer on the program said, "When Ms. Fisher
copped a plea and went to jail she robbed the
public of a trial, leaving behind many unan-
swered questions. Tonight we will try to . . .
complete the unwritten chapter" ("Trial").
Buttafuoco's lawyer from the trial served as a
consultant on this program (Thaler 84). This is

also a good example of how tabloid TV reinforces people's beliefs and plays on people's
feelings. Had her trial not been televised, the
excitement surrounding her case would not have
been so high. Tabloid TV played off the audience's expectation for what a televised trial
should and could reveal. Thus in-court television becomes one more ingredient in the mix of
docudramas, mock trials, talk shows, and
tabloid journalism. This limits the public's
"right to know" by making it difficult to keep
fact separate from storytelling.

In-court TV also affects the quality of
print journalism. Proponents like to claim that
"[f]rom the standpoint of the public's right to
know, there is no good reason why TV journalists should be barred from trials while print
reporters are not" (Zoglin 62). But when TV is
present, there is no level playing field among
the media. Because it provides images, sound,
and movement and a greater sense of speed and
immediacy, TV can easily out-compete other
media for audience attention and thus for advertising dollars. In attempts to keep pace,
newspapers and magazines offer more and more of
the kinds of stories that once were beneath
their standards, such as elaborate focus both
on sensational aspects of the case and on "per-
sonalities, analysis, and prediction" rather
than news (Thaler 45). While these attributes
have always been part of TV and the tabloid
print press, this trend is increasingly apparent in supposedly reputable papers like the New

Useful analysis of
effect of TV.

Square brackets to
indicate author
has altered text
from capital to
lowercase letter.

Washington 10

York Times. During the Smith trial, for example, the Times violated previously accepted
boundaries of propriety by not only identifying
the rape victim but also giving lots of intimate details about her past (Thaler 45).

  Because the media are, for the most part,
commercial, slow periods--and all trials have
them--must always be filled with some "story."
One such story is increasingly the media self-
consciously watching and analyzing itself, to
see how it is handling (or mishandling) coverage of the trial (Thaler 43). At the Smith
trial, for example, one group of reporters was
covering the trial while another group covered
the other reporters (Thaler 44).[5] As bizarre as
this "media watching" is, there would be no
"story" if the trial itself had not been televised.

  Last but not least, televising trials dis-
tracts viewers from other important issues.
Some of these are abstract and thus hard to understand (like the savings-and-loan scandal in
the mid-1980s or the causes of lingering unemployment in the 1990s), while others are
painful to contemplate (like overseas wars and
famines). Yet we have to stay aware of these
issues if we are to function as active citizens
in a democracy.

  Altogether, televising trials is a bad
idea. Not only does it provide deceptive im-
pressions about what's happening in particular
trials; it also doesn't reveal much about our
judicial system. In addition, televising trials

No citation
needed for a point
that can be
considered
common
knowledge, but
notice that point
in the second
sentence *is*
documented.

Useful summary
of main points.

Washington 11

helps to lower the quality of trial coverage
outside of court, thus increasingly depriving
the public of neutral, fact-based reporting. A
healthy free press depends on balance and knowing when to accept limits. Saturating viewers
with extended media coverage of sensational
trials oversteps those limits. In this case,
more is not better.

Yet it is unlikely that TV coverage will
be legally removed from the courtroom, now that
it is here. Only one state (New York) has ever
legislated a return to nontelevised trials (in
1991), and even it changed its mind in 1992
(Thaler 78). Perhaps the best we can do is to
educate ourselves about the pitfalls of televising the judicial system, as we struggle to
do so with the televised electoral process.

Realistic appraisal
of the current
situation and a
suggestion of what
the reader can do.

1″   ↕ ¹/₂″

Washington 12   Double-space
between heading
Notes   and notes, and
throughout notes.

¹ Useful discussions of this history can
be found in Clark (829–32) and Thaler (19–31).

² Cable networks have been showing trial   Superscript
footage to national audiences since at least   number followed
by one space.
1982, when Cable News Network (CNN) covered the
trial of Claus von Bulow (Thaler 33). It continues to show trials. In the first week of
February 1995, four to five million homes accounted for the top fifteen most-watched shows
on cable TV; all were CNN segments of the O. J.
Simpson trial ("Cable TV"). In July 1991,
Steven Brill founded the Courtroom Television
Network, or "Court TV" (Clark 821). Like CNN,
it broadcasts around the clock, showing gavel-
to-gavel coverage. It now claims over fourteen
million cable subscribers (Clark 821) and, as
of January 1994, had televised over 280 trials
("In Camera" 27).

³ Thaler's study The Watchful Eye is a   Each note begins
with ¹/₂″ indent
thoughtful examination of the subtle ways in   (five typewriter
which TV in court can affect trial partici-   spaces), but
subsequent notes
pants, inhibiting witnesses from coming for-   of each line are
ward, provoking grandstanding in attorneys and   flush left.
judges, and pressuring juries to come up with
verdicts acceptable to a national audience.

⁴ Sometimes legal restrictions determine
camera angles. For example, in the Steinberg
trial (1988), the audience and the jury were
not allowed to be televised by New York state
law. This required placing the camera so that
the judge and witnesses were seen in "full
frontal view" (generally a more neutral or pos-

itive stance). The lawyers could only be seen
from the rear when questioning witnesses, and
the defendant was shot in profile (Thaler
110-11). These camera angles, though not chosen
for dramatic effect, still resulted in emotionally laden viewpoints not experienced by the
jury. George W. Trammell, a Los Angeles Superior Court Judge, has written on how technology
can interfere with the fairness of the trial
system. He claims that "Technology, well managed, can be a great benefit. Technology poorly
managed benefits no one."

    5 At the Smith trial a journalist from one
German newspaper inadvertently filmed another
German reporter from a competing newspaper
watching the Smith trial in the pressroom outside the courtroom (Thaler 44).

Washington 14

Works Cited

Altheide, David. "TV News and the Social Construction of Justice." <u>Justice and the Media: Issues and Research</u>. Ed. Ray Surette. Springfield, IL: Thomas, 1984. 292–304.

Bianculli, David. "Shame on You, CNN." <u>New York Post</u> 11 Dec. 1992: 60.

"Cable TV Squeezes High Numbers and Aces Competition." <u>All Things Considered</u>. Natl. Public Radio. 9 Feb. 1994. Unedited transcript. Segment 12. NPR Audience Services. Washington.

Clark, Charles S. "Courts and the Media." <u>CQ Researcher</u> 23 Sept. 1994: 817–40.

Cole, Lewis. "Court TV." <u>Nation</u> 21 Feb. 1994: 243–45.

Entner, Roberta. "Encoding the Image of the American Judiciary Institution: A Semiotic Analysis of Broadcast Trials to Ascertain Its Definition of the Court System." Diss. New York U, 1993.

"Former Panamanian Leader Noriega Sentenced." <u>Facts on File</u> 16 July 1992: 526. <u>InfoTrac: Magazine Index Plus 1992–Feb. 1995</u>. CD-ROM. Information Access. Feb. 1995.

"In Camera with Court TV." <u>New Yorker</u> 24 Jan. 1994: 27–28.

Quindlen, Anna. "The Glass Eye." <u>New York Times</u> 18 Dec. 1991: A29.

"A Tale of a Rug." <u>Economist</u> 15 Jan. 1994: 28–29.

Marginal annotations:

Alphabetical by author's last name.

Indent turnovers ¹/₂″ (five typewriter spaces).

Transcript of radio program.

The title of an unpublished work is not italicized but enclosed within quotation marks.

CD-ROM source.

Anonymous source alphabetized under first word (or second if first is *A, An,* or *The*).

Washington 15

Thaler, Paul. <u>The Watchful Eye: American Justice in the Age of the Television Trial</u>.
Westport: Praeger, 1994.

"The Trial That Had to Happen: The People versus Amy Fisher." <u>A Current Affair</u>. Fox.
WFXT, Boston. 1-4 Feb. 1993.

Trammell, George W. "Cirque du O. J." <u>Court
Technology Bulletin</u> July/Aug. 1995. World
Wide Web. 12 Sept. 1995 <http://
www.ncsc.dni.us/ncsc/bulletin/v07n04.htm>.

Zoglin, Richard. "Justice Faces a Screen Test."
<u>Time</u> 17 June 1991: 62.

Television pro-
gram.

No page reference
for this in-text
Internet citation.

Part Three

FURTHER VIEWS
ON ARGUMENT

7

A Philosopher's View: The Toulmin Model

In Chapter 3, we explained the contrast between *deductive* and *inductive* arguments in order to focus on the two main ways in which we reason, either

making explicit something concealed in what we already accept (**deduction**), or

using what we have observed as a basis for asserting or proposing something new (**induction**).

Both types of reasoning share some structural features, as we also noticed. Thus, all reasoning is aimed at establishing some **thesis** (or conclusion) and does so by means of some **reasons**. These are two basic characteristics that any argument contains.

After a little scrutiny we can in fact point to several features shared by all arguments, deductive and inductive, good and bad alike. Using the vocabulary popularized by Stephen Toulmin in his book *An Introduction to Reasoning* (1979; second edition 1984), they are as follows:

THE CLAIM

Every argument has a purpose, goal, or aim, namely to establish a **claim** (*conclusion* or *thesis*). Suppose you were arguing in favor of equal rights for women. You might state your thesis or claim as follows:

    Men and women ought to have equal rights.

A more precise formulation of the claim might be

    Men and women ought to have equal legal rights.

A still more precise formulation might be

> Equal legal rights for men and women ought to be pro-
> tected by our Constitution.

The third version of this claim states what the controversy in the 1970s over the Equal Rights Amendment was all about.

Consequently, in reading or analyzing someone else's argument, your first question should naturally be: What is the argument intended to prove or establish? *What claim is it making?* Has this claim been clearly and precisely formulated, so that it unambiguously asserts what its advocate wants to assert?

GROUNDS

Once we have the argument's purpose or point clearly in mind and thus know what the arguer is claiming to establish, then we can ask for the evidence, reasons, support, in short, for the **grounds** on which that claim is based. In a deductive argument these grounds are the premises from which the claim is deduced; in an inductive argument the grounds are the evidence—a sample, observation, or experiment—that makes the claim plausible or probable.

Obviously not every kind of claim can be supported by every kind of ground, and conversely, not every kind of ground gives equally good support for every kind of claim. Suppose I claim that half the students in the classroom are women. I can ground this claim in any of several ways.

(1) I can count all the women and all the men. Suppose the total equals fifty. If the number of women is twenty-five, and the number of men is twenty-five, I have vindicated my claim.

(2) I can count a sample of, say, ten students, and find that in the sample, five of the students are women, and thus have inductive—plausible but not conclusive—grounds for my claim.

(3) I can point out that the students in the college divide equally into men and women, and claim that this class is a representative sample of the whole college.

Obviously ground (1) is stronger than ground (2), and (2) is far stronger than ground (3).

So far we have merely restated points about premises and conclusions covered in Chapter 3. But now we want to consider four additional features of arguments.

WARRANTS

Once we have the claim or the point of an argument fixed in mind, and the evidence or reasons offered in its support, the next question to ask is *why* these reasons support this conclusion. What is the **warrant**, or guarantee, that the reasons proffered do support the claim or lead to the conclusion? In simple deductive arguments, the warrant takes different forms, as we shall see. In the simplest cases, we can point to the way in which the *meanings* of the key terms are really equivalent. Thus, if John is taller than Bill, then Bill must be shorter than John because of the meaning in English of "is shorter than" and "is taller than." In this case, the warrant is something we can state quite literally and explicitly.

In other cases, we may need to be more resourceful. A reliable tactic is to think up a simple *parallel argument*, that is, an argument exactly parallel in form and structure to the argument we are trying to defend. We then point out that if we are ready to accept the simpler argument then we must accept the more complex argument because both arguments have exactly the same structure. For example, in her much-discussed essay of 1972 on the abortion controversy, "A Defense of Abortion," philosopher Judith Thomson argues that a pregnant woman has the right to an abortion to save her life, even if it involves the death of her unborn child. She anticipates that some readers may balk at her reasoning, and so she offers this parallel argument: Suppose you were locked in a tiny room with another human being, which through no fault of its own is growing uncontrollably, with the result that it is slowly crushing you to death. Of course it would be morally permissible to kill the other person to save your own life. With the reader's presumed agreement on that conclusion, the parallel argument concerning the abortion situation—so Thomson hopes—is obvious and convincing.

In simple inductive arguments, we are likely to point to the way in which observations or sets of data constitute a *representative sample* of a whole (unexamined) population. Here, the warrant is the representativeness of the sample. For instance, in projecting a line on a graph through a set of points, we defend one projection over alternatives on the ground that it makes the smoothest fit through most of the points. In this case, the warrant is *simplicity* and *inclusiveness*. Or in defending one explanation against competing explanations of a phenomenon, we appeal to the way in which the preferred explanation can be seen as a *special case* of generally accepted physical laws. Examples of such warrants for inductive reasoning will be offered in following pages (see Chapter 8, "A Logician's View," p. 260).

Establishing the warrants for our reasoning—that is, explaining why our grounds really support our claims—can quickly become a highly technical and exacting procedure that goes far beyond what we can hope to explain in this book. Only a solid course or two in formal deductive logic and statistical methods can do justice to our current state of knowledge about these warrants. Developing a "feel" for why reasons or grounds are or are not relevant to what they are alleged to support is the most we can hope to do here without recourse to more rigorous techniques.

Even without formal training, however, one can sense that something is wrong with many bad arguments. Here is an example. British professor C. E. M. Joad found himself standing on a station platform, annoyed because he had just missed his train, when another train, making an unscheduled stop, pulled up to the platform in front of him. He decided to jump aboard, only to hear the porter say "I'm afraid you'll have to get off, sir. This train doesn't stop here." "In that case," replied Joad, "don't worry. I'm not on it."

BACKING

The kinds of reasons appropriate to support an amendment to the Constitution are completely different from the kinds appropriate to settle the question of what caused the defeat of Napoleon's invasion of Russia. Arguments for the amendment might be rooted in an appeal to fairness, whereas arguments about the military defeat might be rooted in letters and other documents in the French and Russian archives. The canons of good argument in each case derive from the ways in which the scholarly communities in law and history, respectively, have developed over the years to support, defend, challenge, and undermine a given kind of argument. Thus, the support or **backing** appropriate for one kind of argument might be quite inappropriate for another kind of argument.

Another way of stating this point is to recognize that once you have given reasons for a claim, you are then likely to be challenged to explain why these reasons are good reasons—why, that is, one should believe these reasons rather than regard them skeptically. Why (a simple example) should we accept the testimony of Dr. X when Dr. Y, equally renowned, supports the opposite side? Or: Why is it safe to rest a prediction on a small though admittedly carefully selected sample? Or: Why is it legitimate to argue that (a) if I dream I am the King of France then I must exist, whereas it is illegitimate to argue that (b) if I dream I am the King of France, then the King of France must exist? To answer these kinds of challenges is to *back up* one's reasoning, and no argument is any better than its backing.

MODAL QUALIFIERS

As we have seen, all arguments are made up of assertions or propositions, which can be sorted into four categories:

the **claim** (conclusion, thesis to be established),

the **grounds** (explicit reasons advanced),

the **warrant** (the principle that connects the ground to the claim), and

the **backing** (implicit assumptions).

All these kinds of propositions have an explicit or tacit **modality,** in which they are asserted, indicating the scope and character with which they are believed to hold true. Is the claim, for instance, believed to be *necessary*—or only *probable*? Is the claim believed to be *plausible*—or only *possible*? Of two reasons for a claim, both may be *good*, but one may be *better* than the other. Indicating the modality with which an assertion is advanced is crucial to any argument for or against it.

Empirical generalizations are typically *contingent* on various factors, and it is important to indicate such contingencies to protect the generalization against obvious counterexamples. Thus, consider this empirical generalization:

Students do best on final examinations if they study hard for them.

Are we really to believe that students who study regularly throughout the whole course and so do not need to cram for the final will do less well than students who neglect regular work in favor of several all-nighters at the last minute? Probably not; what is really meant is that *all other things being equal* (in Latin, *caeteris paribus*), concentrated study just before an exam will yield good results. Alluding to the contingencies in this way shows that the writer is aware of possible exceptions and that they are conceded right from the start.

Assertions also have varying **scope,** and indicating their scope is equally crucial to the role that an assertion plays in argument. Thus, suppose you are arguing against smoking, and the ground for your claim is this:

Heavy smokers cut short their life span.

Such an assertion will be clearer, as well as more likely to be true, if it is explicitly **quantified**. Here, there are three obvious alternative quantifications to choose among: *all* smokers cut short their life span, or *most* do, or only *some* do. Until the assertion is quantified in one of these ways, we really do not know what is being asserted—and so we do not know what degree and kind of evidence and counterevidence is relevant.

In sum, sensitivity to the quantifiers and qualifiers appropriate for each of our assertions, whatever their role in an argument, will help prevent you from asserting exaggerations and other misguided generalizations.

REBUTTALS

Very few arguments of any interest are beyond dispute, conclusively knockdown affairs, in which the claim of the argument is so rigidly tied to its grounds, warrants, and backing, and its quantifiers and qualifiers so precisely orchestrated that it really proves its conclusion beyond any possibility of doubt. On the contrary, most arguments have many counterarguments, and sometimes it is one of these counterarguments that is the more convincing.

Suppose one has taken a sample that appears to be random—an interviewer on your campus accosts the first ten students whom she sees, and seven of them happen to be fraternity or sorority members. She is now ready to argue: Seven-tenths of the student body belong to Greek organizations.

You believe, however, that the Greeks are in the minority and point out that she happens to have conducted her interview around the corner from the Panhellenic Society's office just off Sorority Row. Her random sample is anything but. The ball is now back in her court as you await her response to your rebuttal.

As this example illustrates, it is safe to say that we do not understand our own arguments very well until we have tried to get a grip on the places in which they are vulnerable to criticism, counterattack, or refutation. Edmund Burke (quoted in Chapter 3 but worth repeating) said, "He that wrestles with us strengthens our nerves, and sharpens our skill. Our antagonist is our helper." Therefore, cultivating alertness to such weak spots, girding one's loins to defend at these places, always helps strengthen one's position.

A MODEL ANALYSIS USING THE TOULMIN METHOD

In order to see how the Toulmin method can be used, let's apply it to an argument in this book, Susan Jacoby's "A First Amendment Junkie," on page 29.

The Claim   Jacoby's central thesis or claim is this: Any form of *censorship*—including feminist censorship of pornography in particular— *is wrong.*

Grounds   Jacoby offers six main reasons or grounds for her claim, roughly in this sequence (but arguably not in this order of importance).

First, feminists exaggerate the harm caused by pornography because they confuse expression of offensive ideas with harmful conduct.

Second, letting the government censor the expression of ideas and attitudes is the wrong response to the failure of parents to control the printed materials that get into the hands of their children.

Third, there is no unanimity even among feminists over what is pornography and what isn't.

Fourth, permitting censorship of pornography, in order to please feminists, could well lead to censorship on many issues of concern to feminists ("rape, abortion, menstruation, contraception, lesbianism").

Fifth, censorship under law shows a lack of confidence in the democratic process.

Finally, censorship of words and pictures is suppression of self-expression, and that violates the First Amendment.

Warrants   The grounds Jacoby has offered provide support for her central claim in three ways, although Jacoby (like most writers) is not so didactic as to make these warrants explicit.

First, since the First Amendment protects speech in the broadest sense, the censorship that the feminist attack on pornography advocates is *inconsistent* with the First Amendment.

Second, if feminists want to be consistent, then they must advocate censorship of *all* offensive self-expression; but such a radical interference with free speech (amounting virtually to repeal of the First Amendment) is indefensible.

Third, feminists ought to see that *they risk losing more than they can hope to gain* if they succeed in censoring pornography, because antifeminists will have equal right to censor the things they find offensive but that many feminists seek to publish.

Backing   Why should the reader agree with Jacoby's grounds? She does not appeal to expert authority, the results of experimental tests or other statistical data, or the support of popular opinion. Instead, she relies principally on two things—but without saying so explicitly.

First, she assumes that the reader accepts the propositions that *freedom of self-expression is valuable* and that *censoring self-expression requires the strongest of reasons.* If there is no fundamental agreement on these propositions, several of her reasons cease to support her claim.

Second, she relies on the reader's open-mindedness and willingness to evaluate commonsense (untechnical, ordinary, familiar) considerations at each step of the way. She relies also on the reader having had some personal experience with erotica, pornography, and art. Without that open-mindedness and experience, a reader is not likely to be persuaded by her rejection of the feminist demand for censorship.

Modal Qualifiers   Jacoby defends what she calls an "absolute interpretation" of the First Amendment, that is, the view that *all* censorship of words, pictures, ideas is not only inconsistent with the First Amendment, it is also politically unwise and morally objectionable. She allows that *some* pornography is highly offensive (it offends her, she insists); she allows that *some* pornography ("kiddie porn") may even be harmful to *some* viewers. But she also insists that *more* harm than good would result from the censorship of pornography. She points out that *some* paintings of nude women are art, not pornography; she implies that it is *impossible* to draw a sharp line between permissible erotic pornography and impermissible offensive pornography. She clearly believes that *all* Americans ought to understand and defend the First Amendment under the "absolute interpretation" she favors.

Rebuttals   Jacoby mentions several objections to her views, and perhaps the most effective aspect of her entire argument is her skill in identifying possible objections and meeting them effectively. (Notice the diversity of the objections and the various ways in which she replies.)

Objection: Some of her women friends tell her she is wrong.

Rebuttal: She admits she's a "First Amendment junkie" and she doesn't apologize for it.

Objection: "Kiddie porn" is harmful and deserves censorship.

Rebuttal: Such material is *not* protected by the First Amendment, because it is an "abuse of power" of adults over children.

Objection: Pornography is a form of violence against women, and therefore it is especially harmful.

Rebuttal: (a) No, it really isn't harmful, but it is disgusting and offensive. (b) In any case, it's surely not as harmful as allowing American neo-Nazis to parade in Jewish neighborhoods. (Jacoby is referring to the march in Skokie, Illinois, in 1977, upheld by the courts as permissible political expression under the First Amendment despite its offensiveness to survivors of the Nazi concentration camps.)

Objection: Censoring pornography advances public respect for women.

Rebuttal: Censoring *Ms.* magazine, which antifeminists have already done, undermines women's freedom and self-expression.

Objection: Reasonable people can tell pornography when they see it, so censoring it poses no problems.

Rebuttal: Yes, there are clear cases of gross pornography; but there are lots of borderline cases, as women themselves prove when they disagree over whether a photo in *Penthouse* is offensively erotic or "lovely" and "sensuous."

A CHECKLIST FOR
USING THE TOULMIN METHOD

✓ What claim does the argument make?

✓ What grounds are offered for the claim?

✓ What warrants the inferences from the grounds to the claim?

✓ What backing supports the claims?

✓ With what modalities are the claim and grounds asserted?

✓ To what rebuttals are the claims, grounds, and backing vulnerable?

8

A Logician's View:
Deduction, Induction,
Fallacies

In Chapter 3 we introduced these terms. Now we will discuss them in greater detail.

DEDUCTION

The basic aim of deductive reasoning is to start with some assumption or premise, and extract from it consequences that are concealed but implicit in it. Thus, taking the simplest case, if I assert

    1. The cat is on the mat,

it is a matter of simple deduction to infer that

    2. The mat is under the cat.

Everyone would grant that (2) is entailed by, or follows from (1)—or, that (2) can be validly deduced from (1)—because of the meaning of the key connective concepts in each proposition. Anyone who understands English knows that, whatever A and B are, if A is *on* B, then B must be *under* A. Thus, in this and all other cases of valid deductive reasoning, we can say not only that we are entitled to *infer* the conclusion from the premise—in this case, infer (2) from (1)—but that the premise *implies* or entails the conclusion. Remember, too, the inference of (2) from (1) does not depend on the truth of (1). (2) follows from (1) whether or not (1) is true; consequently, if (1) is true then so is (2); but if (1) is false then (2) is false, also.

    Let's take another example—more interesting, but comparably simple:

3. President Truman was underrated by his critics.

Given (3), a claim amply verified by events of the 1950s, one is entitled to infer

4. The critics underrated President Truman.

On what basis can we argue that (3) implies (4)? The two propositions are equivalent because a rule of English grammar assures us that we can convert the position of subject and predicate phrases in a sentence by shifting from the passive to the active voice (or vice versa) without any change in the conditions that make the proposition true (or false).

Both pairs of examples illustrate that in deductive reasoning, our aim is to transform, reformulate, or restate in our conclusion some (or, as in the two examples above, all) of the information contained in our premises.

Remember, even though a proposition or statement follows from a previous proposition or statement, the statements need not be true. We can see why if we consider another example. Suppose someone asserts or claims that

5. The Hudson River is longer than the Mississippi.

As every student of American geography knows, (5) is false. But, false or not, we can validly deduce from it:

6. The Mississippi is shorter than the Hudson.

This inference is valid (even though the conclusion is untrue) because the conclusion follows logically (more precisely, deductively) from (5): In English, as we know, the meaning of "A is shorter than B," which appears in (6), is simply the converse of "B is longer than A," which appears in (5).

The deductive relation between (5) and (6) reminds us again that the idea of *validity*, which is so crucial to deduction, is not the same as the idea of *truth*. False propositions have implications—logical consequences—too, every bit as precisely as do true propositions.

In the three pairs of examples so far, what can we point to as the *warrant* for our claims? Well, look at the reasoning in each case; the arguments rely on rules of ordinary English. In the first and third pairs of examples, it is a rule of English semantics; in the second pair it is a rule of English syntax. Change those rules and the inferences will no longer be valid; fail to comply with those rules and one will not trust the inferences.

In many cases, of course, the deductive inference or pattern of reasoning is much more complex than that which we have seen in the examples so far. When we introduced the idea of deduction in Chapter 3, we gave as our primary example the *syllogism*. Here is another example:

> 7. Texas is larger than California; California is larger than Arizona; therefore, Texas is larger than Arizona.

The conclusion in this syllogism is derivable from the two premises; that is, anyone who asserts the two premises is committed to accepting the conclusion as well, whether or not one thinks of it.

Notice again that the *truth* of the conclusion is not established merely by validity of the inference. The conclusion in this syllogism happens to be true. And the premises of this syllogism imply the conclusion. But the argument *proves* the conclusion only because both of the premises on which the conclusion depends are true. Even a Californian admits that Texas is larger than California, which in turn is larger than Arizona. In other words, argument (7) is a *sound* argument, because (as we explained in Chapter 3) it is valid and all its premises are true. All—and only—arguments that *prove* their conclusions have these two traits.

How might we present the warrant for the argument in (7)? Short of a crash course in formal logic, either of two strategies might suffice. One is to argue from the fact that the validity of the inference depends on the meaning of a key concept, *being larger than,* which has the property of *transitivity,* a property that many concepts share (for example, *is equal to, is to the right of, is smarter than*—all are transitive concepts). Consequently, whatever A, B, and C are, if A is larger than B, and B is larger than C, then A will be larger than C. The final step is to substitute "Texas," "California," and "Arizona" for A, B, and C, respectively.

A second strategy is to think of representing Texas, California, and Arizona by concentric circles, with the largest for Texas, a smaller circle inside it for California, and a smaller one inside California for Arizona. (This is an adaptation of the technique used in elementary formal logic known as Venn diagrams.) In this manner one can give graphic display to the important fact that the conclusion follows from the premises, because one can literally *see* the conclusion represented by nothing more than a representation of the premises.

Both of these strategies bring out the fact that validity of deductive inference is a purely *formal* property of argument. Each strategy abstracts the form from the content of the propositions involved to show how the concepts in the premises are related to the concepts in the conclusion.

Not all deductive reasoning occurs in syllogisms, however, or at least not in syllogisms like the one in (7). (The term *syllogism* is sometimes used to refer to any deductive argument of whatever form, provided only that it has two premises.) In fact, syllogisms such as (7) are not the commonest form of our deductive reasoning at all. Nor are they the simplest (and of course not the most complex). For an argument that is even simpler, consider this:

> 8. If the horses are loose, then the barn door was left unlocked. The horses are loose. Therefore, the barn door was left unlocked.

Here the pattern of reasoning is called **modus ponens,** which means positing or laying down the minor premise ("the horses are loose"). It is also called **hypothetical syllogism,** because its major premise ("if the horses are loose, then the barn door was left unlocked") is a hypothetical or conditional proposition. The argument has the form: If A then B; A; therefore, B. Notice that the content of the assertions represented by A and B do not matter; any set of expressions having the same form or structure will do equally well, including assertions built out of meaningless terms, as in this example:

9. If the slithy toves, then the gyres gimble. The slithy toves. Therefore, the gyres gimble.

Argument (9) has exactly the same form as argument (8), and as a piece of deductive inference it is every bit as good. Unlike (8), however, (9) is of no interest to us because none of its assertions make any sense (unless you are a reader of Lewis Carroll's "Jabberwocky," and even then the sense of (9) is doubtful). You cannot, in short, use a valid deductive argument to prove anything unless the premises and the conclusion are *true,* but they can't be true unless they *mean* something in the first place.

This parallel between arguments (8) and (9) shows once again that deductive validity in an argument rests on the *form* or structure of the argument, and not on its content or meaning. If all one can say about an argument is that it is valid—that is, its conclusion follows from the premises—one has not given a sufficient reason for accepting the argument's conclusion. It has been said that the Devil can quote Scripture; similarly, an argument can be deductively valid and of no further interest or value whatever, because valid (but false) conclusions can be drawn from false or even meaningless assumptions. Nevertheless, although validity by itself is not enough, it is a necessary condition of any deductive argument that purports to *prove* its conclusion.

Now let us consider another argument with the same form as (8) and (9), only more interesting.

10. If President Truman knew the Japanese were about to surrender, then it was immoral of him to order that atom bombs be dropped on Hiroshima and Nagasaki. Truman knew the Japanese were about to surrender. Therefore, it was immoral of him to order dropping those bombs.

As in the two previous examples, anyone who assents to the premises in argument (10) must assent to the conclusion; the form of arguments (8), (9), and (10) is identical. But do the premises of argument (10) *prove* the conclusion? That depends on whether both premises are true. Well, are they? This turns on a number of considerations, and it is worthwhile pausing to examine this argument closely to illustrate the kinds of things that are involved in answering this question.

Let us begin by examining the second (minor) premise. Its truth is controversial even to this day. Autobiography, memoranda, other documentary evidence—all are needed to assemble the evidence to back up the grounds for the thesis or claim made in the conclusion of this valid argument. Evaluating this material effectively will probably involve not only further deductions, but inductive reasoning as well.

Now consider the first (major) premise in argument (10). Its truth doesn't depend on what history shows, but on the moral principles one accepts. The major premise has the form of a hypothetical proposition ("if . . . then . . ."), and asserts a connection between two very different kinds of things. The antecedent of the hypothetical (the clause following "if") mentions facts about Truman's *knowledge,* and the consequent of the hypothetical (the clause following "then") mentions facts about the *morality* of his conduct in light of such knowledge. The major premise as a whole can thus be seen as expressing a principle of *moral responsibility.*

Such principles can, of course, be controversial. In this case, for instance, is the principle peculiarly relevant to the knowledge and conduct of a president of the United States? Probably not; it is far more likely that this principle is merely a special case of a more general proposition about anyone's moral responsibility. (After all, we know a great deal more about the conditions of our own moral responsibility than we do about those of high government officials.) We might express this more general principle in this way: If we have knowledge that would make our violent conduct unnecessary, then we are immoral if we deliberately act violently anyway. Thus, accepting this general principle can serve as a basis for defending the major premise of argument (10).

We have examined this argument in some detail because it illustrates the kinds of considerations needed to test whether a given argument is not only valid but whether its premises are true—that is, whether its premises really prove the conclusion.

The great value of the form of argument known as hypothetical syllogism, exemplified by arguments (8), (9), and (10), is that the structure of the argument is so simple and so universally applicable in reasoning that it is often both easy and worthwhile to formulate one's claims so that they can be grounded by an argument of this sort.

Before leaving the subject of deductive inference, consider three other forms of argument, each of which can be found in actual use elsewhere in the readings in this volume. The simplest of these is **disjunctive syllogism,** so called because, again, it has two premises, and its major premise is a **disjunction.** That is, a disjunctive syllogism is a complex assertion built from two or more alternatives joined by the conjunction "or"; each of these alternatives is called a **disjunct.** For example,

11. Either censorship of television shows is overdue, or our society is indifferent to the education of its youth. Our society is not indif-

ferent to the education of its youth. Therefore, censorship of television is overdue.

Notice, by the way, that the validity of an argument, as in this case, does not turn on pedantic repetition of every word or phrase as the argument moves along; nonessential elements can be dropped, or equivalent expressions substituted for variety without adverse effect on the reasoning. Thus, in conversation, or in writing, the argument in (11) might actually be presented like this:

12. Either censorship of television is overdue, or our society is indifferent to the education of its youth. But, of course, we aren't indifferent; it's censorship that's overdue.

The key feature of disjunctive syllogism, as example (12) suggests, is that the conclusion is whichever of the disjuncts is left over after the others have been negated in the minor premise. Thus, we could easily have a very complex disjunctive syllogism, with a dozen disjuncts in the major premise, and seven of them denied in the minor premise, leaving a conclusion of the remaining five. Usually, however, a disjunctive argument is formulated in this manner: Assert a disjunction with two or more disjuncts in the major premise; then *deny all but one* in the minor premise; and infer validly the remaining disjunct as the conclusion. That was the form of argument (12).

Another type of argument, especially favored by orators and rhetoricians, is the **dilemma.** Ordinarily we use the term *dilemma* in the sense of an awkward predicament, as when we say, "His dilemma was that he didn't have enough money to pay the waiter." But when logicians refer to a dilemma, they mean a forced choice between two or more equally unattractive alternatives. For example, the predicament of the U.S. government during the mid-1980s as it faced the crisis brought on by terrorist attacks on American civilian targets, which were believed, during that time, to be inspired and supported by the Libyan government, can be formulated in a dilemma:

13. If the United States bombs targets in Libya, innocent people will be killed and the Arab world will be angered. If the United States doesn't bomb Libyan targets, then terrorists will go unpunished and the United States will lose respect among other governments. Either the United States bombs Libyan targets or it doesn't. Therefore, in either case unattractive consequences will follow: The innocent will be killed or terrorists will go unpunished.

Notice first the structure of the argument: two conditional propositions asserted as premises, followed by another premise that states a **necessary truth.** (The premise, "Either we bomb the Libyans or we don't," is a disjunction of two exhaustive alternatives, and so one of the two alternatives must be true. Such a statement is often called analytically true, or a *tautology*.) No doubt the conclusion of this dilemma follows from its premises.

But does the argument prove, as it purports to do, that whatever the U.S. government does, it will suffer undesirable consequences? If the two conditional premises failed to exhaust the possibilities, then one can escape from the dilemma by going "between the horns"; that is, by finding a third alternative. If (as in this case) that is not possible, one can still ask whether both of the main premises are true. (In this argument, it should be clear that neither of these main premises spells out all or even most of the consequences that could be foreseen.) Even so, in cases where both these conditional premises are true, it may be that the consequences of one alternative are nowhere nearly so bad as those of the other. If that is true, but our reasoning stops before evaluating that fact, we may be guilty of failing to distinguish between the greater and the lesser of two admitted evils. The logic of the dilemma itself cannot decide this choice for us. Instead, we must bring to bear empirical inquiry and imagination to the evaluation of the grounds of the dilemma itself.

Writers commonly use the term *dilemma* without explicitly formulating the dilemma to which they refer, leaving it for the readers to do. And sometimes, what is called a dilemma really isn't one. (Remember the dog's tail? Calling it a leg doesn't make it one.) As an example, consider Elizabeth Whelan's reference in her essay on teenage drinking (p. 84) to her "daughter's dilemma." Like most writers, Whelan does not trouble to formulate the dilemma with any precision. With a little effort, one can see that it must read more or less as follows:

> Either the law ought to treat teenagers as adults, or it ought not. If they are going to be treated as adults, then they ought to be allowed to purchase alcoholic beverages as other adults are. If they are not to be treated as adults, then there is no good reason for permitting them to vote, make contracts, and so on. Either way, the current laws affecting teenage behavior need to be reformed.

What this formulation shows is that, strictly speaking, Whelan's daughter does *not* face a dilemma at all. Why? She doesn't face a dilemma because we cannot formulate a conclusion to Whelan's argument consisting of two alternatives, both of which are repellant. What Whelan has done, under the term *dilemma*, is to point to the *inconsistency* in current law, under which teenagers are sometimes treated as full adults and at other times not treated as adults. This behavior may be a problem, but not every problem is a dilemma.

Finally, one of the most powerful and dramatic forms of argument is **reductio ad absurdum** (from the Latin, meaning "reduction to absurdity"). The idea of a reductio argument is to establish a conclusion by refuting its opposite, and it is an especially attractive tactic when you can use it to refute your opponent's position in order to prove your own. For example, in Plato's *Republic,* Socrates asks an old gentleman, Cephalus, to define what right conduct is. Cephalus says that it is paying your debts and keeping your word. Socrates rejects this answer by showing that it leads to a contradiction. He argues that Cephalus cannot have given the correct answer because if we assume that he did, we will be quickly led into contradictions; in some cases when you keep your word you will nonetheless be doing the wrong thing. For suppose, says Socrates, that you borrowed a weapon from a man, promising to return it when he asks for it. One day he comes to your door, demanding his weapon and swearing angrily that he intends to murder a neighbor. Keeping your word under those circumstances is absurd, Socrates implies; and the reader of the dialogue is left to infer that Cephalus's definition, which led to this result, is refuted.

Let's take a closer look at another example. Suppose you are opposed to any form of gun control, whereas I am in favor of gun control. I might try to refute your position by attacking it with a reductio argument. To do that, I start out by assuming the very opposite of what I believe or favor, and try to establish a contradiction that results from following out the consequences of this initial assumption. My argument might look like this:

14. Let's assume your position, namely, that there ought to be no legal restrictions whatever on the sale and ownership of guns. That means that you'd permit having every neighborhood hardware store sell pistols and rifles to whoever walks in the door. But that's not all. You apparently also would permit selling machine guns to children, antitank weapons to lunatics, small-bore cannons to the near-sighted, as well as guns and the ammunition to go with them to anyone with a criminal record. But this is utterly preposterous. No one could favor such a dangerous policy. So the only question worth debating is what *kind* of gun control is necessary.

Now in this example, my reductio of your position on gun control is not based on claiming to show that you have strictly contradicted yourself, for there is no purely logical contradiction in opposing all forms of gun control. Instead, what I have tried to do (just as Socrates did) is to show that there is a contradiction between what you profess—no gun controls whatever—and what you probably really believe, if only you will stop to think about it—no lunatic should be allowed to buy a loaded machine gun.

My refutation of your position rests on whether I succeed in establishing an inconsistency among your own beliefs. If it turns out that you really believe lunatics should be free to purchase guns and ammunition, then my attempted refutation fails.

In explaining reductio ad absurdum, we have had to rely on another idea fundamental to logic, that of **contradiction,** or inconsistency. (We used this idea, remember, to define validity in Chapter 3. A deductive argument is valid if and only if affirming the premises and denying the conclusion results in a contradiction.) The opposite of contradiction is **consistency,** a notion of hardly less importance to good reasoning than validity. These concepts deserve a few words of further explanation and illustration. Consider this pair of assertions:

15. Abortion is homicide.
16. Racism is unfair.

No one would plausibly claim that we can infer or deduce (16) from (15), or, for that matter, (15) from (16). This almost goes without saying, because there is no evident connection between (15) and (16). They are unrelated assertions; logically speaking, they are *independent* of each other. In such cases the two assertions are mutually consistent; that is, both could be true—or both could be false. But now consider another proposition:

17. Euthanasia is not murder.

Could a person assert (15) *abortion is homicide* and also assert (17), and be consistent? This question is equivalent to asking whether one could assert the **conjunction** of these two propositions, namely,

18. Abortion is homicide and euthanasia is not murder.

It is not so easy to say whether (18) is consistent or inconsistent. The kinds of moral scruples that might lead a person to assert one of these conjuncts (that is, one of the two initial propositions, *Abortion is homicide* and *Euthanasia is not murder*) might lead to the belief that the other one must be false, and thus to the conclusion that (18) is inconsistent. (Notice that if [15] were the assertion that *Abortion is murder,* instead of *Abortion is homicide,* the problem of asserting consistently both [15] and [17] would be more acute.) Yet, if we think again, we might imagine someone being convinced that there is no inconsistency in asserting that *Abortion is homicide,* say, and that *Euthanasia is not murder,* or even the reverse. (For instance, suppose you believed that the unborn deserve a chance to live, and that putting elderly persons to death in a painless manner and with their consent confers a benefit on them.)

Let us generalize: We can say of any set of propositions that they are *consistent* if and only if *all could be true together.* (Notice that it follows from this definition that propositions that mutually imply each other, as do *The cat is on the mat* and *The mat is under the cat,* are consistent.) Remember that, once again, the truth of the assertions in question does not matter. Propositions can be consistent or not, quite apart from whether they are true. Not so their falsehood: It follows from our definition of consistency that an *inconsistent* proposition must be *false.* (We have relied on this idea in explaining how a reductio ad absurdum works.)

Assertions or claims that are not consistent can take either of two forms. Suppose you assert proposition (15), that abortion is homicide, early in an essay you are writing, but after you say

19. Abortion is harmless.

You have now asserted a position on abortion that is strictly **contrary** to the one with which you began; contrary in the sense that both assertions (15) and (19) cannot be true. It is simply not true that if an abortion involves killing a human being (which is what *homicide* strictly means) then it causes no one any harm (killing a person always causes harm — even if it is excusable, or justifiable, or not wrong, or the best thing to do in the circumstances, and so on). Notice that although (15) and (19) cannot both be true, they can both be false. In fact, many people who are perplexed about the morality of abortion believe precisely this. They concede that abortion does harm the fetus, so (19) must be false; but they also believe that abortion doesn't kill a person, so (15) must also be false.

Or consider another, simpler case. If you describe the glass as half empty and I describe it as half full, both of us can be right; the two assertions are consistent, even though they sound vaguely incompatible. (This is the reason that disputing over whether the glass is half full or half empty has become the popular paradigm of a futile, purely *verbal disagreement*.) But if I describe the glass as half empty whereas you insist that it is two-thirds empty, then we have a real disagreement; your description and mine are strictly contrary, in that both cannot be true — although both can be false. (Both are false if the glass is only one-quarter full.)

This, by the way, enables us to define the difference between a pair of contradictory propositions and a pair of contrary propositions. Two propositions are contrary if and only if both cannot be true (though both can be false); two propositions are contradictory if and only if they are such that if one is true the other must be false, and vice versa. Thus, if Jack says that Alice Walker's *The Color Purple* is a better novel than Mark Twain's *Huckleberry Finn*, and Jill says, "No, *Huckleberry Finn* is better than *The Color Purple*," she is contradicting Jack. If what either one of them says is true, then what the other says must be false. A more subtle case of contradiction arises when two or more of one's own beliefs implicitly contradict each other. We may find ourselves saying "Travel is broadening," and saying an hour later, "People don't really change." Just beneath the surface of these two beliefs lies a self-contradiction: How can travel broaden us unless it influences — and changes — our beliefs, values, and outlook? But if we can't really change ourselves, then traveling to new places won't change us, either. (Indeed, there is a Roman saying to the effect that travelers change the skies above them, not their hearts.) "Travel is broadening" and "People don't change" collide with each other; something has to give.

Our point, of course, is not that you must never say today something that contradicts something you said yesterday. Far from it; if you think you were mistaken yesterday, of course you will take a different position today. But what you want to avoid is what George Orwell called *doublethink* in his novel *1984*: "*Doublethink* means the power of holding two contradictory beliefs in one's mind simultaneously, and accepting them both."

Genuine contradiction, and not merely contrary assertion, is the situation we should expect to find in some disputes. Someone advances a thesis—such as the assertion in (15), *Abortion is homicide*—and someone else flatly contradicts it by the simple expedient of negating it, thus:

20. Abortion is not homicide.

If we can trust public opinion polls, many of us are not sure whether to agree with (15) or with (20). But we should agree that whichever is true, *both* cannot be true, and *both* cannot be false. The two assertions, between them, exclude all other possibilities; they pose a forced choice for our belief. (Again, we have met this idea, too, in a reductio ad absurdum.)

Now it is one thing for Jack and Jill in a dispute or argument to contradict each other. It is quite another matter for Jack to contradict himself. One wants (or should want) to avoid self-contradiction because of the embarrassing position in which one then finds oneself. Once I have contradicted myself, what are others to believe I really believe? What, indeed, *do* I believe, for that matter?

It may be, as Emerson observed, that a "foolish consistency is the hobgoblin of little minds"—that is, it may be shortsighted to purchase a consistency in one's beliefs at the expense of flying in the face of common sense. But making an effort to avoid a foolish inconsistency is the hallmark of serious thinking.

While we are speaking of inconsistency, we should spend a moment on **paradox.** The word refers to two different things: (1) an assertion that is essentially self-contradictory and therefore cannot be true, and (2) a seemingly contradictory assertion that nevertheless may be true. An example of the first might be, "Evaluations concerning quality in literature are all a matter of personal judgment, but Shakespeare is the world's greatest writer." It is hard to make any sense out of this assertion. Contrast it with a paradox of the second sort, a *seeming* contradiction that may make sense, such as "The longest way round is the shortest way home," or "Work is more fun than fun," or "The best way to find happiness is not to look for it." Here we have assertions that are striking because as soon as we hear them we realize that although they seem inconsistent and self-defeating, they contain (or may contain) profound truths. Paradoxes of this second sort are especially common in religious texts, where they may imply a mysterious reality concealed by a world of contradictory appearances. Examples are "Some who are last shall be first, and some who are first shall be last" (Jesus, quoted in Luke 13.30), and "Death, thou shalt die" (the poet John Donne, alluding to the idea that the person who has faith in Jesus dies to this world but lives eternally). If you use the word *paradox* in your own writing—for instance, to characterize an argument that you are reading—be sure that your reader will understand in which sense you are using the word. (And, of course, you will not want to write paradoxes of the first, self-contradictory sort.)

INDUCTION

Deduction involves logical thinking that applies to any assertion or claim whatever—because every possible statement, true or false, has its deductive logical consequences. Induction is relevant to one kind of assertion only; namely, to **empirical** or *factual* claims. Other kinds of assertions (such as definitions, mathematical equations, and moral or legal norms) simply are not the product of inductive reasoning and cannot serve as a basis for further inductive thinking.

And so, in studying the methods of induction, we are exploring tactics and strategies useful in gathering and then using **evidence**—empirical, observational, experimental—in support of a belief as its ground. Modern scientific knowledge is the product of these methods, and they differ somewhat from one science to another because they depend on the theories and technology appropriate to each of the sciences. Here, all we can do is discuss generally the more abstract features common to inductive inquiry generally. For fuller details, you must eventually consult your local physicist, chemist, geologist, or their colleagues and counterparts in other scientific fields.

Observation and Inference

Let us begin with a simple example. Suppose we have evidence (actually we don't, but that will not matter for our purposes) in support of the claim that

1. Two hundred and thirty persons observed in a sample of 500 smokers have cardiovascular disease.

The basis for asserting (1)—the evidence or ground—would be, presumably, straightforward physical examination of the 500 persons in the sample, one by one.

With this claim in hand, we can think of the purpose and methods of induction as being pointed in both of two opposite directions: toward establishing the basis or ground of the very empirical proposition with which we start, in this example the observation stated in (1); or toward understanding what that observation indicates or suggests as a more general, inclusive, or fundamental fact of nature.

In each case, we start from something we *do* know (or take for granted and treat as a sound starting point) — some fact of nature, perhaps a striking or commonplace event that we have observed and recorded — and then go on to something we do *not* fully know and perhaps cannot directly observe. In example (1), only the second of these two orientations is of any interest, and so let us concentrate exclusively on it. Let us also generously treat as a *method* of induction any regular pattern or style of nondeductive reasoning that we could use to support a claim such as that in (1).

Anyone truly interested in the observed fact that (1) *230 of 500 smokers have cardiovascular disease* is likely to start speculating about, and thus be interested in finding out, whether any or all of several other propositions are also true. For example, one might wonder whether

2. *All* smokers have cardiovascular disease or will develop it during their lifetimes.

This claim is a straightforward generalization of the original observation as reported in claim (1). When we think inductively about the linkage between (1) and (2), we are reasoning from an observed sample (some smokers, that is, 230 of the 500 *observed*) to the entire membership of a more inclusive class (*all* smokers, whether observed or not). The fundamental question raised by reasoning from the narrower claim (1) to the broader claim (2) is whether we have any ground for believing that what is true of *some* members of a class is true of them *all*. So the difference between (1) and (2) is that of *quantity* or scope.

We can also think inductively about the *relation* between the factors mentioned in (1). Having observed data as reported in (1), we may be tempted to assert a different and profounder kind of claim:

3. Smoking *causes* cardiovascular disease.

Here our interest is not merely in generalizing from a sample to a whole class; it is the far more important one of *explaining* the observation with which we began in claim (1). Certainly the preferred, even if not the only, mode of explanation for a natural phenomenon is a *causal* explanation. In proposition (3), we propose to explain the presence of one phenomenon (cardiovascular disease) by the prior occurrence of an independent phenomenon (smoking). The observation reported in (1) is now being used as evidence or support for this new conjecture stated in (3).

Our original claim in (1) asserted no causal relation between anything and anything else; whatever the cause of cardiovascular disease may be, that cause is not observed, mentioned, or assumed in assertion (1). Similarly, the observation asserted in claim (1) is consistent with many explanations. For example, the explanation of (1) might not be (3), but some other, undetected, carcinogenic factor unrelated to smoking, for instance, exposure to high levels of radon. The question one now faces is what can be added to (1), or teased out of it, in order to produce an adequate ground for claiming (3). (We shall return to this example for closer scrutiny.)

But there is a third way to go beyond (1). Instead of a straightforward generalization, as we had in (2), or a pronouncement on the cause of a phenomenon, as in (3), we might have a somewhat more complex and cautious further claim in mind, such as this:

4. Smoking is a factor in the causation of cardiovascular disease in some persons.

This proposition, like (3), advances a claim about causation. But (4) is obviously a weaker claim than (3). That is, other observations, theories, or evidence that would require us to reject (3) might be consistent with (4); evidence that would support (4) could easily fail to be enough to support (3). Consequently, it is even possible that (4) is true although (3) is false, because (4) allows for other (unmentioned) factors in the causation of cardiovascular disease (genetic or dietary factors, for example) which may not be found in all smokers.

Propositions (2), (3), and (4) differ from proposition (1) in an important respect. We began by assuming that (1) states an empirical fact based on direct observation, whereas these others do not. Instead, they state empirical *hypotheses* or conjectures—tentative generalizations not fully confirmed—each of which goes beyond the observed facts asserted in (1). Each of (2), (3), and (4) can be regarded as an *inductive inference* from (1). We can also say that (2), (3), and (4) are hypotheses relative to (1), even if relative to some other starting point (such as all the information that scientists today really have about smoking and cardiovascular disease) they are not.

Probability

Another way of formulating the last point is to say that whereas proposition (1), a statement of observed fact, has a **probability** of 1.0— that is, it is absolutely certain—the probability of each of the hypotheses stated in (2), (3), and (4), *relative* to (1) is smaller than 1.0. (We need not worry here about how much smaller than 1.0 the probabilities are, nor about how to calculate these probabilities precisely.) Relative to some starting point other than (1), however, the probability of these same three hypotheses might be quite different. Of course, it still would not be 1.0, absolute certainty. But it takes only a moment's reflection to realize that, whatever may be the probability of (2) or (3) or (4) relative to (1), those probabilities in each case will be quite different relative to different information, such as this:

5. Ten persons observed in a sample of 500 smokers have cardiovascular disease.

The idea that a given proposition can have different probabilities relative to different bases is fundamental to all inductive reasoning. It can be convincingly illustrated by the following example. Suppose we want to consider the probability of this proposition being true:

6. Susanne Smith will live to be eighty.

Taken as an abstract question of fact, we cannot even guess what the probability is with any assurance. But we can do better than guess; we can in fact even calculate the answer, if we are given some further information. Thus, suppose we are told that

7. Susanne Smith is seventy-nine.

Our original question then becomes one of determining the probability that (6) is true given (7); that is, relative to the evidence contained in proposition (7). No doubt, if Susanne Smith really is seventy-nine, then the probability that she will live to be eighty is greater than if we know only that

8. Susanne Smith is more than nine years old.

Obviously, a lot can happen to Susanne in the seventy years between nine and seventy-nine that is not very likely to happen to her in the one year between seventy-nine and eighty. And so, proposition (6) is more probable relative to proposition (7) than it is relative to proposition (8).

Let us disregard (7) and instead further suppose for the sake of the argument that the following is true:

9. Ninety percent of the women alive at seventy-nine live to be eighty.

Given this additional information, we now have a basis for answering our original question about proposition (6) with some precision. But suppose, in addition to (8), we are also told that

10. Susanne Smith is suffering from inoperable cancer.

and also that

11. The survival rate for women suffering from inoperable cancer is 0.6 years (that is, the average life span for women after a diagnosis of inoperable cancer is about seven months).

With this new information, the probability that (6) will be true has dropped significantly, all because we can now estimate the probability in relation to a new body of evidence.

The probability of an event, thus, is not a fixed number, but one that varies, because it is always relative to some evidence—and given different evidence, one and the same event can have different probabilities. In other words, the probability of any event is always relative to how much is known (assumed, believed), and because different persons may know different things about a given event, or the same person may know different things at different times, one and the same event can have two or more probabilities. This conclusion is not a paradox but a logical consequence of the concept of what it is for an event to have (that is, to be assigned) a probability.

If we shift to the *calculation* of probabilities, we find that generally we have two ways to calculate them. One way to proceed is by the method of **a priori** or **equal probabilities,** that is, by reference to the relevant possibilities taken abstractly and apart from any other information. Thus, in an election contest with only two candidates, A and B, each of the candidates has a fifty-fifty chance of winning (whereas in a three-candidate race, each candidate would have one chance in three of winning). Therefore the probability that candidate A will win is 0.5, and the probability that candidate B will win is also 0.5. (The sum of the probabilities of all possible independent outcomes must always equal 1.0, which is obvious enough if you think about it.)

But in politics the probabilities are not reasonably calculated so abstractly. We know that many empirical factors affect the outcome of an election, and that a calculation of probabilities in ignorance of those factors is likely to be drastically misleading. In our example of the two-candidate election, suppose candidate A has strong party support and is the incumbent, whereas candidate B represents a party long out of power and is further handicapped by being relatively unknown. No one who knows anything about electoral politics would give B the same chance of winning as A. The two events are not equiprobable in relation to all the information available.

Not only that, a given event can have more than one probability. This happens whenever we calculate a probability by relying on different bodies of data that report how often the event in question has been observed to happen. Probabilities calculated in this way are **relative frequencies.** Our earlier hypothetical example of Susanne Smith provides an illustration. If she is a smoker and we have observed that 100 out of a random set of 500 smokers are observed to have cardiovascular disease, we have a basis for claiming that she has a probability of 100 in 500, or 0.2 (one-fifth), of having this disease. However, if we had other data showing that 250 out of 500 women smokers aged eighty or older have cardiovascular disease, we have a basis for believing that there is a probability of 250 in 500, or 0.5 (one-half), that she has this disease. Notice, of course, that in both calculations we assume that Susanne Smith is not among the persons we have examined. In both cases we infer the probability with which she has this disease from observing its frequency in populations that exclude her.

Both methods of calculating probabilities are legitimate; in each case the calculation is relative to observed circumstances. But, as the examples show, it is most reasonable to have recourse to the method of equiprobabilities only when few or no other factors affecting possible outcomes are known.

Mill's Methods

Let us return to our earlier discussion of smoking and cardiovascular disease, and consider in greater detail the question of a causal connection between the two phenomena. We began thus:

1. Two hundred and thirty persons observed in a sample of 500 smokers have cardiovascular disease.

We regarded (1) as an observed fact, though in truth, of course, it is mere supposition. Our question now is, how might we augment this information so as to strengthen our confidence that

3. Smoking causes cardiovascular disease,

or at least

4. Smoking is a factor in the causation of cardiovascular disease in some persons.

Suppose further examination showed that

12. In the sample of 230 smokers with cardiovascular disease, no other suspected factor (such as genetic predisposition, lack of physical exercise, age over fifty) was also observed.

Such an observation would encourage us to believe (3) or (4) is true. Why? We are encouraged to believe it because we are inclined to believe also that whatever the cause of a phenomenon is, it must *always* be present when its effect is present. Thus, the inference from (1) to (3) or (4) is supported by (12), using **Mill's Method of Agreement,** named after the British philosopher, John Stuart Mill (1806–1873), who first formulated it. It is called a method of agreement because of the way in which the inference relies on *agreement* among the observed phenomena where a presumed cause is thought to be *present.*

Let us now suppose that in our search for evidence to support (3) or (4) we conduct additional research, and discover:

13. In a sample of 500 nonsmokers, selected to be representative of both sexes, different ages, dietary habits, exercise patterns, and so on, none is observed to have cardiovascular disease.

This observation would further encourage us to believe that we had obtained significant additional confirmation of (3) or (4). Why? Because we now know that factors present (such as male sex, lack of exercise, family history of cardiovascular disease) in cases where the effect is absent (no cardiovascular disease observed) cannot be the cause. This is an example of **Mill's Method of Difference,** so called because the cause or causal factor of an effect must be *different* from whatever the factors are that are present when the effect is *absent.*

Suppose now that, increasingly confident we have found the cause of cardiovascular disease, we study our first sample of 230 smokers ill with the disease, and discover this:

14. Those who smoke two or more packs of cigarettes daily for ten or more years have cardiovascular disease either much younger or much more severely than those who smoke less.

This is an application of **Mill's Method of Concomitant Variation,** perhaps the most convincing of the three methods. Here we deal not merely with the presence of the conjectured cause (smoking) or the absence of the effect we are studying (cardiovascular disease), as we were previously, but with the more interesting and subtler matter of the *degree and regularity of the correlation* of the supposed cause and effect. According to the observations reported in (14), it strongly appears that the more we have of the "cause" (smoking) the sooner or the more intense the onset of the "effect" (cardiovascular disease).

Notice, however, what happens to our confirmation of (3) and (4) if, instead of the observation reported in (14), we had observed:

15. In a representative sample of 500 nonsmokers, cardiovascular disease was observed in 34 cases.

(Let us not pause here to explain what makes a sample more or less representative of a population, although the representativeness of samples is vital to all statistical reasoning.) Such an observation would lead us almost immediately to suspect some other or additional causal factor: Smoking might indeed be *a* factor in causing cardiovascular disease, but it can hardly be *the* cause, because (using Mill's Method of Difference) we cannot have the effect, as we do in the observed sample reported in (15), unless we also have the cause.

An observation such as the one in (15), however, is likely to lead us to think our hypothesis that *smoking causes cardiovascular disease* has been disconfirmed. But we have a fall-back position ready; we can still defend a weaker hypothesis, namely (4), *Smoking is a factor in the causation of cardiovascular disease in some persons.* Even if (3) stumbles over the evidence in (15), (4) does not. It is still quite possible that smoking is a factor in causing this disease, even if it is not the *only* factor—and if it is, then (4) is true.

Confirmation, Mechanism, and Theory

Notice that in the discussion so far, we have spoken of the *confirmation* of a hypothesis, such as our causal claim in (4), but not of its *verification.* (Similarly, we have imagined very different evidence, such as that stated in [15], leading us to speak of the *dis*confirmation of [3], though not of its *falsi*fication.) Confirmation (getting some evidence for) is weaker than verification (getting sufficient evidence to regard as true);

and our (imaginary) evidence so far in favor of (4) falls well short of conclusive support. Further research—the study of more representative or much larger samples, for example—might yield very different observations. It might lead us to conclude that although initial research had confirmed our hypothesis about smoking as the cause of cardiovascular disease, the additional information obtained subsequently disconfirmed the hypothesis. For most interesting hypotheses, both in detective stories and in modern science, there is both confirming and disconfirming evidence simultaneously. The challenge is to evaluate the hypothesis by considering such conflicting evidence.

As long as we confine our observations to *correlations* of the sort reported in our several (imaginary) observations, such as proposition (1), *230 smokers in a group of 500 have cardiovascular disease,* or (12), *230 smokers with the disease share no other suspected factors,* such as lack of exercise, any defense of a *causal* hypothesis such as claim (3), *Smoking causes cardiovascular disease,* or claim (4), *Smoking is a factor in causing the disease,* is not likely to convince the skeptic or lead those with beliefs alternative to (3) and (4) to abandon them and agree with us. Why is that? It is because a causal hypothesis without any account of the *underlying mechanism* by means of which the (alleged) cause produces the effect will seem superficial. Only when we can specify in detail *how* the (alleged) cause produces the effect will the causal hypothesis be convincing.

In other cases, in which no mechanism can be found, we seek instead to embed the causal hypothesis in a larger *theory,* one that rules out as incompatible any causal hypothesis except the favored one. (That is, we appeal to the test of consistency and thereby bring deductive reasoning to bear on our problem.) Thus, perhaps we cannot specify any mechanism—any underlying structure that generates a regular sequence of events, one of which is the effect we are studying—to explain why, for example, the gravitational mass of a body causes it to attract other bodies. But we can embed this claim in a larger body of physical theory that rules out as inconsistent any alternative causal explanation. To do that convincingly in regard to any given causal hypothesis, as this example suggests, requires detailed knowledge of the current state of the relevant body of scientific theory, something far beyond our aim or need to consider in further detail here.

FALLACIES

The straight road on which sound reasoning proceeds gives little latitude for cruising about. Irrationality, carelessness, passionate attachment to one's unexamined beliefs, and the sheer complexity of some issues, not to mention Original Sin, occasionally spoil the reasoning of even the best of us. Although in this book we reprint many varied voices and arguments, we hope we have reprinted no readings that exhibit the most flagrant errors or commit the graver abuses against the canons of good reasoning. Nevertheless, an inventory of those abuses and their close examination can be an instructive (as well as an amusing) exercise. Instructive, because the diagnosis and repair of error helps to fix more clearly the principles of sound reasoning on which such remedial labors depend. Amusing, because we are so constituted that our perception of the nonsense of others can stimulate our mind, warm our heart, and give us comforting feelings of superiority.

The discussion that follows, then, is a quick tour through the twisting lanes, mudflats, forests, and quicksands of the faults that one sometimes encounters in reading arguments that stray from the highway of clear thinking.

We can and do apply the term *fallacy* to many types of errors, mistakes, and confusions in oral and written discourse, in which our reasoning has gone awry. For convenience, we can group the fallacies by referring to the six aspects of reasoning identified in the Toulmin Method, described earlier (p. 251). Let us take up first those fallacies that spoil our *claims* or our *grounds* for them. These are errors in the meaning, clarity, or sense of a sentence, or of some word or phrase in a sentence, being used in the role of a claim or ground. They are thus not so much errors of *reasoning* as they are errors in *reasons* or in the *claims* that our reasons are intended to support or criticize.

Many Questions

The old saw, "Have you stopped beating your wife?" illustrates the **fallacy of many questions.** This question, as one can readily see, is unanswerable unless both of its implicit presuppositions are true. The questioner presupposes that (a) the addressee has or had a wife, and that (b) he used to beat her. If either of these presuppositions is false, then the question is pointless; it cannot be answered strictly and simply either with a yes or a no.

Ambiguity

Near the center of the town of Concord, Massachusetts, is an empty field with a sign reading "Old Calf Pasture." Hmm. A pasture in former times in which calves grazed? A pasture now in use for old calves? An erstwhile pasture for old calves? These alternative readings arise because of **ambiguity;** brevity in the sign has produced a group of words that give rise to more than one possible interpretation, confusing the reader and (presumably) frustrating the sign-writer's intentions.

Consider a more complex example. Suppose someone asserts *People have equal rights* and also *Everyone has a right to property*. Many people believe both these claims, but their combination involves an ambiguity. On one interpretation, the two claims entail that everyone has an *equal right* to property. (That is, you and I each have an equal right to whatever property we have.) But the two claims can also be interpreted to mean that everyone has a *right to equal property*. (That is, whatever property you have a right to, I have a right to the same, or at least equivalent, property.) The latter interpretation is radically revolutionary, whereas the former is not. Arguments over equal rights often involve this ambiguity.

Death by a Thousand Qualifications

In a letter of recommendation, sent in support of an applicant for a job on your newspaper, you find this sentence: "Young Smith was the best student I've ever taught in an English course." Pretty strong endorsement, you think, except that you do not know, because you have not been told, the letter writer is a very junior faculty member, has been teaching for only two years, is an instructor in the history department, and taught a section of freshman English as a courtesy for a sick colleague, and only eight students were enrolled in the course. Thanks to these implicit qualifications, the letter writer did not lie or exaggerate in his praise; but the effect of his sentence on you, the unwitting reader, is quite misleading. The explicit claim in the letter, and its impact on you, is quite different from the tacitly qualified claim in the mind of the writer.

Death by a thousand qualifications gets its name from the ancient torture of death by a thousand small cuts. Thus, a bold assertion can be virtually killed, its true content reduced to nothing, bit by bit, as all the appropriate or necessary qualifications are added to it. Consider another example. Suppose you hear a politician describing another country (let's call it Ruritania so as not to offend anyone) as a "democracy"—except it turns out that Ruritania doesn't have regular elections, lacks a written constitution, has no independent judiciary, prohibits religious worship except of the state-designated deity, and so forth. So what is left of the original claim that Ruritania is a democracy is little or nothing. The qualifications have taken all the content out of the original description.

Oversimplification

"Poverty causes crime," "Taxation is unfair," "Truth is stranger than fiction"—these are examples of generalizations that exaggerate and therefore oversimplify the truth. Poverty as such can't be the sole cause of crime, because many poor people do not break the law. Some taxes may be unfairly high, others unfairly low—but there is no reason to believe that *every* tax is unfair to all those who have to pay it. Some true stories do amaze us as much or more than some fictional stories, but the reverse is true, too. (In the language of the Toulmin Method, **oversimplification** is the result of a failure to use suitable modal qualifiers in formulating one's claims or grounds or backing.)

False Dichotomy

Sometimes oversimplification takes a more complex form, in which contrary possibilities are wrongly presented as though they were exhaustive and exclusive. "Either we get tough with drug users or we must surrender and legalize all drugs." Really? What about doing neither, and instead offering education and counseling, detoxification programs and incentives to "Say No"? A favorite of debaters, the either/or assertion always runs the risk of ignoring a third (or fourth) possibility. Some disjunctions are indeed exhaustive: "Either we get tough with drug users or we do not." This proposition, though vague (what does "get tough" really mean?), is a tautology; it cannot be false, and there is no third alternative. But most disjunctions do not express a pair of *contradictory* alternatives—they offer only a pair of *contrary* alternatives, and mere contraries do not exhaust the possibilities (recall our discussion of contraries versus contradictories, on pp. 269–70).

An example of **false dichotomy** can be found in the essay by Jeff Jacoby on flogging (p. 119). His entire discussion is built on the relative superiority of whipping over imprisonment, as though there was no alternative punishment worth considering. But of course there is, notably community service (especially for white-collar offenders, juveniles, and many first offenders).

Equivocation

In a delightful passage in Lewis Carroll's *Through the Looking Glass*, the king asks his messenger, "Who did you pass on the road?" and the messenger replies, "Nobody." This prompts the king to observe, "Of course, nobody walks slower than you," provoking the messenger's sullen response: "I do my best. I'm sure nobody walks much faster than I do." At this the king remarks with surprise, "He can't do that or else he'd have been here first!" (This, by the way, is the classic predecessor of the famous comic dialogue "Who's on First?" between the comedians Bud Abbott and Lou Costello.) The king and the messenger are equivocating on the term *nobody*. The messenger uses it in the normal way as an indefinite pronoun equivalent to "not anyone." But the king uses the word as though it were a proper noun, *Nobody*, the rather odd name of some person. No wonder the king and the messenger talk right past each other.

Equivocation (from the Latin for "equal voice," that is, giving utterance to two meanings at the same time in one word or phrase) can ruin otherwise good reasoning, as in this example: *Euthanasia is a good death; one dies a good death when one dies peacefully in old age; therefore euthanasia is dying peacefully in old age.* The etymology of *euthanasia* is literally "a good death," and so the first premise is true. And the second premise is certainly plausible. But the conclusion of this syllogism is false. Euthanasia cannot be defined as a peaceful death in one's old age, for two reasons. First, euthanasia requires the intervention of another person who kills someone (or lets the person die); second, even a very young person can be given euthanasia. The problem arises because "a good death" is used in the second premise in a manner that does not apply to euthanasia. Both meanings of "a good death" are legitimate, but when used together they constitute an equivocation that spoils the argument.

The fallacy of equivocation takes us from the discussion of confusions in individual claims or grounds to the more troublesome fallacies that infect the linkages between the claims we make and the grounds (or reasons) for them. These are the fallacies that occur in statements that, following the vocabulary of the Toulmin Method, are called the *warrant* of reasoning. Each fallacy is an example of reasoning that involves a **non sequitur** (Latin for "It does not follow"). That is, the *claim* (the conclusion) does not follow from the *grounds* (the premises).

For a start, here is an obvious *non sequitur:* "He went to the movies on three consecutive nights, so he must love movies." Why doesn't the claim ("he must love movies") follow from the grounds ("He went to the movies on three consecutive nights")? Perhaps the person was just fulfilling an assignment in a film course (maybe he even hated movies so much that he had postponed three assignments to see films, and now had to see them all in quick succession), or maybe he went with a girlfriend who was a movie buff, or maybe . . . , well, one can think of any number of other possible reasons.

Composition

Could an all-star team of professional basketball players beat the Boston Celtics in their heyday, say the team of 1985–1986? Perhaps in one game or two, but probably not in seven out of a dozen games in a row. As students of the game know, teamwork is an indispensable part of outstanding performance, and the 1985–1986 Celtics were famous for their self-sacrificing style of play.

The **fallacy of composition** can be convincingly illustrated, therefore, in this argument: *A team of five NBA all-stars is the best team in basketball if each of the five players is the best at his position.* The fallacy is called composition because the reasoning commits the error of arguing from the true premise that each member of a group has a certain property to the false conclusion that the group (the composition) itself has the property. (That is, because A is the best player at forward, B is the best center, and so on, therefore the team of A, B . . . is the best team.)

Division

In the Bible, we are told that the apostles of Jesus were twelve and that Matthew was an apostle. Does it follow that Matthew was twelve? No. To argue in this way from a property of a group to a property of a member of that group is to commit the **fallacy of division.** The example of the apostles may not be a very tempting instance of this error; here is a classic version that is a bit more interesting. If it is true that the average American family has 1.8 children, does it follow that your brother and sister-in-law are likely to have 1.8 children? If you think it does, you have committed the fallacy of division.

Poisoning the Well

During the 1970s some critics of the Equal Rights Amendment (ERA) argued against it by pointing out that Marx and Engels, in their *Communist Manifesto,* favored equality of women and men—and therefore the ERA is immoral, or undesirable, and perhaps even a communist plot. This kind of reasoning is an attempt to **poison the well;** that is, an attempt to shift attention from the merits of the argument—the validity of the reasoning, the truth of the claims—to the source or origin of the argument. Such criticism nicely deflects attention from the real issue; namely, whether the view in question is true and what the quality of evidence is in its support. The mere fact that Marx (or Hitler, for that matter) believed something does not show that the belief is false or immoral; just because some scoundrel believes the world is round, that is no reason for you to believe it is flat.

Ad Hominem

Closely allied to poisoning the well is another fallacy, **ad hominem** argument (from the Latin for "against the person"). Since arguments and theories are not natural occurrences but are the creative products of particular persons, a critic can easily yield to the temptation to attack an argument or theory by trying to impeach or undercut the credentials of its advocates.

The Genetic Fallacy

Another member of the family of related fallacies that includes poisoning the well and ad hominem is the **genetic fallacy.** Here the error takes the form of arguing against some claim by pointing out that its origin (genesis) is tainted or that it was invented by someone deserving our contempt. Thus, one might attack the ideas of the Declaration of Independence by pointing out that its principal author, Thomas Jefferson, was a slaveholder. Assuming that it is not anachronistic and inappropriate to criticize a public figure of two centuries ago for practicing slavery,

and conceding that slavery is morally outrageous, it is nonetheless fallacious to attack the ideas or even the sincerity of the Declaration by attempting to impeach the credentials of its author. Jefferson's moral faults
do not by themselves falsify, make improbable, or constitute counterevidence to the truth or other merits of the claims made in his writings. At
most, one's faults cast doubt on one's integrity or sincerity if one makes
claims at odds with one's practice.

The genetic fallacy can take other forms less closely allied to ad
hominem argument. For example, an opponent of the death penalty
might argue:

> Capital punishment arose in barbarous times; but we claim to be civi-
> lized; therefore we should discard this relic of the past.

Such reasoning shouldn't be persuasive, because the question of the
death penalty for our society must be decided by the degree to which it
serves our purposes—justice and defense against crime, presumably—
to which its historic origins are irrelevant. The practices of beer- and
wine-making are as old as human civilization, but their origin in antiquity is no reason to outlaw them in our time. The curious circumstances
in which something originates usually play no role whatever in its validity. Anyone who would argue that nothing good could possibly come
from molds and fungi is refuted by Sir Alexander Fleming's discovery of
penicillin in 1928.

Appeal to Authority

The example of Jefferson can be turned around to illustrate another
fallacy. One might easily imagine someone from the South in 1860 defending the slavocracy of that day by appealing to the fact that no less a
person than Jefferson—a brilliant public figure, thinker, and leader by
any measure—owned slaves. Or, today, one might defend capital punishment on the ground that Abraham Lincoln, surely one of the nation's
greatest presidents, signed many death warrants during the Civil War,
authorizing the execution of Union soldiers. No doubt the esteem in
which such figures as Jefferson and Lincoln are deservedly held amounts
to impressive endorsement for whatever acts and practices, policies and
institutions, they supported. But the **authority** of these figures in itself
is not *evidence* for the truth of their views, and so their authority cannot
be a reason for anyone to agree with them. Obviously, Jefferson and
Lincoln themselves could not support their beliefs by pointing to the fact
that they held them. Because their own authority is no reason for them
to believe what they believe, it is no reason for anyone else, either.

Sometimes the appeal to authority is fallacious because the authoritative person is not an expert on the issue in dispute. The fact that a
high-energy physicist has won the Nobel Prize is no reason for attaching
any special weight to her views on the causes of cancer, the reduction of

traffic accidents, or the legalization of marijuana. On the other hand, one would be well advised to attend to her views on the advisability of ballistic missile-defense systems. For there may be a connection between the kind of research for which she received the prize and the defense research projects.

All of us depend heavily on the knowledge of various experts and authorities, and so it ill-behooves us to ignore their views. Conversely, we should resist the temptation to accord their views on diverse subjects the same respect that we grant them in the area of their expertise.

The Slippery Slope

One of the most familiar arguments against any type of government regulation is that if it is allowed, then it will be just the first step down the path that leads to ruinous interference, overregulation, and totalitarian control. Fairly often we encounter this mode of argument in the public debates over handgun control, the censorship of pornography, and physician-assisted suicide. The argument is called the **slippery slope argument** (or the **wedge argument,** from the way we use the thin end of a wedge to split solid things apart; it is also called, rather colorfully, "letting the camel's nose under the tent"). The fallacy here is in implying that the first step necessarily leads to the second, and so on down the slope to disaster, when in fact there is no necessary slide from the first step to the second at all. (Would handgun registration lead to a police state? Well, it hasn't in Switzerland.) Sometimes the argument takes the form of claiming that a seemingly innocent or even attractive principle that is being applied in a given case (censorship of pornography, to avoid promoting sexual violence) requires one for the sake of consistency to apply the same principle in other cases, only with absurd and catastrophic results (censorship of everything in print, to avoid hurting anyone's feelings).

Here's an extreme example of this fallacy in action:

> Automobiles cause more deaths than handguns do. If you oppose handguns on the ground that doing so would save lives of the innocent, you'll soon find yourself wanting to outlaw the automobile.

Does opposition to handguns have this consequence? Not necessarily. Most people accept without dispute the right of society to regulate the operation of motor vehicles by requiring drivers to have a license, a greater restriction than many states impose on gun ownership. Besides, a gun is a lethal weapon designed to kill whereas an automobile or truck is a vehicle designed for transportation. Private ownership and use in both cases entail risks of death to the innocent. But there is no inconsistency in a society's refusal to tolerate this risk in the case of guns and its willingness to do so in the case of automobiles.

Closely related to the slippery slope is what lawyers call a **parade of horrors,** an array of examples of terrible consequences that will or might follow if we travel down a certain path. A good example appears in Justice William Brennan's opinion for the Supreme Court in *Texas v. Johnson* (p. 316), concerned with a Texas law against burning the American flag in political protest. If this law is allowed to stand, Brennan suggests, we may next find laws against burning the presidential seal, state flags, and the Constitution.

Appeal to Ignorance

In the controversy over the death penalty, the issues of deterrence and executing the innocent are bound to be raised. Because no one knows how many innocent persons have been convicted for murder and wrongfully executed, it is tempting for abolitionists to argue that the death penalty is too risky. It is equally tempting for the proponent of the death penalty to argue that since no one knows how many people have been deterred from murder by the threat of execution, we abolish it at our peril.

Each of these arguments suffers from the same flaw: the **fallacy of appeal to ignorance.** Each argument invites the audience to draw an inference from a premise that is unquestionably true—but what is that premise? It asserts that there is something "we don't know." But what we *don't* know cannot be *evidence* for (or against) anything. Our ignorance is no reason for believing anything, except perhaps that we ought to try to undertake an appropriate investigation in order to reduce our ignorance and replace it with reliable information.

Begging the Question

The argument we have just considered also illustrates another fallacy. From the fact that you were not murdered yesterday, we cannot infer that the death penalty was a deterrent. Yet it is tempting to make this inference, perhaps because—all unawares—we are relying on the **fallacy of begging the question.** If someone tacitly assumes from the start that the death penalty is an effective deterrent, then the fact that you weren't murdered yesterday certainly looks like evidence for the truth of that assumption. But it isn't, so long as there are competing but unexamined alternative explanations, as in this case. (The fallacy is called "begging the question," *petitio principii* in Latin, because the conclusion of the argument is hidden among its assumptions—and so the conclusion, not surprisingly, follows from the premises.)

Of course, the fact that you weren't murdered is *consistent* with the claim that the death penalty is an effective deterrent, just as someone else's being murdered is also consistent with that claim (for an effective deterrent need not be a *perfect* deterrent). In general, from the fact that two propositions are consistent with each other, we cannot infer that either is evidence for the other.

False Analogy

Argument by analogy, as we have pointed out in Chapter 3, and as many of the selections in this book show, is a familiar and even indispensable mode of argument. But it can be treacherous, because it runs the risk of the **fallacy of false analogy.** Unfortunately, we have no simple or foolproof way of distinguishing between the useful and legitimate analogies, and the others. The key question to ask yourself is this: Do the two things put into analogy differ in any essential and relevant respect, or are they different only in unimportant and irrelevant aspects?

In a famous example from his discussion in support of suicide, philosopher David Hume rhetorically asked: "It would be no crime in me to divert the Nile or Danube from its course, were I able to effect such purposes. Where then is the crime of turning a few ounces of blood from their natural channel?" This is a striking analogy, except that it rests on a false assumption. No one has the right to divert the Nile or the Danube or any other major international watercourse; it would be a catastrophic crime to do so without the full consent of people living in the region, their government, and so forth. Therefore, arguing by analogy, one might well say that no one has the right to take his or her own life, either. Thus, Hume's own analogy can be used to argue against his thesis that suicide is no crime. But let us ignore the way in which his example can be turned against him. The analogy is a terrible one in any case. Isn't it obvious that the Nile, whatever its exact course, would continue to nourish Egypt and the Sudan, whereas the blood flowing out of someone's veins will soon leave that person dead? The fact that the blood is the same blood, whether in one's body or in a pool on the floor (just as the water of the Nile is the same body of water whatever path it follows to the sea) is, of course, irrelevant to the question of whether one has the right to commit suicide.

Let us look at a more complex example. During the 1960s, when the nation was convulsed over the purpose and scope of our military involvement in Southeast Asia, advocates of more vigorous United States military participation appealed to the so-called domino effect, supposedly inspired by a passing remark from President Eisenhower in the 1950s. The analogy refers to the way in which a row of standing dominoes will collapse, one after the other, if the first one is pushed. If Vietnam turns communist, according to this analogy, so too will its neighbors, Laos and Cambodia, followed by Thailand and then Burma, until the whole region is as communist as China to the north. The domino analogy (or metaphor) provided, no doubt, a vivid illustration, and effectively portrayed the worry of many anticommunists. But did it really shed any light on the likely pattern of political and military developments in the region? The history of events there during the 1970s and 1980s did not bear out the domino analogy.

Post Hoc Ergo Propter Hoc

One of the most tempting errors in reasoning is to ground a claim about causation on an observed temporal sequence; that is, to argue "after this therefore because of this" (which is what the phrase **post hoc ergo propter hoc** means in Latin). About thirty-five years ago, when the medical community first announced that smoking tobacco caused lung cancer, advocates for the tobacco industry replied that the doctors were guilty of this fallacy.

These industry advocates argued the medical researchers had merely noticed that in some people, lung cancer developed *after* considerable smoking, indeed, years after; but (they insisted) this correlation was not at all the same as a causal relation between smoking and lung cancer. True enough. The claim that A *causes* B is not the same as the claim that B comes after A. After all, it was possible that smokers as a group had some other common trait and that this factor was the true cause of their cancer.

As the long controversy over the truth about the causation of lung cancer shows, to avoid the appearance of fallacious *post hoc* reasoning one needs to find some way to link the observed phenomena (the correlation of smoking and the onset of lung cancer). This step requires some further theory, and preferably some experimental evidence for the exact sequence or physical mechanism, in full detail, of how ingestion of tobacco smoke is a crucial factor—and is not merely an accidental or happenstance prior event—in the subsequent development of the cancer.

Protecting the Hypothesis

In Chapter 3, we contrast *reasoning* and *rationalization* (or the finding of bad reasons for what one intends to believe anyway). Rationalization can take subtle forms, as the following example indicates. Suppose you're standing with a friend on the shore or on a pier, and you watch as a ship heads out to sea. As it reaches the horizon, it slowly disappears—first the hull, then the upper decks, and finally the tip of the mast. Because the ship (you both assume) isn't sinking, it occurs to you that you have in this sequence of observations convincing evidence that the earth's surface is curved. Nonsense, says your companion. Light waves sag, or bend down, over distances of a few miles, and so a flat surface (such as the ocean) can intercept them. Hence the ship, which appears to be going "over" the horizon, really isn't—it's just moving steadily farther and farther away in a straight line. Your friend, you discover to your amazement, is a card-carrying member of the Flat Earth Society (yes, there really is such an organization). Now most of us would regard the idea that light rays bend down in the manner required by the Flat Earther's argument as a rationalization whose sole purpose is to protect the flat-earth doctrine against counterevidence. We would be convinced it was a rationalization, and not a very good one at that, if the Flat Earther held to it despite a patient and thorough explanation from a physicist that showed modern optical theory to be quite incompatible with the view that light waves sag.

This example illustrates two important points about the *backing* of arguments. First, it is always possible to protect a hypothesis by abandoning adjacent or connected hypotheses; this is the tactic our Flat Earth friend has used. This maneuver is possible, however, only because—and this is the second point—whenever we test a hypothesis, we do so by taking for granted (usually quite unconsciously) many other hypotheses as well. So the evidence for the hypothesis we think we are confirming is impossible to separate entirely from the adequacy of the connected hypotheses. As long as we have no reason to doubt that light rays travel in straight lines (at least over distances of a few miles), our Flat Earth friend's argument is unconvincing. But once that hypothesis is itself put in doubt, the idea that looked at first to be a pathetic rationalization takes on an even more troublesome character.

There are, then, not one but two fallacies exposed by this example. The first and perhaps graver is in rigging your hypothesis so that *no matter what* observations are brought against it, you will count nothing as falsifying it. The second and subtler is in thinking that as you test one hypothesis, all of your other background beliefs are left safely to one side, immaculate and uninvolved. On the contrary, our beliefs form a corporate structure, intertwined and connected to each other with great complexity, and no one of them can ever be singled out for unique and isolated application, confirmation, or disconfirmation, to the world around us.

A CHECKLIST FOR EVALUATING AN ARGUMENT FROM A LOGICAL POINT OF VIEW

✓ Is the argument purely deductive, purely inductive, or a mixture of the two?

✓ If it is deductive, is it valid?

✓ If it is valid, are all its premises and assumptions true?

✓ If it is not valid, what fallacy does it commit?

✓ If it is not valid, are the claims at least consistent with each other?

✓ If it is not valid, can you think of additional assumptions that would make it valid?

✓ If the argument is inductive, on what observations is it based?

✓ If the argument is inductive, how probable are its premises and its conclusion?

✓ In any case, can you think of evidence that would further confirm the conclusion? Disconfirm the conclusion?

Max Shulman

Having read about proper and improper arguments, you are now well equipped to read a short story on the topic.

Max Shulman (1919–1988) began his career as a writer when he was a journalism student at the University of Minnesota. Later he wrote humorous novels, stories, and plays. One of his novels, Barefoot Boy with Cheek *(1943), was made into a musical and another,* Rally Round the Flag, Boys! *(1957), was made into a film starring Paul Newman and Joanne Woodward.* The Tender Trap *(1954), a play he wrote with Robert Paul Smith, still retains its popularity with theater groups.*

"Love Is a Fallacy" was first published in 1951, when demeaning stereotypes about women and minorities were widely accepted in the marketplace as well as the home. Thus, jokes about domineering mothers-in-law or about dumb blondes routinely met with no objection.

Love Is a Fallacy

Cool was I and logical. Keen, calculating, perspicacious, acute, and astute—I was all of these. My brain was as powerful as a dynamo, as precise as a chemist's scales, as penetrating as a scalpel. And—think of it!—I was only eighteen.

It is not often that one so young has such a giant intellect. Take, for example, Petey Bellows, my roommate at the university. Same age, same background, but dumb as an ox. A nice enough fellow, you understand, but nothing upstairs. Emotional type. Unstable. Impressionable. Worst of all, a faddist. Fads, I submit, are the very negation of reason. To be swept up in every new craze that comes along, to surrender yourself to idiocy just because everybody else is doing it—this, to me, is the acme of mindlessness. Not, however, to Petey.

One afternoon I found Petey lying on his bed with an expression of such distress on his face that I immediately diagnosed appendicitis. "Don't move," I said. "Don't take a laxative. I'll call a doctor."

"Raccoon," he mumbled thickly.

"Raccoon?" I said, pausing in my flight.   5

"I want a raccoon coat," he wailed.

I perceived that his trouble was not physical, but mental. "Why do you want a raccoon coat?"

"I should have known it," he cried, pounding his temples. "I should have known they'd come back when the Charleston came back. Like a fool I spent all my money for textbooks, and now I can't get a raccoon coat."

"Can you mean," I said incredulously, "that people are actually wearing raccoon coats again?"

"All the Big Men on Campus are wearing them. Where've you 10 been?"

"In the library," I said, naming a place not frequented by Big Men on Campus.

He leaped from the bed and paced the room. "I've got to have a raccoon coat," he said passionately. "I've got to!"

"Petey, why? Look at it rationally. Raccoon coats are unsanitary. They shed. They smell bad. They weigh too much. They're unsightly. They——"

"You don't understand," he interrupted impatiently. "It's the thing to do. Don't you want to be in the swim?"

"No," I said truthfully.   15

"Well, I do," he declared. "I'd give anything for a raccoon coat. Anything!"

My brain, that precision instrument, slipped into high gear. "Anything?" I asked, looking at him narrowly.

"Anything," he affirmed in ringing tones.

I stroked my chin thoughtfully. It so happened that I knew where to get my hands on a raccoon coat. My father had had one in his undergraduate days; it lay now in a trunk in the attic back home. It also happened that Petey had something I wanted. He didn't *have* it exactly, but at least he had first rights on it. I refer to his girl, Polly Espy.

I had long coveted Polly Espy. Let me emphasize that my desire for   20
this young woman was not emotional in nature. She was, to be sure, a girl who excited the emotions, but I was not one to let my heart rule my head. I wanted Polly for a shrewdly calculated, entirely cerebral reason.

I was a freshman in law school. In a few years I would be out in practice. I was well aware of the importance of the right kind of wife in furthering a lawyer's career. The successful lawyers I had observed were, almost without exception, married to beautiful, gracious, intelligent women. With one omission, Polly fitted these specifications perfectly.

Beautiful she was. She was not yet of pin-up proportions, but I felt sure that time would supply the lack. She already had the makings.

Gracious she was. By gracious I mean full of graces. She had an erectness of carriage, an ease of bearing, a poise that clearly indicated the best of breeding. At table her manners were exquisite. I had seen her at the Kozy Kampus Korner eating the specialty of the house—a sandwich that contained scraps of pot roast, gravy, chopped nuts, and a dipper of sauerkraut—without even getting her fingers moist.

Intelligent she was not. In fact, she veered in the opposite direction. But I believed that under my guidance she would smarten up. At any rate, it was worth a try. It is, after all, easier to make a beautiful dumb girl smart than to make an ugly smart girl beautiful.

"Petey," I said, "are you in love with Polly Espy?"   25

"I think she's a keen kid," he replied, "but I don't know if you'd call it love. Why?"

"Do you," I asked, "have any kind of formal arrangement with her? I mean are you going steady or anything like that?"

"No. We see each other quite a bit, but we both have other dates. Why?"

"Is there," I asked, "any other man for whom she has a particular fondness?"

"Not that I know of. Why?"   30

I nodded with satisfaction. "In other words, if you were out of the picture, the field would be open. Is that right?"

"I guess so. What are you getting at?"

"Nothing, nothing," I said innocently, and took my suitcase out of the closet.

"Where you going?" asked Petey.

"Home for the week end." I threw a few things into the bag.   35

"Listen," he said, clutching my arm eagerly, "while you're home, you couldn't get some money from your old man, could you, and lend it to me so I can buy a raccoon coat?"

"I may do better than that," I said with a mysterious wink and closed my bag and left.

"Look," I said to Petey when I got back Monday morning. I threw open the suitcase and revealed the huge, hairy, gamy object that my father had worn in his Stutz Bearcat in 1925.

"Holy Toledo!" said Petey reverently. He plunged his hands into the raccoon coat and then his face. "Holy Toledo!" he repeated fifteen or twenty times.

"Would you like it?" I asked.   40

"Oh yes!" he cried, clutching the greasy pelt to him. Then a canny look came into his eyes. "What do you want for it?"

"Your girl," I said, mincing no words.

"Polly?" he said in a horrified whisper. "You want Polly?"

"That's right."

He flung the coat from him. "Never," he said stoutly.   45

I shrugged. "Okay. If you don't want to be in the swim, I guess it's your business."

I sat down in a chair and pretended to read a book, but out of the corner of my eye I kept watching Petey. He was a torn man. First he looked at the coat with the expression of a waif at a bakery window. Then he turned away and set his jaw resolutely. Then he looked back at the coat, with even more longing in his face. Then he turned away, but with not so much resolution this time. Back and forth his head swiveled, desire waxing, resolution waning. Finally he didn't turn away at all; he just stood and stared with mad lust at the coat.

"It isn't as though I was in love with Polly," he said thickly. "Or going steady or anything like that."

"That's right," I murmured.

"What's Polly to me, or me to Polly?"   50

"Not a thing," said I.

"It's just been a casual kick—just a few laughs, that's all."

"Try on the coat," said I.

He complied. The coat bunched high over his ears and dropped all the way down to his shoe tops. He looked like a mound of dead raccoons. "Fits fine," he said happily.

I rose from my chair. "Is it a deal?" I asked, extending my hand. 55

He swallowed. "It's a deal," he said and shook my hand.

I had my first date with Polly the following evening. This was in the nature of a survey; I wanted to find out just how much work I had to do to get her mind up to the standard I required. I took her first to dinner. "Gee, that was a delish dinner," she said as we left the restaurant. Then I took her to a movie. "Gee, that was a marvy movie," she said as we left the theater. And then I took her home. "Gee, I had a sensaysh time," she said as she bade me good night.

I went back to my room with a heavy heart. I had gravely underestimated the size of my task. This girl's lack of information was terrifying. Nor would it be enough merely to supply her with information. First she had to be taught to *think*. This loomed as a project of no small dimensions, and at first I was tempted to give her back to Petey. But then I got to thinking about her abundant physical charms and about the way she entered a room and the way she handled a knife and fork, and I decided to make an effort.

I went about it, as in all things, systematically. I gave her a course in logic. It happened that I, as a law student, was taking a course in logic myself, so I had all the facts at my fingertips. "Polly," I said to her when I picked her up on our next date, "tonight we are going over to the Knoll and talk."

"Oo, terrif," she replied. One thing I will say for this girl: You would 60 go far to find another so agreeable.

We went to the Knoll, the campus trysting place, and we sat down under an old oak, and she looked at me expectantly: "What are we going to talk about?" she asked.

"Logic."

She thought this over for a minute and decided she liked it. "Magnif," she said.

"Logic," I said, clearing my throat, "is the science of thinking. Before we can think correctly, we must first learn to recognize the common fallacies of logic. These we will take up tonight."

"Wow-dow!" she cried, clapping her hands delightedly. 65

I winced, but went bravely on. "First let us examine the fallacy called Dicto Simpliciter."

"By all means," she urged, batting her lashes eagerly.

"Dicto Simpliciter means an argument based on an unqualified generalization. For example: Exercise is good. Therefore everybody should exercise."

"I agree," said Polly earnestly. "I mean exercise is wonderful. I mean it builds the body and everything."

"Polly," I said gently, "the argument is a fallacy. *Exercise is good* is an 70 unqualified generalization. For instance, if you have heart disease, exercise is bad, not good. Many people are ordered by their doctors *not* to exercise. You must *qualify* the generalization. You must say exercise is *usually* good, or exercise is good *for most people.* Otherwise you have committed a Dicto Simpliciter. Do you see?"

"No," she confessed. "But this is marvy. Do more! Do more!"

"It will be better if you stop tugging at my sleeve," I told her, and when she desisted, I continued. "Next we take up a fallacy called Hasty Generalization. Listen carefully: You can't speak French. I can't speak French. Petey Bellows can't speak French. I must therefore conclude that nobody at the University of Minnesota can speak French."

"Really?" said Polly, amazed. "*Nobody?*"

I hid my exasperation. "Polly, it's a fallacy. The generalization is reached too hastily. There are too few instances to support such a conclusion."

"Know any more fallacies?" she asked breathlessly. "This is more fun 75 than dancing even."

I fought off a wave of despair. I was getting nowhere with this girl, absolutely nowhere. Still, I am nothing if not persistent. I continued. "Next comes Post Hoc. Listen to this: Let's not take Bill on our picnic. Every time we take him out with us, it rains."

"I know somebody just like that," she exclaimed. "A girl back home—Eula Becker, her name is. It never fails. Every single time we take her on a picnic——"

"Polly," I said sharply, "it's a fallacy. Eula Becker doesn't *cause* the rain. She has no connection with the rain. You are guilty of Post Hoc if you blame Eula Becker."

"I'll never do it again," she promised contritely. "Are you mad at me?"

I sighed. "No, Polly, I'm not mad." 80

"Then tell me some more fallacies."

"All right. Let's try Contradictory Premises."

"Yes, let's," she chirped, blinking her eyes happily.

I frowned, but plunged ahead. "Here's an example of Contradictory Premises: If God can do anything, can He make a stone so heavy that He won't be able to lift it?"

"Of course," she replied promptly. 85

"But if He can do anything, He can lift the stone," I pointed out.

"Yeah," she said thoughtfully. "Well, then I guess He can't make the stone."

"But He can do anything," I reminded her.

She scratched her pretty, empty head. "I'm all confused," she admitted.

"Of course you are. Because when the premises of an argument con- 90 tradict each other, there can be no argument. If there is an irresistible force, there can be no immovable object. If there is an immovable object, there can be no irresistible force. Get it?"

"Tell me some more of this keen stuff," she said eagerly.

I consulted my watch. "I think we'd better call it a night. I'll take you home now, and you go over all the things you've learned. We'll have another session tomorrow night."

I deposited her at the girl's dormitory, where she assured me that she had had a perfectly terrif evening, and I went glumly home to my room. Petey lay snoring in his bed, the raccoon coat huddled like a great hairy beast at his feet. For a moment I considered waking him and telling him that he could have his girl back. It seemed clear that my project was doomed to failure. The girl simply had a logic-proof head.

But then I reconsidered. I had wasted one evening; I might as well waste another. Who knew? Maybe somewhere in the extinct crater of her mind a few embers still smoldered. Maybe somehow I could fan them into flame. Admittedly it was not a prospect fraught with hope, but I decided to give it one more try.

Seated under the oak the next evening I said, "Our first fallacy 95 tonight is called Ad Misericordiam."

She quivered with delight.

"Listen closely," I said. "A man applies for a job. When the boss asks him what his qualifications are, he replies that he has a wife and six children at home, the wife is a helpless cripple, the children have nothing to eat, no clothes to wear, no shoes on their feet, there are no beds in the house, no coal in the cellar, and winter is coming."

A tear rolled down each of Polly's pink cheeks. "Oh, this is awful, awful," she sobbed.

"Yes, it's awful," I agreed, "but it's no argument. The man never answered the boss's question about his qualifications. Instead he appealed to the boss's sympathy. He committed the fallacy of Ad Misericordiam. Do you understand?"

"Have you got a handkerchief?" she blubbered.   100

I handed her a handkerchief and tried to keep from screaming while she wiped her eyes. "Next," I said in a carefully controlled tone, "we will discuss False Analogy. Here is an example: Students should be allowed to look at their textbooks during examinations. After all, surgeons have X rays to guide them during an operation, lawyers have briefs to guide them during a trial, carpenters have blueprints to guide them when they are building a house. Why, then, shouldn't students be allowed to look at their textbooks during an examination?"

"There now," she said enthusiastically, "is the most marvy idea I've heard in years."

"Polly," I said testily, "the argument is all wrong. Doctors, lawyers, and carpenters aren't taking a test to see how much they have learned, but students are. The situations are altogether different, and you can't make an analogy between them."

"I still think it's a good idea," said Polly.

"Nuts," I muttered. Doggedly I pressed on. "Next we'll try Hypothe- 105 sis Contrary to Fact."

"Sounds yummy," was Polly's reaction.

"Listen: If Madame Curie had not happened to leave a photographic plate in a drawer with a chunk of pitchblende, the world today would not know about radium."

"True, true," said Polly, nodding her head. "Did you see the movie? Oh, it just knocked me out. That Walter Pidgeon is so dreamy. I mean he fractures me."

"If you can forget Mr. Pidgeon for a moment," I said coldly, "I would like to point out that the statement is a fallacy. Maybe Madame Curie would have discovered radium at some later date. Maybe somebody else would have discovered it. Maybe any number of things would have happened. You can't start with a hypothesis that is not true and then draw any supportable conclusions from it."

"They ought to put Walter Pidgeon in more pictures," said Polly. "I 110 hardly ever see him any more."

One more chance, I decided. But just one more. There is a limit to what flesh and blood can bear. "The next fallacy is called Poisoning the Well."

"How cute!" she gurgled.

"Two men are having a debate. The first one gets up and says, 'My opponent is a notorious liar. You can't believe a word that he is going to say.' . . . Now, Polly, think. Think hard. What's wrong?"

I watched her closely as she knit her creamy brow in concentration. Suddenly a glimmer of intelligence—the first I had seen—came into her eyes. "It's not fair," she said with indignation. "It's not a bit fair. What chance has the second man got if the first man calls him a liar before he even begins talking?"

"Right!" I cried exultantly. "One hundred percent right. It's not fair. 115 The first man has *poisoned the well* before anybody could drink from it. He has hamstrung his opponent before he could even start. . . . Polly, I'm proud of you."

"Pshaw," she murmured, blushing with pleasure.

"You see, my dear, these things aren't so hard. All you have to do is concentrate. Think—examine—evaluate. Come now, let's review everything we have learned."

"Fire away," she said with an airy wave of her hand.

Heartened by the knowledge that Polly was not altogether a cretin, I began a long, patient review of all I had told her. Over and over and over again I cited instances, pointed out flaws, kept hammering away without letup. It was like digging a tunnel. At first everything was work, sweat, and darkness. I had no idea when I would reach the light, or even *if* I would. But I persisted. I pounded and clawed and scraped, and finally I was rewarded. I saw a chink of light. And then the chink got bigger and the sun came pouring in and all was bright.

Five grueling nights this took, but it was worth it. I had made a logi- 120 cian out of Polly; I had taught her to think. My job was done. She was worthy of me at last. She was a fit wife for me, a proper hostess for my many mansions, a suitable mother for my well-heeled children.

It must not be thought that I was without love for this girl. Quite the contrary. Just as Pygmalion loved the perfect woman he had fashioned, so I loved mine. I decided to acquaint her with my feelings at our very next meeting. The time had come to change our relationship from academic to romantic.

"Polly," I said when next we sat beneath our oak, "tonight we will not discuss fallacies."

"Aw, gee," she said, disappointed.

"My dear," I said, favoring her with a smile, "we have now spent five evenings together. We have gotten along splendidly. It is clear that we are well matched."

"Hasty Generalization," said Polly brightly.   125

"I beg your pardon," said I.

"Hasty Generalization," she repeated. "How can you say that we are well matched on the basis of only five dates?"

I chuckled with amusement. The dear child had learned her lessons well. "My dear," I said, patting her hand in a tolerant manner, "five dates is plenty. After all, you don't have to eat a whole cake to know that it's good."

"False Analogy," said Polly promptly. "I'm not a cake. I'm a girl."

I chuckled with somewhat less amusement. The dear child had 130 learned her lesson perhaps too well. I decided to change tactics. Obviously the best approach was a simple, strong, direct declaration of love. I paused for a moment while my massive brain chose the proper words. Then I began:

"Polly, I love you. You are the whole world to me, and the moon and the stars and the constellations of outer space. Please, my darling, say that you will go steady with me, for if you will not, life will be meaningless. I will languish. I will refuse my meals. I will wander the face of the earth, a shambling, hollow-eyed hulk."

There, I thought, folding my arms, that ought to do it.

"Ad Misericordiam," said Polly.

I ground my teeth. I was not Pygmalion; I was Frankenstein, and my monster had me by the throat. Frantically I fought back the tide of panic surging through me. At all costs I had to keep cool.

"Well, Polly," I said, forcing a smile, "you certainly have learned 135 your fallacies."

"You're darn right," she said with a vigorous nod.

"And who taught them to you, Polly?"

"You did."

"That's right. So you do owe me something, don't you, my dear? If I hadn't come along you never would have learned about fallacies."

"Hypothesis Contrary to Fact," she said instantly.   140

I dashed perspiration from my brow. "Polly," I croaked, "You mustn't take all these things so literally. I mean this is just classroom stuff. You know that the things you learn in school don't have anything to do with life."

"Dicto Simpliciter," she said, wagging her finger at me playfully.

That did it. I leaped to my feet, bellowing like a bull. "Will you or will you not go steady with me?"

"I will not," she replied.

"Why not?" I demanded.   145

"Because this afternoon I promised Petey Bellows that I would go steady with him."

I reeled back, overcome with the infamy of it. After he promised, after he made a deal, after he shook my hand! "That rat!" I shrieked, kicking up great chunks of turf. "You can't go with him, Polly. He's a liar. He's a cheat. He's a rat."

"Poisoning the Well," said Polly, "and stop shouting. I think shouting must be a fallacy too."

With an immense effort of will, I modulated my voice. "All right," I said. "You're a logician. Let's look at this thing logically. How could you choose Petey Bellows over me? Look at me—a brilliant student, a tremendous intellectual, a man with an assured future. Look at Petey—a knothead, a jitterbug, a guy who'll never know where his next meal is coming from. Can you give me one logical reason why you should go steady with Petey Bellows?"

"I certainly can," declared Polly. "He's got a raccoon coat."   150

Topic for Critical Thinking and Writing

After you have finished reading "Love Is a Fallacy," you may want to write an argumentative essay of 500–750 words on one of the following topics: (1) the story, rightly understood, is not antiwoman; (2) if the story is anti-woman, it is equally antiman; (3) the story is antiwoman but nevertheless belongs in this book; or (4) the story is antiwoman and does not belong in the book.

9

A Psychologist's View: Rogerian Argument

Carl R. Rogers (1902–1987), perhaps best known for his book entitled *On Becoming a Person* (1961), was a psychotherapist, not a teacher of writing. This short essay by Rogers has, however, exerted much influence on instructors who teach argument. Written in the 1950s, this essay reflects the political climate of the cold war between the United States and the USSR, which dominated headlines for more than forty years (1947–1989). Several of Rogers's examples of bias and frustrated communication allude to the tensions of that era.

On the surface, many arguments seem to show A arguing with B, presumably seeking to change B's mind; but A's argument is really directed not to B but to C. This attempt to persuade a nonparticipant is evident in the courtroom, where neither the prosecutor (A) nor the defense lawyer (B) is really trying to convince the opponent. Rather, both are trying to convince a third party, the jury (C). Prosecutors do not care whether they convince defense lawyers; they don't even mind infuriating defense lawyers, because their only real goal is to convince the jury. Similarly, the writer of a letter to a newspaper, taking issue with an editorial, does not expect to change the paper's policy. Rather, the writer hopes to convince a third party, the reader of the newspaper.

But suppose A really does want to bring B around to A's point of view. Suppose Mary really wants to persuade the teacher to allow her little lamb to stay in the classroom. Rogers points out that when we engage in an argument, if we feel our integrity or our identity is threatened, we will stiffen our position. (The teacher may feel that his or her dignity is compromised by the presence of the lamb, and will scarcely attend to Mary's argument.) The sense of threat may be so great that we are unable to consider the alternative views being offered, and we therefore remain unpersuaded. Threatened, we may defend ourselves rather than our argument, and little communication takes place. Of course a third party might say that we or our opponent presented the more convincing case, but we, and perhaps the opponent, have scarcely listened to each other, and so the two of us remain apart.

Rogers suggests, therefore, that a writer who wishes to communicate with someone (as opposed to convincing a third party) needs to reduce the threat. In a sense, the participants in the argument need to become partners rather than adversaries. Rogers writes, "Mutual communication tends to be pointed toward solving a problem rather than toward attacking a person or group." Thus, an essay on whether schools should test students for use of drugs, need not—and probably should not—see the issue as black or white, *either/or*. Such an essay might indicate that testing is undesirable because it may have bad effects, *but in some circumstances* it may be acceptable. This qualification does not mean that one must compromise. Thus, the essayist might argue that the potential danger to liberty is so great that no circumstances justify testing students for drugs. But even such an essayist should recognize the merit (however limited) of the opposition, and should grant that the position being advanced itself entails great difficulties and dangers.

A writer who wishes to reduce the psychological threat to the opposition, and thus facilitate the partnership in the study of some issue, can do several things: One can show sympathetic understanding of the opposing argument; one can recognize what is valid in it; and one can recognize and demonstrate that those who take the other side are nonetheless persons of goodwill.

Thus a writer who takes Rogers seriously will, usually, in the first part of an argumentative essay

1. state the problem,
2. give the opponent's position, and
3. grant whatever validity the writer finds in that position—for instance, will recognize the circumstances in which the position would indeed be acceptable.

Next, the writer will, if possible,

4. attempt to show how the opposing position will be improved if the writer's own position is accepted.

Sometimes, of course, the differing positions may be so far apart that no reconciliation can be proposed, in which case the writer will probably seek to show how the problem can best be solved by adopting the writer's own position. We have discussed these matters in Chapter 5, but not from the point of view of a psychotherapist, and so we reprint Rogers's essay here.

Carl R. Rogers

Communication: Its Blocking and Its Facilitation

It may seem curious that a person whose whole professional effort is devoted to psychotherapy should be interested in problems of communication. What relationship is there between providing therapeutic help to individuals with emotional maladjustments and the concern of this conference with obstacles to communication? Actually the relationship is very close indeed. The whole task of psychotherapy is the task of dealing with a failure in communication. The emotionally maladjusted person, the "neurotic," is in difficulty first because communication within himself has broken down, and second because as a result of this his communication with others has been damaged. If this sounds somewhat strange, then let me put it in other terms. In the "neurotic" individual, parts of himself which have been termed unconscious, or repressed, or denied to awareness, become blocked off so that they no longer communicate themselves to the conscious or managing part of himself. As long as this is true, there are distortions in the way he communicates himself to others, and so he suffers both within himself, and in his interpersonal relations. The task of psychotherapy is to help the person achieve, through a special relationship with a therapist, good communication within himself. Once this is achieved he can communicate more freely and more effectively with others. We may say then that psychotherapy is good communication, within and between men. We may also turn that statement around and it will still be true. Good communication, free communication, within or between men, is always therapeutic.

It is, then, from a background of experience with communication in counseling and psychotherapy that I want to present here two ideas. I wish to state what I believe is one of the major factors in blocking or impeding communication, and then I wish to present what in our experience has proven to be a very important way to improving or facilitating communication.

I would like to propose, as an hypothesis for consideration, that the major barrier to mutual interpersonal communication is our very natural tendency to judge, to evaluate, to approve or disapprove, the statement of the person, or the other group. Let me illustrate my meaning with some very simple examples. As you leave the meeting tonight, one of the statements you are likely to hear is, "I didn't like that man's talk." Now what do you respond? Almost invariably your reply will be either approval or disapproval of the attitude expressed. Either you respond, "I didn't either. I thought it was terrible," or else you tend to reply, "Oh, I thought it was really good." In other words, your primary reaction is to evaluate what has just been said to you, to evaluate it from *your* point of view, your own frame of reference.

Or take another example. Suppose I say with some feeling, "I think the Republicans are behaving in ways that show a lot of good sound sense these days," what is the response that arises in your mind as you listen? The overwhelming likelihood is that it will be evaluative. You will find yourself agreeing, or disagreeing, or making some judgment about me such as "He must be a conservative," or "He seems solid in his thinking." Or let us take an illustration from the international scene. Russia says vehemently, "The treaty with Japan is a war plot on the part of the United States." We rise as one person to say "That's a lie!"

This last illustration brings in another element connected with my   5
hypothesis. Although the tendency to make evaluations is common in almost all interchange of language, it is very much heightened in those situations where feelings and emotions are deeply involved. So the stronger our feelings, the more likely it is that there will be no mutual element in the communication. There will be just two ideas, two feelings, two judgments, missing each other in psychological space. I'm sure you recognize this from your own experience. When you have not been emotionally involved yourself, and have listened to a heated discussion, you often go away thinking, "Well, they actually weren't talking about the same thing." And they were not. Each was making a judgment, an evaluation, from his own frame of reference. There was really nothing which could be called communication in any genuine sense. This tendency to react to any emotionally meaningful statement by forming an evaluation of it from our own point of view, is, I repeat, the major barrier to interpersonal communication.

But is there any way of solving this problem, of avoiding this barrier? I feel that we are making exciting progress toward this goal and I would like to present it as simply as I can. Real communication occurs, and this evaluative tendency is avoided, when we listen with understanding. What does that mean? It means *to see the expressed idea and attitude from the other person's point of view, to sense how it feels to him, to achieve his frame of reference in regard to the thing he is talking about.*

Stated so briefly, this may sound absurdly simple, but it is not. It is an approach which we have found extremely potent in the field of psychotherapy. It is the most effective agent we know for altering the basic personality structure of an individual, and improving his relationships and his communications with others. If I can listen to what he can tell me, if I can understand how it seems to him, if I can see its personal meaning for him, if I can sense the emotional flavor which it has for him, then I will be releasing potent forces of change in him. If I can really understand how he hates his father, or hates the university, or hates communists—if I can catch the flavor of his fear of insanity, or his fear of atom bombs, or of Russia—it will be of the greatest help to him in altering those very hatreds and fears, and in establishing realistic and harmonious relationships with the very people and situations toward which he has felt hatred and fear. We know from our research that such empathic understanding—understanding *with* a person, not *about* him—is such an effective approach that it can bring about major changes in personality.

Some of you may be feeling that you listen well to people, and that you have never seen such results. The chances are very great indeed that your listening has not been of the type I have described. Fortunately I can suggest a little laboratory experiment which you can try to test the quality of your understanding. The next time you get into an argument with your wife, or your friend, or with a small group of friends, just stop the discussion for a moment and for an experiment, institute this rule. "Each person can speak up for himself only *after* he has first restated the ideas and feelings of the previous speaker accurately, and to that speaker's satisfaction." You see what this would mean. It would simply mean that before presenting your own point of view, it would be necessary for you to really achieve the other speaker's frame of reference—to understand his thoughts and feelings so well that you could summarize them for him. Sounds simple, doesn't it? But if you try it you will discover it one of the most difficult things you have ever tried to do. However, once you have been able to see the other's point of view, your own comments will have to be drastically revised. You will also find the emotion going out of the discussion, the differences being reduced, and those differences which remain being of a rational and understandable sort.

Can you imagine what this kind of an approach would mean if it were projected into larger areas? What would happen to a labor-management dispute if it was conducted in such a way that labor, without necessarily agreeing, could accurately state management's point of view in a way that management could accept; and management, without approving labor's stand, could state labor's case in a way that labor agreed was accurate? It would mean that real communication was established, and one could practically guarantee that some reasonable solution would be reached.

If then this way of approach is an effective avenue to good communication and good relationships, as I am quite sure you will agree if you try the experiment I have mentioned, why is it not more widely tried and used? I will try to list the difficulties which keep it from being utilized.

In the first place it takes courage, a quality which is not too widespread. I am indebted to Dr. S. I. Hayakawa, the semanticist, for pointing out that to carry on psychotherapy in this fashion is to take a very real risk, and that courage is required. If you really understand another person in this way, if you are willing to enter his private world and see the way life appears to him, without any attempt to make evaluative judgments, you run the risk of being changed yourself. You might see it his way, you might find yourself influenced in your attitudes or your personality. This risk of being changed is one of the most frightening prospects most of us can face. If I enter, as fully as I am able, into the private world of a neurotic or psychotic individual, isn't there a risk that I might become lost in that world? Most of us are afraid to take that risk. Or if we had a Russian communist speaker here tonight, or Senator Joe McCarthy, how many of us would dare to try to see the world from each of these points of view? The great majority of us could not *listen;* we would find ourselves compelled to *evaluate,* because listening would seem too dangerous. So the first requirement is courage, and we do not always have it.

But there is a second obstacle. It is just when emotions are strongest that it is most difficult to achieve the frame of reference of the other person or group. Yet it is the time the attitude is most needed, if communication is to be established. We have not found this to be an insuperable obstacle in our experience in psychotherapy. A third party, who is able to lay aside his own feelings and evaluations, can assist greatly by listening with understanding to each person or group and clarifying the views and attitudes each holds. We have found this very effective in small groups in which contradictory or antagonistic attitudes exist. When the parties to a dispute realize that they are being understood, that someone sees how the situation seems to them, the statements grow less exaggerated and less defensive, and it is no longer necessary to maintain the attitude, "I am 100 percent right and you are 100 percent wrong." The influence of such an understanding catalyst in the group permits the members to come closer and closer to the objective truth involved in the relationship. In this way mutual communication is established and some type of agreement becomes much more possible. So we may say that though heightened emotions make it much more difficult to understand *with* an opponent, our experience makes it clear that a neutral, understanding, catalyst type of leader or therapist can overcome this obstacle in a small group.

This last phrase, however, suggests another obstacle to utilizing the approach I have described. Thus far all our experience has been with small face-to-face groups—groups exhibiting industrial tensions, religious tensions, racial tensions, and therapy groups in which many personal tensions are present. In these small groups our experience, confirmed by a limited amount of research, shows that this basic approach leads to improved communication, to greater acceptance of others and by others, and to attitudes which are more positive and more problem-solving in nature. There is a decrease in defensiveness, in exaggerated statements, in evaluative and critical behavior. But these findings are from small groups. What about trying to achieve understanding between larger groups that are geographically remote? Or between face-to-face groups who are not speaking for themselves, but simply as representatives of others, like the delegates at Kaesong?[1] Frankly we do not know the answers to these questions. I believe the situation might be put this way. As social scientists we have a tentative test-tube solution of the problem of breakdown in communication. But to confirm the validity of this test-tube solution, and to adapt it to the enormous problems of communication breakdown between classes, groups, and nations, would involve additional funds, much more research, and creative thinking of a high order.

Even with our present limited knowledge we can see some steps which might be taken, even in large groups, to increase the amount of listening *with*, and to decrease the amount of evaluation *about*. To be imaginative for a moment, let us suppose that a therapeutically oriented international group went to the Russian leaders and said, "We want to achieve a genuine understanding of your views and even more important, of your attitudes and feelings, toward the United States. We will summarize and resummarize the views and feelings if necessary, until you agree that our description represents the situation as it seems to you." Then suppose they did the same thing with the leaders in our own country. If they then gave the widest possible distribution to these two views, with the feelings clearly described but not expressed in name-calling, might not the effect be very great? It would not guarantee the type of understanding I have been describing, but it would make it much more possible. We can understand the feelings of a person who hates us much more readily when his attitudes are accurately described to us by a neutral third party, than we can when he is shaking his fist at us.

But even to describe such a first step is to suggest another obstacle to this approach of understanding. Our civilization does not yet have enough faith in the social sciences to utilize their findings. The opposite is true of the physical sciences. During the war[2] when a test-tube solution was found to the problem of synthetic rubber, millions of dollars and an army of talent was turned loose on the problem of using that finding. If synthetic rubber could be made in milligrams, it could and would be made in the thousands of tons. And it was. But in the social science realm, if a way is found of facilitating communication and mutual understanding in small groups, there is no guarantee that the finding will be utilized. It may be a generation or more before the money and the brains will be turned loose to exploit that finding. 15

In closing, I would like to summarize this small-scale solution to the problem of barriers in communication, and to point out certain of its characteristics.

---

[1] **the delegates at Kaesong** Representatives of North and South Korea met at the border town of Kaesong to arrange terms for an armistice to hostilities during the Korean War (1950–1953). [All notes are the editors'.]
[2] **the war** World War II.

I have said that our research and experience to date would make it appear that breakdowns in communication, and the evaluative tendency which is the major barrier to communication, can be avoided. The solution is provided by creating a situation in which each of the different parties come to understand the other from the *other's* point of view. This has been achieved, in practice, even when feelings run high, by the influence of a person who is willing to understand each point of view empathically, and who thus acts as a catalyst to precipitate further understanding.

This procedure has important characteristics. It can be initiated by one party, without waiting for the other to be ready. It can even be initiated by a neutral third person, providing he can gain a minimum of cooperation from one of the parties.

This procedure can deal with the insincerities, the defensive exaggerations, the lies, the "false fronts" which characterize almost every failure in communication. These defensive distortions drop away with astonishing speed as people find that the only intent is to understand, not judge.

This approach leads steadily and rapidly toward the discovery of the 20 truth, toward a realistic appraisal of the objective barriers to communication. The dropping of some defensiveness by one party leads to further dropping of defensiveness by the other party, and truth is thus approached.

This procedure gradually achieves mutual communication. Mutual communication tends to be pointed toward solving a problem rather than toward attacking a person or group. It leads to a situation in which I see how the problem appears to you, as well as to me, and you see how it appears to me, as well as to you. Thus accurately and realistically defined, the problem is almost certain to yield to intelligent attack, or if it is in part insoluble, it will be comfortably accepted as such.

This then appears to be a test-tube solution to the breakdown of communication as it occurs in small groups. Can we take this small-scale answer, investigate it further, refine it; develop it and apply it to the tragic and well-nigh fatal failures of communication which threaten the very existence of our modern world? It seems to me that this is a possibility and a challenge which we should explore.

A CHECKLIST FOR ANALYZING ROGERIAN ARGUMENT

✓ Have I stated the problem and indicated that a dialogue is possible?

✓ Have I stated at least one other point of view in a way that would satisfy its proponents?

✓ Have I been courteous to those who hold views other than mine?

✓ Have I enlarged my own understanding, to the extent that I can grant validity, at least in some circumstances, to at least some aspects of other positions?

✓ Have I stated my position and indicated the contexts in which I believe it is valid?

✓ Have I pointed out the ground that we share?

✓ Have I shown how other positions will be strengthened by accepting some aspects of my position?

10

A Lawyer's View: Steps toward Civic Literacy

When John Adams in 1774 said that ours is "a government of law, and not of men," he meant that much of public conduct is regulated, rightly, by principles of law that by general agreement ought to be enforced and that can be altered only by our duly elected representatives, whose power is derived from our consent. In a democracy it is laws, not individuals (for instance, kings or tyrants), that govern. Adams and other early Americans rejected the view attributed to Louis XIV, "I am the state" (*L'état c'est moi*).

But what exactly the law in a given situation is often causes hot debate (as we know from watching the TV news). Whether we are ever personally called on to decide the law—as are legislators, judges, jurors, or lawyers—all of us find our daily lives constantly affected by the law. It is fitting, therefore, even necessary that we develop **civic literacy,** the ability to understand the principles by which our government and its courts operate so that we can act appropriately. (In today's global community, our civic literacy must also include a knowledge of the ways our and others' governments function.)

From the time of Plato's *Apology*, reporting Socrates' trial before the Athenian assembly in 399 B.C. on charges of corrupting the young and preaching false gods, courtroom argument has been a staple of dramatic verbal cut-and-thrust. (Think of popular television shows such as *The Practice* and *Law and Order*.) Probably no profession prides itself more on the ability of its members to argue than does the legal profession. The uninitiated are easily intimidated by the skill with which a lawyer can marshal relevant considerations to support a client's interests. But legal argument is, after all, *argument,* and so its main features are those already discussed in Chapter 3 (such as definition, assumption, premise, deduction, conclusion, evidence, validity). What is distinctive about legal reasoning is fairly straightforward in all but the most unusual cases.

CIVIL AND CRIMINAL CASES

Legal cases are divided into civil and criminal. In a *civil* case one party (the plaintiff) brings suit against another party (the defendant), claiming that he or she has suffered some wrong at the hands of the defendant and deserves some remedy (for instance, due to a dispute over a property boundary or over fault in a multicar accident). The judge or jury decides for or against the plaintiff based on the evidence and the relevant law. All crimes are wrongs, but not all wrongs are crimes. For instance, an automobile accident that involves negligence on the part of one of the drivers and results in harm to another is surely a wrong, but the driver responsible for the accident, even if found guilty, does not face a prison sentence (that could happen only if the accident were in fact the result of driving with gross recklessness, or driving while intoxicated, or were no "accident" at all). Why? Because the harm inflicted was not criminal; that is, it was not intentional, deliberate, malicious, or premeditated.

Criminal cases involve someone (the defendant) charged either with a *felony* (a serious crime like assault or battery) or with a *misdemeanor* (a less serious crime, as in *Texas v. Johnson*, p. 316). In criminal cases the state, through its prosecutor, seeks to convict the defendant as charged; the defendant, through his or her attorney, seeks an acquittal or, at worst, a conviction on a lesser charge (manslaughter instead of murder) and a milder punishment. The decision to convict or acquit on the basis of the facts submitted in evidence and the relevant law is the duty of the jury (or the judge, if there is no jury). The prosecutor and defense lawyer present what they believe are the relevant facts. Defining the relevant law is the responsibility of the trial judge. Public interest in criminal cases is often high, especially when the crime is particularly heinous. (Think of the 1995 trial of O. J. Simpson, charged with the murder of his wife and one of her friends, and the 1997 trial of Timothy McVeigh for the Oklahoma City federal building bombing.)

As you begin reading a legal case, therefore, you will want to be sure you can answer this question:

- Is the court trying to decide whether someone accused of a crime is guilty as charged, or is the court trying to resolve some non-criminal (civil) dispute?

TRIAL AND APPEAL

Most cases (civil or criminal) never go to *trial* at all. Most civil cases are settled out of court, and most criminal cases are settled with a plea bargain in which the prosecutor and the defense attorney persuade the judge to accept the defendant's guilty plea in exchange for a less severe sentence. Of the cases that are settled by trial, the losing party usually does not try to reopen, or *appeal*, the case. If, however, the losing party believes that he or she should have won, the case may be appealed for review by a higher appellate court (provided, of course, the loser can finance the appeal). The party bringing the appeal (the appellant) typically argues that because the relevant law was misstated or misapplied during the trial, the decision must be reversed and a new trial ordered. On rare occasion the issue in dispute is appealed all the way to the highest court in the nation—the U.S. Supreme Court—for a final decision. (The cases we reprint for discussion in this book are all cases decided by the Supreme Court.)

A pair of useful questions to answer as you work your way through a reported case are these:

- What are the events that give rise to the legal controversy in this case?

- What are the intermediate steps the case went through before reaching the final court of appeal?

DECISION AND OPINION

With rare exceptions, only cases decided by the appellate courts are *reported*, that is, written up and published. A reported case consists of two very different elements: (1) the court's decision, or *holding* and (2) the court's *opinion* in support of its decision. Typically, a court's decision can be stated in a sentence; it amounts to the conclusion of the court's argument. The opinion, however, is more complex and lengthy; as with most arguments, the premises of judicial reasoning and their linkages with each other involve several steps.

To illustrate, in *Texas v. Johnson* (p. 316), the Supreme Court considered a Texas statute that made it a crime to burn the American flag in political protest. The Court decided that the statute was an unconstitutional interference with freedom of speech. (The decision, as you see, can be stated concisely.)

The Court's opinion, however, runs to several pages. The gist is this: The purpose of the First Amendment (reprinted on p. 316) prohibiting abridgment of speech by the government is to protect personal expression, especially where there is a political intention or significance to the speech. Previous decisions of the Court interpreting the amendment have established that the protection of "speech" applies also to nonverbal acts; flag burning in political protest is such an act. Under certain conditions the state may regulate "speech," but in no case may the state prohibit "speech" because of its content or meaning. The Texas statute did not merely regulate the circumstances of "speech"; rather, it regulated the content or meaning of the "speech." Therefore, the statute is unconstitutional.

Thus, in reading the report of a decided case, you will want to be able to answer these two questions:

- What did the court decide?
- What reasons did the court offer to justify its decision?

MAJORITY, CONCURRING, AND DISSENTING OPINIONS

Not all appellate court decisions are unanimous ones. A court's *majority opinion* contains the ruling and reasoning of a majority of its judges. In *Texas v. Johnson*, for example, Justice William Brennan wrote the majority opinion in which four of his colleagues joined. Occasionally one or more of the judges in the majority files a *concurring opinion*; in such cases the judge agrees with the majority's decision but disagrees with its reasoning. Justice John Paul Stevens wrote a concurring opinion in *Johnson*.

In any appellate court decision, at least one judge is likely to dissent from the majority opinion and file a *dissenting opinion* explaining why. (Throughout this book we make the point that intelligent, honorable people may differ on issues of importance.) In the *Johnson* case, four judges dissented but joined in one dissenting opinion. Minority opinions have much to offer for reflection, and in many instances today's dissenting opinion becomes tomorrow's law. The most famous example is Justice John Marshall Harlan's solitary dissent in *Plessy v. Ferguson* (1896), the case that upheld "separate but equal" racial segregation; Harlan's dissent was eventually vindicated by a unanimous vote of the Supreme Court in *Brown v. Board of Education* (1954).

Thus, where there are majority, concurring, and minority opinions, you will want to think about these questions:

- On what issues do the majority and concurring opinions agree?
- On what issues do they disagree?
- Where does the minority in its dissenting opinion(s) disagree with the majority?
- Which opinion is more convincing, the majority or the minority?

FACTS AND LAW

Every court's decision is based on the relevant facts and the relevant law. What the relevant facts are is often in dispute at the trial but not on appeal; appellate court judges rarely reexamine the facts as decided by the trial court. The appellate court, however, usually restates the relevant facts in the opening paragraphs of its opinion. An old joke told among lawyers is appropriate here: "Argue the facts if the facts are on your side, argue the law if the law is on your side; if neither the law nor the facts are on your side, pound the table!"

Unfortunately, a sharp distinction between facts and law cannot always be maintained. For example, if we describe the defendant's conduct as "careless," is that a matter of fact? Or is it in part a matter of law, because "careless" conduct may also be judged "negligent" conduct, and the law defines what counts as negligence?

As you read through the reported case, keep in mind these two questions:

- What are the relevant facts in the case, insofar as they can be determined by what the appellate court reported?
- Are there issues of fact omitted or ignored by the appellate court that, had they been addressed, might have shed light on the decision?

For instance, consider a case in which a cattle rancher finds one of her cows dead after it collided with a railroad train. She decides to sue for negligence, wins, and the defendant (the railroad company) appeals. Why did she sue the railroad in the first place, rather than the engineer of the train that killed her cow? Suppose the appellate court's opinion fails to mention whether there was a fence at the edge of the field to keep her cattle off the tracks; wouldn't that be relevant to deciding whether she was partly at fault for the accident? (Ought the railroad to have erected a fence on its property parallel to the track?) Information about such facts could well shed light on the strength and correctness of the court's opinion and decision.

Appellate court judges are almost entirely preoccupied with what they believe is the relevant law to deciding the case at hand. The law can come in any of several different forms: common law principles ("No one may enlist the courts to assist him in profiting from his own wrong"), statutes enacted by a legislature ("As of January 1, 1998, income taxes shall be levied according to the following formula . . ."), ordinances enacted by a town council ("Dogs must be leashed in public places"), a precedent found in a prior case decided by some appellate court ("The decision in the case before us is governed by the Supreme Court's earlier holding in . . ."), executive orders ("All persons of Japanese extraction currently resident in California shall be removed inland to a relocation center"), administrative regulations ("Milk shipped interstate must have a butterfat content not less than . . ."), as well as constitutional interpretations ("Statements critical of a public official but not malicious or uttered by one who knows they are false are not libelous and are permitted under the First Amendment"). Not all laws are of equal weight; as *Texas v. Johnson* shows, a state statute inconsistent with the federal Bill of Rights will be nullified, not the other way around.

Appellate court judges devote much of their attention to **interpretation,** trying to decide exactly what the relevant statute, regulation, or prior decision really means and whether it applies to the case before the court. For example, does a local ordinance prohibiting "four-wheeled vehicles" in the park apply to a nanny pushing a baby carriage? The answer often turns on what was the *purpose* of the law or the *intention* of the lawmaker.

It is not easy to decide what the lawmakers' **intention** was; lawmakers are rarely available to state for the courts what their intention was. Can we confidently infer what a legislature's intention was from the legislative history left behind in the form of debates or hearings? From what the relevant committee chairperson says it was? What if (as is typically true) the legislature never declared its intentions when it enacted a law? When a legislature creates a statute, do all those who vote for it act with the same intention? If not, which of the many intentions involved should dominate? How do we find out what those intentions were? What counts as relevant evidence for ascribing this rather than that as someone's intention?

Accordingly, as you read a reported legal case, your study of the court's opinion should lead you to ask such questions as this:

- Exactly what law or laws is the court trying to interpret?
- What evidence does the court cite in favor of its interpretation?

BALANCING INTERESTS

In Supreme Court cases, the decision often turns on how competing interests are to be *balanced* or weighed. This pattern of reasoning is especially relevant when one of the conflicting interests is apparently protected by the Constitution. The majority opinion in *New Jersey v. T.L.O.* (1985) (p. 332) is a good example of such balancing; there, the privacy interests of high school students are weighed (metaphorically speaking, of course—no one can literally "weigh" or "balance" anyone's interests) against the competing interest of school officials responsible for maintaining an orderly environment for teaching. The Court decided that the latter ought to prevail and concluded that "reasonable" searches are not forbidden under the Fourth Amendment's prohibition of "unreasonable searches and seizures."

This leads directly to several other questions you will want to try to answer in the legal cases you study:

- In a constitutional case, what are the conflicting interests?
- How does the Supreme Court propose to balance them?
- Why does it strike the balance one way rather than the other?

A WORD OF CAUTION

Lawyers are both officers of the court and champions for their clients' causes. In the first role they share with judges and other officials the duty to seek justice by honorable means. But in the second role lawyers often see their job as one in which they ought to bend every rule as far as they can in pursuit of their clients' interests (after all, it is the client who pays the bills). This attitude is nicely conveyed in the title of a recent book, *How to Argue and Win Every Time* (1995), by Gerry Spence, one of the nation's leading trial lawyers. And it is reinforced by a comment from defense attorney Alan Dershowitz: "All sides in a trial want to hide at least some of the truth."

Yet it would be wrong to see lawyers as motivated only by a ruthless desire to win at any cost. Lawyers have a civic duty to present their clients' cases in the most favorable light and to challenge whatever evidence and testimony is offered in court against them. (If you were hiring a lawyer to defend you, would you settle for anything less?) In a society such as ours—a society of law rather than of powerful individuals—it is right that accused persons be found guilty as charged only after the strongest defenses have been mounted.

To be sure, everyone concerned to argue on behalf of any claim, whether in or out of court, whether as a lawyer or in some other capacity, ought to take the challenge seriously. But it is too much to hope to "win every time"—and in fact winning is not the only, much less the highest, goal. Sometimes the other side does have the better argument, and in such cases we should be willing, indeed eager, to see the merits and to enlarge our minds.

In any case, in this book we think of argument not as a weapon for use in mortal combat but as a device for exploring the controversy or dispute under discussion, a tool for isolating the issues in contention and for helping in the evaluation of different possible outcomes. We expect you will use argument to persuade your audience to accept your views, just as a lawyer typically does; but we hope you will use argument sometimes—even often—to clarify your ideas *for yourself;* when you develop arguments for effective presentation to your colleagues and associates, you will probably improve the quality of your ideas.

A CHECKLIST FOR ANALYZING
LEGAL ARGUMENTS

✓ Is the court trying to decide whether someone accused of a crime is guilty as charged, or is the court trying to resolve some noncriminal (civil) dispute?

✓ What events gave rise to the legal controversy in this case?

✓ What intermediate steps did the case go through before reaching the final court of appeal?

✓ What did the court decide?

✓ What reasons did the court offer to justify its decision?

✓ On what issues do the majority and concurring opinions agree?

✓ On what issues do they disagree?

✓ Where does the minority in its dissenting opinion(s) disagree with the majority?

✓ Which opinion is more convincing, the majority or the minority?

✓ What are the relevant facts in the case, insofar as they can be determined by what the appellate court reported?

✓ Are there issues of fact omitted or ignored by the appellate court that, had they been addressed, might have shed light on the decision?

✓ Exactly what law or laws is the court trying to interpret?

✓ What evidence does the court cite in favor of its interpretation?

✓ In constitutional cases, what are the conflicting interests?

✓ How does the Supreme Court propose to balance them?

✓ Why does it strike the balance one way rather than the other?

A CASEBOOK ON THE LAW AND SOCIETY: What Rights Do the First and Fourth Amendments Protect?

William J. Brennan, Jr. and William H. Rehnquist

William J. Brennan, Jr. (1906–1990), appointed to the Supreme Court in 1956 by President Dwight D. Eisenhower, established himself as a strong supporter of individual liberties. William H. Rehnquist (b. 1924), appointed in 1971 by President Richard M. Nixon because of his emphasis on law and order, came to be regarded as the most conservative member of the Court.

Texas v. Johnson (1989) concerns the right to burn the American flag in political protest. (Recall that the First Amendment to the Constitution holds that "Congress shall make no law respecting an establishment of religion, or prohibiting the free exercise thereof; or abridging the freedom of speech, or of the press; or the right of the people peaceably to assemble, and to petition the government for a redress of grievances.") The case was decided by a vote of 5 to 4. Immediately after the Court's decision was announced, a resolution was drafted and filed in Congress to condemn the Court's decision. Also filed was the Flag Protection Act of 1989, making it a criminal offense to "knowingly mutilate, deface, burn, or trample upon" the flag. Another bill was designed to amend the Constitution so that criminal penalties for desecration of the flag would not violate the First Amendment. As of the spring of 1998, none of these bills has left the congressional committees charged with examining them. In the excerpt that follows, legal citations have been deleted and portions of the text omitted.

Texas v. Johnson

Associate Justice Brennan delivered the opinion of the Court.

After publicly burning an American flag as a means of political protest, Gregory Lee Johnson was convicted of desecrating a flag in violation of Texas law. This case presents the question whether his conviction is consistent with the First Amendment. We hold that it is not.

I

While the Republican National Convention was taking place in Dallas in 1984, respondent Johnson participated in a political demonstration dubbed the "Republican War Chest Tour." As explained in literature distributed by the demonstrators and in speeches made by them, the purpose of this event was to protest the policies of the Reagan administration and of certain Dallas-based corporations. The demonstrators marched through the Dallas streets, chanting political slogans and stopping at several corporate locations to stage "die-ins" intended to dramatize the consequences of nuclear war. On several occasions they spray-painted the walls of buildings and overturned potted plants, but Johnson himself took no part in such activities. He did, however, accept an American flag handed to him by a fellow protestor who had taken it from a flag pole outside one of the targeted buildings.

The demonstration ended in front of Dallas City Hall, where Johnson unfurled the American flag, doused it with kerosene, and set it on fire. While the flag burned, the protestors chanted, "America, the red, white, and blue, we spit on you." After the demonstrators dispersed, a witness to the flag burning collected the flag's remains and buried them in his backyard. No one was physically injured or threatened with injury, though several witnesses testified that they had been seriously offended by the flag burning.

Of the approximately 100 demonstrators, Johnson alone was charged with a crime. The only criminal offense with which he was charged was the desecration of a venerated object in violation of Tex. Penal Code Ann.[1] After a trial, he was convicted, sentenced to one year in prison, and fined $2,000. The Court of Appeals for the Fifth District of Texas at Dallas affirmed Johnson's conviction, but the Texas Court of Criminal Appeals reversed, holding that the state could not, consistent with the First Amendment, punish Johnson for burning the flag in these circumstances. . . .

II

. . . The First Amendment literally forbids the abridgement only of "speech," but we have long recognized that its protection does not end at the spoken or written word. While we have rejected "the view that an apparently limitless variety of conduct can be labeled 'speech' whenever the person engaging in the conduct intends thereby to express an idea," we have acknowledged that conduct may be "sufficiently imbued with the elements of communication to fall within the scope of the First and Fourteenth Amendments." . . .

[1]Tex. Penal Code Ann. §42.09 (1989) ["Desecration of a Venerated Object"] provides in full:

"(a) A person commits an offense if he intentionally or knowingly desecrates: (1) a public monument; (2) a place of worship or burial; or (3) a state or national flag.

"(b) For purposes of this section, 'desecrate' means deface, damage, or otherwise physically mistreat in a way that the actor knows will seriously offend one or more persons likely to observe or discover his action.

"(c) An offense under this section is a Class A misdemeanor." [Court's note.]

IV

It remains to consider whether the state's interest in preserving the flag as a symbol of nationhood and national unity justifies Johnson's conviction.

As in *Spence* [*v. Washington*], "we are confronted with a case of prosecution for the expression of an idea through activity," and "accordingly, we must examine with particular care the interests advanced by [petitioner] to support its prosecution." Johnson was not, we add, prosecuted for the expression of just any idea; he was prosecuted for his expression of dissatisfaction with the policies of this country, expression situated at the core of our First Amendment values.

Moreover, Johnson was prosecuted because he knew that his politically charged expression would cause "serious offense." If he had burned the flag as a means of disposing of it because it was dirty or torn, he would not have been convicted of flag desecration under this Texas law: Federal law designates burning as the preferred means of disposing of a flag "when it is in such condition that it is no longer a fitting emblem for display," and Texas has no quarrel with this means of disposal. The Texas law is thus not aimed at protecting the physical integrity of the flag in all circumstances, but is designed instead to protect it only against impairments that would cause serious offense to others. Texas concedes as much: "Section 42.09(b) reaches only those severe acts of physical abuse of the flag carried out in a way likely to be offensive. The statute mandates intentional or knowing abuse, that is, the kind of mistreatment that is not innocent, but rather is intentionally designed to seriously offend other individuals."

Whether Johnson's treatment of the flag violated Texas law thus depended on the likely communicative impact of his expressive conduct. Our decision in *Boos v. Barry* tells us that this restriction on Johnson's expression is content based. In *Boos,* we considered the constitutionality of a law prohibiting "the display of any sign within 500 feet of a foreign embassy if that sign tends to bring that foreign government into 'public odium' or 'public disrepute.'" Rejecting the argument that the law was content neutral because it was justified by "our international law obligation to shield diplomats from speech that offends their dignity," we held that "the emotive impact of speech on its audience is not a 'secondary effect'" unrelated to the content of the expression itself. . . .

Texas argues that its interest in preserving the flag as a symbol of na- 10
tionhood and national unity survives this close analysis. Quoting extensively from the writings of this Court chronicling the flag's historic and symbolic role in our society, the state emphasizes the "'special place'" reserved for the flag in our nation. The state's argument is not that it has an interest simply in maintaining the flag as a symbol of something, no matter what it symbolizes; indeed, if that were the state's position, it

would be difficult to see how that interest is endangered by highly symbolic conduct such as Johnson's. Rather, the state's claim is that it has an interest in preserving the flag as a symbol of *nationhood* and *national unity*, a symbol with a determinate range of meanings. According to Texas, if one physically treats the flag in a way that would tend to cast doubt on either the idea that nationhood and national unity are the flag's referents or that national unity actually exists, the message conveyed thereby is a harmful one and therefore may be prohibited.

If there is a bedrock principle underlying the First Amendment, it is that the government may not prohibit the expression of an idea simply because society finds the idea itself offensive or disagreeable.

We have not recognized an exception to this principle even where our flag has been involved. In *Street v. New York*, we held that a state may not criminally punish a person for uttering words critical of the flag. Rejecting the argument that the conviction could be sustained on the ground that Street had "failed to show the respect for our national symbol which may properly be demanded of every citizen," we concluded that "the constitutionally guaranteed 'freedom to be intellectually . . . diverse or even contrary,' and the 'right to differ as to things that touch the heart of the existing order,' encompass the freedom to express publicly one's opinions about our flag, including those opinions which are defiant or contemptuous." Nor may the government, we have held, compel conduct that would evince respect for the flag. "To sustain the compulsory flag salute we are required to say that a Bill of Rights which guards the individual's right to speak his own mind, left it open to public authorities to compel him to utter what is not in his mind." . . .

Texas's focus on the precise nature of Johnson's expression, moreover, misses the point of our prior decisions: their enduring lesson, that the government may not prohibit expression simply because it disagrees with its message, is not dependent on the particular mode in which one chooses to express an idea. If we were to hold that a state may forbid flag burning wherever it is likely to endanger the flag's symbolic role, but allow it wherever burning a flag promotes that role—as where, for example, a person ceremoniously burns a dirty flag—we would be saying that when it comes to impairing the flag's physical integrity, the flag itself may be used as a symbol—as a substitute for the written or spoken word or a "short cut from mind to mind"—only in one direction. We would be permitting a state to "prescribe what shall be orthodox" by saying that one may burn the flag to convey one's attitude toward it and its referents only if one does not endanger the flag's representation of nationhood and national unity.

We never before have held that the government may ensure that a symbol be used to express only one view of that symbol or its referents. Indeed, in *Schacht v. United States*, we invalidated a federal statute permitting an actor portraying a member of one of our armed forces to "'wear the uniform of that armed force if the portrayal does not tend to discredit that armed force.'" This proviso, we held, "which leaves Americans free to praise the war in Vietnam but can send persons like Schacht to prison for opposing it, cannot survive in a country which has the First Amendment."

We perceive no basis on which to hold that the principle underlying 15 our decision in *Schacht* does not apply to this case. To conclude that the government may permit designated symbols to be used to communicate only a limited set of messages would be to enter territory having no discernible or defensible boundaries. Could the government, on this theory, prohibit the burning of state flags? Of copies of the presidential seal? Of the Constitution? In evaluating these choices under the First Amendment, how would we decide which symbols were sufficiently special to warrant this unique status? To do so, we would be forced to consult our own political preferences, and impose them on the citizenry, in the very way that the First Amendment forbids us to do.

There is, moreover, no indication—either in the text of the Constitution or in our cases interpreting it—that a separate juridical category exists for the American flag alone. Indeed, we would not be surprised to learn that the persons who framed our Constitution and wrote the Amendment that we now construe were not known for their reverence for the Union Jack. The First Amendment does not guarantee that other concepts virtually sacred to our nation as a whole—such as the principle that discrimination on the basis of race is odious and destructive—will go unquestioned in the marketplace of ideas. We decline, therefore, to create for the flag an exception to the joust of principles protected by the First Amendment.

It is not the state's ends, but its means, to which we object. It cannot be gainsaid that there is a special place reserved for the flag in this nation, and thus we do not doubt that the government has a legitimate interest in making efforts to "preserve the national flag as an unalloyed symbol of our country." We reject the suggestion, urged at oral argument by counsel for Johnson, that the government lacks "any state interest whatsoever" in regulating the manner in which the flag may be displayed. Congress has, for example, enacted precatory regulations describing the proper treatment of the flag, and we cast no doubt on the legitimacy of its interest in making such recommendations. To say that the government has an interest in encouraging proper treatment of the flag, however, is not to say that it may criminally punish a person for burning a flag as a means of political protest. "National unity as an end which officials may foster by persuasion and example is not in question. The problem is whether under our Constitution compulsion as here employed is a permissible means for its achievement." . . .

We are tempted to say, in fact, that the flag's deservedly cherished place in our community will be strengthened, not weakened, by our holding today. Our decision is a reaffirmation of the principles of freedom and inclusiveness that the flag best reflects, and of the conviction that our toleration of criticism such as Johnson's is a sign and source of our strength. Indeed, one of the proudest images of our flag, the one immortalized in our own national anthem, is of the bombardment it survived at Fort McHenry. It is the nation's resilience, not its rigidity, that Texas sees reflected in the flag—and it is that resilience that we reassert today.

The way to preserve the flag's special role is not to punish those who feel differently about these matters. It is to persuade them that they are wrong. "To courageous, self-reliant men, with confidence in the power of free and fearless reasoning applied through the processes of popular government, no danger flowing from speech can be deemed clear and present, unless the incidence of the evil apprehended is so imminent that it may befall before there is opportunity for full discussion. If there be time to expose through discussion the falsehood and fallacies, to avert the evil by the processes of education, the remedy to be applied is more speech, not enforced silence." And, precisely because it is our flag that is involved, one's response to the flag burner may exploit the uniquely persuasive power of the flag itself. We can imagine no more appropriate response to burning a flag than waving one's own, no better way to counter a flag burner's message than by saluting the flag that burns, no surer means of preserving the dignity even of the flag that burned than by—as one witness here did—according its remains a respectful burial. We do not consecrate the flag by punishing its desecration, for in doing so we dilute the freedom that this cherished emblem represents. . . .

Chief Justice Rehnquist dissented.

. . . Both Congress and the states have enacted numerous laws regu- 20 lating misuse of the American flag. Until 1967, Congress left the regulation of misuse of the flag up to the states. Now, however, Title 18 U.S.C. §700(a) provides that:

> Whoever knowingly casts contempt upon any flag of the United States by publicly mutilating, defacing, defiling, burning, or trampling upon it shall be fined not more than $1,000 or imprisoned for not more than one year, or both.

Congress has also prescribed, inter alia, detailed rules for the design of the flag, the time and occasion of flag's display, the position and manner of its display, respect for the flag, and conduct during hoisting, lowering, and passing of the flag. With the exception of Alaska and Wyoming, all of the states now have statutes prohibiting the burning of the flag. Most of the state statutes are patterned after the Uniform Flag Act of 1917, which in §3 provides: "No person shall publicly mutilate, deface, defile, defy, trample upon, or by word or act cast contempt upon any such flag, standard, color, ensign or shield." Most were passed by the states at about the time of World War I. . . .

The American flag, then, throughout more than two hundred years of our history, has come to be the visible symbol embodying our nation. It does not represent the views of any particular political party, and it does not represent any particular political philosophy. The flag is not simply another "idea" or "point of view" competing for recognition in the marketplace of ideas. Millions and millions of Americans regard it with an almost mystical reverence regardless of what sort of social, political, or philosophical beliefs they may have. I cannot agree that the First Amendment invalidates the act of Congress, and the laws of forty-eight of the fifty states, which make criminal the public burning of the flag.

More than eighty years ago in *Halter v. Nebraska*, this Court upheld the constitutionality of a Nebraska statute that forbade the use of representations of the American flag for advertising purposes upon articles of merchandise. The Court there said:

> For that flag every true American has not simply an appreciation but a deep affection. . . . Hence, it has often occurred that insults to a flag have been the cause of war, and indignities put upon it, in the presence of those who revere it, have often been resented and sometimes punished on the spot. . . .

But the Court insists that the Texas statute prohibiting the public burning of the American flag infringes on respondent Johnson's freedom of expression. Such freedom, of course, is not absolute. In *Chaplinsky v. New Hampshire*, a unanimous Court said:

> Allowing the broadest scope to the language and purpose of the Fourteenth Amendment, it is well understood that the right of free speech is not absolute at all times and under all circumstances. There are certain well-defined and narrowly limited classes of speech, the prevention and punishment of which have never been thought to raise any Constitutional problem. These include the lewd and obscene, the profane, the libelous, and the insulting or 'fighting' words—those which by their very utterance inflict injury or tend to incite an immediate breach of the peace. It has been well observed that such utterances are no essential part of any exposition of ideas, and are of such slight social value as a step to truth that any benefit that may be derived from them is clearly outweighed by the social interest in order and morality. . . .

The result of the Texas statute is obviously to deny one in Johnson's frame of mind one of many means of "symbolic speech." Far from being a case of "one picture being worth a thousand words," flag burning is the equivalent of an inarticulate grunt or roar that, it seems fair to say, is most likely to be indulged in not to express any particular idea, but to antagonize others. . . . The Texas statute deprived Johnson of only one rather inarticulate symbolic form of protest—a form of protest that was profoundly offensive to many—and left him with a full panoply of other symbols and every conceivable form of verbal expression to express his deep disapproval of national policy. Thus, in no way can it be said that Texas is punishing him because his hearers—or any other group of people—were profoundly opposed to the message that he sought to convey. Such opposition is no proper basis for restricting speech or expression under the First Amendment. It was Johnson's use of this particular symbol, and not the idea that he sought to convey by it or by his many other expressions, for which he was punished.

Our prior cases dealing with flag desecration statutes have left open 25 the question that the Court resolves today. In *Street v. New York*, the defendant burned a flag in the street, shouting "We don't need no damned flag" and, "if they let that happen to Meredith we don't need an American flag." The Court ruled that since the defendant might have been convicted solely on the basis of his words, the conviction could not stand, but it expressly reserved the question whether a defendant could constitutionally be convicted for burning the flag. . . .

In *Spence v. Washington*, the Court reversed the conviction of a college student who displayed the flag with a peace symbol affixed to it by means of removable black tape from the window of his apartment. Unlike the instant case, there was no risk of a breach of the peace, no one other than the arresting officers saw the flag, and the defendant owned the flag in question. The Court concluded that the student's conduct was protected under the First Amendment, because "no interest the state may have in preserving the physical integrity of a privately owned flag was significantly impaired on these facts." The Court was careful to note, however, that the defendant "was not charged under the desecration statute, nor did he permanently disfigure the flag or destroy it."

In another related case, *Smith v. Goguen*, the appellee, who wore a small flag on the seat of his trousers, was convicted under a Massachusetts flag-misuse statute that subjected to criminal liability anyone who "publicly . . . treats contemptuously the flag of the United States." The Court affirmed the lower court's reversal of appellee's conviction, because the phrase "treats contemptuously" was unconstitutionally broad and vague. The Court was again careful to point out that "certainly nothing prevents a legislature from defining with substantial specificity what constitutes forbidden treatment of United States flags." ("The flag is a national property, and the Nation may regulate those who would make, imitate, sell, possess, or use it. I would not question those statutes which proscribe mutilation, defacement, or burning of the flag or which otherwise protect its physical integrity, without regard to whether such conduct might provoke violence. . . . There would seem to be little question about the power of Congress to forbid the mutilation of the Lincoln Memorial. . . . The flag is itself a monument, subject to similar protection"); ("Goguen's punishment was constitutionally permissible for harming the physical integrity of the flag by wearing it affixed to the seat of his pants").

But the Court today will have none of this. The uniquely deep awe and respect for our flag felt by virtually all of us are bundled off under the rubric of "designated symbols" that the First Amendment prohibits the government from "establishing." But the government has not "established" this feeling; two hundred years of history have done that. The government is simply recognizing as a fact the profound regard for the American flag created by that history when it enacts statutes prohibiting the disrespectful public burning of the flag.

The Court concludes its opinion with a regrettably patronizing civics lecture, presumably addressed to the members of both houses of Congress, the members of the forty-eight state legislatures that enacted prohibitions against flag burning, and the troops fighting under that flag in Vietnam who objected to its being burned: "The way to preserve the flag's special role is not to punish those who feel differently about these matters. It is to persuade them that they are wrong." The Court's role as the final expositor of the Constitution is well established, but its role as a platonic guardian admonishing those responsible to public opinion as if they were truant school children has no similar place in our system of government. The cry of "no taxation without representation" animated those who revolted against the English Crown to found our nation — the idea that those who submitted to government should have some say as to what kind of laws would be passed. Surely one of the high purposes of a democratic society is to legislate against conduct that is regarded as evil and profoundly offensive to the majority of people — whether it be murder, embezzlement, pollution, or flag burning.

Our Constitution wisely places limits on powers of legislative majorities to act, but the declaration of such limits by this Court "is, at all times, a question of much delicacy, which ought seldom, if ever, to be decided in the affirmative, in a doubtful case." Uncritical extension of constitutional protection to the burning of the flag risks the frustration of the very purpose for which organized governments are instituted. The Court decides that the American flag is just another symbol, about which not only must opinions pro and con be tolerated, but for which the most minimal public respect may not be enjoined. The government may conscript men into the armed forces where they must fight and perhaps die for the flag, but the government may not prohibit the public burning of the banner under which they fight. I would uphold the Texas statute as applied in this case.

Topics for Critical Thinking and Writing

1. State the facts of this case describing Johnson's illegal conduct and the events in court, beginning with his arrest and culminating in the decision of the Supreme Court.

2. What does Justice Brennan state are the interests in conflict?

3. Why does Brennan (para. 10) describe Johnson's conduct as "highly symbolic"? What would count as less symbolic, or nonsymbolic, conduct having the same purpose as flag burning?

4. Chief Justice Rehnquist suggests (para. 24) that Johnson's flag burning is "equivalent" to "an inarticulate grunt or roar," with the intention "not to express any particular idea, but to antagonize others." Explain why you agree or disagree with these judgments.

5. Brennan cites the prior cases of *Street v. New York* and *Schacht v. United States* in his favor; Rehnquist cites several cases supporting his dissenting opinion. Which of these precedents (if any) do you find most relevant to the proper outcome of this case, and why?

6. Would it be a desecration of the flag to print the Stars and Stripes on paper towels to be sold for Fourth of July picnics? On toilet paper? Write a 250-word essay on the topic: "Desecration of the Flag: What It Is and What It Isn't."

7. In paragraph 15, Brennan uses a version of the slippery slope argument (see p. 285) in support of striking down the Texas statute. Explain whether you think this argument is effective and relevant.

8. In First Amendment cases, it is often said that the government may not restrict "speech" because of its "content," but it may be restricted in the "time, place, and manner" of expression. What might be plausible restrictions of these sorts on flag burning for political purposes?

John Marshall Harlan and Harry A. Blackmun

During the 1960s, draft-age men often protested against the Selective Service System on grounds that it was administered unfairly and that it was being used to provide troops to fight an unjust war in Vietnam. Protest took varied forms, including civil disobedience and violent resistance. Peaceful objections were far more frequent, but in some cases it was hard to tell whether the protest was lawful or not. The conduct of Paul Robert Cohen is one of these borderline cases. Cohen was convicted in 1968 in Los Angeles of a misdemeanor for behaving in a manner that violated a California statute forbidding "tumultuous or offensive conduct." Cohen argued that his conduct was protected by the U.S. Constitution as an act of "free speech," but the California Court of Appeals disagreed and upheld his conviction. He appealed to the U.S. Supreme Court and won by a vote of 6 to 3. Excerpted here is the majority opinion, written by Associate Justice John Marshall Harlan (1899–1971), one of the most respected jurists to sit on the Court during the past generation. The facts of the case are briefly set out by Harlan in his opening paragraphs. We also reprint the main argument of the brief dissenting opinion, written by Associate Justice Harry A. Blackmun (b. 1908). Legal citations have been omitted.

Cohen v. California

Justice Harlan delivered the opinion of the Court.

This case may seem at first blush too inconsequential to find its way into our books, but the issue it presents is of no small constitutional significance.

Appellant Paul Robert Cohen was convicted in the Los Angeles Municipal Court of violating that part of California Penal Code §415 which prohibits "maliciously and willfully disturb[ing] the peace or quiet of any neighborhood or person, . . . by . . . offensive conduct. . . ." He was given thirty days' imprisonment. The facts upon which his conviction rests are detailed in the opinion of the Court of Appeal of California, Second Appellate District, as follows:

> On April 26, 1968 the defendant was observed in the Los Angeles County Courthouse in the corridor outside of Division 20 of the Municipal Court wearing a jacket bearing the words "Fuck the Draft" which were plainly visible. There were women and children present in the corridor. The defendant was arrested. The defendant testified that he wore the jacket as a means of informing the public of the depth of his feelings against the Vietnam War and the draft.
>
> The defendant did not engage in, nor threaten to engage in, nor did anyone as the result of his conduct in fact commit or threaten to commit any act of violence. The defendant did not make any loud or unusual noise, nor was there any evidence that he uttered any sound prior to his arrest.

In affirming the conviction the Court of Appeal held that "offensive conduct" means "behavior which has a tendency to provoke *others* to acts of violence or to in turn disturb the peace," and that the state had proved this element because, on the facts of this case, "[i]t was certainly reasonably foreseeable that such conduct might cause others to rise up to commit a violent act against the person of the defendant or attempt to forcibly remove his jacket." The California Supreme Court declined review by a divided vote. We brought the case here, postponing the consideration of the question of our jurisdiction over this appeal to a hearing of the case on the merits. We now reverse.

The question of our jurisdiction need not detain us long. Throughout the proceedings below, Cohen consistently claimed that, as construed to apply to the facts of this case, the statute infringed his rights to freedom of expression guaranteed by the First and Fourteenth Amendments of the federal Constitution. That contention has been rejected by the highest California state court in which review could be had. Accordingly, we are fully satisfied that Cohen has properly invoked our jurisdiction by this appeal. 5

I

In order to lay hands on the precise issue which this case involves, it is useful first to canvass various matters which this record does *not* present.

The conviction quite clearly rests upon the asserted offensiveness of the *words* Cohen used to convey his message to the public. The only "conduct" which the state sought to punish is the fact of communication. Thus, we deal here with a conviction resting solely upon "speech," not upon any separately identifiable conduct which allegedly was intended by Cohen to be perceived by others as expressive of particular views but which, on its face, does not necessarily convey any message and hence arguably could be regulated without effectively repressing Cohen's ability to express himself. Further, the state certainly lacks power to punish Cohen for the underlying content of the message the inscription conveyed. At least so long as there is no showing of an intent to incite disobedience to or disruption of the draft. Cohen could not, consistently with the First and Fourteenth Amendments, be punished for asserting the evident position on the inutility or immorality of the draft his jacket reflected.

Appellant's conviction, then, rests squarely upon his exercise of the "freedom of speech" protected from arbitrary governmental interference by the Constitution and can be justified, if at all, only as a valid regulation of the manner in which he exercised that freedom, not as a permissible prohibition on the substantive message it conveys. This does not end the inquiry, of course, for the First and Fourteenth Amendments have never been thought to give absolute protection to every individual to speak whenever or wherever he pleases, or to use any form of address in any circumstance that he chooses. In this vein, too, however, we think it important to note that several issues typically associated with such problems are not presented here.

In the first place, Cohen was tried under a statute applicable throughout the entire state. Any attempt to support this conviction on the ground that the statute seeks to preserve an appropriately decorous atmosphere in the courthouse where Cohen was arrested must fail in the absence of any language in the statute that would have put appellant on notice that certain kinds of otherwise permissible speech or conduct would nevertheless, under California law, not be tolerated in certain places. No fair reading of the phrase "offensive conduct" can be said sufficiently to inform the ordinary person that distinctions between certain locations are thereby created.[1]

In the second place, as it comes to us, this case cannot be said to fall 10 within those relatively few categories of instances where prior decisions

---

[1] It is illuminating to note what transpired when Cohen entered a courtroom in the building. He removed his jacket and stood with it folded over his arm. Meanwhile, a policeman sent the presiding judge a note suggesting that Cohen be held in contempt of court. The judge declined to do so and Cohen was arrested by the officer only after he emerged from the courtroom. [All notes are the Court's.]

have established the power of government to deal more comprehensively with certain forms of individual expression simply upon a showing that such a form was employed. This is not, for example, an obscenity case. Whatever else may be necessary to give rise to the states' broader power to prohibit obscene expression, such expression must be, in some significant way, erotic. It cannot plausibly be maintained that this vulgar allusion to the Selective Service System would conjure up such psychic stimulation in anyone likely to be confronted with Cohen's crudely defaced jacket.

This Court has also held that the states are free to ban the simple use, without a demonstration of additional justifying circumstances, of so-called "fighting words," those personally abusive epithets which, when addressed to the ordinary citizen, are, as a matter of common knowledge, inherently likely to provoke violent reaction. While the four-letter word displayed by Cohen in relation to the draft is not uncommonly employed in a personally provocative fashion, in this instance it was clearly not "directed to the person of the hearer." No individual actually or likely to be present could reasonably have regarded the words on appellant's jacket as a direct personal insult. Nor do we have here an instance of the exercise of the state's police power to prevent a speaker from intentionally provoking a given group to hostile reaction. There is, as noted above, no showing that anyone who saw Cohen was in fact violently aroused or that appellant intended such a result.

Finally, in arguments before this Court much has been made of the claim that Cohen's distasteful mode of expression was thrust upon unwilling or unsuspecting viewers, and that the state might therefore legitimately act as it did in order to protect the sensitive from otherwise unavoidable exposure to appellant's crude form of protest. Of course, the mere presumed presence of unwitting listeners or viewers does not serve automatically to justify curtailing all speech capable of giving offense. While this Court has recognized that government may properly act in many situations to prohibit intrusion into the privacy of the home of unwelcome views and ideas which cannot be totally banned from the public dialogue, we have at the same time consistently stressed that "we are often 'captives' outside the sanctuary of the home and subject to objectionable speech." The ability of government, consonant with the Constitution, to shut off discourse solely to protect others from hearing it is, in other words, dependent upon a showing that substantial privacy interests are being invaded in an essentially intolerable manner. Any broader view of this authority would effectively empower a majority to silence dissidents simply as a matter of personal predilections.

In this regard, persons confronted with Cohen's jacket were in a quite different posture than, say, those subjected to the raucous emissions of sound trucks blaring outside their residences. Those in the Los Angeles courthouse could effectively avoid further bombardment of their sensibilities simply by averting their eyes. And, while it may be that one has a more substantial claim to a recognizable privacy interest when walking through a courthouse corridor than, for example, strolling through Central Park, surely it is nothing like the interest in being free from unwanted expression in the confines of one's own home. Given the subtlety and complexity of the factors involved, if Cohen's "speech" was otherwise entitled to constitutional protection, we do not think the fact that some unwilling "listeners" in a public building may have been briefly exposed to it can serve to justify this breach of the peace conviction where, as here, there was no evidence that persons powerless to avoid appellant's conduct did in fact object to it, and where that portion of the statute upon which Cohen's conviction rests evinces no concern, either on its face or as construed by the California courts, with the special plight of the captive auditor, but, instead, indiscriminately sweeps within its prohibitions all "offensive conduct" that disturbs "any neighborhood or person."[2]

II

Against this background, the issue flushed by this case stands out in bold relief. It is whether California can excise, as "offensive conduct," one particular scurrilous epithet from the public discourse, either upon the theory of the court below that its use is inherently likely to cause violent reaction or upon a more general assertion that the states, acting as guardians of public morality, may properly remove this offensive word from the public vocabulary.

The rationale of the California court is plainly untenable. At most it reflects an "undifferentiated fear or apprehension of disturbance [which] is not enough to overcome the right to freedom of expression." We have been shown no evidence that substantial numbers of citizens are standing ready to strike out physically at whoever may assault their sensibilities with execrations like that uttered by Cohen. There may be some persons about with such lawless and violent proclivities, but that is an insufficient base upon which to erect, consistently with constitutional values, a governmental power to force persons who wish to ventilate their dissident views into avoiding particular forms of expression. The argument amounts to little more than the self-defeating proposition that to avoid physical censorship of one who has not sought to provoke such

[2]In fact, other portions of the same statute do make some such distinctions. For example, the statute also prohibits disturbing "the peace or quiet . . . by loud or unusual noise" and using "vulgar, profane or indecent language within the presence or hearing of women or children, in a loud and boisterous manner." . . . This second quoted provision in particular serves to put the actor on much fairer notice as to what is prohibited. It also buttresses our view that the "offensive conduct" portion, as construed and applied in this case, cannot legitimately be justified in this Court as designed or intended to make fine distinctions between differently situated recipients.

a response by a hypothetical coterie of the violent and lawless, the states may more appropriately effectuate that censorship themselves.

Admittedly, it is not so obvious that the First and Fourteenth Amendments must be taken to disable the states from punishing public utterance of this unseemly expletive in order to maintain what they regard as a suitable level of discourse within the body politic. We think, however, that examination and reflection will reveal the shortcoming of a contrary viewpoint.

At the outset, we cannot overemphasize that, in our judgment, most situations where the state has a justifiable interest in regulating speech will fall within one or more of the various established exceptions, discussed above but not applicable here, to the usual rule that governmental bodies may not prescribe the form or content of individual expression. Equally important to our conclusion is the constitutional backdrop against which our decision must be made. The constitutional right of free expression is powerful medicine in a society as diverse and populous as ours. It is designed and intended to remove governmental restraints from the arena of public discussion, putting the decision as to what views shall be voiced largely into the hands of each of us, in the hope that use of such freedom will ultimately produce a more capable citizenry and more perfect polity and in the belief that no other approach would comport with the premise of individual dignity and choice upon which our political system rests.

To many, the immediate consequence of this freedom may often appear to be only verbal tumult, discord, and even offensive utterance. These are, however, within established limits, in truth necessary side effects of the broader enduring values which the process of open debate permits us to achieve. That the air may at times seem filled with verbal cacophony is, in this sense, not a sign of weakness but of strength. We cannot lose sight of the fact that, in what otherwise might seem a trifling and annoying instance of individual distasteful abuse of a privilege, these fundamental societal values are truly implicated. That is why "[w]holly neutral futilities . . . come under the protection of free speech as fully as do Keats's poems or Donne's sermons," and why "so long as the means are peaceful, the communication need not meet standards of acceptability."

Against this perception of the constitutional policies involved, we discern certain more particularized considerations that peculiarly call for reversal of this conviction. First, the principle contended for by the state seems inherently boundless. How is one to distinguish this from any other offensive word? Surely the state has no right to cleanse public debate to the point where it is grammatically palatable to the most squeamish among us. Yet no readily ascertainable general principle exists for stopping short of that result were we to affirm the judgment below. For, while the particular four-letter word being litigated here is perhaps more distasteful than most others of its genre, it is nevertheless often true that one man's vulgarity is another's lyric. Indeed, we think it is largely because governmental officials cannot make principled distinctions in this area that the Constitution leaves matters of taste and style so largely to the individual.

Additionally, we cannot overlook the fact, because it is well illus- 20
trated by the episode involved here, that much linguistic expression serves a dual communicative function: It conveys not only ideas capable of relatively precise, detached explication, but otherwise inexpressible emotions as well. In fact, words are often chosen as much for their emotive as their cognitive force. We cannot sanction the view that the Constitution, while solicitous of the cognitive content of individual speech, has little or no regard for that emotive function which, practically speaking, may often be the more important element of the overall message sought to be communicated. Indeed, as Mr. Justice Frankfurter has said, "One of the prerogatives of American citizenship is the right to criticize public men and measures—and that means not only informed and responsible criticism but the freedom to speak foolishly and without moderation."

Finally, and in the same vein, we cannot indulge the facile assumption that one can forbid particular words without also running a substantial risk of suppressing ideas in the process. Indeed, governments might soon seize upon the censorship of particular words as a convenient guise for banning the expression of unpopular views. We have been able, as noted above, to discern little social benefit that might result from running the risk of opening the door to such grave results.

It is, in sum, our judgment that, absent a more particularized and compelling reason for its actions, the state may not, consistently with the First and Fourteenth Amendments, make the simple public display here involved of this single four-letter expletive a criminal offense. Because that is the only arguably sustainable rationale for the conviction here at issue, the judgment below must be reversed.

Justice Blackmun, with whom the Chief Justice and Justice Black join.

I dissent:

Cohen's absurd and immature antic, in my view, was mainly con- 25
duct and little speech. The California Court of Appeal appears so to have described it, and I cannot characterize it otherwise. . . .

Topics for Critical Thinking and Writing

1. After reading the facts of the case, do you agree with the dissenting opinion that what Cohen did was "mainly conduct and little speech"? Does it matter if this evaluation is correct?

2. State briefly and in your own words the several kinds of issues that, in the majority's opinion, the Cohen case does *not* involve. If the case doesn't involve them, why does the majority discuss them?

3. In Part II of the majority opinion, the Court gives its reasons for reversing Cohen's conviction. State those reasons in your own words, perhaps in three or four sentences.

4. Suppose Cohen's behavior and arrest had occurred in a neighborhood office of the Selective Service System (a local draft board), rather than in the county courthouse. Do you think this circumstance might have affected the Court's judgment? Explain in an essay of 250 words.

5. Suppose, contrary to fact, there had been evidence that Cohen's conduct actually had provoked others to acts of violence or to disturb the peace (para. 4). In an essay of 250 to 500 words, explain whether you think this evidence should have led the majority to uphold his conviction, and why.

Byron R. White
and John Paul Stevens

In January 1985, a majority of the U.S. Supreme Court, in a case called New Jersey v. T.L.O. *(a student's initials), ruled 6 to 3 that a school official's search of a student who was suspected of disobeying a school regulation does not violate the Fourth Amendment's protection against unreasonable searches and seizures.*

The case originated thus: An assistant principal in a New Jersey high school opened the purse of a fourteen-year-old girl who had been caught violating school rules by smoking in the lavatory. The girl denied that she ever smoked, and the assistant principal thought that the contents of her purse would show whether or not she was lying. The purse was found to contain cigarettes, marijuana, and some notes that seemed to indicate that she sold marijuana to other students. The school then called the police.

The case went through three lower courts; almost five years after the event occurred, the case reached the Supreme Court. Associate Justice Byron R. White wrote the majority opinion, joined by Chief Justice Warren E. Burger and by Associate Justices Lewis F. Powell, Jr., William H. Rehnquist, and Sandra Day O'Connor. Associate Justice Harry A. Blackmun concurred in a separate opinion. Associate Justices William J. Brennan, Jr., John Paul Stevens, and Thurgood Marshall dissented in part. In the excerpt that follows, legal citations have been omitted.

New Jersey v. T.L.O.

Justice White delivered the opinion of the Court.

In determining whether the search at issue in this case violated the Fourth Amendment, we are faced initially with the question whether that amendment's prohibition on unreasonable searches and seizures applies to searches conducted by public school officials. We hold that it does.

It is now beyond dispute that "the Federal Constitution, by virtue of the Fourteenth Amendment, prohibits unreasonable searches and seizures by state officers." Equally indisputable is the proposition that the Fourteenth Amendment protects the rights of students against encroachment by public school officials.

On reargument, however, the State of New Jersey has argued that the history of the Fourth Amendment indicates that the amendment was intended to regulate only searches and seizures carried out by law enforcement officers; accordingly, although public school officials are concededly state agents for purposes of the Fourteenth Amendment, the Fourth Amendment creates no rights enforceable against them.

But this Court has never limited the amendment's prohibition on unreasonable searches and seizures to operations conducted by the police. Rather, the Court has long spoken of the Fourth Amendment's strictures as restraints imposed upon "governmental action"—that is, "upon the activities of sovereign authority." Accordingly, we have held the Fourth Amendment applicable to the activities of civil as well as criminal authorities: building inspectors, OSHA inspectors, and even firemen entering privately owned premises to battle a fire, are all subject to the restraints imposed by the Fourth Amendment.

Notwithstanding the general applicability of the Fourth Amendment to the activities of civil authorities, a few courts have concluded that school officials are exempt from the dictates of the Fourth Amendment by virtue of the special nature of their authority over schoolchildren. Teachers and school administrators, it is said, act *in loco parentis* [that is, in place of a parent] in their dealings with students: Their authority is that of the parent, not the state, and is therefore not subject to the limits of the Fourth Amendment.

Such reasoning is in tension with contemporary reality and the teachings of this Court. We have held school officials subject to the commands of the First Amendment, and the Due Process Clause of the Fourteenth Amendment. If school authorities are state actors for purposes of the constitutional guarantees of freedom of expression and due process, it is difficult to understand why they should be deemed to be exercising parental rather than public authority when conducting searches of their students.

In carrying out searches and other disciplinary functions pursuant to such policies, school officials act as representatives of the state, not merely as surrogates for the parents, and they cannot claim the parents' immunity from the strictures of the Fourth Amendment.

To hold that the Fourth Amendment applies to searches conducted by school authorities is only to begin the inquiry into the standards governing such searches. Although the underlying command of the Fourth Amendment is always that searches and seizures be reasonable, what is reasonable depends on the context within which a search takes place.

[STANDARD OF REASONABLENESS]

The determination of the standard of reasonableness governing any specific class of searches requires balancing the need to search against the invasion which the search entails. On one side of the balance are arrayed the individual's legitimate expectations of privacy and personal security; on the other, the government's need for effective methods to deal with breaches of public order.

We have recognized that even a limited search of the person is a substantial invasion of privacy. A search of a child's person or of a closed purse or other bag carried on her person, no less than a similar search carried out on an adult, is undoubtedly a severe violation of subjective expectations of privacy.

Of course, the Fourth Amendment does not protect subjective expectations of privacy that are unreasonable or otherwise "illegitimate." The State of New Jersey has argued that because of the pervasive supervision to which children in the schools are necessarily subject, a child has virtually no legitimate expectation of privacy in articles of personal property "unnecessarily" carried into a school. This argument has two factual premises: (1) the fundamental incompatibility of expectations of privacy with the maintenance of a sound educational environment; and (2) the minimal interest of the child in bringing any items of personal property into the school. Both premises are severely flawed.

Although this Court may take notice of the difficulty of maintaining discipline in the public schools today, the situation is not so dire that students in the schools may claim no legitimate expectations of privacy.

[PRIVACY AND DISCIPLINE]

Against the child's interest in privacy must be set the substantial interest of teachers and administrators in maintaining discipline in the classroom and on school grounds. Maintaining order in the classroom has never been easy, but in recent years, school disorder has often taken particularly ugly forms; drug use and violent crime in the schools have become major social problems. Accordingly, we have recognized that maintaining security and order in the schools requires a certain degree of flexibility in school disciplinary procedures, and we have respected the value of preserving the informality of the student-teacher relationship.

How, then, should we strike the balance between the schoolchild's legitimate expectations of privacy and the school's equally legitimate need to maintain an environment in which learning can take place? It is evident that the school setting requires some easing of the restrictions to which searches by public authorities are ordinarily subject. The warrant requirement, in particular, is unsuited to the school environment; requiring a teacher to obtain a warrant before searching a child suspected of an infraction of school rules (or of the criminal law) would unduly interfere with the maintenance of the swift and informal disciplinary procedures needed in the schools. We hold today that school officials need not obtain a warrant before searching a student who is under their authority.

The school setting also requires some modification of the level 15 of suspicion of illicit activity needed to justify a search. Ordinarily, a search—even one that may permissibly be carried out without a warrant—must be based upon "probable cause" to believe that a violation of the law has occurred. However, "probable cause" is not an irreducible requirement of a valid search.

[BALANCING OF INTERESTS]

The fundamental command of the Fourth Amendment is that searches and seizures be reasonable, and although "both the concept of probable cause and the requirement of a warrant bear on the reasonableness of a search, . . . in certain limited circumstances neither is required." Thus, we have in a number of cases recognized the legality of searches and seizures based on suspicions that, although "reasonable," do not rise to the level of probable cause. Where a careful balancing of governmental and private interests suggests that the public interest is best served by a Fourth Amendment standard of reasonableness that stops short of probable cause, we have not hesitated to adopt such a standard.

We join the majority of courts that have examined this issue in concluding that the accommodation of the privacy interests of schoolchildren with the substantial need of teachers and administrators for freedom to maintain order in the schools does not require strict adherence to the requirement that searches be based on probable cause to believe that the subject of the search has violated or is violating the law.

Rather, the legality of a search of a student should depend simply on the reasonableness, under all the circumstances, of the search. Determining the reasonableness of any search involves a twofold inquiry; first, one must consider "whether the . . . action was justified at its inception," second, one must determine whether the search as actually conducted "was reasonably related in scope to the circumstances which justified the interference in the first place."

Under ordinary circumstances, a search of a student by a teacher or other school official will be "justified at its inception" when there are reasonable grounds for suspecting that the search will turn up evidence that the student has violated or is violating either the law or the rules of the school. Such a search will be permissible in its scope when the measures adopted are reasonably related to the objectives of the search and not excessively intrusive in light of the age and sex of the student and the nature of the infraction.

This standard will, we trust, neither unduly burden the efforts of 20 school authorities to maintain order in their schools nor authorize unrestrained intrusions upon the privacy of schoolchildren. By focusing attention on the question of reasonableness, the standard will spare teachers and school administrators the necessity of schooling themselves in the niceties of probable cause and permit them to regulate their conduct according to the dictates of reason and common sense. At the same time, the reasonableness standard should insure that the interests of students will be invaded no more than is necessary to achieve the legitimate end of preserving order in the schools.

There remains the question of the legality of the search in this case. We recognize that the "reasonable grounds" standard applied by the New Jersey Supreme Court in its consideration of this question is not substantially different from the standard that we have adopted today. Nonetheless, we believe that the New Jersey court's application of that standard to strike down the search of T.L.O.'s purse reflects a somewhat crabbed notion of reasonableness. Our review of the facts surrounding the search leads us to conclude that the search was in no sense unreasonable for Fourth Amendment purposes.

Justice Stevens, dissenting.

The majority holds that "a search of a student by a teacher or other school official will be 'justified at its inception' when there are reasonable grounds for suspecting that the search will turn up evidence *that the student has violated or is violating either the law or the rules of the school.*"

This standard will permit teachers and school administrators to search students when they suspect that the search will reveal evidence of [violation of] even the most trivial school regulation or precatory guideline for students' behavior. For the Court, a search for curlers and sunglasses in order to enforce the school dress code is apparently just as important as a search for evidence of heroin addiction or violent gang activity.

A standard better attuned to this concern would permit teachers and school administrators to search a student when they have reason to believe that the search will uncover *evidence that the student is violating the law or engaging in conduct that is seriously disruptive of school order, or the educational process.*

A standard that varies the extent of the permissible intrusion with 25 the gravity of the suspected offense is also more consistent with common-law experience and this Court's precedent. Criminal law has traditionally recognized a distinction between essentially regulatory offenses and serious violations of the peace, and graduated the response of the criminal justice system depending on the character of the violation.

Topics for Critical Thinking and Writing

1. In the majority opinion Justice White says (para. 14) that it is "evident that the school setting requires some easing of the restrictions to which searches by public authorities are ordinarily subject." Does White offer evidence supporting what he says is "evident"? List any evidence that White gives or any that you can think of.

2. What argument does White give to show that the Fourth Amendment prohibition against "unreasonable searches and seizures" applies to the behavior of school officials? Do you think his argument is reasonable, or not? Explain.

3. On what ground does White argue (para. 14) that school students have "legitimate expectations of privacy" and so New Jersey is wrong in arguing the contrary?

4. What are the conflicting interests involved in the case, according to White? How does the Supreme Court resolve this conflict?

5. Why does White argue (para. 15) that school authorities may search students without first obtaining a search warrant? (By the way, who issues a search warrant? Who seeks one?) What does he mean when he says that the requirement of "probable cause" is "not an irreducible requirement of a valid search" (para. 15)?

6. Could a search undertaken on the principle enunciated by the Court's majority mean that whenever authorities perceive what they choose to call "disorder" — perhaps in the activity of an assembly of protesters in the streets of a big city — they may justify otherwise unlawful searches and seizures?

7. Some forty years before this case, Justice Robert H. Jackson argued that the schools have a special responsibility for adhering to the Constitution: "That they are educating the young for citizenship is reason for scrupulous protection of constitutional freedoms of the individual, if we are not to strangle the free mind at its source and teach youth to discount important principles of our government as mere platitudes." Similarly, in 1967 in an analogous case involving another female pupil, Justice Brennan argued that "schools cannot expect their students to learn the lessons of good citizenship when the school authorities themselves disregard the fundamental principles underpinning our constitutional freedoms." Do you find these arguments compelling? Why, or why not?

8. Let's admit that maintaining order in schools may be extremely difficult. In your opinion, does the difficulty justify diminishing the rights

of citizens? Smoking is not an illegal activity, yet in this instance a student suspected of smoking—that is, merely of violating a school rule—was searched. In an essay of 250 words, consider whether the maintenance of school discipline in such a matter justifies a search.

9. White relies on a standard of "reasonableness." Do you think this criterion is too subjective to be a proper standard to distinguish between permissible and impermissible searches? Write a 500-word essay on the standard of reasonable searches and seizures, giving a hypothetical but plausible example of a reasonable search and seizure and then of an unreasonable search and seizure.

11

A Literary Critic's View: Arguing about Literature

You might think that literature—fiction, poetry (including songs), drama—is meant only to be enjoyed, not to be argued about. Yet literature is constantly the subject of argumentative writing—not all of it by teachers of English. For instance, if you glance at the current issue of *Time* or *Newsweek* you probably will find a review of a play, suggesting that the play is worth seeing or is not worth seeing. Or, in the same magazine, you may find an article reporting that a senator or member of Congress argued that the National Endowment for the Humanities wasted its grant money by funding research on such-and-such an author, or that the National Endowment for the Arts insulted taxpayers by making an award to a writer who defamed the American family.

Probably most writing about literature, whether done by college students, their professors, journalists, members of Congress, or whomever, is devoted to interpreting, judging (evaluating), and theorizing. Let's look at each of these, drawing our examples chiefly from Shakespeare's *Macbeth*.

INTERPRETING

Interpreting is a matter of setting forth the *meaning* or the meanings of a work. For some readers, a work has *a* meaning, the one intended by the writer, which we may or may not perceive. For most critics today, however, a work has *many* meanings, for instance the meaning it had for the writer, the meanings it has accumulated over time, and the meanings it has for each of today's readers. Take *Macbeth*, a play about a Scottish king, written soon after a Scot—James VI of Scotland—had been installed as James I, King of England. The play must have meant something special to the king—we know that it was presented at court—and something a little different to the ordinary English citizen. And surely it means something different to us. For instance, few if any people today believe in the divine right of kings, although James I certainly did; and few if any people today believe in malignant witches, although witches play an important role in the tragedy. What *we* see in the play must be rather different from what Shakespeare's audience saw in it.

Many interpretations of *Macbeth* have been offered. Let's take two fairly simple and clearly opposed views.

1. Macbeth is a villain who, by murdering his lawful king, offends God's rule, so he is overthrown by God's earthly instruments, Malcolm and Macduff. Macbeth is justly punished; the reader or spectator rejoices in his defeat.

One can offer a good deal of evidence—and if one is taking this position in an essay of course one must *argue* it—by giving supporting reasons rather than merely assert the position. Here is a second view.

2. Macbeth is a hero-villain, a man who commits terrible crimes, but who never completely loses the reader's sympathy; although he is justly punished, the reader believes that with the death of Macbeth the world has become a smaller place.

Again, one *must* offer evidence in an essay that presents this thesis, or indeed presents any interpretation. For instance, one might offer as evidence the fact that the survivors, especially Macduff and Malcolm, have not interested us nearly as much as Macbeth has. One might argue, too, that although Macbeth's villainy is undeniable, his conscience never deserts him—here one would point to specific passages, and would offer some brief quotations. Macbeth's pained awareness of what he has done, it can be argued, enables the reader to sympathize with him continually.

Or consider an interpretation of Lady Macbeth. Is she simply evil through and through, or are there mitigating reasons for her actions? Might one argue, perhaps in a feminist interpretation, that despite her intelligence and courage she had no outlet for expression except through her husband? In order to make this argument, the writer might want to go beyond the text of the play, offering as evidence Elizabethan comments about the proper role of women.

JUDGING (OR EVALUATING)

Literary criticism is also concerned with such questions as these: Is *Macbeth* a great tragedy? Is *Macbeth* a greater tragedy than *Romeo and Juliet*? The writer offers an opinion about the worth of the literary work, but the opinion must be supported by an argument, expressed in sentences that offer supporting evidence.

Let's pause for a moment to think about evaluation in general. When we say "This is a great play," are we in effect saying only "I like this play"? That is, are we merely *expressing* our taste rather than *asserting* anything about something out there—something independent of our tastes and feelings? (The next few paragraphs will not answer this question, but they may start you thinking about your own answer.) Consider these three sentences.

1. It's raining outside.
2. I like vanilla.
3. This is a really good book.

If you are indoors and you say that it is raining outside, a hearer may ask for verification. Why do you say what you say? "Because," you reply, "I'm looking out the window." Or "Because Jane just came in, and she is drenched." Or "Because I just heard a weather report." If, on the other hand, you say that you like vanilla, it's almost unthinkable that anyone would ask you why. No one expects you to justify—to support, to give a reason for—an expression of taste.

Now consider the third statement, "This is a really good book." It is entirely reasonable, we think, for someone to ask you why you say that. And you reply, "Well, the characters are realistic, and the plot held my interest," or "It really gave me an insight into what life among the rich [or the poor] must be like," or some such thing. That is, statement 3 at least seems to be stating a fact, and it seems to be something we can discuss, even argue about, in a way that we cannot argue about a personal preference for vanilla. Almost everyone would agree that when we offer an aesthetic judgment we ought to be able to give reasons for it. At the very least, we might say, we hope to show *why* we evaluate the work as we do, and to suggest that if our readers try to see it from our point of view they may then accept our evaluation.

Evaluations are always based on assumptions, although these assumptions may be unstated, and in fact the writer may even be unaware of them. Some of these assumptions play the role of criteria; they control the sort of evidence the writer believes is relevant to the evaluation. What sorts of assumptions may underlie value judgments? We will mention a few, merely as examples. Other assumptions are possible, and all of these assumptions can themselves become topics of dispute:

1. A good work of art, although fictional, says something about real life.
2. A good work of art is complex yet unified.
3. A good work of art sets forth a wholesome view of life.
4. A good work of art is original.
5. A good work of art deals with an important subject.

Let's look briefly at these views, one by one.

1. *A good work of art, although fictional, says something about real life.* If you hold this view, that literature is connected to life, and you believe that human beings behave in fairly consistent ways, that is, that each of us has an enduring "character," you probably will judge as inferior a work in which the figures behave inconsistently or seem not to be adequately motivated. (The point must be made, however, that different literary forms or genres are governed by different rules. For instance, consistency of character is usually expected in tragedy but not in melodrama or in comedy, where last-minute reformations may be welcome and greeted with applause. The novelist Henry James said, "You will not write a good novel unless you possess the sense of reality." He is probably right—but does his view hold for the writer of farces?) In the case of *Macbeth* you might well find that the characters are consistent: Although the play begins by showing Macbeth as a loyal defender of King Duncan, Macbeth's later treachery is understandable, given the temptation and the pressure. Similarly, Lady Macbeth's descent into madness, although it may come as a surprise, may strike you as entirely plausible: At the beginning of the play she is confident that she can become an accomplice to a murder, but she has overestimated herself (or, we might say, she has underestimated her own humanity, the power of her guilty conscience, which drives her to insanity).

2. *A good work of art is complex yet unified.* If Macbeth is only a "tyrant" (Macduff's word) or a "butcher" (Malcolm's word), he is a unified character but he may be too simple and too uninteresting a character to be the subject of a great play. But, one argument holds, Macbeth in fact is a complex character, not simply a villain but a hero-villain, and the play as a whole is complex. *Macbeth* is a good work of art, one might argue, partly because it shows us so many aspects of life (courage, fear, loyalty, treachery, for a start) through a richly varied language (the diction ranges from a grand passage in which Macbeth says that his bloody hands will "incarnadine," or make red, "the multitudinous seas" to colloquial passages such as the drunken porter's "Knock, knock"). The play shows us the heroic Macbeth tragically destroying his own life, and it shows us the comic porter making coarse jokes about deceit and damnation, jokes that (although the porter doesn't know it) connect with Macbeth's crimes.

3. *A good work of art sets forth a wholesome view of life.* The idea that a work should be judged partly or largely on the moral view that it contains is widely held by the general public. (It has also been held by esteemed philosophers, notably Plato.) Thus, a story that demeans women—perhaps one that takes a casual view of rape—would be given a low rating and so would a play that treats a mass murderer as a hero.

Implicit in this approach is what is called an *instrumentalist* view— the idea that a work of art is an instrument, a means, to some higher value. Thus, many people hold that reading great works of literature makes us better—or at least does not make us worse. In this view, a work that is pornographic or in some other way thought to be immoral will be given a low value. At the time we are writing this chapter, a law requires the National Endowment for the Arts to take into account standards of decency when making awards.

Moral judgments, it should be noted, do not come only from the conservative right; the liberal left has been quick to detect political incorrectness. In fact, except for those people who subscribe to the now unfashionable view that a work of art is an independent aesthetic object with little or no connection to the real world—something like a pretty floral arrangement, or a wordless melody—most people judge works of literature largely by their content, by what the works seem to say about life. Marxist critics, for instance, have customarily held that literature should make the reader aware of the political realities of life; feminist critics are likely to hold that literature should make us aware of gender relationships—for example, aware of patriarchal power and of female accomplishments. Later in this chapter you will be asked to think about whether the militaristic passages in "The Star-Spangled Banner" perhaps stir the wrong sorts of sentiments in us.

4. *A good work of art is original.* This assumption puts special value on new techniques and new subject matter. Thus, the *first* playwright who introduces a new subject (say, AIDS) gets extra credit, so to speak. Or, to return to Shakespeare, one sign of his genius, it is held, is that he was so highly varied; none of his tragedies seems merely to duplicate another, each is a world of its own, a new kind of achievement. Compare, for instance, *Romeo and Juliet,* with its two youthful and innocent heroes, with *Macbeth,* with its deeply guilty hero. Both plays are tragedies, but we can hardly imagine two more different plays—even if a reader perversely argues that the young lovers are guilty of impetuosity and of disobeying appropriate authorities.

5. *A good work of art deals with an important subject.* Here we are concerned with theme: Great works, in this view, must deal with great themes. Love, death, patriotism, and God, say, are great themes; a work that deals with these may achieve a height, an excellence, that, say, a work describing a dog scratching for fleas may not. (Of course if the reader feels that the dog is a symbol of humanity plagued by invisible enemies, then the poem about the dog may reach the heights, but then, too, it is *not* a poem about a dog and fleas—it is really a poem about humanity and the invisible.)

The point: In writing an evaluation you must let your reader know *why* you value the work as you do. Obviously it is not enough just to keep saying that *this* work is great whereas *that* work is not so great; the reader wants to know *why* you offer the judgments that you do, which means that you will have to set forth your criteria and then offer evidence that is in accord with them.

THEORIZING

Some literary criticism is concerned with such theoretical questions as these:

> What is tragedy? Can the hero be a villain? How does tragedy differ from melodrama?
>
> Why do tragedies—works showing good or at least interesting people destroyed—give us pleasure?
>
> Does a work of art—a play or a novel, say, a made-up world with imagined characters—offer anything that can be called "truth"? Does an experience of a work of art affect our character?
>
> Does a work of art have meaning in itself, or is the meaning simply whatever anyone wishes to say it is? Does *Macbeth* tell us anything about life, or is it just an invented story?

And, yet again, one hopes that anyone asserting a thesis concerned with any of these topics will offer evidence, will, indeed, *argue* rather than merely assert.

A CHECKLIST FOR AN ARGUMENT ABOUT LITERATURE

✓ Is your imagined reader like a typical classmate of yours, someone who is not a specialist in literature but who is open-minded and interested in hearing your point of view about a work?

✓ Is the essay supported with evidence, usually from the text itself, but conceivably from other sources (such as a statement by the author, or a statement by a person regarded as an authority, or perhaps the evidence of comparable works)?

✓ Is the essay inclusive? Does it take into account all relevant details (which is not to say that it includes everything the writer knows about the work—for instance, that it was made into a film or that the author died poor)?

✓ Is the essay focused? Does the thesis stay steadily before the reader?

✓ Does the essay use quotations, but as evidence, not as padding? Whenever possible, does it abridge or summarize long quotations?

✓ Are all sources fully acknowledged? (For the form of documentation, see pp. 210–26.)

EXAMPLES:
Two Students Interpret
Robert Frost's "Mending Wall"

Let's consider two competing interpretations of a poem, Robert Frost's "Mending Wall." We say "competing" because these interpretations clash head-on. Differing interpretations need not be incompatible, of course. For instance, a historical interpretation of *Macbeth*, arguing that an understanding of the context of English-Scottish politics around 1605 helps us to appreciate the play, need not be incompatible with a psychoanalytic interpretation that tells us that Macbeth's murder of King Duncan is rooted in an Oedipus complex, the king being a father figure. Different approaches thus can illuminate different aspects of the work, just as they can emphasize or subordinate different elements in the plot or characters portrayed. But, again, in the next few pages we will deal with mutually incompatible interpretations of the meaning of Frost's poem—of what Frost's poem is about.

After reading the poem and the two interpretations written by students, spend a few minutes thinking about the questions that we raise after the second interpretation.

Robert Frost

Robert Frost (1874–1963) studied for part of one term at Dartmouth College in New Hampshire, then did odd jobs (including teaching), and from 1897 to 1899 was enrolled as a special student at Harvard. He then farmed in New Hampshire, published a few poems in newspapers, did some more teaching, and in 1912 left for England, where he hoped to achieve success as a writer. By 1915 he was known in England, and he returned to the United States. By the time of his death he was the nation's unofficial poet laureate. "Mending Wall" was first published in 1914.

Mending Wall

Something there is that doesn't love a wall,
That sends the frozen-ground-swell under it,
And spills the upper boulders in the sun;
And makes gaps even two can pass abreast.
The work of hunters is another thing: 5
I have come after them and made repair
Where they have left not one stone on a stone,
But they would have the rabbit out of hiding,
To please the yelping dogs. The gaps I mean,

No one has seen them made or heard them made,   10
But at spring mending-time we find them there.
I let my neighbor know beyond the hill;
And on a day we meet to walk the line
And set the wall between us once again.
We keep the wall between us as we go.   15
To each the boulders that have fallen to each.
And some are loaves and some so nearly balls
We have to use a spell to make them balance:
"Stay where you are until our backs are turned!"
We wear our fingers rough with handling them.   20
Oh, just another kind of outdoor game,
One on a side. It comes to little more:
There where it is we do not need the wall:
He is all pine and I am apple orchard.
My apple trees will never get across   25
And eat the cones under his pines, I tell him.
He only says, "Good fences make good neighbors."
Spring is the mischief in me, and I wonder
If I could put a notion in his head:
"*Why* do they make good neighbors? Isn't it   30
Where there are cows? But here there are no cows.
Before I built a wall I'd ask to know
What I was walling in or walling out,
And to whom I was like to give offense.
Something there is that doesn't love a wall,   35
That wants it down." I could say "Elves" to him,
But it's not elves exactly, and I'd rather
He said it for himself. I see him there
Bringing a stone grasped firmly by the top
In each hand, like an old-stone savage armed.   40
He moves in darkness as it seems to me,
Not of woods only and the shade of trees.
He will not go behind his father's saying,
And he likes having thought of it so well
He says again, "Good fences make good neighbors."   45

Jonathan Deutsch

Professor Walton

English 102

March 3, 1998

   The Deluded Speaker in Frost's "Mending Wall"

   Our discussions of "Mending Wall" in high
school showed that most people think Frost is
saying that walls between people are a bad
thing, and that we should not try to separate
ourselves from each other unnecessarily. Perhaps
the wall, in this view, is a symbol for race
prejudice or religious differences, and Frost is
suggesting that these differences are minor and
that they should not keep us apart. In this common view, the neighbor's words, "Good fences
make good neighbors" (lines 27 and 45) show that
the neighbor is shortsighted. I disagree with
this view, but first I want to present the evidence that might be offered for it, so that we
can then see whether it really is substantial.

   First of all, someone might claim that in
lines 23 to 26 Frost offers a good argument
against walls:

      There where it is we do not need the wall:
      He is all pine and I am apple orchard.
      My apple trees will never get across
      And eat the cones under his pines, I tell
         him.

The neighbor does not offer a valid reply to
this argument; in fact, he doesn't offer any
argument at all but simply says, "Good fences
make good neighbors."

Deutsch 2

Another piece of evidence supposedly showing that the neighbor is wrong, it is said, is
found in Frost's description of him as "an old-
stone savage," and someone who "moves in darkness" (40, 41). And a third piece of evidence
is said to be that the neighbor "will not go
behind his father's saying" (43), but he merely
repeats the saying.

There is, however, another way of looking
at the poem. As I see it, the speaker is a very
snide and condescending person. He is confident
that he knows it all and that his neighbor is
an ignorant savage; he is even willing to tease
his supposedly ignorant neighbor. For instance,
the speaker admits to "the mischief in me"
(28), and he is confident that he could tell
the truth to the neighbor but he arrogantly
thinks that it would be a more effective form
of teaching if the neighbor "said it for himself" (38).

The speaker is not only unpleasantly mis-
chievous and condescending toward his neighbor,
but he is also shallow, for he does not see the
great wisdom that there is in proverbs. The
American Heritage Dictionary of the English
Language, third edition, defines a proverb as
"A short, pithy saying in frequent and widespread use that expresses a basic truth."
Frost, or at least the man who speaks this
poem, does not seem to realize that proverbs
express truths. He just dismisses them, and
he thinks the neighbor is wrong not to "go behind his father's saying" (43). But there is

a great deal of wisdom in the sayings of our
fathers. For instance, in the Bible (in the Old
Testament) there is a whole book of proverbs,
filled with wise sayings such as "Reprove
not a scorner, lest he hate thee: rebuke a
wise man, and he will love thee" (9:8); "He
that trusteth in his riches shall fall"
(11:28); "The way of a fool is right in his
own eyes" (12:15; this might be said of the
speaker of "Mending Wall"); "A soft answer
turneth away wrath" (15:1); and (to cut
short what could be a list many pages long),
"Whoso diggeth a pit shall fall therein"
(26:27).

The speaker is confident that walls are unnecessary and probably bad, but he doesn't realize that even where there are no cattle, walls
serve the valuable purpose of clearly marking
out our territory. They help us to preserve our
independence and our individuality. Walls--man-
made structures--are a sign of civilization. A
wall more or less says, "This is mine, but I respect that as yours." Frost's speaker is so confident of his shallow view that he makes fun of
his neighbor for repeating that "Good fences
make good neighbors" (27, 45). But he himself
repeats his own saying, "Something there is that
doesn't love a wall" (1, 35). And at least the
neighbor has age-old tradition on his side,
since the proverb is the saying of his father.
On the other hand, the speaker has only his own
opinion, and he can't even say what the "something" is.

It may be that Frost meant for us to laugh at
the neighbor, and to take the side of the
speaker, but I think it is much more likely
that he meant for us to see that the speaker is
mean-spirited (or at least given to unpleasant
teasing), too self-confident, foolishly dismissing the wisdom of the old times, and entirely unaware that he has these unpleasant
characteristics.

Felicia Alonso

Professor Walton

English 102

March 3, 1998

The Debate in Robert Frost's "Mending Wall"

I think the first thing to say about Frost's "Mending Wall" is this: The poem is not about a debate over whether good fences do or do not make good neighbors. It is about two debaters: One of the debaters is on the side of vitality, and the other is on the side of an unchanging, fixed--dead, we might say--tradition.

How can we characterize the speaker? For one thing, he is neighborly. Interestingly, it is <u>he</u>, and not the neighbor, who initiates the repairing of the wall: "I let my neighbor know beyond the hill" (line 12). This seems strange, since the speaker doesn't see any point in this wall, whereas the neighbor is all in favor of walls. Can we explain this apparent contradiction? Yes; the speaker is a good neighbor, willing to do his share of the work, and willing (perhaps in order not to upset his neighbor) to maintain an old tradition even though he doesn't see its importance. It may not be important, he thinks, but it is really rather pleasant, "another kind of outdoor game" (21). In fact, sometimes he even repairs fences on his own, after hunters have destroyed them.

Second, we can say that the speaker is on the side of nature. "Something there is that doesn't love a wall," he says (1, 35), and of course the "something" is nature itself. Nature "sends the frozen-ground-swell" under the wall and "spills the upper boulders in the sun; / And makes gaps even two can pass abreast" (2-4). Notice that nature itself makes the gaps, and that "two can pass abreast," that is, people can walk together in a companionable way. It is hard to imagine the neighbor walking side by side with anyone.

Third, we can say that the speaker has a sense of humor. When he thinks of trying to get his neighbor interested in the issue, he admits that "the mischief" is in him (28), and he amusingly attributes his playfulness to a natural force, the spring. He playfully toys with the obviously preposterous idea of suggesting to his neighbor that elves caused the stones to fall, but he stops short of making this amusing suggestion to his very serious neighbor. Still, the mere thought assures us that he has a playful, genial nature, and the idea also again implies that not only the speaker but also some sort of mysterious natural force dislikes walls.

Finally, though of course he thinks he is right and that his neighbor is mistaken, he at least is cautious in his view. He does <u>not</u> call his neighbor "an old-stone savage"; rather, he uses a simile ("like") and he then adds that this is only his opinion, so the opinion is softened quite a bit. Here is the description of the neighbor, with underlining added in order to clarify my point. The neighbor is

> . . . <u>like</u> an old-stone savage armed.
> He moves in darkness <u>as it seems to me</u> . . .
> (40-41)

Of course the only things we know about
the neighbor are those things that the speaker
chooses to tell us, so it is not surprising
that the speaker comes out ahead. He comes out
ahead not because he is right about walls (real
or symbolic) and his neighbor is wrong--that's
an issue that is not settled in the poem. He
comes out ahead because he is a more interesting figure, someone who is neighborly, thoughtful, playful. Yes, maybe he seems to us to feel
superior to his neighbor, but we can be certain
that he doesn't cause his neighbor any embarrassment. Take the very end of the poem. The
speaker tells us that the neighbor

> . . . will not go behind his father's say-
>   ing,
> And he likes having thought of it so well
> He says again, "Good fences make good
>   neighbors."

The speaker is telling <u>us</u> that the neighbor
is utterly unoriginal and that the neighbor confuses <u>remembering</u> something with <u>thinking</u>. But
the speaker doesn't get into an argument; he
doesn't rudely challenge his neighbor and demand
reasons, which might force the neighbor to see
that he can't think for himself. And in fact we
probably like the neighbor just as he is, and we
don't want him to change his mind. The words

```
                                              Alonso 4


    that ring in our ears are not the speaker's but
    the neighbor's: "Good fences make good neigh-
    bors." The speaker of the poem is a good
    neighbor. After all, one can hardly be more
    neighborly than to let the neighbor have the
    last word.
```

Topics for Critical Thinking and Writing

1. State the thesis of each essay. Do you believe the theses are sufficiently clear and appear sufficiently early in the essays?

2. Consider the evidence that each essay offers by way of supporting its thesis. Do you find some of the evidence unconvincing? Explain.

3. Putting aside the question of which interpretation you prefer, comment on the organization of each essay. Is the organization clear? Do you want to propose some other pattern that you think might be more effective?

4. Consult the Checklist for Peer Review on pages 182–83, and offer comments on one of the two essays. Or: If you were the instructor in the course in which these two essays were submitted, what might be your final comments on each of them? Or: Write an analysis (250–500 words) of the strengths and weaknesses of either essay.

EXERCISES: Reading a Poem and Reading Two Stories

Andrew Marvell

Marvell (1621–1678), born in Hull, England, and educated at *…e, Cambridge, was traveling in Europe when the civil war be-* *…lists and the puritans broke out in England in 1642. The pu-*

ritans were victorious and established the Commonwealth (the monarchy was restored later, in 1660), and Marvell became a tutor to the daughter of the victorious Lord-General. In 1657 he became an assistant to the blind poet John Milton, who held the title of Latin Secretary (Latin was the language of international diplomacy). In 1659 Marvell was elected to represent Hull in Parliament. As a man of letters, during his lifetime he was known chiefly for some satiric prose and poetry; most of the writings for which he is now esteemed were published posthumously. The following poem was first published in 1681.

To His Coy Mistress°

Had we but world enough, and time,
This coyness,° Lady, were no crime.
We would sit down, and think which way
To walk, and pass our long love's day.
Thou by the Indian Ganges' side   5
Shouldst rubies find; I by the tide
Of Humber° would complain. I would
Love you ten years before the Flood,
And you should, if you please, refuse
Till the Conversion of the Jews.°   10
My vegetable° love should grow
Vaster than empires and more slow;
An hundred years should go to praise
Thine eyes, and on thy forehead gaze;
Two hundred to adore each breast,   15
But thirty thousand to the rest;
An age at least to every part,
And the last age should show your heart.
For, Lady, you deserve this state,°
Nor would I love at lower rate.   20
    But at my back I always hear
Time's wingèd chariot hurrying near;
And yonder all before us lie
Deserts of vast eternity.
Thy beauty shall no more be found,   25
Nor, in thy marble vault, shall sound

---

1 Mistress Beloved woman.   **3 coyness** Reluctance.   **7 Humber** An estuary at Hull, Marvell's birthplace.   **10 the Conversion of the Jews** Something that would take place in the remote future, at the end of history.   **11 vegetable** Vegetative or growing.   **19 state** Ceremonious treatment.

My echoing song; then worms shall try°
That long-preserved virginity,
And your quaint° honour turn to dust,
And into ashes all my lust: 30
The grave's a fine and private place,
But none, I think, do there embrace.
   Now therefore, while the youthful hue
Sits on thy skin like morning dew,
And while thy willing soul transpires   35
At every pore with instant fires,
Now let us sport us while we may,
And now, like amorous birds of prey,
Rather at once our time devour
Than languish in his slow-chapt° power.   40
Let us roll all our strength and all
Our sweetness up into one ball,
And tear our pleasures with rough strife
Thorough° the iron gates of life:
Thus, though we cannot make our sun   45
Stand still, yet we will make him run.°

Topics for Critical Thinking and Writing

1. The motif that life is short and that we should seize the day (Latin: *carpe diem*) is old. Marvell's poem, in fact, probably has its ultimate source in a classical text called *The Greek Anthology*, a collection of about six thousand short Greek poems composed between the first century B.C. and the tenth century A.D. One poem goes thus, in a fairly literal translation:

   > You spare your maidenhead, and to what profit? For when you come to Hades you will not find your lover, girl. Among the living are the delights of Venus, but, maiden, we shall lie in the underworld mere bones and dust.

   If you find Marvell's poem more impressive, offer reasons for your belief.

2. A student, working from the translation just given, produced this rhyming version:

   > You keep your virginity, but to what end?
   > Below, in Hades, you won't find your friend.

---

27 try Test.   **29 quaint** Fastidious or finicky, with a pun on a coarse word defined in an Elizabethan dictionary as "a woman's privities."   **40 slow-chapt** Slow-jawed.
44 Thorough Through.   **45–46 we cannot . . . still** An allusion to Joshua, the ancient Hebrew who, according to the Book of Joshua (10.12–13), made the sun stand still.

> On earth we enjoy Venus' sighs and moans;
> Buried below, we are senseless bones.

What do you think of this version? Why? Prepare your own version—your instructor may divide the class into groups of four, and each group can come up with a collaborative version—and then compare it with other versions, giving reasons for your preferences.

3. Marvell's poem takes the form of a syllogism (see pp. 58–62). It can be divided into three parts:

   1. "Had we" (line 1), a supposition, or suppositional premise;
   2. "But at my back" (line 21), a refutation;
   3. "Now, therefore" (line 33), a deduction.

   Look closely at the poem and develop the argument using these three parts, devoting a few sentences to each part.

4. A student wrote of this poem:

   > As a Christian I can't accept the lover's statement that "yonder all before us lie / Deserts of vast eternity" (lines 23–24). The poem may contain beautiful lines, and it may offer clever reasoning, but the reasoning is based on what my religion tells me is wrong. I not only cannot accept the idea of the poem, but I also cannot enjoy the poem, since it presents a false view of reality.

   What assumptions is this student making about a reader's response to a work of literature? Do you agree or disagree? Why?

5. Here are three additional comments by students. For each, list the writer's assumptions, and then evaluate each comment. You may agree or disagree, in whole or in part, with any comment, but give your reasons.

   > A. The poem is definitely clever, and that is part of what is wrong with it. It is a blatant attempt at seduction. The man seems to think he is smarter than the woman he is speaking to, and he "proves" that she should go to bed with him. Since we don't hear her side of the argument, Marvell implies that she has nothing to say and that his argument is sound. What the poet doesn't seem to understand is that there is such a thing as virtue, and a woman need not sacrifice virtue just because death is inevitable.

   > B. On the surface, "To His Coy Mistress" is an attempt to persuade a woman to go to bed with the speaker, but the poem is really less about sex than it is about the terrifying shortness of life.

   > C. This is not a love poem. The speaker admits that his impulse is "lust" (line 30), and he makes fun of the girl's conception of honor and virginity. If we enjoy this poem at all, our enjoyment must be in the hope that this would-be date-rapist is unsuccessful.

6. Read the poem several times slowly, perhaps even aloud. Do certain lines seem especially moving, especially memorable? If so, which ones? Give reasons for your belief.

7. In *On Deconstruction* (1982), a study of contemporary literary theory, Jonathan Culler remarks that feminist criticism has often stressed "read-

ing as a woman." This concept, Culler says, affirms the "continuity between women's experience of social and familial structures and their experiences as readers." Do you agree with his suggestion that men and women often interpret literary works differently? Consider Marvell's poem in particular: Identify and discuss phrases and images in it to which men and women readers might (or might not) respond very differently.

8. A small point, but perhaps one of some interest. In the original text, line 34 ends with *glew*, not with *dew*. Most editors assume that the printer made an error, and—looking for a word to rhyme with *hue*—they replace *glew* with *dew*. Another possible emendation is *lew*, an archaic word meaning "warmth." But the original reading has been defended, as a variant of the word *glow*. Your preference? Your reasons?

Jean Rhys

Jean Rhys (1890–1979) was the pseudonym used by Ella Gwendolen Rees Williams. She was born in the West Indies, in Dominica (at that time a British colony) and educated there and in England. In 1927, in England, she began to publish stories and novels (we reprint a story of 1931), but she did not achieve wide recognition until 1966 with the publication of Wide Sargasso Sea, *a retelling of Charlotte Bronte's* Jane Eyre *from the point of view of Rochester's first wife, the madwoman confined to the attic. In addition to stories and five novels, she wrote an autobiography,* Smile Please: An Unfinished Autobiography *(1979).*

I Used to Live Here Once

She was standing by the river looking at the stepping stones and remembering each one. There was the round unsteady stone, the pointed one, the flat one in the middle—the safe stone where you could stand and look round. The next wasn't so safe for when the river was full the water flowed over it and even when it showed dry it was slippery. But after that it was easy and soon she was standing on the other side.

The road was much wider than it used to be but the work had been done carelessly. The felled trees had not been cleared away and the bushes looked trampled. Yet it was the same road and she walked along feeling extraordinarily happy.

It was a fine day, a blue day. The only thing was that the sky had a glassy look that she didn't remember. That was the only word she could think of. Glassy. She turned the corner, saw that what had been the old pavé[1] had

---

[1]**pavé** Paved road. [Editors' note.]

been taken up, and there too the road was much wider, but it had the same unfinished look.

She came to the worn stone steps that led up to the house and her heart began to beat. The screw pine was gone, so was the mock summer house called the ajoupa, but the clove tree was still there and at the top of the steps the rough lawn stretched away, just as she remembered it. She stopped and looked towards the house that had been added to and painted white. It was strange to see a car standing in front of it.

There were two children under the big mango tree, a boy and a little girl, and she waved to them and called "Hello" but they didn't answer her or turn their heads. Very fair children, as Europeans born in the West Indies so often are: as if the white blood is asserting itself against all odds.

The grass was yellow in the hot sunlight as she walked towards them. When she was quite close she called again, shyly: "Hello." Then, "I used to live here once," she said.

Still they didn't answer. When she said for the third time "Hello" she was quite near them. Her arms went out instinctively with the longing to touch them.

It was the boy who turned. His gray eyes looked straight into hers. His expression didn't change. He said: "Hasn't it gone cold all of a sudden. D'you notice? Let's go in." "Yes, let's," said the girl.

Her arms fell to her sides as she watched them running across the grass to the house. That was the first time she knew.

Topics for Critical Thinking and Writing

1. What do you make of the following details? (1) The sky (para. 3) has an unfamiliar "glassy" look. (2) The children don't reply. (3) The narrator speaks of "hot sunlight" (para. 6), but the boy comments (para. 8) on a sudden chilliness.

2. It is commonplace for adults to revisit the neighborhoods of their youth and to wistfully declare, "You can't go back again." Is this a plausible thesis to ascribe to Rhys's story? Why, or why not?

3. Rhys ends the story with the narrator saying, "That was the first time she knew." What is it that the speaker now knows for the first time? Make clear your answer by rewriting the final sentence as follows: "That was the first time that she knew that . . ."

4. Do you think the title is effective? If not, suggest a better title.

5. Write a short essay *evaluating* the story. Do you think the story is very good, pretty good, fair, or poor? Support your evaluation with reasons. You may want to devote a paragraph to each reason, in between an opening and a concluding paragraph. Thus, if you think the story is

good for two reasons (for instance, because it is brief and because the setting is sharply depicted) but is weak for one reason (for instance, because not much happens), you may find that five paragraphs are a convenient way of setting forth your views.

Kate Chopin

Kate Chopin (1851–1904) was born in St. Louis and named Katherine O'Flaherty. At the age of nineteen she married a cotton broker in New Orleans, Oscar Chopin (the name is pronounced something like "show pan"), who was descended from the early French settlers in Louisiana. After her husband's death in 1883, Kate Chopin turned to writing fiction. The following story was first published in 1894.

The Story of an Hour

Knowing that Mrs. Mallard was afflicted with a heart trouble, great care was taken to break to her as gently as possible the news of her husband's death.

It was her sister Josephine who told her, in broken sentences, veiled hints that revealed in half concealing. Her husband's friend Richards was there, too, near her. It was he who had been in the newspaper office when intelligence of the railroad disaster was received, with Brently Mallard's name leading the list of "killed." He had only taken the time to assure himself of its truth by a second telegram, and had hastened to forestall any less careful, less tender friend in bearing the sad message.

She did not hear the story as many women have heard the same, with a paralyzed inability to accept its significance. She wept at once, with sudden, wild abandonment, in her sister's arms. When the storm of grief had spent itself she went away to her room alone. She would have no one follow her.

There stood, facing the open window, a comfortable, roomy armchair. Into this she sank, pressed down by a physical exhaustion that haunted her body and seemed to reach into her soul.

She could see in the open square before her house the tops of trees   5 that were all aquiver with the new spring life. The delicious breath of rain was in the air. In the street below a peddler was crying his wares. The notes of a distant song which some one was singing reached her faintly, and countless sparrows were twittering in the eaves.

There were patches of blue sky showing here and there through the clouds that had met and piled one above the other in the west facing her window.

She sat with her head thrown back upon the cushion of the chair, quite motionless, except when a sob came up into her throat and shook her, as a child who has cried itself to sleep continues to sob in its dreams.

She was young, with a fair, calm face, whose lines bespoke repression and even a certain strength. But now there was a dull stare in her eyes, whose gaze was fixed away off yonder on one of those patches of blue sky. It was not a glance of reflection, but rather indicated a suspension of intelligent thought.

There was something coming to her and she was waiting for it, fearfully. What was it? She did not know; it was too subtle and elusive to name. But she felt it, creeping out of the sky, reaching toward her through the sounds, the scents, the color that filled the air.

Now her bosom rose and fell tumultuously. She was beginning to 10 recognize this thing that was approaching to possess her, and she was striving to beat it back with her will—as powerless as her two white slender hands would have been.

When she abandoned herself a little whispered word escaped her slightly parted lips. She said it over and over under her breath: "Free, free, free!" The vacant stare and the look of terror that had followed it went from her eyes. They stayed keen and bright. Her pulses beat fast, and the coursing blood warmed and relaxed every inch of her body.

She did not stop to ask if it were not a monstrous joy that held her. A clear and exalted perception enabled her to dismiss the suggestion as trivial.

She knew that she would weep again when she saw the kind, tender hands folded in death; the face that had never looked save with love upon her, fixed and gray and dead. But she saw beyond that bitter moment a long procession of years to come that would belong to her absolutely. And she opened and spread her arms out to them in welcome.

There would be no one to live for her during those coming years; she would live for herself. There would be no powerful will bending her in that blind persistence with which men and women believe they have a right to impose a private will upon a fellow creature. A kind intention or a cruel intention made the act seem no less a crime as she looked upon it in that brief moment of illumination.

And yet she had loved him—sometimes. Often she had not. What 15 did it matter! What could love, the unsolved mystery, count for in face of this possession of self-assertion which she suddenly recognized as the strongest impulse of her being.

"Free! Body and soul free!" she kept whispering.

Josephine was kneeling before the closed door with her lips to the keyhole, imploring for admission. "Louise, open the door! I beg; open the door—you will make yourself ill. What are you doing, Louise? For heaven's sake open the door."

"Go away. I am not making myself ill." No; she was drinking in a very elixir of life through that open window.

Her fancy was running riot along those days ahead of her. Spring days, and summer days, and all sorts of days that would be her own. She breathed a quick prayer that life might be long. It was only yesterday she had thought with a shudder that life might be long.

She arose at length and opened the door to her sister's importuni- 20
ties. There was a feverish triumph in her eyes, and she carried herself unwittingly like a goddess of Victory. She clasped her sister's waist, and together they descended the stairs. Richards stood waiting for them at the bottom.

Some one was opening the front door with a latchkey. It was Brently Mallard who entered, a little travel-stained, composedly carrying his gripsack and umbrella. He had been far from the scene of accident, and did not even know there had been one. He stood amazed at Josephine's piercing cry; at Richards' quick motion to screen him from the view of his wife.

But Richards was too late.

When the doctors came they said she had died of heart disease — of joy that kills.

Topic for Critical Thinking and Writing

Read the following assertions, and consider whether you agree or disagree, and why. For each assertion, draft a paragraph with your arguments.

1. The railroad accident is a symbol of the destructiveness of the industrial revolution.
2. The story claims that women rejoice in the deaths of their husbands.
3. Mrs. Mallard's death at the end is a just punishment for the joy she takes in her husband's death.
4. The story is rich in irony. Some examples: (1) The other characters think she is grieving, but she is rejoicing; (2) she prays for a long life, but she dies almost immediately; (3) the doctors say she died of "the joy that kills," but they think her joy was seeing her husband alive.
5. The story is excellent because it has a surprise ending.

THINKING ABOUT
THE EFFECTS OF LITERATURE

Works of art are artifacts — things constructed, made up, fashioned, just like houses and automobiles. In analyzing works of literature it is therefore customary to keep one's eye on the complex, constructed object, and not simply tell the reader how one feels about it. Instead of reporting their feelings, critics usually analyze the relationships between the parts and the relationship of the parts to the whole.

For instance, in talking about literature we can examine the relationship of plot to character, or of one character to another, or the relationship of one stanza in a poem to the next. Still, although we may try to engage in this sort of analysis as dispassionately as possible, we all know that inevitably we are not only examining something out there, but are also examining our own responses. Why? Because literature has an effect on us. Indeed, it probably has several kinds of effects, ranging from short-range emotional responses ("I really enjoyed this," "I burst out laughing," "It revolted me") to long-range effects ("I have always tried to live up to a line in *Hamlet*, 'This above all, to thine own self be true'"). Let's talk first, very briefly, about immediate emotional responses.

Analysis usually begins with a response: "This is marvelous," or "What a bore," and we then go on to try to account for our response. A friend mentions a book or a film to us, and we say, "I couldn't stay with it for five minutes." The friend expresses surprise, and we then go on to explain, giving reasons (to the friend and also to ourselves) why we couldn't stay with it. Perhaps the book seemed too remote from life, or perhaps, on the other hand, it seemed to be nothing more than a transcript of the boring talk that we can overhear on a bus or in an elevator.

In such discussions, when we draw on our responses, as we must, the work may disappear; we find ourselves talking about ourselves. Let's take two extreme examples: "I can't abide *Huckleberry Finn*. How am I expected to enjoy a so-called masterpiece that has a character in it called 'Nigger Jim.'" Or: "T. S. Eliot's anti-Semitism is too much for me to take. Don't talk to me about Eliot's skill with meter, when he has such lines as 'Rachel, *née* Rabinovitch / Tears at the grapes with murderous paws."

Although everyone agrees that literature can evoke this sort of strong emotional response, not everyone agrees on how much value we should put on our personal experience. Several of the Topics for Critical Thinking and Writing on page 364 invite you to reflect on this issue.

What about the *consequences of the effects* of literature? Does literature shape our character and therefore influence our behavior? It is fairly widely believed that literature does have an effect. One hears, for example, that literature (like travel) is broadening, which is to say that it makes us aware of, and tolerant of, kinds of behavior that differ from our own and from what we see around us. One of the chief arguments against pornography, for instance, is that it desensitizes us, makes us too tolerant of abusive relationships, relationships in which people (usually men) use other people (usually women) as mere things or instruments for pleasure. (A contrary view should be mentioned: Some people argue that pornography provides a relatively harmless outlet for fantasies that otherwise might be given release in the real world. In this view, pornography acts as a sort of safety valve.) Discussions of the effects of literature that get into the popular press almost always involve pornography, but other topics are also the subjects of controversy. For instance, in recent decades parents and educators have been much concerned with fairy tales. Does the violence in some fairy tales ("Little Red Riding Hood," "The Three Little Pigs") have a bad effect on children? Do some of the stories teach the wrong lessons, implying that women should be passive, men active ("Sleeping Beauty," for instance, in which the sleeping woman is brought to life by the action of the handsome prince)? The Greek philosopher Plato (427–347 B.C.) strongly believed that the literature we hear or read shapes our later behavior, and since most of the ancient Greek traditional stories (notably Homer's *Odyssey* and *Iliad*) celebrate acts of love and war rather than of justice, he prohibited the reading of such material in his ideal society. (We reprint a relevant passage from Plato on p. 365.)

Topics for Critical Thinking and Writing

1. If you have responded strongly (favorably or unfavorably) to some aspect of the social content of a literary work, for instance its depiction of women or of a particular minority group, in an essay of 250 to 500 words analyze the response, and try to determine whether you are talking chiefly about yourself or the work. (Two works widely regarded as literary masterpieces but nonetheless often banned from classrooms are Shakespeare's *The Merchant of Venice* and Mark Twain's *Huckleberry Finn*. If you have read either of these, you may want to write about it and your response.) Can we really see literary value—*really* see it—in a work that deeply offends us?

2. Most people believe that literature influences life—that in some perhaps mysterious way it helps to shape character. Certainly anyone who believes that some works should be censored, or at least should be made unavailable to minors, assumes that they can have a bad influence, so why not assume that other works can have a good influence?

   Read the following brief claims about literature, then choose one and write a 250-word essay offering support or taking issue with it.

   The pen is mightier than the sword. — ANONYMOUS

   The writer isn't made in a vacuum. Writers are witnesses. The reason we need writers is because we need witnesses to this terrifying century. — E. L. DOCTOROW

   When we read of human beings behaving in certain ways, with the approval of the author, who gives his benedictions to this behavior by his attitude towards the result of the behavior arranged by himself, we can be influenced towards behaving in the same way. — T. S. ELIOT

   Poetry makes nothing happen. — W. H. AUDEN

   Literature is *without proofs*. By which it must be understood that it cannot prove, not only *what* it says, but even that it is worth the trouble of saying it. — ROLAND BARTHES

> Of course the illusion of art is to make one believe that great literature is very close to life, but exactly the opposite is true. Life is amorphous, literature is formal. — FRANÇOISE SAGAN

3. At least since the time of Plato (see the piece directly following) some thoughtful people have wanted to ban certain works of literature because they allegedly stimulate the wrong sorts of pleasure or cause us to take pleasure in the wrong sorts of things. Consider, by way of comparison, bullfighting and cockfighting. Of course they cause pain to the animals, but branding animals also causes pain and it is not banned. Bullfighting and cockfighting probably are banned in the United States largely because most of us believe that people should not take pleasure in these activities. Now to return to literature: Should some kinds of writing be prohibited because they offer the wrong sorts of pleasure?

Plato

Plato (427–347 B.C.), an Athenian aristocrat by birth, was the student of one great philosopher (Socrates) and the teacher of another (Aristotle). His legacy of more than two dozen dialogues — imaginary discussions between Socrates and one or more other speakers, usually young Athenians — has been of such influence that the whole of Western philosophy can be characterized, A. N. Whitehead wrote, as "a series of footnotes to Plato." Plato's interests encompassed the full range of topics in philosophy: ethics, politics, logic, metaphysics, epistemology, aesthetics, psychology, and education.

This selection from Plato's Republic, *one of his best-known and longest dialogues, is about the education suitable for the rulers of an ideal society. Re-*public *begins, typically, with an investigation into the nature of justice. Socrates (who speaks for Plato) convincingly explains to Glaucon that we cannot reasonably expect to achieve a just society unless we devote careful attention to the moral education of the young men who are scheduled in later life to become the rulers. (Here as elsewhere, Plato's elitism and aristocratic bias shows itself; as readers of* Republic *soon learn, Plato is no admirer of democracy or of a classless society.) Plato cares as much about what the educational curriculum should exclude as what it should include. His special target was the common practice in his day of using for pedagogy the Homeric tales and other stories about the gods. He readily embraces the principle of censorship, as the excerpt explains, because he thinks it is a necessary means to achieve the ideal society.*

"The Greater Part of the Stories Current Today We Shall Have to Reject"

"What kind of education shall we give them then? We shall find it difficult to improve on the time-honored distinction between the physical training we give to the body and the education we give to the mind and character."

"True."

"And we shall begin by educating mind and character, shall we not?"

"Of course."

"In this education you would include stories, would you not?"   5

"Yes."

"These are of two kinds, true stories and fiction.[1] Our education must use both, and start with fiction."

"I don't know what you mean."

"But you know that we begin by telling children stories. These are, in general, fiction, though they contain some truth. And we tell children stories before we start them on physical training."

"That is so."   10

"That is what I meant by saying that we must start to educate the mind before training the body."

"You are right," he said.

"And the first step, as you know, is always what matters most, particularly when we are dealing with those who are young and tender. That is the time when they are easily molded and when any impression we choose to make leaves a permanent mark."

"That is certainly true."

"Shall we therefore readily allow our children to listen to any   15
stories made up by anyone, and to form opinions that are for the most part the opposite of those we think they should have when they grow up?"

"We certainly shall not."

"Then it seems that our first business is to supervise the production of stories, and choose only those we think suitable, and reject the rest. We shall persuade mothers and nurses to tell our chosen stories to their children, and by means of them to mold their minds and characters which are more important than their bodies. The greater part of the stories current today we shall have to reject."

"Which are you thinking of?"

"We can take some of the major legends as typical. For all, whether major or minor, should be cast in the same mold and have the same effect. Do you agree?"

"Yes: but I'm not sure which you refer to as major."   20

"The stories in Homer and Hesiod and the poets. For it is the poets who have always made up fictions and stories to tell to men."

---

[1]The Greek word *pseudos* and its corresponding verb meant not only "fiction"—stories, tales—but also "what is not true" and so, in suitable contexts, "lies": and this ambiguity should be borne in mind. [Editors' note: All footnotes are by the translator, but some have been omitted.]

"What sort of stories do you mean and what fault do you find in them?"

"The worst fault possible," I replied, "especially if the fiction is an ugly one."

"And what is that?"

"Misrepresenting the nature of gods and heroes, like a portrait 25 painter whose portraits bear no resemblance to their originals."

"That is a fault which certainly deserves censure. But give me more details."

"Well, on the most important of subjects, there is first and foremost the foul story about Ouranos[2] and the things Hesiod says he did, and the revenge Cronos took on him. While the story of what Cronos did, and what he suffered at the hands of his son, is not fit as it is to be lightly repeated to the young and foolish, even if it were true; it would be best to say nothing about it, or if it must be told, tell it to a select few under oath of secrecy, at a rite which required, to restrict it still further, the sacrifice not of a mere pig but of something large and difficult to get."

"These certainly are awkward stories."

"And they shall not be repeated in our state, Adeimantus," I said. "Nor shall any young audience be told that anyone who commits horrible crimes, or punishes his father unmercifully, is doing nothing out of the ordinary but merely what the first and greatest of the gods have done before."

"I entirely agree," said Adeimantus, "that these stories are un- 30 suitable."

"Nor can we permit stories of wars and plots and battles among the gods; they are quite untrue, and if we want our prospective guardians to believe that quarrelsomeness is one of the worst of evils, we must certainly not let them be told the story of the Battle of the Giants or embroider it on robes, or tell them other tales about many and various quarrels between gods and heroes and their friends and relations. On the contrary, if we are to persuade them that no citizen has ever quarreled with any other, because it is sinful, our old men and women must tell children stories with this end in view from the first, and we must compel our poets to tell them similar stories when they grow up. But we can admit to our state no stories about Hera being tied up by her son, or Hephaestus being flung out of Heaven by his father for trying to help his mother when she was getting a beating, nor any of Homer's Battles of the Gods, whether their intention is allegorical or not. Children

---

[2]**Ouranos** (the sky), the original supreme god, was castrated by his son Cronos to separate him from Gaia (mother earth). Cronos was in turn deposed by Zeus in a struggle in which Zeus was helped by the Titans.

cannot distinguish between what is allegory and what isn't, and opinions formed at that age are usually difficult to eradicate or change; we should therefore surely regard it as of the utmost importance that the first stories they hear shall aim at encouraging the highest excellence of character."

"Your case is a good one," he agreed, "but if someone wanted details, and asked what stories we were thinking of, what should we say?"

To which I replied, "My dear Adeimantus, you and I are not engaged on writing stories but on founding a state. And the founders of a state, though they must know the type of story the poet must produce, and reject any that do not conform to that type, need not write them themselves."

"True: but what are the lines on which our poets must work when they deal with the gods?"

"Roughly as follows," I said. "God must surely always be represented 35 as he really is, whether the poet is writing epic, lyric, or tragedy."

"He must."

"And in reality of course god is good, and he must be so described."

"Certainly."

"But nothing good is harmful, is it?"[3]

"I think not."   40

"Then can anything that is not harmful do harm?"

"No."

"And can what does no harm do evil?"

"No again."

"And can what does no evil be the cause of any evil?"   45

"How could it?"

"Well then; is the good beneficial?"

"Yes."

"So it must be the cause of well-being."

"Yes."   50

"So the good is not the cause of everything, but only of states of well-being and not of evil."

"Most certainly," he agreed.

"Then god, being good, cannot be responsible for everything, as is commonly said, but only for a small part of human life, for the greater part of which he has no responsibility. For we have a far smaller share of good than of evil, and while god must be held to be the sole cause of good, we must look for some factors other than god as cause of the evil."

"I think that's very true," he said.

---

[3]The reader of the following passage should bear the following ambiguities in mind: (1) the Greek word for good (*agathos*) can mean (a) morally good, (b) beneficial or advantageous; (2) the Greek word for evil (*kakos*) can also mean harm or injury; (3) the adverb of *agathos* (*eu*—the well) can imply either morally right or prosperous. The word translated "cause of" could equally well be rendered "responsible for."

"So we cannot allow Homer or any other poet to make such a stupid 55 mistake about the gods, as when he says that

> Zeus has two jars standing on the floor of his palace, full of fates, good in one and evil in the other

and that the man to whom Zeus allots a mixture of both has 'varying fortunes sometimes good and sometimes bad,' while the man to whom he allots unmixed evil is 'chased by ravening despair over the face of the earth.'[4] Nor can we allow references to Zeus as 'dispenser of good and evil.' And we cannot approve if it is said that Athene and Zeus prompted the breach of solemn treaty and oath by Pandarus, or that the strife and contentions of the gods were due to Themis and Zeus. Nor again can we let our children hear from Aeschylus that

> God implants a fault in man, when he wishes to destroy a house utterly.

No: We must forbid anyone who writes a play about the sufferings of Niobe (the subject of the play from which these last lines are quoted), or the house of Pelops, or the Trojan war, or any similar topic, to say they are acts of god; or if he does he must produce the sort of interpretation we are now demanding, and say that god's acts were good and just, and that the sufferers were benefited by being punished. What the poet must not be allowed to say is that those who were punished were made wretched through god's action. He may refer to the wicked as wretched because they needed punishment, provided he makes it clear that in punishing them god did them good. But if a state is to be run on the right lines, every possible step must be taken to prevent anyone, young or old, either saying or being told, whether in poetry or prose, that god, being good, can cause harm or evil to any man. To say so would be sinful, inexpedient, and inconsistent."

"I should approve of a law for this purpose and you have my vote for it," he said.

"Then of our laws laying down the principles which those who write or speak about the gods must follow, one would be this: *God is the cause, not of all things, but only of good.*"

"I am quite content with that," he said.

Topics for Critical Thinking and Writing

1. In the beginning of the dialogue Plato says that adults recite fictions to very young children, and that these fictions help to mold character.

---

[4]Quotations from Homer are generally taken from the translations by Dr. Rieu in the Penguin series. At times (as here) the version quoted by Plato differs slightly from the accepted text.

Think of some stories that you heard or read when young, such as "Snow White and the Seven Dwarfs" or "Ali Baba and the Forty Thieves." Try to think of a story that, in the final analysis, is not in accord with what you consider to be proper morality, such as a story in which a person triumphs through trickery, or a story in which evil actions—perhaps murders—are set forth without unfavorable comment. (Was it naughty of Jack to kill the giant?) Upon reflection, do you think children should not be told such stories? Why, or why not? Or think of the early film westerns, in which, on the whole, the Indians (except for an occasional Uncle Tonto) are depicted as bad guys and the whites (except for an occasional coward or rustler) are depicted as good guys. Many people who now have gray hair enjoyed such films in their childhood. Are you prepared to say that such films are not damaging? Or, on the other hand, are you prepared to say they are damaging and should be prohibited?

2. It is often objected that censorship of reading matter and of television programs available to children underrates their ability to think for themselves and to discount the dangerous, obscene, and tawdry. Do you agree with this objection? Does Plato?

3. Plato says that allowing poets to say what they please about the gods in his ideal state would be "inconsistent." Explain what he means by this criticism, and then explain why you agree or disagree with it.

4. Do you believe that parents should censor the "fiction" their children encounter (literature, films, pictures, music), but that the community should not censor the "fiction" of adults? Write an essay of 500 words on one of these topics: "Censorship and Rock Lyrics"; "X-rated Films"; "Ethnic Jokes." (These topics are broadly worded; you can narrow one, and offer whatever thesis you wish.)

5. Were you taught that any of the founding fathers ever acted disreputably, or that any American hero had any serious moral flaw? Or that America ever acted immorally in its dealings with other nations? Do you think it appropriate for children to hear such things?

THINKING ABOUT
GOVERNMENT FUNDING FOR THE ARTS

Our government supports the arts, including writers, by giving grants to numerous institutions. On the other hand, the amount that the government contributes is extremely small when compared to the amounts given to the arts by most European governments. Consider the following questions.

1. Should taxpayers' dollars be used to support the arts? Why, or why not?

2. What possible public benefit can come from supporting the arts? Can one argue that we should support the arts for the same reasons that we support the public schools, that is, to have a civilized society?

3. If dollars are given to the arts, should the political content of the works be taken into account, or only the aesthetic merit? Can we separate content from aesthetic merit? (The best way to approach this issue probably is to begin by thinking of a strongly political work.)

4. Is it censorship not to award public funds to writers whose work is not approved of, or is it simply a matter of refusing to reward them with taxpayers' dollars?

5. Should decisions about grants to writers be made chiefly by government officials or chiefly by experts in the field? Why?

A CASEBOOK ON LITERATURE AND SOCIETY: What Should Be Our National Anthem?

Caldwell Titcomb

Caldwell Titcomb (b. 1926), a professor emeritus of music at Brandeis University, has composed stage and film music scores. This essay first appeared in The New Republic, *1985.*

Star-Spangled Earache: What So Loudly We Wail

Not long ago Representative Andrew Jacobs, Jr., of Indiana filed a bill to replace "The Star-Spangled Banner" with "America the Beautiful" as our national anthem. Many people have long advocated just such a change, and for a number of reasons the bill deserves wide support.

"The Star-Spangled Banner" has been the official national anthem only since March 3, 1931. Most people assume that it has been the anthem virtually from time immemorial and that it is thus now sacrosanct. But clearly there is nothing wrong with supplanting something that has been in effect for only fifty-odd years.

The music is by an Englishman, John Stafford Smith (1750–1836), who wrote it as a drinking song for a London social club, the Anacreontic Society. Is our nation so poverty-stricken that we must rule out homegrown music?

The tune is a constant stumbling block. Technically, it covers a span of a twelfth—that is, an octave plus a perfect fifth. Not only is it difficult for the general public to sing, but it has repeatedly caused trouble even for professional opera singers. Some people assert that this problem could be solved by selecting the right key for performance. But the point is that *all* twelve possible keys are poor. No matter what the key, the tune goes either too high or too low (and both, for some people). What's more, the tune is irregular in its phrasing, and does not always fit the text well. In "Whose broad stripes," for instance, assigning "broad" to a tiny sixteenth note is bad.

Finally, Francis Scott Key's poem (1814) is not suitable. It is of low 5 quality as poetry, and its subject matter is too specific and too militaristic, dealing with a one-day incident in a war. Are glaring rockets and bursting bombs the essence of the nation? I wonder how many people have really read through all four stanzas and thought about the words. The third stanza is particularly offensive: "Their blood has wash'd out their foul foot-steps' pollution. / No refuge could save the hireling and slave / From the terror of flight or the gloom of the grave." When a bank celebrated the last Independence Day by buying a full page in the *New York Times* to print the tune and text of the anthem, not surprisingly the dreadful third stanza was entirely omitted. The poem has little to recommend it except for the single line, "The land of the free and the home of the brave."

Why choose "America the Beautiful" in its place?

Both the text and music are by citizens of the United States. And now that we have overcome the notion that this is mainly a man's world, it is additionally fitting that the poem was written by a woman, Katharine Lee Bates (1859–1929), and the music by a man, Samuel Augustus Ward (1848–1903).

The music (composed in 1882) is simple and dignified, and exhibits balanced phrasing. The tune has a range of only a ninth—that is, an oc-tave plus one step—which means that almost anyone, trained or un-trained, can sing it. For the musically sophisticated, there is also a neat touch in the four-voice harmonization that has been standard since its first publication in 1888: The soprano tune of the first line becomes the bass part of the third line.

The poem—originally written in 1893, and by a happy coincidence first printed in the Fourth of July issue of a periodical in 1895 (and twice somewhat revised by its author)—is in its final form an admirable text of broad scope. It is not bellicose or geographically restricted, and all four stanzas can be sung without embarrassment. It was inspired by a trip taken by an Easterner through the Midwest (with a visit to the Chicago World's Columbian Exposition: "alabaster cities gleam") and on across "the fruited plain" and "amber waves of grain" to the Rocky Mountains (Pikes Peak in Colorado: "purple mountain majesties").

It acknowledges both urban and rural life. It pays homage to our na- 10 tion's past and to those who have sacrificed themselves for their country (without glorifying war), it points to present virtues, and it voices a goal that our nation should aspire to ("brotherhood / From sea to shining sea"). Even a celebrated foreign historian was impelled to comment: "Few patriotic songs breathe such broad, humane idealism as this."

This joining of words and music has stood the test of time. The piece is taught and learned in school throughout the country, and is known and loved by the populace at large, which can sing it effectively, confidently, and with pride.

There has long been widespread advocacy for making it our national anthem. When the selection of an anthem was before Congress in 1931, several organizations, acting independently, took a strong stand in favor of "America the Beautiful" and against "The Star-Spangled Banner," including the National Federation of Music Clubs, the National Hymn Society, the Music Supervisors National Conference, and education experts at Columbia Teachers College.

When the controversy resurfaced in Boston in 1977 (as it periodically does here and there), a poll of *Boston Globe* readers revealed that they favored "America the Beautiful" over "The Star-Spangled Banner" by a vote of 493 to 220. And it has already been adopted as the official song of the National Federation of Women's Clubs.

From time to time people have expressed a preference for other choices, but these can easily be shown unsuitable. "The Battle Hymn of the Republic" (1861), like "The Star-Spangled Banner," is too warlike, and its tune belongs to "John Brown's Body Lies A-Mould'ring in the Grave." The music of Irving Berlin's "God Bless America" (1918) is insufficiently dignified, and the text setting is faulty. "My Country 'Tis of Thee" uses the music of the British national anthem, and thus cannot be seriously considered. John Philip Sousa's "The Stars and Stripes Forever" (1897) is as great a march as anyone has ever composed, but it lacks a text and only its refrain would lend itself to singing. The idea of having a nationwide contest for a new anthem has been tried, without success. If tried again, there would surely be no agreement.

When one takes all factors into account, "America the Beautiful" is   15
by far the outstanding candidate. It would indeed be fortunate if the entire country could sing "America the Beautiful" as the official national anthem when it celebrates the two-hundredth anniversary of the Constitution on September 17, 1987. We have less than two years to accomplish this worthy task.

Topics for Critical Thinking and Writing

1. Evaluate Titcomb's title and first paragraph. How effective do you think they are? How would you defend (or criticize) them?

2. List, in order, Titcomb's arguments for replacing the anthem. Do you think the sequence is reasonable and effective? Why, or why not?

3. Suppose someone were to argue, by analogy, that since the national bird is the bald eagle, not exactly a gentle creature, it is appropriate that the national anthem be similarly vigorous and even warlike. Write a 100-word essay supporting or attacking the analogy.

4. Titcomb asserts in paragraph 5 that "The poem has little to recommend it except for the single line, 'The land of the free and the home of the brave.'" Do you agree with his evaluation? And, whether you agree or not, do you think he should have *argued* that Key's poem is weak rather than merely asserting that it is?

5. As his final paragraph indicates, Titcomb wrote the essay in 1985, two years before the two-hundredth anniversary of the Constitution. We have now passed that landmark, and so his final paragraph is no longer appropriate. Regardless of the merits of Titcomb's position, write a new concluding paragraph for his essay.

Hendrik Hertzberg

Hendrik Hertzberg (b. 1943) is the editorial director of The New Yorker, *where this essay originally appeared in 1997.*

Star-Spangled Banter

Ted Turner set off a firecracker of his own this Fourth of July. Speaking in front of Independence Hall, in Philadelphia, he argued that it's time to dump "The Star-Spangled Banner." Over the years, Mr. Turner has had many capital ideas—CNN, Turner Classic Movies, and interrupting Jane Fonda's career as a serial monogamist, to name three. Now he has come up with another, and one cannot but agree with him. By all means, let us ease the old chestnut into well-deserved retirement. But not for the reason he offers, and not to make way for the alternative he recommends.

Mr. T notes that the national anthem is warlike, whereas the age we live in is (relatively) peaceful. He is right on both counts, but his second point makes his first less compelling. Just as gun control is more urgent in Detroit than in Lausanne, bellicose songs are more worrying in bellicose times than in times of tranquillity. "The Star-Spangled Banner" is warlike, yes. But so are a lot of first-rate national anthems. ("The Marseillaise," with its ghoulish call to "drench our fields" in "impure blood," makes its American counterpart sound like a Joni Mitchell ditty.) In any case, there are plenty of better reasons for getting rid of "The Star-Spangled Banner." Its tonal range corresponds to that of the electric guitar, as Jimi Hendrix proved, but not to that of the human voice. The lyrics include some fine phrases—"the twilight's last gleaming," "the ramparts we watched"—that are a reliable source of titles for the type of potboiler novel that goes in for raised lettering on the jacket, but on the whole the words don't convey what politicians call core American values. Francis Scott Key's poem was written to immortalize the siege of Fort McHenry, Maryland, during the War of 1812—a silly war, a minor war, a war that ended in what was at best a tie. (The British torched the White House and smashed our hopes of gobbling up Canada. We got to keep our independence.) The poem lends itself to mishearing, from the traditional "José, can you see" opening, through "O, sadists that stars spank," to the closing "Orlando D. Free and Homer D. Brave."

Congress designated "The Star-Spangled Banner" our national anthem during the Hoover Administration, when the country's judgment was impaired by clinical depression. The relevant bill—whose sponsor hoped to promote the tourist trade in his district, which included Fort McHenry—was rejected three times by the House before it finally passed, on a slow day. It was supported by the "Americanism" busybodies of the Daughters of the American Revolution and the American Legion but opposed by music teachers—an important group at a time when pianos were more common than phonographs. The complaints then were identical to the complaints now: too martial, too irritating, too hard to sing.

What's the alternative? Mr. T suggests "America the Beautiful"—the music teachers' choice back in 1930, by the way. It's nice, but, like so many nice things, it's also wimpy. The best that can be said for it is that it's more singable than the incumbent. A third contender—"America (My Country, 'Tis of Thee)"—has O.K. words, but the tune is the same as that of "God Save the Queen." This would make for an unusually severe "Is there an echo in here?" problem during joint appearances by Bill Clinton and Tony Blair. How about "This Land Is Your Land"? Plenty of progressive-school pupils already think Woody Guthrie's populist jingle is the national anthem, but the tune is a little too Barney the Dinosaurish, and the lyrics have a musty, Popular Front feeling about them.

Our country has at hand what is perhaps the greatest patriotic hymn   5
ever written: "The Battle Hymn of the Republic." But secularists would object that it is too God-filled, and Southerners—white Southerners, at least—would complain that the vineyards it advocates trampling were their vineyards. ("The Star-Spangled Banner" was also popular with the Union Army, but never mind.) Perhaps "The Battle Hymn of the Republic" could be twinned with "Dixie," as in the Elvis Presley version, but "Dixie" has its own problems. Anyhow, serious countries do not have national medleys.

This space would like to offer a recommendation of its own: "Lift Ev'ry Voice and Sing." James Weldon Johnson, a poet of the Harlem Renaissance, wrote it, in 1900, for a Lincoln's Birthday celebration. It is already a national anthem of sorts; its alternative title, in fact, is "The Negro National Anthem." Its tune (by J. Rosamond Johnson, the poet's brother) is stirring, and so are its words. The opening verse, the one that would be sung at ballgames, goes, in part:

> Lift ev'ry voice and sing,
> Till earth and heaven ring,
> Ring with the harmonies of liberty . . .
> Sing a song full of the faith that the dark past has taught us,
> Sing a song full of the hope that the present has brought us;
> Facing the rising sun of our new day begun,
> Let us march on till victory is won.

No bombast, no boasting, no wimpishness—just good, solid values that are both American and universal. How about it, Ted?

Topics for Critical Thinking and Writing

1. List the reasons that Hertzberg gives for replacing "The Star-Spangled Banner" with "Lift Ev'ry Voice and Sing." (We give the full text of "The Star-Spangled Banner" on p. 377, and of "Lift Ev'ry Voice and Sing" on pp. 380–81.) Which of his reasons (if any) seem especially strong? Which (if any) seem especially weak? Explain your evaluations.

2. In paragraph 2 Hertzberg says that the French national anthem is first-rate even though it includes a "ghoulish call to 'drench our fields' in 'impure blood.'" If you are familiar with "The Marseillaise," evaluate Hertzberg's view of it. Even if you are not familiar with the anthem, indicate whether you think such phrases ought to disqualify the song from high praise as a national anthem.

3. Read or reread Caldwell Titcomb's essay (p. 371). In 500 words, write Titcomb's imagined response to Hertzberg. Might Titcomb be convinced by Hertzberg's argument? Or would Titcomb reject Hertzberg's nomination? In any case, write a response that you can imagine Titcomb offering.

Francis Scott Key

Francis Scott Key (1779–1843), a lawyer who practiced in Washington, wrote "The Star-Spangled Banner" while aboard a British ship, seeking the release of an American who had been taken prisoner during the War of 1812. After Key boarded the ship, the British force began bombarding Fort McHenry, in Baltimore Harbor, and Key was forced to remain on the ship throughout the night of September 13, 1814. Released the next morning, he drafted the poem while being taken ashore, and revised it in his Baltimore hotel on the night of September 14. It was published anonymously on September 20. The tune is that of a popular drinking song by John Stafford Smith whose first words are "To Anacreon in Heaven." In 1916 President Wilson issued an executive order designating "The Star-Spangled Banner" as the national anthem, but it did not officially achieve this status until Congress confirmed Wilson's order in 1931.

The Star-Spangled Banner

O say, can you see, by the dawn's early light,
    What so proudly we hailed at the twilight's last gleaming?
Whose broad stripes and bright stars, through the perilous fight,
    O'er the ramparts we watched, were so gallantly streaming!
And the rockets' red glare, the bombs bursting in air,   5
Gave proof through the night that our flag was still there:
    O say, does that star-spangled banner yet wave
    O'er the land of the free and the home of the brave?

On the shore, dimly seen through the mists of the deep,
    Where the foe's haughty host in dread silence reposes,   10
What is that which the breeze, o'er the towering steep,
    As it fitfully blows, now conceals, now discloses?
Now it catches the gleam of the morning's first beam,
In full glory reflected now shines on the stream:
    'Tis the star-spangled banner! O long may it wave   15
    O'er the land of the free and the home of the brave!

And where is the band who so vauntingly swore
    That the havoc of war and the battle's confusion
A home and a country would leave us no more?
    Their blood has washed out their foul footsteps' pollution.   20
No refuge could save the hireling and slave
From the terror of flight, or the gloom of the grave:
    And the star-spangled banner in triumph doth wave
    O'er the land of the free and the home of the brave!

    Oh! thus be it ever, when freemen shall stand   25
    Between their loved homes and the war's desolation!
Blest with victory and peace, may the heaven-rescued land
    Praise the Power that hath made and preserved us a nation.
Then conquer we must, for our cause it is just,
And this be our motto: "In God is our trust."   30
    And the star-spangled banner in triumph shall wave
    O'er the land of the free and the home of the brave!

Samuel Francis Smith

Samuel Francis Smith (1808–1895), a Boston Baptist clergyman, wrote "America" in 1831, when he was a student at Andover Theological Seminary. It was first sung on July 4, 1931, to the tune of the British "God Save the King."

America

My country! 'tis of thee,
Sweet land of liberty!
Of thee I sing;
Land where my fathers died,
Land of the pilgrim's pride,   5
From ev'ry mountain side
Let freedom ring.

My native country! thee,
Land of the noble free,
Thy name I love;   10
I love thy rocks and rills,
Thy woods and templed hills,
My heart with rapture thrills,
Like that above.

Our Father's God! to thee,   15
Author of liberty!
To thee we sing;
Long may our land be bright,
With freedom's holy light,
Protect us by Thy might,   20
Great God, our King.

Katharine Lee Bates

Katharine Lee Bates (1859–1929), a professor of English at Wellesley College, Massachusetts, wrote children's books and scholarly works as well as poems. "America the Beautiful," first published on July 4, 1895, was later set to music by Samuel Ward.

America the Beautiful

Oh beautiful for spacious skies,
For amber waves of grain,
For purple mountain majesties
Above the fruited plain.
America! America!   5
God shed His grace on thee,
And crown thy good with brotherhood
From sea to shining sea.

Oh beautiful for pilgrim feet
Whose stern impassioned stress
A thoroughfare for freedom beat   10
Across the wilderness.
America! America!
God mend thine ev'ry flaw,
Confirm thy soul in self-control,   15
Thy liberty in law.

Oh beautiful for heroes proved
In liberating strife,
Who more than self their country loved,
And mercy more than life.   20
America! America!
May God thy gold refine,
Till all success be nobleness,
And every gain divine.

Oh beautiful for patriot dream   25
That sees beyond the years,
Thine alabaster cities gleam,
Undimmed by human tears.
America! America!
God shed His grace on thee,   30
And crown thy good with brotherhood
From sea to shining sea.

James Weldon Johnson

*James Weldon Johnson (1871–1938), born in Jacksonville, Florida, was the
first African American lawyer to be admitted to the Florida bar, the founder
in 1895 of the first black daily newspaper (the* Daily American), *and a
diplomat of distinction. He was also an accomplished poet, novelist, and essayist. "Lift Ev'ry Voice and Sing," written in 1900 to celebrate Lincoln's
birthday, is well known among African Americans but not among other
Americans. Johnson's poem was set to music composed by his brother,
J. Rosamond Johnson.*

Lift Ev'ry Voice and Sing

1 Lift ev-ery voice and sing, till earth and heav - en ring, ring with the
2 Ston-y the road we trod, bit - ter the chas - tening rod, felt in the
3 God of our wea - ry years, God of our si - lent tears, God who has

har - mo - nies of lib - er - ty; Let our re - joic - ing
days when hope un - born had died; Yet with a stead - y
brought us thus far on the way; God, who by your

rise, high as the lis - tening skies, let it re - sound loud as the
beat, have not our wea - ry feet, come to the place for which our
might, led us in - to the light, keep us for - ev - er in the

roll - ing sea. Sing a song full of the
peo - ple sighed? We have come o - ver a
path, we pray. Lest our feet stray from the

Topics for Critical Thinking and Writing

1. Which song do you consider the best as a poem, and which the weakest? Compare the two, indicating the reasons for your preference. *Suggestion*: You may want to begin by finding lines in each poem that you consider especially memorable or quotable. For instance, some students have cited, in "The Star-Spangled Banner," "The land of the free and the home of the brave." Which phrases particularly appeal to you? Try to explain *why* certain lines appeal. Probably your answers will have to do not only with the subject matter but also with the distinctive *way* in which it is expressed. For instance, do you agree that "The land of the free and the home of the brave" owes some of its effectiveness to the parallelism? Test this assertion by comparing it with "The land of the free, and brave people's home," or "The land of the free, where brave people live," or some such formulation.

2. Next turn to the overall content of the two poems you chose and discuss it in terms of suitability for the national anthem. If you are discussing "The Star-Spangled Banner," how much weight do you give to the argument that it is militaristic (especially in the third and fourth stanzas), too much so to be our anthem?

3. "The Star-Spangled Banner" asserts that "In God is our trust." It also says that our nation is "heaven-rescued" and it speaks of "the Power that hath made and preserved us a nation." Smith's "America" ends by referring to "Great God, our King"; Bates's "America the Beautiful" and Johnson's "Lift Ev'ry Voice and Sing" also speak of God. Americans hold a variety of faiths, and some Americans do not believe in God. Are the quoted expressions inappropriate in the anthem of a nation that does not have a national church? Explain your reasoning.

4. If you are familiar with a national anthem other than "The Star-Spangled Banner," evaluate it (1) as a poem or song, and (2) as a national anthem. (Bring at least a few copies of the work to class.)

Part Four

CURRENT ISSUES: PRO-CON DEBATES

A CHECKLIST FOR ANALYZING A DEBATE

✓ What is the writer's thesis?
  ✓ What claim is asserted?
  ✓ What assumptions are made?
  ✓ Are key terms defined satisfactorily?
✓ What support is offered on behalf of the claim?
  ✓ Are examples relevant and convincing?
  ✓ Are statistics relevant, accurate, and convincing?
  ✓ Are the authorities appropriate?
  ✓ Is the logic—deductive and inductive—valid?
  ✓ If there is an appeal to emotion, is this appeal acceptable?
✓ Does the writer seem fair?
  ✓ Are counterarguments considered?
  ✓ Is there any evidence of dishonesty?

Next, ask yourself the following additional questions:

✓ Do the disputants differ in
  ✓ assumptions?
  ✓ interpretations of relevant facts?
  ✓ selection of and emphasis on these facts?
  ✓ definitions of key terms?
  ✓ values and norms?
✓ What common ground do the disputants share?
✓ Which disputant seems to you to have the better overall argument? Why?

12

Abortion: Whose Right to Life Is It Anyway?

In reading essays debating a given issue, keep in mind the questions given on page 76, "A Checklist for Analyzing an Argument." On the facing page they are listed again with a few additional points of special relevance to debates.

Ellen Willis

Ellen Willis (b. 1941) was educated at Barnard College and the University of California at Berkeley. She has been a freelance writer since 1966, publishing in such journals as The New Yorker, Rolling Stone, *and* The Village Voice, *where this essay first appeared on July 16, 1985.*

Putting Women Back into the Abortion Debate

Some years ago I attended a New York Institute for the Humanities seminar on the new right. We were a fairly heterogeneous group of liberals and lefties, feminists and gay activists, but on one point nearly all of us agreed: The right-to-life movement was a dangerous antifeminist crusade. At one session I argued that the attack on abortion had significance far beyond itself, that it was the linchpin of the right's social agenda. I got a lot of supporting comments and approving nods. It was too much for Peter Steinfels, a liberal Catholic, author of *The Neoconservatives,* and executive editor of *Commonweal*. Right-to-lifers were not all right-wing fanatics, he protested. "You have to understand," he said plaintively, "that many of us see abortion as a *human life issue*." What I remember best was his air of frustrated isolation. I don't think he came back to the seminar after that.

Things are different now. I often feel isolated when I insist that abortion is, above all, a *feminist issue*. Once people took for granted that abortion was an issue of sexual politics and morality. Now, abortion is most often discussed as a question of "life" in the abstract. Public concern over abortion centers almost exclusively on fetuses; women and their bodies are merely the stage on which the drama of fetal life and death takes place. Debate about abortion—if not its reality—has become sexlessly scholastic. And the people most responsible for this turn of events are, like Peter Steinfels, on the left.

The left wing of the right-to-life movement is a small, seemingly eccentric minority in both "progressive" and antiabortion camps. Yet it has played a critical role in the movement: By arguing that opposition to abortion can be separated from the right's antifeminist program, it has given antiabortion sentiment legitimacy in left-symp and (putatively) profeminist circles. While left antiabortionists are hardly alone in emphasizing fetal life, their innovation has been to claim that a consistent "pro-life" stand involves opposing capital punishment, supporting disarmament, demanding government programs to end poverty, and so on. This is of course a leap the right is neither able nor willing to make. It's been liberals—from Garry Wills to the Catholic bishops—who have supplied the mass media with the idea that prohibiting abortion is part of a "seamless garment" of respect for human life.

Having invented this countercontext for the abortion controversy, left antiabortionists are trying to impose it as the only legitimate context for debate. Those of us who won't accept their terms and persist in seeing opposition to abortion, antifeminism, sexual repression, and religious sectarianism as the real seamless garment have been accused of obscuring the issue with demagoguery. Last year *Commonweal*—perhaps the most important current forum for left antiabortion opinion—ran an editorial demanding that we shape up: "Those who hold that abortion is immoral believe that the biological dividing lines of birth or viability should no more determine whether a developing member of the species is denied or accorded essential rights than should the biological dividing lines of sex or race or disability or old age. This argument is open to challenge. Perhaps the dividing lines are sufficiently different. Pro-choice advocates should state their reasons for believing so. They should meet the argument on its own grounds. . . ."

In other words, the only question we're allowed to debate—or the   5
only one *Commonweal* is willing to entertain—is "Are fetuses the moral equivalent of born human beings?" And I can't meet the argument on its own grounds because I don't agree that this is the key question, whose answer determines whether one supports abortion or opposes it. I don't doubt that fetuses are alive, or that they're biologically human—what else would they be? I do consider the life of a fertilized egg less precious

than the well-being of a woman with feelings, self-consciousness, a history, social ties; and I think fetuses get closer to being human in a moral sense as they come closer to birth. But to me these propositions are intuitively self-evident. I wouldn't know how to justify them to a "nonbeliever," nor do I see the point of trying.

I believe the debate has to start in a different place—with the recognition that fertilized eggs develop into infants inside the bodies of women. Pregnancy and birth are active processes in which a woman's body shelters, nourishes, and expels a new life; for nine months she is immersed in the most intimate possible relationship with another being. The growing fetus makes considerable demands on her physical and emotional resources, culminating in the cataclysmic experience of birth. And childbearing has unpredictable consequences; it always entails some risk of injury or death.

For me all this has a new concreteness: I had a baby last year. My much-desired and relatively easy pregnancy was full of what antiabortionists like to call "inconveniences." I was always tired, short of breath; my digestion was never right; for three months I endured a state of hormonal siege; later I had pains in my fingers, swelling feet, numb spots on my legs, the dread hemorrhoids. I had to think about everything I ate. I developed borderline glucose intolerance. I gained fifty pounds and am still overweight; my shape has changed in other ways that may well be permanent. Psychologically, my pregnancy consumed me—though I'd happily bought the seat on the roller coaster, I was still terrified to be so out of control of my normally tractable body. It was all bearable, even interesting—even, at times, transcendent—because I wanted a baby. Birth was painful, exhausting, and wonderful. If I hadn't wanted a baby it would only have been painful and exhausting—or worse. I can hardly imagine what it's like to have your body and mind taken over in this way when you not only don't look forward to the result, but positively dread it. The thought appalls me. So as I see it, the key question is "Can it be moral, under any circumstances, to make a woman bear a child against her will?"

From this vantage point, *Commonweal*'s argument is irrelevant, for in a society that respects the individual, no "member of the species" in *any* stage of development has an "essential right" to make use of someone else's body, let alone in such all-encompassing fashion, without that person's consent. You can't make a case against abortion by applying a general principle about everybody's human rights; you have to show exactly the opposite—that the relationship between fetus and pregnant woman is an exception, one that justifies depriving women of their right to bodily integrity. And in fact all antiabortion ideology rests on the premise—acknowledged or simply assumed—that women's unique capacity to bring life into the world carries with it a unique obligation that women cannot be allowed to "play God" and launch only the lives they welcome.

Yet the alternative to allowing women this power is to make them impotent. Criminalizing abortion doesn't just harm individual women with unwanted pregnancies, it affects all women's sense of themselves. Without control of our fertility we can never envision ourselves as free, for our biology makes us constantly vulnerable. Simply because we are female our physical integrity can be violated, our lives disrupted and transformed, at any time. Our ability to act in the world is hopelessly compromised by our sexual being.

Ah, sex—it does have a way of coming up in these discussions, de-   10
spite all. When pressed, right-to-lifers of whatever political persuasion invariably point out that pregnancy doesn't happen by itself. The leftists often give patronizing lectures on contraception (though some find only "natural birth control" acceptable), but remain unmoved when reminded that contraceptives fail. Openly or implicitly they argue that people shouldn't have sex unless they're prepared to procreate. (They are quick to profess a single standard—men as well as women should be sexually "responsible." Yes, and the rich as well as the poor should be allowed to sleep under bridges.) Which amounts to saying that if women want to lead heterosexual lives they must give up any claim to self-determination, and that they have no right to sexual pleasure without fear.

Opposing abortion, then, means accepting that women must suffer sexual disempowerment and a radical loss of autonomy relative to men: If fetal life is sacred, the self-denial basic to women's oppression is also basic to the moral order. Opposing abortion means embracing a conservative sexual morality, one that subordinates pleasure to reproduction: If fetal life is sacred, there is no room for the view that sexual passion—or even sexual love—for its own sake is a human need and a human right. Opposing abortion means tolerating the inevitable double standard, by which men may accept or reject sexual restrictions in accordance with their beliefs, while women must bow to them out of fear . . . or defy them at great risk. However much *Commonweal*'s editors and those of like mind want to believe their opposition to abortion is simply about saving lives, the truth is that in the real world they are shoring up a particular sexual culture, whose rules are stacked against women. I have yet to hear any left right-to-lifers take full responsibility for that fact or deal seriously with its political implications.

Unfortunately, their fuzziness has not lessened their appeal—if anything it's done the opposite. In increasing numbers liberals and leftists, while opposing antiabortion laws, have come to view abortion as an "agonizing moral issue" with some justice on both sides, rather than an issue—however emotionally complex—of freedom versus repression, or equality versus hierarchy, that affects their political self-definition. This above-the-battle stance is attractive to leftists who want to be feminist good guys but are uneasy or ambivalent about sexual issues, not to mention those who want to ally with "progressive" factions of the

Catholic church on Central America, nuclear disarmament, or populist economics without that sticky abortion question getting in the way.

Such neutrality is a way of avoiding the painful conflict over cultural issues that continually smolders on the left. It can also be a way of coping with the contradictions of personal life at a time when liberation is a dream deferred. To me the fight for abortion has always been the cutting edge of feminism, precisely because it denies that anatomy is destiny, that female biology dictates women's subordinate status. Yet recently I've found it hard to focus on the issue, let alone summon up the militance needed to stop the antiabortion tanks. In part that has to do with second-round weariness—do we really have to go through all these things twice?—in part with my life now.

Since my daughter's birth my feelings about abortion—not as a political demand but as a personal choice—have changed. In this society, the difference between the situation of a childless woman and of a mother is immense; the fear that having a child will dislodge one's tenuous hold on a nontraditional life is excruciating. This terror of being forced into the sea-change of motherhood gave a special edge to my convictions about abortion. Since I've made that plunge voluntarily, with consequences still unfolding, the terror is gone; I might not want another child, for all sorts of reasons, but I will never again feel that my identity is at stake. Different battles with the culture absorb my energy now. Besides, since I've experienced the primal, sensual passion of caring for an infant, there will always be part of me that does want another. If I had an abortion today, it would be with conflict and sadness unknown to me when I had an abortion a decade ago. And the antiabortionists' imagery of dead babies hits me with new force. Do many women—left, feminist women—have such feelings? Is this the sort of "ambivalence about abortion" that in the present atmosphere slides so easily into self-flagellating guilt?

Some left antiabortionists, mainly pacifists—Juli Loesch, Mary Meehan, and other "feminists for life"; Jim Wallis and various writers for Wallis's radical evangelical journal *Sojourners*—have tried to square their position with concern for women. They blame the prevalence of abortion on oppressive conditions—economic injustice, lack of child care and other social supports for mothers, the devaluation of childrearing, men's exploitative sexual behavior and refusal to take equal responsibility for children. They disagree on whether to criminalize abortion now (since murder is intolerable no matter what the cause) or to build a long-term moral consensus (since stopping abortion requires a general social transformation), but they all regard abortion as a desperate solution to desperate problems, and the women who resort to it as more sinned against than sinning.

This analysis grasps an essential feminist truth: that in a male-supremacist society no choice a woman makes is genuinely free or entirely in her interest. Certainly many women have had abortions they didn't want or wouldn't have wanted if they had any plausible means of caring for a child; and countless others wouldn't have gotten pregnant in the first place were it not for inadequate contraception, sexual confusion and guilt, male pressure, and other stigmata of female powerlessness. Yet forcing a woman to bear a child she doesn't want can only add injury to insult, while refusing to go through with such a pregnancy can be a woman's first step toward taking hold of her life. And many women who have abortions are "victims" only of ordinary human miscalculation, technological failure, or the vagaries of passion, all bound to exist in any society, however utopian. There will always be women who, at any given moment, want sex but don't want a child; some of these women will get pregnant; some of them will have abortions. Behind the victim theory of abortion is the implicit belief that women are always ready to be mothers, if only conditions are right, and that sex for pleasure rather than procreation is not only "irresponsible" (i.e., bad) but something men impose on women, never something women actively seek. Ironically, left right-to-lifers see abortion as always coerced (it's "exploitation" and "violence against women"), yet regard motherhood—which for most women throughout history has been inescapable, and is still our most socially approved role—as a positive choice. The analogy to the feminist antipornography movement goes beyond borrowed rhetoric: the antiporners, too, see active female lust as surrender to male domination and traditionally feminine sexual attitudes as expressions of women's true nature.

This Orwellian version of feminism, which glorifies "female values" and dismisses women's struggles for freedom—particularly sexual freedom—as a male plot, has become all too familiar in recent years. But its use in the abortion debate has been especially muddleheaded. Somehow we're supposed to leap from an oppressive patriarchal society to the egalitarian one that will supposedly make abortion obsolete without ever allowing women to see themselves as people entitled to control their reproductive function rather than be controlled by it. How women who have no power in this most personal of areas can effectively fight for power in the larger society is left to our imagination. A "New Zealand feminist" quoted by Mary Meehan in a 1980 article in *The Progressive* says, "Accepting short-term solutions like abortion only delays the implementation of real reforms like decent maternity and paternity leaves, job protection, high-quality child care, community responsibility for dependent people of all ages, and recognition of the economic contribution of childminders"—as if these causes were progressing nicely before legal abortion came along. On the contrary, the fight for reproductive freedom is the foundation of all the others, which is why antifeminists resist it so fiercely.

As "pro-life" pacifists have been particularly concerned with refuting charges of misogyny, the liberal Catholics at *Commonweal* are most exercised by the claim that antiabortion laws violate religious freedom. The editorial quoted above hurled another challenge at the proabortion forces:

> It is time, finally, for the pro-choice advocates and editorial writers to abandon, once and for all, the argument that abortion is a religious "doctrine" of a single or several churches being imposed on those of other persuasions in violation of the First Amendment. . . . Catholics and their bishops are accused of imposing their "doctrine" on abortion, but not their "doctrine" on the needs of the poor, or their "doctrine" on the arms race, or their "doctrine" on human rights in Central America. . . .
>
> The briefest investigation into Catholic teaching would show that the church's case against abortion is utterly unlike, say, its belief in the Real Presence, known with the eyes of faith alone, or its insistence on a Sunday obligation, applicable only to the faithful. The church's moral teaching on abortion . . . is for the most part like its teaching on racism, warfare, and capital punishment, based on ordinary reasoning common to believers and nonbelievers. . . .

This is one more example of right-to-lifers' tendency to ignore the sexual ideology underlying their stand. Interesting, isn't it, how the editorial neglects to mention that the church's moral teaching on abortion jibes neatly with its teaching on birth control, sex, divorce, and the role of women. The traditional, patriarchal sexual morality common to these teachings is explicitly religious, and its chief defenders in modern times have been the more conservative churches. The Catholic and evangelical Christian churches are the backbone of the organized right-to-life movement and—a few Nathansons and Hentoffs notwithstanding—have provided most of the movement's activists and spokespeople.

Furthermore, the Catholic hierarchy has made opposition to abor- 20 tion a litmus test of loyalty to the church in a way it has done with no other political issue—witness Archbishop O'Connor's harassment of Geraldine Ferraro during her vice-presidential campaign. It's unthinkable that a Catholic bishop would publicly excoriate a Catholic officeholder or candidate for taking a hawkish position on the arms race or Central America or capital punishment. Nor do I notice anyone trying to read William F. Buckley out of the church for his views on welfare. The fact is there is no accepted Catholic "doctrine" on these matters comparable to the church's absolutist condemnation of abortion. While differing attitudes toward war, racism, and poverty cut across religious and secular lines, the sexual values that mandate opposition to abortion are the bedrock of the traditional religious world view, and the source of the most bitter conflict with secular and religious modernists. When churches devote their considerable political power, organizational resources, and money to translating those values into law, I call that imposing their religious beliefs on me—whether or not they're technically violating the First Amendment.

Statistical studies have repeatedly shown that people's views on abortion are best predicted by their opinions on sex and "family" issues, not on "life" issues like nuclear weapons or the death penalty. That's not because we're inconsistent but because we comprehend what's really at stake in the abortion fight. It's the antiabortion left that refuses to face the contradiction in its own position: you can't be wholeheartedly for "life" — or for such progressive aspirations as freedom, democracy, equality — and condone the subjugation of women. The seamless garment is full of holes.

Topics for Critical Thinking and Writing

1. What does Willis mean when she insists, in her second paragraph, that abortion is "a *feminist issue*"? Whether or not you agree, write a paragraph explaining her point. You may want to begin simply by saying, "When Ellen Willis says abortion is a '*feminist issue*,' she means . . ."

2. After describing the physical and psychological difficulties of pregnancy, Willis says (para. 8):

   > in a society that respects the individual, no "member of the species" in *any* stage of development has an "essential right" to make use of someone else's body, let alone in such all-encompassing fashion, without that person's consent. You can't make a case against abortion by applying a general principle about everybody's human rights; you have to show exactly the opposite — that the relationship between fetus and pregnant woman is an exception, one that justifies depriving women of their right to bodily integrity.

   Do you accept all of Willis's declarations? Any of them? Why, or why not? And (another topic) consider the expression, "without that person's consent." Suppose a woman takes no precautions against becoming pregnant — possibly she even wants to become pregnant — but at a late stage in pregnancy decides she does not wish to bear a child. Can she withdraw her "consent" at any time?

3. In the previous question we asked you to consider Willis's expression "without that person's consent." Here is a related problem: The relationship between fetus and pregnant woman is different from all other relationships, but is it relevant to point out that women are not alone in having their bodies possessed, so to speak, by others? In time of war, men — but not women — are drafted; the interruption of their normal career causes considerable hardship. At the very least, a draftee is required to give up months or even several years of his life, and to live in circumstances that severely interfere with his privacy and his autonomy. And of course he may in fact be required to yield his life.

4. Do you think (in contrast to Willis) that persons who are opposed to capital punishment and to increased military spending — persons who are, so to speak, "pro-life" — must, if they are to be consistent, also oppose abortion? Why, or why not?

Randall A. Terry

Randall A. Terry is the founder of the antiabortion organization Operation Rescue. This essay originally appeared in the Boston Globe, *January 9, 1995.*

The Abortion Clinic Shootings: Why?

As the nation heard with sorrow the news of the deplorable shooting spree at abortion facilities in Brookline,[1] the question is asked: Why? Why this sudden rise of violence in this arena?

I have been intricately involved in the antiabortion movement for more than a decade. I have led thousands of people in peaceful antiabortion activism via Operation Rescue. Hence, I enjoy a perspective few have. So I submit these answers to the question "Why?"

Enemies of the babies and the antiabortion movement will argue that the conviction that abortion is murder, and the call to take nonviolent direct action to save children from death, inevitably leads to the use of lethal force. This argument is ludicrous — unless one is prepared to argue that Gandhi's nonviolent civil disobedience in India during the 1930s led to the murder of British officials; or that Dr. Martin Luther King's nonviolent civil disobedience led to the violent actions that accompanied the civil rights movement in the United States during the 1960s.

So why, then, this recent violent outburst? Law enforcement officials need look no further than *Roe v. Wade;* abortion providers need look no further than their own instruments of death; and Congress and the president need look no further than the Freedom of Access to Clinic Entrances Act to understand the roots of the shootings.

The Supreme Court's attempt to overthrow Law (capital "L") in order to legalize and legitimize murder has led to the inevitable — a disregard of or contempt for law. I say the court's attempt, for the court can no more overturn Law and legalize murder than it can overturn the law of gravity. God's immutable commandment "Thou shalt not murder" has forever made murder illegal. The court's lawlessness is breeding lawlessness. The court cannot betray the foundation of law and civilization — the Ten Commandments — and then expect a people to act "lawful" and "civilized."

Let us look at the abortion industry itself. Abortion is murder. And just as segregation and the accompanying violence possess the seeds for further violence, likewise it appears that the Law of sowing and reaping is being visited upon the abortion industry. A society cannot expect to

---

[1]On December 30, 1994, a gunman opened fire at two abortion facilities in Brookline, Massachusetts, wounding several people, two of them fatally. [Editors' note.]

tear 35 million innocent babies from their mothers' wombs without reaping horrifying consequences. Was it perhaps inevitable that the violent abortion industry should itself reap a portion of what it has so flagrantly and callously sown?

Now to Congress and the judiciary. Similar to the civil rights activists, antiabortion activists have often been brutalized at the hands of police and then subjected to vulgar injustices in sundry courts of law. Add to this the Freedom of Access to Clinic Entrances Act, which turns peaceful antiabortion activists into federal felons and perhaps one can understand the frustration and anger that is growing in Americans.

The abortion industry can partly blame itself for the recent shootings. It clamored for harsh treatment of peaceful antiabortion activists, and it usually got it. Now it has to deal with an emerging violent fringe. John F. Kennedy stated, "Those who make peaceful revolution impossible will make violent revolution inevitable." One would think the pro-choice crowd would belatedly heed the late president's warning, but they haven't. They're urging an all too political Justice Department to launch a witch hunt into the lives of peaceful antiabortion activists and leaders. Make no mistake—what the pro-choice people want is to pressure law enforcement and the courts to intimidate anyone who condemns abortion as murder. Their recent public relations scam is to blame all antiabortion people for the shootings. And they will not be content until they have crushed all dissent against abortion. We must not allow them to cause us to cower in silence.

To those who support the recent shootings or herald John Salvi as a hero, I ask you: Has God authorized one person to be policeman, judge, jury, and executioner? Is it logical to leap from nonviolent life-saving activities to lethal force? Read your history! Remember the principles of Calvin, Knox, and Cromwell concerning lower magistrates. Are you likening John Salvi and Co. to Knox or Cromwell? Are you calling for revolution? Please consider these questions before calling someone who walks into a clinic and starts randomly shooting people a hero.

So what can be done to curtail this trend? First, the Freedom of Access to Clinic Entrances Act should be repealed immediately. This oppressive law is an outrage. The crushing weight of the federal government punishing peaceful protesters is the kind of thing we would expect in Communist China against political dissidents.   10

Second, the courts must stop abusing antiabortion activists. We must be accorded the same tolerance and leniency that every politically correct protester receives nationwide, i.e., small fines, two days in jail, charges dismissed, etc.

Finally, and this is most urgent, child killing must be brought to an immediate end. Whether the Supreme Court declares the personhood and inalienable right to life of preborn children or the Constitution is amended or the president signs an emancipation proclamation for children or Congress outlaws abortion outright, we must bring a swift end to the murder of innocent children.

Topics for Critical Thinking and Writing

1. In his third paragraph, Terry draws a parallel between Operation Rescue and the nonviolent civil disobedience campaigns in India, led by Gandhi, and in the United States, led by Martin Luther King, Jr. Is the analogy a good one?

2. Does Terry think that the Supreme Court's decision in *Roe v. Wade* (upholding a woman's right to have an abortion) *causes* violent disruption of abortion clinics? Or that it *justifies* that violence? If so, spell out the details of this causation or justification. If not, what does he mean when he says in paragraph 4 that "Law enforcement officials need look no further than *Roe v. Wade*"?

3. Why does Terry think (see paras. 5 and 6) that "abortion is murder"?

4. In paragraph 8 Terry cites a remark of President Kennedy: "'Those who make peaceful revolution impossible will make violent revolution inevitable.'" Evaluate the aptness of this quotation as an explanation of violent disruption of medical services at an abortion clinic.

5. What is the purpose and the effect of Terry's choice of words when he writes, in paragraph 8, of a "public relations scam," "crush[ing] all dissent," "not . . . cower[ing] in silence"?

6. In the library, get some information about the Freedom of Access to Clinic Entrances Act (mentioned by Terry in paras. 7 and 10). Do you think its repeal, which Terry advocates, would help reduce violence at abortion clinics? Why, or why not? Why do you think this law was enacted by Congress in the first place?

7. Terry describes abortion as "child killing" (para. 12). Do you think that is a fair description? Why, or why not?

8. At the end of his essay (paras. 10–12), Terry proposes three things government ought to do to end the trend toward violence in the antiabortion movement. Do you think the pro-choice advocates can accept any of these policies? Why, or why not?

9. Terry asserts that "preborn children" have an "inalienable right to life" (para. 12). What does "inalienable" mean? Suppose a pregnant woman would die because of medical complications if she carried her unborn child to birth. Do you think Terry would favor the mother dying because we must respect "the inalienable right to life" of the unborn? Does the mother, too, have such a right? How do you think he ought to resolve this conflict of rights, and why?

13

Affirmative Action:
Is It Fair?

Terry Eastland

Terry Eastland, born in Dallas, Texas, and educated at Vanderbilt Univer-
sity, Tennessee, and Balliol College, Oxford, is a frequent contributor to con-
servative journals such as The National Review, American Spectator,
Commentary, *and* The Public Interest. *He is the author of several books,*
including Religious Liberty in the Supreme Court: The Cases that Define the Debate over Church and State *(1995) and* Ending Affirmative Action: The Case for Colorblind Justice *(1996), from which this ex-*
cerpt is taken.

Ending Affirmative Action

One of the central and hard-won lessons of the fight for colorblindness, lasting more than a century and a quarter, was that distinctions
drawn on the basis of race inevitably lead to racial discrimination. That is
why the advocates of colorblindness sought the elimination of racial distinctions in the law. They sought to end the source, the raw material, of
racial discrimination. The nation was the better for their efforts when,
starting in the 1940s, our legal system was strengthened by the addition
of a variety of antidiscrimination laws, culminating in the Civil Rights
Act of 1964. Soon afterward, the founders of affirmative action, searching for ways to improve the material condition of black Americans and
make amends for slavery and segregation, found the constraints of colorblind law inconvenient. They managed to loosen the colorblind strictures
of the Civil Rights Act of 1964, and the federal judiciary failed to tighten
them in turn. Once preferential treatment was made possible, it spread

throughout the public and private sectors, and the targets of numerical affirmative action became more numerous, coming to include Hispanics, Asians, and women.

Defenders of the policy initially promised that it would be temporary—a position that implicitly recognized that it is better not to sort people on the basis of race, that colorblindness is a worthy guide. But with the first step away from colorblindness, further steps came more easily, and in time we heard less often the promise that someday we would renew our previous commitment.

Nonetheless, more than a quarter century of thinking by race and counting by race has served only to confirm and strengthen the case for colorblind law.

We now know that when government has the power to sort people on the basis of race, racial discrimination often results. Preferential treatment is never benign. Whoever would have been admitted to a school, or won the promotion or the contract, but for race, has suffered discrimination—and there is no good discrimination. The nation owes a debt of gratitude to people like Allan Bakke, Brian Weber, Randy Pech, and Cheryl Hopwood, who have brought lawsuits challenging preferential affirmative action. They have courageously kept alive the question of the legality and morality of preferential treatment, providing often lonely witness to the principle at the heart of colorblind law—that no one in America should be discriminated against on account of race.

We know, too, that the effort to regulate on the basis of race can have unanticipated consequences. Where the old advocates of colorblind law were pessimists about the very idea of racial regulation, the founders of affirmative action were optimists, confident of their ability to distinguish between benign and invidious racial classifications. They thought the world could be divided into good and bad people. The bad discriminated against blacks, either intentionally or through seemingly neutral procedures that produced adverse effects. The good—and the founders of affirmative action included themselves in this category—sought to do well by blacks. They were pure in heart, and so they could be trusted not to harm blacks.

But now we know better. It was weak-minded and dangerously naive to think that taking race into account would produce unambiguously good results for those in whose behalf it was done. Many ostensible beneficiaries of affirmative action have testified that preferential treatment often leads to self-doubt, dependency, and entitlement. To be sure, affirmative action doesn't always do that. Sometimes it "works," though the paradox of affirmative action is that its "working" is a function of how soon the recipient quits it entirely and labors under the same rules as everyone else, a sign of genuine equality that is possible only among individuals. But, as the practice of affirmative action has shown, no one knows enough confidently to predict in advance of an act of preferential treatment which effects, for better or worse, it will have upon a given recipient. This negative experience of affirmative action does not constitute an unanswerable argument against it; patients do undergo risky operations. But we do have a choice in the matter; that is, we do not have to take the risk of affirmative action. And once free of it, those now eligible for it would be able to compete and achieve on the same terms as everyone else.

There have been other unanticipated consequences as well, chief among them the stigma produced by affirmative action. Wherever affirmative action operates, the very existence of such a program will lead some people to think that every minority student or every minority employee would not have won opportunity without preferential treatment, a judgment that strips people of the respect due them as individuals. Consider, in the context of higher education, the case of the minority student admitted under affirmative action who would not have won the place without it. This student very well might have been admitted to another school, without the "help" of affirmative action. The problem, however, is that the student admitted under affirmative action is unable to erase its stigma until the individual succeeds in a nonpreferential environment. Even then, however, the number of those who know the nature of the student's achievement is likely to be very small. And the formal, pervasive nature of affirmative action, encouraged and required by so many local, state, and federal government agencies, means that the public will continue to make generalizations about minority advancement simply because it is easy to do so in the absence of particular knowledge. The generalization is that "minority" equals "affirmative action" equals "lower standards." The inference drawn is that affirmative action explains minority success. Tragically, this process of generalization and inference trails the many minorities—perhaps the majority—who make their way without the "help" of any preferential treatment.

Here the negative experience of affirmative action makes a powerful argument for colorblind law. Because affirmative action is stigmatizing, even for those who do not "benefit" from it, it is better to forego affirmative action altogether in favor of procedures for admitting students or hiring workers or awarding contracts that do not brand their targets as inferior and do not provide a basis for generalizing about minority achievement. Such procedures, of course, are those that do not distinguish on the basis of race, that do not "take race into account" in deciding who gets ahead.

Sports, fortunately, is still a world governed by such colorblind rules. No one receives preferential treatment in sports, so no one has self-doubts induced by affirmative action, no one has to "transcend" affirmative action, and no one is stigmatized by affirmative action. No one ever thinks, "Williams is in center field because of affirmative action," or "Lopez is catching because he is Hispanic." Outside of sports—which is to say, in the rest of society—the deeply human desire to be known for individual accomplishment explains why some minorities have made a point of declining participation in programs for which their race or ethnicity makes them eligible. The Hispanic law student at the University of Texas School of Law, whose academic qualifications were good enough to be admitted under the standards governing "white and others," was making an important point when he said that sometimes he wished he was wearing a shirt indicating his academic credentials. Ending affirmative action will create circumstances in which individuals will shine and, just as importantly, be seen to shine, quite on their own merits.

The longer affirmative action remains in place, the more reasons there are to bring it to an end. Of course, past advocates of colorblind law could have told us how hard it would be to quit thinking and counting by race once the racial license had been granted. They knew that the human mind is creative, remarkably capable of coming up with reasons, even quite attractive ones, for why we ought to "take race into account." The founding rationale of affirmative action was to remedy the ill effects of past discrimination against blacks, but this rationale did not easily fit the other groups. So affirmative action was redefined and rejustified in terms of overcoming "underrepresentation" and achieving "diversity." We have also heard the argument that affirmative action is necessary to prevent future discrimination. There have been other reasons offered: Affirmative action is needed to create minority role models, to stimulate the creation of minority businesses, to jump-start economic development in minority communities. With the advent at the local level of minority-dominated governments, minorities have discriminated against nonminorities by fashioning affirmative action programs that, while publicly touted in terms of one or another of the usual rationales, realistically are little more than expressions of racial politics, the ignoble triumph of minority majorities.

The use of race now threatens to produce some truly bizarre results. In large cities where new immigrants congregate, blacks who hold disproportionately more public-sector jobs stand to lose some of those jobs to "underrepresented" Hispanics. Diversity, meanwhile, is a rationale that may allow discrimination against members of traditional minority groups. Even President Clinton has said he would support laying off a black teacher instead of a white teacher if doing so would promote diversity. We cannot escape the fact that by drawing racial and ethnic lines, affirmative action—whatever its rationale—encourages Americans to think of themselves in racial and ethnic terms. That has been a recipe for resentment and chauvinism, neither of which promotes the good health of our democracy.

Fortunately, the Supreme Court has kept the light on, letting us know where home is, even in those cases where it has ruled in support of affirmative action. Those justices of the Supreme Court who consistently voted for affirmative action programs nonetheless refused to endorse group rights or to break in principle with the colorblind tradition. Equality under the Constitution, Justice Brennan wrote, is linked "with the proposition that differences in color or creed, birth or status, are neither significant nor relevant to the way in which such persons are treated." Justice Marshall declared his desire to live in a society "in which the color of a person's skin will not determine the opportunities available to him or her." And Justice Blackmun endorsed a society in which "persons will be regarded as persons," without regard to race or ethnicity.[1]

In recent years the Court has been shining the home light much more brightly. Its decisions in the *Croson* and *Adarand* cases, which speak to every government in the United States, impose strict conditions on the use of racial preferences. These decisions point us in the right direction. Citing Justice Harlan's dissent in *Plessy v. Ferguson* and the opinions in the Japanese Relocation Cases, *Croson* and *Adarand* raise the standard of colorblind law in a context that makes colorblindness even more compelling today than Harlan could have known. He made his argument for colorblind law in the context of a society made up of two races—black and white. Ours today consists of many races and ethnic groups, thanks especially to recent waves of immigration. Law that tries to distinguish among the groups and to favor one over another is bound to fail the country. Instead, we need law that can discourage the natural tendency people have to seek their own kind, law that invites people to minimize and transcend racial and ethnic differences. The best protection for every individual—of whatever race or ethnic background—is to be found in law that does not give effect to any racial views, but, as Harlan put it, provides for "equality before the law of all citizens of the United States, without regard to race."

The Supreme Court, however, has left much of the task of ending affirmative action to the American people.[2] That is just as well. Decisions by the elective branches of government to end programs containing preferences would be reached consequent to public debate, not after legal briefs have been submitted. We can take major steps toward recovering colorblind law and principle by enacting measures at the federal and state levels that would deny government the power to favor or slight anyone on account of race. If we do not take such steps, of course, the uncertain political tides may turn back to favor the supporters of affirmative action. Progress toward colorblind law will be much slower, if not impossible, if we rely exclusively on judicial decisions, for the defenders

---

[1]See Lawrence H. Fuchs, *The American Kaleidoscope: Race, Ethnicity, and the Civic Culture* (Hanover, N.H.: Wesleyan University Press, 1995), p. 456. [All notes are the author's.]

[2]As for whether the Court should declare the Constitution flatly colorblind—a position endorsed by Justices Antonin Scalia and Clarence Thomas—the issue involves complicated and controversial questions, starting with the original meaning of the Fourteenth Amendment. See Jeff Rosen, "The Colorblind Court," *The New Republic,* July 31, 1995, and Andrew Kull, *The Color-Blind Constitution* (Cambridge, Mass.: Harvard University Press, 1992), pp. 221–24.

of affirmative action will respond by "mending" programs in ways that better disguise preferences but do not eliminate them. It is possible, too, that judicial progress toward colorblind law could be arrested or even reversed, if there are new Supreme Court appointees with views at odds with those of the majorities in *Croson* and *Adarand*. It falls to us to take action now.

The choice for colorblindness is the choice our own best tradition invites us to make. Our founding charter declares that "all men are created equal" and are "endowed by their Creator with certain unalienable rights," among them "life, liberty, and the pursuit of happiness." We are thereby committed to the proposition that it is individuals who have rights, not groups, and that all individuals enjoy a fundamental equality of rights. The startling character of the United States—and what it has modeled to the rest of the world—is that the individuals who have equal rights may be of any race or ethnic background.

Few Americans have stated the case for equality as cogently as Abraham Lincoln, who did so in an 1858 speech he gave in Chicago in observation of Independence Day. The challenge before Lincoln was to show that the truths of the Declaration of Independence were relevant to the audience before him, which included European immigrants who were not descended from those who wrote the Declaration, fought the Revolution, and framed the Constitution. Having paid honor to the "men living in that day whom we claim as our fathers and grandfathers," and having linked the principle they contended for to the nation's subsequent prosperity, Lincoln told the audience that "we hold this annual celebration to remind ourselves of all the good done . . . and how it was done and who did it, and how we are historically connected with it." He added that "we go from these meetings in better humor with ourselves—we feel more attached the one to the other, and more firmly bound to the country we inhabit." And, yes, those he was addressing were as much a part of this country as anyone else:

> We have [besides those descended from the founders] . . . among us perhaps half our people who are not descendants at all of these men, they are men who have come from Europe—German, Irish, French, and Scandinavian—men that have come from Europe themselves, or whose ancestors have come hither and settled here, finding themselves our equals in all things. If they look back through this history to trace their connection with those days by blood, they find they have none, they cannot carry themselves back into that glorious epoch and make themselves feel that they are part of us, but when they look through that old Declaration of Independence they find that those old men say that "We hold these truths to be self-evident, that all men are created equal," and then they feel that moral sentiment taught in that day evidences their relation to those men, that it is the father of all moral principle in them, and that they have a right to claim it as though they were

blood of the blood, and flesh of the flesh of the men who wrote that Declaration, and so they are.[3]

As Lincoln reminds us, the Declaration included any person from anywhere — the Germans and Swedes and other Europeans whom Lincoln addressed, the slaves Lincoln freed, the Asians who began arriving on our shores just before the nation was about to rend itself in a civil war, the Hispanics from all parts of the globe, Englishmen, American Indians, Jews — in sum, everyone. The Declaration is the great leveler, teaching that the rights of one are the rights of all. It puts us all on the same footing, and it implies the necessity of colorblind law because only that kind of law fully respects the equal rights of all persons, as individuals.

Affirmative action has always been an aberration from our best principles. The time has come to end it.

Topics for Critical Thinking and Writing

1. Find out, with the help of the reference librarian, what Allan Bakke, Brian Weber, Randy Pech, or Cheryl Hopwood did to warrant commendation from Eastland (para. 4), and write a 250-word essay on what you discover.

2. What, if any, particular programs of affirmative action does Eastland mention and criticize?

3. When Eastland writes (para. 6) that "we do not have to take the risk of affirmative action," what does he mean? How do you think he would reply to someone who disagrees with him?

4. Eastland concentrates on the objections to affirmative action for African Americans; he says little about affirmative action for women. Do you think his objections apply equally well to both groups? Why, or why not?

5. Suppose one argued that affirmative action is a necessary tactic to achieve more racial and cultural diversity on campus among students, faculty, and staff, and that such diversity is an end good in itself. How do you think Eastland might reply to such an argument?

6. Head Start programs, established under the Economic Opportunity Act of 1964, help prepare economically disadvantaged students to meet the rigors of academic life in school and college. Do Eastland's criticisms of affirmative action apply to Head Start?

[3]Roy P. Basler, ed., *The Collected Works of Abraham Lincoln* (New Brunswick, N.J.: Rutgers University Press, 1953), vol. 2, pp. 499–500.

7. Which statement do you think best characterizes Eastland's position? (a) We do not have a problem with racism, so affirmative action was never needed to solve it. (b) We do have a problem with racism, but affirmative action is not the way to solve it. (c) Affirmative action creates a problem of racism where none existed.

8. Read the essay by Stanley Fish (directly following) in defense of affirmative action programs, and write a 1,000-word essay explaining why you think Fish or Eastland has the better argument overall.

Stanley Fish

Stanley Fish, born in Providence, Rhode Island, in 1938, holds degrees from the University of Pennsylvania and Yale University. His first career was as a professor of English at the University of California at Berkeley and then at the Johns Hopkins University. He moved next to Duke University, where in 1986 he became not only the chair of the Department of English but also a professor of law. He has written increasingly on a variety of social and political topics. Among his publications are Doing What Comes Naturally: Change, Rhetoric, and the Practice of Theory in Literary and Legal Studies *(1989) and* There's No Such Thing as Free Speech: And It's a Good Thing, Too *(1994). The essay was originally published in the* Atlantic Monthly *November 1993 issue.*

Reverse Racism, or How the Pot Got to Call the Kettle Black

I take my text from George Bush, who, in an address to the United Nations on September 23, 1991, said this of the UN resolution equating Zionism with racism: "Zionism . . . is the idea that led to the creation of a home for the Jewish people. . . . And to equate Zionism with the intolerable sin of racism is to twist history and forget the terrible plight of Jews in World War II and indeed throughout history." What happened in the Second World War was that 6 million Jews were exterminated by people who regarded them as racially inferior and a danger to Aryan purity. What happened after the Second World War was that the survivors of that Holocaust established a Jewish state — that is, a state centered on Jewish history, Jewish values, and Jewish traditions: in short, a Jewo-centric state. What President Bush objected to was the logical sleight of hand by which these two actions were declared equivalent because they were both expressions of racial exclusiveness. Ignored, as Bush said, was the *historical* difference between them — the difference between a program of genocide and the determination of those who escaped it to establish a community in which they would be the makers, not the victims, of the laws.

Only if racism is thought of as something that occurs principally in the mind, a falling-away from proper notions of universal equality, can the desire of a victimized and terrorized people to band together be declared morally identical to the actions of their would-be executioners. Only when the actions of the two groups are detached from the historical conditions of their emergence and given a purely abstract description can they be made interchangeable. Bush was saying to the United Nations, "Look, the Nazis' conviction of racial superiority generated a policy of systematic genocide; the Jews' experience of centuries of persecution in almost every country on earth generated a desire for a homeland of their own. If you manage somehow to convince yourself that these are the same, it is you, not the Zionists, who are morally confused, and the reason you are morally confused is that you have forgotten history."

A KEY DISTINCTION

What I want to say, following Bush's reasoning, is that a similar forgetting of history has in recent years allowed some people to argue, and argue persuasively, that affirmative action is reverse racism. The very phrase "reverse racism" contains the argument in exactly the form to which Bush objected: In this country whites once set themselves apart from blacks and claimed privileges for themselves while denying them to others. Now, on the basis of race, blacks are claiming special status and reserving for themselves privileges they deny to others. Isn't one as bad as the other? The answer is no. One can see why by imagining that it is not 1993 but 1955, and that we are in a town in the South with two more or less distinct communities, one white and one black. No doubt each community would have a ready store of dismissive epithets, ridiculing stories, self-serving folk myths, and expressions of plain hatred, all directed at the other community, and all based in racial hostility. Yet to regard their respective racisms—if that is the word—as equivalent would be bizarre, for the hostility of one group stems not from any wrong done to it but from its wish to protect its ability to deprive citizens of their voting rights, to limit access to educational institutions, to prevent entry into the economy except at the lowest and most menial levels, and to force members of the stigmatized group to ride in the back of the bus. The hostility of the other group is the result of these actions, and whereas hostility and racial anger are unhappy facts wherever they are found, a distinction must surely be made between the ideological hostility of the oppressors and the experience-based hostility of those who have been oppressed.

Not to make that distinction is, adapting George Bush's words, to twist history and forget the terrible plight of African Americans in the more than two hundred years of this country's existence. Moreover, to equate the efforts to remedy that plight with the actions that produced it is to twist history even further. Those efforts, designed to redress the imbalances caused by long-standing discrimination, are called affirmative action; to argue that affirmative action, which gives preferential treatment to disadvantaged minorities as part of a plan to achieve social equality, is no different from the policies that created the disadvantages in the first place is a travesty of reasoning. "Reverse racism" is a cogent description of affirmative action only if one considers the cancer of racism to be morally and medically indistinguishable from the therapy we apply to it. A cancer is an invasion of the body's equilibrium, and so is chemotherapy; but we do not decline to fight the disease because the medicine we employ is also disruptive of nominal functioning. Strong illness, strong remedy: The formula is as appropriate to the health of the body politic as it is to that of the body proper.

At this point someone will always say, "But two wrongs don't make   5
a right; if it was wrong to treat blacks unfairly, it is wrong to give blacks preference and thereby treat whites unfairly." This objection is just another version of the forgetting and rewriting of history. The work is done by the adverb "unfairly," which suggests two more or less equal parties, one of whom has been unjustly penalized by an incompetent umpire. But blacks have not simply been treated unfairly; they have been subjected first to decades of slavery, and then to decades of second-class citizenship, widespread legalized discrimination, economic persecution, educational deprivation, and cultural stigmatization. They have been bought, sold, killed, beaten, raped, excluded, exploited, shamed, and scorned for a very long time. The word "unfair" is hardly an adequate description of their experience, and the belated gift of "fairness" in the form of a resolution no longer to discriminate against them legally is hardly an adequate remedy for the deep disadvantages that the prior discrimination has produced. When the deck is stacked against you in more ways than you can even count, it is small consolation to hear that you are now free to enter the game and take your chances.

A TILTED FIELD

The same insincerity and hollowness of promise infect another formula that is popular with the anti-affirmative-action crowd: the formula of the level playing field. Here the argument usually takes the form of saying "It is undemocratic to give one class of citizens advantages at the expense of other citizens; the truly democratic way is to have a level playing field to which everyone has access and where everyone has a fair and equal chance to succeed on the basis of his or her merit." Fine words—but they conceal the facts of the situation as it has been given to us by history: The playing field is already tilted in favor of those by whom and for whom it was constructed in the first place. If mastery of the requirements for entry depends upon immersion in the cultural experiences of the mainstream majority, if the skills that make for success are nurtured by institutions and cultural practices from which the disadvantaged minority has been systematically excluded, if the language and ways of comporting oneself that identify a player as "one of us" are alien to the lives minorities are forced to live, then words like "fair" and "equal" are cruel jokes, for what they promote and celebrate is an institutionalized unfairness and a perpetuated inequality. The playing field is already tilted, and the resistance to altering it by the mechanisms of affirmative action is in fact a determination to make sure that the present imbalances persist as long as possible.

One way of tilting the field is the Scholastic Aptitude Test. This test figures prominently in Dinesh D'Souza's book *Illiberal Education* (1991), in which one finds many examples of white or Asian students denied admission to colleges and universities even though their SAT scores were higher than the scores of some others—often African Americans—who were admitted to the same institution. This, D'Souza says, is evidence that as a result of affirmative-action policies colleges and universities tend "to depreciate the importance of merit criteria in admissions." D'Souza's assumption—and it is one that many would share—is that the test does in fact measure *merit*, with merit understood as a quality objectively determined in the same way that body temperature can be objectively determined.

In fact, however, the test is nothing of the kind. Statistical studies have suggested that test scores reflect income and socioeconomic status. It has been demonstrated again and again that scores vary in relation to cultural background; the test's questions assume a certain uniformity in educational experience and lifestyle and penalize those who, for whatever reason, have had a different experience and lived different kinds of lives. In short, what is being measured by the SAT is not absolutes like native ability and merit but accidents like birth, social position, access to libraries, and the opportunity to take vacations or to take SAT prep courses.

Furthermore, as David Owen notes in *None of the Above: Behind the Myth of Scholastic Aptitude* (1985), the "correlation between SAT scores and college grades . . . is lower than the correlation between weight and height; in other words you would have a better chance of predicting a person's height by looking at his weight than you would of predicting his freshman grades by looking only at his SAT scores." Everywhere you look in the SAT story, the claims of fairness, objectivity, and neutrality fall away, to be replaced by suspicions of specialized measures and unfair advantages.

Against this background a point that in isolation might have a questionable force takes on a special and even explanatory resonance: The principal deviser of the test was an out-and-out racist. In 1923 Carl Campbell Brigham published a book called *A Study of American Intelligence*, in which, as Owen notes, he declared, among other things, that we faced in America "a possibility of racial admixture . . . infinitely worse than that faced by any European country today, for we are incorporating the Negro into our racial stock, while all of Europe is compara-   10 tively free of this taint." Brigham had earlier analyzed the Army Mental Tests using classifications drawn from another racist text, Madison Grant's *The Passing of the Great Race*, which divided American society into four distinct racial strains, with Nordic, blue-eyed, blond people at the pinnacle and the American Negro at the bottom. Nevertheless, in 1925 Brigham became a director of testing for the College Board, and developed the SAT. So here is the great SAT test, devised by a racist in order to confirm racist assumptions, measuring not native ability but cultural advantage, an uncertain indicator of performance, an indicator of very little except what money and social privilege can buy. And it is in the name of this mechanism that we are asked to reject affirmative action and reaffirm "the importance of merit criteria in admissions."

THE REALITY OF DISCRIMINATION

Nevertheless, there is at least one more card to play against affirmative action, and it is a strong one. Granted that the playing field is not level and that access to it is reserved for an already advantaged elite, the disadvantages suffered by others are less racial—at least in 1993—than socioeconomic. Therefore shouldn't, as D'Souza urges, "universities . . . retain their policies of preferential treatment, but alter their criteria of application from race to socioeconomic disadvantage," and thus avoid the unfairness of current policies that reward middle-class or affluent blacks at the expense of poor whites? One answer to this question is given by D'Souza himself when he acknowledges that the overlap between minority groups and the poor is very large—a point underscored by the former Secretary of Education Lamar Alexander, who said, in response to a question about funds targeted for black students, "Ninety-eight percent of race-specific scholarships do not involve constitutional problems." He meant, I take it, that 98 percent of race-specific scholarships were also scholarships to the economically disadvantaged.

Still, the other 2 percent—nonpoor, middle-class, economically favored blacks—are receiving special attention on the basis of disadvantages they do not experience. What about them? The force of the question depends on the assumption that in this day and age race could not possibly be a serious disadvantage to those who are otherwise well positioned in the society. But the lie was given dramatically to this assumption in a 1991 broadcast of the ABC program "PrimeTime Live." In a stunning fifteen-minute segment reporters and a camera crew followed two young men of equal education, cultural sophistication, level of apparent affluence, and so forth around St. Louis, a city where neither was known. The two differed in only a single respect: one was white, the other black. But that small difference turned out to mean everything. In a series of encounters with shoe salesmen, record-store employees, rental agents, landlords, employment agencies, taxicab drivers, and ordinary citizens, the black member of the pair was either ignored or given a special and suspicious attention. He was asked to pay more for the same goods or come up with a larger down payment for the same car, was turned away as a prospective tenant, was rejected as a prospective taxi-cab fare, was treated with contempt and irritation by clerks and bureau-crats, and in every way possible was made to feel inferior and unwanted.

The inescapable conclusion was that alike though they may have been in almost all respects, one of these young men, because he was black, would lead a significantly lesser life than his white counterpart: He would be housed less well and at greater expense; he would pay more for services and products when and if he was given the opportunity to buy them; he would have difficulty establishing credit; the first emotions he would inspire on the part of many people he met would be distrust and fear; his abilities would be discounted even before he had a chance to display them; and, above all, the treatment he received from minute to minute would chip away at his self-esteem and self-confidence with consequences that most of us could not even imagine. As the young man in question said at the conclusion of the broadcast, "You walk down the street with a suit and tie and it doesn't matter. Someone will make de-terminations about you, determinations that affect the quality of your life."

Of course, the same determinations are being made quite early on by kindergarten teachers, grade school principals, high school guidance counselors, and the like, with results that cut across socioeconomic lines and place young black men and women in the ranks of the disadvan-taged no matter what the bank accounts of their parents happen to show. Racism is a cultural fact, and although its effects may to some ex-tent be diminished by socioeconomic variables, those effects will still be sufficiently great to warrant the nation's attention and thus the continu-ation of affirmative-action policies. This is true even of the field thought to be dominated by blacks and often cited as evidence of the equal op-portunities society now affords them. I refer, of course, to professional athletics. But national self-congratulation on this score might pause in the face of a few facts: A minuscule number of African Americans ever receive a paycheck from a professional team. Even though nearly sixteen hundred daily newspapers report on the exploits of black athletes, they employ only seven full-time black sports columnists. Despite repeated pledges and resolutions, major-league teams have managed to put only a handful of blacks and Hispanics in executive positions.

WHY ME?

When all is said and done, however, one objection to affirmative ac-tion is unanswerable on its own terms, and that is the objection of the individual who says, "Why me? Sure, discrimination has persisted for many years, and I acknowledge that the damage done has not been re-moved by changes in the law. But why me? I didn't own slaves; I didn't vote to keep people on the back of the bus; I didn't turn water hoses on civil-rights marchers. Why, then, should I be the one who doesn't get the job or who doesn't get the scholarship or who gets bumped back to the waiting list?"

I sympathize with this feeling, if only because in a small way I have had the experience that produces it. I was recently nominated for an administrative post at a large university. Early signs were encouraging, but after an interval I received official notice that I would not be included at the next level of consideration, and subsequently I was told unofficially that at some point a decision had been made to look only in the direction of women and minorities. Although I was disappointed, I did not conclude that the situation was "unfair," because the policy was obviously not directed at me—at no point in the proceedings did someone say, "Let's find a way to rule out Stanley Fish." Nor was it directed even at persons of my race and sex—the policy was not intended to disenfranchise white males. Rather, the policy was driven by other considerations, and it was only as a by-product of those considerations—not as the main goal—that white males like me were rejected. Given that the institution in question has a high percentage of minority students, a very low percentage of minority faculty, and an even lower percentage of minority administrators, it made perfect sense to focus on women and minority candidates, and within that sense, not as the result of prejudice, my whiteness and maleness became disqualifications.

I can hear the objection in advance: "What's the difference? Unfair is unfair: you didn't get the job; you didn't even get on the short list." The difference is not in the outcome but in the ways of thinking that led up to the outcome. It is the difference between an unfairness that befalls one as the unintended effect of a policy rationally conceived and an unfairness that is pursued as an end in itself. It is the difference between the awful unfairness of Nazi extermination camps and the unfairness to Palestinian Arabs that arose from, but was not the chief purpose of, the founding of a Jewish state.

THE NEW BIGOTRY

The point is not a difficult one, but it is difficult to see when the unfairness scenarios are presented as simple contrasts between two decontextualized persons who emerge from nowhere to contend for a job or a place in a freshman class. Here is student A; he has a board score of 1,300. And here is student B; her board score is only 1,200, yet she is admitted and A is rejected. Is that fair? Given the minimal information provided, the answer is of course no. But if we expand our horizons and consider fairness in relation to the cultural and institutional histories that have brought the two students to this point, histories that weigh on them even if they are not the histories' authors, then both the question and the answer suddenly grow more complicated.

The sleight-of-hand logic that first abstracts events from history and then assesses them from behind a veil of willed ignorance gains some of its plausibility from another key word in the anti-affirmative-action lexicon. That word is "individual," as in "The American way is to focus on the rights of individuals rather than groups." Now, "individual" and "individualism" have been honorable words in the American political vocabulary, and they have often been well employed in the fight against various tyrannies. But like any other word or concept, individualism can be perverted to serve ends the opposite of those it originally served, and this is what has happened when in the name of individual rights, millions of individuals are enjoined from redressing historically documented wrongs. How is this managed? Largely in the same way that the invocation of fairness is used to legitimize an institutionalized inequality. First one says, in the most solemn of tones, that the protection of individual rights is the chief obligation of society. Then one defines individuals as souls sent into the world with equal entitlements as guaranteed either by their Creator or by the Constitution. Then one pretends that nothing has happened to them since they stepped onto the world's stage. And then one says of these carefully denatured souls that they will all be treated in the same way, irrespective of any of the differences that history has produced. Bizarre as it may seem, individualism in this argument turns out to mean that everyone is or should be the same. This dismissal of individual difference in the name of the individual would be funny were its consequences not so serious: It is the mechanism by which imbalances and inequities suffered by millions of people through no fault of their own can be sanitized and even celebrated as the natural workings of unfettered democracy.

"Individualism," "fairness," "merit"—these three words are continu-   20
ally misappropriated by bigots who have learned that they need not put on a white hood or bar access to the ballot box in order to secure their ends. Rather, they need only clothe themselves in a vocabulary plucked from its historical context and made into the justification for attitudes and policies they would not acknowledge if frankly named.

Topics for Critical Thinking and Writing

1. Fish opens his essay (paras. 1–2) by explaining why claims that Zionism is a form of racism are wrong. Explain whether you think this beginning is or is not effective.

2. Explain as precisely and concisely as you can exactly what racism is and what reverse racism is.

3. What, if any, particular programs of affirmative action does Fish mention? Defend? Are there some that he overlooks? Does this omission trouble you? Why?

4. Evaluate Fish's analogy between fighting racism with affirmative action and fighting cancer with chemotherapy (para. 4).

5. Why does Fish dispute any claim that tests measuring scholastic aptitude also measure a college applicant's merit for admission (paras. 7–10)? Under what conditions, if any, do you think an applicant to your college deserves to be admitted?

6. How does Fish deal with the objection that, under affirmative action, too many affluent middle-class African American students are admitted to the most competitive colleges on the basis of their race, thereby displacing more needy students who are white (paras. 11–12)?

7. If possible, compare your own experience with Fish's in being discriminated against because of your age, gender, or race to make room for someone from an underrepresented group (paras. 16–17). Did your reaction differ from his, or was it similar? Explain your experience and your reflections on it in an essay of 250 words.

14

Gay Marriages: Should They Be Legalized?

Thomas B. Stoddard

Thomas B. Stoddard (1948–1997) was executive director of the Lambda Legal Defense and Education Fund, a gay rights organization. In 1995 New York University School of Law established a fellowship in Stoddard's name, honoring him for his work on behalf of gay and lesbian rights.

This article is from the Op-Ed section of the New York Times, *March 4, 1988.*

Gay Marriages: Make Them Legal

"In sickness and in health, 'til death do us part." With those familiar words, millions of people each year are married, a public affirmation of a private bond that both society and the newlyweds hope will endure. Yet for nearly four years, Karen Thompson was denied the company of the one person to whom she had pledged lifelong devotion. Her partner is a woman, Sharon Kowalski, and their home state of Minnesota, like every other jurisdiction in the United States, refuses to permit two individuals of the same sex to marry.

Karen Thompson and Sharon Kowalski are spouses in every respect except the legal. They exchanged vows and rings; they lived together until November 13, 1983 — when Ms. Kowalski was severely injured when her car was struck by a drunk driver. She lost the capacity to walk or to speak more than several words at a time, and needed constant care.

Ms. Thompson sought a court ruling granting her guardianship over her partner, but Ms. Kowalski's parents opposed the petition and obtained sole guardianship. They moved Ms. Kowalski to a nursing home three-hundred miles away from Ms. Thompson and forbade all visits be-

412

tween the two women. Last month, as part of a reevaluation of Ms. Kowalski's mental competency, Ms. Thompson was permitted to visit her partner again. But the prolonged injustice and anguish inflicted on both women hold a moral for everyone.

Marriage, the Supreme Court declared in 1967, is "one of the basic civil rights of man" (and, presumably, of woman as well). The freedom to marry, said the Court, is "essential to the orderly pursuit of happiness."

Marriage is not just a symbolic state. It can be the key to survival,   5
emotional and financial. Marriage triggers a universe of rights, privileges, and presumptions. A married person can share in a spouse's estate even when there is no will. She is typically entitled to the group insurance and pension programs offered by the spouse's employer, and she enjoys tax advantages. She cannot be compelled to testify against her spouse in legal proceedings.

The decision whether or not to marry belongs properly to individuals — not the government. Yet at present, all fifty states deny that choice to millions of gay and lesbian Americans. While marriage has historically required a male partner and a female partner, history alone cannot sanctify injustice. If tradition were the only measure, most states would still limit matrimony to partners of the same race.

As recently as 1967, before the Supreme Court declared miscegenation statutes unconstitutional, sixteen states still prohibited marriages between a white person and a black person. When all the excuses were stripped away, it was clear that the only purpose of those laws was, in the words of the Supreme Court, "to maintain white supremacy."

Those who argue against reforming the marriage statutes because they believe that same sex marriage would be "antifamily" overlook the obvious: Marriage creates families and promotes social stability. In an increasingly loveless world, those who wish to commit themselves to a relationship founded upon devotion should be encouraged, not scorned. Government has no legitimate interest in how that love is expressed.

And it can no longer be argued — if it ever could — that marriage is fundamentally a procreative unit. Otherwise, states would forbid marriage between those who, by reason of age or infertility, cannot have children, as well as those who elect not to.

As the case of Sharon Kowalski and Karen Thompson demonstrates,   10
sanctimonious illusions lead directly to the suffering of others. Denied the right to marry, these two women are left subject to the whims and prejudices of others, and of the law.

Depriving millions of gay American adults the marriages of their choice, and the rights that flow from marriage, denies equal protection of the law. They, their families and friends, together with fair-minded people everywhere, should demand an end to this monstrous injustice.

Topics for Critical Thinking and Writing

1. Study the essay as an example of ways to argue. What sorts of arguments does Stoddard offer? Obviously he does not offer statistics or cite authorities, but what *does* he do in an effort to convince the reader?

2. Stoddard draws an analogy between laws that used to prohibit marriage between persons of different races and laws that still prohibit marriage between persons of the same sex. Evaluate this analogy in an essay of 100 words.

3. Stoddard cites Karen Thompson and Sharon Kowalski. Presumably he could have found, if he had wished, a comparable example using two men rather than two women. Do you think the effect of his essay would be better, worse, or the same if his example used men rather than women? Why?

4. Do you find adequate Stoddard's response to the charge (para. 8) that "same sex marriage would be 'antifamily'"? Why?

5. One widespread assumption is that the family exists in order to produce children. Stoddard mentions this, but he does not mention that although gay couples cannot produce children they can (where legally permitted to do so) rear children, and thus fulfill a social need. (Further, if the couple is lesbian, one of the women can even be the natural mother.) Do you think he was wise to omit this argument in behalf of same sex marriages? Why?

6. Think about what principal claims one might make to contradict Stoddard's claims, and then write a 500-word essay defending this proposition: Lawful marriage should be limited to heterosexual couples. Or, if you believe that gay marriages should be legitimized, write an essay offering additional support to Stoddard's essay.

7. Stoddard's whole purpose is to break down the prejudice against same sex marriages, but he seems to take for granted the appropriateness of monogamy. Yet one might argue against Stoddard that if society opened the door to same sex marriages, it would be hard to keep the door closed to polygamy or polyandry. Write a 500-word essay exploring this question.

8. Would Stoddard's argument require him to allow marriage between a brother and a sister? A parent and a child? A human being and an animal? Why, or why not?

Lisa Schiffren

Lisa Schiffren was a speechwriter for former Vice President Dan Quayle. We reprint an essay that originally was published in the New York Times *on March 23, 1996.*

Gay Marriage, an Oxymoron

As study after study and victim after victim testify to the social devastation of the sexual revolution, easy divorce, and out-of-wedlock motherhood, marriage is fashionable again. And parenthood has transformed many baby boomers into advocates of bourgeois norms.

Indeed, we have come so far that the surprise issue of the political season is whether homosexual "marriage" should be legalized. The Hawaii courts will likely rule that gay marriage is legal, and other states will be required to accept those marriages as valid.

Considering what a momentous change this would be — a radical redefinition of society's most fundamental institution — there has been almost no real debate. This is because the premise is unimaginable to many, and the forces of political correctness have descended on the discussion, raising the cost of opposition. But one may feel the same affection for one's homosexual friends and relatives as for any other and be genuinely pleased for the happiness they derive from relationships while opposing gay marriage for principled reasons.

"Same-sex marriage" is inherently incompatible with our culture's understanding of the institution. Marriage is essentially a lifelong compact between a man and woman committed to sexual exclusivity and the creation and nurture of offspring. For most Americans, the marital union — as distinguished from other sexual relationships and legal and economic partnerships — is imbued with an aspect of holiness. Though many of us are uncomfortable using religious language to discuss social and political issues, Judeo-Christian morality informs our view of family life.

Though it is not polite to mention it, what the Judeo-Christian tradi- 5
tion has to say about homosexual unions could not be clearer. In a diverse, open society such as ours, tolerance of homosexuality is a necessity. But for many, its practice depends on a trick of cognitive dissonance that allows people to believe in the Judeo-Christian moral order while accepting, often with genuine regard, the different lives of homosexual acquaintances. That is why, though homosexuals may believe that they are merely seeking a small expansion of the definition of marriage, the majority of Americans perceive this change as a radical deconstruction of the institution.

Some make the conservative argument that making marriage a civil right will bring stability, an end to promiscuity, and a sense of fairness to gay men and women. But they miss the point. Society cares about stability in heterosexual unions because it is critical for raising healthy children and transmitting the values that are the basis of our culture.

Whether homosexual relationships endure is of little concern to society. That is also true of most childless marriages, harsh as it is to say. Society has wisely chosen not to differentiate between marriages, because it would require meddling into the motives and desires of everyone who applies for a license.

In traditional marriage, the tie that really binds for life is shared responsibility for the children. (A small fraction of gay couples may choose to raise children together, but such children are offspring of one partner and an outside contributor.) What will keep gay marriages together when individuals tire of each other?

Similarly, the argument that legal marriage will check promiscuity by gay males raises the question of how a "piece of paper" will do what the threat of AIDS has not. Lesbians seem to have little problem with monogamy or the rest of what constitutes "domestication," despite the absence of official status.

Finally, there is the so-called fairness argument. The government gives   10
tax benefits, inheritance rights, and employee benefits only to the married. Again, these financial benefits exist to help couples raise children. Tax reform is an effective way to remove distinctions among earners.

If the American people are interested in a radical experiment with same-sex marriages, then subjecting it to the political process is the right route. For a court in Hawaii to assume that it has the power to radically redefine marriage is a stunning abuse of power. To present homosexual marriage as a fait accompli, without national debate, is a serious political error. A society struggling to recover from thirty years of weakened norms and broken families is not likely to respond gently to having an institution central to most people's lives altered.

Topics for Critical Thinking and Writing

1. What is an oxymoron, and why does Schiffren think the phrases "gay marriage" and "same sex marriage" are oxymorons?

2. In paragraph 3 Schiffren refers to "political correctness." How would you define that term? So defined, do you think political correctness is sometimes objectionable? Always objectionable? Sometimes justifiable? Always justifiable?

3. Schiffren defines marriage in paragraph 4 in such a way that a man and woman who marry with no intention of having children are deviant. She does not imply, however, that such marriages should be prohibited by law or otherwise nullified. Does consistency require her to grant that while same sex marriages are no doubt deviant—in the sense of atypical or relatively rare—they are nonetheless legitimate?

4. Schiffren refers to "cognitive dissonance" (para. 5). What does she mean by this term, and how does she think it plays a role in our society's prevailing attitude toward homosexuality?

5. Schiffren says (para. 7), "Whether homosexual relationships endure is of little concern to society," because such relationships do not involve

nurturing children. By the same token, does society have little concern for heterosexual marriages to endure where there are no children involved? Or do you think that there are other considerations that make stable intimate relations between consenting adults important to society?

6. List the reasons for same sex marriage unions that Schiffren mentions. Which, if any, do you think are significant? Are there reasons you can think of that she fails to mention?

7. In her final paragraph, Schiffren deplores the federal court in Hawaii that ratified same sex marriage. Is it the process or the result of this decision to which she mostly objects? Do you agree with her objection? Go to your college library, find out the current status in the courts of this issue, and write a 500-word paper on the Hawaiian same sex marriage law, how it became law, and what it provides.

8. If gay marriage is recognized as legal, are we necessarily on a slippery slope (see p. 285) that will bring us to recognition of polygamy or polyandry (perhaps heterosexual, but perhaps a marriage of a bisexual to a man and also to a woman) and incest. Why, or why not?

9. Schiffren was not replying directly to Thomas Stoddard (p. 412), but she probably knew his arguments. Does he make any points that you wish she had faced? If so, what are they? If she were asked to comment on these points by Stoddard, what do you think her responses would be?

10. How would you characterize Schiffren's tone? Haughty? Earnest? Smart-alecky? (You need not come up with a one-word answer; you might say, "She is chiefly X, but also sometimes Y.") Do you think her tone will help her to persuade people to accept her views?

15

Gun Control: Would It Really Help?

J. Warren Cassidy

When J. Warren Cassidy wrote this article, he was the National Rifle Association's executive vice president. The article was originally published in Time *(January 29, 1990).*

The Case for Firearms

The American people have a right "to keep and bear arms." This right is protected by the Second Amendment to the Constitution, just as the right to publish editorial comment in this magazine is protected by the First Amendment. Americans remain committed to the constitutional right to free speech even when their most powerful oracles have, at times, abused the First Amendment's inherent powers. Obviously the American people believe no democracy can survive without a free voice.

In the same light, the authors of the Bill of Rights knew that a democratic republic has a right—indeed, a need—to keep and bear arms. Millions of American citizens just as adamantly believe the Second Amendment is crucial to the maintenance of the democratic process. Many express this belief through membership in the National Rifle Association of America.

Our cause is neither trendy nor fashionable, but a basic American belief that spans generations. The NRA's strength has never originated in Washington but instead has reached outward and upward from Biloxi, Albuquerque, Concord, Tampa, Topeka—from every point on the compass and from communities large and small. Those who fail to grasp this widespread commitment will never understand the depth of political and philosophical dedication symbolized by the letters NRA.

Scholars who have devoted careers to the study of the Second Amendment agree in principle that the right to keep and bear arms is fundamental to our concept of democracy. No high-court decision has yet found grounds to challenge this basic freedom. Yet some who oppose this freedom want to waive the constitutionality of the "gun control" question for the sake of their particular—and sometimes peculiar— brand of social reform.

In doing so they seem ready, even eager, to disregard a constitu-   5 tional right exercised by at least 70 million Americans who own firearms. Contrary to current antigun evangelism, these gun owners are not bad people. They are hard working, law abiding, tax paying. They are safe, sane, and courteous in their use of guns. They have never been, nor will they ever be, a threat to law and order.

History repeatedly warns us that human character cannot be scrubbed free of its defects through vain attempts to regulate inanimate objects such as guns. What has worked in the past, and what we see working now, are tough, NRA-supported measures that punish the incorrigible minority who place themselves outside the law.

As a result of such measures, violent crimes with firearms, like assault and robbery, have stabilized or are actually declining. We see proof that levels of firearm ownership cannot be associated with levels of criminal violence, except for their deterrent value. On the other hand, tough laws designed to incarcerate violent offenders offer something gun control cannot: swift, sure justice meted out with no accompanying erosion of individual liberty.

Violent crime continues to rise in cities like New York and Washington even after severe firearm-control statutes were rushed into place. Criminals, understandably, have illegal ways of obtaining guns. Antigun laws—the waiting periods, background checks, handgun bans, et al.—only harass those who obey them. Why should an honest citizen be deprived of a firearm for sport or self-defense when, for a gangster, obtaining a gun is just a matter of showing up on the right street corner with enough money?

Antigun opinion steadfastly ignores these realities known to rank-and-file police officers—men and women who face crime firsthand, not police administrators who face mayors and editors. These law-enforcement professionals tell us that expecting firearm restrictions to act as crime-prevention measures is wishful thinking. They point out that proposed gun laws would not have stopped heinous crimes committed by the likes of John Hinckley, Jr., Patrick Purdy, Laurie Dann,[1] or mentally

---

[1]**John Hinckley, Jr., Patrick Purdy, Laurie Dann** Hinckley attempted to assassinate President Ronald Reagan in Washington, D.C., in March 1981, wounding the president and three others. Purdy fired a hundred bullets from his AK-47 at children in a Stockton, California, schoolyard in January 1989. He killed five and then killed himself. Dann, firing three guns, shot six schoolchildren in a Chicago suburb in May 1988, killing one and herself as well. [Editors' note.]

disturbed, usually addicted killers. How can such crimes be used as examples of what gun control could prevent?

There are better ways to advance our society than to excuse criminal 10
behavior. The NRA initiated the first hunter-safety program, which has
trained millions of young hunters. We are the shooting sports' leading
safety organization, with more than 26,000 certified instructors training
750,000 students and trainees last year alone. Through 1989 there were
9,818 NRA-certified law-enforcement instructors teaching marksman-
ship to thousands of peace officers.

Frankly, we would rather keep investing NRA resources in such
worthwhile efforts instead of spending our time and members' money
debunking the failed and flawed promises of gun prohibitionists.

If you agree, I invite you to join the NRA.

Topics for Critical Thinking and Writing

1. Cassidy opens his essay by drawing a parallel between abuse of the First
   Amendment (speech that harms) and abuse of the Second Amendment
   (using guns to commit crimes), arguing that no sensible person would
   conclude that these abuses show the Bill of Rights ought to be revised.
   Do you agree? Is his parallel fair and instructive? Explain.

2. In his first paragraph Cassidy says, "The American people have a right
   'to keep and bear arms.' This right is protected by the Second Amendment to the Constitution." The Second Amendment says this: "A well-
   regulated militia being necessary to the security of a free State, the right
   of the people to keep and bear arms shall not be infringed." Has Cassidy
   quoted a passage out of context? Support your answer.

3. In the second paragraph Cassidy says that there is not only a "right"
   but also a "need" in "a democratic republic . . . to keep and bear arms."
   Does he indicate what the need is? Or is it self-evident? Support your
   answer.

4. In paragraph 6 Cassidy says, "History repeatedly warns us that human
   character cannot be scrubbed free of its defects through vain attempts to
   regulate inanimate objects such as guns." He does not give examples.
   What examples can you offer to help make this generalization convincing? (If you cannot give any examples, do you think Cassidy should
   himself have provided them?)

5. Cassidy asserts (para. 7) that "violent crimes with firearms . . . have stabilized or are actually declining." Visit your college library, locate recent
   issues of *Uniform Crime Reports* (published annually by the FBI), and see
   whether you can verify Cassidy's claim.

6. Cassidy claims that "antigun laws," including "waiting periods [and]
   background checks," only "harass" law-abiding citizens (para. 8). Do
   you think it is unfair or futile to try to keep legally purchased guns out

of the hands of ex-felons, or the mentally disturbed, by such laws? Explain your position in an essay of 250 words.

Nan Desuka

Nan Desuka (1957–1985) was born in Japan but at age two was brought by her parents to Los Angeles, where she was educated. Although she most often wrote about ecology, she occasionally wrote about other controversial topics.

Why Handguns Must Be Outlawed

"Guns don't kill people—criminals do." That's a powerful slogan, much more powerful than its alternate version: "Guns don't kill people—people kill people." But this second version, though less effective, is much nearer to the whole truth. Although accurate statistics are hard to come by, and even harder to interpret, it seems indisputable that large numbers of people, not just criminals, kill, with a handgun, other people. Scarcely a day goes by without a newspaper in any large city reporting that a child has found a gun, kept by the child's parents for self-protection, and has, in playing with this new-found toy, killed himself or a playmate. Or we read of a storekeeper, trying to protect himself during a robbery, who inadvertently shoots an innocent customer. These killers are not, in any reasonable sense of the word, criminals. They are just people who happen to kill people. No wonder the gun lobby prefers the first version of the slogan, "Guns don't kill people—criminals do." This version suggests that the only problem is criminals, not you or me, or our children, and certainly not the members of the National Rifle Association.

Those of us who want strict control of handguns—for me that means the outlawing of handguns, except to the police and related service units—have not been able to come up with a slogan equal in power to "Guns don't kill people—criminals do." The best we have been able to come up with is a mildly amusing bumper sticker showing a teddy bear, with the words "Defend your right to arm bears." Humor can be a powerful weapon (even in writing *on behalf* of gun control, one slips into using the imagery of force), and our playful bumper sticker somehow deflates the self-righteousness of the gun lobby, but doesn't equal the power (again the imagery of force) of "Guns don't kill people—criminals do." For one thing, the effective alliteration of "*c*riminals" and "*k*ill" binds the two words, making everything so terribly simple. Criminals kill; when there are no criminals, there will be no deaths from guns.

But this notion won't do. Despite the uncertainty of some statistical evidence, everyone knows, or should know, that only about 30 percent of murders are committed by robbers or rapists (Kates, 1978). For the most part the victims of handguns know their assailants well. These victims are women killed by jealous husbands, or they are the women's lovers; or they are drinking buddies who get into a violent argument; or they are innocent people who get shot by disgruntled (and probably demented) employees or fellow workers who have (or imagine) a grudge. Or they are, as I've already said, bystanders at a robbery, killed by a storekeeper. Or they are children playing with their father's gun.

Of course this is not the whole story. Hardened criminals also have guns, and they use them. The murders committed by robbers and rapists are what give credence to Barry Goldwater's quip, "We have a crime problem in this country, not a gun problem" (1975, p. 186). But here again the half-truth of a slogan is used to mislead, used to direct attention away from a national tragedy. Different sources issue different statistics, but a conservative estimate is that handguns annually murder at least fifteen thousand Americans, accidentally kill at least another three thousand and wound at least another hundred thousand. Handguns are easily available, both to criminals and to decent people who believe they need a gun in order to protect themselves from criminals. The decent people, unfortunately, have good cause to believe they need protection. Many parts of many cities are utterly unsafe, and even the tiniest village may harbor a murderer. Senator Goldwater is right in saying there is a crime problem (that's the truth of his half-truth), but he is wrong in saying there is not also a gun problem.

Surely the homicide rate would markedly decrease if handguns were   5 outlawed. The FBI reports (Federal Bureau of Investigation, 1985) that more than 60 percent of all murders are caused by guns, and handguns are involved in more than 70 percent of these. Surely many, even most, of these handgun killings would not occur if the killer had to use a rifle, club, or knife. Of course violent lovers, angry drunks, and deranged employees would still flail out with knives or baseball bats, but some of their victims would be able to run away, with few or no injuries, and most of those who could not run away would nevertheless survive, badly injured but at least alive. But if handguns are outlawed, we are told, responsible citizens will have no way to protect themselves from criminals. First, one should remember that at least 90 percent of America's burglaries are committed when no one is at home. The householder's gun, if he or she has one, is in a drawer of the bedside table, and the gun gets lifted along with the jewelry, adding one more gun to the estimated hundred thousand handguns annually stolen from law-abiding citizens (Shields, 1981). Second, if the householder is at home, and attempts to use the gun, he or she is more likely to get killed or wounded than to kill or deter the intruder. Another way of looking at this last point is to recall that for every burglar who is halted by the sight of a handgun, four innocent people are killed by handgun accidents.

Because handguns are not accurate beyond ten or fifteen feet, they are not the weapons of sportsmen. Their sole purpose is to kill or at least to disable a person at close range. But only a minority of persons killed with these weapons are criminals. Since handguns chiefly destroy the innocent, they must be outlawed—not simply controlled more strictly, but outlawed—to all except to law-enforcement officials. Attempts to control handguns are costly and ineffective, but even if they were cheap and effective stricter controls would not take handguns out of circulation among criminals, because licensed guns are stolen from homeowners and shopkeepers, and thus fall into criminal hands. According to Wright, Rossi, and Daly (1983, p. 181), about 40 percent of the handguns used in crimes are stolen, chiefly from homes that the guns were supposed to protect.

The National Rifle Association is fond of quoting a University of Wisconsin study that says, "gun control laws have no individual or collective effect in reducing the rate of violent crime" (cited in Smith, 1981, p. 17). Agreed—but what if handguns were not available? What if the manufacturer of handguns is severely regulated, and if the guns may be sold only to police officers? True, even if handguns are outlawed, some criminals will manage to get them, but surely fewer petty criminals will have guns. It is simply untrue for the gun lobby to assert that all criminals—since they are by definition lawbreakers—will find ways to get handguns. For the most part, if the sale of handguns is outlawed, guns won't be available, and fewer criminals will have guns. And if fewer criminals have guns, there is every reason to believe that violent crime will decline. A youth armed only with a knife is less likely to try to rob a store than if he is armed with a gun. This commonsense reasoning does not imply that if handguns are outlawed crime will suddenly disappear, or even that an especially repulsive crime such as rape will decrease markedly. A rapist armed with a knife probably has a sufficient weapon. But *some* violent crime will almost surely decrease. And the decrease will probably be significant if in addition to outlawing handguns, severe mandatory punishments are imposed on a person who is found to possess one, and even severer mandatory punishments are imposed on a person who uses one while committing a crime. Again, none of this activity will solve "the crime problem," but neither will anything else, including the "get tough with criminals" attitude of Senator Goldwater. And of course any attempt to reduce crime (one cannot realistically talk of "solving" the crime problem) will have to pay attention to our systems of bail, plea bargaining, and parole, but outlawing handguns will help.

What will the cost be? First, to take "cost" in its most literal sense, there will be the cost of reimbursing gun owners for the weapons they surrender. Every owner of a handgun ought to be paid the fair market value of the weapon. Since the number of handguns is estimated to be between 50 million and 90 million, the cost will be considerable, but it will be far less than the costs—both in money and in sorrow—that result from deaths due to handguns.

Second, one may well ask if there is another sort of cost, a cost to our liberty, to our constitutional rights. The issue is important, and persons who advocate abolition of handguns are blind or thoughtless if they simply brush it off. On the other hand, opponents of gun control do all of us a disservice by insisting over and over that the Constitution guarantees "the right to bear arms." The Second Amendment in the Bill of Rights says this: "A well-regulated militia being necessary to the security of a free State, the right of the people to keep and bear arms shall not be infringed." It is true that the founding fathers, mindful of the British attempt to disarm the colonists, viewed the presence of "a well-regulated militia" as a safeguard of democracy. Their intention is quite clear, even to one who has not read Stephen P. Halbrook's *That Every Man Be Armed,* an exhaustive argument in favor of the right to bear arms. There can be no doubt that the framers of the Constitution and the Bill of Rights believed that armed insurrection was a justifiable means of countering oppression and tyranny. The Second Amendment may be fairly paraphrased thus: "*Because* an organized militia is necessary to the security of the State, the people have the right to possess weapons." But the owners of handguns are not members of a well-regulated militia. Furthermore, nothing in the proposal to ban handguns would deprive citizens of their rifles or other long-arm guns. All handguns, however, even large ones, should be banned. "Let's face it," Guenther W. Bachmann (a vice president of Smith and Wesson) admits, "they are all concealable" (Kennedy, 1981, p. 6). In any case, it is a fact that when gun control laws have been tested in the courts, they have been found to be constitutional. The constitutional argument was worth making, but the question must now be regarded as settled, not only by the courts but by anyone who reads the Second Amendment.

Still, is it not true that "If guns are outlawed, only outlaws will have 10 guns"? This is yet another powerful slogan, but it is simply not true. First, we are talking not about "guns" but about handguns. Second, the police will have guns—handguns and others—and these trained professionals are the ones on whom we must rely for protection against criminals. Of course the police have not eradicated crime; and of course we must hope that in the future they will be more successful in protecting all citizens. But we must also recognize that the efforts of private citizens to protect themselves with handguns have chiefly taken the lives not of criminals but of innocent people.

REFERENCES

Federal Bureau of Investigation (1985). *Uniform crime reports for the United States.* Washington, DC: U.S. Department of Justice.

Goldwater, B. (1975, December). Why gun control laws don't work. *Reader's Digest, 107,* 183–188.

Halbrook, S. P. (1985). *That every man be armed: The evolution of a constitutional right.* Albuquerque: University of New Mexico Press.

Kates, D. B., Jr. (1978, September). Against civil disarming. *Harper's, 257*, 28–33.

Kennedy, E. (1981, October 5). Handguns: Preferred instruments of criminals. *Congressional Record*. Washington, DC: U.S. Government Printing Office.

Shields, P. (1981). *Guns don't die—people do*. New York: Arbor House.

Smith, A. (1981, April). Fifty million handguns. *Esquire, 96*, 16–18.

Wright, J. D., Rossi, P. H., & Daly, K. (1983). *Under the gun*. New York: Aldine.

Topics for Critical Thinking and Writing

1. Reread the first and last paragraphs, and then in a sentence or two comment on the writer's strategy for opening and closing her essay.

2. On the whole, does the writer strike you as a person who is fair, or who at least is trying to be fair? Support your answer by citing specific passages that lead you to your opinion.

3. Many opponents of gun control argue that control of handguns will be only a first move down the slippery slope that leads to laws prohibiting private ownership of any sort of gun. Even if you hold this view, state as best you can the arguments that one might offer against it. (Notice that you are asked to offer arguments, not merely an assertion that it won't happen.)

4. Do you agree with Desuka that a reasonable reading of the Second Amendment reveals that individuals do not have a constitutional right to own handguns, even though the founding fathers said that "the right of the people to keep and bear arms shall not be infringed"?

5. Write a 500-word analysis of Desuka's essay (for a sample analysis see p. 110), or write a 500-word reply to her essay, responding to her main points.

6. Do you think the prohibition of handguns is feasible? Could it be enforced? Would the effort to enforce it result in worse problems than we already have? Write a 500-word essay defending or attacking the feasibility of Desuka's proposal.

16

Sex Education:
Should Condoms Be
Distributed in Schools?

Rush H. Limbaugh III

Rush Limbaugh, born in Cape Girardeau, Missouri, became a Top 40 deejay in the 1960s before becoming a radio talk show host in Sacramento. In 1988 his show went national. We reprint a passage from his book The Way Things Ought To Be *(1992).*

Condoms: The New Diploma

The logic and motivation behind this country's mad dash to distribute free condoms in our public schools is ridiculous and misguided. Worse, the message conveyed by mass condom distribution is a disservice and borders on being lethal. Condom distribution sanctions, even encourages, sexual activity, which in teen years tends to be promiscuous and relegates to secondary status the most important lesson to be taught: abstinence. An analysis of the entire condom distribution logic also provides a glimpse into just what is wrong with public education today.

First things first. Advocates of condom distribution say that kids are going to have sex, that try as we might we can't stop them. Therefore they need protection. Hence, condoms. Well, hold on a minute. Just whose notion is it that "kids are going to do it anyway, you can't stop them"? Why limit the application of that brilliant logic to sexual activity? Let's just admit that kids are going to do drugs and distribute safe, untainted drugs every morning in homeroom. Kids are going to smoke, too, we can't stop them, so let's provide packs of low-tar cigarettes to the students for their after-sex smoke. Kids are going to get guns and shoot them, you can't stop them, so let's make sure that teachers have bulletproof vests. I mean, come on! If we are really concerned about safe sex, why stop at condoms? Let's convert study halls to Safe Sex Centers where students can go to actually have sex on nice double beds with clean sheets under the watchful and approving eye of the school nurse, who will be on hand to demonstrate, along with the principal, just how to use a condom. Or even better: If kids are going to have sex, let's put disease-free hookers in these Safe Sex Centers. Hey, if safe sex is the objective, why compromise our standards?

There is something else very disturbing about all this. Let's say that Johnnie and Susie are on a date in Johnny's family sedan. Johnny pulls in to his town's designated Teen Parking Location hoping to score a little affection from Susie. They move to the backseat and it isn't long before Johnny, on the verge of bliss, whips out his trusty high school-distributed condom and urges Susie not to resist him. She is hesitant, being a nice girl and all, and says she doesn't think the time is right.

"Hey, everything is okay. Nothing will go wrong. Heck, the *school gave me this condom,* they know what they're doing. You'll be fine," coos the artful and suave Johnny.

Aside from what is obviously wrong here, there is something you   5
probably haven't thought of which to me is profound. Not that long ago, school policy, including that on many college campuses, was designed to protect the girls from the natural and instinctive aggressive pursuit of young men. Chaperones, for example, were around to make sure the girls were not in any jeopardy. So much for that thinking now. The schools may just as well endorse and promote these backseat affairs. The kids are going to do it anyway.

Well, here's what's wrong. There have always been consequences to having sex. Always. Now, however, some of these consequences are severe: debilitating venereal diseases and AIDS. You can now die from having sex. It is that simple. If you look, the vast majority of adults in America have made adjustments in their sexual behavior in order to protect themselves from some of the dire consequences floating around out there. For the most part, the sexual revolution of the sixties is over, a miserable failure. Free love and rampant one-night stands are tougher to come by because people are aware of the risks. In short, we have modified our behavior. Now, would someone tell me what is so difficult about sharing this knowledge and experience with kids? The same stakes are involved. Isn't that our responsibility, for crying out loud, to teach them what's best for them? If we adults aren't responding to these new dangers by having condom-protected sex anytime, anywhere, why should such folly be taught to our kids?

Let me try the Magic Johnson example for you who remain unconvinced. Imagine that you are in the Los Angeles Lakers locker room after a game and you and Magic are getting ready to go hit the town. Outside the locker room are a bunch of young women, as there always are, and as Magic had freely admitted there always were, and that you know that the woman Magic is going to pick up and take back to the hotel has

AIDS. You approach Magic and say, "Hey, Magic! Hold on! That girl you're going to take back to the hotel with you has AIDS. Here, don't worry about it. Take these condoms, you'll be fine."

Do you think Magic would have sex with that woman? Ask yourself: Would you knowingly have sex with *anyone* who has AIDS with only a condom to protect you from getting the disease? It doesn't take Einstein to answer that question. So, why do you think it's okay to send kids out into the world to do just that? Who is to know who carries the HIV virus, and on the chance your kid runs into someone who does have it, are you confident that a condom will provide all the protection he or she needs?

Doesn't it make sense to be honest with kids and tell them the best thing they can do to avoid AIDS or any of the other undesirable consequences is to abstain from sexual intercourse? It is the best way—in fact, it is the only surefire way—to guard against sexual transmission of AIDS, pregnancy, and venereal diseases. What's so terrible about saying so?

Yet, there are those who steadfastly oppose the teaching of absti- 10 nence, and I think they should be removed from any position of authority where educating children is concerned. In New York, the City Board of Education *narrowly won* (4–3) the passage of a resolution requiring the inclusion of teaching abstinence in the AIDS education program in the spring of 1992. No one was trying to eliminate anything from the program, such as condom distribution or anal sex education (which does occur in New York public school sex education classes). All they wanted was that abstinence also be taught. Yet, the Schools Chancellor, Joseph Fernandez, vigorously fought the idea, saying it would do great damage to their existing program! Well, just how is that? The fact is that abstinence works every time it is tried. As this book went to press, the New York Civil Liberties Union was considering filing a lawsuit to stop this dangerous new addition to the curriculum. Now what in the name of God is going on here? This is tantamount to opposing a drug education program which instructs students not to use drugs because it would not be useful.

The Jacksonville, Florida, school board also decided that abstinence should be the centerpiece of their sexual education curriculum, and the liberals there were also outraged about this. What is so wrong with this? Whose agenda is being denied by teaching abstinence and just what is that agenda?

Jacksonville teachers are telling seventh-graders that "the only safe sex is no sex at all." Sex education classes provide some information about birth control and sexually transmitted diseases, but these areas are not the primary focus of the classes. Nancy Corwin, a member of the school board, admits the paradox when she says that the schools send a nonsensical message when they teach kids not to have sex but then give them condoms.

Instead of this twaddle, the Jacksonville school board has decided to teach real safe sex, which is abstinence. However, six families, along with Planned Parenthood and the ACLU, are suing the schools over this program. This bunch of curious citizens says that teaching abstinence puts the children at a greater risk of catching AIDS or other sexually transmitted diseases. Greater risk? !£#$£@! How can that be? What kind of contaminated thinking is this? The suit alleges that the schools are providing a "fear-based program that gives children incomplete, inaccurate, biased, and sectarian information." You want more? Try this: Linda Lanier of Planned Parenthood says, "It's not right to try to trick our students." Trick the students? #£&@£!? If anyone is trying to trick students, it's Planned Parenthood and this band of hedonists who try to tell kids that a condom will protect them from any consequences of sex.

Folks, here you have perhaps the best example of the culture war being waged in our country today. To say that "teaching abstinence is a trick" is absurd. Is Ms. Lanier having sex every night of the week? What adjustments has she made in her sex life because of AIDS? Does she think that a little sheath of latex will be enough to protect her?

This is terribly wrong. The Jacksonville public school system is at- 15 tempting to teach right from wrong, as opposed to teaching that sex does not have any consequences, which I believe is the selfish agenda these people hold dear. I have stated elsewhere in this book, and I state it again here, that there are many people who wish to go through life guilt-free and engage in behavior they know to be wrong and morally vacant. In order to assuage their guilt they attempt to construct and impose policies which not only allow them to engage in their chosen activities but encourage others to do so as well. There is, after all, strength in numbers.

Promiscuous and self-gratifying, of-the-moment sex is but one of these chosen lifestyles. Abortions on demand and condom distribution are but two of the policies and programs which, as far as these people are concerned, ensure there are no consequences. As one disgusted member of the Jacksonville school board said, "Every yahoo out there has a social program that they want to run through the school system. We are here for academic reasons and we cannot cure the social evils of the world."

The worst of all of this is the lie that condoms really protect against AIDS. The condom failure rate can be as high as 20 percent. Would you get on a plane—or put your children on a plane—if one in five passengers would be killed on the flight? Well, the statistic holds for condoms, folks.

Ah, but there is even more lunacy haunting the sacred halls of academe. According to the *Los Angeles Times*, administrators in the Los Angeles public schools have regretfully acknowledged that the sex education courses undertaken in the early 1970s "might" have a correlation to the rising teen pregnancy rates in their schools which can be traced to the same years. They have devised an enlightened and marvelous new approach to modernize and correct the sex education curriculum. It is called Outercourse. I am not making this up. Outercourse is, in essence, instruction in creative methods of masturbation.

"Hi, class, and welcome to Outercourse 101. I am your instructor, Mr. Reubens, from Florida, and I want to remind you that this is a hands-on course." We will know the graduates of Outercourse 101 in about forty years. They will be the people walking around with seeing-eye dogs.

Topics for Critical Thinking and Writing

1. In his second paragraph Limbaugh attempts to give a reductio ad absurdum of the proposal to distribute condoms in high school. (We discuss reductio on pp. 266–67.) Do you think this tactic of criticism as used here is successful or not? Explain.

2. Limbaugh thinks that distributing condoms in high school will encourage sex among adolescents as well as give premarital sex a stamp of approval by school authorities. Do you agree? Why, or why not?

3. In paragraph 17 Limbaugh says, "The condom failure rate can be as high as 20 percent." What do you take this statement to mean?

4. Limbaugh says that those who favor condom distribution "try to tell kids that a condom will protect them from *any* consequences of sex" (para. 13, emphasis added). Inquire at your campus health office to find out what current medical practice advises about the likelihood of condom failure, resulting in unwanted pregnancy or in acquiring a sexually transmitted disease.

5. Make a list of the *reasons* Limbaugh gives for opposing the distribution of condoms; evaluate those reasons.

6. Limbaugh quotes (para. 16) with evident approval the public school official who complained, " 'Every yahoo out there has a social program that they want to run through the school system. We are here for academic reasons....' " Yet elsewhere Limbaugh supports prayer in the public schools. Do you think he is inconsistent or not? Explain.

Anna Quindlen

From 1986 to 1994, Anna Quindlen regularly wrote a column for the New York Times, *where this essay appeared on January 8, 1994. She is also the author of several books, including* One True Thing *(1994) and* Black and Blue *(1998).*

A Pyrrhic Victory

Pop quiz: A sixteen-year-old is appropriately treated at a school clinic after he is advised that the reason it feels as if he is going to die when he urinates is because he has a sexually transmitted disease. Told that condoms could have protected him from infection, he asks for some. A nurse tells him to wait while she looks for his name on the list of students whose parents have confidentially requested that their sons and daughters not receive them.

The student replies: (a) "No problem"; (b) "Hmmm—an interesting way to balance the reproductive health of adolescents and the rights of parents"; (c) Nothing. He sidles out of the office and not long afterward gets a whopping case of chlamydia.

Condoms, condoms, condoms. As those who oppose condom distribution in the schools gloated over an appellate court decision that said the program violated parents' rights, Alwyn Cohall, the pediatrician who oversees several school-based clinics in New York, quoted Yogi Berra. "It's déjà vu all over again," said Dr. Cohall, who has to clean up the messes made when sexually active kids don't use condoms. And he wasn't smiling.

Over the last two years the Board of Education has wasted time better spent on instructional issues giving and receiving lectures on latex. The opt-out provision its members are now likely to adopt is the "let me see if you're on the list, dear" scenario outlined above, and if you think it might have a chilling effect on a young man too self-conscious to ask for Trojans in a drugstore, then you get an A in adolescent psychology.

You get extra credit if you figure that being on the list will be scant   5 protection against disease if the young man has sex anyhow. "A victory for parents," some have called the provision. But is it Pyrrhic?

Dr. Cohall, a champion of condom distribution, agrees that it is best if teenagers abstain from sexual activity and talk to their parents about issues of sex, morality, and health. But he also notes that in 1992 his three high school clinics saw around 150 cases of sexually transmitted diseases like condyloma, chlamydia, and the better-known gonorrhea and syphilis.

He has a sixteen-year-old in the hospital right now who got AIDS from her second sexual partner. And he recalls a girl who broke her leg jumping out an apartment window because her mother found her birth control pills, seized her by the throat, and said, according to the kid, "I brought you into the world; I can take you out of it."

Don't you just love those little mother-daughter sex talks?

He also knows that at the heart of the balancing act between keeping kids healthy and keeping parents involved there has always been a covert place in which many opponents of condom distribution really settle. It's called Fantasyland.

You could see that in the response to the rather mild commercials on   10
condom use and abstinence that the Department of Health and Human
Services unveiled this week. The general secretary of the National Conference of Catholic Bishops immediately said the ads "promote promiscuity"
and the networks should reject them. At the same time ABC said it would
not run the spots during its prime-time "family-oriented" programs.

So foolish. ABC's own *Roseanne* has been far more candid about sexuality than any of the new government public-service spots. And what
could be a better way to foment conversation with the children of the
video age than a television advertisement? Right there in your living
room you have a goad to the kind of discussion that opponents of condom distribution have always argued is the purview of parents. And you
put the ads on late at night? Do we really want to talk with our kids? Or
do we just want to talk about talking to them?

The Board of Education could do a great good if it found ways to
truly foster parent-child communication in all things, not just matters
sexual. But instead its members argue about condoms. This isn't really
about condoms, of course, but about control and the shock of adolescent
sexuality and the difficulty parents have communicating with their kids
and a deep and understandable yearning for simpler times.

While we yearn and argue, Dr. Cohall visits his sixteen-year-old
AIDS patient. Her parents' involvement may someday consist of visiting
the cemetery. Imagine how they'd feel if they put her on the no-condom
list, then put her in the hospital, then put her in the ground. Some
victory.

Topics for Critical Thinking and Writing

1. Exactly what is a Pyrrhic victory?

2. Quindlen offers three possible responses for her sixteen-year-old male
   student (para. 2). Write a fourth and (if possible) a fifth response.

3. As paragraph 3 indicates, some parents argue that the distribution of
   condoms violates parents' rights. What parental right is at stake in the
   dispute over whether high schools should distribute condoms to students who seek them? Or is there no such right, but instead a parental
   duty involved?

4. Quindlen mentions four sexually transmitted diseases. What are their
   names, their symptoms, and the cure in each case? (You will probably
   need to talk to a physician or nurse, or do some library research, to answer this question.)

5. Some people argue that any discussion of condoms, even in a context
   that advocates abstinence, in effect promotes promiscuity. Do you agree
   or disagree? Why?

6. Evaluate Quindlen's final paragraph as a piece of persuasive writing.

Part Five

CURRENT ISSUES: CASEBOOKS

17

Censoring the Internet:
Is It Necessary?

J. James Exon

J. James Exon, after serving two terms as the Democratic governor of Ne-braska, was elected in 1978 to the U.S. Senate. He sponsored the Communi-cations Decency Act (CDA), which was passed by Congress in 1996 but found unconstitutional later in 1996. Here we give his argument on behalf of the legislation, and we immediately follow it with the court decision.

Keep the Internet Safe for Families

When a youngster logs onto a computer terminal, he or she is wel-comed into a vast new world of information that will revolutionize how we all learn and work in the future. This World Wide Web of compu-ter connections represents an information explosion unprecedented in world history. This information revolution may rival the invention of the printing press and broadcasting in terms of how it will affect our daily lives.

The evolving telecommunications infrastructure known as the Inter-net will link homes, businesses, schools, hospitals, and libraries to each other and to a vast array of electronic information resources. Imagine a student in Hastings, Nebraska, being able to tap into the computer data-base of a university in Budapest, Hungary, more easily than walking down to the local library.

But there are some dark side roads on the information superhigh-way that contain material that would be considered unacceptable by any reasonable standard.

The U.S. Senate will consider my proposal, the Communications Decency Amendment, to lay down some basic guidelines on the information superhighway. I want to make this exciting new highway as safe as possible for kids and families to travel. Just as we have laws against dumping garbage on the interstate, we ought to have similar laws for the information superhighway.

My amendment to the Telecommunications Reform Bill will   5
toughen penalties for people who actively "transmit" pornographic and harassing material, boosting the maximum fine from $50,000 to $100,000 and increasing the maximum jail sentence from six months to two years. We need this added deterrent so that those who would pervert the network will think twice. We already have laws to prohibit obscenity over the telephone or pornography through the mail. My amendment extends to computer users the very same protections against obscenity or harassment that now partially protect telephone users.

The legislation does not make innocent "carriers" of electronic messages liable for inappropriate messages, nor does it by any stretch of the imagination require system operators to "eavesdrop" on electronic messages. To do so would be the equivalent of holding the mailman liable for the packages he delivers.

Many critics say that on the Internet, anything should go, no matter how outrageous. I say the framers of the Constitution never intended for the First Amendment to protect pornographers and pedophiles.

There are documented cases of computer misuse all over the country. These include incidents of electronic stalking, inappropriate contact with children, and computer breaking and entering.

Last summer, the *Los Angeles Times* reported that a computer at the Lawrence Livermore National Laboratory in California was being used to store and distribute hard-core pornography. Despite the lab's elaborate security precautions, investigators found more than one thousand pornographic pictures. The computer was shut down and the FBI called in.

The *Washington Post* reported on a case where a group of investiga-   10
tors signed on to a major computer service with false identifications and pretended to be children. They posted a few innocuous messages on teen bulletin boards and the next day they had "solicitations for nude pictures, phone sex, and offers to meet in person for sex."

Computers are a unique medium because children often have much more knowledge about how they operate than their parents. My amendment would pass the standard outlined by the U.S. Supreme Court that Congress may take action to protect children from obscenity, pornography and indecency in areas like radio or television broadcasts where youngsters have unique access.

Does anyone really think that a parent can stand over their child's shoulder and monitor them all of their waking hours of every day? If anyone thinks that this material is hard for youngsters to come by, they don't know youngsters.

We have laws against murder and we have laws against speeding. We still have murder and we still have speeding. But I think most reasonable people would agree that we very likely would have more murders and more speeders if we didn't have laws as a deterrent.

In a recent newspaper article, a computer "hacker" who viewed some of this pornography on the Internet said 98 percent of it is no worse than you might find in an "adult video rental store." That weird admission makes my point. Is material that is okay for an adult video store okay for kids to see on their home computers?

To those who are critical of my suggestions I say, "Come, let us reason together." Nothing is etched in stone and I am open to any constructive proposals. I have suggested, for example, a parental lockout mechanism as a possible solution to make certain areas of the Internet inaccessible to youngsters.

We are talking about our most important and precious commodity — our children. We cannot simply throw up our hands and say a solution is impossible or the First Amendment is so sacrosanct that we must stand idly by while our children are inundated with pornography and smut on the Internet. The public needs to be aware of the problem and direct its correction.

Topics for Critical Thinking and Writing

1. In paragraph 4 Exon says that the act is concerned with laying down "some basic guidelines on the information superhighway. I want to make this exciting new highway as safe as possible for kids and families to travel. Just as we have laws against dumping garbage on the interstate, we ought to have similar laws for the information superhighway." Evaluate Senator Exon's analogy. (On analogies, see pp. 67–68 and 287–88). How compelling is this analogy? Why?

2. In paragraph 12 Exon says that his proposed regulation is needed because it is clearly impossible for parents to supervise their children "all of their waking hours of every day." And it is, of course, true that even if parents keep watch over children at home, they cannot exert supervision when children go elsewhere. Is this, then, a compelling reason for some sort of regulation of the Internet? Explain.

3. Does Exon explain how the proposed Internet censorship he favors to protect children will also affect what adults may choose to view? (See para. 14.)

Stewart Dalzell

We reprint here a portion of the opinion, written by Judge Stewart Dalzell of the Court of Appeals for the Third Circuit, in the case of American Civil Liberties Union v. Reno *(1996).*

We abridge the decision, indicating ellipses with three spaced periods. We do not, however, indicate the omission of legal citations within or at the ends of sentences.

American Civil Liberties Union v. Reno

INTRODUCTION

I begin with first principles: As a general rule, the Constitution forbids the Government from silencing speakers because of their particular message. This general rule is subject only to "narrow and well-understood exceptions." A law that, as here, regulates speech on the basis of its content, is "presumptively invalid."

Two of the exceptions to this general rule deal with obscenity (commonly understood to include so-called hardcore pornography). The government can and does punish with criminal sanction people who engage in these forms of speech. Indeed, the government could punish these forms of speech on the Internet even without the CDA.

The Government could also completely ban obscenity and child pornography from the Internet. No Internet speaker has a right to engage in these forms of speech, and no Internet listener has a right to receive them. Child pornography and obscenity have "no constitutional protection, and the government may ban [them] outright in certain media, or in all."

The cases before us, however, are *not* about obscenity or child pornography. Plaintiffs in these actions claim no right to engage in these forms of speech in the future, nor does the government intimate that plaintiffs have engaged in these forms of speech in the past.

This case is about "indecency," as that word has come to be understood since the Supreme Court's decisions in *FCC v. Pacifica Foundation,* and *Sable Communications v. FCC.* The legal difficulties in these actions arise because of the special place that indecency occupies in the Supreme Court's First Amendment jurisprudence. While adults have a First Amendment right to engage in indecent speech, the Supreme Court has also held that the government may, consistent with the Constitution, regulate indecency on radio and television, and in the "dial-a-porn" context, as long as the regulation does not operate as a complete ban. Thus, any regulation of indecency in these areas must give adults access to indecent speech, which is their right.

The government may only regulate indecent speech for a compelling reason, and in the least restrictive manner. "It is not enough to show

5

that the government's ends are compelling; the means must be carefully tailored to achieve those ends." This "most exacting scrutiny" requires the government to "demonstrate that the recited harms are real, not merely conjectural, and that the regulation will in fact alleviate these harms in a direct and material way."

The government argues that this case is really about pornography on the Internet. Apart from hardcore and child pornography, however, the word *pornography* does not have a fixed legal meaning. . . .

PLAINTIFFS' LIKELIHOOD OF PROSECUTION UNDER THE ACT

The government has consistently argued that the speech of many of the plaintiffs here is almost certainly not indecent. They point, for example, to the educational and political content of plaintiffs' speech, and they also suggest that the occasional curse word in a card catalogue will probably not result in prosecution. In this section I address that argument.

I agree with the government that some of plaintiffs' claims are somewhat exaggerated, but hyperbolic claims do not in themselves weigh in the government's favor. In recent First Amendment challenges, the Supreme Court has itself paid close attention to extreme applications of content-based laws.

In *Simon & Schuster, Inc. v. Members of the New York State Crime Victims* 10 *Board*, the Court addressed the constitutionality of a law that required criminals to turn over to their victims any income derived from books, movies, or other commercial exploitation of their crimes. In its opinion, the Court evaluated the argument of an *amicus curiae* that the law's reach could include books such as *The Autobiography of Malcolm X, Civil Disobedience*, and *Confessions of Saint Augustine*, and authors such as Emma Goldman, Martin Luther King, Jr., Sir Walter Raleigh, Jesse Jackson, and Bertrand Russell. The Court credited the argument even while recognizing that it was laced with "hyperbole." . . .

Putting aside hyperbolic application, I also have little doubt that some communities could well consider plaintiffs' speech indecent, and these plaintiffs could—perhaps should—have a legitimate fear of prosecution. In *Action for Children's Television v. FCC*, the District of Columbia Court of Appeals summarized three broadcasts that the FCC found indecent in the late 1980s:

> The offending morning broadcast . . . contained "explicit references to masturbation, ejaculation, breast size, penis size, sexual intercourse, nudity, urination, oral-genital contact, erections, sodomy, bestiality, menstruation, and testicles." The remaining two were similarly objectionable.

In *Infinity Broadcasting*, one of the broadcasts that the FCC found indecent was an excerpt of a play about AIDS, finding that the excerpts "contained the concentrated and repeated use of vulgar and shocking
language to portray graphic and lewd depictions of excretion, anal intercourse, ejaculation, masturbation, and oral-genital sex." To the FCC,
even broadcasts with "public value . . . addressing the serious problems
posed by AIDS" can be indecent if "that material is presented in a *manner*
that is patently offensive."

Yet, this is precisely the kind of speech that occurs, for example, on
Critical Path AIDS Project's Web site, which includes safer sex instructions written in street language for easy comprehension. The Web site
also describes the risk of HIV transmission for particular sexual practices.
The FCC's implication in *In the Matter of King Broadcasting Co.* that a "candid discussion . . . of sexual topics" on television was decent in part because it was "not presented in a pandering, titillating, or vulgar manner"
would be unavailing to Critical Path, other plaintiffs, and some *amici*.
These organizations *want* to pander and titillate on their Web sites, at
least to a degree, to attract a teen audience and deliver their message in
an engaging and coherent way.

In *In re letter to Merrell Hansen*, the FCC found indecent a morning
discussion between two announcers regarding Jim Bakker's alleged rape
of Jessica Hahn. Here, too, the FCC recognized that the broadcast had
public value. Yet, under the FCC's interpretation of *Pacifica*, "the merit
of a work is 'simply one of the many variables' that make up a work's
context."

One of the plaintiffs here, Stop Prisoner Rape, Inc., has as its core
purpose the issue of prison rape. The organization creates chat rooms in
which members can discuss their experiences. Some *amici* have also organized Web sites dedicated to survivors of rape, incest, and other sexual
abuse. These Web sites provide fora for the discussion and contemplation
of shared experiences. The operators of these sites, and their participants,
could legitimately fear prosecution under the CDA. . . .

A MEDIUM-SPECIFIC ANALYSIS

The Internet is a new medium of mass communication. As such, the 15
Supreme Court's First Amendment jurisprudence compels us to consider
the special qualities of this new medium in determining whether the
CDA is a constitutional exercise of governmental power. Relying on
these special qualities, which we have described at length in our findings
of fact above, I conclude that the CDA is unconstitutional and that the
First Amendment denies Congress the power to regulate protected
speech on the Internet. . . .

We cannot simply assume that the government has the power to
regulate protected speech over the Internet, devoting our attention
solely to the issue of whether the CDA is a constitutional exercise of that

power. Rather, we must also decide the validity of the underlying assumption as well, to wit, whether the government has the power to regulate protected speech at all. . . .

Over the course of five days of hearings and many hundreds of pages of declarations, deposition transcripts, and exhibits, we have learned about the special attributes of Internet communication. Our findings of fact—many of them undisputed—express our understanding of the Internet. These findings lead to the conclusion that Congress may not regulate indecency on the Internet at all.

Four related characteristics of Internet communication have a transcendent importance to our shared holding that the CDA is unconstitutional on its face. . . . First, the Internet presents very low barriers to entry. Second, these barriers to entry are identical for both speakers and listeners. Third, as a result of these low barriers, astoundingly diverse content is available on the Internet. Fourth, the Internet provides significant access to all who wish to speak in the medium, and even creates a relative parity among speakers. . . .

The CDA will, without doubt, undermine the substantive, speech-enhancing benefits that have flowed from the Internet. Barriers to entry to those speakers affected by the Act would skyrocket, especially for noncommercial and not-for-profit information providers. Such costs include those attributable to age or credit card verification (if possible), tagging (if tagging is even a defense under the Act), and monitoring or review of one's content.

The diversity of the content will necessarily diminish as a result. The 20 economic costs associated with compliance with the Act will drive from the Internet speakers whose content falls within the zone of possible prosecution. Many Web sites, newsgroups, and chat rooms will shut down, since users cannot discern the age of other participants. In this respect, the Internet would ultimately come to mirror broadcasting and print, with messages tailored to a mainstream society from speakers who could be sure that their message was likely decent in every community in the country. . . .

Perversely, commercial pornographers would remain relatively unaffected by the Act, since we learned that most of them already use credit card or adult verification anyway. Commercial pornographers normally provide a few free pictures to entice a user into proceeding further into the Web site. To proceed beyond these teasers, users must provide a credit card number or adult verification number. The CDA will force these businesses to remove the teasers (or cover the most salacious content with cgi scripts), but the core, commercial product of these businesses will remain in place. . . .

It is no exaggeration to conclude that the Internet has achieved, and continues to achieve, the most participatory marketplace of mass speech that this country—and indeed the world—has yet seen. The plaintiffs in these actions correctly describe the "democratizing" effects of Internet communication: Individual citizens of limited means can speak to a worldwide audience on issues of concern to them. Federalists and Anti-Federalists may debate the structure of their government nightly, but these debates occur in newsgroups or chat rooms rather than in pamphlets. Modern-day Luthers still post their theses, but to electronic bulletin boards rather than the door of the Wittenberg Schlosskirche. . . .

Indeed, the government's asserted "failure" of the Internet rests on the implicit premise that *too much* speech occurs in that medium, and that speech there is *too available* to the participants. This is *exactly* the benefit of Internet communication, however. The government, therefore, implicitly asks this court to limit both the amount of speech on the Internet and the availability of that speech. This argument is profoundly repugnant to First Amendment principles. . . .

Finally, if the goal of our First Amendment jurisprudence is the "individual dignity and choice" that arises from "putting the decision as to what views shall be voiced largely into the hands of each of us," then we should be especially vigilant in preventing content-based regulation of a medium that every minute allows individual citizens actually to make those decisions. Any content-based regulation of the Internet, no matter how benign the purpose, could burn the global village to roast the pig.

Protection of children from pornography. I accept without 25 reservation that the government has a compelling interest in protecting children from pornography. The proposition finds one of its clearest expressions in Mill, who recognized that his exposition regarding liberty itself "is meant to apply only to human beings in the maturity of their faculties":

> We are not speaking of children or of young persons below the age which the law may fix as that of manhood or womanhood. Those who are still in a state to require being taken care of by others must be protected against their own actions as well as against external injury.

This rationale, however, is as dangerous as it is compelling. Laws regulating speech for the protection of children have no limiting principle, and a well-intentioned law restricting protected speech on the basis of its content is, nevertheless, state-sponsored censorship. Regulations that "drive certain ideas or viewpoints from the marketplace" for children's benefit risk destroying the very "political system and cultural life" that they will inherit when they come of age.

I therefore have no doubt that a Newspaper Decency Act, passed because Congress discovered that young girls had read a front page article in the *New York Times* on female genital mutilation in Africa, would be unconstitutional. Nor would a Novel Decency Act, adopted after legislators had seen too many pot-boilers in convenience store book racks, pass constitutional muster. There is no question that a Village Green Decency Act, the fruit of a Senator's overhearing of a ribald conversation between two adolescent boys on a park bench, would be unconstitutional. A Postal Decency Act, passed because of constituent complaints about unsolicited lingerie catalogues, would also be unconstitutional. In these forms of communication, regulations on the basis of decency simply would not survive First Amendment scrutiny.

The Internet is a far more speech-enhancing medium than print, the village green, or the mails. Because it would necessarily affect the Internet itself, the CDA would necessarily reduce the speech available for adults on the medium. This is a constitutionally intolerable result.

Some of the dialogue on the Internet surely tests the limits of conventional discourse. Speech on the Internet can be unfiltered, unpolished, and unconventional, even emotionally charged, sexually explicit, and vulgar—in a word, "indecent" in many communities. But we should expect such speech to occur in a medium in which citizens from all walks of life have a voice. We should also protect the autonomy that such a medium confers to ordinary people as well as media magnates.

Moreover, the CDA will almost certainly fail to accomplish the government's interest in shielding children from pornography on the Internet. Nearly half of Internet communications originate outside the United States, and some percentage of that figure represents pornography. Pornography from, say, Amsterdam will be no less appealing to a child on the Internet than pornography from New York City, and residents of Amsterdam have little incentive to comply with the CDA.

My analysis does not deprive the government of all means of protecting children from the dangers of Internet communication. The government can continue to protect children from pornography on the Internet through vigorous enforcement of existing laws criminalizing obscenity and child pornography. As we learned at the hearing, there is also a compelling need for public education about the benefits and dangers of this new medium, and the government can fill that role as well. In my view, our action today should only mean that the government's permissible supervision of Internet content stops at the traditional line of unprotected speech.

Parents, too, have options available to them. As we learned at the hearing, parents can install blocking software on their home computers, or they can subscribe to commercial online services that provide parental controls. It is quite clear that powerful market forces are at work to expand parental options to deal with these legitimate concerns. More fundamentally, parents can supervise their children's use of the Internet or deny their children the opportunity to participate in the medium until they reach an appropriate age.

CONCLUSION

Cutting through the acronyms and *argot* that littered the hearing testimony, the Internet may fairly be regarded as a neverending worldwide conversation. The government may not, through the CDA, interrupt that conversation. As the most participatory form of mass speech yet developed, the Internet deserves the highest protection from governmental intrusion.

True it is that many find some of the speech on the Internet to be offensive, and amid the din of cyberspace many hear discordant voices that they regard as indecent. The absence of governmental regulation of Internet content has unquestionably produced a kind of chaos, but as one of plaintiffs' experts put it with such resonance at the hearing:

> What achieved success was the very chaos that the Internet is. The strength of the Internet is that chaos.

Just as the strength of the Internet is chaos, so the strength of our liberty depends upon the chaos and cacophony of the unfettered speech the First Amendment protects.

For these reasons, I without hesitation hold that the CDA is unconstitutional on its face. 35

Topics for Critical Thinking and Writing

1. Dalzell says that the "cases before us . . . are *not* about obscenity or child pornography" (para. 4). Yet the sponsor of the CDA, Senator Exon (see p. 435), defends this legislation on the ground that it will properly censor obscenity and child pornography. Can you explain this discrepancy?

2. Do you think it is possible for speech to be "indecent" as well as educational? Or is it rather that once speech is seen to be educational, it cannot be "indecent"? What is Dalzell's view on this issue?

3. The Court of Appeals judged the CDA to be unconstitutional on four grounds. What are they? (See para. 18.) Do you think they are equally important? Explain.

4. Dalzell argues that the Constitution prohibits any "content-based regulation" of speech on the Internet (para. 24). What do you think his view would be about regulations based wholly on time, place, or manner — for example, prohibiting a teacher from putting indecent material on the Internet on display in a school classroom for young children?

5. What is Dalzell's point in using hypothetical censorship laws — a Newspaper Decency Act, a Novel Decency Act, a Village Green Decency Act, a Postal Decency Act (para. 27)? What do you think his view would be about a Child Decency Act, designed solely to protect minors from exposure to indecent materials in print or on screen?

6. Is it a good argument against the CDA, or any other such legislation, that it will do nothing to stop indecent material on the Internet that originates outside this country (para. 30)?

7. In paragraph 32 Dalzell says that "parents can install blocking software on their home computers, or they can subscribe to commercial online services that provide parental controls." True, but Gary Bauer, a supporter of the CDA, in *USA Today* (June 14, 1996) wrote that "this logic says people are free to pollute the air, and parents must buy gas masks for their children." Evaluate his comment, paying special attention to the analogy drawn between pornography and air pollution. (On analogies, see pp. 67–68 and 287–88.)

Julia Wilkins

Julia Wilkins is the author of two books on educating children, Math Activities for Young Children: A Resource Guide for Parents and Teachers *and* Non-Competitive Motor Activities: A Guide for Elementary Classroom Teachers. *This essay originally appeared in the journal* The Humanist *in 1997.*

Protecting Our Children from Internet Smut: Moral Duty or Moral Panic?

The term *moral panic* is one of the more useful concepts to have emerged from sociology in recent years. A moral panic is characterized by a wave of public concern, anxiety, and fervor about something, usually perceived as a threat to society. The distinguishing factors are a level of interest totally out of proportion to the real importance of the subject, some individuals building personal careers from the pursuit and magnification of the issue, and the replacement of reasoned debate with witch-hunts and hysteria.

Moral panics of recent memory include the Joseph McCarthy anti-communist witch-hunts of the 1950s and the satanic ritual abuse allegations of the 1980s. And, more recently, we have witnessed a full-blown moral panic about pornography on the Internet. Sparked by the July 3, 1995, *Time* cover article "On a Screen Near You: Cyberporn," this moral panic has been perpetuated and intensified by a raft of subsequent media reports. As a result, there is now a widely held belief that pornography is easily accessible to all children using the Internet. This was also the judgment of Congress, which, proclaiming to be "protecting the children," voted overwhelmingly in 1996 for legislation to make it a criminal offense to send "indecent" material over the Internet into people's computers.

The original *Time* article was based on its exclusive access to Marty Rimm's *Georgetown University Law Journal* paper, "Marketing

Pornography on the Information Superhighway." Although published, the article had not received peer review and was based on an undergraduate research project concerning descriptions of images on adult bulletin board systems in the United States. Using the information in this paper, *Time* discussed the type of pornography available online, such as "pedophilia (nude pictures of children), hebephelia (youths) and . . . images of bondage, sadomasochism, urination, defecation, and sex acts with a barnyard full of animals." The article proposed that pornography of this nature is readily available to anyone who is even remotely computer literate and raised the stakes by offering quotes from worried parents who feared for their children's safety. It also presented the possibility that pornographic material could be mailed to children without their parents' knowledge. *Time*'s example was of a ten-year-old boy who supposedly received pornographic images in his e-mail showing "10 thumbnail size pictures showing couples engaged in various acts of sodomy, heterosexual intercourse, and lesbian sex." Naturally, the boy's mother was shocked and concerned, saying, "Children should not be subject to these images." *Time* also quoted another mother who said that she wanted her children to benefit from the vast amount of knowledge available on the Internet but was inclined not to allow access, fearing that her children could be "bombarded with X-rated pornography and [she] would know nothing about it."

From the outset, Rimm's report generated a lot of excitement—not only because it was reportedly the first published study of online pornography but also because of the secrecy involved in the research and publication of the article. In fact, the *New York Times* reported on July 24, 1995, that Marty Rimm was being investigated by his university, Carnegie Mellon, for unethical research and, as a result, would not be giving testimony to a Senate hearing on Internet pornography. Two experts from *Time* reportedly discovered serious flaws in Rimm's study involving gross misrepresentation and erroneous methodology. His work was soon deemed flawed and inaccurate, and *Time* recanted in public. With Rimm's claims now apologetically retracted, his original suggestion that 83.5 percent of Internet graphics are pornographic was quietly withdrawn in favor of a figure less than 1 percent.

Time admitted that grievous errors had slipped past their editorial 5 staff, as their normally thorough research succumbed to a combination of deadline pressure and exclusivity agreements that barred them from showing the unpublished study to possible critics. But, by then, the damage had been done: The study had found its way to the Senate.

GOVERNMENT INTERVENTION

Senator Charles Grassley (Republican–Iowa) jumped on the pornography bandwagon by proposing a bill that would make it a criminal offense to supply or permit the supply of "indecent" material to minors over the Internet. Grassley introduced the entire *Time* article into the congressional record, despite the fact that the conceptual, logical, and methodological flaws in the report had already been acknowledged by the magazine.

On the Senate floor, Grassley referred to Marty Rimm's undergraduate research as "a remarkable study conducted by researchers at Carnegie Mellon University" and went on to say:

> The university surveyed 900,000 computer images. Of these 900,000 images, 83.5 percent of all computerized photographs available on the Internet are pornographic. . . . With so many graphic images available on computer networks, I believe Congress must act and do so in a constitutional manner to help parents who are under assault in this day and age.

Under the Grassley bill, later known as the Protection of Children from Pornography Act of 1995, it would have been illegal for anyone to knowingly or recklessly transmit indecent material to minors. This bill marked the beginning of a stream of Internet censorship legislation at various levels of government in the United States and abroad.

The most extreme and fiercely opposed of these was the Communications Decency Act, sponsored by former Senator James Exon (Democrat–Nebraska) and Senator Dan Coats (Republican–Indiana). The CDA labeled the transmission of "obscene, lewd, lascivious, filthy, indecent, or patently offensive" pornography over the Internet a crime. It was attached to the Telecommunications Reform Act of 1996, which was then passed by Congress on February 1, 1996. One week later, it was signed into law by President Clinton. On the same day, the American Civil Liberties Union filed suit in Philadelphia against the U.S. Department of Justice and Attorney General Janet Reno, arguing that the statute would ban free speech protected by the First Amendment and subject Internet users to far greater restrictions than exist in any other medium. Later that month, the Citizens Internet Empowerment Coalition initiated a second legal challenge to the CDA, which formally consolidated with *ACLU v. Reno*. Government lawyers agreed not to prosecute "indecent" or "patently offensive" material until the three-judge court in Philadelphia ruled on the case.

Although the purpose of the CDA was to protect young children 10 from accessing and viewing material of sexually explicit content on the Internet, the wording of the act was so broad and poorly defined that it could have deprived many adults of information they needed in the areas of health, art, news, and literature—information that is legal in print form. Specifically, certain medical information available on the Internet includes descriptions of sexual organs and activities which might have been considered "indecent" or "patently offensive" under the act— for example, information on breastfeeding, birth control, AIDS, and gynecological and urological information. Also, many museums and art galleries now have Web sites. Under the act, displaying art like the Sistine Chapel nudes could be cause for criminal prosecution. Online newspapers would not be permitted to report the same information as is available in the print media. Reports on combatants in war, at the scenes of crime, in the political arena, and outside abortion clinics often provoke images or language that could be constituted "offensive" and therefore illegal on the Net. Furthermore, the CDA provided a legal basis for banning books which had been ruled unconstitutional to ban from school libraries. These include many of the classics as well as modern literature containing words that may be considered "indecent."

The act also expanded potential liability for employers, service providers, and carriers that transmit or otherwise make available restricted communications. According to the CDA, "knowingly" allowing obscene material to pass through one's computer system was a criminal offense. Given the nature of the Internet, however, making service providers responsible for the content of the traffic they pass on to other Internet nodes is equivalent to holding a telephone carrier responsible for the content of the conversations going over that carrier's lines. So, under the terms of the act, if someone sent an indecent electronic comment from a workstation, the employer, the e-mail service provider, and the carrier all could be potentially held liable and subject to up to $100,000 in fines or two years in prison.

On June 12, 1996, after experiencing live tours of the Internet and hearing arguments about the technical and economical infeasibility of complying with the censorship law, the three federal judges in Philadelphia granted the request for a preliminary injunction against the CDA. The court determined that "there is no evidence that sexually oriented material is the primary type of content on this new medium" and proposed that "communications over the Internet do not 'invade' an individual's home or appear on one's computer screen unbidden. Users seldom encounter content 'by accident.'" In a unanimous decision, the judges ruled that the Communications Decency Act would unconstitutionally restrict free speech on the Internet.

The government appealed the judges' decision and, on March 19, 1997, the U.S. Supreme Court heard oral arguments in the legal challenge to the CDA, now known as *Reno v. ACLU*. Finally, on June 26, the decision came down. The Court voted unanimously that the act violated the First Amendment guarantee of freedom of speech and would have threatened "to torch a large segment of the Internet community."

Is the panic therefore over? Far from it. The July 7, 1997, *Newsweek*, picking up the frenzy where *Time* left off, reported the Supreme Court decision in a provocatively illustrated article featuring a color photo of a woman licking her lips and a warning message taken from the Web site of the House of Sin. Entitled "On the Net, Anything Goes," the opening words by Steven Levy read, "Born of a hysteria triggered by a genuine problem—the ease with which wired-up teenagers can get hold of nasty pictures on the Internet—the Communications Decency Act (CDA) was never really destined to be a companion piece to the Bill of Rights." At the announcement of the Court's decision, antiporn protesters were on the street outside brandishing signs which read, "Child Molesters Are Looking for Victims on the Internet."

Meanwhile, government talk has shifted to the development of a universal Internet rating system and widespread hardware and software filtering. Referring to the latter, White House Senior Adviser Rahm Emanuel declared, "We're going to get the V-chip for the Internet. Same goal, different means."

But it is important to bear in mind that children are still a minority of Internet users. A contract with an Internet service provider typically needs to be paid for by credit card or direct debit, therefore requiring the intervention of an adult. Children are also unlikely to be able to view any kind of porn online without a credit card.

In addition to this, there have been a variety of measures developed to protect children on the Internet. The National Center for Missing and Exploited Children has outlined protective guidelines for parents and children in its pamphlet, *Child Safety on the Information Superhighway*. A number of companies now sell Internet newsfeeds and Web proxy accesses that are vetted in accordance with a list of forbidden topics. And, of course, there remain those blunt software instruments that block access to sexually oriented sites by looking for keywords such as *sex*, *erotic*, and *X-rated*. But one of the easiest solutions is to keep the family computer in a well-traveled space, like a living room, so that parents can monitor what their children download.

FACT OR MEDIA FICTION?

In her 1995 *CMC* magazine article, "Journey to the Centre of Cybersmut," Lisa Schmeiser discusses her research into online pornography. After an exhaustive search, she was unable to find any pornography, apart from the occasional commercial site (requiring a credit card for access), and concluded that one would have to undertake extensive searching to find quantities of explicit pornography. She suggested that, if children were accessing pornography online, they would not have been doing it by accident. Schmeiser writes: "There will be children who circumvent passwords, Surfwatch software, and seemingly innocuous links to find the 'adult' material. But these are the same kids who would visit every convenience store in a five-mile radius to find the one stocking *Playboy*." Her argument is simply that, while there is a certain amount of pornography online, it is not freely and readily available. Contrary to what the media often report, pornography is not that easy to find.

There *is* pornography in cyberspace (including images, pictures, movies, sounds, and sex discussions) and several ways of receiving pornographic material on the Internet (such as through private bulletin board systems, the World Wide Web, newsgroups, and e-mail). However, many sites just contain reproduced images from hardcore magazines and videos available from other outlets, and registration fee restrictions make them inaccessible to children. And for the more contentious issue of pedophilia, a recent investigation by the *Guardian* newspaper in Britain revealed that the majority of pedophilic images distributed on the Internet are simply electronic reproductions of the small output of legitimate pedophile magazines, such as *Lolita*, published in the 1970s.

Clearly the issue of pornography on the Internet is a moral panic— 20 an issue perpetuated by a sensationalistic style of reporting and misleading content in newspaper and magazine articles. And probably the text from which to base any examination of the possible link between media reporting and moral panics is Stanley Cohen's 1972 book, *Folk Devils and Moral Panic*, in which he proposes that the mass media are ultimately responsible for the creation of such panics. Cohen describes a moral panic as occurring when "a condition, episode, person or group of persons emerges to become a threat to societal values and interests; . . . the moral barricades are manned by editors . . . politicians and other 'right thinking' people." He feels that, while problematical elements of society can pose a threat to others, this threat is realistically far less than the perceived image generated by mass media reporting.

Cohen describes how the news we read is not necessarily the truth; editors have papers to sell, targets to meet, and competition from other publishers. It is in their interest to make the story "a good read"—the sensationalist approach sells newspapers. The average person is likely to be drawn in with the promise of scandal and intrigue. This can be seen in the reporting of the *National Enquirer* and *People*, with their splashy pictures and sensationalistic headlines, helping them become two of the largest circulation magazines in the United States.

Cohen discusses the "inventory" as the set of criteria inherent in any reporting that may be deemed as fueling a moral panic. This inventory consists of the following:

Exaggeration in reporting. Facts are often overblown to give the story a greater edge. Figures that are not necessarily incorrect but have been quoted out of context, or have been used incorrectly to shock, are two forms of this exaggeration.

Looking back at the original *Time* cover article, "On a Screen Near You: Cyberporn," this type of exaggeration is apparent. Headlines such as "The Carnegie Mellon researchers found 917,410 sexually explicit pictures, short stories, and film clips online" make the reader think that there really is a problem with the quantity of pornography in cyberspace. It takes the reader a great deal of further exploration to find out how this figure was calculated. Also, standing alone and out of context, the oft-quoted figure that 83.5 percent of images found on Usenet newsgroups are pornographic could be seen as cause for concern. However, if one looks at the math associated with this figure, one would find that this is a sampled percentage with a research leaning toward known areas of pornography.

The repetition of fallacies. This occurs when a writer reports in- 25 formation that seems perfectly believable to the general public, even though those who know the subject are aware it is wildly incorrect. In the case of pornography, the common fallacy is that the Internet is awash with nothing but pornography and that all you need to obtain it is a computer and a modem. Such misinformation is integral to the fueling of moral panics.

Take, for example, the October 18, 1995, *Scotland on Sunday*, which reports that, to obtain pornographic material, "all you need is a personal computer, a phone line with a modem attached, and a connection via a specialist provider to the Internet." What the article fails to mention is that the majority of pornography is found on specific Usenet sites not readily available from the major Internet providers, such as America Online and Compuserve. It also fails to mention that this pornography needs to be downloaded and converted into a viewable form, which requires certain skills and can take considerable time.

Misleading pictures and snappy titles. Media representation often exaggerates a story through provocative titles and flashy pictorials — all in the name of drawing in the reader. The titles set the tone for the rest of the article; the headline is the most noticeable and important part of any news item, attracting the reader's initial attention. The recent *Newsweek* article is a perfect example. Even if the headline has little relevance to the article, it sways the reader's perception of the topic. The symbolization of images further increases the impact of the story. *Time*'s own images in its original coverage — showing a shocked little boy on the cover and, inside, a naked man hunched over a computer monitor — added to the article's ability to shock and to draw the reader into the story.

Through sensationalized reporting, certain forms of behavior become classified as *deviant*. Specifically, those who put pornography online or those who download it are seen as being deviant in nature. This style of reporting benefits the publication or broadcast by giving it the aura of "moral guardian" to the rest of society. It also increases revenue.

In exposing deviant behavior, newspapers and magazines have the ability to push for reform. So, by classifying a subject and its relevant activities as deviant, they can stand as crusaders for moral decency, championing the cause of "normal" people. They can report the subject and call for something to be done about it, but this power is easily abused. The *Time* cyberporn article called for reform on the basis of Rimm's findings, proclaiming, "A new study shows us how pervasive and wild [pornography on the Internet] really is. Can we protect our kids—and free speech?" These cries to protect our children affected the likes of Senators James Exon and Robert Dole, who took the *Time* article with its "shocking" revelations (as well as a sample of pornographic images) to the Senate floor, appealing for changes to the law. From this response it is clear how powerful a magazine article can be, regardless of the integrity and accuracy of its reporting.

The *Time* article had all of Cohen's elements relating to the fueling of 30 a moral panic: exaggeration, fallacies, and misleading pictures and titles. Because certain publications are highly regarded and enjoy an important role in society, anything printed in their pages is consumed and believed by a large audience. People accept what they read because, to the best of their knowledge, it is the truth. So, even though the *Time* article was based on a report by an undergraduate student passing as "a research team from Carnegie Mellon," the status of the magazine was great enough to launch a panic that continues unabated—from the halls of Congress to the pulpits of churches, from public schools to the offices of software developers, from local communities to the global village.

Topics for Critical Thinking and Writing

1. Wilkins introduces us to the idea of a "moral panic" in paragraph 1 and gives a couple of examples in paragraph 2. Can you think of others? Would any of the following qualify: the Missile Gap (1960), the Cuban Missile Crisis (1962), the AIDS epidemic (1982–), alarm over El Niño (1997–98), or global warming (present)? Choose one of these events and, after consulting with your reference librarian for necessary information, write a 500-word essay explaining your answer.

2. Citing examples from Wilkins's essay, how would you define *pornography*? If "less than 1 percent" (para. 4) of graphics on the Internet are pornographic, is there much reason to worry about censoring it—or will a policy of no censorship result in the percent of pornography on the Internet steadily growing?

3. Wilkins judges the *Time* article of July 3, 1995, to be riddled with "conceptual, logical, and methodological flaws" (para. 6). Cite an example of each kind of flaw, based on her account.

4. Consult your college library for the text of the U.S. Supreme Court's opinion in *ACLU v. Reno* (excerpts appeared in the *New York Times* for June 27, 1997). Summarize the reasoning of the Court in a paper of no more than 500 words.

5. Does Wilkins make out a convincing case for her conclusion that "clearly the issue of pornography on the Internet is a moral panic" (para. 20)? How would she meet the objection that she underestimates the likely rate of growth of pornography on the Internet—and that it will be matched by

ever greater access to it by impressionable children—unless some form of censorship is introduced very soon?

Cathleen A. Cleaver

Cathleen A. Cleaver is director of legal studies at the Family Research Council, a Washington-based research and educational organization. She delivered this speech at Boston University on October 29, 1997, as part of a College of Communication Great Debate.

The Internet: A Clear and Present Danger?

- Someone breaks through your firewall and steals proprietary information from your computer systems. You find out and contact a lawyer who says, "Man, you shouldn't have had your stuff online." The thief becomes a millionaire using your ideas, and you go broke, if laws against copyright violation don't protect material on the Internet.

- You visit the Antiques Anonymous Web site and decide to pay their hefty subscription fee for a year's worth of exclusive estate sale previews in their private online monthly magazine. They never deliver and, in fact, never intended to—they don't even have a magazine. You have no recourse, if laws against fraud don't apply to online transactions.

- Bob Guccione decides to branch out into the lucrative child porn market and creates a Teen Hustler Web site featuring nude adolescents and preteens. You find out and complain, but nothing can be done, if child pornography distribution laws don't apply to computer transmissions.

- A major computer software vendor who dominates the market develops his popular office software so that it works only with his browser. You're a small browser manufacturer who is completely squeezed out of the market, but you have to find a new line of work, if antitrust laws don't apply online.

- Finally, a pedophile e-mails your son, misrepresenting himself as a twelve-year-old named Jenny. They develop an online relationship and one day arrange to meet after school, where he intends to rape your son. Thankfully, you learn in advance about the meeting and go there yourself, where you find a forty-year-old man instead of Jenny. You flee to the police, who'll tell you there's nothing they can do, if child-stalking laws don't apply to the Internet.

THE ISSUE

The awesome advances in interactive telecommunication that we've witnessed in just the last few years have changed the way in which many Americans communicate and interact. No one can doubt that the Internet is a technological revolution of enormous proportion, with outstanding possibilities for human advancement.

As lead speaker for the affirmative, I'm asked to argue that the Internet poses a "clear and present danger," but the Internet, as a whole, isn't dangerous. In fact, it continues to be a positive and highly beneficial tool, which will undoubtedly improve education, information exchange, and commerce in years to come. In other words, the Internet will enrich many aspects of our daily life. Thus, instead of defending this rather apocalyptic view of the Internet, I'll attempt to explain why some industry and government regulation of certain aspects of the Internet is necessary — or, stated another way, why people who use the Internet should not be exempt from many of the laws and regulations that govern their conduct elsewhere. My opening illustrations were meant to give examples of some illegal conduct which should not become legal simply because someone uses the Internet. In looking at whether Internet regulation is a good idea, I believe we should consider whether regulation is in the public interest. In order to do that, we have to ask the question: Who is the public? More specifically, does the "public" whose interests we care about tonight include children?

CHILDREN AND THE INTERNET

Dave Barry describes the Internet as a "worldwide network of university, government, business, and private computer systems, run by a thirteen-year-old named Jason." This description draws a smile precisely because we acknowledge the highly advanced computer literacy of our children. Most children demonstrate computer proficiency that far surpasses that of their parents, and many parents know only what their children have taught them about the Internet, which gives new relevance to Wordsworth's insight: "The child is father of the man." In fact, one could go so far as to say that the Internet is as accessible to many children as it is inaccessible to many adults. This technological evolution is new in many ways, not the least of which is its accessibility to children, wholly independent of their parents.

When considering what's in the public interest, we must consider the whole public, including children, as individual participants in this new medium.

PORNOGRAPHY AND THE INTERNET

This new medium is unique in another way. It provides, through a   5
single avenue, the full spectrum of pornographic depictions, from the

more familiar convenience store fare to pornography of such violence and depravity that it surpasses the worst excesses of the normal human imagination. Sites displaying this material are easily accessible, making pornography far more freely available via the Internet than from any other communications medium in the United States. Pornography is the third largest sector of sales on the Internet, generating $1 billion annually. There are an estimated seventy-two-thousand pornographic sites on the World Wide Web alone, with approximately thirty-nine new explicit sex sites every day. Indeed, the *Washington Post* has called the Internet the largest pornography store in the history of mankind.

There is little restriction of pornography-related activity in cyberspace. While there are some porn-related laws, the specter of those laws does not loom large in cyberspace. There's an implicit license there that exists nowhere else with regard to pornography—an environment where people are free to exploit others for profit and be virtually untroubled by legal deterrent. Indeed, if we consider cyberspace to be a little world of its own, it's the type of world for which groups like the ACLU have long fought but, so far, fought in vain.

I believe it will not remain this way, but until it changes, we should take the opportunity to see what this world looks like, if for no other reason than to reassure ourselves that our decades-old decisions to control pornography were good ones.

With a few clicks of the mouse, anyone, any child, can get graphic and often violent sexual images—the kind of stuff it used to be difficult to find without exceptional effort and some significant personal risk. Anyone with a computer and a modem can set up public sites featuring the perversion of their choice, whether it's mutilation of female genitals, eroticized urination and defecation, bestiality, or sites featuring depictions of incest. These pictures can be sold for profit, they can be sent to harass others, or posted to shock people. Anyone can describe the fantasy rape and murder of a specific person and display it for all to read. Anyone can meet children in chat rooms or via e-mail and send them pornography and find out where they live. An adult who signs onto an AOL chat room as a thirteen-year-old girl is hit on thirty times within the first half hour.

All this can be done from the seclusion of the home, with the feeling of near anonymity and with the comfort of knowing that there's little risk of legal sanction.

The phenomenon of this kind of pornography finding such a welcome home in this new medium presents abundant opportunities for social commentary. What does Internet pornography tell us about human sexuality? Photographs, videos, and virtual games that depict rape and the dehumanization of women in sexual scenes send powerful messages about human dignity and equality. Much of the pornography freely available without restriction on the Internet celebrates unhealthy and antisocial kinds of sexual activity, such as sadomasochism, abuse, 10 and degradation. Of course, by its very nature, pornography encourages voyeurism.

Beyond the troubling social aspects of unrestricted porn, we face the reality that children are accessing it and that predators are accessing children. We have got to start considering what kind of society we'll have when the next generation learns about human sexuality from what the Internet teaches. What does unrestricted Internet pornography teach children about relationships, about the equality of women? What does it teach little girls about themselves and their worth?

Opponents of restrictions are fond of saying that it's up to the parents to deal with the issue of children's exposure. Well, of course it is, but placing the burden solely on parents is illogical and ineffective. It's far easier for a distributor of pornography to control his material than it is for parents, who must, with the help of software, search for and find the pornographic sites, which change daily, and then attempt to block them. Any pornographer who wants to can easily subvert these efforts, and a recent Internet posting from a teenager wanting to know how to disable the filtering software on his computer received several effective answers. Moreover, it goes without saying that the most sophisticated software can only be effective where it's installed, and children will have access to many computers that don't have filtering software, such as those in libraries, schools, and at neighbors' houses.

INTERNET TRANSACTIONS
SHOULD NOT BE EXEMPT

Opponents of legal restrictions often argue simply that the laws just cannot apply in this new medium, but the argument that old laws can't apply to changing technology just doesn't hold. We saw this argument last in the early '80s with the advent of the videotape. Then, certain groups tried to argue that, since you can't view videotapes without a VCR, you can't make the sale of child porn videos illegal, because, after all, they're just plastic boxes with magnetic tape inside. Technological change mandates legal change only insofar as it affects the justification for a law. It just doesn't make sense that the government may take steps to restrict illegal material in *every* medium—video, television, radio, the private telephone, *and* print—but that it may do *nothing* where people distribute the material by the Internet. While old laws might need redefinition, the old principles generally stand firm.

The question of enforcement usually is raised here, and it often comes in the form of: "How are you going to stop people from doing it?" Well, no law stops people from doing things—a red light at an intersection doesn't force you to stop but tells you that you should stop and that there could be legal consequences if you don't. Not everyone who runs a red light is caught, but that doesn't mean the law is futile. The same concept holds true for Internet laws. Government efforts to temper harmful conduct online will never be perfect, but that doesn't mean they shouldn't undertake the effort at all.

There's clearly a role for industry to play here. Search engines don't have to run ads for porn sites or prioritize search results to highlight porn. One new search engine even has *sex* as the default search term. Internet service providers can do something about unsolicited e-mail with hotlinks to porn, and they can and should carefully monitor any chat rooms designed for kids. 15

Some charge that industry standards or regulations that restrict explicit pornography will hinder the development of Internet technology. But that is to say that its advancement *depends upon* unrestricted exhibition of this material, and this cannot be true. The Internet does not belong to pornographers, and it's clearly in the public interest to see that they don't usurp this great new technology. We don't live in a perfect society, and the Internet is merely a reflection of the larger social community. Without some mitigating influences, the strong will exploit the weak, whether a Bill Gates or a child predator.

CONCLUSION:
TECHNOLOGY MUST SERVE MAN

To argue that the strength of the Internet is chaos or that our liberty depends upon chaos is to misunderstand not only the Internet but also the fundamental nature of our liberty. It's an illusion to claim social or moral neutrality in the application of technology, even if its development may be neutral. It can be a valuable resource only when placed at the service of humanity and when it promotes our integral development for the benefit of all.

Guiding principles simply cannot be inferred from mere technical efficiency or from the usefulness accruing to some at the expense of others. Technology by its very nature requires unconditional respect for the fundamental interests of society.

Internet technology must be at the service of humanity and of our inalienable rights. It must respect the prerogatives of a civil society, among which is the protection of children.

Topics for Critical Thinking and Writing

1. Cleaver begins her essay with a list of five hypothetical anecdotes. Do you think it would have been more or less effective if she had dropped those anecdotes and started directly with the text following the list? Why, or why not?

2. Cleaver says she will argue for the thesis that "people who use the Internet should not be exempt from many of the laws and regulations that govern their conduct elsewhere" (para. 2). Read the opinion of Judge

Dalzell (p. 438). Does it argue against this thesis of Cleaver's? If so, what is the argument? If not, then on what issue or issues does she disagree?

3. In paragraph 6, speaking of cyberspace, Cleaver says, "There's an implicit license there that exists nowhere else with regard to pornography—an environment where people are free to exploit others for profit and be virtually untroubled by legal deterrent." Do you agree that pornographers "exploit others for profit"? If they do, are they doing something different from what, say, automobile manufacturers, farmers, and the owners of corner convenience stores do, all of whom seek to reduce their costs and to sell to a market? Explain what you think Cleaver means. Then indicate whether or not you agree with her, and why.

4. Cleaver talks about the depiction of "rape and the dehumanization of women in sexual scenes" (para. 10). What do you imagine her response would be to tender scenes of lesbian love? Have we any basis for conjecturing about her response? Explain.

5. In paragraph 13 Cleaver correctly notices that restrictions govern television and radio, and she suggests that they should also govern the Internet. In fact, the restrictions on television and radio derive from the scarcity of bandwidth. Because the available number of television and radio channels is limited, the government assigns them to broadcasters and is thought to have the right to control them in some respects. But the government does not assign any privilege to a server, and therefore, some people hold, the argument that the government should monitor the Internet just as it monitors television and radio is invalid. Your view in an essay of 500 words?

6. Some supporters of regulation argue that regulation is needed because innocent children may accidentally encounter disturbing material. Cleaver does not make this point, and, in fact, she assumes that at least some children will actively seek (and easily find) this material. Can it be argued that although a case for regulation might be made if there really is a likelihood that innocents will stumble across offensive material, no case for regulation can be made if people—obviously not innocent—have to seek it?

7. Is it a sufficient response to Cleaver to say that parents should guide their children and that the government should play no role in monitoring the Internet? Explain.

8. Compare the arguments used by Senator Exon (p. 435) and Cleaver in favor of censorship. On what points do they agree? On what, if any, do they seem to disagree? Write a 750-word essay on the topic "Two Votes for Internet Censorship: Exon and Cleaver."

18

Cloning: Dare We Replicate Human Beings?

Laurence H. Tribe

Laurence H. Tribe (b. 1941), a graduate of Harvard College and Harvard Law School, teaches constitutional law at Harvard. In addition to writing for the legal profession, Tribe writes for the general public. Among the books written for all of us are Constitutional Choices *(1985),* On Reading the Constitution *(1991), and* Abortion: The Clash of Absolutes *(1992). We reprint an Op-Ed piece that he published in the* New York Times *on December 5, 1997, and we follow it with a letter written in response.*

Second Thoughts on Cloning

Some years ago, long before human cloning became a near-term prospect, I was among those who urged that human cloning be assessed not simply in terms of concrete costs and benefits but in terms of what the technology might do to the very meaning of human reproduction, child rearing, and individuality. I leaned toward prohibition as the safest course.

Today, with the prospect of a renewed push for sweeping prohibition rather than mere regulation, I am inclined to say, "Not so fast."

When scientists announced in February that they had created a clone of an adult sheep—a genetically identical copy named Dolly, created in the laboratory from a single cell of the "parent"—ethicists, theologians, and others passionately debated the pros and cons of trying to clone a human being.

People spoke of the plight of infertile couples; the grief of someone who has lost a child whose biological "rebirth" might offer solace; the prospect of using cloning to generate donors for tissues and organs; the possibility of creating genetically enhanced clones with a particular talent or a resistance to some dread disease.

But others saw a nightmarish and decidedly unnatural perversion of human reproduction. California enacted a ban on human cloning, and the President's National Bioethics Advisory Commission recommended making the ban nationwide.

That initial debate has cooled, however, and many in the scientific field now seem to be wondering what all the fuss was about.

They are asking whether human cloning isn't just an incremental step beyond what we are already doing with artificial insemination, in vitro fertilization, fertility enhancing drugs, and genetic manipulation. That casual attitude is sure to give way before long to yet another wave of prohibitionist outrage — a wave that I no longer feel comfortable riding.

I certainly don't subscribe to the view that whatever technology permits us to do we ought to do. Nor do I subscribe to the view that the Constitution necessarily guarantees every individual the right to reproduce through whatever means become technically possible.

Rather, my concern is that the very decision to use the law to condemn, and then outlaw, patterns of human reproduction — especially by invoking vague notions of what is "natural" — is at least as dangerous as the technologies such a decision might be used to control.

Human cloning has been condemned by some of its most articulate detractors as the ultimate embodiment of the sexual revolution, severing sex from the creation of babies and treating gender and sexuality as socially constructed.

But to ban cloning as the technological apotheosis of what some see as culturally distressing trends may, in the end, lend credence to strikingly similar objections to surrogate motherhood or gay marriage and gay adoption.

Equally scary, when appeals to the natural, or to the divinely ordained, lead to the criminalization of some method for creating human babies, we must come to terms with the inevitable: The prohibition will not be airtight.

Just as was true of bans on abortion and on sex outside marriage, bans on human cloning are bound to be hard to enforce. And that, in turn, requires us to think in terms of a class of potential outcasts — people whose very existence society will have chosen to label as a misfortune and, in essence, to condemn.

One need only think of the long struggle to overcome the stigma of "illegitimacy" for the children of unmarried parents. How much worse might be the plight of being judged morally incomplete by virtue of one's man-made origin?

There are some black markets (in narcotic drugs, for instance) that may be worth risking when the evils of legalization would be even worse. But when the contraband we are talking of creating takes the form of human beings, the stakes become enormous.

There are few evils as grave as that of creating a caste system, one in which an entire category of persons, while perhaps not labeled untouchable, is marginalized as not fully human.

And even if one could enforce a ban on cloning, or at least insure that clones would not be a marginalized caste, the social costs of prohibition could still be high. For the arguments supporting an ironclad prohibition of cloning are most likely to rest on, and reinforce, the notion that it is unnatural and intrinsically wrong to sever the conventional links between heterosexual unions sanctified by tradition and the creation and upbringing of new life.

The entrenchment of that notion cannot be a welcome thing for lesbians, gay men, and perhaps others with unconventional ways of linking erotic attachment, romantic commitment, genetic replication, gestational mothering, and the joys and responsibilities of child rearing.

And, from the perspective of the wider community, straight no less than gay, a society that bans acts of human creation for no better reason than that their particular form defies nature and tradition is a society that risks cutting itself off from vital experimentation, thus losing a significant part of its capacity to grow. If human cloning is to be banned, then, the reasons had better be far more compelling than any thus far advanced.

Topics for Critical Thinking and Writing

1. Construct an outline of Tribe's essay.

2. What is the distinction Tribe has in mind when he contrasts "prohibition" of cloning, in contrast to "mere regulation" (para. 2)? Which do you favor, and why?

3. Some observers suggest, Tribe writes, that human cloning is "just an incremental step beyond what we are already doing with artificial insemination, in vitro fertilization, fertility enhancing drugs, and genetic manipulation" (para. 7). Take one of these four technological developments and write a 500-word paper comparing and contrasting it with human cloning.

4. In your library, with the help of the reference librarian, obtain a copy of the President's National Bioethics Advisory Commission report and recommendations. Summarize its findings and recommendations in a paper of 250 words.

5. Why does Tribe worry that banning human cloning may lead to legal attacks on surrogate motherhood, gay marriage, or gay adoption?

6. If human cloning is prohibited by law, and some persons defy the law, why does Tribe worry about where that would leave their cloned offspring?

Holly Finn

The following letter was published as a response to Laurence Tribe's Op-Ed piece (directly preceding). The title above the letter presumably was created by the editor of the letters section of the New York Times.

Romance of Childbirth

To the Editor:

Laurence H. Tribe's "Second Thoughts on Cloning" (Op-Ed, Dec. 5) was masterfully written, and sneaky. The emotional whammy was tucked in at the end, where he said, "A society that bans acts of human creation . . . is a society that risks cutting itself off from vital experimentation, thus losing a significant part of its capacity to grow." What a taunt. All good Americans want to grow, after all.

Mr. Tribe asks for better reasons to oppose human cloning. How about this? I have not yet had children, but I hope to have many. I don't want just to replicate mine and another's genes (that seems a bit perfunctory); I want to feel as my mother did after giving birth: "Very clever," she says. There's romance, delight, and mystery in that. Call me a Luddite, but I believe in the ancient means of production.

Holly Finn
New York, Dec. 5, 1997

Topics for Critical Thinking and Writing

1. In her final sentence Finn says that some people may think of her as a Luddite. She uses the word in an unusual way. (If you are unfamiliar with the word, check a dictionary.) Is her use effective? Why, or why not?

2. Do you agree that cloning takes the "romance, delight, and mystery" out of birth? Explain.

3. Pretend you are Laurence Tribe, and write—but don't mail—a response to Finn's letter.

James Q. Wilson

James Q. Wilson is Collins Professor of Management and Public Policy at the University of California at Los Angeles. Among his books are Bureaucracy *(1989),* The Moral Sense *(1994),* Moral Judgment *(1997), and, with Leon Kass,* The Ethics of Human Cloning *(1998). We reprint an essay that originally appeared in* The Weekly Standard, *May 26, 1997.*

The Paradox of Cloning

Let us suppose that it becomes possible to clone human beings. The creation of Dolly the cloned sheep makes this more likely than anyone once suspected. How should we react to this event?

Like most people, I instinctively recoil from the idea. There is, I think, a natural sentiment that is offended by the mental picture of identical babies being produced in some biological factory. When we hear a beautiful model say that she would like to have a clone of herself, we are puzzled. When we recall *The Boys from Brazil*, a story of identical offspring of Adolf Hitler being raised in order to further his horrible work, we are outraged.

But before deciding what we think about cloning, we ought to pause and identify more precisely what it is about the process that is so distressing. My preliminary view is that the central problem is not creating an identical twin but creating it without parents.

Happily, we need not react immediately to human cloning. The task of moving from one sheep to many sheep, and from sheep to other animals, and from animals to humans, will be long and difficult. Dolly was the only lamb to emerge out of 277 attempts, and we still do not know how long she will live or what diseases, if any, she might contract.

And the risks attendant on a hasty reaction are great. A premature ban on any scientific effort moving in the direction of cloning could well impede useful research on the genetic basis of diseases or on opportunities for improving agriculture. Already a great deal of work is underway on modifying the genetic structure of laboratory animals in order to study illnesses and to generate human proteins and antibodies. Aware of the value of genetic research, several members of Congress have expressed reservations about quick legislative action. Nevertheless, bills to ban cloning research have been introduced.

But even if such bills pass, the argument will be far from over. Congress may regulate or even block cloning research in the United States, but other countries are free to pursue their own strategies. If cloning is illegal in America but legal in Japan or China, Americans will go to those countries as cloning techniques are perfected. Science cannot be stopped. We should have learned this from the way we regulate drug treatments. We can ban a risky but useful drug, but the only effect is to limit its use to those who are willing and able to pay the airfare to Hong Kong.

There are both philosophical and utilitarian objections to cloning. Two philosophical objections exist. The first is that cloning violates God's will by creating an infant in a way that does not depend on human sexual congress or make possible the divine inculcation of a soul. That is true, but so does in vitro fertilization. An egg and a sperm are united outside the human body in a glass container. The fertilized egg is then put into the body of either the woman who produced it or another woman hired to bear the infant. When first proposed, in vitro fertilization was ethically suspect. Today, it is generally accepted, and for good reason. Science supplies what one or both human bodies lack, namely, a reasonable chance to produce an infant. Surely God can endow that infant with a soul. Cloning, of course, removes one of the conjugal partners, but it is hard to imagine that God's desire to bestow a unique soul can be blocked by the fact that the infant does not result from an egg and sperm's joining but instead arises from an embryonic egg's reproducing itself.

The other philosophical objection is that cloning is contrary to nature. This is often asserted by critics of cloning who do not believe in an active God. I sympathize with this reaction, but few critics have yet made clear to me what compelling aspect of nature cloning violates. To the extent this objection has meaning, I think it must arise from the danger that the cloned child will be put to various harmful uses. If so, it cannot easily be distinguished from the more practical problems.

One set of those problems requires us to imagine scientists' cloning children in order to harvest organs and body parts or producing for later use many Adolf Hitlers or Saddam Husseins. I have no doubt that there will arise mad scientists willing to do these things. After all, they have already created poison gas and conducted grisly experiments on prisoners of war and concentration-camp inmates.

But under what circumstances will such abuses occur? Largely, I   10
think, when the cloned child has no parents. Parents, whether they acquire a child by normal birth, artificial insemination, or adoption, will, in the overwhelming majority of cases, become deeply attached to the infant and care for it without regard to its origin. The parental tie is not infallible—infanticide occurs, and some neonates are abandoned in trash bins—but it is powerful and largely independent of the origin of the child. If cloning is to occur, the central problem is to ensure that it be done only for two-parent families who want a child for their own benefit. We should remember that a clone must be borne by a female; it cannot be given birth in a laboratory. A human mother will carry a human clone; she and her husband will determine its fate. Hardly any parents, I think, would allow their child to be used as an organ bank for defective adults or as the next-generation proxy for a malevolent dictator. If the cloned child is born in the same way as a child resulting from marital congress, can it matter to the parents how it was conceived? And if it does not matter to the parents, should it matter to us?

We already have a kind of clone: identical twins. They are genetically identical humans. I have not heard of any twin being used against its will as an unwitting organ bank for its brother or sister. Some may surrender a kidney or bone marrow to their sibling; many may give blood; but none, I think, has been "harvested." The idea that a cloned infant, born to its mother, would be treated differently is, I think, quite far-fetched.

At some time in the future, science may discover a way to produce a clone entirely in the laboratory. That we should ban. Without human birth, the parents' attitude toward the infant will be deeply compromised. Getting a clone from a laboratory would be like getting a puppy from a pet store: Both creatures might be charming, but neither would belong in any meaningful emotional sense to the owner. And unclaimed clones would be disposed of the same way as unclaimed puppies— killed.

There may be parents who, out of fear or ideology, can be persuaded to accept a clone of a Hussein in hopes that they can help produce an unending chain of vicious leaders. This is less far-fetched. We already know from the study of identical twins reared in different families that they are remarkably similar. A cloned Hussein would have an IQ close to that of his father and a personality that (insofar as we can measure these things) would have roughly a 50 percent chance of being like his. Each clone would be like an identical twin: nearly the same in appearance, very similar in intelligence and manner, and alike (but not a duplicate) in personality. We know that the environment will have some effect on each twin's personality, but it is easy to overestimate this. I am struck by how many scientists interested in cloning have reflexively adopted the view that the environment will have a powerful effect on a cloned child. (Cloning seems to have given a large boost to environmentalists.) But that reaction is exaggerated. From the work of Dr. Thomas Bouchard at the University of Minnesota, we know that giving identical twins different environments produces only slightly greater differences in character.

Our best hope for guarding against the duplication of a Saddam Hussein is a practical one. Any cloned offspring would reach maturity forty or so years after his father was born, and by then so much would have changed—Hussein, Sr., would probably not even be in power, his country's political system might have been profoundly altered—that it is unlikely Hussein, Jr., could do what his father did.

We do not know how many parents will request cloning, but some 15 will. Suppose the father cannot provide sperm or the mother is unable to produce a fertilizable egg. Such a family now has only two choices—remain childless or adopt. Cloning would create a third choice: duplicate the father or the mother. Some parents who do not want to remain childless will find this more attractive than adoption, which introduces a wholly new and largely unknown genetic factor into their family tree. Cloning guarantees that the child's genetic makeup will be identical to that of whichever parent is cloned.

There is, of course, a risk that cloning may increase the number of surrogate mothers, with all of the heartbreak and legal complexities that this entails, but I suspect that surrogates would be no more common for clones than they are for babies conceived in vitro.

More troubling is the possibility that a lesbian couple will use cloning to produce a child. Do we wish to make it easy for a homosexual pair to have children? Governments have different policies on this; let me set aside discussion of this matter for another occasion.

There is one important practical objection to the widespread use of cloning. As every evolutionary scientist knows, the survival of a species depends on two forces—environmental change that rewards some creatures and penalizes others, and sufficient diversity among the species that no matter what the environment, some members of the species will benefit.

Cloning creates the opportunity for people to maximize a valued trait. Suppose we wish to have children with a high IQ, an athletic physique, easily tanned skin, or freedom from a particular genetic disease. By cloning persons who have the desired trait, we can guarantee that the trait will appear in the infant.

This may make good sense to parents, but it is bad news for the species. We have no way of knowing what environmental challenges will confront us in the future. Traits that today are desirable may become irrelevant or harmful in the future; traits that now are unappealing may become essential for human survival in the centuries ahead.

This problem is one for which there is no obvious individual solution. People maximizing the welfare of their infant can inhibit the welfare of the species. One way to constrain a couple's efforts to secure the "perfect" child would be to restrict their choice of genes to either the father or the mother. They could secure a specific genetic product, but they could not obtain what they might think is the ideal product.

But the real constraint on the misuse of cloning comes from a simple human tendency. Many parents do not want a child with particular traits. Conception is a lottery. It produces an offspring that gets roughly half of its genes from its father and half from its mother, but the mixture occurs in unpredictable and fascinating combinations. All parents spend countless delightful hours wondering whether the child has its mother's eyes or its father's smile or its grandfather's nose or its grandmother's personality. And they watch in wonder as the infant becomes an adult with its own unique personality and mannerisms.

I think that most people prefer the lottery to certainty. (I know they prefer sex to cloning.) Lured by the lottery, they help meet the species's need for biological diversity. Moreover, if parents are tempted by certainty but limited to cells taken from either the father or the mother, they will have to ask themselves hard questions.

Do I want another man like the father, who is smart and earns a lot—but whose hair is receding, who has diabetes, and who is so obsessed with work that he is not much fun on weekends? Or do I want another woman like the mother, who is bright and sweet—but who has bad teeth, a family risk of breast cancer, and sleeps too late in the morning?

Not many of us know perfect people, least of all our own parents. If we want to clone a person, most of us will think twice about cloning somebody we already know well. And if we can clone only from among our own family, our desire to do it at all will be much weakened. Perhaps parents' love of entering the reproductive lottery is itself a revelation of evolution at work, one designed to help maintain biological diversity.

In one special case we may want to clone a creature well known to us. My friend Heather Higgins has said that cloning our pets—or at least some pets—may make sense. I would love to have another Labrador retriever just like Winston and another pair of cats exactly like Sarah and Clementine.

The central question facing those who approach cloning with an open mind is whether the gains from human cloning—a remedy for infertility and substitute for adoption—are worth the risks of farming organs, propagating dictators, and impeding evolution. I think that, provided certain conditions are met, the gains will turn out to exceed the risks.

The conditions are those to which I have already referred. Cloning should be permitted only on behalf of two married partners, and the mother should—absent some special medical condition that doctors must certify—carry the fertile tissue to birth. Then the offspring would belong to the parents. This parental constraint would prevent organ farming and the indiscriminate or political misuse of cloning technology.

The major threat cloning produces is a further weakening of the two-parent family. Cloning humans, if it can occur at all, cannot be prevented, but cloning unmarried persons will expand the greatest cultural problem our country now faces. A cloned child, so far as we now know, cannot be produced in a laboratory. A mother must give it birth. Dolly had a mother, and if humans are produced the same way, they will have mothers, also. But not, I hope, unmarried mothers. Indeed, given the likely expense and difficulty of cloning, and the absence from it of any sexual pleasure, we are unlikely to see many unmarried teenage girls choosing that method. If unmarried cloning occurs, it is likely to be among affluent persons who think they are entitled to act without the restraints and burdens of family life. They are wrong.

Of course an unmarried or unscrupulous person eager for a cloned 30 offspring may travel from the United States to a place where there are no restrictions of the sort I suggest. There is no way to prevent this. We can try to curtail it by telling anyone who returns to this country with a child born abroad to an American citizen that one of two conditions must be met before the child will be regarded as an American citizen. The parent bringing it back must show by competent medical evidence either that the child is the product of a normal (noncloned) birth or adoption or that the child, though the product of cloning, belongs to a married couple who will be responsible for it. Failing this, the child could not become an American citizen. But of course some people would evade any restrictions. There is, in short, no way that American law can produce a fail-safe restraint on undesirable cloning.

My view—that cloning presents no special ethical risks if society does all in its power to establish that the child is born to a married woman and is the joint responsibility of the married couple—will not satisfy those whose objections to cloning are chiefly religious. If man is made in the image of God, can man make himself (by cloning) and still be in God's image? I would suggest that producing a fertilized egg by sexual contact does not uniquely determine that image and therefore that nonsexual, in vitro fertilization is acceptable. And if this is so, then nonsexually transplanting cell nuclei into enucleated eggs might also be acceptable.

This is not a view that will commend itself to many devout Christians or Jews. I would ask of them only that they explain what it is about sexual fertilization that so affects God's judgment about the child that results.

Topics for Critical Thinking and Writing

1. What is the "paradox of cloning" to which Wilson refers in the title of his essay? (Consult pp. 270–71 for an explanation of paradox.)

2. What does Wilson isolate as "the central problem" about cloning (para. 3)? Are you inclined to agree or disagree? Why?

3. Both Wilson (para. 5) and Laurence Tribe (p. 459) favor no legal ban on cloning, yet their reasons are very different. Write a 100-word essay on their reasons.

4. Wilson mentions two "philosophical objections" to human cloning (paras. 7–8). Which of the two do you think is the more persuasive? Would you accept either, both, or neither?

5. What is the difference between a pair of identical twins and a pair of persons one of whom is the clone of the other? If we have no moral problems with identical twins, why should we have any with clones?

6. Explain why Wilson says, in passing, "Cloning seems to have given a large boost to environmentalists" (para. 13).

7. Wilson seems not to be very worried about the possibility that cloning might be used to produce a race of Adolf Hitlers or Saddam Husseins (paras. 13–14). Explain whether you share his view and why or why not.

8. Wilson confesses that as he weighs the costs and benefits of cloning, he thinks the benefits prevail (para. 27). Write a 500-word essay in which you briefly set forth his views of the costs and benefits, and then give your own views, indicating why you agree or disagree with Wilson.

Charles Krauthammer

Charles Krauthammer (b. 1950) was educated at McGill, Oxford, and Harvard Universities. He is a medical doctor and a licensed psychiatrist, but he is chiefly known as a writer. His essays appear regularly in Time *magazine and in* The New Republic. *The article reprinted here originally appeared in* Time *on January 19, 1998.*

Of Headless Mice . . . and Men

Last year Dolly the cloned sheep was received with wonder, titters, and some vague apprehension. Last week the announcement by a Chicago physicist that he is assembling a team to produce the first human clone occasioned yet another wave of Brave New World anxiety. But the scariest news of all—and largely overlooked—comes from two obscure labs, at the University of Texas and at the University of Bath. During the past four years, one group created headless mice; the other, headless tadpoles.

For sheer Frankenstein wattage, the purposeful creation of these animal monsters has no equal. Take the mice. Researchers found the gene that tells the embryo to produce the head. They deleted it. They did this in a thousand mice embryos, four of which were born. I use the term loosely. Having no way to breathe, the mice died instantly.

Why then create them? The Texas researchers want to learn how genes determine embryo development. But you don't have to be a genius to see the true utility of manufacturing headless creatures: for their organs—fully formed, perfectly useful, ripe for plundering.

Why should you be panicked? Because humans are next. "It would almost certainly be possible to produce human bodies without a forebrain," Princeton biologist Lee Silver told the London *Sunday Times*. "These human bodies without any semblance of consciousness would not be considered persons, and thus it would be perfectly legal to keep them 'alive' as a future source of organs."

"Alive." Never have a pair of quotation marks loomed so ominously.   5
Take the mouse-frog technology, apply it to humans, combine it with cloning, and you are become a god: With a single cell taken from, say, your finger, you produce a headless replica of yourself, a mutant twin, arguably lifeless, that becomes your own personal, precisely tissue-matched organ farm.

There are, of course, technical hurdles along the way. Suppressing the equivalent "head" gene in man. Incubating tiny infant organs to grow into larger ones that adults could use. And creating artificial wombs (as per Aldous Huxley), given that it might be difficult to recruit sane women to carry headless fetuses to their birth/death.

It won't be long, however, before these technical barriers are breached. The ethical barriers are already cracking. Lewis Wolpert,

professor of biology at University College, London, finds producing headless humans "personally distasteful" but, given the shortage of organs,
does not think distaste is sufficient reason not to go ahead with something
that would save lives. And Professor Silver not only sees "nothing wrong,
philosophically or rationally," with producing headless humans for organ
harvesting; he wants to convince a skeptical public that it is perfectly O.K.

When prominent scientists are prepared to acquiesce in—or indeed
encourage—the deliberate creation of deformed and dying quasi-human
life, you know we are facing a bioethical abyss. Human beings are ends,
not means. There is no grosser corruption of biotechnology than creating
a human mutant and disemboweling it at our pleasure for spare parts.

The prospect of headless human clones should put the whole debate
about "normal" cloning in a new light. Normal cloning is less a treatment
for infertility than a treatment for vanity. It is a way to produce an exact
genetic replica of yourself that will walk the earth years after you're
gone.

But there is a problem with a clone. It is not really you. It is but a   10
twin, a perfect John Doe, Jr., but still a junior. With its own independent
consciousness, it is, alas, just a facsimile of you.

The headless clone solves the facsimile problem. It is a gateway to
the ultimate vanity: immortality. If you create a real clone, you cannot
transfer your consciousness into it to truly live on. But if you create a
headless clone of just your body, you have created a ready source of replacement parts to keep you—your consciousness—going indefinitely.

Which is why one form of cloning will inevitably lead to the other.
Cloning is the technology of narcissism, and nothing satisfies narcissism
like immortality. Headlessness will be cloning's crowning achievement.

The time to put a stop to this is now. Dolly moved President Clinton
to create a commission that recommended a temporary ban on human
cloning. But with physicist Richard Seed threatening to clone humans,
and with headless animals already here, we are past the time for tooth-
less commissions and meaningless bans.

Clinton banned federal funding of human-cloning research, of
which there is none anyway. He then proposed a five-year ban on
cloning. This is not enough. Congress should ban human cloning now.
Totally. And regarding one particular form, it should be draconian: The
deliberate creation of headless humans must be made a crime, indeed a
capital crime. If we flinch in the face of this high-tech barbarity, we'll deserve to live in the hell it heralds.

Topics for Critical Thinking and Writing

1. With the help of a reference librarian, find out about the Chicago physicist Dr. Richard Seed and his proposal to clone human beings (para. 1).
   Write a 250-word report of your investigations.

2. Why is the prospect of cloning a headless zombie for the purpose of one's own private "organ farm" (para. 5) so scary? Are we just being squeamish? Or is there some deep moral objection to such a practice? Does Krauthammer show clearly what moral principle his objection to such a practice relies on? Write a 250-word essay on the topic "Krauthammer's Ethical Objections to Cloning One's Own Headless Organ Farm."

3. When Krauthammer says "Human beings are ends, not means" (para. 8), what does he mean?

4. Why does Krauthammer describe a desire for immortality as "the ultimate vanity" (para. 11)?

5. Krauthammer says that with one's own headless clone available, thanks to organ transplants, one could "keep going indefinitely" (para. 11). How long is "indefinitely"? Suppose one argued that Krauthammer's worry is unfounded: He gives no evidence for his claim, and there is every reason to believe a human brain (however propped up by transplants of other organs) will remain just as vulnerable to Alzheimer's disease and other debilitating and fatal illnesses as it is now. How might he reply?

Jean Bethke Elshtain

Jean Bethke Elshtain, a professor of political science at the University of Chicago, publishes regularly in such journals as The New Republic *and* Commonweal. *Among her recent books are* Democracy on Trial *(1995) and* Women and War *(1995). The essay that we reprint was originally published in* The New Republic *on March 31, 1997.*

Ewegenics

For a change, there was no waffling. The president acted decisively and boldly, and, what's more, rightly, when he called for a moratorium on all cloning experiments involving humans. The alarm and moral clarity behind the president's action, however, has been absent in much of the media. The newspapers' ubiquitous search for "balance" is unbalanced when the matter at hand is as extraordinarily unsettling as cloning. I read a half-dozen pieces pairing a techno-enthusiast against a hand-wringing theologian. A professional ethicist is usually brought onstage as an arbiter between two obviously one-sided points of view. A comforting sense of moderation is achieved. The article ends.

But listen to the radio call-in shows and you get a rather different picture. For every wild-eyed optimist there are, by my count, a good half-dozen alarmists. Talk to the man and woman on the street and you hear murmurs and rumblings and dark portents of the "end-of-times" and "now we've gone too far." The airwaves and the street win this one hands down. They represent a humane and sobering contrast to the celebratory glitz of, say, *USA Today*, which trumpeted "HELLO DOLLY!"—the name of the fetching ewe staring at us in a front-page color photo. The subhead read: "SHEEP CLONING PROMPTS ETHICAL DEBATE." The sheep looks perfectly normal, of course, and not terribly exercised about her historic significance. That she is the child of no one will probably not haunt her nights and days. But we—we humans, that is—should be haunted, by Dolly and all the Dollies to come and by the prospect others will appear on this earth as the progeny of our omnipotent striving, our yearning to create without pausing to reflect on what we are simultaneously destroying.

A few nights ago, I watched the Chicago Bulls clobber the San Antonio Spurs. Michael Jordan performed one of his typically superhuman feats, an assist that suggested he had eyes in the back of his head and two sets of arms. To one citizen who called a local program, the prospect of "more Michael Jordans" made the whole "cloning thing" not only palatable but desirable. "Can you imagine a whole basketball team of Michael Jordans?" he asked giddily.

Unfortunately, I can. It's a nightmare. If there were basketball teams fielding Jordans against Jordans, we wouldn't be able to recognize the one, the only, Michael Jordan. It's like suggesting that forty Mozarts are better than one. There would be no Mozart if there were forty Mozarts. We know the singularity of the one, the extraordinary genius—a Jordan, a Mozart—because they stand apart from and above the rest. Absent that irreducible singularity, their gifts and glorious accomplishments would mean nothing. They would be the norm, commonplace: another dunk, another concerto. In fact, lots of callers made this point, or one similar to it, in reacting to the Michael Jordan Clonetopia scenario.

A research librarian at a small college in Indiana, who had given me   5
a drive to her campus for the purpose of delivering a lecture, offered a spontaneous, sustained, and troubling critique of cloning that rivals the best dystopian fictions. Her cloning nightmare was a veritable army of Hitlers, ruthless and remorseless bigots who kept reproducing themselves until they had finished what the historic Hitler had failed to do: annihilate us. It occurred to me that an equal number of Mother Teresas would probably not be a viable deterrent, not if the Hitler clones were behaving like, well, Hitler.

But I had my own nightmare scenario: a society that clones human beings to serve as spare parts for the feeble. Because the cloned entities are not fully human, our moral queasiness is somewhat disarmed. We could then "harvest" organs to our heart's content—organs from human beings of every age, race, and phenotype. Anencephalic newborns, whose organs are now "harvested," would, in that world, be the equivalent of the Model T—an early and, it turns out, very rudimentary prototype of glorious, gleaming things to come.

Far-fetched? No longer. Besides, the far-fetched often gets us nearer to the truth than the cautious, persnickety pieces that fail to come anywhere close to the pity and terror this topic evokes.

Consider Stanislaw Lem's science fiction classic, *The Star Diaries*, in which his protagonist, Ijon Tichy, described as a "hapless Candide of the Cosmos," ventures into space and encounters one weird situation after another. Lem's "Thirteenth Voyage" takes Tichy to a planet called Panta, where he runs afoul of local custom and is accused of the worst of crimes, "the crime of personal differentiation." The evidence against him is incriminating. Nonetheless, Tichy is given an opportunity to conform. A planet spokesman instructs Tichy on the benefits of his planet, on which there are no separate entities—"only the collective."

The denizens of Panta have come to understand that the source of all "the cares, sufferings and misfortunes to which beings, gathered together in societies, are prone" lies in the individual, "in his private identity." The individual, by contrast to the collective, is "characterized by uncertainty, indecision, inconsistency of action, and above all—by impermanence." Having "completely eliminated individuality," the people of planet Panta have achieved "the highest degree of social interchangeability." It works rather the way the Marxist utopia was to function: Everyone at any moment can be anything else. Functions or roles are commutable. On Panta you occupy a role for twenty-four hours only: one day a gardener, the next an engineer, then a mason, now a judge.

The same principle holds with families. "Each is composed of relatives—there's a father, mother, children. Only the functions remain constant; the ones who perform them are changed every day." All feelings and emotions are entirely abstract. One never needs to grieve or to mourn as everyone is infinitely replaceable. "Affection, respect, love were at one time gnawed by constant anxiety, by the fear of losing the person held dear," Lem writes. "This dread we have conquered. For in point of fact whatever upheavals, diseases or calamities may be visited upon us, we shall always have a father, a mother, a spouse and children." Indeed, there is no "I." And there can be no death, "where there are no individuals." In this commutable void, we do not die. Tichy, like most of us, can't quite get with the program. Brought before a court, he is "found guilty and condemned to life identification." He blasts off and sets his course for Earth.

Only this time, if Lem were writing an addendum to his brilliant tale, Tichy would probably land on terra firma—in both the literal and metaphorical sense—only to discover the greeting party at the rocket-port a bit strange: There are forty very tall basketball players all wearing identical number 23 jerseys, dribbling on one side and, on the other side, forty men in powdered wigs, suited up in breeches and satin frock coats, all playing *The Marriage of Figaro*.

Topics for Critical Thinking and Writing

1. If human cloning is morally wrong, there must be some important moral principle, standard, or ideal that cloning violates. Does Elshtain mention any such norm? Can you think of any? Write a 350-word essay on the topic "Moral Norms and Human Cloning."

2. Do you agree with Elshtain's argument that genius (on the court or at the piano) vanishes as soon as it becomes the standard performance?

3. Elshtain worries that if cloning is permitted, we will use cloned humans for harvesting organs for the rest of us. Do you think that could be made illegal and thus prevented once human cloning for other purposes was allowed?

4. Suppose someone argued that Elshtain's lengthy review of Stanislaw Lem's sci-fi classic, *The Star Diaries*, is just a scare tactic designed to frighten us into believing that nature will imitate art. How might she reply to such a criticism?

5. Julia Wilkins (p. 445) describes what she calls a "moral panic." Are the current "alarmists" that Elshtain mentions (including herself) in her second paragraph suffering from a moral panic? Why, or why not?

19

The Death Penalty:
Can It Ever Be Justified?

Edward I. Koch

Edward I. Koch (b. 1924), long active in Democratic politics, was mayor of New York from 1978 to 1989. This essay first appeared in The New Republic *on April 15, 1985.*

Death and Justice:
How Capital Punishment Affirms Life

Last December a man named Robert Lee Willie, who had been convicted of raping and murdering an eighteen-year-old woman, was executed in the Louisiana state prison. In a statement issued several minutes before his death, Mr. Willie said: "Killing people is wrong. . . . It makes no difference whether it's citizens, countries, or governments. Killing is wrong." Two weeks later in South Carolina, an admitted killer named Joseph Carl Shaw was put to death for murdering two teenagers. In an appeal to the governor for clemency, Mr. Shaw wrote: "Killing was wrong when I did it. Killing is wrong when you do it. I hope you have the courage and moral strength to stop the killing."

It is a curiosity of modern life that we find ourselves being lectured on morality by cold-blooded killers. Mr. Willie previously had been convicted of aggravated rape, aggravated kidnapping, and the murders of a Louisiana deputy and a man from Missouri. Mr. Shaw committed another murder a week before the two for which he was executed, and admitted mutilating the body of the fourteen-year-old girl he killed. I can't help wondering what prompted these murderers to speak out against killing as they entered the deathhouse door. Did their newfound reverence for life stem from the realization that they were about to lose their own?

Life is indeed precious, and I believe the death penalty helps to affirm this fact. Had the death penalty been a real possibility in the minds of these murderers, they might well have stayed their hand. They might have shown moral awareness before their victims died, and not after. Consider the tragic death of Rosa Velez, who happened to be home when a man named Luis Vera burglarized her apartment in Brooklyn. "Yeah, I shot her," Vera admitted. "She knew me, and I knew I wouldn't go to the chair."

During my twenty-two years in public service, I have heard the pros and cons of capital punishment expressed with special intensity. As a district leader, councilman, congressman, and mayor, I have represented constituencies generally thought of as liberal. Because I support the death penalty for heinous crimes of murder, I have sometimes been the subject of emotional and outraged attacks by voters who find my position reprehensible or worse. I have listened to their ideas. I have weighed their objections carefully. I still support the death penalty. The reasons I maintain my position can be best understood by examining the arguments most frequently heard in opposition.

1. The death penalty is "barbaric." Sometimes opponents of 5 capital punishment horrify with tales of lingering death on the gallows, of faulty electric chairs, or of agony in the gas chamber. Partly in response to such protests, several states such as North Carolina and Texas switched to execution by lethal injection. The condemned person is put to death painlessly, without ropes, voltage, bullets, or gas. Did this answer the objections of death penalty opponents? Of course not. On June 22, 1984, the *New York Times* published an editorial that sarcastically attacked the new "hygienic" method of death by injection, and stated that "execution can never be made humane through science." So it's not the method that really troubles opponents. It's the death itself they consider barbaric.

Admittedly, capital punishment is not a pleasant topic. However, one does not have to like the death penalty in order to support it any more than one must like radical surgery, radiation, or chemotherapy in order to find necessary these attempts at curing cancer. Ultimately we may learn how to cure cancer with a simple pill. Unfortunately, that day has not yet arrived. Today we are faced with the choice of letting the cancer spread or trying to cure it with the methods available, methods that one day will almost certainly be considered barbaric. But to give up and do nothing would be far more barbaric and would certainly delay the discovery of an eventual cure. The analogy between cancer and murder is imperfect, because murder is not the "disease" we are trying to cure. The disease is injustice. We may not like the death penalty, but it must be available to punish crimes of cold-blooded murder, cases in which any other form of punishment would be inadequate and, therefore, unjust. If we create a society in which injustice is not tolerated, incidents of murder — the most flagrant form of injustice — will diminish.

2. No other major democracy uses the death penalty. No other major democracy — in fact, few other countries of any description — are plagued by a murder rate such as that in the United States. Fewer and fewer Americans can remember the days when unlocked doors were the norm and murder was a rare and terrible offense. In America the murder rate climbed 122 percent between 1963 and 1980. During that same period, the murder rate in New York City increased by almost 400 percent, and the statistics are even worse in many other cities. A study at M.I.T. showed that based on 1970 homicide rates a person who lived in a large American city ran a greater risk of being murdered than an American soldier in World War II ran of being killed in combat. It is not surprising that the laws of each country differ according to differing conditions and traditions. If other countries had our murder problem, the cry for capital punishment would be just as loud as it is here. And I dare say that any other major democracy where 75 percent of the people supported the death penalty would soon enact it into law.

3. An innocent person might be executed by mistake. Consider the work of Hugo Adam Bedau, one of the most implacable foes of capital punishment in this country. According to Mr. Bedau, it is "false sentimentality to argue that the death penalty should be abolished because of the abstract possibility that an innocent person might be executed." He cites a study of the seven thousand executions in this country from 1892 to 1971, and concludes that the record fails to show that such cases occur. The main point, however, is this. If government functioned only when the possibility of error didn't exist, government wouldn't function at all. Human life deserves special protection, and one of the best ways to guarantee that protection is to assure that convicted murderers do not kill again. Only the death penalty can accomplish this end. In a recent case in New Jersey, a man named Richard Biegenwald was freed from prison after serving eighteen years for murder; since his release he has been convicted of committing four murders. A prisoner named Lemuel Smith, who, while serving four life sentences for murder (plus two life sentences for kidnapping and robbery) in New York's Green Haven Prison, lured a woman corrections officer into the chaplain's office and strangled her. He then mutilated and dismembered her body. An additional life sentence for Smith is meaningless. Because New York has no death penalty statute, Smith has effectively been given a license to kill.

But the problem of multiple murder is not confined to the nation's penitentiaries. In 1981, ninety-one police officers were killed in the line of duty in this country. Seven percent of those arrested in the cases that have been solved had a previous arrest for murder. In New York City in 1976 and 1977, eighty-five persons arrested for homicide had a previous arrest for murder. Six of these individuals had two previous arrests for murder, and one had four previous murder arrests. During those two years the New York police were arresting for murder persons with a previous arrest for murder on the average of one every eight and a half days. This is not surprising when we learn that in 1975, for example, the median time served in Massachusetts for homicide was less than two and a half years. In 1976 a study sponsored by the Twentieth Century Fund found that the average time served in the United States for first-degree murder is ten years. The median time served may be considerably lower.

4. Capital punishment cheapens the value of human life. 10
On the contrary, it can be easily demonstrated that the death penalty strengthens the value of human life. If the penalty for rape were lowered, clearly it would signal a lessened regard for the victim's suffering, humiliation, and personal integrity. It would cheapen their horrible experience, and expose them to an increased danger of recurrence. When we lower the penalty for murder, it signals a lessened regard for the value of the victim's life. Some critics of capital punishment, such as columnist Jimmy Breslin, have suggested that a life sentence is actually a harsher penalty for murder than death. This is sophistic nonsense. A few killers may decide not to appeal a death sentence, but the overwhelming majority make every effort to stay alive. It is by exacting the highest penalty for the taking of human life that we affirm the highest value of human life.

5. The death penalty is applied in a discriminatory manner. This factor no longer seems to be the problem it once was. The appeals process for a condemned prisoner is lengthy and painstaking. Every effort is made to see that the verdict and sentence were fairly arrived at. However, assertions of discrimination are not an argument for ending the death penalty but for extending it. It is not justice to exclude everyone from the penalty of the law if a few are found to be so favored. Justice requires that the law be applied equally to all.

6. Thou Shalt Not Kill. The Bible is our greatest source of moral inspiration. Opponents of the death penalty frequently cite the sixth of the Ten Commandments in an attempt to prove that capital punishment is divinely proscribed. In the original Hebrew, however, the Sixth Commandment reads "Thou Shalt Not Commit Murder," and the Torah specifies capital punishment for a variety of offenses. The biblical viewpoint has been upheld by philosophers throughout history. The greatest thinkers of the nineteenth century—Kant, Locke, Hobbes, Rousseau, Montesquieu, and Mill—agreed that natural law properly authorizes the sovereign to take life in order to vindicate justice. Only Jeremy Bentham was ambivalent. Washington, Jefferson, and Franklin endorsed it. Abraham Lincoln authorized executions for deserters in wartime. Alexis de Tocqueville, who expressed profound respect for American institutions, believed that the death penalty was indispensable to the support of social order. The United States Constitution, widely admired as one of the seminal achievements in the history of humanity, condemns cruel and inhuman punishment, but does not condemn capital punishment.

7. The death penalty is state-sanctioned murder. This is the defense with which Messrs. Willie and Shaw hoped to soften the resolve of those who sentenced them to death. By saying in effect, "You're no better than I am," the murderer seeks to bring his accusers down to his own level. It is also a popular argument among opponents of capital punishment, but a transparently false one. Simply put, the state has rights that the private individual does not. In a democracy, those rights are given to the state by the electorate. The execution of a lawfully condemned killer is no more an act of murder than is legal imprisonment an act of kidnapping. If an individual forces a neighbor to pay him money under threat of punishment, it's called extortion. If the state does it, it's called taxation. Rights and responsibilities surrendered by the individual are what give the state its power to govern. This contract is the foundation of civilization itself.

Everyone wants his or her rights, and will defend them jealously. Not everyone, however, wants responsibilities, especially the painful responsibilities that come with law enforcement. Twenty-one years ago a woman named Kitty Genovese was assaulted and murdered on a street in New York. Dozens of neighbors heard her cries for help but did nothing to assist her. They didn't even call the police. In such a climate the criminal understandably grows bolder. In the presence of moral cowardice, he lectures us on our supposed failings and tries to equate his crimes with our quest for justice.

The death of anyone—even a convicted killer—diminishes us all. But we are diminished even more by a justice system that fails to function. It is an illusion to let ourselves believe that doing away with capital punishment removes the murderer's deed from our conscience. The rights of society are paramount. When we protect guilty lives, we give up innocent lives in exchange. When opponents of capital punishment say to the state, "I will not let you kill in my name," they are also saying to murderers: "You can kill in your *own* name as long as I have an excuse for not getting involved."

It is hard to imagine anything worse than being murdered while neighbors do nothing. But something worse exists. When those same neighbors shrink back from justly punishing the murderer, the victim dies twice.

Topics for Critical Thinking and Writing

1. In paragraph 6 Koch draws an analogy between cancer and murder, and observes that imperfect as today's cures for cancer are, "to give up and do nothing would be far more barbaric." What is the relevance of this comment in the context of the analogy and the dispute over the death penalty?

2. In paragraph 8 Koch describes a convicted but unexecuted recidivist murderer as someone who "has effectively been given a license to kill." But a license to kill, as in a deer-hunter's license, entitles the holder to engage in lawful killing. (Think of the fictional hero James Bond — Agent 007 — who, we are told, had a real "license to kill.") What is the difference between really having a license and "effectively" having one? How might the opponent of the death penalty reply to Koch's position here?

3. Koch distinguishes between the "median" time served by persons convicted of murder but not sentenced to death, and the "average" time they serve, and he adds that the former "may be considerably longer" than the latter. Explain the difference between a "median" and an "average" (review the section on statistics, pp. 70–72). Is knowing one of these more important for certain purposes than the other? Why?

4. Koch identifies seven arguments against the death penalty, and he rejects them all. Which of the seven arguments seems to you to be the strongest objection to the death penalty? Which the weakest? Why? Does Koch effectively refute the strongest argument? Can you think of any argument(s) against the death penalty that he neglects?

5. Koch says he supports the death penalty "for heinous crimes of murder" (para. 4). Does he imply that all murders are heinous crimes, or only some? If the latter, what criteria seem to you to be the appropriate ones to distinguish the heinous murders from the rest? Why these criteria?

6. Koch asserts that the death penalty helps to "affirm" the idea that "life is indeed precious." Yet opponents of the death penalty often claim the reverse, arguing that capital punishment undermines the idea that human life is precious. Write an essay of 500 words in which you explain what it means to assert that life is precious, and why one of the two positions — support for or opposition to the death penalty — best supports (or is consistent with) this principle.

David Bruck

David Bruck (b. 1949) graduated from Harvard College and received his law degree from the University of South Carolina. His practice is devoted almost entirely to the defense of persons under death sentence, through the South Carolina Office of Appellate Defense. The essay reprinted here originally appeared on May 20, 1985, in The New Republic *as a response to the essay by Edward I. Koch (p. 475).*

The Death Penalty

Mayor Ed Koch contends that the death penalty "affirms life." By failing to execute murderers, he says, we "signal a lessened regard for the value of the victim's life." Koch suggests that people who oppose the death penalty are like Kitty Genovese's neighbors, who heard her cries for help but did nothing while an attacker stabbed her to death.

This is the standard "moral" defense of death as punishment: Even if executions don't deter violent crime any more effectively than imprisonment, they are still required as the only means we have of doing justice in response to the worst of crimes.

Until recently, this "moral" argument had to be considered in the abstract, since no one was being executed in the United States. But the death penalty is back now, at least in the southern states, where every one of the more than thirty executions carried out over the last two years has taken place. Those of us who live in those states are getting to see the difference between the death penalty in theory, and what happens when you actually try to use it.

South Carolina resumed executing prisoners in January with the electrocution of Joseph Carl Shaw. Shaw was condemned to death for helping to murder two teenagers while he was serving as a military policeman at Fort Jackson, South Carolina. His crime, propelled by mental illness and PCP, was one of terrible brutality. It is Shaw's last words ("Killing was wrong when I did it. It is wrong when you do it. . . .") that so outraged Mayor Koch: He finds it "a curiosity of modern life that we are being lectured on morality by cold-blooded killers." And so it is.

But it was not "modern life" that brought this curiosity into being. It was capital punishment. The electric chair was J. C. Shaw's platform. (The mayor mistakenly writes that Shaw's statement came in the form of a plea to the governor for clemency: Actually Shaw made it only seconds before his death, as he waited, shaved and strapped into the chair, for the switch to be thrown.) It was the chair that provided Shaw with celebrity and an opportunity to lecture us on right and wrong. What made this weird moral reversal even worse is that J. C. Shaw faced his own death with undeniable dignity and courage. And while Shaw died, the TV crews recorded another "curiosity" of the death penalty—the crowd gathered outside the death-house to cheer on the executioner. Whoops of elation greeted the announcement of Shaw's death. Waiting at the penitentiary gates for the appearance of the hearse bearing Shaw's remains, one demonstrator started yelling, "Where's the beef?"

For those who had to see the execution of J. C. Shaw, it wasn't easy to keep in mind that the purpose of the whole spectacle was to affirm life. It will be harder still when Florida executes a cop-killer named Alvin Ford. Ford has lost his mind during his years of death-row confinement, and now spends his days trembling, rocking back and forth, and muttering unintelligible prayers. This has led to litigation over whether Ford meets a centuries-old legal standard for mental competency. Since the Middle Ages, the Anglo-American legal system has generally prohibited the execution of anyone who is too mentally ill to understand what is about to be done to him and why. If Florida wins its case, it will have earned the right to electrocute Ford in his present condition. If it loses, he will not be executed until the state has first nursed him back to some semblance of mental health.[1]

We can at least be thankful that this demoralizing spectacle involves a prisoner who is actually guilty of murder. But this may not always be so. The ordeal of Lenell Jeter—the young black engineer who recently served more than a year of a life sentence for a Texas armed robbery that he didn't commit—should remind us that the system is quite capable of making the very worst sort of mistake. That Jeter was eventually cleared is a fluke. If the robbery had occurred at 7 P.M. rather than 3 P.M., he'd have had no alibi, and would still be in prison today. And if someone had been killed in that robbery, Jeter probably would have been sentenced to death. We'd have seen the usual execution-day interviews with state officials and the victim's relatives, all complaining that Jeter's appeals took too long. And Jeter's last words from the gurney would have taken their place among the growing literature of death-house oration that so irritates the mayor.

Koch quotes Hugo Adam Bedau, a prominent abolitionist, to the effect that the record fails to establish that innocent defendants have been executed in the past. But this doesn't mean, as Koch implies, that it hasn't happened. All Bedau was saying was that doubts concerning executed prisoners' guilt are almost never resolved. Bedau is at work now on an effort to determine how many wrongful death sentences may have been imposed: His list of murder convictions since 1900 in which the state eventually *admitted* error is some four hundred cases long. Of course, very few of these cases involved actual executions: The mistakes that Bedau documents were uncovered precisely because the prisoner was alive and able to fight for his vindication. The cases where someone is executed are the very cases in which we're least likely to learn that we got the wrong man.

I don't claim that executions of entirely innocent people will occur very often. But they will occur. And other sorts of mistakes already have. Roosevelt Green was executed in Georgia two days before J. C. Shaw. Green and an accomplice kidnapped a young woman. Green swore that his companion shot her to death after Green had left, and that he knew nothing about the murder. Green's claim was supported by a statement that his accomplice made to a witness after the crime. The

[1]Florida lost its case to execute Ford. On June 26, 1986, the Supreme Court barred execution of convicted murderers who have become so insane that they do not know they are about to be executed nor the reason for it. If Ford regains his sanity, however, he can be executed. [Editors' note.]

jury never resolved whether Green was telling the truth, and when he tried to take a polygraph examination a few days before his scheduled execution, the state of Georgia refused to allow the examiner into the prison. As the pressure for symbolic retribution mounts, the courts, like the public, are losing patience with such details. Green was electrocuted on January 9, while members of the Ku Klux Klan rallied outside the prison.

Then there is another sort of arbitrariness that happens all the 10 time. Last October, Louisiana executed a man named Ernest Knighton. Knighton had killed a gas station owner during a robbery. Like any murder, this was a terrible crime. But it was not premeditated, and is the sort of crime that very rarely results in a death sentence. Why was Knighton electrocuted when almost everyone else who committed the same offense was not? Was it because he was black? Was it because his victim and all twelve members of the jury that sentenced him were white? Was it because Knighton's court-appointed lawyer presented no evidence on his behalf at his sentencing hearing? Or maybe there's no reason except bad luck. One thing is clear: Ernest Knighton was picked out to die the way a fisherman takes a cricket out of a bait jar. No one cares which cricket gets impaled on the hook.

Not every prisoner executed recently was chosen that randomly. But many were. And having selected these men so casually, so blindly, the death penalty system asks us to accept that the purpose of killing each of them is to affirm the sanctity of human life.

The death penalty states are also learning that the death penalty is easier to advocate than it is to administer. In Florida, where executions have become almost routine, the governor reports that nearly a third of his time is spent reviewing the clemency requests of condemned prisoners. The Florida Supreme Court is hopelessly backlogged with death cases. Some have taken five years to decide, and the rest of the Court's work waits in line behind the death appeals. Florida's death row currently holds more than 230 prisoners. State officials are reportedly considering building a special "death prison" devoted entirely to the isolation and electrocution of the condemned. The state is also considering the creation of a special public defender unit that will do nothing else but handle death penalty appeals. The death penalty, in short, is spawning death agencies.

And what is Florida getting for all of this? The state went through almost all of 1983 without executing anyone: Its rate of intentional homicide declined by 17 percent. Last year Florida executed eight people—the most of any state, and the sixth highest total for any year since Florida started electrocuting people back in 1924. Elsewhere in the United States last year, the homicide rate continued to decline. But in Florida, it actually rose by 5.1 percent.

But these are just the tiresome facts. The electric chair has been a centerpiece of each of Koch's recent political campaigns, and he knows better than anyone how little the facts have to do with the public's support for capital punishment. What really fuels the death penalty is the justifiable frustration and rage of people who see that the government is not coping with violent crime. So what if the death penalty doesn't work? At least it gives us the satisfaction of knowing that we got one or two of the sons of bitches.

Perhaps we want retribution on the flesh and bone of a handful of   15
convicted murderers so badly that we're willing to close our eyes to all of the demoralization and danger that come with it. A lot of politicians think so, and they may be right. But if they are, then let's at least look honestly at what we're doing. This lottery of death both comes from and encourages an attitude toward human life that is not reverent, but reckless.

And that is why the mayor is dead wrong when he confuses such fury with justice. He suggests that we trivialize murder unless we kill murderers. By that logic, we also trivialize rape unless we sodomize rapists. The sin of Kitty Genovese's neighbors wasn't that they failed to stab her attacker to death. Justice does demand that murderers be punished. And common sense demands that society be protected from them. But neither justice nor self-preservation demands that we kill men whom we have already imprisoned.

The electric chair in which J. C. Shaw died earlier this year was built in 1912 at the suggestion of South Carolina's governor at the time, Cole Blease. Governor Blease's other criminal justice initiative was an impassioned crusade in favor of lynch law. Any lesser response, the governor insisted, trivialized the loathsome crimes of interracial rape and murder. In 1912, a lot of people agreed with Governor Blease that a proper regard for justice required both lynching and the electric chair. Eventually we are going to learn that justice requires neither.

Topics for Critical Thinking and Writing

1. After three introductory paragraphs, Bruck devotes two paragraphs to Shaw's execution. In a sentence or two, state the point he is making in his discussion of this execution. Then, in another sentence or two (or three), indicate the degree to which this point refutes Koch's argument.

2. In paragraph 7, Bruck refers to the case of Lenell Jeter, an innocent man who was condemned to a life sentence. Evaluate this point as a piece of evidence used to support an argument against the death penalty.

3. In paragraph 8, Bruck says that "the state eventually *admitted* error" in some four hundred cases. He goes on: "Of course, very few of these cases involved actual executions." How few is "very few"? Why do you suppose Bruck doesn't specify the number? If, say, it is only two, in your opinion does that affect Bruck's point?

4. Discussing the case of Roosevelt Green (para. 9), Bruck points out that Green offered to take a polygraph test but "the state of Georgia refused to allow the examiner into the prison." In a paragraph evaluate the state's position on this matter.

5. In paragraph 13 Bruck points out that although "last year" (1984) the state executed eight people, the homicide rate in Florida rose 5.1 percent, whereas elsewhere in the United States the homicide rate declined. What do you make of these figures? What do you think Edward Koch (p. 475) would make of them?

6. In his next-to-last paragraph Bruck says that Koch "suggests that we trivialize murder unless we kill murderers. By that logic, we also trivialize rape unless we sodomize rapists." Do you agree that this statement brings out the absurdity of Koch's thinking?

7. Evaluate Bruck's final paragraph (a) as a concluding paragraph, and (b) as a piece of argumentation.

8. Bruck, writing early in 1985, stresses that all the "more than thirty" executions in the nation "in the last two years" have taken place in the South. Why does he think this figure points to a vulnerability in Koch's argument? Would Bruck's argument here be spoiled if some executions were to occur outside of the South? (By the way, where exactly have most of the recent executions in the nation occurred?)

9. Bruck argues that the present death-penalty system—in practice even if not in theory—utterly fails to "affirm the sanctity of human life" (para. 11). Do you think Bruck would, or should, concede that at least in theory it is possible for a death-penalty system to be no more offensive to the value of human life than, say, a system of imprisonment is offensive to the value of human liberty, or a system of fines is offensive to the value of human property?

10. Can Bruck be criticized for implying that cases like those he cites— Shaw, Ford, Green, and Knightson in particular—are the rule, rather than the exception? Does either Bruck or Koch cite any evidence to help settle this question?

11. Write a paragraph explaining which of these events seems to you to be the more unseemly: a condemned prisoner, on the threshold of execution, lecturing the rest of us on the immorality of killing; or the crowd that bursts into cheers outside a prison when it learns that a scheduled execution has been carried out.

William J. Brennan, Jr.

In 1972, after a five-year moratorium on executions, the U.S. Supreme Court confronted the constitutionality of the death penalty in the case of Furman v. Georgia. *The Court divided 5 to 4, with the majority holding that the death penalty as administered violated the Eighth Amendment prohibition against "cruel and unusual punishment" and the Fourteenth Amendment requirement of "equal protection of the law." Each of the nine justices wrote his own opinion; the result was 243 pages of judicial reasoning, at the time the longest set of opinions in one case in the history of the Court.*

The five in the majority were divided into two groups: Associate Justices William J. Brennan, Jr., and Thurgood Marshall argued that the death penalty was unconstitutional under any conditions; Associate Justices Byron R. White, Potter Stewart, and William O. Douglas argued for the narrower conclusion that fault lay in the way the death penalty was actually administered under statutes like the one in Georgia under which Furman was convicted and sentenced to death. Accordingly, the decision did not rule the death penalty as such to be unconstitutional; rather, it left room for legislatures to craft new death penalty statutes that would significantly reduce, if not entirely eliminate, the "arbitrariness" that all the justices in the majority agreed was unconstitutional. We reprint only portions of the lengthy opinion by Justice Brennan (1899–1997). Four years later, in 1976, in Gregg v. Georgia *(p. 494), the Supreme Court ruled that the death penalty as such was not unconstitutional under the Eighth and Fourteenth Amendments.*

In the following opinion, the citations referring to legal documents have been omitted.

Furman v. Georgia

. . . We have very little evidence of the Framers' intent in including the Cruel and Unusual Punishments Clause among those restraints upon the new government enumerated in the Bill of Rights. . . .

[T]he Framers were well aware that the reach of the Clause was not limited to the proscription of unspeakable atrocities. Nor did they intend simply to forbid punishments considered "cruel and unusual" at the time. The "import" of the Clause is, indeed, "indefinite," and for good reason. A constitutional provision "is enacted, it is true, from an experience of evils, but its general language should not, therefore, be necessarily confined to the form that evil had theretofore taken. Time works changes, brings into existence new conditions and purposes. Therefore a principle to be vital must be capable of wider application than the mischief which gave it birth."

There are . . . four principles by which we may determine whether a particular punishment is "cruel and unusual." The primary principle, which I believe supplies the essential predicate for the application of the others, is that a punishment must not by its severity be degrading to human dignity. The paradigm violation of this principle would be the infliction of a torturous punishment of the type that the Clause has always prohibited. Yet "[i]t is unlikely that any State at this moment in history" would pass a law providing for the infliction of such a punishment. Indeed, no such punishment has ever been before this Court. The same may be said of the other principles. It is unlikely that this Court will confront a severe punishment that is obviously inflicted in wholly arbitrary fashion; no state would engage in a reign of blind terror. Nor is it likely that this Court will be called upon to review a severe punishment that is clearly and totally rejected throughout society; no legislature would be able even to authorize the infliction of such a punishment. Nor, finally, is it likely that this Court will have to consider a severe punishment that is patently unnecessary; no state today would inflict a severe punishment knowing that there was no reason whatever for doing so. In short, we are unlikely to have occasion to determine that a punishment is fatally offensive under any one principle.

Since the Bill of Rights was adopted, this Court has adjudged only three punishments to be within the prohibition of the Clause. See *Weems v. United States* (12 years in chains at hard and painful labor); *Trop v. Dulles* (expatriation); *Robinson v. California* (imprisonment for narcotics addiction). Each punishment, of course, was degrading to human dignity, but of none could it be said conclusively that it was fatally offensive under one or the other of the principles. Rather, these "cruel and unusual punishments" seriously implicated several of the principles, and it was the application of the principles in combination that supported the judgment. That, indeed, is not surprising. The function of these principles, after all, is simply to provide means by which a court can determine whether a challenged punishment comports with human dignity. They are, therefore, interrelated, and in most cases it will be their convergence that will justify the conclusion that a punishment is "cruel and unusual." The test, then, will ordinarily be a cumulative one: If a punishment is unusually severe, if there is a strong probability that it is inflicted arbitrarily, if it is substantially rejected by contemporary society, and if there is no reason to believe that it serves any penal purpose more effectively than some less severe punishment, then the continued infliction of that punishment violates the command of the Clause that the State may not inflict inhuman and uncivilized punishments upon those convicted of crimes.

. . . I will analyze the punishment of death in terms of the principles set out above and the cumulative test to which they lead: It is a denial of human dignity for the State arbitrarily to subject a person to an unusually severe punishment that society has indicated it does not regard as acceptable, and that cannot be shown to serve any penal purpose more effectively than a significantly less drastic punishment. Under these principles and this test, death is today a "cruel and unusual" punishment.   5

I

Death is a unique punishment in the United States. In a society that so strongly affirms the sanctity of life, not surprisingly the common view is that death is the ultimate sanction. This natural human feeling appears all about us. There has been no national debate about punishment, in general or by imprisonment, comparable to the debate about the punishment of death. No other punishment has been so continuously restricted. . . . And those states that still inflict death reserve it for the most heinous crimes. Juries, of course, have always treated death cases differently, as have governors exercising their commutation powers. Criminal defendants are of the same view. . . . This Court, too, almost always treats death cases as a class apart. And the unfortunate effect of this punishment upon the functioning of the judicial process is well known; no other punishment has a similar effect.

The only explanation for the uniqueness of death is its extreme severity. Death is today an unusually severe punishment, unusual in its pain, in its finality, and in its enormity. No other existing punishment is comparable to death in terms of physical and mental suffering. . . .

The unusual severity of death is manifested most clearly in its finality and enormity. Death, in these respects, is in a class by itself. Expatriation, for example, is a punishment that "destroys for the individual the political existence that was centuries in the development," that "strips the citizen of his status in the national and international political community," and that puts "[h]is very existence" in jeopardy. Expatriation thus inherently entails "the total destruction of the individual's status in organized society." "In short, the expatriate has lost the right to have rights." Yet, demonstrably, expatriation is not "a fate worse than death." . . . Although death, like expatriation, destroys the individual's "political existence" and his "status in organized society," it does more, for, unlike expatriation, death also destroys "[h]is very existence." There is, too, at least the possibility that the expatriate will in the future regain "the right to have rights." Death forecloses even that possibility.

Death is truly an awesome punishment. The calculated killing of a human being by the state involves, by its very nature, a denial of the executed person's humanity. The contrast with the plight of a person punished by imprisonment is evident. An individual in prison does not lose "the right to have rights." A prisoner retains, for example, the constitutional rights to the free exercise of religion, to be free of cruel and unusual punishments, and to treatment as a "person" for purposes of due process of law and the equal protection of the laws. A prisoner remains a member of the human family. Moreover, he retains the right of access to the courts. His punishment is not irrevocable. Apart from the common charge, grounded upon the recognition of human fallibility, that the punishment of death must inevitably be inflicted upon innocent men, we know that death has been the lot of men whose convictions were unconstitutionally secured in view of later, retroactively applied, holdings of this Court. The punishment itself may have been unconstitutionally inflicted, yet the finality of death precludes relief. An executed person has indeed "lost the right to have rights." As one nineteenth-century proponent of punishing criminals by death declared, "When a man is hung, there is an end of our relations with him. His execution is a way of saying, 'You are not fit for this world, take your chance elsewhere.'"[1]

In comparison to all other punishments today, then, the deliberate 10 extinguishment of human life by the state is uniquely degrading to human dignity. I would not hesitate to hold, on that ground alone, that death is today a "cruel and unusual" punishment, were it not that death is a punishment of long-standing usage and acceptance in this country. I therefore turn to the second principle—that the state may not arbitrarily inflict an unusually severe punishment.

II

The outstanding characteristic of our present practice of punishing criminals by death is the infrequency with which we resort to it. The evidence is conclusive that death is not the ordinary punishment for any crime. . . .

When a country of over 200 million people inflicts an unusually severe punishment no more than fifty times a year, the inference is strong that the punishment is not being regularly and fairly applied. To dispel it would indeed require a clear showing of nonarbitrary infliction.

Although there are no exact figures available, we know that thousands of murders and rapes are committed annually in states where death is an authorized punishment for those crimes. However the rate of infliction is characterized—as "freakishly" or "spectacularly" rare, or simply as rare—it would take the purest sophistry to deny that death is inflicted in only a minute fraction of these cases. How much rarer, after all, could the infliction of death be?

When the punishment of death is inflicted in a trivial number of the cases in which it is legally available, the conclusion is virtually inescapable that it is being inflicted arbitrarily. Indeed, it smacks of little more than a lottery system. The states claim, however, that this rarity is evidence not of arbitrariness, but of informed selectivity: Death is inflicted, they say, only in "extreme" cases.

Informed selectivity, of course, is a value not to be denigrated. Yet pre- 15 sumably the states could make precisely the same claim if there were ten executions per year, or five, or even if there were but one. That there may be as many as fifty per year does not strengthen the claim. When the rate of infliction is at this low level, it is highly implausible that only the worst criminals or the criminals who commit the worst crimes are selected for this punishment. No one has yet suggested a rational basis that could differentiate in those terms the few who die from the many who go to prison. Crimes and criminals simply do not admit of a distinction that can be

---

[1]Stephen, Capital Punishments, 69 *Fraser's Magazine* 753, 763 (1864). [All notes are the Court's.]

drawn so finely as to explain, on that ground, the execution of such a tiny sample of those eligible. Certainly the laws that provide for this punishment do not attempt to draw that distinction; all cases to which the laws apply are necessarily "extreme." Nor is the distinction credible in fact. . . .

Furthermore, our procedures in death cases, rather than resulting in the selection of "extreme" cases for this punishment, actually sanction an arbitrary selection. For this Court has held that juries may, as they do, make the decision whether to impose a death sentence wholly unguided by standards governing that decision. In other words, our procedures are not constructed to guard against the totally capricious selection of criminals for the punishment of death.

III

. . . From the beginning of our nation, the punishment of death has stirred acute public controversy. Although pragmatic arguments for and against the punishment have been frequently advanced, this longstanding and heated controversy cannot be explained solely as the result of differences over the practical wisdom of a particular government policy. At bottom, the battle has been waged on moral grounds. The country has debated whether a society for which the dignity of the individual is the supreme value can, without a fundamental inconsistency, follow the practice of deliberately putting some of its members to death. In the United States, as in other nations of the Western world, "the struggle about this punishment has been one between ancient and deeply rooted beliefs in retribution, atonement or vengeance on the one hand, and, on the other, beliefs in the personal value and dignity of the common man that were born of the democratic movement of the eighteenth century, as well as beliefs in the scientific approach to an understanding of the motive forces of human conduct, which are the result of the growth of the sciences of behavior during the nineteenth and twentieth centuries."[2] It is this essentially moral conflict that forms the backdrop for the past changes in and the present operation of our system of imposing death as a punishment for crime. . . .

The progressive decline in, and the current rarity of, the infliction of death demonstrate that our society seriously questions the appropriateness of this punishment today. The states point out that many legislatures authorize death as the punishment for certain crimes and that substantial segments of the public, as reflected in opinion polls and referendum votes, continue to support it. Yet the availability of this punishment through statutory authorization, as well as the polls and referenda, which amount simply to approval of that authorization, simply underscores the extent to which our society has in fact rejected this punish-

[2]T. Sellin, The Death Penalty, A Report for the Model Penal Code Project of the American Law Institute 15 (1959).

ment. When an unusually severe punishment is authorized for wide-scale application but not, because of society's refusal, inflicted save in a few instances, the inference is compelling that there is a deepseated reluctance to inflict it. Indeed, the likelihood is great that the punishment is tolerated only because of its disuse. The objective indicator of society's view of an unusually severe punishment is what society does with it, and today society will inflict death upon only a small sample of the eligible criminals. Rejection could hardly be more complete without becoming absolute. At very least, I must conclude that contemporary society views this punishment with substantial doubt.

IV

The final principle to be considered is that an unusually severe and degrading punishment may not be excessive in view of the purposes for which it is inflicted. This principle, too, is related to the others. When there is a strong probability that the state is arbitrarily inflicting an unusually severe punishment that is subject to grave societal doubts, it is likely also that the punishment cannot be shown to be serving any penal purpose that could not be served equally well by some less severe punishment.

The states' primary claim is that death is a necessary punishment because it prevents the commission of capital crimes more effectively than any less severe punishment. . . .

We are not presented with the theoretical question whether under any imaginable circumstances the threat of death might be a greater deterrent to the commission of capital crimes than the threat of imprisonment. We are concerned with the practice of punishing criminals by death as it exists in the United States today. Proponents of this argument necessarily admit that its validity depends upon the existence of a system in which the punishment of death is invariably and swiftly imposed. Our system, of course, satisfies neither condition. A rational person contemplating a murder or rape is confronted, not with the certainty of a speedy death, but with the slightest possibility that he will be executed in the distant future. The risk of death is remote and improbable; in contrast, the risk of long-term imprisonment is near and great. In short, whatever the speculative validity of the assumption that the threat of death is a superior deterrent, there is no reason to believe that as currently administered the punishment of death is necessary to deter the commission of capital crimes. . . .

There is, however, another aspect to the argument that the punishment of death is necessary for the protection of society. The infliction of death, the states urge, serves to manifest the community's outrage at the commission of the crime. It is, they say, a concrete public expression of moral indignation that inculcates respect for the law and helps assure a more peaceful community. Moreover, we are told, not only does the punishment of death exert this widespread moralizing influence upon community values, it also satisfies the popular demand for grievous condemnation of abhorrent crimes and thus prevents disorder, lynching, and attempts by private citizens to take the law into their own hands.

The question, however, is not whether death serves these supposed purposes of punishment, but whether death serves them more effectively than imprisonment. There is no evidence whatever that utilization of imprisonment rather than death encourages private blood feuds and other disorders. Surely if there were such a danger, the execution of a handful of criminals each year would not prevent it. The assertion that death alone is a sufficiently emphatic denunciation for capital crimes suffers from the same defect. If capital crimes require the punishment of death in order to provide moral reinforcement for the basic values of the community, those values can only be undermined when death is so rarely inflicted upon the criminals who commit the crimes. Furthermore, it is certainly doubtful that the infliction of death by the state does in fact strengthen the community's moral code; if the deliberate extinguishment of human life has any effect at all, it more likely tends to lower our respect for life and brutalize our values. That, after all, is why we no longer carry out public executions. . . .

There is, then, no substantial reason to believe that the punishment of death, as currently administered, is necessary for the protection of society. The only other purpose suggested, one that is independent of protection for society, is retribution. . . .

Obviously, concepts of justice change; no immutable moral order requires death for murderers and rapists. The claim that death is a just punishment necessarily refers to the existence of certain public beliefs. The claim must be that for capital crimes death alone comports with society's notion of proper punishment. As administered today, however, the punishment of death cannot be justified as a necessary means of exacting retribution from criminals. When the overwhelming number of criminals who commit capital crimes go to prison, it cannot be concluded that death serves the purpose of retribution more effectively than imprisonment. The asserted public belief that murderers and rapists deserve to die is flatly inconsistent with the execution of a random few. As the history of the punishment of death in this country shows, our society wishes to prevent crime; we have no desire to kill criminals simply to get even with them.

In sum, the punishment of death is inconsistent with all four principles: Death is an unusually severe and degrading punishment; there is a strong probability that it is inflicted arbitrarily; its rejection by contemporary society is virtually total; and there is no reason to believe that it serves any penal purpose more effectively than the less severe punishment of imprisonment. The function of these principles is to enable a court to determine whether a punishment comports with human dignity. Death, quite simply, does not. . . .

Topics for Critical Thinking and Writing

1. Justice Brennan identifies "four principles" that together, he claims, express the meaning of the Eighth Amendment prohibition against "cruel and unusual punishment." What are these principles? Can you think of objections to any of them? Can you think of any relevant principles that he overlooks?

2. What is the logic of Brennan's argument against the death penalty? Write out the steps of the argument, one by one. (*Hint*: Think of logic as involving a minimum of two premises and a conclusion. Let the major premise define what "cruel and unusual punishment" means; let the minor premise express Brennan's beliefs about the facts regarding the death penalty; let the conclusion state that the death penalty is unconstitutional.)

3. Brennan rests much weight in his argument on the idea of "human dignity." In a sentence or two, state what you think human dignity consists of. How, if at all, does the death penalty violate that dignity?

4. What is Brennan's evidence for the claim that the death penalty system "is little more than a lottery system" (para. 14)? Write a 500-word essay on this topic: What, if anything, is morally wrong with a (hypothetical) death-penalty system deliberately based on a lottery in which the losers get sentenced to death and executed and the winners get sentenced to life in prison?

5. Statistics published by the FBI show that there are more than twenty-thousand criminal homicides annually in the 1990s, but far fewer arrests and convictions. Thus, many who are eligible for the death penalty in fact are never sentenced and executed. Does this mean that it is unfair to execute the relatively few who happen to be caught and convicted? Explain your reasoning.

6. Brennan denies that the death penalty is "necessary for the protection of society" (para. 22). How might he have replied to the following two objections? (1) It *is* necessary—for the purpose of retribution. (2) Even though it may not be necessary for public protection in a few states (Michigan abolished the death penalty in 1847, Wisconsin in 1853), it surely is necessary in many others (for instance, California, Florida, Texas).

Potter Stewart

After the Supreme Court decided Furman v. Georgia *in 1972 (p. 486, requiring states either to abolish the death penalty or revise their statutes to avoid the "arbitrariness" to which the Court objected in* Furman, *state legislatures reacted in one of two ways. A few states enacted mandatory death penalties, giving the trial court no alternative to a death sentence once the defendant was convicted. Most states, including Georgia, tightened up their procedures by imposing new requirements on the trial and appellate courts*

*in death penalty cases. In 1976 these new statutes were challenged, and in a
series of decisions the Court (by a 7 to 2 majority) settled two crucial questions. (1) The death penalty was not per se ("as such") in violation of the
Eighth Amendment (prohibiting "cruel and unusual punishments") and
the Fourteenth Amendment (guaranteeing "equal protection of the laws"),
and (2) several kinds of new death penalty statutes were constitutionally un-
objectionable. The most important of these cases was* Gregg v. Georgia; *we
reprint excerpts from the majority opinion by Associate Justice Potter Stewart
(1915–1985). (Justice Stewart had voted against the death penalty in* Furman, *but four years later he switched sides, evidently believing that his objections of 1972 were no longer relevant.)*

*In the following opinion, the citations referring to legal documents have
been omitted.*

Gregg v. Georgia

The Georgia statute, as amended after our decision in *Furman v. Georgia*, retains the death penalty for six categories of crime: murder, kidnapping for ransom or where the victim is harmed, armed robbery, rape,
treason, and aircraft hijacking. The capital defendant's guilt or innocence
is determined in the traditional manner, either by a trial judge or a jury,
in the first stage of a bifurcated trial. . . .

After a verdict, finding, or plea of guilty to a capital crime, a presen-
tence hearing is conducted before whoever made the determination of
guilt. The sentencing procedures are essentially the same in both bench
and jury trials. At the hearing:

> [T]he judge [or jury] shall hear additional evidence in extenuation, mit-
> igation, and aggravation of punishment, including the record of any
> prior criminal convictions and pleas of guilty or pleas of nolo con-
> tendere of the defendant, or the absence of any prior conviction and
> pleas: Provided, however, that only such evidence in aggravations as
> the State has made known to the defendant prior to his trial shall be ad-
> missible. The judge [or jury] shall also hear argument by the defendant
> or his counsel and the prosecuting attorney . . . regarding the punish-
> ment to be imposed.

The defendant is accorded substantial latitude as to the types of evidence
that he may introduce. Evidence considered during the guilt stage may
be considered during the sentencing stage without being resubmitted.

In the assessment of the appropriate sentence to be imposed the
judge is also required to consider or to include in his instructions to the
jury "any mitigating circumstances or aggravating circumstances otherwise authorized by law and any of [ten] statutory aggravating circumstances which may be supported by the evidence. . . ." The scope of the
nonstatutory aggravating or mitigating circumstances is not delineated in
the statute. Before a convicted defendant may be sentenced to death,
however, except in cases of treason or aircraft hijacking, the jury, or the
trial judge in cases tried without a jury, must find beyond a reasonable

doubt one of the ten aggravating circumstances specified in the statute.[1] The sentence of death may be imposed only if the jury (or judge) finds one of the statutory aggravating circumstances and then elects to impose that sentence. If the verdict is death the jury or judge must specify the aggravating circumstance(s) found. In jury cases, the trial judge is bound by the jury's recommended sentence.

In addition to the conventional appellate process available in all criminal cases, provision is made for special expedited direct review by the Supreme Court of Georgia of the appropriateness of imposing the sentence of death in the particular case. The court is directed to consider "the punishment as well as any errors enumerated by way of appeal," and to determine

1. whether the sentence of death was imposed under the influence of passion, prejudice, or any other arbitrary factor, and
2. whether, in cases other than treason or aircraft hijacking, the evidence supports the jury's or judge's finding of a statutory aggravating circumstance as enumerated in §27.2534.1 (b), and
3. whether the sentence of death is excessive or disproportionate to the penalty imposed in similar cases, considering both the crime and the defendant.

If the court affirms a death sentence, it is required to include in its decision reference to similar cases that it has taken into consideration.

. . . We now consider specifically whether the sentence of death for the crime of murder is a per se violation of the Eighth and Fourteenth Amendments to the Constitution. We note first that history and precedent strongly support a negative answer to this question.

The imposition of the death penalty for the crime of murder has a long history of acceptance both in the United States and in England. The common-law rule imposed a mandatory death sentence on all convicted murderers. And the penalty continued to be used into the twentieth century by most American states, although the breadth of the common-law rule was diminished, initially by narrowing the class of murders to be punished by death and subsequently by widespread adoption of laws expressly granting juries the discretion to recommend mercy.

It is apparent from the text of the Constitution itself that the existence of capital punishment was accepted by the Framers. At the time the Eighth Amendment was ratified, capital punishment was a common sanction in every state. Indeed, the First Congress of the United States enacted legislation providing death as the penalty for specified crimes. The Fifth Amendment, adopted at the same time as the Eighth, contemplated the continued existence of the capital sanction by imposing certain limits on the prosecution of capital cases:

No person shall be held to answer for a capital, or otherwise infamous crime, unless on a presentment or indictment of a Grand Jury . . . ; nor shall any person be subject for the same offense to be twice put in jeopardy of life or limb; . . . nor be deprived of life, liberty, or property, without due process of law. . . .

And the Fourteenth Amendment, adopted over three-quarters of a century later, similarly contemplates the existence of the capital sanction in providing that no state shall deprive any person of "life, liberty, or property" without due process of law.

Four years ago, the petitioners in *Furman* and its companion cases predicated their argument primarily upon the asserted proposition that standards of decency had evolved to the point where capital punishment no longer could be tolerated. The petitioners in those cases said, in effect, that the evolutionary process had come to an end, and that standards of decency required that the Eighth Amendment be construed finally as prohibiting capital punishment for any crime regardless of its depravity and impact on society. This view was accepted by two Justices. Three other Justices were unwilling to go so far; focusing on the procedures by which convicted defendants were selected for the death penalty rather than on the actual punishment inflicted, they joined in the conclusion that the statutes before the Court were constitutionally invalid.

The petitioners in the capital cases before the Court today renew the "standards of decency" argument, but developments during the four years since *Furman* have undercut substantially the assumptions upon which their argument rested. Despite the continuing debate, dating back to the nineteenth century, over the morality and utility of capital punishment, it is now evident that a large proportion of American society continues to regard it as an appropriate and necessary criminal sanction.

The most marked indication of society's endorsement of the death [10] penalty for murder is the legislative response to *Furman*. The legislatures of at least thirty-five states have enacted new statutes that provide for the death penalty for at least some crimes that result in the death of another person. And the Congress of the United States, in 1974, enacted a statute providing the death penalty for aircraft piracy that results in death. . . .

In the only statewide referendum occurring since *Furman* and brought to our attention, the people of California adopted a constitutional amendment that authorized capital punishment, in effect negating a prior ruling by the Supreme Court of California in *People v. Anderson*, that the death penalty violated the California Constitution.

The jury also is a significant and reliable objective index of contemporary values because it is so directly involved. . . .

It may be true that evolving standards have influenced juries in recent decades to be more discriminating in imposing the sentence of death. But the relative infrequency of jury verdicts imposing the death sentence does not indicate rejection of capital punishment per se. Rather, the reluctance of juries in many cases to impose the sentence may well reflect the humane feeling that this most irrevocable of sanctions should be reserved for a small number of extreme cases. Indeed, the actions of juries in many states since *Furman* are fully compatible with the legislative judgments, reflected in the new statutes, as to the continued utility and necessity of capital punishment in appropriate cases. At the close of 1974 at least 254 persons had been sentenced to death since *Furman*, and by the end of March 1976, more than 460 persons were subject to death sentences. . . .

The death penalty is said to serve two principal social purposes; retribution and deterrence of capital crimes by prospective offenders.

In part, capital punishment is an expression of society's moral outrage at particularly offensive conduct. This function may be unappealing to many, but it is essential in an ordered society that asks its citizens to rely on legal processes rather than self-help to vindicate their wrongs.

> The instinct for retribution is part of the nature of man, and channeling that instinct in the administration of criminal justice serves an important purpose in promoting the stability of a society governed by law. When people begin to believe that organized society is unwilling or unable to impose upon criminal offenders the punishment they "deserve," then there are sown the seeds of anarchy—of self-help, vigilante justice, and lynch law. *Furman v. Georgia* (Stewart, J., concurring).

"Retribution is no longer the dominant objective of the criminal law," *Williams v. New York*, but neither is it a forbidden objective nor one inconsistent with our respect for the dignity of men. . . . Indeed, the decision that capital punishment may be the appropriate sanction in extreme cases is an expression of the community's belief that certain crimes are themselves so grievous an affront to humanity that the only adequate response may be the penalty of death.[2]

Statistical attempts to evaluate the worth of the death penalty as a deterrent to crimes by potential offenders have occasioned a great deal of debate. The results simply have been inconclusive. As one opponent of capital punishment has said:

> [A]fter all possible inquiry, including the probing of all possible methods of inquiry, we do not know, and for systematic and easily visible reasons cannot know, what the truth about this "deterrent" effect may be. . . .
> The inescapable flaw is . . . that social conditions in any state are not constant through time, and that social conditions are not the same in any two states. If an effect were observed (and the observed effects, one way or another, are not large) then one could not at all tell whether any of this effect is attributable to the presence or absence of capital punishment. A "scientific"—that is to say, a soundly based—conclusion is simply impossible, and no methodological path out of this tangle suggests itself. C. Black, *Capital Punishment: The Inevitability of Caprice and Mistake* 25–26 (1974).

Although some of the studies suggest that the death penalty may not function as a significantly greater deterrent than lesser penalties, there is no convincing empirical evidence either supporting or refuting this view. We may nevertheless assume safely that there are murderers, such as those who act in passion, for whom the threat of death has little or no deterrent effect. But for many others, the death penalty undoubtedly is a significant deterrent. There are carefully contemplated murders, such as murder for hire, where the possible penalty of death may well enter into the cold calculus that precedes the decision to act.[3] And there are some categories of murder, such as murder by a life prisoner, where other sanctions may not be adequate. . . .

In sum, we cannot say that the judgment of the Georgia legislature that capital punishment may be necessary in some cases is clearly wrong. Considerations of federalism, as well as respect for the ability of a legislature to evaluate, in terms of its particular state, the moral consensus concerning the death penalty and its social utility as a sanction, require us to conclude, in the absence of more convincing evidence, that the infliction of death as a punishment for murder is not without justification and thus is not unconstitutionally severe.

Finally, we must consider whether the punishment of death is disproportionate in relation to the crime for which it is imposed. There is no question that death as a punishment is unique in its severity and irrevocability. But we are concerned here only with the imposition of capital punishment for the crime of murder, and when a life has been taken deliberately by the offender,[4] we cannot say that the punishment is invariably disproportionate to the crime. It is an extreme sanction, suitable to the most extreme of crimes.

We hold that the death penalty is not a form of punishment that may never be imposed, regardless of the circumstances of the offense, regardless of the character of the offender, and regardless of the procedure followed in reaching the decision to impose it. . . .   20

While some have suggested that standards to guide a capital jury's sentencing deliberations are impossible to formulate, the fact is that such standards have been developed. When the drafters of the Model Penal Code faced this problem, they concluded "that it is within the realm of possibility to point to the main circumstances of aggravation and of mitigation that should be weighed *and weighed against each other* when they are presented in a concrete case" (emphasis in original). While such standards are by necessity somewhat general, they do provide guidance to the sentencing authority and thereby reduce the likelihood that it will impose a sentence that fairly can be called capricious or arbitrary. Where the sentencing authority is required to specify the factors it relied upon in reaching its decision, the further safeguard of meaningful appellate review is available to ensure that death sentences are not imposed capriciously or in a freakish manner.

In summary, the concerns expressed in *Furman* that the penalty of death not be imposed in an arbitrary or capricious manner can be met by a carefully drafted statute that ensures that the sentencing authority is given adequate information and guidance. As a general proposition these concerns are best met by a system that provides for a bifurcated proceeding at which the sentencing authority is apprised of the information relevant to the imposition of sentence and provided with standards to guide its use of the information.

For the reasons expressed in this opinion, we hold that the statutory system under which Gregg was sentenced to death does not violate the Constitution. Accordingly, the judgment of the Georgia Supreme Court is affirmed.

NOTES

1. The statute provides in part:
   (a) The death penalty may be imposed for the offenses of aircraft hijacking or treason, in any case.
   (b) In all cases of other offenses for which the death penalty may be authorized, the judge shall consider, or he shall include in his instructions to the jury for it to consider, any mitigating circumstances or aggravating circumstances otherwise authorized by law and any of the following statutory aggravating circumstances which may be supported by the evidence:
      (1) The offense of murder, rape, armed robbery, or kidnapping was committed by a person with a prior record of conviction for a capital felony, or the offense of murder was committed by a person who has a substantial history of serious assaultive criminal convictions.
      (2) The offense of murder, rape, armed robbery, or kidnapping was committed while the offender was engaged in the commission of another capital felony, or aggravated battery, or the offense of murder was committed while the offender was engaged in the commission of burglary or arson in the first degree.
      (3) The offender by his act of murder, armed robbery, or kidnapping knowingly created a great risk of death to more than one person in a public place by means of a weapon or device which would normally be hazardous to the lives of more than one person.
      (4) The offender committed the offense of murder for himself or another, for the purpose of receiving money or any other thing of monetary value.
      (5) The murder of a judicial officer, former judicial officer, district attorney or solicitor or former district attorney or solicitor during or because of the exercise of his official duty.
      (6) The offender caused or directed another to commit murder or committed murder as an agent or employee of another person.
      (7) The offense of murder, rape, armed robbery, or kidnapping was outrageously or wantonly vile, horrible or inhuman in that it involved torture, depravity of mind, or an aggravated battery to the victim.
      (8) The offense of murder was committed against any peace officer, corrections employee or fireman while engaged in the performance of his official duties.

(9) The offense of murder was committed by a person in, or who has escaped from, the lawful custody of a peace officer or place of lawful confinement.

(10) The murder was committed for the purpose of avoiding, interfering with, or preventing a lawful arrest or custody in a place of lawful confinement, of himself or another.

(c) The statutory instructions as determined by the trial judge to be warranted by the evidence shall be given in charge and in writing to the jury for its deliberation. The jury, if its verdict be a recommendation of death, shall designate in writing, signed by the foreman of the jury, the aggravating circumstance or circumstances which it found beyond a reasonable doubt. In non-jury cases the judge shall make such designation. Except in cases of treason or aircraft hijacking, unless at least one of the statutory aggravating circumstances enumerated is so found, the death penalty shall not be imposed.

The Supreme Court of Georgia recently held unconstitutional the portion of the first circumstance encompassing persons who have a "substantial history of serious assaultive criminal convictions" because it did not set "sufficiently 'clear and objective standards.'"

2. Lord Justice Denning, Master of the Rolls of the Court of Appeal in England, spoke to this effect before the British Royal Commission on Capital Punishment:

> Punishment is the way in which society expresses its denunciation of wrong doing: and, in order to maintain respect for law, it is essential that the punishment inflicted for grave crimes should adequately reflect the revulsion felt by the great majority of citizens for them. It is a mistake to consider the objects of punishment as being deterrent or reformative or preventive and nothing else. . . . The truth is that some crimes are so outrageous that society insists on adequate punishment, because the wrong-doer deserves it, irrespective of whether it is a deterrent or not.

A contemporary writer has noted more recently that opposition to capital punishment "has much more appeal when the discussion is merely academic than when the community is confronted with a crime, or a series of crimes, so gross, so heinous, so cold-blooded that anything short of death seems an inadequate response." Raspberry, Death Sentence, *Washington Post*, Mar. 12, 1976, p. A27, cols. 5–6.

3. Other types of calculated murders, apparently occurring with increasing frequency, include the use of bombs or other means of indiscriminate killings, the extortion murder of hostages or kidnap victims, and the execution-style killing of witnesses to a crime.

4. We do not address here the question whether the taking of the criminal's life is a proportionate sanction where no victim has been deprived of life—for example, when capital punishment is imposed for rape, kidnapping, or armed robbery that does not result in the death of any human being.

Topics for Critical Thinking and Writing

1. What features of Georgia's new death penalty statute does Justice Stewart point to in arguing that the new statute will prevent the problems found in the old statute?

2. Reread Stewart's opinion carefully, keeping in mind the four principles Justice Brennan announced in *Furman* (p. 486). Precisely where do Brennan and Stewart disagree? Is it over Brennan's four principles? Over the facts about the death penalty as a deterrent or protection for society? Both? Or something else entirely? Write a 750-word essay on the topic "The Disagreement between Justices Stewart and Brennan on the Constitutionality of the Death Penalty."

3. Since the new Georgia statute upheld by the Supreme Court in its *Gregg* decision does nothing to affect the discretion the prosecutor has in deciding whether to seek the death penalty in a murder case, and nothing to affect the complete discretion the governor has in deciding whether to extend clemency, can it be argued that despite the new death penalty statutes like Georgia's, the problems that gave rise to the decision in *Furman* will probably reappear?

4. How important do you think public opinion is in determining what the Bill of Rights means? Does it matter to the meaning of "cruel and unusual punishment" that most Americans profess to favor the death penalty? (Think of parallel cases: Does it matter to the meaning of "due process of law," "the right to bear arms," "an impartial jury"—all protected in the Bill of Rights—what a majority of the public thinks?)

5. In 1976, when the Supreme Court decided *Gregg*, it also decided *Woodson v. North Carolina*; in that case the Court held unconstitutional under the Eighth and Fourteenth Amendments a *mandatory* death penalty for anyone convicted of first-degree murder. Do you think North Carolina's statute was a reasonable response to objections to the death penalty at the time of *Furman* based on the alleged arbitrary and discriminatory administration of that penalty? Why, or why not?

6. Stewart mentions the kinds of murder where he thinks the death penalty might be a better deterrent than life imprisonment. What are they? What reasons might be given for or against agreeing with him?

7. A year after *Gregg* was decided, the Supreme Court ruled in *Coker v. Georgia* that the death penalty for rape was unconstitutional under the Eighth and Fourteenth Amendments. Do you think that Stewart's opinion in *Gregg* silently implies that *only* murder is punishable by death? (What about a death penalty for treason? Espionage? Kidnapping for ransom? Large-scale illegal drug trafficking?) In an essay of 500 words, argue either for or against that conclusion.

Ernest van den Haag

Ernest van den Haag (b. 1914) is a professor (retired) of jurisprudence at Fordham University Law School. He is the author of several books, including Punishing Criminals *(1975). His essay here is excerpted from* The Death Penalty Pro and Con: A Debate *(1983).*

The Deterrent Effect of the Death Penalty

Crime is going to be with us as long as there is any social order articulated by laws. There is no point making laws that prohibit some action or other (e.g., murder or theft) unless there is some temptation to commit it. And however harsh the threats of the law, they will not restrain some people, whether because they discount the risk of punishment or because they are exposed to extraordinary temptation. They may hope for an immense profit; or be passionately angry or vindictive; or be in such misery that they feel they have nothing to lose. Thus, I repeat, the problem every society must attempt to solve (in part by means of punishment) is not eliminating crime but controlling it.

That threats will not deter everybody all the time must be expected. And it must also be expected that persons committed to criminal activity—career criminals—are not likely to be restrained by threats; nor are persons strongly under the influence of drugs or intoxicated by their own passions. However, if threats are not likely to deter habitual offenders, they are likely to help deter people from *becoming* habitual offenders.

People are not deterred by exactly calculating the size of the threat and the actual risk of suffering punishment against the likely benefit of the crime they consider committing. Few people calculate at all. Rather, the effect of threats is to lead most people to ignore criminal opportunities most of the time. One just does not consider them—any more than the ordinary person sitting down for lunch starts calculating whether he could have Beluga caviar and champagne instead of his usual hamburger and beer. He is not accustomed to caviar, and one reason he is not accustomed to it is that it costs too much. He does not have to calculate every time to know as much. Similarly, he is not accustomed to breaking the law, and one reason is that it costs too much. He does not need to calculate.

It is quite a different matter if one asks, not: "Do threats deter?" but rather: "How much does one threat deter compared to another?" Does the more severe threat deter significantly more? Does the added deterrence warrant the added severity? Thus, no one pondering the death penalty will contend that it does not deter. The question is: Does it deter more than alternative penalties proposed, such as life imprisonment or any lengthy term of imprisonment?

In the past many attempts were made to determine whether the $\quad$ 5 death penalty deters the crimes for which it was threatened—capital crimes—more than other penalties, usually life imprisonment, mitigated by parole (and amounting therefore to something like ten years in prison in most cases). Most of these attempts led to ambiguous results, often rendered more ambiguous by faulty procedures and research methods. Frequently, contiguous states—one with and the other without the death penalty—were compared. Or states were compared before and after abolition. Usually these comparisons were based on the legal avail ability or unavailability of the death penalty rather than on the presence or absence of executions and on their frequency. But what matters is whether the death penalty is practiced, not whether theoretically it is available. Finally, nobody would assert that the death penalty—or any crime-control measure—is the only determinant of the frequency of the crime. The number of murders certainly depends as well on the proportion of young males in the population, on income distribution, on education, on the proportion of various races in the population, on local cultural traditions, on the legal definition of murder, and on other such factors.

Comparisons must take all of these matters into account if they are to evaluate the effect threatened penalties may have in deterring crimes. In contiguous states, influential factors other than the death penalty may differ; they may even differ in the same state before and after abolition. Hence, differences (or equalities) in capital crime frequencies cannot simply be ascribed to the presence or absence of the death penalty. Moreover, one does not know how soon a change in penalties will make a difference, if it ever does, or whether prospective murderers will know that the death penalty has been abolished in Maine and kept in Vermont. They certainly will know whether or not there is a death penalty in the United States. But in contiguous states? Or within a short time after abolition or reinstatement?

Theoretically, experiments to avoid all these difficulties are possible. But they face formidable obstacles in practice. If, for instance, the death penalty were threatened for murders committed on Monday, Wednesday, and Friday, and life imprisonment for murders committed on Tuesday, Thursday, and Saturday, we would soon see which days murderers prefer, i.e., how much the death penalty deters on Monday, Wednesday, and Friday over and above life imprisonment threatened for murders committed on the other days. If we find no difference, the abolitionist thesis that the death penalty adds no deterrence over and above the threat of life imprisonment would be confirmed.

In the absence of such experiments, none of the available studies seems conclusive. Recently such studies have acquired considerable mathematical sophistication, and some of the more sophisticated studies have concluded, contrary to what used to be accepted scholarly opinion, that the death penalty can be shown to deter over and above life imprisonment. Thus, Isaac Ehrlich, in a study published in the *American Economic Review* (June 1975), concluded that, over the period 1933–69, "an additional execution per year . . . may have resulted on the average in seven or eight fewer murders."

Other studies published since Ehrlich's contend that his results are due to the techniques and periods he selected, and that different techniques and periods yield different results. Despite a great deal of research on all sides, one cannot say that the statistical evidence is conclusive. Nobody has claimed to have *disproved* that the death penalty may deter more than life imprisonment. But one cannot claim, either, that it has been proved statistically in a conclusive manner that the death penalty does deter more than alternative penalties. This lack of proof does not amount to disproof. However, abolitionists insist that there ought to be proof positive.

Unfortunately, there is little proof of the sort sought by those who 10 oppose the death penalty, for the deterrent effect of any sort of punishment. Nobody has statistically shown that four years in prison deter more than two, or twenty more than ten. We assume as much. But I know of no statistical proof. One may wonder why such proof is demanded for the death penalty but not for any other. To be sure, death is more serious a punishment than any other. But ten years in prison are not exactly trivial either. . . .

If it is difficult, perhaps impossible, to prove statistically—and just as hard to disprove—that the death penalty deters more from capital crimes than available alternative punishments do (such as life imprisonment), why do so many people believe so firmly that the death penalty is a more effective deterrent?

Some are persuaded by irrelevant arguments. They insist that the death penalty at least makes sure that the person who suffered it will not commit other crimes. True. Yet this confuses incapacitation with a specific way to bring it about: death. Death is the surest way to bring about the most total incapacitation, and it is irrevocable. But does incapacitation need to be that total? And is irrevocability necessarily an advantage? Obviously it makes correcting mistakes and rehabilitation impossible. What is the advantage of execution, then, over alternative ways of achieving the desired incapacitation?

More important, the argument for incapacitation confuses the elimination of one murderer (or of any number of murderers) with a reduction in the homicide rate. But the elimination of any specific number of actual or even of potential murderers—and there is some doubt that the actual murderers of the past are the most likely future (potential) murderers—will not affect the homicide rate, except through deterrence. There are enough potential murderers around to replace all those incapacitated. Deterrence may prevent the potential from becoming actual murderers. But incapacitation of some or all actual murderers is not likely to have much effect by itself. Let us then return to the question: Does capital punishment deter more than life imprisonment?

Science, logic, or statistics often have been unable to prove what common sense tells us to be true. Thus, the Greek philosopher Zeno some two thousand years ago found that he could not show that motion is possible; indeed, his famous paradoxes appear to show that motion is impossible. Though nobody believed them to be true, nobody succeeded in showing the fallacy of these paradoxes until the rise of mathematical logic less than a hundred years ago. But meanwhile, the world did not stand still. Indeed, nobody argued that motion should stop because it had not been shown to be logically possible. There is no more reason to abolish the death penalty than there was to abolish motion simply because the death penalty has not been, and perhaps cannot be, shown statistically to be a deterrent over and above other penalties. Indeed, there are two quite satisfactory, if nonstatistical, indications of the marginal deterrent effect of the death penalty.

In the first place, our experience shows that the greater the threatened penalty, the more it deters. Ceteris paribus, the threat of fifty lashes, deters more than the threat of five; a $1,000 fine deters more than a $10 fine; ten years in prison deter more than one year in prison—just as, conversely, the promise of a $1,000 reward is a greater incentive than the promise of a $10 reward, etc. There may be diminishing returns. Once a reward exceeds, say, $1 million, the additional attraction may diminish. Once a punishment exceeds, say, ten years in prison (net of parole), there may be little additional deterrence in threatening additional years. We know hardly anything about diminishing returns of penalties. It would still seem likely, however, that the threat of life in prison deters more than any other term of imprisonment.

The threat of death may deter still more. For it is a mistake to regard the death penalty as though it were of the same kind as other penalties. If it is not, then diminishing returns are unlikely to apply. And death differs significantly, in kind, from any other penalty. Life in prison is still life, however unpleasant. In contrast, the death penalty does not just threaten to make life unpleasant—it threatens to take life altogether. This difference is perceived by those affected. We find that when they have the choice between life in prison and execution, 99 percent of all prisoners under sentence of death prefer life in prison. By means of appeals, pleas for commutation, indeed by all means at their disposal, they indicate that they prefer life in prison to execution.

From this unquestioned fact a reasonable conclusion can be drawn in favor of the superior deterrent effect of the death penalty. Those who have the choice in practice, those whose choice has actual and immediate effects on their life and death, fear death more than they fear life in prison or any other available penalty. If they do, it follows that the threat of the death penalty, all other things equal, is likely to deter more than the threat of life in prison. One is most deterred by what one fears most. From which it follows that whatever statistics fail, or do not fail, to show, the death penalty is likely to be more deterrent than any other.

Suppose now one is not fully convinced of the superior deterrent effect of the death penalty. I believe I can show that even if one is genuinely uncertain as to whether the death penalty adds to deterrence, one should still favor it, from a purely deterrent viewpoint. For if we are not sure, we must choose either to (1) trade the certain death, by execution, of a convicted murderer for the probable survival of an indefinite number of murder victims whose future murder is less likely (whose survival is more likely)—if the convicted murderer's execution deters prospective murderers, as it might, or to (2) trade the certain survival of the convicted murderer for the probable loss of the lives of future murder victims more likely to be murdered because the convicted murderer's nonexecution might not deter prospective murderers, who could have been deterred by executing the convicted murderer.

To restate the matter: If we were quite ignorant about the marginal deterrent effects of execution, we would have to choose—like it or not—between the certainty of the convicted murderer's death by execution and the likelihood of the survival of future victims of other murderers on the one hand, and on the other his certain survival and the likelihood of the death of new victims. I'd rather execute a man convicted of having murdered others than to put the lives of innocents at risk. I find it hard to understand the opposite choice.

Topics for Critical Thinking and Writing

1. Van den Haag mentions (para. 5) several factors relevant to the volume of murder. Easy availability of handguns (not to mention automatic rifles) is not one of them. Read the essays by J. Warren Cassidy (p. 418) and Nan Desuka (p. 421) and explain in 100 words whether you think effective gun control would reduce the volume of murder in the United States.

2. Van den Haag proposes (para. 7) an ideal but impractical experiment that he thinks would settle the question whether the death penalty deters. Modifying his example, suppose there was conclusive evidence that the police were ineffective in catching murderers who commit their crimes on Mondays, Wednesdays, and Fridays but were effective in arresting those who murder on Tuesdays, Thursdays, and Saturdays. If you planned to murder someone, which day(s) of the week would you choose for the crime, and why?

3. Van den Haag distinguishes (para. 13) between the death penalty as a *deterrent* and as *incapacitative,* and argues that in the latter role the death penalty cannot reduce the crime rate. What is his argument, and do you agree?

4. Van den Haag defends the death penalty as a deterrent, not because of strong evidence but by appeal to "common sense" (para. 14). How reliable are appeals to common sense, anyway? Suppose someone defended the proposition that the sun moves around the earth, and not the earth around the sun, because it's obvious, common sense, as anyone can see. Why should we reject this appeal to common sense (if we should) and accept van den Haag's (if we should)?

5. Van den Haag implies (paras. 16–17) that because death row prisoners prefer to have their sentences commuted to life in prison, the threat of death in general may be a better deterrent than the threat of even a long prison sentence. Lay out this argument, step by step, and explain

whether you think it is sound. On what assumptions does it rest? Are they vulnerable to criticism?

6. Van den Haag's final argument (para. 18) appears to assume that the convicted murderer whose execution is in question is really guilty. But suppose he's not, or that the evidence against him is not really conclusive. Do you think this affects the force of van den Haag's argument? Why, or why not?

Vivian Berger

Vivian Berger (b. 1944), a professor of law at Columbia University in New York, is a founding member of the New York Lawyers against the Death Penalty. She wrote this article for the October 1988 issue of the New York State Bar Journal. *Footnotes, chiefly legal citations, have been omitted.*

Rolling the Dice to Decide Who Dies

Since 1984, when the Court of Appeals held unconstitutional the last vestige of the death penalty in New York State, New York has been one of fewer than a third of the states in this country that do not provide for capital punishment. In each of the past few years, however, our legislature has passed bills reauthorizing death as the sanction for certain types of murder. Governor Cuomo, a committed opponent of capital punishment as was Governor Carey before him, has consistently vetoed these efforts. But sooner or later the governor will relinquish office. Surely, therefore, a time will come when the state acquires as chief executive someone who either supports execution or declines to counter the lawmakers' wishes. Then New Yorkers, acting through their elected officials, will have to regard the death penalty as more than a mere symbolic gesture—a banner to wave in the war against crime.

Because that point may be in the offing, the New York Bar, whose collective opinion should weigh heavily in the final decision whether we remain an abolitionist state, must begin to think seriously about the issues. I, like our governor, fervently oppose capital punishment; and I do so based on considerable experience with how it operates, not just with the rhetoric that surrounds it. I hope to persuade those of you who have no opinion on the subject and perhaps even some who currently favor reviving the death sentence in New York that such a course has nothing to commend it. To the contrary, reinstatement would amount to a giant step backward in this state's historical march toward a decent and efficient system of justice.

To plunge yourself right into the reality of capital punishment, imagine that you are sitting on a jury in Georgia or Florida or some other death-penalty state in the following cases. Your awesome task is to determine whether the defendant should receive life imprisonment or death. Even if you could in fact never sentence a person to die, you must try to envision that possibility—for the prosecution would have struck you for cause unless you had indicated on voir-dire that you would consider the option of death. Here are the five cases in cameo:

1. A nineteen-year-old man, John, and his companion stole a young woman's purse on the street, pushed her to the ground, and jumped into their nearby car. A taxi driver, observing the theft, sought to block their getaway with his cab. The defendant, John, shot and killed him. It was his first violent offense.

2. A nineteen-year-old man, Joe, tried to grab the purse of a fifty-four-year-old woman in a shopping center parking lot. She resisted and began screaming. They struggled for the purse and Joe shot her once in the side, killing her. He had prior misdemeanor convictions for shoplifting and simple battery as well as a felony conviction for theft.

3. A twenty-one-year-old man, Robert, drove up to an all-night self-service station and filled his tank. He was paying for the gas with a "hot" credit card when the attendant, a college student, became suspicious that the card was stolen. Robert then shot the attendant once, killing him instantly, in order to avoid being arrested for the credit-card theft. Robert had previous convictions for an unarmed juvenile robbery and the burglary of a store.

4. A twenty-year-old man, Nickie, who was under the influence of drugs, broke into a neighbor's apartment and bludgeoned her and her eight-year-old daughter to death with a hammer. He said later that he had done it because he liked to see blood. Nickie had past convictions for robbery and attempted aggravated rape.

5. A twenty-six-year-old man, Stephen, together with a seventeen-year-old friend, burglarized the home of an elderly widow for whom the friend had done yard work. They were planning to rob her. The woman ended by being raped, beaten, and strangled as well as robbed. The defendant, Stephen, admitted that the two of them had raped and robbed her. He insisted, however (and no witness supported or contradicted his story) that only the friend had killed the victim and that he, Stephen, had tried in vain to stop the murder. He had previously committed an unarmed "date rape."

Ask yourself which, if any, of these men you would have sentenced to life in prison and which to death. Next, try to guess how the actual jurors decided these cases. In fact, #1, John, the purse-snatcher who shot the cabbie, received life. #2, Joe, the other purse-snatcher who shot the fifty-four-year-old woman, was sentenced to die. #3, Robert, the credit-card thief who shot the attendant at the gas service station, got death as well; he is one of my clients. #4, Nickie, the hammer-bludgeoner who liked to see blood, got life imprisonment. Finally, #5, Stephen, who robbed and raped and may (or may not) have strangled the widow, was sentenced to death; he is also my client.

Whether or not you called any of the cases correctly, you might want to ask yourself: "Did the divergent results make sense?" If there was a pattern, I must say it eludes me. But for the moment, taking some liberties with the facts and treating my examples as hypothetical instead of the true accounts which they are, I want the reader to consider the possibility that jurors in a couple of the cases that ended in death might likelier have opted for life imprisonment if they had received some more information. For example, suppose the sentencing jurors had heard that Joe had been the incredibly abused child of a violent alcoholic father and a battered, helpless, incompetent mother? That the father had made a game of placing Joe and his siblings in a tight circle and throwing heavy objects like glass ashtrays into the air for the pleasure of seeing who would be hit? That Joe had at last run away from home at the age of twelve, camped for some months in a Dempsey dumpster, and then been taken in by a man who sheltered him in return for homosexual favors? That during his one, too-brief experience in foster care when he was nine, Joe responded with great affection and excellent behavior to the love and attention of his foster mother? Or, to take another example, suppose the jury had known that Stephen had an IQ in the high fifties or low sixties? That confronted once with a power mower that wasn't running, Stephen put water from a hose inside it because he had seen others fill the machine but never realized that not *any* type of liquid would do?

Of course, no one knows how real jurors would have reacted to the scenarios I described. But experts in capital defense work agree that no matter how appalling the crime, twelve not unduly sentimental jurors may well decide to spare a defendant when shown that he is a human being with some explanation if not excuse for his horrible acts. Yet while the jurors routinely hear the worst things about the defendant, including usually his criminal record, what is shocking is that in so many cases they hear *nothing* else about him that might be deemed relevant to sentence. (Why this occurs, and what it means for the operation of capital punishment, I will explore further shortly.) What they *do* necessarily learn is the race of both defendant and victim. If I had recounted some more examples of the type I asked you to judge as a juror and told you the race of the persons involved, or at least the victim's, you might have begun to detect a pattern that did not emerge from the *pertinent* data. To this topic, too, I will soon return. But what I hope I have done thus far is to give the reader a "slice of death." At the very least, by relating these sadly prosaic stories, I wanted to scotch the notion which so many people have that death is reserved for special cases: the serial killers, the depraved torturers, the Mafia hit men. In New York we deal with the Joes and Stephens each week by the hundreds.

A bit of history sheds some light on how Capital Punishment U.S.A. acquired its present salient features. The watershed came when the

United States Supreme Court handed down the landmark *Furman v. Georgia* [decision] in 1972. *Furman* invalidated all existing death sentence statutes as violative of the Eighth Amendment's ban on cruel and unusual punishment and thus depopulated state death rows of their 629 occupants. Although there was no majority opinion and only Justices Brennan and Marshall would have held execution to be intrinsically cruel and unusual, Justice Stewart captured the essence of the centrist justices' view—that the death penalty *as actually applied* was unconstitutionally arbitrary—in his famous analogy between the imposition of a capital sentence and the freakishness of a strike of lightning. Being "struck" by a capital sentence was cruel and unusual in the same way as being hit by a lightning bolt: The event was utterly capricious and random.

But worse, if possible, than death sentences that are entirely arbitrary in the sense that a strike of lightning is freakish are those imposed on invidious grounds: where the lightning rod is race, religion, gender, or class. As Justice Douglas trenchantly remarked: "The Leopolds and Loebs are given prison terms, not sentenced to death." Blacks, however, were disproportionately sentenced to die, especially for the rape of white females. Indeed, the abolitionist campaign, which culminated in the *Furman* decision, had its genesis in the effort to eliminate capital punishment for rape. So perhaps, historically, the death penalty was really less "unusual" than "cruel": An invisible hand, and clearly a white one, was sorting out whites from blacks and thereby creating a pattern of results that many decent people abhorred.

Probably the justices hoped and believed that after *Furman* the death penalty in the United States would remain dead; if so, they were wrong. Many legislatures simply determined to try until they got it right. And in 1976, in *Gregg v. Georgia* and its four companion cases, a majority of the Court upheld the post-*Furman* capital punishment statutes of Georgia, Florida, and Texas against a challenge to their facial validity, while simultaneously nullifying the revised laws of two other states. Those states had sought to resolve the randomness problem identified in *Furman* by ensuring that lightning would strike *all* persons convicted of murder in the first degree, rather than just a hapless few. In rejecting this tack, the Court noted that mandatory death sentence laws did not really resolve the problem but instead "simply papered [it] over" since juries responded by refusing to convict certain arbitrarily chosen defendants of first-degree murder.

More importantly, though, the justices ratified the so-called guided discretion statutes at issue in three of the five cases. The Court specifically approved some features of the new statutes which it expected would reduce the capriciousness of capital punishment and at the same time further the goal of individualization in sentencing. Thus, to take Georgia's law as a sample, the *Gregg* majority endorsed its provision for separate trials on guilt and penalty and automatic appellate review of sentences of death. The bifurcated trial innovation permitted the admission of evidence relevant only to sentence (for instance, the defendant's prior convictions) in a way that would not prejudice the jury in deciding guilt or innocence. The Court also emphasized that, at the penalty trial, not only did the state have to prove some aggravating circumstances beyond the fact of the murder itself (for example, torture or a previous record of criminal violence) but also defendants had the opportunity to offer evidence in mitigation—brave-conduct medals, or thrown ashtrays and waterlogged mowers.

It is basically under these post-*Gregg* schemes that Capital Punishment U.S.A. has been operating for over a decade. Until recently, however, only a handful of executions occurred every year. But in the mid-1980s, in the wake of four adverse Supreme Court decisions—after a period in which the Court had overturned the capital sentence in fourteen out of fifteen cases, the engine of death acquired new steam. In 1984 alone, there were twenty-one executions (almost twice as many as in all of the years following *Gregg*); 1985 and 1986 saw eighteen apiece, and the body count continues to grow. Thus, *Furman II* is hardly on the horizon now. That being so, if our next governor permits the enactment of capital statutes, the Court will surely not "veto" them: Members of the Bar should understand that New York will have not dead-letter laws but dying defendants.

Why should New Yorkers oppose this result? Some believe that capital punishment inherently violates human dignity. But because many disagree with that view and my expertise is only lawyering, not moral philosophy, I leave it to others to debate the ultimate ethical issues. I take my stand with an eminent colleague, Professor Charles L. Black, Jr. Like me, refusing to resolve the basic clash of values, he reminds us wisely that there is "no abstract capital punishment." Asked how he would feel about the death penalty if only its administration were perfected, the professor replies: "What would you do if an amoeba were taught to play the piano?" In other words, it's a silly question; capital punishment *is* as it *does*. Therefore, the often high-flown rhetoric bandied about by the pros and antis assumes, in my view, second place to the homely facts that make the American "legal system not good enough to choose people to die." I end with a few of the reasons why, which I hope that those who support or are open to reviving the death sentence in New York take deeply to heart.

Consider, first, the arbitrariness of the death penalty—how, in the real world, capital punishment must be forever married to caprice. From the initial decision to charge through the determination of sentence, the criminal justice system in general is rife with unreviewable discretion. The capital setting provides all of the same opportunities (and several more) for virtually unconstrained choice: The players roll the dice in a game where the stakes consist of life or death. Nonexhaustively, the prosecutor must decide such things as whether to charge capital murder instead a lesser degree of homicide; whether to plea bargain with the accused or, in a multidefendant case, whether to grant one of the defendants immunity or some other concession in return for cooperating with the state; and whether, if the defendant is convicted of a potentially capital charge, to move the case to the penalty phase and attempt to obtain a verdict of death. Many of those choices and especially the likelihood of plea bargaining will be dramatically affected by factors that have little or nothing to do with the nature of the crime or the strength of the evidence. These factors include geography (district attorneys have different policies on capital punishment, not to speak of varying amounts of dollars to spend on costly capital litigation); political concerns like the proximity of an election; the perceived acumen and aggressiveness of defense counsel; and the desires of the victim's family.

Other players than the prosecutor occupy key roles, too, of course. These include the judge and jury and, depending on local practice, the governor, administrative board, or both, who may be requested to grant clemency. Jurors, it is worth noting, not only possess the completely unreviewable discretion to acquit or compromise on lesser charges; they are also asked, in penalty trials, to determine such intrinsically fuzzy questions as "Will the defendant kill again?" or "Was this murder especially heinous, atrocious, or cruel?" or "Do the aggravating circumstances outweigh the proof in mitigation?" The latter inquiry forces jurors to try to assess how, for instance, the fact that the murder occurred during the course of a robbery and was committed to eliminate a witness should be balanced against the facts that the defendant was high on crack, is a first offender, and has a wife and three children who love him. Could *you* meaningfully weigh such factors?

Consider, second, that these sources of arbitrariness are exacerbated [20] by extreme variations in the performance of defense counsel. Ineffective assistance of counsel completely permeates the penalty phase of capital trials in the post-*Gregg* era. With regard to cases like Stephen's and Joe's and the others with which I began this piece, I pointed out how often the jury hears nothing personal about the defendant even when substantial mitigating proof is readily available, yet I did not explain this phenomenon. The explanation is simply that many defense attorneys do little or nothing by way of investigation geared to sentencing issues and hence do not themselves learn what they should be spreading before the jury. Why do attorneys drop the ball at the penalty phase with such depressing regularity? Some lack the knowledge, experience, or will to assume the role demanded of them in the unique capital setting. Lawyers find it easier to hunt for what one whom I know called "eyeball witnesses" than to construct a psychodrama about a protagonist who is frequently hostile, uncommunicative, beset with mental or emotional problems, or all of the above—especially when to do so involves searching out potential witnesses (family, friends, neighbors, teachers) who, like the client, usually hail from a different racial or socioeconomic milieu from counsel. Others curtail their investigations on account of shockingly low compensation. Still others "throw in the towel" once the verdict of guilt is in. Whatever the causes of these derelictions, most or all can be expected both to cross jurisdictional lines and to continue into the future.

Consider, finally, the last but hardly the least point in my brief against the death penalty—racial discrimination in sentencing. In its modern guise, racial bias focuses primarily on the race of the *victim*, not the defendant. Sophisticated studies by social scientists have demonstrated that murderers of whites are much likelier to be sentenced to death than murderers of blacks. In Georgia, for instance, Professor David Baldus's prizewinning study revealed that, after one accounted for dozens of variables that might legitimately affect punishment, the killer of a white stood a *4.3 times* greater chance of receiving death than did a person who killed a black! The reason for these results is clear and as firmly rooted in our history as prejudice against the black defendant: White society places a premium upon white life. New Yorkers inclined to discount such division on grounds of race as a regional Southern phenomenon need only recall the tensions evoked by the Howard Beach and Goetz trials to see how very wrong they are. In any event, capital punishment only magnifies inequalities of race that persist in the criminal justice system and in American society generally.

Last term, the Supreme Court rejected a challenge, grounded on the damning Baldus statistics, to the death penalty as applied in Georgia. Assuming the validity of the study, the court nonetheless held 5–4 in *McCleskey v. Kemp* that unless a capital defendant could prove that some specific actor or actors purposely discriminated in his case, thereby causing his sentence of death, neither the Eighth Amendment nor Equal Protection was offended. I hope, however, that New Yorkers will be offended by, and wary of, the prospect of even risking racially tainted sentencing where a person's life is at stake.

There is no good reason to take that risk. The death penalty has not been shown to deter murder. Administering it with even the minimum amount of decency will further increase the logjams in our crowded courts and will likely cost more in the end than the alternative of long-term imprisonment. At worst, some innocent men and women will be executed as time goes by. At best, the guilty we choose to kill will be morally indistinguishable from the rest whose lives we opt to spare. New York cannot—in any sense of the word—afford to resurrect such a bankrupt system. Thoughtful citizens should be proud that our last two governors have resisted the siren call of capital "justice." The Bar, therefore, should strongly support the principled and pragmatic stance of opposition to capital punishment.

Topics for Critical Thinking and Writing

1. Write a 100-word essay on the question whether a state governor should veto a death penalty law if he or she is personally opposed to capital punishment.

2. During the presidential campaign of 1988, the death penalty was frequently mentioned by then Vice President Bush, who was for it, and by his opponent, Governor Michael Dukakis of Massachusetts, who was against it. Do some research on the campaign and write a 100-word essay on the question whether the pro–capital punishment position of the Republicans was largely what Berger calls "a mere symbolic gesture" (para. 1).

3. Relying only on the information Berger gives in paragraphs 4–8 about those five cases, decide how you would sentence each defendant; then compare your results with those that actually occurred (para. 9). Write a 500-word essay defending your proposed sentences whether or not they agree with those the juries actually handed down.

4. Take into account the additional information Berger supplies in paragraph 10 about the five cases she discusses, and write a 250-word essay explaining why this additional evidence would or would not cause you to change your proposed sentences.

5. Defenders of the death penalty often arouse support for capital punishment by describing murderers as "savage beasts" or as "hopeless recidivists" and the like, whereas Berger (para. 11) arouses opposition to it by telling the reader "sadly prosaic stories" about "the Joes and the Stephens." To what extent do you think such techniques shed light on the morality of the death penalty? On the appropriate legal punishment for the crime of murder?

6. Berger quotes (para. 13) Justice Douglas's reference to Leopold and Loeb. Who were they, and why are their cases relevant to the death penalty controversy? Do some library research to find out, and write a 500-word essay on the lessons of the Leopold and Loeb case. (*Hint:* The case occurred in Chicago in the 1920s, and involved the famous defense attorney Clarence Darrow.)

7. In response to Berger's point about the "arbitrariness" of the death-penalty system (paras. 18–19), a death penalty advocate might reply: Since all murderers really deserve to die anyway, why make so much out of the arbitrary way in which only some are actually sentenced to death and executed? What's so unfair about the good luck of all those who aren't executed even though they deserve to die? How might Berger reply?

8. In response to Berger's point about the "racial discrimination" in sentencing (para. 21), a defender of the death penalty might object: The solution to the problem of racial discrimination in death sentencing is not abolishing the death penalty; it is sentencing and executing more whites who kill blacks and more blacks who kill blacks. How might Berger reply?

20

Drugs: Should Their Sale and Use Be Legalized?

William J. Bennett

William Bennett, born in Brooklyn in 1943, was educated at Williams College, the University of Texas, and Harvard Law School. Today he is most widely known as the author of an immensely popular book, The Book of Virtues: A Treasury of Great Moral Stories *(1993), but he has also been a public servant, Secretary of Education, and a director of the National Drug Control Policy. In 1989, during his tenure as "drug czar," he delivered at Harvard the address that we reprint.*

Drug Policy and the Intellectuals

. . . The issue I want to address is our national drug policy and the intellectuals. Unfortunately, the issue is a little one-sided. There is a very great deal to say about our national drug policy, but much less to say about the intellectuals—except that by and large, they're against it. Why they should be against it is an interesting question, perhaps more a social-psychological question than a properly intellectual one. But whatever the reasons, I'm sorry to say that on properly intellectual grounds the arguments mustered against our current drug policy by America's intellectuals make for very thin gruel indeed.

I should point out, however, that in the fields of medical and scientific research, there is indeed serious and valuable drug-related work going on. But in the great public policy debate over drugs, the academic and intellectual communities have by and large had little to contribute, and little of that has been genuinely useful or for that matter mentally distinguished.

The field of national drug policy is wide open for serious research and serious thinking on both the theoretical and the practical levels; treatment and prevention; education; law enforcement and the criminal-justice system; the proper role of the federal government versus state and local jurisdictions; international diplomacy and foreign intelligence—these are only a few of the areas in which complex questions of policy and politics need to be addressed and resolved if our national drug strategy is to be successful. But apart from a handful of exceptions—including Mark Moore and Mark Kleiman here at the Kennedy School, and Harvard's own, or ex-own, James Q. Wilson—on most of these issues the country's major ideas factories have not just shut down, they've hardly even tooled up.

It's not that most intellectuals are indifferent to the drug issue, though there may be some of that, too. Rather, they seem complacent and incurious. They've made up their minds, and they don't want to be bothered with further information or analysis, further discussion or debate, especially when it comes from Washington. What I read in the opinion columns of my newspaper or in my monthly magazine or what I hear from the resident intellectual on my favorite television talk show is something like a developing intellectual consensus on the drug question. That consensus holds one or both of these propositions to be self-evident: (a) *that the drug problem in America is absurdly simple, and easily solved;* and (b) *that the drug problem in America is a lost cause.*

As it happens, each of these apparently contradictory propositions is   5
false. As it also happens, both are disputed by the *real* experts on drugs in the United States—and there are many such experts, though not the kind the media like to focus on. And both are disbelieved by the American people, whose experience tells them, emphatically, otherwise.

The consensus has a political dimension, which helps account for its seemingly divergent aspect. In some quarters of the far Right there is a tendency to assert that the drug problem is essentially a problem of the inner city, and therefore that what it calls for, essentially, is quarantine. "If those people want to kill themselves off with drugs, let them kill themselves off with drugs," would be a crude but not too inaccurate way of summarizing this position. But this position has relatively few adherents. On the Left, it is something else, something much more prevalent. There we see whole cadres of social scientists, abetted by whole armies of social workers, who seem to take it as catechism that the problem facing us isn't drugs at all, it's poverty, or racism, or some other equally large and intractable social phenomenon. If we want to eliminate the drug problem, these people say, we must first eliminate the "root causes" of drugs, a hopelessly daunting task at which, however, they also happen to make their living. Twenty-five years ago, no one would have suggested that we must first address the root causes of racism before fighting segregation. We fought it, quite correctly, by passing laws against unacceptable conduct. The causes of racism was an interesting question, but the moral imperative was to end it as soon as possible and by all reasonable means: education, prevention, the media and not least of all, the law. So too with drugs.

What unites these two views of the drug problem from opposite sides of the political spectrum is that they issue, inevitably, in a policy of neglect. To me that is a scandalous position, intellectually as well as morally scandalous. For I believe, along with those I have named as the real experts on drugs, and along with most Americans, that the drug problem is not easy but difficult—very difficult in some respects. But at the same time, and again along with those same experts and with the American people, I believe it is not a lost cause but a solvable one. I will return to this theme, but let me pause here to note one specific issue on which the Left/Right consensus has lately come to rest; a position around which it has been attempting to build national sentiment. That position is legalization.

It is indeed bizarre to see the likes of Anthony Lewis and William F. Buckley lining up on the same side of an issue; but such is the perversity that the so-called legalization debate engenders. To call it a "debate," though, suggests that the arguments in *favor* of drug legalization are rigorous, substantial, and serious. They are not. They are, at bottom, a series of superficial and even disingenuous ideas that more sober minds recognize as a recipe for a public policy disaster. Let me explain.

Most conversations about legalization begin with the notion of "taking the profit out of the drug business." But has anyone bothered to examine carefully how the drug business works? As a recent *New York Times* article vividly described, instances of drug dealers actually earning huge sums of money are relatively rare. There are some who do, of course, but most people in the crack business are the low-level "runners" who do not make much money at all. Many of them work as prostitutes or small-time criminals to supplement their drug earnings. True, a lot of naive kids are lured into the drug world by visions of a life filled with big money and fast cars. That's what they think the good life holds for them. But the reality is far different. Many dealers, in the long run, wind up smoking more crack than they sell. Their business becomes a form of slavery: long hours, dangerous work, small pay, and, as the *Times* pointed out, no health benefits either. In many cases, steady work at McDonald's over time would in fact be a step *up* the income scale for these kids. What does straighten them out, it seems, is not a higher minimum wage, or less stringent laws, but the dawning realization that dealing drugs invariably leads to murder or to prison. And that's exactly why we have drug laws—to make drug use a wholly unattractive choice.

Legalization, on the other hand, removes that incentive to stay away   10 from a life of drugs. Let's be honest—there are some people who are going to smoke crack whether it is legal or illegal. But by keeping it illegal, we maintain the criminal sanctions that persuade most people that the good life cannot be reached by dealing drugs.

The big lie behind every call for legalization is that making drugs legally available would "solve" the drug problem. But has anyone actually thought about what that kind of legalized regime would look like? Would crack be legal? How about PCP? Or smokable heroin? Or ice? Would they all be stocked at the local convenience store, perhaps just a few blocks from an elementary school? And how much would they cost? If we taxed drugs and made them expensive, we would still have the black market and crime problems that we have today; if we sold them cheap to eliminate the black market cocaine at, say, $10 a gram—then we would succeed in making a daily dose of cocaine well within the allowance budget of most sixth-graders. When pressed, the advocates of legalization like to sound courageous by proposing that we begin by legalizing marijuana. But they have absolutely nothing to say on the tough questions of controlling other, more powerful drugs, and how they would be regulated.

As far as marijuana is concerned, let me say this: I didn't have to become drug czar to be opposed to legalized marijuana. As Secretary of Education I realized that, given the state of American education, the last thing we needed was a policy that made widely available a substance that impairs memory, concentration, and attention span; why in God's name foster the use of a drug that makes you stupid?

Now what would happen if drugs were suddenly made legal? Legalization advocates deny that the amount of drug use would be affected. I would argue that if drugs are easier to obtain, drug use will soar. In fact, we have just undergone a kind of cruel national experiment in which drugs became cheap and widely available: That experiment is called the crack epidemic. When powder cocaine was expensive and hard to get, it was found almost exclusively in the circles of the rich, the famous, or the privileged. Only when cocaine was dumped into the country, and a $3 vial of crack could be bought on street corners did we see cocaine use skyrocket, this time largely among the poor and disadvantaged. The lesson is clear: If you're in favor of drugs being sold in stores like aspirin, you're in favor of boom times for drug users and drug addicts. With legalization, drug use will go up, way up.

When drug use rises, who benefits and who pays? Legalization advocates think that the cost of enforcing drug laws is too great. But the real question—the question they never ask—is what does it cost not to enforce those laws. The price that American society would have to pay for legalized drugs, I submit, would be intolerably high. We would have more drug-related accidents at work, on the highways, and in the airways. We would have even bigger losses in worker productivity. Our hospitals would be filled with drug emergencies. We would have more school kids on dope, and that means more dropouts. More pregnant women would buy legal cocaine, and then deliver tiny, premature infants. I've seen them in hospitals across the country. It's a horrid form of child abuse, and under a legalization scheme, we will have a lot more of it. For those women and those babies, crack has the same effect whether it's legal or not. Now, if you add to that the costs of treatment, social welfare, and insurance, you've got the price of legalization. So I ask you again, who benefits, who pays?

What about crime? To listen to legalization advocates, one might 15 think that street crime would disappear with the repeal of our drug laws. They haven't done their homework. Our best research indicates that most drug criminals were into crime well before they got into drugs. Making drugs legal would just be a way of subsidizing their habit. They would continue to rob and steal to pay for food, for clothes, for entertainment. And they would carry on with their drug trafficking by undercutting the legalized price of drugs and catering to teenagers, who, I assume, would be nominally restricted from buying drugs at the corner store.

All this should be old news to people who understand one clear lesson of prohibition. When we had laws against alcohol, there was less consumption of alcohol, less alcohol-related disease, fewer drunken brawls, and a lot less public drunkenness. And contrary to myth, there is no evidence that Prohibition caused big increases in crime. No one is suggesting that we go back to Prohibition. But at least we should admit that legalized alcohol, which is responsible for some 100,000 deaths a year, is hardly a model for drug policy. As Charles Krauthammer has pointed out, the question is not which is worse, alcohol or drugs. The question is can we accept both legalized alcohol *and* legalized drugs? The answer is no.

So it seems to me that on the merits of their arguments, the legalizers have no case at all. But there is another, crucial point I want to make on this subject, unrelated to costs or benefits. Drug use—especially heavy drug use—destroys human character. It destroys dignity and autonomy, it burns away the sense of responsibility, it subverts productivity, it makes a mockery of virtue. As our Founders would surely recognize, a citizenry that is perpetually in a drug-induced haze doesn't bode well for the future of self-government. Libertarians don't like to hear this, but it is a truth that everyone knows who has seen drug addiction up close. And don't listen to people who say drug users are only hurting themselves: They hurt parents, they destroy families, they ruin friendships. And let me remind this audience, here at a great university, that drugs are a threat to the life of the mind; anyone who values that life should have nothing but contempt for drugs. Learned institutions should regard drugs as the plague.

That's why I find the surrender of many of America's intellectuals to arguments for drug legalization so odd and so scandalous. For the past three months, I have been traveling the country, visiting drug-ridden neighborhoods, seeing treatment and prevention programs in action, talking to teachers, cops, parents, kids. These, it seems, are the real drug experts—they've witnessed the problem firsthand. But unlike some prominent residents of Princeton, Madison, Cambridge, or Palo Alto, they refuse to surrender. They are in the community, reclaiming their neighborhoods, working with police, setting up community activities, getting addicts into treatment, saving their children.

Too many American intellectuals don't know about this and seem not to want to know. Their hostility to the national war on drugs is, I think, partly rooted in a general hostility to law enforcement and criminal justice. That's why they take refuge in pseudosolutions like legalization, which stress only the treatment side of the problem. Whenever discussion turns to the need for more police and stronger penalties, they cry that our constitutional liberties are in jeopardy. Well, yes, they are in jeopardy, but not from drug *policy:* On this score, the guardians of our Constitution can sleep easy. Constitutional liberties are in jeopardy, instead, from drugs themselves, which every day scorch the earth of our common freedom. Yes, sometimes cops go too far, and when they do they should be held accountable. But these excursions from the law are the exception. Meanwhile drug dealers violate our rights everyday as a rule, as a norm, as their modus operandi. Why can't our civil libertarians see that?

When we are not being told by critics that law enforcement threat- 20 ens our liberties, we are being told that it won't work. Let me tell you that law enforcement does work and why it must work. Several weeks ago I was in Wichita, Kansas, talking to a teenage boy who was now in his fourth treatment program. Every time he had finished a previous round of treatment, he found himself back on the streets, surrounded by the same cheap dope and tough hustlers who had gotten him started in the first place. He was tempted, he was pressured, and he gave in. Virtually any expert on drug treatment will tell you that, for most people, no therapy in the world can fight temptation on that scale. As long as drugs are found on any street corner, no amount of treatment, no amount of education can finally stand against them. Yes, we need drug treatment and drug education. But drug treatment and drug education need law enforcement. And that's why our strategy calls for a bigger criminal justice system: as a form of drug *prevention*.

To the Americans who are waging the drug war in their own front yards every day, this is nothing new, nothing startling. In the San Jose section of Albuquerque, New Mexico, just two weeks ago, I spoke to Rudy Chavez and Jack Candelarla, and police chief Sam Baca. They had wanted to start a youth center that would keep their kids safe from the depredations of the street. Somehow it never worked—until together they set up a police station right in the heart of drug-dealing territory. Then it worked. Together with the cops, the law-abiding residents cleared the area, and made it safe for them and their children to walk outside their homes. The youth center began to thrive.

Scenes like this are being played out all across the country. I've seen them in Tulsa, Dallas, Tampa, Omaha, Des Moines, Seattle, New York.

Americans—many of them poor, black, or Hispanic—have figured out what the armchair critics haven't. Drugs may threaten to destroy their neighborhoods, but *they* refuse to stand by and let it happen. *They* have discovered that it is possible not only to fight back, but to win. In some elite circles, the talk may be only of the sad state of the helpless and the hopeless, but while these circles talk on, the helpless and the hopeless themselves are carrying out a national drug policy. They are fighting back.

When I think of these scenes I'm reminded of what John Jacob, president of the Urban League, said recently: Drugs are destroying more black families than poverty ever did. And I'm thankful that many of these poor families have the courage to fight drugs now, rather than declaring themselves passive victims of root causes.

America's intellectuals—and here I think particularly of liberal intellectuals—have spent much of the last nine years decrying the social programs of two Republican administrations in the name of the defenseless poor. But today, on the one outstanding issue that disproportionately hurts the poor—that is wiping out many of the poor—where are the liberal intellectuals to be found? They are on the editorial and op-ed pages, and in magazines like this month's *Harper's*, telling us with an ignorant sneer that our drug policy won't work. Many universities, too, which have been quick to take on the challenges of sexism, racism, and ethnocentrism, seem content on the drug issue to wag a finger at us, or to point it mindlessly at American society in general. In public policy schools, there is no shortage of arms control scholars. Isn't it time we had more drug control scholars?

The current situation won't do. The failure to get serious about the 25 drug issue is, I think, a failure of civic courage—the kind of courage shown by many who have been among the main victims of the drug scourge. But it betokens as well a betrayal of the self-declared mission of intellectuals as the bearers of society's conscience. There may be reasons for this reluctance, this hostility, this failure. But I would remind you that not all crusades led by the U.S. government, enjoying broad popular support, are brutish, corrupt, and sinister. What is brutish, corrupt, and sinister is the murder and mayhem being committed in our cities' streets. One would think that a little more concern and serious thought would come from those who claim to care so deeply about America's problems.

So I stand here this afternoon with a simple message for America's pundits and academic cynics: Get serious about drug policy. We are grappling with complicated, stubborn policy issues, and I encourage you to join us. Tough work lies ahead, and we need serious minds to focus on how we should use the tools that we have in the most effective way.

I came to this job with realistic expectations. I am not promising a drug-free America by next week, or even by next year. But that doesn't mean that success is out of reach. Success will come—I've seen a lot of it already—in slow, careful steps. Its enemies are timidity, petulance, false expectations. But its three greatest foes remain surrender, despair, and neglect. So, for the sake of their fellow citizens, I invite America's deep thinkers to get with the program, or at the very least, to get in the game.

Topics for Critical Thinking and Writing

1. In paragraph 6, Bennett draws a parallel between racism and drug abuse, and suggests that society ought to fight the one (drug abuse) as it successfully fought the other (racism). What do you think of this parallel? Explain.

2. Bennett identifies two propositions on the issue of drug abuse that he believes are accepted by "consensus" thinking in America (para. 4). What are these propositions, and what is Bennett's view of them? How does he try to convince the reader to agree with him?

3. What are Bennett's main objections to solving the problem of drug abuse by legalizing drugs?

4. At the time he gave this lecture, Bennett was a confirmed cigarette smoker trying to break the habit. Do you see any inconsistency in his opposing legalized marijuana and tolerating (and even using) legalized tobacco?

5. What measures besides stricter law enforcement does Bennett propose for wide-scale adoption, in the belief they will reduce drug abuse? Why does he object to relying only on such measures?

James Q. Wilson

James Q. Wilson is Collins Professor of Management and Public Policy at the University of California at Los Angeles. He is the author of Thinking about Crime *(1975) and* Bureaucracy *(1989), the coauthor of* Crime and Human Nature *(1985), and the coeditor of* Drugs and Crime *(1990). The essay that we reprint appeared originally in February 1990 in* Commentary, *a conservative magazine.*

Against the Legalization of Drugs

In 1972, the president appointed me chairman of the National Advisory Council for Drug Abuse Prevention. Created by Congress, the Council was charged with providing guidance on how best to coordinate the national war on drugs. (Yes, we called it a war then, too.) In those days, the drug we were chiefly concerned with was heroin. When I took office, heroin use had been increasing dramatically. Everybody was worried that this increase would continue. Such phrases as "heroin epidemic" were commonplace.

That same year, the eminent economist Milton Friedman published an essay in *Newsweek* in which he called for legalizing heroin. His argument was on two grounds: As a matter of ethics, the government has no right to tell people not to use heroin (or to drink or to commit suicide); as a matter of economics, the prohibition of drug use imposes costs on society that far exceed the benefits. Others, such as the psychoanalyst Thomas Szasz, made the same argument.

We did not take Friedman's advice. (Government commissions rarely do.) I do not recall that we even discussed legalizing heroin, though we did discuss (but did not take action on) legalizing a drug, cocaine, that many people then argued was benign. Our marching orders were to figure out how to win the war on heroin, not to run up the white flag of surrender.

That was 1972. Today, we have the same number of heroin addicts that we had then — half a million, give or take a few thousand. Having that many heroin addicts is no trivial matter; these people deserve our attention. But not having had an increase in that number for over fifteen years is also something that deserves our attention. What happened to the "heroin epidemic" that many people once thought would overwhelm us?

The facts are clear: A more or less stable pool of heroin addicts has 5 been getting older, with relatively few new recruits. In 1976 the average age of heroin users who appeared in hospital emergency rooms was about twenty-seven; ten years later it was thirty-two. More than two-thirds of all heroin users appearing in emergency rooms are now over the age of thirty. Back in the early 1970s, when heroin got onto the national political agenda, the typical heroin addict was much younger, often a teenager. Household surveys show the same thing — the rate of opiate use (which includes heroin) has been flat for the better part of two decades. More fine-grained studies of inner-city neighborhoods confirm this. John Boyle and Ann Brunswick found that the percentage of young blacks in Harlem who use heroin fell from 8 percent in 1970–71 to about 3 percent in 1975–76.

Why did heroin lose its appeal for young people? When the young blacks in Harlem were asked why they stopped, more than half mentioned "trouble with the law" or "high cost" (and high cost is, of course, directly the result of law enforcement). Two-thirds said that heroin hurt their health; nearly all said they had had a bad experience with it. We need not rely, however, simply on what they said. In New York City in 1973–75, the street price of heroin rose dramatically and its purity sharply declined, probably as a result of the heroin shortage caused by the success of the Turkish government in reducing the supply of opium base and of the French government in closing down heroin-processing laboratories located in and around Marseilles. These were short-lived gains for, just as Friedman predicted, alternative sources of supply — mostly in Mexico — quickly emerged. But the three-year heroin shortage interrupted the easy recruitment of new users.

Health and related problems were no doubt part of the reason for the reduced flow of recruits. Over the preceding years, Harlem youth had watched as more and more heroin users died of overdoses, were poisoned by adulterated doses, or acquired hepatitis from dirty needles. The word got around: Heroin can kill you. By 1974 new hepatitis cases and drug-overdose deaths had dropped to a fraction of what they had been in 1970.

Alas, treatment did not seem to explain much of the cessation in drug use. Treatment programs can and do help heroin addicts, but treatment did not explain the drop in the number of *new* users (who by definition had never been in treatment) nor even much of the reduction in the number of experienced users.

No one knows how much of the decline to attribute to personal observation as opposed to high prices or reduced supply. But other evidence suggests strongly that price and supply played a large role. In 1972 the National Advisory Council was especially worried by the prospect that U.S. servicemen returning to this country from Vietnam would bring their heroin habits with them. Fortunately, a brilliant study by Lee Robins of Washington University in St. Louis put that fear to rest. She measured drug use of Vietnam veterans shortly after they had returned home. Though many had used heroin regularly while in Southeast Asia, most gave up the habit when back in the United States. The reason: Here, heroin was less available and sanctions on its use were more pronounced. Of course, if a veteran had been willing to pay enough—which might have meant traveling to another city and would certainly have meant making an illegal contact with a disreputable dealer in a threatening neighborhood in order to acquire a (possibly) dangerous dose—he could have sustained his drug habit. Most veterans were unwilling to pay this price, and so their drug use declined or disappeared.

RELIVING THE PAST

Suppose we had taken Friedman's advice in 1972. What would have happened? We cannot be entirely certain, but at a minimum we would have placed the young heroin addicts (and, above all, the prospective addicts) in a very different position from the one in which they actually found themselves. Heroin would have been legal. Its price would have been reduced by 95 percent (minus whatever we chose to recover in taxes). Now that it could be sold by the same people who make aspirin, its quality would have been assured—no poisons, no adulterants. Sterile hypodermic needles would have been readily available at the neighborhood drugstore, probably at the same counter where the heroin was sold. No need to travel to big cities or unfamiliar neighborhoods—heroin could have been purchased anywhere, perhaps by mail order.

There would no longer have been any financial or medical reason to avoid heroin use. Anybody could have afforded it. We might have tried to prevent children from buying it, but as we have learned from our efforts to prevent minors from buying alcohol and tobacco, young people have a way of penetrating markets theoretically reserved for adults. Returning Vietnam veterans would have discovered that Omaha and Raleigh had been converted into the pharmaceutical equivalent of Saigon.

Under these circumstances, can we doubt for a moment that heroin use would have grown exponentially? Or that a vastly larger supply of new users would have been recruited? Professor Friedman is a Nobel Prize–winning economist whose understanding of market forces is profound. What did he think would happen to consumption under his legalized regime? Here are his words: "Legalizing drugs might increase the number of addicts, but it is not clear that it would. Forbidden fruit is attractive, particularly to the young."

Really? I suppose that we should expect no increase in Porsche sales if we cut the price by 95 percent, no increase in whiskey sales if we cut the price by a comparable amount—because young people only want fast cars and strong liquor when they are "forbidden." Perhaps Friedman's uncharacteristic lapse from the obvious implications of price theory can be explained by a misunderstanding of how drug users are recruited. In his 1972 essay he said that "drug addicts are deliberately made by pushers, who give likely prospects their first few doses free." If drugs were legal it would not pay anybody to produce addicts, because everybody would buy from the cheapest source. But as every drug expert knows, pushers do not produce addicts. Friends or acquaintances do. In fact, pushers are usually reluctant to deal with nonusers because a nonuser could be an undercover cop. Drug use spreads in the same way any fad or fashion spreads: Somebody who is already a user urges his friends to try, or simply shows already-eager friends how to do it.

But we need not rely on speculation, however plausible, that lowered prices and more abundant supplies would have increased heroin usage. Great Britain once followed such a policy and with almost exactly those results. Until the mid-1960s, British physicians were allowed to prescribe heroin to certain classes of addicts. (Possessing these drugs without a doctor's prescription remained a criminal offense.) For many years this policy worked well enough because the addict patients were typically middle-class people who had become dependent on opiate painkillers while undergoing hospital treatment. There was no drug culture. The British system worked for many years, not because it prevented drug abuse but because there was no problem of drug abuse that would test the system.

All that changed in the 1960s. A few unscrupulous doctors began 15 passing out heroin in wholesale amounts. One doctor prescribed almost six hundred thousand heroin tablets—that is, over thirteen pounds — in just one year. A youthful drug culture emerged with a demand for drugs far different from that of the older addicts. As a result, the British government required doctors to refer users to government-run clinics to receive their heroin.

But the shift to clinics did not curtail the growth in heroin use. Throughout the 1960s the number of addicts increased—the late John Kaplan of Stanford estimated by fivefold—in part as a result of the diversion of heroin from clinic patients to new users on the streets. An addict would bargain with the clinic doctor over how big a dose he would receive. The patient wanted as much as he could get, the doctor wanted to give as little as was needed. The patient had an advantage in this conflict because the doctor could not be certain how much was really needed. Many patients would use some of their "maintenance" dose and sell the remaining part to friends, thereby recruiting new addicts. As the clinics learned of this, they began to shift their treatment away from heroin and toward methadone, an addictive drug that, when taken orally, does not produce a "high" but will block the withdrawal pains associated with heroin abstinence.

Whether what happened in England in the 1960s was a miniepidemic or an epidemic depends on whether one looks at numbers or at rates of change. Compared to the United States, the numbers were small. In 1960 there were sixty-eight heroin addicts known to the British government; by 1968 there were two thousand in treatment and many more who refused treatment. (They would refuse in part because they did not want to get methadone at a clinic if they could get heroin on the street.) Richard Hartnoll estimates that the actual number of addicts in England is five times the number officially registered. At a minimum, the number of British addicts increased by thirtyfold in ten years; the actual increase may have been much larger.

In the early 1980s the numbers began to rise again, and this time nobody doubted that a real epidemic was at hand. The increase was estimated to be 40 percent a year. By 1982 there were thought to be twenty thousand heroin users in London alone. Geoffrey Pearson reports that many cities—Glasgow, Liverpool, Manchester, and Sheffield among them—were now experiencing a drug problem that once had been largely confined to London. The problem, again, was supply. The country was being flooded with cheap, high-quality heroin, first from Iran and then from Southeast Asia.

The United States began the 1960s with a much larger number of heroin addicts and probably a bigger at-risk population than was the case in Great Britain. Even though it would be foolhardy to suppose that the British system, if installed here, would have worked the same way or with the same results, it would be equally foolhardy to suppose that a combination of heroin available from leaky clinics and from street dealers who faced only minimal law-enforcement risks would not have produced a much greater increase in heroin use than we actually experienced. My guess is that if we had allowed either doctors or clinics to prescribe heroin, we would have had far worse results than were produced in Britain, if for no other reason than the vastly larger number of addicts with which we began. We would have had to find some way to police thousands (not scores) of physicians and hundreds (not dozens) of clinics. If the British civil service found it difficult to keep heroin in the hands of addicts and out of the hands of recruits when it was dealing with a few hundred people, how well would the American civil service have accomplished the same tasks when dealing with tens of thousands of people?

BACK TO THE FUTURE

Now cocaine, especially in its potent form, crack, is the focus of at-   20
tention. Now as in 1972 the government is trying to reduce its use. Now as then some people are advocating legalization. Is there any more reason to yield to those arguments today than there was almost two decades ago?[1]

I think not. If we had yielded in 1972 we almost certainly would have had today a permanent population of several million, not several hundred thousand, heroin addicts. If we yield now we will have a far more serious problem with cocaine.

Crack is worse than heroin by almost any measure. Heroin produces a pleasant drowsiness and, if hygienically administered, has only the physical side effects of constipation and sexual impotence. Regular heroin use incapacitates many users, especially poor ones, for any productive work or social responsibility. They will sit nodding on a street corner, helpless but at least harmless. By contrast, regular cocaine use leaves the user neither helpless nor harmless. When smoked (as with crack) or injected, cocaine produces instant, intense, and short-lived euphoria. The experience generates a powerful desire to repeat it. If the drug is readily available, repeat use will occur. Those people who progress to "bingeing" on cocaine become devoted to the drug and its effects to the exclusion of almost all other considerations—job, family, children, sleep, food, even sex. Dr. Frank Gawin at Yale and Dr. Everett Ellinwood at Duke report that a substantial percentage of all high-dose, binge users become uninhibited, impulsive, hypersexual, compulsive, irritable, and hyperactive. Their moods vacillate dramatically, leading at times to violence and homicide.

Women are much more likely to use crack than heroin, and if they are pregnant, the effects on their babies are tragic. Douglas Besharov, who has been following the effects of drugs on infants for twenty years,

---

[1]I do not here take up the question of marijuana. For a variety of reasons—its widespread use and its lesser tendency to addict—it presents a different problem from cocaine or heroin. For a penetrating analysis, see Mark Kleiman, *Marijuana: Costs of Abuse, Costs of Control* (Greenwood Press, 217 pp.). [Wilson's note.]

writes that nothing he learned about heroin prepared him for the devastation of cocaine. Cocaine harms the fetus and can lead to physical deformities or neurological damage. Some crack babies have for all practical purposes suffered a disabling stroke while still in the womb. The long-term consequences of this brain damage are lowered cognitive ability and the onset of mood disorders. Besharov estimates that about thirty thousand to fifty thousand such babies are born every year, about seven thousand in New York City alone. There may be ways to treat such infants, but from everything we now know the treatment will be long, difficult, and expensive. Worse, the mothers who are most likely to produce crack babies are precisely the ones who, because of poverty or temperament, are least able and willing to obtain such treatment. In fact, anecdotal evidence suggests the crack mothers are likely to abuse their infants.

The notion that abusing drugs such as cocaine is a "victimless crime" is not only absurd but dangerous. Even ignoring the fetal drug syndrome, crack-dependent people are, like heroin addicts, individuals who regularly victimize their children by neglect, their spouses by improvidence, their employers by lethargy, and their co-workers by carelessness. Society is not and could never be a collection of autonomous individuals. We all have a stake in ensuring that each of us displays a minimal level of dignity, responsibility, and empathy. We cannot, of course, coerce people into goodness, but we can and should insist that some standards must be met if society itself—on which the very existence of the human personality depends—is to persist. Drawing the line that defines those standards is difficult and contentious, but if crack and heroin use do not fall below it, what does?

The advocates of legalization will respond by suggesting that my picture is overdrawn. Ethan Nadelmann of Princeton argues that the risk of legalization is less than most people suppose. Over twenty million Americans between the ages of eighteen and twenty-five have tried cocaine (according to a government survey), but only a quarter million use it daily. From this Nadelmann concludes that at most 3 percent of all young people who try cocaine develop a problem with it. The implication is clear: Make the drug legal and we only have to worry about 3 percent of our youth.

The implication rests on a logical fallacy and a factual error. The fallacy is this: The percentage of occasional cocaine users who become binge users *when the drug is illegal* (and thus expensive and hard to find) tells us nothing about the percentage who will become dependent when the drug is legal (and thus cheap and abundant). Drs. Gawin and Ellinwood report, in common with several other researchers, that controlled or occasional use of cocaine changes to compulsive and frequent use "when access to the drug increases" or when the user switches from snorting to smoking. More cocaine more potently administered alters, perhaps sharply, the proportion of "controlled" users who become heavy users.

The factual error is this: The federal survey Nadelmann quotes was done in 1985, *before* crack had become common. Thus the probability of becoming dependent on cocaine was derived from the responses of users who snorted the drug. The speed and potency of cocaine's action increases dramatically when it is smoked. We do not yet know how greatly the advent of crack increases the risk of dependency, but all the clinical evidence suggests that the increase is likely to be large.

It is possible that some people will not become heavy users even when the drug is readily available in its most potent form. So far there are no scientific grounds for predicting who will and who will not become dependent. Neither socioeconomic background nor personality traits differentiate between casual and intensive users. Thus, the only way to settle the question of who is correct about the effect of easy availability on drug use, Nadelmann or Gawin and Ellinwood, is to try it and see. But the social experiment is so risky as to be no experiment at all, for if cocaine is legalized and if the rate of its abusive use increases dramatically, there is no way to put the genie back in the bottle, and it is not a kindly genie.

HAVE WE LOST?

Many people who agree that there are risks in legalizing cocaine or heroin still favor it because, they think, we have lost the war on drugs. "Nothing we have done has worked" and the current federal policy is just "more of the same." Whatever the costs of greater drug use, surely they would be less than the costs of our present, failed efforts.

That is exactly what I was told in 1972 — and heroin is not quite as 30 bad a drug as cocaine. We did not surrender and we did not lose. We did not win, either. What the nation accomplished then was what most efforts to save people from themselves accomplish: The problem was contained and the number of victims minimized, all at a considerable cost in law enforcement and increased crime. Was the cost worth it? I think so, but others may disagree. What are the lives of would-be addicts worth? I recall some people saying to me then, "Let them kill themselves." I was appalled. Happily, such views did not prevail.

Have we lost today? Not at all. High-rate cocaine use is not commonplace. The National Institute of Drug Abuse (NIDA) reports that less than 5 percent of high-school seniors used cocaine within the last thirty days. Of course this survey misses young people who have dropped out of school and miscounts those who lie on the questionnaire, but even if we inflate the NIDA estimate by some plausible percentage, it is still not much above 5 percent. Medical examiners reported in 1987 that about 1,500 died from cocaine use; hospital emergency rooms reported about 30,000 admissions related to cocaine abuse.

These are not small numbers, but neither are they evidence of a nationwide plague that threatens to engulf us all. Moreover, cities vary greatly in the proportion of people who are involved with cocaine. To get city-level data we need to turn to drug tests carried out on arrested persons, who obviously are more likely to be drug users than the average citizen. The National Institute of Justice, through its Drug Use Forecasting (DUF) project, collects urinalysis data on arrestees in twenty-two cities. As we have already seen, opiate (chiefly heroin) use has been flat or declining in most of these cities over the last decade. Cocaine use has gone up sharply, but with great variation among cities. New York, Philadelphia, and Washington, D.C., all report that two-thirds or more of their arrestees tested positive for cocaine, but in Portland, San Antonio, and Indianapolis the percentage was one-third or less.

In some neighborhoods, of course, matters have reached crisis proportions. Gangs control the streets, shootings terrorize residents, and drug dealing occurs in plain view. The police seem barely able to contain matters. But in these neighborhoods—unlike at Palo Alto cocktail parties—the people are not calling for legalization, they are calling for help. And often not much help has come. Many cities are willing to do almost anything about the drug problem except spend more money on it. The federal government cannot change that; only local voters and politicians can. It is not clear that they will.

It took about ten years to contain heroin. We have had experience with crack for only about three or four years. Each year we spend perhaps $11 billion on law enforcement (and some of that goes to deal with marijuana) and perhaps $2 billion on treatment. Large sums, but not sums that should lead anyone to say, "We just can't afford this any more."

The illegality of drugs increases crime, partly because some users turn 35 to crime to pay for their habits, partly because some users are stimulated by certain drugs (such as crack or PCP) to act more violently or ruthlessly than they otherwise would, and partly because criminal organizations seeking to control drug supplies use force to manage their markets. These also are serious costs, but no one knows how much they would be reduced if drugs were legalized. Addicts would no longer steal to pay black-market prices for drugs, a real gain. But some, perhaps a great deal, of that gain would be offset by the great increase in the number of addicts. These people, nodding on heroin or living in the delusion-ridden high of cocaine, would hardly be ideal employees. Many would steal simply to support themselves, since snatch-and-grab, opportunistic crime can be managed even by people unable to hold a regular job or plan an elaborate crime. Those British addicts who get their supplies from government clinics are not models of law-abiding decency. Most are in crime, and though their per-capita rate of criminality may be lower thanks to the cheapness of their drugs, the total volume of crime they produce may be quite large. Of course, society could decide to support all unemployable addicts on welfare, but that would mean that gains from lowered rates of crime would have to be offset by large increases in welfare budgets.

Proponents of legalization claim that the costs of having more addicts around would be largely if not entirely offset by having more money available with which to treat and care for them. The money would come from taxes levied on the sale of heroin and cocaine.

To obtain this fiscal dividend, however, legalization's supporters must first solve an economic dilemma. If they want to raise a lot of money to pay for welfare and treatment, the tax rate on the drugs will have to be quite high. Even if they themselves do not want a high rate, the politicians' love of "sin taxes" would probably guarantee that it would be high anyway. But the higher the tax, the higher the price of the drug, and the higher the price the greater the likelihood that addicts will turn to crime to find the money for it and that criminal organizations will be formed to sell tax-free drugs at below-market rates. If we managed to keep taxes (and thus prices) low, we would get that much less money to pay for welfare and treatment and more people could afford to become addicts. There may be an optimal tax rate for drugs that maximizes revenue while minimizing crime, bootlegging, and the recruitment of new addicts, but our experience with alcohol does not suggest that we know how to find it.

THE BENEFITS OF ILLEGALITY

The advocates of legalization find nothing to be said in favor of the current system except, possibly, that it keeps the number of addicts smaller than it would otherwise be. In fact, the benefits are more substantial than that.

First, treatment. All the talk about providing "treatment on demand" implies that there is a demand for treatment. That is not quite right. There are some drug-dependent people who genuinely want treatment and will remain in it if offered; they should receive it. But there are far more who want only short-term help after a bad crash; once stabilized and bathed, they are back on the street again, hustling. And even many of the addicts who enroll in a program honestly wanting help drop out after a short while when they discover that help takes time and commitment. Drug-dependent people have very short time horizons and a weak capacity for commitment. These two groups—those looking for a quick fix and those unable to stick with a long-term fix—are not easily helped. Even if we increase the number of treatment slots—as we should—we would have to do something to make treatment more effective.

One thing that can often make it more effective is compulsion. 40 Douglas Anglin of UCLA, in common with many other researchers, has found that the longer one stays in a treatment program, the better the chances of a reduction in drug dependency. But he, again like most other researchers, has found that dropout rates are high. He has also found, however, that patients who enter treatment under legal compulsion stay in the program longer than those not subject to such pressure. His research on the California civil commitment program, for example, found that heroin users involved with its required drug-testing program had over the long term a lower rate of heroin use than similar addicts who were free of such constraints. If for many addicts compulsion is a useful component of treatment, it is not clear how compulsion could be achieved in a society in which purchasing, possessing, and using the drug were legal. It could be managed, I suppose, but I would not want to have to answer the challenge from the American Civil Liberties Union that it is wrong to compel a person to undergo treatment for consuming a legal commodity.

Next, education. We are now investing substantially in drug-education programs in the schools. Though we do not yet know for certain what will work, there are some promising leads. But I wonder how credible such programs would be if they were aimed at dissuading children from doing something perfectly legal. We could, of course, treat drug education like smoking education: Inhaling crack and inhaling tobacco are both legal, but you should not do it because it is bad for you. That tobacco is bad for you is easily shown; the Surgeon General has seen to that. But what do we say about crack? It is pleasurable, but devoting yourself to so much pleasure is not a good idea (though perfectly legal)? Unlike tobacco, cocaine will not give you cancer or emphysema, but it will lead you to neglect your duties to family, job, and neighborhood? Everybody is doing cocaine, but you should not?

Again, it might be possible under a legalized regime to have effective drug-prevention programs, but their effectiveness would depend heavily, I think, on first having decided that cocaine use, like tobacco use, is purely a matter of practical consequences; no fundamental moral significance attaches to either. But if we believe—as I do—that dependency on certain mind-altering drugs *is* a moral issue and that their illegality rests in part on their immorality, then legalizing them undercuts, if it does not eliminate altogether, the moral message.

That message is at the root of the distinction we now make between nicotine and cocaine. Both are highly addictive; both have harmful physical effects. But we treat the two drugs differently, not simply because nicotine is so widely used as to be beyond the reach of effective prohibition, but because its use does not destroy the user's essential humanity. Tobacco shortens one's life, cocaine debases it. Nicotine alters one's habits, cocaine alters one's soul. The heavy use of crack, unlike the heavy use of tobacco, corrodes those natural sentiments of sympathy and duty that constitute our human nature and make possible our social life. To say, as does Nadelmann, that distinguishing morally between tobacco and cocaine is "little more than a transient prejudice" is close to saying that morality itself is but a prejudice.

THE ALCOHOL PROBLEM

Now we have arrived where many arguments about legalizing drugs begin: Is there any reason to treat heroin and cocaine differently from the way we treat alcohol?

There is no easy answer to that question because, as with so many 45 human problems, one cannot decide simply on the basis either of moral principles or of individual consequences; one has to temper any policy by a commonsense judgment of what is possible. Alcohol, like heroin, cocaine, PCP, and marijuana, is a drug—that is, a mood-altering substance—and consumed to excess it certainly has harmful consequences: auto accidents, barroom fights, bedroom shootings. It is also, for some people, addictive. We cannot confidently compare the addictive powers of these drugs, but the best evidence suggests that crack and heroin are much more addictive than alcohol.

Many people, Nadelmann included, argue that since the health and financial costs of alcohol abuse are so much higher than those of cocaine or heroin abuse, it is hypocritical folly to devote our efforts to preventing cocaine or drug use. But as Mark Kleiman of Harvard has pointed out, this comparison is quite misleading. What Nadelmann is doing is showing that a *legalized* drug (alcohol) produces greater social harm than *illegal* ones (cocaine and heroin). But of course. Suppose that in the 1920s we had made heroin and cocaine legal and alcohol illegal. Can anyone doubt that Nadelmann would now be writing that it is folly to continue our ban on alcohol because cocaine and heroin are so much more harmful?

And let there be no doubt about it—widespread heroin and cocaine use are associated with all manner of ills. Thomas Bewley found that the mortality rate of British heroin addicts in 1968 was twenty-eight times as high as the death rate of the same age group of nonaddicts, even though in England at the time an addict could obtain free or low-cost heroin and clean needles from British clinics. Perform the following mental experiment: Suppose we legalized heroin and cocaine in this country. In what proportion of auto fatalities would the state police report that the driver was nodding off on heroin or recklessly driving on a coke high? In what proportion of spouse-assault and child-abuse cases would the local police report that crack was involved? In what proportion of industrial accidents would safety investigators report that the forklift or drill-press operator was in a drug-induced stupor or frenzy? We do not know exactly what the proportion would be, but anyone who asserts that it would not be much higher than it is now would have to believe that these drugs have little appeal except when they are illegal. And that is nonsense.

An advocate of legalization might concede that social harm—perhaps harm equivalent to that already produced by alcohol—would follow from making cocaine and heroin generally available. But at least, he might add, we would have the problem "out in the open" where it could be treated as a matter of "public health." That is well and good, *if* we knew how to treat—that is, cure—heroin and cocaine abuse. But we do not know how to do it for all the people who would need such help. We are having only limited success in coping with chronic alcoholics. Addictive behavior is immensely difficult to change, and the best methods for changing it—living in drug-free therapeutic communities, becoming faithful members of Alcoholics Anonymous or Narcotics Anonymous—require great personal commitment, a quality that is, alas, in short supply among the very persons—young people, disadvantaged people—who are often most at risk for addiction.

Suppose that today we had, not fifteen million alcohol abusers, but half a million. Suppose that we already knew what we have learned from our long experience with the widespread use of alcohol. Would we make whiskey legal? I do not know, but I suspect there would be a lively debate. The surgeon general would remind us of the risks alcohol poses to pregnant women. The National Highway Traffic Safety Administration would point to the likelihood of more highway fatalities caused by drunk drivers. The Food and Drug Administration might find that there is a nontrivial increase in cancer associated with alcohol consumption. At the same time the police would report great difficulty in keeping illegal whiskey out of our cities, officers being corrupted by bootleggers, and alcohol addicts often resorting to crime to feed their habit. Libertarians, for their part, would argue that every citizen has a right to drink anything he wishes and that drinking is, in any event, a "victimless crime."

However the debate might turn out, the central fact would be that 50 the problem was still, at that point, a small one. The government cannot legislate away the addictive tendencies in all of us, nor can it remove completely even the most dangerous addictive substances. But it can cope with harms when the harms are still manageable.

SCIENCE AND ADDICTION

One advantage of containing a problem while it is still containable is that it buys time for science to learn more about it and perhaps to discover a cure. Almost unnoticed in the current debate over legalizing drugs is that basic science has made rapid strides in identifying the underlying neurological processes involved in some forms of addiction. Stimulants such as cocaine and amphetamines alter the way certain brain cells communicate with one another. That alteration is complex and not entirely understood, but in simplified form it involves modifying the way in which a neurotransmitter called dopamine sends signals from one cell to another.

When dopamine crosses the synapse between two cells, it is in effect carrying a message from the first cell to activate the second one. In certain parts of the brain that message is experienced as pleasure. After the message is delivered, the dopamine returns to the first cell. Cocaine apparently blocks this return, or "reuptake," so that the excited cell and others nearby continue to send pleasure messages. When the exaggerated high produced by cocaine-influenced dopamine finally ends, the brain cells may (in ways that are still a matter of dispute) suffer from an extreme lack of dopamine, thereby making the individual unable to experience any pleasure at all. This would explain why cocaine users often feel so depressed after enjoying the drug. Stimulants may also affect the way in which other neurotransmitters, such as serotonin and noradrenaline, operate.

Whatever the exact mechanism may be, once it is identified it becomes possible to use drugs to block either the effect of cocaine or its tendency to produce dependency. There have already been experiments using desipramine, imipramine, bromocriptine, carbamazepine, and other chemicals. There are some promising results.

Tragically, we spend very little on such research, and the agencies funding it have not in the past occupied very influential or visible posts in the federal bureaucracy. If there is one aspect of the "war on drugs" metaphor that I dislike, it is its tendency to focus attention almost exclusively on the troops in the trenches, whether engaged in enforcement or treatment, and away from the research-and-development efforts back on the home front where the war may ultimately be decided.

I believe that the prospects of scientists in controlling addiction will 55 be strongly influenced by the size and character of the problem they face. If the problem is a few hundred thousand chronic, high-dose users of an illegal product, the chances of making a difference at a reasonable cost will be much greater than if the problem is a few million chronic users of legal substances. Once a drug is legal, not only will its use increase but many of those who then use it will prefer the drug to the treatment: They will want the pleasure, whatever the cost to themselves or their families, and they will resist—probably successfully—any effort to wean them away from experiencing the high that comes from inhaling a legal substance.

IF I AM WRONG . . .

No one can know what our society would be like if we changed the law to make access to cocaine, heroin, and PCP easier. I believe, for reasons given, that the result would be a sharp increase in use, a more widespread degradation of the human personality, and a greater rate of accidents and violence.

I may be wrong. If I am, then we will needlessly have incurred heavy costs in law enforcement and some forms of criminality. But if I am right, and the legalizers prevail anyway, then we will have consigned millions of people, hundreds of thousands of infants, and hundreds of neighborhoods to a life of oblivion and disease. To the lives and families destroyed by alcohol we will have added countless more destroyed by cocaine, heroin, PCP, and whatever else a basement scientist can invent.

Human character is formed by society; indeed, human character is inconceivable without society, and good character is less likely in a bad society. Will we, in the name of an abstract doctrine of radical individualism, and with the false comfort of suspect predictions, decide to take the chance that somehow individual decency can survive amid a more general level of degradation?

I think not. The American people are too wise for that, whatever the academic essayists and cocktail-party pundits may say. But if Americans today are less wise than I suppose, then Americans at some future time will look back on us now and wonder, what kind of people were they that they could have done such a thing?

Topics for Critical Thinking and Writing

1. Wilson objects to the idea that drug abuse with cocaine is a "victimless crime" (para. 24; see also para. 49). A crime is said to be "victimless" when the offender consents to the act and those who do not consent are not harmed. Why does it matter to Wilson, do you think, whether drug abuse is a victimless crime?

2. Wilson accuses Ethan Nadelmann, an advocate of legalization, of committing "a logical fallacy and a factual error" (para. 26). What is the fallacy, and what is the error?

3. Wilson raises the question whether we "won" or "lost" the war on heroin in the 1970s, and whether we will do any better with the current war on cocaine (paras. 30 and 31). What would you regard as convincing evidence that we are winning the war on drugs? Or losing it?

4. In his criticism of those who would legalize drugs, Wilson points to what he regards as an inescapable "economic dilemma" (para. 37). What is this dilemma? Do you see any way around it?

5. Economists tell us that we can control the use of some good or service either by controlling the cost (thus probably reducing the demand) or by ignoring the cost and controlling the supply, or by doing both. In the war on drugs, which of these three strategies does Wilson apparently favor, and why?

Milton Friedman

Milton Friedman, winner of a Nobel Prize in economics, was born in Brooklyn in 1912. Educated at Rutgers University, the University of Chicago, and Columbia University, Friedman, a leading conservative economist, has had considerable influence on economic thought in America through his academic and popular writings. We reprint a piece that appeared in the New York Times *in 1998.*

There's No Justice in the War on Drugs

Twenty-five years ago, President Richard M. Nixon announced a "War on Drugs." I criticized the action on both moral and expediential grounds in my *Newsweek* column of May 1, 1972, "Prohibition and Drugs":

> On ethical grounds, do we have the right to use the machinery of government to prevent an individual from becoming an alcoholic or a drug addict? For children, almost everyone would answer at least a qualified yes. But for responsible adults, I, for one, would answer no. Reason with the potential addict, yes. Tell him the consequences, yes. Pray for and with him, yes. But I believe that we have no right to use force, directly or indirectly, to prevent a fellow man from committing suicide, let alone from drinking alcohol or taking drugs.

That basic ethical flaw has inevitably generated specific evils during the past quarter century, just as it did during our earlier attempt at alcohol prohibition.

1. The use of informers. Informers are not needed in crimes like robbery and murder because the victims of those crimes have a strong incentive to report the crime. In the drug trade, the crime consists of a transaction between a willing buyer and willing seller. Neither has any incentive to report a violation of law. On the contrary, it is in the self-interest of both that the crime not be reported. That is why informers are needed. The use of informers and the immense sums of money at stake inevitably generate corruption—as they did during Prohibition. They also lead to violations of the civil rights of innocent people, to the shameful practices of forcible entry and forfeiture of property without due process.

As I wrote in 1972: "Addicts and pushers are not the only ones corrupted. Immense sums are at stake. It is inevitable that some relatively low-paid police and other government officials—and some high-paid ones as well—will succumb to the temptation to pick up easy money."

2. Filling the prisons. In 1970, 200,000 people were in prison. 5
Today, 1.6 million people are. Eight times as many in absolute number, six times as many relative to the increased population. In addition, 2.3 million are on probation and parole. The attempt to prohibit drugs is by far the major source of the horrendous growth in the prison population.

There is no light at the end of that tunnel. How many of our citizens do we want to turn into criminals before we yell "enough"?

3. Disproportionate imprisonment of blacks. Sher Hosonko, at the time Connecticut's director of addiction services, stressed this effect of drug prohibition in a talk given in June 1995:

> Today in this country, we incarcerate 3,109 black men for every 100,000 of them in the population. Just to give you an idea of the drama in this number, our closest competitor for incarcerating black men is South Africa. South Africa—and this is pre–Nelson Mandela and under an overt public policy of apartheid—incarcerated 729 black men for every 100,000. Figure this out: In the land of the Bill of Rights, we jail over four times as many black men as the only country in the world that advertised a political policy of apartheid.

4. Destruction of inner cities. Drug prohibition is one of the most important factors that have combined to reduce our inner cities to their present state. The crowded inner cities have a comparative advantage for selling drugs. Though most customers do not live in the inner cities, most sellers do. Young boys and girls view the swaggering, affluent drug dealers as role models. Compared with the returns from a traditional career of study and hard work, returns from dealing drugs are tempting to young and old alike. And many, especially the young, are not dissuaded by the bullets that fly so freely in disputes between competing drug dealers—bullets that fly only because dealing drugs is illegal. Al Capone epitomizes our earlier attempt at Prohibition; the Crips and Bloods epitomize this one.

5. Compounding the harm to users. Prohibition makes drugs exorbitantly expensive and highly uncertain in quality. A user must associate with criminals to get the drugs, and many are driven to become criminals themselves to finance the habit. Needles, which are hard to get, are often shared, with the predictable effect of spreading disease. Finally, an addict who seeks treatment must confess to being a criminal in order to qualify for a treatment program. Alternatively, professionals who treat addicts must become informers or criminals themselves.

6. Undertreatment of chronic pain. The Federal Department of Health and Human Services has issued reports showing that two-thirds of all terminal cancer patients do not receive adequate pain medication, and the numbers are surely higher in nonterminally ill patients. Such serious undertreatment of chronic pain is a direct result of the Drug Enforcement Agency's pressures on physicians who prescribe narcotics.

7. Harming foreign countries. Our drug policy has led to thousands of deaths and enormous loss of wealth in countries like Colombia, Peru, and Mexico, and has undermined the stability of their governments. All because we cannot enforce our laws at home. If we did, there would be no market for imported drugs. There would be no Cali cartel. The foreign countries would not have to suffer the loss of sovereignty involved in letting our "advisers" and troops operate on their soil, search their vessels, and encourage local militaries to shoot down their planes. They could run their own affairs, and we, in turn, could avoid the diversion of military forces from their proper function.

Can any policy, however high-minded, be moral if it leads to widespread corruption, imprisons so many, has so racist an effect, destroys our inner cities, wreaks havoc on misguided and vulnerable individuals, and brings death and destruction to foreign countries?

Topics for Critical Thinking and Writing

1. State in one sentence the thesis of Friedman's essay.

2. Which of the seven reasons Friedman cites in favor of revising our "war on drugs" do you find most convincing? Explain why, in a short essay of 100 words.

3. Friedman distinguishes between "moral" and "expediential" objections to current drug policy (para. 1). What does he mean by this distinction? Which kind of objection do you think is the most persuasive? Why?

4. If a policy, practice, or individual act is unethical or immoral, then it must be because it violates some ethical standard or moral norm. What norms or standards does Friedman think our current drug policy violates?

5. Does Friedman favor a policy toward addictive (and currently illegal) drugs like our policy toward alcohol? Explain how the two policies might differ in an essay of 250 words.

Michael Tooley

Michael Tooley, author of Abortion and Infanticide *(1983), is a professor of philosophy at the University of Colorado. The selection reprinted here first appeared in the Spring 1994 issue of the newsletter of the Center for Values and Social Policy, University of Colorado.*

Our Current Drug Legislation: Grounds for Reconsideration

Why is the American policy debate not focused more intensely on the relative merits or demerits of our current approach to drugs and of possible alternatives to it? The lack of discussion of this issue is rather striking, given that America has the most serious drug problem in the world, that alternatives to a prohibitionist approach are under serious consideration in other countries, and that the grounds for reconsidering our current approach are, I shall argue, so weighty.

One consideration that tells against our present approach to drugs is that prohibition simply does not work. For we have, after all, been pursuing this approach in the case of heroin since the Harrison Narcotic Act of 1914, and what has been the outcome? We have the worst heroin problem in the world. Our brief experiment in banning the consumption of what is undoubtedly our most harmful drug, alcohol, turned out to be an utter failure.

A second consideration, often noted, is the striking difference in our treatment of drugs such as alcohol and nicotine, on the one hand, and drugs such as marijuana, heroin, and LSD, on the other. This difference is so familiar that it may no longer seem strange. If so, it is worth asking the following question. If you were on a desert island, with a plentiful supply of both tobacco plants and opium poppies, and you knew that your son or daughter was going to wind up addicted either to nicotine or to heroin, which would you prefer? If your choice is nicotine, you have chosen the drug that, according to the testimony of most heroin addicts, is the more addictive of the two drugs. In addition, given access to heroin that has not been combined with dangerous chemicals, your son or daughter could be a lifelong addict without suffering serious organ damage. But a lifelong addiction to tobacco is often, of course, a very different story.

I want now to turn in detail to perhaps the two most important reasons for reconsidering our current drug policy: first, the difficulty of providing any adequate justification for the restrictions that prohibitive laws place on people's liberty; and second, the enormous social and personal costs associated with a prohibitionist approach.

JUSTIFYING LAWS

Under what conditions is a law justified? To answer this question, 5 one needs to determine what purposes may justifiably be pursued by means of legislation and what goals justify attaching penalties to certain actions. Particular laws can then be justified by reference to the relevant purpose or purposes—although one may also need to show that the costs associated with the law in question do not outweigh the relevant benefits. For the present, however, I shall defer discussion of costs, so that we can focus on what positive rationale might be offered for a prohibitionist approach to certain drugs.

What purpose, or purposes, then, may legislation justifiably serve? One very important answer—defended by John Stuart Mill in his *On Liberty*—is that the only actions that may be made illegal are actions that harm others against their will. (Philosophers of a less utilitarian sort would say that a law is justified if, and only if, it is necessary to protect people's rights.) If this answer were accepted, how would the case for prohibition stand? Not very well. For the laws in question prevent people from buying drugs that they want to consume from people who want to sell them those drugs, and provided that there is no misrepresentation, nor lack of relevant information—such as information about the potential for addiction—then no one is harmed against his or her will, and no one's rights are being violated. On a classical libertarian conception of the purpose of the law, then, prohibition cannot be justified.

Others have argued, however, that the law may serve other purposes beyond protecting the rights of individuals. Often, for example, it is suggested that an important function of the law is to enforce morality, thereby helping to ensure that people do not come to feel that, because certain actions do not violate anyone's rights, they are therefore morally acceptable. Such an appeal is often made, for example, to justify the laws against various types of noncoercive sexual activity which exist in most American states. For given that the behavior in question is voluntary, the laws in question could not be justified if the criterion was whether they were necessary to protect the rights of individuals. So if one is to justify such laws, one must be prepared to argue both that the actions in question are morally wrong, and that an appropriate function of the law is to enforce morality.

Would this view of the function of the law provide a justification of laws prohibiting the distribution and use of drugs? And if so, how?

Illegal drugs produce changes in one's state of consciousness, thereby providing interesting and/or pleasurable experiences. Might one argue, then, that it is morally wrong to consume substances that have such effects? Such a conclusion would be a very strong one, since many things that most people eat and drink produce interesting and/or pleasurable experiences. So unless one can show that illegal drugs are different in some important and morally relevant way, this line of argument will surely not be very plausible.

An alternative approach would be to argue, instead, that it is morally 10 wrong to become addicted to a drug. But this line of argument also seems problematic. First, caffeine and nicotine are addictive, and alcohol is addictive for some people, so the present line of thought would catch more than illegal drugs in its net: Tobacco products, alcoholic beverages, together with tea, coffee, and many soft drinks would also have to go. Second, many illegal drugs—including major hallucinogenic drugs, such as LSD, mescaline, and peyote—are not addicting, and so this line of argument would fail to justify a good deal of current legislation. And third, surely it is appropriate here to weigh pros and cons. Other things being equal, it is preferable not to be addicted to something. But if the substance to which one is addicted provides interesting or pleasurable experiences, might that not outweigh any disvalue associated with addiction? Are people who enjoy coffee, for example, really worse off for being addicted to caffeine?

A third purpose which people sometimes argue that legislation may legitimately serve is that of preventing people from harming themselves. Compulsory seat belt legislation, for example, is sometimes supported by an appeal to paternalistic considerations. But, aside from laws that are concerned with the well being of children, the idea that legislation can justifiably impose restrictions upon people so that they do not act contrary to their own interests is widely rejected. For consider the ways in which people can harm themselves: by being overweight; by not getting enough exercise; by eating diets that are high in fat, or low in fiber, or full of empty calories, etc. And even if one were prepared to embrace laws whose only justification is paternalistic, that would not serve to justify our current policies, since many illegal drugs are either not harmful or only marginally so.

SOME COSTS OF OUR CURRENT APPROACH

Setting justificatory questions aside, we must turn next to the significant costs associated with our present approach. Those costs can be divided into two categories: those borne by members of society as a whole and those that fall upon those who are addicted to, or who choose to use, illegal drugs.

Let us begin with the former. What are some of the ways in which a policy of prohibition affects all members of society, including those of us who do not use illegal drugs? One obvious first effect is increased crime and violence in society. When a drug is illegal, its cost may be one hundred times as great than the cost if it was legal. So many addicts need to steal to be able to buy drugs, generating many more crimes against property and against persons. In addition, the high cost of illegal drugs has the same effect that prohibition had for alcohol. Distribution of the illegal substance becomes an enormously profitable business, and violence is often necessary, both to discourage competitors from trying to take over one's markets, and to ward off interference by law enforcement agencies in one's business activities.

Second, the cost of enforcing drug laws is very great indeed. Detection is difficult, because we are dealing with crimes where there are no complainants, no victims to draw attention to the crimes in question. After arrests have been made, we must bear the substantial costs of prosecution, which slows down an already overloaded legal system still further. Then come the substantial costs associated with incarceration of convicted drug offenders, who often must serve lengthy mandatory sentences.

Third, given the heavy involvement of the criminal justice system 15 in enforcing drug legislation, a much smaller proportion of law enforcement effort can be given over to the prevention and solution of crimes that do involve victims. And because our prisons are crowded past their capacity with drug offenders, violent criminals are often released after strikingly short terms, free once again to inflict serious harm upon people.

What about the impact of a prohibitionist policy on those who use illegal drugs? One obvious consequence is that one may be convicted of using an illegal drug, thereby suffering a serious and extended loss of one's freedom. But bad as this is, other consequences may be much more serious. One, which results from the exorbitantly inflated costs of illegal drugs, is the degradation of addicts who are forced into a life of crime and/or prostitution in order to be able to purchase the drug that they need. Another arises from the fact that illegal drugs are not typically subject to quality control, and so may contain impurities and may vary dramatically in dose and concentration, and thus may lead to illness or premature death. Finally, the fact that a drug is illegal may encourage both the intravenous use of that drug and the sharing of needles. In a time of AIDS, and other serious diseases such as hepatitis B, the implications of this are ominous indeed, not only for those who use drugs, but for others as well. The rapid spread of AIDS into the heterosexual community, in this country, has been mainly via intravenous drug users.

CONCLUSION

It is difficult not to conclude that the costs of a prohibitionist approach are enormous—in terms of money, but even more so in terms of suffering and deaths. This, together with the difficulty, even ignoring those costs, of offering a satisfactory justification for our present drug legislation, strongly suggests that there are excellent reasons for thinking seriously about alternative approaches.

Topics for Critical Thinking and Writing

1. Tooley argues that "prohibition simply does not work" (para. 2). Despite the 1914 narcotic act that made heroin an illegal drug, he says we "have the worst heroin problem in the world." Suppose one were to reply, "So what? It would be much worse if we hadn't made it illegal in 1914." How do you think Tooley might reply?

2. Tooley cites two important objections to current drug policy. What are they? What is his argument in support of each of these objections?

3. Tooley concludes, "On a classical libertarian conception of the purpose of the law, . . . prohibition cannot be justified" (para. 6). What exactly is his argument for this conclusion?

4. Tooley thinks it is futile to argue against taking drugs such as heroin on the ground that the drug is addictive. What is his argument for this conclusion? Do you find it persuasive? Why, or why not?

5. Tooley concedes that "other things being equal, it is preferable not to be addicted to something" (para. 10). But why? What do you think Tooley thinks is wrong with being addicted to something? If you liked coffee, say, but were not addicted to caffeine, do you think you'd be better off, worse off, or neither if you became addicted to it?

6. Construct an outline of Tooley's overall essay, making sure that each of his seventeen paragraphs is represented in the outline with its own number or letter, and that you sharply contrast his main from his subordinate points (for guidance on how to construct an outline, see pp. 177–78).

21

The Environment: Natural Resource or Raw Material?

Leila L. Kysar

Leila L. Kysar is the business manager of a tree-farm-management enter-prise in the state of Washington. Her essay originally appeared as a "My Turn" column in Newsweek *(October 22, 1990).*

A Logger's Lament

My father was a logger. My husband is a logger. My sons will not be loggers. Loggers are an endangered species, but the environmental groups, which so righteously protect endangered species in the animal kingdom, have no concern for their fellow human beings under siege. Loggers are a much misunderstood people, pictured as brutal rapists of our planet, out to denude it of trees and, as a result, of wildlife.

It is time to set the record straight. Loggers take great pride in the old-growth trees, the dinosaurs of the forests, and would be sorry to see them all cut. There are in the national forests in Washington and Oregon (not to mention other states) approximately 8.5 million acres of forested land, mostly old growth set aside, never to be used for timber production. In order to see it all, a man would have to spend every weekend and holiday for sixty years looking at timber at a rate of more than one-thousand acres per day. This does not include acreage to be set aside for spotted-owl protection.

In addition to this huge amount of forested land never to be logged, the State of Washington Forest Practices Act, established in 1973, speci-fies that all land that is clear-cut of trees must be replanted unless con-verted to some other use. As a tree farmer generally plants more trees per acre than he removes, more trees are being planted than are being cut. In the last twenty years in Clark County, Washington, alone, the Department of Natural Resources has overseen the planting of at least 15,000 acres of previously unforested private lands.

The term *logger* applies to the person harvesting trees. A tree farmer is the one who owns the land and determines what is to be done with it. To a tree farmer, clear-cutting is no more than the final harvest of that generation of trees. The next spring, he reforests the land. To the public, clear-cutting is a bad word. Does the public cry shame when a wheat farmer harvests his crop and leaves a field of stubble in place of the beautiful wheat?

In the Pacific Northwest, in five years, the newly planted trees will   5 grow taller than the farmer's head; in ten years, more than fifteen feet tall; and in twenty to thirty years, the trees will be ready for the first commercial harvest. The farmer then thins the trees to make room for better growth. In forty to fifty years, he will be ready to clear-cut his farm and replant again. Contrary to public opinion, it does *not* take three hundred to four hundred years to grow a Douglas fir tree to harvestable age.

Tree farming keeps us in wood products. We build with wood, write on paper, and even use the unmentionable in the bathroom. But in order to keep this flow of wood products available, we need to keep it economically feasible to grow trees. If we restrict the tree-farming practices because we do not like clear-cuts or because some animal might (and probably might not) become extinct, or we restrict markets for the timber by banning log exports or overtax the farmer, we are creating a situation where the farmer will no longer grow trees. If he cannot make money, he will not tree-farm. He will sell his tree farm so that it can grow houses. The *land* that grows trees is the natural resource; the *trees* are just a crop.

Legislation is constantly being introduced to take away the private-property rights of tree farmers. They are beleaguered by the public, who believe that any forest belongs to the public. Who, after all, buys the land and pays the taxes? Who invests money in property that will yield them an income only once every twenty to thirty years? Would John Q. Public picnic in a farmer's wheat field?

The tree farmer must have a diversified market. When there is a building slump in this country, it is vital to the industry to have an export market. Earlier recessions were devastating to tree farmers until markets were developed overseas. Some trees have little market value in the United States. The logs China and Korea bought in the late 1980s could not be sold here to cover the cost of delivery.

As to the wildlife becoming extinct, that is a joke that is not very funny. Animals thrive in clear-cuts better than in old-growth timber. Look at the Mount St. Helens blast area. Nature created an immense clearing and now deer, elk, and other wildlife are returning in numbers.

Why? Because there is more food growing in an open area than under the tall trees. And as for the spotted owl, surely the 8.5 million acres set aside is enough to maintain quite a respectable owl population. Numerous recent observations show that the owl lives in second-growth timber as well as in old growth. In the Wenatchie National Forest there are more than two hundred fifty examples of spotted owls living in other than old-growth timber. The owl is a tool of the environmentalist groups to get what they want: the complete eradication of the species *Logger*.

BEAUTIFUL NEW TREES

Consider the scenic value of a preserved old-growth forest versus a 10 managed stand of timber. In Glacier National Park, Montana, for example, which is totally untouched, one sees the old trees, the dead and dying trees, the windfalls crisscrossing the forest. In a managed forest, one sees the older stands with the forest floor cleared of the dead windfalls, leaving a more parklike setting. In the younger stands, one sees the beautiful new trees with their brilliant greens thrusting their tops to the sky and, in the clear-cuts, before the new trees obscure the view, one sees the huckleberry bushes with their luscious-tasting berries, the bright pink of fireweed and deer and elk feeding. True environmentalists husband the land; they do not let the crops stagnate and rot. Tree farming regenerates the trees *and* utilizes the product.

A tree farmer from Sweden (where they are fined if they do *not* tree-farm their forests) asked me recently why we do not just explain these facts to the environmental groups so that they will work *with* us instead of *against* us. Well, do you know the difference between a terrorist and an environmentalist? It is easier to reason with the terrorist.

Topics for Critical Thinking and Writing

1. In a few sentences summarize Kysar's essay.

2. What, exactly, is Kysar's thesis?

3. Kysar makes a comparison between the tree farmer clear-cutting his timber and the wheat farmer harvesting his crop (para. 4). Do you think this is a fair comparison? Why, or why not?

4. In the next-to-last paragraph, Kysar argues that national parks, with their "managed forest[s]," have more "scenic value" (as well as economic value) than untended natural forests. Can you think of any respects in which the reverse is true? Write a 500-word essay arguing for or against this proposition: All public natural forests in the United States ought to be turned into managed forests.

5. Kysar ends her essay by comparing "environmentalists" with "terrorists." What would it take to convince you that she was not exaggerating for rhetorical effect, but fairly describing the plight of the logger and tree farmer?

6. Kysar does not assert, but she does (through her silence) imply, that there are no adverse environmental effects from clear-cutting timber in part because as soon as the trees are cut, the tree farmer "reforests the land" (para. 4). Do some research in your college library on the practice of clear-cutting, and write a 500-word essay with the title "The Truth about Clear-Cutting for Timber."

Donella Meadows

Donella Meadows is an adjunct professor of environmental studies at Dartmouth College in New Hampshire. This essay originally appeared in Valley News, *a regional newspaper, on June 30, 1990.*

Not Seeing the Forest for the Dollar Bills

The U.S. Fish and Wildlife Service has finally declared the spotted owl an endangered species. The decision will, if the administration enforces the law of the land, drastically cut back logging in the owl's habitat—old-growth forest in the Pacific Northwest.

The logging companies are fighting back. They will go to court to "dispute the science" behind the finding. Knowing that the science is not on their side, they have also leaned on the administration not to enforce the law. And they are trying to get the law changed.

The law in question is the Endangered Species Act. The companies want it to take into account economic considerations. If it did, they say over and over to the press, the politicians, and the public, we would never choose to sacrifice 28,000 jobs for an owl.

That is not the choice at all, of course. The choice is not between an owl and jobs, but between a forest and greed.

The spotted owl is, like every other species, the holder of a unique 5
genetic code that is millions of years old and irreplaceable. Even more important, the owl is a canary, in the old miners' sense—a sign that all is well. It is an indicator species, a creature high up the food chain that depends upon a large area of healthy land for its livelihood.

Every thriving family of spotted owls means that 4,000 acres of forest are well. The trees are living their full lives and returning stored nutrients to the soil when they die. Two hundred other vertebrates that live in the forest are well, as are 1,500 insects and spiders and untold numbers of smaller creatures. The spongy soil under the trees is storing and filtering rain, controlling floods and droughts, keeping the streams clear and pure.

When old-growth is clear-cut, the trees and the owls disappear and so does everything else. Burned slash releases to the sky nutrients that have been sequestered and recycled by living things for 500 years. What's left of the soil bleeds downhill as from an open wound. Waters cloud and silt, flood and dry up. The temperature goes up, the humidity goes down. It will take hundreds of years to regather the nutrients, rebuild the soil, and restore the complex system of the intact forest, *if* there is still old-growth forest around to recolonize, and *if* the forest companies stay away.

They are unlikely to stay away. On their own land, they replant with a single, commercially valuable, fast-growing species and call it a forest. It bears as much resemblance to a 500-year-old natural forest as a suburb of identical ticky-tacky houses bears to a Renaissance cathedral. Ecologists call such plantations "cornfields." It's not at all certain how many cycles of these cornfields will be possible, given the loss of soil and nutrients when they are cut every fifty years or so.

In the past ten years, 13,000 forest-related jobs were lost in Oregon alone, though the annual cut increased. The jobs were lost to automation and to moving mills offshore, not to the Endangered Species Act.

The forest companies are interested not in jobs or forests, but in multiplying money. Old-growth forests yield higher profit than second-growth plantations. Therefore 85 percent of the old growth is already gone. The companies have stripped it from their own lands. Nearly all that remains is on federal land, owned by you and me. In Washington and Oregon, 2.4 million acres of old growth are left, of which 800,000 are protected in national parks. The rest, in national forests, is marked for cutting.

Our elected representatives are selling off old-growth logging rights in national forests at a rate of about 100,000 acres per year, and at a loss. Taxpayers are subsidizing this process. At the present cutting rate, all but the last protected bits will be gone in about twenty years. The owls will be on their way out—the 800,000 acres remaining will be too fragmented to sustain them. The jobs will be gone, not because of owls, but because of rapacious forestry.

If loggers and their communities cannot be sustained by second-growth cutting on private lands, then they were in trouble anyway. A compassionate nation would look for a dignified way to help them build a viable economy. It wouldn't sacrifice the biological treasure of an intact forest to keep them going twenty more years. That's the kind of behavior we are righteously telling the Brazilians to stop.

The Endangered Species Act should not take into account economic considerations. Economics doesn't know how to value a species or a forest. Its logic drives people to exploit resources to the point of extinction. The Endangered Species Act tells us that extinction is morally unacceptable. It was enacted by a Congress and president in a wise mood, to express a higher value than a bottom line. It should not be weakened. It should be enforced.

Topics for Critical Thinking and Writing

1. In a few sentences summarize Meadows's essay.

2. In a sentence or two state her thesis.

3. In paragraphs 3 and 13 Meadows refers to the Endangered Species Act. What, exactly, does the act provide? Write a 250-word summary of the act. (You probably will want to consult with your college reference librarian to find the text of this law and some details concerning its enactment by Congress.)

4. In paragraphs 3 and 4 Meadows says that the choice is not between 28,000 jobs and an owl, but "between a forest and greed." Do you think she has properly formulated the choice? Or do you think the choice *is* between the owl and jobs? Or would you put the choice differently? Explain.

5. What do you think are Meadows's strongest points? Her weakest points?

6. In paragraph 5 Meadows says that the spotted owl is "the holder of a unique genetic code that is millions of years old and irreplaceable." In her final paragraph she says that "extinction is morally unacceptable." Suppose someone were to reply, "Extinction is nature's way. Countless species—all of the dinosaurs, for instance—have become extinct." What reply might Meadows offer?

Sally Thane Christensen

Sally Thane Christensen was a thirty-eight-year-old resident of Missoula, Montana, and a lawyer for the Forest Service when she published this essay in Newsweek *on October 22, 1990. She died in early 1992.*

Is a Tree Worth a Life?

For most of the last decade, federal timberlands in the West have been held hostage in a bitter fight between environmental groups and the timber industry. The environmentalists want to save the forests and their wildlife occupants. The timber industry wants to cut trees and provide jobs in a depressed economy. Caught in the middle is the United States Forest Service, which must balance the conflicting concepts of sustained yield and multiple use of national forest land.

The latest pawn in this environmental chess match is the Pacific yew tree, a scrubby conifer found from southern Alaska to central California and in Washington, Oregon, Idaho, and Montana. Historically the yew has not been harvested for value but often has been treated as logging slash and washed. Not any longer. An extract of the bark of the Pacific yew known as taxol has been found to have cancer-fighting properties, particularly with ovarian cancer. As many as 30 percent of those treated with taxol have shown significant responses. Some researchers call taxol the most significant new cancer drug to emerge in fifteen years.

For the first time, the environmental debate over the use of a natural resource involves more than a question of the priority of the resource versus economic considerations. At stake is the value of a species of tree and the habitat it provides for wildlife as opposed to the value of the greatest of all natural resources, human life.

When I was first diagnosed three years ago, no one had an inkling that I would become caught in the center of what may become the most significant environmental debate of my generation. Although as early as 1979 researchers had discovered that taxol killed cancer in a unique way, imprisoning malignant cells in a cage of scaffoldlike rods called microtubules, lab tests on animals were inconclusive. By 1985, however, a woman with terminal ovarian cancer was treated with taxol and had a dramatic response. Six years later, the once lowly yew tree is at the threshold of a controversy that challenges the fundamental precepts of even the most entrenched environmentalist.

MY FATE

It takes about three one-hundred-year-old Pacific yew trees, or 5 roughly sixty pounds of bark, to produce enough taxol to treat one patient. When the bark is removed, the tree dies. Environmental groups like the Oregon Natural Resources Council and the Audubon Society are concerned that the Pacific yew as a species may be decimated by the demand for taxol. But this year alone, twelve thousand women will die from ovarian cancer. Breast cancer will kill forty-five thousand women. Is preservation of the Pacific yew worth the price?

It is sublimely ironic that my fate hinges so directly on the Pacific yew. As a federal attorney representing the Forest Service, I have witnessed the environmental movement in the West from its embryonic stages. I have seen such diverse groups as the National Wildlife Federation and the Sierra Club challenge the Forest Service's ability to sell and harvest its trees. Win or lose, the forests are often locked up during the lengthy legal process.

The viability of the national forests does not rise or fall with the Pacific yew. But, unfortunately for cancer victims, the tree is most abundant on national-forest lands which are subject to environmental review by the public. Already challenges to the federal harvest of the yew have begun. In Montana, the Save the Yaak Committee has protested the Kootenai National Forest's intention to harvest yew trees and make them available for experimental use. The committee contends that the yew may be endangered by overharvesting.

I have news for the Save the Yaak Committee. I am endangered, too. I've had four major abdominal surgeries in two years. I've had the conventional chemotherapy for ovarian cancer, and it didn't work. Though I was in remission for almost a year, last August my cancer returned with a vengeance. Taxol may be my last hope.

Because of the scarcity of supply, taxol is not commercially available. It is available only in clinical trials at a number of institutions. Bristol-Myers, working with the National Cancer Institute in Bethesda, Maryland, asked the Forest Service to provide 750,000 pounds of bark for clinical studies this year.

The ultimate irony of my story is that I am one of the lucky ones. This May I was accepted by the National Cancer Institute for one of its clinical trials. On May 8 I was infused with my first treatment of taxol. Hospitalized in intensive care at NCI, I watched the precious, clear fluid drip into my veins and prayed for it to kill the cancer that has ravaged my body. I thought about the thousands of women who will die of cancer this year, who will not have my opportunity.

Every effort should be made to ensure that the yew tree is made available for the continued research and development of taxol. Environmental groups, the timber industry, and the Forest Service must recognize that the most important value of the Pacific yew is as a treatment for cancer. At the same time, its harvest can be managed in a way that allows for the production of taxol without endangering the continued survival of the yew tree.

The yew may be prime habitat for spotted owls. It may be esthetically appealing. But certainly its most critical property is its ability to treat a fatal disease. Given a choice between trees or people, people must prevail. No resource can be more valuable or more important than a human life. Ask my husband. Ask my two sons. Ask me.

Topics for Critical Thinking and Writing

1. News reports in 1994 informed the world that scientists had succeeded in synthesizing taxol. Does this success in creating synthetic taxol undermine Christensen's entire argument for harvesting the Pacific yew? Why, or why not?

2. Assume that taxol is, indeed, effective as a remedy for ovarian cancer. But assume also that the demand far exceeds the supply. How do you think it ought to be rationed to those who need it? By some form of random lottery? By raising the price so high that only a few can afford it? By some other method? Present your responses in an essay of 500 words.

3. Christensen says, "Given a choice between trees or people, people must prevail" (para. 12). Suppose all the yew trees were owned by private corporations who refused to sell to the highest bidder. Do you think Christensen ought to argue that, given a choice between someone's private property and someone else's life, human life must prevail? Why, or why not?

Sallie Tisdale

Sallie Tisdale, a resident of Portland, Oregon, is a writer. Her most recent books are Stepping Westward: The Long Search for Home in the Pacific Northwest *(1991) and* Talk Dirty to Me: An Intimate Philosophy of Sex *(1994). The essay that we reprint originally appeared as an Op-Ed piece in the* New York Times *(October 26, 1991).*

Save a Life, Kill a Tree?

Land wars are a constant in the West.

The latest battle concerns the Pacific yew tree, an unassuming conifer scattered throughout the Pacific Northwest. The yew's bark contains taxol, a chemical with potent anticancer effects. Taxol seems to work best against ovarian cancer, a devastating and often fatal disease.

No one knows how many yews there are here. Until last year loggers considered the humble Pacific yew a "trash tree." It was typically cut and burned with other logging debris. But suddenly it is invaluable.

In current taxol laboratory trials, it takes about 60 pounds of yew bark to treat one person. The National Cancer Institute expects to collect 750,000 pounds of yew bark this year, the bark of approximately thirty-eight thousand trees. And thus is the battle born: People versus Trees. Sally Thane Christensen, a cancer patient in a taxol trial, wrote recently in *Newsweek*, "Given a choice between trees or people, people must prevail."

Ms. Christensen is a lawyer for the Forest Service. She's used to arguing against environmental protection lawsuits. She wants her drug now—forget the future. But forgetting the future is exactly what uncontrolled yew harvesting will do. 5

The slow-growing yew requires shade. With rare exceptions, it lives its whole life in the understory, under the high canopy of Douglas fir and Western hemlock, which are themselves rapidly disappearing. The Forest Service, in response to the outcry of preservationists, has said that the nearly forty thousand yews killed this year for taxol had already been logged or were destined for logging anyway.

Perhaps I sound battle-weary. We've seen these same equations so many times before: people versus the old growth, people versus the spotted owl, people versus wild rivers, versus wetlands, the snail darter, caribou, wolves, salmon. But all of these battles are really just between us. There is one war and it is people versus people—a kind of civil war in which trees and rivers and owls are the innocent bystanders, taking stray bullets.

The real battle lies outside the few remaining forests. What does it mean that the Pacific yew was burned by the tens of thousands until last winter? Far from trash, the lowly yew is a beautiful hardwood. The problem is greed: The yew occurs too sparely in any given area to make logging it worthwhile. Its casual destruction in the course of more lucrative harvests was profiteering and nothing more.

Greed has gotten us here, to where one more loss is more than the forest can sustain. Loggers are desperate for work partly because we are running out of old-growth trees; we are running out of trees because the managers of the trees, including the Forest Service, hold a peculiarly narrow view of their job. They see the forest as a pile of goods first to be inventoried and then passed out. Loggers have a telling term for the commercial value of a forest stand: They call it "stumpage." You can't miss the results of that thinking. The clear-cuts crowd every road.

The worth of the Pacific yew is now dependent only on the demand 10 for taxol. Another product. If taxol were synthesized tomorrow, the Pacific yew would be back on the slash pile.

People versus people. The salmon are squeezed in the dams, between fishermen and the power companies. The spotted owl is driven from one shrinking island to another. The loggers are hurting, like the fishermen, like the cancer patients. My mother died of cancer a few years ago and both my sister and I are at risk for a death like hers. I would welcome almost any cure—but I reject the notion that our human future requires the sacrifice of the human habitat, the earth.

"People must prevail." Such comments degrade all we know of biology. God help us if people do finally prevail. Do we really think the undisturbed forest has nothing to offer the human race? Do we think we stand alone, separate, independent?

The forest, like any ecosystem, is an organism greater than the sum of its parts. Take away all the tall trees, or all the spotted owls, and it slowly bleeds to death. Whole, the forest makes and keeps great secrets: secrets like taxol, going up in smoke.

Topics for Critical Thinking and Writing

1. When Tisdale declares, "God help us if people do finally prevail" (para. 12), how is she interpreting the slogan "People must prevail"?

2. Suppose some environmentalist declared, "Human beings have never done anything good for the environment—and never will." Do you think Tisdale would agree? Why, or why not?

3. Tisdale seems unsympathetic to the plight of Christensen and others who suffer from a form of cancer that taxol from yew trees might cure. Do you think she really believes that it is better for Christensen to die of cancer than to cure her by cutting down yew trees to get taxol? If Tisdale doesn't believe this, what does she believe? What is your view? In an essay of 500 words, set forth what you take to be Tisdale's view in 100 to 200 words and your own view in the remainder of the essay.

22

Euthanasia:
Should Doctors Intervene
at the End of Life?

Barbara Huttman

Barbara Huttman, born in Oakland, California, in 1935, earned nursing degrees in 1976 and 1978. She is the author of numerous articles and of several books, including Code Blue: A Nurse's True-Life Story *(1982). The essay that we reprint originally appeared in* Newsweek *(August 8, 1983).*

A Crime of Compassion

"Murderer," a man shouted. "God help patients who get *you* for a nurse."

"What gives you the right to play God?" another one asked.

It was the Phil Donahue show where the guest is a fatted calf and the audience a two-hundred-strong flock of vultures hungering to pick up the bones. I had told them about Mac, one of my favorite cancer patients. "We resuscitated him fifty-two times in just one month. I refused to resuscitate him again. I simply sat there and held his hand while he died."

There wasn't time to explain that Mac was a young, witty, macho cop who walked into the hospital with thirty-two pounds of attack equipment, looking as if he could single-handedly protect the whole city, if not the entire state. "Can't get rid of this cough," he said. Otherwise, he felt great.

Before the day was over, tests confirmed that he had lung cancer. And   5
before the year was over, I loved him, his wife, Maura, and their three kids as if they were my own. All the nurses loved him. And we all battled his disease for six months without ever giving death a thought. Six months

isn't such a long time in the whole scheme of things, but it was long enough to see him lose his youth, his wit, his macho, his hair, his bowel and bladder control, his sense of taste and smell, and his ability to do the slightest thing for himself. It was also long enough to watch Maura's transformation from a young woman into a haggard, beaten old lady.

When Mac had wasted away to a sixty-pound skeleton kept alive by liquid food we poured down a tube, IV solutions we dripped into his veins, and oxygen we piped to a mask on his face, he begged us: "Mercy . . . for God's sake, please just let me go."

The first time he stopped breathing, the nurse pushed the button that calls a "code blue" throughout the hospital and sends a team rushing to resuscitate the patient. Each time he stopped breathing, sometimes two or three times in one day, the code team came again. The doctors and technicians worked their miracles and walked away. The nurses stayed to wipe the saliva that drooled from his mouth, irrigate the big craters of bedsores that covered his hips, suction the lung fluids that threatened to drown him, clean the feces that burned his skin like lye, pour the liquid food down the tube attached to his stomach, put pillows between his knees to ease the bone-on-bone pain, turn him every hour to keep the bedsores from getting worse, and change his gown and linen every two hours to keep him from being soaked in perspiration.

At night I went home and tried to scrub away the smell of decaying flesh that seemed woven into the fabric of my uniform. It was in my hair, the upholstery of my car—there was no washing it away. And every night I prayed that his agonized eyes would never again plead with me to let him die.

Every morning I asked the doctor for a "no code" order. Without that order, we had to resuscitate every patient who stopped breathing. His doctor was one of the several who believe we must extend life as long as we have the means and knowledge to do it. To not do it is to be liable for negligence, at least in the eyes of many people, including some nurses. I thought about what it would be like to stand before a judge, accused of murder, if Mac stopped breathing and I didn't call a code.

And after the fifty-second code, when Mac was still lucid enough to 10 beg for death again, and Maura was crumbled in my arms again, and when no amount of pain medication stilled his moaning and agony, I wondered about a spiritual judge. Was all this misery and suffering supposed to be building character or infusing us all with the sense of humility that comes from impotence?

Had we, the whole medical community, become so arrogant that we believed in the illusion of salvation through science? Had we become so self-righteous that we thought meddling in God's work was our duty, our moral imperative, and our legal obligation? Did we really believe that we had the right to force "life" on a suffering man who had begged for the right to die?

Such questions haunted me more than ever early one morning when Maura went home to change her clothes and I was bathing Mac. He had been still for so long, I thought he at last had the blessed relief of coma. Then he opened his eyes and moaned, "Pain . . . no more . . . Barbara . . . do something . . . God, let me go."

The desperation in the eyes and voice riddled me with guilt. "I'll stop," I told him as I injected the pain medication.

I sat on the bed and held Mac's hands in mine. He pressed his bony fingers against my hand and muttered, "Thanks." Then there was the one soft sigh and I felt his hands go cold in mine. "Mac?" I whispered, as I waited for his chest to rise and fall again.

A clutch of panic banded my chest, drew my finger to the code button, urged me to do something, anything . . . but sit there alone with death. I kept one finger on the button, without pressing it, as a waxen pallor slowly transformed his face from person to empty shell. Nothing I've ever done in my forty-seven years has taken so much effort as it took *not* to press that code button.   15

Eventually, when I was as sure as I could be that the code team would fail to bring him back, I entered the legal twilight zone and pushed the button. The team tried. And while they were trying, Maura walked in the room and shrieked, "No . . . don't let them do this to him . . . for God's sake . . . please, no more."

Cradling her in my arms was like cradling myself, Mac, and all those patients and nurses who had been in this place before who do the best they can in a death-denying society.

So a TV audience accused me of murder. Perhaps I am guilty. If a doctor had written a no-code order, which is the only *legal* alternative, would he have felt any less guilty? Until there is legislation making it a criminal act to code a patient who has requested the right to die, we will all of us risk the same fate as Mac. For whatever reason, we developed the means to prolong life, and now we are forced to use it. We do not have the right to die.

Topics for Critical Thinking and Writing

1. If you think that Huttman's title sounds somewhat familiar—if it seems to echo a familiar phrase—you are right. What does it echo, and how effective do you think the title is?

2. In order to advance a thesis Huttman narrates an experience. That is, she draws on her authority as a person who has undergone something. In a sentence or two state her thesis.

3. What persona does Huttman convey? How important is the persona to the argument?

4. Huttman's closing sentence is, "We do not have the right to die." Taking her words in the context of her essay, what do they mean?

5. Huttman obviously believes that euthanasia (mercy killing) is sometimes justified. Reflecting the argument of her essay, complete the following criterion: "A person is justified in killing another person, as an act of mercy, if and only if . . ." Cite examples of three hypothetical cases of so-called mercy killing that this criterion would exclude—that is, that this criterion implies are *not* justified.

6. Huttman's patient, Mac, clearly wanted to die (see paras. 6 and 12). But suppose you do not know whether the patient wants to die, because, say, she arrives at the hospital in a coma, and is thus unable from the start to indicate to her family or the hospital staff whether she wants to be allowed to die. Write a 500- to 750-word essay exploring what you think Huttman would argue we ought to do in such a case.

7. As Huttman's final paragraph indicates, when she wrote her essay (1983) the only legal alternative to resuscitation was a physician's written no-code order. Today many states recognize *living wills*, documents in which a person indicates his or her desires concerning resuscitation. Find out the legal status in your state of living wills expressing a "right to die." If such documents are recognized, study one and evaluate it.

Ellen Goodman

Ellen Goodman, educated at Radcliffe College, worked as a reporter for Newsweek *and the* Detroit Free Press. *Since 1967 she has written for the* Boston Globe, *and since 1972 her column has been nationally syndicated. This column appeared in the* Boston Globe *in February 1980, the year she won a Pulitzer Prize for journalism.*

Who Lives? Who Dies? Who Decides?

Some have called it a Right to Die case. Others have labeled it a Right to Live case. One group of advocates has called for "death with dignity." Others have responded accusingly, "euthanasia."

At the center of the latest controversy about life and death, medicine and law, is a seventy-eight-year-old Massachusetts man whose existence hangs on a court order.

On one point, everyone agrees: Earle Spring is not the man he used to be. Once a strapping outdoorsman, he is now strapped to a wheelchair. Once a man with a keen mind, he is now called senile by many, and mentally incompetent by the courts. He is, at worst, a member of the living dead; at best, a shriveled version of his former self.

For more than two years, since his physical and then mental health began to deteriorate, Earle Spring has been kept alive by spending five hours on a kidney dialysis machine three times a week. Since January

1979, his family has pleaded to have him removed from the life-support system.

They believe deeply that the Earle Spring who was would not want to live as the Earle Spring who is. They believe they are advocates for the right to die in peace.

In the beginning, the courts agreed. Possibly for the first time, they ruled last month in favor of withdrawing medical care from an elderly patient whose mind had deteriorated. The dialysis was stopped.

But then, in a sudden intervention, an outside nurse and doctor visited Earle Spring and testified that he was alert enough to "make a weak expression of his desire to live." And so the treatments were resumed.

Now, while the courts are waiting for new and more thorough evidence about Spring's mental state, the controversy rages about legal procedures; no judge ever visited Spring, no psychiatrist ever testified. And even more important, we are again forced to determine one person's right to die or to live.

This case makes the Karen Ann Quinlan story seem simple in comparison. Quinlan today hangs onto her "life" long after her "plug was pulled." But when the New Jersey court heard that case, Quinlan had no will. She had suffered brain death by any definition.

The Spring story is different. He is neither competent nor comatose. He lives in a gray area of consciousness. So the questions also range over the gray area of our consciences.

What should the relationship be between mental health and physical treatment? Should we treat the incompetent as aggressively as the competent? Should we order heart surgery for one senile citizen? Should we take another off a kidney machine? What is the mental line between a life worth saving and the living dead? Who is to decide?

Until recently, we didn't have the technology to keep an Earle Spring alive. Until recently, the life-and-death decisions about the senile elderly or the retarded or the institutionalized were made privately between families and medical people. Now, increasingly, in states like Massachusetts, they are made publicly and legally.

Clearly there are no absolutes in this case. No right to die. No right to live. We have to take into account many social as well as medical factors. How much of the resources of a society or a family should be allotted to a member who no longer recognizes it? How many sacrifices should the healthy and vital make for the terminally or permanently ill and disabled?

In England, where kidney dialysis machines are scarce, Earle Spring would never have remained on one. In America, one Earle Spring can decimate the energy and income of an entire family.

But the Spring case is a crucial, scary one that could affect all those living under that dubious sentence "incompetent" or that shaky diagnosis "senile." So it seems to me that if there is one moment a week when the fog lifts and when this man wants to live, if there is any mental activity at all, then disconnecting him from life would be a dangerous precedent, far more dangerous than letting him continue.

The court ruled originally in favor of taking Spring off the machine. It ruled that this is what Earle Spring would have wanted. I have no doubt that his family believes it. I have no doubt of their affection or their pain.

But I remember, too, what my grandfather used to say: No one wants to live to be one hundred until you ask the man who is ninety-nine. Well, no one, including Earle Spring, wants to live to be senile. But once senile, he may well want to live. We simply have to give him the benefit of the doubt. Any doubt.

Topics for Critical Thinking and Writing

1. Suppose you were in the condition of Earle Spring, as described by Goodman (paras. 3, 4, and 10). Would you want to be kept alive, or not? In an essay of 250 words, explain why.

2. Goodman invites us to think about the relationship between "mental health and physical treatment" (para. 11). She concludes that we have to give everyone, no matter what mental condition he or she is in, "the benefit of the doubt" (para. 17). Does she give any argument for this conclusion? If so, what is it and what do you think of it? If not, invent an argument that you think she might accept.

3. Goodman declares, "Clearly there are no absolutes in this case. No right to die. No right to live" (para. 13). Why does she hold this view, do you think? Could there be a right to die (or to live) that is not "absolute"? What sort of right to die, or to live, do you think *you* have—if any? Explain your view in an essay of 500 words.

James Rachels

James Rachels, professor of philosophy at the University of Alabama at Birmingham, is the author of several books, including The End of Life: Euthanasia and Morality *(1986) and* Can Ethics Provide Answers? And Other Essays in Moral Philosophy *(1997). The article reprinted here appeared in the* New England Journal of Medicine *in 1975.*

Active and Passive Euthanasia

The distinction between active and passive euthanasia is thought to be crucial for medical ethics. The idea is that it is permissible, at least in some cases, to withhold treatment and allow a patient to die, but it is never permissible to take any direct action designed to kill the patient. This doctrine seems to be accepted by most doctors, and it is endorsed in a statement adopted by the House of Delegates of the American Medical Association on December 4, 1973:

> The intentional termination of the life of one human being by another—mercy killing—is contrary to that for which the medical profession stands and is contrary to the policy of the American Medical Association. The cessation of the employment of extraordinary means to prolong the life of the body when there is irrefutable evidence that biological death is imminent is the decision of the patient and/or his immediate family. The advice and judgment of the physician should be freely available to the patient and/or his immediate family.

However, a strong case can be made against this doctrine. In what follows I will set out some of the relevant arguments, and urge doctors to reconsider their views on this matter.

To begin with a familiar type of situation, a patient who is dying of incurable cancer of the throat is in terrible pain, which can no longer be satisfactorily alleviated. He is certain to die within a few days, even if present treatment is continued, but he does not want to go on living for those days since the pain is unbearable. So he asks the doctor for an end to it, and his family joins in the request.

Suppose the doctor agrees to withhold treatment, as the conventional doctrine says he may. The justification for his doing so is that the patient is in terrible agony, and since he is going to die anyway, it would be wrong to prolong his suffering needlessly. But now notice this. If one simply withholds treatment, it may take the patient longer to die, and so he may suffer more than he would if more direct action were taken and a lethal injection given. This fact provides strong reason for thinking that, once the initial decision not to prolong his agony has been made, active euthanasia is actually preferable to passive euthanasia, rather than the reverse. To say otherwise is to endorse the option that leads to more suffering rather than less, and is contrary to the humanitarian impulse that prompts the decision not to prolong his life in the first place.

Part of my point is that the process of being "allowed to die" can be relatively slow and painful, whereas being given a lethal injection is relatively quick and painless. Let me give a different sort of example. In the United States about one in six hundred babies is born with Down's syndrome. Most of these babies are otherwise healthy—that is, with only the usual pediatric care, they will proceed to an otherwise normal infancy. Some, however, are born with congenital defects such as intestinal obstructions that require operations if they are to live. Sometimes, the parents and the doctor will decide not to operate, and let the infant die. Anthony Shaw describes what happens then:

> When surgery is denied [the doctor] must try to keep the infant from suffering while natural forces sap the baby's life away. As a surgeon

whose natural inclination is to use the scalpel to fight off death, standing by and watching a salvageable baby die is the most emotionally exhausting experience I know. It is easy at a conference, in a theoretical
discussion to decide that such infants should be allowed to die. It is altogether different to stand by in the nursery and watch as dehydration
and infection wither a tiny being over hours and days. This is a terrible
ordeal for me and the hospital staff—much more so than for the parents who never set foot in the nursery.[1]

I can understand why some people are opposed to all euthanasia, and
insist that such infants must be allowed to live. I think I can also understand why other people favor destroying these babies quickly and painlessly. But why should anyone favor letting "dehydration and infection
wither a tiny being over hours and days"? The doctrine that says that a
baby may be allowed to dehydrate and wither, but may not be given an
injection that would end its life without suffering, seems so patently
cruel as to require no further refutation. The strong language is not intended to offend, but only to put the point in the clearest possible way.

My second argument is that the conventional doctrine leads to deci-   5
sions concerning life and death made on irrelevant grounds.

Consider again the case of the infants with Down's syndrome who
need operations for congenital defects unrelated to the syndrome to live.
Sometimes, there is no operation, and the baby dies, but when there is
no such defect, the baby lives on. Now, an operation such as that to remove an intestinal obstruction is not prohibitively difficult. The reason
why such operations are not performed in these cases is, clearly, that the
child has Down's syndrome and the parents and the doctor judge that
because of that fact it is better for the child to die.

But notice that this situation is absurd, no matter what view one
takes of the lives and potentials of such babies. If the life of such an infant is worth preserving, what does it matter if it needs a simple operation? Or, if one thinks it better that such a baby should not live on, what
difference does it make that it happens to have an unobstructed intestinal tract? In either case, the matter of life and death is being decided on
irrelevant grounds. It is the Down's syndrome, and not the intestines,
that is the issue. The matter should be decided, if at all, on that basis, and
not be allowed to depend on the essentially irrelevant question of
whether the intestinal tract is blocked.

What makes this situation possible, of course, is the idea that when
there is an intestinal blockage, one can "let the baby die," but when
there is no such defect there is nothing that can be done, for one must
not "kill" it. The fact that this idea leads to such results as deciding life or

---

[1]Anthony Shaw, "Doctor, Do We Have a Choice?" *New York Times Magazine*, January 30,
1972, p. 54. [Rachels's note.]

death on irrelevant grounds is another good reason why the doctrine would be rejected.

One reason why so many people think that there is an important moral difference between active and passive euthanasia is that they think killing someone is morally worse than letting someone die. But is it? Is killing, in itself, worse than letting die? To investigate this issue, two cases may be considered that are exactly alike except that one involves killing whereas the other involves letting someone die. Then, it can be asked whether this difference makes any difference to the moral assessments. It is important that the cases be exactly alike, except for this one difference, since otherwise one cannot be confident that it is this difference and not some other that accounts for any variation in the assessments of the two cases. So, let us consider this pair of cases:

In the first, Smith stands to gain a large inheritance if anything should happen to his six-year-old cousin. One evening while the child is taking his bath, Smith sneaks into the bathroom and drowns the child, and then arranges things so that it will look like an accident.

In the second, Jones also stands to gain if anything should happen to his six-year-old cousin. Like Smith, Jones sneaks in planning to drown the child in his bath. However, just as he enters the bathroom Jones sees the child slip and hit his head, and fall face down in the water. Jones is delighted; he stands by, ready to push the child's head back under if it is necessary, but it is not necessary. With only a little thrashing about, the child drowns all by himself, "accidentally," as Jones watches and does nothing.

Now Smith killed the child, whereas Jones "merely" let the child die. That is the only difference between them. Did either man behave better, from a moral point of view? If the difference between killing and letting die were in itself a morally important matter, one should say that Jones's behavior was less reprehensible than Smith's. But does one really want to say that? I think not. In the first place, both men acted from the same motive, personal gain, and both had exactly the same end in view when they acted. It may be inferred from Smith's conduct that he is a bad man, although the judgment may be withdrawn or modified if certain further facts are learned about him—for example, that he is mentally deranged. But would not the very same thing be inferred about Jones from his conduct? And would not the same further considerations also be relevant to any modification of this judgment? Moreover, suppose Jones pleaded, in his own defense, "After all, I didn't do anything except just stand there and watch the child drown. I didn't kill him; I only let him die." Again, if letting die were in itself less bad than killing, this defense should have at least some weight. But it does not. Such a "defense" can only be regarded as a grotesque perversion of moral reasoning. Morally speaking, it is no defense at all.

Now, it may be pointed out, quite properly, that the cases of euthanasia with which doctors are concerned are not like this at all. They do not involve personal gain or the destruction of normal healthy children. Doctors are concerned only with cases in which the patient's life is of no further use to him, or in which the patient's life has become or will soon become a terrible burden. However, the point is the same in these cases: The bare difference between killing and letting die does not, in itself, make a moral difference. If a doctor lets a patient die, for humane reasons, he is in the same moral position as if he had given the patient a lethal injection for humane reasons. If his decision was wrong—if, for example, the patient's illness was in fact curable—the decision would be equally regrettable no matter which method was used to carry it out. And if the doctor's decision was the right one, the method used is not in itself important.

The AMA policy statement isolates the crucial issue very well; the crucial issue is "the intentional termination of the life of one human being by another." But after identifying this issue, and forbidding "mercy killing," the statement goes on to deny that the cessation of treatment is the intentional termination of life. This is where the mistake comes in, for what is the cessation of treatment, in these circumstances, if it is not "the intentional termination of the life of one human being by another?" Of course it is exactly that, and if it were not, there would be no point to it.

Many people will find this judgment hard to accept. One reason, I   15
think, is that it is very easy to conflate the question of whether killing is, in itself, worse than letting die, with the very different question of whether most actual cases of killing are more reprehensible than most actual cases of letting die. Most actual cases of killing are clearly terrible (think, for example, of all the murders reported in the newspapers), and one hears of such cases every day. On the other hand, one hardly ever hears of a case of letting die, except for the actions of doctors who are motivated by humanitarian reasons. So one learns to think of killing in a much worse light than of letting die. But this does not mean that there is something about killing that makes it in itself worse than letting die, for it is not the bare difference between killing and letting die that makes the difference in these cases. Rather, the other factors—the murderer's motive of personal gain, for example, contrasted with the doctor's humanitarian motivation—account for different reactions to the different cases.

I have argued that killing is not in itself any worse than letting die; if my contention is right, it follows that active euthanasia is not any worse than passive euthanasia. What arguments can be given on the other side? The most common, I believe, is the following:

> The important difference between active and passive euthanasia is that, in passive euthanasia, the doctor does not do anything to bring about the patient's death. The doctor does nothing, and the patient dies of whatever ills already afflict him. In active euthanasia, however, the doctor does something to bring about the patient's death: He kills him.

> The doctor who gives the patient with cancer a lethal injection has himself caused his patient's death; whereas if he merely ceases treatment, the cancer is the cause of the death.

A number of points need to be made here. This first is that it is not exactly correct to say that in passive euthanasia the doctor does nothing, for he does do one thing that is very important: He lets the patient die. "Letting someone die" is certainly different, in some respects, from other types of action—mainly in that it is a kind of action that one may perform by way of not performing certain other actions. For example, one may let a patient die by way of not giving medication, just as one may insult someone by way of not shaking his hand. But for any purpose of moral assessment, it is a type of action nonetheless. The decision to let a patient die is subject to moral appraisal in the same way that a decision to kill him would be subject to moral appraisal: It may be assessed as wise or unwise, compassionate or sadistic, right or wrong. If a doctor deliberately let a patient die who was suffering from a routinely curable illness, the doctor would certainly be to blame for what he had done, just as he would be to blame if he had needlessly killed the patient. Charges against him would then be appropriate. If so, it would be no defense at all for him to insist that he didn't "do anything." He would have done something very serious indeed, for he let his patient die.

Fixing the cause of death may be very important from a legal point of view, for it may determine whether criminal charges are brought against the doctor. But I do not think that this notion can be used to show a moral difference between active and passive euthanasia. The reason why it is considered bad to be the cause of someone's death is that death is regarded as a great evil—and so it is. However, if it has been decided that euthanasia—even passive euthanasia—is desirable in a given case, it has also been decided that in this instance death is not greater an evil than the patient's continued existence. And if this is true, the usual reason for not wanting to be the cause of someone's death simply does not apply.

Finally, doctors may think that all of this is only of academic interest—the sort of thing that philosophers may worry about but that has no practical bearing on their own work. After all, doctors must be concerned about the legal consequences of what they do, and active euthanasia is clearly forbidden by the law. But even so, doctors should also be concerned with the fact that the law is forcing upon them a moral doctrine that may be indefensible, and has a considerable effect on their practices. Of course, most doctors are not now in the position of being coerced in this matter, for they do not regard themselves as merely going along with what the law requires. Rather, in statements such as the AMA policy statement that I have quoted, they are endorsing this doctrine as a central point of medical ethics. In that statement, active euthanasia is condemned not merely as illegal but as "contrary to that for which the medical profession stands," whereas passive euthanasia is approved. However, the preceding considerations suggest that there is really no moral difference between the two, considered in themselves (there may be important moral differences in some cases in their *consequences*, but, as I pointed out, these differences may make active euthanasia, and not passive euthanasia, the morally preferable option). So, whereas doctors may have to discriminate between active and passive euthanasia to satisfy the law, they should not do any more than that. In particular, they should not give the distinction any added authority and weight by writing it into official statements of medical ethics.

Topics for Critical Thinking and Writing

1. Explain the distinction between "active" and "passive" euthanasia. Why do you think the American Medical Association attaches importance to the distinction?

2. Rachels argues that in certain cases, "active euthanasia is actually preferable to passive euthanasia" (para. 3). What is his argument? Do you think it ought to persuade a person who already favors "passive" euthanasia to perform "active" euthanasia in cases of the sort Rachels describes? Why, or why not?

3. What is Rachels's "second argument" (para. 5) and what is it supposed to prove? Do you think it succeeds, or not? Explain.

4. Rachels asks whether "killing" is worse, as many people think, than "letting someone die" (para. 9). He argues that it is not; what is his argument? Does it persuade you? Why, or why not?

5. Rachels opens his essay by discussing a genuine case of a newborn with Down's syndrome (para. 4); but eventually he is forced to construct purely hypothetical cases (paras. 10 and 11). Do you think that the persuasive power of his argument suffers when he shifts to hypothetical cases? Or does it improve? Or doesn't it matter whether he is discussing actual or only hypothetical cases? Explain.

6. The principal thesis of Rachels's essay is that "the bare difference between killing and letting die does not, in itself, make a moral difference" (para. 13). Summarize his argument for this thesis.

Timothy M. Quill

Timothy M. Quill, born in 1949, was educated at Amherst College and at the University of Rochester School of Medicine. He now teaches at the University of Rochester and is division head of internal medicine at the Genesee Hospital in Rochester, New York. The essay here first appeared on March 7, 1991, in the New England Journal of Medicine, *a publication read chiefly by*

physicians. Dr. Quill later expanded on the ideas in this essay in a book entitled Death and Dignity: Making Choices and Taking Charge *(1993).
In 1996 he published* A Midwife Through the Dying Process: Stories of
Healing and Hard Choices at the End of Life.

Death and Dignity: A Case
of Individualized Decision Making

Diane was feeling tired and had a rash. A common scenario, though
there was something subliminally worrisome that prompted me to check
her blood count. Her hematocrit was 22, and the white-cell count was
4.3 with some metamyelocytes and unusual white cells. I wanted it to be
viral, trying to deny what was staring me in the face. Perhaps in a repeated count it would disappear. I called Diane and told her it might be
more serious than I had initially thought—that the test needed to be repeated and that if she felt worse, we might have to move quickly. When
she pressed for the possibilities, I reluctantly opened the door to leukemia. Hearing the word seemed to make it exist. "Oh, shit!" she said.
"Don't tell me that." Oh, shit! I thought, I wish I didn't have to.

Diane was no ordinary person (although no one I have ever come to
know has been really ordinary). She was raised in an alcoholic family
and had felt alone for much of her life. She had vaginal cancer as a
young woman. Through much of her adult life, she had struggled with
depression and her own alcoholism. I had come to know, respect, and
admire her over the previous eight years as she confronted these problems and gradually overcame them. She was an incredibly clear, at times
brutally honest, thinker and communicator. As she took control of her
life, she developed a strong sense of independence and confidence. In
the previous three and a half years, her hard work had paid off. She was
completely abstinent from alcohol, she had established much deeper
connections with her husband, college-age son, and several friends, and
her business and her artistic work were blossoming. She felt she was
really living fully for the first time.

Not surprisingly, the repeated blood count was abnormal, and detailed examination of the peripheral-blood smear showed myelocytes. I
advised her to come into the hospital, explaining that we needed to do a
bone marrow biopsy and make some decisions relatively rapidly. She
came to the hospital knowing what we would find. She was terrified,
angry, and sad. Although we knew the odds, we both clung to the
thread of possibility that it might be something else.

The bone marrow confirmed the worst: acute myelomonocytic
leukemia. In the face of this tragedy, we looked for signs of hope. This is
an area of medicine in which technological intervention has been successful, with cures 25 percent of the time—long-term cures. As I probed
the costs of these cures, I heard about induction chemotherapy (three

weeks in the hospital, prolonged neutropenia, probable infectious complications, and hair loss; 75 percent of patients respond, 25 percent do
not). For the survivors, this is followed by consolidation chemotherapy
(with similar side effects; another 25 percent die, for a net survival of 50
percent). Those still alive, to have a reasonable chance of long-term survival, then need bone marrow transplantation (hospitalization for two
months and whole-body irradiation, with complete killing of the bone
marrow, infectious complications, and the possibility for graft-versus-
host disease — with a survival of approximately 50 percent, to 25 percent
of the original group). Though hematologists may argue over the exact
percentages, they don't argue about the outcome of no treatment — certain death in days, weeks, or at most a few months.

Believing that delay was dangerous, our oncologist broke the news   5
to Diane and began making plans to insert a Hickman catheter and begin
induction chemotherapy that afternoon. When I saw her shortly thereafter, she was enraged at his presumption that she would want treatment, and devastated by the finality of the diagnosis. All she wanted to
do was go home and be with her family. She had no further questions
about treatment and in fact had decided that she wanted none. Together
we lamented her tragedy and the unfairness of life. Before she left, I felt
the need to be sure that she and her husband understood that there was
some risk in delay, that the problem was not going to go away, and that
we needed to keep considering the options over the next several days.
We agreed to meet in two days.

She returned in two days with her husband and son. They had
talked extensively about the problem and the options. She remained
very clear about her wish not to undergo chemotherapy and to live
whatever time she had left outside the hospital. As we explored her
thinking further, it became clear that she was convinced she would die
during the period of treatment and would suffer unspeakably in the
process (from hospitalization, from lack of control over her body, from
the side effects of chemotherapy, and from pain and anguish). Although
I could offer support and my best effort to minimize her suffering if she
chose treatment, there was no way I could say any of this would not
occur. In fact, the last four patients with acute leukemia at our hospital
had died very painful deaths in the hospital during various stages of
treatment (a fact I did not share with her). Her family wished she would
choose treatment but sadly accepted her decision. She articulated very
clearly that it was she who would be experiencing all the side effects of
treatment and that odds of 25 percent were not good enough for her
to undergo so toxic a course of therapy, given her expectations of
chemotherapy and hospitalization and the absence of a closely matched
bone marrow donor. I had her repeat her understanding of the treatment, the odds, and what to expect if there were no treatment. I clarified
a few misunderstandings, but she had a remarkable grasp of the options
and implications.

I have been a long-time advocate of active, informed patient choice of treatment or nontreatment, and of a patient's right to die with as much control and dignity as possible. Yet there was something about her giving up a 25 percent chance of long-term survival in favor of almost certain death that disturbed me. I had seen Diane fight and use her considerable inner resources to overcome alcoholism and depression, and I half expected her to change her mind over the next week. Since the window of time in which effective treatment can be initiated is rather narrow, we met several times that week. We obtained a second hematology consultation and talked at length about the meaning and implications of treatment and nontreatment. She talked to a psychologist she had seen in the past. I gradually understood the decision from her perspective and became convinced that it was the right decision for her. We arranged for home hospice care (although at that time Diane felt reasonably well, was active, and looked healthy), left the door open for her to change her mind, and tried to anticipate how to keep her comfortable in the time she had left.

Just as I was adjusting to her decision, she opened up another area that would stretch me profoundly. It was extraordinarily important to Diane to maintain control of herself and her own dignity during the time remaining to her. When this was no longer possible, she clearly wanted to die. As a former director of a hospice program, I know how to use pain medicines to keep patients comfortable and lessen suffering. I explained the philosophy of comfort care, which I strongly believe in. Although Diane understood and appreciated this, she had known of people lingering in what was called relative comfort, and she wanted no part of it. When the time came, she wanted to take her life in the least painful way possible. Knowing of her desire for independence and her decision to stay in control, I thought this request made perfect sense. I acknowledged and explored this wish but also thought that it was out of the realm of currently accepted medical practice and that it was more than I could offer or promise. In our discussion, it became clear that preoccupation with her fear of a lingering death would interfere with Diane's getting the most out of the time she had left until she found a safe way to ensure her death. I feared the effects of a violent death on the family, the consequences of an ineffective suicide that would leave her lingering in precisely the state she dreaded so much, and the possibility that a family member would be forced to assist her, with all the legal and personal repercussions that would follow. She discussed this at length with her family. They believed that they should respect her choice. With this in mind, I told Diane that information was available from the Hemlock Society that might be helpful to her.

A week later she phoned me with a request for barbiturates for sleep. Since I knew that this was an essential ingredient in a Hemlock Society suicide, I asked her to come to the office to talk things over. She was more than willing to protect me by participating in a superficial conversation about her insomnia, but it was important to me to know how she planned to use the drugs and to be sure that she was not in despair or overwhelmed in a way that might color her judgment. In our discussion, it was apparent that she was having trouble sleeping, but it was also evident that the security of having enough barbiturates available to commit suicide when and if the time came would leave her secure enough to live fully and concentrate on the present. It was clear that she was not despondent and that in fact she was making deep, personal connections with her family and close friends. I made sure that she knew how to use the barbiturates for sleep, and also that she knew the amount needed to commit suicide. We agreed to meet regularly, and she promised to meet with me before taking her life, to ensure that all other avenues had been exhausted. I wrote the prescription with an uneasy feeling about the boundaries I was exploring—spiritual, legal, professional, and personal. Yet I also felt strongly that I was setting her free to get the most out of the time she had left and to maintain dignity and control on her own terms until her death.

The next several months were very intense and important for Diane. 10 Her son stayed home from college, and they were able to be with one another and say much that had not been said earlier. Her husband did his work at home so that he and Diane could spend more time together. She spent time with her closest friends. I had her come into the hospital for a conference with our residents, at which she illustrated in a most profound and personal way the importance of informed decision making, the right to refuse treatment, and the extraordinarily personal effects of illness and interaction with the medical system. There were emotional and physical hardships as well. She had periods of intense sadness and anger. Several times she became very weak, but she received transfusions as an outpatient and responded with marked improvement of symptoms. She had two serious infections that responded surprisingly well to empirical courses of oral antibiotics. After three tumultuous months, there were two weeks of relative calm and well-being, and fantasies of a miracle began to surface.

Unfortunately, we had no miracle. Bone pain, weakness, fatigue, and fevers began to dominate her life. Although the hospice workers, family members, and I tried our best to minimize the suffering and promote comfort, it was clear that the end was approaching. Diane's immediate future held what she feared the most—increasing discomfort, dependence, and hard choices between pain and sedation. She called up her closest friends and asked them to come over to say goodbye, telling them that she would be leaving soon. As we had agreed, she let me know as well. When we met, it was clear that she knew what she was doing, that she was sad and frightened to be leaving, but that she would be even more terrified to stay and suffer. In our tearful goodbye, she promised a reunion in the future at her favorite spot on the edge of Lake Geneva, with dragons swimming in the sunset.

Two days later her husband called to say that Diane had died. She had said her final goodbyes to her husband and son that morning and asked them to leave her alone for an hour. After an hour, which must have seemed an eternity, they found her on the couch, lying very still and covered by her favorite shawl. There was no sign of struggle. She seemed to be at peace. They called me for advice about how to proceed. When I arrived at their house, Diane indeed seemed peaceful. Her husband and son were quiet. We talked about what a remarkable person she had been. They seemed to have no doubts about the course she had chosen or about their cooperation, although the unfairness of her illness and the finality of her death were overwhelming to us all.

I called the medical examiner to inform him that a hospice patient had died. When asked about the cause of death, I said, "acute leukemia." He said that was fine and that we should call a funeral director. Although acute leukemia was the truth, it was not the whole story. Yet any mention of suicide would have given rise to a police investigation and probably brought the arrival of an ambulance crew for resuscitation. Diane would have become a "coroner's case," and the decision to perform an autopsy would have been made at the discretion of the medical examiner. The family or I could have been subject to criminal prosecution, and I to professional review, for our roles in support of Diane's choices. Although I truly believe that the family and I gave her the best care possible, allowing her to define her limits and directions as much as possible, I am not sure the law, society, or the medical profession would agree. So I said "acute leukemia" to protect all of us, to protect Diane from an invasion into her past and her body, and to continue to shield society from the knowledge of the degree of suffering that people often undergo in the process of dying. Suffering can be lessened to some extent, but in no way eliminated or made benign, by the careful intervention of a competent, caring physician, given current social constraints.

Diane taught me about the range of help I can provide if I know people well and if I allow them to say what they really want. She taught me about life, death, and honesty and about taking charge and facing tragedy squarely when it strikes. She taught me that I can take small risks for people that I really know and care about. Although I did not assist in her suicide directly, I helped indirectly to make it possible, successful, and relatively painless. Although I know we have measures to help control pain and lessen suffering, to think that people do not suffer in the process of dying is an illusion. Prolonged dying can occasionally be peaceful, but more often the role of the physician and family is limited to lessening but not eliminating severe suffering.

I wonder how many families and physicians secretly help patients over the edge into death in the face of such severe suffering. I wonder how many severely ill or dying patients secretly take their lives, dying alone in despair. I wonder whether the image of Diane's final aloneness will persist in the minds of her family, or if they will remember more the intense, meaningful months they had together before she died. I wonder whether Diane struggled in that last hour, and whether the Hemlock Society's way of death by suicide is the most benign. I wonder why Diane, who gave so much to so many of us, had to be alone for the last hour of her life. I wonder whether I will see Diane again, on the shore of Lake Geneva at sunset, with dragons swimming on the horizon.

Topics for Critical Thinking and Writing

1. Do you think Diane's refusal to fight her leukemia (para. 5) shows— dare we say it?—that she was a coward in the face of death? When Dr. Quill says (para. 7) that her refusal "disturbed me," is he tacitly and evasively making just such a judgment? Or do his reservations have another source and meaning?

2. Dr. Quill refers to his belief that a patient has the "right to die with as much control and dignity as possible" (para. 7). How would you define human dignity? What do you think are appropriate criteria for dying with dignity? What is an undignified death—and how can it be avoided? Write an essay of 500 words explaining these ideas.

3. The reader is told that Diane wanted to "maintain control of herself and her own dignity during the time remaining to her" (para. 8; cf. para. 11, end). What is the evidence that she succeeded or failed? Explain in an essay of 250 words whether you think she succeeded, or not.

4. Did Dr. Quill lie to the county medical examiner when he reported Diane's death as caused by "acute leukemia" (para. 13)? If not, why not? If he did, do you think the lie was justified? Why, or why not? Write an essay of 500 words in which you argue for your position on these questions.

Ronald Pies

Ronald Pies, associate professor of psychiatry at Tufts University, is the author of a textbook on psychiatry. This essay appeared in the journal Tufts Medicine *(Spring 1994).*

Does Clinical Depression Undermine Physician-Assisted Suicide?

An article published this winter in the *Boston Globe* concerned an eighty-eight-year-old woman who attempted suicide. The essay was written by the woman's niece and, in essence, argued that her aunt's suicide attempt was an understandable, if not laudable, expression of personal autonomy. As the writer put it, her aunt "was simply striving to put the period at the end of a very run-on sentence." The author argued for what has come to be termed *physician-assisted suicide,* suggesting that those of us who wish to end our lives "when our bodies fail us" ought to have the benefit of a family physician's assistance. Curiously, the author's aunt *did not seem to have any severe or incapacitating physical illness,* other than arthritis. Rather, her aunt felt that she had "had enough," had "overstayed her welcome" and "wasn't contributing anything."

I found this essay disturbing on several levels. As a writer and physician, I objected to the misuse of a literary metaphor: A human life, even at age eighty-eight, is not a run-on sentence in need of terminal punctuation. As a psychiatrist specializing in mood disorders, I was distressed by the writer's apparent inability to recognize that her aunt may have been clinically depressed—she had shown some of the classic symptoms, and had been taking corticosteroids, a common organic cause of major depression. I also was uneasy with the notion that the medical profession should actively participate in ending the life of another human being— though I am not entirely opposed to "euthanasia" under certain carefully proscribed circumstances.

But first things first: Surely any discussion of physician-assisted suicide must be prefaced by the distinction between *treatable* and *untreatable* (more accurately, incurable) illness. Let us stipulate that patients who wish to end their lives during, say, the final stages of metastatic pancreatic carcinoma have an untreatable illness and might conceivably benefit from some form of assisted suicide. This is by no means the situation with respect to major depression—*a highly treatable* illness that often presents with *reversible* suicidal ideation. The recognition and aggressive treatment of major depression is the physician's first responsibility, long before any notion of "honoring" the patient's suicidal wishes.

Dr. James Jefferson of the University of Wisconsin Department of Psychiatry has spoken of the staggering human costs of depression—a condition he describes as "underdiagnosed, misdiagnosed, undertreated, and mistreated." Each year, major depression costs our economy nearly $30 billion in medical care and absenteeism. The Medical Outcomes Study (Wells and Burnam 1991) found that depression had more associated morbidity than any chronic medical condition except heart disease. Yet depression in primary care and nursing home settings often goes undetected and untreated. Why?

I believe that many physicians still are reluctant to give their patients   5 a "psychiatric" diagnosis, which is perceived as both stigmatizing and threatening—often as much to the physician as to the patient. Sometimes the well-meaning physician will overidentify with the patient, rationalizing away the signs of depression with the old saw "I'd be depressed, too, if I were in Mrs. Jones' shoes." This sort of fallacious reasoning often appears in nursing home settings, where it is expected that patients will be depressed. In reality, major depression is *less* prevalent among the elderly than among the middle-aged; when it shows up in an older person, it is not a normal development, but an illness. Clinical depression, of course, is different from unhappiness, of which there is no short supply in nursing homes, hospitals or anywhere else. But when that telltale cluster of signs and symptoms appears—*hopelessness, loss of pleasure, poor appetite, sleep disturbance, inappropriate guilt, social withdrawal, and suicidal ideation*—we must recognize it as major depression and begin vigorous treatment. More than 70 percent of patients will respond to adequate antidepressant medication, usually in combination with some form of psychotherapy. What seemed a hard-and-fast decision to die often melts into a renewed commitment to life. Incidentally, the elderly do benefit from psychotherapy, contrary to the unfortunate adage about "old dogs" and "new tricks."

But what about cases of untreatable or incurable illness, particularly when extreme pain or suffering is present? Should the physician then directly participate in a patient's wish to commit suicide? Easy answers don't leap to mind, but one thing seems clear to me: The one-man-army approach of Dr. Jack Kevorkian is not consonant with my understanding of medical ethics. (I often wonder how frequently Dr. Kevorkian seeks psychiatric consultation in order to rule out major depression in his suicidal patients.)

Recently, a Seattle-based group of physicians and clergy initiated an unusual service for those who wish to end their own lives. This group developed a strict set of guidelines for deciding whether to assist suicide, including a mandatory review of the case by a team of group members. Furthermore, patients must be able to obtain lethal drugs from their own doctor and be able to administer them. Group members will not do so. I find this sort of thoughtful, multidisciplinary approach infinitely more responsible than that of Dr. Kevorkian. But I still am not persuaded that physicians should be directly involved in assisted suicides. Perhaps we do need some segment of society to perform such a function, under scrupulous regulation, but I am not eager for physicians to step forward. We already have our hands full simply trying to detect and treat reversible illness—including that underdiagnosed and undertreated condition, depression.

Topics for Critical Thinking and Writing

1. Pies refers in his opening paragraph to "personal autonomy." How would you define this concept? Do a person's physical handicaps constitute an obstacle to personal autonomy? Why, or why not?

2. After reading Pies's essay, how would you define "clinical depression"—its symptoms, especially?

3. Pies explains the unwillingness of doctors to diagnose their patients as in need of "psychiatric" help on the ground that it is "stigmatizing and threatening" (para. 5). Would you agree? Why, or why not?

4. Pies obviously disapproves of the "one-man-army approach of Dr. Jack Kevorkian" (para. 6). What grounds does Pies give to persuade the reader to agree with this judgment? (You might check in the *New York Times Index* for newspaper articles on Kevorkian and see whether such further information you can obtain confirms or disconfirms your prior judgment.)

5. Read the essay by Timothy Quill (p. 566) and decide whether you agree with Pies in implicitly criticizing Quill for his failure to adopt a "thoughtful, multidisciplinary approach" (para. 7) to physician-assisted suicide.

23

Multiculturalism: What Is It, and Is It Good or Bad?

Henry Louis Gates, Jr.

Henry Louis Gates, Jr., was born in West Virginia in 1950 and educated at Yale University, where he received his bachelor's degree summa cum laude in 1973. He earned his M.A. and Ph.D. degrees at Cambridge University. The author of several books, including Black Literature and Literary Theory *(1984),* Figures in Black *(1987), and* Loose Canons: Notes on the Culture Wars *(1992), Gates has taught at Yale, Cornell, and Duke Universities and now is chairman of the Afro-American Studies Department and a professor of English at Harvard. The article reprinted here was first published in the* Boston Globe Magazine *(October 13, 1991), paired with the following essay by Kenneth T. Jackson.*

The Debate Has Been Miscast from the Start

What is multiculturalism and why are they saying such terrible things about it?

We've been told that it threatens to fragment American culture into a warren of ethnic enclaves, each separate and inviolate. We've been told that it menaces the Western tradition of literature and the arts. We've been told that it aims to politicize the school curriculum, replacing honest historical scholarship with a "feel-good" syllabus designed solely to bolster the self-esteem of minorities. The alarm has been sounded, and many scholars and educators—liberals as well as conservatives—have responded to it. After all, if multiculturalism is just a pretty name for ethnic chauvinism, who needs it?

But I don't think that's what multiculturalism is—at least, I don't think that's what it ought to be. And because the debate has been miscast from the beginning, it may be worth setting the main issues straight.

To both proponents and antagonists, multiculturalism represents—either refreshingly or frighteningly—a radical departure. Like most claims for cultural novelty, this one is more than a little exaggerated. For the challenges of cultural pluralism—and the varied forms of official resistance to it—go back to the very founding of our republic.

In the university today, it must be admitted, the challenge has taken on a peculiar inflection. But the underlying questions are time-tested. What does it mean to be an American? Must academic inquiry be subordinated to the requirements of national identity? Should scholarship and education reflect our actual diversity, or should they, rather, forge a communal identity that may not yet have been achieved?

For answers, you can, of course, turn to the latest jeremiad on the subject from, say, George Will, Dinesh D'Souza, or Roger Kimball. But in fact these questions have always occasioned lively disagreement among American educators. In 1917, William Henry Hulme decried "the insidious introduction into our scholarly relations of the political propaganda of a wholly narrow, selfish, and vicious nationalism and false patriotism." His opponents were equally emphatic in their beliefs. "More and more clearly," Fred Lewis Pattee ventured in 1919, "is it seen now that the American soul, the American conception of democracy, Americanism, should be made prominent in our school curriculums, as a guard against the rising spirit of experimental lawlessness." Sound familiar?

Given the political nature of the debate over education and the national interest, the conservative penchant for charging the multiculturalists with "politics" is a little perplexing. For conservative critics, to their credit, have never hesitated to provide a political defense of what they consider to be the "traditional" curriculum: The future of the republic, they argue, depends on the inculcation of proper civic virtues. What these virtues are is a matter of vehement dispute. But to imagine a curriculum untouched by political concerns is to imagine—as no one does—that education can take place in a vacuum.

So where's the beef? Granted, multiculturalism is no panacea for our social ills. We're worried when Johnny can't read. We're worried when Johnny can't add. But shouldn't we be worried, too, when Johnny tramples gravestones in a Jewish cemetery or scrawls racial epithets on a dormitory wall? And it's because we've entrusted our schools with the fashioning of a democratic polity that education has never been exempt from the kind of debate that marks every other aspect of American political life.

Perhaps this isn't altogether a bad thing. As the political theorist Amy Gutmann has argued: "In a democracy, political disagreement is not something that we should generally seek to avoid. Political controversies over our educational problems are a particularly important source of social progress because they have the potential for educating so many citizens."

And while I'm sympathetic to what Robert Nisbet once dubbed the 10 "academic dogma"—the ideal of knowledge for its own sake—I also believe that truly humane learning, unblinkered by the constraints of narrow ethnocentrism, can't help but expand the limits of human understanding and social tolerance. Those who fear that "Balkanization" and social fragmentation lie this way have got it exactly backward. Ours is a world that already is fissured by nationality, ethnicity, race, and gender. And the only way to transcend those divisions—to forge, for once, a civic culture that respects both differences and commonalities—is through education that seeks to comprehend the diversity of human culture. Beyond the hype and the high-flown rhetoric is a pretty homely truth: There is no tolerance without respect—and no respect without knowledge.

The historical architects of the university always understood this. As Cardinal Newman wrote more than a century ago, the university should promote "the power of viewing many things at once as one whole, of referring them severally to their true place in the universal system, of understanding their respective values, and determining their mutual dependence." In just this vein, the critic Edward Said has recently suggested that "our model for academic freedom should therefore be the migrant or traveler: for if, in the real world outside the academy, we must needs be ourselves and only ourselves, inside the academy we should be able to discover and travel among other selves, other identities, other varieties of the human adventure. But, most essentially, in this joint discovery of self and other, it is the role of the academy to transform what might be conflict, or context, or assertion into reconciliation, mutuality, recognition, creative interaction."

But if multiculturalism represents the culmination of an age-old ideal—the dream known in the seventeenth century, as *mathesis universalis*[1]—why has it been the target of such ferocious attacks? On this point, I'm often reminded of a wonderfully wicked piece of nineteenth-century student doggerel about Benjamin Jowett, the great Victorian classicist and master of Balliol College, Oxford:

> Here stand I, my name is Jowett,
> If there's knowledge, then I know it;
> I am the master of this college,
> What I know not, is not knowledge.

Of course, the question of how we determine what is worth knowing is now being raised with uncomfortable persistence. So that in the

---

[1]*mathesis universalis* Knowledge of all things. [All notes are the editors'.]

most spirited attacks on multiculturalism in the academy today, there's a nostalgic whiff of the old sentiment: We are the masters of this college; what we know not is not knowledge.

I think this explains the conservative desire to cast the debate in terms of the West vs. the Rest. And yet that's the very opposition that the pluralist wants to challenge. Pluralism sees cultures as porous, dynamic, and interactive, rather than the fixed property of particular ethnic groups. Thus the idea of a monolithic, homogenous "West" itself comes into question (nothing new here: Literary historians have pointed out that the very concept of "Western culture" may date back only to the eighteenth century). But rather than mourning the loss of some putative ancestral purity, we can recognize what's valuable, resilient, even cohesive, in the hybrid and variegated nature of our modernity.

Genuine multiculturalism is not, of course, everyone's cup of tea. Vulgar cultural nationalists—like Allan Bloom or Leonard Jeffries[2]—correctly identify it as the enemy. These polemicists thrive on absolute partitions: between "civilization" and "barbarism," between "black" and "white," between a thousand versions of Us and Them. But they are whistling in the wind. 15

For whatever the outcome of the culture wars in the academy, the world we live in is multicultural already. Mixing and hybridity is the rule, not the exception. As a student of African American culture, of course, I've come to take this kind of cultural palimpsest for granted. Duke Ellington, Miles Davis, John Coltrane have influenced popular musicians the world over. Wynton Marsalis is as comfortable with Mozart as he is with jazz; Anthony Davis writes operas in a musical idiom that combines Bartok with the blues.

In dance, Judith Jamison, Alvin Ailey, Katherine Dunham all excelled at "Western" cultural forms, melding these with African American styles to produce performances that were neither, and both. In painting, Romare Bearden and Jacob Lawrence, Martin Puryear and Augusta Savage learned to paint and sculpt by studying Western masters, yet each has pioneered the construction of a distinctly African American visual art.

And in literature, of course, the most formally complex and compelling black writers—such as Jean Toomer, Sterling Brown, Langston Hughes, Zora Hurston, Richard Wright, Ralph Ellison, James Baldwin, and Gwendolyn Brooks—have always blended forms of Western literature with African American vernacular and written traditions. Then,

---

[2]**Allan Bloom ... Leonard Jeffries** Bloom, a white professor at the University of Chicago, was known for his emphasis on the traditional Eurocentric curriculum; Jeffries, an African American professor at the City College of New York, is known for his belief that African Americans ("sun people") are superior to whites ("ice people").

again, even a vernacular form such as the spiritual took for its texts the King James version of the Old and New Testaments. Toni Morrison's master's thesis was on Virginia Woolf and Faulkner; Rita Dove is as comfortable with German literature as she is with the blues.

Indeed, the greatest African American art can be thought of as an exploration of that hyphenated space between the African and the American. As James Baldwin once reflected during his long European sojourn, "I would have to appropriate these white centuries, I would have to make them mine. I would have to accept my special attitude, my special place in this scheme, otherwise I would have no place in any scheme."

"Pluralism," the American philosopher John Dewey insisted early in 20 this century, "is the greatest philosophical idea of our times." But he recognized that it was also the greatest problem of our times: "How are we going to make the most of the new values we set on variety, difference, and individuality—how are we going to realize their possibilities in every field, and at the same time not sacrifice that plurality to the cooperation we need so much?" It has the feel of a scholastic conundrum: How can we negotiate between the one and the many?

Today, the mindless celebration of difference has proven as untenable as that bygone model of monochrome homogeneity. If there is an equilibrium to be struck, there's no guarantee we will ever arrive at it. The worst mistake we can make, however, is not to try.

Topics for Critical Thinking and Writing

1. How does Gates define "multiculturalism"? Does he use "cultural pluralism" as a synonym?

2. If before reading Gates's essay you had heard of multiculturalism, in a few sentences explain what you took the word to mean. If Gates's multiculturalism differs from your earlier understanding, how do you account for the difference?

3. Gates says we must face anew the "time-tested" question "What does it mean to be an American?" (para. 5). After reading Gates's essay, how would you answer this question? Set forth your answer in an essay of no more than 500 words.

4. In paragraph 7 Gates says that it is impossible "to imagine a curriculum untouched by political concerns" because it is impossible to imagine "that education can take place in a vacuum." Consider your experience in secondary school or in college, and set forth in 500 words evidence supporting or refuting Gates's assertion.

5. In his final paragraph Gates speaks of "the mindless celebration of difference." What does he mean? What examples might he (or you) cite?

Kenneth T. Jackson

Kenneth T. Jackson was born in Memphis, Tennessee, in 1939 and educated at Memphis State University and the University of Chicago. Since 1968 he has taught history at Columbia University. Among his books is Crabgrass Frontier: The Suburbanization of the United States *(1985), which has won several prizes. This article first appeared in the* Boston Globe Magazine *(October 13, 1991), along with the selection by Henry Louis Gates, Jr., that appears on page 576.*

Too Many Have Let Enthusiasm Outrun Reason

In June, after almost a year of deliberation, the New York State Social Studies Syllabus Review Committee released its report "One Nation, Many Peoples: A Declaration of Cultural Interdependence." In July, the state Board of Regents adopted the document as a blueprint for educational change in the schools.

The report occasioned a firestorm of controversy, perhaps because the committee recommended, among other things, that Christopher Columbus be viewed from the perspective of the natives already resident in North America, that Thanksgiving be understood as a day of mourning as well as of celebration, and that slaves be referred to as "enslaved persons." Most important, however, was the realization that "One Nation, Many Peoples" is about the purpose of social studies, the nature of community, and the meaning of the United States itself.

Along with Arthur Schlesinger and Paul A. Gagnon, I was one of three dissenters to the report. I agonized over my decision, in part because I have spent most of the past three decades, almost my entire adult life, studying the very topics that the committee suggests should receive more attention—ethnicity, racism, discrimination, inequality, and civil rights—and in part because I do believe that we should celebrate the cultural diversity that has made the United States unique among the world's nations. We should acknowledge the heterogeneity that has made this land rich and creative, and we should give our young people a varied and challenging multicultural education.

But too many of those who wave the flag for multiculturalism have let enthusiasm outrun reason. In particular, I believe four major issues deserve more debate and consideration before we embrace the brave new world of multicultural education.

First, we should not confuse moral judgment with historical judg-   5
ment. To study a subject is not necessarily to endorse it. As William Shakespeare reminded us in a line in *Henry IV*, there is history in all men's lives. Because we cannot study all men's lives, however, the curriculum should emphasize those people, places, and events that have

disproportionately influenced the world in which we live. Thus, Europe should be an academic focus not because it has been morally good or even because it is the ancestral home of most Americans, but because, for the last five hundred years or so, it has been much more influential than any other place, and it has had a particularly heavy impact on the political, legal, and religious institutions of the United States.

This is a historical judgment, not a moral one. Quite simply, Europe has generated most of the political values which we hold dear, democracy and freedom prominent among them. It has also experienced more bloodletting, more intolerance, more terror, and more general nastiness than any other place. To analyze the Spanish Inquisition or the Thirty Years War or the Holocaust is not to wish we could have been there. Similarly, students need to know about Hitler because he may reasonably be held to account for 30 million or 40 million or 50 million deaths, not because anyone seeks to elevate the significance of Europe. Should the people of Africa, Asia, or South America feel historically slighted because they have not yet produced an approximation of Nazi Germany?

My second point is that in state after state across the country, a new social studies curriculum is already in place, and teachers have barely had time to familiarize themselves with the new guidelines. Why not give those revisions some time to percolate through the classrooms? In New York State, the focus of so much recent controversy, the entire social studies curriculum was revised just four years ago with the expressed purpose of making it more multicultural. The major consultants for the effort were Eric Foner, Hazel Hertzberg, and Christopher Lasch, three of the most respected historians in the United States. Their efforts to adjust classroom materials and objectives to the new social realities of our time were largely successful, and the current New York State curriculum in American history already reflects the latest social studies scholarship.

To hear multiculturalists talk, however, one would think that our teachers have changed not at all since the Eisenhower era. In fact, they are better prepared and more sophisticated than their critics allege, and most of them are already teaching a multicultural curriculum. In my quarter century of teaching, for example, I have encountered students who did not know whether Boston was northeast or southwest of New York City, whether the Soviet Union fought Germany in World War II, or whether Tammany Hall was a billiard parlor. But I have never met a person, of any age or circumstance, who thought that Columbus discovered an uninhabited world, or that the natives he encountered ultimately received a fair shake from the white invaders.

Meanwhile, the "Eurocentric" curriculum is itself a myth, largely because European history, so much reviled by multiculturalists, has practically disappeared from the nation's classrooms. Before 1970, the history of Western civilization was a standard part of the American educational experience. Since that time, its decline has been precipitous. A general trend has been to substitute an introductory course in world history for the traditional course in Western civilization. An even greater trend has been to substitute other social studies courses for history.

In 1987, for example, fewer than half of all American high school graduates had taken a year of either European or world history. New York State again illustrates the trend. This year, under a curriculum presumed to be Eurocentric, students in New York spend no more time on Britain and Western Europe than they do on Africa, Asia, Latin America, or the Soviet Union. Equally important, they have little time to consider the history of any of the regions, whatever their location on the globe. Most students get around to Europe only in the last quarter of their sophomore year, and then the focus is on contemporary problems, not history. Only 1 percent of students take a year-long course in European history, and those are the kids in advanced placement classes. Everyone else must make do with an ahistorical concoction known as global studies.

My third reservation about multicultural education is the allegation of its supporters that a major purpose of the effort is to raise self-esteem, to make students feel good about themselves, and to make the curriculum reflect the demography of the classroom. These are questionable propositions that often lead to complications. One particularly dispiriting tendency is a willingness to teach controversial theories as facts. A favored theme of Afrocentrism at the moment is an insistence that ancient Egypt be regarded as a part of Africa, that many or most Egyptians were black or multiracial, and that residents of the Nile River Valley were largely responsible for the later glories of Greece and Rome in particular and of the West in general.

The specifics of the argument need not concern us here. The argument may indeed be correct. But this interpretation remains very much in dispute. Some distinguished scholars accept such claims; others ridicule them. Would it not be better to let the historians fight it out before we introduce such material in the classroom? Other, more generally accepted, examples could advance the argument that no one race, no one continent, and no one religion has a corner on human achievement. All students, for example, should know that Africa was once the home of many advanced civilizations, that Timbuktu, in what is now Mali, was a thriving center of learning and trade when Paris was a dump, and that Europe was a backwater for a thousand years while China was in its glory.

Another problem with the "feel-good" approach is that it can reduce history to a list of "firsts" by each ethnic or racial group. This type of teaching strategy is the main reason that students habitually list the social studies as the most boring and irrelevant of all their courses. Alternatively, the feel-good approach might simply replace one myth (e.g., slavery was a benign institution that actually benefited many of its victims) with another (slavery was a uniquely Western institution).

My final reservation is with the notion of cultural interdependence, the idea that all cultures are equal, and the proposition that no one tradition should have special status in the United States. I disagree. Every viable nation has to have a common culture to survive in peace. Precisely because we lack a common religion, a common race, and a common ethnicity, we need a common denominator of another sort. We can find it in our history, in our values, in our aspirations — in short, in our common culture. That common culture should be and has been ever changing. It began, in most Colonies, with the English language and with British legal and political institutions, but it has since metamorphosed over the centuries, and it is now an amalgam of every group that came here. Our food, our music, our holidays, our literature, our traditions, even our language, reflect this distinctive "American" culture.

This issue has special relevance in 1991, when ethnic, racial, religious, and nationality fault lines are creating earthquakes around the world. Canada, Yugoslavia, the Soviet Union, India, and a dozen other places are examples of a powerful sentiment, which I regard as pernicious, that suggests that a country is a country only if it is ethnically pure. Citizenship thus becomes less a function of residence than of blood. Thus, the Baltic countries may deny the vote to Russians who have lived there for decades because they lack the proper pedigree. As more and more people begin to regard loyalty to group as more important than loyalty to country, we get a chilling preview of what the United States might be like if each of us maintains our own culture, if we reject mainstreaming and assimilation, and if in fact there is no mainstream. 15

Fortunately, the United States does not have the massive cultural divides that are bringing other nations to separation and even to civil war. But we are not immune to the problem. Too often today there is an ugliness associated with feelings of pride, the development of an "us vs. them" mentality. Across the United States, the concept of community, the idea of the melting pot, the feeling that we are all Americans — all seem quaintly out of date. The consensus-building institutions that once held us together, especially the big-city public systems, are in decline. Increasingly, Americans are retreating into private realms.

Nothing is wrong with being proud of one's family heritage, of wanting to remember and treasure the traditions handed down from parents. The United States has prospered and grown rich from its vibrant, vital, multiethnic and multiracial culture. But the maintenance of distinctive cultures should be the function of synagogues, churches, music festivals, ethnic celebrations, and, most especially, dinner tables. The public schools should emphasize common traditions and common values.

Topics for Critical Thinking and Writing

1. Jackson says (para. 3) that "we should celebrate the cultural diversity that has made the United States unique among the world's nations." Does he make clear, to your satisfaction, how he proposes to practice

what he preaches? Do you think there are aspects of "cultural diversity" about which he is silent? Support your answer.

2. Jackson declares we must address "four major issues" before embracing "the brave new world of multicultural education" (para. 4). What are these four issues? Where does Jackson stand on each?

3. In paragraph 5 Jackson explains why, in his opinion, "Europe should be an academic focus." What response might someone who differs from Jackson make?

4. Jackson contrasts "historical" and "moral" judgments (paras. 5 and 6). Write a paragraph explaining the difference and giving an example of each kind of judgment.

5. In paragraph 9 Jackson says that "the 'Eurocentric' curriculum is itself a myth." Drawing on your experience in secondary school or college, indicate whether you think Jackson's assertion is true. Explain.

6. In paragraphs 11–13 Jackson attacks the idea that education should raise the self-esteem of students ("the 'feel-good' approach"). Do you share his reservations about this aspect of education? Explain.

7. In paragraph 15 Jackson looks at other countries, and he suggests that they offer "a chilling preview of what the United States might be like if each of us maintains our own culture." Are you chilled? Why, or why not?

8. In his final sentence Jackson speaks of "common traditions and common values." What (if any) examples might he have given?

9. After rereading this essay by Jackson, (re)read carefully the essay by Henry Louis Gates, Jr. (p. 576). On what (if anything) do these two writers seem to disagree? Agree?

Linda Chavez

Linda Chavez, director of the Center for the New American Community, is John M. Olin Fellow at the Manhattan Institute and the author of Out of the Barrio *(1991). This essay first appeared in* The National Review *(February 21, 1994).*

Demystifying Multiculturalism

Multiculturalism is on the advance, everywhere from President Clinton's Cabinet to corporate boardrooms to public-school classrooms. If you believe the multiculturalists' propaganda, whites are on the verge of becoming a minority in the United States. The multiculturalists predict that this demographic shift will fundamentally change American culture—indeed destroy the very idea that America *has* a single, unified culture. They aren't taking any chances, however. They have enlisted the help of government, corporate leaders, the media, and the education establishment in waging a cultural revolution. But has America truly become a multicultural nation? And if not, will those who capitulate to these demands create a self-fulfilling prophecy?

At the heart of the argument is the assumption that the white population is rapidly declining in relation to the nonwhite population. A 1987 Hudson Institute report helped catapult this claim to national prominence. The study, *Workforce 2000,* estimated that by the turn of the century only 15 percent of new workers would be white males. The figure was widely interpreted to mean that whites were about to become a minority in the workplace — and in the country.

In fact, white males will still constitute about 45 percent — a plurality — of the workforce in the year 2000. The proportion of white men in the workforce *is* declining — it was nearly 51 percent in 1980 — but primarily because the proportion of white women is growing. They will make up 39 percent of the workforce within ten years, according to government projections, up from 36 percent in 1980. Together, white men and women will account for 84 percent of all workers by 2000 — hardly a minority share.

But the business world is behaving as if a demographic tidal wave is about to hit. A whole new industry of "diversity professionals" has emerged to help managers cope with the expected deluge of nonwhite workers. These consultants are paid as much as $10,000 a day to train managers to "value diversity," a term so ubiquitous that it has appeared in more than seven hundred articles in major newspapers in the last three years. According to Heather MacDonald in *The New Republic,* about half of Fortune 500 corporations now employ someone responsible for "diversity."

What precisely does valuing diversity mean? The underlying assumptions seem to be that nonwhites are so different from whites that employers must make major changes to accommodate them, and that white workers will be naturally resistant to including nonwhites in their ranks. Public-opinion polls don't bear out the latter. They show that support among whites for equal job opportunity for blacks is extraordinarily high, exceeding 90 percent as early as 1975. As for accommodating different cultures, the problem is not culture — or race, or ethnicity — but education. Many young people, in particular, are poorly prepared for work, and the problem is most severe among those who attended inner-city schools, most of them blacks and Hispanics. 5

Nevertheless, multiculturalists insist on treating race and ethnicity as if they were synonymous with culture. They presume that skin color and national origin, which are immutable traits, determine values, mores, language, and other cultural attributes, which, of course, are learned. In the multiculturalists' world view, African Americans, Puerto Ricans, or Chinese Americans living in New York City have more in common with persons of their ancestral group living in Lagos or San Juan or Hong

Kong than they do with other New Yorkers who are white. Culture becomes a fixed entity, transmitted, as it were, in the genes, rather than through experience. Thus, "Afrocentricity," a variant of multiculturalism, is "a way of being," its exponents claim. According to a leader of the Afrocentric education movement, Molefi Kete Asante, there is "one African Cultural System manifested in diversities," whether one speaks of Afro-Brazilians, Cubans, or Nigerians (or, presumably, African Americans). Exactly how this differs from the traditional racist notion that all blacks (Jews, Mexicans, Chinese, etc.) think alike is unclear. What is clear is that the multiculturalists have abandoned the ideal that all persons should be judged by the content of their character, not the color of their skin. Indeed, the multiculturalists seem to believe that a person's character is *determined* by the color of his skin and by his ancestry.

Such convictions lead multiculturalists to conclude that, again in the words of Asante, "[T]here is no common American culture." The logic is simple, but wrongheaded: Since Americans (or more often, their forebears) hail from many different places, each of which has its own specific culture, the argument goes, America must be multicultural. And it is becoming more so every day as new immigrants bring their cultures with them.

Indeed, multiculturalists hope to ride the immigrant wave to greater power and influence. They have certainly done so in education. Some 2.3 million children who cannot speak English well now attend public school, an increase of 1 million in the last seven years. Multicultural advocates cite the presence of such children to demand bilingual education and other multicultural services. The Los Angeles Unified School District alone currently offers instruction in Spanish, Armenian, Korean, Cantonese, Tagalog, Russian, and Japanese. Federal and state governments now spend literally billions of dollars on these programs.

Ironically, the multiculturalists' emphasis on education undercuts their argument that culture is inextricable from race or national origin. They are acutely aware just how fragile cultural identification is; why else are they so adamant about reinforcing it? Multiculturalists insist on teaching immigrant children in their native language, instructing them in the history and customs of their native land and imbuing them with reverence for their ancestral heroes, lest these youngsters be seduced by American culture. Far from losing faith in the power of assimilation, they seem to believe that without a heavy dose of multicultural indoctrination, immigrants won't be able to resist it. And they're right, though it remains to be seen whether anything, including the multiculturalists' crude methods, will ultimately detour immigrants from the assimilation path.

The urge to assimilate has traditionally been overpowering in the 10 United States, especially among the children of immigrants. Only groups that maintain strict rules against intermarriage with persons outside the group, such as Orthodox Jews and the Amish, have ever succeeded in preserving distinct, full-blown cultures within American society. (It is interesting to note that religion seems to be a more effective deterrent to full assimilation than the secular elements of culture, including language.) Although many Americans worry that Hispanic immigrants, for example, are not learning English and will therefore fail to assimilate into the American mainstream, little evidence supports the case. By the third generation in the United States, a majority of Hispanics, like other ethnic groups, speak only English and are closer to other Americans on most measures of social and economic status than they are to Hispanic immigrants. On one of the most rigorous gauges of assimilation — intermarriage — Hispanics rank high. About one-third of young third-generation Hispanics marry non-Hispanic whites, a pattern similar to that of young Asians. Even for blacks, exogamy rates, which have been quite low historically, are going up; about 3 percent of blacks now marry outside their group.

The impetus for multiculturalism is not coming from immigrants, but from their more affluent and assimilated native-born counterparts. The proponents are most often the elite — the best educated and most successful members of their respective racial and ethnic groups. College campuses, where the most radical displays of multiculturalism take place, are fertile recruiting grounds. Last May, for example, a group of Mexican American students at UCLA, frustrated that the university would not elevate the school's twenty-three-year-old Chicano studies program to full department status, stormed the faculty center, breaking windows and furniture and causing half a million dollars in damage. The same month, a group of Asian American students at UC Irvine went on a hunger strike to pressure administrators into hiring more professors of Asian American studies. These were not immigrants, or even, by and large, disadvantaged students, but middle-class beneficiaries of their parents' or grandparents' successful assimilation to the American mainstream.

The protestors' quest had almost nothing to do with any effort to maintain their ethnic identity. For the most part, such students probably never thought of themselves as anything but American before they entered college. A recent study of minority students at the University of California at Berkeley found that most Hispanic and Asian students "discovered" their ethnic identity after they arrived on campus — when they also discovered that they were victims of systematic discrimination. As one Mexican American freshman summed it up, she was "unaware of the things that have been going on with our people, all the injustice we've suffered, how the world really is. I thought racism didn't exist and here, you know, it just comes to light." The researchers added that "students of color" had difficulty pinpointing exactly what constituted this "subtle form of the new racism. . . . There was much talk about certain facial expressions, or the way people look, and how white students 'take over the class' and speak past you."

Whatever their new-found victim status, these students look amazingly like other Americans on most indices. For example, the median family income of Mexican American students at Berkeley in 1989 was $32,500, slightly above the national median for all Americans that year, $32,191; and 17 percent of those students came from families that earned more than $75,000 a year, even though they were admitted to the university under affirmative-action programs (presumably because they suffered some educational disadvantage attributed to their ethnicity).

Affirmative-action programs make less and less sense as discrimination diminishes in this society—which it indisputably has—and as minorities improve their economic status. Racial and ethnic identity, too, might wane if there weren't such aggressive efforts to ensure that this not happen. The multiculturalists know they risk losing their constituency if young blacks, Hispanics, Asians, and others don't maintain strong racial and ethnic affiliations. Younger generations must be *trained* to think of themselves as members of oppressed minority groups entitled to special treatment. And the government provides both the incentives and the money to ensure that this happens. Meanwhile, the main beneficiaries are the multicultural professionals, who often earn exorbitant incomes peddling identity.

One particularly egregious example occurred in the District of Columbia last fall. The school system paid $250,000 to a husband-and-wife consultant team to produce an Afrocentric study guide to be used in a single public elementary school. Controversy erupted after the two spent three years and produced only a five-page outline. Although the husband had previously taught at Howard University, the wife's chief credential was a master's degree from an unaccredited "university" which she and her husband had founded. When the *Washington Post* criticized the school superintendent for his handling of the affair, he called a press conference to defend the couple, who promptly claimed they were the victims of a racist vendetta.

D.C. students rank lowest in the nation in math and fourth-lowest in verbal achievement; one can only wonder what $250,000 in tutoring at one school might have done. Instead, the students were treated to bulletin boards in the classrooms proclaiming on their behalf: "We are the sons and daughters of The Most High. We are the princes and princesses of African kings and queens. We are the descendants of our black ancestors. We are black and we are proud." This incident is not unique. Thousands of consultants with little or no real expertise sell feel-good programs to school systems across the nation.

Multiculturalism is not a grassroots movement. It was created, nurtured, and expanded through government policy. Without the expenditure of vast sums of public money, it would wither away and die. That is not to say that ethnic communities would disappear from the American scene or that groups would not retain some attachment to their ancestral roots. American assimilation has always entailed some give and take, and American culture has been enriched by what individual groups brought to it. The distinguishing characteristic of American culture is its ability to incorporate so many disparate groups, creating a new whole from the many parts. What could be more American, for example, than jazz and film, two distinctive art forms created, respectively, by blacks and immigrant Jews but which all Americans think of as their own? But in the past, government—especially public schools—saw it as a duty to try to bring newcomers into the fold by teaching them English, by introducing them to the great American heroes as their own, by instilling respect for American institutions. Lately, we have nearly reversed course, treating each group, new and old, as if what is most important is to preserve its separate identity and space.

It is easy to blame the ideologues and radicals who are pushing the disuniting of America, to use Arthur Schlesinger's phrase, but the real culprits are those who provide multiculturalists the money and the access to press their cause. Without the acquiescence of policy-makers and ordinary citizens, multiculturalism would be no threat. Unfortunately, most major institutions have little stomach for resisting the multicultural impulse—and many seem eager to comply with whatever demands the multiculturalists make. Americans should have learned by now that policy matters. We have only to look at the failure of our welfare and crime policies to know that providing perverse incentives can change the way individuals behave—for the worse. Who is to say that if we pour enough money into dividing Americans we won't succeed?

Topics for Critical Thinking and Writing

1. In her first paragraph Chavez asks whether America has "truly become a multicultural nation." How would you define *multiculturalism*, and what would you take as strong evidence that the nation is, or is about to become, or will not become, multicultural?

2. Chavez implies (para. 6) that it is a grave error to treat "race and ethnicity as if they were synonymous with culture." Can you define all three terms so that they are distinct? (Consulting an encyclopedia or unabridged dictionary might be of help.) Is there some overlap in the criteria for each?

3. Chavez introduces the idea of "assimilation" as the opposite of multiculturalism (see paras. 9–11 and 17) and implies that it was the traditional goal of all but a tiny minority of immigrant groups to this country. Does she indicate why this traditional goal is no longer so popular with recent immigrant groups? Does she (and can you) consider a third alternative to either assimilation and multiculturalism?

4. Chavez writes as if she believes there is a conspiracy afoot across the nation, fueled by "government policy" (para. 17), to impose multiculturalism on us whether we want it or not. She thinks that colleges and universities are among the worst offenders (see para. 11). Do some research on your own campus and write a 500-word essay on the subject "The Nature and Extent of Multiculturalism on Our Campus."

Nathan Glazer

Nathan Glazer, born in 1923 in New York City, is a professor of education and sociology at Harvard University. He is the author of several books, including Ethnic Dilemmas *(1983), and the editor or coeditor of several books, including* Clamor at the Gates: The New American Immigration *(1985). This essay originally appeared on September 2, 1991, in* The New Republic.

In Defense of Multiculturalism

I served as a member of the committee appointed by New York's commissioner of education, Thomas Sobol, to review the social studies syllabi in the state's elementary and high schools. Our committee, composed of academics and teachers, was not particularly biased toward strong advocates of multiculturalism. It included critics of the multicultural trend—Arthur Schlesinger, Kenneth Jackson, Paul Gagnon, and myself. Nevertheless, the report that emerged, "One Nation, Many Peoples: A Declaration of Cultural Interdependence," called for further acknowledgment of American diversity, and was severely attacked by some members of the committee, and in many editorials (see "Mr. Sobol's Planet," *The New Republic,* July 15 and 22), for further dissolving the common bonds that make us a nation. I also appended critical remarks to the report, yet had reservations in joining in a frontal attack. The report needs its sharp critics (it was undoubtedly the criticism that subsequently led Mr. Sobol to make recommendations to the Regents of New York State that most critics of multiculturalism would agree with). But we also need to see why the demand for something called multiculturalism is now so widespread, and why American education will have to respond to it.

Multiculturalism can mean many things, and no one argues with a curriculum that gives proper weight to the role of American Indians, blacks, Asians, and European immigrant and ethnic groups in American history. But as currently used, the word "multiculturalism" is something of a misnomer. It suggests a general desire or need for students to have something in the curriculum that relates to their own ethnic traits, if these exist, or to those of their parents or ancestors. I don't think this desire is particularly widespread among many ethnic groups. "We are all immigrants" is nice rhetoric, but in fact we are not all immigrants. Some of us came in the last decade, some of our parents came long before that, many millions of us have only the haziest idea of how many ancestors came from where. Since 1980 the Census has included a new question, "What is your ancestry?" The great majority of respondents report two, three, or more ancestries. Tens of millions simply insist on being "American," and nothing else.

Nor does multiculturalism reflect the increased immigration of recent decades, particularly to some of our largest cities, such as New York, Los Angeles, San Francisco, and Miami. It is not the new immigrants who are arguing for multiculturalism. Most of them would be content with the education provided to the previous waves of European immigrants, which paid not a whit of attention to their ethnic or racial background, or to their distinct culture or language. A product of that kind of education, I was also quite content with it.

But if it is not the new immigration that is driving the multicultural demands, what is? Multiculturalism in its present form derives basically from black educators. It is one of the longest settled elements in the American population that makes the sharpest case for multiculturalism. Asians, who make up half of current immigrants, are not much concerned. Nor are Spanish-speaking immigrants from Central and South America. Puerto Ricans and Mexican Americans do tend to support bilingual education and the maintenance of the Spanish language. But they are definitely junior partners in the fight for multiculturalism.

I'm convinced that were it not for the pattern of poor achievement   5
among blacks in the schools, the multicultural movement would lose much of its force. Even taking into account recent progress among blacks, shown in NAEP (National Assessment of Educational Progress) scores, SAT scores, and high school graduation rates, blacks still regularly score below whites, often below Hispanics and Native Americans, and far below Asians. Multiculturalism, and one of its variants, Afrocentrism, is presented to us by black educators and leaders as one of the means whereby this deficiency may be overcome.

It is not a new proposal, though it has achieved greater force and notoriety in the past few years. Many of us are simply not aware how far advanced our schools already are on the road to a black-oriented version of multiculturalism. The SATs, according to David Reich in the *New York Times*, are now thoroughly multicultural, the questions requiring knowledge of Zora Neale Hurston, Ralph Ellison, Richard Wright, Gwendolyn Brooks, Lorraine Hansberry, and Jackie Robinson (he comes up twice). The fiction reading is from Maya Angelou. Diane Ravitch and Chester Finn, in *What Do Our 17-Year-Olds Know?*, report that in a national sample of seventeen-year-olds more could identify Harriet Tubman than Winston Churchill or Joseph Stalin, more knew Tubman than knew that George Washington commanded the American Army during the Revolution, or that Lincoln wrote the Emancipation Proclamation.

The mass of materials that flowed in on us as we worked on our report showed how established multiculturalism was in New York State. One of the documents listed teachers' guides available from the State Education Department, in addition to the social studies syllabi. Of the seven publications available, four dealt with minorities and women. One of them, the most substantial, was a three-volume publication on the teaching of the Holocaust. A survey of in-service workshops completed by New York State teachers in 1990–91 showed that far more had taken workshops on African history, black studies, ethnic studies, multicultural education, and cultural diversity than on American and European history.

One of the reasons all this is so agitating to so many is historical. After all, when Jewish and Italian American students dominated the public schools of New York City, George Washington and Abraham Lincoln were still on the walls, not Herzl and Garibaldi, and students were told that the Anglo-American forefathers of the American commonwealth were their forefathers. The students and their parents did not object, and most embraced the new identity. This background dominates much of the argument over multiculturalism. "We didn't get it, why should they? We didn't need it, why do they? We didn't want it, why do they?" But things change. They—and by that I mean primarily American blacks—may need it. I say "may" because we don't know. Nor are we clear on how many want it, but there are certainly a good number.

Multiculturalism today is in the same class as the proposals for schools for black boys, another desperate try to help black high school achievement. Or vouchers to permit black students to attend private black schools. In view of the extensive failure among low-income blacks, it is not easy to stand four-square against these proposals, particularly when advanced by black advocates aiming to overcome black school failure.

I do not see how school systems with a majority of black and Latino 10 students, with black or Latino leadership at the top, as is true of almost all our big-city school systems, can stand firmly against the multicultural thrust. The new president of the New York City Board of Education, H. Carl McCall, is reported by the *New York Times* as saying he could support a school "focusing primarily, but not exclusively, on black male students" and that "an Afrocentric curriculum . . . can be positive." One could add other testimonials, from members of other big-city school boards, and from school superintendents. In the big cities, in many schools, an unbalanced, indeed distorted view of American and world history and culture is prevailing. We should fight its excesses. Yet when set against the reality of majorities of black and Latino students in these schools, the political dominance of black and Latino administrators, the weak preparation of teachers and administrators in history, and the responsiveness of textbook publishers to organized pressure, the weight of the truth of history, as determined by the best scholars, is reduced to only one interest.

This may appear shocking, but it is not an entirely new phenomenon. In the elementary and high schools, a properly nuanced historical truth based on the best available evidence has always been only one interest among many. History in the schools has always played a socializing, nationalizing function (sometimes a regional pride function, as in the Southern versions of some texts). That function was the inculcation of patriotism in immigrants, and their assimilation to a culture deriving from England, and the experience of English-speaking colonists.

Some recent trends, even without the pressure of multiculturalists, are already changing that pattern. The most important is the general challenge to an unquestioning, simple, and direct American patriotism. After the past twenty years, with the relative decline of American power and the doubts about an unblemished American virtue, we will not have the triumphalist history that prevailed until a few decades ago. Our little war in Iraq will not turn around this tendency to be skeptical about the American past and present. (The worst of all histories, except for all the others, we might say.)

What does one do in the face of these trends? One thing is to fight the errors, distortions, untruths, imbalances. Some of the comments attached to the report did that, and the report fortunately did not add further weight to the more extreme claims. But the sharper critics of the report, I believe, have failed to recognize that demographic and political pressures change the history that is to be taught. They direct us to look for things we could not have noticed before. Assertions that are at first glance fantastic may have to be given some modest acquiescence. Yes, it seems that there were some Egyptian pharaohs who were racially black. (What one makes of it is another matter.) Yes, it seems that some ancient Greeks believed that they got their gods, myths, mystical knowledge from ancient Egypt. Martin Bernal's *Black Athena* will eventually leave some deposit in textbook accounts. (It will be ironic if one consequence of Afrocentrism is that our students, who know nothing of ancient Greece and less of ancient Egypt, will now be forced to learn something in order to accommodate the argument of African influences!) Yes, there is another side to the story of the expansion of Europe and imperialism. Yes, it is possible that, as the economic historian Barbara Solow argues, the weight of slave-produced plantation products was much greater in shaping the economy of the American colonies than is generally understood. Yes, there is a Mexican perspective on the Mexican-American War, and when one deals with classes that are dominantly Latin American it would be best to know it. And so on.

Black and Hispanic advocates will call for these new perspectives; historians, attracted by new ideas, politicized by new trends, looking for new topics, will explore them, and their researches will over time change weight and nuance in the treatment of various issues in the textbooks. It's happened before; it will happen again.

Yet another development bears on the multicultural problem. This is   15 the push for more choice in the public school system. That effort, supported by conservatives today, was first introduced as a policy alternative in American education in the late 1960s by liberals and radicals. Choice bears upon this debate because it implies diversity of curricula, because there should be something to choose among. It implies that quite a range of emphases may be offered, from Afrocentrism to Eurocentrism—perhaps, some have noted in alarm, the spectrum will run all the way from black Muslims to white racists.

In Milwaukee today hundreds of low-income black students attend, with state grants, inner-city black private schools, some of which emphasize Afrocentrism or black nationalism in their curricula. This program, under strong attack by the local teachers' union and others, has been adopted less because Milwaukee black leaders want to promote Afrocentrism than because they are fed up with the poor education their children receive in the public schools and hope that private schools, whatever their orientation, will do better—a view bolstered by the researches of James Coleman, John Chubb, and Terry Moe.

The movement for choice means the acceptance of more diversity in school curricula. At the margin, this diversity can be limited, if public funds are to be provided to assist choice. But there seems to me a kind of contradiction in simultaneously insisting on a strong, common, assimilationist curriculum in the public schools and accepting a wide range of diversity in the nonpublic school system. The line between the two systems and the two functions will not be easily maintained.

Inevitably, the current debate is focused on high-profile reports, large statements. But much of it ignores the reality of what goes on in American schooling. While multiculturalism and Afrocentrism race ahead in some schools and systems, others may happily continue to be the schools many of us remember and approve of, with only some modest modifications to prepare students for tests with a surprisingly high content of questions dealing with blacks and women, and particularly black women. The New York State report is only one step in a process that is far from concluded. The syllabi we reviewed are not required or imposed. The specific curricula of the classrooms are developed by hundreds of school districts, thousands of schools, many thousands of administrators and teachers. The syllabi are themselves broad outlines with examples. Many schools in the state already do more in the way of "multiculturalism" than the syllabi call for, many do less, and this ragged pattern will continue.

Whatever the strength of the multicultural thrust, I believe that American history in its main lineaments will have to be what it has been, and will not become completely alien to those of us educated in another time. We will find the story of the settlement by the English, but students will also be told that the Spaniards got to New Mexico and Florida first. The description of colonial America will place more emphasis on blacks, slave and free. The War for Independence will still play a large role, but we will now certainly find the blacks who fought in the war, along with Pulaski, von Steuben, Lafayette, and Haym Solomon. The Constitution will maintain its centrality, but we will now emphasize the argument over slavery, the references to the Indians. The expansion westward will emphasize how nasty we were to the Indians and the Mexicans. The struggle over slavery leading to the Civil War will emphasize even more strongly the criminal failure of Reconstruction and the importance of the postwar amendments and their role. The story of industrialization and the rise of the city will include more about the immigrants and the black migration north. And so on.

The skeletal structure will remain, because we still live under the   20
polity established by the Constitution, and it is in that polity, under that Constitution, that radical and ethnic and minority groups and women seek to expand their rights. It will be quite a job to keep nonsense and exaggeration and mindless ethnic and racial celebration out of the schools, but the basic structure of instruction in history will survive.

In my own comments, attached to the report, I took issue with the attempt to turn the United States into a congeries of ethnic and racial groups, and nothing more. Assimilation is a reality; scores of millions of unhyphenated Americans, who owe no allegiance to any identity other than American, are evidence of that. And assimilation continues to work its way, through the processes of work and of entertainment, with less help from the schools than before.

In this respect, present-day immigrants will not be very different from previous immigrants. They will assimilate. But one group, because of its experience of cruel, centuries-long ill treatment, is not yet fully incorporated in this generally successful process of nation-building. Present-day multiculturalism is a product of that apartness. Most of those who embrace it, I believe, do so in the hope that it will overcome that apartness. They want, in some key respects, to become more like other Americans—for example, in educational achievement—not different from them, and believe that the way to becoming more like them is to take more account of difference, and yes, of ill-treatment, of past and current achievement, even if exaggerated.

That is where we stand, and while some parts of this phenomenon are alarming enough, the proper parallel is not with Serbia and Croatia, or even Quebec. It is with our own American past, and the varying ways over time in which people of different race, religion, and ethnic background have become one nation.

Topics for Critical Thinking and Writing

1. Glazer implicitly asks two questions: (a) Who really wants "multicultur-alism" in the schools? (b) Why do they want it? What are his answers? From your experience in school and college, do you agree with him, or not—or does your experience so far provide no evidence one way or the other? Explain.

2. In paragraph 2 Glazer expresses his doubt that there is a widespread "desire or need for students to have something in the curriculum that relates to their own ethnic traits." Does your experience confirm or re-fute his doubt? Explain.

3. In paragraph 6 Glazer apparently accepts the view that the SATs are "thoroughly multicultural." If you are familiar with the SATs, indicate to what degree you share Glazer's belief on this point.

4. Glazer reports (para. 6) that more American seventeen-year-olds can identify Harriet Tubman than Winston Churchill or Joseph Stalin and that more know who Tubman was than know who wrote the Emanci-pation Proclamation. Does Glazer imply that this is regrettable? Do you think it is regrettable? Explain.

5. Glazer says (para. 11), "History in the schools has always played a so-cializing, nationalizing function." (Reread the entire paragraph to make sure you understand Glazer's point.) Does your experience (or, to your knowledge, the experience of your parents or grandparents) confirm Glazer's view? Explain.

24

Sexual Harassment: Is There Any Doubt about What It Is?

Tufts University

Many colleges and universities have drawn up statements of policy concerning sexual harassment. The following statement is fairly typical in that it seeks to define sexual harassment, to suggest ways of stopping it (these range from informal discussion to a formal grievance procedure), and to indicate resources that can provide help.

What Is Sexual Harassment?

Sexual harassment is a form of sex discrimination and violates federal and state law and university policy. Tufts University, its agents, supervisory employees, employees, and students shall be held liable for their acts of sexual harassment and are subject to appropriate university disciplinary action and personal liability. Sexual harassment is prohibited at Tufts University.

Sexual harassment, whether between people of different sexes or the same sex, is defined to include but is not limited to, unwanted sexual advances, unwelcome requests for sexual favors, and other behavior of a sexual nature when:

1. submission to such conduct is made either explicitly or implicitly a term and condition of an individual's employment or academic status; or

2. submission to, or rejection of, such conduct by an individual is used as a basis for employment or academic decisions affecting him or her; or

3. such conduct, whether verbal or physical, has the purpose or effect of unreasonably interfering with the individual's work or academic performance or of creating an intimidating, hostile, or offensive environment in which to work or to learn.

Any member of the Tufts community who feels that he or she has been sexually harassed should feel free to use the procedure described in this pamphlet without threat of intimidation, retaliation, or harassment.

WHO ARE THE PARTICIPANTS?

Sexual harassment can involve

- instructor and instructor
- professor and student
- teaching assistant and student
- supervisor and employee
- student and student
- staff member and student
- other relationships among colleagues, peers, and co-workers

The following behavior may constitute sexual harassment:

- lewd remarks, whistles, or personal reference to one's anatomy
- unwanted physical contact such as patting, pinching, or constant brushing against a person's body
- subtle or overt pressure for sexual favors
- persistent and offensive sexual jokes and comments
- display of pictures of a sexual nature
- persistent and unwanted requests for dates
- e-mail messages of an offensive sexual nature

The consequences to a person responsible for sexual harassment can include

- termination
- demotion
- denial of a promotion
- suspension
- letter of reprimand

It is unlawful to retaliate against an employee or student for filing a complaint of sexual harassment or for cooperating in an investigation of a complaint of sexual harassment.

HOW TO STOP SEXUAL HARASSMENT

If you are experiencing some form of sexual harassment, you need to know that Tufts provides several options to assist you. Since each situation is as distinct as the persons involved, the preferences of the complainant—including the need for confidentiality—will determine which option is most appropriate. Both informal and formal resolution options are available at Tufts. The only alternative we do not recommend is that you do nothing.

If you believe you are being or have been sexually harassed, you should consider taking the following steps immediately:

1. You may want to keep track of dates, places, times, witnesses, and the nature of the harassment. Save any letters, cards, or notes in a safe place.
2. Seek the advice of or report the incident to any of the individuals listed as sexual harassment resource persons. You may also seek the assistance of the Counseling Center, campus chaplains, Health Services psychiatrist, or Health Services counselor.

You may also consider using the following strategies: 10

1. Say "no" to your harasser. Say it firmly without smiling and apologizing.
2. Tell your harasser, in writing, that you object to this behavior. Describe the specific behaviors which are offensive or threatening, and keep a copy.
3. Utilize the Tufts University sexual harassment grievance procedure.

WHERE TO FIND HELP?

On each campus there are university sexual harassment resource persons who are available to provide informal and formal resolution options. Efforts will be made to protect your confidentiality. Each, however, has a duty to assure resolution and report the incident to the Office of Equal Opportunity, which may limit the ability to maintain confidentiality. The Tufts University sexual harassment resource persons are: [At this point the brochure gives a list of names of Tufts deans and organizations (for instance, Asian American Center; Health Education Program; Lesbian, Gay, Bisexual Resource Center) as well as outside organizations (for instance, Equal Employment Opportunity Commission), with telephone numbers.]

RESOLUTION BY INFORMAL DISCUSSION

Any student or employee who believes that he/she has been sexually harassed should first attempt to resolve the problem through discussion with the other party. In cases in which discussing the problem with that person presents particular stress or difficulties, the complainant has the right to consult on an informal basis with a supervisor, an administrator, the Office of Equal Opportunity, Human Resources, or a sexual harassment resource person. Efforts will be made to protect your confidentiality. The complainant may bring an associate to that meeting if desired. If there has been no resolution within a reasonable period of time, the sexual harassment grievance procedure shall then be instituted if desired.

SEXUAL HARASSMENT
GRIEVANCE PROCEDURE

If the problem has not been resolved to the satisfaction of the complainant through informal discussion, she/he has the right to file a grievance in accordance with the following procedure.

A. Where to File the Grievance?

If the person alleged to be responsible for the harassment is:

1. a staff member or an administrator—file with the vice president for Human Resources or campus Human Resources manager;
2. a faculty member—file with the appropriate dean of college/school or provost;
3. a student—file with the appropriate dean of students or dean of the college/school.

B. What Should Be Filed?

The grievance should be in writing and should summarize the ha- 15
rassment complained of, the person alleged to be responsible, and the resolution sought.

C. When Should the Grievance Be Filed?

The grievance should normally be filed within ninety (90) days of the incident(s) giving rise to the complaint. The university may extend this period if it finds that there are extenuating circumstances.

D. How Will the Grievance Be Processed?

1. If the person alleged to be responsible for the harassment is a student, the grievance will be processed through the discipline procedure applicable to that student.
2. If the person alleged to be responsible for the harassment is a staff member, administrator, or faculty member, the person with whom the grievance is filed will notify the special assistant to the president for affirmative action, who will attempt to resolve it by discussion, investigation, or other steps that he/she deems

appropriate. The special assistant to the president for affirmative action may appoint a hearing panel to review the matter. The complainant will be informed by the special assistant to the president for affirmative action or his/her designee of the action taken.

3. If a hearing panel is appointed, it will conduct an investigation which may, if the panel deems appropriate, include a hearing. The findings and recommendations of the panel will be sent to the president.

4. The president or his/her designee will review the findings and recommendations of the panel and may review other facts relating to the grievance. The decision of the president or his/her designee is binding and shall not be subject to review under any other grievance procedure in effect at Tufts University.

Topics for Critical Thinking and Writing

1. Where, if at all, would you draw the line between harmless, inoffensive flirtation and sexual harassment?

2. Is it, or should it be, a necessary condition for an act to qualify as sexual harassment that the aggressor persist in behavior the victim doesn't want after the victim has said "Stop!"? What position does the Tufts policy take on this issue?

3. Evaluate the four-part grievance procedure described in the Tufts statement. Can you think of ways it might be improved to be fairer? More efficient? Should the accused have the right to face his or her accusers? Should the victim's testimony require corroboration? Explain your answers to these questions in an essay of 500 words.

4. The list headed "Who Are the Participants?" does not include "student and instructor" or "student and staff member," though of course it includes the reverse relationships. Can you conceive of situations in which a student harasses an instructor or a staff member?

5. If your school has a comparable statement of policy, study it closely, partly by comparing it with the Tufts policy. Then (assuming that your school's statement does not in every respect satisfy you), set forth (with supporting reasons) the revisions you might make in it.

Ellen Goodman

Ellen Goodman, educated at Radcliffe College, worked as a reporter for Newsweek *and the* Detroit Free Press. *Since 1967 she has written for the* Boston Globe, *and since 1972 her column has been nationally syndicated. The essay that we reprint appeared in the* Boston Globe *in October 1991.*

The Reasonable Woman Standard

Since the volatile mix of sex and harassment exploded under the Capitol dome, it hasn't just been senators scurrying for cover. The case of the professor and judge has left a gender gap that looks more like a crater.[1]

We have discovered that men and women see this issue differently. Stop the presses. Sweetheart, get me rewrite.

On the "Today" show, Bryant Gumbel asks something about a man's right to have a pinup on the wall and Katie Couric says what she thinks of that. On the normally sober "MacNeil/Lehrer" hour the usual panel of legal experts doesn't break down between left and right but between male and female.

On a hundred radio talk shows, women are sharing experiences and men are asking for proof. In ten thousand offices, the order of the day is the nervous joke. One boss asks his secretary if he can still say "good morning," or is that sexual harassment. Heh, heh. The women aren't laughing.

Okay boys and girls, back to your corners. Can we talk? Can we hear?   5

The good news is that women have stopped rolling their eyes at each other and started speaking out. The bad news is that we may each assume the other gender not only doesn't understand but can't understand. "They don't get it" becomes "they can't get it."

Let's start with the fact that sexual harassment is a concept as new as date rape. Date rape, that should-be oxymoron, assumes a different perspective on the part of the man and the woman. His date, her rape. Sexual harassment comes with some of the same assumptions. What he labels sexual, she labels harassment.

This produces what many men tend to darkly call a "murky" area of the law. Murky however is a step in the right direction. When everything was clear, it was clearly biased. The old single standard was [a] male standard. The only options a working woman had were to grin, bear it, or quit.

Sexual harassment rules are based on the point of view of the victim, nearly always a woman. The rules ask, not just whether she has been physically assaulted, but whether the environment in which she works is intimidating or coercive. Whether she feels harassed. It says that her feelings matter.

---

[1]Goodman is alluding to the charges that Professor Anita Hill, of the University of Oklahoma law school, made during the Senate hearings before confirmation of Justice Clarence Thomas to a seat on the Supreme Court. The hearings were televised nationally, and several senators on the Judiciary Committee were widely regarded as having treated Hill very badly. [Editors' note.]

This, of course, raises all sorts of hackles about women's *feelings*, 10 women's *sensitivity*. How can you judge the sensitivity level of every single woman you work with? What's a poor man to do?

But the law isn't psychiatry. It doesn't adapt to individual sensitivity levels. There is a standard emerging by which the courts can judge these cases and by which people can judge them as well. It's called "the reasonable woman standard." How would a reasonable woman interpret this? How would a reasonable woman behave?

This is not an entirely new idea, although perhaps the law's belief in the reasonableness of women is. There has long been a "reasonable man" in the law not to mention a "reasonable pilot," a "reasonable innkeeper," a "reasonable train operator."

Now the law is admitting that a reasonable woman may see these situations differently than a man. That truth—available in your senator's mailbag—is also apparent in research. We tend to see sexualized situations from our own gender's perspective. Kim Lane Scheppele, a political science and law professor at the University of Michigan, summarizes the miscues this way: "Men see the sex first and miss the coercion. Women see the coercion and miss the sex."

Does that mean that we are genetically doomed to our double vision? Scheppele is quick to say no. Our justice system rests on the belief that one person can get in another's head, walk in her shoes, see things from another perspective. And so does our hope for change.

If a jury of car drivers can understand how a "reasonable pilot" 15 would see one situation, a jury of men can see how a reasonable woman would see another event. The crucial ingredient is empathy.

Check it out in the office tomorrow. He's coming on, she's backing off, he keeps coming. Read the body language. There's a *Playboy* calendar on the wall and a PMS joke in the boardroom and the boss is just being friendly. How would a reasonable woman feel?

At this moment, when the air is crackling with hostility and consciousness-raising has the hair sticking up on the back of many necks, guess what? Men can "get it." Reasonable men.

Topics for Critical Thinking and Writing

1. Goodman is a journalist, which means in part that her writing is lively. Point to two or three sentences that you would not normally find in a textbook, and evaluate them. (*Example*: "Okay boys and girls, back to your corners," para. 5.) Are the sentences you have selected effective? Why, or why not?

2. Why does Goodman describe date rape as a "should-be oxymoron" (para. 7)?

3. In paragraphs 11 and 12 Goodman speaks of "the reasonable woman standard." In recent years several cases have come to the courts in which women have said that they are harassed by posters of nude women in the workplace. Such posters have been said to create an "intimidating, hostile, or offensive environment." (a) What do you think Goodman's opinion would be? (b) Imagine that you are a member of the jury deciding such a case. What is your verdict? Why?

4. According to Goodman's account of the law (paras. 8–13), the criterion for sexual harassment is whether the "reasonable woman" would regard the "environment" in which she works (or studies) as "intimidating" or "coercive," thus causing her to "feel harassed." In a 500-word essay describe three hypothetical cases, one of which you believe clearly involves sexual harassment, a second that clearly does not, and a third that is a borderline case.

5. Given what Goodman says about sexual harassment, can men be victims of sexual harassment? Why, or why not?

Catharine A. MacKinnon

Catharine A. MacKinnon, a professor of law at the University of Michigan, is widely regarded as the nation's leading lawyer concerned with fighting sexual harassment and with outlawing pornography. The essay originally appeared in Aegis, *a magazine devoted to ending violence against women, and was later reprinted in MacKinnon's* Feminism Unmodified *(1987), where it was accompanied by this note: "This early synthesis was framed in part to respond to panel members' concerns with cooptation at the National Conference on Women and the Law, Boston, Massachusetts, April 5, 1981."*

Sex and Violence: A Perspective

I want to raise some questions about the concept of this panel's title, "Violence against Women," as a concept that may coopt us as we attempt to formulate our own truths. I want to speak specifically about four issues: rape, sexual harassment, pornography, and battery. I think one of the reasons we say that each of these issues is an example of violence against women is to reunify them. To say that aggression against women has this unity is to criticize the divisions that have been imposed on that aggression by the legal system. What I see to be the danger of the analysis, what makes it potentially cooptive, is formulating it—and it *is* formulated this way—these are issues of violence, *not* sex: Rape is a crime of violence, not sexuality; sexual harassment is an abuse of power, not sexuality; pornography is violence against women; it is not erotic. Although battering is not categorized so explicitly, it is usually treated as though there is nothing sexual about a man beating up a woman so long as it is with his fist. I'd like to raise some questions about that as well.

I hear in the formulation that these issues are violence against women, not sex, that we are in the shadow of Freud, intimidated at being called repressive Victorians. We're saying we're *op*pressed and they say we're *re*pressed. That is, when we say we're against rape, the immediate response is, "Does that mean you're against sex?" "Are you attempting to impose neo-Victorian prudery on sexual expression?" This comes up with sexual harassment as well. When we say we're against sexual harassment, the first thing people want to know is, "What's the difference between that and ordinary male-to-female sexual initiation?" That's a good question. . . . The same is also true of criticizing pornography. "You can't be against erotica?" It's the latest version of the accusation that feminists are antimale. To distinguish ourselves from this, and in reaction to it, we call these abuses violence. The attempt is to avoid the critique—we're not against sex—and at the same time retain our criticism of these practices. So we rename as violent those abuses that have been seen to be sexual, without saying that we have a very different perspective on violence and on sexuality and their relationship. I also think a reason we call these experiences violence is to avoid being called lesbians, which for some reason is equated with being against sex. In order to avoid that, yet retain our opposition to sexual violation, we put this neutral, objective, abstract word *violence* on it all.

To me this is an attempt to have our own perspective on these outrages without owning up to having one. To have our point of view but present it as *not* a particular point of view. Our problem has been to label something as rape, as sexual harassment, as pornography in the face of a suspicion that it might be intercourse, it might be ordinary sexual initiation, it might be erotic. To say that these purportedly sexual events violate us, to be against them, we call them not sexual. But the attempt to be objective and neutral avoids owning up to the fact that women do have a specific point of view on these events. It avoids saying that from women's point of view, intercourse, sex roles, and eroticism can be and at times are violent to us as women.

My approach would claim our perspective; we are not attempting to be objective about it, we're attempting to represent the point of view of women. The point of view of men up to this time, called objective, has been to distinguish sharply between rape on the one hand and intercourse on the other; sexual harassment on the one hand and normal, ordinary sexual initiation on the other; pornography or obscenity on the one hand and eroticism on the other. The male point of view defines them by distinction. What women experience does not so clearly distinguish the normal, everyday things from those abuses from which they have been defined by distinction. Not just "Now we're going to take what *you* say is rape and call it violence"; "Now we're going to take what *you* say is sexual harassment and call it violence"; "Now we're going to take what *you* say is pornography and call it violence." We have a deeper critique of what has been done to women's sexuality and who controls access to it. What we are saying is that sexuality in exactly these normal forms often *does* violate us. So long as we say that those things are abuses of violence, not sex, we fail to criticize what has been made of *sex,* what has been done to us *through* sex, because we leave the line between rape and intercourse, sexual harassment and sex roles, pornography and eroticism, right where it is.

I think it is useful to inquire how women and men (I don't use the 5 term *persons,* I guess, because I haven't seen many lately) live through the meaning of their experience with these issues. When we ask whether rape, sexual harassment, and pornography are questions of violence or questions of sexuality, it helps to ask, to whom? What is the perspective of those who are involved, whose experience it is—to rape or to have been raped, to consume pornography or to be consumed through it. As to what these things *mean* socially, it is important whether they are about sexuality to women and men or whether they are instead about "violence"—or whether violence and sexuality can be distinguished in that way, as they are lived out.

The crime of rape—this is a legal and observed, not a subjective, individual, or feminist definition—is defined around penetration. That seems to me a very male point of view on what it means to be sexually violated. And it is exactly what heterosexuality as a social institution is fixated around, the penetration of the penis into the vagina. Rape is defined according to what men think violates women, and that is the same as what they think of as the sine qua non of sex. What women experience as degrading and defiling when we are raped includes as much that is distinctive to us as is our experience of sex. Someone once termed penetration a "peculiarly resented aspect" of rape—I don't know whether that meant it was peculiar that it was resented or that it was resented with heightened peculiarity. Women who have been raped often do resent having been penetrated. But that is not all there is to what was intrusive or expropriative of a woman's sexual wholeness.

I do think the crime of rape focuses more centrally on what men define as sexuality than on women's experience of our sexual being, hence its violation. A common experience of rape victims is to be unable to feel good about anything heterosexual thereafter—or anything sexual at all, or men at all. The minute they start to have sexual feelings or feel sexually touched by a man, or even a woman, they start to relive the rape. I had a client who came in with her husband. She was a rape victim, a woman we had represented as a witness. Her husband sat the whole time and sobbed. They couldn't have sex anymore because every time he started to touch her, she would flash to the rape scene and see his face change into the face of the man who had raped her. That, to me, is sexual. When a woman has been raped, and it is sex that she then cannot experience without connecting it to that, it was her sexuality that was violated.

Similarly, men who are in prison for rape think it's the dumbest thing that ever happened. . . . It isn't just a miscarriage of justice; they were put in jail for something very little different from what most men do most of the time and call it sex. The only difference is they got caught. That view is nonremorseful and not rehabilitative. It may also be true. It seems to me we have here a convergence between the rapist's view of what he has done and the victim's perspective on what was done to her. That is, for both, their ordinary experiences of heterosexual intercourse and the act of rape have something in common. Now this gets us into intense trouble, because that's exactly how judges and juries see it who refuse to convict men accused of rape. A rape victim has to prove that it was not intercourse. She has to show that there was force and she resisted, because if there was sex, consent is inferred. Finders of fact look for "more force than usual during the preliminaries." Rape is defined by distinction from intercourse — not nonviolence, intercourse. They ask, does this event look more like fucking or like rape? But what is their standard for sex, and is this question asked from the *woman's point of view?* The level of force is not adjudicated at her point of violation; it is adjudicated at the standard of the normal level of force. Who sets this standard?

In the criminal law, we can't put everybody in jail who does an ordinary act, right? Crime is supposed to be deviant, not normal. Women continue not to report rape, and a reason is that they believe, and they are right, that the legal system will not see it from their point of view. We get very low conviction rates for rape.[1] We also get many women who believe they have never been raped, although a lot of force was involved. They mean that they were not raped in a way that is legally provable. In other words, in all these situations, there was not *enough* violence against them to take it beyond the category of "sex"; they were not coerced enough. Maybe they were forced-fucked for years and put up with it, maybe they tried to get it over with, maybe they were coerced by something other than battery, something like economics, maybe even something like love.

What I am saying is that unless you make the point that there is much violence in intercourse, as a usual matter, none of that is changed. Also we continue to stigmatize the women who claim rape as having experienced a deviant violation and allow the rest of us to go through life feeling violated but thinking we've never been raped, when there were a great many times when we, too, have had sex and didn't want it. What

---

[1]Gerald D. Robin, "Forcible Rape: Institutionalized Sexism in the Criminal Justice System," *Crime and Delinquency* (April 1977), 136–53. "Forcible rape is unique among crimes in the manner in which its victims are dealt with by the criminal justice system. Raped women are subjected to an institutionalized sexism that begins with the treatment by the police, continues through a male-dominated criminal justice system influenced by pseudoscientific notions of victim precipitation, and ends with the systematic acquittal of many de facto rapists." Lorenne M. G. Clark and Debra Lewis, *Rape: The Price of Coercive Sexuality* 57 (1977). [All notes are the author's.]

this critique does that is different from the "violence, not sex" critique is ask a series of questions about normal, heterosexual intercourse and attempt to move the line between heterosexuality on the one hand—intercourse—and rape on the other, rather than allow it to stay where it is.

Having done that so extensively with rape, I can consider sexual harassment more briefly. The way the analysis of sexual harassment is sometimes expressed now (and it bothers me) is that it is an abuse of power, not sexuality. That does not allow us to pursue whether sexuality, as socially constructed in our society through gender roles, is *itself* a power structure. If you look at sexual harassment as power, not sex, what is power supposed to be? Power is employer/employee, not because courts are marxist but because this is a recognized hierarchy. Among men. Power is teacher/student, because courts recognize a hierarchy there. Power is on one side and sexuality on the other. Sexuality is ordinary affection, everyday flirtation. Only when ordinary, everyday affection and flirtation and "I was just trying to be friendly" come into the context of *another* hierarchy is it considered potentially an abuse of power. What is not considered to be hierarchy is women and men—men on top and women on the bottom. That is not considered to be a question of power or social hierarchy, legally or politically. A feminist perspective suggests that it is.

When we have examples of coequal sexual harassment (within these other hierarchies), worker to worker on the same level, involving women and men, we have a lot of very interesting, difficult questions about sex discrimination, which is supposed to be about gender difference, but does not conceive of gender as a social hierarchy. I think that implicit in race discrimination cases for a brief moment of light was the notion that there is a social hierarchy between blacks and whites. So that presumptively it's an exercise of power for a white person to do something egregious to a black person or for a white institution to do something egregious systematically to many black people. Situations of coequal power—among coworkers or students or teachers—are difficult to see as examples of sexual harassment unless you have a notion of male power. I think we lie to women when we call it not power when a woman is come onto by a man who is not her employer, not her teacher. What do we labor under, what do we feel, when a man—any man—comes and hits on us? I think we require women to feel fine about turning down male-initiated sex so long as the man doesn't have some *other* form of power over us. Whenever—every and any time—a woman feels conflicted and wonders what's wrong with her that she can't decline although she has no inclination, and she feels open to male accusations, whether they come from women or men, of "Why didn't you just tell him to buzz off?" we have sold her out, not named her experience. We are taught that we exist for men. We should be flattered or at least act as if we are—be careful about a man's ego because you never know what he can do to you. To flat out say to him, "You?" or "I don't want to" is not *in* most women's sex-role learning. To say it is, is bravado. And that's because he's a man, not just because you never know what he can do to you because he's your boss (that's two things— he's a man and he's the boss) or your teacher or in some other hierarchy. It seems to me that we haven't talked very much about gender *as* a hierarchy, as a division of power, in the way that's expressed and acted out, primarily I think sexually. And therefore we haven't expanded the definition according to women's experience of sexuality, including our own sexual intimidation, of what things are sexual in this world. So men have also defined what can be called sexual about us. They say, "I was just trying to be affectionate, flirtatious, and friendly," and we were just all felt up. We criticize the idea that rape comes down to her word against his—but it really *is* her perspective against his perspective, and the law has been written from *his* perspective. If he didn't mean it to be sexual, it's not sexual. If he didn't see it as forced, it wasn't forced.[2] Which is to say, only male sexual violations, that is, only male ideas of what sexually violates us as women, are illegal. We buy into this when we say our sexual violations are abuses of power, not sex.

Just as rape is supposed to have nothing against intercourse, just as sexual harassment is supposed to have nothing against normal sexual initiation (men initiate, women consent—that's mutual?), the idea that pornography is violence against women, not sex, seems to distinguish artistic creation on the one hand from what is degrading to women on the other. It is candid and true but not enough to say of pornography, as Justice Stewart said, "I know it when I see it."[3] *He* knows what he thinks it is when he sees it—but is that what *I* know? Is that the same "it"? Is he going to know what I know when I see it? I think pretty much not, given what's on the newsstand, given what is not considered hard-core pornography. Sometimes I think what is obscene is what does *not* turn on the Supreme Court—or what revolts them more. Which is uncommon, since revulsion is eroticized. We have to admit that pornography turns men on; it is therefore erotic. It is a lie to say that pornography is not erotic. When we say it is violence, not sex, we are saying, there is this degrading to women, over here, and this erotic, over there, without saying to whom. It is overwhelmingly disproportionately men to whom pornography is erotic. It is women, on the whole, to whom it is violent, among other things. And this is not just a matter of perspective, but a matter of reality.

---

[2]Examples are particularly clear in England, Canada, and California. *Director of Public Prosecutions v. Morgan*, 2411 E.R.H.L. 347 (1975); *Pappajohn v. The Queen*, 11 D.L.R. 3d 1 (1980); *People v. Mayberry*, 15 Cal. 3d 143, 542 P. 2d 1337 (1975). But cf. *People v. Barnes*, 228 Cal. Rptr. 228 (Cal. 1986).
[3]*Jacobellis v. Ohio*, 378 U.S. 184, 197 (1964) (Stewart, J., concurring).

Pornography turns primarily men on. Certainly they are getting something out of it. They pay incredible amounts of money for it; it's one of the largest industries in the country. If women got as much out of it as men do, we would buy it instead of cosmetics. It's a massive industry, cosmetics. We are poor but we have *some* money; we are some market. We spend our money to set ourselves up as the objects that emulate those images that are sold as erotic to men. What pornography says about us is that we enjoy degradation, that we are sexually turned on by being degraded. For me that obliterates the line, as a line at all, between pornography on one hand and erotica on the other, if what turns men on, what men find beautiful, is what degrades women. It is pervasively present in art, also, and advertising. But it is definitely present in eroticism, if that is what it is. It makes me think that women's sexuality as such is a stigma. We also sometimes have an experience of sexuality authentic somehow in all this. We are not allowed to have it; we are not allowed to talk about it; we are not allowed to speak of it or image it as from our own point of view. And, to the extent we try to assert that we are beings equal with men, we have to be either asexual or virgins.

To worry about cooptation is to realize that lies make bad politics. It 15 is ironic that cooptation often results from an attempt to be "credible," to be strategically smart, to be "effective" on existing terms. Sometimes you become what you're fighting. Thinking about issues of sexual violation as issues of violence not sex could, if pursued legally, lead to opposing sexual harassment and pornography through morals legislation and obscenity laws. It is actually interesting that this theoretical stance has been widely embraced but these legal strategies have not been. Perhaps women realize that these legal approaches would not address the subordination of women to men, specifically and substantively. These approaches are legally as abstract as the "violence not sex" critique is politically abstract. They are both not enough and too much of the wrong thing. They deflect us from criticizing everyday behavior that is pervasive and normal and concrete and fuses sexuality with gender in violation and it is not amenable to existing legal approaches. I think we need to think more radically in our legal work here.

Battering is called violence, rather than something sex-specific: This is done to women. I also think it is sexually done to women. Not only in where it is done — over half of the incidents are in the bedroom.[4] Or the surrounding events — precipitating sexual jealousy. But when violence against women is eroticized as it is in this culture, it is very difficult to say that there is a major distinction in the level of sex involved between being assaulted by a penis and being assaulted by a fist, especially when the perpetrator is a man. If women as gender female are defined as sexual beings, and violence is eroticized, then men violating women has a

---

[4] R. Emerson Dobash and Russell Dobash, *Violence against Wives* (1979) at 14–21.

sexual component. I think men rape women because they get off on it in a way that fuses dominance with sexuality. (This is different in emphasis from what Susan Brownmiller says.[5]) I think that when men sexually harass women it expresses male control over sexual access to us. It doesn't mean they all want to fuck us, they just want to hurt us, dominate us, and control us, and that *is* fucking us. They want to be able to have that and to be able to say when they can have it, to *know* that. That is in itself erotic. The idea that opposing battering is about saving the family is, similarly, abstracted, gender-neutral. There are gender-neutral formulations of all these issues: law and order as opposed to derepression, Victorian morality as opposed to permissiveness, obscenity as opposed to art and freedom of expression. Gender-neutral, objective formulations like these avoid asking *whose* expression, from whose point of view? Whose law and whose order? It's not just a question of who is free to express ourselves; it's not just that there is almost no, if any, self-respecting women's eroticism. The fact is that what we do see, what we are allowed to experience, even in our own suffering, even in what we are to complain about, is overwhelmingly constructed from the male point of view. Laws against sexual violation express what men see and do when they engage in sex with women; laws against obscenity center on the display of women's bodies in ways that men are turned on by viewing. To me, it not only makes us cooptable to define such abuses in gender-neutral terms like violence; when we fail to assert that we are fighting for the affirmative definition and control of our own sexuality, of our own lives as women, and that these experiences violate *that*, we have already been bought.

Topics for Critical Thinking and Writing

1. Suppose a fellow student told you that he or she did not understand MacKinnon's first three paragraphs. In a few sentences summarize these paragraphs as clearly as possible.

2. In paragraph 4 MacKinnon sharply distinguishes between "the point of view of women" and "the point of view of men" concerning the experience of rape, sexual harassment, pornography, and battery. Do you agree that it is useful to make this clear-cut distinction? Support your answer.

3. In paragraph 14 MacKinnon notes that men far outnumber women as purchasers of pornography. How might you account for this fact?

4. MacKinnon's thesis might be formulated this way: Describing rape, sexual harassment, pornography, and battery as "violence against women,"

---

[5]Susan Brownmiller, *Against Our Will: Men, Women and Rape* (1975).

as distinct from *sexual* abuse, distorts the reality as experienced by women. (See especially MacKinnon's opening and closing paragraphs.) State as succinctly as you can what the reality is, and why "violence against women," distinguished from "sexual violence," distorts that reality.

5. Read the essay by Ellen Goodman on sexual harassment (p. 602), and write a 500-word essay explaining the similarities and differences between Goodman's view and MacKinnon's on this topic. Which view do you prefer? Why?

Sarah J. McCarthy

As Sarah J. McCarthy indicates in this essay, she is the owner of a small restaurant. The essay originally appeared in the December 9, 1991, issue of Forbes, *a business-oriented magazine.*

Cultural Fascism

On the same day that Ted Kennedy asked forgiveness for his personal "shortcomings," he advocated slapping lottery-size punitive damages on small-business owners who may be guilty of excessive flirting or whose employees may be guilty of talking dirty. Senator Kennedy expressed regrets that the new civil rights bill caps punitive damages for sexual harassment as high as $300,000 (depending on company size), and he promises to push for increases next year. Note that the senators have voted to exempt themselves from punitive damages.

I am the owner of a small restaurant/bar that employs approximately twenty young males whose role models range from Axl Rose to John Belushi. They work hard in a high-stress, fast-paced job in a hot kitchen and at times they are guilty of colorful language. They have also been overheard telling Pee-Wee Herman jokes and listening to obnoxious rock lyrics. They have discussed pornography and they have flirted with waitresses. One chef/manager has asked out a pretty blonde waitress probably a hundred times in three years. She seems to enjoy the game, but always says no. Everyone calls everyone else "Honey"—it's a ritual, a way of softening what sound like barked orders: "I need the medium-rare shish kebab *now!*"

"Honey" doesn't mean the same thing here as it does in women's studies departments or at the EEOC.[1] The auto body shop down the street has pinups. Perhaps under the vigilant eyes of the feminist political correctness gestapo we can reshape our employees' behavior so they act more like nerds from the Yale women's studies department. The gestapo

---

[1]**EEOC** Equal Employment Opportunity Commission. [Editors' note.]

will not lack for potential informers seeking punitive damages and instant riches.

With the Civil Rights Bill of 1991 we are witnessing the most organized and systematic assault on free speech and privacy since the McCarthy era. The vagueness of the sexual harassment law, combined with our current litigation explosion, is a frightening prospect for small businesses. We are now financially responsible for sexually offensive verbal behavior, even if we don't know it is occurring, under a law that provides no guidelines to define "offensive" and "harassment." This is a cultural fascism unmatched since the Chinese communists outlawed handholding, decorative clothing, and premarital sex.

This law is detrimental even to the women it professes to help. I am   5
a feminist, but the law has made me fearful of hiring women. If one of our cooks or managers—or my husband or sons—offends someone, it could cost us $100,000 in punitive damages and legal expenses. There will be no insurance fund or stockholders or taxpayers to pick up the tab.

When I was a feminist activist in the 1970s, we knew the dangers of a pedestal—it was said to be as confining as any other small place. As we were revolted and outraged by the woman-hatred in violent pornography, we reminded each other that education, not laws, was the solution to our problems. In Women Against Sexist Violence in Pornography and Media, in Pittsburgh, we were well aware of the dangers of encroaching on the First Amendment. Free speech was, perhaps more than anything else, what made our country grow into a land of enlightenment and diversity. The lesbians among us were aware that the same laws used to censor pornography could be used against them if their sexual expressions were deemed offensive.

We admired powerful women writers such as Marge Piercy and poets like Robin Morgan who swooped in from nowhere, writing break-your-chains poems about women swinging from crystal chandeliers like monkeys on vines and defecating in punch bowls. Are we allowed to talk about these poems in the current American workplace?

The lawyers—the prim women and men who went to the politically correct law schools—believe with sophomoric arrogance that the solution to all the world's problems is tort litigation. We now have eternally complicated questions of sexual politics judged by the shirting standards of the reasonable prude.

To the leadership of the women's movement: You do women a disservice. You ladies—and I use that term intentionally—have trivialized the women's movement. You have made us ladies again. You have not considered the unintended effects of your sexual harassment law. You are saying that too many things men say and do with each other are too rough-and-tumble for us. Wielding the power of your $300,000 lawsuits, you are frightening managers into hiring men over women. I know that I am so frightened. You have installed a double pane of glass on the glass ceiling with the help of your white knight and protector, Senator Kennedy.

You and your allies tried to lynch Clarence Thomas. You alienate 10 your natural allies. Men and women who wanted to work shoulder to shoulder with you are now looking over their shoulders. You have made women into china dolls that if broken come with a $300,000 price tag. The games, intrigue, nuances, and fun of flirting have been made into criminal activity.

We women are not as delicate and powerless as you think. We do not want victim status in the workplace. Don't try to foist it on us.

Topics for Critical Thinking and Writing

1. Reread McCarthy's opening paragraph. What is her point? How effective do you think this paragraph is as the opening of an argumentative essay?

2. In her third paragraph McCarthy speaks of "the feminist political correctness gestapo." What does she mean by this phrase, and why does she use it?

3. In paragraph 8 McCarthy refers to "tort litigation." Explain the phrase.

4. In her second paragraph McCarthy suggests that in "a high-stress, fast-paced" environment with young (and presumably not highly educated) males, "colorful language and dirty jokes" and "obnoxious rock lyrics" are to be expected. Would you agree that a woman who takes a job in such an environment cannot reasonably complain that this sort of behavior constitutes sexual harassment? Explain.

5. How do you think McCarthy would define sexual harassment? That is, how according to her views should we complete the following sentence: Person A sexually harasses person B if and only if . . . ?

6. Read the essay by Ellen Goodman (p. 602) and explain in a brief essay of 100 words where she and Sarah J. McCarthy differ. With whom do you agree? Why?

25

Violence on TV:
Do Children Need
to Be Protected?

Leonard D. Eron

Leonard D. Eron, professor of psychology at the University of Michigan and a student of TV violence since 1957, is chair of the American Psychological Association's Commission on Violence and Youth. This essay originated in a panel discussion sponsored by the Harvard School of Public Health in 1992.

The Television Industry
Must Police Itself

A recent summary of over two hundred studies, published in 1990, offers convincing evidence that the observation of violence, as seen in standard everyday television entertainment, does affect the aggressive behavior of the viewer. . . .

What can be done? As soon as the suggestion for action comes up, the TV industry raises the issue of censorship, violation of First Amendment rights, and abrogation of the Constitution. For many years now Western European countries have monitored TV and films and have not permitted the showing of excess violence, especially during child viewing hours. I have never heard of any complaints by citizens in those democratic countries that their rights have been violated. But in the United States, youth violence is a public health problem, so designated by the Centers for Disease Control [and Prevention]. . . . No one is claiming that TV violence is the sole cause of the epidemic. However, it is certainly *one* of the causes, and one which we at least can do something about. Is it too much to ask the industry to police itself? It has done so before with some success.

I don't favor censorship and I am jealous of my First Amendment rights. But I don't think some serious self-regulation and monitoring by the TV and film industry is a threat to our constitutional rights.

It would be appropriate for the FCC to require stations to document what they have done to lower the violence in their programming before their licenses are renewed. . . .

In the spring [of 1992] we had to face the implications of the uncon- 5 trolled violence in Los Angeles. TV cannot escape its share of the responsibility for this outburst. We know that children living in the inner city watch more TV than other children. Children living in the inner city are increasingly surrounded by violence—at home, in the neighborhood, on the way to and from school. They are constantly dodging bullets, cowering in hallways, hiding under tables, because the streets are so dangerous from drive-by shootings and other violence. They spend more and more time indoors watching TV.

And what do they see on TV? More violence. This validates what the children have seen in the neighborhood. It makes violence normative—everyone's doing it, not just in their neighborhood but all over. TV represents violence as an appropriate way to solve interpersonal problems, to get what you want out of life, avenge slights and insults, and make up for perceived injustices.

Topics for Critical Thinking and Writing

1. In his first paragraph Eron asserts that a summary of studies shows "convincing evidence that the observation of violence . . . does affect the aggressive behavior of the viewer." Design a study that you think might show the effects of observing violence.

2. Eron says (para. 2) that censorship of violence on TV in Western European countries has led to no complaints "in those democratic countries that their rights have been violated." How might Eron respond if you pointed out to him that those countries do not have a First Amendment that guarantees their citizens "freedom of speech" and "freedom of the press"?

3. Eron thinks (para. 4) that TV stations ought to be required to show "what they have done to lower the violence" in their programs. How do you think the quantity or quality of violence ought to be measured?

4. If, as Eron admits (para. 5), inner-city children live in a world "surrounded by violence," why does he think that reducing fictional portrayals of violence on television will have a beneficial effect?

5. Violence on television is of many kinds—for instance, fictional stories of police, news images of war or murder, nature films of animals preying on other animals, and cartoons of animals knocking other animals around. Do you think episodes in cartoons such as *Bugs Bunny* and *Tom and Jerry* may stimulate children to act violently? Explain.

6. Get a copy of the week's *TV Guide*, turn on your television set, and devote twelve hours (from 10 A.M. to 10 P.M.) gathering your own data firsthand on TV violence. Then write an essay of 750 words explaining your methodology and your conclusions for or against this thesis: "There Is Too Much Violence Shown on Television during Prime-Time Viewing Hours."

Del Reisman

Del Reisman is a former president of the Writers Guild of America, West. Like the preceding essay, this one originated in a panel discussion sponsored by the Harvard School of Public Health in 1992.

Additional Guidelines for Violence Are Not Called For

The only way to significantly reduce violence, or the threat of violence, in storytelling is for networks and cable to simply not order series or special films which are, virtually by definition, inherently violent, such as action-adventure, crime, futuristic melodrama, etc., and use instead the softer genres, such as we see on the networks now, shows such as *Homefront, Sisters, Northern Exposure,* and so on. Not a very realistic possibility, however.

Networks, as you know, follow. They do not lead. Networks react to social change and community standards. I *know*. I have served as a story editor on many weekly series. Story editors scan the headlines, searching for ways to paraphrase the truth and put it into fictional form. . . .

I believe that additional guidelines for violence should not be called for because they will simply reduce the actual sights of some violence but not the threatening storytelling that builds to it, and therefore such guidelines would be a crumb thrown to those who believe in a causal relationship.

I believe that writers should continue to tell the stories of our time. Abuse in the home toward children, or parents, or grandparents is out of the closet now, thanks to its dramatization on television. Child custody struggles, in which the losing parent literally kidnaps a child, at last is before the American public as the serious social problem that it is. Fictional television has seen this dramatized frequently. Gay bashing has found its way from the dark alleys of our cities to the films of both weekly series and movies-of-the-week. The violence on the home screen *follows* the violence in our lives.

We've lived with Broadcast Standards for forty years, fighting the departments frequently, losing most of the fights, but reacting positively as networks followed changes in community standards from the days of no "hells" and no "damns" to today's relatively explicit language, frank relationships, and open dramatizations of dysfunctional families. Writers want to involve audiences in our stories. Writers are family people, too. We're parents and children and siblings and grandparents and grandchildren. We are community-minded and we care deeply about the world around us. We are as shocked and concerned by what is happening on our streets, on our schoolyards, in our classrooms, and in our homes as any of you. We agree on very little but we do agree on fundamentals, such as freedom of expression and freedom from censorship, the official kind and the unofficial kind which induces self-censorship.

Topics for Critical Thinking and Writing

1. Reisman contrasts (para. 1) "inherently violent" TV films and series with those of "softer genres." Why does he think it is "not a very realistic possibility" that TV networks will shift from screening the former in favor of the latter?

2. Think further about the "inherently violent" genres, such as "action-adventure, crime, [and] futuristic melodrama." If we are convinced that watching such films does indeed make viewers more prone to acts of violence, should we not suppress these programs? Explain.

3. Reisman argues, in paragraph 4, that television tells "the stories of our time." How strong an argument against curbing depictions of violence do you find this? Explain.

4. In his closing paragraph Reisman reminds the reader that writers, too, are people ("parents and children and siblings and grandparents and grandchildren"). What does Reisman hope to accomplish by reminding us of this obvious fact?

Ernest F. Hollings

Ernest F. Hollings is the ranking Democrat of the Senate Committee on Commerce, Science, and Transportation. This essay was originally published in the New York Times *(November 23, 1993) as part of a dialogue called "TV Violence: Survival vs. Censorship," along with an essay by Floyd Abrams (p. 622).*

Save the Children

Imagine an intruder entering your home, seizing your children, and forcing them to watch 8,000 murders and 100,000 acts of violence. A monstrous crime? Yes. A crime that would do untold psychological harm to your children? No question about it.

Wake up, parents. Chances are that your child is the victim I just described. The statistics come from the American Psychological Association, which reported in 1992 that by the end of elementary school, the average American child has watched that many acts of violence on television.

Saturday morning children's programming leads the way in mayhem and gore, showing an average of thirty-two violent acts per hour.

Enough! It is time for decent Americans to rescue our children from this threat. To that end, I have co-sponsored with Senator Daniel K. Inouye the Children's Protection from Violent Programming Act of 1993, which would ban the broadcast or cable transmission of violent programming during hours when children make up a substantial share of the audience.

At a hearing before the committee in October, TV executives claimed that they have cleaned up their prime-time programming, created monitoring committees, and shown good faith. But we've heard these same hollow pledges for four decades.

Testifying, Attorney General Janet Reno remarked, "Don't things   5
seem upside-down when violent programming is turning television into one more obstacle that parents and teachers have to overcome in order to raise their children?"

First and foremost, the bill to fight TV violence is intended to benefit children—many of them unsupervised, all of them impressionable and vulnerable.

More than one thousand studies—including reports by the Surgeon General, the National Institute of Mental Health, and others—have demonstrated a direct link between exposure to violence in the media and aggressive, violent behavior.

Shamefully, Hollywood and the TV networks have thumbed their nose at this crisis. And they have mobilized to defeat the bill. Many media executives acknowledge the harmful effects of violent programming on children, but insist it isn't their responsibility. Their solution: Parents should supervise children's viewing.

But what about the millions of kids whose viewing is unsupervised? A civic leader from South Central Los Angeles told the Commerce Committee that 80 percent of children in inner-city neighborhoods are latchkey kids—kids who return from school to parentless homes, where they spend four to five hours an afternoon, unsupervised, in front of the electronic baby sitter.

Some TV executives claim the bill infringes on their First Amend-   10
ment right to free speech. Not so, responded Attorney General Reno, testifying that the Supreme Court has upheld a "compelling state interest" in protecting the physical and psychological well-being of children. Under this principle, we have restricted sexual indecency on TV for decades. The same principle applies to violence.

Bear in mind that the legislation in no way seeks to control what adults watch. Premium cable channels such as HBO and Showtime are not covered. Networks and cable channels would remain free to broadcast violent programming during hours when children are not a substantial part of the audience.

For Hollywood, violence and sex translate into profits and market share. This is its corporate bottom line. But our society has a different bottom line. The proposed legislation gives concerned Americans a chance to fight back. If the TV and cable industries have no sense of shame, we must take it upon ourselves to stop licensing their violence-saturated programming.

Topics for Critical Thinking and Writing

1. In his first paragraph Hollings speaks of the 8,000 murders and the 100,000 acts of violence that children are likely to see by the time they complete elementary school. Drawing on your own experience, what sorts of people are treated violently on television?

2. Do you think that the murders and acts of violence you saw on television when you were young influenced your behavior? Often? Sometimes? Rarely? Never? Explain.

3. If you do not think you were influenced by seeing violence on television, do you think that other young people were? If so, why were they influenced but not you?

4. Some researchers argue that although televised violence may increase aggressiveness, it may also have other effects. For instance, it may increase fearfulness of becoming a victim, or it may increase callousness toward violence directed at others. Drawing on your own experience, can you support these views? Explain.

5. Hollings reports (para. 2) that a typical Saturday morning's worth of television for children shows "an average of thirty-two violent acts per hour." On a convenient Saturday morning, turn on your television and do some channel surfing between 8 A.M. and noon. How many "violent acts" did you see? What was your criterion of a "violent act"? Does your research incline you to agree or disagree with the data that Hollings reported?

6. If, as Hollings says in paragraph 9, "80 percent of children in inner-city neighborhoods are latchkey kids," and if we assume that many of their households have not only a TV set but also a VCR, and that children know how to operate a VCR, what's to keep these children from watching all the violence they want by the simple expedient of plugging in a suitable videocassette?

Floyd Abrams

Floyd Abrams, a lawyer, has represented the New York Times, *other newspapers, and broadcasters. This essay was first published, along with the preceding essay by Senator Ernest F. Hollings (p. 619), in the* New York Times *(November 23, 1993), as part of a dialogue called "TV Violence: Survival vs. Censorship."*

Save Free Speech

As the Senate Commerce Committee's hearings on television violence drew to a close, two Senators argued about a movie.

Senator Conrad Burns had just seen *Rudy* in a theater. Although the movie was violent, he thought it was a "wonderful" and "delightful" story about a Notre Dame football player that the entire family should see on TV.

Senator Byron L. Dorgan disagreed. Seeing the movie in a theater was one thing, he said. Allowing it to come out of "a television box in the living room" was something else.

The exchange was illuminating. We cannot even agree on which violence children should not see. Should it include *Roots* and *Lonesome Dove*? *The War of the Roses* and *True Grit*? Or is the problem only "bad" violence, the sordid and frightening depiction, cited by Senator Paul Simon, of some fiend on the attack with a chainsaw?

Laws don't have vocabularies that distinguish between good and bad   5
violence. Adjectives help when we speak to each other—words like "sordid" and "frightening." Even a word like "bad." But these are not and cannot be the words of legislation.

If they were, we would need a constantly monitoring Federal Communications Commission deciding on matters of subjective taste and psychological reality: which violence is constructive, which gratuitous. We would, in short, need a national censorship board. But that is the world of the Ayatollah, not ours.

Even objective criteria would not help. How many bullets are too many? How much violence is too much? Does it matter if the movie is *Glory* or *Gettysburg*? Or the latest remake of *Nightmare on Elm Street*? Or if the characters are Tom or Jerry?

One proposal is that Congress should bar the showing of *any* act of violence on TV in the evening before, say, 11 P.M. That is the heart of the legislation proposed by Senators Ernest F. Hollings and Daniel K. Inouye.

No program or film with any violence, whatever its artistic value or potential social benefit, could thus be shown at a time when most adults and most children watch TV. Not *Rudy*. Not *A Streetcar Named Desire*. We could watch *Married With Children* but not *War and Remembrance*, *Star Search* but not *Star Wars*.

This is censorship, plain and simple. It is no less so because the legis-   10
lation is designed to protect children. As the Supreme Court Justice Felix Frankfurter put it in a 1957 opinion, we may not "reduce the adult population" to material "fit for children."

Justice Lewis Powell added a related conclusion in an opinion seventeen years later: "Speech that is neither obscene as to youths nor subject to some other legitimate prescription cannot be suppressed solely to protect the young from ideas or images that a legislative body thinks unsuitable for them."

That is precisely what all of the antiviolence legislation before Congress seeks to do. Much of it is justified on the ground that since Congress can regulate "indecency" on TV, it should be permitted to regulate violence as well.

But the depiction of violence, some of which is contained in the greatest works of literature and film, is hardly equivalent to that of "indecent material"—material that a much disputed 5–4 Supreme Court opinion in 1978 concluded "surely lies at the periphery of First Amendment concern."

Whatever the correctness of that ruling, there is nothing peripheral to the First Amendment of much of the TV programming that so many in Congress seek to regulate. Senator Burns was right: It is not for Congress to choose whether or when we see *Rudy* on TV. And he was right about something else. Legislation in this area cannot be passed "that would stay within the Constitution."

Topics for Critical Thinking and Writing

1. Abrams argues that reasonable people cannot agree on how to distinguish between "good and bad violence" (para. 5). Try to formulate a distinction—perhaps working with three or four of your classmates. Begin with examples that seem obvious and then work toward a grayer area but where you still think a line can be drawn. If you can think of an example that in your opinion could go on either side, briefly summarize the example and explain why you think it cannot be firmly classified.

2. Abrams argues that just because "Congress can regulate 'indecency,'" it doesn't follow that Congress can or ought to regulate violence (para. 12). How would Abrams reply to these objections: (1) Surely, depictions of violence can be far more harmful to the young than any depictions of indecency. (2) If publishers can comply with regulations against indecency, there is no good reason why movie and television producers cannot also comply with regulations against violence. (3) Censorship of violence is no more unreasonable than censorship of indecency—and since we have the latter, why not have the former, too?

3. How might Hollings reply to Abrams's point that under the Hollings-Inouye plan, families could not watch, say, *A Streetcar Named Desire* before 11 P.M.?

Dale Kunkel

Dale Kunkel teaches communication at the University of California at Santa Barbara. His special interest is television and children, and he has published widely on this topic, for instance in the Journal of Clinical Child Psychology *and the* Journal of Broadcasting and Electronic Media. *We reprint an article originally published in* The Chronicle of Higher Education *in 1997.*

Why Content, Not the Age of Viewers, Should Control What Children Watch on TV

After rancorous debate, the "V-chip" television-rating system is now in place. But controversy persists over the way in which the industry has chosen to rate its programs.

Among the most vocal opponents of the new system have been parents and educators concerned that the ratings do not provide adequate information to families worried about the impact of television on children. Their concern is well grounded, given the compelling academic research on the effects of TV violence. As the new system undergoes formal review by the Federal Communications Commission, researchers who have studied the effects of television on children should join efforts by parent groups and child advocates to emphasize to the FCC the need for improvements.

To those outside of the entertainment and news media, the debate over the rating system may be confusing. A year ago, the president and Congress said parents deserved a V-chip—an electronic means of screening out content, particularly violence, that they deem inappropriate for their children's viewing. In December, the television industry delivered on its promise to the president to implement, rather than oppose, the V-chip. The industry introduced a rating system and began using it even as it was undergoing FCC review.

Although the actual V-chip won't be installed in new TV sets until 1998, parents will soon be able to buy an add-on device for about fifty dollars that will allow them to block programs using the V-chip system. So parents can now enter the twenty-first century using the latest electronic technology to help them supervise the more than one-thousand hours a year that most children spend watching television.

There's only one problem. The linchpin of the V-chip system is the   5 framework of categories that the industry will use to rate television programs; a parent can't block out TV content that isn't categorized. And under the new system, the ratings will not indicate whether any given show actually contains violence, sex, or adult language, thereby conveniently avoiding the controversies that would result from clearly labeling violent content with a "V" designation. It's a clever arrangement that succeeds in taking the "V" out of the V-chip.

It's a bit like offering a weather forecast that says, "Warning: severe weather approaching," without telling you whether to expect rain, snow, wind, or fog. The details aren't important; just be careful out there.

Further, because Congress left entirely up to the television industry the decision about what categories to use, the plan will rely solely on the program producer's judgment about the suitability of a show's content for children of different ages.

This approach deprives parents of the information that they need to make intelligent decisions about what their children should view. Providing specific information to parents was the initial premise of the V-chip, so it is not surprising that advocates for children and the V-chip proponents are now fighting hard to pressure the television industry for a better approach.

Although billed as a twenty-first-century tool for parents, the new V-chip ratings are suspiciously similar to the movie-rating system created in 1968 by Jack Valenti, president of the Motion Picture Association of America. Not coincidentally, he led the TV industry's effort to devise the new V-chip ratings. Like the film ratings, the new TV ratings employ age-based advisories, which indicate nothing more than the television programmer's overall judgment about the acceptability of content for specific age groups.

Ironically, by labeling programs with age designations rather than 10 indicating how much violence, sex, or adult language the shows contain, the TV industry may create a boomerang effect in which *more* children will end up watching the programs with sensitive content. Research conducted by Joanne Cantor, a professor of communications at the University of Wisconsin at Madison, indicates that young children, boys in particular, are more attracted to program listings that include age-based "parental guidance" warnings than they are to the identical programs when they carry a descriptive label — for example, "contains violent content." Professor Cantor labels this pattern the "forbidden fruit" effect, suggesting that children typically want whatever their parents think they shouldn't have, or what is intended for children older than themselves.

The television industry knows this. Mr. Valenti has spent the last year meeting with research experts, parent groups, and child advocates to discuss the development of the TV-rating system. I've participated in several of these meetings and consulted with dozens of other people who also have attended. The advice the industry received was virtually unanimous but nonetheless ignored.

The ratings approach that people want is a content-based descriptive system, not a system grounded in age-based advisories that are determined solely by television producers. With a descriptive system, programs would be labeled for the type and degree of violence, sex, and adult language they contain, without applying any value judgments about what material is appropriate for whom. Using this information and applying their own values, parents could then judge what material was most suitable for their children. In contrast, the age-based advisory system hides the descriptive information from the public by "filtering" it with the television industry's judgment of what content is suitable for all children within a given age range.

A recent study by the National Parent Teacher Association found that 80 percent of parents preferred the content-based, descriptive system to age-based categories. A replication study conducted several weeks later for the Media Studies Center by the University of Connecticut's Roper Center for Public Opinion Research produced an almost identical figure: 79 percent of parents favored content information over age-based categories.

In addition, Children Now, a national advocacy group, conducted a survey of leading child advocates and media researchers and found that seventeen out of eighteen respondents judged the descriptive approach an essential aspect of any useful ratings system.

Knowledge that a program contains violence is especially important, given what research has shown about the psychological effects of TV violence on children. A compelling body of evidence demonstrates that exposure to televised violence contributes to aggressive attitudes and behaviors, to desensitization to the victims of violence, and to fear among children. Scientific studies by the U.S. Surgeon General, the National Academy of Sciences, and the National Institute of Mental Health, as well as by numerous professional organizations such as the American Psychological Association, the American Medical Association, and the American Academy of Pediatrics, have found clear evidence that media violence has harmful effects. 15

Just as with cigarette smoking, exposure to violent media is a risk factor. Not everyone who smokes contracts cancer, but the more one smokes, the greater the risk. So too with viewing violence. Simply put, the pervasiveness of media violence is a serious public-health and societal concern.

While parents are concerned about violence, sexual messages, and adult language, not all parents are concerned to the same degree about the same types of material. Different families have different concerns that are unique to their values or specific to the needs of their children. No one universal standard is appropriate for all children of the same age.

That is why it is important to be clear in conveying why a program is rated as it is. TV producers' claims that the sheer volume of programs broadcast weekly would preclude rating them for content are disingenuous: The judgments necessary for a content-based system also have to be made for the present age-based advisories; the only difference is in how those judgments are reported.

The video-game industry reports such judgments in clear and descriptive content ratings that indicate to parents the levels of violence, sex, and profane language included in each product. The video-game ratings, which are currently being extended to Web sites on the Internet, are administered by an independent body known as the Recreational

Software Advisory Council, which includes research experts, teachers, and teenagers, as well as industry representatives.

Are the parents of children who use video games supposed to be 20 smarter than the parents of children who just watch television? Does the TV industry think parents can't handle program-content information in raw form—that judgments about sex and violence on TV have to be interpreted for them?

I suspect an ulterior motive. By clouding the reasons why a program is rated in a certain way, as well as by providing only the vaguest information about what types of violence or sex are shown, the controversies surrounding actual program ratings can be minimized. Imagine the economic implications for broadcasters if people who didn't want their children to see violence on TV actually had an effective way of blocking all violent programs. Ratings would go down and advertising dollars would decline.

That's an unacceptable outcome for the broadcasters. So the strategy is to deliver a ratings system, but to limit it to categories so imprecise that they never really reduce viewership of a program. If parents can't figure out why a program has been rated in a given way, perhaps neither will sponsors who otherwise might be scared away from programs clearly identified as violent or sex-laden.

A system of age-based ratings for television thus serves the needs of the television industry, but not the needs of America's children and families. The V-chip technology holds the potential to empower parents to make choices based on their own value judgments. But the potential can be realized only with a rating system grounded in content-based information.

President Clinton has asked that the new system be given a trial, so it seems unlikely that the FCC will reject it at this point. Yet given the volume of objections since the plan was announced, the industry has agreed to reevaluate its system at the end of 1997, once parents have had experience with it.

The most important consideration now is that the FCC select a tech- 25 nological standard that allows for future refinements in the ratings. If TV sets begin rolling off assembly lines with a V-chip capable of operating only on the age-based advisory system, what the president now calls a "trial" will become a fait accompli.

The overwhelming evidence about the risks from children's exposure to media violence warrants the clear identification of this type of content. What information do parents gain when they review the prime-time schedule and discover that virtually everything is rated TV-PG, from an incident of rape on "New York Undercover" to the double-entendres on "Seinfield"?

When the television industry first agreed to the V-chip at a White House meeting almost one year ago, Jack Valenti issued a statement on behalf of the television industry that acknowledged, "We have a civic obligation to offer as much parental guidance and information as is humanly possible to provide." Researchers should join with parents' groups and child advocates to make sure the industry delivers on that promise. It hasn't yet.

Topics for Critical Thinking and Writing

1. What is the V-chip?

2. Why does Kunkel think that the rating system used with the V-chip "may create a boomerang effect in which *more* children will end up watching the programs with sensitive content" (para. 10)?

3. Kunkel claims to know what type of rating system the public wants (paras. 11–14). On what evidence does he base his claim to this knowledge?

4. Kunkel draws an analogy in paragraph 16 between smoking and watching violence on TV. In a short essay of 250 words state and evaluate this analogy.

5. Why does Kunkel think that the TV broadcasting industry has favored a flawed rating system (paras. 20–22)? Do you think his reasons are cynical or plausible? Set forth your answer in an essay of 500 words.

Part Six

ENDURING QUESTIONS: ESSAYS, STORIES, POEMS, AND PLAYS

26

What Is the
Ideal Society?

Thomas More

*The son of a prominent London lawyer, More (1478–1535) served as a page
in the household of the Archbishop of Canterbury, went to Oxford, and then
studied law in London. More's charm, brilliance, and gentle manner caused
Erasmus, the great Dutch humanist who became his friend during a visit to
London, to write to a friend: "Did nature ever create anything kinder,
sweeter, or more harmonious than the character of Thomas More?"*

*More served in Parliament, became a diplomat, and after holding sev-
eral important positions in the government of Henry VIII, rose to become
Lord Chancellor. But when Henry married Anne Boleyn, broke from the
Church of Rome, and established himself as head of the Church of England,
More refused to subscribe to the Act of Succession and Supremacy. Condemned to death as a traitor, he still refused to accept Henry as head of the
church and so was executed in 1535, nominally for treason but really because he would not recognize the king rather than the pope as the head of
his church. A moment before the ax fell, More displayed a bit of the whimsy
for which he was known: When he put his head on the block, he brushed his
beard aside, commenting that his beard had done no offense to the king. In
1886 the Roman Catholic Church beatified More, and in 1935, the four-
hundredth anniversary of his death, it canonized him as St. Thomas More.*

More wrote Utopia *(1514–15) in Latin, the international language of
the day. The book's name, however, is Greek for "no place" (ou topos),
with a pun on "good place" (eu topos).* Utopia *owes something to Plato's*
Republic, *and something to then-popular accounts of voyagers such as
Amerigo Vespucci.* Utopia *purports to record an account given by a traveler
named Hytholodaeus (Greek for "learned in nonsense"), who allegedly visited Utopia. The work is playful, but it is also serious. In truth, it is hard to
know exactly where it is serious, and how serious it is. One inevitably wonders, for example, if More the devoted Roman Catholic could really have advocated euthanasia. And could More the persecutor of heretics really have*

approved of the religious tolerance practiced in Utopia? Is he perhaps in ef-
fect saying, "Let's see what reason, unaided by Christian revelation, can tell
us about an ideal society"? But if so is he nevertheless also saying, very
strongly, that Christian countries, though blessed with the revelation of
Christ's teachings, are far behind these unenlightened pagans? Utopia *has*
been widely praised by all sorts of readers—from Roman Catholics to com-
munists—but for all sorts of reasons.
    The selection here is about one-twelfth of the book.

From *Utopia*

[A DAY IN UTOPIA]

And now for their working conditions. Well, there's one job they all
do, irrespective of sex, and that's farming. It's part of every child's education. They learn the principles of agriculture at school, and they're taken
for regular outings into the fields near the town, where they not only
watch farm work being done, but also do some themselves, as a form of
exercise.

Besides farming which, as I say, is everybody's job, each person is
taught a special trade of his own. He may be trained to process wool or
flax, or he may become a stonemason, a blacksmith, or a carpenter.
Those are the only trades that employ any considerable quantity of
labor. They have no tailors or dressmakers, since everyone on the island
wears the same sort of clothes—except that they vary slightly according
to sex and marital status—and the fashion never changes. These clothes
are quite pleasant to look at, they allow free movement of the limbs,
they're equally suitable for hot and cold weather—and the great thing
is, they're all home-made. So everybody learns one of the other trades I
mentioned, and by everybody I mean the women as well as the men—
though the weaker sex are given the lighter jobs, like spinning and
weaving, while the men do the heavier ones.

Most children are brought up to do the same work as their parents,
since they tend to have a natural feeling for it. But if a child fancies some
other trade, he's adopted into a family that practices it. Of course, great
care is taken, not only by the father, but also by the local authorities, to
see that the foster father is a decent, respectable type. When you've
learned one trade properly, you can, if you like, get permission to
learn another—and when you're an expert in both, you can practice
whichever you prefer, unless the other one is more essential to the
public.

The chief business of the Stywards[1]—in fact, practically their only
business—is to see that nobody sits around doing nothing, but that

---

[1]**Stywards** In Utopia, each group of thirty households elects a styward; each town has
two hundred stywards, who elect the mayor. [All notes are the editors'.]

everyone gets on with his job. They don't wear people out, though, by keeping them hard at work from early morning till late at night, like cart horses. That's just slavery—and yet that's what life is like for the working classes nearly everywhere else in the world. In Utopia they have a six-hour working day—three hours in the morning, then lunch—then a two-hour break—then three more hours in the afternoon, followed by supper. They go to bed at 8 P.M., and sleep for eight hours. All the rest of the twenty-four they're free to do what they like—not to waste their time in idleness or self-indulgence, but to make good use of it in some congenial activity. Most people spend these free periods on further education, for there are public lectures first thing every morning. Attendance is quite voluntary, except for those picked out for academic training, but men and women of all classes go crowding in to hear them—I mean, different people go to different lectures, just as the spirit moves them. However, there's nothing to stop you from spending this extra time on your trade, if you want to. Lots of people do, if they haven't the capacity for intellectual work, and are much admired for such public-spirited behavior.

After supper they have an hour's recreation, either in the gardens   5
or in the communal dining-halls, according to the time of year. Some people practice music, others just talk. They've never heard of anything so silly and demoralizing as dice, but they have two games rather like chess. The first is a sort of arithmetical contest, in which certain numbers "take" others. The second is a pitched battle between virtues and vices, which illustrates most ingeniously how vices tend to conflict with one another, but to combine against virtues. It also shows which vices are opposed to which virtues, how much strength vices can muster for a direct assault, what indirect tactics they employ, what help virtues need to overcome vices, what are the best methods of evading their attacks, and what ultimately determines the victory of one side or the other.

But here's a point that requires special attention, or you're liable to get the wrong idea. Since they only work a six-hour day, you may think there must be a shortage of essential goods. On the contrary, those six hours are enough, and more than enough to produce plenty of everything that's needed for a comfortable life. And you'll understand why it is, if you reckon up how large a proportion of the population in other countries is totally unemployed. First you have practically all the women—that gives you nearly 50 percent for a start. And in countries where the women *do* work, the men tend to lounge about instead. Then there are all the priests, and members of so-called religious orders—how much work do they do? Add all the rich, especially the landowners, popularly known as nobles and gentlemen. Include their domestic staffs—I mean those gangs of armed ruffians that I mentioned before. Finally, throw in all the beggars who are perfectly hale and hearty, but pretend to be ill as an excuse for being lazy. When you've counted them up, you'll be surprised to find how few people actually produce what the human race consumes.

And now just think how few of these few people are doing essential work—for where money is the only standard of value, there are bound to be dozens of unnecessary trades carried on, which merely supply luxury goods or entertainment. Why, even if the existing labor force were distributed among the few trades really needed to make life reasonably comfortable, there'd be so much overproduction that prices would fall too low for the workers to earn a living. Whereas, if you took all those engaged in nonessential trades, and all who are too lazy to work—each of whom consumes twice as much of the products of other people's labor as any of the producers themselves—if you put the whole lot of them on to something useful, you'd soon see how few hours' work a day would be amply sufficient to supply all the necessities and comforts of life—to which you might add all real and natural forms of pleasure.

[THE HOUSEHOLD]

But let's get back to their social organization. Each household, as I said, comes under the authority of the oldest male. Wives are subordinate to their husbands, children to their parents, and younger people generally to their elders. Every town is divided into four districts of equal size, each with its own shopping center in the middle of it. There the products of every household are collected in warehouses, and then distributed according to type among various shops. When the head of a household needs anything for himself or his family, he just goes to one of these shops and asks for it. And whatever he asks for, he's allowed to take away without any sort of payment, either in money or in kind. After all, why shouldn't he? There's more than enough of everything to go round, so there's no risk of his asking for more than he needs—for why should anyone want to start hoarding, when he knows he'll never have to go short of anything? No living creature is naturally greedy, except from fear of want—or in the case of human beings, from vanity, the notion that you're better than people if you can display more superfluous property than they can. But there's no scope for that sort of thing in Utopia.

[UTOPIAN BELIEFS]

The Utopians fail to understand why anyone should be so fascinated by the dull gleam of a tiny bit of stone, when he has all the stars in the sky to look at—or how anyone can be silly enough to think himself better than other people, because his clothes are made of finer woollen thread than theirs. After all, those fine clothes were once worn by a sheep, and they never turned it into anything better than a sheep.

Nor can they understand why a totally useless substance like gold 10 should now, all over the world, be considered far more important than human beings, who gave it such value as it has, purely for their own convenience. The result is that a man with about as much mental agility as a lump of lead or a block of wood, a man whose utter stupidity is paralleled only by his immorality, can have lots of good, intelligent people at his beck and call, just because he happens to possess a large pile of gold coins. And if by some freak of fortune or trick of the law — two equally effective methods of turning things upside down — the said coins were suddenly transferred to the most worthless member of his domestic staff, you'd soon see the present owner trotting after his money, like an extra piece of currency, and becoming his own servant's servant. But what puzzles and disgusts the Utopians even more is the idiotic way some people have of practically worshipping a rich man, not because they owe him money or are otherwise in his power, but simply because he's rich — although they know perfectly well that he's far too mean to let a single penny come their way, so long as he's alive to stop it.

They get these ideas partly from being brought up under a social system which is directly opposed to that type of nonsense, and partly from their reading and education. Admittedly, no one's allowed to become a full-time student, except for the very few in each town who appear as children to possess unusual gifts, outstanding intelligence, and a special aptitude for academic research. But every child receives a primary education, and most men and women go on educating themselves all their lives during those free periods that I told you about. . . .

In ethics they discuss the same problems as we do. Having distinguished between three types of "good," psychological, physiological, and environmental, they proceed to ask whether the term is strictly applicable to all of them, or only to the first. They also argue about such things as virtue and pleasure. But their chief subject of dispute is the nature of human happiness — on what factor or factors does it depend? Here they seem rather too much inclined to take a hedonistic view, for according to them human happiness consists largely or wholly in pleasure. Surprisingly enough, they defend this self-indulgent doctrine by arguments drawn from religion — a thing normally associated with a more serious view of life, if not with gloomy asceticism. You see, in all their discussions of happiness they invoke certain religious principles to supplement the operations of reason, which they think otherwise ill-equipped to identify true happiness.

The first principle is that every soul is immortal, and was created by a kind God, Who meant it to be happy. The second is that we shall be rewarded or punished in the next world for our good or bad behavior in this one. Although these are religious principles, the Utopians find rational grounds for accepting them. For suppose you didn't accept them? In that case, they say, any fool could tell you what you ought to do. You should go all out for your own pleasure, irrespective of right and wrong. You'd merely have to make sure that minor pleasures didn't interfere with major ones, and avoid the type of pleasure that has painful aftereffects. For what's the sense of struggling to be virtuous, denying yourself the pleasant things of life, and deliberately making yourself uncomfortable, if there's nothing you hope to gain by it? And what *can* you hope to gain by it, if you receive no compensation after death for a thoroughly unpleasant, that is, a thoroughly miserable life?

Not that they identify happiness with every type of pleasure—only with the higher ones. Nor do they identify it with virtue—unless they belong to a quite different school of thought. According to the normal view, happiness is the *summmum bonum*[2] toward which we're naturally impelled by virtue—which in their definition means following one's natural impulses, as God meant us to do. But this includes obeying the instinct to be reasonable in our likes and dislikes. And reason also teaches us, first to love and reverence Almighty God, to Whom we owe our existence and our potentiality for happiness, and secondly to get through life as comfortably and cheerfully as we can, and help all other members of our species to do so too.

The fact is, even the sternest ascetic tends to be slightly inconsistent 15 in his condemnation of pleasure. He may sentence *you* to a life of hard labor, inadequate sleep, and general discomfort, but he'll also tell you to do your best to ease the pains and privations of others. He'll regard all such attempts to improve the human situation as laudable acts of humanity—for obviously nothing could be more humane, or more natural for a human being, than to relieve other people's sufferings, put an end to their miseries, and restore their *joie de vivre,* that is, their capacity for pleasure. So why shouldn't it be equally natural to do the same thing for oneself?

Either it's a bad thing to enjoy life, in other words, to experience pleasure—in which case you shouldn't help anyone to do it, but should try to save the whole human race from such a frightful fate—or else, if it's good for other people, and you're not only allowed, but positively obliged to make it possible for them, why shouldn't charity begin at home? After all, you've a duty to yourself as well as to your neighbor, and, if Nature says you must be kind to others, she can't turn round the next moment and say you must be cruel to yourself. The Utopians therefore regard the enjoyment of life—that is, pleasure—as the natural object of all human efforts, and natural, as they define it, is synonymous with virtuous. However, Nature also wants us to help one another to enjoy life, for the very good reason that no human being has a monopoly of her affections. She's equally anxious for the welfare of every member of the species. So of course she tells us to make quite sure that we don't pursue our own interests at the expense of other people's.

On this principle they think it right to keep one's promises in private life, and also to obey public laws for regulating the distribution of

---

[2]*summum bonum* Latin for "the highest good."

"goods"—by which I mean the raw materials of pleasure—provided such laws have been properly made by a wise ruler, or passed by common consent of a whole population, which has not been subjected to any form of violence or deception. Within these limits they say it's sensible to consult one's own interests, and a moral duty to consult those of the community as well. It's wrong to deprive someone else of a pleasure so that you can enjoy one yourself, but to deprive yourself of a pleasure so that you can add to someone else's enjoyment is an act of humanity by which you always gain more than you lose. For one thing, such benefits are usually repaid in kind. For another, the mere sense of having done somebody a kindness, and so earned his affection and goodwill, produces a spiritual satisfaction which far outweighs the loss of a physical one. And lastly—a belief that comes easily to a religious mind—God will reward us for such small sacrifices of momentary pleasure, by giving us an eternity of perfect joy. Thus they argue that, in the final analysis, pleasure is the ultimate happiness which all human beings have in view, even when they're acting most virtuously.

Pleasure they define as any state or activity, physical or mental, which is naturally enjoyable. The operative word is *naturally*. According to them, we're impelled by reason as well as an instinct to enjoy ourselves in any natural way which doesn't hurt other people, interfere with greater pleasures, or cause unpleasant aftereffects. But human beings have entered into an idiotic conspiracy to call some things enjoyable which are naturally nothing of the kind—as though facts were as easily changed as definitions. Now the Utopians believe that, so far from contributing to happiness, this type of thing makes happiness impossible—because, once you get used to it, you lose all capacity for real pleasure, and are merely obsessed by illusory forms of it. Very often these have nothing pleasant about them at all—in fact, most of them are thoroughly disagreeable. But they appeal so strongly to perverted tastes that they come to be reckoned not only among the major pleasures of life, but even among the chief reasons for living.

In the category of illusory pleasure addicts they include the kind of person I mentioned before, who thinks himself better than other people because he's better dressed than they are. Actually he's just as wrong about his clothes as he is about himself. From a practical point of view, why is it better to be dressed in fine woollen thread than in coarse? But he's got it into his head that fine thread is naturally superior, and that wearing it somehow increases his own value. So he feels entitled to far more respect than he'd ever dare to hope for, if he were less expensively dressed, and is most indignant if he fails to get it.

Talking of respect, isn't it equally idiotic to attach such importance to 20 a lot of empty gestures which do nobody any good? For what real pleasure can you get out of the sight of a bared head or a bent knee? Will it cure the rheumatism in your own knee, or make you any less weak in the head? Of course, the great believers in this type of artificial pleasure are those who pride themselves on their "nobility." Nowadays that merely means that they happen to belong to a family which has been rich for several generations, preferably in landed property. And yet they feel every bit as "noble" even if they've failed to inherit any of the said property, or if they have inherited it and then frittered it all away.

Then there's another type of person I mentioned before, who has a passion for jewels, and feels practically superhuman if he manages to get hold of a rare one, especially if it's a kind that's considered particularly precious in his country and period—for the value of such things varies according to where and when you live. But he's so terrified of being taken in by appearances that he refuses to buy any jewel until he's stripped off all the gold and inspected it in the nude. And even then he won't buy it without a solemn assurance and a written guarantee from the jeweler that the stone is genuine. But my dear sir, why shouldn't a fake give you just as much pleasure, if you can't, with your own eyes, distinguish it from a real one? It makes no difference to you whether it's genuine or not—any more than it would to a blind man!

And now, what about those people who accumulate superfluous wealth, for no better purpose than to enjoy looking at it? Is their pleasure a real one, or merely a form of delusion? The opposite type of psychopath buries his gold, so that he'll never be able to use it, and may never even see it again. In fact, he deliberately loses it in his anxiety not to lose it—for what can you call it but lost, when it's put back into the earth, where it's no good to him, or probably to anyone else? And yet he's tremendously happy when he's got it stowed away. Now, apparently, he can stop worrying. But suppose the money is stolen, and ten years later he dies without ever knowing it has gone. Then for a whole ten years he has managed to survive his loss, and during that period what difference has it made to him whether the money was there or not? It was just as little use to him either way.

Among stupid pleasures they include not only gambling—a form of idiocy that they've heard about but never practiced—but also hunting and hawking. What on earth is the fun, they ask, of throwing dice onto a table? Besides, you've done it so often that, even if there was some fun in it at first, you must surely be sick of it by now. How can you possibly enjoy listening to anything so disagreeable as the barking and howling of dogs? And why is it more amusing to watch a dog chasing a hare than to watch one dog chasing another? In each case the essential activity is running—if running is what amuses you. But if it's really the thought of being in at the death, and seeing an animal torn to pieces before your eyes, wouldn't pity be a more appropriate reaction to the sight of a weak, timid, harmless little creature like a hare being devoured by something so much stronger and fiercer?

So the Utopians consider hunting below the dignity of free men, and leave it entirely to butchers, who are, as I told you, slaves. In their view hunting is the vilest department of butchery, compared with which all the others are relatively useful and honorable. An ordinary butcher slaughters livestock far more sparingly, and only because he has to, whereas a hunter kills and mutilates poor little creatures purely for his own amusement. They say you won't find that type of blood lust even among animals, unless they're particularly savage by nature, or have become so by constantly being used for this cruel sport.

There are hundreds of things like that, which are generally regarded as pleasures, but everyone in Utopia is quite convinced that they've got nothing to do with real pleasure, because there's nothing naturally enjoyable about them. Nor is this conviction at all shaken by the argument that most people do actually enjoy them, which would seem to indicate an appreciable pleasure content. They say this is a purely subjective reaction caused by bad habits, which can make a person prefer unpleasant things to pleasant ones, just as pregnant women sometimes lose their sense of taste, and find suet or turpentine more delicious than honey. But however much one's judgment may be impaired by habit or ill health, the nature of pleasure, as of everything else, remains unchanged.

Real pleasures they divide into two categories, mental and physical. Mental pleasures include the satisfaction that one gets from understanding something, or from contemplating truth. They also include the memory of a well-spent life, and the confident expectation of good things to come. Physical pleasures are subdivided into two types. First there are those which fill the whole organism with a conscious sense of enjoyment. This may be the result of replacing physical substances which have been burnt up by the natural heat of the body, as when we eat or drink. Or else it may be caused by the discharge of some excess, as in excretion, sexual intercourse, or any relief of irritation by rubbing or scratching. However, there are also pleasures which satisfy no organic need, and relieve no previous discomfort. They merely act, in a mysterious but quite unmistakable way, directly on our senses, and monopolize their reactions. Such is the pleasure of music.

Their second type of physical pleasure arises from the calm and regular functioning of the body—that is, from a state of health undisturbed by any minor ailments. In the absence of mental discomfort, this gives one a good feeling, even without the help of external pleasures. Of course, it's less ostentatious, and forces itself less violently on one's attention than the cruder delights of eating and drinking, but even so it's often considered the greatest pleasure in life. Practically everyone in Utopia would agree that it's a very important one, because it's the basis of all the others. It's enough by itself to make you enjoy life, and unless you have it, no other pleasure is possible. However, mere freedom from pain, without positive health, they would call not pleasure but anesthesia.

Some thinkers used to maintain that a uniformly tranquil state of health couldn't properly be termed a pleasure since its presence could only be detected by contrast with its opposite—oh yes, they went very thoroughly into the whole question. But that theory was exploded long ago, and nowadays nearly everybody subscribes to the view that health is most definitely a pleasure. The argument goes like this—illness involves pain, which is the direct opposite of pleasure, and illness is the direct opposite of health, therefore health involves pleasure. They don't think it matters whether you say that illness *is* or merely *involves* pain. Either way it comes to the same thing. Similarly, whether health *is* a pleasure, or merely *produces* pleasure as inevitably as fire produces heat, it's equally logical to assume that where you have an uninterrupted state of health you cannot fail to have pleasure.

Besides, they say, when we eat something, what really happens is this. Our failing health starts fighting off the attacks of hunger, using the food as an ally. Gradually it begins to prevail, and, in this very process of winning back its normal strength, experiences the sense of enjoyment which we find so refreshing. Now, if health enjoys the actual battle, why shouldn't it also enjoy the victory? Or are we to suppose that when it has finally managed to regain its former vigor—the one thing that it has been fighting for all this time—it promptly falls into a coma, and fails to notice or take advantage of its success? As for the idea that one isn't conscious of health except through its opposite, they say that's quite untrue. Everyone's perfectly aware of feeling well, unless he's asleep or actually feeling ill. Even the most insensitive and apathetic sort of person will admit that it's delightful to be healthy—and what is delight, but a synonym for pleasure?

They're particularly fond of mental pleasures, which they consider of 30 primary importance, and attribute mostly to good behavior and a clear conscience. Their favorite physical pleasure is health. Of course, they believe in enjoying food, drink, and so forth, but purely in the interests of health, for they don't regard such things as very pleasant in themselves—only as methods of resisting the stealthy onset of disease. A sensible person, they say, prefers keeping well to taking medicine, and would rather feel cheerful than have people trying to comfort him. On the same principle it's better not to need this type of pleasure than to become addicted to it. For, if you think that sort of thing will make you happy, you'll have to admit that your idea of perfect felicity would be a life consisting entirely of hunger, thirst, itching, eating, drinking, rubbing, and scratching—which would obviously be most unpleasant as well as quite disgusting. Undoubtedly these pleasures should come right at the bottom of the list, because they're so impure. For instance, the pleasure of eating is invariably diluted with the pain of hunger, and not in equal proportions either—for the pain is both more intense and more prolonged. It starts before the pleasure, and doesn't stop until the pleasure has stopped too.

So they don't think much of pleasures like that, except insofar as they're necessary. But they enjoy them all the same, and feel most grateful to Mother Nature for encouraging her children to do things that have to be done so often, by making them so attractive. For just think how dreary life would be, if those chronic ailments, hunger and thirst, could only be cured by foul-tasting medicines, like the rarer types of disease!

They attach great value to special natural gifts such as beauty, strength, and agility. They're also keen on the pleasures of sight, hearing, and smell, which are peculiar to human beings—for no other species admires the beauty of the world, enjoys any sort of scent, except as a method of locating food, or can tell the difference between a harmony and a discord. They say these things give a sort of relish to life.

However, in all such matters they observe the rule that minor pleasures mustn't interfere with major ones, and that pleasure mustn't cause pain—which they think is bound to happen, if the pleasure is immoral. But they'd never dream of despising their own beauty, overtaxing their strength, converting their agility into inertia, ruining their physique by going without food, damaging their health, or spurning any other of Nature's gifts, unless they were doing it for the benefit of other people or of society, in the hope of receiving some greater pleasure from God in return. For they think it's quite absurd to torment oneself in the name of an unreal virtue, which does nobody any good, or in order to steel oneself against disasters which may never occur. They say such behavior is merely self-destructive, and shows a most ungrateful attitude toward Nature—as if one refused all her favors, because one couldn't bear the thought of being indebted to her for anything.

Well, that's their ethical theory, and short of some divine revelation, they doubt if the human mind is capable of devising a better one. We've no time to discuss whether it's right or wrong—nor is it really necessary, for all I undertook was to describe their way of life, not to defend it.

[TREATMENT OF THE DYING]

As I told you, when people are ill, they're looked after most sympa- 35
thetically, and given everything in the way of medicine or special food that could possibly assist their recovery. In the case of permanent invalids, the nurses try to make them feel better by sitting and talking to them, and do all they can to relieve their symptoms. But if, besides being incurable, the disease also causes constant excruciating pain, some priests and government officials visit the person concerned, and say something like this:

"Let's face it, you'll never be able to live a normal life. You're just a nuisance to other people and a burden to yourself—in fact you're really leading a sort of posthumous existence. So why go on feeding germs? Since your life's a misery to you, why hesitate to die? You're imprisoned in a torture chamber—why don't you break out and escape to a better world? Or say the word, and we'll arrange for your release. It's only common sense to cut your losses. It's also an act of piety to take the advice of a priest, because he speaks for God."

If the patient finds these arguments convincing, he either starves himself to death, or is given a soporific and put painlessly out of his misery. But this is strictly voluntary, and, if he prefers to stay alive, everyone will go on treating him as kindly as ever.

[THE SUMMING UP]

Well, that's the most accurate account I can give you of the Utopian Republic. To my mind, it's not only the best country in the world, but the only one that has any right to call itself a republic. Elsewhere, people are always talking about the public interest, but all they really care about is private property. In Utopia, where's there's no private property, people take their duty to the public seriously. And both attitudes are perfectly reasonable. In other "republics" practically everyone knows that, if he doesn't look out for himself, he'll starve to death, however prosperous his country may be. He's therefore compelled to give his own interests priority over those of the public; that is, of other people. But in Utopia, where everything's under public ownership, no one has any fear of going short, as long as the public storehouses are full. Everyone gets a fair share, so there are never any poor men or beggars. Nobody owns anything, but everyone is rich—for what greater wealth can there be than cheerfulness, peace of mind, and freedom from anxiety? Instead of being worried about his food supply, upset by the plaintive demands of his wife, afraid of poverty for his son, and baffled by the problem of finding a dowry for his daughter, the Utopian can feel absolutely sure that he, his wife, his children, his grandchildren, his great-grandchildren, his great-great-grandchildren, and as long a line of descendants as the proudest peer could wish to look forward to, will always have enough to eat and enough to make them happy. There's also the further point that those who are too old to work are just as well provided for as those who are still working.

Now, will anyone venture to compare these fair arrangements in Utopia with the so-called justice of other countries?—in which I'm damned if I can see the slightest trace of justice or fairness. For what sort of justice do you call this? People like aristocrats, goldsmiths, or money-lenders, who either do no work at all, or do work that's really not essential, are rewarded for their laziness or their unnecessary activities by a splendid life of luxury. But laborers, coachmen, carpenters, and farmhands, who never stop working like cart horses, at jobs so essential that, if they *did* stop working, they'd bring any country to a standstill within twelve months—what happens to them? They get so little to eat, and have such a wretched time, that they'd be almost better off if they *were* cart horses. Then at least, they wouldn't work quite such long hours, their food wouldn't be very much worse, they'd enjoy it more, and they'd have no fears for the future. As it is, they're not only ground down by unrewarding toil in the present, but also worried to death by the prospect of a poverty-stricken old age—since their daily wages aren't enough to support them for one day, let alone leave anything over to be saved up when they're old.

Can you see any fairness or gratitude in a social system which lav- 40 ishes such great rewards on so-called noblemen, goldsmiths, and people like that, who are either totally unproductive or merely employed in producing luxury goods or entertainment, but makes no such kind provision for farmhands, coal heavers, laborers, carters, or carpenters, without whom society couldn't exist at all? And the climax of ingratitude comes when they're old and ill and completely destitute. Having taken advantage of them throughout the best years of their lives, society now forgets all the sleepless hours they've spent in its service, and repays them for all the vital work they've done, by letting them die in misery. What's more, the wretched earnings of the poor are daily whittled away by the rich, not only through private dishonesty, but through public legislation. As if it weren't unjust enough already that the man who contributes most to society should get the least in return, they make it even worse, and then arrange for injustice to be legally described as justice.

In fact, when I consider any social system that prevails in the modern world, I can't, so help me God, see it as anything but a conspiracy of the rich to advance their own interests under the pretext of organizing society. They think up all sorts of tricks and dodges, first for keeping safe their ill-gotten gains, and then for exploiting the poor by buying their labor as cheaply as possible. Once the rich have decided that these tricks and dodges shall be officially recognized by society—which includes the poor as well as the rich—they acquire the force of law. Thus an unscrupulous minority is led by its insatiable greed to monopolize what would have been enough to supply the needs of the whole population. And yet how much happier even these people would be in Utopia! There, with the simultaneous abolition of money and the passion for money, how many other social problems have been solved, how many crimes eradicated! For obviously the end of money means the end of all those types of criminal behavior which daily punishments are powerless to check: fraud, theft, burglary, brawls, riots, disputes, rebellion, murder, treason, and black magic. And the moment money goes, you can also say goodbye to fear, tension, anxiety, overwork, and sleepless nights. Why, even poverty itself, the one problem that has always seemed to need money for its solution, would promptly disappear if money ceased to exist.

Let me try to make this point clearer. Just think back to one of the years when the harvest was bad, and thousands of people died of starvation. Well, I bet if you'd inspected every rich man's barn at the end of that lean period you'd have found enough corn to have saved all the lives that were lost through malnutrition and disease, and prevented anyone from suffering any ill effects whatever from the meanness of the weather and the soil. Everyone could so easily get enough to eat, if it weren't for that blessed nuisance, money. There you have a brilliant invention which was designed to make food more readily available. Actually it's the only thing that makes it unobtainable.

I'm sure that even the rich are well aware of all this, and realize how much better it would be to have everything one needed, than lots of things one didn't need—to be evacuated altogether from the danger area, than to dig oneself in behind a barricade of enormous wealth. And I've no doubt that either self-interest, or the authority of our Savior Christ—Who was far too wise not to know what was best for us, and far too kind to recommend anything else—would have led the whole world to adopt the Utopian system long ago, if it weren't for that beastly root of all evils, pride. For pride's criterion of prosperity is not what you've got yourself, but what other people haven't got. Pride would refuse to set foot in paradise, if she thought there'd be no underprivileged classes there to gloat over and order about—nobody whose misery could serve as a foil to her own happiness, or whose poverty she could make harder to bear, by flaunting her own riches. Pride, like a hellish serpent gliding through human hearts—or shall we say, like a sucking-fish that clings to the ship of state?—is always dragging us back, and obstructing our progress toward a better way of life.

But as this fault is too deeply ingrained in human nature to be easily eradicated, I'm glad that at least one country has managed to develop a system which I'd like to see universally adopted. The Utopian way of life provides not only the happiest basis for a civilized community, but also one which, in all human probability, will last forever. They've eliminated the root causes of ambition, political conflict, and everything like that. There's therefore no danger of internal dissension, the one thing that has destroyed so many impregnable towns. And as long as there's unity and sound administration at home, no matter how envious neighboring kings may feel, they'll never be able to shake, let alone to shatter, the power of Utopia. They've tried to do so often enough in the past, but have always been beaten back.

Topics for Critical Thinking and Writing

1. More, writing early in the sixteenth century, of course was living in a primarily agricultural society. Laborers were needed on farms; but might More have had any other reason for insisting (para. 1) that all people should do some farming, and that farming should be part of "every child's education"? Do you think everyone should put in some time as a farmer? Why, or why not?

2. More indicates that in the England of his day many people loafed or engaged in unnecessary work (producing luxury goods, for one thing),

putting an enormous burden on those who engaged in useful work. Is this condition, or any part of it, true of our society? Explain.

3. The Utopians cannot understand why the people of other nations value gems, gold, and fine clothes. If you value any of these, can you offer an explanation?

4. What arguments can you offer against the Utopians' treatment of persons who are incurably ill and in pain? (You may get some ideas from the essays by Ellen Goodman, p. 558, and Ronald Pies, p. 572.)

5. Summarize More's report of the Utopians' idea of pleasure. (This summary will probably take three or four paragraphs.)

6. More's Utopians cannot understand why anyone takes pleasure in gambling or in hunting. If either activity gives you pleasure, in an essay of 500 words explain why, and offer an argument on behalf of your view.

7. As More makes clear in the part we entitle "The Summing Up," in Utopia there is no private property. In a sentence or two summarize the reasons he gives for this principle, and then in a paragraph evaluate them.

Niccolò Machiavelli

Niccolò Machiavelli (1469–1527) was born in Florence at a time when Italy was divided into five major states: Venice, Milan, Florence, the Papal States, and Naples. Although these states often had belligerent relations with one another as well as with lesser Italian states, under the Medici family in Florence they achieved a precarious balance of power. In 1494, however, Lorenzo de' Medici, who had ruled from 1469 to 1492, died, and two years later Lorenzo's successor was exiled when the French army arrived in Florence. Italy became a field where Spain, France, and Germany competed for power. From 1498 to 1512 Machiavelli held a high post in the diplomatic service of the Florentine Republic, but when the French army reappeared and the Florentines in desperation recalled the Medici, Machiavelli lost his post, was imprisoned, tortured, and then exiled. Banished from Florence, he nevertheless lived in fair comfort on a small estate nearby, writing his major works and hoping to obtain an office from the Medici. In later years he was employed in a few minor diplomatic missions, but even after the collapse and expulsion of the Medici in 1527, and the restoration of the republic, he did not regain his old position of importance. He died shortly after the restoration.

Our selection comes from The Prince, *which Machiavelli wrote in 1513 during his banishment hoping that it would interest the Medici and thus restore him to favor; but the book was not published until 1532, five years after his death. In this book of twenty-six short chapters, Machiavelli begins by examining different kinds of states, but the work's enduring power resides in the discussions (in Chapters 15–18, reprinted here) of qualities necessary to a prince, that is, a head of state. Any such examination obviously is based in part on assumptions about the nature of the citizens of the realm.*

From *The Prince*

ON THOSE THINGS FOR WHICH MEN, AND PARTICULARLY PRINCES, ARE PRAISED OR BLAMED

Now there remains to be examined what should be the methods and procedures of a prince in dealing with his subjects and friends. And because I know that many have written about this, I am afraid that by writing about it again I shall be thought of as presumptuous, since in discussing this material I depart radically from the procedures of others. But since my intention is to write something useful for anyone who understands it, it seemed more suitable to me to search after the effectual truth of the matter rather than its imagined one. And many writers have imagined for themselves republics and principalities that have never been seen nor known to exist in reality; for there is such a gap between how one lives and how one ought to live that anyone who abandons what is done for what ought to be done learns his ruin rather than his preservation: for a man who wishes to make a vocation of being good at all times will come to ruin among so many who are not good. Hence it is necessary for a prince who wishes to maintain his position to learn how not to be good, and to use this knowledge or not to use it according to necessity.

Leaving aside, therefore, the imagined things concerning a prince, and taking into account those that are true, I say that all men, when they are spoken of, and particularly princes, since they are placed on a higher level, are judged by some of these qualities which bring them either blame or praise. And this is why one is considered generous, another miserly (to use a Tuscan word, since "avaricious" in our language is still used to mean one who wishes to acquire by means of theft; we call "miserly" one who excessively avoids using what he has); one is considered a giver, the other rapacious; one cruel, another merciful; one treacherous, another faithful; one effeminate and cowardly, another bold and courageous; one humane, another haughty; one lascivious, another chaste; one trustworthy, another cunning; one harsh, another lenient; one serious, another frivolous; one religious, another unbelieving; and the like. And I know that everyone will admit that it would be a very praiseworthy thing to find in a prince, of the qualities mentioned above, those that are held to be good; but since it is neither possible to have them nor to observe them all completely, because human nature does not permit it, a prince must be prudent enough to know how to escape the bad reputation of those vices that would lose the state for him, and must protect himself from those that will not lose it for him, if this is possible; but if he cannot, he need not concern himself unduly if he ignores these less serious vices. And, moreover, he need not worry about incurring the bad reputation of those vices without which it would be difficult to hold his state; since, carefully taking everything into account, one will discover that something which appears to be a virtue, if pursued, will end in his destruction; while some other thing which seems to be a vice, if pursued, will result in his safety and his well-being.

ON GENEROSITY AND MISERLINESS

Beginning, therefore, with the first of the above-mentioned qualities, I say that it would be good to be considered generous; nevertheless, generosity used in such a manner as to give you a reputation for it will harm you; because if it is employed virtuously and as one should employ it, it will not be recognized and you will not avoid the reproach of its opposite. And so, if a prince wants to maintain his reputation for generosity among men, it is necessary for him not to neglect any possible means of lavish display; in so doing such a prince will always use up all his resources and he will be obliged, eventually, if he wishes to maintain his reputation for generosity, to burden the people with excessive taxes and to do everything possible to raise funds. This will begin to make him hateful to his subjects, and, becoming impoverished, he will not be much esteemed by anyone; so that, as a consequence of his generosity, having offended many and rewarded few, he will feel the effects of any slight unrest and will be ruined at the first sign of danger; recognizing this and wishing to alter his policies, he immediately runs the risk of being reproached as a miser.

A prince, therefore, unable to use this virtue of generosity in a manner which will not harm himself if he is known for it, should, if he is wise, not worry about being called a miser; for with time he will come to be considered more generous once it is evident that, as a result of his parsimony, his income is sufficient, he can defend himself from anyone who makes war against him, and he can undertake enterprises without overburdening his people, so that he comes to be generous with all those from whom he takes nothing, who are countless, and miserly with all those to whom he gives nothing, who are few. In our times we have not seen great deeds accomplished except by those who were considered miserly; all others were done away with. Pope Julius II, although he made use of his reputation for generosity in order to gain the papacy, then decided not to maintain it in order to be able to wage war; the present King of France has waged many wars without imposing extra taxes on his subjects, only because his habitual parsimony has provided for the additional expenditures; the present King of Spain, if he had been considered generous, would not have engaged in nor won so many campaigns.

Therefore, in order not to have to rob his subjects, to be able to defend himself, not to become poor and contemptible, and not to be forced to become rapacious, a prince must consider it of little importance if he incurs the name of miser, for this is one of those vices that permits him to rule. And if someone were to say: Caesar with his generosity came to rule the empire, and many others, because they were generous and known to be so, achieved very high positions; I reply: You are either already a prince or you are on the way to becoming one; in the first instance such generosity is damaging; in the second it is very necessary to be thought generous. And Caesar was one of those who wanted to gain the principality of Rome; but if, after obtaining this, he had lived and had not moderated his expenditures, he would have destroyed that empire. And if someone were to reply: There have existed many princes who have accomplished great deeds with their armies who have been reputed to be generous; I answer you: A prince either spends his own money and that of his subjects or that of others; in the first case he must be economical; in the second he must not restrain any part of his generosity. And for that prince who goes out with his soldiers and lives by looting, sacking, and ransoms, who controls the property of others, such generosity is necessary; otherwise he would not be followed by his troops. And with what does not belong to you or to your subjects you can be a more liberal giver, as were Cyrus, Caesar, and Alexander; for spending the wealth of others does not lessen your reputation but adds to it; only the spending of your own is what harms you. And there is nothing that uses itself up faster than generosity, for as you employ it you lose the means of employing it, and you become either poor or despised or, in order to escape poverty, rapacious and hated. And above all other things a prince must guard himself against being despised and hated; and generosity leads you to both one and the other. So it is wiser to live with the reputation of a miser, which produces reproach without hatred, than to be forced to incur the reputation of rapacity, which produces reproach along with hatred, because you want to be considered as generous.

ON CRUELTY AND MERCY AND WHETHER IT IS BETTER TO BE LOVED THAN TO BE FEARED OR THE CONTRARY

Proceeding to the other qualities mentioned above, I say that every prince must desire to be considered merciful and not cruel; nevertheless, he must take care not to misuse this mercy. Cesare Borgia[1] was considered cruel; nonetheless, his cruelty had brought order to Romagna, united it, restored it to peace and obedience. If we examine this carefully, we shall see that he was more merciful than the Florentine people,

---

[1]**Cesare Borgia** The son of Pope Alexander VI, Cesare Borgia (1476–1507) was ruthlessly opportunistic. Encouraged by his father, in 1499 and 1500 he subdued the cities of **Romagna**, the region including Ferrara and Ravenna. [All notes are the editors' unless otherwise specified.]

who, in order to avoid being considered cruel, allowed the destruction of Pistoia.[2] Therefore, a prince must not worry about the reproach of cruelty when it is a matter of keeping his subjects united and loyal; for with a very few examples of cruelty he will be more compassionate than those who, out of excessive mercy, permit disorders to continue, from which arise murders and plundering; for these usually harm the community at large, while the executions that come from the prince harm one individual in particular. And the new prince, above all other princes, cannot escape the reputation of being called cruel, since new states are full of dangers. And Virgil, through Dido, states: "My difficult condition and the newness of my rule make me act in such a manner, and to set guards over my land on all sides."[3]

Nevertheless, a prince must be cautious in believing and in acting, nor should he be afraid of his own shadow; and he should proceed in such a manner, tempered by prudence and humanity, so that too much trust may not render him imprudent nor too much distrust render him intolerable.

From this arises an argument: whether it is better to be loved than to be feared, or the contrary. I reply that one should like to be both one and the other; but since it is difficult to join them together, it is much safer to be feared than to be loved when one of the two must be lacking. For one can generally say this about men: that they are ungrateful, fickle, simulators and deceivers, avoiders of danger, greedy for gain; and while you work for their good they are completely yours, offering you their blood, their property, their lives, and their sons, as I said earlier, when danger is far away; but when it comes nearer to you they turn away. And that prince who bases his power entirely in their words, finding himself stripped of other preparations, comes to ruin; for friendships that are acquired by a price and not by greatness and nobility of character are purchased but are not owned, and at the proper moment they cannot be spent. And men are less hesitant about harming someone who makes himself loved than one who makes himself feared because love is held together by a chain of obligation which, since men are a sorry lot, is broken on every occasion in which their own self-interest is concerned; but fear is held together by a dread of punishment which will never abandon you.

A prince must nevertheless make himself feared in such a manner that he will avoid hatred, even if he does not acquire love; since to be feared and not to be hated can very well be combined; and this will always be so when he keeps his hands off the property and the women of his citizens and his subjects. And if he must take someone's life, he

---

[2]**Pistoia** A town near Florence; Machiavelli suggests that the Florentines failed to treat dissenting leaders with sufficient severity.
[3]In *Aeneid* I, 563–64, **Virgil** (70–19 B.C.) puts this line into the mouth of **Dido,** the queen of Carthage.

should do so when there is proper justification and manifest cause; but, above all, he should avoid the property of others; for men forget more quickly the death of their father than the loss of their patrimony. More-over, the reasons for seizing their property are never lacking; and he who begins to live by stealing always finds a reason for taking what be-longs to others; on the contrary, reasons for taking a life are rarer and disappear sooner.

But when the prince is with his armies and has under his command 10 a multitude of troops, then it is absolutely necessary that he not worry about being considered cruel; for without that reputation he will never keep an army united or prepared for any combat. Among the praise-worthy deeds of Hannibal[4] is counted this: that, having a very large army, made up of all kinds of men, which he commanded in foreign lands, there never arose the slightest dissension, neither among themselves nor against their prince, both during his good and his bad fortune. This could not have arisen from anything other than his inhuman cruelty, which, along with his many other abilities, made him always respected and terri-fying in the eyes of his soldiers; and without that, to attain the same ef-fect, his other abilities would not have sufficed. And the writers of his-tory, having considered this matter very little, on the one hand admire these deeds of his and on the other condemn the main cause of them.

And that it be true that his other abilities would not have been suffi-cient can be seen from the example of Scipio,[5] a most extraordinary man not only in his time but in all recorded history, whose armies in Spain rebelled against him; this came about from nothing other than his exces-sive compassion, which gave to his soldiers more liberty than military discipline allowed. For this he was censured in the senate by Fabius Maximus, who called him the corruptor of the Roman militia. The Locri-ans, having been ruined by one of Scipio's officers, were not avenged by him, nor was the arrogance of that officer corrected, all because of his tolerant nature; so that someone in the senate who tried to apologize for him said that there were many men who knew how not to err better than they knew how to correct errors. Such a nature would have, in time, damaged Scipio's fame and glory if he had maintained it during the empire; but, living under the control of the senate, this harmful charac-teristic of his not only concealed itself but brought him fame.

I conclude, therefore, returning to the problem of being feared and loved, that since men love at their own pleasure and fear at the pleasure of the prince, a wise prince should build his foundation upon that which belongs to him, not upon that which belongs to others: He must strive only to avoid hatred, as has been said.

---

[4]**Hannibal** The Carthaginian general (247–183 B.C.) whose crossing of the Alps with ele-phants and full baggage train is one of the great feats of military history.
[5]**Scipio** Publius Cornelius Scipio Africanus the Elder (235–183 B.C.), the conqueror of Hannibal in the Punic Wars. The mutiny of which Machiavelli speaks took place in 206 B.C.

HOW A PRINCE SHOULD KEEP HIS WORD

How praiseworthy it is for a prince to keep his word and to live by integrity and not by deceit everyone knows; nevertheless, one sees from the experience of our times that the princes who have accomplished great deeds are those who have cared little for keeping their promises and who have known how to manipulate the minds of men by shrewdness; and in the end they have surpassed those who laid their foundations upon honesty.

You must, therefore, know that there are two means of fighting: one according to the laws, the other with force; the first way is proper to man, the second to beasts; but because the first, in many cases, is not sufficient, it becomes necessary to have recourse to the second. Therefore, a prince must know how to use wisely the natures of the beast and the man. This policy was taught to princes allegorically by the ancient writers, who described how Achilles and many other ancient princes were given to Chiron[6] the Centaur to be raised and taught under his discipline. This can only mean that, having a half-beast and half-man as a teacher, a prince must know how to employ the nature of the one and the other; and the one without the other cannot endure.

Since, then, a prince must know how to make good use of the nature of the beast, he should choose from among the beasts the fox and the lion; for the lion cannot defend itself from traps and the fox cannot protect itself from wolves. It is therefore necessary to be a fox in order to recognize the traps and a lion in order to frighten the wolves. Those who play only the part of the lion do not understand matters. A wise ruler, therefore, cannot and should not keep his word when such an observance of faith would be to his disadvantage and when the reasons which made him promise are removed. And if men were all good, this rule would not be good; but since men are a sorry lot and will not keep their promises to you, you likewise need not keep yours to them. A prince never lacks legitimate reasons to break his promises. Of this one could cite an endless number of modern examples to show how many pacts, how many promises have been made null and void because of the infidelity of princes; and he who has known best how to use the fox has come to a better end. But it is necessary to know how to disguise this nature well and to be a great hypocrite and a liar: and men are so simpleminded and so controlled by their present necessities that one who deceives will always find another who will allow himself to be deceived.

I do not wish to remain silent about one of these recent instances. Alexander VI[7] did nothing else, he thought about nothing else, except to

---

[6]**Chiron** (Kī′ron) A centaur (half man, half horse), who was said in classical mythology to have been the teacher not only of Achilles but also of Theseus, Jason, Hercules, and other heroes.
[7]**Alexander VI** Pope from 1492 to 1503; father of Cesare Borgia.

deceive men, and he always found the occasion to do this. And there never was a man who had more forcefulness in his oaths, who affirmed a thing with more promises, and who honored his word less; nevertheless, his tricks always succeeded perfectly since he was well acquainted with this aspect of the world.

Therefore, it is not necessary for a prince to have all of the above-mentioned qualities, but it is very necessary for him to appear to have them. Furthermore, I shall be so bold as to assert this; that having them and practicing them at all times is harmful; and appearing to have them useful; for instance, to seem merciful, faithful, humane, forthright, religious, and to be so; but his mind should be disposed in such a way that should it become necessary not to be so, he will be able and know how to change to the contrary. And it is essential to understand this: that a prince, and especially a new prince, cannot observe all those things by which men are considered good, for in order to maintain the state he is often obliged to act against his promise, against charity, against humanity, and against religion. And therefore, it is necessary that he have a mind ready to turn itself according to the way the winds of Fortune and the changeability of affairs require him; and, as I said above, as long as it is possible, he should not stray from the good, but he should know how to enter into evil when necessity commands.

A prince, therefore, must be very careful never to let anything slip from his lips which is not full of the five qualities mentioned above: He should appear, upon seeing and hearing him, to be all mercy, all faithfulness, all integrity, all kindness, all religion. And there is nothing more necessary than to seem to possess this last quality. And men in general judge more by their eyes than their hands; for everyone can see but few can feel. Everyone sees what you seem to be, few perceive what you are, and those few do not dare to contradict the opinion of the many who have the majesty of the state to defend them; and in the actions of all men, and especially of princes, where there is no impartial arbiter, one must consider the final result.[8] Let a prince therefore act to seize and to maintain the state; his methods will always be judged honorable and will be praised by all; for ordinary people are always deceived by appearances and by the outcome of a thing; and in the world there is nothing but ordinary people; and there is no room for the few, while the many have a place to lean on. A certain prince of the present day, whom I shall refrain from naming, preaches nothing but peace and faith, and to both one and the other he is entirely opposed; and both, if he had put them into practice, would have cost him many times over either his reputation or his state.

---

[8]The Italian original, *si guarda al fine,* has often been mistranslated as "the ends justify the means," something Machiavelli never wrote. [Translators' note.]

Topics for Critical Thinking and Writing

1. In the opening paragraph, Machiavelli claims that a ruler who wishes to keep in power must "learn how not to be good" — that is, must know where and when to ignore the demands of conventional morality. In the rest of the excerpt, does he give any convincing evidence to support this claim? Can you think of any recent political event in which a political leader violated the requirements of morality, as Machiavelli advises?

2. Machiavelli says in paragraph 1 that "a man who wishes to make a vocation of being good at all times will come to ruin among so many who are not good." (By the way, the passage is ambiguous. "At all times" is, in the original, a squinting modifier. It may look backward, to "being good," or forward, to "will come to ruin," but probably Machiavelli means, "A man who at all times wishes to make a vocation of being good will come to ruin among so many who are not good.") Is this view realistic or cynical? (What is the difference between these two?) Assume for the moment that the view is realistic. Does it follow that society requires a ruler who must act according to the principles Machiavelli sets forth?

3. In his second paragraph Machiavelli claims that it is impossible for a ruler to exhibit *all* the conventional virtues (trustworthiness, liberality, and so on). Why does he make this claim? Do you agree with it?

4. In paragraph 4 Machiavelli cites as examples Pope Julius II, the King of France, the King of Spain, and other rulers. Is he using these examples to illustrate his generalizations, or to provide evidence for them? If you think he is using them to provide evidence, how convincing do you find the evidence? (*Consider:* Could Machiavelli be arguing from a biased sample?)

5. In paragraphs 6–10 Machiavelli argues that it is sometimes necessary for a ruler to be cruel, and so he praises Cesare Borgia and Hannibal. What is it about human nature, according to Machiavelli, that explains this need to have recourse to cruelty? (By the way, how do you think *cruelty* should be defined here?)

6. Machiavelli says that Cesare Borgia's cruelty brought peace to Romagna, and that, on the other hand, the Florentines who sought to avoid being cruel in fact brought pain to Pistoia. Can you think of recent episodes supporting the view that cruelty can be beneficial to society? If so, restate Machiavelli's position, using these examples from recent history. Then go on to write two paragraphs, arguing on behalf of your two examples. Or, if you believe that Machiavelli's point here is fundamentally wrong, explain why, again using current examples.

7. In *The Prince*, Machiavelli is writing about how to be a successful ruler. He explicitly says he is dealing with things as they are, not things as they should be. Do you think that in fact one can write usefully about statecraft without considering ethics? Explain. Or you may want to think about it in this way: The study of politics is often called *political science*. Machiavelli can be seen as a sort of scientist, objectively analyzing the

nature of governing—without offering any moral judgments. In an essay of 500 words argue for or against the view that the study of politics is rightly called *political science.*

8. In paragraph 18 Machiavelli declares that "one must consider the final result." Taking account of the context, do you think the meaning is that (a) any end, goal, or purpose of anyone justifies using any means to reach it, or (b) the end of governing the state, nation, or country justifies using any means to achieve it? Or do you think Machiavelli means both, or something else entirely?

9. Take some important contemporary political figure and in 500 words argue that he or she does or does not act according to Machiavelli's principles.

10. If you have read the selection from Thomas More's *Utopia* (p. 632), write an essay of 500 words on one of these two topics: (1) Why More's book is or is not wiser than Machiavelli's, or (2) why one of the books is more interesting than the other.

11. More and Machiavelli wrote their books at almost exactly the same time. Write a dialogue of two or three double-spaced typed pages, in which the two men argue about the nature of the state. (During the argument, they will have to reveal their assumptions about the nature of human beings, and the role of government.)

Thomas Jefferson

Thomas Jefferson (1743–1826) was a congressman, the governor of Virginia, the first secretary of state, and the president of the United States, but he said he wished to be remembered for only three things: drafting the Declaration of Independence, writing the Virginia Statute for Religious Freedom, and founding the University of Virginia. All three were efforts to promote freedom.

Jefferson was born in Virginia and educated at William and Mary College in Williamsburg, Virginia. After graduating he studied law, was admitted to the bar, and in 1769 was elected to the Virginia House of Burgesses, his first political office. In 1776 he went to Philadelphia as a delegate to the second Continental Congress, where he was elected to a committee of five to write the Declaration of Independence. Jefferson drafted the document, which was then subjected to some changes by the other members of the committee and by the Congress. Although he was unhappy with the changes (especially with the deletion of a passage against slavery), his claim to have written the Declaration is just.

The Declaration of Independence

When in the course of human events, it becomes necessary for one people to dissolve the political bands which have connected them with another, and to assume among the Powers of the earth, the separate and equal station to which the Laws of Nature and of Nature's God entitle them, a decent respect to the opinions of mankind requires that they should declare the causes which impel them to the separation.

We hold these truths to be self-evident, that all men are created equal, that they are endowed by their Creator with certain unalienable Rights, that among these are Life, Liberty and the pursuit of Happiness.

That to secure these rights, Governments are instituted among Men, deriving their just powers from the consent of the governed.

That whenever any Form of Government becomes destructive of these ends, it is the Right of the People to alter or to abolish it, and to institute a new Government, laying its foundation on such principles and organizing its powers in such form, as to them shall seem most likely to effect their Safety and Happiness. Prudence, indeed, will dictate that Governments long established should not be changed for light and transient causes; and accordingly all experience hath shown that mankind are more disposed to suffer, while evils are sufferable, than to right themselves by abolishing the forms to which they are accustomed. But when a long train of abuses and usurpations pursuing invariably the same Object evinces a design to reduce them under absolute Despotism, it is their right, it is their duty, to throw off such government, and to provide new Guards for their future security.

Such has been the patient sufferance of these Colonies; and such is   5
now the necessity which constrains them to alter their former Systems of Government. The history of the present King of Great Britain is a history of repeated injuries and usurpations, all having in direct object the establishment of an absolute Tyranny over these States. To prove this, let Facts be submitted to a candid world.

He has refused his Assent to Laws, the most wholesome and necessary for the public good.

He has forbidden his Governors to pass Laws of immediate and pressing importance, unless suspended in their operation till his Assent should be obtained; and when so suspended, he has utterly neglected to attend to them.

He has refused to pass over Laws for the accommodation of large districts of people, unless those people would relinquish the right of Representation in the Legislature, a right inestimable to them and formidable to tyrants only.

He has called together legislative bodies at places unusual, uncomfortable, and distant from the depository of their Public Records, for the sole purpose of fatiguing them into compliance with his measures.

He has dissolved Representative Houses repeatedly, for opposing   10
with manly firmness his invasions on the rights of the people.

He has refused for a long time, after such dissolutions, to cause others to be elected; whereby the Legislative Powers, incapable of Annihilation, have returned to the People at large for their exercise; the State remaining in the mean time exposed to all the dangers of invasion from without, and convulsions within.

He has endeavored to prevent the population of these States, for that purpose obstructing the Laws of Naturalization of Foreigners; refusing to pass others to encourage their migration hither, and raising the conditions of new Appropriations of Lands.

He has obstructed the Administration of Justice, by refusing his Assent to Laws for establishing Judiciary Powers.

He has made Judges dependent on his Will alone, for the tenure of their offices, and the amount and payment of their salaries.

He has erected a multitude of New Offices, and sent hither swarms 15 of Officers to harass our People, and eat out their substance.

He has kept among us, in time of peace, Standing Armies without the consent of our Legislature.

He has affected to render the Military independent of and superior to the Civil Power.

He has combined with others to subject us to jurisdictions foreign to our constitution, and unacknowledged by our laws; giving his Assent to their acts of pretended Legislation:

For quartering large bodies of armed troops among us:

For protecting them, by a mock Trial, from Punishment for any Mur- 20 ders which they should commit on the Inhabitants of these States:

For cutting off our Trade with all parts of the world:

For imposing Taxes on us without our Consent:

For depriving us in many cases, of the benefits of Trial by Jury:

For transporting us beyond Seas to be tried for pretended offenses:

For abolishing the free System of English Laws in a Neighbouring 25 Province, establishing therein an Arbitrary government, and enlarging its boundaries so as to render it at once an example and fit instrument for introducing the same absolute rule into these Colonies:

For taking away our Charters, abolishing our most valuable Laws, and altering fundamentally the Forms of our Governments.

For suspending our own Legislatures, and declaring themselves invested with Power to legislate for us in all cases whatsoever.

He has abdicated Government here, by declaring us out of his Protection and waging War against us.

He has plundered our seas, ravaged our Coasts, burnt our towns and destroyed the Lives of our people.

He is at this time transporting large Armies of foreign Mercenaries to 30 compleat the works of death, desolation and tyranny, already begun with circumstances of Cruelty & perfidy scarcely paralleled in the most barbarous ages, and totally unworthy the Head of a civilized nation.

He has constrained our fellow Citizens taken Captive on the high Seas to bear Arms against their Country, to become the executioners of their friends and Brethren, or to fall themselves by their Hands.

He has excited domestic insurrections amongst us, and has endeavored to bring on the inhabitants of our frontiers, the merciless Indian Savages, whose known rule of warfare is an undistinguished destruction of all ages, sexes and conditions.

In every stage of these Oppressions We Have Petitioned for Redress in the most humble terms: Our repeated petitions have been answered only by repeated injury. A Prince, whose character is thus marked by every act which may define a Tyrant, is unfit to be the ruler of a free People.

Nor have We been wanting in attention to our British brethren. We have warned them from time to time of attempts by their legislature to extend an unwarrantable jurisdiction over us. We have reminded them of the circumstances of our emigration and settlement here. We have appealed to their native justice and magnanimity and we have conjured them by the ties of our common kindred to disavow these usurpations, which would inevitably interrupt our connections and correspondence. They too have been deaf to the voice of justice and of consanguinity. We must, therefore, acquiesce in the necessity, which denounces our Separation, and hold them, as we hold the rest of mankind, Enemies in War, in Peace Friends.

We, therefore, the Representatives of the United States of America, 35 in General Congress, Assembled, appealing to the Supreme Judge of the world of the rectitude of our intentions, do, in the Name, and by Authority of the good People of these Colonies, solemnly publish and declare, That these United Colonies are, and of Right ought to be, Free and Independent States; that they are Absolved from all Allegiance to the British Crown, and that all political connection between them and the State of Great Britain, is and ought to be totally dissolved; and that as Free and Independent States, they have full power to levy War, conclude Peace, contract Alliances, establish Commerce, and so all the other Acts and Things which Independent States may of right do. And for the support of this Declaration, with a firm reliance on the protection of Divine Providence, we mutually pledge to each other our lives, our Fortunes and our sacred Honor.

Topics for Critical Thinking and Writing

1. According to the first paragraph, for what audience was the Declaration written? What other audiences do you think the document was (in one way or another) addressed to?

2. The Declaration states that it is intended to "prove" that the acts of the government of George III had as their "direct object the establishment of an absolute Tyranny" in the American colonies (para. 5). Write an essay of 500 to 750 words showing whether the evidence offered in the

Declaration "proves" this claim to your satisfaction. (You will, of course, want to define *absolute tyranny*.) If you think further evidence is needed to "prove" the colonists' point, indicate what this evidence might be.

3. Paying special attention to the paragraphs beginning "That whenever any Form of Government" (para. 4), "In every stage" (para. 33), and "Nor have We been wanting" (para. 34), in a sentence or two set forth the image of themselves that the colonists seek to convey.

4. In the Declaration of Independence it is argued that the colonists are entitled to certain things, and that under certain conditions they may behave in a certain way. Make explicit the syllogism that Jefferson is arguing.

5. What evidence does Jefferson offer to support his major premise? His minor premise?

6. In paragraph 2 the Declaration cites "certain unalienable Rights" and mentions three: "Life, Liberty and the pursuit of Happiness." What is an unalienable right? If someone has an unalienable (or inalienable) right, does that imply that he or she also has certain duties? If so, what are these duties? John Locke, a century earlier (1690), asserted that all men have a natural right to "life, liberty, and property." Do you think the decision to drop "property" from this list and substitute "pursuit of Happiness" made an improvement? Explain.

7. The Declaration ends thus: "We mutually pledge to each other our lives, our Fortunes and our sacred Honor." Is it surprising that Honor is put in the final, climactic position? Is this a better ending than "our Fortunes, our sacred Honor, and our lives," or than "our sacred Honor, our lives, and our Fortunes?" Why?

8. King George III has asked you to reply, on his behalf, to the colonists, in 500 to 750 words. Write his reply. (*Caution:* A good reply will probably require you to do some reading about the period.)

9. Write a declaration of your own, setting forth in 500 to 750 words why some group is entitled to independence. You may want to argue that adolescents should not be compelled to attend school, or that animals should not be confined in zoos, or that persons who use drugs should be able to buy them legally. Begin with a premise, then set forth facts illustrating the unfairness of the present condition, and conclude by stating what the new condition will mean to society.

Elizabeth Cady Stanton

Elizabeth Cady Stanton (1815–1902), a lawyer's daughter and journalist's wife, proposed in 1848 a convention to address the "social, civil, and religious condition and rights of women." Responding to Stanton's call, women from all over the Northeast convened in the village of Seneca Falls, New York. Her Declaration, adopted by the Seneca Falls Convention—but only after vigorous debate and some amendments by others—became the platform for the women's movement in this country.

Declaration of Sentiments and Resolutions

When, in the course of human events, it becomes necessary for one portion of the family of man to assume among the people of the earth a position different from that which they have hitherto occupied, but one to which the laws of nature and of nature's God entitle them, a decent respect to the opinions of mankind requires that they should declare the causes that impel them to such a course.

We hold these truths to be self-evident: that all men and women are created equal; that they are endowed by their Creator with certain inalienable rights; that among these are life, liberty and the pursuit of happiness; that to secure these rights governments are instituted, deriving their just powers from the consent of the governed. Whenever any form of government becomes destructive of these ends, it is the right of those who suffer from it to refuse allegiance to it, and to insist upon the institution of a new government, laying its foundation on such principles, and organizing its powers in such form, as to them shall seem most likely to effect their safety and happiness. Prudence, indeed, will dictate that governments long established should not be changed for light and transient causes; and accordingly all experience hath shown that mankind are more disposed to suffer, while evils are sufferable, than to right themselves by abolishing the forms to which they were accustomed. But when a long train of abuses and usurpations, pursuing invariably the same object, evinces a design to reduce them under absolute despotism, it is their duty to throw off such government, and to provide new guards for their future security. Such has been the patient sufferance of the women under this government, and such is now the necessity which constrains them to demand the equal station to which they are entitled.

The history of mankind is a history of repeated injuries and usurpations on the part of man toward woman, having in direct object the establishment of an absolute tyranny over her. To prove this, let facts be submitted to a candid world.

He has never permitted her to exercise her inalienable right to the elective franchise.

He has compelled her to submit to laws, in the formation of which 5 she had no voice.

He has withheld from her rights which are given to the most ignorant and degraded men — both natives and foreigners.

Having deprived her of this first right of a citizen, the elective franchise, thereby leaving her without representation in the halls of legislation, he has oppressed her on all sides.

He has made her, if married, in the eye of the law, civilly dead.

He has taken from her all right in property, even to the wages she earns.

He has made her, morally, an irresponsible being, as she can commit 10 many crimes with impunity, provided they be done in the presence of her husband. In the covenant of marriage, she is compelled to promise obedience to her husband, he becoming to all intents and purposes, her master—the law giving him power to deprive her of her liberty, and to administer chastisement.

He has so framed the laws of divorce, as to what shall be the proper causes, and in case of separation, to whom the guardianship of the children shall be given, as to be wholly regardless of the happiness of women—the law, in all cases, going upon a false supposition of the supremacy of man, and giving all power into his hands.

After depriving her of all rights as a married woman, if single, and the owner of property, he has taxed her to support a government which recognizes her only when her property can be made profitable to it.

He has monopolized nearly all the profitable employments, and from those she is permitted to follow, she receives but a scanty remuneration. He closes against her all the avenues to wealth and distinction which he considers most honorable to himself. As a teacher of theology, medicine, or law, she is not known.

He has denied her the facilities for obtaining a thorough education, all colleges being closed against her.

He allows her in Church, as well as State, but a subordinate position, 15 claiming Apostolic authority for her exclusion from the ministry, and, with some exceptions, from any public participation in the affairs of the Church.

He has created a false public sentiment by giving to the world a different code of morals for men and women, by which moral delinquencies which exclude women from society, are not only tolerated, but deemed of little account in man.

He has usurped the prerogative of Jehovah himself, claiming it as his right to assign for her a sphere of action, when that belongs to her conscience and to her God.

He has endeavored, in every way that he could, to destroy her confidence in her own powers, to lessen her self-respect, and to make her willing to lead a dependent and abject life.

Now, in view of this entire disfranchisement of one-half the people of this country, their social and religious degradation—in view of the unjust laws above mentioned, and because women do feel themselves aggrieved, oppressed, and fraudulently deprived of their most sacred rights, we insist that they have immediate admission to all the rights and privileges which belong to them as citizens of the United States.

In entering upon the great work before us, we anticipate no small 20 amount of misconception, misrepresentation, and ridicule; but we shall use every instrumentality within our power to effect our object. We shall employ agents, circulate tracts, petition the State and National legislatures, and endeavor to enlist the pulpit and the press in our behalf. We hope this Convention will be followed by a series of Conventions embracing every part of the country.

[The following resolutions were discussed by Lucretia Mott, Thomas and Mary Ann McClintock, Amy Post, Catharine A. F. Stebbins, and others, and were adopted:]

Whereas, The great precept of nature is conceded to be, that "man shall pursue his own true and substantial happiness." Blackstone in his Commentaries remarks, that this law of Nature being coeval with mankind, and dictated by God himself, is of course superior in obligation to any other. It is binding over all the globe, in all countries, and at all times; no human laws are of any validity if contrary to this, and such of them as are valid, derive all their force, and all their validity, and all their authority, mediately and immediately, from this original; therefore,

Resolved, That such laws as conflict, in any way, with the true and substantial happiness of woman, are contrary to the great precept of nature and of no validity, for this is "superior in obligation to any other."

Resolved, That all laws which prevent woman from occupying such a station in society as her conscience shall dictate, or which place her in a position inferior to that of man, are contrary to the great precept of nature, and therefore of no force or authority.

Resolved, That woman is man's equal—was intended to be so by the Creator, and the highest good of the race demands that she should be recognized as such.

Resolved, That the women of this country ought to be enlightened in 25 regard to the laws under which they live, that they may no longer publish their degradation by declaring themselves satisfied with their present position, nor their ignorance, by asserting that they have all the rights they want.

Resolved, That inasmuch as man, while claiming for himself intellectual superiority, does accord to woman moral superiority, it is preeminently his duty to encourage her to speak and teach, as she has an opportunity, in all religious assemblies.

Resolved, That the same amount of virtue, delicacy, and refinement of behavior that is required of woman in the social state, should also be required of man, and the same transgressions should be visited with equal severity on both man and woman.

Resolved, That the objection of indelicacy and impropriety, which is so often brought against woman when she addresses a public audience, comes with a very ill-grace from those who encourage, by their attendance, her appearance on the stage, in the concert, or in feats of the circus.

Resolved, That woman has too long rested satisfied in the circumscribed limits which corrupt customs and a perverted application of the Scriptures have marked out for her, and that it is time she should move in the enlarged sphere which her great Creator has assigned her.

Resolved, That it is the duty of the women of this country to secure to 30 themselves their sacred right to the elective franchise.

Resolved, That the equality of human rights results necessarily from the fact of the identity of the race in capabilities and responsibilities.

Resolved, therefore, That, being invested by the Creator with the same capabilities, and the same consciousness of responsibility for their exercise, it is demonstrably the right and duty of woman, equally with man, to promote every righteous cause by every righteous means; and especially in regard to the great subjects of morals and religion, it is self-evidently her right to participate with her brother in teaching them, both in private and in public, by writing and by speaking, by any instrumentalities proper to be used, and in any assemblies proper to be held; and this being a self-evident truth growing out of the divinely implanted principles of human nature, any custom or authority adverse to it, whether modern or wearing the hoary sanction of antiquity, is to be regarded as a self-evident falsehood, and at war with mankind.

[At the last session Lucretia Mott offered and spoke to the following resolution:]

Resolved, That the speedy success of our cause depends upon the zealous and untiring efforts of both men and women, for the overthrow of the monopoly of the pulpit, and for the securing to woman an equal participation with men in the various trades, professions, and commerce.

Topics for Critical Thinking and Writing

1. Stanton echoes the Declaration of Independence because she wishes to associate her ideas and the movement she supports with a document and a movement that her readers esteem. And of course she must have believed that if readers esteem the Declaration of Independence, they must grant the justice of her goals. Does her strategy work, or does it backfire by making her essay seem strained?

2. When Stanton insists that women have an "inalienable right to the elective franchise" (para. 4), what does she mean by "inalienable"?

3. Stanton complains that men have made women, "in the eye of the law, civilly dead" (para. 8). What does she mean by "civilly dead"? How is it possible for a person to be biologically alive yet civilly dead?

4. Stanton objects that women are "not known" as teachers of "theology, medicine, or law" (para. 13). Is this still true today? Do some research in your library, and then write three 100-word biographical sketches, one each on a well-known woman professor of theology, medicine, and law.

5. How might you go about proving (rather than merely asserting) that, as paragraph 24 says, "woman is man's equal — was intended to be so by the Creator"?

6. The Declaration claims that women have "the same capabilities" as men (para. 32). Yet in 1848 Stanton and the others at Seneca Falls knew, or should have known, that history recorded no example of an outstanding woman philosopher to compare with Plato or Kant, a great composer to compare with Beethoven or Chopin, a scientist to compare with Galileo or Newton, or a creative mathematician to compare with Euclid or Descartes. Do these facts contradict the Declaration's claim? If not, why not? How else but by different intellectual capabilities do you think such facts are to be explained?

7. Stanton's Declaration is about one-hundred-fifty years old. Have all of the issues she raised been satisfactorily resolved? If not, which ones remain?

8. In our society, children have very few rights. For instance, a child cannot decide to drop out of elementary school or high school, and a child cannot decide to leave his or her parents to reside with some other family that he or she finds more compatible. Whatever your view of children's rights, compose the best Declaration of the Rights of Children that you can.

Martin Luther King, Jr.

Martin Luther King, Jr. (1929–1968), was born in Atlanta and educated at Morehouse College, Crozer Theological Seminary, and Boston University. In 1954 he was called to serve as a Baptist minister in Montgomery, Alabama. During the next two years he achieved national fame when, using a policy of nonviolent resistance, he successfully led the boycott against segregated bus lines in Montgomery. He then organized the Southern Christian Leadership Conference, which furthered civil rights, first in the South and then nationwide. In 1964 he was awarded the Nobel Peace Prize. Four years later he was assassinated in Memphis, Tennessee, while supporting striking garbage workers.

"I Have a Dream" was delivered from the steps of the Lincoln Memorial, in Washington, D.C., in 1963, the hundredth anniversary of the Emancipation Proclamation. King's immediate audience consisted of more than two hundred thousand people who had come to demonstrate for civil rights.

I Have a Dream

I am happy to join with you today in what will go down in history as the greatest demonstration for freedom in the history of our nation.

Five score years ago, a great American, in whose symbolic shadow we stand today, signed the Emancipation Proclamation. This momentous decree came as a great beacon light of hope to millions of Negro slaves who had been seared in the flames of withering injustice. It came as a joyous daybreak to end the long night of their captivity. But one hundred years later, the Negro still is not free. One hundred years later, the life of the Negro is still sadly crippled by the manacles of segregation and the chains of discrimination. One hundred years later, the Negro lives on a lonely island of poverty in the midst of a vast ocean of material prosperity. One hundred years later, the Negro is still anguished in the corners of American society and finds himself in exile in his own land. And so we have come here today to dramatize a shameful condition.

In a sense we have come to our nation's capital to cash a check. When the architects of our republic wrote the magnificent words of the Constitution and the Declaration of Independence, they were signing a promissory note to which every American was to fall heir. This note was the promise that all men—yes, black men as well as white men—would be guaranteed the inalienable rights of life, liberty, and the pursuit of happiness.

It is obvious today that America has defaulted on this promissory note insofar as her citizens of color are concerned. Instead of honoring this sacred obligation, America has given the Negro people a bad check, a check which has come back marked "insufficient funds." But we refuse to believe that the bank of justice is bankrupt. We refuse to believe that there are insufficient funds in the great vaults of opportunity of this nation; and so we have come to cash this check, a check that will give us upon demand the riches of freedom and the security of justice.

We have also come to this hallowed spot to remind America of the   5
fierce urgency of *now*. This is no time to engage in the luxury of cooling off or to take the tranquilizing drug of gradualism. *Now* is the time to make real promises of democracy. *Now* is the time to rise from the dark and desolate valley of segregation to the sunlit path of racial justice. *Now* is the time to lift our nation from the quicksands of racial injustice to the solid rock of brotherhood. *Now* is the time to make justice a reality for all of God's children.

It would be fatal for the nation to overlook the urgency of the moment. This sweltering summer of the Negro's legitimate discontent will not pass until there is an invigorating autumn of freedom and equality. Nineteen sixty-three is not an end, but a beginning. And those who hope that the Negro needed to blow off steam and will now be content will have a rude awakening if the nation returns to business as usual. There will be neither rest nor tranquility in America until the Negro is granted his citizenship rights. The whirlwinds of revolt will continue to shake the foundations of our nation until the bright day of justice emerges.

But there is something that I must say to my people who stand on the warm threshold which leads into the palace of justice. In the process of gaining our rightful place, we must not be guilty of wrongful deeds. Let us not seek to satisfy our thirst for freedom by drinking from the cup of bitterness and hatred. We must forever conduct our struggle on the high plane of dignity and discipline. We must not allow our creative protest to degenerate into physical violence. Again and again we must rise to the majestic heights of meeting physical force with soul force. And the marvelous new militancy which has engulfed the Negro community must not lead us to a distrust of all white people; for many of our white brothers, as evidenced by their presence here today, have come to realize that their destiny is tied up with our destiny, and they have come to realize that their freedom is inextricably bound to our freedom.

We cannot walk alone. And as we walk we must make the pledge that we shall always march ahead. We cannot turn back. There are those who are asking the devotees of civil rights, "When will you be satisfied?" We can never be satisfied as long as the Negro is the victim of the unspeakable horrors of police brutality. We can never be satisfied as long as our bodies, heavy with the fatigue of travel, cannot gain lodging in the motels of the highways and the hotels of the cities. We cannot be satisfied as long as the Negro's basic mobility is from a smaller ghetto to a larger one. We can never be satisfied as long as our children are stripped of their selfhood and robbed of their dignity by signs stating "For Whites Only." We cannot be satisfied as long as the Negro in Mississippi cannot vote and a Negro in New York believes he has nothing for which to vote. No, no, we are not satisfied, and we will not be satisfied until justice rolls down like waters and righteousness like a mighty stream.[1]

I am not unmindful that some of you have come here out of great trials and tribulations. Some of you have come fresh from narrow jail cells. Some of you have come from areas where your quest for freedom left you battered by the storms of persecution and staggered by the winds of police brutality. You have been the veterans of creative suffering. Continue to work with the faith that unearned suffering is redemptive.

Go back to Mississippi, and go back to Alabama. Go back to South　10 Carolina. Go back to Georgia. Go back to Louisiana. Go back to the slums and ghettos of our Northern cities, knowing that somehow this situation can and will be changed. Let us not wallow in the valley of despair.

I say to you today, my friends, even though we face the difficulties of today and tomorrow, I still have a dream. It is a dream deeply rooted in the American dream. I have a dream that one day this nation will rise up and live out the true meaning of its creed: "We hold these truths to be self-evident, that all men are created equal." I have a dream that one day, on the red hills of Georgia, sons of former slaves and the sons of former slave owners will be able to sit down together at the table of brotherhood. I have a dream that one day even the state of Mississippi, a state sweltering with the heat of injustice, sweltering with the heat of oppression, will be transformed into an oasis of freedom and justice. I have a dream that my four little children will one day live in a nation where they will not be judged by the color of their skin, but by the content of their character.

---

[1]**justice . . . stream** A quotation from the Hebrew Bible: Amos 5:24. [All notes are the editors'.]

I have a dream today. I have a dream that one day down in Alabama—with its vicious racists, with its governor's lips dripping with the words of interposition and nullification—one day right there in Alabama, little black boys and black girls will be able to join hands with little white boys and white girls as sisters and brothers.

I have a dream today. I have a dream that one day every valley shall be exalted and every hill and mountain shall be made low, the rough places will be made plain and the crooked places will be made straight, and the glory of the Lord shall be revealed, and all flesh shall see it together.[2]

This is our hope. This is the faith that I go back to the South with. And with this faith we will be able to hew out of the mountain of despair a stone of hope. With this faith we will be able to transform the jangling discords of our nation into a beautiful symphony of brotherhood. With this faith we will be able to work together, to play together, to struggle together, to go to jail together, to stand up for freedom together, knowing that we will be free one day.

And this will be the day—this will be the day when all of God's chil-   15
dren will be able to sing with new meaning:

> My country, 'tis of thee,
> Sweet land of liberty,
>   Of thee I sing;
> Land where my fathers died,
> Land of the Pilgrim's pride,
> From every mountainside
>   Let freedom ring.

And if America is to be a great nation, this must become true.

And so let freedom ring from the prodigious hilltops of New Hampshire. Let freedom ring from the mighty mountains of New York. Let freedom ring from the heightening Alleghenies of Pennsylvania. Let freedom ring from the snow-capped Rockies of Colorado. Let freedom ring from the curvaceous slopes of California.

But not only that. Let freedom ring from Stone Mountain of Georgia. Let freedom ring from Lookout Mountain of Tennessee. Let freedom ring from every hill and molehill of Mississippi. "From every mountainside let freedom ring."

And when this happens—when we allow freedom to ring, when we let it ring from every village and every hamlet, from every state and every city—we will be able to speed up that day when all of God's children, Black men and white men, Jews and Gentiles, Protestants and Catholics, will be able to join hands and sing in the words of the old Negro spiritual: "Free at last! Free at last! Thank God Almighty. We are free at last!"

---

[2]**every valley . . . see it together** Another quotation from the Hebrew Bible: Isaiah 40:4–5.

Topics for Critical Thinking and Writing

1. Analyze the rhetoric—the oratorical art—of the second paragraph. What, for instance, is gained by saying "five score years ago" instead of "a hundred years ago"? By metaphorically calling the Emancipation Proclamation "a great beacon light?" By saying that "Negro slaves . . . had been seared in the flames of withering injustice"? And what of the metaphors "daybreak" and "the long night of . . . captivity"?

2. Do the first two paragraphs make an effective opening? Why?

3. In the third and fourth paragraphs King uses the metaphor of a bad check. Rewrite the third paragraph *without* using any of King's metaphors, and then in a paragraph evaluate the difference between King's version and yours.

4. King's highly metaphoric speech of course appeals to emotions. But it also offers *reasons*. What reason(s), for instance, does King give to support his belief that blacks should not resort to physical violence?

5. When King delivered the speech, his audience at the Lincoln Memorial was primarily black. Do you think that the speech is also addressed to whites? Explain.

6. The speech can be divided into three parts: paragraphs 1 through 6; paragraphs 7 ("But there is") through 10; and paragraph 11 ("I say to you today, my friends") to the end. Summarize each of these three parts in a sentence or two, so that the basic organization is evident.

7. King says (para. 11) that his dream is "deeply rooted in the American dream." First, what is the American dream, as King seems to understand it? Second, how does King establish his point—that is, what evidence does he use to convince us—that his dream is the American dream? (On this second issue, for a start one might point out that in the second paragraph King refers to the Emancipation Proclamation. What other relevant documents does he refer to?)

8. King delivered his speech in 1963, more than thirty-five years ago. In an essay of 500 words argue that the speech still is—or is not—relevant. Or write an essay of 500 words in which you state what you take to be the "American dream," and argue that it now is or is not readily available to blacks.

Richard Rorty

Richard Rorty (b. 1927), University Professor of the Humanities at the University of Virginia, is the author of several books, including Contingency, Irony, and Solidarity *(1989). The essay that we reprint was originally published in the September 29, 1996, issue of the* New York Times Magazine.

Fraternity Reigns

Our long, hesitant, painful recovery, over the last five decades, from the breakdown of democratic institutions during the Dark Years (2014–2044) has changed our political vocabulary, as well as our sense of the relation between the moral order and the economic order. Just as twentieth-century Americans had trouble imagining how their pre–Civil War ancestors could have stomached slavery, so we at the end of the twenty-first century have trouble imagining how our great-grandparents could have legally permitted a CEO to get twenty times more than her lowest-paid employees. We cannot understand how Americans a hundred years ago could have tolerated the horrific contrast between a childhood spent in the suburbs and one spent in the ghettos. Such inequalities seem to us evident moral abominations, but the vast majority of our ancestors took them to be regrettable necessities.

As long as their political discourse was dominated by the notion of "rights"—whether "individual" or "civil"—it was hard for Americans to think of the results of unequal distribution of wealth and income as immoral. Such rights talk, common among late-twentieth-century liberals, gave conservative opponents of redistributionist policies a tremendous advantage: "The right to a job" (or "to a decent wage") had none of the resonance of "the right to sit in the front of the bus" or "the right to vote" or even "the right to equal pay for equal work." Rights in the liberal tradition were, after all, powers and privileges to be wrested from the state, not from the economy.

Of course socialists had, since the mid-nineteenth century, urged that the economy and the state be merged to guarantee economic rights. But it had become clear by the middle of the twentieth century that such merging was disastrous. The history of the pre-1989 "socialist" countries—bloody dictatorships that paid only lip service to the fraternity for which the socialist revolutionaries had yearned—made it plausible for conservatives to argue that extending the notion of rights to the economic order would be a step down the road to serfdom. By the end of the twentieth century, even left-leaning American intellectuals agreed that "socialism, no wave of the future, now looks (at best) like a temporary historical stage through which various nations passed before reaching the great transition to capitalist democracy."[1]

---

[1]From the article "Socialism," by the labor historian Sean Wilentz, in the first edition of *A Companion to American Thought*, eds. Richard Fox and James Kloppenberg (London and New York: Blackwell, 1995). That edition appeared exactly one hundred years before the current one, which contains the article "Fraternity" excerpted here. Whereas the first edition contained no essay on fraternity, the latest edition has neither an essay on socialism nor one on rights. For the full text of "Fraternity," see pp. 247–98 of *A Companion to American Thought*, seventh edition, eds. Cynthia Rodriguez, S.J., and Youzheng Patel (London and New York: Blackwell, 2095). [Rorty's note.]

The realization by those on the left that a viable economy required free markets did not stop them from insisting that capitalism would be compatible with American ideals of human brotherhood only if the state were able to redistribute wealth. Yet this view was still being criticized as "un-American" and "socialist" at the beginning of the present century, even as, under the pressures of a globalized world economy, the gap between most Americans' incomes and those of the lucky one-third at the top widened. Looking back, we think how easy it would have been for our great-grandfathers to have forestalled the social collapse that resulted from these economic pressures. They could have insisted that all classes had to confront the new global economy together. In the name of our common citizenship, they could have asked everybody, not just the bottom two-thirds, to tighten their belts and make do with less. They might have brought the country together by bringing back its old pride in fraternal ideals.

But as it happened, decades of despair and horror were required to 5 impress Americans with lessons that now seem blindingly obvious.

The apparent incompatibility of capitalism and democracy is, of course, an old theme in American political and intellectual life. It began to be sounded more than two centuries ago. Historians divide our history into the one hundred years before the coming of industrial capitalism and the more than two hundred years since. During the first period, the open frontier made it possible for Americans to live in ways that became impossible for their descendants. If you were white in nineteenth-century America, you always had a second chance: Something was always opening up out West.

So the first fault line in American politics was not between the rich and the poor. Instead, it was between those who saw chattel slavery as incompatible with American fraternity and those who did not. (Abolitionist posters showed a kneeling slave asking, "Am I not a man, and a brother?") But only forty years after the Civil War, reformers were already saying that the problem of chattel slavery had been replaced by that of wage slavery.

The urgency of that problem dominates Herbert Croly's progressivist manifesto of 1909, "The Promise of American Life." Croly argued that the Constitution, and a tradition of tolerant individualism, had kept America hopeful and filled with what he called "genuine good-fellowship" during its first hundred years. But beginning with the first wave of industrialization in the 1870s and 1880s, things began to change. Wage slavery—a life of misery and toil, without a sense of participation in the national life, and without any trace of the frontiersman's proud independence—became the fate of more and more Americans. Alexis de Tocqueville had rejoiced that an opulent merchant and his shoemaker, when they met on the streets of Philadelphia in 1840, would exchange political opinions. "These two citizens," he wrote, "are concerned with affairs of state, and they do not part without shaking hands." Croly feared that this kind of unforced fraternity was becoming impossible.

From Croly to John Kenneth Galbraith and Arthur Schlesinger in the 1960s, reformers urged that we needed some form of redistribution to bring back Tocquevillian comity. They battled with conservatives who claimed that redistributive measures would kill economic prosperity. The reformers insisted that what Theodore Roosevelt had called "the money power" and Dwight Eisenhower "the military-industrial complex" was the true enemy of American ideals. The conservatives rejoined that the only enemy of democracy was the state and that the economy must be shielded from do-gooders.

This debate simmered through the first two decades following the   10
Second World War. During that relatively halcyon period, most Americans could get fairly secure, fairly well-paying jobs and could count on their children having a better life than theirs. White America seemed to be making slow but steady progress toward a classless society. Only the growth of the increasingly miserable black underclass reminded white Americans that the promise of American life was still far from being fulfilled.

The sense that this promise was still alive was made possible, in part, by what the first edition of the "Companion" called the "rights revolution." Most of the moral progress that took place in the second half of the twentieth century was brought about by the Supreme Court's invocation of constitutional rights, in such decisions as *Brown v. Board of Education* (1954) and *Romer v. Evans* (1996), the first Supreme Court decision favorable to homosexuals. But this progress was confined almost entirely to improvements in the situation of groups identified by race, ethnicity, or sexuality. The situation of women and of homosexuals changed radically in this period. Indeed, it is now clear that those changes, which spread from America around the world, were the most lasting and significant moral achievements of the twentieth century.

But though such groups could use the rhetoric of rights to good effect, the trade unions, the unemployed, and those employed at the ludicrously low minimum wage ($174 an hour, in 2095 dollars, compared with the present minimum of $400) could not. Perhaps no difference between present-day American political discourse and that of one hundred years ago is greater than our assumption that the first duty of the state is to prevent gross economic and social inequality, as opposed to our ancestors' assumption that the government's only *moral* duty was to insure "equal protection of the laws" — laws that, in their majestic impartiality, allowed the rich and the poor to receive the same hospital bills.

The Supreme Court, invoking this idea of equal protection, began the great moral revival we know as the Civil Rights Movement. The *Brown* decision initiated both an explosion of violence and an upsurge of fraternal feeling. Some white Americans burned crosses and black churches. Many more had their eyes opened to the humiliations being inflicted on their fellow citizens: If they did not join civil rights marches, they at least felt relieved of guilt when the Court threw out miscegenation laws and when Congress began to protect black voting rights. For a decade or so there was an uplifting sense of moral improvement. For the first time, white and black Americans started to think of each other as fellow citizens.

By the beginning of the 1980s, however, this sense of fraternity was only a faint memory. A burst of selfishness had produced tax revolts in the '70s, stopping in its tracks the fairly steady progress toward a full-fledged welfare state that had been under way since the New Deal. The focus of racial hate was transferred from the rural South to the big cities, where a criminal culture of unemployed (and, in the second generation, virtually unemployable) black youths grew up—a culture of near constant violence, made possible by the then-famous American "right to bear arms." All the old racial prejudices were revived by white suburbanites' claims that their tax money was being used to coddle criminals. Politicians gained votes by promising to spend what little money could be squeezed from their constituents on prisons rather than on day care.

Tensions between the comfortable middle-class suburbs and the rest 15 of the country grew steadily in the closing decades of the twentieth century, as the gap between the educated and well paid and the uneducated and ill paid steadily widened. Class division came into existence between those who made "professional" salaries and those whose hourly wage kept sinking toward the minimum. But the politicians pretended to be unaware of this steady breakdown of fraternity.

Our nation's leaders, in the last decade of the old century and the first of the new, seemed never to have thought that it might be dangerous to make automatic weapons freely and cheaply available to desperate men and women—people without hope—living next to the centers of transportation and communication. Those weapons burst into the streets in 2014, in the revolution that, leaving the cities in ruins and dislocating American economic life, plunged the country into the Second Great Depression.

The insurgency in the ghettos, coming at a time when all but the wealthiest Americans felt desperately insecure, led to the collapse of trust in government. The collapse of the economy produced a war of all against all, as gasoline and food became harder and harder to buy, and as even the suburbanites began to brandish guns at their neighbors. As the generals never stopped saying throughout the Dark Years, only the military saved the country from utter chaos.

Here, in the late twenty-first century, as talk of fraternity and unselfishness has replaced talk of rights, American political discourse has come to be dominated by quotations from Scripture and literature, rather than from political theorists or social scientists. Fraternity, like friendship, was not a concept that either philosophers or lawyers knew how to handle. They could formulate principles of justice, equality, and liberty, and invoke these principles when weighing hard moral or legal issues. But how to formulate a "principle of fraternity"? Fraternity is an inclination of the heart, one that produces a sense of shame at having much when others have little. It is not the sort of thing that anybody can have a theory about or that people can be argued into having.

Perhaps the most vivid description of the American concept of fraternity is found in a passage from John Steinbeck's 1939 novel, *The Grapes of Wrath*. Steinbeck describes a desperately impoverished family, dispossessed tenant farmers from Oklahoma, camped out at the edge of Highway 66, sharing their food with an even more desperate migrant family. Steinbeck writes: "'I have a little food' plus 'I have none.' If from this problem the sum is 'We have a little food,' the movement has direction." As long as people in trouble can sacrifice to help people who are in still worse trouble, Steinbeck insisted, there is fraternity, and therefore social hope.

The movement Steinbeck had in mind was the revolutionary social- 20 ism that he, like many other leftists of the 1930s, thought would be required to bring the First Great Depression to an end. "The quality of owning," he wrote, "freezes you forever into the 'I,' and cuts you off forever from the 'we.'" Late-twentieth-century liberals no longer believed in getting rid of private ownership, but they agreed that the promise of American life could be redeemed only as long as Americans were willing to sacrifice for the sake of fellow Americans—only as long as they could see the government not as stealing their tax money but as needing it to prevent unnecessary suffering.

The Democratic Vistas Party, the coalition of trade unions and churches that toppled the military dictatorship in 2044, has retained control of Congress by successfully convincing the voters that its opponents constitute "the parties of selfishness." The traditional use of "brother" and "sister" in union locals and religious congregations is the principal reason why "fraternity" (or, among purists, "siblinghood") is now the name of our most cherished ideal.

In the first two centuries of American history Jefferson's use of rights had set the tone for political discourse, but now political argument is not about who has the right to what but about what can best prevent the reemergence of hereditary castes—either racial or economic. The old union slogan "An injury to one is an injury to all" is now the catch phrase of American politics. "Solidarity Forever" and "This Land Is Your Land" are sung at least as often as "The Star-Spangled Banner."

Until the last fifty years, moral instruction in America had inculcated personal responsibility, and most sermons had focused on individual salvation. Today morality is thought of neither as a matter of applying the moral law nor as the acquisition of virtues but as fellow feeling, the ability to sympathize with the plight of others.

In the churches, the "social gospel" theology of the early twentieth century has been rediscovered. Walter Rauschenbusch's "Prayer against the servants of Mammon" ("Behold the servants of Mammon, who defy thee and drain their fellow-men for gain . . . who have made us ashamed of our dear country by their defilements and have turned our holy freedom into a hollow name. . . .") is familiar to most churchgoers. In the schools, students learn about our country's history from social novels describing our past failures to hang together when we needed to, the novels of Steinbeck, Upton Sinclair, Theodore Dreiser, Richard Wright and, of course, Russel Banks's samizdat[2] novel, *Trampling the Vineyards* (2021).

Historians unite in calling the twentieth the "American" century. Cer- 25 tainly it was in the twentieth century that the United States was richest, most powerful, most influential, and most self-confident. Our ancestors one hundred years ago still thought of the country as destined to police, inform, and inspire the world. Compared with the Americans of one hundred years ago, we are citizens of an isolationist, unambitious, middle-grade nation.

Our products are only now becoming competitive again in international markets, and Democratic Vistas politicians continue to urge that our consistently low productivity is a small price to pay for union control of the workplace and worker ownership of the majority of firms. We continue to lag behind the European Community, which was able to withstand the pressures of a globalized labor market by having a full-fledged welfare state already in place, and which (except for Austria and Great Britain) was able to resist the temptation to impoverish the most vulnerable in order to keep its suburbanites affluent. Spared the equivalent of our own Dark Years, Europe still, despite all that China can do, holds the position we lost in 2014: It still dominates both the world's economy and its culture.

For two centuries Americans believed that they were as far ahead of Europe, in both virtue and promise, as Europe was ahead of the rest of the world. But American exceptionalism did not survive the Dark Years: We no longer think of ourselves as singled out by divine favor. We are now, once again, a constitutional democracy, but we have proved as vulnerable as Germany, Russia, and India to dictatorial takeovers. We have a sense of fragility, of susceptibility to the vicissitudes of time and chance, which Walt Whitman and John Dewey may never have known.

Perhaps no American writer will ever again begin a book, as Croly did, by saying, "The faith of Americans in their own country is religious,

---

[2]**samizdat** Literature that was clandestinely printed and distributed contrary to the wishes of the government of the former Soviet Union and its republics. [Editors' note.]

if not in its intensity, at any rate in its almost absolute and universal authority." But our chastened mood, our lately learned humility, may have made us better able to realize that everything depends on keeping our fragile sense of American fraternity intact.

Topics for Critical Thinking and Writing

1. Rorty claims that "rights talk" has given "conservative opponents of re-distributionist policies a tremendous advantage" (para. 2). Explain what he means and why he says this. Do you agree?

2. Why would someone criticize the power of the state to "redistribute wealth" as " 'un-American' " (para. 4)?

3. Explain the differences between "chattel slavery" and "wage slavery" (para. 7).

4. Rorty says that the decision in *Romer v. Evans* (1996) was the "first Supreme Court decision favorable to homosexuals" (para. 11). Consult with your college's reference librarian, find out more about this deci-sion, and write a 500-word essay explaining whether you agree or dis-agree with it.

5. Rorty thinks that "the first duty of the state is to prevent gross economic and social inequality" (para. 12). Do you agree? Or can you think of other tasks for the government of a constitutional democracy such as ours that have a higher priority?

6. What are the "miscegenation laws" that Rorty mentions in passing (para. 13)? What did they provide, when and where were they enacted, and what penalties were imposed for their violation?

7. Throughout his essay, Rorty attaches great weight to the value of "fra-ternity." (Along with "Liberty" and "Equality," it was the great slogan of the French Revolution in 1789.) What, according to Rorty, is fraternity, and why does he think it is so important? Do you agree?

8. When Rorty refers to the "revolution" of 2014 (para. 16) and the "mili-tary dictatorship" of 2044 (para. 21), is he predicting a revolution and a dictatorship in those years? If not, what role do his references to the fu-ture play in his overall argument?

W. H. Auden

Wystan Hugh Auden (1907–1973) was born in York, England, and edu-cated at Oxford University. In the 1930s his witty left-wing poetry earned him wide acclaim as the leading poet of his generation. In 1939 he came to the United States, becoming a citizen in 1946, though he returned to En-gland for his last years.

Much of Auden's poetry is characterized by a combination of colloquial diction and technical dexterity. The poem reprinted here was originally published in 1940.

The Unknown Citizen

(To JS/07/M/378
This Marble Monument
Is Erected by the State)

He was found by the Bureau of Statistics to be
One against whom there was no official complaint,
And all the reports on his conduct agree
That, in the modern sense of an old-fashioned word, he was a saint,
For in everything he did he served the Greater Community.   5
Except for the War till the day he retired
He worked in a factory and never got fired,
But satisfied his employers, Fudge Motors Inc.
Yet he wasn't a scab or odd in his views,
For his Union reports that he paid his dues,   10
(Our report on his Union shows it was sound)
And our Social Psychology workers found
That he was popular with his mates and liked a drink.
The Press are convinced that he bought a paper every day
And that his reactions to advertisements were normal in every way.   15
Policies taken out in his name prove that he was fully insured,
And his Health-card shows he was once in hospital but left it cured.
Both Producers Research and High-Grade Living declare
He was fully sensible to the advantages of the Installment Plan
And had everything necessary to the Modern Man,   20
A phonograph, radio, a car and a frigidaire.
Our researches into Public Opinion are content
That he held the proper opinions for the time of year;
When there was peace, he was for peace; when there was war, he went.
He was married and added five children to the population,   25
Which our Eugenist says was the right number for a parent of his
    generation,
And our teachers report that he never interfered with their education.
Was he free? Was he happy? The question is absurd:
Had anything been wrong, we should certainly have heard.

Topics for Critical Thinking and Writing

1. Who is the narrator in Auden's poem, and on what sort of occasion is he
   speaking? How do you know?

2. France, Great Britain, and the United States all have monuments to "The Unknown" (formerly "The Unknown Soldier"). How is Auden's proposed monument like and unlike these war memorials?

3. The poem ends by asking "Was he free? Was he happy?" and the questions are dismissed summarily. Is that because the answers are so obvious? What answers (obvious or subtle) do you think the poem offers to these questions?

4. Evaluate the poem, making clear the reasons behind your evaluation. (On literary evaluations, see pp. 340–43.)

5. If you have read the selection from Thomas More's *Utopia* (p. 632), write an essay of 500 to 750 words—in More's voice—setting forth More's response to Auden's poem.

Langston Hughes

Langston Hughes (1902–1967), an African American writer, was born in Joplin, Missouri, but after his parents were divorced he lived for a while with his grandmother in Lawrence, Kansas, then in Cleveland, and then for fifteen months in Mexico with his father. He returned to the United States in 1921 and spent a year at Columbia University, served as a merchant seaman, and worked in a Paris nightclub, where he showed some of his poems to Dr. Alain Locke, a strong advocate of African American literature. Encouraged by Locke, when Hughes returned to the United States he studied at the University of Pennsylvania and Lincoln University, where he earned a bachelor's degree. He continued to write, publishing fiction, plays, essays, and biographies; he also founded theaters, gave public readings, and was, in short, a highly visible presence.

Esquire magazine first published an abridged version of "Let America Be America Again" in 1936.

Let America Be America Again

Let America be America again.
Let it be the dream it used to be.
Let it be the pioneer on the plain
Seeking a home where he himself is free.

(America never was America to me.)   5

Let America be the dream the dreamers dreamed—
Let it be that great strong land of love
Where never kings connive nor tyrants scheme
That any man be crushed by one above.

(It never was America to me.)   10

O, let my land be a land where Liberty
Is crowned with no false patriotic wreath,
But opportunity is real, and life is free,
Equality is in the air we breathe.

(There's never been equality for me,   15
Nor freedom in this "homeland of the free.")

Say, who are you that mumbles in the dark?
And who are you that draws your veil across the stars?

I am the poor white, fooled and pushed apart,
I am the Negro bearing slavery's scars.   20
I am the red man driven from the land,
I am the immigrant clutching the hope I seek—
And finding only the same old stupid plan
Of dog eat dog, of mighty crush the weak.

I am the young man, full of strength and hope,   25
Tangled in that ancient endless chain
Of profit, power, gain, of grab the land!
Of grab the gold! Of grab the ways of satisfying need!
Of work the men! Of take the pay!
Of owning everything for one's own greed!   30

I am the farmer, bondsman to the soil.
I am the worker sold to the machine.
I am the Negro, servant to you all.
I am the people, humble, hungry, mean—
Hungry yet today despite the dream.   35
Beaten yet today—O, Pioneers!
I am the man who never got ahead,
The poorest worker bartered through the years.

Yet I'm the one who dreamt our basic dream
In that Old World while still a serf of kings,   40
Who dreamt a dream so strong, so brave, so true,
That even yet its mighty daring sings
In every brick and stone, in every furrow turned
That's made America the land it has become.
O, I'm the man who sailed those early seas   45
In search of what I meant to be my home—
For I'm the one who left dark Ireland's shore,
And Poland's plain, and England's grassy lea,
And torn from Black Africa's strand I came
To build a "homeland of the free."   50

The free?

Who said the free? Not me?
Surely not me? The millions on relief today?
The millions shot down when we strike?
The millions who have nothing for our pay?   55
For all the dreams we've dreamed
And all the songs we've sung
And all the hopes we've held
And all the flags we've hung,
The millions who have nothing for our pay—   60
Except the dream that's almost dead today.

O, let America be America again—
The land that never has been yet—
And yet must be—the land where *every* man is free.
The land that's mine—the poor man's, Indian's, Negro's, ME—   65
Who made America,
Whose sweat and blood, whose faith and pain,
Whose hand at the foundry, whose plow in the rain,
Must bring back our mighty dream again.

Sure, call me any ugly name you choose—   70
The steel of freedom does not stain.
From those who live like leeches on the people's lives,
We must take back our land again,
America!

O, yes,   75
I say it plain,
America never was America to me,
And yet I swear this oath—
America will be!

Out of the rack and ruin of our gangster death,   80
The rape and rot of graft, and stealth, and lies,
We, the people, must redeem
The land, the mines, the plants, the rivers.
The mountains and the endless plain—
All, all the stretch of these great green states—   85
And make America again!

Topics for Critical Thinking and Writing

1. Hughes says in line 1, "Let America be America again," but do you suppose America ever was what he seems to assume that it once was? For instance, might not his "pioneer" (line 3) have been a sexist and a racist? Or is it evident that contemporary society is morally inferior to early American society?

2. In line 24 Hughes speaks of a system "of dog eat dog," where the "mighty crush the weak," and in line 27 he speaks of a system of "profit, power, gain, of grab the land." Do you believe that this charge can be lodged today against our system of capitalism? Explain.

3. When *Esquire* magazine bought the poem, it bought only the first fifty lines. Why do you suppose the magazine declined to publish the remainder? Because the latter part is less good as poetry? Because it is too radical? In an essay of 500 words compare the two versions (lines 1–50 and 1–86), and indicate which version you would publish if you were an editor today and why.

Ursula K. Le Guin

Ursula K. Le Guin was born in 1929 in Berkeley, California, the daughter of a distinguished mother (Theodora Kroeber, a folklorist) and father (Alfred L. Kroeber, an anthropologist). After graduating from Radcliffe College, she earned a master's degree at Columbia University; in 1952 she held a Fulbright Fellowship for study in Paris, where she met and married Charles Le Guin, a historian. She began writing in earnest while bringing up three children. Although her work is most widely known to buffs of science fiction, because it usually has larger moral or political dimensions it interests many other readers who normally do not care for sci-fi.

Le Guin has said that she was prompted to write the following story by a remark she encountered in William James's "The Moral Philosopher and the Moral Life." James suggests there that if millions of people could be "kept permanently happy on the one simple condition that a certain lost soul on the far-off edge of things should lead a life of lonely torment," our moral sense "would make us immediately feel" it would be "hideous" to accept such a bargain. This story first appeared in New Dimensions 3 *(1973).*

The Ones Who Walk Away from Omelas

With a clamor of bells that set the swallows soaring, the Festival of Summer came to the city Omelas, bright-towered by the sea. The rigging of the boats in harbor sparkled with flags. In the streets between houses with red roofs and painted walls, between old moss-grown gardens and under avenues of trees, past great parks and public buildings, processions moved. Some were decorous: old people in long stiff robes of mauve and gray, grave master workmen, quiet, merry women carrying their babies and chatting as they walked. In other streets the music beat faster, a shimmering of gong and tambourine, and the people went dancing, the procession was a dance. Children dodged in and out, their high calls rising like the swallows' crossing flights over the music and the singing. All the processions wound towards the north side of the city, where on the great water-meadow called the Green Fields boys and girls, naked in the bright air, with mudstained feet and ankles and long, lithe arms, exercised their restive horses before the race. The horses wore no gear at all but a halter without bit. Their manes were braided with streamers of silver, gold, and green. They flared their nostrils and pranced and boasted to one another; they were vastly excited, the horse being the only animal who has adopted our ceremonies as his own. Far off to the north and west the mountains stood up half encircling Omelas on her bay. The air of morning was so clear that the snow still crowning the Eighteen Peaks burned with white-gold fire across the miles of sunlit air, under the dark blue of the sky. There was just enough wind to make the banners that marked the racecourse snap and flutter now and then. In the silence of the broad green meadows one could hear the music winding through the city streets, farther and nearer and ever approaching, a cheerful faint sweetness of the air that from time to time trembled and gathered together and broke out into the great joyous clanging of the bells.

Joyous! How is one to tell about joy? How describe the citizens of Omelas?

They were not simple folk, you see, though they were happy. But we do not say the words of cheer much any more. All smiles have become archaic. Given a description such as this one tends to make certain assumptions. Given a description such as this one tends to look next for the King, mounted on a splendid stallion and surrounded by his noble knights, or perhaps in a golden litter borne by great-muscled slaves. But there was no king. They did not use swords, or keep slaves. They were not barbarians. I do not know the rules and laws of their society, but I suspect that they were singularly few. As they did without monarchy and slavery, so they also got on without the stock exchange, the advertisement, the secret police, and the bomb. Yet I repeat that these were not simple folk, not dulcet shepherds, noble savages, bland utopians. They were not less complex than us. The trouble is that we have a bad habit, encouraged by pedants and sophisticates, of considering happiness as something rather stupid. Only pain is intellectual, only evil interesting. This is the treason of the artist: a refusal to admit the banality of evil and the terrible boredom of pain. If you can't lick 'em, join 'em. If it hurts, repeat it. But to praise despair is to condemn delight, to embrace violence is to lose hold of everything else. We have almost lost hold, we can no longer describe a happy man, nor make any celebration of joy. How can I tell you about the people of Omelas? They were not naïve and happy children—though their children were, in fact, happy. They were mature, intelligent, passionate adults whose lives were not wretched. O miracle! But I wish I could describe it better. I wish I could convince you. Omelas sounds in my words like a city in a fairy tale, long ago and far away, once upon a time. Perhaps it would be best if you imagined it as your own fancy bids, assuming it will rise to the occasion, for certainly I cannot suit you all. For instance, how about technology? I think that there would be no cars or helicopters in and above the streets; this follows from the fact that the people of Omelas are happy people. Happiness is based on a just discrimination of what is necessary, what is neither necessary nor destructive, and what is destructive. In the middle category, however—that of the unnecessary but undestructive, that of comfort, luxury, exuberance, etc.—they could perfectly well have central heating, subway trains, washing machines, and all kinds of marvelous devices not yet invented here, floating light-sources, fuelless power, a cure for the common cold. Or they could have none of that: it doesn't matter. As you like it. I incline to think that people from towns up and down the coast have been coming in to Omelas during the last days before the Festival on very fast little trains and double-decked trams, and that the train station of Omelas is actually the handsomest building in town, though plainer than the magnificent Farmers' Market. But even granted trains, I fear that Omelas so far strikes some of you as goody-goody. Smiles, bells, parades, horses, bleh. If so, please add an orgy. If an orgy would help, don't hesitate. Let us not, however, have temples from which issue beautiful nude priests and priestesses already half in ecstasy and ready to copulate with any man or woman, lover or stranger, who desires union with the deep godhead of the blood, although that was my first idea. But really it would be better not to have any temples in Omelas—at least, not manned temples. Religion yes, clergy no. Surely the beautiful nudes can just wander about, offering themselves like divine soufflés to the hunger of the needy and the rapture of the flesh. Let them join the processions. Let tambourines be struck above the copulations, and the glory of desire be proclaimed upon the gongs, and (a not unimportant point) let the offspring of these delightful rituals be beloved and looked after by all. One thing I know there is none of in Omelas is guilt. But what else should there be? I thought that first there were no drugs, but that is puritanical. For those who like it, the faint insistent sweetness of *drooz* may perfume the ways of the city, *drooz* which first brings a great lightness and brilliance to the mind and limbs, and then after some hours a dreamy languor, and wonderful visions at last of the very arcana and inmost secrets of the Universe, as well as exciting the pleasure of sex beyond all belief; and it is not habit-forming. For more modest tastes I think there ought to be beer. What else, what else belongs in the joyous city? The sense of victory, surely, the celebration of courage. But as we did without clergy, let us do without soldiers. The joy built upon successful slaughter is not the right kind of joy; it will not do; it is fearful and it is trivial. A boundless and generous contentment, a magnanimous triumph felt not against some outer enemy but in communion with the finest and fairest in the souls of all men everywhere and the splendor of the world's summer: this is what swells the hearts of the people of Omelas, and the victory they celebrate is that of life. I really don't think many of them need to take *drooz*.

Most of the processions have reached the Green Fields by now. A marvelous smell of cooking goes forth from the red and blue tents of the provisioners. The faces of small children are amiably sticky; in the benign grey beard of a man a couple of crumbs of rich pastry are entangled. The youths and girls have mounted their horses and are beginning to group around the starting line of the course. An old woman, small, fat, and laughing, is passing out flowers from a basket, and tall young men wear her flowers in their shining hair. A child of nine or ten sits at the edge of the crowd, alone, playing on a wooden flute. People pause to listen, and they smile, but they do not speak to him, for he never ceases playing and never sees them, his dark eyes wholly rapt in the sweet, thin magic of the tune.

He finishes, and slowly lowers his hands holding the wooden flute.   5

As if that little private silence were the signal, all at once a trumpet sounds from the pavilion near the starting line: imperious, melancholy, piercing. The horses rear on their slender legs, and some of them neigh in answer. Sober-faced, the young riders stroke the horses' necks and soothe them, whispering, "Quiet, quiet, there my beauty, my hope. . . ." They begin to form in rank along the starting line. The crowds along the racecourse are like a field of grass and flowers in the wind. The Festival of Summer has begun.

Do you believe? Do you accept the festival, the city, the joy? No? Then let me describe one more thing.

In a basement under one of the beautiful public buildings of Omelas, or perhaps in the cellar of one of its spacious private homes, there is a room. It has one locked door, and no window. A little light seeps in dustily between cracks in the boards, secondhand from a cobwebbed window somewhere across the cellar. In one corner of the little room a couple of mops, with stiff, clotted, foul-smelling heads, stand near a rusty bucket. The floor is dirt, a little damp to the touch, as cellar dirt usually is. The room is about three paces long and two wide: a mere broom closet or disused tool room. In the room a child is sitting. It could be a boy or a girl. It looks about six, but actually is nearly ten. It is feeble-minded. Perhaps it was born defective, or perhaps it has become imbecile through fear, malnutrition, and neglect. It picks its nose and occasionally fumbles vaguely with its toes or genitals, as it sits hunched in the corner farthest from the bucket and the two mops. It is afraid of the mops. It finds them horrible. It shuts its eyes, but it knows the mops are still standing there; and the door is locked; and nobody will come. The door is always locked; and nobody ever comes, except that sometimes—the child has no understanding of time or interval—sometimes the door rattles terribly and opens, and a person, or several people, are there. One of them may come in and kick the child to make it stand up. The others never come close, but peer in at it with frightened, disgusted eyes. The food bowl and the water jug are hastily filled, the door is locked, the eyes disappear. The people at the door never say anything, but the child, who has not always lived in the tool room, and can remember sunlight and its mother's voice, sometimes speaks. "I will be good," it says. "Please let me out. I will be good!" They never answer. The child used to scream for help at night, and cry a good deal, but now it only makes a kind of whining, "eh-haa, eh-haa," and it speaks less and less often. It is so thin there are no calves to its legs; its belly protrudes; it lives on a half-bowl of corn meal and grease a day. It is naked. Its buttocks and thighs are a mass of festered sores, as it sits in its own excrement continually.

They all know it is there, all the people of Omelas. Some of them have come to see it, others are content merely to know it is there. They all know that it has to be there. Some of them understand why, and some do not, but they all understand that their happiness, the beauty of their city, the tenderness of their friendships, the health of their children, the wisdom of their scholars, the skill of their makers, even the abundance of their harvest and the kindly weathers of their skies, depend wholly on this child's abominable misery.

This is usually explained to children when they are between eight 10 and twelve, whenever they seem capable of understanding; and most of those who come to see the child are young people, though often enough an adult comes, or comes back, to see the child. No matter how well the matter has been explained to them, these young spectators are always shocked and sickened at the sight. They feel disgust, which they had thought themselves superior to. They feel anger, outrage, impotence, despite all the explanations. They would like to do something for the child. But there is nothing they can do. If the child were brought up into the sunlight out of that vile place, if it were cleaned and fed and comforted, that would be a good thing, indeed; but if it were done, in that day and hour all the prosperity and beauty and delight of Omelas would wither and be destroyed. Those are the terms. To exchange all the goodness and grace of every life in Omelas for that single, small improvement: to throw away the happiness of thousands for the chance of the happiness of one: that would be to let guilt within the walls indeed.

The terms are strict and absolute; there may not even be a kind word spoken to the child.

Often the young people go home in tears, or in a tearless rage, when they have seen the child and faced this terrible paradox. They may brood over it for weeks or years. But as time goes on they begin to realize that even if the child could be released, it would not get much good of its freedom: a little vague pleasure of warmth and food, no doubt, but little more. It is too degraded and imbecile to know any real joy. It has been afraid too long ever to be free of fear. Its habits are too uncouth for it to respond to humane treatment. Indeed, after so long it would probably be wretched without walls about it to protect it, and darkness for its eyes, and its own excrement to sit in. Their tears at the bitter injustice dry when they begin to perceive the terrible justice of reality, and to accept it. Yet it is their tears and anger, the trying of their generosity and the acceptance of their helplessness, which are perhaps the true source of the splendor of their lives. Theirs is no vapid, irresponsible happiness. They know that they, like the child, are not free. They know compassion. It is the existence of the child, and their knowledge of its existence, that makes possible the nobility of their architecture, the poignancy of their music, the profundity of their science. It is because of the child that they are so gentle with children. They know that if the wretched one were not there snivelling in the dark, the other one, the flute-player, could make no joyful music as the young riders line up in their beauty for the race in the sunlight of the first morning of summer.

Now do you believe in them? Are they not more credible? But there is one more thing to tell, and this is quite incredible.

At times one of the adolescent girls or boys who go to see the child does not go home to weep or rage, does not, in fact, go home at all. Sometimes also a man or woman much older falls silent for a day or two, and then leaves home. These people go out into the street, and walk down the street alone. They keep walking, and walk straight out of the city of Omelas, through the beautiful gates. They keep walking across the farmlands of Omelas. Each one goes alone, youth or girl, man or woman. Night falls; the traveler must pass down village streets, between the houses with yellow-lit windows, and on out into the darkness of the fields. Each alone, they go west or north, towards the mountains. They go on. They leave Omelas, they walk ahead into the darkness, and they do not come back. The place they go towards is a place even less imaginable to most of us than the city of happiness. I cannot describe it at all. It is possible that it does not exist. But they seem to know where they are going, the ones who walk away from Omelas.

Topics for Critical Thinking and Writing

1. Summarize the point of the story—not the plot, but what the story adds up to, what the author is getting at. Next, set forth what you would probably do (and why) if you were born in Omelas.

2. Consider the narrator's assertion (para. 3) that happiness "is based on a just discrimination of what is necessary."

3. Do you think the story implies a criticism of contemporary American society? Explain.

27

How Free Is the Will
of the Individual
within Society?

Plato

Plato (427–347 B.C.), an Athenian aristocrat by birth, was the student of one great philosopher (Socrates) and the teacher of another (Aristotle). His legacy of more than two dozen dialogues—imaginary discussions between Socrates and one or more other speakers, usually young Athenians—has been of such influence that the whole of Western philosophy can be characterized, A. N. Whitehead wrote, as "a series of footnotes to Plato." Plato's interests encompassed the full range of topics in philosophy: ethics, politics, logic, metaphysics, epistemology, aesthetics, psychology, and education.

The selection reprinted here, Crito, *is the third of four dialogues telling the story of the final days of Socrates (469–399 B.C.). The first in the sequence,* Euthyphro, *portrays Socrates in his typical role, questioning someone about his beliefs (in this case, the young aristocrat, Euthyphro). The discussion is focused on the nature of piety, but the conversation breaks off before a final answer is reached—perhaps none is possible—because Socrates is on his way to stand trial before the Athenian assembly. He has been charged with "preaching false gods" (heresy) and "corrupting the youth" by causing them to doubt or disregard the wisdom of their elders. (How faithful to any actual event or discussion* Euthyphro *and Plato's other Socratic dialogues really are, scholars cannot say with assurance.)*

In Apology, *the second dialogue in the sequence, Plato (who remains entirely in the background, as he does in all the dialogues) recounts Socrates' public reply to the charges against him. During the speech, Socrates explains his life, reminding his fellow citizens that if he is (as the oracle had pronounced) "the wisest of men," then it is only because he knows that he doesn't know what others believe or pretend they do know. The dialogue ends with Socrates being found guilty and duly sentenced to death.*

The third in the series is Crito, *but we will postpone comment on it for a moment, and glance at the fourth dialogue,* Phaedo, *in which Plato portrays Socrates' final philosophical discussion. The topic, appropriately, is whether the soul is immortal. It ends with Socrates, in the company of his closest friends, bidding them a last farewell and drinking the fatal cup of hemlock.*

Crito, the whole text of which is reprinted here, is the debate provoked by Crito, an old friend and admirer of Socrates. He visits Socrates in prison and urges him to escape while he still has the chance. After all, Crito argues, the guilty verdict was wrong and unfair, few Athenians really want to have Socrates put to death, his family and friends will be distraught, and so forth. Socrates will not have it. He patiently but firmly examines each of Crito's arguments and explains why it would be wrong to follow his advice.

Plato's Crito thus ranks with Sophocles' tragedy Antigone as one of the first explorations in Western literature of the perennial theme of our responsibility for obeying laws that challenge our conscientious moral convictions. Antigone concludes that she must disobey the law of Creon, tyrant of Thebes; Socrates concludes that he must obey the law of democratic Athens.

In Crito, we have not only a superb illustration of Socratic dialogue and argument, but also a portrait of a virtuous thinker at the end of a long life, reflecting on its course and on the moral principles that have guided him. We see Socrates living an "examined life," the only life he thought was worth living.

Crito

(**SCENE:** *A room in the State prison at Athens in the year 399 B.C. The time is half an hour before dawn, and the room would be almost dark but for the light of a little oil lamp. There is a pallet bed against the back wall. At the head of it a small table supports the lamp; near the foot of it Crito is sitting patiently on a stool. He is an old man, kindly, practical, simple-minded; at present he is suffering from acute emotional strain. On the bed lies Socrates asleep. He stirs, yawns, opens his eyes and sees Crito.)*

SOCRATES: Here already, Crito? Surely it is still early?

CRITO: Indeed it is.

SOCRATES: About what time?

CRITO: Just before dawn.

SOCRATES: I wonder that the warder paid any attention to you.   5

CRITO: He is used to me now, Socrates, because I come here so often; besides, he is under some small obligation to me.

SOCRATES: Have you only just come, or have you been here for long?

CRITO: Fairly long.

SOCRATES: Then why didn't you wake me at once, instead of sitting by my bed so quietly?

CRITO: I wouldn't dream of such a thing, Socrates. I only wish I were   10
not so sleepless and depressed myself. I have been wondering at you, because I saw how comfortably you were sleeping; and I deliberately didn't wake you because I wanted you to go on being as comfortable as you could. I have often felt before in the course of my life how fortunate you are in your disposition, but I feel it more than ever now in your present misfortune when I see how easily and placidly you put up with it.

SOCRATES: Well, really, Crito, it would be hardly suitable for a man of my age to resent having to die.

CRITO: Other people just as old as you are get involved in these misfortunes, Socrates, but their age doesn't keep them from resenting it when they find themselves in your position.

SOCRATES: Quite true. But tell me, why have you come so early?

CRITO: Because I bring bad news, Socrates; not so bad from your point of view, I suppose, but it will be very hard to bear for me and your other friends, and I think that I shall find it hardest of all.

SOCRATES: Why, what is this news? Has the boat come in from Delos— 15 the boat which ends my reprieve when it arrives?[1]

CRITO: It hasn't actually come in yet, but I expect that it will be here today, judging from the report of some people who have just arrived from Sunium and left it there. It's quite clear from their account that it will be here today; and so by tomorrow, Socrates, you will have to—to end your life.

SOCRATES: Well, Crito, I hope that it may be for the best; if the gods will it so, so be it. All the same, I don't think it will arrive today.

CRITO: What makes you think that?

SOCRATES: I will try to explain. I think I am right in saying that I have to die on the day after the boat arrives?

CRITO: That's what the authorities say, at any rate. 20

SOCRATES: Then I don't think it will arrive on this day that is just beginning, but on the day after. I am going by a dream that I had in the night, only a little while ago. It looks as though you were right not to wake me up.

CRITO: Why, what was the dream about?

SOCRATES: I thought I saw a gloriously beautiful woman dressed in white robes, who came up to me and addressed me in these words: "Socrates, to the pleasant land of Phthia on the third day thou shalt come."

CRITO: Your dream makes no sense, Socrates.

SOCRATES: To my mind, Crito, it is perfectly clear. 25

CRITO: Too clear, apparently. But look here, Socrates, it is still not too late to take my advice and escape. Your death means a double calamity for me. I shall not only lose a friend whom I can never possibly replace, but besides a great many people who don't know you and me very well will be sure to think that I let you down, because I could have saved you if I had been willing to spend the money; and what could be more contemptible than to get a name for thinking more of money than of your

---

[1]**Delos . . . arrives** Ordinarily execution was immediately carried out, but the day before Socrates' trial was the first day of an annual ceremony that involved sending a ship to Delos. When the ship was absent—in this case for about a month—executions could not be performed. As Crito goes on to say, Socrates could easily escape, and indeed he could have left the country before being tried. [All notes are the editors'.]

hot polie.

friends? Most people will never believe that it was you who refused to leave this place although we tried our hardest to persuade you.

SOCRATES: But my dear Crito, why should we pay so much attention to what "most people" think? The really reasonable people, who have more claim to be considered, will believe that the facts are exactly as they are.

CRITO: You can see for yourself, Socrates, that one has to think of popular opinion as well. Your present position is quite enough to show that the capacity of ordinary people for causing trouble is not confined to petty annoyances, but has hardly any limits if you once get a bad name with them.

SOCRATES: I only wish that ordinary people *had* unlimited capacity for doing harm; then they might have an unlimited power for doing good; which would be a splendid thing, if it were so. Actually they have neither. They cannot make a man wise or stupid; they simply act at random.

CRITO: Have it that way if you like; but tell me this, Socrates. I hope   30 that you aren't worrying about the possible effects on me and the rest of your friends, and thinking that if you escape we shall have trouble with informers for having helped you to get away, and have to forfeit all our property or pay an enormous fine, or even incur some further punishment? If any idea like that is troubling you, you can dismiss it altogether. We are quite entitled to run that risk in saving you, and even worse, if necessary. Take my advice, and be reasonable.

SOCRATES: All that you say is very much in my mind, Crito, and a great deal more besides.

CRITO: Very well, then, don't let it distress you. I know some people who are willing to rescue you from here and get you out of the country for quite a moderate sum. And then surely you realize how cheap these informers are to buy off; we shan't need much money to settle them; and I think you've got enough of my money for yourself already. And then even supposing that in your anxiety for my safety you feel that you oughtn't to spend my money, there are these foreign gentlemen staying in Athens who are quite willing to spend theirs. One of them, Simmias of Thebes, has actually brought the money with him for this very purpose; and Cebes and a number of others are quite ready to do the same. So as I say, you mustn't let any fears on these grounds make you slacken your efforts to escape; and you mustn't feel any misgivings about what you said at your trial, that you wouldn't know what to do with yourself if you left this country. Wherever you go, there are plenty of places where you will find a welcome; and if you choose to go to Thessaly, I have friends there who will make much of you and give you complete protection, so that no one in Thessaly can interfere with you.

Besides, Socrates, I don't even feel that it is right for you to try to do what you are doing, throwing away your life when you might save it.

You are doing your best to treat yourself in exactly the same way as your enemies would, or rather did, when they wanted to ruin you. What is more, it seems to me that you are letting your sons down too. You have it in your power to finish their bringing up and education, and instead of that you are proposing to go off and desert them, and so far as you are concerned they will have to take their chance. And what sort of chance are they likely to get? The sort of thing that usually happens to orphans when they lose their parents. Either one ought not to have children at all, or one ought to see their upbringing and education through to the end. It strikes me that you are taking the line of least resistance, whereas you ought to make the choice of a good man and a brave one, considering that you profess to have made goodness your object all through life. Really, I am ashamed, both on your account and on ours your friends'; it will look as though we had played something like a coward's part all through this affair of yours. First, there was the way you came into court when it was quite unnecessary—that was the first act; than there was the conduct of the defense—that was the second; and finally, to complete the farce, we get this situation, which makes it appear that we have let you slip out of our hands through some lack of courage and enterprise on our part, because we didn't save you, and you didn't save yourself, when it would have been quite possible and practicable, if we had been any use at all.

There, Socrates; if you aren't careful, besides the suffering there will be all this disgrace for you and us to bear. Come, make up your mind. Really it's too late for that now; you ought to have it made up already. There is no alternative; the whole thing must be carried through during this coming night. If we lose any more time, it can't be done, it will be too late. I appeal to you, Socrates, on every ground; take my advice and please don't be unreasonable!

SOCRATES: My dear Crito, I appreciate your warm feelings very 35 much—that is, assuming that they have some justification; if not, the stronger they are, the harder they will be to deal with. Very well, then; we must consider whether we ought to follow your advice or not. You know that this is not a new idea of mine; it has always been my nature never to accept advice from any of my friends unless reflection shows that it is the best course that reason offers. I cannot abandon the principles which I used to hold in the past simply because this accident has happened to me; they seem to me to be much as they were, and I respect and regard the same principles now as before. So unless we can find better principles on this occasion, you can be quite sure that I shall not agree with you; not even if the power of the people conjures up fresh hordes of bogies to terrify our childish minds, by subjecting us to chains and executions and confiscations of our property.

Well, then, how can we consider the question most reasonably? Suppose that we begin by reverting to this view which you hold about people's opinions. Was it always right to argue that some opinions should be taken seriously but not others? Or was it always wrong? Perhaps it was right before the question of my death arose, but now we can see clearly that it was a mistaken persistence in a point of view which was really irresponsible nonsense. I should like very much to inquire into this problem, Crito, with your help, and to see whether the argument will appear in any different light to me now that I am in this position, or whether it will remain the same; and whether we shall dismiss it or accept it.

doxa (greek)

Serious thinkers, I believe, have always held some such view as the one which I mentioned just now: that some of the opinions which people entertain should be respected, and others should not. Now I ask you, Crito, don't you think that this is a sound principle?—You are safe from the prospect of dying tomorrow, in all human probability; and you are not likely to have your judgment upset by this impending calamity. Consider, then; don't you think that this is a sound enough principle, that one should not regard all the opinions that people hold, but only some and not others? What do you say? Isn't that a fair statement?

CRITO: Yes, it is.

SOCRATES: In other words, one should regard the good ones and not the bad?

CRITO: Yes.

SOCRATES: The opinions of the wise being good, and the opinions of the foolish bad?

CRITO: Naturally.

SOCRATES: To pass on, then: What do you think of the sort of illustration that I used to employ? When a man is in training, and taking it seriously, does he pay attention to all praise and criticism and opinion indiscriminately, or only when it comes from the one qualified person, the actual doctor or trainer?

one who knows

CRITO: Only when it comes from the one qualified person.

SOCRATES: Then he should be afraid of the criticism and welcome the praise of the one qualified person, but not those of the general public.

CRITO: Obviously.

SOCRATES: So he ought to regulate his actions and exercises and eating and drinking by the judgment of his instructor, who has expert knowledge, rather than by the opinions of the rest of the public.

CRITO: Yes, that is so.

SOCRATES: Very well. Now if he disobeys the one man and disregards his opinion and commendations, and pays attention to the advice of the many who have no expert knowledge, surely he will suffer some bad effect?

CRITO: Certainly.

SOCRATES: And what is this bad effect? Where is it produced?—I mean, in what part of the disobedient person?

CRITO: His body, obviously; that is what suffers.

pleasant trust

40

45

50

SOCRATES: Very good. Well now, tell me, Crito—we don't want to go through all the examples one by one—does this apply as a general rule, and above all to the sort of actions which we are trying to decide about: just and unjust, honorable and dishonorable, good and bad? Ought we to be guided and intimidated by the opinion of the many or by that of the one—assuming that there is someone with expert knowledge? Is it true that we ought to respect and fear this person more than all the rest put together; and that if we do not follow his guidance we shall spoil and mutilate that part of us which, as we used to say, is improved by right conduct and destroyed by wrong? Or is this all nonsense?

CRITO: No, I think it is true, Socrates.

SOCRATES: Then consider the next step. There is a part of us which is 55 improved by healthy actions and ruined by unhealthy ones. If we spoil it by taking the advice of nonexperts, will life be worth living when this part is once ruined? The part I mean is the body; do you accept this?

CRITO: Yes.

SOCRATES: Well, is life worth living with a body which is worn out and ruined by health?

CRITO: Certainly not.

SOCRATES: What about the part of us which is mutilated by wrong actions and benefited by right ones? Is life worth living with this part ruined? Or do we believe that this part of us, whatever it may be, in which right and wrong operate, is of less importance than the body?

CRITO: Certainly not. 60

SOCRATES: It is really more precious?

CRITO: Much more.

SOCRATES: In that case, my dear fellow, what we ought to consider is not so much what people in general will say about us but how we stand with the expert in right and wrong, the one authority, who represents the actual truth. So in the first place your proposition is not correct when you say that we should consider popular opinion in questions of what is right and honorable and good, or the opposite. Of course one might object "All the same, the people have the power to put us to death."

CRITO: No doubt about that! Quite true, Socrates; it is a possible objection.

SOCRATES: But so far as I can see, my dear fellow, the argument 65 which we have just been through is quite unaffected by it. At the same time I should like you to consider whether we are still satisfied on this point: that the really important thing is not to live, but to live well.

CRITO: Why, yes.

SOCRATES: And that to live well means the same thing as to live honorably or rightly?

CRITO: Yes.

SOCRATES: Then in the light of this agreement we must consider whether or not it is right for me to try to get away without an official discharge. If it turns out to be right, we must make the attempt; if not, we must let it drop. As for the considerations you raise about expense and reputation and bringing up children, I am afraid, Crito, that they represent the reflections of the ordinary public, who put people to death, and would bring them back to life if they could, with equal indifference to reason. Our real duty, I fancy, since the argument leads that way, is to consider one question only, the one which we raised just now: Shall we be acting rightly in paying money and showing gratitude to these people who are going to rescue me, and in escaping or arranging the escape ourselves, or shall we really be acting wrongly in doing all this? If it becomes clear that such conduct is wrong, I cannot help thinking that the question whether we are sure to die, or to suffer any other ill effect for that matter, if we stand our ground and take no action, ought not to weigh with us at all in comparison with the risk of doing what is wrong.

CRITO: I agree with what you say, Socrates; but I wish you would 70 consider what we ought to *do*.

SOCRATES: Let us look at it together, my dear fellow; and if you can challenge any of my arguments, do so and I will listen to you; but if you can't, be a good fellow and stop telling me over and over again that I ought to leave this place without official permission. I am very anxious to obtain your approval before I adopt the course which I have in mind; I don't want to act against your convictions. Now give your attention to the starting point of this inquiry—I hope that you will be satisfied with my way of stating it—and try to answer my questions to the best of your judgment.

CRITO: Well, I will try.

SOCRATES: Do we say that one must never willingly do wrong, or does it depend upon circumstance? Is it true, as we have often agreed before, that there is no sense in which wrongdoing is good or honorable? Or have we jettisoned all our former convictions in these last few days? Can you and I at our age, Crito, have spent all these years in serious discussions without realizing that we were no better than a pair of children? Surely the truth is just what we have always said. Whatever the popular view is, and whether the alternative is pleasanter than the present one or even harder to bear, the fact remains that to do wrong is in every sense bad and dishonorable for the person who does it. Is that our view, or not?

CRITO: Yes, it is.

SOCRATES: Then in no circumstances must one do wrong.   75

CRITO: No.

SOCRATES: In that case one must not even do wrong when one is wronged, which most people regard as the natural course.

CRITO: Apparently not.

SOCRATES: Tell me another thing, Crito: Ought one to do injuries or not?

CRITO: Surely not, Socrates.   80

SOCRATES: And tell me: Is it right to do an injury in retaliation, as most people believe, or not?

CRITO: No, never.

SOCRATES: Because, I suppose, there is no difference between injuring people and wronging them.

CRITO: Exactly.   *passive resistance*

SOCRATES: So one ought not to return a wrong or an injury to any   85 person, whatever the provocation is. Now be careful, Crito, that in making these single admissions you do not end by admitting something contrary to your real beliefs. I know that there are and always will be few people who think like this; and consequently between those who do think so and those who do not there can be no agreement on principle; they must always feel contempt when they observe one another's decisions. I want even you to consider very carefully whether you share my views and agree with me, and whether we can proceed with our discussion from the established hypothesis that it is never right to do a wrong or return a wrong or defend one's self against injury by retaliation; or whether you dissociate yourself from any share in this view as a basis for discussion. I have held it for a long time, and still hold it; but if you have formed any other opinion, say so and tell me what it is. If, on the other hand, you stand by what we have said, listen to my next point.

CRITO: Yes, I stand by it and agree with you. Go on.

SOCRATES: Well, here is my next point, or rather question. Ought one to fulfill all one's agreements, provided that they are right, or break them?

CRITO: One ought to fulfill them.

SOCRATES: Then consider the logical consequence. If we leave this place without first persuading the State to let us go, are we or are we not doing an injury, and doing it in a quarter where it is least justifiable? Are we or are we not abiding by our just agreements?

CRITO: I can't answer your question, Socrates; I am not clear in my   90 mind.

SOCRATES: Look at it in this way. Suppose that while we were preparing to run away from here (or however one should describe it) the Laws and Constitution of Athens were to come and confront us and ask this question: "Now, Socrates, what are you proposing to do?   *sleepy* Can you deny that by this act which you are contemplating you in-   *slope.* tend, so far as you have the power, to destroy us, the Laws, and the whole State as well? Do you imagine that a city can continue to exist and not be turned upside down, if the legal judgments which are pronounced in it have no force but are nullified and destroyed by private persons?"—how shall we answer this question, Crito, and others of the same kind? There is much that could be said, especially by a professional advocate, to protest against the invalidation of this law which enacts that judgments once pronounced shall be binding. Shall we say "Yes, I do intend to destroy the laws, because the State wronged me by passing a faulty judgment at my trial"? Is this to be our answer, or what?

CRITO: What you have just said, by all means, Socrates.

SOCRATES: Then what supposing the Laws say, "Was there provision for this in the agreement between you and us, Socrates? Or did you undertake to abide by whatever judgments the State pronounced?" If we expressed surprise at such language, they would probably say: "Never mind our language, Socrates, but answer our questions; after all, you are accustomed to the method of question and answer. Come now, what charge do you bring against us and the State, that you are trying to destroy us? Did we not give you life in the first place? Was it not through us that your father married your mother and begot you? Tell us, have you any complaint against those of us Laws that deal with marriage?" "No, none," I should say. "Well, have you any against the laws which deal with children's upbringing and education, such as you had yourself? Are you not grateful to those of us Laws which were instituted for this end, for requiring your father to give you a cultural and physical education?" "Yes," I should say. "Very good. Then since you have been born and brought up and educated, can you deny, in the first place, that you were our child and servant, both you and your ancestors? And if this is so, do you imagine that what is right for us is equally right for you, and that whatever we try to do to you, you are justified in retaliating? You did not have equality of rights with your father, or your employer (supposing that you had had one), to enable you to retaliate; you were not allowed to answer back when you were scolded or to hit back when you were beaten, or to do a great many other things of the same kind. Do you expect to have such license against your country and its laws that if we try to put you to death in the belief that it is right to do so, you on your part will try your hardest to destroy your country and us its Laws in return? And will you, the true devotee of goodness, claim that you are justified in doing so? Are you so wise as to have forgotten that compared with your mother and father and all the rest of your ancestors your country is something far more precious, more venerable, more sacred, and held in greater honor both among gods and among all reasonable men? Do you not realize that you are even more bound to respect and placate the anger of your country than your father's anger? That if you cannot persuade your country you must do whatever it orders, and patiently submit to any punishment that it imposes, whether it be flogging or imprisonment? And if it leads you out to war, to be wounded or killed, you must comply, and it is right that you should do so; you must not give way or retreat or abandon your position. Both in war and in the law courts and everywhere else you must do whatever your city and your country commands, or else persuade it in accordance with universal justice; but violence is a sin even against your parents, and it is a far greater sin against your country"—What shall we say to this, Crito?—that what the Laws say is true, or not?

CRITO: Yes, I think so.

SOCRATES: "Consider, then, Socrates," the Laws would probably con-   95
tinue, "whether it is also true for us to say that what you are now trying to do to us is not right. Although we have brought you into the
world and reared you and educated you, and given you and all your fellow citizens a share in all the good things at our disposal, nevertheless
by the very fact of granting our permission we openly proclaim this
principle: that any Athenian, on attaining to manhood and seeing for
himself the political organization of the State and us its Laws, is permitted, if he is not satisfied with us, to take his property and go away wherever he likes. If any of you chooses to go to one of our colonies, supposing that he should not be satisfied with us and the State, or to
emigrate to any other country, not one of us Laws hinders or prevents
him from going away wherever he likes, without any loss of property.
On the other hand, if any one of you stands his ground when he can
see how we administer justice and the rest of our public organization,
we hold that by so doing he has in fact undertaken to do anything that
we tell him; and we maintain that anyone who disobeys is guilty of
doing wrong on three separate counts: first because we are his parents,
and secondly because we are his guardians; and thirdly because, after
promising obedience, he is neither obeying us nor persuading us to
change our decision if we are at fault in any way; and although all our
orders are in the form of proposals, not of savage commands, and we
give him the choice of either persuading us or doing what we say, he is
actually doing neither. These are the charges, Socrates, to which we say
that you will be liable if you do what you are contemplating; and you
will not be the least culpable of your fellow countrymen, but one of the
most guilty." If I said "Why do you say that?" they would no doubt
pounce upon me with perfect justice and point out that there are very
few people in Athens who have entered into this agreement with them
as explicitly as I have. They would say "Socrates, we have substantial evidence that you are satisfied with us and with the State. You would not
have been so exceptionally reluctant to cross the borders of your country if you had not been exceptionally attached to it. You have never left
the city to attend a festival or for any other purpose, except on some
military expedition; you have never traveled abroad as other people do,
and you have never felt the impulse to acquaint yourself with another
country or constitution; you have been content with us and with our
city. You have definitely chosen us, and undertaken to observe us in all
your activities as a citizen; and as the crowning proof that you are satisfied with our city, you have begotten children in it. Furthermore, even
at the time of your trial you could have proposed the penalty of banishment, if you had chosen to do so; that is, you could have done then
with the sanction of the State what you are now trying to do without it.
But whereas at that time you made a noble show of indifference if you
had to die, and in fact preferred death, as you said, to banishment, now
you show no respect for your earlier professions, and no regard for us,

the Laws, whom you are trying to destroy; you are behaving like the lowest type of menial, trying to run away in spite of the contracts and undertakings by which you agreed to live as a member of our State. Now first answer this question: Are we or are we not speaking the truth when we say that you have undertaken, in deed if not in word, to live your life as a citizen in obedience to us?" What are we to say to that, Crito? Are we not bound to admit it?

CRITO: We cannot help it, Socrates.

SOCRATES: "It is a fact, then," they would say, "that you are breaking covenants and undertakings made with us, although you made them under no compulsion or misunderstanding, and were not compelled to decide in a limited time; you had seventy years in which you could have left the country, if you were not satisfied with us or felt that the agreements were unfair. You did not choose Sparta or Crete—your favorite models of good government—or any other Greek or foreign state; you could not have absented yourself from the city less if you had been lame or blind or decrepit in some other way. It is quite obvious that you stand by yourself above all other Athenians in your affection for this city and for us its Laws;—who would care for a city without laws? And now, after all this, are you not going to stand by your agreement? Yes, you are, Socrates, if you will take our advice; and then you will at least escape being laughed at for leaving the city.

"We invite you to consider what good you will do to yourself or your friends if you commit this breach of faith and stain your conscience. It is fairly obvious that the risk of being banished and either losing their citizenship or having their property confiscated will extend to your friends as well. As for yourself, if you go to one of the neighboring states, such as Thebes or Megara, which are both well governed, you will enter them as an enemy to their constitution[2] and all good patriots will eye you with suspicion as a destroyer of law and order. Incidentally you will confirm the opinion of the jurors who tried you that they gave a correct verdict; a destroyer of laws might very well be supposed to have a destructive influence upon young and foolish human beings. Do you intend, then, to avoid well governed states and the higher forms of human society? And if you do, will life be worth living? Or will you approach these people and have the impudence to converse with them? What arguments will you use, Socrates? The same which you used here, that goodness and integrity, institutions and laws, are the most precious possessions of mankind? Do you not think that Socrates and everything about him will appear in a disreputable light? You certainly ought to think so. But perhaps you will retire from this part of the world and go to Crito's friends in Thessaly? That is the home of indiscipline and laxity, and no doubt they would enjoy hearing the amusing story of how you

---

[2]**as an enemy to their constitution** As a lawbreaker.

managed to run away from prison by arraying yourself in some costume or putting on a shepherd's smock or some other conventional runaway's disguise, and altering your personal appearance. And will no one comment on the fact that an old man of your age, probably with only a short time left to live, should dare to cling so greedily to life, at the price of violating the most stringent laws? Perhaps not, if you avoid irritating anyone. Otherwise, Socrates, you will hear a good many humiliating comments. So you will live as the toady and slave of all the populace, literally 'roistering in Thessaly,' as though you had left this country for Thessaly to attend a banquet there; and where will your discussions about goodness and uprightness be then, we should like to know? But of course you want to live for your children's sake, so that you may be able to bring them up and educate them. Indeed! by first taking them off to Thessaly and making foreigners of them, so that they may have that additional enjoyment? Or if that is not your intention, supposing that they are brought up here with you still alive, will they be better cared for and educated without you, because of course your friends will look after them? Will they look after your children if you go away to Thessaly, and not if you go away to the next world? Surely if those who profess to be your friends are worth anything, you must believe that they would care for them.

"No, Socrates; be advised by us your guardians, and do not think more of your children or of your life or of anything else than you think of what is right; so that when you enter the next world you may have all this to plead in your defense before the authorities there. It seems clear that if you do this thing, neither you nor any of your friends will be the better for it or be more upright or have a cleaner conscience here in this world, nor will it be better for you when you reach the next. As it is, you will leave this place, when you do, as the victim of a wrong done not by us, the Laws, but by your fellow men. But if you leave in that dishonorable way, returning wrong for wrong and evil for evil, breaking your agreements and covenants with us, and injuring those whom you least ought to injure—yourself, your friends, your country, and us—then you will have to face our anger in your lifetime, and in that place beyond when the laws of the other world know that you have tried, so far as you could, to destroy even us their brothers, they will not receive you with a kindly welcome. Do not take Crito's advice, but follow ours."

That, my dear friend Crito, I do assure you, is what I seem to hear them saying, just as a mystic seems to hear the strains of music; and the sound of their arguments rings so loudly in my head that I cannot hear the other side. I warn you that, as my opinion stands at present, it will be useless to urge a different view. However, if you think that you will do any good by it, say what you like.

CRITO: No, Socrates, I have nothing to say.

SOCRATES: Then give it up, Crito, and let us follow this course, since God points out the way.

Topics for Critical Thinking and Writing

1. State as precisely as you can all the arguments Crito uses to try to convince Socrates that he ought to escape. Which of these arguments seems to you to be the best? The worst? Why?

2. Socrates says to Crito, "I cannot abandon the principles which I used to hold in the past simply because this accident [the misfortune of being convicted by the Athenian assembly and then sentenced to death] has happened to me" (para. 35). Does this remark strike you as self-righteous? Stubborn? Smug? Stupid? Explain.

3. Socrates declares that "serious thinkers" have always held the view that "some of the opinions which people entertain should be respected, and others should not" (para. 37). There are two main alternatives to this principle: (a) One should respect *all* the opinions that others hold, and (b) one should respect *none* of the opinions of others. Socrates attacks (a) but he ignores (b).What are his objections to (a)? Do you find them convincing? Can you think of any convincing arguments against (b)?

4. As Socrates shows in his reply to Crito, he seems ready to believe (para. 63) that there are "expert[s] in right and wrong"—that is, persons with expert opinion or even authoritative knowledge on matters of right and wrong conduct—and that their advice should be sought and followed. Do you agree? Consider the thesis that there are no such experts, and write a 500-word essay defending or attacking it.

5. Socrates, as he comments to Crito, believes that "it is never right to do a wrong or return a wrong or defend one's self against injury by retaliation" (para. 85). He does not offer any argument for this thesis in the dialogue (although he does elsewhere). It was a very strange doctrine in his day, and even now it is not generally accepted. Write a 1,000-word essay defending or attacking this thesis.

6. Socrates seems to argue: Because (a) no one ought to do wrong, and because (b) it would injure the state for someone in Socrates' position to escape, because (c) this act would break a "just agreement" between the citizen and his state, therefore (d) no one in Socrates' position should escape. Do you think this argument is valid? If not, what further assumptions would be needed to make it valid? Do you think the argument is sound (that is, both valid and true in all its premises)? If not, explain. If you had to attack premise (b) or (c), which do you think is the more vulnerable, and why?

7. In the imaginary speech by the Laws of Athens to Socrates, especially in paragraph 93, the Laws convey a picture of the supremacy of the state over the individual—and Socrates seems to assent to this picture. Do you? Why, or why not?

8. The Laws (para. 95) claim that if Socrates were to escape, he would be "guilty of doing wrong on three separate counts." What are they? Do you agree with all or any? Why, or why not? Read the essay by Martin Luther King, Jr., "Letter from Birmingham Jail" (p. 717), and decide how King would have responded to the judgment of the Laws of Athens.

9. At the end of their peroration (para. 99), the Laws of Athens say to Socrates: Take your punishment as prescribed, and at your death "you will leave this place . . . as the victim of wrong done not by us, the Laws, but by your fellow men." To what wrong do the Laws allude? Do you agree that it is men and not laws who perpetrated this wrong? If you were in Socrates' position, would it matter to you if you were being wronged not by laws but only by men? Explain.

Samuel Johnson and James Boswell

James Boswell (1740–1795), Scottish lawyer and author, is known chiefly as the author of one of the world's great biographies, The Life of Samuel Johnson, LL.D. *(1791), in which he reports the conversations of England's leading man of letters at the time. Samuel Johnson (1709–1784) was a poet, essayist, and critic of distinction, but he lives chiefly in Boswell's biography; the anecdotes and conversations that Boswell reports are better known than Johnson's own writings.*

We reprint a page from Boswell's Life, *in which Johnson and Boswell, along with a clergyman named Dr. Mayo, discuss prescience (knowledge of actions before they occur). The discussion, which took place on April 15, 1778, begins with Mayo asking Johnson if he has read the writings of Jonathan Edwards (1703–1758), the American theologian who had written on freedom of the will and on grace (usually defined as God's all-powerful gift enabling human beings—all of whom are sinful at birth—to enjoy eternal life).*

Do We Have Free Will?

DR. MAYO (TO DR. JOHNSON): Pray, Sir, have you read Edwards, of New England, on grace?

JOHNSON: No, sir.

BOSWELL: It puzzled me so much as to the freedom of the will, by stating, with wonderful acute ingenuity, our being actuated by a series of motives which we cannot resist, that the only relief I had was to forget it.

MAYO: But he makes the proper distinction between moral and physical necessity.

BOSWELL: Alas, sir, they come both to the same thing. You may be   5
bound as hard by chains when covered by leather, as when the iron appears. The argument for the moral necessity of human actions is always, I observe, fortified by supposing universal prescience to be one of the attributes of the Deity.

JOHNSON: You are surer that you are free, than you are of prescience; you are surer that you can lift up your finger or not as you please, than you are of any conclusion from a deduction of reasoning. But let us consider a little the objection from prescience. It is certain I am either to go home tonight or not; that does not prevent my freedom.

BOSWELL: That it is certain you are *either* to go home or not, does not prevent your freedom; because the liberty of choice between the two is compatible with that certainty. But if *one* of these events be certain *now*, you have no *future* power of volition. If it be certain you are to go home tonight, you *must* go home.

JOHNSON: If I am well acquainted with a man, I can judge with great probability how he will act in any case, without his being restrained by my judging. God may have this probability increased to certainty.

BOSWELL: When it is increased to certainty, freedom ceases, because that cannot be certainly foreknown, which is not certain at the time; but if it be certain at the time, it is a contradiction in terms to maintain that there can be afterwards any *contingency* dependent upon the exercise of will or anything else.

JOHNSON: All theory is against the freedom of the will; all experience   10 for it.

Topics for Critical Thinking and Writing

1. What does Dr. Mayo mean in paragraph 4 by "the proper distinction between moral and physical necessity"? What does Boswell mean in the following paragraph when he says "they come both to the same thing"?

2. Do you think that if "universal prescience" (that is, the ability to predict with certainty everything that we will do) is "one of the attributes of the Deity" (para. 5), then we must lack free will?

3. Johnson observes in the final paragraph that "all theory is against the freedom of the will; all experience for it." Theory of what? Experience of what? Explain in no more than 100 words what Johnson means.

4. Boswell says, "If it be certain you are to go home tonight, you *must* go home" (para. 7). Do you agree? Would Walter Stace (see p. 707)? When Boswell says this, is he implying that in such cases one has no free will? If not, what do you think he means?

George Orwell

George Orwell was the pen name adopted by Eric Blair (1903–1950), an Englishman born in India. Orwell was educated at Eton, in England, but in 1921 he went back to the East and served for five years as a police officer in Burma (now Myanmar). Disillusioned with the colonial imperialism, he returned to Europe, doing odd jobs while writing novels and stories. In 1936 he fought in the Spanish Civil War on the side of the Republicans, an experience he reported in Homage to Catalonia *(1938). His last years were spent writing in England. His best known work probably is the satiric allegory* 1984 *(1949), showing a totalitarian state in which the citizens are perpetu-*

ally under the eye of Big Brother. The following essay is from Shooting an Elephant and Other Essays *(1950).*

Shooting an Elephant

In Moulmein, in Lower Burma, I was hated by large numbers of people—the only time in my life that I have been important enough for this to happen to me. I was sub-divisional police officer of the town, and in an aimless, petty kind of way anti-European feeling was very bitter. No one had the guts to raise a riot, but if a European woman went through the bazaars alone somebody would probably spit betel juice over her dress. As a police officer I was an obvious target and was baited whenever it seemed safe to do so. When a nimble Burman tripped me up on the football field and the referee (another Burman) looked the other way, the crowd yelled with hideous laughter. This happened more than once. In the end the sneering yellow faces of young men that met me everywhere, the insults hooted after me when I was at a safe distance, got badly on my nerves. The young Buddhist priests were the worst of all. There were several thousands of them in the town and none of them seemed to have anything to do except stand on street corners and jeer at Europeans.

All this was perplexing and upsetting. For at that time I had already made up my mind that imperialism was an evil thing and the sooner I chucked up my job and got out of it the better. Theoretically—and secretly, of course—I was all for the Burmese and all against their oppressors, the British. As for the job I was doing, I hated it more bitterly than I can perhaps make clear. In a job like that you see the dirty work of Empire at close quarters. The wretched prisoners huddling in the stinking cages of the lock-ups, the grey, cowed faces of the long-term convicts, the scarred buttocks of the men who had been flogged with bamboos— all these oppressed me with an intolerable sense of guilt. But I could get nothing into perspective. I was young and ill-educated and I had had to think out my problems in the utter silence that is imposed on every Englishman in the East. I did not even know that the British Empire is dying, still less did I know that it is a great deal better than the younger empires that are going to supplant it. All I knew was that I was stuck between my hatred of the empire I served and my rage against the evil-spirited little beasts who tried to make my job impossible. With one part of my mind I thought of the British Raj[1] as an unbreakable tyranny, as something clamped down, in *saecula saeculorum,*[2] upon the will of prostrate peoples; with another part I thought that the greatest joy in the world would be to drive a bayonet into a Buddhist priest's guts. Feelings

---

[1]**British Raj** British imperial government in India and Burma. [All notes are the editors'.]
[2]**in *saecula saeculorum*** Forever.

like these are the normal by-products of imperialism; ask any Anglo-Indian official, if you can catch him off duty.

One day something happened which in a roundabout way was enlightening. It was a tiny incident in itself, but it gave me a better glimpse than I had had before of the real nature of imperialism—the real motives for which despotic governments act. Early one morning the sub-inspector at a police station the other end of the town rang me up on the 'phone and said that an elephant was ravaging the bazaar. Would I please come and do something about it? I did not know what I could do, but I wanted to see what was happening and I got on to a pony and started out. I took my rifle, an old .44 Winchester and much too small to kill an elephant, but I thought the noise might be useful *in terrorem.*[3] Various Burmans stopped me on the way and told me about the elephant's doings. It was not, of course, a wild elephant, but a tame one which had gone "must."[4] It had been chained up, as tame elephants always are when their attack of "must" is due, but on the previous night it had broken its chain and escaped. Its mahout, the only person who could manage it when it was in that state, had set out in pursuit, but had taken the wrong direction and was now twelve hours' journey away, and in the morning the elephant had suddenly reappeared in the town. The Burmese population had no weapons and were quite helpless against it. It had already destroyed somebody's bamboo hut, killed a cow and raided some fruit-stalls and devoured the stock; also it had met the municipal rubbish van and, when the driver jumped out and took to his heels, had turned the van over and inflicted violences upon it.

The Burmese sub-inspector and some Indian constables were waiting for me in the quarter where the elephant had been seen. It was a very poor quarter, a labyrinth of squalid bamboo huts, thatched with palm-leaf, winding all over a steep hillside. I remember that it was a cloudy, stuffy morning at the beginning of the rains. We began questioning the people as to where the elephant had gone and, as usual, failed to get any definite information. That is invariably the case in the East; a story always sounds clear enough at a distance, but the nearer you get to the scene of events the vaguer it becomes. Some of the people said that the elephant had gone in one direction, some said that he had gone in another, some professed not even to have heard of any elephant. I had almost made up my mind that the whole story was a pack of lies, when we heard yells a little distance away. There was a loud, scandalized cry of "Go away, child! Go away this instant!" and an old woman with a switch in her hand came round the corner of a hut, violently shooing away a crowd of naked children. Some more women followed, clicking their tongues and exclaiming; evidently there was something that the children ought not to have seen. I rounded the hut and saw a man's

---

[3]*in terrorem* As a warning.
[4]**"must"** Into sexual heat.

dead body sprawling in the mud. He was an Indian, a black Dravidian coolie, almost naked, and he could not have been dead many minutes. The people said that the elephant had come suddenly upon him round the corner of the hut, caught him with its trunk, put its foot on his back and ground him into the earth. This was the rainy season and the ground was soft, and his face had scored a trench a foot deep and a couple of yards long. He was lying on his belly with arms crucified and head sharply twisted to one side. His face was coated with mud, the eyes wide open, the teeth bared and grinning with an expression of unendurable agony. (Never tell me, by the way, that the dead look peaceful. Most of the corpses I have seen looked devilish.) The friction of the great beast's foot had stripped the skin from his back as neatly as one skins a rabbit. As soon as I saw the dead man I sent an orderly to a friend's house nearby to borrow an elephant rifle. I had already sent back the pony, not wanting it to go mad with fright and throw me if it smelt the elephant.

The orderly came back in a few minutes with a rifle and five cartridges, and meanwhile some Burmans had arrived and told us that the elephant was in the paddy fields below, only a few hundred yards away. As I started forward practically the whole population of the quarter flocked out of the houses and followed me. They had seen the rifle and were all shouting excitedly that I was going to shoot the elephant. They had not shown much interest in the elephant when he was merely ravaging their homes, but it was different now that he was going to be shot. It was a bit of fun to them, as it would be to an English crowd; besides they wanted the meat. It made me vaguely uneasy. I had no intention of shooting the elephant—I had merely sent for the rifle to defend myself if necessary—and it is always unnerving to have a crowd following you. I marched down the hill, looking and feeling a fool, with the rifle over my shoulder and an ever-growing army of people jostling at my heels. At the bottom, when you got away from the huts, there was a metalled road and beyond that a miry waste of paddy fields a thousand yards across, not yet ploughed but soggy from the first rains and dotted with coarse grass. The elephant was standing eight yards from the road, his left side towards us. He took not the slightest notice of the crowd's approach. He was tearing up bunches of grass, beating them against his knees to clean them and stuffing them into his mouth.

I had halted on the road. As soon as I saw the elephant I knew with perfect certainty that I ought not to shoot him. It is a serious matter to shoot a working elephant—it is comparable to destroying a huge and costly piece of machinery—and obviously one ought not to do it if it can possibly be avoided. And at that distance, peacefully eating, the elephant looked no more dangerous than a cow. I thought then and I think now that his attack of "must" was already passing off; in which case he would merely wander harmlessly about until the mahout came back and caught him. Moreover, I did not in the least want to shoot him. I decided that I would watch him for a little while to make sure that he did not turn savage again, and then go home.

But at that moment I glanced round at the crowd that had followed me. It was an immense crowd, two thousand at the least and growing every minute. It blocked the road for a long distance on either side. I looked at the sea of yellow faces above the garish clothes—faces all happy and excited over this bit of fun, all certain that the elephant was going to be shot. They were watching me as they would watch a conjurer about to perform a trick. They did not like me, but with the magical rifle in my hands I was momentarily worth watching. And suddenly I realized that I should have to shoot the elephant after all. The people expected it of me and I had got to do it; I could feel their two thousand wills pressing me forward, irresistibly. And it was at this moment, as I stood there with the rifle in my hands, that I first grasped the hollowness, the futility of the white man's dominion in the East. Here was I, the white man with his gun, standing in front of the unarmed native crowd—seemingly the leading actor of the piece; but in reality I was only an absurd puppet pushed to and fro by the will of those yellow faces behind. I perceived in this moment that when the white man turns tyrant it is his own freedom that he destroys. He becomes a sort of hollow, posing dummy, the conventionalized figure of a sahib. For it is the condition of his rule that he shall spend his life in trying to impress the "natives," and so in every crisis he has got to do what the "natives" expect of him. He wears a mask, and his face grows to fit it. I had got to shoot the elephant. I had committed myself to doing it when I sent for the rifle. A sahib has got to act like a sahib; he has got to appear resolute, to know his own mind and do definite things. To come all that way, rifle in hand, with two thousand people marching at my heels, and then to trail feebly away, having done nothing—no, that was impossible. The crowd would laugh at me. And my whole life, every white man's life in the East, was one long struggle not to be laughed at.

But I did not want to shoot the elephant. I watched him beating his bunch of grass against his knees, with that preoccupied grandmotherly air that elephants have. It seemed to me that it would be murder to shoot him. At that age I was not squeamish about killing animals, but I had never shot an elephant and never wanted to. (Somehow it always seems worse to kill a *large* animal.) Besides, there was the beast's owner to be considered. Alive, the elephant was worth at least a hundred pounds; dead, he would only be worth the value of his tusks, five pounds, possibly. But I had got to act quickly. I turned to some experienced-looking Burmans who had been there when we arrived, and asked them how the elephant had been behaving. They all said the same thing; he took no notice of you if you left him alone, but he might charge if you went too close to him.

It was perfectly clear to me what I ought to do. I ought to walk up to within, say, twenty-five yards of the elephant and test his behavior.

If he charged, I could shoot; if he took no notice of me, it would be safe to leave him until the mahout came back. But also I knew that I was going to do no such thing. I was a poor shot with a rifle and the ground was soft mud into which one would sink at every step. If the elephant charged and I missed him, I should have about as much chance as a toad under a steam-roller. But even then I was not thinking particularly of my own skin, only of the watchful yellow faces behind. For at that moment, with the crowd watching me, I was not afraid in the ordinary sense, as I would have been if I had been alone. A white man mustn't be frightened in front of "natives"; and so, in general, he isn't frightened. The sole thought in my mind was that if anything went wrong those two thousand Burmans would see me pursued, caught, trampled on and reduced to a grinning corpse like that Indian up the hill. And if that happened it was quite probable that some of them would laugh. That would never do. There was only one alternative. I shoved the cartridges into the magazine and lay down on the road to get a better aim.

The crowd grew very still, and a deep, low, happy sigh, as of people 10 who see the theatre curtain go up at last, breathed from innumerable throats. They were going to have their bit of fun after all. The rifle was a beautiful German thing with cross-hair sights. I did not then know that in shooting an elephant one would shoot to cut an imaginary bar running from ear-hole to ear-hole. I ought, therefore, as the elephant was sideways on, to have aimed straight at his ear-hole; actually I aimed several inches in front of this, thinking the brain would be further forward.

When I pulled the trigger I did not hear the bang or feel the kick—one never does when a shot goes home—but I heard the devilish roar of glee that went up from the crowd. In that instant, in too short a time, one would have thought, even for the bullet to get there, a mysterious, terrible change had come over the elephant. He neither stirred nor fell, but every line of his body had altered. He looked suddenly stricken, shrunken, immensely old, as though the frightful impact of the bullet had paralyzed him without knocking him down. At last, after what seemed a long time—it might have been five seconds, I dare say—he sagged flabbily to his knees. His mouth slobbered. An enormous senility seemed to have settled upon him. One could have imagined him thousands of years old. I fired again into the same spot. At the second shot he did not collapse but climbed with desperate slowness to his feet and stood weakly upright, with legs sagging and head dropping. I fired a third time. That was the shot that did for him. You could see the agony of it jolt his whole body and knock the last remnant of strength from his legs. But in falling he seemed for a moment to rise, for as his hind legs collapsed beneath him he seemed to tower upward like a huge rock toppling, his trunk reaching skywards like a tree. He trumpeted, for the first and only time. And then down he came, his belly towards me, with a crash that seemed to shake the ground even where I lay.

I got up. The Burmans were already racing past me across the mud. It was obvious that the elephant would never rise again, but he was not dead. He was breathing very rhythmically with long rattling gasps, his great mound of a side painfully rising and falling. His mouth was wide open—I could see far down into caverns of pale pink throat. I waited a long time for him to die, but his breathing did not weaken. Finally I fired my two remaining shots into the spot where I thought his heart must be. The thick blood welled out of him like red velvet, but still he did not die. His body did not even jerk when the shots hit him, the tortured breathing continued without a pause. He was dying, very slowly and in great agony, but in some world remote from me where not even a bullet could damage him further. I felt that I had got to put an end to that dreadful noise. It seemed dreadful to see the great beast lying there, powerless to move and yet powerless to die, and not even to be able to finish him. I sent back for my small rifle and poured shot after shot into his heart and down his throat. They seemed to make no impression. The tortured gasps continued as steadily as the ticking of a clock.

In the end I could not stand it any longer and went away. I heard later that it took him half an hour to die. Burmans were bringing dahs[5] and baskets even before I left, and I was told they had stripped his body almost to the bones by the afternoon.

Afterwards, of course, there were endless discussions about the shooting of the elephant. The owner was furious, but he was only an Indian and could do nothing. Besides, legally I had done the right thing, for a mad elephant has to be killed, like a mad dog, if its owner fails to control it. Among the Europeans opinion was divided. The older men said I was right, the younger men said it was a damn shame to shoot an elephant for killing a coolie, because an elephant was worth more than any damn Coringhee coolie. And afterwards I was very glad that the coolie had been killed; it put me legally in the right and it gave me a sufficient pretext for shooting the elephant. I often wondered whether any of the others grasped that I had done it solely to avoid looking a fool.

Topics for Critical Thinking and Writing

1. Did Orwell shoot the elephant of his own free will? Or did he shoot the elephant because he *had* to shoot it? What does he say about this? Do you find his judgment convincing, or not? Write a 500-word essay explaining your answer.

2. Was Orwell justified in shooting the elephant? Did he do the right thing in killing it? In the aftermath, did he think he did the right thing? Do you? Write a 500-word essay explaining your answers.

[5]**dahs** Large knives.

3. Orwell says that "as soon as I saw the elephant I knew with perfect certainty that I ought not to shoot him" (para. 6). How could he claim to "know" this, when moments later he did shoot the elephant?

4. Orwell says in passing, "Somehow it always seems worse to kill a *large* animal" (para. 8). Explain why you think Orwell says this and whether you agree.

5. A biographer who did research on Orwell in Burma reported that he could find no supporting documentation, either in the local newspapers or in the files of the police, that this episode ever occurred. Suppose that Orwell made it up. If so, is your response different? Explain.

6. If, pressured by circumstances, you have ever acted against what you might think is your reason or your nature, report the experience, and your present evaluation of your behavior.

Walter T. Stace

Walter T. Stace (1886–1967), a professor of philosophy at Princeton for many years, was the author of several books, including Religion and the Modern Mind *(1952), from which this selection is taken.*

Is Determinism Inconsistent with Free Will?[1]

The second great problem which the rise of scientific naturalism has created for the modern mind concerns the foundations of morality. The old religious foundations have largely crumbled away, and it may well be thought that the edifice built upon them by generations of men is in danger of collapse. A total collapse of moral behavior is, as I pointed out before, very unlikely. For a society in which this occurred could not survive. Nevertheless the danger to moral standards inherent in the virtual disappearance of their old religious foundations is not illusory.

I shall first discuss the problem of free will, for it is certain that if there is no free will there can be no morality. Morality is concerned with what men ought and ought not to do. But if a man has no freedom to choose what he will do, if whatever he does is done under compulsion, then it does not make sense to tell him that he ought not to have done what he did and that he ought to do something different. All moral precepts would in such case be meaningless. Also if he acts always under compulsion, how can he be held morally responsible for his actions? How can he, for example, be punished for what he could not help doing?

---

[1]The title is the editors'.

It is to be observed that those learned professors of philosophy or psychology who deny the existence of free will do so only in their professional moments and in their studies and lecture rooms. For when it comes to doing anything practical, even of the most trivial kind, they invariably behave as if they and others were free. They inquire from you at dinner whether you will choose this dish or that dish. They will ask a child why he told a lie, and will punish him for not having chosen the way of truthfulness. All of which is inconsistent with a disbelief in free will. This should cause us to suspect that the problem is not a real one; and this, I believe, is the case. The dispute is merely verbal, and is due to nothing but a confusion about the meanings of words. It is what is now fashionably called a semantic problem.

How does a verbal dispute arise? Let us consider a case which, although it is absurd in the sense that no one would ever make the mistake which is involved in it, yet illustrates the principle which we shall have to use in the solution of the problem. Suppose that someone believed that the word "man" means a certain sort of five-legged animal; in short that "five-legged animal" is the correct *definition* of man. He might then look around the world, and rightly observing that there are no five-legged animals in it, he might proceed to deny the existence of men. This preposterous conclusion would have been reached because he was using an incorrect definition of "man." All you would have to do to show him his mistake would be to give him the correct definition; or at least to show him that his definition was wrong. Both the problem and its solution would, of course, be entirely verbal. The problem of free will, and its solution, I shall maintain, is verbal in exactly the same way. The problem has been created by the fact that learned men, especially philosophers, have assumed an incorrect definition of free *will*, and then finding that there is nothing in the world which answers to their definition, have denied its existence. As far as logic is concerned, their conclusion is just as absurd as that of the man who denies the existence of men. The only difference is that the mistake in the latter case is obvious and crude, while the mistake which the deniers of free will have made is rather subtle and difficult to detect.

Throughout the modern period, until quite recently, it was assumed, both by the philosophers who denied free will and by those who defended it, that *determinism is inconsistent with free will*. If a man's actions were wholly determined by chains of causes stretching back into the remote past, so that they could be predicted beforehand by a mind which knew all the causes, it was assumed that they could not in that case be free. This implies that a certain definition of actions done from free will was assumed, namely that they are actions *not* wholly determined by causes or predictable beforehand. Let us shorten this by saying that free will was defined as meaning indeterminism. This is the incorrect definition which has led to the denial of free will. As soon as we see what the true definition is we shall find that the question whether the world is deterministic, as Newtonian science implied, or in a measure indeterministic, as current physics teaches, is wholly irrelevant to the problem.

Of course there is a sense in which one can define a word arbitrarily in any way one pleases. But a definition may nevertheless be called correct or incorrect. It is correct if it accords with a *common usage* of the word defined. It is incorrect if it does not. And if you give an incorrect definition, absurd and untrue results are likely to follow. For instance, there is nothing to prevent you from arbitrarily defining a man as a five-legged animal, but this is incorrect in the sense that it does not accord with the ordinary meaning of the word. Also it has the absurd result of leading to a denial of the existence of men. This shows that *common usage is the criterion for deciding whether a definition is correct or not*. And this is the principle which I shall apply to free will. I shall show that indeterminism is not what is meant by the phrase "free will" *as it is commonly used*. And I shall attempt to discover the correct definition by inquiring how the phrase is used in ordinary conversation.

Here are a few samples of how the phrase might be used in ordinary conversation. It will be noticed that they include cases in which the question whether a man acted with free will is asked in order to determine whether he was morally and legally responsible for his acts.

JONES: I once went without food for a week.
SMITH: Did you do that of your own free will?
JONES: No. I did it because I was lost in a desert and could find no food.

But suppose that the man who had fasted was Mahatma Gandhi. The conversation might then have gone:

GANDHI: I once fasted for a week.
SMITH: Did you do that of your own free will?
GANDHI: Yes. I did it because I wanted to compel the British Government to give India its independence.

Take another case. Suppose that I had stolen some bread, but that I was as truthful as George Washington. Then, if I were charged with the crime in court, some exchange of the following sort might take place:

JUDGE: Did you steal the bread of your own free will?
STACE: Yes. I stole it because I was hungry.

Or in different circumstances the conversation might run: 10

JUDGE: Did you steal of your own free will?
STACE: No. I stole because my employer threatened to beat me if I did not.

At a recent murder trial in Trenton some of the accused had signed confessions, but afterwards asserted that they had done so under police duress. The following exchange might have occurred:

JUDGE: Did you sign this confession of your own free will?
PRISONER: No. I signed it because the police beat me up.

Now suppose that a philosopher had been a member of the jury. We could imagine this conversation taking place in the jury room.

FOREMAN OF THE JURY: The prisoner says he signed the confession because he was beaten, and not of his own free will.
PHILOSOPHER: This is quite irrelevant to the case. There is no such thing as free will.
FOREMAN: Do you mean to say that it makes no difference whether he signed because his conscience made him want to tell the truth or because he was beaten?
PHILOSOPHER: None at all. Whether he was caused to sign by a beating or by some desire of his own—the desire to tell the truth, for example—in either case his signing was causally determined, and therefore in neither case did he act of his own free will. Since there is no such thing as free will, the question whether he signed of his own free will ought not to be discussed by us.

The foreman and the rest of the jury would rightly conclude that the philosopher must be making some mistake. What sort of a mistake could it be? There is only one possible answer. The philosopher must be using the phrase "free will" in some peculiar way of his own which is not the way in which men usually use it when they wish to determine a question of moral responsibility. That is, he must be using an incorrect definition of it as implying action not determined by causes.

Suppose a man left his office at noon, and were questioned about it. Then we might hear this:

JONES: Did you go out of your own free will?
SMITH: Yes. I went out to get my lunch.

But we might hear:

15

JONES: Did you leave your office of your own free will?
SMITH: No. I was forcibly removed by the police.

We have now collected a number of cases of actions which, in the ordinary usage of the English language, would be called cases in which people have acted of their own free will. We should also say in all these cases that they *chose* to act as they did. We should also say that they could have acted otherwise, if they had chosen. For instance, Mahatma Gandhi was not compelled to fast; he chose to do so. He could have eaten if he had wanted to. When Smith went out to get his lunch, he chose to do so. He could have stayed and done some more work, if he had wanted to. We have also collected a number of cases of the opposite kind. They are cases in which men were not able to exercise their free will. They had no choice. They were compelled to do as they did. The man in the desert did not fast of his own free will. He had no choice in the matter. He was compelled to fast because there was nothing for him to eat. And so with the other cases. It ought to be quite easy, by an inspection of these cases, to tell what we ordinarily mean when we say that a man did or did not exercise free will. We ought therefore to be able to extract from them the proper definition of the term. Let us put the cases in a table:

Free Acts	*Unfree Acts*
Gandhi fasting because he wanted to free India.	The man fasting in the desert because there was no food.
Stealing bread because one is hungry.	Stealing because one's employer threatened to beat one.
Signing a confession because one wanted to tell the truth.	Signing because the police beat one.
Leaving the office because one wanted one's lunch.	Leaving because forcibly removed.

It is obvious that to find the correct definition of free acts we must discover what characteristic is common to all the acts in the left-hand column, and is, at the same time, absent from all the acts in the right-hand column. This characteristic which all free acts have, and which no unfree acts have, will be the defining characteristic of free will.

Is being uncaused, or not being determined by causes, the characteristic of which we are in search? It cannot be, because although it is true that all the acts in the right-hand column have causes, such as the beating by the police or the absence of food in the desert, so also do the acts in the left-hand column. Mr. Gandhi's fasting was caused by his desire to free India, the man leaving his office by his hunger, and so on. Moreover there is no reason to doubt that these causes of the free acts were in turn caused by prior conditions, and that these were again the results of causes, and so on back indefinitely into the past. Any physiologist can tell us the causes of hunger. What caused Mr. Gandhi's tremendously powerful desire to free India is no doubt more difficult to discover. But it must have had causes. Some of them may have lain in peculiarities of his glands or brain, others in his past experiences, others in his heredity, others in his education. Defenders of free will have usually tended to deny such facts. But to do so is plainly a case of special pleading, which is unsupported by any scrap of evidence. The only reasonable view is that all human actions, both those which are freely done and those which are not, are either wholly determined by causes, or at least as much determined as other events in nature. It may be true, as the physicists tell us, that nature is not as deterministic as was once thought. But whatever degree of determinism prevails in the world, human actions appear to be as much determined as anything else. And if this is so, it cannot be the case that what distinguishes actions freely chosen from those which are not free is that the latter are determined by causes while the former are not. Therefore, being uncaused or being undetermined by causes, must be an incorrect definition of free will.

What, then, is the difference between acts which are freely done and those which are not? What is the characteristic which is present to all the acts in the left-hand column and absent from all those in the right-hand column? It is not obvious that, although both sets of actions have causes, the causes of those in the left-hand column are *of a different kind* from the causes of those in the right-hand column? The free acts are all caused by desires, or motives, or by some sort of internal psychological states of the agent's mind. The unfree acts, on the other hand, are all caused by physical forces or physical conditions, outside the agent. Police arrest means physical force exerted from the outside; the absence of food in the desert is a physical condition of the outside world. We may therefore frame the following rough definitions. *Acts freely done are those whose immediate causes are psychological states in the agent. Acts not freely done are those whose immediate causes are states of affairs external to the agent.*

It is plain that if we define free will in this way, then free will cer- 20 tainly exists, and the philosopher's denial of its existence is seen to be what it is—nonsense. For it is obvious that all those actions of men which we should ordinarily attribute to the exercise of their free will, or of which we should say that they freely chose to do them, are in fact actions which have been caused by their own desires, wishes, thoughts, emotions, impulses, or other psychological states.

In applying our definition we shall find that it usually works well, but that there are some puzzling cases which it does not seem exactly to fit. These puzzles can always be solved by paying careful attention to the ways in which words are used, and remembering that they are not always used consistently. I have space for only one example. Suppose that a thug threatens to shoot you unless you give him your wallet, and suppose that you do so. Do you, in giving him your wallet, do so of your own free will or not? If we apply our definition, we find that you acted freely, since the immediate cause of the action was not an actual outside force but the fear of death, which is a psychological cause. Most people, however, would say that you did not act of your own free will but under compulsion. Does this show that our definition is wrong? I do not think so. Aristotle, who gave a solution of the problem of free will substantially the same as ours (though he did not use the term "free will") admitted that there are what he called "mixed" or borderline cases in which it is difficult to know whether we ought to call the acts free or compelled. In the case under discussion, though no actual force was used, the gun at your forehead so nearly approximated to actual force that we tend to say the case was one of compulsion. It is a borderline case.

Here is what may seem like another kind of puzzle. According to our view an action may be free though it could have been predicted beforehand with certainty. But suppose you told a lie, and it was certain beforehand that you would tell it. How could one then say, "You could have told the truth"? The answer is that it is perfectly true that you could have told the truth *if* you had wanted to. In fact you would have done so, for in that case the causes producing your action, namely your desires, would have been different, and would therefore have produced different effects. It is a delusion that predictability and free will are incompatible. This agrees with common sense. For if, knowing your character, I predict that you will act honorably, no one would say when you do act honorably, that this shows you did not do so of your own free will.

Since free will is a condition of moral responsibility, we must be sure that our theory of free will gives a sufficient basis for it. To be held morally responsible for one's actions means that one may be justly punished or rewarded, blamed or praised, for them. But it is not just to punish a man for what he cannot help doing. How can it be just to punish him for an action which it was certain beforehand that he would do? We have not attempted to decide whether, as a matter of fact, all events, including human actions, are completely determined. For that question is irrelevant to the problem of free will. But if we assume for the purposes of argument that complete determinism is true, but that we are nevertheless free, it may then be asked whether such a deterministic free will is compatible with moral responsibility. For it may seem unjust to punish a man for an action which it could have been predicted with certainty beforehand that he would do.

But that determinism is incompatible with moral responsibility is as much a delusion as that it is incompatible with free will. You do not excuse a man for doing a wrong act because, knowing his character, you felt certain beforehand that he would do it. Nor do you deprive a man of a reward or prize because, knowing his goodness or his capabilities, you felt certain beforehand that he would win it.

Volumes have been written on the justification of punishment. But 25 so far as it affects the question of free will, the essential principles involved are quite simple. The punishment of a man for doing a wrong act is justified, either on the ground that it will correct his own character, or that it will deter other people from doing similar acts. The instrument of punishment has been in the past, and no doubt still is, often unwisely used; so that it may often have done more harm than good. But that is not relevant to our present problem. Punishment, if and when it is justified, is justified only on one or both of the grounds just mentioned. The question then is how, if we assume determinism, punishment can correct character or deter people from evil actions.

Suppose that your child develops a habit of telling lies. You give him a mild beating. Why? Because you believe that his personality is such that the usual motives for telling the truth do not cause him to do so. You therefore supply the missing cause, or motive, in the shape of pain and the fear of future pain if he repeats his untruthful behavior. And you hope that a few treatments of this kind will condition him to the habit of truth-telling, so that he will come to tell the truth without the infliction of pain. You assume that his actions are determined by causes, but that the usual causes of truth-telling do not in him produce their usual effects. You therefore supply him with an artificially injected motive, pain and fear, which you think will in the future cause him to speak truthfully.

The principle is exactly the same where you hope, by punishing one man, to deter others from wrong actions. You believe that the fear of punishment will cause those who might otherwise do evil to do well.

We act on the same principle with nonhuman, and even with inanimate, things, if they do not behave in the way we think they ought to behave. The rose bushes in the garden produce only small and poor blooms, whereas we want large and rich ones. We supply a cause which will produce large blooms, namely fertilizer. Our automobile does not go properly. We supply a cause which will make it go better, namely oil in the works. The punishment for the man, the fertilizer for the plant, and the oil for the car are all justified by the same principle and in the same way. The only difference is that different kinds of things require different kinds of causes to make them do what they should. Pain may be the appropriate remedy to apply, in certain cases, to human beings, and oil to the machine. It is, of course, of no use to inject motor oil into the boy or to beat the machine.

Thus we see that moral responsibility is not only consistent with determinism, but requires it. The assumption on which punishment is based is that human behavior is causally determined. If pain could not be a cause of truth-telling there would be no justification at all for punishing lies. If human actions and volitions were uncaused, it would be useless either to punish or reward, or indeed to do anything else to correct people's bad behavior. For nothing that you could do would in any way influence them. Thus moral responsibility would entirely disappear. If there were no determinism of human beings at all, their actions would be completely unpredictable and capricious, and therefore irresponsible. And this is in itself a strong argument against the common view of philosophers that free will means being undetermined by causes.

Topics for Critical Thinking and Writing

1. Stace asserts that "if there is no free will there can be no morality" (para. 2). What is his reasoning (see para. 23)? Do you agree?

2. "The dispute is merely verbal," Stace proclaims in paragraph 3. What "dispute"? Why "merely verbal"? What would Stace say to someone who insists that, no, whether we have free will is—as it seems to be—a question of *fact*?

3. What is *determinism* (para. 5)? Why does Stace seem to think that philosophers are strongly inclined to believe in it?

4. Stace claims that he will show that "indeterminism is not what is meant by . . . 'free will' *as it is commonly used*" (para. 6). What is his argument? What does he think *free will* means as the term is "commonly used"? Are you convinced? Why, or why not? Write a 500-word paper answering these questions.

5. Stace insists that "all human actions . . . are . . . at least as much determined as other events in nature" (para. 18). How might one argue against this?

6. Complete the following definition so that it captures Stace's view: "When Smith did *X*, he acted freely if and only if . . ."

7. Stace mentions some "puzzling cases" (para. 21) that do not quite fit, he admits, his analysis of free will. Give an example of such a case and explain why it is puzzling.

8. Why does Stace conclude in paragraph 22 that "it is a delusion that predictability and free will are incompatible"? Do you agree? Why, or why not?

9. It seems paradoxical to assert, as Stace does in his last paragraph, that "moral responsibility is not only consistent with determinism, but requires it." Explain Stace's view here in no more than 250 words.

Martin Luther King, Jr.

Martin Luther King, Jr. (1929–1968) was born in Atlanta and educated at Morehouse College, Crozer Theological Seminary, and Boston University. In 1954 he was called to serve as a Baptist minister in Montgomery, Alabama. During the next two years he achieved national fame when, using a policy of nonviolent resistance, he successfully led the boycott against segregated bus lines in Montgomery. He then organized the Southern Christian Leadership Conference, which furthered civil rights, first in the South and then nationwide. In 1964 he was awarded the Nobel Peace Prize. Four years later he was assassinated in Memphis, Tennessee, while supporting striking garbage workers.

In 1963 Dr. King was arrested in Birmingham, Alabama, for participating in a march for which no parade permit had been issued by the city officials. In jail he wrote a response to a letter that eight local clergymen had published in a newspaper. Their letter, titled "A Call for Unity," is printed here, followed by King's response.

Letter from Birmingham Jail

A CALL FOR UNITY

April 12, 1963

We the undersigned clergymen are among those who, in January, issued "An Appeal for Law and Order and Common Sense," in dealing with racial problems in Alabama. We expressed understanding that honest convictions in racial matters could properly be pursued in the courts, but urged that decisions of those courts should in the meantime be peacefully obeyed.

Since that time there had been some evidence of increased forebearance and a willingness to face facts. Responsible citizens have undertaken to work on various problems which cause racial friction and unrest. In Birmingham, recent public events have given indication that we all have opportunity for a new constructive and realistic approach to racial problems.

However, we are now confronted by a series of demonstrations by some of our Negro citizens, directed and led in part by outsiders. We recognize the natural impatience of people who feel that their hopes are slow in being realized. But we are convinced that these demonstrations are unwise and untimely.

We agree rather with certain local Negro leadership which has called for honest and open negotiation of racial issues in our area. And we believe this kind of facing of issues can best be accomplished by citizens of our own metropolitan area, white and Negro, meeting with their knowledge and experience of the local situation. All of us need to face that responsibility and find proper channels for its accomplishment.

Just as we formerly pointed out that "hatred and violence have no   5
sanction in our religious and political traditions," we also point out that such actions as incite to hatred and violence, however technically peaceful those actions may be, have not contributed to the resolution of our local problems. We do not believe that these days of new hope are days when extreme measures are justified in Birmingham.

We commend the community as a whole, and the local news media and law enforcement officials in particular, on the calm manner in which these demonstrations have been handled. We urge the public to continue to show restraint should the demonstrations continue, and the law enforcement officials to remain calm and continue to protect our city from violence.

We further strongly urge our own Negro community to withdraw support from these demonstrations, and to unite locally in working peacefully for a better Birmingham. When rights are consistently denied, a cause should be pressed in the courts and in negotiations among local leaders, and not in the streets. We appeal to both our white and Negro citizenry to observe the principles of law and order and common sense.

C.C.J. Carpenter, D.D., L.L.D., Bishop of Alabama; Joseph A. Durick, D.D., Auxiliary Bishop, Diocese of Mobile-Birmingham; Rabbi Milton L. Grafman, Temple Emanu-El, Birmingham, Alabama; Bishop Paul Hardin, Bishop of the Alabama–West Florida Conference of the Methodist Church; Bishop Nolan B. Harmon, Bishop of the North Alabama Conference of the Methodist Church; George M. Murray, D.D., L.L.D., Bishop Coadjutor, Episcopal Diocese of Alabama; Edward V. Ramage, Moderator, Synod of the Alabama Presbyterian Church in the United

States; Earl Stallings, Pastor, First Baptist Church, Birmingham, Alabama.

LETTER FROM BIRMINGHAM JAIL

April 16, 1963

My Dear Fellow Clergymen:

While confined here in the Birmingham city jail, I came across your recent statement calling my present activities "unwise and untimely."[1] Seldom do I pause to answer criticism of my work and ideas. If I sought to answer all the criticisms that cross my desk, my secretaries would have little time for anything other than such correspondence in the course of the day, and I would have no time for constructive work. But since I feel that you are men of genuine good will and that your criticisms are sincerely set forth, I want to try to answer your statement in what I hope will be patient and reasonable terms.

I think I should indicate why I am here in Birmingham, since you have been influenced by the view which argues against "outsiders coming in." I have the honor of serving as president of the Southern Christian Leadership Conference, an organization operating in every southern state, with headquarters in Atlanta, Georgia. We have some eighty-five affiliated organizations across the South, and one of them is the Alabama Christian Movement for Human Rights. Frequently we share staff, educational, and financial resources with our affiliates. Several months ago the affiliate here in Birmingham asked us to be on call to engage in a nonviolent direct-action program if such were deemed necessary. We readily consented, and when the hour came we lived up to our promise. So I, along with several members of my staff, am here because I was invited here. I am here because I have organizational ties here.

But more basically, I am in Birmingham because injustice is here. Just as the prophets of the eighth century B.C. left their villages and carried their "thus saith the Lord" far beyond the boundaries of their home towns, and just as the Apostle Paul left his village of Tarsus and carried the gospel of Jesus Christ to the far corners of the Greco-Roman world, so am I compelled to carry the gospel of freedom beyond my own home town. Like Paul, I must constantly respond to the Macedonian call for aid.

---

[1] This response to a published statement by eight fellow clergymen from Alabama (Bishop C.C.J. Carpenter, Bishop Joseph A. Durick, Rabbi Milton L. Grafman, Bishop Paul Hardin, Bishop Nolan B. Harmon, the Reverend George M. Murray, the Reverend Edward V. Ramage, and the Reverend Earl Stallings) was composed under somewhat constricting circumstances. Begun on the margins of the newspaper in which the statement appeared while I was in jail, the letter was continued on scraps of writing paper supplied by a friendly Negro trusty, and concluded on a pad my attorneys were eventually permitted to leave me. Although the text remains in substance unaltered, I have indulged in the author's prerogative of polishing it for publication. [King's note.]

Moreover, I am cognizant of the interrelatedness of all communities and states. I cannot sit idly by in Atlanta and not be concerned about what happens in Birmingham. Injustice anywhere is a threat to justice everywhere. We are caught in an inescapable network of mutuality; tied in a single garment of destiny. Whatever affects one directly, affects all indirectly. Never again can we afford to live with the narrow, provincial "outside agitator" idea. Anyone who lives inside the United States can never be considered an outsider anywhere within its bounds.

You deplore the demonstrations taking place in Birmingham. But your statement, I am sorry to say, fails to express a similar concern for the conditions that brought about the demonstrations. I am sure that none of you would want to rest content with the superficial kind of social analysis that deals merely with effects and does not grapple with underlying causes. It is unfortunate that demonstrations are taking place in Birmingham, but it is even more unfortunate that the city's white power structure left the Negro community with no alternative.

In any nonviolent campaign there are four basic steps: collection of the facts to determine whether injustices exist; negotiation; self-purification; and direct action. We have gone through all these steps in Birmingham. There can be no gainsaying the fact that racial injustice engulfs this community. Birmingham is probably the most thoroughly segregated city in the United States. Its ugly record of brutality is widely known. Negroes have experienced grossly unjust treatment in the courts. There have been more unsolved bombings of Negro homes and churches in Birmingham than in any other city in the nation. These are the hard, brutal facts of the case. On the basis of these conditions, Negro leaders sought to negotiate with the city fathers. But the latter consistently refused to engage in good-faith negotiation.

Then, last September, came the opportunity to talk with leaders of Birmingham's economic community. In the course of the negotiations, certain promises were made by the merchants—for example, to remove the stores' humiliating racial signs. On the basis of these promises, the Reverend Fred Shuttleworth and the leaders of the Alabama Christian Movement for Human Rights agreed to a moratorium on all demonstrations. As the weeks and months went by, we realized that we were the victims of a broken promise. A few signs, briefly removed, returned; the others remained.

As in so many past experiences, our hopes had been blasted, and the shadow of deep disappointment settled upon us. We had no alternative except to prepare for direct action, whereby we would present our very bodies as a means of laying our case before the conscience of the local and the national community. Mindful of the difficulties involved, we decided to undertake a process of self-purification. We began a series of workshops on nonviolence, and we repeatedly asked ourselves: "Are you able to accept blows without retaliating?" "Are you able to endure the ordeal of jail?" We decided to schedule our direct-action program for the Easter season, realizing that except for Christmas, this is the main shopping period of the year. Knowing that a strong economic-withdrawal program would be the by-product of direct action, we felt that this would be the best time to bring pressure to bear on the merchants for the needed change.

Then it occurred to us that Birmingham's mayoralty election was coming up in March, and we speedily decided to postpone action until after election day. When we discovered that the Commissioner of Public Safety, Eugene "Bull" Connor, had piled up enough votes to be in the run-off, we decided again to postpone action until the day after the run-off so that the demonstrations could not be used to cloud the issues. Like many others, we waited to see Mr. Connor defeated, and to this end we endured postponement after postponement. Having aided in this community need, we felt that our direct-action program could be delayed no longer.

You may well ask: "Why direct action? Why sit-ins, marches, and so 10 forth? Isn't negotiation a better path?" You are quite right in calling for negotiation. Indeed, this is the very purpose of direct action. Nonviolent direct action seeks to create such a crisis and foster such a tension that a community which has constantly refused to negotiate is forced to confront the issue. It seeks so to dramatize the issue that it can no longer be ignored. My citing the creation of tension as part of the work of the nonviolent-resister may sound rather shocking. But I must confess that I am not afraid of the word "tension." I have earnestly opposed violent tension, but there is a type of constructive, nonviolent tension which is necessary for growth. Just as Socrates felt that it was necessary to create a tension in the mind so that individuals could rise from the bondage of myths and half-truths to the unfettered realm of creative analysis and objective appraisal, so must we see the need for nonviolent gadflies to create the kind of tension in society that will help men rise from the dark depths of prejudice and racism to the majestic heights of understanding and brotherhood.

The purpose of our direct-action program is to create a situation so crisis-packed that it will inevitably open the door to negotiation. I therefore concur with you in your call for negotiation. Too long has our beloved Southland been bogged down in a tragic effort to live in monologue rather than dialogue.

One of the basic points in your statement is that the action that I and my associates have taken in Birmingham is untimely. Some have asked: "Why didn't you give the new city administration time to act?" The only answer that I can give to this query is that the new Birmingham administration must be prodded about as much as the outgoing one, before it will act. We are sadly mistaken if we feel that the election of Albert Boutwell as mayor will bring the millennium to Birmingham. While Mr. Boutwell is a much more gentle person than Mr. Connor, they are both segregationists, dedicated to maintenance of the status quo. I have hope that Mr. Boutwell will be reasonable enough to see the futility of massive resistance to desegregation. But he will not see this without pressure from devotees of civil rights. My friends, I must say to you that we have not made a single gain in civil rights without determined legal and nonviolent pressure. Lamentably, it is an historical fact that privileged groups seldom give up their privileges voluntarily. Individuals may see the moral light and voluntarily give up their unjust posture; but as Reinhold Niebuhr[2] has reminded us, groups tend to be more immoral than individuals.

We know through painful experience that freedom is never voluntarily given by the oppressor; it must be demanded by the oppressed. Frankly, I have yet to engage in a direct-action campaign that was "well timed" in the view of those who have not suffered unduly from the disease of segregation. For years now I have heard the word "Wait!" It rings in the ear of every Negro with piercing familiarity. This "Wait" has almost always meant "Never." We must come to see, with one of our distinguished jurists, that "justice too long delayed is justice denied."[3]

We have waited for more than 340 years for our constitutional and God-given rights. The nations of Asia and Africa are moving with jetlike speed toward gaining political independence, but we still creep at horse-and-buggy pace toward gaining a cup of coffee at a lunch counter. Perhaps it is easy for those who have never felt the stinging darts of segregation to say, "Wait." But when you have seen vicious mobs lynch your mothers and fathers at will and drown your sisters and brothers at whim; when you have seen hate-filled policemen curse, kick, and even kill your black brothers and sisters; when you see the vast majority of your twenty million Negro brothers smothering in an airtight cage of poverty in the midst of an affluent society; when you suddenly find your tongue twisted and your speech stammering as you seek to explain to your six-year-old daughter why she can't go to the public amusement park that has just been advertised on television, and see tears welling up in her eyes when she is told that Funtown is closed to colored children, and see ominous clouds of inferiority beginning to form in her little mental sky, and see her beginning to distort her personality by developing an unconscious bitterness toward white people; when you have to concoct an answer for a five-year-old son who is asking: "Daddy, why do white people treat colored people so mean?"; when you take a cross-country drive and find it necessary to sleep night after night in the uncomfortable corners of your automobile because no motel will accept you; when you are humiliated day in and day out by nagging signs reading "white" and "colored"; when your first name be-

[2]**Reinhold Niebuhr** Niebuhr (1892–1971) was a minister, political activist, author, and professor of applied Christianity at Union Theological Seminary. [All notes are the editors' unless otherwise specified.]

[3]**justice . . . denied** A quotation attributed to William E. Gladstone (1809–1898), British statesman and prime minister.

comes "nigger," your middle name becomes "boy" (however old you are) and your last name becomes "John," and your wife and mother are never given the respected title "Mrs."; when you are harried by day and haunted by night by the fact that you are a Negro, living constantly at tiptoe stance, never quite knowing what to expect next, and are plagued with inner fears and outer resentments; when you are forever fighting a degenerating sense of "nobodiness" — then you will understand why we find it difficult to wait. There comes a time when the cup of endurance runs over, and men are no longer willing to be plunged into the abyss of despair. I hope, sirs, you can understand our legitimate and unavoidable impatience.

You express a great deal of anxiety over our willingness to break 15 laws. This is certainly a legitimate concern. Since we so diligently urge people to obey the Supreme Court's decision of 1954 outlawing segregation in the public schools, at first glance it may seem rather paradoxical for us consciously to break laws. One may well ask: "How can you advocate breaking some laws and obeying others?" The answer lies in the fact that there are two types of laws: just and unjust. I would be the first to advocate obeying just laws. One has not only a legal but a moral responsibility to obey just laws. Conversely, one has a moral responsibility to disobey unjust laws. I would agree with St. Augustine that "an unjust law is no law at all."

Now, what is the difference between the two? How does one determine whether a law is just or unjust? A just law is a man-made code that squares with the moral law or the law of God. An unjust law is a code that is out of harmony with the moral law. To put it in the terms of St. Thomas Aquinas: An unjust law is a human law that is not rooted in eternal law and natural law. Any law that uplifts human personality is just. Any law that degrades human personality is unjust. All segregation statutes are unjust because segregation distorts the soul and damages the personality. It gives the segregator a false sense of superiority and the segregated a false sense of inferiority. Segregation, to use the terminology of the Jewish philosopher Martin Buber, substitutes an "I-it" relationship for an "I-thou" relationship and ends up relegating persons to the status of things. Hence segregation is not only politically, economically, and sociologically unsound, it is morally wrong and sinful. Paul Tillich[4] has said that sin is separation. Is not segregation an existential expression of man's tragic separation, his awful estrangement, his terrible sinfulness? Thus it is that I can urge men to obey the 1954 decision of the Supreme Court, for it is morally right; and I can urge them to disobey segregation ordinances, for they are morally wrong.

---

[4]**Paul Tillich** Tillich (1886–1965), born in Germany, taught theology at several German universities, but in 1933 he was dismissed from his post at the University of Frankfurt because of his opposition to the Nazi regime. At the invitation of Reinhold Niebuhr, he came to the United States and taught at Union Theological Seminary.

Let us consider a more concrete example of just and unjust laws. An unjust law is a code that a numerical or power majority group compels a minority group to obey but does not make binding on itself. This is *difference* made legal. By the same token, a just law is a code that a majority compels a minority to follow and that it is willing to follow itself. This is *sameness* made legal.

Let me give another explanation. A law is unjust if it is inflicted on a minority that, as a result of being denied the right to vote, had no part in enacting or devising the law. Who can say that the legislature of Alabama which set up that state's segregation laws was democratically elected? Throughout Alabama all sorts of devious methods are used to prevent Negroes from becoming registered voters, and there are some counties in which, even though Negroes constitute a majority of the population, not a single Negro is registered. Can any law enacted under such circumstances be considered democratically structured?

Sometimes a law is just on its face and unjust in its application. For instance, I have been arrested on a charge of parading without a permit. Now, there is nothing wrong in having an ordinance which requires a permit for a parade. But such an ordinance becomes unjust when it is used to maintain segregation and to deny citizens the First Amendment privilege of peaceful assembly and protest.

I hope you are able to see the distinction I am trying to point out. In no sense do I advocate evading or defying the law, as would the rabid segregationist. That would lead to anarchy. One who breaks an unjust law must do so openly, lovingly, and with a willingness to accept the penalty. I submit that an individual who breaks a law that conscience tells him is unjust, and who willingly accepts the penalty of imprisonment in order to arouse the conscience of the community over its injustice, is in reality expressing the highest respect for law.

Of course, there is nothing new about this kind of civil disobedience. It was evidenced sublimely in the refusal of Shadrach, Meshach, and Abednego to obey the laws of Nebuchadnezzar, on the ground that a higher moral law was at stake. It was practiced superbly by the early Christians, who were willing to face hungry lions and the excruciating pain of chopping blocks rather than submit to certain unjust laws of the Roman Empire. To a degree, academic freedom is a reality today because Socrates practiced civil disobedience. In our own nation, the Boston Tea Party represented a massive act of civil disobedience.

We should never forget that everything Adolf Hitler did in Germany was "legal" and everything the Hungarian freedom fighters did in Hungary was "illegal." It was "illegal" to aid and comfort a Jew in Hitler's Germany. Even so, I am sure that, had I lived in Germany at the time, I would have aided and comforted my Jewish brothers. If today I lived in a Communist country where certain principles dear to the Christian faith are suppressed, I would openly advocate disobeying that country's anti-religious laws.

I must make two honest confessions to you, my Christian and Jewish brothers. First, I must confess that over the past few years I have been gravely disappointed with the white moderate. I have almost reached the regrettable conclusion that the Negro's great stumbling block in his stride toward freedom is not the White Citizen's Counciler or the Ku Klux Klanner, but the white moderate, who is more devoted to "order" than to justice; who prefers a negative peace which is the absence of tension to a positive peace which is the presence of justice; who constantly says: "I agree with you in the goal you seek, but I cannot agree with your methods or direct action"; who paternalistically believes he can set the timetable for another man's freedom; who lives by a mythical concept of time and who constantly advises the Negro to wait for a "more convenient season." Shallow understanding from people of good will is more frustrating than absolute misunderstanding from people of ill will. Lukewarm acceptance is much more bewildering than outright rejection.

I had hoped that the white moderate would understand that law and order exist for the purpose of establishing justice and that when they fail in this purpose they become the dangerously structured dams that block the flow of social progress. I had hoped that the white moderate would understand that the present tension in the South is a necessary phase of the transition from an obnoxious negative peace, in which the Negro passively accepted his unjust plight, to a substantive and positive peace, in which all men will respect the dignity and worth of human personality. Actually, we who engage in nonviolent direct action are not the creators of tension. We merely bring to the surface the hidden tension that is already alive. We bring it out in the open, where it can be seen and dealt with. Like a boil that can never be cured so long as it is covered up but must be opened with all its ugliness to the natural medicines of air and light, injustice must be exposed, with all the tension its exposure creates, to the light of human conscience and the air of national opinion before it can be cured.

In your statement you assert that our actions, even though peaceful, 25 must be condemned because they precipitate violence. But is this a logical assertion? Isn't this like condemning a robbed man because his possession of money precipitated the evil act of robbery? Isn't this like condemning Socrates because his unswerving commitment to truth and his philosophical inquiries precipitated the act by the misguided populace in which they made him drink hemlock? Isn't this like condemning Jesus because his unique God-consciousness and never-ceasing devotion to God's will precipitated the evil act of crucifixion? We must come to see that, as the federal courts have consistently affirmed, it is wrong to urge an individual to cease his efforts to gain his basic constitutional rights because the quest may precipitate violence. Society must protect the robbed and punish the robber.

I had also hoped that the white moderate would reject the myth concerning time in relation to the struggle for freedom. I have just received a letter from a white brother in Texas. He writes: "All Christians know that the colored people will receive equal rights eventually, but it is possible that you are in too great a religious hurry. It has taken Christianity almost two thousand years to accomplish what it has. The teachings of Christ take time to come to earth." Such an attitude stems from a tragic misconception of time, from the strangely irrational notion that there is something in the very flow of time that will inevitably cure all ills. Actually, time itself is neutral; it can be used either destructively or constructively. More and more I feel that the people of ill will have used time much more effectively than have the people of good will. We will have to repent in this generation not merely for the hateful words and actions of the bad people but for the appalling silence of the good people. Human progress never rolls in on wheels of inevitability; it comes through the tireless efforts of men willing to be co-workers with God, and without this hard work, time itself becomes an ally of the forces of social stagnation. We must use time creatively, in the knowledge that the time is always ripe to do right. Now is the time to make real the promise of democracy and transform our pending national elegy into a creative psalm of brotherhood. Now is the time to lift our national policy from the quicksand of racial injustice to the solid rock of human dignity.

You speak of our activity in Birmingham as extreme. At first I was rather disappointed that fellow clergymen would see my nonviolent efforts as those of an extremist. I began thinking about the fact that I stand in the middle of two opposing forces in the Negro community. One is a force of complacency, made up in part of Negroes who, as a result of long years of oppression, are so drained of self-respect and a sense of "somebodiness" that they have adjusted to segregation; and in part of a few middle-class Negroes who, because of a degree of academic and economic security and because in some ways they profit by segregation, have become insensitive to the problems of the masses. The other force is one of bitterness and hatred, and it comes perilously close to advocating violence. It is expressed in the various black nationalist groups that are springing up across the nation, the largest and best-known being Elijah Muhammad's Muslim movement. Nourished by the Negro's frustration over the continued existence of racial discrimination, this movement is made up of people who have lost faith in America, who have absolutely repudiated Christianity, and who have concluded that the white man is an incorrigible "devil."

I have tried to stand between these two forces, saying that we need emulate neither the "do-nothingism" of the complacent nor the hatred and despair of the black nationalist. For there is the more excellent way of love and nonviolent protest. I am grateful to God that, through the influence of the Negro church, the way of nonviolence became an integral part of our struggle.

If this philosophy had not emerged, by now many streets of the South should, I am convinced, be flowing with blood. And I am further convinced that if our white brothers dismiss as "rabble-rousers" and "outside agitators" those of us who employ nonviolent direct action, and if they refuse to support our nonviolent efforts, millions of Negroes will, out of frustration and despair, seek solace and security in black-nationalist ideologies—a development that would inevitably lead to a frightening racial nightmare.

Oppressed people cannot remain oppressed forever. The yearning 30 for freedom eventually manifests itself, and that is what has happened to the American Negro. Something within has reminded him of his birthright of freedom, and something without has reminded him that it can be gained. Consciously or unconsciously, he has been caught up by the *Zeitgeist*,[5] and with his black brothers of Africa and his brown and yellow brothers of Asia, South America, and the Caribbean, the United States Negro is moving with a sense of great urgency toward the promised land of racial justice. If one recognizes this vital urge that has engulfed the Negro community, one should readily understand why public demonstrations are taking place. The Negro has many pent-up resentments and latent frustrations, and he must release them. So let him march; let him make prayer pilgrimages to the city hall; let him go on freedom rides—and try to understand why he must do so. If his repressed emotions are not released in nonviolent ways, they will seek expression through violence; this is not a threat but a fact of history. So I have not said to my people: "Get rid of your discontent." Rather, I have tried to say that this normal and healthy discontent can be channeled into the creative outlet of nonviolent direct action. And now this approach is being termed extremist.

But though I was initially disappointed at being categorized as an extremist, as I continued to think about the matter I gradually gained a measure of satisfaction from the label. Was not Jesus an extremist for love: "Love your enemies, bless them that curse you, do good to them that hate you, and pray for them which despitefully use you, and persecute you." Was not Amos an extremist for justice: "Let justice roll down like waters and righteousness like an ever-flowing stream." Was not Paul an extremist for the Christian gospel: "I bear in my body the marks of the Lord Jesus." Was not Martin Luther an extremist: "Here I stand; I cannot do otherwise, so help me God." And John Bunyan: "I will stay in jail to the end of my days before I make a butchery of my conscience." And Abraham Lincoln: "This nation cannot survive half slave and half free." And Thomas Jefferson: "We hold these truths to be self-evident, that all men are created equal. . . ." So the question is not whether we will be extremists, but what kind of extremists we will be. Will we be extremists for hate or for love? Will we be extremists for the preservation of injustice or for the extension of justice? In that dramatic scene on Calvary's hill three men were crucified. We must never forget that all three

---

[5]***Zeitgeist*** German for "spirit of the age."

were crucified for the same crime—the crime of extremism. Two were extremists for immorality, and thus fell below their environment. The other, Jesus Christ, was an extremist for love, truth, and goodness, and thereby rose above his environment. Perhaps the South, the nation, and the world are in dire need of creative extremists.

I had hoped that the white moderate would see this need. Perhaps I was too optimistic; perhaps I expected too much. I suppose I should have realized that few members of the oppressor race can understand the deep groans and passionate yearnings of the oppressed race, and still fewer have the vision to see that injustice must be rooted out by strong, persistent, and determined action. I am thankful, however, that some of our white brothers in the South have grasped the meaning of this social revolution and committed themselves to it. They are still all too few in quantity, but they are big in quality. Some—such as Ralph McGill, Lillian Smith, Harry Golden, James McBride Dabbs, Ann Braden, and Sarah Patton Boyle—have written about our struggle in eloquent and prophetic terms. Others have marched with us down nameless streets of the South. They have languished in filthy, roach-infested jails, suffering the abuse and brutality of policemen who view them as "dirty nigger-lovers." Unlike so many of their moderate brothers and sisters, they have recognized the urgency of the moment and sensed the need for powerful "action" antidotes to combat the disease of segregation.

Let me take note of my other major disappointment. I have been so greatly disappointed with the white church and its leadership. Of course, there are some notable exceptions. I am not unmindful of the fact that each of you has taken some significant stands on this issue. I commend you, Reverend Stallings, for your Christian stand on this past Sunday, in welcoming Negroes to your worship service on a nonsegregated basis. I commend the Catholic leaders of this state for integrating Spring Hill College several years ago.

But despite these notable exceptions, I must honestly reiterate that I have been disappointed with the church. I do not say this as one of those negative critics who can always find something wrong with the church. I say this as a minister of the gospel, who loves the church; who was nurtured in its bosom; who has been sustained by its spiritual blessings and who will remain true to it as long as the cord of life shall lengthen.

When I was suddenly catapulted into the leadership of the bus   35 protest in Montgomery, Alabama, a few years ago, I felt we would be supported by the white church. I felt that the white ministers, priests, and rabbis of the South would be among our strongest allies. Instead, some have been outright opponents, refusing to understand the freedom movement and misrepresenting its leaders; all too many others have been more cautious than courageous and have remained silent behind the anesthetizing security of stained-glass windows.

In spite of my shattered dreams, I came to Birmingham with the hope that the white religious leadership of this community would see the justice of our cause and, with deep moral concern, would serve as the channel through which our just grievances could reach the power structure. I had hoped that each of you would understand. But again I have been disappointed.

I have heard numerous southern religious leaders admonish their worshipers to comply with a desegregation decision because it is the law, but I have longed to hear white ministers declare: "Follow this decree because integration is morally right and because the Negro is your brother." In the midst of blatant injustices inflicted upon the Negro, I have watched white churchmen stand on the sideline and mouth pious irrelevancies and sanctimonious trivialities. In the midst of a mighty struggle to rid our nation of racial and economic injustice, I have heard many ministers say: "Those are social issues, with which the gospel has no real concern." And I have watched many churches commit themselves to a completely otherworldly religion which makes a strange, unbiblical distinction between body and soul, between the sacred and the secular.

I have traveled the length and breadth of Alabama, Mississippi, and all the other southern states. On sweltering summer days and crisp autumn mornings I have looked at the South's beautiful churches with their lofty spires pointing heavenward. I have beheld the impressive outlines of her massive religious-education buildings. Over and over I have found myself saying: "What kind of people worship here? Who is their God? Where were their voices when the lips of Governor Barnett dripped with words of interposition and nullification? Where were they when Governor Wallace gave a clarion call for defiance and hatred? Where were their voices of support when bruised and weary Negro men and women decided to rise from the dark dungeons of complacency to the bright hills of creative protest?"

Yes, these questions are still in my mind. In deep disappointment I have wept over the laxity of the church. But be assured that my tears have been tears of love. There can be no deep disappointment where there is not deep love. Yes, I love the church. How could I do otherwise? I am in the rather unique position of being the son, the grandson, and the great-grandson of preachers. Yes, I see the church as the body of Christ. But, Oh! How we have blemished and scarred that body through social neglect and through fear of being nonconformists.

There was a time when the church was very powerful—in the time 40 when the early Christians rejoiced at being deemed worthy to suffer for what they believed. In those days the church was not merely a thermometer that recorded the ideas and principles of popular opinion; it was a thermostat that transformed the mores of society. Whenever the early Christians entered a town, the people in power became disturbed and immediately sought to convict the Christians for being "disturbers of the peace" and "outside agitators." But the Christians pressed on, in the conviction that they were "a colony of heaven," called to obey God rather than man. Small in number, they were big in commitment. They were too God-intoxicated to be "astronomically intimidated." By their effort and example they brought an end to such ancient evils as infanticide and gladiatorial contests.

Things are different now. So often the contemporary church is a weak, ineffectual voice with an uncertain sound. So often it is an archdefender of the status quo. Far from being disturbed by the presence of the church, the power structure of the average community is consoled by the church's silent—and often even vocal—sanction of things as they are.

But the judgment of God is upon the church as never before. If today's church does not recapture the sacrificial spirit of the early church, it will lose its authenticity, forfeit the loyalty of millions, and be dismissed as an irrelevant social club with no meaning for the twentieth century. Every day I meet young people whose disappointment with the church has turned into outright disgust.

Perhaps I have once again been too optimistic. Is organized religion too inextricably bound to the status quo to save our nation and the world? Perhaps I must turn my faith to the inner spiritual church, the church within the church, as the true *ekklesia* and the hope of the world. But again I am thankful to God that some noble souls from the ranks of organized religion have broken loose from the paralyzing chains of conformity and joined us as active partners in the struggle for freedom. They have left their secure congregations and walked the streets of Albany, Georgia, with us. They have gone down the highways of the South on tortuous rides for freedom. Yes, they have gone to jail with us. Some have been dismissed from their churches, have lost the support of their bishops and fellow ministers. But they have acted in the faith that right defeated is stronger than evil triumphant. Their witness has been the spiritual salt that has preserved the true meaning of the gospel in these troubled times. They have carved a tunnel of hope through the dark mountain of disappointment.

I hope the church as a whole will meet the challenge of this decisive hour. But even if the church does not come to the aid of justice, I have no despair about the future. I have no fear about the outcome of our struggle in Birmingham, even if our motives are at present misunderstood. We will reach the goal of freedom in Birmingham and all over the nation, because the goal of America is freedom. Abused and scorned though we may be, our destiny is tied up with America's destiny. Before the pilgrims landed at Plymouth, we were here. Before the pen of Jefferson etched the majestic words of the Declaration of Independence across the pages of history, we were here. For more than two centuries our forebears labored in this country without wages; they made cotton king; they built the homes of their masters while suffering gross injustice and shameful humiliation—and yet out of a bottomless vitality they continue to thrive and develop. If the inexpressible cruelties of slavery could not stop us, the opposition we now face will surely fail. We will win our freedom because the sacred heritage of our nation and the eternal will of God are embodied in our echoing demands.

Before closing I feel impelled to mention one other point in your 45 statement that has troubled me profoundly. You warmly commended the Birmingham police force for keeping "order" and "preventing violence." I doubt that you would have so warmly commended the police force if you had seen its dogs sinking their teeth into unarmed, nonviolent Negroes. I doubt that you would so quickly commend the policemen if you were to observe their ugly and inhumane treatment of Negroes here in the city jail; if you were to watch them push and curse old Negro women and young Negro girls; if you were to see them slap and kick old Negro men and young boys; if you were to observe them, as they did on two occasions, refuse to give us food because we wanted to sing our grace together. I cannot join you in your praise of the Birmingham police department.

It is true that the police have exercised a degree of discipline in handling the demonstrators. In this sense they have conducted themselves rather "nonviolently" in public. But for what purpose? To preserve the evil system of segregation. Over the past few years I have consistently preached that nonviolence demands that the means we use must be as pure as the ends we seek. I have tried to make clear that it is wrong to use immoral means to attain moral ends. But now I must affirm that it is just as wrong, or perhaps even more so, to use moral means to preserve immoral ends. Perhaps Mr. Connor and his policemen have been rather nonviolent in public, as was Chief Pritchett in Albany, Georgia, but they used the moral means of nonviolence to maintain the immoral end of racial injustice. As T. S. Eliot has said: "The last temptation is the greatest treason: To do the right deed for the wrong reason."

I wish you had commended the Negro sit-inners and demonstrators of Birmingham for their sublime courage, their willingness to suffer, and their amazing discipline in the midst of great provocation. One day the South will recognize its real heroes. They will be the James Merediths, with the noble sense of purpose that enables them to face jeering and hostile mobs, and with the agonizing loneliness that characterizes the life of the pioneer. They will be old, oppressed, battered Negro women, symbolized in a seventy-two-year-old woman in Montgomery, Alabama, who rose up with a sense of dignity and with her people decided not to ride segregated buses, and who responded with ungrammatical profundity to one who inquired about her weariness: "My feets is tired, but my soul is at rest." They will be the young high school and college students, the young ministers of the gospel and a host of their elders, courageously and nonviolently sitting in at lunch counters and willingly going to jail for conscience' sake. One day the South will know that when these disinherited children of God sat down at lunch counters, they were in reality standing up for what is best in the American dream and for the most sacred values in our Judaeo-Christian heritage, thereby bringing our nation back to those great wells of democracy which were dug deep by the founding fathers in their formulation of the Constitution and the Declaration of Independence.

Never before have I written so long a letter. I'm afraid it is much too long to take your precious time. I can assure you that it would have been much shorter if I had been writing from a comfortable desk, but what else can one do when he is alone in a narrow jail cell, other than write long letters, think long thoughts, and pray long prayers?

If I have said anything in this letter that overstates the truth and indicates an unreasonable impatience, I beg you to forgive me. If I have said anything that understates the truth and indicates my having a patience that allows me to settle for anything less than brotherhood, I beg God to forgive me.

I hope this letter finds you strong in the faith. I also hope that cir- 50
cumstances will soon make it possible for me to meet each of you, not as an integrationist or a civil-rights leader but as a fellow clergyman and a Christian brother. Let us all hope that the dark clouds of racial prejudice will soon pass away and the deep fog of misunderstanding will be lifted from our fear-drenched communities, and in some not too distant tomorrow the radiant stars of love and brotherhood will shine over our great nation with all their scintillating beauty.

Yours for the cause of Peace and Brotherhood,
Martin Luther King, Jr.

Topics for Critical Thinking and Writing

1. In his first five paragraphs, how does King assure his audience that he is not a meddlesome intruder but a man of good will?

2. In paragraph 3 King refers to Hebrew prophets and to the Apostle Paul, and later (para. 10) to Socrates. What is the point of these references?

3. In paragraph 11 what does King mean when he says that "our beloved Southland" has long tried to "live in monologue rather than dialogue"?

4. King begins paragraph 23 with "I must make two honest confessions to you, my Christian and Jewish brothers." What would have been gained or lost if he had used this paragraph as his opening?

5. King's last three paragraphs do not advance his argument. What do they do?

6. Why does King advocate breaking unjust laws "openly, lovingly" (para. 20)? What does he mean by these words? What other motives or attitudes do these words rule out?

7. Construct two definitions of "civil disobedience," and explain whether and to what extent it is easier (or harder) to justify civil disobedience, depending on how you have defined the expression.

8. If you feel that you wish to respond to King's letter on some point, write a letter nominally addressed to King. You may, if you wish, adopt the persona of one of the eight clergymen whom King initially addressed.

9. King writes (para. 46) that "nonviolence demands that the means we use must be as pure as the ends we seek." How do you think King would evaluate the following acts of civil disobedience: (a) occupying a college administration building in order to protest the administration's unsatisfactory response to a racial incident on campus, or in order to protest the failure of the administration to hire minority persons as staff and faculty; (b) sailing on a collision course with a whaling ship to protest against whaling; (c) trespassing on an abortion clinic to protest abortion? Set down your answer in an essay of 500 words.

Stanley Milgram

Stanley Milgram (1933–1984) taught at Yale and Harvard Universities and at the Graduate Center, City University of New York. In 1963, while at Yale, he devised an experiment that tested the willingness of people to submit to the authority of an experimenter even if it meant they would violate their conscience by inflicting pain on another person during the course of the experiment. He published his research on conformity in a book, Obedience to Authority *(1974), which was nominated for the National Book Award.*

The Perils of Obedience

Obedience is as basic an element in the structure of social life as one can point to. Some system of authority is a requirement of all communal living, and it is only the person dwelling in isolation who is not forced to respond, with defiance or submission, to the commands of others. For many people, obedience is a deeply ingrained behavior tendency, indeed a potent impulse overriding training in ethics, sympathy, and moral conduct.

The dilemma inherent in submission to authority is ancient, as old as the story of Abraham, and the question of whether one should obey when commands conflict with conscience has been argued by Plato, dramatized in *Antigone*, and treated to philosophic analysis in almost every historical epoch. Conservative philosophers argue that the very fabric of society is threatened by disobedience, while humanists stress the primacy of the individual conscience.

The legal and philosophic aspects of obedience are of enormous import, but they say very little about how most people behave in concrete situations. I set up a simple experiment at Yale University to test how much pain an ordinary citizen would inflict on another person simply because he was ordered to by an experimental scientist. Stark authority was pitted against the subjects' strongest moral imperatives against hurting others, and, with the subjects' ears ringing with the screams of the victims, authority won more often than not. The extreme willingness of adults to go to almost any lengths on the command of an authority constitutes the chief finding of the study and the fact most urgently demanding explanation.

In the basic experimental design, two people come to a psychology laboratory to take part in a study of memory and learning. One of them is designated as a "teacher" and the other a "learner." The experimenter explains that the study is concerned with the effects of punishment on learning. The learner is conducted into a room, seated in a kind of miniature electric chair; his arms are strapped to prevent excessive movement, and an electrode is attached to his wrist. He is told that he will be read lists of simple word pairs, and that he will then be tested on his ability to remember the second word of a pair when he hears the first one again. Whenever he makes an error, he will receive electric shocks of increasing intensity.

The real focus of the experiment is the teacher. After watching the   5 learner being strapped into place, he is seated before an impressive shock generator. The instrument panel consists of thirty lever switches set in a horizontal line. Each switch is clearly labeled with a voltage designation ranging from 15 to 450 volts. The following designations are clearly indicated for groups of four switches, going from left to right: Slight Shock, Moderate Shock, Strong Shock, Very Strong Shock, Intense Shock, Extreme Intensity Shock, Danger: Severe Shock. (Two switches after this last designation are simply marked XXX.)

When a switch is depressed, a pilot light corresponding to each switch is illuminated in bright red; an electric buzzing is heard; a blue light, labeled "voltage energizer," flashes; the dial on the voltage meter swings to the right; and various relay clicks sound off.

The upper left-hand corner of the generator is labeled SHOCK GENERATOR, TYPE ZLB, DYSON INSTRUMENT COMPANY, WALTHAM, MASS. OUTPUT 15 VOLTS– 450 VOLTS.

Each subject is given a sample 45-volt shock from the generator before his run as teacher, and the jolt strengthens his belief in the authenticity of the machine.

The teacher is a genuinely naïve subject who has come to the laboratory for the experiment. The learner, or victim, is actually an actor who receives no shock at all. The point of the experiment is to see how far a person will proceed in a concrete and measurable situation in which he is ordered to inflict increasing pain on a protesting victim.

Conflict arises when the man receiving the shock begins to show   10 that he is experiencing discomfort. At 75 volts, he grunts; at 120 volts, he complains loudly; at 150, he demands to be released from the experiment. As the voltage increases, his protests become more vehement and emotional. At 285 volts, his response can be described only as an agonized scream. Soon thereafter, he makes no sound at all.

For the teacher, the situation quickly becomes one of gripping tension. It is not a game for him; conflict is intense and obvious. The manifest suffering of the learner presses him to quit; but each time he hesitates to administer a shock, the experimenter orders him to continue. To extricate himself from this plight, the subject must make a clear break with authority.

The subject, Gretchen Brandt, is an attractive thirty-one-year-old medical technician who works at the Yale Medical School. She had emigrated from Germany five years before.[1]

On several occasions when the learner complains, she [Gretchen] turns to the experimenter coolly and inquires, "Shall I continue?" She promptly returns to her task when the experimenter asks her to do so. At the administration of 210 volts, she turns to the experimenter, remarking firmly, "Well, I'm sorry, I don't think we should continue."

EXPERIMENTER: The experiment requires that you go on until he has learned all the word pairs correctly.

BRANDT: He has a heart condition, I'm sorry. He told you that before. 15

EXPERIMENTER: The shocks may be painful but they are not dangerous.

BRANDT: Well, I'm sorry, I think when shocks continue like this, they *are* dangerous. You ask him if he wants to get out. It's his free will.

EXPERIMENTER: It is absolutely essential that we continue. . . .

BRANDT: I'd like you to ask him. We came here of our free will. If he wants to continue I'll go ahead. He told you he had a heart condition. I'm sorry. I don't want to be responsible for anything happening to him. I wouldn't like it for me either.

EXPERIMENTER: You have no other choice. 20

BRANDT: I think we are here on our own free will. I don't want to be responsible if anything happens to him. Please understand that.

She refuses to go further and the experiment is terminated.

The woman is firm and resolute throughout. She indicates in the interview that she was in no way tense or nervous, and this corresponds to her controlled appearance during the experiment. She feels that the last shock she administered to the learner was extremely painful and reiterates that she "did not want to be responsible for any harm to him."

The woman's straightforward, courteous behavior in the experiment, lack of tension, and total control of her own action seem to make disobedience a simple and rational deed. Her behavior is the very embodiment of what I envisioned would be true for almost all subjects.

---

[1]Names of subjects described in this piece have been changed. [Milgram's note.]

AN UNEXPECTED OUTCOME

Before the experiments, I sought predictions about the outcome from 25 various kinds of people—psychiatrists, college sophomores, middle-class adults, graduate students, and faculty in the behavioral sciences. With remarkable similarity, they predicted that virtually all subjects would refuse to obey the experimenter. The psychiatrists, specifically, predicted that most subjects would not go beyond 150 volts, when the victim makes his first explicit demand to be freed. They expected that only 4 percent would reach 300 volts, and that only a pathological fringe of about one in a thousand would administer the highest shock on the board.

These predictions were unequivocally wrong. Of the forty subjects in the first experiment, twenty-five obeyed the orders of the experimenter to the end, punishing the victim until they reached the most potent shock available on the generator. After 450 volts were administered three times, the experimenter called a halt to the session. Many obedient subjects then heaved sighs of relief, mopped their brows, rubbed their fingers over their eyes, or nervously fumbled cigarettes. Others displayed only minimal signs of tension from beginning to end.

When the very first experiments were carried out, Yale undergraduates were used as subjects, and about 60 percent of them were fully obedient. A colleague of mine immediately dismissed these findings as having no relevance to "ordinary" people, asserting that Yale undergraduates are a highly aggressive, competitive bunch who step on each other's necks on the slightest provocation. He assured me that when "ordinary" people were tested, the results would be quite different. As we moved from the pilot studies to the regular experimental series, people drawn from every stratum of New Haven life came to be employed in the experiment: professionals, white-collar workers, unemployed persons, and industrial workers. *The experiment's total outcome was the same as we had observed among the students.*

Moreover, when the experiments were repeated in Princeton, Munich, Rome, South Africa, and Australia, the level of obedience was invariably somewhat *higher* than found in the investigation reported in this article. Thus one scientist in Munich found 85 percent of his subjects obedient.

Fred Prozi's reactions, if more dramatic than most, illuminate the conflicts experienced by others in less visible form. About fifty years old and unemployed at the time of the experiment, he has a good-natured, if slightly dissolute, appearance, and he strikes people as a rather ordinary fellow. He begins the session calmly but becomes tense as it proceeds. After delivering the 180-volt shock, he pivots around in his chair and, shaking his head, addresses the experimenter in agitated tones:

PROZI: I can't stand it. I'm not going to kill that man in there. You 30 hear him hollering?

EXPERIMENTER: As I told you before, the shocks may be painful, but . . .

PROZI: But he's hollering. He can't stand it. What's going to happen to him?

EXPERIMENTER (his voice is patient, matter-of-fact): The experiment requires that you continue, Teacher.

PROZI: Aaah, but, unh, I'm not going to get that man sick in there— know what I mean?

EXPERIMENTER: Whether the learner likes it or not, we must go on, 35 through all the word pairs.

PROZI: I refuse to take the responsibility. He's in there hollering!

EXPERIMENTER: It's absolutely essential that you continue, Prozi.

PROZI: (indicating the unused questions): There's too many left here, I mean, Jeez, if he gets them wrong, there's too many of them left. I mean, who's going to take the responsibility if anything happens to that gentleman?

EXPERIMENTER: I'm responsible for anything that happens to him. Continue, please.

PROZI: All right. (Consults list of words.) The next one's "Slow— 40 walk, truck, dance, music." Answer, please. (A buzzing sound indicates the learner has signaled his answer.) Wrong. A hundred and ninety-five volts. "Dance." (Zzumph!)

LEARNER (yelling): Let me out of here! My heart's bothering me! (Teacher looks at experimenter.)

EXPERIMENTER: Continue, please.

LEARNER (screaming): Let me out of here! You have no right to keep me here! Let me out of hear, my heart's bothering me, let me out!

PROZI (shakes head, pats the table nervously): You see, he's hollering. Hear that? Gee, I don't know.

EXPERIMENTER: The experiment requires . . . 45

PROZI (interrupting): I know it does, sir, but I mean—hunh! He don't know what he's getting in for. He's up to 195 volts! (Experiment continues, through 210 volts, 225 volts, 240 volts, 255 volts, 270 volts, at which point Prozi, with evident relief, runs out of word-pair questions.)

EXPERIMENTER: You'll have to go back to the beginning of that page and go through them again until he's learned them all correctly.

PROZI: Aw, no. I'm not going to kill that man. You mean I've got to keep going up with the scale? No sir. He's hollering in there. I'm not going to give him 450 volts.

EXPERIMENTER: The experiment requires that you go on.

LEARNER: Ohhh. I absolutely refuse to answer anymore. (Shouting 50 urgently now.) Let me out of here! You can't hold me here! Get me out. Get-me-out-of-here!

EXPERIMENTER: Continue. The next word is "Green," please.

PROZI: "Green—grass, hat, ink, apple." (Nothing happens. No answering buzz. Just gloomy silence.)

PROZI: I don't think he is going to answer.

EXPERIMENTER: If the learner doesn't answer in a reasonable time, about four or five seconds, consider the answer wrong. And follow the same procedures you have been doing for wrong answers. Say, "Wrong," tell him the number of volts, give him the punishment, read him the correct answer. Continue, please.

PROZI: "Green—grass, hat, ink, apple." Answer, please. (More si-   55
lence. Subject just sits there.)

EXPERIMENTER: Go on with the procedure, please.

PROZI: Three hundred and fifteen volts. The answer is "ink." (Zzumph!)

LEARNER: Ohh. Ooohh.

PROZI (relieved to hear response): Next one . . .

LEARNER: I absolutely refuse to answer.   60

PROZI: You got to. You get a shock if you don't answer. (Experiment continues with learner refusing to answer, and, finally, failing even to grunt or groan. At 375 volts, the subject stands up.)

PROZI: I think something's happened to that fellow in there. I don't get no answer. He was hollering at less voltage. Can't you check in and see if he's all right, please?

EXPERIMENTER (with same detached calm): Not once we've started. Please continue, Teacher.

PROZI (sits down, sighs deeply): "Cool—day, shade, water, paint." Answer, please. Are you all right in there? Are you all right?

EXPERIMENTER: Please continue, Teacher. Continue, please. (Subject   65
pushes lever. Zzumph!)

PROZI (swiveling around in his chair): Something's happened to that man in there. (Swiveling back.) Next one. "Low—dollar, necklace, moon, paint." (Turning around again.) Something's happened to that man in there. You better check in on him, sir. He won't answer or nothing.

EXPERIMENTER: Continue. Go on, please.

PROZI: You accept all responsibility?

EXPERIMENTER: The responsibility is mine. Correct. Please go on. (Subject returns to his list, starts running through words as rapidly as he can read them, works through to 450 volts.)

PROZI: That's that.   70

EXPERIMENTER: Continue using the 450 switch for each wrong answer. Continue, please.

PROZI: But I don't get anything!

EXPERIMENTER: Please continue. The next word is "white."

PROZI: Don't you think you should look in on him, please?

EXPERIMENTER: Not once we've started the experiment.   75

PROZI: What if he's dead in there? (Gestures toward the room with the electric chair.) I mean, he told me he can't stand the shock, sir. I don't mean to be rude, but I think you should look in on him. All you have to do is look in on him. All you have to do is look in the door. I don't get no answer, no noise. Something might have happened to the gentleman in there, sir.

EXPERIMENTER: We must continue. Go on, please.

PROZI: You mean keep giving him what? Four-hundred-fifty volts, what he's got now?

EXPERIMENTER: That's correct. Continue. The next word is "white."

PROZI (now at a furious pace): "White—cloud, horse, rock, house." 80 Answer, please. The answer is "horse." Four hundred and fifty volts. (Zzumph!) Next word, "Bag—paint, music, clown, girl." The answer is "paint." Four hundred and fifty volts. (Zzumph!) Next word is "Short— sentence, movie . . ."

EXPERIMENTER: Excuse me, Teacher. We'll have to discontinue the experiment.

PECULIAR REACTIONS

Morris Braverman, another subject, is a thirty-nine-year-old social worker. He looks older than his years because of his bald head and serious demeanor. His brow is furrowed, as if all the world's burdens were carried on his face. He appears intelligent and concerned.

When the learner refuses to answer and the experimenter instructs Braverman to treat the absence of an answer as equivalent to a wrong answer, he takes his instruction to heart. Before administering 300 volts he asserts officiously to the victim, "Mr. Wallace, your silence has to be considered as a wrong answer." Then he administers the shock. He offers half-heartedly to change places with the learner, then asks the experimenter, "Do I have to follow these instructions literally?" He is satisfied with the experimenter's answer that he does. His very refined and authoritative manner of speaking is increasingly broken up by wheezing laughter.

The experimenter's notes on Mr. Braverman at the last few shocks are:

- Almost breaking up now each time gives shock. Rubbing face to hide laughter.
- Squinting, trying to hide face with hand, still laughing.
- Cannot control his laughter at this point no matter what he does.
- Clenching fist, pushing it onto table.

In an interview after the session, Mr. Braverman summarizes the ex- 85 periment with impressive fluency and intelligence. He feels the experiment may have been designed also to "test the effects on the teacher of being in an essentially sadistic role, as well as the reactions of a student to a learning situation that was authoritative and punitive." When asked how painful the last few shocks administered to the learner were, he indicates that the most extreme category on the scale is not adequate (it read EXTREMELY PAINFUL) and places his mark at the edge of the scale with an arrow carrying it beyond the scale.

It is almost impossible to convey the greatly relaxed, sedate quality of his conversation in the interview. In the most relaxed terms, he speaks about his severe inner tension.

EXPERIMENTER: At what point were you most tense or nervous?

MR. BRAVERMAN: Well, when he first began to cry out in pain, and I realized this was hurting him. This got worse when he just blocked and refused to answer. There was I. I'm a nice person, I think, hurting somebody, and caught up in what seemed a mad situation . . . and in the interest of science, one goes through with it.

When the interviewer pursues the general question of tension, Mr. Braverman spontaneously mentions his laughter.

"My reactions were awfully peculiar. I don't know if you were 90 watching me, but my reactions were giggly, and trying to stifle laughter. This isn't the way I usually am. This was a sheer reaction to a totally impossible situation. And my reaction was to the situation of having to hurt somebody. And being totally helpless and caught up in a set of circumstances where I just couldn't deviate and I couldn't try to help. This is what got me."

Mr. Braverman, like all subjects, was told the actual nature and purpose of the experiment, and a year later he affirmed in a questionnaire that he had learned something of personal importance: "What appalled me was that I could possess this capacity for obedience and compliance to a central idea, i.e., the value of a memory experiment, even after it became clear that continued adherence to this value was at the expense of violation of another value, i.e., don't hurt someone who is helpless and not hurting you. As my wife said, 'You can call yourself Eichmann.' I hope I deal more effectively with any future conflicts of values I encounter."

THE ETIQUETTE OF SUBMISSION

One theoretical interpretation of this behavior holds that all people harbor deeply aggressive instincts continually pressing for expression, and that the experiment provides institutional justification for the release of these impulses. According to this view, if a person is placed in a situation in which he has complete power over another individual, whom he may punish as much as he likes, all that is sadistic and bestial in man comes to the fore. The impulse to shock the victim is seen to flow from the potent aggressive tendencies, which are part of the motivational life of the individual, and the experiment, because it provides social legitimacy, simply opens the door to their expression.

It becomes vital, therefore, to compare the subject's performance when he is under orders and when he is allowed to choose the shock level.

The procedure was identical to our standard experiment, except that the teacher was told that he was free to select any shock level on any of the trials. (The experimenter took pains to point out that the teacher could use the highest levels on the generator, the lowest, any in between, or any combination of levels.) Each subject proceeded for thirty critical trials. The learner's protests were coordinated to standard shock levels, his first grunt coming at 75 volts, his first vehement protest at 150 volts.

The average shock used during the thirty critical trials was less than 95 60 volts—lower than the point at which the victim showed the first signs of discomfort. Three of the forty subjects did not go beyond the very lowest level on the board, twenty-eight went no higher than 75 volts, and thirty-eight did not go beyond the first loud protest at 150 volts. Two subjects provided the exception, administering up to 325 and 450 volts, but the overall result was that the great majority of people delivered very low, usually painless, shocks when the choice was explicitly up to them.

This condition of the experiment undermines another commonly offered explanation of the subjects' behavior—that those who shocked the victim at the most severe levels came only from the sadistic fringe of society. If one considers that almost two-thirds of the participants fall into the category of "obedient" subjects, and that they represented ordinary people drawn from working, managerial, and professional classes, the argument becomes very shaky. Indeed, it is highly reminiscent of the issue that arose in connection with Hannah Arendt's 1963 book, *Eichmann in Jerusalem*. Arendt contended that the prosecution's effort to depict Eichmann as a sadistic monster was fundamentally wrong, that he came closer to being an uninspired bureaucrat who simply sat at his desk and did his job. For asserting her views, Arendt became the object of considerable scorn, even calumny. Somehow, it was felt that the monstrous deeds carried out by Eichmann required a brutal, twisted personality, evil incarnate. After witnessing hundreds of ordinary persons submit to the authority in our own experiments, I must conclude that Arendt's conception of the banality of evil comes closer to the truth than one might dare imagine. The ordinary person who shocked the victim did so out of a sense of obligation—an impression of his duties as a subject—and not from any peculiarly aggressive tendencies.

This is, perhaps, the most fundamental lesson of our study: Ordinary people, simply doing their jobs, and without any particular hostility on their part, can become agents in a terrible destructive process. Moreover, even when the destructive effects of their work become patently clear, and they are asked to carry out actions incompatible with fundamental standards of morality, relatively few people have the resources needed to resist authority.

Many of the people were in some sense against what they did to the learner, and many protested even while they obeyed. Some were totally convinced of the wrongness of their actions but could not bring themselves to make an open break with authority. They often derived satisfaction from their thoughts and felt that—within themselves, at least—they had been on the side of the angels. They tried to reduce strain by obeying the experimenter but "only slightly," encouraging the learner, touching the generator switches gingerly. When interviewed, such a subject would stress that he had "asserted my humanity" by administering the briefest shock possible. Handling the conflict in this manner was easier than defiance.

The situation is constructed so that there is no way the subject can stop shocking the learner without violating the experimenter's definitions of his own competence. The subject fears that he will appear arrogant, untoward, and rude if he breaks off. Although these inhibiting emotions appear small in scope alongside the violence being done to the learner, they suffuse the mind and feelings of the subject who is miserable at the prospect of having to repudiate the authority to his face. (When the experiment was altered so that the experimenter gave his instructions by telephone instead of in person, only a third as many people were fully obedient through 450 volts.) It is a curious thing that a measure of compassion on the part of the subject—an unwillingness to "hurt" the experimenter's feelings—is part of those binding forces inhibiting his disobedience. The withdrawal of such deference may be as painful to the subject as to the authority he defies.

DUTY WITHOUT CONFLICT

The subjects do not derive satisfaction from inflicting pain, but they often like the feeling they get from pleasing the experimenter. They are proud of doing a good job, obeying the experimenter under difficult circumstances. While the subjects administered only mild shocks on their own initiative, one experimental variation showed that, under orders, 30 percent of them were willing to deliver 450 volts even when they had to forcibly push the learner's hand down on the electrode.

Bruno Batta is a thirty-seven-year-old welder who took part in the variation requiring the use of force. He was born in New Haven, his parents in Italy. He has a rough-hewn face that conveys a conspicuous lack of alertness. He has some difficulty in mastering the experimental procedure and needs to be corrected by the experimenter several times. He shows appreciation for the help and willingness to do what is required. After the 150-volt level, Batta has to force the learner's hand down on the shock plate, since the learner himself refuses to touch it.

When the learner first complains, Mr. Batta pays no attention to him. His face remains impassive, as if to dissociate himself from the learner's disruptive behavior. When the experimenter instructs him to force the learner's hand down, he adopts a rigid, mechanical procedure. He tests the generator switch. When it fails to function, he immediately forces the learner's hand onto the shock plate. All the while he maintains the same rigid mask. The learner, seated alongside him, begs him to stop, but with robotic impassivity he continues the procedure.

What is extraordinary is his apparent total indifference to the learner; he hardly takes cognizance of him as a human being. Meanwhile, he relates to the experimenter in a submissive and courteous fashion.

At the 330-volt level, the learner refuses not only to touch the shock plate but also to provide any answers. Annoyed, Batta turns to him, and chastises him: "You better answer and get it over with. We can't stay here all night." These are the only words he directs to the learner in the course of an hour. Never again does he speak to him. The scene is brutal and depressing, his hard, impassive face showing total indifference as he subdues the screaming learner and gives him shocks. He seems to derive no pleasure from the act itself, only quiet satisfaction at doing his job properly.

When he administers 450 volts, he turns to the experimenter and asks, "Where do we go from here, Professor?" His tone is deferential and expresses his willingness to be a cooperative subject, in contrast to the learner's obstinacy. 105

At the end of the session he tells the experimenter how honored he has been to help him, and in a moment of contrition, remarks, "Sir, sorry it couldn't have been a full experiment."

He has done his honest best. It is only the deficient behavior of the learner that has denied the experimenter full satisfaction.

The essence of obedience is that a person comes to view himself as the instrument for carrying out another person's wishes, and he therefore no longer regards himself as responsible for his actions. Once this critical shift of viewpoint has occurred, all of the essential features of obedience follow. The most far-reaching consequence is that the person feels responsible *to* the authority directing him but feels no responsibility *for* the content of the actions that the authority prescribes. Morality does not disappear—it acquires a radically different focus: The subordinate person feels shame or pride depending on how adequately he has performed the actions called for by authority.

Language provides numerous terms to pinpoint this type of morality: *Loyalty, duty, discipline* all are terms heavily saturated with moral meaning and refer to the degree to which a person fulfills his obligations to authority. They refer not to the "goodness" of the person per se but to the adequacy with which a subordinate fulfills his socially defined role. The most frequent defense of the individual who has performed a heinous act under command of authority is that he has simply done his duty. In asserting this defense, the individual is not introducing an alibi concocted for the moment but is reporting honestly on the psychological attitude induced by submission to authority.

For a person to feel responsible for his actions, he must sense that [110] the behavior has flowed from "the self." In the situation we have studied, subjects have precisely the opposite view of their actions—namely, they see them as originating in the motives of some other person. Subjects in the experiment frequently said, "If it were up to me, I would not have administered shocks to the learner."

Once authority has been isolated as the cause of the subject's behavior, it is legitimate to inquire into the necessary elements of authority and how it must be perceived in order to gain his compliance. We conducted some investigations into the kinds of changes that would cause the experimenter to lose his power and to be disobeyed by the subject. Some of the variations revealed that

- *The experimenter's physical presence has a marked impact on his authority.* As cited earlier, obedience dropped off sharply when orders were given by telephone. The experimenter could often induce a disobedient subject to go on by returning to the laboratory.

- *Conflicting authority severely paralyzes action.* When two experimenters of equal status, both seated at the command desk, gave incompatible orders, no shocks were delivered past the point of their disagreement.

- *The rebellious action of others severely undermines authority.* In one variation, three teachers (two actors and a real subject) administered a test and shocks. When the two actors disobeyed the experimenter and refused to go beyond a certain shock level, thirty-six of forty subjects joined their disobedient peers and refused as well.

Although the experimenter's authority was fragile in some respects, it is also true that he had almost none of the tools used in ordinary command structures. For example, the experimenter did not threaten the subjects with punishment—such as loss of income, community ostracism, or jail—for failure to obey. Neither could he offer incentives. Indeed, we should expect the experimenter's authority to be much less than that of someone like a general, since the experimenter has no power to enforce his imperatives, and since participation in a psychological experiment scarcely evokes the sense of urgency and dedication found in warfare. Despite these limitations, he still managed to command a dismaying degree of obedience.

I will cite one final variation of the experiment that depicts a dilemma that is more common in everyday life. The subject was not ordered to pull the lever that shocked the victim, but merely to perform a subsidiary task (administering the word-pair test) while another person administered the shock. In this situation, thirty-seven of forty adults continued to the highest level on the shock generator. Predictably, they excused their behavior by saying that the responsibility belonged to the man who actually pulled the switch. This may illustrate a dangerously typical arrangement in a complex society: It is easy to ignore responsibility when one is only an intermediate link in a chain of action.

The problem of obedience is not wholly psychological. The form and shape of society and the way it is developing have much to do with it. There was a time, perhaps, when people were able to give a fully human response to any situation because they were fully absorbed in it as human beings. But as soon as there was a division of labor things changed. Beyond a certain point, the breaking up of society into people carrying out narrow and very special jobs takes away from the human quality of work and life. A person does not get to see the whole situation but only a small part of it, and is thus unable to act without some kind of overall direction. He yields to authority but in doing so is alienated from his own actions.

Even Eichmann was sickened when he toured the concentration 115 camps, but he had only to sit at a desk and shuffle papers. At the same time the man in the camp who actually dropped Cyclon-b into the gas chambers was able to justify *his* behavior on the ground that he was only following orders from above. Thus there is a fragmentation of the total human act; no one is confronted with the consequences of his decision to carry out the evil act. The person who assumes responsibility has evaporated. Perhaps this is the most common characteristic of socially organized evil in modern society.

Topics for Critical Thinking and Writing

1. Milgram says that "the dilemma inherent in submission to authority is ancient, as old as the story of Abraham" (para. 2). What is the story of Abraham to which he refers? And what is the "dilemma inherent in submission"? (Review the section on dilemmas, p. 266.)

2. Describe the Milgram experiments in an essay of 150 words. In a sentence, what conclusion does Milgram himself draw from the experiments?

3. Read the essay by Walter Stace (p. 707) and decide whether he would regard the dialogue between the experimenter and Ms. Brandt (paras. 14–21) as a good example of people acting of their own "free will." Is the experimenter correct when he tells her "You have no other choice"?

4. Milgram explains that prior to the experiment he asked various people to predict the results; these predictions were "unequivocally wrong" (para. 26). Explain, if you can, why these groups predicted a very different outcome from what actually happened.

5. Did the experimenter ever threaten the subjects in the experiments? Use coercion? What is your evidence, one way or the other?

6. Milgram eventually offers "one theoretical interpretation" of the behavior of the experimenters (para. 92). What is that interpretation? Do you think it is plausible, or not?

7. What, according to Milgram (para. 108), is "the essence of obedience"? Does an obedient person, in this sense of the term, cease to act of his own free will? Explain why or why not in an essay of 250 words.

8. Suppose someone were to criticize Milgram for his experiments, arguing that they were unethical because they were based fundamentally on deceiving the subjects about what they were really doing. How might Milgram reply?

Sophocles

One of the three great tragic dramatists of ancient Greece, Sophocles (496?–406 B.C.) was born in Colonus, near Athens. He is said to have written 120 plays, but only 7 tragedies are extant.

Antigone, probably written about 441 B.C., is one play in Sophocles' so-called Theban Trilogy, three plays about the family of Oedipus, King of Thebes. In fact, however, the three plays were written at widely separated intervals; King Oedipus *is usually dated about 430 B.C., and the third play,* Oedipus at Colonus, *written at the very end of Sophocles' life, was not produced until 401 B.C., five years after his death. Further, although* Antigone *is the first in terms of date of composition, in terms of the narrative it is the last, taking place after the death of Oedipus.*

Just as today someone writing a novel, play, or film script on the Civil War can assume that we know the roles of characters with the names of Lincoln, Grant, Lee, Jackson, and Booth and yet can still offer fresh characterizations of these figures, so Sophocles could assume that his audience knew the outlines of the story of Oedipus and his family, and yet he could to some degree make it his own story. The gist is this: When Oedipus, King of Thebes, learned that he had unknowingly killed his father and married his mother, he blinded himself and left Thebes. Ultimately he died in Colonus. His sons, Polyneices and Eteocles, quarreled; Polyneices was driven out, went to Argos, and returned with the Argive army to assault Thebes, and in the battle each brother killed the other. Creon became king (this is the situation in Antigone*) and ordered that Polyneices' body be left to rot unburied on the battlefield because he attacked his own city.*

Antigone

An English Version by Dudley Fitts and Robert Fitzgerald

LIST OF CHARACTERS
ANTIGONE
ISMENE
EURYDICE

CREON
HAIMON
TEIRESIAS
A SENTRY
A MESSENGER
CHORUS

SCENE: *Before the palace of Creon, King of Thebes. A central double door, and two lateral doors. A platform extends the length of the façade, and from this platform three steps lead down into the "orchestra," or chorus-ground.*

TIME: *Dawn of the day after the repulse of the Argive army from the assault on Thebes.*

Prologue

Antigone and Ismene enter from the central door of the palace.

ANTIGONE. Ismene, dear sister,
    You would think that we had already suffered enough
    For the curse on Oedipus.°
    I cannot imagine any grief
    That you and I have not gone through. And now—   5
    Have they told you of the new decree of our King Creon?
ISMENE. I have heard nothing: I know
    That two sisters lost two brothers, a double death
    In a single hour; and I know that the Argive army
    Fled in the night; but beyond this, nothing.   10
ANTIGONE. I thought so. And this is why I wanted you
    To come out here with me. There is something we must do.
ISMENE. Why do you speak so strangely?
ANTIGONE. Listen, Ismene:
    Creon buried our brother Eteocles   15
    With military honors, gave him a soldier's funeral,
    And it was right that he should; but Polyneices,
    Who fought as bravely and died as miserably,—
    They say that Creon has sworn
    No one shall bury him, no one mourn for him,   20
    But his body must lie in the fields, a sweet treasure
    For carrion birds to find as they search for food.
    That is what they say, and our good Creon is coming here

---

3 Oedipus once King of Thebes, was the father of Antigone and Ismene, and of their brothers Polyneices and Eteocles. Oedipus unwittingly killed his father, Laïos, and married his own mother, Iocaste. When he learned what he had done, he blinded himself and left Thebes. Eteocles and Polyneices quarreled; Polyneices was driven out but returned to assault Thebes. In the battle each brother killed the other; Creon became king and ordered that Polyneices be left to rot unburied on the battlefield as a traitor. [All notes are the editors'.]

To announce it publicly; and the penalty —
Stoning to death in the public square!

                               There it is,   25
And now you can prove what you are:
A true sister, or a traitor to your family.

ISMENE. Antigone, you are mad! What could I possibly do?

ANTIGONE. You must decide whether you will help me or not.

ISMENE. I do not understand you. Help you in what?   30

ANTIGONE. Ismene. I am going to bury him. Will you come?

ISMENE. Bury him! You have just said the new law forbids it.

ANTIGONE. He is my brother. And he is your brother, too.

ISMENE. But think of the danger! Think what Creon will do!

ANTIGONE. Creon is not strong enough to stand in my way.   35

ISMENE. Ah sister!

Oedipus died, everyone hating him
For what his own search brought to light, his eyes
Ripped out by his own hand; and Iocaste died,
His mother and wife at once: she twisted the cords   40
That strangled her life; and our two brothers died,
Each killed by the other's sword. And we are left:
But oh, Antigone,
Think how much more terrible than these
Our own death would be if we should go against Creon   45
And do what he has forbidden! We are only women,
We cannot fight with men, Antigone!
The law is strong, we must give in to the law
In this thing, and in worse. I beg the Dead
To forgive me, but I am helpless: I must yield   50
To those in authority. And I think it is dangerous business
To be always meddling.

ANTIGONE.   If that is what you think,
I should not want you, even if you asked to come.
You have made your choice, you can be what you want to be.
But I will bury him; and if I must die,   55
I say that this crime is holy: I shall lie down
With him in death, and I shall be as dear
To him as he to me.

                It is the dead,
Not the living, who make the longest demands:
We die for ever. . . .

                      You may do as you like.   60
Since apparently the laws of the gods mean nothing to you.

ISMENE. They mean a great deal to me; but I have no strength
To break laws that were made for the public good.

ANTIGONE. That must be your excuse, I suppose. But as for me,
I will bury the brother I love.

ISMENE.   Antigone,   65
    I am so afraid for you!
ANTIGONE.   You need not be:
    You have yourself to consider, after all.
ISMENE. But no one must hear of this, you must tell no one!
    I will keep it a secret, I promise!
ANTIGONE.   O tell it! Tell everyone!
    Think how they'll hate you when it all comes out   70
    If they learn that you knew about it all the time!
ISMENE. So fiery! You should be cold with fear.
ANTIGONE. Perhaps. But I am doing only what I must.
ISMENE. But can you do it? I say that you cannot.
ANTIGONE. Very well: when my strength gives out, I shall do no more.   75
ISMENE. Impossible things should not be tried at all.
ANTIGONE. Go away, Ismene:
    I shall be hating you soon, and the dead will too,
    For your words are hateful. Leave me my foolish plan:
    I am not afraid of the danger; if it means death,   80
    It will not be the worst of deaths—death without honor.
ISMENE. Go then, if you feel that you must.
    You are unwise,
    But a loyal friend indeed to those who love you.

Exit into the palace. Antigone goes off, left. Enter the Chorus.

Parodos

CHORUS. Now the long blade of the sun, lying   *Strophe° 1*
    Level east to west, touches with glory
    Thebes of the Seven Gates. Open, unlidded
    Eye of golden day! O marching light
    Across the eddy and rush of Dirce's stream,°   5
    Striking the white shields of the enemy
    Thrown headlong backward from the blaze of morning!
CHORAGOS.° Polyneices their commander
    Roused them with windy phrases,
    He the wild eagle screaming   10
    Insults above our land,
    His wings their shields of snow,
    His crest their marshalled helms.

CHORUS. Against our seven gates in a yawning ring   *Antistrophe° 1*
    The famished spears came onward in the night: 15

---

1 Strophe Literally, "turn," a stanza of a choral song, sung as the chorus moves in one direction. **5 Dirce's stream** A stream west of Thebes. **8 Choragos** Leader of the Chorus.
14 Antistrophe Sung as the chorus moves in the opposite direction.

But before his jaws were sated with our blood,
Or pine fire took the garland of our towers,
He was thrown back; and as he turned, great Thebes—
No tender victim for his noisy power—
Rose like a dragon behind him, shouting war.   20

CHORAGOS. For God hates utterly
The bray of bragging tongues;
And when he beheld their smiling,
Their swagger of golden helms,
The frown of his thunder blasted   25
Their first man from our walls.

CHORUS. We heard his shout of triumph high in the air   *Strophe 2*
Turn to a scream; far out in a flaming arc
He fell with his windy torch, and the earth struck him.
And others storming in fury no less than his   30
Found shock of death in the dusty joy of battle.

CHORAGOS. Seven captains at seven gates
Yielded their clanging arms to the god
That bends the battle-line and breaks it.
These two only, brothers in blood,   35
Face to face in matchless rage,
Mirroring each the other's death,
Clashed in long combat.

CHORUS. But now in the beautiful morning of victory   *Antistrophe 2*
Let Thebes of the many chariots sing for joy!   40
With hearts for dancing we'll take leave of war:
Our temples shall be sweet with hymns of praise,
And the long nights shall echo with our chorus.

Scene I

CHORAGOS. But now at last our new King is coming:
Creon of Thebes, Menoikeus' son.
In this auspicious dawn of his reign
What are the new complexities
That shifting Fate has woven for him?   5
What is his counsel? Why has he summoned
The old men to hear him?

Enter Creon from the palace, center. He addresses the Chorus from the top step.

CREON. Gentlemen: I have the honor to inform you that our Ship of State, which recent storms have threatened to destroy, has come safely to harbor at last, guided by the merciful wisdom of Heaven. I have sum- 10
moned you here this morning because I know that I can depend upon you: your devotion to King Laïos was absolute; you never hesitated in your duty to our late ruler Oedipus; and when Oedipus died, your loy-

alty was transferred to his children. Unfortunately, as you know, his two sons, the princes Eteocles and Polyneices, have killed each other in 15 battle; and I, as the next in blood, have succeeded to the full power of the throne.

I am aware, of course, that no Ruler can expect complete loyalty from his subjects until he has been tested in office. Nevertheless, I say to you at the very outset that I have nothing but contempt for the kind of 20 Governor who is afraid, for whatever reason, to follow the course that he knows is best for the State; and as for the man who sets private friendship above the public welfare,—I have no use for him, either. I call God to witness that if I saw my country headed for ruin, I should not be afraid to speak out plainly; and I need hardly remind you that I would 25 never have any dealings with an enemy of the people. No one values friendship more highly than I: but we must remember that friends made at the risk of wrecking our Ship are not real friends at all.

These are my principles, at any rate, and that is why I have made the following decision concerning the sons of Oedipus: Eteocles, who died as 30 a man should die, fighting for his country, is to be buried with full military honors, with all the ceremony that is usual when the greatest heroes die; but his brother Polyneices, who broke his exile to come back with fire and sword against his native city and the shrines of his fathers' gods, whose one idea was to spill the blood of his blood and sell his own 35 people into slavery—Polyneices, I say, is to have no burial: no man is to touch him or say the least prayer for him; he shall lie on the plain, unburied; and the birds and the scavenging dogs can do with him whatever they like.

This is my command, and you can see the wisdom behind it. As long 40 as I am King, no traitor is going to be honored with the loyal man. But whoever shows by word and deed that he is on the side of the State— he shall have my respect while he is living and my reverence when he is dead.

CHORAGOS. If that is your will, Creon son of Menoikeus, 45
You have the right to enforce it: we are yours.

CREON. That is my will. Take care that you do your part.

CHORAGOS. We are old men: let the younger ones carry it out.

CREON. I do not mean that: the sentries have been appointed.

CHORAGOS. Then what is it that you would have us do? 50

CREON. You will give no support to whoever breaks the law.

CHORAGOS. Only a crazy man is in love with death!

CREON. And death it is; yet money talks, and the wisest
Have sometimes been known to count a few coins too many.

Enter Sentry from left.

SENTRY. I'll not say that I'm out of breath from running, King, because 55 every time I stopped to think about what I have to tell you, I felt like going back. And all the time a voice kept saying, "You fool, don't you

know you're walking straight into trouble?"; and then another voice:
"Yes, but if you let somebody else get the news to Creon first, it will be
even worse than that for you!" But good sense won out, at least I hope it   60
was good sense, and here I am with a story that makes no sense at all;
but I'll tell it anyhow, because, as they say, what's going to happen's
going to happen and—

CREON. Come to the point. What have you to say?

SENTRY. I did not do it. I did not see who did it. You must not punish me   65
     for what someone else has done.

CREON. A comprehensive defense! More effective, perhaps,
     If I knew its purpose. Come: what is it?

SENTRY. A dreadful thing . . . I don't know how to put it—

CREON. Out with it!

SENTRY.   Well, then;   70
     The dead man—
                    Polyneices—

Pause. The Sentry is overcome, fumbles for words. Creon waits impassively.

                    out there—
                                someone,—

New dust on the slimy flesh!

Pause. No sign from Creon.

Someone has given it burial that way, and
Gone . . .

Long pause. Creon finally speaks with deadly control.

CREON. And the man who dared do this?

SENTRY.   I swear I   75
     Do not know! You must believe me!
                              Listen:
The ground was dry, not a sign of digging, no,
Not a wheeltrack in the dust, no trace of anyone.
It was when they relieved us this morning: and one of them,
The corporal, pointed to it.
                    There it was,   80
The strangest—
          Look:
The body, just mounded over with light dust: you see?
Not buried really, but as if they'd covered it
Just enough for the ghost's peace. And no sign
Of dogs or any wild animal that had been there.   85

And then what a scene there was! Every man of us
Accusing the other: we all proved the other man did it,
We all had proof that we could not have done it.
We were ready to take hot iron in our hands,

Walk through fire, swear by all the gods,   90
It was not I!
I do not know who it was, but it was not I!

*Creon's rage has been mounting steadily, but the sentry is too intent upon his
story to notice it.*

And then, when this came to nothing, someone said
A thing that silenced us and made us stare
Down at the ground: you had to be told the news,   95
And one of us had to do it! We threw the dice,
And the bad luck fell to me. So here I am,
No happier to be here than you are to have me:
Nobody likes the man who brings bad news.

CHORAGOS. I have been wondering, King: can it be that the gods have 100
done this?

CREON (*furiously*). Stop!
Must you doddering wrecks
Go out of your heads entirely? "The gods"!
Intolerable!   105
The gods favor this corpse? Why? How had he served them?
Tried to loot their temples, burn their images,
Yes, and the whole State, and its laws with it!
Is it your senile opinion that the gods love to honor bad men?
A pious thought! —
                        No, from the very beginning   110
There have been those who have whispered together,
Stiff-necked anarchists, putting their heads together,
Scheming against me in alleys. These are the men,
And they have bribed my own guard to do this thing.
(*Sententiously.*) Money!   115
There's nothing in the world so demoralizing as money.
Down go your cities,
Homes gone, men gone, honest hearts corrupted.
Crookedness of all kinds, and all for money!
(*To Sentry.*)   But you —!
I swear by God and by the throne of God,   120
The man who has done this thing shall pay for it!
Find that man, bring him here to me, or your death
Will be the least of your problems: I'll string you up
Alive, and there will be certain ways to make you
Discover your employer before you die;   125
And the process may teach you a lesson you seem to have missed:
The dearest profit is sometimes all too dear:
That depends on the source. Do you understand me?
A fortune won is often misfortune.

SENTRY. King, may I speak?

CREON.   Your very voice distresses me.   130
SENTRY. Are you sure that it is my voice, and not your conscience?
CREON. By God, he wants to analyze me now!
SENTRY. It is not what I say, but what has been done, that hurts you.
CREON. You talk too much.
SENTRY.   Maybe; but I've done nothing.
CREON. Sold your soul for some silver: that's all you've done.   135
SENTRY. How dreadful it is when the right judge judges wrong!
CREON. Your figures of speech
    May entertain you now; but unless you bring me the man,
    You will get little profit from them in the end.

Exit Creon into the palace.

SENTRY. "Bring me the man"—!   140
    I'd like nothing better than bringing him the man!
    But bring him or not, you have seen the last of me here.
    At any rate, I am safe!

(Exit Sentry.)

Ode I

CHORUS. Numberless are the world's wonders, but none   *Strophe 1*
    More wonderful than man; the stormgray sea
    Yields to his prows, the huge crests bear him high;
    Earth, holy and inexhaustible, is graven
    With shining furrows where his plows have gone   5
    Year after year, the timeless labor of stallions.

    The lightboned birds and beasts that cling to cover,   *Antistrophe 1*
    The lithe fish lighting their reaches of dim water,
    All are taken, tamed in the net of his mind;
    The lion on the hill, the wild horse windy-maned,   10
    Resign to him; and his blunt yoke has broken
    The sultry shoulders of the mountain bull.

    Words also, and thought as rapid as air,   *Strophe 2*
    He fashions to his good use; statecraft is his,
    And his the skill that deflects the arrows of snow,   15
    The spears of winter rain: from every wind
    He has made himself secure—from all but one:
    In the late wind of death he cannot stand.

    O clear intelligence, force beyond all measure!   *Antistrophe 2*
    O fate of man, working both good and evil!   20
    When the laws are kept, how proudly his city stands!
    When the laws are broken, what of his city then?

Never may the anarchic man find rest at my hearth,
Never be it said that my thoughts are his thoughts.

Scene II

Reenter Sentry leading Antigone.

CHORAGOS. What does this mean? Surely this captive woman
    Is the Princess, Antigone. Why should she be taken?
SENTRY. Here is the one who did it! We caught her
    In the very act of burying him. — Where is Creon?
CHORAGOS. Just coming from the house.

Enter Creon, center.

CREON.   What has happened?   5
    Why have you come back so soon?
SENTRY (*expansively*).   O King,
    A man should never be too sure of anything:
    I would have sworn
    That you'd not see me here again: your anger
    Frightened me so, and the things you threatened me with;   10
    But how could I tell then
    That I'd be able to solve the case so soon?
    No dice-throwing this time: I was only too glad to come!
    Here is this woman. She is the guilty one:
    We found her trying to bury him.   15
    Take her, then; question her; judge her as you will.
    I am through with the whole thing now, and glad of it.
CREON. But this is Antigone! Why have you brought her here?
SENTRY. She was burying him, I tell you!
CREON (*severely*).   Is this the truth?
SENTRY. I saw her with my own eyes. Can I say more?   20
CREON. The details: come, tell me quickly!
SENTRY.   It was like this:
    After those terrible threats of yours, King,
    We went back and brushed the dust away from the body.
    The flesh was soft by now, and stinking,
    So we sat on a hill to windward and kept guard.   25
    No napping this time! We kept each other awake.
    But nothing happened until the white round sun
    Whirled in the center of the round sky over us:
    Then, suddenly,
    A storm of dust roared up from the earth, and the sky   30
    Went out, the plain vanished with all its trees
    In the stinging dark. We closed our eyes and endured it.
    The whirlwind lasted a long time, but it passed;
    And then we looked, and there was Antigone!

I have seen   35
A mother bird come back to a stripped nest, heard
Her crying bitterly a broken note or two
For the young ones stolen. Just so, when this girl
Found the bare corpse, and all her love's work wasted,
She wept, and cried on heaven to damn the hands   40
That had done this thing.
                    And then she brought more dust
And sprinkled wine three times for her brother's ghost.

We ran and took her at once. She was not afraid,
Not even when we charged her with what she had done.
She denied nothing.
                 And this was a comfort to me,   45
And some uneasiness: for it is a good thing
To escape from death, but it is no great pleasure
To bring death to a friend.
              Yet I always say
There is nothing so comfortable as your own safe skin!
CREON (*slowly, dangerously*). And you, Antigone,   50
You with your head hanging,—do you confess this thing?
ANTIGONE. I do. I deny nothing.
CREON (*to Sentry*).   You may go.

(Exit Sentry.)

(To Antigone.) Tell me, tell me briefly:
Had you heard my proclamation touching this matter?
ANTIGONE. It was public. Could I help hearing it?   55
CREON. And yet you dared defy the law.
ANTIGONE.   I dared.
It was not God's proclamation. That final Justice
That rules the world below makes no such laws.

Your edict, King, was strong.
But all your strength is weakness itself against   60
The immortal unrecorded laws of God.
They are not merely now: they were, and shall be,
Operative for ever, beyond man utterly.
I knew I must die, even without your decree:
I am only mortal. And if I must die   65
Now, before it is my time to die,
Surely this is no hardship: can anyone
Living, as I live, with evil all about me,
Think Death less than a friend? This death of mine
Is of no importance; but if I had left my brother   70
Lying in death unburied, I should have suffered.

Now I do not.
                You smile at me. Ah Creon,
Think me a fool, if you like; but it may well be
That a fool convicts me of folly.
CHORAGOS. Like father, like daughter: both headstrong, deaf to reason!   75
    She has never learned to yield.
CREON.   She has much to learn.
    The inflexible heart breaks first, the toughest iron
Cracks first, and the wildest horses bend their necks
At the pull of the smallest curb.
                       Pride? In a slave?
This girl is guilty of a double insolence,   80
Breaking the given laws and boasting of it.
Who is the man here,
She or I, if this crime goes unpunished?
Sister's child, or more than sister's child,
Or closer yet in blood—she and her sister   85
Win bitter death for this!
(*To Servants.*)   Go, some of you,
Arrest Ismene. I accuse her equally.
Bring her: you will find her sniffling in the house there.

Her mind's a traitor: crimes kept in the dark
Cry for light, and the guardian brain shudders;   90
But how much worse than this
Is brazen boasting of barefaced anarchy!
ANTIGONE. Creon, what more do you want than my death?
CREON.   Nothing.
    That gives me everything.
ANTIGONE.   Then I beg you: kill me.
    This talking is a great weariness: your words   95
Are distasteful to me, and I am sure that mine
Seem so to you. And yet they should not seem so:
I should have praise and honor for what I have done.
All these men here would praise me
Were their lips not frozen shut with fear of you.   100
(*Bitterly.*) Ah the good fortune of kings,
Licensed to say and do whatever they please!
CREON. You are alone here in that opinion.
ANTIGONE. No, they are with me. But they keep their tongues in leash.
CREON. Maybe. But you are guilty, and they are not.   105
ANTIGONE. There is no guilt in reverence for the dead.
CREON. But Eteocles—was he not your brother too?
ANTIGONE. My brother too.
CREON.   And you insult his memory?
ANTIGONE (*softly*). The dead man would not say that I insult it.

CREON. He would: for you honor a traitor as much as him.　　　　110
ANTIGONE. His own brother, traitor or not, and equal in blood.
CREON. He made war on his country. Eteocles defended it.
ANTIGONE. Nevertheless, there are honors due all the dead.
CREON. But not the same for the wicked as for the just.
ANTIGONE. Ah Creon, Creon,　　　　115
　　　Which of us can say what the gods hold wicked?
CREON. An enemy is an enemy, even dead.
ANTIGONE. It is my nature to join in love, not hate.
CREON (*finally losing patience*). Go join them then; if you must have your love,
　　　Find it in hell!　　　　120
CHORAGOS. But see, Ismene comes:

Enter Ismene, guarded.

　　　Those tears are sisterly, the cloud
　　　That shadows her eyes rains down gentle sorrow.
CREON. You too, Ismene,
　　　Snake in my ordered house, sucking my blood　　　　125
　　　Stealthily—and all the time I never knew
　　　That these two sisters were aiming at my throne!

　　　　　　　　　　　　　　　　　　　Ismene,
　　　Do you confess your share in this crime, or deny it?
　　　Answer me.
ISMENE. Yes, if she will let me say so. I am guilty.　　　　130
ANTIGONE (*coldly*). No, Ismene. You have no right to say so.
　　　You would not help me, and I will not have you help me.
ISMENE. But now I know what you meant; and I am here
　　　To join you, to take my share of punishment.
ANTIGONE. The dead man and the gods who rule the dead　　　　135
　　　Know whose act this was. Words are not friends.
ISMENE. Do you refuse me, Antigone? I want to die with you:
　　　I too have a duty that I must discharge to the dead.
ANTIGONE. You shall not lessen my death by sharing it.
ISMENE. What do I care for life when you are dead?　　　　140
ANTIGONE. Ask Creon. You're always hanging on his opinions.
ISMENE. You are laughing at me. Why, Antigone?
ANTIGONE. It's a joyless laughter, Ismene.
ISMENE.　　　　　　　　　　　　But can I do nothing?
ANTIGONE. Yes. Save yourself. I shall not envy you.
　　　There are those who will praise you; I shall have honor, too.　　　　145
ISMENE. But we are equally guilty!
ANTIGONE.　　　　　　　　　　No more, Ismene.
　　　You are alive, but I belong to Death.
CREON (*to the Chorus*). Gentlemen, I beg you to observe these girls:
　　　One has just now lost her mind; the other,
　　　It seems, has never had a mind at all.　　　　150

ISMENE. Grief teaches the steadiest minds to waver, King.

CREON. Yours certainly did, when you assumed guilt with the guilty!

ISMENE. But how could I go on living without her?

CREON.   You are.

    She is already dead.

ISMENE.   But your own son's bride!

CREON. There are places enough for him to push his plow.   155

    I want no wicked women for my sons!

ISMENE. O dearest Haimon, how your father wrongs you!

CREON. I've had enough of your childish talk of marriage!

CHORAGOS. Do you really intend to steal this girl from your son?

CREON. No; Death will do that for me.

CHORAGOS.   Then she must die?   160

CREON (*ironically*). You dazzle me.

               —But enough of this talk!

(*To Guards.*) You, there, take them away and guard them well:

For they are but women, and even brave men run

When they see Death coming.

Exeunt Ismene, Antigone, and Guards.

Ode II

CHORUS. Fortunate is the man who has never tasted God's

    vengeance!   *Strophe 1*

Where once the anger of heaven has struck, that house is shaken

For ever: damnation rises behind each child

Like a wave cresting out of the black northeast,

When the long darkness under sea roars up   5

And bursts drumming death upon the windwhipped sand.

I have seen this gathering sorrow from time long past   *Antistrophe 1*

Loom upon Oedipus' children: generation from generation

Takes the compulsive rage of the enemy god.

So lately this last flower of Oedipus' line   10

Drank the sunlight! but now a passionate word

And a handful of dust have closed up all its beauty.

What mortal arrogance   *Strophe 2*

Transcends the wrath of Zeus°?

Sleep cannot lull him nor the effortless long months   15

Of the timeless gods: but he is young for ever,

And his house is the shining day of high Olympos.

All that is and shall be,

And all the past, is his.

14 Zeus Chief Greek deity.

No pride on earth is free of the curse of heaven.   20

The straying dreams of men   *Antistrophe 2*
    May bring them ghosts of joy:
But as they drowse, the waking embers burn them;
Or they walk with fixed eyes, as blind men walk.
But the ancient wisdom speaks for our own time: 25
    Fate works most for woe
    With Folly's fairest show.
Man's little pleasure is the spring of sorrow.

                              Scene III

CHORAGOS. But here is Haimon, King, the last of all your sons.
        Is it grief for Antigone that brings him here,
        And bitterness at being robbed of his bride?

        Enter Haimon.

CREON. We shall soon see, and no need of diviners.
                                               —Son,
        You have heard my final judgment on that girl: 5
        Have you come here hating me, or have you come
        With deference and with love, whatever I do?
HAIMON. I am your son, father. You are my guide.
        You make things clear for me, and I obey you.
        No marriage means more to me than your continuing wisdom.   10
CREON. Good. That is the way to behave: subordinate
        Everything else, my son, to your father's will.
        This is what a man prays for, that he may get
        Sons attentive and dutiful in his house,
        Each one hating his father's enemies,   15
        Honoring his father's friends. But if his sons
        Fail him, if they turn out unprofitably,
        What has he fathered but trouble for himself
        And amusement for the malicious?
                                        So you are right
        Not to lose your head over this woman.   20
        Your pleasure with her would soon grow cold, Haimon,
        And then you'd have a hellcat in bed and elsewhere.
        Let her find her husband in Hell!
        Of all the people in this city, only she
        Has had contempt for my law and broken it.   25

        Do you want me to show myself weak before the people?
        Or to break my sworn word? No, and I will not.

The woman dies.
I suppose she'll plead "family ties." Well, let her.
If I permit my own family to rebel,   30
How shall I earn the world's obedience?
Show me the man who keeps his house in hand,
He's fit for public authority.
                              I'll have no dealings
With lawbreakers, critics of the government:
Whoever is chosen to govern should be obeyed—   35
Must be obeyed, in all things, great and small,
Just and unjust! O Haimon,
The man who knows how to obey, and that man only,
Knows how to give commands when the time comes.
You can depend on him, no matter how fast   40
The spears come: he's a good soldier, he'll stick it out.

Anarchy, anarchy! Show me a greater evil!
This is why cities tumble and the great houses rain down,
This is what scatters armies!
No, no: good lives are made so by discipline.   45
We keep the laws then, and the lawmakers,
And no woman shall seduce us. If we must lose,
Let's lose to a man, at least! Is a woman stronger than we?
CHORAGOS. Unless time has rusted my wits,
    What you say, King, is said with point and dignity.   50
HAIMON (*boyishly earnest*). Father:
    Reason is God's crowning gift to man, and you are right
To warn me against losing mine. I cannot say—
I hope that I shall never want to say!—that you
Have reasoned badly. Yet there are other men   55
Who can reason, too; and their opinions might be helpful.
You are not in a position to know everything
That people say or do, or what they feel:
Your temper terrifies—everyone
Will tell you only what you like to hear.   60
But I, at any rate, can listen; and I have heard them
Muttering and whispering in the dark about this girl.
They say no woman has ever, so unreasonably,
Died so shameful a death for a generous act:
"She covered her brother's body. Is this indecent?   65
She kept him from dogs and vultures. Is this a crime?
Death?—She should have all the honor that we can give her!"

This is the way they talk out there in the city.

You must believe me:

Nothing is closer to me than your happiness.   70
What could be closer? Must not any son
Value his father's fortune as his father does his?
I beg you, do not be unchangeable:
Do not believe that you alone can be right.
The man who thinks that,   75
The man who maintains that only he has the power
To reason correctly, the gift to speak, the soul—
A man like that, when you know him, turns out empty.

It is not reason never to yield to reason!
In flood time you can see how some trees bend,   80
And because they bend, even their twigs are safe,
While stubborn trees are torn up, roots and all.
And the same thing happens in sailing:
Make your sheet fast, never slacken,—and over you go,
Head over heels and under: and there's your voyage.   85
Forget you are angry! Let yourself be moved!
I know I am young; but please let me say this:
The ideal condition
Would be, I admit, that men should be right by instinct;
But since we are all too likely to go astray,   90
The reasonable thing is to learn from those who can teach.
CHORAGOS. You will do well to listen to him, King,
    If what he says is sensible. And you, Haimon,
    Must listen to your father.—Both speak well.
CREON. You consider it right for a man of my years and experience   95
    To go to school to a boy?
HAIMON.   It is not right
    If I am wrong. But if I am young, and right,
    What does my age matter?
CREON. You think it right to stand up for an anarchist?
HAIMON. Not at all. I pay no respect to criminals.   100
CREON. Then she is not a criminal?
HAIMON. The City would deny it, to a man.
CREON. And the City proposes to teach me how to rule?
HAIMON. Ah. Who is it that's talking like a boy now?
CREON. My voice is the one voice giving orders in this City!   105
HAIMON. It is no City if it takes orders from one voice.
CREON. The State is the King!
HAIMON.   Yes, if the State is a desert.

    Pause.

CREON. This boy, it seems, has sold out to a woman.
HAIMON. If you are a woman: my concern is only for you.
CREON. So? Your "concern"! In a public brawl with your father!   110

HAIMON. How about you, in a public brawl with justice?

CREON. With justice, when all that I do is within my rights?

HAIMON. You have no right to trample on God's right.

CREON (*completely out of control*). Fool, adolescent fool! Taken in by a woman!

HAIMON. You'll never see me taken in by anything vile. 115

CREON. Every word you say is for her!

HAIMON. (*quietly, darkly*). And for you.
And for me. And for the gods under the earth.

CREON. You'll never marry her while she lives.

HAIMON. Then she must die. — But her death will cause another.

CREON. Another? 120
Have you lost your senses? Is this an open threat?

HAIMON. There is no threat in speaking to emptiness.

CREON. I swear you'll regret this superior tone of yours!
You are the empty one!

HAIMON. If you were not my father,
I'd say you were perverse. 125

CREON. You girlstruck fool, don't play at words with me!

HAIMON. I am sorry. You prefer silence.

CREON. Now, by God — !
I swear, by all the gods in heaven above us,
You'll watch it, I swear you shall!
(*To the Servants.*) Bring her out!
Bring the woman out! Let her die before his eyes! 130
Here, this instant, with her bridegroom beside her!

HAIMON. Not here, no; she will not die here, King.
And you will never see my face again.
Go on raving as long as you've a friend to endure you.

(*Exit Haimon.*)

CHORAGOS. Gone, gone. 135
Creon, a young man in a rage is dangerous!

CREON. Let him do, or dream to do, more than a man can.
He shall not save these girls from death.

CHORAGOS. These girls?
You have sentenced them both?

CREON. No, you are right.
I will not kill the one whose hands are clean. 140

CHORAGOS. But Antigone?

CREON (*somberly*). I will carry her far away
Out there in the wilderness, and lock her
Living in a vault of stone. She shall have food,
As the custom is, to absolve the State of her death.
And there let her pray to the gods of hell: 145
They are her only gods:

Perhaps they will show her an escape from death,
Or she may learn,
                        though late,
That piety shown the dead is piety in vain.

(Exit Creon.)

Ode III

CHORUS. Love, unconquerable   *Strophe*
        Waster of rich men, keeper
        Of warm lights and all-night vigil
        In the soft face of a girl:
        Sea-wanderer, forest-visitor!   5
        Even the pure Immortals cannot escape you,
        And mortal man, in his one day's dusk,
        Trembles before your glory.

        Surely you swerve upon ruin   *Antistrophe*
        The just man's consenting heart,   10
        As here you have made bright anger
        Strike between father and son—
        And none has conquered but Love!
        A girl's glance working the will of heaven:
        Pleasure to her alone who mocks us,   15
        Merciless Aphrodite.°

Scene IV

CHORAGOS (*as Antigone enters guarded*).   But I can no longer stand in awe of this,
        Nor, seeing what I see, keep back my tears.
        Here is Antigone, passing to that chamber
        Where all find sleep at last.

ANTIGONE. Look upon me, friends, and pity me   *Strophe 1* 5
        Turning back at the night's edge to say
        Good-by to the sun that shines for me no longer;
        Now sleepy Death
        Summons me down to Acheron,° that cold shore:
        There is no bridesong there, nor any music.   10
CHORUS. Yet not unpraised, not without a kind of honor,
        You walk at last into the underworld;
        Untouched by sickness, broken by no sword.

---

16 Aphrodite Goddess of love.   **Scene IV 9 Acheron** A river of the underworld,
which was ruled by Hades.

What woman has ever found your way to death?

ANTIGONE. How often I have heard the story of Niobe,°   *Antistrophe 1* 15
    Tantalos' wretched daughter, how the stone
    Clung fast about her, ivy-close: and they say
    The rain falls endlessly
    And sifting soft snow; her tears are never done.
    I feel the loneliness of her death in mine.   20
CHORUS. But she was born of heaven, and you
    Are woman, woman-born. If her death is yours,
    A mortal woman's, is this not for you
    Glory in our world and in the world beyond?

ANTIGONE. You laugh at me. Ah, friends, friends,   *Strophe 2* 25
    Can you not wait until I am dead? O Thebes,
    O men many-charioted, in love with Fortune,
    Dear springs of Dirce, sacred Theban grove,
    Be witnesses for me, denied all pity,
    Unjustly judged! and think a word of love   30
    For her whose path turns
    Under dark earth, where there are no more tears.
CHORUS. You have passed beyond human daring and come at last
    Into a place of stone where Justice sits.
    I cannot tell   35
    What shape of your father's guilt appears in this.
ANTIGONE. You have touched it at last: that bridal bed   *Antistrophe 2*
    Unspeakable, horror of son and mother mingling:
    Their crime, infection of all our family!
    O Oedipus, father and brother!   40
    Your marriage strikes from the grave to murder mine.
    I have been a stranger here in my own land:
    All my life
    The blasphemy of my birth has followed me.
CHORUS. Reverence is a virtue, but strength   45
    Lives in established law: that must prevail.
    You have made your choice,
    Your death is the doing of your conscious hand.
ANTIGONE. Then let me go, since all your words are bitter,   *Epode*°
    And the very light of the sun is cold to me.   50
    Lead me to my vigil, where I must have
    Neither love nor lamentation; no song, but silence.

---

15 Niobe Niobe boasted of her numerous children, provoking Leto, the mother of Apollo, to destroy them. Niobe wept profusely, and finally was turned to stone on Mount Sipylus, whose streams are her tears.   **49 Epode** The third unit of a triad following the strophe and antistrophe.

Creon interrupts impatiently.

CREON. If dirges and planned lamentations could put off death,
Men would be singing for ever.
(*To the Servants.*)   Take her, go!
You know your orders: take her to the vault   55
And leave her alone there. And if she lives or dies,
That's her affair, not ours: our hands are clean.

ANTIGONE. O tomb, vaulted bride-bed in eternal rock,
Soon I shall be with my own again
Where Persephone° welcomes the thin ghosts underground: 60
And I shall see my father again, and you, mother,
And dearest Polyneices—
                          dearest indeed
To me, since it was my hand
That washed him clean and poured the ritual wine:
And my reward is death before my time!   65

And yet, as men's hearts know, I have done no wrong,
I have not sinned before God. Or if I have,
I shall know the truth in death. But if the guilt
Lies upon Creon who judged me, then, I pray,
May his punishment equal my own.
CHORAGOS.   O passionate heart,   70
Unyielding, tormented still by the same winds!
CREON. Her guards shall have good cause to regret their delaying.
ANTIGONE. Ah! That voice is like the voice of death!
CREON. I can give you no reason to think you are mistaken.
ANTIGONE. Thebes, and you my fathers' gods,   75
And rulers of Thebes, you see me now, the last
Unhappy daughter of a line of kings,
Your kings, led away to death. You will remember
What things I suffer, and at what men's hands,
Because I would not transgress the laws of heaven.   80
(*To the Guards, simply.*) Come: let us wait no longer.

(*Exit Antigone, left, guarded.*)

Ode IV

CHORUS. All Danae's° beauty was locked away   *Strophe 1*
In a brazen cell where the sunlight could not come:

---

60 Persephone Queen of the underworld.   **1 Danae** In Greek mythology, she was imprisoned in a tower, but Zeus so lusted for her that he visited in a shower of gold.

A small room still as any grave, enclosed her.
Yet she was a princess too,
And Zeus in a rain of gold poured love upon her.   5
O child, child,
No power in wealth or war
Or tough sea-blackened ships
Can prevail against untiring Destiny!

And Dryas' son° also, that furious king,   *Antistrophe 1* 10
Bore the god's prisoning anger for his pride:
Sealed up by Dionysos in deaf stone,
His madness died among echoes.
So at the last he learned what dreadful power
His tongue had mocked: 15
For he had profaned the revels,
And fired the wrath of the nine
Implacable Sisters° that love the sound of the flute.

And old men tell a half-remembered tale   *Strophe 2*
Of horror where a dark ledge splits the sea   20
And a double surf beats on the gray shores:
How a king's new woman,° sick
With hatred for the queen he had imprisoned,
Ripped out his two sons' eyes with her bloody hands
While grinning Ares° watched the shuttle plunge   25
Four times: four blind wounds crying for revenge,

Crying, tears and blood mingled. — Piteously born,   *Antistrophe 2*
Those sons whose mother was of heavenly birth!
Her father was the god of the North Wind
And she was cradled by gales,   30
She raced with young colts on the glittering hills
And walked untrammeled in the open light:
But in her marriage deathless Fate found means
To build a tomb like yours for all her joy.

Scene V

Enter blind Teiresias, led by a boy. The opening speeches of Teiresias should be in singsong contrast to the realistic lines of Creon.

---

10 Dryas' son Lycurgus, King of Thrace.   **18 Sisters** The Muses.   **22 king's new woman** Eidothea, second wife of King Phineus, blinded her stepsons. Their mother, Cleopatra, had been imprisoned in a cave. Phineus was the son of a king, and Cleopatra, his first wife, was the daughter of Boreas, the North Wind, but this illustrious ancestry could not protect his sons from violence and darkness.   **25 Ares** God of war.

TEIRESIAS. This is the way the blind man comes, Princes, Princes,
    Lock-step, two heads lit by the eyes of one.
CREON. What new thing have you to tell us, old Teiresias?
TEIRESIAS. I have much to tell you: listen to the prophet, Creon.
CREON. I am not aware that I have ever failed to listen. 5
TEIRESIAS. Then you have done wisely, King, and ruled well.
CREON. I admit my debt to you. But what have you to say?
TEIRESIAS. This, Creon: you stand once more on the edge of fate.
CREON. What do you mean? Your words are a kind of dread.
TEIRESIAS. Listen, Creon: 10
    I was sitting in my chair of augury, at the place
    Where the birds gather about me. They were all a-chatter,
    As is their habit, when suddenly I heard
    A strange note in their jangling, a scream, a
    Whirring fury; I knew that they were fighting, 15
    Tearing each other, dying
    In a whirlwind of wings clashing. And I was afraid.
    I began the rites of burnt-offering at the altar,
    But Hephaistos° failed me: instead of bright flame,
    There was only the sputtering slime of the fat thigh-flesh 20
    Melting: the entrails dissolved in gray smoke,
    The bare bone burst from the welter. And no blaze!

    This was a sign from heaven. My boy described it,
    Seeing for me as I see for others.

    I tell you, Creon, you yourself have brought 25
    This new calamity upon us. Our hearths and altars
    Are stained with the corruption of dogs and carrion birds
    That glut themselves on the corpse of Oedipus' son.
    The gods are deaf when we pray to them, their fire
    Recoils from our offering, their birds of omen 30
    Have no cry of comfort, for they are gorged
    With the thick blood of the dead.
                  O my son,
    These are no trifles! Think: all men make mistakes,
    But a good man yields when he knows his course is wrong,
    And repairs the evil. The only crime is pride. 35

    Give in to the dead man, then: do not fight with a corpse—
    What glory is it to kill a man who is dead?
    Think, I beg you:

19 Hephaistos God of fire.

It is for your own good that I speak as I do.
You should be able to yield for your own good. 40
CREON. It seems that prophets have made me their especial province.
All my life long
I have been a kind of butt for the dull arrows
Of doddering fortune-tellers!
                              No, Teiresias:
If your birds—if the great eagles of God himself 45
Should carry him stinking bit by bit to heaven,
I would not yield. I am not afraid of pollution:
No man can defile the gods.
                              Do what you will,
Go into business, make money, speculate
In India gold or that synthetic gold from Sardis, 50
Get rich otherwise than by my consent to bury him.
Teiresias, it is a sorry thing when a wise man
Sells his wisdom, lets out his words for hire!
TEIRESIAS. Ah Creon! Is there no man left in the world—
CREON. To do what?—Come, let's have the aphorism! 55
TEIRESIAS. No man who knows that wisdom outweighs any wealth?
CREON. As surely as bribes are baser than any baseness.
TEIRESIAS. You are sick, Creon! You are deathly sick!
CREON. As you say: it is not my place to challenge a prophet.
TEIRESIAS. Yet you have said my prophecy is for sale. 60
CREON. The generation of prophets has always loved gold.
TEIRESIAS. The generation of kings has always loved brass.
CREON. You forget yourself! You are speaking to your King.
TEIRESIAS. I know it. You are a king because of me.
CREON. You have a certain skill; but you have sold out. 65
TEIRESIAS. King, you will drive me to words that—
CREON.   Say them, say them!
Only remember: I will not pay you for them.
TEIRESIAS. No, you will find them too costly.
CREON.   No doubt. Speak:
Whatever you say, you will not change my will.
TEIRESIAS. Then take this, and take it to heart! 70
The time is not far off when you shall pay back
Corpse for corpse, flesh of your own flesh.
You have thrust the child of this world into living night,
You have kept from the gods below the child that is theirs:
The one in a grave before her death, the other, 75
Dead, denied the grave. This is your crime:
And the Furies and the dark gods of Hell
Are swift with terrible punishment for you.

Do you want to buy me now, Creon?

Not many days,
And your house will be full of men and women weeping,   80
And curses will be hurled at you from far
Cities grieving for sons unburied, left to rot
Before the walls of Thebes.

These are my arrows, Creon: they are all for you.

(*To Boy.*) But come, child: lead me home.   85
Let him waste his fine anger upon younger men.
Maybe he will learn at last
To control a wiser tongue in a better head. (*Exit Teiresias.*)
CHORAGOS. The old man has gone, King, but his words
   Remain to plague us. I am old, too,   90
But I cannot remember that he was ever false.
CREON. That is true. . . . It troubles me.
   Oh it is hard to give in! but it is worse
To risk everything for stubborn pride.
CHORAGOS. Creon: take my advice.
CREON.   What shall I do?   95
CHORAGOS. Go quickly: free Antigone from her vault
   And build a tomb for the body of Polyneices.
CREON. You would have me do this!
CHORAGOS.   Creon, yes!
   And it must be done at once: God moves
Swiftly to cancel the folly of stubborn men.   100
CREON. It is hard to deny the heart! But I
   Will do it: I will not fight with destiny.
CHORAGOS. You must go yourself, you cannot leave it to others.
CREON. I will go.
      —Bring axes, servants:
Come with me to the tomb. I buried her, I   105
Will set her free.
      Oh quickly!
My mind misgives—
The laws of the gods are mighty, and a man must serve them
To the last day of his life!

(*Exit Creon.*)

Paean°

CHORAGOS. God of many names   *Strophe 1*

Paean A hymn (here dedicated to Iacchos, also called Dionysos. His father was Zeus, his mother was Semele, daughter of Kadmos. Iacchos's worshipers were the Maenads, whose cry was "*Evohe evohe*").

CHORUS.   O Iacchos

                       son

of Kadmeian Semele

           O born of the Thunder!

Guardian of the West

          Regent

of Eleusis' plain

        O Prince of maenad Thebes

and the Dragon Field by rippling Ismenos:°   5

CHORAGOS. God of many names   *Antistrophe 1*

CHORUS.   the flame of torches

flares on our hills

        the nymphs of Iacchos

dance at the spring of Castalia:°

from the vine-close mountain

          come ah come in ivy:

Evohe evohe! sings through the streets of Thebes   10

CHORAGOS. God of many names   *Strophe 2*

CHORUS.   Iacchos of Thebes

heavenly Child

       of Semele bride of the Thunderer!

The shadow of plague is upon us:

         come

with clement feet

       oh come from Parnassos

down the long slopes

        across the lamenting water   15

CHORAGOS. Io Fire! Chorister of the throbbing stars!   *Antistrophe 2*

O purest among the voices of the night!

Thou son of God, blaze for us!

CHORUS. Come with choric rapture of circling Maenads

Who cry *Io Iacche!*

      God of many names!   20

           Exodos°

Enter Messenger from left.

MESSENGER. Men of the line of Kadmos,° you who live

Near Amphion's citadel,°

       I cannot say

---

5 Ismenos A river east of Thebes. From a dragon's teeth, sown near the river, there
sprang men who became the ancestors of the Theban nobility.   **8 Castalia** A spring on
Mount Parnassos.   **Exodos** The final scene in a Greek tragedy.   **1 Kadmos,** who
sowed the dragon's teeth, was founder of Thebes.   **2 Amphion's citadel** Amphion
played so sweetly on his lyre that he charmed stones to form a wall around Thebes.

Of any condition of human life "This is fixed.
This is clearly good, or bad." Fate raises up,
And Fate casts down the happy and unhappy alike: 5
No man can foretell his Fate.
                                        Take the case of Creon:
Creon was happy once, as I count happiness:
Victorious in battle, sole governor of the land,
Fortunate father of children nobly born.
And now it has all gone from him! Who can say   10
That a man is still alive when his life's joy fails?
He is a walking dead man. Grant him rich,
Let him live like a king in his great house:
If his pleasure is gone, I would not give
So much as the shadow of smoke for all he owns.   15
CHORAGOS. Your words hint at sorrow: what is your news for us?
MESSENGER. They are dead. The living are guilty of their death.
CHORAGOS. Who is guilty? Who is dead? Speak!
MESSENGER.   Haimon.
    Haimon is dead; and the hand that killed him
    Is his own hand.
CHORAGOS. His father's? or his own?   20
MESSENGER. His own, driven mad by the murder his father had done.
CHORAGOS. Teiresias, Teiresias, how clearly you saw it all!
MESSENGER. This is my news: you must draw what conclusions you can
    from it.
CHORAGOS. But look: Eurydice, our Queen:
    Has she overheard us?   25

Enter Eurydice from the palace, center.

EURYDICE. I have heard something, friends:
    As I was unlocking the gate of Pallas'° shrine,
    For I needed her help today, I heard a voice
    Telling of some new sorrow. And I fainted
    There at the temple with all my maidens about me.   30
    But speak again: whatever it is, I can bear it:
    Grief and I are no strangers.
MESSENGER.   Dearest Lady,
    I will tell you plainly all that I have seen.
    I shall not try to comfort you: what is the use,
    Since comfort could lie only in what is not true?   35
    The truth is always best.
                                        I went with Creon

_____

27 **Pallas'** Pallas Athene, goddess of wisdom.

To the outer plain where Polyneices was lying,
No friend to pity him, his body shredded by dogs.
We made our prayers in the place to Hecate
And Pluto,° that they would be merciful. And we bathed   40
The corpse with holy water, and we brought
Fresh-broken branches to burn what was left of it,
And upon the urn we heaped up a towering barrow
Of the earth of his own land.
                      When we were done, we ran
To the vault where Antigone lay on her couch of stone.   45
One of the servants had gone ahead,
And while he was yet far off he heard a voice
Grieving within the chamber, and he came back
And told Creon. And as the King went closer,
The air was full of wailing, the words lost,   50
And he begged us to make all haste. "Am I a prophet?"
He said, weeping, "And must I walk this road,
The saddest of all that I have gone before?
My son's voice calls me on. Oh quickly, quickly!
Look through the crevice there, and tell me   55
If it is Haimon, or some deception of the gods!"

We obeyed: and in the cavern's farthest corner
We saw her lying:
She had made a noose of her fine linen veil
And hanged herself. Haimon lay beside her,   60
His arms about her waist, lamenting her,
His love lost under ground, crying out
That his father had stolen her away from him.
When Creon saw him the tears rushed to his eyes
And he called to him: "What have you done, child? Speak to me.   65
What are you thinking that makes your eyes so strange?
O my son, my son, I come to you on my knees!"
But Haimon spat in his face. He said not a word,
Staring—
            And suddenly drew his sword
And lunged. Creon shrank back, the blade missed; and the boy,   70
Desperate against himself, drove it half its length
Into his own side, and fell. And as he died
He gathered Antigone close in his arms again,
Choking, his blood bright red on her white cheek.
And now he lies dead with the dead, and she is his   75

39–40 Hecate / And Pluto Hecate and Pluto (also known as Hades) were deities of the underworld.

At last, his bride in the house of the dead.

Exit Eurydice into the palace.

CHORAGOS. She has left us without a word. What can this mean?
MESSENGER. It troubles me, too; yet she knows what is best,
    Her grief is too great for public lamentation,
    And doubtless she has gone to her chamber to weep   80
    For her dead son, leading her maidens in his dirge.

    Pause.

CHORAGOS. It may be so: but I fear this deep silence.
MESSENGER. I will see what she is doing. I will go in.

    Exit Messenger into the palace.

    Enter Creon with attendants, bearing Haimon's body.

CHORAGOS. But here is the king himself: oh look at him,
    Bearing his own damnation in his arms.   85
CREON. Nothing you say can touch me any more.
    My own blind heart has brought me
    From darkness to final darkness. Here you see
    The father murdering, the murdered son —
    And all my civic wisdom!   90

    Haimon my son, so young, so young to die,
    I was the fool, not you; and you died for me.
CHORAGOS. That is the truth; but you were late in learning it.
CREON. This truth is hard to bear. Surely a god
    Has crushed me beneath the hugest weight of heaven,   95
    And driven me headlong a barbaric way
    To trample out the thing I held most dear.

    The pains that men will take to come to pain!

    Enter Messenger from the palace.

MESSENGER. The burden you carry in your hands is heavy,
    But it is not all: you will find more in your house.   100
CREON. What burden worse than this shall I find there?
MESSENGER. The Queen is dead.
CREON. O port of death, deaf world,
    Is there no pity for me? And you, Angel of evil,
    I was dead, and your words are death again.   105
    Is it true, boy? Can it be true?
    Is my wife dead? Has death bred death?
MESSENGER. You can see for yourself.

    The doors are opened and the body of Eurydice is disclosed within.

CREON. Oh pity!
    All true, all true, and more than I can bear!   110

O my wife, my son!
MESSENGER. She stood before the altar, and her heart
    Welcomed the knife her own hand guided,
    And a great cry burst from her lips for Megareus° dead,
    And for Haimon dead, her sons; and her last breath   115
    Was a curse for their father, the murderer of her sons.
    And she fell, and the dark flowed in through her closing eyes.
CREON. O God, I am sick with fear.
    Are there no swords here? Has no one a blow for me?
MESSENGER. Her curse is upon you for the deaths of both.   120
CREON. It is right that it should be. I alone am guilty.
    I know it, and I say it. Lead me in,
    Quickly, friends.
    I have neither life nor substance. Lead me in.
CHORAGOS. You are right, if there can be right in so much wrong.   125
    The briefest way is best in a world of sorrow.
CREON. Let it come,
    Let death come quickly, and be kind to me.
    I would not ever see the sun again.
CHORAGOS. All that will come when it will; but we, meanwhile,   130
    Have much to do. Leave the future to itself.
CREON. All my heart was in that prayer!
CHORAGOS. Then do not pray any more: the sky is deaf.
CREON. Lead me away. I have been rash and foolish.
    I have killed my son and my wife.   135
    I look for comfort; my comfort lies here dead.
    Whatever my hands have touched has come to nothing.
    Fate has brought all my pride to a thought of dust.

As Creon is being led into the house, the Choragos advances and speaks directly to the audience.

CHORAGOS. There is no happiness where there is no wisdom;
    No wisdom but in submission to the gods.   140
    Big words are always punished,
    And proud men in old age learn to be wise.

Topics for Critical Thinking and Writing

1. In the prologue, on page 746, Ismene insists, "we must give in to the law" (line 48), and Antigone replies, "apparently the laws of the gods mean nothing to you" (line 61). Can you reconcile this apparent contradiction?

2. In scene II Ismene says that she and Antigone are "equally guilty," but Antigone coldly (nastily?) refuses to let Ismene share her martyrdom.

---

114 Megareus Megareus, brother of Haimon, had died in the assault on Thebes.

What do you make of her behavior? In a 500-word essay write on Ismene's assertion that the two are equally guilty, and on Antigone's response.

3. The play includes several references to Fate or Destiny. At the beginning of scene IV, Ode IV, for example, the chorus, speaking of Danae, says that nothing "can prevail against untiring Destiny" (p. 765, line 9). How seriously are we to take these references to Fate? Do you think they reflect the dominant theme of the play, or are they to be explained as merely the utterances of this or that dramatic character? As instances of a human tendency to blame ill fortune on some mysterious external force? Do you think that, as we see them in the play, Antigone and Creon act of their own free will? Explain.

4. Throughout the play, Creon bewails the risk of "anarchy." What is anarchy? Is it reasonable for Creon to condemn Antigone's behavior for its anarchistic tendencies?

5. When the Chorus in scene IV declares "strength Lives in established law" (p. 763, lines 45–46), is this said in support of Creon, Antigone, both, or neither? Which law should be enforced, do you think — Creon's edict or the customary law of Thebes, on which Antigone relies? In a 500-word essay support your view.

6. At the end of the play Creon says, "I alone am guilty" (p. 773, line 121). Do you share his view? Or do you think that in some ways Antigone too is guilty? Are the words *hero* and *villain* of some use in talking about this play, or should they be discarded? In an essay of 500 words discuss some aspect of these related issues.

7. In scene V, p. 766, line 35, Teiresias says, "The only crime is pride." Is Antigone as guilty of this crime as Creon? How much of the terrible harms done throughout the play can be explained by excessive pride?

8. The play obviously deals with a clash between a citizen who feels she has familial and religious duties and a political leader who believes it is his duty to govern the state. Do you think that in addition to the conflict between feeling and law there are also significant conflicts between a male and a female? Between an old person and a young one?

9. If you were staging the play today, would you use modern dress? What might be gained, and what might be lost, by using modern dress?

Thomas Hardy

Thomas Hardy (1840–1928) was born in Dorset, England, the son of a stonemason. Despite great obstacles he studied the classics and architecture, and in 1862 he moved to London to study and practice as an architect. Ill health forced him to return to Dorset, where he continued to work as an architect and to write. Best known for his novels, Hardy ceased writing fiction after the hostile reception of Jude the Obscure *in 1896 and turned to writing lyric poetry. We print a poem of 1902.*

The Man He Killed

"Had he and I but met
By some old ancient inn,
We should have sat us down to wet
Right many a nipperkin°!

"But ranged an infantry,   5
And staring face to face,
I shot at him as he at me,
And killed him in his place.

"I shot him dead because—
Because he was my foe,   10
Just so: my foe of course he was;
That's clear enough; although

"He thought he'd 'list, perhaps,
Off-hand like—just as I—
Was out of work—had sold his traps°—   15
No other reason why.

"Yes; quaint and curious war is!
You shoot a fellow down
You'd treat if met where any bar is,
Or help to half-a-crown."   20

Topics for Critical Thinking and Writing

1. Hardy published this poem in 1902, at the conclusion of the Boer War (1899–1902, also called the South African War), a war between the Boers (Dutch) and the British for possession of part of Africa. The speaker of the poem is an English veteran of the war. Do you think such a poem might just as well have been written by an English (or American) soldier in World War II? Explain.

2. Characterize the speaker. What sort of man does he seem to be? Pay special attention to the punctuation in the third and fourth stanzas— what do the pauses indicated by the dashes, the colons, and the semi-colon tell us about him?—and pay special attention to the final stanza, in which he speaks of war as "quaint and curious" (line 17). Do you think that Hardy too would speak of war this way? Why, or why not? Can you imagine an American soldier in the Vietnam War speaking of the war as "quaint and curious"? Explain.

4 nipperkin Cup.   **15 traps** Personal belongings.

T. S. Eliot

Thomas Stearns Eliot (1888–1965) was born into a New England family that had moved to St. Louis. He attended a preparatory school in Massachu-setts, graduated from Harvard University, and then continued his studies in literature in France, Germany, and England. In 1914 he began working for Lloyds Bank in London, and three years later he published his first book of poems, which included "Prufrock." In 1925 he joined a publishing firm, and in 1927 he became a British citizen and a member of the Church of England. In 1948 he received the Nobel Prize for Literature.

The Love Song of J. Alfred Prufrock

> *S'io credesse che mia risposta fosse*
> *A persona che mai tornasse al mondo,*
> *Questa fiamma staria senza più scosse.*
> *Ma perciocchè giammai di questo fondo*
> *Non torno vivo alcun, s' i' odo il vero,*
> *Senza tema d'infamia ti rispondo.°*

Let us go then, you and I,
When the evening is spread out against the sky
Like a patient etherised upon a table;
Let us go, through certain half-deserted streets,
The muttering retreats   5
Of restless nights in one-night cheap hotels
And sawdust restaurants with oyster-shells:
Streets that follow like a tedious argument
Of insidious intent
To lead you to an overwhelming question . . .   10
Oh, do not ask, "What is it?"
Let us go and make our visit.

In the room the women come and go
Talking of Michelangelo.

The yellow fog that rubs its back upon the window-panes,   15
The yellow smoke that rubs its muzzle on the window-panes
Licked its tongue into the corners of the evening,
Lingered upon the pools that stand in drains,
Let fall upon its back the soot that falls from chimneys,
Slipped by the terrace, made a sudden leap,   20

The Italian epigraph that begins the poem is a quotation from Dante's *Divine Comedy* (1321). In this passage, a damned soul in Hell who had sought absolution before commit-ting a crime addresses Dante, thinking that his words will never reach the earth. He says: "If I thought that my answer were to someone who could ever return to the world, this flame would be still, without further motion. But because no one has ever returned alive from this depth, if what I hear is true, without fear of shame I answer you." [All notes are the editors'.]

And seeing that it was a soft October night,
Curled once about the house, and fell asleep.

And indeed there will be time
For the yellow smoke that slides along the street,
Rubbing its back upon the window-panes;   25
There will be time, there will be time
To prepare a face to meet the faces that you meet;
There will be time to murder and create,
And time for all the works and days° of hands
That lift and drop a question on your plate;   30
Time for you and time for me,
And time yet for a hundred indecisions,
And for a hundred visions and revisions,
Before the taking of a toast and tea.

In the room the women come and go   35
Talking of Michelangelo
And indeed there will be time
To wonder, "Do I dare?" and, "Do I dare?"
Time to turn back and descend the stair,
With a bald spot in the middle of my hair—   40
[They will say: "How his hair is growing thin!"]
My morning coat, my collar mounting firmly to the chin,
My necktie rich and modest, but asserted by a simple pin—
[They will say: "But how his arms and legs are thin!"]
Do I dare   45
Disturb the universe?
In a minute there is time
For decisions and revisions which a minute will reverse.

For I have known them all already, known them all:—
Have known the evenings, mornings, afternoons,   50
I have measured out my life with coffee spoons;
I know the voices dying with a dying fall°
Beneath the music from a farther room.
        So how should I presume?

And I have known the eyes already, known them all—   55
The eyes that fix you in a formulated phrase,
And when I am formulated, sprawling on a pin,
When I am pinned and wriggling on the wall,
Then how should I begin
To spit out all the butt-ends of my days and ways?   60

---

29 works and days The title of a poem on farm life by Hesiod (Greek, eighth century B.C.).   **52 dying fall** Echoes Shakespeare's *Twelfth Night* 1.1.4.

And how should I presume?

And I have known the arms already, known them all—
Arms that are braceleted and white and bare
[But in the lamplight, downed with light brown hair!]
Is it perfume from a dress   65
That makes me so digress?
Arms that lie along a table, or wrap about a shawl.
       And should I then presume?
       And how should I begin?

          . . . . .

Shall I say, I have gone at dusk through narrow streets   70
And watched the smoke that rises from the pipes
Of lonely men in shirt-sleeves, leaning out of windows? . . .

I should have been a pair of ragged claws
Scuttling across the floors of silent seas.

          . . . . .

And the afternoon, the evening, sleeps so peacefully!   75
Smoothed by long fingers,
Asleep . . . tired . . . or it malingers,
Stretched on the floor, here beside you and me.
Should I, after tea and cakes and ices,
Have the strength to force the moment to its crisis?   80
But though I have wept and fasted, wept and prayed,
Though I have seen my head [grown slightly bald]
      brought in upon a platter,°
I am no prophet—and here's no great matter;
I have seen the moment of my greatness flicker,
And I have seen the eternal Footman hold my coat, and
      snicker,   85
And in short, I was afraid.

And would it have been worth it, after all,
After the cups, the marmalade, the tea,
Among the porcelain, among some talk of you and me,
Would it have been worth while,   90
To have bitten off the matter with a smile,
To have squeezed the universe into a ball
To roll° it toward some overwhelming question,

81–83 head . . . platter Alludes to John the Baptist, whose head was delivered on a platter to Salome.   **92–93 ball to roll** Echoes Andrew Marvell's "To His Coy Mistress," lines
41–42 (see p. 355).

To say: "I am Lazarus,° come from the dead,
Come back to tell you all, I shall tell you all"—   95
If one, settling a pillow by her head,
     Should say: "That is not what I meant at all.
     That is not it, at all."

And would it have been worth it, after all,
Would it have been worth while,   100
After the sunsets and the dooryards and the sprinkled streets,
After the novels, after the teacups, after the skirts
     that trail along the floor—
And this, and so much more?—
It is impossible to say just what I mean!
But as if a magic lantern threw the nerves in patterns
     on a screen: 105
Would it have been worth while
If one, settling a pillow or throwing off a shawl,
And turning toward the window, should say:
     "That is not it at all,
     That is not what I meant, at all."   110

        . . . . .

No! I am not Prince Hamlet,° nor was meant to be;
Am an attendant lord, one that will do
To swell a progress, start a scene or two,
Advise the prince; no doubt, an easy tool.
Deferential, glad to be of use,   115
Politic, cautious, and meticulous;
Full of high sentence,° but a bit obtuse;
At times, indeed, almost ridiculous—
Almost, at times, the Fool.

I grow old . . . I grow old . . .   120
I shall wear the bottoms of my trousers rolled.

Shall I part my hair behind? Do I dare to eat a peach?
I shall wear white flannel trousers, and walk upon the beach.
I have heard the mermaids singing, each to each.

---

94 Lazarus Mentioned twice in the New Testament: Luke 16.19–31 tells of a poor man named Lazarus, who is carried by angels to Abraham's bosom, whereas a rich man is tormented in the underworld; the rich man, concerned about his brothers who are still on earth, asks Abraham to send Lazarus back to earth to warn them, but Abraham refuses. The other reference to Lazarus—possibly but not certainly the same man—is in John 11; this Lazarus rises from the dead at the command of Jesus.   **111 Prince Hamlet** The next few lines allude to lesser figures in Shakespeare's tragedy, specifically to Polonius, a self-satisfied fatuous courtier.   **117 full of high sentence** Full of thoughtful sayings; comes from Chaucer's description of the Oxford student in *The Canterbury Tales*.

I do not think that they will sing to me.   125

I have seen them riding seaward on the waves
Combing the white hair of the waves blown back
When the wind blows the water white and black.

We have lingered in the chambers of the sea
By sea-girls wreathed with seaweed red and brown   130
Till human voices wake us, and we drown.

Topics for Critical Thinking and Writing

1. One of the most famous images of the poem compares the evening to "a patient etherised upon a table" (lines 2–3). Does the image also suggest that individuals—for instance, Prufrock—may not be fully conscious and therefore are not responsible for their actions or their inactions?

2. Are lines 57–60 meant to evoke the reader's pity for the speaker? If not, what (if any) response are these lines intended to evoke?

3. The speaker admits he is "At times, indeed, . . . / Almost . . . the Fool" (lines 118–19). Where, if at all, in the poem do we see him not at all as a fool?

4. Do you take the poem to be a criticism of an individual, a society, neither, or both? Why?

5. "The poem is obscure—it begins in Italian, and it includes references that most readers can't know—and it is not at all uplifting. In fact, in so far as it is comprehensible, it is depressing. These are not the characteristics of a great poem." Evaluate this critical judgment, offering evidence to support your view.

6. The poem is chiefly concerned with the thoughts of a man, J. Alfred Prufrock. Do you think it therefore is of more interest to men than to women? Explain.

7. The speaker describes the streets he walks as "follow[ing] like a tedious argument" (line 8). Is the simile apt? When do you think an argument becomes tedious?

Susan Glaspell

Susan Glaspell (1882–1948) was born in Davenport, Iowa, and educated at Drake University in Des Moines. In 1903 she married George Cram Cook and, with Cook and other writers, actors, and artists, in 1915 founded the Provincetown Players, a group that remained vital until 1929. Glaspell wrote Trifles *(1916) for the Provincetown Players, but she also wrote stories, novels, and a biography of her husband. In 1931 she won the Pulitzer Prize for* Alison's House, *a play about the family of a deceased poet who in some ways resembles Emily Dickinson.*

Trifles

(**SCENE:** *The kitchen in the now abandoned farmhouse of John Wright, a gloomy kitchen, and left without having been put in order—unwashed pans under the sink, a loaf of bread outside the breadbox, a dish towel on the table—other signs of incompleted work. At the rear the outer door opens, and the Sheriff comes in, followed by the County Attorney and Hale. The Sheriff and Hale are men in middle life, the County Attorney is a young man; all are much bundled up and go at once to the stove. They are followed by the two women—the Sheriff's Wife first; she is a slight wiry woman, a thin nervous face. Mrs. Hale is larger and would ordinarily be called more comfortable looking, but she is disturbed now and looks fearfully about as she enters. The women have come in slowly and stand close together near the door.*)

COUNTY ATTORNEY *(rubbing his hands).* This feels good. Come up to the fire, ladies.

MRS. PETERS *(after taking a step forward).* I'm not—cold.

SHERIFF *(unbuttoning his overcoat and stepping away from the stove as if to the beginning of official business).* Now, Mr. Hale, before we move things about, you explain to Mr. Henderson just what you saw when you came here yesterday morning.

COUNTY ATTORNEY. By the way, has anything been moved? Are things just as you left them yesterday?

SHERIFF *(looking about).* It's just the same. When it dropped below zero last   5
night, I thought I'd better send Frank out this morning to make a fire for us—no use getting pneumonia with a big case on; but I told him not to touch anything except the stove—and you know Frank.

COUNTY ATTORNEY. Somebody should have been left here yesterday.

SHERIFF. Oh—yesterday. When I had to send Frank to Morris Center for that man who went crazy—I want you to know I had my hands full yesterday. I knew you could get back from Omaha by today, and as long as I went over everything here myself—

COUNTY ATTORNEY. Well, Mr. Hale, tell just what happened when you came here yesterday morning.

HALE. Harry and I had started to town with a load of potatoes. We came along the road from my place; and as I got here, I said, "I'm going to see if I can't get John Wright to go in with me on a party telephone." I spoke to Wright about it once before, and he put me off, saying folks talked too much anyway, and all he asked was peace and quiet—I guess you know about how much he talked himself; but I thought maybe if I went to the house and talked about it before his wife, though I said to Harry that I didn't know as what his wife wanted made much difference to John—

COUNTY ATTORNEY. Let's talk about that later, Mr. Hale. I do want to talk 10
about that, but tell now just what happened when you got to the
house.

HALE. I didn't hear or see anything; I knocked at the door, and still it was
all quiet inside. I knew they must be up, it was past eight o'clock. So
I knocked again, and I thought I heard somebody say, "Come in." I
wasn't sure, I'm not sure yet, but I opened the door—this door (indicating the door by which the two women are still standing), and there
in that rocker—(pointing to it) sat Mrs. Wright. (They all look at the
rocker.)

COUNTY ATTORNEY. What—was she doing?

HALE. She was rockin' back and forth. She had her apron in her hand
and was kind of—pleating it.

COUNTY ATTORNEY. And how did she—look?

HALE. Well, she looked queer.   15

COUNTY ATTORNEY. How do you mean—queer?

HALE. Well, as if she didn't know what she was going to do next. And
kind of done up.

COUNTY ATTORNEY. How did she seem to feel about your coming?

HALE. Why, I don't think she minded—one way or other. She didn't pay
much attention. I said, "How do, Mrs. Wright, it's cold, ain't it?" And
she said, "Is it?"—and went on kind of pleating at her apron. Well, I
was surprised; she didn't ask me to come up to the stove, or to set
down, but just sat there, not even looking at me, so I said, "I want
to see John." And then she—laughed. I guess you would call it a
laugh. I thought of Harry and the team outside, so I said a little
sharp: "Can't I see John?" "No," she says, kind o' dull like. "Ain't he
home?" says I. "Yes," says she, "he's home." "Then why can't I see
him?" I asked her, out of patience. "'Cause he's dead," says she.
"Dead?" says I. She just nodded her head, not getting a bit excited,
but rockin' back and forth. "Why—where is he?" says I, not knowing what to say. She just pointed upstairs—like that (himself pointing
to the room above). I got up, with the idea of going up there. I walked
from there to here—then I says, "Why, what did he die of?" "He
died of a rope around his neck," says she, and just went on pleatin'
at her apron. Well, I went out and called Harry. I thought I might—
need help. We went upstairs, and there he was lyin'—

COUNTY ATTORNEY. I think I'd rather have you go into that upstairs, where 20
you can point it all out. Just go on now with the rest of the story.

HALE. Well, my first thought was to get that rope off. I looked . . . (Stops,
his face twitches.) . . . but Harry, he went up to him, and he said, "No,
he's dead all right, and we'd better not touch anything." So we went
back downstairs. She was still sitting that same way. "Has anybody
been notified?" I asked. "No," says she, unconcerned. "Who did this,
Mrs. Wright?" said Harry. He said it businesslike—and she stopped
pleatin' of her apron. "I don't know," she says. "You don't know?"
says Harry. "No," says she. "Weren't you sleepin' in the bed with

him?" says Harry. "Yes," says she, "but I was on the inside." "Somebody slipped a rope round his neck and strangled him, and you
didn't wake up?" says Harry. "I didn't wake up," she said after him.
We must 'a looked as if we didn't see how that could be, for after a
minute she said, "I sleep sound." Harry was going to ask her more
questions, but I said maybe we ought to let her tell her story first to
the coroner, or the sheriff, so Harry went fast as he could to Rivers'
place, where there's a telephone.

COUNTY ATTORNEY. And what did Mrs. Wright do when she knew that you
had gone for the coroner?

HALE. She moved from that chair to this over here . . . *(Pointing to a small
chair in the corner.)* . . . and just sat there with her hands held together
and looking down. I got a feeling that I ought to make some conversation, so I said I had come in to see if John wanted to put in a telephone, and at that she started to laugh, and then she stopped and
looked at me—scared. *(The County Attorney, who has had his notebook
out, makes a note.)* I dunno, maybe it wasn't scared. I wouldn't like to
say it was. Soon Harry got back, and then Dr. Lloyd came, and you,
Mr. Peters, and so I guess that's all I know that you don't.

COUNTY ATTORNEY *(looking around).* I guess we'll go upstairs first—and then
out to the barn and around there. *(To the Sheriff.)* You're convinced
that there was nothing important here—nothing that would point
to any motive?

SHERIFF. Nothing here but kitchen things. *(The County Attorney, after again* 25
*looking around the kitchen, opens the door of a cupboard closet. He gets up
on a chair and looks on a shelf. Pulls his hand away, sticky.)*

COUNTY ATTORNEY. Here's a nice mess. *(The women draw nearer.)*

MRS. PETERS *(to the other woman).* Oh, her fruit; it did freeze. *(To the Lawyer.)*
She worried about that when it turned so cold. She said the fire'd go
out and her jars would break.

SHERIFF. Well, can you beat the women! Held for murder and worryin'
about her preserves.

COUNTY ATTORNEY. I guess before we're through she may have something
more serious than preserves to worry about.

HALE. Well, women are used to worrying over trifles. *(The two women* 30
move a little closer together.)

COUNTY ATTORNEY *(with the gallantry of a young politician).* And yet, for all
their worries, what would we do without the ladies? *(The women do
not unbend. He goes to the sink, takes a dipperful of water from the pail and,
pouring it into a basin, washes his hands. Starts to wipe them on the roller
towel, turns it for a cleaner place.)* Dirty towels! *(Kicks his foot against
the pans under the sink.)* Not much of a housekeeper, would you say,
ladies?

MRS. HALE *(stiffly).* There's a great deal of work to be done on a farm.

COUNTY ATTORNEY. To be sure. And yet . . . *(With a little bow to her.)* . . . I
know there are some Dickson county farmhouses which do not have
such roller towels. *(He gives it a pull to expose its full length again.)*

MRS. HALE. Those towels get dirty awful quick. Men's hands aren't always as clean as they might be.

COUNTY ATTORNEY. Ah, loyal to your sex. I see. But you and Mrs. Wright 35 were neighbors. I suppose you were friends, too.

MRS. HALE *(shaking her head).* I've not seen much of her of late years. I've not been in this house—it's more than a year.

COUNTY ATTORNEY. And why was that? You didn't like her?

MRS. HALE. I liked her all well enough. Farmers' wives have their hands full, Mr. Henderson. And then—

COUNTY ATTORNEY. Yes—?

MRS. HALE *(looking about).* It never seemed a very cheerful place.   40

COUNTY ATTORNEY. No—it's not cheerful. I shouldn't say she had the homemaking instinct.

MRS. HALE. Well, I don't know as Wright had, either.

COUNTY ATTORNEY. You mean they didn't get on very well?

MRS. HALE. No, I don't mean anything. But I don't think a place'd be any cheerfuller for John Wright's being in it.

COUNTY ATTORNEY. I'd like to talk more of that a little later. I want to get 45 the lay of things upstairs now. *(He goes to the left, where three steps lead to a stair door.)*

SHERIFF. I suppose anything Mrs. Peters does'll be all right. She was to take in some clothes for her, you know, and a few little things. We left in such a hurry yesterday.

COUNTY ATTORNEY. Yes, but I would like to see what you take, Mrs. Peters, and keep an eye out for anything that might be of use to us.

MRS. PETERS. Yes, Mr. Henderson. *(The women listen to the men's steps on the stairs, then look about the kitchen.)*

MRS. HALE. I'd hate to have men coming into my kitchen, snooping around and criticizing. *(She arranges the pans under the sink which the Lawyer had shoved out of place.)*

MRS. PETERS. Of course it's no more than their duty.   50

MRS. HALE. Duty's all right, but I guess that deputy sheriff that came out to make the fire might have got a little of this on. *(Gives the roller towel a pull.)* Wish I'd thought of that sooner. Seems mean to talk about her for not having things slicked up when she had to come away in such a hurry.

MRS. PETERS *(who has gone to a small table in the left rear corner of the room, and lifted one end of a towel that covers a pan).* She had bread set. *(Stands still.)*

MRS. HALE *(eyes fixed on a loaf of bread beside the breadbox, which is on a low shelf at the other side of the room. Moves slowly toward it).* She was going to put this in there. *(Picks up loaf, then abruptly drops it. In a manner of returning to familiar things.)* It's a shame about her fruit. I wonder if it's all gone. *(Gets up on the chair and looks.)* I think there's some here that's all right, Mrs. Peters. Yes—here; *(Holding it toward the window.)* this is cherries, too. *(Looking again.)* I declare I believe that's the only one. *(Gets down, bottle in her hand. Goes to the sink and wipes it off on the outside.)* She'll feel awful bad after all her hard work in the hot weather. I remember the afternoon I put up my cherries last summer. *(She puts the bottle on the big kitchen table, center of the room. With a sigh, is about to sit down in the rocking chair. Before she is seated realizes what chair it is; with a slow look at it, steps back. The chair, which she has touched, rocks back and forth.)*

MRS. PETERS. Well, I must get those things from the front room closet. *(She goes to the door at the right, but after looking into the other room steps back.)* You coming with me, Mrs. Hale? You could help me carry them. *(They go into the other room; reappear, Mrs. Peters carrying a dress and skirt, Mrs. Hale following with a pair of shoes.)*

MRS. PETERS. My, it's cold in there. *(She puts the cloth on the big table, and* 55 *hurries to the stove.)*

MRS. HALE *(examining the skirt)*. Wright was close. I think maybe that's why she kept so much to herself. She didn't even belong to the Ladies' Aid. I suppose she felt she couldn't do her part, and then you don't enjoy things when you feel shabby. She used to wear pretty clothes and be lively, when she was Minnie Foster, one of the town girls singing in the choir. But that — oh, that was thirty years ago. This all you was to take in?

MRS. PETERS. She said she wanted an apron. Funny thing to want, for there isn't much to get you dirty in jail, goodness knows. But I suppose just to make her feel more natural. She said they was in the top drawer in this cupboard. Yes, here. And then her little shawl that always hung behind the door. *(Opens stair door and looks.)* Yes, here it is. *(Quickly shuts door leading upstairs.)*

MRS. HALE *(abruptly moving toward her)*. Mrs. Peters?

MRS. PETERS. Yes, Mrs. Hale?

MRS. HALE. Do you think she did it?   60

MRS. PETERS *(in a frightened voice)*. Oh, I don't know.

MRS. HALE. Well, I don't think she did. Asking for an apron and her little shawl. Worrying about her fruit.

MRS. PETERS *(starts to speak, glances up, where footsteps are heard in the room above. In a low voice)*. Mr. Peters says it looks bad for her. Mr. Henderson is awful sarcastic in speech, and he'll make fun of her sayin' she didn't wake up.

MRS. HALE. Well, I guess John Wright didn't wake when they was slipping that rope under his neck.

MRS. PETERS. No, it's strange. It must have been done awful crafty and 65 still. They say it was such a — funny way to kill a man, rigging it all up like that.

MRS. HALE. That's just what Mr. Hale said. There was a gun in the house. He says that's what he can't understand.

MRS. PETERS. Mr. Henderson said coming out that what was needed for the case was a motive; something to show anger or — sudden feeling.

MRS. HALE *(who is standing by the table).* Well, I don't see any signs of anger around here. *(She puts her hand on the dish towel which lies on the table, stands looking down at the table, one half of which is clean, the other half messy.)* It's wiped here. *(Makes a move as if to finish work, then turns and looks at loaf of bread outside the breadbox. Drops towel. In that voice of coming back to familiar things.)* Wonder how they are finding things upstairs? I hope she had it a little more red-up there. You know, it seems kind of *sneaking.* Locking her up in town and then coming out here and trying to get her own house to turn against her!

MRS. PETERS. But, Mrs. Hale, the law is the law.

MRS. HALE. I s'pose 'tis. *(Unbuttoning her coat.)* Better loosen up your 70 things, Mrs. Peters. You won't feel them when you go out. *(Mrs. Peters takes off her fur tippet, goes to hang it on hook at the back of room, stands looking at the under part of the small corner table.)*

MRS. PETERS. She was piecing a quilt. *(She brings the large sewing basket, and they look at the bright pieces.)*

MRS. HALE. It's log cabin pattern. Pretty, isn't it? I wonder if she was goin' to quilt or just knot it? *(Footsteps have been heard coming down the stairs. The Sheriff enters, followed by Hale and the County Attorney.)*

SHERIFF. They wonder if she was going to quilt it or just knot it. *(The men laugh, the women look abashed.)*

COUNTY ATTORNEY *(rubbing his hands over the stove).* Frank's fire didn't do much up there, did it? Well, let's go out to the barn and get that cleared up. *(The men go outside.)*

MRS. HALE *(resentfully).* I don't know as there's anything so strange, our 75 takin' up our time with little things while we're waiting for them to get the evidence. *(She sits down at the big table, smoothing out a block with decision.)* I don't see as it's anything to laugh about.

MRS. PETERS *(apologetically).* Of course they've got awful important things on their minds. *(Pulls up a chair and joins Mrs. Hale at the table.)*

MRS. HALE *(examining another block).* Mrs. Peters, look at this one. Here, this is the one she was working on, and look at the sewing! All the rest of it has been so nice and even. And look at this! It's all over the place! Why, it looks as if she didn't know what she was about! *(After she has said this, they look at each other, then start to glance back at the door. After an instant Mrs. Hale has pulled at a knot and ripped the sewing.)*

MRS. PETERS. Oh, what are you doing, Mrs. Hale?

MRS. HALE *(mildly).* Just pulling out a stitch or two that's not sewed very good. *(Threading a needle.)* Bad sewing always made me fidgety.

MRS. PETERS *(nervously).* I don't think we ought to touch things.   80

MRS. HALE. I'll just finish up this end. *(Suddenly stopping and leaning forward.)* Mrs. Peters?

MRS. PETERS. Yes, Mrs. Hale?

MRS. HALE. What do you suppose she was so nervous about?

MRS. PETERS. Oh—I don't know. I don't know as she was nervous. I sometimes sew awful queer when I'm just tired. *(Mrs. Hale starts to say something, looks at Mrs. Peters, then goes on sewing.)* Well, I must get these things wrapped up. They may be through sooner than we think. *(Putting apron and other things together.)* I wonder where I can find a piece of paper, and string.

MRS. HALE. In that cupboard, maybe.   85

MRS. PETERS *(looking in cupboard).* Why, here's a birdcage. *(Holds it up.)* Did she have a bird, Mrs. Hale?

MRS. HALE. Why, I don't know whether she did or not—I've not been here for so long. There was a man around last year selling canaries cheap, but I don't know as she took one; maybe she did. She used to sing real pretty herself.

MRS. PETERS *(glancing around).* Seems funny to think of a bird here. But she must have had one, or why should she have a cage? I wonder what happened to it?

MRS. HALE. I s'pose maybe the cat got it.

MRS. PETERS. No, she didn't have a cat. She's got that feeling some people 90 have about cats—being afraid of them. My cat got in her room, and she was real upset and asked me to take it out.

MRS. HALE. My sister Bessie was like that. Queer, ain't it?

MRS. PETERS *(examining the cage).* Why, look at this door. It's broke. One hinge is pulled apart.

MRS. HALE *(looking, too).* Looks as if someone must have been rough with it.

MRS. PETERS. Why, yes. *(She brings the cage forward and puts it on the table.)*

MRS. HALE. I wish if they're going to find any evidence they'd be about it. 95 I don't like this place.

MRS. PETERS. But I'm awful glad you came with me, Mrs. Hale. It would be lonesome for me sitting here alone.

MRS. HALE. It would, wouldn't it? *(Dropping her sewing.)* But I tell you what I do wish, Mrs. Peters. I wish I had come over sometimes when *she* was here. I—*(Looking around the room.)*—wish I had.

MRS. PETERS. But of course you were awful busy, Mrs. Hale—your house and your children.

MRS. HALE. I could've come. I stayed away because it weren't cheerful—and that's why I ought to have come. I—I've never liked this place. Maybe because it's down in a hollow, and you don't see the road. I dunno what it is, but it's a lonesome place and always was. I wish I had come over to see Minnie Foster sometimes. I can see now—*(Shakes her head.)*

MRS. PETERS. Well, you musn't reproach yourself, Mrs. Hale. Somehow we 100 just don't see how it is with other folks until—something comes up.

MRS. HALE. Not having children makes less work—but it makes a quiet house, and Wright out to work all day, and no company when he did come in. Did you know John Wright, Mrs. Peters?

MRS. PETERS. Not to know him; I've seen him in town. They say he was a good man.

MRS. HALE. Yes—good; he didn't drink, and kept his word as well as
most, I guess, and paid his debts. But he was a hard man, Mrs. Peters. Just to pass the time of day with him. *(Shivers.)* Like a raw wind
that gets to the bone. *(Pauses, her eye falling on the cage.)* I should think
she would 'a' wanted a bird. But what do you suppose went with it?

MRS. PETERS. I don't know, unless it got sick and died. *(She reaches over and
swings the broken door, swings it again; both women watch it.)*

MRS. HALE. You weren't raised around here, were you? *(Mrs. Peters shakes* 105
her head.) You didn't know—her?

MRS. PETERS. Not till they brought her yesterday.

MRS. HALE. She—come to think of it, she was kind of like a bird herself—
real sweet and pretty, but kind of timid and—fluttery. How—
she—did—change. *(Silence; then as if struck by a happy thought and relieved to get back to everyday things.)* Tell you what, Mrs. Peters, why
don't you take the quilt in with you? It might take up her mind.

MRS. PETERS. Why, I think that's a real nice idea, Mrs. Hale. There couldn't
possible be any objection to it, could there? Now, just what would I
take? I wonder if her patches are in here—and her things. *(They look
in the sewing basket.)*

MRS. HALE. Here's some red. I expect this has got sewing things in it.
(Brings out a fancy box.) What a pretty box. Looks like something
somebody would give you. Maybe her scissors are in here. *(Opens
box. Suddenly puts her hand to her nose.)* Why—*(Mrs. Peters bends nearer,
then turns her face away.)* There's something wrapped up in this piece
of silk.

MRS. PETERS. Why, this isn't her scissors.   110

MRS. HALE *(lifting the silk)*. Oh, Mrs. Peters—it's—*(Mrs. Peters bends closer.)*

MRS. PETERS. It's the bird.

MRS. HALE *(jumping up)*. But, Mrs. Peters—look at it. Its neck! Look at its
neck! It's all—other side *to*.

MRS. PETERS. Somebody—wrung—its neck. *(Their eyes meet. A look of growing comprehension of horror. Steps are heard outside. Mrs. Hale slips box
under quilt pieces, and sinks into her chain. Enter Sheriff and County Attorney, Mrs. Peters rises.)*

COUNTY ATTORNEY *(as one turning from serious things to little pleasantries)*. Well, 115
ladies, have you decided whether she was going to quilt it or knot it?

MRS. PETERS. We think she was going to—knot it.

COUNTY ATTORNEY. Well, that's interesting, I'm sure. *(Seeing the birdcage.)*
Has the bird flown?

MRS. HALE *(putting more quilt pieces over the box)*. We think the—cat got it.

COUNTY ATTORNEY *(preoccupied)*. Is there a cat? *(Mrs. Hale glances in a quick
covert way at Mrs. Peters.)*

MRS. PETERS. Well, not now. They're superstitious, you know. They leave. 120

COUNTY ATTORNEY *(to Sheriff Peters, continuing an interrupted conversation)*. No
sign at all of anyone having come from the outside. Their own rope.
Now let's go up again and go over it piece by piece. *(They start up-*

stairs.) It would have to have been someone who knew just the— *(Mrs. Peters sits down. The two women sit there not looking at one another, but as if peering into something and at the same time holding back. When they talk now, it is the manner of feeling their way over strange ground, as if afraid of what they are saying, but as if they cannot help saying it.)*

MRS. HALE. She liked the bird. She was going to bury it in that pretty box.

MRS. PETERS *(in a whisper).* When I was a girl—my kitten—there was a boy took a hatchet, and before my eyes—and before I could get there—*(Covers her face an instant.)* If they hadn't held me back, I would have—*(Catches herself, looks upstairs where steps are heard, falters weakly.)*—hurt him.

MRS. HALE *(with a slow look around her).* I wonder how it would seem never to have had any children around. *(Pause.)* No, Wright wouldn't like the bird—a thing that sang. She used to sing. He killed that, too.

MRS. PETERS *(moving uneasily).* We don't know who killed the bird. 125

MRS. HALE. I knew John Wright.

MRS. PETERS. It was an awful thing was done in this house that night, Mrs. Hale. Killing a man while he slept, slipping a rope around his neck that choked the life out of him.

MRS. HALE. His neck. Choked the life out of him. *(Her hand goes out and rests on the birdcage.)*

MRS. PETERS *(with a rising voice).* We don't know who killed him. We don't know.

MRS. HALE *(her own feeling not interrupted).* If there'd been years and years 130 of nothing, then a bird to sing to you, it would be awful—still, after the bird was still.

MRS. PETERS *(something within her speaking).* I know what stillness is. When we homesteaded in Dakota, and my first baby died—after he was two years old, and me with no other then—

MRS. HALE *(moving).* How soon do you suppose they'll be through, looking for evidence?

MRS. PETERS. I know what stillness is. *(Pulling herself back.)* The law has got to punish crime, Mrs. Hale.

MRS. HALE *(not as if answering that).* I wish you'd seen Minnie Foster when she wore a white dress with blue ribbons and stood up there in the choir and sang. *(A look around the room.)* Oh, I *wish* I'd come over here once in a while! That was a crime! That was a crime! Who's going to punish that?

MRS. PETERS *(looking upstairs).* We mustn't—take on. 135

MRS. HALE. I might have known she needed help! I know how things can be—for women. I tell you, it's queer, Mrs. Peters. We live close together and we live far apart. We all go through the same things—it's all just a different kind of the same thing. *(Brushes her eyes, noticing the bottle of fruit, reaches out for it.)* If I was you, I wouldn't tell her her fruit was gone. Tell her it *ain't.* Tell her it's all right. Take this in to prove it to her. She—she may never know whether it was broke or not.

MRS. PETERS *(takes the bottle, looks about for something to wrap it in; takes petti-coat from the clothes brought from the other room, very nervously begins winding this around the bottle. In a false voice).* My, it's a good thing the men couldn't hear us. Wouldn't they just laugh! Getting all stirred up over a little thing like a—dead canary. As if that could have any-thing to do with—with—wouldn't they *laugh!* *(The men are heard coming downstairs.)*

MRS. HALE *(under her breath).* Maybe they would—maybe they wouldn't.

COUNTY ATTORNEY. No, Peters, it's all perfectly clear except a reason for doing it. But you know juries when it comes to women. If there was some definite thing. Something to show—something to make a story about—a thing that would connect up with this strange way of doing it. *(The women's eyes meet for an instant. Enter Hale from outer door.)*

HALE. Well, I've got the team around. Pretty cold out there.   140

COUNTY ATTORNEY. I'm going to stay here a while by myself. *(To the Sheriff.)* You can send Frank out for me, can't you? I want to go over every-thing. I'm not satisfied that we can't do better.

SHERIFF. Do you want to see what Mrs. Peters is going to take in? *(The Lawyer goes to the table, picks up the apron, laughs.)*

COUNTY ATTORNEY. Oh, I guess they're not very dangerous things the ladies have picked up. *(Moves a few things about, disturbing the quilt pieces which cover the box. Steps back.)* No, Mrs. Peters doesn't need supervis-ing. For that matter, a sheriff's wife is married to the law. Ever think of it that way, Mrs. Peters?

MRS. PETERS. Not—just that way.

SHERIFF *(chuckling).* Married to the law. *(Moves toward the other room.)* I just 145 want you to come in here a minute, George. We ought to take a look at these windows.

COUNTY ATTORNEY *(scoffingly).* Oh, windows!

SHERIFF. We'll be right out, Mr. Hale. *(Hale goes outside. The Sheriff follows the County Attorney into the other room. Then Mrs. Hale rises, hands tight together, looking intensely at Mrs. Peters, whose eyes take a slow turn, finally meeting Mrs. Hale's. A moment Mrs. Hale holds her, then her own eyes point the way to where the box is concealed. Suddenly Mrs. Peters throws back quilt pieces and tries to put the box in the bag she is carrying. It is too big. She opens box, starts to take the bird out, cannot touch it, goes to pieces, stands there helpless. Sound of a knob turning in the other room. Mrs. Hale snatches the box and puts it in the pocket of her big coat. Enter County Attor-ney and Sheriff.)*

COUNTY ATTORNEY *(facetiously).* Well, Henry, at least we found out that she was not going to quilt it. She was going to—what is it you call it, ladies?

MRS. HALE *(her hand against her pocket).* We call it—knot it, Mr. Hen-derson.

Topics for Critical Thinking and Writing

1. Obviously the dead canary in the box isn't evidence that Mrs. Wright has killed her husband. So what is the point of the dead canary in the play?

2. Do you think the play is immoral? Explain.

3. Assume that Minnie is indicted for murder, and assume that you are a lawyer. Assume also that you somehow know that the evidence of the canary has been suppressed. You are asked to serve as Minnie's defense lawyer. Do you accept the case? Why, or why not? (It is unlawful for *prosecutors* to withhold or suppress evidence, but it is not unlawful for defense lawyers to keep quiet about incriminating evidence that they are aware of. Still, would you be comfortable taking this case?)

4. Assume that you have accepted Minnie's case. In 500 words set forth the defense you will offer for her. (Take any position that you wish. You may, for example, argue that she committed justifiable homicide, or that—on the basis of her behavior as reported by Mr. Hale—she is innocent by reason of insanity.)

5. Assume that Minnie has been found guilty and convicted. Compose the speech she might give before being sentenced.

6. "*Trifles* is badly dated. It cannot speak to today's audience." In an essay of 500 words evaluate this view—offer an argument supporting or rejecting it—or you may want to take a middle position.

Mitsuye Yamada

Mitsuye Yamada, the daughter of Japanese immigrants to the United States, was born in Japan in 1923, during her mother's return visit to her native land. Yamada was raised in Seattle, but in 1942 she and her family were incarcerated and then relocated in a camp in Idaho, when Executive Order 9066 (signed by President Franklin D. Roosevelt in 1941) gave military authorities the right to remove any and all persons from "military areas." In 1954 she became an American citizen. A professor of English at Cypress Junior College in San Luis Obispo, California, Yamada is the author of poems and stories.

Yamada's poem concerns the compliant response to Executive Order 9066, which brought about the incarceration and relocation of the entire Japanese and Japanese American population on the Pacific coast—about 112,000 people. More than two-thirds of the people moved were native-born citizens of the United States. (The 158,000 Japanese residents of the Territory of Hawaii were not affected.) There was virtually no protest at the time, but in recent years the order has been widely regarded as an outrageous infringement on liberty, and some younger Japanese Americans cannot fathom why their parents and grandparents complied with it. This poem first appeared in Camp Notes and Other Poems *in 1976.*

To the Lady

The one in San Francisco who asked:
Why did the Japanese Americans let
the government put them in
those camps without protest?

Come to think of it I   5
    should've run off to Canada
    should've hijacked a plane to Algeria
    should've pulled myself up from my
    bra straps
    and kicked'm in the groin   10
    should've bombed a bank
    should've tried self-immolation
    should've holed myself up in a
    woodframe house
    and let you watch me   15
    burn up on the six o'clock news
    should've run howling down the street
    naked and assaulted you at breakfast
    by AP wirephoto
    should've screamed bloody murder   20
    like Kitty Genovese°

    Then
YOU would've
    come to my aid in shining armor
    laid yourself across the railroad track   25
    marched on Washington
    tattooed a Star of David on your arm
    written six million enraged
    letters to Congress

    But we didn't draw the line   30
    anywhere
    law and order Executive Order 9066
    social order moral order internal order

    YOU let'm
    I let'm   35
    All are punished.

---

21 Kitty Genovese In 1964 Kitty Genovese of Kew Gardens, New York, was stabbed to death when she left her car and walked toward her home. Thirty-eight persons heard her screams, but no one came to her assistance.

Topics for Critical Thinking and Writing

1. Has the lady's question (lines 2–4) ever crossed your mind? If so, what answers did you think of?

2. What, in effect, is the speaker really saying in lines 5–21? And in lines 22–29?

3. What possible arguments can you offer for and against the removal of Japanese Americans in 1942?

4. Do you think the survivors of the relocation are entitled to some sort of redress? Why? And if you think they merit compensation, what should the compensation be?

28

What Are the Grounds
of Religious Faith?

The Hebrew Bible

Among the books in the Hebrew Bible (usually called the Old Testament by Christians) is the Book of Psalms (psalm is from the Greek psalmoi, songs of praise), or the Psalter (Greek, psalterion, a stringed instrument). The Book of Psalms contains about 150 songs, prayers, and meditations. The number is a bit imprecise for several reasons: For instance, in the Hebrew Bible the numbering from Psalm 10 to Psalm 148 is one digit ahead of the numbering in Bibles used in the Christian church, which joins 9 and 10, and 114 and 115, but which divides both 116 and 147 into two.

The Hebrew text attributes seventy-three of the psalms to David, who reigned circa 1010–970 B.C. David is said to have been a musician (1 Samuel 16:23; Amos 6:5), but these attributions are no longer accepted by scholars, who point out that although some of the psalms may indeed go back to the tenth century B.C., some others may be as late as 200 B.C. The book in fact is a compilation of earlier collections from hundreds of years of Hebrew history.

The psalms are of various types, for instance lamentations, songs of thanksgiving, songs of sacred history, and songs of praise. Psalm 19 is a song of praise. We give it in the King James Version (1611); later translations are recognized as more accurate, but none is regarded as the literary equal of the King James Version.

Psalm 19

The heavens declare the glory of God; and the firmament[1] sheweth his handywork.

---

[1]**firmament** Dome of the sky. [All notes are the editors'.]

2 Day unto day uttereth speech, and night unto night sheweth knowledge.

3 There is no speech nor language, where their voice is not heard.

4 Their line is gone out through all the earth, and their words to the end of the world. In them hath he set a tabernacle for the sun,

5 Which is as a bridegroom coming out of his chamber, and rejoiceth as a strong man to run a race.

6 His going forth is from the end of the heaven, and his circuit unto the ends of it: and there is nothing hid from the heat thereof.

7 The law of the Lord is perfect, converting the soul: the testimony of the Lord is sure, making wise the simple.

8 The statutes of the Lord are right, rejoicing the heart: the commandment of the Lord is pure, enlightening the eyes.

9 The fear[2] of the Lord is clean, enduring for ever: the judgments of the Lord are true and righteous altogether.

10 More to be desired are they than gold, yea, than much fine gold: sweeter also than honey and the honeycomb.

11 Moreover by them is thy servant warned: and in keeping of them there is great reward.

12 Who can understand his errors? cleanse thou me from secret faults.[3]

13 Keep back thy servant also from presumptuous sins; let them not have dominion over me: then shall I be upright, and I shall be innocent from the great transgression.

14 Let the words of my mouth, and the meditation of my heart, be acceptable in thy sight, O Lord, my strength, and my redeemer.

Topics for Critical Thinking and Writing

1. In Psalm 19, probably most readers will agree about the structure of the poem: 1–6 are on nature, 7–11 are on the Law, and 12–14 are a prayer. How might you state the *argument* of lines 1–6? Of lines 7–11?

2. Do you think these three units cohere into a whole? For instance, does it make sense to say that the second unit is connected to the first by the idea that just as nothing is hidden from the heat of the sun (6), in like manner "the law of the Lord" is everywhere? Is such a reading appropriate, or is it strained? Explain.

[2]**fear** Often emended in later translations to *word*.
[3]**secret faults** Unconscious violations of God's will.

Paul

Paul (A.D. 5?–67?), known as Saul before his conversion from Judaism to Christianity, was a native of Tarsus, a commercial town in the land that is now Turkey. Tarsus was part of the Roman Empire, and Saul, though a Jew, was a Roman citizen. After attending a rabbinical school in Jerusalem, Saul set out for Damascus in A.D. 33 or 34 to suppress Christianity there, but on the way he saw a blinding light, heard the voice of Jesus, and experienced a conversion, described in Acts of the Apostles 9:1–22. In later years he traveled widely, preaching Christianity to Jews and gentiles. Between 59 and 61 he was imprisoned in Rome, and he may have been convicted and executed, but nothing certain is known about his death.

Paul seems to have been the first Christian missionary to Corinth, a Roman colony in Greece, a little to the west of Athens. After his initial visit, probably from 50 to 52, he is reported to have gone to Judea, Syria, Ephesus, and elsewhere. While at Ephesus, however, he heard reports of disorders in Corinth. His letter of response, probably written in about 54, was incorporated into the New Testament as 1 Corinthians, one of his two extant epistles addressed to the Christian community at Corinth. From this letter we reprint Chapter 15.

It is not entirely clear what doctrine(s) of resurrection Paul is opposing in this passage. Perhaps some members of the church did not believe in any form of life after death; perhaps others believed that the resurrection took place at baptism; and perhaps others debated the nature of the resurrection body.

The Interpreter's Bible, 10:12, outlines the fifty-eight verses of Chapter 15 thus:

    A. *The resurrection of Jesus (1–19)*
        1. *The tradition concerning the fact (1–11)*
        2. *The significancy of the resurrection (12–19)*
    B. *The eschatological drama [i.e., concern with ultimate things, such as death and heaven] (20–34)*
        1. *The order of events (20–28)*
        2. *Ad hominem rebuttal (29–34)*
    C. *The resurrection body (35–50)*
        1. *Various types of body (35–41)*
        2. *A spiritual body (42–50)*
    D. *The Christian confidence (51–58)*

The translation used here is the Authorized Version (1611), also known as the King James Version.

1 Corinthians 15

Moreover, brethren, I declare unto you the gospel which I preached unto you, which also ye have received, and wherein ye stand;

2 By which also ye are saved, if we keep in memory what I preached unto you, unless ye have believed in vain.

3 For I delivered unto you first of all that which I also received, how that Christ died for our sins according to the scriptures;

4 And that he was buried, and that he rose again the third day according to the scriptures:

5 And that he was seen of Cephas, then of the twelve:

6 After that, he was seen of above five hundred brethren at once; of whom the greater part remain unto this present, but some are fallen asleep.

7 After that, he was seen of James; then of all the apostles.

8 And last of all he was seen of me also, as of one born out of due time.

9 For I am the least of the apostles, that am not meet to be called an apostle, because I persecuted the church of God.

10 But by the grace of God I am what I am: and his grace which was bestowed upon me was not in vain; but I laboured more abundantly than they all: yet not I, but the grace of God which was with me.

11 Therefore whether it were I or they, so we preach, and so ye believed.

12 Now if Christ be preached that he rose from the dead, how say some among you that there is no resurrection of the dead?

13 But if there be no resurrection of the dead, then is Christ not risen:

14 And if Christ be not risen, then is our preaching vain, and your faith is also vain.

15 Yea, and we are found false witnesses of God; because we have testified of God that he raised up Christ: whom he raised not up, if so be that the dead rise not.

16 For if the dead rise not, then is not Christ raised:

17 And if Christ be not raised, your faith is vain; ye are yet in your sins.

18 Then they also which are fallen asleep in Christ are perished.

19 If in this life only we have hope in Christ, we are of all men most miserable.

20 But now is Christ risen from the dead, and become the first fruits of them that slept.

21 For since by man came death, by man came also the resurrection of the dead.

22 For as in Adam all die, even so in Christ shall all be made alive.

23 But every man in his own order: Christ the first fruits; afterward they that are Christ's at his coming.

24 Then cometh the end, when he shall have delivered up the kingdom to God, even the Father; when he shall have put down all rule and all authority and power.

25 For he must reign, till he hath put all enemies under his feet.

26 The last enemy that shall be destroyed is death.

27 For he hath put all things under his feet. But when he saith all things are put under him, it is manifest that he is excepted, which did put all things under him.

28 And when all things shall be subdued unto him, then shall the Son also himself be subject unto him that put all things under him, that God may be all in all.

29 Else what shall they do which are baptized for the dead, if the dead rise not at all? why are they then baptized for the dead?

30 And why stand we in jeopardy every hour?

31 I protest by your rejoicing which I have in Christ Jesus our Lord, I die daily.

32 If after the manner of men I have fought with beasts at Ephesus, what advantageth it me, if the dead rise not? let us eat and drink; for to-morrow we die.

33 Be not deceived: evil communications corrupt good manners.

34 Awake to righteousness, and sin not; for some have not the knowledge of God: I speak this to your shame.

35 But some man will say, How are the dead raised up? and with what body do they come?

36 Thou fool, that which thou sowest is not quickened, except it die:

37 And that which thou sowest, thou sowest not that body that shall be, but bare grain, it may chance of wheat, or of some other grain:

38 But God giveth it a body as it hath pleased him, and to every seed his own body.

39 All flesh is not the same flesh: but there is one kind of flesh of men, another flesh of beasts, another of fishes, and another of birds.

40 There are also celestial bodies, and bodies terrestrial: but the glory of the celestial is one, and the glory of the terrestrial is another.

41 There is one glory of the sun, and another glory of the moon, and another glory of the stars: for one star differeth from another star in glory.

42 So also is the resurrection of the dead. It is sown in corruption; it is raised in incorruption:

43 It is sown in dishonour; it is raised in glory: it is sown in weakness; it is raised in power:

44 It is sown a natural body; it is raised a spiritual body. There is a natural body, and there is a spiritual body.

45 And so it is written, The first man Adam was made a living soul; the last Adam was made a quickening spirit.

46 Howbeit that was not first which is spiritual, but that which is natural; and afterward that which is spiritual.

47 The first man is of the earth, earthy: the second man is the Lord from heaven.

48 As is the earthy, such are they also that are earthy: and as is the heavenly, such are they also that are heavenly.

49 And as we have borne the image of the earthy, we shall also bear the image of the heavenly.

50 Now this I say, brethren, that flesh and blood cannot inherit the kingdom of God; neither doth corruption inherit incorruption.

51 Behold, I shew you a mystery; We shall not all sleep, but we shall all be changed,

52 In a moment, in the twinkling of an eye, at the last trump: for the trumpet shall sound, and the dead shall be raised incorruptible, and we shall be changed.

53 For this corruptible must put on incorruption, and this mortal must put on immortality.

54 So when this corruptible shall have put on incorruption, and this mortal shall have put on immortality, then shall be brought to pass the saying that is written, Death is swallowed up in victory.

55 O death, where is thy sting? O grave, where is thy victory?

56 The sting of death is sin; and the strength of sin is the law.

57 But thanks be to God, which giveth us the victory through our Lord Jesus Christ.

58 Therefore, my beloved brethren, be ye stedfast, unmoveable, always abounding in the work of the Lord, forasmuch as ye know that your labour is not in vain in the Lord.

Topics for Critical Thinking and Writing

1. Why is belief in the Resurrection of Christ important to Paul? What evidence does he offer to support his belief in it?

2. What leads Paul to the conclusion that the dead are resurrected? What evidence does he offer to support this belief? What conclusion, according to Paul, follows if the dead are not resurrected?

3. In verse 22 Paul speaks of people who are "in Adam," and of others who are "in Christ." Explain the distinction to someone who finds it puzzling. (If you find it puzzling, check a guide to the Bible, such as *The Interpreter's Bible,* or *A New Catholic Commentary on Holy Scripture,* ed. Reginald C. Fuller et al.)

4. What mistaken belief, according to Paul, leads people to conclude that we should (as he says in verse 32) "eat and drink; for tomorrow we die"?

5. In verses 35–50 Paul insists again on bodily resurrection of human beings. In 35–44 he uses an analogy to explain that the body that dies and the body that is resurrected are continuous and yet also are different. Put his analogy into your own words. Do you think analogy is an effective way of making this point? Why? In verse 45 Paul uses a different argument, contrasting Adam ("the first man Adam") with Christ ("the last Adam"). Why do you think he drops the analogy and now offers this evidence? How in verses 46–47 does Paul bring the two points together?

6. In verse 55 Paul says, "O death, where is thy sting? O grave, where is thy victory?" In a paragraph summarize the beliefs (expressed in this selection) that lead Paul to the conclusion that death and the grave are conquered.

C. S. Lewis

Clive Staples Lewis (1898–1963), a professor of English literature at Oxford and later at Cambridge, wrote several important books on literature, but he is most widely known for his writings on Christianity (he converted to Christianity from atheism) and for his children's stories. The material reprinted here was originally delivered to the British public in a series of radio addresses in the early 1940s.

What Christians Believe

1. THE RIVAL CONCEPTIONS OF GOD

I have been asked to tell you what Christians believe, and I am going to begin by telling you one thing that Christians do not need to believe. If you are a Christian you do not have to believe that all the other religions are simply wrong all through. If you are an atheist you do have to believe that the main point in all the religions of the whole world is simply one huge mistake. If you are a Christian, you are free to think that all these religions, even the queerest ones, contain at least some hint of the truth. When I was an atheist I had to try to persuade myself that most of the human race have always been wrong about the question that mattered to them most; when I became a Christian I was able to take a more liberal view. But, of course, being a Christian does mean thinking that where Christianity differs from other religions, Christianity is right and they are wrong. As in arithmetic—there is only one right answer to a sum, and all other answers are wrong: but some of the wrong answers are much nearer being right than others.

The first big division of humanity is into the majority, who believe in some kind of God or gods, and the minority who do not. On this point, Christianity lines up with the majority—lines up with ancient Greeks and Romans, modern savages, Stoics, Platonists, Hindus, Mohammedans, etc., against the modern Western European materialist.

Now I go on to the next big division. People who all believe in God can be divided according to the sort of God they believe in. There are two very different ideas on this subject. One of them is the idea that He is beyond good and evil. We humans call one thing good and another thing bad. But according to some people that is merely our human point of view. These people would say that the wiser you become the less you would want to call anything good or bad, and the more clearly you would see that everything is good in one way and bad in another, and that nothing could have been different. Consequently, these people think that long before you got anywhere near the divine point of view the distinction would have disappeared altogether. We call a cancer bad, they would say, because it kills a man; but you might just as well call a successful surgeon bad because he kills a cancer. It all depends on the point of view. The other and opposite idea is that God is quite definitely "good" or "righteous," a God who takes sides, who loves love and hates hatred, who wants us to behave in one way and not in another. The first of these views—the one that thinks God beyond good and evil—is called Pantheism. It was held by the great Prussian philosopher Hegel and, as far as I can understand them, by the Hindus. The other view is held by Jews, Mohammedans, and Christians.

And with this big difference between Pantheism and the Christian 4
idea of God, there usually goes another. Pantheists usually believe that God, so to speak, animates the universe as you animate your body: that the universe almost *is* God, so that if it did not exist He would not exist either, and anything you find in the universe is a part of God. The Christian idea is quite different. They think God invented and made the universe—like a man making a picture or composing a tune. A painter is not a picture, and he does not die if his picture is destroyed. You may say, "He's put a lot of himself into it," but you only mean that all its beauty and interest has come out of his head. His skill is not in the picture in the same way that it is in his head, or even in his hands. I expect you see how this difference between Pantheists and Christians hangs together with the other one. If you do not take the distinction between good and bad very seriously, then it is easy to say that anything you find in this world is a part of God. But, of course, if you think some things really bad, and God really good, then you cannot talk like that. You must believe that God is separate from the world and that some of the things we see in it are contrary to His will. Confronted with a cancer or a slum the Pantheist can say, "If you could only see it from the divine point of view, you would realize that this also is God." The Christian replies, "Don't talk damned nonsense."[1] For Christianity is a fighting religion. It thinks God made the world—that space and time, heat and cold, and all the colors and tastes, and all the animals and vegetables, are things that God "made up out of His head" as a man makes up a story. But it also thinks that a great many things have gone wrong with the world that God made and that God insists, and insists very loudly, on our putting them right again.

And, of course, that raises a very big question. If a good God made 5
the world why has it gone wrong? And for many years I simply refused to listen to the Christian answers to this question, because I kept on feeling "whatever you say, and however clever your arguments are, isn't it much simpler and easier to say that the world was not made by any intelligent power? Aren't all your arguments simply a complicated attempt to avoid the obvious?" But then that threw me back into another difficulty.

---

[1]One listener complained of the word *damned* as frivolous swearing. But I mean exactly what I say—nonsense that is *damned* is under God's curse, and will (apart from God's grace) lead those who believe it to eternal death. [Lewis's note.]

My argument against God was that the universe seemed so cruel and   6
unjust. But how had I got this idea of *just* and *unjust*? A man does not call
a line crooked unless he has some idea of a straight line. What was I comparing this universe with when I called it unjust? If the whole show was
bad and senseless from A to Z, so to speak, why did I, who was supposed to
be part of the show, find myself in such violent reaction against it? A man
feels wet when he falls into water, because man is not a water animal: A
fish would not feel wet. Of course I could have given up my idea of justice
by saying it was nothing but a private idea of my own. But if I did that, then
my argument against God collapsed too—for the argument depended on
saying that the world was really unjust, not simply that it did not happen
to please my private fancies. Thus in the very act of trying to prove that
God did not exist—in other words, that the whole of reality was senseless
—I found I was forced to assume that one part of reality—namely my idea
of justice—was full of sense. Consequently atheism turns out to be too
simple. If the whole universe has no meaning, we should never have
found out that it has no meaning: Just as, if there were no light in the universe and therefore no creatures with eyes, we should never know it was
dark. *Dark* would be without meaning.

2. THE INVASION

Very well then, atheism is too simple. And I will tell you another   7
view that is also too simple. It is the view I call Christianity-and-water,
the view which simply says there is a good God in Heaven and everything is all right—leaving out all the difficult and terrible doctrines
about sin and hell and the devil, and the redemption. Both these are
boys' philosophies.

It is no good asking for a simple religion. After all, real things are not   8
simple. They look simple, but they are not. The table I am sitting at looks
simple: But ask a scientist to tell you what it is really made of—all about
the atoms and how the light waves rebound from them and hit my eye and
what they do to the optic nerve and what it does to my brain—and, of
course, you find that what we call "seeing a table" lands you in mysteries
and complications which you can hardly get to the end of. A child saying a
child's prayer looks simple. And if you are content to stop there, well and
good. But if you are not—and the modern world usually is not—if you
want to go on and ask what is really happening—then you must be prepared for something difficult. If we ask for something more than simplicity, it is silly then to complain that the something more is not simple.

Very often, however, this silly procedure is adopted by people who   9
are not silly, but who, consciously or unconsciously, want to destroy
Christianity. Such people put up a version of Christianity suitable for a
child of six and make that the object of their attack. When you try to explain the Christian doctrine as it is really held by an instructed adult,
they then complain that you are making their heads turn round and that

it is all too complicated and that if there really were a God they are sure He would have made "religion" simple, because simplicity is so beautiful, etc. You must be on your guard against these people for they will change their ground every minute and only waste your time. Notice, too, their idea of God "making religion simple": as if "religion" were something God invented, and not His statement to us of certain quite unalterable facts about His own nature.

Besides being complicated, reality, in my experience, is usually odd. 10 It is not neat, not obvious, not what you expect. For instance, when you have grasped that the earth and the other planets all go round the sun, you would naturally expect that all the planets were made to match — all at equal distances from each other, say, or distances that regularly increased, or all the same size, or else getting bigger or smaller as you go farther from the sun. In fact, you find no rhyme or reason (that we can see) about either the sizes or the distances; and some of them have one moon, one has four, one has two, some have none, and one has a ring.

Reality, in fact, is usually something you could not have guessed. 11 That is one of the reasons I believe Christianity. It is a religion you could not have guessed. If it offered us just the kind of universe we had always expected, I should feel we were making it up. But, in fact, it is not the sort of thing anyone would have made up. It has just that queer twist about it that real things have. So let us leave behind all these boys' philosophies — these oversimple answers. The problem is not simple and the answer is not going to be simple either.

What is the problem? A universe that contains much that is obvi- 12 ously bad and apparently meaningless, but containing creatures like ourselves who know that it is bad and meaningless. There are only two views that face all the facts. One is the Christian view that this is a good world that has gone wrong, but still retains the memory of what it ought to have been. The other is the view called Dualism. Dualism means the belief that there are two equal and independent powers at the back of everything, one of them good and the other bad, and that this universe is the battlefield in which they fight out an endless war. I personally think that next to Christianity Dualism is the manliest and most sensible creed on the market. But it has a catch in it.

The two powers, or spirits, or gods — the good one and the bad 13 one — are supposed to be quite independent. They both existed from all eternity. Neither of them made the other, neither of them has any more right than the other to call itself God. Each presumably thinks it is good and thinks the other bad. One of them likes hatred and cruelty, the other likes love and mercy, and each backs its own view. Now what do we mean when we call one of them the Good Power and the other the Bad Power? Either we are merely saying that we happen to prefer the one to the other — like preferring beer to cider — or else we are saying that, whatever the two powers think about it, and whichever we humans, at the moment, happen to like, one of them is actually wrong, actually mistaken, in regarding itself as good. Now if we mean merely that we happen to prefer the first, then we must give up talking about good and evil at all. For good means what you ought to prefer quite regardless of what you happen to like at any given moment. If "being good" meant simply joining the side you happened to fancy, for no real reason, then good would not deserve to be called good. So we must mean that one of the two powers is actually wrong and the other actually right.

But the moment you say that, you are putting into the universe a 14 third thing in addition to the two Powers: some law or standard or rule of good which one of the powers conforms to and the other fails to conform to. But since the two powers are judged by this standard, then this standard, or the Being who made this standard, is farther back and higher up than either of them, and He will be the real God. In fact, what we meant by calling them good and bad turns out to be that one of them is in a right relation to the real ultimate God and the other in a wrong relation to Him.

The same point can be made in a different way. If Dualism is true, 15 then the Bad Power must be a being who likes badness for its own sake. But in reality we have no experience of anyone liking badness just because it is bad. The nearest we can get to it is in cruelty. But in real life people are cruel for one of two reasons — either because they are sadists, that is, because they have a sexual perversion which makes cruelty a cause of sensual pleasure to them, or else for the sake of something they are going to get out of it — money, or power, or safety. But pleasure, money, power, and safety are all, as far as they go, good things. The badness consists in pursuing them by the wrong method, or in the wrong way, or too much. I do not mean, of course, that the people who do this are not desperately wicked. I do mean that wickedness, when you examine it, turns out to be the pursuit of some good in the wrong way. You can be good for the mere sake of goodness; you cannot be bad for the mere sake of badness. You can do a kind action when you are not feeling kind and when it gives you no pleasure, simply because kindness is right; but no one ever did a cruel action simply because cruelty is wrong — only because cruelty was pleasant or useful to him. In other words badness cannot succeed even in being bad in the same way in which goodness is good. Goodness is, so to speak, itself: Badness is only spoiled goodness. And there must be something good first before it can be spoiled. We called sadism a sexual perversion; but you must first have the idea of a normal sexuality before you can talk of its being perverted: and you can see which is the perversion, because you can explain the perverted from the normal, and cannot explain the normal from the perverted. It follows that this Bad Power, who is supposed to be on an equal footing with the Good Power, and to love badness in the same way as the Good Power loves goodness, is a mere bogy. In order to be bad he must have good things to want and then to pursue in the wrong way: He must have impulses which were originally good in order to be able to pervert them. But if he is bad he cannot supply himself either with good things to desire or with good impulses to pervert. He must be getting both from the Good Power. And if so, then he is not independent. He is part of the Good Power's world: He was made either by the Good Power or by some power above them both.

Put it more simply still. To be bad, he must exist and have intelli- 16
gence and will. But existence, intelligence, and will are in themselves good. Therefore he must be getting them from the Good Power: Even to be bad he must borrow or steal from his opponent. And do you now begin to see why Christianity has always said that the devil is a fallen angel? That is not a mere story for the children. It is a real recognition of the fact that evil is a parasite, not an original thing. The powers which enable evil to carry on are powers given it by goodness. All the things which enable a bad man to be effectively bad are in themselves good things—resolution, cleverness, good looks, existence itself. That is why Dualism, in a strict sense, will not work.

But I freely admit that real Christianity (as distinct from Christianity- 17
and-water) goes much nearer to Dualism than people think. One of the things that surprised me when I first read the New Testament seriously was that it talked so much about a Dark Power in the universe—a mighty evil spirit who was held to be the Power behind death and disease, and sin. The difference is that Christianity thinks this Dark Power was created by God, and was good when he was created, and went wrong. Christianity agrees with Dualism that this universe is at war. But it does not think this is a war between independent powers. It thinks it is a civil war, a rebellion, and that we are living in a part of the universe occupied by the rebel.

Enemy-occupied territory—that is what this world is. Christianity is 18
the story of how the rightful king has landed, you might say landed in disguise, and is calling us all to take part in a great campaign of sabotage. When you go to church you are really listening in to the secret wireless from our friends: That is why the enemy is so anxious to prevent us from going. He does it by playing on our conceit and laziness and intellectual snobbery. I know someone will ask me, "Do you really mean, at this time of day, to reintroduce our old friend the devil—hoofs and horns and all?" Well, what the time of day has to do with it I do not know. And I am not particular about the hoofs and horns. But in other respects my answer is "Yes, I do." I do not claim to know anything about his personal appearance. If anybody really wants to know him better I would say to that person, "Don't worry. If you really want to, you will. Whether you'll like it when you do is another question."

3. THE SHOCKING ALTERNATIVE

Christians, then, believe that an evil power has made himself for the 19
present the Prince of this World. And, of course, that raises problems. Is this state of affairs in accordance with God's will or not? If it is, He is a

strange God, you will say: And if it is not, how can anything happen contrary to the will of a being with absolute power?

But anyone who has been in authority knows how a thing can be in 20 accordance with your will in one way and not in another. It may be quite sensible for a mother to say to the children, "I'm not going to go and make you tidy the schoolroom every night. You've got to learn to keep it tidy on your own." Then she goes up one night and finds the Teddy bear and the ink and the French Grammar all lying in the grate. That is against her will. She would prefer the children to be tidy. But on the other hand, it is her will which has left the children free to be untidy. The same thing arises in any regiment, or trade union, or school. You make a thing voluntary and then half the people do not do it. That is not what you willed, but your will has made it possible.

It is probably the same in the universe. God created things which 21 had free will. That means creatures which can go either wrong or right. Some people think they can imagine a creature which was free but had no possibility of going wrong; I cannot. If a thing is free to be good it is also free to be bad. And free will is what has made evil possible. Why, then, did God give them free will? Because free will, though it makes evil possible, is also the only thing that makes possible any love or goodness or joy worth having. A world of automata—of creatures that worked like machines—would hardly be worth creating. The happiness which God designs for His higher creatures is the happiness of being freely, voluntarily united to Him and to each other in an ecstasy of love and delight compared with which the most rapturous love between a man and a woman on this earth is mere milk and water. And for that they must be free.

Of course God knew what would happen if they used their freedom 22 the wrong way: Apparently He thought it worth the risk. Perhaps we feel inclined to disagree with him. But there is a difficulty about disagreeing with God. He is the source from which all your reasoning power comes: You could not be right and He wrong any more than a stream can rise higher than its own source. When you are arguing against Him you are arguing against the very power that makes you able to argue at all: It is like cutting off the branch you are sitting on. If God thinks this state of war in the universe a price worth paying for free will—that is, for making a live world in which creatures can do real good or harm and something of real importance can happen, instead of a toy world which only moves when He pulls the strings—then we may take it it is worth paying.

When we have understood about free will, we shall see how silly it 23 is to ask, as somebody once asked me: "Why did God make a creature of such rotten stuff that it went wrong?" The better stuff a creature is made of—the cleverer and stronger and freer it is—then the better it will be if it goes right, but also the worse it will be if it goes wrong. A cow cannot be very good or very bad; a dog can be both better and worse; a child better and worse still; an ordinary man, still more so; a man of genius, still more so; a superhuman spirit best — or worst — of all.

How did the Dark Power go wrong? Here, no doubt, we ask a ques- 24 tion to which human beings cannot give an answer with any certainty. A reasonable (and traditional) guess, based on our own experiences of going wrong, can, however, be offered. The moment you have a self at all, there is a possibility of putting yourself first — wanting to be the center — wanting to be God, in fact. That was the sin of Satan: And that was the sin he taught the human race. Some people think the fall of man had something to do with sex, but that is a mistake. (The story in the Book of Genesis rather suggests that some corruption in our sexual nature followed the fall and was its result, not its cause.) What Satan put into the heads of our remote ancestors was the idea that they could "be like gods" — could set up on their own as if they had created them-selves — be their own masters — invent some sort of happiness for them-selves outside God, apart from God. And out of that hopeless attempt has come nearly all that we call human history — money, poverty, ambition, war, prostitution, classes, empires, slavery — the long terrible story of man trying to find something other than God which will make him happy.

The reason why it can never succeed is this. God made us: invented 25 us as a man invents an engine. A car is made to run on gasoline, and it would not run properly on anything else. Now God designed the human machine to run on Himself. He Himself is the fuel our spirits were de-signed to burn, or the food our spirits were designed to feed on. There is no other. That is why it is just no good asking God to make us happy in our own way without bothering about religion. God cannot give us a happiness and peace apart from Himself, because it is not there. There is no such thing.

That is the key to history. Terrific energy is expended — civilizations 26 are built up — excellent institutions devised; but each time something goes wrong. Some fatal flaw always brings the selfish and cruel people to the top and it all slides back into misery and ruin. In fact, the machine conks. It seems to start up all right and runs a few yards, and then it breaks down. They are trying to run it on the wrong juice. That is what Satan has done to us humans.

And what did God do? First of all He left us conscience, the sense of 27 right and wrong: And all through history there have been people trying (some of them very hard) to obey it. None of them ever quite succeeded. Secondly, he sent the human race what I call good dreams: I mean those queer stories scattered all through the heathen religions about a god who dies and comes to life again and, by his death, has somehow given new life to men. Thirdly, He selected one particular people and spent several centuries hammering into their heads the sort of God He was — that there was only one of Him and that He cared about right conduct. Those people were the Jews, and the Old Testament gives an account of the hammering process.

Then comes the real shock. Among these Jews there suddenly turns 28
up a man who goes about talking as if He was God. He claims to forgive
sins. He says He has always existed. He says He is coming to judge the
world at the end of time. Now let us get this clear. Among Pantheists,
like the Indians, anyone might say that he was a part of God, or one
with God: There would be nothing very odd about it. But this man, since
He was a Jew, could not mean that kind of God. God, in their language,
meant the Being outside the world Who had made it and was infinitely
different from anything else. And when you have grasped that, you will
see that what this man said was, quite simply, the most shocking thing
that has ever been uttered by human lips.

One part of the claim tends to slip past us unnoticed because we 29
have heard it so often that we no longer see what it amounts to. I
mean the claim to forgive sins: any sins. Now unless the speaker is
God, this is really so preposterous as to be comic. We can all understand how a man forgives offenses against himself. You tread on my
toe and I forgive you, you steal my money and I forgive you. But what
should we make of a man, himself unrobbed and untrodden on, who
announced that he forgave you for treading on other men's toes and
stealing other men's money? Asinine fatuity is the kindest description
we should give of his conduct. Yet this is what Jesus did. He told
people that their sins were forgiven, and never waited to consult all
the other people whom their sins had undoubtedly injured. He unhesitatingly behaved as if He was the party chiefly concerned, the person
chiefly offended in all offenses. This makes sense only if He really was
the God whose laws are broken and whose love is wounded in every
sin. In the mouth of any speaker who is not God, these words would
imply what I can only regard as a silliness and conceit unrivaled by any
other character in history.

Yet (and this is the strange, significant thing) even His enemies, 30
when they read the Gospels, do not usually get the impression of silliness and conceit. Still less do unprejudiced readers. Christ says that He is
"humble and meek" and we believe Him; not noticing that, if He were
merely a man, humility and meekness are the very last characteristics
we could attribute to some of His sayings.

I am trying here to prevent anyone saying the really foolish thing 31
that people often say about Him: "I'm ready to accept Jesus as a great
moral teacher, but I don't accept His claim to be God." That is the one
thing we must not say. A man who was merely a man and said the sort
of things Jesus said would not be a great moral teacher. He would either
be a lunatic—on a level with the man who says he is a poached egg—or
else he would be the Devil of Hell. You must make your choice. Either
this man was, and is, the Son of God: or else a madman or something
worse. You can shut Him up for a fool, you can spit at Him and kill Him
as a demon; or you can fall at His feet and call Him Lord and God. But let

us not come with any patronizing nonsense about His being a great human teacher. He has not left that open to us. He did not intend to.

4. THE PERFECT PENITENT

We are faced, then, with a frightening alternative. This man we are 32 talking about either was (and is) just what He said or else a lunatic, or something worse. Now it seems to me obvious that He was neither a lunatic nor a fiend: And consequently, however strange or terrifying or unlikely it may seem, I have to accept the view that he was and is God. God has landed on this enemy-occupied world in human form.

And now, what was the purpose of it all? What did He come to do? 33 Well, to teach, of course; but as soon as you look into the New Testament or any other Christian writing you will find they are constantly talking about something different—about His death and His coming to life again. It is obvious that Christians think the chief point of the story lies here. They think the main thing He came to earth to do was to suffer and be killed.

Now before I became a Christian I was under the impression that 34 the first thing Christians had to believe was one particular theory as to what the point of this dying was. According to that theory God wanted to punish men for having deserted and joined the Great Rebel, but Christ volunteered to be punished instead, and so God let us off. Now I admit that even this theory does not seem to me quite so immoral and so silly as it used to; but that is not the point I want to make. What I came to see later on was that neither this theory nor any other is Christianity. The central Christian belief is that Christ's death has somehow put us right with God and given us a fresh start. Theories as to how it did this are another matter. A good many different theories have been held as to how it works: What all Christians are agreed on is that it does work. I will tell you what I think it is like. All sensible people know that if you are tired and hungry a meal will do you good. But the modern theory of nourishment—all about the vitamins and proteins—is a different thing. People ate their dinners and felt better long before the theory of vitamins was ever heard of: And if the theory of vitamins is some day abandoned they will go on eating their dinners just the same. Theories about Christ's death are not Christianity: They are explanations about how it works. Christians would not all agree as to how important these theories are. My own church—the Church of England—does not lay down any one of them as the right one. The Church of Rome goes a bit further. But I think they will all agree that the thing itself is infinitely more important than any explanations that theologians have produced. I think they would probably admit that no explanation will ever be quite adequate to the reality. But as I said in the preface to this book, I am only a layman, and at this point we are getting into deep water. I can only tell you, for what it is worth, how I, personally, look at the matter.

On my view the theories are not themselves the thing you are asked 35 to accept. Many of you no doubt have read Jeans or Eddington.[2] What they do when they want to explain the atom, or something of that sort, is to give you a description out of which you can make a mental picture. But then they warn you that this picture is not what the scientists actually believe. What the scientists believe is a mathematical formula. The pictures are there only to help you to understand the formula. They are not really true in the way the formula is; they do not give you the real thing but only something more or less like it. They are only meant to help, and if they do not help you can drop them. The thing itself cannot be pictured, it can only be expressed mathematically. We are in the same boat here. We believe that the death of Christ is just that point in history at which something absolutely unimaginable from outside shows through into our own world. And if we cannot picture even the atoms of which our own world is built, of course we are not going to be able to picture this. Indeed, if we found that we could fully understand it, that very fact would show it was not what it professes to be—the inconceivable, the uncreated, the thing from beyond nature, striking down into nature like lightning. You may ask what good will it be to us if we do not understand it. But that is easily answered. A man can eat his dinner without understanding exactly how food nourishes him. A man can accept what Christ has done without knowing how it works; indeed, he certainly would not know how it works until he has accepted it.

We are told that Christ was killed for us, that His death has washed 36 out our sins, and that by dying He disabled death itself. That is the formula. That is Christianity. That is what has to be believed. Any theories we build up as to how Christ's death did all this are, in my view, quite secondary: mere plans or diagrams to be left alone if they do not help us, and, even if they do help us, not to be confused with the thing itself. All the same, some of these theories are worth looking at.

The one most people have heard is the one I mentioned before—the 37 one about our being let off because Christ had volunteered to bear a punishment instead of us. Now on the face of it that is a very silly theory. If God was prepared to let us off, why on earth did He not do so? And what possible point could there be in punishing an innocent person instead? None at all that I can see, if you are thinking of punishment in the police-court sense. On the other hand, if you think of a debt, there is plenty of point in a person who has some assets paying it on behalf of someone who has not. Or if you take "paying the penalty," not in the sense of being punished, but in the more general sense of "standing the racket" or "footing the bill," then, of course, it is a matter of common ex-

[2]**Jeans or Eddington** Sir James Hopwood Jeans (1877–1946), English physicist, astronomer, and author.   Sir Arthur Stanley Eddington (1822–1944), English astronomer.

perience that, when one person has got himself into a hole, the trouble of getting him out usually falls on a kind friend.

Now what was the sort of "hole" man had got himself into? He had 38 tried to set up on his own, to behave as if he belonged to himself. In other words, fallen man is not simply an imperfect creature who needs improvement: He is a rebel who must lay down his arms. Laying down your arms, surrendering, saying you are sorry, realizing that you have been on the wrong track and getting ready to start life over again from the ground floor—that is the only way out of a "hole." This process of surrender—this movement full speed astern—is what Christians call repentance. Now repentance is no fun at all. It is something much harder than merely eating humble pie. It means unlearning all the self-conceit and self-will that we have been training ourselves into for thousands of years. It means killing part of yourself, undergoing a kind of death. In fact, it needs a good man to repent. And here comes the catch. Only a bad person needs to repent: Only a good person can repent perfectly. The worse you are the more you need it and the less you can do it. The only person who could do it perfectly would be a perfect person—and he would not need it.

Remember, this repentance, this willing submission to humiliation 39 and a kind of death, is not something God demands of you before He will take you back and which He could let you off if He chose: It is simply a description of what going back to Him is like. If you ask God to take you back without it, you are really asking Him to let you go back without going back. It cannot happen. Very well, then, we must go through with it. But the same badness which makes us need it, makes us unable to do it. Can we do it if God helps us? Yes, but what do we mean when we talk of God helping us? We mean God putting into us a bit of Himself, so to speak. He lends us a little of His reasoning powers and that is how we think: He puts a little of His love into us and that is how we love one another. When you teach a child writing, you hold its hand while it forms the letters: That is, it forms the letters because you are forming them. We love and reason because God loves and reasons and holds our hand while we do it. Now if we had not fallen, that would be all plain sailing. But unfortunately we now need God's help in order to do something which God, in His own nature, never does at all—to surrender, to suffer, to submit, to die. Nothing in God's nature corresponds to this process at all. So that the one road for which we now need God's leadership most of all is a road God, in His own nature, had never walked. God can share only what He has: This thing, in His own nature, He has not.

But supposing God became a man—suppose our human nature 40 which can suffer and die was amalgamated with God's nature in one person—then that person could help us. He could surrender His will, and suffer and die, because He was man; and He could do it perfectly because He was God. You and I can go through this process only if God does it in us; but God can do it only if He becomes man. Our attempts at this dying will succeed only if we men share in God's dying, just as our thinking can succeed only because it is a drop out of the ocean of His intelligence: But we cannot share God's dying unless God dies; and He cannot die except by being a man. That is the sense in which He pays our debt, and suffers for us what He Himself need not suffer at all.

I have heard some people complain that if Jesus was God as well as 41 man, then His sufferings and death lose all value in their eyes, "because it must have been so easy for him." Others may (very rightly) rebuke the ingratitude and ungraciousness of this objection; what staggers me is the misunderstanding it betrays. In one sense, of course, those who make it are right. They have even understated their own case. The perfect submission, the perfect suffering, the perfect death were not only easier to Jesus because He was God, but were possible only because He was God. But surely that is a very odd reason for not accepting them? The teacher is able to form the letters for the child because the teacher is grown-up and knows how to write. That, of course, makes it easier for the teacher; and only because it is easier for him can he help the child. If it rejected him because "it's easy for grown-ups" and waited to learn writing from another child who could not write itself (and so had no "unfair" advantage), it would not get on very quickly. If I am drowning in a rapid river, a man who still has one foot on the bank may give me a hand which saves my life. Ought I to shout back (between my gasps) "No, it's not fair! You have an advantage! You're keeping one foot on the bank"? That advantage—call it "unfair" if you like—is the only reason why he can be of any use to me. To what will you look for help if you will not look to that which is stronger than yourself?

Such is my own way of looking at what Christians call the Atone- 42 ment. But remember this is only one more picture. Do not mistake it for the thing itself: And if it does not help you, drop it.

5. THE PRACTICAL CONCLUSION

The perfect surrender and humiliation were undergone by Christ: 43 perfect because He was God, surrender and humiliation because He was man. Now the Christian belief is that if we somehow share the humility and suffering of Christ we shall also share in His conquest of death and find a new life after we have died and in it become perfect, and perfectly happy, creatures. This means something much more than our trying to follow His teaching. People often ask when the next step in evolution— the step to something beyond man—will happen. But on the Christian view, it has happened already. In Christ a new kind of man appeared: And the new kind of life which began in Him is to be put into us.

How is this to be done? Now, please remember how we acquired the 44 old, ordinary kind of life. We derived it from others, from our father and mother and all our ancestors, without our consent—and by a very curious process, involving pleasure, pain, and danger. A process you would never have guessed. Most of us spend a good many years in childhood trying to guess it: And some children, when they are first told, do not believe it—and I am not sure that I blame them, for it is very odd. Now the God who arranged that process is the same God who arranges how the new kind of life—the Christ life—is to spread. We must be prepared for it being odd too. He did not consult us when He invented sex: He has not consulted us either when He invented this.

There are three things that spread the Christ life to us: baptism, belief, and that mysterious action which different Christians call by different names—Holy Communion, the Mass, the Lord's Supper. At least, those are the three ordinary methods. I am not saying there may not be special cases where it is spread without one or more of these. I have not time to go into special cases, and I do not know enough. If you are trying in a few minutes to tell a man how to get to Edinburgh you will tell him the trains: He can, it is true, get there by boat or by a plane, but you will hardly bring that in. And I am not saying anything about which of these three things is the most essential. My Methodist friend would like me to say more about belief and less (in proportion) about the other two. But I am not going into that. Anyone who professes to teach you Christian doctrine will, in fact, tell you to use all three, and that is enough for our present purpose. 45

I cannot myself see why these things should be the conductors of the new kind of life. But then, if one did not happen to know, I should never have seen any connection between a particular physical pleasure and the appearance of a new human being in the world. We have to take reality as it comes to us: There is no good jabbering about what it ought to be like or what we should have expected it to be like. But though I cannot see why it should be so, I can tell you why I believe it is so. I have explained why I have to believe that Jesus was (and is) God. And it seems plain as a matter of history that He taught His followers that the new life was communicated in this way. In other words, I believe it on His authority. Do not be scared by the word *authority*. Believing things on authority only means believing them because you have been told them by someone you think trustworthy. Ninety-nine percent of the things you believe are believed on authority. I believe there is such a place as New York. I have not seen it myself. I could not prove by abstract reasoning that there must be such a place. I believe it because reliable people have told me so. The ordinary man believes in the Solar System, atoms, evolution, and the circulation of the blood on authority—because the scientists say so. Every historical statement in the world is believed on authority. None of us has seen the Norman Conquest or the defeat of the Armada. None of us could prove them by pure logic as you prove a thing in mathematics. We believe them simply because people who did see them have left writings that tell us about them: in fact, on authority. A man who jibbed at authority in other things as some people do in religion would have to be content to know nothing all his life. 46

Do not think I am setting up baptism and belief and the Holy Communion as things that will do instead of your own attempts to copy Christ. Your natural life is derived from your parents; that does not mean it will stay there if you do nothing about it. You can lose it by neglect, or you can drive it away by committing suicide. You have to feed it and look after it: But always remember you are not making it, you are only keeping up a life you got from someone else. In the same way a Christian can lose the Christ-life which has been put into him, and he has to make efforts to keep it. But even the best Christian that ever lived is not acting on his own steam—he is only nourishing or protecting a life he could never have acquired by his own efforts. And that has practical consequences. As long as the natural life is in your body, it will do a lot toward repairing that body. Cut it, and up to a point it will heal, as a dead body would not. A live body is not one that never gets hurt, but one that can to some extent repair itself. In the same way a Christian is not a man who never goes wrong, but a man who is enabled to repent and pick himself up and begin over again after each stumble—because the Christ-life is inside him, repairing him all the time, enabling him to repeat (in some degree) the kind of voluntary death which Christ Himself carried out. 47

That is why the Christian is in a different position from other people who are trying to be good. They hope, by being good, to please God if there is one; or—if they think there is not—at least they hope to deserve approval from good men. But the Christian thinks any good he does comes from the Christ-life inside him. He does not think God will love us because we are good, but that God will make us good because He loves us; just as the roof of a greenhouse does not attract the sun because it is bright, but becomes bright because the sun shines on it. 48

And let me make it quite clear that when Christians say the Christ-life is in them, they do not mean simply something mental or moral. When they speak of being "in Christ" or of Christ being "in them," this is not simply a way of saying that they are thinking about Christ or copying Him. They mean that Christ is actually operating through them; that the whole mass of Christians are the physical organism through which Christ acts—that we are His fingers and muscles, the cells of His body. And perhaps that explains one or two things. It explains why this new life is spread not only by purely mental acts like belief, but by bodily acts like baptism and Holy Communion. It is not merely the spreading of the idea; it is more like evolution—a biological or superbiological fact. There is no good trying to be more spiritual than God. God never meant man to be a purely spiritual creature. That is why He uses material things like bread and wine to put the new life into us. We may think this rather crude and unspiritual. God does not: He invented eating. He likes matter. He invented it. 49

Here is another thing that used to puzzle me. Is it not frightfully unfair that this new life should be confined to people who have heard of Christ 50 and been able to believe in Him? But the truth is God has not told us what His arrangements about the other people are. We do know that no man can be saved except through Christ; we do not know that only those who know Him can be saved through Him. But in the meantime, if you are worried about the people outside, the most unreasonable thing you can do is to remain outside yourself. Christians are Christ's body, the organism through which He works. Every addition to that body enables Him to do more. If you want to help those outside you must add your own little cell to the body of Christ who alone can help them. Cutting off a man's fingers would be an odd way of getting him to do more work.

Another possible objection is this. Why is God landing in this enemy- 51 occupied world in disguise and starting a sort of secret society to undermine the devil? Why is He not landing in force, invading it? Is it that He is not strong enough? Well, Christians think He is going to land in force; we do not know when. But we can guess why He is delaying. He wants to give us the chance of joining His side freely. I do not suppose you and I would have thought much of a Frenchman who waited till the Allies were marching into Germany and then announced he was on our side. God will invade. But I wonder whether people who ask God to interfere openly and directly in our world quite realize what it will be like when He does. When that happens, it is the end of the world. When the author walks on to the stage the play is over. God is going to invade, all right: But what is the good of saying you are on His side then, when you see the whole natural universe melting away like a dream and something else—something it never entered your head to conceive—comes crashing in; something so beautiful to some of us and so terrible to others that none of us will have any choice left? For this time it will be God without disguise; something so overwhelming that it will strike either irresistible love or irresistible horror into every creature. It will be too late then to choose your side. There is no use saying you choose to lie down when it has become impossible to stand up. That will not be the time for choosing: It will be the time when we discover which side we really have chosen, whether we realized it before or not. Now, today, this moment, is our chance to choose the right side. God is holding back to give us that chance. It will not last forever. We must take it or leave it.

Topics for Critical Thinking and Writing

1. What is Lewis's argumentative strategy in his opening paragraph? Why does he bother to tell us about his atheistic days?

2. Lewis often seeks to clarify his points by giving rather simple examples—of a painter (para. 4), of straight and crooked lines (para. 6), of a fish (para. 6), and of a car (para. 25). Reread the paragraphs in which these examples are given, and see if you find the examples helpful—or do you find them too simple?

3. In paragraph 44 Lewis talks about sex. Exactly why does he introduce this point?

4. In part 3 of his essay, Lewis refers to "the Dark Power." Reflect on this metaphor: Why "dark"? Why "power"? How much power does Lewis allow that the Dark Power has over us?

5. Lewis accepts Jesus as God because he finds only three alternatives, and rejects all of them. What are these alternatives, and what is Lewis's argument for rejecting each? Do you find this a convincing argument— identifying four possible positions, rejecting three, and concluding that the remaining one must be true?

6. Put yourself in the shoes of Lewis's original audience—persons listening to a radio in the 1940s. Let's assume you were not a believer at the start, and you remained a nonbeliever at the finish. Do you think that you have learned anything—other than, of course, what Lewis believed? And, second, do you think, as a nonbeliever, that you have been addressed courteously and fairly?

7. Lewis says (para. 11) one of his reasons for believing Christianity is that "it is a religion you could not have guessed." In an essay of 500 words explain what he means by this comment, and discuss whether, in general, inability to guess something is a good reason for believing in it.

Bertrand Russell

Bertrand Russell (1872–1970), born in England, made his academic reputation as a mathematician and logician, but he won a popular reputation as a philosopher and social critic. Among his highly readable books are History of Western Philosophy *(1945) and* Why I Am Not a Christian *(1957).*

A pacifist during World War I, Russell was imprisoned in 1916 and deprived of his teaching position at Cambridge University. His unorthodox opinions continued to cause him personal difficulties. In 1938 he was offered a post at the City College of New York, but a judge refused to grant him a visa because of Russell's allegedly dangerous views on sex. During the last two decades of his life, Russell's criticism of American foreign policy made him an especially provocative figure in this country.

Reprinted here is one of his most famous essays on religion, delivered as a lecture on March 6, 1927, to the National Secular Society, South London Branch, at Battersea Town Hall. An amusing note: On one occasion when he was imprisoned, the jailer asked him his religion. Russell replied that he was an atheist, a remark that puzzled the jailer, but the man, wishing to be friendly, replied, "Ah well, we all believe in the same God, don't we?"

Why I Am Not a Christian

As your Chairman has told you, the subject about which I am going   1
to speak to you tonight is "Why I Am Not a Christian." Perhaps it would
be as well, first of all, to try to make out what one means by the word

Christian. It is used these days in a very loose sense by a great many people. Some people mean no more by it than a person who attempts to live a good life. In that sense I suppose there would be Christians in all sects and creeds; but I do not think that that is the proper sense of the word, if only because it would imply that all the people who are not Christians—all the Buddhists, Confucians, Mohammedans, and so on— are not trying to live a good life. I do not mean by a Christian any person who tries to live decently according to his lights. I think that you must have a certain amount of definite belief before you have a right to call yourself a Christian. The word does not have quite such a full-blooded meaning now as it had in the times of St. Augustine and St. Thomas Aquinas. In those days, if a man said that he was a Christian it was known what he meant. You accepted a whole collection of creeds which were set out with great precision, and every single syllable of those creeds you believed with the whole strength of your convictions.

WHAT IS A CHRISTIAN?

Nowadays it is not quite that. We have to be a little more vague in   2
our meaning of Christianity. I think, however, that there are two differ- ent items which are quite essential to anybody calling himself a Chris- tian. The first is one of a dogmatic nature—namely, that you must be- lieve in God and immortality. If you do not believe in those two things, I do not think that you can properly call yourself a Christian. Then, fur- ther than that, as the name implies, you must have some kind of be- lief about Christ. The Mohammedans, for instance, also believe in God and in immortality, and yet they would not call themselves Christians. I think you must have at the very lowest the belief that Christ was, if not divine, at least the best and wisest of men. If you are not going to believe that much about Christ, I do not think you have any right to call your- self a Christian. Of course, there is another sense, which you find in *Whitaker's Almanack* and in geography books, where the population of the world is said to be divided into Christians, Mohammedans, Bud- dhists, fetish worshipers, and so on; and in that sense we are all Chris- tians. The geography books count us all in, but that is a purely geograph- ical sense, which I suppose we can ignore. Therefore I take it that when I tell you why I am not a Christian I have to tell you two different things: first, why I do not believe in God and in immortality; and, secondly, why I do not think that Christ was the best and wisest of men, although I grant him a very high degree of moral goodness.

But for the successful efforts of unbelievers in the past, I could not   3
take so elastic a definition of Christianity as that. As I said before, in olden days it had a much more full-blooded sense. For instance, it in- cluded the belief in hell. Belief in eternal hell-fire was an essential item of Christian belief until pretty recent times. In this country, as you know, it ceased to be an essential item because of a decision of the Privy

Council, and from that decision the Archbishop of Canterbury and the Archbishop of York dissented; but in this country our religion is settled by Act of Parliament, and therefore the Privy Council was able to override their Graces and hell was no longer necessary to a Christian. Consequently I shall not insist that a Christian must believe in hell.

THE EXISTENCE OF GOD

To come to this question of the existence of God: It is a large and serious question, and if I were to attempt to deal with it in any adequate manner I should have to keep you here until Kingdom Come, so that you will have to excuse me if I deal with it in a somewhat summary fashion. You know, of course, that the Catholic Church has laid it down as a dogma that the existence of God can be proved by the unaided reason. That is a somewhat curious dogma, but it is one of their dogmas. They had to introduce it because at one time the freethinkers adopted the habit of saying that there were such and such arguments which mere reason might urge against the existence of God, but of course they knew as a matter of faith that God did exist. The arguments and the reasons were set out at great length, and the Catholic Church felt that they must stop it. Therefore they laid it down that the existence of God can be proved by the unaided reason and they had to set up what they considered were arguments to prove it. There are, of course, a number of them, but I shall take only a few. 4

THE FIRST CAUSE ARGUMENT

Perhaps the simplest and easiest to understand is the argument of the First Cause. (It is maintained that everything we see in this world has a cause, and as you go back in the chain of causes further and further you must come to a First Cause, and to that First Cause you give the name of God.) That argument, I suppose, does not carry very much weight nowadays, because, in the first place, cause is not quite what it used to be. The philosophers and the men of science have got going on cause, and it has not anything like the vitality it used to have; but, apart from that, you can see that the argument that there must be a First Cause is one that cannot have any validity. I may say that when I was a young man and was debating these questions very seriously in my mind, I for a long time accepted the argument of the First Cause, until one day, at the age of eighteen, I read John Stuart Mill's *Autobiography,* and I there found this sentence: "My father taught me that the question 'Who made me?' cannot be answered, since it immediately suggests the further question 'Who made God?'" That very simple sentence showed me, as I still think, the fallacy in the argument of the First Cause. If everything must have a cause, then God must have a cause. If there can be everything without a cause, it may just as well be the world as God, so that 5 there cannot be any validity in that argument. It is exactly of the same nature as the Hindu's view that the world rested upon an elephant and the elephant rested upon a tortoise; and when they said, "How about the tortoise?" the Indian said, "Suppose we change the subject." The argument is really no better than that. There is no reason why the world could not have come into being without a cause; nor, on the other hand, is there any reason why it should not have always existed. There is no reason to suppose that the world had a beginning at all. The idea that things must have a beginning is really due to the poverty of our imagination. Therefore, perhaps, I need not waste any more time upon the argument about the First Cause.

THE NATURAL LAW ARGUMENT

Then there is a very common argument from natural law. That was   6
a favorite argument all through the eighteenth century, especially under the influence of Sir Isaac Newton and his cosmogony. People observed the planets going around the sun according to the law of gravitation, and they thought that God had given a behest to these planets to move in that particular fashion, and that was why they did so. That was, of course, a convenient and simple explanation that saved them the trouble of looking any further for explanations of the law of gravitation. Nowadays we explain the law of gravitation in a somewhat complicated fashion that Einstein has introduced. I do not propose to give you a lecture on the law of gravitation, as interpreted by Einstein, because that again would take some time; at any rate, you no longer have the sort of natural law that you had in the Newtonian system, where, for some reason that nobody could understand, nature behaved in a uniform fashion. We now find that a great many things we thought were natural laws are really human conventions. You know that even in the remotest depths of stellar space there are still three feet to a yard. That is, no doubt, a very remarkable fact, but you would hardly call it a law of nature. And a great many things that have been regarded as laws of nature are of that kind. On the other hand, where you can get down to any knowledge of what atoms actually do, you will find they are much less subject to law than people thought, and that the laws at which you arrive are statistical averages of just the sort that would emerge from chance. There is, as we all know, a law that if you throw dice you will get double sixes only about once in thirty-six times, and we do not regard that as evidence that the fall of the dice is regulated by design; on the contrary, if the double sixes came every time we should think that there was design. The laws of nature are of that sort as regards a great many of them. They are statistical averages such as would emerge from the laws of chance; and that makes this whole business of natural law much less impressive than it formerly was. Quite apart from that, which represents the momentary state of science that may change tomorrow, the whole idea that

natural laws imply a lawgiver is due to a confusion between natural and human laws. Human laws are behests commanding you to behave a certain way, in which way you may choose to behave, or you may choose not to behave; but natural laws are a description of how things do in fact behave, and being a mere description of what they in fact do, you cannot argue that there must be somebody who told them to do that, because even supposing that there were, you are then faced with the question "Why did God issue just those natural laws and no others?" If you say that he did it simply from his own good pleasure, and without any reason, you then find that there is something which is not subject to law, and so your train of natural law is interrupted. If you say, as more orthodox theologians do, that in all the laws which God issues he had a reason for giving those laws rather than others—the reason, of course, being to create the best universe, although you would never think it to look at it—if there were a reason for the laws which God gave, then God himself was subject to law, and therefore you do not get any advantage by introducing God as an intermediary. You have really a law outside and anterior to the divine edicts, and God does not serve your purpose, because he is not the ultimate lawgiver. In short, this whole argument about natural law no longer has anything like the strength that it used to have. I am traveling on in time in my review of the arguments. The arguments that are used for the existence of God change their character as time goes on. They were at first hard intellectual arguments embodying certain quite definite fallacies. As we come to modern times they become less respectable intellectually and more and more affected by a kind of moralizing vagueness.

THE ARGUMENT FROM DESIGN

The next step in this process brings us to the argument from design. 7 You all know the argument from design: Everything in the world is made just so that we can manage to live in the world, and if the world was ever so little different, we could not manage to live in it. That is the argument from design. It sometimes takes a rather curious form; for instance, it is argued that rabbits have white tails in order to be easy to shoot. I do not know how rabbits would view that application. It is an easy argument to parody. You all know Voltaire's remark, that obviously the nose was designed to be such as to fit spectacles. That sort of parody has turned out to be not nearly so wide of the mark as it might have seemed in the eighteenth century, because since the time of Darwin we understand much better why living creatures are adapted to their environment. It is not that their environment was made to be suitable to them but that they grew to be suitable to it, and that is the basis of adaptation. There is no evidence of design about it.

When you come to look into this argument from design, it is a most 8 astonishing thing that people can believe that this world, with all the things that are in it, with all its defects, should be the best that omnipotence and omniscience have been able to produce in millions of years. I really cannot believe it. Do you think that, if you were granted omnipotence and omniscience and millions of years in which to perfect your world, you could produce nothing better than the Ku Klux Klan or the Fascists? Moreover, if you accept the ordinary laws of science, you have to suppose that human life and life in general on this planet will die out in due course: It is a stage in the decay of the solar system; at a certain stage of decay you get the sort of conditions of temperature and so forth which are suitable to protoplasm, and there is life for a short time in the life of the whole solar system. You see in the moon the sort of thing to which the earth is tending—something dead, cold, and lifeless.

I am told that that sort of view is depressing, and people will some- 9 times tell you that if they believed that, they would not be able to go on living. Do not believe it; it is all nonsense. Nobody really worries much about what is going to happen millions of years hence. Even if they think they are worrying much about that, they are really deceiving themselves. They are worried about something much more mundane, or it may merely be a bad digestion; but nobody is really seriously rendered unhappy by the thought of something that is going to happen to this world millions and millions of years hence. Therefore, although it is of course a gloomy view to suppose that life will die out—at least I suppose we may say so, although sometimes when I contemplate the things that people do with their lives I think it is almost a consolation—it is not such as to render life miserable. It merely makes you turn your attention to other things.

THE MORAL ARGUMENTS FOR DEITY

Now we reach one stage further in what I shall call the intellectual 10 descent that the Theists have made in their argumentations, and we come to what are called the moral arguments for the existence of God. You all know, of course, that there used to be in the old days three intellectual arguments for the existence of God, all of which were disposed of by Immanuel Kant in the *Critique of Pure Reason;* but no sooner had he disposed of those arguments than he invented a new one, a moral argument, and that quite convinced him. He was like many people: In intellectual matters he was skeptical, but in moral matters he believed implicitly in the maxims that he had imbibed at his mother's knee. That illustrates what the psychoanalysts so much emphasize—the immensely stronger hold upon us that our very early associations have than those of later times.

Kant, as I say, invented a new moral argument for the existence of 11 God, and that in varying forms was extremely popular during the nineteenth century. It has all sorts of forms. One form is to say that there would be no right or wrong unless God existed. I am not for the moment concerned with whether there is a difference between right and wrong, or whether there is not: That is another question. The point I am concerned with is that, if you are quite sure there is a difference between right and wrong, you are then in this situation: Is that difference due to God's fiat or is it not? If it is due to God's fiat, then for God himself there is no difference between right and wrong, and it is no longer a significant statement to say that God is good. If you are going to say, as theologians do, that God is good, you must then say that right and wrong have some meaning which is independent of God's fiat, because God's fiats are good and not bad independently of the mere fact that he made them. If you are going to say that, you will then have to say that it is not only through God that right and wrong came into being, but that they are in their essence logically anterior to God. You could, of course, if you liked, say that there was a superior deity who gave orders to the God who made this world, or could take up the line that some of the gnostics took up—a line which I often thought was a very plausible one—that as a matter of fact this world that we know was made by the devil at a moment when God was not looking. There is a good deal to be said for that, and I am not concerned to refute it.

THE ARGUMENT FOR THE REMEDYING
OF INJUSTICE

Then there is another very curious form of moral argument, which is 12 this: They say that the existence of God is required in order to bring justice into the world. In the part of this universe that we know there is great injustice, and often the good suffer, and often the wicked prosper, and one hardly knows which of those is the more annoying; but if you are going to have justice in the universe as a whole you have to suppose a future life to redress the balance of life here on earth. So they say that there must be a God, and there must be heaven and hell in order that in the long run there may be justice. That is a very curious argument. If you looked at the matter from a scientific point of view, you would say, "After all, I know only this world. I do not know about the rest of the universe, but so far as one can argue at all on probabilities one would say that probably this world is a fair sample, and if there is injustice here the odds are that there is injustice elsewhere also." Supposing you got a crate of oranges that you opened, and you found all the top layer of oranges bad, you would not argue, "The underneath ones must be good, so as to redress the balance." You would say, "Probably the whole lot is a bad consignment"; and that is really what a scientific person would argue about the universe. He would say, "Here we find in this world a great deal of injustice, and so far as that goes that is a reason for supposing that justice does not rule in the world; and therefore so far as it goes it affords a moral argument against deity and not in favor of one." Of course I know that the sort of intellectual arguments that I have been talking to you about are not what really moves people. What really moves people to believe in God is not any intellectual argument at all. Most people believe in God because they have been taught from early infancy to do it, and that is the main reason.

Then I think that the next most powerful reason is the wish for safety, a sort of feeling that there is a big brother who will look after you. That plays a very profound part in influencing people's desire for a belief in God. 13

THE CHARACTER OF CHRIST

I now want to say a few words upon a topic which I often think is not quite sufficiently dealt with by Rationalists, and that is the question whether Christ was the best and the wisest of men. It is generally taken for granted that we should all agree that that was so. I do not myself. I think that there are a good many points upon which I agree with Christ a great deal more than the professing Christians do. I do not know that I could go with Him all the way, but I could go with Him much further than most professing Christians can. You will remember that He said, "Resist not evil: But whosoever shall smite thee on thy right cheek, turn to him the other also." That is not a new precept or a new principle. It was used by Lao-tse and Buddha some 500 or 600 years before Christ, but it is not a principle which as a matter of fact Christians accept. I have no doubt that the present Prime Minister,[1] for instance, is a most sincere Christian, but I should not advise any of you to go and smite him on one cheek. I think you might find that he thought this text was intended in a figurative sense. 14

Then there is another point which I consider excellent. You will remember that Christ said, "Judge not lest ye be judged." That principle I do not think you would find was popular in the law courts of Christian countries. I have known in my time quite a number of judges who were very earnest Christians, and none of them felt that they were acting contrary to Christian principles in what they did. Then Christ says, "Give to him that asketh of thee, and from him that would borrow of thee turn not thou away." That is a very good principle. Your Chairman has reminded you that we are not here to talk politics, but I cannot help observing that the last general election was fought on the question of how desirable it was to turn away from him that would borrow of thee, so that one must assume that the Liberals and Conservatives of this country are composed of people who do not agree with the teaching of Christ, because they certainly did very emphatically turn away on that occasion. 15

[1]Stanley Baldwin (1867–1947). [Editors' note.]

Then there is one other maxim of Christ which I think has a great 16 deal in it, but I do not find that it is very popular among some of our Christian friends. He says, "If thou wilt be perfect, go and sell that which thou hast, and give to the poor." That is a very excellent maxim, but, as I say, it is not much practiced. All these, I think, are good maxims, although they are a little difficult to live up to. I do not profess to live up to them myself; but then, after all, it is not quite the same thing as for a Christian.

DEFECTS IN CHRIST'S TEACHING

Having granted the excellence of these maxims, I come to certain 17 points in which I do not believe that one can grant either the superlative wisdom or the superlative goodness of Christ as depicted in the Gospels; and here I may say that one is not concerned with the historical question. Historically it is quite doubtful whether Christ ever existed at all, and if He did we do not know anything about Him, so that I am not concerned with the historical question, which is a very difficult one. I am concerned with Christ as He appears in the Gospels, taking the Gospel narrative as it stands, and there one does find some things that do not seem to be very wise. For one thing, He certainly thought that His second coming would occur in clouds of glory before the death of all the people who were living at that time. There are a great many texts that prove that. He says, for instance, "Ye shall not have gone over the cities of Israel till the Son of Man be come." Then He says, "There are some standing here which shall not taste death till the Son of Man comes into His kingdom"; and there are a lot of places where it is quite clear that He believed that His second coming would happen during the lifetime of many then living. That was the belief of His earlier followers, and it was the basis of a good deal of His moral teaching. When He said, "Take no thought for the morrow," and things of that sort, it was very largely because He thought that the second coming was going to be very soon, and that all ordinary mundane affairs did not count. I have, as a matter of fact, known some Christians who did believe that the second coming was imminent. I knew a parson who frightened his congregation terribly by telling them that the second coming was very imminent indeed, but they were much consoled when they found that he was planting trees in his garden. The early Christians did really believe it, and they did abstain from such things as planting trees in their gardens, because they did accept from Christ the belief that the second coming was imminent. In that respect, clearly He was not so wise as some other people have been, and He was certainly not superlatively wise.

THE MORAL PROBLEM

Then you come to moral questions. There is one very serious defect 18 to my mind in Christ's moral character, and that is that He believed in

hell. I do not myself feel that any person who is really profoundly humane can believe in everlasting punishment. Christ certainly as depicted
in the Gospels did believe in everlasting punishment, and one does find
repeatedly a vindictive fury against those people who would not listen to
His preaching—an attitude which is not uncommon with preachers, but
which does somewhat detract from superlative excellence. You do not,
for instance, find that attitude in Socrates. You find him quite bland and
urbane toward the people who would not listen to him; and it is, to my
mind, far more worthy of a sage to take that line than to take the line of
indignation. You probably all remember the sort of things that Socrates
was saying when he was dying, and the sort of things that he generally
did say to people who did not agree with him.

19   You will find that in the Gospels Christ said, "Ye serpents, ye generation of vipers, how can ye escape the damnation of hell." That was said
to people who did not like His preaching. It is not really to my mind
quite the best tone, and there are a great many of these things about
hell. There is, of course, the familiar text about the sin against the Holy
Ghost: "Whosoever speaketh against the Holy Ghost it shall not be forgiven him neither in this World nor in the world to come." That text has
caused an unspeakable amount of misery in the world, for all sorts of
people have imagined that they have committed the sin against the Holy
Ghost, and thought that it would not be forgiven them either in this
world or in the world to come. I really do not think that a person with a
proper degree of kindliness in his nature would have put fears and ter-
rors of that sort into the world.

20   Then Christ says, "The Son of Man shall send forth His angels, and
they shall gather out of His kingdom all things that offend, and them
which do iniquity, and shall cast them into a furnace of fire; there shall
be wailing and gnashing of teeth"; and He goes on about the wailing and
gnashing of teeth. It comes in one verse after another, and it is quite
manifest to the reader that there is a certain pleasure in contemplating
wailing and gnashing of teeth, or else it would not occur so often. Then
you all, of course, remember about the sheep and the goats; how at the
second coming He is going to divide the sheep from the goats, and He is
going to say to the goats, "Depart from me, ye cursed, into everlasting
fire." He continues, "And these shall go away into everlasting fire." Then
He says again, "If thy hand offend thee, cut it off; it is better for thee to
enter into life maimed, than having two hands to go into hell, into the
fire that never shall be quenched; where the worm dieth not and the fire
is not quenched." He repeats that again and again also. I must say that I
think all this doctrine, that hell-fire is a punishment for sin, is a doctrine
of cruelty. It is a doctrine that put cruelty into the world and gave the
world generations of cruel torture; and the Christ of the Gospels, if you
could take Him as His chroniclers represent Him, would certainly have to
be considered partly responsible for that.

21   There are other things of less importance. There is the instance of
the Gadarene swine, where it certainly was not very kind to the pigs to

put the devils into them and make them rush down the hill to the sea. You must remember that He was omnipotent, and He could have made the devils simply go away; but He chose to send them into the pigs. Then there is the curious story of the fig tree, which always rather puzzled me. You remember what happened about the fig tree. "He was hungry; and seeing a fig tree afar off having leaves, He came if haply He might find anything thereon; and when He came to it He found nothing but leaves, for the time of figs was not yet. And Jesus answered and said unto it: 'No man eat fruit of thee hereafter for ever' . . . and Peter . . . saith unto Him: 'Master, behold the fig tree which thou cursedst is withered away.'" This is a very curious story, because it was not the right time of year for figs, and you really could not blame the tree. I cannot myself feel that either in the matter of wisdom or in the matter of virtue Christ stands quite as high as some other people known to history. I think I should put Buddha and Socrates above Him in those respects.

THE EMOTIONAL FACTOR

As I said before, I do not think that the real reason why people ac-   22
cept religion has anything to do with argumentation. They accept religion on emotional grounds. One is often told that it is a very wrong thing to attack religion, because religion makes men virtuous. So I am told; I have not noticed it. You know, of course, the parody of that argument in Samuel Butler's book, *Erewhon Revisited.* You will remember that in *Erewhon* there is a certain Higgs who arrives in a remote country, and after spending some time there he escapes from that country in a balloon. Twenty years later he comes back to that country and finds a new religion in which he is worshipped under the name of the "Sun Child," and it is said that he ascended into heaven. He finds that the Feast of the Ascension is about to be celebrated, and he hears Professors Hanky and Panky say to each other that they never set eyes on the man Higgs, and they hope they never will; but they are the high priests of the religion of the Sun Child. He is very indignant, and he comes up to them, and he says, "I am going to expose all this humbug and tell the people of Erewhon that it was only I, the man Higgs, and I went up in a balloon." He was told, "You must not do that, because all the morals of this country are bound round this myth, and if they once know that you did not ascend into heaven they will all become wicked"; and so he is persuaded of that and he goes quietly away.

That is the idea—that we should all be wicked if we did not hold to   23
the Christian religion. It seems to me that the people who have held to it have been for the most part extremely wicked. You find this curious fact, that the more intense has been the religion of any period and the more profound has been the dogmatic belief, the greater has been the cruelty and the worse has been the state of affairs. In the so-called ages of faith, when men really did believe the Christian religion in all its complete-

ness, there was the Inquisition, with its tortures; there were millions of unfortunate women burned as witches; and there was every kind of cruelty practiced upon all sorts of people in the name of religion.

You find as you look around the world that every single bit of 24 progress in humane feeling, every improvement in the criminal law, every step toward the diminution of war, every step toward better treatment of the colored races, or every mitigation of slavery, every moral progress that there has been in the world, has been consistently opposed by the organized churches of the world. I say quite deliberately that the Christian religion, as organized in its churches, has been and still is the principal enemy of moral progress in the world.

HOW THE CHURCHES HAVE RETARDED PROGRESS

You may think that I am going too far when I say that that is still so. 25 I do not think that I am. Take one fact. You will bear with me if I mention it. It is not a pleasant fact, but the churches compel one to mention facts that are not pleasant. Supposing that in this world that we live in today an inexperienced girl is married to a syphilitic man; in that case the Catholic Church says, "This is an indissoluble sacrament. You must endure celibacy or stay together. And if you stay together, you must not use birth control to prevent the birth of syphilitic children." Nobody whose natural sympathies have not been warped by dogma, or whose moral nature was not absolutely dead to all sense of suffering, could maintain that it is right and proper that that state of things should continue.

That is only an example. There are a great many ways in which, at 26 the present moment, the church, by its insistence upon what it chooses to call morality, inflicts upon all sorts of people undeserved and unnecessary suffering. And of course, as we know, it is in its major part an opponent still of progress and of improvement in all the ways that diminish suffering in the world, because it has chosen to label as morality a certain narrow set of rules of conduct which have nothing to do with human happiness; and when you say that this or that ought to be done because it would make for human happiness, they think that has nothing to do with the matter at all. "What has human happiness to do with morals? The object of morals is not to make people happy."

FEAR, THE FOUNDATION OF RELIGION

Religion is based, I think, primarily and mainly upon fear. It is partly 27 the terror of the unknown and partly, as I have said, the wish to feel that you have a kind of elder brother who will stand by you in all your troubles and disputes. Fear is the basis of the whole thing—fear of the mysterious, fear of defeat, fear of death. Fear is the parent of cruelty, and therefore it is no wonder if cruelty and religion have gone hand in hand. It is because fear is at the basis of those two things. In this world we can now begin a little to understand things, and a little to master them by help of science, which has forced its way step by step against the Christian religion, against the churches, and against the opposition of all the old precepts. Science can help us to get over this craven fear in which mankind has lived for so many generations. Science can teach us, and I think our own hearts can teach us, no longer to look around for imaginary supports, no longer to invent allies in the sky, but rather to look to our own efforts here below to make this world a fit place to live in, instead of the sort of place that the churches in all these centuries have made it.

WHAT WE MUST DO

We want to stand upon our own feet and look fair and square at the world—its good facts, its bad facts, its beauties, and its ugliness; see the world as it is and be not afraid of it. Conquer the world by intelligence and not merely by being slavishly subdued by the terror that comes from it. The whole conception of God is a conception derived from the ancient Oriental despotisms. It is a conception quite unworthy of free men. When you hear people in church debasing themselves and saying that they are miserable sinners, and all the rest of it, it seems contemptible and not worthy of self-respecting human beings. We ought to stand up and look the world frankly in the face. We ought to make the best we can of the world, and if it is not so good as we wish, after all it will still be better than what these others have made of it in all these ages. A good world needs knowledge, kindliness, and courage; it does not need a regretful hankering after the past or a fettering of the free intelligence by the words uttered long ago by ignorant men. It needs a fearless outlook and a free intelligence. It needs hope for the future, not looking back all the time toward a past that is dead, which we trust will be far surpassed by the future that our intelligence can create.

Topics for Critical Thinking and Writing

1. Russell's talk was originally delivered to the National Secular Society. What sort of a group do you think this Society was? Do you imagine that the audience approved or disapproved of the talk? Do you think that to some extent the talk was geared to the taste of this audience? What evidence can you offer for your view?

2. In a sentence summarize Russell's first paragraph, and in another sentence summarize his second paragraph. Finally, write a third sentence, this one describing and evaluating Russell's strategy in beginning his essay with these two paragraphs.

3. Read and reread Russell's third paragraph, about hell. In the last sentence of this paragraph, he says, "Consequently I shall not insist that a Christian must believe in hell." "Consequently," of course, suggests that what follows is logically derived from what precedes. State in your own words the reason that Russell offers for the conclusion here. What do you think Russell thought of that reason?

4. In paragraph 8 Russell wonders why an omnipotent and omniscient creator would "produce nothing better than the Ku Klux Klan or the Fascists." Even if you do not believe in an omnipotent and omniscient creator, try to write a one-paragraph response to this point.

5. Many Christians would say that they believe in God because Jesus believed in God. (This point is made by C. S. Lewis, in the preceding essay.) They would add that because historical evidence supports their belief that Jesus did indeed live and die and was resurrected, there can be no reason to doubt Jesus' teachings. Why, in your opinion, does Russell not comment on this argument?

6. Russell discusses the meaning of the term "Christian," and offers his own definition. Look up in two unabridged dictionaries the definitions of this term, and explain whether Russell's definition agrees with all or any of those in the dictionaries. (By the way, do the dictionaries fully agree with each other?)

7. In paragraph 15 Russell says that many Christians do not practice certain teachings of Jesus. Suppose he is right; does this failing show that Jesus' teachings are wrong? Or that it is unreasonable to believe in Jesus? What, exactly, does Russell's argument prove?

8. In paragraph 21, setting forth what he takes to be some of Jesus' unpleasant teachings and doings, Russell refers to one episode in which exorcised devils entered into swine (Matthew 8:28–34; Mark 5:1–20) and another in which Jesus cursed a fig tree (Matthew 21:19; Mark 11:13–14). In the library examine several Christian commentaries on the Bible (for instance, D. E. Nineham's *The Gospel of St. Mark,* or even *The Interpreter's One-Volume Commentary on the Bible*) to see what explanations believers have offered. Do you find any of these explanations adequate? Why, or why not?

9. In paragraph 24 Russell asserts that "every single bit of progress in humane feeling . . . has been consistently opposed by the organized churches of the world." What evidence does he offer? What evidence can you offer to support or to refute this view?

10. Russell states and criticizes five arguments for God's existence. Whether or not you find any of these arguments wholly convincing, which of them seems to you to be the strongest or the most likely to be sound, and which the weakest? In an essay of 500 words explain your evaluation. Optional: If you believe in God's existence, does it matter to you whether any of these arguments survived Russell's criticisms? Explain.

11. In paragraph 27 Russell says that "fear" is the basis of religion. Many Christians would disagree and would insist that love is the basis of Christianity. On this issue, where do you stand? Why?

12. In his final paragraph Russell says that people who debase themselves and call themselves "miserable sinners" in fact are "contemptible." If you have done things of which you have been deeply ashamed, do you think your confession (even if only to yourself) is "contemptible"?

13. Putting aside your own views of Christianity, in an essay of 500 to 750 words assess the strengths and the weaknesses of Russell's essay as an argument.

Joseph Addison

*Joseph Addison (1672–1719), an English essayist and poet, was perhaps the most influential literary critic of his day. His essays, written chiefly for two newspapers (*The Tatler *and* The Spectator*), were immensely popular and they remain highly esteemed today, at least by teachers of English.*

In one issue of The Spectator *(#465, August 23, 1712) Addison published the poem that we reprint here, a version of Psalm 19. He called it simply "Ode." (An ode is a song of praise, specifically of an exalted subject such as heroism, or one's nation, or God.) In the essay he introduced the poem thus:*

> *The Supreme Being has made the best Arguments for his own Existence, in the Formation of the Heavens and the Earth, and these are Arguments which a Man of Sense cannot forbear attending to, who is out of the Noise and Hurry of Human Affairs. Aristotle says, that should a Man live under Ground, and there converse with Works of Art and Mechanism, and should afterwards be brought up into the open Day, and see the several Glories of the Heav'n and Earth, he would immediately pronounce them the Works of such a Being as we define God to be.*

What Addison is here offering is his version of the Argument from Design, the argument that the world obviously is a designed thing, like, say, a watch, and therefore there must be a designer, God.

Ode

> The Spacious Firmament on high,
> With all the blue Etherial Sky,
> And spangled Heav'ns, a Shining Frame,
> Their great Original proclaim:
> Th'unwearied Sun, from Day to Day,   5
> Does his Creator's Power display,
> And publishes to every land
> The Work of an Almighty Hand.
>
> Soon as the Evening Shades prevail,
> The Moon takes up the wondrous Tale,   10
> And nightly to the listning Earth
> Repeats the Story of her Birth:
> Whilst all the Stars that round her burn,

And all the Planets, in their turn,
Confirm the Tidings as they rowl, 15
And spread the truth from Pole to Pole.

What though, in solemn Silence, all
Move round the dark terrestrial Ball?
What tho' nor real Voice nor Sound
Amid their radiant Orbs be found? 20
In Reason's Ear they all rejoice,
And utter forth a glorious Voice,
For ever singing, as they shine,
"The Hand that made us is Divine."

Topics for Critical Thinking and Writing

1. In a sentence or two summarize Addison's argument for the existence of God.

2. In the biographical note we mention the Argument from Design—the idea that the universe is a complex, functioning thing and therefore it must have been made by a creator. Some Christian theologians argued that because the universe functions perfectly, we can infer the perfection of the creator. What objections, if any, can be offered against the basic argument, and against the amplified argument that we can infer the qualities of the creator from the creation?

Emily Dickinson

Emily Dickinson (1830–1886) was born into a proper New England family in Amherst, Massachusetts. Although she spent her seventeenth year a few miles away, at Mount Holyoke Seminary (now Mount Holyoke College), in the next twenty years she left Amherst only five or six times, and in the following twenty years she may never have left her house.

Dickinson's attitude toward religion seems to have been decidedly untraditional. She apparently disliked the patriarchal deity of the Hebrew Bible, whom she calls "Burglar! Banker—Father!"; she mentioned to a correspondent that the members of her family were all religious, except for her, and that they "address an Eclipse every morning—whom they call their 'Father.'"

Papa above!

Papa above!
Regard a Mouse
O'erpowered by the Cat!
Reserve within thy kingdom
A "Mansion" for the Rat! 5

Snug in seraphic Cupboards
To nibble all the day,
While unsuspecting Cycles°
Wheel solemnly away!

Topics for Critical Thinking and Writing

1. In the Gospel according to St. John, 14:2, Jesus says, "In my Father's house are many mansions." What does this mean, and is it relevant to this poem?

2. Some readers take the poem to be a satire on religious faith. Do you agree? Explain.

Emily Dickinson

Those—dying, then

Those—dying, then
Knew where they went
They went to God's Right Hand—
The Hand is amputated now
And God cannot be found—   5

The abdication of Belief
Makes the Behavior small—
Better an ignis fatuus
Than no illume at all—

Topics for Critical Thinking and Writing

1. In a sentence or two, state the point of the poem.

2. Is the image in line 4 in poor taste? Explain.

3. What is an *ignis fatuus*? In what ways does it connect visually with traditional images of hell and heaven?

8 Cycles Long periods, eons. [Editors' note.]

Gerard Manley Hopkins

*Gerard Manley Hopkins (1844–1889) was born near London and was edu-
cated at Oxford University, where he studied the classics. A convert from An-
glicanism to Roman Catholicism, he was ordained a Jesuit priest in 1877.
Hopkins published only a few poems during his lifetime, partly because he
believed that the pursuit of literary fame was incompatible with his vocation
as a priest, and partly because he was aware that his highly individual style
might puzzle readers.*

*Especially in the last few years of his short life Hopkins experienced
what religious mystics call "the dark night of the soul," agonizing sensations
of weakness or unworthiness. "I cannot produce anything at all," he wrote,
in a note typical of this period, "not only the luxuries like poetry, but the duties almost of my position." We cannot, of course, speak confidently about
Hopkins's state of mind, but his doubt seems to have centered not in belief in
God but in Hopkins's own ability to live up to the faith that he held.*

*Hopkins wrote "Thou Art Indeed Just, Lord" shortly before he died. He
prefaces the poem with a quotation from a Latin translation of the Hebrew
Bible, Jeremiah 12, which he translates in the first two and a half lines of
his poem. But the "&c" at the end of the Latin quotation indicates that Hopkins had additional biblical verses in mind. In this chapter, Jeremiah accuses God of injustice. We quote part of the chapter, from the New Jerusalem
Bible, a Roman Catholic translation. (Yahweh, regarded by many modern
scholars as the best approximation of the Hebrew YHWH, is more usually
given as Jehovah.)*

> *Your uprightness is too great, Yahweh,*
> *for me to dispute with you.*
> *But I should like to discuss some points of justice with you:*
> *Why is it that the way of the wicked prospers?*
> *Why do all treacherous people thrive?*
> *You plant them, they take root,*
> *they flourish, yes, and bear fruit.*
> *You are on their lips,*
> *yet far from their heart.*
> *You know me, Yahweh, you see me,*
> *you probe my heart, which is close to yours. . . .*

Thou Art Indeed Just, Lord

> *Justus quidem tu es, Domine, si disputem tecum; verumtamen
> justa loquar ad te: Quare via impiorum prosperatur? &c.*

Thou art indeed just, Lord, if I contend
With thee; but, sir, so what I plead is just.
Why do sinners' ways prosper? and why must
Disappointment all I endeavor end?

Wert thou my enemy, O thou my friend,   5
How wouldst thou worse, I wonder, than thou dost

Defeat, thwart me? Oh, the sots and thralls of lust
Do in spare hours more thrive than I that spend,

Sir, life upon thy cause. See, banks and brakes°
Now, leavèd how thick! lacèd they are again   10
With fretty chervil, look, and fresh wind shakes

Them; birds build—but not I build; no, but strain,
Time's eunuch, and not breed one work that wakes.
Mine, O thou lord of life, send my roots rain.

Topics for Critical Thinking and Writing

1. Do you find it inappropriate for a priest to "contend" with God (line 1)? To suggest (line 3) that "sinners' ways prosper"? Explain.

2. The title and first line assure us the poet thinks the Lord is "just," yet the poet offers no evidence to support that judgment. Is this a flaw in the poem? Why, or why not?

3. In lines 9–12 Hopkins comments excitedly about natural phenomena that are flourishing all around him—the leafy thickets, the abundant chervil (an aromatic plant used in soups and stews), the birds building nests—and suggests that he is less productive than they. Does it make sense for human beings to compare their productivity with that of other living things?

Robert Frost

Robert Frost (1874–1963) studied for part of one term at Dartmouth College in New Hampshire, then did odd jobs (including teaching), and from 1897 to 1899 was enrolled as a special student at Harvard. He then farmed in New Hampshire, published a few poems in newspapers, did some more teaching, and in 1912 left for England, where he hoped to achieve success as a writer. By 1915 he was known in England, and he returned to the United States. By the time of his death he was the nation's unofficial poet laureate. This poem was first published in 1936.

Design

I found a dimpled spider, fat and white,
On a white heal-all,° holding up a moth
Like a white piece of rigid satin cloth—

---

9 brakes Thickets.
2 heal-all A flower, which is normally blue. [Editors' note.]

Assorted characters of death and blight
Mixed ready to begin the morning right, 5
Like the ingredients of a witches' broth —
A snow-drop spider, a flower like froth,
And dead wings carried like a paper kite.

What had that flower to do with being white,
The wayside blue and innocent heal-all? 10
What brought the kindred spider to that height,
Then steered the white moth thither in the night?
What but design of darkness to appall? —
If design govern in a thing so small.

Topics for Critical Thinking and Writing

1. The poem is a sonnet, divided into an octave (the first eight lines) and a sestet (the next six). How does the structure shape the thought?

2. What meanings of the word *design* come to your mind? Which of these meanings are relevant to the poem?

Leslie Marmon Silko

Leslie Marmon Silko characterizes herself as "Laguna, Mexican, white." She was born in 1948 in Albuquerque, New Mexico, and grew up on the Laguna Pueblo Reservation some fifty miles to the west. After graduating from the University of New Mexico in 1969, Silko entered law school but soon left to become a writer. She taught for two years at Navajo Community College at Many Farms, Arizona, and then went to Alaska for two years where she studied Eskimo-Aleut culture and worked on a novel, Ceremony. *After returning to the Southwest, she taught at the University of Arizona and then at the University of New Mexico.*

In addition to writing stories, novels, and poems, Silko has written the screenplay for Marlon Brando's film, Black Elk. *In 1981 she was awarded one of the so-called genius grants from the MacArthur Foundation, which supports "exceptionally talented individuals." This story was first published by the* New Mexico Quarterly *in 1969.*

The Man to Send Rain Clouds

ONE

They found him under a big cottonwood tree. His Levi jacket and pants were faded light-blue so that he had been easy to find. The big cottonwood tree stood apart from a small grove of winterbare cottonwoods which grew in the wide, sandy arroyo. He had been dead for a day or

more, and the sheep had wandered and scattered up and down the arroyo. Leon and his brother-in-law, Ken, gathered the sheep and left
them in the pen at the sheep camp before they returned to the cottonwood tree. Leon waited under the tree while Ken drove the truck
through the deep sand to the edge of the arroyo. He squinted up at the
sun and unzipped his jacket—it sure was hot for this time of year. But
high and northwest the blue mountains were still deep in snow. Ken
came sliding down the low, crumbling bank about fifty yards down, and
he was bringing the red blanket.

Before they wrapped the old man, Leon took a piece of string out of
his pocket and tied a small gray feather in the old man's long white hair.
Ken gave him the paint. Across the brown wrinkled forehead he drew a
streak of white and along the high cheekbones he drew a strip of blue
paint. He paused and watched Ken throw pinches of corn meal and
pollen into the wind that fluttered the small gray feather. Then Leon
painted with yellow under the old man's broad nose, and finally, when
he had painted green across the chin, he smiled.

"Send us rain clouds, Grandfather." They laid the bundle in the back
of the pickup and covered it with a heavy tarp before they started back
to the pueblo.

They turned off the highway onto the sandy pueblo road. Not long
after they passed the store and post office they saw Father Paul's car
coming toward them. When he recognized their faces he slowed his car
and waved for them to stop. The young priest rolled down the car
window.

"Did you find old Teofilo?" he asked loudly.   5

Leon stopped the truck. "Good morning, Father. We were just out to
the sheep camp. Everything is O.K. now."

"Thank God for that. Teofilo is a very old man. You really shouldn't
allow him to stay at the sheep camp alone."

"No, he won't do that any more now."

"Well, I'm glad you understand. I hope I'll be seeing you at Mass
this week—we missed you last Sunday. See if you can get old Teofilo
to come with you." The priest smiled and waved at them as they drove
away.

TWO

Louise and Teresa were waiting. The table was set for lunch, and the   10
coffee was boiling on the black iron stove. Leon looked at Louise and
then at Teresa.

"We found him under a cottonwood tree in the big arroyo near the
sheep camp. I guess he sat down to rest in the shade and never got up
again." Leon walked toward the old man's bed. The red plaid shawl had
been shaken and spread carefully over the bed, and a new brown flannel
shirt and pair of stiff new Levis were arranged neatly beside the pillow.

Louise held the screen door open while Leon and Ken carried in the red blanket. He looked small and shriveled, and after they dressed him in the new shirt and pants he seemed more shrunken.

It was noontime now because the church bells rang the Angelus.[1] They ate the beans with hot bread, and nobody said anything until after Teresa poured the coffee.

Ken stood up and put on his jacket. "I'll see about the gravediggers. Only the top layer of soil is frozen. I think it can be ready before dark."

Leon nodded his head and finished his coffee. After Ken had been gone for a while, the neighbors and clanspeople came quietly to embrace Teofilo's family and to leave food on the table because the gravediggers would come to eat when they were finished.

THREE

The sky in the west was full of pale-yellow light. Louise stood out- 15 side with her hands in the pockets of Leon's green army jacket that was too big for her. The funeral was over, and the old men had taken their candles and medicine bags and were gone. She waited until the body was laid into the pickup before she said anything to Leon. She touched his arm, and he noticed that her hands were still dusty from the corn meal that she had sprinkled around the old man. When she spoke, Leon could not hear her.

"What did you say? I didn't hear you."

"I said that I had been thinking about something."

"About what?"

"About the priest sprinkling holy water for Grandpa. So he won't be thirsty."

Leon stared at the new moccasins that Teofilo had made for the 20 ceremonial dances in the summer. They were nearly hidden by the red blanket. It was getting colder, and the wind pushed gray dust down the narrow pueblo road. The sun was approaching the long mesa where it disappeared during the winter. Louise stood there shivering and watching his face. Then he zipped up his jacket and opened the truck door. "I'll see if he's there."

FOUR

Ken stopped the pickup at the church, and Leon got out; and then Ken drove down the hill to the graveyard where people were waiting. Leon knocked at the old carved door with its symbols of the Lamb.

---

[1]**Angelus** A devotional prayer commemorating the Annunciation (the angel Gabriel's announcement of the Incarnation of God in the human form of Jesus). [Editors' note.]

While he waited he looked up at the twin bells from the king of Spain with the last sunlight pouring around them in their tower.

The priest opened the door and smiled when he saw who it was. "Come in! What brings you here this evening?"

The priest walked toward the kitchen, and Leon stood with his cap in his hand, playing with the earflaps and examining the living room—the brown sofa, the green armchair, and the brass lamp that hung down from the ceiling by links of chain. The priest dragged a chair out of the kitchen and offered it to Leon.

"No thank you, Father. I only came to ask you if you would bring your holy water to the graveyard."

The priest turned away from Leon and looked out the window at the 25 patio full of shadows and the dining-room windows of the nuns' cloister across the patio. The curtains were heavy, and the light from within faintly penetrated; it was impossible to see the nuns inside eating supper. "Why didn't you tell me he was dead? I could have brought the Last Rites anyway."

Leon smiled. "It wasn't necessary, Father."

The priest stared down at his scuffed brown loafers and the worn hem of his cassock. "For a Christian burial it was necessary."

His voice was distant, and Leon thought that his blue eyes looked tired.

"It's O.K., Father, we just want him to have plenty of water."

The priest sank down in the green chair and picked up a glossy mis- 30 sionary magazine. He turned the colored pages full of lepers and pagans without looking at them.

"You know I can't do that, Leon. There should have been the Last Rites and a funeral Mass at the very least."

Leon put on his green cap and pulled the flaps down over his ears. "It's getting late, Father. I've got to go."

When Leon opened the door Father Paul stood up and said, "Wait." He left the room and came back wearing a long brown overcoat. He followed Leon out the door and across the dim churchyard to the adobe steps in front of the church. They both stooped to fit through the low adobe entrance. And when they started down the hill to the graveyard only half of the sun was visible above the mesa.

The priest approached the grave slowly, wondering how they had managed to dig into the frozen ground; and then he remembered that this was New Mexico, and saw the pile of cold loose sand beside the hole. The people stood close to each other with little clouds of steam puffing from their faces. The priest looked at them and saw a pile of jackets, gloves, and scarves in the yellow, dry tumbleweeds that grew in the graveyard. He looked at the red blanket, not sure that Teofilo was so small, wondering if it wasn't some perverse Indian trick—something they did in March to ensure a good harvest—wondering if maybe old

Teofilo was actually at sheep camp corraling the sheep for the night. But there he was, facing into a cold dry wind and squinting at the last sunlight, ready to bury a red wool blanket while the faces of the parishioners were in shadow with the last warmth of the sun on their backs.

His fingers were stiff, and it took them a long time to twist the lid off 35 the holy water. Drops of water fell on the red blanket and soaked into dark icy spots. He sprinkled the grave and the water disappeared almost before it touched the dim, cold sand; it reminded him of something—he tried to remember what it was, because he thought if he could remember he might understand this. He sprinkled more water; he shook the container until it was empty, and the water fell through the light from sundown like August rain that fell while the sun was still shining, almost evaporating before it touched the wilted squash flowers.

The wind pulled at the priest's brown Franciscan robe and swirled away the corn meal and pollen that had been sprinkled on the blanket. They lowered the bundle into the ground, and they didn't bother to untie the stiff pieces of new rope that were tied around the ends of the blanket. The sun was gone, and over on the highway the eastbound lane was full of headlights. The priest walked away slowly. Leon watched him climb the hill, and when he had disappeared within the tall, thick walls, Leon turned to look up at the high blue mountains in the deep snow that reflected a faint red light from the west. He felt good because it was finished, and he was happy about the sprinkling of the holy water; now the old man could send them big thunderclouds for sure.

Topics for Critical Thinking and Writing

1. Why do Leon and Ken decorate the body of the old man (para. 2)? Why do they conceal this from Father Paul?

2. Why do Catholic priests sprinkle holy water on the body of a person about to be buried? Why does Louise (para. 19) think it is to keep her grandfather from being thirsty? Why does Leon think (para. 36) sprinkling the grave will bring "big thunderclouds for sure"? Are we to suppose that she and Leon don't understand the Christian ritual? Or that they reject it? (See especially paras. 24–29.)

3. How well does Leon understand the priest? How well does the priest understand Leon? Have the Indians made an unwitting fool of Father Paul? What do you think he would think if he knew what the Indians had said to one another behind his back?

4. Do you think the story is in any way offensive to Christians, specifically to Catholics? Explain.

5. Did you enjoy the story? If so, presumably you think it is a good story, *good* here being an aesthetic judgment and probably having nothing

to do with moral judgment. In any case, evaluate the story, supporting your evaluation with reasons.

Judith Ortiz Cofer

Born in Puerto Rico in 1952 of a Puerto Rican mother and a United States mainland father who served in the Navy, Judith Ortiz Cofer was educated both in Puerto Rico and on the mainland. After earning a bachelor's and a master's degree in English, she did further graduate work at Oxford University and then taught English in Florida. She has published seven volumes of poetry. This poem first appeared in Triple Crown: Chicano, Puerto Rican, and Cuban American Poetry *(1987).*

Latin Women Pray

Latin women pray
In incense sweet churches
They pray in Spanish to an Anglo God
With a Jewish heritage.
And this Great White Father   5
Imperturbable in his marble pedestal
Looks down upon his brown daughters
Votive candles shining like lust
In his all seeing eyes
Unmoved by their persistent prayers.   10

Yet year after year
Before his image they kneel
Margarita Josefina Maria and Isabel
All fervently hoping
That if not omnipotent   15
At least he be bilingual

Topics for Critical Thinking and Writing

1. The Hebrew Bible tells us (Genesis 1:26) that "God said, Let us make man in our image." Some cynic, reversing the idea, has observed that men make God in their own image. (Montesquieu, the eighteenth-century French philosopher, put it a bit differently: "If triangles made a god, they would give him three sides.") Is this poem with its reference to "an Anglo God" and a "Great White Father" spoken in the same spirit? Is the poem at all serious, or is it just a mildly amusing joke? Support your answer with reasons.

2. C. S. Lewis (whose essay expressing his religious faith is found on p. 800) in *A Grief Observed* (1961) wrote, "Can a mortal ask questions which God finds unanswerable? Quite easily, I think. All nonsense questions are unanswerable." Do you imagine that a devout person who believes that God has not answered his or her prayers might find this comment acceptable? Explain.

Appendix:
World Wide Web Sources
for Current Issues

If you use the Internet for research, you may have difficulty knowing where to begin. The following list can help by pointing you toward some useful sources of information on the World Wide Web covering many of the current issues in this book. Many of these topics have hundreds, even thousands, of Web pages dedicated to them, pages of highly varied quality and reliability. This list is hardly complete or definitive; it is merely a place to start, so you are not overwhelmed by the available choices. Many of the sources listed should be useful for the early stages of your research because they often contain extensive links and pointers to other sources of information: further Web sites, newsgroups and discussion lists, archived electronic documents, and traditional print sources. We have tried to indicate whether the author or sponsoring organization for a Web site takes sides in the debate.

Please note that although we tried to include only stable and up-to-date sources, the Internet changes from day to day. It is possible that some of these sources are no longer available at the specified address, or that the content of the pages has changed significantly.

General Information/Current Events

CNN Interactive and the *New York Times Online* are two excellent sources of late-breaking information on current topics, essentially any story that would be covered in print or broadcast news. Of course, there are many other reputable news organizations with online components, and if you are researching a very timely topic, you may want to expand your search or use another source (such as the newspaper for a particular city) that seems appropriate.

CNN Interactive. <http://www.cnn.com>
A very elaborate site, with many visuals, audio and video clips, and user-friendly site navigation. Its extensive coverage of current news is revised several times daily, as news breaks, and it also includes features, commentaries, and related stories.

New York Times Online. <http://www.nytimes.com>
Contains text and pictures from the day's edition of the *Times*, the nation's "newspaper of record." You must register the first time you use the site, but registration is free for users within the United States.

Abortion

Abortion Law Homepage. <http://members.aol.com/abtrbng/index.htm>
One of the few relatively "neutral" sites in a divisive online battle over the abortion issue. It includes the full (and edited) text of important court decisions (including *Roe v. Wade* and *Planned Parenthood v. Casey*), information on state and federal laws, and a glossary of abortion-related legal terms.

Affirmative Action

The Affirmative Action and Diversity Project: A Web Page for Research. <http://humanitas.ucsb.edu/aa.html>
Because the project is run out of the University of California at Santa Barbara, some information is California-specific, though an effort is made to include wider coverage. It includes news, economic perspectives, pending legislation, and bibliographies of print sources, as well as links to legal and administrative documents and the text of articles from various perspectives.

Alcohol Abuse

Rutgers University Center of Alcohol Studies. <http://www.rci.rutgers.edu/~cas2>
Site maintained by a multidisciplinary research institute. Includes fact sheets on topics such as drunk driving, the effects of alcohol, alcohol and domestic violence, and women and alcohol. Also provides links to pages of other major organizations and government agencies.

Animal Rights

People for the Ethical Treatment of Animals (PETA). <http://www.peta-online.org>
A comprehensive site run by the largest animal rights organization in America. Includes answers to frequently asked questions on PETA philosophy, links to news articles on animal rights, and an "activists library" pointing to publications, videos, images of animal research labs, and so on.

Critiques of Animal Rights. <http://www.animalrights.net>
A site favoring animal use. The "Links" section connects to the pages of antianimal rights groups, as well as to online articles on "animal rights terrorism," animal testing, hunting, and education.

Bilingual Education

"Bilingual Education." *Education Week.* <http://www.edweek.org/context/topics/biling.htm>
Provides an overview of the debate on bilingual education in the United States. Discusses various theories of and methods for bilingual education and

gives links to articles from the *Education Week* archives on various aspects of bilingual education — legal, financial, and social.

Bilingual Education Resources on the Internet.
<http://www.edb.utexas.edu/coe/depts/ci/bilingue/resources.html>
Although this site favors bilingual education, it gives links to broadly useful sources, including government documents, journals, and an online discussion list.

Cloning

Biotechnology and Genetic Engineering.
<http://www.anselm.edu/homepage/jpitocch/resbiotech.html>
A list of links to reputable general information on biotechnology, related ethical questions, regulations, and patents.

Cloning and Genetic Engineering Frequently Asked Questions.
<http://www.u.arizona.edu/~ahk/cloning/index.html>
Considers cloning and other forms of genetic engineering. The site clearly favors cloning, but it relies on solid facts and provides links to other online sources containing such material as scientific data and ethical arguments.

Death Penalty

"Focus on the Death Penalty." *Justice Center Web Site.* 1998.
<http://www.uaa.alaska.edu/just/death>
Provides a brief historical overview and information from both sides of the current debate, including statistics and summaries of court decisions. Good links are available to bibliographies and further online and traditional sources.

Divorce

Divorce Reform Page. <http://adams.patriot.net/~crouch/divorce.html>
Although page has a bias in favor of making divorce more difficult, it includes links to both pro- and antireform articles and editorials in reputable online periodicals as well as to divorce statistics and news about laws in various states.

Drug Legalization

Drug Enforcement Administration.
<http://www.usdoj.gov/dea/index.htm>
The U.S. Drug Enforcement Administration's home page gives the government's official line on drug policy and an overview of the agency. The "pub-

lications" page provides information about specific drugs and antidrug legalization.

"Recent Articles in the Media." *Drug Reform Coordination Network.*
<http://druglibrary.org/schaffer/media/MAG_ART.HTM>
Favors decriminalization. Provides links to text of online articles favoring drug law reform.

Environment

United States Environmental Protection Agency.
<http://www.epa.gov/index.html>
The Environmental Protection Agency's official home page provides up-to-date information on official programs and policies as well as the link between the environment and the U.S. economy.

Foundation for Research on Economics and the Environment.
<http://www.free-eco.org/links.html>
Home page of a group describing itself as "an educational and research foundation, established to support environmental goals based on individual liberty and responsibility and harmonized with economic prosperity." It gives links to think tanks, environmental groups, and government organizations.

Euthanasia

Euthanasia World Directory. <http://www.efn.org/~ergo>
Generally advocating the right to die, the site includes many links to groups favoring that perspective, as well as texts of euthanasia-related laws. The "news" link is updated daily and points to sources of world news on all aspects of euthanasia and assisted suicide.

First Amendment

"Some Freedom of Expression WWW Sources." *MIT Student Association for Freedom of Expression (SAFE) Home Page.*
<http://www.mit.edu:8001/activities/safe/resources.html>
Provides an annotated list of links to many reliable sites and sources, including the American Civil Liberties Union Archive, the Electronic Frontier Foundation, and the text of Supreme Court decisions.

Fourth Amendment

The Privacy Pages. <http://www.2020tech.com/maildrop/privacy.html>
Includes links to breaking news, privacy organizations, and articles from worldwide periodicals. Provides much information on privacy issues online, including encryption, anonymous servers, and privacy software.

Gay Marriage

Domestic Partnerships and Same Sex Marriages.
<http://www.cs.cmu.edu/afs/cs.cmu.edu/user/scotts/
domestic-partners/mainpage.html>
Includes links to many resources — for example, personal essays, opinion pieces, legal cases, and news stories — related to same sex marriages and domestic partnerships as law and policy.

Gun Control

Handgun Control, Inc. and The Center To Prevent Handgun Violence.
<http://www.handguncontrol.org>
Provides useful information on state and national laws, as well as links to pro-gun control articles (the site's bias).

Immigration

Yahoo! News.
<http://headlines.yahoo.com/Full_Coverage/US/Immigration>
Part of the *Yahoo!* Web search "Full Coverage" series. Provides links to recent immigration-related stories in major U.S. newspapers and magazines as well as additional Web sites screened for reliability.

Siskind, Susser, Haas & Chang Documents Collection.
<http://www.telalink.net/~gsiskind/docs>
Site of large immigration law firm. The collection includes text of recent and pending state and national immigration legislation, reports, and related documents.

Internet Censorship

"Internet Censorship." *Electronic Privacy Information Center.*
<http://www.epic.org/free_speech/censorship>
Links to text of current Internet censorship legislation and to other groups interested in free speech on the Net, including the Electronic Freedom Forum and the American Civil Liberties Union.

Juvenile Justice

Juvenile Justice Center.
<http://www.abanet.org/crimjust/juvjus/home.html>
The American Bar Association's Juvenile Justice Center exists "to monitor and influence juvenile justice policy and practice." Web site provides links to information on state and national law and the full text of articles from law journals.

Multiculturalism

National MultiCultural Institute. <http://www.nmci.org>
Organization dedicated to promoting multiculturalism in American education and business. "Facts" page provides reliable statistics about demographic diversity in America.

Pornography

Computer Mediate Communications Magazine.
<http://sunsite.unc.edu/cmc/mag/1995/aug/toc.html>
The August 1995 issue of this online magazine is dedicated to an analysis of the debate over pornography on the Internet. Several thoughtful articles are included, many with links to other sources. Links from "Editor's Page" are especially useful.

Racist Speech

"Internet Resources on Hate Speech." *University of Iowa Libraries Gateway to the Internet.*
<http://www.arcade.uiowa.edu:80/gw/journalism/mediaLaw/hateSpeech.html>
Links to a number of reputable articles on racist and other forms of hate speech, especially emphasizing speech online and on college campuses.

Sex Education

Birth Control and Sex Education: Pro.
<http://www.nonline.com/ProCon/html/proSexEd.htm>
Reprint of an article from The Planned Parenthood Federation of America. Lays out the basic goals of sex education and makes a case in favor of its inclusion in the school curriculum.

Birth Control and Sex Education: Con.
<http://www.nonline.com/ProCon/html/conSexEd.htm>
Reprint of an article by an evangelical Christian. Provides a history of sex education in America, arguing that, while sex education prior to around 1960 stressed abstinence and created healthy attitudes, current sex education methods promote immorality.

Sexual Harassment

"Sexual Harassment: Myths and Realities." *American Psychological Association.* <http://www.apa.org/pubinfo/harass.html>
One of the American Psychological Association's online brochures on topics related to mental health and psychology. Includes overview of issues and summary of relevant research, focusing on harassment in the workplace.

"Sexual Harassment Bibliography." *University of Maryland Sexual Harassment Page.*
<http://www.inform.umd.edu/EdRes/Topic/WomensStudies/GenderIssues/SexualHarassment/sexual-harassment-bibliography>
Annotated bibliography of print books and magazines covering various aspects of sexual harassment, on campus and in the workplace.

Smokers' Rights

CDC's Tobacco Information and Prevention Source.
<http://www.cdc.gov/tobacco>
Part of the U.S. Centers for Disease Control's antismoking education effort, this site includes the text of Surgeon General's reports, research and statistics, and information on smoking and tobacco legislation in the news.

Fight Ordinances & Restrictions to Control and Eliminate Smoking (FORCES).
<http://forces.org>
Site demonstrates a strong bias in favor of smoker's rights. Provides links to the pages of like-minded groups, the text of recent antismoking legislation, and articles downplaying the dangers of smoking and arguing against restrictions.

Teenage Pregnancy

Boston University Community Outreach Health Information System.
<http://web.bu.edu:80/COHIS/teenpreg/teenpreg.htm>
Part of a clearinghouse of information on public health issues. Provides general statistics about teen pregnancy and information on risks, pregnancy prevention, maternal and infant health, and related topics.

National Campaign to Prevent Teen Pregnancy.
<http://www.teenpregnancy.org>
The stated goal of the sponsoring organization is "to reduce the teen pregnancy rate by one-third by the year 2005." The site provides recent statistics and facts, as well as an annotated page of "related sites," linking to other organizations with an interest in teen pregnancy.

Television Violence

Television and Violence. <http://www.ksu.edu/humec/tele.htm>
Reprints of several articles and book excerpts (some with good bibliographies) on the impact of television violence.

"Children and Media/TV Violence Resource List." *Center for Media Education.*
<http://www.cme.org/cme/cta/bib-viol.html>
Bibliography of print sources on the link between television violence and violent behavior in children.

Acknowledgments continued from page ii

Robert Bork, "Addicted to Health" [editors' title] from *The National Review* (July 28, 1997). Copyright © 1997 by National Review, Inc. Reprinted with the permission of National Review, Inc., 215 Lexington Avenue, New York, NY 10016.

Judy Brady, "I Want a Wife" from *Ms.* (1971). Copyright © 1971 by Judy Brady. Reprinted with the permission of the author.

Lois M. Brenner, "Take the Pain Away" from *The New York Times* (February 21, 1996), "Letters to the Editor." Reprinted with the permission of the author.

Susan Brownmiller, "Let's Put Pornography Back in the Closet" from *Newsday* (1979). Copyright © 1979 by Susan Brownmiller. Reprinted with the permission of the author.

David Bruck, "The Death Penalty" from *The New Republic* (May 20, 1985). Copyright © 1985 by The New Republic, Inc. Reprinted with the permission of *The New Republic*.

J. Warren Cassidy, "The Case for Firearms" from *Time* (January 29, 1990). Copyright © 1990 by Time, Inc. Reprinted with the permission of *Time*.

Linda Chavez, "Demystifying Multiculturalism" from *The National Review* (February 21, 1994). Copyright © 1994 by The National Review, Inc. Reprinted with the permission of *The National Review*, 215 Lexington Avenue, New York, NY 10016.

Sally Thane Christensen, "Is a Tree Worth a Life?" from *Newsweek* (October 22, 1990). Reprinted with the permission of Michael Christensen.

Judith H. Christie, "What About the Faculty?" from *The New York Times* (May 14, 1996), "Letters to the Editor." Reprinted with the permission of the author.

Cathleen A. Cleaver, "The Internet: A Clear and Present Danger?" Reprinted with the permission of the author.

Judith Ortiz Cofer, "Latin Women Pray" from *Reaching for the Mainland and Selected New Poems*. Copyright © 1985 by Judith Ortiz Cofer. Reprinted with the permission of Bilingual Press/Editorial Bilingue, Arizona State University, Box 872702, Tempe, AZ 85287-2702.

David Cole, "Five Myths About Immigration" from *The Nation* (October 17, 1994). Copyright © 1994 by The Nation Company, L.P. Reprinted with the permission of *The Nation*.

Emily Dickinson, "Papa above!" and "Those—dying, then" from *The Poems of Emily Dickinson*, edited by Thomas H. Johnson. Copyright © 1951, © 1955, 1979, 1983 by the President and Fellows of Harvard College. Reprinted with the permission of the publishers and the Trustees of Amherst College.

"The Divorce Debate" from *The New York Times* (February 5, 1996). Copyright © 1996 by The New York Times Company. Reprinted with the permission of *The New York Times*.

Terry Eastland, "Ending Affirmative Action" from *Ending Affirmative Action*. Copyright © 1996 by Terry Eastland. Reprinted with the permission of BasicBooks, a subsidiary of Perseus Books Group, LLC.

T. S. Eliot, "The Love Song of J. Alfred Prufrock" from *Collected Poems 1909–1962* (New York: Harcourt Brace & World, 1963). Copyright © 1917 and renewed 1945 by T. S. Eliot. Reprinted with the permission of Faber and Faber Limited.

Jean Bethke Elshtain, "Ewegenics" from *The New Republic* (1997). Copyright © 1997 by The New Republic, Inc. Reprinted with the permission of *The New Republic*.

Leonard D. Eron, "The Television Industry Must Police Itself" from Harvard School of Public Health panel discussion, 1992. Copyright © 1992 by Leonard D. Eron. Reprinted with the permission of the author.

J. James Exon, "Keep the Internet Safe for Families" from *The Dallas Morning News* (April 9, 1995). Copyright © 1995. Reprinted with the permission of *The Dallas Morning News*.

Holly Finn, "Romance of Childbirth" from *The New York Times* (December 7, 1997), "Letter to the Editor." Reprinted with the permission of the author.

Stanley Fish, "Reverse Racism, Or How the Pot Got to Call the Kettle Black" from *Atlantic Monthly* (November 1993). Reprinted with the permission of the author.

Milton Friedman, "There's No Justice in the War on Drugs" from *The New York Times* (January 17, 1998). Copyright © 1998 by The New York Times Company. Reprinted with the permission of *The New York Times*.

Robert Frost, "The Flood" and "Design" from *The Poetry of Robert Frost*, edited by Edward Connery Lathem. Copyright 1936, © 1956 by Robert Frost, © 1964 by Lesley Frost Ballantine. Copyright 1928, © 1969 by Henry Holt and Co., Inc. "Mending Wall" from *The Poetry of Robert Frost*, edited by John Connery Lathem. Copyright © 1936 by Robert Frost. Copyright © 1964 by Leslie Frost Ballantine. Copyright © 1969 by Henry Holt and Co., Inc. Reprinted with the permission of Henry Holt and Co., Inc.

Maggie Gallagher, "Why Make Divorce Easy?" from *The New York Times* (February 20, 1996). Copyright © 1996 by The New York Times Company. Reprinted with the permission of *The New York Times*.

Lisa M. Garcia, "Economics Are a Factor" from *The New York Times* (September 9, 1997), "Letter to the Editor." Reprinted with the permission of the author.

Henry Louis Gates, Jr., "The Debate Has Been Miscast from the Start" from *The Boston Globe* (October 13, 1991). Copyright © 1991 by Henry Louis Gates, Jr. Reprinted with the permission of Brandt and Brandt Literary Agents, Inc.

Nathan Glazer, "In Defense of Multiculturalism" from *The New Republic* (September 2, 1991). Copyright © 1991 by The New Republic, Inc. Reprinted with the permission of *The New Republic*.

Ellen Goodman, "The Reasonable Woman Standard" from *The Boston Globe* (October 1991). Copyright © 1991 by The Boston Globe Newspaper Co./The Washington Post Writer's Group. "Who Lives? Who Dies? Who Decides?" from *The Boston Globe* (February 1980). Copyright © 1980 by The Boston Globe Newspaper Co./The Washington Post Writer's Group. Reprinted with the permission of The Washington Post Writer's Group.

Hendrik Hertzberg, "Star Spangled Banter" from *The New Yorker* (July 21, 1997). Copyright © 1997 by Hendrik Hertzberg. Reprinted with the permission of the author.

Ernest F. Hollings, "Save the Children" from *The New York Times* (November 23, 1993). Copyright © 1993 by The New York Times Company. Reprinted with the permission of *The New York Times*.

Mathilda Holzman, "Immersion Won't Work" from *The New York Times* (September 9, 1997), "Letter to the Editor." Reprinted with the permission of the author.

Langston Hughes, "Let America Be America Again" from *Collected Poems*. Originally published in *Esquire* (July 1936). Copyright 1936 and renewed © 1964 by Langston Hughes. Copyright © 1994 by the Estate of Langston Hughes. Reprinted with the permission of Alfred A. Knopf, Inc.

Barbara Huttman, "A Crime of Compassion" from *Newsweek* (August 8, 1983). Copyright © 1983 by Barbara Huttman. Reprinted with the permission of the author.

Kenneth T. Jackson, "Too Many Have Let Enthusiasm Outrun Reason" from *The Boston Globe* (October 13, 1991). Copyright © 1991 by Kenneth T. Jackson. Reprinted with the permission of the author.

Jeff Jacoby, "Bring Back Flogging" from *The Boston Globe* (February 26, 1997). Copyright © 1997. Reprinted with the permission of *The Boston Globe*.

Susan Jacoby, "A First Amendment Junkie" from *The New York Times* (January 26, 1978). Copyright © 1978 by Susan Jacoby. Reprinted with the permission of Georges Borchardt, Inc. for the author.

Jeffrey O. Jones, "A Young Man's Success" from *The New York Times* (September 9, 1997), "Letter to the Editor." Reprinted with the permission of the author.

Kendall A. King, "Bilingual Education Keeps Students in School" from *The New York Times* (September 9, 1997), "Letter to the Editor." Reprinted with the permission of the author.

Martin Luther King, Jr., "I Have a Dream." Copyright © 1963 by Martin Luther King, Jr., copyright renewed 1991 by Coretta Scott King. Reprinted with the permission of the Heirs to the Estate of Martin Luther King, Jr., c/o Writers House, Inc. as the agent for the proprietor. "Letter from Birmingham Jail." Copyright © 1963, 1964 by Martin Luther King, Jr., copyright renewed 1991, 1992 by Coretta Scott King. Reprinted with the permission of the Heirs to the Estate of Martin Luther King, Jr., c/o Writers House, Inc. as the agent for the proprietor.

Edward I. Koch, "Death and Justice: How Capital Punishment Affirms Life" from *The New Republic* (April 15, 1985). Copyright © 1985 by The New Republic, Inc. Reprinted with the permission of *The New Republic*.

Rita Kramer, "Juvenile Justice Is Delinquent" from *The Wall Street Journal* (May 27, 1992). Copyright © 1992 by Dow Jones & Company, Inc. Reprinted with the permission of the author and *The Wall Street Journal*. All rights reserved.

Charles Krauthammer, "Of Headless Mice . . . and Men" from *Time* (January 19, 1998). Copyright © 1998 by Time, Inc. Reprinted with the permission of *Time*.

Dale Kunkel, "Why Content, Not the Age of Viewers, Should Control What Children Watch on TV" from *The Chronicle of Higher Education* (January 31, 1997). Copyright © 1997 by The Chronicle of Higher Education, Inc. Reprinted with the permission of *The Chronicle of Higher Education*.

Leila L. Kysar, "A Logger's Lament" from *Newsweek* (October 22, 1990). Copyright © 1990 by Leila L. Kysar. Reprinted with the permission of the author.

Allison Lassieur, "Earn Right to Say 'I Do'" from *The New York Times* (February 21, 1996). Reprinted with the permission of the author.

Charles R. Lawrence III, "On Racist Speech" from *The Chronicle of Higher Education* (October 25, 1989). Copyright © 1989 by Charles R. Lawrence III. Reprinted with the permission of the author.

Ursula K. Le Guin, "The Ones Who Walk Away from Omelas" from *New Dimensions 3*. Copyright © 1973 by Ursula K. Le Guin. Reprinted with the permission of the author and the author's agent, Virginia Kidd.

C. S. Lewis, "What Christians Believe" from *Mere Christianity, A Revised and Enlarged Edition*. Reprinted with the permission of HarperCollins Publishers Ltd.

Rush H. Limbaugh III, "Condoms: The New Diploma" from *The Way Things Ought to Be*. Copyright © 1992 by Rush Limbaugh. Reprinted with the permission of Pocket Books, a division of Simon & Schuster, Inc.

Niccolò Machiavelli, excerpt from *The Prince* from *The Portable Machiavelli*, edited by Peter Bondanella and Mark Musa. Copyright © 1979 by Viking Penguin, Inc. Reprinted with the permission of Viking Penguin, a division of Penguin Books USA, Inc.

Catharine A. MacKinnon, "Sex and Violence: A Perspective" from *Feminism Unmodified*. Copyright © 1987 by the President and Fellows of Harvard College. Reprinted with the permission of Harvard University Press.

Sarah J. McCarthy, "Cultural Fascism" from *Forbes* (December 9, 1991). Copyright © 1991 by Forbes, Inc. Reprinted with the permission of *Forbes* Magazine.

Steven McDonald, "The Laws of Cyberspace: What Colleges Need to Know" from "Academe Today" (*The Chronicle of Higher Education* Web site) (October 28, 1997). Copyright © 1997 by The Chronicle of Higher Education, Inc. Reprinted with the permission of *The Chronicle of Higher Education*.

Bertrand Russell, "Why I Am Not a Christian" from *Why I Am Not a Christian and Other Essays*. Copyright © 1957 by George Allen & Unwin, Ltd. Reprinted with the permission of Simon & Schuster and the Bertrand Russell Peace Foundation, Ltd.

Rebecca Sawyer-Fay, "Letter to the Editor" from *The New York Times* (February 24, 1996). Reprinted with the permission of the author.

Lisa Schiffren, "Gay Marriage, an Oxymoron" from *The New York Times* (March 23, 1996). Copyright © 1996 The New York Times Company. Reprinted with the permission of *The New York Times*.

Stanley S. Scott, "Smokers Get a Raw Deal" from *The New York Times* (December 29, 1984). Copyright © 1984 by The New York Times Company. Reprinted with the permission of *The New York Times*.

Max Shulman, "Love is a Fallacy" from *Love is a Fallacy* (New York: Doubleday, 1951). Copyright 1951 and renewed © 1979 by Max Shulman. Reprinted with the permission of Harold Matson Agency.

John Silber, "Students Should Not Be Above the Law" from *The New York Times* (May 9, 1996). Copyright © 1996 by The New York Times Company. Reprinted with the permission of *The New York Times*.

Leslie Marmon Silko, "The Man to Send Rainclouds" from *Storyteller* (New York: Seaver Books, 1981). Copyright © 1981 by Leslie Marmon Silko. Reprinted with the permission of The Wylie Agency, Inc.

Peter Singer, "Animal Liberation" from *The New York Review of Books* (April 15, 1973). Copyright © 1973 by Peter Singer. Reprinted with the permission of the author.

Sophocles, "Antigone," translated by Dudley Fitts and Robert Fitzgerald, from *The Oedipus Cycle: An English Version*. Copyright 1939 by Dudley Fitts and Robert Fitzgerald. Reprinted with the permission of Harcourt Brace & Company.

Walter T. Stace, "Is Determinism Inconsistent With Free Will?" from *Religion and the Modern Mind*. Copyright 1952 by Walter T. Stace, renewed © 1980 by Blanche Stace. Reprinted with the permission of Lippincott-Raven Publishers.

Thomas Stoddard, "Gay Marriages: Make Them Legal" from *The New York Times* (March 4, 1989). Copyright © 1989 by The New York Times Company. Reprinted with the permission of *The New York Times*.

Ronald Takaki, "The Harmful Myth of Asian Superiority" from *The New York Times* (June 16, 1990). Copyright © 1990 by The New York Times Company. Reprinted with the permission of *The New York Times*.

Randall Terry, "The Abortion Clinic Shootings: Why?" from *The Boston Globe* (January 9, 1995). Copyright © 1995 by Randall Terry. Reprinted with the permission of the author.

Sallie Tisdale, "Save a Life, Kill a Tree?" from *The New York Times* (October 26, 1991). Copyright © 1991 by The New York Times Company. Reprinted with the permission of *The New York Times*.

Caldwell Titcomb, "Star-Spangled Earache: What So Loudly We Wail" from *The New Republic* (1985). Copyright © 1985 by The New Republic, Inc. Reprinted with the permission of *The New Republic*.

Michael Tooley, "Our Current Drug Legislation: Grounds for Reconsideration" from *The Newsletter of the Center for Values and Social Policy* 8, no. 1 (Spring 1994). Copyright © 1994. Reprinted with the permission of the Center for Values and Social Policy.

Lawrence Tribe, "Second Thoughts on Cloning" from *The New York Times* (December 5, 1997). Copyright © 1997 by The New York Times Company. Reprinted with the permission of *The New York Times*.

Tufts University, "What Is Sexual Harassment?" Reprinted with the permission of Tufts University.

Index of Authors
and Titles

Index of Terms

DIRECTORY TO DOCUMENTATION MODELS IN MLA FORMAT

In-Text or Parenthetical Citations, 210

List of Works Cited, 216

Books

Anthologies

Periodical Articles